RESOURCE
RECOVERY
GUIDE

RESOURCE
RECOVERY
GUIDE

James G. Abert

VNR VAN NOSTRAND REINHOLD COMPANY
NEW YORK CINCINNATI TORONTO LONDON MELBOURNE

Manufactured in the United States of America

Published by Van Nostrand Reinhold Company Inc.
135 West 50th Street, New York, N.Y. 10020

Van Nostrand Reinhold Publishing
1410 Birchmount Road
Scarborough, Ontario MIP 2 E7, Canada

Van Nostrand Reinhold
480 Latrobe Street
Melbourne, Victoria 3000, Australia

Van Nostrand Reinhold Company Limited
Molly Millars Lane
Wokingham, Berkshire, England

15 14 13 12 11 10 9 8 7 6 5 4 3 2 1

Library of Congress Cataloging in Publication Data
Main entry under title:

Resource recovery guide.

   Includes index.
   1. Recycling (Waste, etc.) – United States.
I. Abert, James Goodear.
TD794.5.R456 1982   363.7'28   82-8324
ISBN 0-442-20235-0   AACR2

Preface

During the decade of the 1970s the literature on resource recovery from municipal waste expanded. However, by and large, relevant articles appeared in scattered sources, many not readily available in the library community. To some extent this situation improved in the latter half of the decade, with the increased circulation of the *Bulletin of the National Center for Resource Recovery* and with the fonding and, albeit initially limited, circulation of *Resource Recovery and Conservation* and *Conservation and Recycling*. The purpose of this collection is to draw from these divergent sources readings illustrating the relevant issues which underlie recycling of the material values found in municipal discards as well as the potential for a national energy dividend by realizing the energy value inherent in this waste.

Many have contributed to the selection and organization of this collection. These include Harvey Alter, Randy Chrismon, Sharon Bauman, Gwen McNamee, Margaret McVicker, Susan Lane, and Mauryne Brent. Special thanks, of course, go to the authors of the readings. Without them, there would be no collection.

Preface

Contents

Preface   v

**PART 1 NATIONAL CONCERNS FOR RECYCLING AND RESOURCE RECOVERY
OF MUNICIPAL WASTE: POLICY PERSPECTIVES**

1-1 "Municipal Waste and Energy Conservation." Reprinted from NCRR *Resource Recovery Briefs*, July 1979, 4pp. Harvey Alter, author. Adapted from remarks before a joint hearing of the Subcommittee on Energy Development and Applications of the Committee on Science and Technology and the Subcommittee on Transportation and Commerce in Interstate and Foreign Commerce, U.S. House of Representatives.   3

1-2 "Recycling." Reprinted from *Government and the Nation's Resources,* the report of the National Commission on Supplies and Shortages. December 1976, pp. 155-172.   7

1-3 "Comparison of Two Government Reports as to Their Approaches to Recycling." *Resource Recovery and Conservation,* Vol. 2, No. 4 (November 1977), pp. 361-364. David A. Tillman, author. Reprinted with permission of Elsevier Scientific Publishing Company.   20

1-4 "Public Policies Toward the Use of Scrap Materials." Reprinted from the *American Economic Review,* Vol. 67, No. 1 (February 1977), pp. 355-358. Robert C. Anderson, author. Reprinted with permission of the American Economic Association and the author.   23

1-5 "Waste Reduction: Issues and Policies." Reprinted from *Resources Policy,* Vol. 3, No. 1 (March 1977) pp. 23-38. W. David Conn, author.   27

1-6 "Energy Conservation and Fuel Production by Processing Solid Wastes." *"Environmental Conservation,* Vol. 4, No. 1 (Spring 1977), pp. 11-19. Harvey Alter, author. Reprinted with permission of the Foundation for Environmental Conservation.   41

1-7 "Notes on Changes in Energy Economics." Adapted from a paper in the *Proceedings of the Mineral Economics Symposium, A Challenge for the Materials Industry: Changing Energy Economics.* Washington, D.C., November 9, 1976, pp. 95-109. Frank Austin Smith, author.   52

1-8 "Resource Recovery as a Solid Waste Management Option." Adapted from Chapter V of *Solid Waste Management and the Paper Industry: A report for the Solid Waste Council of the Paper Industry* by Franklin Associates, Ltd. and International Research and Technology Corporation, 1979, pp. 64-83. W.E. and M.A. Franklin and M.E. Weber, authors. Reprinted with permission of the American Paper Institute, Inc., Washington, D.C.   58

1-9 "Resource Recovery as a Pollution-Control Device." Reprinted from *Waste Age,* Vol. 10, No. 4 (April 1979), pp. 49-52. Albert Klee and Judith Gordon, authors. Reprinted with permission of the National Solid Wastes Management Association.   80

1-10 *A Handbook on Scrap Futures Markets and Futures Trading.* Adapted from a report prepared for the U.S. Environmental Protection Agency, Cincinnati, Ohio, 1979, 28 pp. Roger Dower and Robert C. Anderson, authors.   85

1-11 "The Treatment of Resource Recovery in Solid Waste Plans." Resource Recovery and Conservation, Vol. 2, No. 4 (November 1977), pp. 365-372. W. David Conn, author. Reprinted with permission of Elsevier Scientific Publishing Company.   101

PART 2 PLANNING, PROCUREMENT, MARKETING, ECONOMICS, AND FINANCE

2-1 "Is there Gold Among the Garbage?" Sky, (April 1979), pp. 10-16. Franchot Buhler, author. Reprinted with the permission of Halsey Publishing Company and the author.   111

2-2 "Five Rules for Resource Recovery." Reprinted from NCRR Bulletin, Vol. VI, No. 4 (Fall 1976), pp. 93-94. Richard W. Chase, author.   116

2-3 "Resource Recovery: Is It for Your City?" Nations Cities, Vol. 15, No. 7 (July 1977), pp. 9-14. Stephen Burks and Clint Page, authors. Reprinted with permission of the National League of Cities.   119

2-4 "Resource Recovery: The Economics and the Risks." Professional Engineer, Vol. 45, No. 11 (November 1975), pp. 29-31. J.G. Abert, author. Reprinted with permission of the National Society of Professional Engineers.   126

2-5 "Waste-to-Energy: Applying the Technology in the Real World." Adapted from two articles in Solid Wastes Management, Vol. 22, No. 5 (May 1979), pp. 20-21, 24, 28, 88, and Vol. 22, No. 6 (June 1979), pp. 56, 58, 60. Glenn A. Swinehart and Whitney A. Sanders. Reprinted with permission of Communication Channels, Inc.   130

2-6 "Resource Recovery: The Management of Technical and Economic Risks." NCRR Bulletin, Vol. 9, No. 4 (December 1979), pp. 80-84. Harvey Alter, author.   141

2-7 "Overcoming Barriers to Resource Recovery." NCRR Bulletin, Vol. 9, No. 2 (June 1979), pp. 28-34. Susan J. Kinney, author.   146

2-8 Flow Control Ordinance: City of Akron. John E. Holcomb and Richard Cohen, authors. Printed with permission of the authors.   153

2-9 "Environmental Impacts of Resource Recovery Facilities Should Be Pre-determined." Solid Waste Management, Vol. 21, No. 2 (February 1978), pp. 20, 22, 46-47; Vol. 21, No. 3 (March 1978), pp. 60, 62, 64, 88. Allen Serper, author. Reprinted with permission of Communication Channels, Inc.   158

2-10 "Marketing Recovered Materials." NCRR Bulletin, Vol. V, No. 4 (Fall 1975), pp. 74-83. Harvey W. Gershman, author.   167

2-11 "How to Buy Resource Recovery." American City & Country, Vol. 94, No. 4 (April 1979), pp. 91-93. Stephen G. Lewis, author. Reprinted with permission of Morgan-Grampian Publishing Company.   178

2-12 "Breakeven Economics of Resource Recovery Systems." Proceedings of the Fifth Mineral Waste Utilization Symposium, Chicago, Illinois, April 13-14, 1976, pp. 53-57. Donald L. Mihelich, author.   181

2-13 Steps to Resource Recovery for the I-95 Complex. Adapted from a report of the same title prepared by the National Center for Resource Recovery, April 1976, 28 pp.   187

2-14 "Elements of Financial Risk." Proceedings of the National Waste Processing Conference, Chicago, Illinois, May 7-10, 1978, pp. 287-293. Jeffrey F. Clunie and Robert G. Taylor, authors. Reprinted with permission of the American Society of Mechanical Engineers.   212

2-15 "Resource Recovery Financing." *NCRR Bulletin,* Vol. VII, No. 3 (Summer 1977), pp. 73–80. Charles A. Ballard, author.   220

PART 3 WASTE AS A SOURCE OF RAW MATERIALS

3-1 "Source Separation: A Resource Recovery Option." Reprinted from *NCRR Bulletin,* Vol. VII, No. 1 (Winter 1977), pp. 3–10. Elizabeth Johnson, author.   231

3-2 "Facilitating Paper Recycling." Reprinted from the *Journal of Applied Behavior Analysis,* Vol. 9, pp. 315–322, J.F. Witmer and E.S. Geller, authors. Reprinted with permission of the Society for the Experimental Analysis of Behavior, Inc.   240

3-3 "What's to be Done with Used Newspapers?" Adapted from article with the same' title published in *Waste Age,* Vol. 8, No. 7 (July 1977), pp. 50–66. Robert Davis and Bruce MacDonald, authors. Reprinted with permission of the National Solid Wastes Management Association.   247

3-4 "Technological Barriers to the Recovery of Secondary Fibers from Municipal Solid Waste." *Proceedings of the 1978 Pulping Conference,* New Orleans, Louisiana, November 5-8, 1978, pp. 333–345. Marc L. Renard, author. Reprinted with permission of the Technical Association of the Pulp and Paper Industry and the author.   254

3-5 "Fiber Recovery from Municipal Solid Waste." Reprinted from *Proceedings of the Sixth Mineral Waste Utilization Symposium,* May 2-3, 1978, Chicago, Illinois; pp. 222–228. G.M. Savage, L.F. Diaz, and G.J. Trezek, authors.   268

3-6 "Recovery of Paper from Municipal Solid Waste." *Proceedings of the 1979 Pulping Conference,* Seattle, Washington, September 24-26, 1979, pp. 275-280. Curt Cederholm and Jorgen G. Hedenhag, authors. Reprinted with permission of the Technical Association of the Pulp and Paper Industry.   275

3-7 "Research into the Hygienic Qualities of Paper Recovered by Mechanical Sorting of Municipal Waste." *Conservation and Recycling,* Vol. 2, No. 3/4, 1979, pp. 263–267. Hubert W. Kindler, author. Reprinted with permission of Pergamon Press, Ltd.   281

3-8 "Selective Dry Processing, Pulp Cleaning and Paper Making Tests on Three Feedstocks from Municipal Solid Wastes." *Proceedings of the 1979 Pulping Conference,* Seattle, Washington, September 24-26, 1979, pp. 247-258. Marc L. Renard, author. Reprinted with permission of the Technical Association of the Pulp and Paper Industry and the author.   286

3-9 "Recovery of Ferrous Scrap from Municipal Solid Waste." Adapted from a presentation to the International Iron and Steel Institute, XI Annual Conference, Rome, Italy, October 12, 1977. 39 pp. Rocco A. Petrone, author.   299

3-10 "Aluminum Recovery: A Status Report." *NCRR Bulletin,* Part 1, Vol. VII, No. 2 (Spring 1977), pp. 37-45; Part 2, Vol. VII, No. 3 (Summer 1977), pp. 68-72. James Abert, author.   308

3-11 "Resource Recovery from Solid Wastes by Water Only Cyclone Process and Heavy Medium Cyclone Process." Adapted from an article with the same title in *Conservation and Recycling,* Vol. 2, No. 3/4, 1979, pp. 233-254. P.C. Reeves, J.H. Absil, H.H. Dreissen, and A.T. Basten, authors. Reprinted with permission of Pergamon Press, Ltd.   323

3-12 "The Recovery of Waste Glass Cullet for Recycling Purposes by Means of Electro-Optical Sorters." Adapted from an article with the same title in *Conservation and Recycling,* Vol. 1, No. 2, 1976, pp. 209-219. H. Stirling, author. Reprinted with permission of Pergamon Press, Ltd.   339

3-13 "Glass and Non-Ferrous Metal Recovery Subsystem at Franklin, Ohio." adapted from a paper published in the *Proceedings of the Fifth Mineral Waste Utilization Symposium,* Chicago, Illinois, April 13-14, 1976, pp. 175-183. John P. Cummings, author.   343

3-14 "Recovery of Glass from Urban Refuse by Froth Flotation." Reprinted from *Proceedings of the Sixth Mineral Waste Utilization Symposium,* Chicago, Illinois, May 2-3, 1978, pp. 230-240. J.H. Heginbotham, author.   350

3-15 "Lightweight Structural Concrete Aggregate from Municipal Waste Glass." Reprinted from *Proceedings of the Fifth Mineral Waste Utilization Symposium,* Chicago, Illinois, April 13-14, 1976, pp. 219-222. K.J. Liles, author.   363

3-16 "Some Observations on the Recycling of Plastics and Rubber." Reprinted with permission from *Conservation and Recycling,* Vol. 1, No. 3/4, 1977, pp. 247-271. A.G. Buekens, author. Reprinted with permission of Pergamon Press, Ltd.   368

3-17 "Tire Recycling: Research Trends and Needs." *Conservation and Recycling,* Vol. 2, No. 2, 1978, pp. 137-143. Arthur H. Purcell, author. Reprinted with permission of Pergamon Press, Ltd.   391

PART 4 WASTE AS AN ENERGY SOURCE

4-1 "Draft Report of a Commercialization Strategy for Energy from Urban Wastes." Adapted from a U.S. Department of Energy publication titled *Commercialization Strategy Report for Energy from Urban Wastes (TID-28852).* Donald Walter, Steve Levy, and Charlotte Rines, authors. 26 pp.   403

4-2 "Energy from Waste: A Report on Mass Burning in Europe." *NCRR Bulletin,* Vol. 10, No. 1 (March 1980), pp. 14-16. Thomas Cunningham, author.   417

4-3 "Energy from Waste Utilization in the Federal Republic of Germany." Adapted from an article by the same title in *Solid Waste,* Vol. LXVIII, No. 2 (February 1978), pp. 64-82. L. Barniske, author. Reprinted with permission of the Institute of Solid Waste Management.   421

4-4 "30 Years of Refuse Fired Boiler Experience." Adapted from an article in *Resource Recovery and Conservation,* Vol. 4, No. 1 (May 1979), 83-98. Charles O. Velzy, author. Reprinted with permission of Elsevier Scientific Publishing Company.   429

4-5 "Energy from Waste: Saugus, Massachusetts." *NCRR Bulletin,* Vol. VII, No. 2 (Spring 1977), pp. 46-52. E. Joseph Duckett, author.   438

4-6 "Air Pollution from Burning Refuse Fuels." *NCRR Bulletin,* Vol. VII, No. 1 (Winter 1977), pp. 15-27. James Abert, author.   445

4-7 "Pre-Burn Separation Should Limit Metal Emissions." *Waste Age,* Vol. 9, No. 9 (September 1978), pp. 51-59. Stephen Law, Benjamin Haynes, and William J. Campbell, authors. Reprinted with permission of the National Solid Wastes Management Association.   460

4-8 "Prepared vs Unprepared Refuse Fired Steam Generators." *First International Conference on Conversion of Refuse to Energy.* Montreux, Switzerland, November 3-5, 1975, pp. 407-415. L.J. Cohan, J.H. Fernandes, M.E. Maguire, and R.C. Shenk, authors. Reprinted with permission of the Joint Engineering Societies.   466

4-9 "The City of Akron's Waste-to-Steam Facility." *NCRR Bulletin,* Vol. 10, No. 2 (June 1980), pp. 36-42. Ronald W. Musselwhite, author.   473

4-10 "Processed Municipal Refuse: A Fuel for Small Power Plant Boilers." Reprinted from *News of Environmental Research in Cincinnati,* (November 15, 1976), 4 pp. U.S. Environmental Protection Agency. Donald A. Oberacker, author.   481

4-11 "District Heating with Refuse Derived Fuel at Wright-Patterson Air Force Base." *Mechanical Engineering,* Vol. 24, No. 11 (December 1977), pp. 35-38. A.J. Buonicone and J.P. Waltz, authors. Reprinted with permission of the American Society of Mechanical Engineers.   485

4-12 "Waste Fuel Densification: Review of the Technology and Applications." Paper presented at the International Conference on Prepared Fuels and Resource Recovery Technology, Nashville, Tennessee, February 10-13, 1981, 19 pp. Jay A. Campbell, author.   493

4-13 "Economic Factors in Refuse Derived Fuel Utilization." *Proceedings of the 1978 National Waste Processing Conference,* Chicago, Illinois, May 7-10, 1978, pp. 277-284. John L. Rose, author. Reprinted with permission of the American Society of Mechanical Engineers.   502

4-14 "Economic and Flow Stream Analyses of the Ames Solid Waste Recovery System." Paper presented at the *1979 AIIE Annual Conference,* San Francisco, California, May 22, 25, 1979, 9 pp. S. Keith Adams, John C. Even, Jr., Petras Gheresus, and Robert A. Olexsey, authors. Reprinted with permission of AIIE.   511

4-15 "RDF: Quality Must Precede Quantity. A Trommel Stage Can Help." *Waste Age,* Vol. 9, No. 4 (April 1978), pp. 100-106. G.M. Savage, L.F. Diaz, and G.J. Trezek, authors. Reprinted with permission of the National Solid Wastes Management Association.   522

4-16 "Eco-Fuel® II: The Third Generation." Paper presented at the *International Conference on Prepared Fuels and Resource Recovery Technology,* Nashville, Tennessee, February 10-13, 1981, 19 pp. F. Hasselriis, H. Master, C. Konheim, H. Betzig, authors.   527

4-17 "RDF as a Kiln Fuel." *Proceedings of 1980 National Waste Processing Conference,* Washington, D.C., May 11-14, 1980, pp. 387-400. E. Joseph Duckett and David Weiss, authors. Reprinted with permission of the American Society of Mechanical Engineers.   539

4-18 "Converting Solid Waste and Residue into Fuel." Adapted from *Chemical Engineering,* Vol. 85, No. 2 (January 2, 1978), pp. 87-94. Jerry Jones, author. Reprinted with permission of McGraw Hill, Inc.   554

4-19 "Pyrolysis in Baltimore: From Failure to Success." *NCRR Bulletin,* Vol. 10, No. 1 (March 1980), pp. 8-13. John C. Even, Jr., author. Reprinted with permission of rhw National Center for Resource Recovery.   564

4-20 "Predicting Gas Generation from Landfills." *Waste Age,* Vol. 10, No. 11 (November 1979), pp. 50-58. Robert H. Ham, author. Reprinted with permission of the National Solid Wastes Management Association.   570

4-21 "The Status of the Pompano Beach Project." Paper presented at the *American Institute of Chemical Engineering, 72nd Annual Conference,* San Francisco, California, November 29, 1979, 16 pp. Peter J. Ware, author. Printed with permission of the author.   575

4-22 "Co-disposal: A Practical Approach to Integrated Waste Management." *NCRR Bulletin,* Vol. 9, No. 3 (September 1979), pp. 64-69. Richard A. Baldwin, et al, authors.   583

Index   591

RESOURCE RECOVERY GUIDE

Part 1
National Concerns for Recycling and for Resource Recovery of Municipal Waste: Policy Perspectives

For many years, the idea of recycling materials discarded by households as waste and the combustion of that part of the waste that would burn gained its chief support from the fact that it would provide an environmentally sound means of disposal. That which could be reused would not have to be landfilled. Combustion reduces the volume of waste and, therefore, conserves landfill space. In recent years the focus has shifted to that of conservation. Recycling of materials retards their extraction from the ground and even from the forest. Wastes' energy value offers a means of decreasing the nation's dependency on overseas energy imports. What more domestic fuel is there than household discards?

In the first reading of this section Harvey Alter presents a brief summary of the status of resource recovery, with the emphasis on the conversion of municipal solid waste to energy. Where do we stand as the nation enters the decade of the 1980s? According to Alter, "The technology is available today to make a significant start, we now need the will." Part 1 of this volume of readings is designed to address the question of motivation. Why should we as a nation be desirous of recycling our waste? And, covered here to a lesser extent, what is the opportunity for waste reduction?

Following Alter's brief status report, the next reading is taken from the report of the National Commission on Supplies and Shortages. Among other topics this "blue ribbon" commission looked at recycling. The reason is that recycling affects the available supply of materials. They concluded that while not all materials can be economically recycled, present rates of recycling can be increased substantially to supply a limited but important fraction of our total needs for materials. The report looks more broadly at recycling than simply household discards. "In plant" recycling and industrial wastes are also considered. In this sense, a purpose of this reading is to place municipal waste in its appropriate perspective. The reading is well referenced, particularly to other governmental studies and the legislation that affects recycling, i.e., procurement specifications, freight rates, tax treatment of virgin materials, etc.

The next reading is a companion piece in the sense that it contrasts and compares the report of the Commission on Supplies and Shortages with a document that appeared three and a half years earlier. This was the report of the National Commission of Materials Policy. In making this comparison, David Tillman finds that "stark contrasts and discontinuities exist between the two reports." The philosophical tenets of the two commissions were quite different. Therefore, it is not surprising to find differences in their findings. The two reports make policy recommendations to change old policies, to implement new ones, and indeed, even to let some alone.

In the next reading Robert C. Anderson looks specifically at public policies toward the use of scrap materials. This is followed by a reading by W. David Conn entitled, "Waste Reduction: Issues and Policies." Anderson's work examines public policy at the national level. By way of contrast, Conn views the issue at the state level by describing the efforts of and the options open to California's Source Reduction and Packaging Policy Committee charged with the task of preparing a background report and recommending alternative methods for reducing solid waste generation. The task here, obtaining concensus, proved difficult as the reading amply illustrates.

Given this policy discussion, the next reading examines the various claims made for waste as a means of energy conservation. It is easy to talk of barrels of oil equivalents, but what does it mean? How does one sort through arithmetic equivalence, conversion equivalence, and substitution equivalence? The reading attempts to do this. Of added benefit is the fact that the literature on this issue is extensively cited.

"Notes on Changes in Energy Economics," the next reading, is included to develop an appropriate context from which to evaluate the extent to which changing energy prices may impact recycling. As pointed out in the text, it is easy to overemphasize the possible impact of the energy price revolution on substitution of secondary for virgin materials.

The next reading summarizes both the state-of-the-art of resource recovery technology and the economics of the principal candidate recovery technologies. Taken from these two perspectives alone, the reading is out of place. Later sections of the text will look in some detail at both technology and economics. The reason the reading appears here is that it develops the national perspective for resource recovery implementation. It presents an accounting of actual and planned resource recovery implementation in 1975 and then extends this through 1990. Contrasted to this forecast is an analysis of the implications of an accelerated resource recovery plant construction program that would target on the processing of 50 percent of the municipal solid waste of the 150 largest cities by 1990. The capital requirements for both the baseline and stimulated resource recovery implementation scenarios are also developed.

As mentioned earlier, a principal reason resource recovery was valued, prior to the current energy situation, was because it appeared to offer a more environmentally sound disposal method than the traditional landfill. Albert Klee and Judith Gordon examine this issue in "Resource Recovery as a Pollution-Control Device." They find in favor of resource recovery.

This is followed by one of the longest readings in this section, a reading entitled, "Handbook for Scrap Futures Markets and Futures Trading." It is a reprint of a report by Roger Dower and Robert C. Anderson prepared for the U.S. Environmental Protection Agency. While the recovery literature contains a good deal of supplementary material for the interested reader concerning most proposed governmental policy actions, this is not so in the case of futures markets, and this is the reason for presenting a fairly extensive survey, actually a "how to do it" reading, here.

In the next part of this volume a good deal of attention will be paid to the idea of planning, i.e., how to improve the resource recovery implementation process. As a lead-in to Part 2, the final reading in this section looks at a case study of state-wide solid waste management planning. California has taken a leadership position among states in this regard. What happens when a state mandates the consideration of resource recovery? Not too much, according to W. David Conn in his reading on "The Treatment of Resource Recovery in Solid Waste Management Plans."

1-1 Municipal Waste and Energy Conservation

Harvey Alter

Source: *Resource Recovery Briefs* (July 1979) National Center for Resource Recovery, 4 pp.
Reprinted with Permission of National Center for Resource Recovery

In spite of recent progress, municipal solid waste (MSW) is a virtually untapped resource, both as a conserver of energy and as a source of fuel. The fuel should be considered for new boiler installations, and can be a low-sulfur supplement to coal in many existing installations. There are also future opportunities for using the waste as a source of fuel gas. Most of the opportunities are here today.

The resource recovery processing of MSW can provide an additional source of raw materials for industries for the remanufacture of paper, steel, aluminum and glass. Today, some post-consumer wastes are used as a raw material, particularly paper of several grades. The use of recovered paper, steel, aluminum and glass saves energy compared to using existing sources of virgin materials. The amount of municipal waste (exclusive of recovered paper) estimated to be in the Standard Metropolitan Statistical Areas (SMSAs) today could provide enough material to save the country 0.4 quad of energy per year. And, the combustible portion of this waste used as fuel could provide the U.S. with nearly 0.9 quad per year. (For thermodynamic reasons, energy savings of this sort should not be expressed as barrels of oil equivalent. However, bowing to popular practice, 0.4 quad is equivalent to approximately 60 million barrels of oil and 0.9 quad is approximately 136 million barrels.)

Municipal solid waste can be used as-received to generate steam and electricity in a device called a waterwall incinerator. Alternatively, the waste can be mechanically processed by a number of schemes to produce a shredded product for use either by itself or as a supplementary fuel with coal, to generate steam. (Perhaps by one scheme, it can be processed to a form called Eco-Fuel® for use with oil in some instances.) The major advantages of processing waste are to enable convenient storage and transport of the new fuel, and to produce daily a specification commodity of constant properties that meets the handling and burning requirements of the boiler.

There is healthy competition among purveyors of various waterwall incinerator designs and of mechanical processing systems. A disadvantage of the competition is present confusion over which system is "best," if indeed such a judgment can be made. The bases for picking a system are initially simple: they are cost and compatibility of the fuel with the intended boiler. For example, if the fuel is to be stored, mixed, and burned with stoker coal, the waste has to be mechanically processed and densified into pellets or other forms to resemble the lump coal used in stoker-fired units.

The development of resource recovery technology, and its consequent cost, have suffered from an initial zeal and lack of R&D. Initially, there was an insufficient technical base for a new industry. The result was that after design, construction, and operation, plans did not meet ordinary industrial objectives for reliability and low maintenance. Also, the materials and fuel products did not always meet specification; consequently, they could not be sold on a consistent basis. As a result, municipalities and industry are now hesitant to invest. Emphasis today is, therefore, on planning — and more planning — rather than on doing.

This overview of available waste-to-energy technologies will hopefully clarify what has been learned from past experiences and how future plants can be improved.

First, waste-to-energy technologies may be divided into what is available now and what is likely to be available sometime in the future. Available now are several methods for processing MSW to solid fuels, broadly termed refuse-derived fuel (RDF). As will be seen, there are several forms of RDF.

Likely to be available in the future are the technologies for biologically digesting MSW to produce methane and pyrolysis (chemical decomposition) to produce a mixture of combustible gases or liquids, or both.

Waste can be burned, as-received and without processing, in a waterwall incinerator. Such installations now in operation are generally copies from similar plants extant in Europe and elsewhere. Plant capital and operating costs are high because this is probably the only industrial application for a non-specification fuel. The plant has to accept waste of a wide range of properties, or that which is discarded as MSW. An advantage might be that the European experiences can be used to extrapolate costs. The technology is generally considered proven, if only because there are many replicate plants.

Waste can be shredded, the magnetic metals removed and the remainder burned, which is the approach used in plants under construction in Albany, N.Y., and operating in Hamilton, Ontario. This relatively inexpensive approach passes a great deal of noncombustible matter through the firebox.

An alternative has been to air classify, or winnow, the waste to remove some of the noncombustible material. The resulting fuel still contains a large fraction of noncombustible material; nonetheless, it can be burned by itself (as in Akron, Ohio, or Niagara Falls, N.Y.) or with coal (as in Ames, Iowa; Milwaukee, Wisc.; Chicago, Ill.; or Monroe County, N.Y.). When burned with coal, the fuel is shredded a second time to reduce the particle size.

In all of the above examples, the waste is shredded and classified dry. In some instances (Hempstead, N.Y., and Dade County, Fla.), shredding and classification are done in a water

suspension and the fuel is squeezed to remove most of the water. (The plant in Hempstead is operating and the one in Dade County is under construction.)

Various processes differ in detail but broadly, not in principle. When possible, implementors seek to co-fire the RDF with coal in a utility boiler because such boilers are generally large enough to accept all of the RDF a community could produce and obviously, resource recovery costs less using an existing boiler. However, there is no technical reason why a purpose-built boiler could not be used to provide steam or electricity, or both, from RDF.

There have been proposals, and some test firings, to use forms of RDF for other than raising steam. Particular proposals have been to use RDF in cement manufacture, aggregate drying and as a fuel for the incineration of sewage sludge (termed co-disposal). The first industrial application will be a plant for co-disposal soon to begin operation in Duluth, Minn.

Fuel users have objected to the high ash (or noncombustible) content of most RDF, and a few installations (Milwaukee and Ames) have retrofitted screens to sieve the RDF at some stage of processing to remove ash. In a different approach, one plant sieves the shredded waste (Madison, Wisc.) as part of producing RDF and two plants (New Orleans, La., and Bridgeport, Conn.) sieve the as-received waste to remove noncombustible material before the first shredding step. This latter approach is reported to be extremely effective in producing a low ash fuel.

Future plants should include some type of screening step in the process flow so as to narrow the range of fuel properties and thus improve the quality of the product sold. Screening is relatively cheap and effective; some day screens may supplant air classifiers. However, more R&D is needed so as to be able to choose one type of screen over another.

The knowledge is available to overcome many of the recognized inadequacies of waste-to-energy plants. Generally, these plants have a poor reputation — sometimes deservedly — but given the chance, the plants can be greatly improved. New ones promise to be much more reliable. The reason waste-to-energy plants have a poor reputation is perhaps because unlike some technologies, resource recovery has not matured through a process of research, pilot plant, semi-works, etc. Rather, it began, and continues, as an art. As a result, technical problems and questions constantly arise, plants do not work as well as they might, and implementors find their investment insufficient to meet technical, sales and cost objectives. Importantly, profitability is not high enough for the private sector to invest large sums in R&D. Several government agencies, notably the Bureau of Mines, EPA, and DOE, have established R&D programs; but at present, the DOE program is the only one essentially functioning.

The DOE program is directed mostly at solving operational and design problems identified in existing plants. It will, however, be a long time before the results of this research can be incorporated into new or existing plants. In the meantime, implementors perceive technical and economic risks and are fearful that the plant they build will not work, and that they will not be able to sell the recovered materials and energy products on a consistent basis. Apparently, implementors are waiting until such risks either disappear or are greatly lessened. In the meantime, few new plants are being built and resources are being buried.

There have been many proposals of programs to alleviate this situation, such as guaranteed loans and construction of demonstration plants. Clearly, we need more plants, incorporating the new designs based on what has been learned from operating the old. *The art cannot advance if there are no new trials, no experimentation, no new facilities.*

At present, implementors of new plants are generally reluctant to incorporate innovation. Understandably, a municipality must be prudent and thus seeks the "proven" technology of processes which are in operation elsewhere. Government support of innovation and R&D is viewed as a federal role, not state or local. Local governments would be hesitant today to invest in a process which merely placed a screen in a different location than as in present plants, or to accept a new kind of screen or other device which maybe has great promise but has not yet been used in resource recovery. A way must be found to encourage what might be termed "prudent innovation" in order to advance the art of resource recovery.

This brief technological overview hopefully communicated that the state-of-the-art today permits construction and operation of waste-to-energy plants. The question at hand is, what can be done to build more and better plants?

First, there is need for more R&D. Then, steps should be taken to reduce some of the risk currently impeding decisions for resource recovery. In the latter case, there have been proposals for guaranteed loans and demonstration grants. Though considered, little has been done.

The time has come to offer some new proposals to address the risks perceived by resource recovery plant owners and fuel users. The owners are concerned if the plants will work to specification and the users are concerned whether the new form of fuel will damage or otherwise interfere with the efficient use of their boilers (or other recovered materials interfere with their production processes).

The owners' concerns can be alleviated by a program which, after review of plans prior to construction, provides a fund (perhaps a maximum percentage of total capital cost), which will be available for repairs and retrofits after construction and start-up, to correct operating deficiencies. After some period of time, operating shortcomings (such as failure of equipment to recover to specification) can be documented and identified and a plan formulated and costed to change equipment, or whatever else is needed, to make the plant fully operable. During the periods of problem identification and correction, the fund may also supplement the revenue shortfall from selling non-specification products at a discount. This feature will encourage continued operation of the plant, even if sub-optimal.

Fuel users are concerned about the long-term effects on their equipment from the new fuel. This may be alleviated by the establishment of a new form of boiler insurance against the extra and unknown risk of premature failure due to the new fuel. Because private carriers could not now estimate the risk, the government may have to participate in the underwriting, so as to bring the premiums within the range of normal types of business or boiler insurance premiums. This program could well be applied to either existing or new plants, so as to expand energy conservation and take greater advantage of existing plant facilities.

New programs of these types are likely to encourage the construction of many new waste-to-energy plants because the owners will be assured that ultimately their plants will work economically and their customers will be assured that the new fuels (or other products) will not cause them large maintenance bills at some future date. In this way, the current state-of-the-art of resource recovery can advance and the nation can achieve greater energy conservation and environmental benefit from what is now a waste. The technology is available today to make a significant start. We now need the will.

1-2 Recycling

Source: Reprinted From *Government and the Nation's Resources:* Report of the National Commission on Supplies and Shortages (December 1976) pp. 155–172. Reprinted with Permission of: None Needed.

Recycling affects the available supply of materials. Sizeable amounts of some major materials already are recycled, but as a percentage of total consumption, recycling has been static or declining in America, and only a small portion of postconsumer waste is recycled. Not all of the materials consumed can be economically recycled but present rates of recycling can be increased substantially, to supply a limited but important fraction of our total needs for materials.

The term "urban ore" has been applied to the materials used up and discarded by consumers. Some economic considerations discourage the recycling of "urban ore" in much the same way that similar considerations discourage the exploitation of virgin ore deposits. Moreover, a number of Government practices effectively (if inadvertently) discourage recycling. Such practices are deviations from the principle that the rate of recycling should reflect informed decisions made on the basis of the true cost of materials. Within the last year, Congress has taken legislative action to eliminate discrimination against recycled materials in procurement specifications, possible discrimination against recyclables in regulated freight rates, and a variety of institutional barriers which cause localities to miss recycling opportunities. Further action should be taken in furtherance of the true-cost-of-materials principle — for example, repeal of tax subsidies to producers of virgin materials and the imposition of disposal charges and refundable deposits on containers and paper products.

THE POTENTIAL FOR RECYCLING

The American economy uses approximately 4.5 billion tons of nonfood materials each year. A large fraction of current consumption of major materials is met from recycling. However, as Table 1 shows, the portion of materials demand met from recycling is static or declining overall — and most recycling comes from scrap created by industrial production and fabrication processes rather than from materials which consumers discard.

Proponents claim four major benefits from increased recycling in the United States.

1. Increasing demands on the world's virgin resources are making their extraction more and more costly in terms of capital requirements and environmental degradation. Recycling material in postconsumer waste can reduce those demands. Once such material is discarded and buried, it becomes much more difficult to recover economically.

2. The production of manufactured products from recycled materials generally results in a significant saving of energy. For example, energy equivalent to 6,700 kwh is required to produce a ton of steel from virgin resources, and only one-third of that amount is required to manufacture a ton from scrap; 70,000 kwh are required to extract a ton of aluminum from virgin resources, and only one-twentieth of that amount to

Table 1. Total Recycling as a Percent of Consumption.

	Steel	Aluminum	Copper	Paper
1955	51	21	53	26
1965	50	17	61	21
1973	51	18	55	21
Postconsumer Waste Recycling as a Percent of Consumption				
1973	16	3	19	14

Sources: Statistics for steel, aluminum, and copper recycling are derived from United States Department of the Interior, Bureau of Mines *Minerals Yearbook;* statistics for aluminum and copper recycling are limited to purchased scrap. Statistics for paper are also limited to purchased scrap; they are taken from American Paper Institute, *Statistics of Paper and Paperboard.*

extract it from scrap; substantially more energy is required to manufacture a ton of paper from virgin resources than from scrap.[1]

3. Recycling provides a domestic source of materials. This reduces the political uncertainties of foreign sources of supply and the adverse impact of the demand for imported materials on the Nation's balance of trade.

4. A fourth major benefit is beyond the narrowly defined bounds of materials policy. Solid waste handling accounts for the second largest expenditure of our major cities; cities can expect a 20 to 30 percent increase in real disposal costs over the next 10 years; landfill sites are becoming scarce in heavily populated areas and disposal presents air and water pollution problems. One potential by-product of recycling is a smaller waste stream whose constituent parts are more easily managed.

To what extent can increased recycling of industrial and postconsumer solid waste provide these benefits?

It has been assumed in the past that all the industrial waste economically available is being recycled. This assumption is based on the fact that much industrial scrap is high-grade and available at convenient locations. There has been relatively little study of actual rates of recycling industrial solid waste, however, and there is a large new source of such waste about which even less is known. Under the Clean Air Act and the Federal Water Pollution Control Act, the Environmental Protection Agency

(EPA) has promulgated regulations which require that materials formerly discharged as air and water pollutants must now be collected and handled as solid waste. The mineral concentrations in many such wastes exceed those in many ores now being processed.[2]

There has been much more study of municipally-collected postconsumer solid waste, including some 80 million tons of metals, paper, and glass. At present less than 10 percent of this material is recycled.[3] Excluding the postconsumer wastes that are discarded in remote locations, lost in litter, or are unusable for technical reasons, it has been estimated that recycling the remainder could contribute significantly to the Nation's supply of materials. Three recent estimates, shown in Table 2, may be regarded as "ball-park" figures.

The estimates in Table 2 are consistent with the independent assessments made by the Commission staff: ferrous scrap potentially recoverable from municipal solid waste has been put at 4 or 5 percent of total consumption by industry sources; skyrocketing costs of plant and equipment, energy, and raw materials will provide substantial incentives to increase the recycling of aluminum; the chances of increased recycling of copper are more modest.[4] It has also been estimated that increased recovery of resources (both materials and energy) from postconsumer solid waste could save energy equivalent to 521,000 barrels of oil per day — 7 percent of all the fuel consumed by utilities in 1970.[5] Balance-of-trade effects would admittedly be modest, but in the right direction. Currently available resource recovery systems can readily reduce by 65 percent the amount of solid waste which must be disposed of.[6]

**Table 2. Potential Additional Materials from Recycling of Postconsumer Waste
(percent of domestic consumption).**

	Steel	Aluminum	Copper	Paper
Postconsumer waste (Population Commission, 1972)	2	15	10	—
Municipal solid waste (EPA, 1974)	7	8	5	14
Municipal solid waste (FEA, 1974)	4	6	—	14

Sources: Fischman and Landsberg, "Adequacy of Nonfuel Minerals and Forest Resources," in Commission on Population Growth and the American Future, *Research Reports* Vol. 3, 98 (1972). These estimates are based on projections of the amounts of materials likely to be in use in the year 2000 and of the useful life (and "retirement" rate) of such materials.

   EPA, *Second Report to Congress: Resource Recovery and Source Reduction* 14 (1974). These estimates are based on EPA calculations of the amounts of materials in municipal solid waste collected in standard metropolitan statistical areas during 1971; recovery efficiencies of 30% for paper and 80% for other materials are assumed.

   Federal Energy Administration, *Report to Congress: Energy Conservation Study* 83 (1974). These estimates are based on calculations by Resource Planning Associates of the amounts of materials in municipal solid waste collected in standard metropolitan statistical areas during 1970; recovery efficiencies of 80% for steel, 60% for aluminum and 30% for paper are assumed.

OBSTACLES AND OPPORTUNITIES

If recycling is economically beneficial, why isn't more material being recycled? The economic value of some material in postconsumer waste is not as high as the cost of exploiting it, often for much the same reasons that value of virgin material is insufficient to justify exploitation. The material in some postconsumer waste may not be sufficiently concentrated to be of economic value — for example, roadside litter. Or the material may be so far removed from processing plants that transportation costs would be prohibitive — for example, waste in remote rural locations. Not only may the positive economic value of material in postconsumer waste be insufficient, but its negative economic value may also be insufficient. The economic value of recycling material in postconsumer waste is the sum of the money realized from recovery of the materials and the money saved from not having to dispose of the material. While actual postcollection disposal costs in the Northeast may run to $15 a ton and provide a strong incentive to recycle rather than dispose, such costs in the West can be as low as $1 or $2 per ton and thus afford little incentive.

   However, quite apart from these market considerations, some Government practices discourage recycling: these practices deviate from the principle that the rate of recycling should reflect informed decisions made on the basis of the true costs of materials. Until 1975, congres-

sional enactments which have dealt explicitly with recycling[7] have been limited to authorizing further study or allocating Federal money for technical research, development and demonstrations.* Recently, the Congress has been giving much closer attention to recycling.

Federal Funding of Demonstration Projects

The 94th Congress considered and rejected several recommendations for Federal funding of projects to demonstrate the recovery of resources from solid waste. A House Committee marked up legislation which would have authorized loan guarantees for projects to demonstrate

---

*The Solid Waste Disposal Act, as amended by the Resource Recovery Act of 1970, does require EPA to establish guidelines for solid waste collection, separation, disposal, and recovery systems. Essentially, the guidelines are binding only on Federal agencies which dispose of solid waste. Under the Act, EPA has promulgated guidelines which:
  (1) Require a deposit of at least 5¢ on all beverage containers sold in Federal facilities;
  (2) Require any Federal facility disposing of 100 tons or more per day of solid waste to separate and recover materials or energy, or both, from it;
  (3) Require Federal facilities to separate at the source, collect and sell high-grade paper for the purpose of recycling (in offices of over 100 workers) used newspapers (on residential facilities of more than 500 families) and corrugated containers (from any commercial establishment generating 10 or more tons per month).
Federal agencies may determine not to comply with these guidelines upon a finding that compliance would be economically impracticable.

the recovery of resources from solid waste in amounts up to $2.5 billion. A House-Senate conference committee recommended an authorization of $300 million in loan guarantees to produce energy from biomass (defined as urban and industrial waste, crops, animal waste, sewage sludge), and an authorization of $5 million for a price-support program to demonstrate the production of fuels and energy-intensive products from solid waste. And four House committees reported a bill authorizing loan guarantees in varying amount up to $3.5 billion for projects to demonstrate the production of synthetic fuels from domestic resources, including solid waste.

None of these bills is an effective approach to the problem of increasing recycling. It does not appear that increased recycling is being thwarted by any lack of government-supported research and development. R&D programs on resource recovery are currently maintained by the Office of Solid Waste Management Programs in EPA (which has an appropriation of $15.7 million for fiscal 1977), by the Solid Waste Division of the Bureau of Mines (which administers programs funded at $5.5 million for fiscal 1977), and by the Energy Research and Development Administration (ERDA), which has appropriations of $4.6 million for its Urban Waste Technology Branch and $5.2 million for its fuels-from-biomass program in fiscal 1977. There are areas which warrant continuing technological research, but there is a broad consensus that inadequate technology is not the major (or even *a* major) restraint on recycling. The House Committee on Government Operations has reported that:

> Representatives of municipalities, of State Government, of the Federal Government, of private industry and of financial institutions are in basic agreement that the technology of resource recovery is now available.[8]

Besides, until recently most recycling of municipal solid waste was accomplished by a low-technology method — requiring users to separate their trash. The preliminary results of demonstration projects currently assisted by EPA suggest that source separation is still a cost-effective means of resource recovery.

The availability of Federal money for demonstration projects can lead local governments to uneconomic decisions: only by adopting new high-technology, capital-intensive systems can cities transfer their costs to the Federal Government. To subsidize the recovery of energy, but not of materials, from solid waste would be to compound pressures for the inefficient use of resources. (For example, use of old newspapers as fuel is signficantly less energy-efficient than recycling of the same newspapers into newsprint.[9]) Furthermore, Federal investment decisions can be uneconomic and counter-productive — a substantial risk in any system which is (necessarily) driven by political considerations.

The EPA demonstration program, perhaps because of its modest size, has been able to avoid political pressures to a large degree; the program appears to be more successful than other Federally-funded demonstration programs included in a recent study sponsored by the Experimental Technology Incentives Program of the National Bureau of Standards. This study concluded that demonstration projects have a narrow scope for effective use and that diffusion of the technology to be demonstrated depends on "market pull" rather than "technology push."[10]

Some high-technology local projects for resource recovery are in operation or under construction without Federal support, and investment bankers have expressed interest in financing other projects.[11] The House Committee on Government Operations has concluded that:

> Congress should not authorize Federal financial assistance . . . (or) Federal guarantees of municipal or State bonds . . . to finance resource recovery or other municipal solid waste disposal systems.[12]

These considerations all suggest that Government funding of resource recovery demonstrations should not be increased substantially above its present modest size. The Resource Conservation and Recovery Act of 1976 recognizes these considerations by providing that EPA may not fund a full-scale resource recovery facility unless it finds:

- that the facility will demonstrate at full scale a new or significantly improved technology or process, a practical and significant improvement in solid waste management practice, or the technical feasibility and cost-effectiveness of an existing but unproven process;
- that the facility will not duplicate any other facility on which construction has already begun; and
- that the facility is not likely to be constructed or operated without such funding.

To the extent that solid waste disposal costs present overwhelming financial problems to cities which justify Federal assistance, these problems would best be met through some form of general revenue sharing, and not through a system of financial assistance which would require a city to adopt something other than the least expensive solution.

The Commission opposes Federal funding of systems to recover energy or materials from waste, whether by means of grants, loan guarantees, or price supports; exception should be made only for the limited number of systems which possess the characteristics of true demonstration projects.

Tax Subsidies

There is a broad consensus that lack of long-term, stable demand is a major deterrent to utilization of resources in postconsumer waste. The degree to which tax preferences to the consumption of virgin over recycled materials undermine long-term, stable demand for recycled materials has not yet been adequately calculated; however, scattered pieces of evidence indicate that such preferences have a substantial undermining effect. The 94th Congress considered proposals to repeal tax subsidies for the consumption of virgin materials and to create countervailing tax subsidies for the consumption of recycled materials.*

The Federal Government gives tax subsidies to the consumption of virgin materials both by allowing the deduction from income of a fixed percentage of the value of mineral production** and by allowing capital gains treatment of in-

come derived from the increase in the value of standing timber.

Minerals. The percentage depletion allowance in particular has been the subject of extensive study. The Treasury Department has estimated that, largely as a result of this tax subsidy, mineral industries have an effective tax rate of about 25 percent of total net income, compared with 43 percent for other manufacturing industries.[13]

Percentage depletion has encouraged the growth of large vertically-integrated materials companies which shelter their income by maintaining high prices for their virgin material input and allocating their profits to virgin material production.[14] The dominant materials companies are structured, both physically and institutionally, to use wholly-owned virgin materials as their primary feed. They also make routine use of high-grade scrap produced in their own plants and the manufacturing and fabricating processes of their customers. But usually they

---

*Amendment No. 1882, proposed by Senator Haskell to H.R. 10612 and rejected by the full Senate, would have effectively repealed a variety of tax subsidies, including the percentage depletion allowance for minerals and capital gains treatment for timber. H.R. 10612, the Tax Reform Act of 1976, as reported by the Senate Finance Committee, would have allowed a taxpayer, as a credit against tax, a percentage of the qualifying amount of recyclable solid waste material which he purchases and recycles in the U.S.; the amount of purchases which qualifies would be the amount which exceeds 75% of annual average purchases in the preceding three years; the percentage allowed would equal ½ of the percent of the depletion allowance for metals (precious metals are excluded), 10% for textile and paper waste, and 5% for glass and plastics; recyclable solid waste materials would be defined as postconsumer solid waste and purchased scrap (if the latter is from fabricators who do not produce their own feed material). The full Senate deleted this provision. A similar tax credit, proposed by the House Ways and Means Committee, in the Resource Conservation and Conversion Act of 1975, was defeated last year.

**Mineral companies have the option of using the same type of cost depletion which is available to other industries — i.e., they may divide the original cost of developing the mineral deposit by the number of tons to be produced, and deduct this amount as part of the cost of each ton mined. In 1960, cost depletion accounted for less than 10% of the depletion taken by the minerals industry. Miller, "Percentage Depletion and the Level of Domestic Mineral Production." 15 *Natural Resources* J. 242 (1975).

purchase postconsumer scrap only to respond to peaks in the demand for their product; accordingly, their demand for recycled material fluctuates over a wide range. Physical reasons alone do not account for such a structure: postconsumer scrap has the advantage over virgin materials of being found in bulk at the point of ultimate consumption; there are certainly substantial problems in preparing lower grades of scrap for industrial use, but there are also substantial problems in preparing lower grades of virgin materials. However, industry has devoted great effort to beneficiating low-grade ores and little or no effort to recovering resources in postconsumer waste.

The American steel industry, for example, is dominated by eight vertically-integrated companies which accounted for 75 percent of production in 1974; more than 85 percent of the ore which they consumed came from company-owned sources.[15] The industry has consistently raised the price at which it sells itself ore, regardless of fluctuations in the demand for steel; on the other hand, the price of scrap purchased has fluctuated sharply with demand (see Table 3). In recent years, the export price of No. 1 heavy melting scrap has regularly exceeded the domestic price; since foreign purchasers must bear transportation charges as well, it is probable that the domestic steel industry substantially under-values scrap. It has been estimated that in the United States the effect of tax preferences more than accounts for the difference between the cost of producing a ton of steel from scrap, and the lower cost of producing it from virgin material.*

Econometric studies (performed for EPA) have concluded that the repeal of tax subsidies for the consumption of virgin materials would increase the current price of virgin materials only slightly; the resulting increases in rates of recycling were estimated at about 1 to 5 percent.[16] However, these studies of marginal price effects are based on an historical record which reveals that there is relatively little price elasticity of demand for postconsumer scrap.** Thus, they assume the continued existence of an historical industry structure based at least in part upon the same tax subsidies. Only time can tell the extent to which repeal of these subsidies would change industry structure.

Recently, materials companies have demonstrated that they will integrate vertically into scrap sources of supply, given the right economic circumstances.[17]

The argument that repeal of tax subsidies will increase the rate of recycling is supported by incomplete evidence. But the evidence to support continuation of such tax subsidies is even weaker.

In the past it has been politically difficult to repeal existing tax subsidies, such as the percentage depletion allowance for minerals. In spite of this history, the Congress terminated the percentage depletion allowance for major oil companies in 1975. (The House voted, 248–163, to repeal the entire allowance; the Senate, by a vote of 47–41, retained the allowance for independent producers)†

---

*See EPA, *Second Report to Congress: Resource Recovery and Source Reduction* 35 (1974). The cost of a ton of steel using pig iron was estimated to be $40.50; the cost of a ton of steel using scrap was $43.00; the tax benefits to virgin iron ore and coal exceed $2.50. This calculation is confirmed by more recent cost estimates in Cosman, "Studies of Recycling Problems in Selected Industries," in Commission Document, *Additional Background Studies.*

**See, e.g., Charles River Associates, Inc. *A Study of the Ferrous Scrap Market During the Shortage Period of 1973-1974* (June 1976), p. 7-4. While the *demand* for postconsumer scrap is relatively inelastic, the *supply* of postconsumer scrap is highly price-elastic. *Ibid.* The Treasury Department has concluded that:

> most scrap or waste that can be economically used is already collected. The cost of substantially expanding collection is prohibitive. Therefore, an increase in recycling is not prevented by any tax incentive-induced reduction in the sale price of competitive virgin materials, but by the costs of collection. Administration Position, Hearings on Certain Provisions of the Tax Reform Bill (H.R. 10612) before the Senate Committee on Finance, July 20, 1976.

The premise of the Treasury Department argument is not supported by the evidence. Industry has historically been capable of recycling far higher percentages of aluminum and paper scrap, for example. See Table 1. An industry-sponsored study estimates that scrap dealers now have in-place capacity to process more than twice the previous record annual demand for ferrous scrap. See Battelle Columbus Laboratories, *The Processing Capacity of the Ferrous Scrap Industry* (August 10, 1976).

†*Cf. The National Democratic Platform 1976,* p. 48: "Economic inequities created by subsidies for virgin materials to the disadvantage of recycled materials must be eliminated. Depletion allowances and unequal freight rates serve to discourage the growing numbers of businesses engaged in recycling efforts."

Table 3. Steel Production and Ore and Scrap Prices, 1950–1975.

Year	Steel Produced (Millions of Tons)	Price of Ore ($/Ton)	Composite Price of No. 1 Heavy Melting Scrap ($/Ton)
1950	72	4.99	35
1951	79	5.46	43
1952	68	6.09	42
1953	80	6.76	40
1954	63	6.99	29
1955	85	7.12	40
1956	83	7.75	53
1957	80	8.33	47
1958	60	8.39	38
1959	69	8.69	38
1960	71	8.79	33
1961	66	8.99	36
1962	71	8.84	28
1963	76	9.22	27
1964	85	9.52	36
1965	93	9.33	34
1966	90	9.49	31
1967	84	9.92	28
1968	92	10.21	26
1969	93	10.34	31
1970	91	10.80	45
1971	87	11.55	35
1972	92	12.20	37
1973	111	12.84	58
1974	110	16.34	109
1975	80	21.41	72

Sources: Figures for steel produced are those of shipments in American Iron & Steel Institute. *Annual Statistical Report.* The price of ore represents the average value of domestic ore at the mme. per gross ton, this price and that of No. 1 heavy melting scrap are derived from United States Department of the Interior. Bureau of Mines *Minerals Yearbook.*

Repeal of the percentage depletion allowance for minerals would probably make little difference in the near-term availability of virgin materials: the allowance may only be taken on one-half of profits; thus, if a mineral deposit is not very profitable, the allowance affords little incentive to produce. It now appears that most depletion is taken at the full statutory rate; i.e., on non-marginal deposits which would be mined without regard to any tax subsidy. (For example, if depletion is taken on a copper mine at the full statutory rate [15 percent], then the profit on the mine must be equal to at least 30 percent of the value of production.)[18]

Repeal of tax subsidies could affect the long-term availability of domestic minerals by lowering the after-tax return on capital from domestic mineral exploitation. Lowering the return on capital of the mineral industries relative to other industries would not be entirely negative: the percentage depletion allowance for minerals currently distorts resource allocation toward capital- (and energy-) intensive exploitation of lower-grade domestic ore. Federal Trade Commission figures suggest that in recent years before- and after-tax rates of profit on stockholders' equity for corporations in the mining industry have been substantially greater than the rate of profit for all manufacturing corporations.[19] The mining industry has urged in defense of the mineral depletion allowance that it will need to raise vast amounts of capital over the coming years.[20] But the industry has made no attempt to demonstrate that the Government should favor *its* efforts to raise capital over the efforts of other industries. Tax equity and economic efficiency would be better served if the Federal Government considered the needs of the mineral industry for tax relief in raising capital* together with the needs of other industries, and not as a class apart.

If tax subsidies were repealed, prices would bear the full burden of stimulating virgin mineral production. Congressional opponents of percentage depletion for oil and gas argued that prices rather than subsidies are the appropriate method of stimulating production.[21]

The mining industry has also urged that the continuation of tax subsidies protects the national interest in an assured supply of minerals.[22] But the cost of tax subsidies is substantial: it has been estimated that the revenue loss from the percentage depletion allowance for minerals will exceed $850 million in fiscal year 1977.[23] Because the percentage depletion allowance for

---

*COMMISSIONER WEINBERG: If the public is to provide capital for private firms through tax subsidies, it (i.e., the government as the representative of the public) should obtain an equity interest in the firm in return for its capital contribution. (See colloquy on this point between Mr. Charles Carlisle, Vice President, St. Joe Mineral Company and myself, Commission Document, *Public Hearings on Problems of Supplies and Shortages.)*

minerals offers the least incentive to the exploitation of marginal deposits, it is not well designed to increase mineral supplies. The Treasury Department estimated in 1969 that the percentage depletion allowance for oil and gas cost about $1.6 billion in tax revenue for additional reserves worth only $0.15 billion.[24] The cost of tax subsidies as a method of protecting the national interest in an assured supply of minerals should be measured against costs of other methods of preventing disruption of foreign supply — such as stockpiling. The latter method may be many times cheaper.*

In sum, the cost of the percentage depletion allowance for minerals is substantial in terms of lost revenue. While the marginal price effect of this tax subsidy appears to be negligible, it is a strong incentive to an industry structure which is inimical to the use of resources in postconsumer waste. The benefits derived from the percentage depletion allowance do not appear to be proportionate to the cost.

Timber. The consequences of capital gains treatment for timber have been studied less thoroughly than the consequences of percentage depletion for minerals. There are some similarities. The Treasury Department has estimated that the lumber industry has a tax rate of only 30 percent, largely as a result of capital gains treatment for timber;[25] the revenue loss from this tax subsidy will be about $200 million in fiscal year 1977.[26] Treasury has identified capital gains treatment for timber as a cause of the shift in ownership of timberland toward large, vertically-integrated corporations which shelter their income by maintaining high timber prices.[27] The twenty largest paper companies accounted for 65 percent of all the paper and paperboard made in the United States during

1974; eighteen of these companies had timber holdings totalling 37 million acres in the United States and 4 million acres in Canada.[28] The Treasury Department reported in 1969 that:

> The tax advantage of capital gains treatment of timber accrues mainly to large corporations and high-income individuals. Small corporations with taxable income less than $25,000 do not benefit from the capital gains provision. In 1965 there were 13,251 corporate returns filed in the lumber and paper industries. Of these, five companies reported 51.3 percent of the long-term capital gains.[29]

Although it is difficult to assign a causal relationship on the present evidence, the rate of paper recycling in the United States has declined from 35 percent to 21 percent since capital gains treatment for timber was enacted (over President Roosevelt's veto) in 1944.[30] The major consumers of recycled paper are, for the most part, not the largest paper companies but a handful of companies without major timber holdings.[31] The industry's demand for recycled paper is so unstable that waste paper prices fell during 1974 from $60 to $5 per ton; sometimes a buyer could not be found at any price.

However, there are complicating factors in assessing the consequences of capital gains treatment for timber, such as industry's extensive cutting of timber from public lands.[32] The matter is further complicated by the fact that capital gains treatment for timber is an extension of a more general provision of the tax code applicable to other long-lived assets; the Commission has not examined the question of equitable application of the capital gains provisions to timber versus other assets. Nonetheless, the Congress should require a thorough justification of this tax subsidy, before determining to continue it.

Countervailing Tax Proposal. During the 94th Congress, the House Ways and Means Committee and the Senate Finance Committee each reported proposals to create a countervailing tax subsidy in the form of a tax credit for purchase of recyclable solid waste materials. These proposals would have substantially increased,

---

*The Commission has sought the views of the Department of the Interior and the Bureau of Mines on this subject. The Assistant Secretary of the Interior for Energy and Minerals has informed the Commission that "quantitative answers will be exceedingly difficult to derive. It is my firm judgment that the depletion allowance is fully justified, notwithstanding the present difficulty in quantitative justification." See letter of November 8, 1976 from Dr. William L. Fisher to Dr. George C. Eads in Commission Document, *Public Hearing on Problems of Materials Supplies and Shortages.*

rather than reduced, the subsidy of materials consumption by the general tax rolls. It has been estimated that the Senate Finance Committee bill would have reduced budget receipts by an estimated $345 million in fiscal 1981.[33] According to past estimates, tax subsidies for virgin material consumption are an inefficient means of expanding the supply of minerals; there is no reason to suppose that a tax credit for the purchase of recycled materials would be a more efficient expenditure of tax dollars. Apart from these general considerations, both proposals would have allowed substantial windfalls in the form of credits for the recycling of high-grade purchased industrial scrap:

In the absence of compelling evidence for its continuation, the Commission recommends the repeal of the percentage depletion allowance for minerals; the Commission opposes the creation of new tax subsidies for the consumption of recycled materials.*

Internalizing Disposal Costs

Governments discourage the recycling of containers and paper products by assessing the cost

---

*COMMISSIONERS GREENSPAN, HOUTHAKKER, LYNN, SEIDMAN, AND SIMON: Repeal of the percentage depletion allowance would improve economic efficiency by eliminating an artificial bias toward virgin material use, but would raise the effective corporation income tax rate. Repeal of percentage depletion should be accompanied by a compensating reduction in general corporation income tax rates sufficient to offset the revenue effect of removing the depletion allowance. However, this does not imply that we believe the present level of corporate taxation to be appropriate.

COMMISSIONER WEINBERG: This recommendation should have included a call for ending the capital gains tax subsidy for standing timber. The only significant argument advanced against such a recommendation was that since capital gains treatment applies generally, timber should not be singled out for its elimination. In my view, favoritism to capital gains income over earned income should be ended across the board. In any event, timber harvesting has never been eligible for capital gains treatment under general provisions of the tax code. Congress singled out timber to receive special capital gains treatment in the Revenue Act of 1943. In his veto message, Franklin Roosevelt (himself a tree farmer) argued that timber should continue to be treated as a crop and its sale treated as ordinary income. I believe he was right, even though his veto was overridden.

of discarding such materials against general revenues rather than against the price of the containers and paper products. As recently as 1960, 95 percent of the soft drinks and 50 percent of the beer were sold in returnable containers; the price of the beverage included the cost of distributing containers, collecting them after use, cleaning them and placing them back in service.[34] Now the most common form of beverage container is the no deposit-no return bottle or can; the price does not reflect collection and disposal costs, which are borne not by the consumer but by society at large.

The 94th Congress considered legislation requiring EPA to establish standards of control for products which "may use an unreasonable amount of energy or of materials identified by the President as critical to national security or in short supply." Another bill would have imposed a schedule of national solid waste disposal charges on the sale or transfer, at the bulk production level, of rigid consumer containers (at 0.5¢ per container), and of flexible consumer packaging and paper (at 1.3¢ per lb.); the charge would have been introduced over a ten-year period, starting at zero and increasing by 10 percent per year; it would have been reduced by the percent of secondary materials content in the product. A third bill would have required a refundable deposit of at least five cents on carbonated beverage containers, to take effect in five years.

The first bill is inconsistent with the general principle that the rate of recycling should reflect the true costs of materials; the bill proposes a regulatory approach similar to that of the Clean Air Act or the Federal Water Pollution Control Act. These acts establish regulatory schemes which require businesses to install the best demonstrated or available control technology. The definition of such technology for a multiplicity of industries and plants has proved a difficult regulatory task. Businesses have delayed substantial costs by engaging in protracted litigation against regulations.[35] Perhaps such an approach should be reserved for those situations where it is difficult, if not impossible, to estimate external costs. It is relatively easy to estimate disposal costs.

The second bill would incorporate disposal costs into the prices of products. It would leave to individual businesses the decision on how to increase recycling or reduce waste in order to obtain the greatest progress at the least cost. Accumulating tax liability would eliminate an incentive to use litigation as a delaying tactic. The bill would cover packaging and paper products which make up almost one-half of the total waste stream and 80 percent of all product-type wastes. A study prepared for EPA suggests that such a system of product charges could double present rates of paper recycling and provide a marginal incentive for more efficient use of materials in production.[36] Administration costs have been projected at about one-half of 1 percent of the revenue raised.[37] Gradual imposition of a disposal charge would allow time for implementing regulations embodying suggested "fine-tuning" changes, such as adding the costs of complying with environmental controls on disposal to the base cost, or establishing a separate rate of charge for plastic containers, such as that proposed by the City of New York. It would also be appropriate to exempt consumer packaging which carried a refundable deposit from such a disposal charge.

A mandatory deposit on carbonated beverage containers, proposed in the third bill, would also internalize external costs. Such a deposit has been tested in the State of Oregon where it has greatly stimulated recycling and reduced the amount of roadside litter while leaving beverage prices essentially unchanged.[38] Detailed projections of the national impact of a mandatory deposit system have been made by the Department of Commerce (which is opposed to such a system), by the Federal Energy Administration (which has not taken a position) and by the Environmental Protection Agency (which favors such a system). The average of capital cost estimates by Commerce and by FEA is $1-$4 billion; all three agencies predict a modest net gain in employment, but with a shift of 40,000 to 80,000 jobs from container industries to retailing and distribution. Given a 90 percent return rate (not unrealistic in light of Oregon's experience), all three agencies predict energy savings of 150–200 billion Btu per year, somewhat less than one day's national energy consumption;

EPA predicts savings of about 13 billion pounds of raw materials. Commerce predicts a reduction in municipal solid waste of slightly less than 5 percent by weight; EPA predicts a reduction of about 20 percent by volume in municipal solid waste; FEA predicts that the value of materials thus removed from the waste stream would have no substantial effect on municipal decisions to landfill or to recover resources.[39] Sweden is putting into effect a similar mandatory deposit system for automobiles: there is a tax of SwKr 300 ($65) on the purchase of a car; the tax is refundable when the car is turned in to a scrap yard. This system merits further study in the United States.*

The Commission recommends that the Government take steps to internalize the cost of disposing of materials; means of accomplishing this include mandatory deposits on beverage containers, excise taxes on non-returnable containers, and product disposal charges on other consumer packaging and on paper.

Freight Rates

Discriminatory freight rates have been cited as a factor depressing the demand for recycled materials. The evidence supporting this assertion is mixed, at best. A 1973 study concluded that freight rates represented a substantial fraction of the cost of using scrap iron and wastepaper, but not of aluminum scrap; and that the ratio of railroad revenue to variable costs was higher for scrap iron than for iron ore, but lower for aluminum scrap than ingots and for wastepaper than woodpulp.[40] A 1974 study concluded that, when directly compared, rates for transporting scrap iron were higher than for iron ore, and rates for wastepaper higher than for wood chips; however, rates were lower for wastepaper and scrap iron when compared on a chemically equivalent basis (*i.e.*, comparing the cost of

---

*Commissioner Weinberg: The logic of the refundable Swedish tax on automobiles is so obvious and compelling that it is not enough to say merely that it "merits further study." Adoption of a similar system in the United States should have been *recommended* to facilitate recycling, to eliminate the eyesores represented by cars abandoned on the streets and to spare public authorities the cost of hauling them to junkyards.

transporting enough virgin materials to make one ton of steel or paperboard against the costs of transporting enough secondary materials to make the same ton).[41]

The Railroad Revitalization and Regulatory Reform Act of 1976 (together with the prior Regional Railroad Reorganization Act) requires the Interstate Commerce Commission to investigate the rate structure for transporting recyclable materials and competing virgin materials: in this investigation the burden of proof is upon the railroads to show that any rate structure is just, reasonable, and non-discriminatory; the ICC must issue orders requiring the removal of any unreasonable or unjustly discriminatory rate; EPA is authorized to participate as a party in such an investigation. The mandated ICC investigation is under way. The draft Environmental Impact Statement of the ICC staff dismisses as insignificant the effects of freight rate changes on recycling. Proposals for further action should await conclusion of the current investigation.

Procurement Specifications

Government procurement specifications can reduce the demand for recycled materials by discriminating against them. For example, the Department of the Army recently cited its procurement specifications to justify rejection of a recommendation by its Audit Agency that it purchase retreaded rather than new tires for its commercial vehicles.[42] GSA (which purchases $1.2 billion in supplies annually) has already made some progress in eliminating such discrimination. However, DoD (which purchases $32.6 billion in supplies annually) has indicated that it would give low priority to anti-discrimination arguments so long as action was discretionary and not mandatory.[43] There is some evidence that the purchasing specifications of private industry also discriminate unnecessarily against recycled materials.[44]

The Resource Conservation and Recovery Act of 1976 addresses the problem of discriminatory procurement specifications. It requires that each agency shall procure items composed of the highest practicable percentage of recovered materials consistent with maintaining a

satisfactory level of competition. The decision not to procure such items must be based on a determination that such items (1) are not reasonably available, (2) fail to meet performance standards set forth in specifications based on guidelines to be issued by the Department of Commerce through the National Bureau of Standards, or (3) are only available at unreasonable prices. Agencies which generate heat or energy from fossil fuels must, to the greatest practicable extent, use any capability for burning recovered material or fuel derived from recovered material. All federal agencies must review and revise procurement specifications to eliminate any exclusion of recovered materials or requirement that an item be manufactured from virgin materials, and to require use of reclaimed materials to the greatest possible extent without jeopardizing the intended end use of the item. EPA must prepare guidelines for the use of procuring agencies in complying with the requirements of the section. The Office of Procurement Policy is to implement the policy of the Act and report annually to Congress on actions taken.

Under this Act, the Department of Commerce (through the National Bureau of Standards) must do more than develop specifications that define the ability of recycled materials to replace virgin materials in various industrial, commercial, and governmental uses. It must also identify potential markets for recycled materials, identify barriers to their use, and encourage the development of new uses for recycled materials. The Department is also authorized to evaluate the commercial feasibility of resource recovery systems, publish the results, and develop a data base to assist persons in choosing such a system. Given the Department's expressed lack of enthusiasm for this legislation, and given the history of inattention to similar legislation (the Mining and Minerals Policy Act) by the Department of the Interior, it is not unreasonable to fear that these provisions of the Act may become a dead letter. A specific dollar authorization for the Department of Commerce to carry out these duties, along with continuing Congressional oversight, are possible remedies. The Government should consider a variety of arrangements to disseminate information to industry. One such promising arrangement is the Industrial Waste Exchange of the St. Louis Regional Commerce and Growth Association, which has just completed its first listing.[44]

Institutional Barriers

Institutional barriers prevent increased recycling of municipal solid wastes. The solid waste of a single metropolitan area is often handled by a number of jurisdictions with conflicting interests. Many cities lack the power to contract for long-term delivery of waste; such contracts are often a precondition to private investment in recycling. Even where cities do have the necessary legal authority and where they face increasing costs for the disposal of waste (especially in the Northeast), they miss opportunities to recycle waste because of the inertia of their solid waste management bureaucracies.*

Widespread awareness of opportunities for resource recovery is the first step toward overcoming bureaucratic inertia and institutional barriers in this field. The Resource Conservation and Recovery Act of 1976 is a promising beginning. The Act directs EPA to provide financial assistance and technical assistance (through teams of experts in finance, marketing, technology, and law) to the States in developing and carrying out plans for solid waste disposal and resource recovery that will identify sources and markets. In order to qualify for assistance, a State plan must identify appropriate regional organizations authorized to deal with common

solid waste disposal and resource recovery problems. The plan also must remove provisions prohibiting any local governments from entering into long-term contracts to supply solid waste to resource recovery facilities.

The Nation's supply of materials will be used most efficiently when decisions about the use of materials are based upon their true costs. Although the recycling of waste material has often been treated as a good per se, the Commission believes that the principle of determining use by true costs applies just as fully to the resources contained in waste material as it does to the resources contained in virgin material. The Congress has already taken a number of commendable steps in the direction of implementing this principle. The Commission urges that it continue in this direction.

REFERENCES

1. National Commission on Materials Policy, *Final Report* 4D-8 (1973), and Cosman, "Studies of Recycling Problems in Selected Industries," in Commission Document, *Additional Background Studies.*
2. Kirby and Prokopovitsh, "Technological Insurance Against Shortages in Minerals and Metals," 191 *Science* 719 (February 20, 1976).
3. EPA, *Third Report to Congress: Resource Recovery and Waste Reduction* 10 (1975).
4. See Cosman, op. cit.
5. House Committee on Foreign and Interstate Commerce, *Materials Relating to the Resource Conservation and Recovery Act of 1976,* 94th Congress, 2d Session, Comm. Print 64 (1976).
6. 41 *Fed. Reg.* 2362 (January 15, 1976).
7. See National Environment Policy Act of 1969, Pub. Law 91-190 (January 1, 1970); 42 USC §§ 4341 et seq.; Mining and Minerals Policy Act of 1970, Pub. Law 91-631 (December 31, 1970), 30 USC § 219; Solid Waste Disposal Act, as amended by Resource Recovery Act of 1970, Pub. Law 89-272 (October 20, 1965), Pub. Law 91-312 (October 16, 1970), 42 USC §§ 3251 et seq.; Federal Nonnuclear Energy and Development Act of 1974, Pub. Law 93-577 (December 31, 1974), 42 USC §§ 5905-5906.
8. House Committee on Government Operation, Report No. 94-1319, 94th Congress, 2d Session 12 (1976). See also Blum, "Tapping Resources in Municipal Solid Waste," 191 *Science* 674 (February 20, 1976), and Spendlove, *Recycling Trends in the United States: A Review* 20 (Bureau of Mines Information Circular/1976).

*For example, it costs Washington, D.C. $15 per ton to dispose of its municipal solid waste after collection. The city had an opportunity to sell collected waste to the Potomac Electric Power Company, where it would have been burned as fuel on a pilot plant scale and its energy value recovered. The city missed this opportunity in large part because no one was willing to contend with bureaucratic obstacles to the proposal; the city is now attempting to negotiate a larger regional energy recovery agreement with PEPCO. Interviews, Dr. James G. Abert, National Center for Resource Recovery, Inc.; J. Robert Holloway, Resource Recovery Division, Office of Solid Waste Management Programs, Environmental Protection Agency. For a more general assessment of bureaucratic inertia in the solid waste field, see the address of Dr. E.S. Savas in House Committee on Interstate and Foreign Commerce, *Symposium on Resource Conservation and Recovery,* Comm. Print, 94th Cong., 2d Sess., 9-12 (1976).

9. See Statement by Talbot Page in Hearings, U.S. Senate Committee on Public Works, Panel on Materials Policy, 94th Congress, 2d Sess., 6 (May 20, 1976) (cited hereafter as *Hearing*), and Statement of Richard B. Scudder in House Committee on Interstate and Foreign Commerce, *Symposium on Resource Conservation and Recovery,* Comm. Print, 94th Cong., 2d Sess. 83 (1976).

10. Baer, Johnson and Morrow, *Analysis of Federally Funded Demonstration Projects,* Experimental Technology Incentives Program, U.S. Department of Commerce, National Bureau of Standards, Vol. 1, iv-v (Apri 1976).

11. House Committee on Interstate and Foreign Commerce, *Materials Relating to the Resource Conservation and Recovery Act of 1976,* 94th Congress, 2d Sess., Comm. Print 70-71 (1976); House Committee on Government Operations, Report No. 94-1319, 94th Congress, 2d Sess. 12 (1976).

12. House Committee on Government Operations, Report No. 94-1319, 94th Congress, 2d Sess. 6 (1976).

13. U.S. Treasury Department, *Tax Reform Studies and Proposals,* House Committee on Ways and Means and U.S. Senate Committee on Finance, 91st Congress, 1st Session, Comm. Print 99-100 (1969) (cited hereafter as Treasury *Tax Reform Studies*).

14. See, *e.g.,* Miller, "Percentage Depletion and the Level of Domestic Mineral Production" 15 *Natural Resources J.* 248 (1975).

15. Interview, Richard Johnson, Federal Trade Commission; also Cosman, "The Threat of an Iron Ore Cartel" (unpublished).

16. See Booz-Allen and Hamilton, *An Evaluation of the Impact of Discriminatory Taxation on the Use of Primary and Secondary Raw Materials,* (1975), and Environmental Law Institute, *Federal Tax Policy and Depletable Resources: Impacts and Alternatives for Recycling and Conservation* (Draft, 1976).

17. See, e.g., Charles River Associates, Inc. "A Study of the Ferrous Scrap Market During the Shortage Period of 1973-1974" in National Commission Supplies and Shortages, *The Commodities Shortages of 1973-74: Case Studies.*

18. Miller, *op cit.* 243-245. See also Mancke, *The Failure of U.S. Energy Policy* 85-87 (1974).

19. See Federal Trade Commission, *Quarterly Financial Reports for Manufacturing, Mining and Trade Corporations,* 1973-1976. FTC reported figures for the lumber industry only 1972-1974, and for the mining industry 1974-1976.

20. J. Allen Overton, President, American Mining Congress, letter to Dr. Eads, with enclosures, August 20, 1976; Simon D. Strauss, Executive Vice President, ASARCO, Inc., letter to Dr. Eads, October 5, 1976.

21. 121 *Cong. Record* H.1163, 1187-1189 (February 27, 1975), S.4233 (March 18, 1975).

22. Simon D. Strauss, Executive Vice President, ASARCO, Inc., letter to Dr. Eads, October 5, 1976.

23. *Budget of the United States Government, Fiscal Year 1977,* Special Analysis F, 123; interview, Cynthia Wallace, Office of Tax Analysis, Treasury Department.

24. Treasury *Tax Reform Studies* 428.

25. Ibid.

26. *Budget of the United States Government, Fiscal Year 1977,* Special Analysis F, 123.

27. Treasury *Tax Reform Studies,* 435-438.

28. Arthur D. Little, Inc., *Analysis of Demand and Supply for Secondary Fiber in the U.S. Paper and Paperboard Industry* IV-7 (1975).

29. Treasury *Tax Reform Studies* 434-435.

30. American Paper Institute, *Statistics of Paper and Paperboard.*

31. Arthur D. Little, Inc., *op. cit.* III-49.

32. See, Greenfield *"The National Forest Service and the Forest and Rangeland Renewable Resources Planning Act of 1974"* 15 *Natural Resources J,* 605-606 (1975).

33. U.S. Senate Committee on Finance, Report No. 94-938, 94th Congress, 2d Session 578 (1976).

34. 122 *Cong. Record* S.11073 (June 30, 1976).

35. See statements of William J. Baumol and Leonard Lee Lane, *Hearing.*

36. Research Triangle Institute, *An Evaluation of the Effectiveness and Costs of Regulatory and Fiscal Policy Instruments on Product Packaging,* Environmental Protection Agency (March 1974).

37. Statement of Sheldon Meyers, *Hearing.*

38. Gudger and Walters "Beverage Container Regulation" 5 *Ecology L.Q.* 265 (1976).

39. U.S. Department of Commerce, Bureau of Domestic Commerce Staff Study, *The Impacts of National Beverage Container Legislation* (October 1975); FEA, *Energy and Economic Impacts of Mandatory Deposits: Executive Summary* (Sept. 1976); EPA, *Third Report to Congress: Resource Recovery and Waste Reduction,* 29-30 (1975).

40. See EPA, *Second Report to Congress: Resource Recovery and Source Reduction* 19-24 (1974).

41. Resources Planning Institute, *Raw Materials Transportation Costs and Their Influence on the Use of Wastepaper and Scrap Iron and Steel,* Environmental Protection Agency (April 1974).

42. General Accounting Office, *Report to the Congress: Policies and Programs Being Developed to Expand Procurement of Products Containing Recycled Materials* 12 (May 18, 1976).

43. Ibid. 1, 22-23.

44. Interview, Henri-Claude Bailly, Resource Planning Associates, Inc.

45. 7 *Solid Waste Report* 76 (May 10, 1976).

1-3 Comparison of Two Government Reports as to Their Approaches to Recycling

David A. Tillman

Source: *Resource Recovery and Conservation,* Vol. 2, No. 4 (November 1977), pp. 361–364.
Reprinted with Permission of Elsevier Scientific Publishing Company.

In June, 1973, the National Commission on Materials Policy made its final report.[1] Some three and a half years later, the National Commission on Supplies and Shortages spoke to many of the same issues – including recycling.[2] Because stark contrasts and discontinuities exist between the two reports, it is important to identify both views on resource recovery. It is also important to consider their implications.

It is useful to point out that the National Commission on Supplies and Shortages was formed in response to the unusual conditions of 1973–1974, when the U.S. and world economies boomed and created unusually high demands on the materials producing industries. By contrast, the National Commission on Materials Policy had a more general objective. It examined the U.S. materials policy in totality a generation after the previous commission on materials policy, the Paley Commission,[3] had reported.

It is also useful to observe differences in philosophy generally which appear in the overall report of the two commissions. The National Commission on Materials Policy concluded that a working and supportive interface between industry and government was required. It concluded that the private marketplace should be the "prime determinant" of the direction of the economy rather than government planning. The Commission on Supplies and Shortages, however, approached these problems with an emphasis on extensive government planning and government activity in both stimulating and reg-

ulating the marketplace. These philosophic differences led to distinct and separate approaches to the problem of resource recovery.

GENERAL APPROACH TO RECYCLING

The National Commission on Supplies and Shortages begins by observing, "Sizeable amounts of some major materials already are recycled but as a percentage of total consumption, recycling has been static or declining in America and only a small portion of postconsumer waste is recycled. Not all of the materials consumed can be economically recycled but present rates of recycling can be increased substantially to supply a limited but important fraction of our total needs for materials." Recycling, then, was viewed first as a supply option.

In contrast, the National Commission on Materials Policy viewed municipal waste recycling primarily as an urban solid waste disposal option. The materials supply option was significant, but of lesser prominence.

Both studies observed that significant amounts of material are being recycled presently. Both studies stated that the amount of materials supplied to the economy by recycling is declining as a percentage of total consumption. As a consequence, both called for increased recycling.

The National Commission on Materials Policy gave more recognition to the technical difficulties associated with the quality of urban waste as a material for utilization. It made several telling observations considering the quality of obsolete municipal waste vis a vis the quality of industrial waste, home scrap, and virgin material. Included in these considerations was the known chemical composition of virgin material and industrial scrap as opposed to the heterogeneity of urban refuse.

TECHNICAL OPTIONS AND ACCEPTANCE

The National Commission on Materials Policy considered all of the technology options available in recycling, including materials recovery and energy recovery. It favored the development of both approaches. In contrast, the National Commission on Supplies and Shortages appeared to resist energy recovery from municipal waste. It stated, "To subsidize recovery of energy, but not of materials, from solid waste would be to compound pressures for the inefficient use of resources. For example, use of old newspapers as fuel is significantly less energy-efficient than recycling of the same newspapers into newsprint." The extension of this philosophy contrasts sharply with the present activity and thinking in the paper fiber resource industries in the U.S.

The report of the National Commission on Materials Policy, which was published in June of 1973, was written at a time when few centralized resource recovery plants had been installed. By the time the National Commission on Supplies and Shortages had written its report, several recycling plants either were committed and under construction or had gone on-line. Thus, the National Commission on Materials Policy recommended, ". . . the Federal Government offer loans at low rates of interest to private firms for recovery of resources from municipal wastes." The National Commission on Supplies and Shortages stated, "The Commission opposes Federal funding of systems to recover energy or materials from waste, whether by means of grants, loan guarantees, or price supports; exceptions should be made only for the limited number of systems which possess the characteristics of true demonstration projects." Sufficient time and economic pressure evolved in the interim to obviate some of the need for

the Federal Government to involve itself in the financing of municipal waste.

DIRECT FEDERAL REGULATORY INVOLVEMENT

Both reports favored the Federal Government eliminating labeling and other procurement barriers which limit markets for recycling. The National Commission on Materials Policy took a very strong stand, as did the National Commission on Supplies and Shortages. Regarding freight rate discrimination, the National Commission on Materials Policy took an equally strong stand. It recommended, ". . . the Federal Government take the necessary steps to correct the existing freight rate differentials between secondary and primary materials." The National Commission on Supplies and Shortages took a wait and see attitude, citing more recent research in the area by the Interstate Commerce Commission. That report states, ". . . the draft environmental impact statement of the ICC staff dismisses as insignificant the effects of freight rate changes on recycling. Proposals for further action should await conclusion of the current investigation."

MARKET DEVELOPMENT

The National Commission on Materials Policy approached market development in a positive manner. Rather than penalize industry for using virgin materials, it sought to encourage industry to use recycled materials. This stemmed from the overall philosophy of the report which was expressed in the first objective contained in the letter of transmittal to the President and the Congress, ". . . provide adequate energy and materials supplies to satisfy not only the basic needs of nutrition, shelter and health, but a dynamic economy without indulgence in waste." In this overall context, the National Commission on Materials Policy saw a need to encourage the development of minerals and timber, not only from secondary sources, but also from virgin sources. It sought equity for both raw materials sources. It also recognized that in addition to operating cost advantages, industries with massive capital investments to assure themselves of a supply of raw material, cannot turn their back on such investments.

Thus, the National Commission on Materials Policy recommended, ". . . the Federal Government give users (scrap consumers, e.g. steel mills) of materials economic incentives in the form of tax credits for expanded use of recycled materials." That Commission also recommended that the Federal Government offer a tax credit for investments in new plants and equipment specifically geared to the production of marketable products from recycled materials. It sought, in short, to encourage the consumption of recycled materials by tax benefits.

Conversely, the National Commission on Supplies and Shortages approach was oriented to disincentives. They stated, in their introductory remarks in the Executive Summary, "The Commission recommends repeal of the percentage depletion allowance for minerals." The National Commission on Supplies and Shortages recommended a higher cost system, taking away percentage depletion, which is analogous to a depreciation allowance provided for other manufacturers. It thereby used a depressant on virgin materials rather than a stimulant for recycled materials. It approached market creation indirectly. The difference is significant for it reflects the philosophic approaches taken by each Commission.

TRUE COST OF MATERIALS

Both Commissions, however, did recommend that the true cost of materials production, in-

cluding the environmental cost, be included in the price of goods. In their report, the National Commission on Supplies and Shortages states, "The nation's supply of materials will be used most effectively when decisions about the use of materials are based upon their true cost. Although the recycling of waste material has often been treated as a good, per se, the Commission believes that the principle of determining use by true cost applies just as fully to the resources contained in waste material as it does to the resources contained in virgin material." The National Commission on Materials Policy made similar statements, although less extensive. While the National Commission on Supplies and Shortages applied this specifically to packaging and, discriminatorily, to beverage containers, the National Commission on Materials Policy stopped far short of such specific arguments.

REFERENCES

1. National Commission on Materials Policy, 1973. Material Needs and the Environment — Today and Tomorrow. Final Report, June. U.S. Government Printing Office, Washington, D.C.
2. National Commission on Supplies and Shortages, 1976. Government and the Nation's Resources. Report, December. U.S. Government Printing Office, Washington, D.C.
3. The President's Materials Policy Commission, 1952. Resources for Freedom, June. U.S. Government Printing Office, Washington, D.C.

1-4 Public Policies Toward the Use of Scrap Materials

Robert C. Anderson

Source: *American Economic Review*, Vol. 67, No. 1 (February 1977) pp. 355–358. Reprinted with Permission of The American Economic Association and the Author.

Numerous proposals to stimulate the flow of recycled materials have been discussed in recent sessions of Congress. The thrust of the proposals is that recycling rates are too low and that the federal government should offer incentives to aid the competitive position of the secondary materials sector. This paper examines the principal economic arguments which have been offered in support of a federal program of recycling incentives and analyzes some of the recent legislative proposals in light of available information on the structure of the secondary materials industry.

I. BACKGROUND

One key argument advanced in support of recycling incentives is that tax equity should be established between recyclers and primary material producers. The depletion allowance for mineral production, expensing provisions for mineral exploration and development, and capital gains treatment of profits on standing timber all contribute to a reduced tax burden for primary material production. Some recent legislative proposals have suggested that similar subsidies be offered to recyclers (e.g., depletion deductions in *H.R.* 148).

A second argument is based upon market failure attributable to external diseconomies in primary material production (air and water pollution and the disruption of scenic natural environments). Because resource recovery would lessen these environmental damages and create few new ones of its own, one may wish to subsidize the secondary materials industry. The force of this argument has been reduced by statutes such as the National Environmental Policy Act, the Federal Water Pollution Control Act, and the Clean Air Act, all of which were designed to reduce environmental degradation.

The existing pattern of municipal subsidization of postconsumer waste disposal constitutes a deterrent to recycling. Most of the nation's households do not pay for their incremental use of waste collection and disposal services. Free disposal for individual users with disposal costs covered out of general tax revenues induces the production of greater quantities of solid residuals than if disposal fees were levied. In addition, free disposal biases the ultimate disposition of solid residuals toward disposal and against recycling. Kenneth Wertz has estimated the price elasticity of demand for municipal waste collection to be $-.15$ and calculated that imposition of disposal fees would reduce the demand for municipal waste collection by about 15 percent. The fraction of this 15 percent which would represent increased resource recovery is unknown.

A final argument is that the existing structure of federal regulation favors primary production over secondary material recovery and should be balanced with incentives for recycling. Specific examples of discriminatory regulations include the General Mining Law of 1872 which grants mineral rights to those making a discovery on open federal lands, the pattern of freight rates which are alleged to favor primary over competing secondary raw materials, and labeling regulations which require source identification for many products which contain recycled materials.

Do the arguments which have been offered provide an economic rationale for the creation of federal recycling subsidies? Here each point is examined in turn. The history of the depletion allowance, as reviewed by Talbot Page (1976a), suggests that legislative desires to promote equity among taxpayers has been the primary force behind the gradual expansion of coverage of the depletion allowance. If depletion is to be allowed for coal, iron, copper, and other minerals, as well as sand, gravel, and sea shells, why not extend it to other exhaustible sources of industrial raw materials, namely the recycling sector? Arnold Harberger has argued that efficiency in the factor market requires that income be taxed at similar rates in all activities. Thus one may argue that extension of tax subsidies to recyclers is desirable. However, this would extend the distortion between investments in material production and investments in general manufacturing. Rather than extend income tax subsidies to recyclers the existing tax subsidies for virgin material production should be eliminated if one is interested in promoting efficiency in the allocation of factors of production.

Recycling may result in less environmental disruption than does production of an equivalent output of virgin raw materials. But to subsidize recycling merely because it produces fewer harmful external effects would not promote efficiency in resource allocation. A subsidized recycling industry may compete more effectively with a polluting primary sector, but the reduction in primary material demand provides little incentive for primary producers to reduce their production of effluents.

Most consumers have free use of municipal solid waste systems, creating a divergence between private and social costs which adversely affects consumer incentives to recycle solid wastes. On the other hand, producers of industrial scrap materials must pay for solid waste disposal. A subsidy to recycling which is intended to offset the effects of free disposal should be designed so that only scrap originating within the municipal waste stream is eligible. No corrective action for industrial scrap is warranted.

Inasmuch as charging for disposal appears to be the obvious solution to this market failure, we should review the case for not pricing disposal services. One argument in favor of free disposal is that littering, another form of free disposal, will become more attractive whenever disposal fees are levied. Because littering involves large social costs, it may be desirable to subsidize disposal. The littering issue is largely unresolved, but it may constitute an important second-best argument in favor of recycling subsidies rather than the imposition of fees for use of the municipal waste system. Another argument is that the costs of administering a system of disposal fees might outweigh the benefits, although the merit of this argument may be questioned since disposal fees have an established history of use in some western cities (e.g., San Francisco).

Recapitulating the discussion to this point, it appears that offsetting free private disposal of postconsumer waste is the only valid justification for a recycling subsidy. In situations of direct discrimination against recycling (e.g., freight rates and labeling requirements), the indicated course of action would be to remove the discriminatory regulation, if not justified by the protection of other interests, rather than grant offsetting subsidies for recycling.

II. LEGISLATIVE ACTION

Congressional interest in augmenting the flow of recycled materials has developed on many fronts. The study of freight rate discrimination was mandated by the Railroad Revitalization and Regulatory Reform Act of 1976. Loan guarantees for facilities to recover energy from solid waste were proposed in *H.R.* 1045 and tax deductions for similar facilities were proposed in *H.R.* 1046. Tax deductions or direct cash subsidies for recycling would be granted under a variety of proposals offered before Congress. In this section we focus on two such proposals.

H.R. 148 would create deductions against taxable income from recycling analogous to depletion allowances for primary raw material production. The deductions would be similar in magnitude to existing depletion deductions: 15 percent for scrap iron and steel, 15 percent

Table 1. Price Elasticities.

Material	Demand[a]	Primary Supply	Secondary Supply[b]
Iron & Steel[c]	.64	—	1.1
Wastepaper	.25	—	.49
Lead	.21	1.0	.48
Copper	.86	1.67	.32

[a]Demand is domestic consumption of all copper and lead, secondary iron and steel, and wastepaper.
[b]Secondary supply is for industrial and postconsumer scrap steel and wastepaper, and for only the postconsumer component of secondary lead and copper flows.
[c]Demand elasticity is from Anderson and Spiegelman; supply elasticities reported by Anderson and Spiegelman and Shriner essentially identical.

for secondary copper, and 22 percent for lead. Some recycled commodities whose virgin material counterpart does not receive a depletion deduction would be granted deductions (e.g., wastepaper at 18 percent). Like depletion deductions, the income tax deductions under H.R. 148 would be limited to one-half of net income.

H.R. 10612 would grant to purchasers of recyclable materials credits against income tax liabilities. The credits would apply to only that portion of materials recycled which exceeded 75 percent of a base-year figure.[1] The credit would equal 7.5 percent of price for recycled ferrous metals, 11 percent for nonferrous metals, and 10 percent for wastepaper, subject to lower and upper bounds of $5.50 and $8.00 for wastepaper.

The remainder of this paper is devoted to the evaluation of recycling subsidies proposed in H.R. 148 and H.R. 10612. The factors which will be considered include the projected impact on the quantity of material recycled and the cost to the Treasury relative to the value of materials which are recovered. The evaluation will be done through the application of econo-

[1]It should be noted that a tax credit which applies to output in excess of some base amount will affect new entrants to the industry quite differently from existing firms in the industry. Although marginal costs for each would be the same, average costs for new entrants would be lower. This could produce incentives for firms to exit and later reenter the industry. Consequently, the costs to the Treasury may be higher than the estimates presented here.

metric models of secondary material markets which have been developed by Franklin Fisher, et al., Robert Shriner, and Robert Anderson and Richard Spiegelman. It is recognized that the econometric approach is not wholly satisfactory for the analysis of permanent changes in factor costs, but as of this writing other, perhaps more satisfactory methodologies (e.g., linear programming) have yet to be applied to an entire secondary material market.

The impacts of the proposals on the quantity of scrap recycled can be derived from the elasticities reported in Table 1. For wastepaper and scrap iron and steel we assumed that demand is dependent on the supply of substitute virgin materials by incorporating the price of pig iron (in its molten state a substitute for scrap steel) and the price of pulp wood (a substitute for wastepaper) in the respective demand equations. For both copper and lead it was assumed that primary and secondary supply substitute freely in satisfying industry demand. Under these assumptions the effects of the various legislative proposals were estimated. They are summarized below in Table 2.

The cost to the Treasury of each of the legislative proposals can be compared to the market value of the material whose recovery would be induced. Such a comparison is reported in Table 3.

How do these costs compare with the subsidy which would offset free disposal? Disposal costs currently average approximately $26 per ton, or some 25 percent of the value of scrap iron and steel, 65 percent of the value of wastepaper, 10 percent of the value of scrap lead, and two percent of the value of scrap copper. For deductions which would apply to all scrap

Table 2. Estimated Increases in Recycling.

Material	H.R. 148	H.R. 10612
Iron & Steel	2.9%	3.0%
Wastepaper	1.4%	1.6%
Lead	3.6%	3.8%
Copper	2.1%	3.2%

Note: These calculations are based on the assumption that profit margins are large enough to support the full deduction. To the extent profit margins fall short of that which would permit the maximum deduction, the estimated impact on recycling would be reduced.

Table 3. Cost to Treasury as Percent of Market Values.

Material	H.R. 148	H.R. 10612
Scrap iron & steel	250%	60%
Wastepaper	620%	160%
Lead	290%	70%
Copper	340%	90%

Note: Treasury costs as a percent of market value are independent of profit margins.

recovered, the cost to the Treasury equals or exceeds ten times the magnitude of the uncharged disposal fee. Because most industrial scrap and much of the easily recovered postconsumer scrap would not be eligible for deductions under the proposed *H.R.* 10612, the cost to the Treasury per incremental ton recovered is less than under legislation permitting deductions for all recovered scrap. Even so, the costs of the subsidy are in excess of twice the cost of disposal for the material recovered under the subsidy.

Rather than subsidize the recovery of postconsumer waste, it has been suggested by Fred Smith, Page (1976b) and William Baumol that disposal costs could be internalized by imposing fees upon material use anywhere in the stream of materials flows. In particular, it has been suggested that these fees be collected at the manufacturing stage, primarily for ease of administration. A product charge levied on material use at the manufacturing stage would internalize the externality caused by free disposal only in the special case where consumers had no choice as to the disposition of waste material. But consumers do have a choice between municipal waste collection and collection by scrap dealers. A product charge which increases the cost of consumer goods in proportion to the costs of disposal would affect demand for consumer goods, and hence, the design practices followed by manufacturers, but it would

not affect the externality which exists when municipal waste collection is a free good.

Other approaches to shaping a materials policy have also received attention recently, particularly loan guarantees for recycling facilities, governmental stockpiling to stabilize supply and demand for secondary materials, and the creation of futures markets for secondary materials to reduce price uncertainty. Although these latter policies would not operate to correct the source of market failure, they, as well as the other policies which have been reviewed, may be deemed socially desirable in the broader context of a national materials policy – a policy which must consider explicitly such problems as the balance of payments, national security, and the resource needs of future generations.

REFERENCES

1. Robert Anderson, and Richard Spiegelman, "Tax Policy and Secondary Material Use," *J. Env. Econ. Mgt.,* forthcoming 1977.
2. William Baumol, "Statement before the Panel on Materials Policy," Senate Public Works Committee, May 1976.
3. Franklin Fisher, Paul Cootner and Martin Baily, "An Econometric Model of the World Copper Industry," *Bell J. Econ. Mgt. Science,* Autumn 1972, **3,** 568–609.
4. Arnold Harberger, "Efficiency Effects of Taxes on Income from Capital," in *Effects of the Corporate Income Tax* (Kryzaniak, ed.), Detroit 1966.
5. Talbot Page, *An Economic Basis for Materials Policy,* Baltimore 1976a.
 ———— , "Statement before the Panel on Materials Policy," Senate Public Works Committee, May 1976b.
6. Robert Shriner, "An Econometric Analysis of Supply and Demand for Scrap Steel," presented at the meetings of Regional Science Association, Chicago, Nov. 1974.
7. Fred Smith, "The Disposal Charge Concept," mimeo, Sept. 23, 1974.
8. Kenneth Wertz, "Economic Factors Influencing Households' Production of Refuse," *J. Env. Econ. Mgt.,* Apr. 1976, **2,** 263–72.

1-5 Waste Reduction: Issues and Policies

W. David Conn

Source: *Resources Policy*, Vol. 3, No. 1 (March 1977) pp. 23–38. Reprinted with Permission of Waiting for Permission

An ever-increasing problem faced by urban areas in our so-called advanced societies' lies in disposing of the residuals from production and consumption processes. In California, for example, nearly 20 million tons of municipal solid wastes are generated each year, and this figure is currently expected to grow at an annual rate of 1-2%.[1] The average resident in a metropolitan area generates between 2-3 lb of household refuse per day, adding to the 2 1/2-3 lb of commercial refuse produced per capita.[2] These figures do not include the vast quantities of agricultural, industrial, and other wastes.

It is becoming increasingly difficult and costly[3] to dispose of such wastes without causing damage to the environment. Suitable landfill sites close to urban areas are scarce; technological processes (such as incineration) which can reduce, although not normally eliminate, the need for landfill space require major capital investments and are expensive to operate; and growing public opposition poses problems for the siting of any solid waste facility. Furthermore, the feeling is increasing that we cannot afford simply to discard our wastes, since they contain potentially valuable resources.

There are three basic approaches to dealing with the solid waste problem. The first is to continue the traditional practice of attempting to assimilate the wastes into the environment without causing unacceptable damage. The second is to seek the recovery of as much energy and materials as possible from the waste stream. The third is to try to reduce the rate at which the wastes are generated in the first place. At present, the first approach is the most widely used, the second is gaining increased support, but attention is only just beginning to focus on the third. This approach, commonly known as 'waste reduction',[4] could have a major impact on the solid waste problem; however, it also has implications of a much wider significance, as will become evident from this paper.

In California, the Nejedly, Z'Berg, Dills Solid Waste Management and Resource Recovery Act of 1972 required the newly established State Solid Waste Management Board to investigate 'changes in current product characteristics, and production and packaging practices, which would reduce the amount of solid waste generated at its source' (Section 66785(b)2). In January 1975 the Board established a Source Reduction and Packaging Policy Committee with the task of preparing a background report and recommending alternative methods for reducing solid waste generation.[5] The Committee, whose findings were communicated to the Board in March 1976, included representatives from civic and environmental groups, government agencies, and industries interested in product packaging.

DEFINING WASTE REDUCTION

The first problem confronting the Committee was that of defining their area of concern. In the US Environmental Protection Agency's Third Report to Congress on Resource Recovery and Waste Reduction,[6] waste reduction is defined as the 'prevention of waste at its source, either by redesigning products or by otherwise changing societal patterns of consumption or waste generation'. However, there has been some confusion over the distinction between waste reduction and resource recovery, both of which are intended to conserve natural resources and reduce the flow of materials requiring disposal. If a refillable bottle is returned to a retailer for a deposit and is subsequently reused, this has generally been considered to be waste reduction; however, if a householder separates out newspapers, glass, or metals from the rest of the garbage and makes them available for recycling (either voluntarily or for payment), this has generally been considered to be resource recovery.

The distinction appears to hinge on the definition of 'waste' or, more precisely, the point at which an item is said to enter the waste stream. The Committee decided that for the purpose of their report, the waste stream would by definition include all items that no longer serve their originally intended purpose. Thus a refillable container, while it continued to be reused, would not be considered a waste, while a non-refillable container would be (even if it is recycled into the manufacture of new containers). It was noted that the latter has value solely because of its content of materials, while the former also has value as a product (although even refillable containers are ultimately discarded, at which time they become waste).[7]

The importance of the distinction should perhaps not be exaggerated, since both waste reduction and resource recovery are simply means to an end. It can be argued that, in comparing policy options, the overriding consideration should be the extent to which benefits are gained (ie objectives are met) at an acceptable level of costs, rather than the way in which the policies happen to be categorized. Studies by the Environmental Protection Agency (EPA) have indicated that a balanced approach using more than one option is likely to be the wisest course to take.[8]

OBJECTIVES OF WASTE REDUCTION

The next problem was to define the objectives of waste reduction. It soon became apparent that a number of different objectives were of concern, including the reduction of solid waste management costs, the reduction of litter, the conservation of natural resources, and the reduction of adverse environmental effects associated with the flow of energy and materials through the economic system.

Solid Waste Management Costs

The primary impetus for waste reduction has come from those concerned with the ever-increasing solid waste problem, their main objective being to reduce the costs (financial, environmental, social, political, etc.) of handling and disposal. A reduction in the weight of the waste stream would be one way of meeting the objective; however, depending on the handling/disposal methods used, the costs are also influenced by the volume and nature of the wastes (eg, their biodegradability, toxicity, combustion characteristics, etc.). The Committee realized that a proposed policy could have a desirable effect on one parameter, but an undesirable effect on another; for example, the weight of the stream could be reduced by substituting containers made of polyvinyl chloride for those made of glass, but if the wastes are disposed of by combustion, the substitution could aggravate air pollution (due to the emission of hydrogen chloride).

Litter

It was recognized that many of the policy options proposed for waste reduction would also reduce litter; indeed, the legislation requiring mandatory refunds on beverage containers, already enacted in some states (eg Oregon and Vermont), was introduced with litter reduction as its prime objective. However, since the Solid Waste Management Board has so far chosen to consider the litter problem separately from the more general issue of waste reduction,[9] the Committee placed it low on the list of priorities.

Conservation of Natural Resources

To the extent that waste reduction measures would reduce the flow of energy and materials through the economic system, they would reduce the need to extract raw materials from the environment and would therefore conserve natural resources. However, the Committee found it difficult to define a satisfactory measure of attainment because priorities in conservation are not well established; most people would consider that it is more important to conserve some resources than others (thus the reduction in weight of raw materials is not by itself a satisfactory measure), but there is no general agreement on the relative values (from a conservation viewpoint) of different resources.

It was pointed out that in establishing priorities, policy makers would almost certainly wish to take into account the relationship between projected resource needs and projected availability, making reasonable assumptions about the likelihood and extent of future discoveries, technological developments, changing economic and political constraints, and the availability of substitutes. A high priority is likely to be assigned to energy resources, savings in which can readily be measured in terms of heat values.

Reduction of Adverse Environmental Impacts

Apart from directly reducing the environmental impacts associated with the handling and disposal of solid wastes, waste reduction measures (to the extent that they would reduce the total energy and materials flow) would also indirectly reduce the impacts at other stages in the economic system, from extraction through processing and distribution to 'consumption' (perhaps better described as 'use'). Once again, the Committee found it difficult to measure attainment of this objective; by itself, the weight of residuals generated is not strictly suitable, since other factors such as the nature of the residuals and the method of their disposal are crucial in determining the environmental impact.

Conflicts Between Objectives

Just as conflicts might arise in meeting a single objective, depending on how its attainment is measured, it was apparent that there might also be conflicts in meeting objectives. For example, a policy designed to increase product durability

and thus reduce the generation of solid waste might result in the use of 'exotic' materials (such as metal alloys) made from resources that are considered more important to conserve than those used in less durable products.

Faced with this problem, the Committee did not attempt to reach agreement in advance on a set of weights reflecting the relative merits of achieving the three major objectives.[10] Instead, they called for a value-free analysis of the likely effectiveness of each proposed policy in meeting each of the objectives, together with a review of other impacts, and subsequently compared policies directly on the basis of each individual's subjective judgment. By doing this it was recognized that the Solid Waste Management Board would have the option either of accepting the Committee's recommendations (implying acceptance of their trade-offs) or of reassessing the information about each policy in the light of their own preferences.

THE COSTS AND BENEFITS OF MEASURES FOR ACHIEVING WASTE REDUCTION

The Distribution of Impacts

The Committee recognized that the introduction of measures designed to achieve waste reduction would undoubtedly impose costs on certain segments of society. Apart from the costs to the government of administering these measures, shifts in production patterns (with a possible reduction in total material output) would impose costs on some industries, some employees might lose their jobs, and some consumers would suffer as the result of involuntary changes in their consumption habits and/or the necessity to pay more to maintain existing habits.

At the same time, the measures would be expected to result in benefits for other segments of society (apart from the overall benefits which provide the main reason for the measures' introduction). Thus some industries would gain rather than lose from shifts in production patterns (eg, a shift to refillable bottles would benefit the manufacturers of bottle-washing equipment), some new job opportunities would open up (eg, handling the refillable bottles), and some consumers would gain (eg, those buying goods whose durability is increased).

Waste Reduction and the Standard of Living

An issue which greatly concerned the Committee was whether waste reduction measures would cause a decrease in the standard of living for society as a whole. It was pointed out that by intention, they would certainly decrease the level of material throughput, but whether this would represent a reduction in the standard of living depends on how the latter is measured. If it is measured by the market value of the flow of goods and services through the economy (ie by their contribution to the Gross National Product), then clearly the standard of living would be reduced to the extent that the value of this flow is reduced.

However, it is now well established that market values frequently fail to reflect many of the factors that govern the welfare of society. Costs such as resource depletion and environmental pollution represent as much of a drain on social welfare as any other costs, but they commonly remain external to economic accounting because, under existing property rights, private individuals and firms are not required to take into account the full consequences of their actions. Thus, for example, manufacturers who design their products with 'built-in obsolescence' do not normally have to consider the resulting implications for solid waste handling and disposal; indeed, since they do not have to pay the extra costs involved, it is often in their interest to design short-lived products. If the standard of living were measured in such a way that it reflected the full social costs and benefits of economic activities, a reduced material throughput might be found to give a higher standard of living.

Another, more fundamental reason was given for this. Conventional economic accounting attaches value to provision of the means of consumption rather than to the actual satisfaction of needs which may take place much later and often over an extended period. Thus an increase in the flow of goods and services for consumption is seen as something desirable. However, it has been argued that welfare is more closely related to a stock than to a flow;[11] in other words, it is the capital stock from which satisfactions are derived, rather than the additons to it

(production) or the subtraction from it (consumption). If this is true, 'consumption, far from being a desideratum, is a deplorable property of the capital stock which necessitates the equally deplorable activities of production'.[12] On this basis, welfare would be best served by minimizing rather than maximizing throughput, for a given level of satisfaction of needs. The notion of waste reduction is clearly consistent with this philosophy.

BASIC APPROACHES TO WASTE REDUCTION

The Committee reviewed the three basic approaches to waste reduction listed in the EPA's Third Report to Congress. The first is to reduce the quantity of material used per unit of product (in the product itself or in its packaging); for example, a milk container has been designed which uses 31% less paper and 16% less plastic than the traditional package, but still contains a half-pint of milk. The second approach is to increase the average lifetime of durable and semi-durable goods to reduce discards and replacement needs; for example, if longer-lasting radial tires were fitted on motor vehicles instead of bias or belted bias tires, there would be a substantial reduction in the quantity of tires wasted. The third approach is to substitute reusable products for single-use 'disposable' products and to increase the number of times that items are reused; for example, it has been demonstrated that considerable material and energy savings could result from replacing paper plates with reusable dishes.

Implied in the first two approaches is the notion that the products/packaging affected would still serve essentially the same function (ie they would still satisfy the same consumer needs); however, they would do this using less material resources. The same is only partially true of the third approach in that a refillable beverage container, for example, does not perform the same 'convenience' function served by a disposal (although both serve the basic function of containing liquid). The Committee agreed that a fourth approach should be added to the list, namely that of directly reducing the consumption of material goods by persuading people to sacrifice having certain functions satisified (ie, to moderate their needs).

THE ANALYSIS OF WASTE REDUCTION POLICIES

A list of proposed policy options was developed by the Committee and the present author, based largely on those mentioned in the existing literature (but also incorporating new ideas). As will be seen below, the policies fall into the three categories of regulations; fiscal incentives; and voluntary efforts.

The analysis attempted, as objectively as possible, to identify the likely effects of each policy option on:

- the solid waste stream;
- materials and energy utilization/environmental impact;
- government revenues/costs;
- industry;
- employment; and
- consumers.

It was recognized that a given policy option typically has many variations and can have (very) different impacts. For example, it makes a considerable difference to the likely effects of a tax on packaging by weight whether or not an exemption is granted for the use of recycled materials. A policy option may be considered acceptable in one variation, but wholly unacceptable in another. For this reason, the analysis examined a set of general approaches but made reference to at least some of the possible variations under each.

It was clearly impossible to identify and describe all the impacts of each policy option and variation thereof. An attempt was made to describe the impacts most likely to be significant, based whenever possible on the results of existing studies. However, there are few of these, and in the absence of tried government policies it was necessary to base much of the analysis on informed speculation. Each of the options and their possible effects are described selectively below.

Regulations

Possible regulatory approaches include the use of standards governing the characteristics (eg, disposability, durability, etc.) of certain products, minimum warranty requirements, and restrictions on government purchasing.

In general, the advantages of regulations stem from the directness with which they attack the problem and the reasonably high predictability of their immediate impacts. However, they can be costly to administer and enforce, difficult to write so as to cover all possible situations, and once written tend to be inflexible. The regulatory approaches considered in the analysis are set out below.

Option 1. Direct Regulation of Individual Products (Non-durables). Designated products (notably packages but possibly also other single-use products such as disposable cutlery, plates, clothing, etc.) would be subject to review by a state agency and would be approved for sale only if they meet pre-specified criteria (based on considerations of solid waste management and environmental protection). Each product under review would be compared with alternatives performing the same or similar function to encourage minimum consumption of resources and minimum adverse environmental impact. The model on which this regulation might be based is that provided by the Minnesota Packaging Law of 1973, under which the Minnesota Pollution Control Agency has issued regulations[13] for the review of new or revised packages.

If exemptions were granted to existing packages, the effects on the present solid waste stream and on resource utilization/environmental impact would probably be small, although future adverse impacts might be reduced. On the other hand, if exemption were not granted, the effects on the waste stream could be much more significant, but the costs of administration and the dislocation suffered by industry could be very severe.

Option 2. Purchasing Regulations for State Agencies, Etc. (Non-durables). State agencies would be prohibited from purchasing designated single-use products and/or products in designated non-returnable containers. Similar purchasing restrictions would govern the use of state funds by other government agencies, contractors, schools, etc. Prohibited items would be designated on the basis that less wasteful alternatives are available to fulfil the same or a similar function at a reasonable cost.

The direct impact of this measure would probably be small; the purpose would be to stimulate markets for reusable products and to serve as an example to others. If successful in this, it could have a significant indirect impact.

Option 3. Direct Regulation of Individual Products (Durables). Certain products such as household appliances, TV sets, etc., specified by their SIC codes,[14] would be subject to regulations affecting such characteristics as their material content, energy requirements, ease of maintenance/repair, and durability. By a designated future date, manufacturers would have to demonstrate to a state review board that their products were designed to meet the requirements and that there was adequate quality control on mass-produced items. Products that failed to meet the requirements could not be offered for sale in California.

This measure could have a significant effect on the durable goods component of the solid waste stream (currently about 10–15% by weight), though not immediately (depending on the lifetimes of the products affected). It is impossible to predict the effect on resource utilization/environmental impact; for example, if durability were given the highest priority in the regulations, the quantity of materials used over time would probably decrease (owing to a decrease in the rate of production of goods[15]) but there might be a shift in the *nature* of materials used, possibly to those which are more scarce and/or whose extraction and utilization involve more adverse environmental impacts. The measure would be costly to administer and is likely to produce an increase in the initial selling price of products, although there might be savings for consumers in the long term due to improved product characteristics.

Option 4. Minimum Warranty Requirements (Durables). For designated durable products

(specified by SIC code), the state would require the manufacturer to provide a complete and unconditional warranty (including parts and labor) on some or all parts of each product for a specified minimum period of time.

The effectiveness of this measure would depend on whether it would in practice lead to increased product durability. It may be noted that in the late 1960s many warranties for television, refrigerators, and other durable goods were extended from a 90-day to a one-year coverage as the result of consumer pressure and competition between manufacturers; there is some evidence[16] to suggest that manufacturers have, as a result, improved the design of their products so that fewer repairs would be needed, at least in the first year of operation.

Initial administrative costs are likely to be high as an agency would have to establish warranty terms that are feasible and reasonable for each designated product. Manufacturers' costs would increase, probably leading to higher product prices; however, consumers would face reduced risks when buying products. There might be problems of enforcing warranties, with consumers having to pay costs in time, inconvenience, legal fees, etc., as well as having to overcome any psychological aversion to 'fighting' with a manufacturer or retailer.

Option 5. Mandatory Disclosure of Environmental Impact (Non-durables and Durables). After a specified future date, designated products (including non-durables such as packaging and/or durables such as household appliances) could not be offered for sale in California unless a satisfactory statement of resource utilization/environmental impact had previously been filed with the State Solid Waste Management Board. The statement would have to include such items as: an assessment of virgin materials use, energy use, water use, industrial solid wastes, post-consumer solid wastes, air pollution emissions, and water pollutant effluents for each stage in the product's life cycle (from the extraction of raw materials through ultimate disposal);[17] the secondary material content of the product; an estimate of its durability under 'reasonable' use conditions; and a list of alternative products serving the same or a similar function. The document or an approved summary thereof would be made available by retailers for public inspection.

This measure would permit consumers to make more informed purchasing decisions. Its effectiveness in attaining waste reduction objectives would depend on whether consumers, as a result, shift their purchasing habits and cause manufacturers to react by changing production methods and specifications, etc. The main cost of the measure would initially fall on manufacturers, who would undoubtedly pass at least some of it on to consumers; there would also be administrative costs associated with reviewing the adequacy of the assessments, etc.

Fiscal Incentives

Possible approaches involving fiscal incentives include the use of deposits on reusable products (notably containers), product charges and other forms of taxation, and subsidies to offset the costs of achieving waste reduction. In principle, taxes or subsidies can be set at levels appropriate to correct the divergence between private and social costs and benefits (discussed earlier) and thus promote efficiency in the allocation of resources; however, in practice it is difficult (if not impossible) to determine what these levels should be. Taxes can be used not only to provide an incentive for waste reduction but also to raise revenue which can be drawn upon to support government activities in waste reduction, resource recovery, and other fields. A major advantage of the tax/subsidy approach is that it permits individuals and firms to re-allocate resources in the most efficient manner, albeit under a new set of constraints; thus, for example, the person who greatly values convenience would still be able to discard his refundable beverage container instead of returning it, but at a price (whereas under a regulation, he would probably have no choice). On the other hand, incentive approaches have the disadvantage that because of their indirect nature, they tend to be more unpredictable in their outcome than regulations, and more difficult to design so as to ensure the achievement of their objective;

futhermore, they too can be costly to administer (although not usually as much as regulations, and costs can be kept to a minimum by the use of existing collection/disbursement channels). Fiscal incentives approaches considered in the analysis are set out below.

Option 6. Mandatory Refunds on Beverage Containers.

All beer and soft drink containers would be required to have a specified refund value, payable on receipt of the containers by all distributors. Certified beverage containers, which are reusable by more than one manufacturer, might carry a smaller refund value. The model for this measure would be Oregon's Minimum Deposit Law, which became effective on 1 October 1972.

Of all the measures considered in the analysis, this has been the most studied.[18] However, the likely impacts remain uncertain, since they would depend on a number of unknown factors, ie, the extent to which there would be a shift in the mix of container types; the extent to which containers would be returned for their refund value and subsequently reused (ie the trippage rate); and the extent to which total beverage sales would be affected. For example, assuming that there is a significant shift to the use of returnables, that the trippage rate is sufficiently high,[19] and that there is some reduction in total beverage sales, there would be a significant reduction in the beverage container portion of the waste stream,[20] significant savings in resources, and reduced environmental impact. On the other hand, if the trippage rate is low (eg if the heavier refillable containers are discarded regardless of their refund value) there might be an increase in the waste stream as well as increased resource utilization and greater environmental impact.

The measure could have a significant impact on industry due to a possible reduction in total beverage sales, a likely reduction in the sales of metal containers, a possible reduction in the sales of glass containers (depending on the trippage rate), and the need for investment in storage, transportation, washing, refilling, etc. The net effect on employment is unknown; although there would be a decrease in the number of skilled jobs in the metal and glass container industries, this would be partially or wholly offset by an increase in the number of lower-paid, unskilled jobs in the beverage production, distribution, and retailing industries, as well as common carrier trucking, due to the need for additional handling of the refillable containers.

Option 7. Disposal Tax by Weight (Non-durables; Possibly Durables Also). A tax would be levied at the manufacturing level on the weight of designated non-durable products sold in the state, such as packaging, single-use disposable goods, etc.; it might also apply to durable goods. The level of the tax could reflect the average costs associated with the collection and disposal of solid wastes (as determined by the Board); alternatively the tax rate could vary according to a product's 'disposability', or it could be set irrespective of collection/disposal costs. A tax reduction or exemption might be provided for the use of returnables and/or recycled materials.

The key factors influencing the likely effectiveness of this measure are the level at which the tax would be set and whether or not an allowance/exemption would be provided for the use of returnables and/or recycled materials. If the tax were set at $26/ton (corresponding to average solid waste collection/disposal costs across the nation), and no allowance/exemption were given, the results of a published study[21] suggest that the measure would have only a slight effect on the solid waste stream, on resource utilization, and on environmental impact. Since a tax by weight would almost certainly cause a shift from the use of heavy products to that of light products serving the same or a similar function (eg from glass bottles to plastic bottles or aluminum cans), the impacts could be adverse. If an exemption for returnables/recycled materials were given, the study predicts a significant reduction in raw materials consumption, although the other impacts would remain small.

Option 8. Tax on Containers. A tax would be levied on each rigid or semi-rigid container (including a semi-rigid toothpaste tube but not a polyethylene bag). The tax would be charged to the container manufacturers, and a reduction or exemption could be given for containers designed for reuse.

There is some evidence[22] that a tax of 1 or 2 cents per container could be significantly effective in attaining the objectives of waste reduction (for example, reducing the packaging component of the waste stream by as much as 11% and the consumption of raw materials by as much as 10%). The tax would have most impact on low-cost containers (such as those made of paper) and might produce a shift in packaging types (eg, from rigid to flexible containers).

Option 9. Disposal Tax Based Partly on Weight, Partly on Units (Non-durables). A tax would be levied on designated products, notably those comprising the major portion of the waste stream (including consumer rigid and flexible packaging and non-packaging paper other than construction grades, but excluding consumer durables). For products other than rigid containers, the tax would be based on weight, while rigid containers would be charged at a fixed rate per unit. The tax would be levied at the bulk production level. This approach, first discussed in detail by Smith,[23] was incorporated in the proposed Solid Waste Utilization Act, considered in the 94th US Congress. The Act provided for an initial tax level of $1 \cdot 3 ¢/lb$ ($26/ton) or $0 \cdot 5 ¢$ per rigid container, a gradual phasing in of the tax over a 10-year period to aid adjustment, and a temporary subsidy for the use of recycled materials, to be phased out over the 10-year period as the tax is phased in.

The likely effectiveness of this measure can only be inferred from the existing study[24] which considers the weight-based and unit-based taxes separately. It would seem that, depending primarily on the tax rate adopted, the measure could significantly reduce the solid waste stream (particularly the packaging component), while also reducing resource utilization/environmental impact.

Option 10. Value-based Tax (Non-durables). A tax would be levied on the value of designated non-durable products such as packaging, single-use disposable goods, etc.[25] The tax would be imposed on the manufacturers of the products covered. A reduction or exemption could possibly be provided for the use of secondary materials and/or for products that are designed for reuse.

The tax would be expected to cause shifts from more expensive to less expensive forms of the products where this is functionally possible, and/or reductions in the overall consumption of these products. Most affected would be consumer goods of whose value a large proportion is taxable (eg cosmetics in expensive packages); however, the high value might in some cases be due to extensive labor input and might not be indicative of a product's solid waste potential or of the resource utilization/environmental impact associated with it. Unless the tax were very high, it was thought unlikely to be very effective.

Option 11. Variable Waste Collection/Disposal Fee. Instead of a flat-rate fee for collection/disposal of post-consumer solid wastes (as is common for municipal collections at the present time), a variable fee based on volume (ie the number of garbage containers) could be charged. Ideally, each collection would be separately metered; alternatively, householders could be charged a fee according to the number of containers that they wish to have collected regularly.[26] Specified source-separated materials, put out for separate collection, could be exempted. The fee could be set at a level just sufficient to cover costs, or at a higher level to act as a greater disincentive to waste generation. The rate could increase with the waste collected.

If the fee were low, this would probably have little effect; if the fee were high, people might avoid putting waste out for collection by delivering it personally to the disposal site or by causing increased litter and other forms of uncontrolled disposal, with their associated environmental impact. If the fee were based on volume, increased compaction of the waste by the householder (including the use of energy-consuming home compactors) might result, giving a reduction in volume but not in weight.

Option 12. Subsidy to Offset Capital Costs of Converting from One-way to Reusable Products. Tax relief or another form of subsidy (eg low interest and/or guaranteed loans) would be provided to manufacturers, distributors, retailers and associated industries to offset the capital costs involved in converting from the production/handling of one-way products (eg beverage containers) to that of reusable products.

This measure was thought unlikely to cause any significant change by itself; however, in combination with one or more other measures it might produce a more rapid and extensive transition to a system employing reusable products, with waste reduction benefits.

Voluntary Efforts

The encouragement and support of voluntary efforts can involve R & D, the provision of technical information, publicity, etc. These activities are not without their costs and their impact is uncertain; however, they tend to be more widely acceptable than other approaches because they interfere the least with existing freedoms and pose little or no direct threat to established interests.

A group of possible measures to encourage voluntary efforts were considered in the analysis under a single heading.

Option 13. Encouragement of Voluntary Waste Reduction Efforts. The state government would conduct research on methods of waste reduction, provide education, technical advice, etc. on waste reduction to industry and consumers (pointing out how it can be in their own interest to reduce waste), and persuade companies and individuals to voluntarily reduce waste.

The effectiveness of these measures would depend on their precise nature and is therefore impossible to predict. At the national level, the Environmental Protection Agency already has a small research program in waste reduction and is disseminating information on the subject; there is no evidence that its efforts have been more than minimally successful so far in actually reducing waste, although the research is vital in providing a basis for the development of controls that are not voluntary (ie regulations and/or fiscal incentives). Industries as profit maximizers actively seek ways of reducing waste as long as it is in their interest to do so (which may not, for example, include making products more durable); government encouragement is not likely to make them go further on a purely voluntary basis. Government efforts might have more effect on consumers who may be motivated to reduce waste but are, in general, less well educated about methods for doing so.

THE COMMITTEE'S CONCLUSIONS

With the analysis before them, members considered the merits of each policy approach in the light of their own judgments. An attempt was made to reach consensus on a policy or policies to recommend to the Board, but this proved difficult due to the wide diversity of interests, some sharp divergencies between the views of members representing these different interests, and disagreements between members representing similar interests.

A poll was conducted in which members were asked to state, for each policy approach (and assuming that the optimum variation, as they perceived it, would be used) whether they were strongly in favor; mildly in favor; mildly against, or strongly against. The results of the poll are given in Table 1. The only policy to obtain unanimous support (although not everyone was convinced that it would be effective) was option 13. Option 11 received broad but not unanimous support, as did option 4. On the other hand, there was nearly unanimous opposition to option 1 and fairly broad opposition to option 7 and option 5.

Opinions regarding the remaining policies were fairly evenly split, with the representatives of industry and the Anti-Litter League generally opposing the policies, while the representatives from the EPA and the civic/environmental groups generally gave their support. The sole representative from local government stood somewhere near the center of the spectrum of recorded views.

On the basis of the poll, the only recommendation that could be made unreservedly was one of encouraging voluntary waste reduction efforts. It was not felt appropriate to translate the views of a simple numerical majority into recommendations from the Committee as a whole;[27] instead, individual members were invited to submit personal statements that were attached to the report.

DISCUSSION

Based on Committee discussions, the preferences registered in the poll, and the personal statements submitted for inclusion in the report, it is possible to identify some major points of disagreement between Committee members. They were:

- whether, for the purpose of waste reduction, there is any need for government intervention in the working of the 'free' market;
- whether the waste reduction concept simply provides an excuse for imposing new controls on the packaging industry; and
- which, if any, of the measures can be significantly effective without incurring unacceptable costs.

The Need for Government Action

The attitude of each member on this fundamental issue was crucial in determining the outcome of the Committee's deliberations. On the whole, the industry representatives were not convinced of the necessity for any government action and therefore their first preference was to oppose all but the voluntary policies. It was only on the basis that the state might take action regardless, that some were prepared to discuss which of the other policies might be the 'least objectionable'.

The industry representatives argued that the market system normally tends to minimize waste and that it should be allowed to operate without government interference. One argued that 'our solid waste problem could be aided best by the operation of the free, open market place and

Table 1. Committee Members' Assessments of Policy Approaches.

Option	Regulations	Environmental	Environmental	Environmental	Civic	Federal Govt. (EPA)	Local Govt.	Anti-litter League	Glass Containers Industry	Glass Containers Industry	Paper Industry	Aluminum Industry	Plastics Industry	Metal Can Industry
	Regulations													
1	Direct regulation of individual products (non-durables)	X	X	O	X	X	XX	X	XX	XX	XX	XX	X	XX
2	Purchasing regulations for state agencies, etc.	OO	OO	OO	OO	OO	OO	X	X	X	X	XX	X	XX
3	Direct regulation of individual products (durables)	O	O	OO	O	O	XX	X	X	X	XX	X	X	XX
4	Minimum warranty requirements	OO	O	O	X	O	X	O	O	O	X	O	O	XX
5	Mandatory disclosure of environment impact	XX	X	OO	O	O	XX	O	XX	XX	X	XX	X	XX
	Financial incentives													
6	Mandatory refunds on beverage containers	OO	OO	OO	OO	OO	X	XX	XX	XX	XX	XX	X	XX
7	Disposal tax by weight	XX	X	O	O	X	OO	X	XX	XX	XX	XX	O	XX
8	Tax on containers	XX	O	O	O	O	X	X	XX	XX	XX	XX	X	XX
9	Disposal tax based partly on weight, partly on units	O	O	OO	OO	OO	X	X	X	X	XX	X	X	XX
10	Value based tax	X	O	O	O	O	O	X	X	X	XX	X	X	XX
11	Variable waste collection/disposal fee	OO	OO	OO	OO	OO	X	O	O	O	O	O	O	XX
12	Subsidy to offset capital costs of converting from one-way to reusable products	OO	O	O	O	O	O	O	XX	XX	OO	XX	X	XX
	Voluntary measures													
13	Encouragement of voluntary waste reduction efforts	O	OO	O	O	OO	OO	OO	O	OO	OO	OO	OO	O

Key
OO   Strongly in favor
O   Mildly in favor
X   Mildly against
XX   Strongly against

Source: Adapted from "Proposed Policies for Waste Reduction in California," prepared for the State Solid Waste Management Board, California 1976.

its various interactions of technology and competition'. Another commented that 'the market place is the most democratic and efficient mechanism for the allocation, conservation, and development of resources needed by the public'. They contended that waste reduction would reduce the standard of living (implying that throughput is the appropriate measure) and doubted 'that a majority of Californians would support the philosophy that our standard of living must be reduced because we consume more per capita than other nations'.

Other Committee members disagreed; they felt that the market currently fails to prevent the generation of excess waste and that the standard of living would not necessarily be lowered by an appropriate waste reduction program.   The local government representative was most concerned about the shortage of landfill sites; he considered waste reduction a 'supplemental strategy to resource recovery as a means of reducing our landfill needs'. Another member commented that 'we know that solid waste is not going to decrease without help'. The environmentalists were deeply concerned with the need not only to reduce solid waste management costs but also to conserve resources and preserve the environment; they argued that government measures are essential 'to alter the throw-away mentality of the present system'.

Waste Reduction and the Packaging Industry

The industry representatives (all of whom were associated with packaging) complained that they were the subjects of unfair discrimination. One viewed the whole exercise as 'nothing more than one attempting to provide a reason for recommending mandatory deposits on beer and soft drink containers'. Another argued that the situation is far more complex than many people imagine, suggesting that the case for packaging controls is anything but clear-cut.

Other Committee members did not feel that the packaging industry was being treated unfairly. They pointed out that containers and packaging materials constitute more than one-third of total post-consumer wastes (by weight) and that these are an inevitable target of waste reduction efforts. Moreover, several of the policies considered by the Committee applied to wastes other than those from packaging.

Cost-effective Policies

As mentioned above, some (though not all) of the industry representatives were prepared to consider which of the policies (other than voluntary efforts) would be the least objectionable, and two options (4 and 11) received mild support from them on this basis.[28] The lack of firm information about likely effects gave both sides (ie, those generally sympathetic with the need for waste reduction and those against) the opportunity to support their respective arguments using the same analysis. Thus one of the industry representatives, in justifying his opposition to most of the policies, interpreted the analysis as signifying that 'the effects of these options on the solid waste stream are minimal to insignificant, while the costs to government, industry and the consumer are significant to high'.

This was not the conclusion drawn by the non-industry members of the Committee, who felt that some of the other options could be significantly effective at an acceptable level of costs. However, since each member had a different set of criteria for selection and a different view of how these criteria might be met, their choices of particular policies differed significantly. The local government representative, for example, looked for policies 'most productive in terms of landfill requirements, easy to implement, and presenting the least difficulty in enforcement and administration'; in his mind, this meant that most of the proposed regulatory approaches were unsatisfactory while option 7 (disposal tax by weight, with an exemption for secondary material content) was the most preferred. The civic group representative, who felt that 'a policy should produce a clear reduction in waste volume . . . with as little direct intervention or regulation as possible' also gave her strongest support to fiscal rather than regulatory measures, but favored other options (6, 9, and 11) over 7.

Several measures emphasized the need for some action to be taken soon. One commented:

'While voluntary reduction measures are widely supported, the overall effect of voluntary efforts in reducing the volume of waste has proved to be extremely minimal. It is time for the state of California to step forward and lead the nation in waste reduction with a series of regulations and financial incentives aimed at the problem'. Another argued that 'it is time to do *something* to reduce waste. The longer decisions are put off, the harder it will be to implement any, and the problem grows worse in the meantime'.

CONCLUSIONS

At first glance, waste reduction may seem a fairly obvious and reasonably straightforward approach to take in tackling the solid waste problem. After all, it is not unusual to hear people complaining that goods are 'over-packaged' or that products wear out too quickly; it may seem a relatively simple matter to eliminate 'excess packaging' and to persuade manufacturers that they should make more durable products. Indeed, in a few instances, waste reduction can be accomplished without fuss: for example, the manufacturer who introduced a new milk container that performs as well (if not better) than the existing one but requires less packaging material, hurt no-one (except, perhaps, the suppliers of the material itself) but benefited both himself and those who have to pay for solid waste disposal. His action, it may be noted, was entirely consistent with the working of the market system.

In general, however, waste reduction cannot be so readily accomplished; the benefits do not come without costs. As mentioned earlier, one argument in favor of waste reduction is based on the existence of market breakdowns; there is fairly wide agreement that many (if not most) production and consumption processes cause externalities, and some waste reduction measures can be justified as a means of restoring market efficiency. Nevertheless, even if this reasoning is accepted, there is still room for disagreement on the nature and scale of the 'corrections' necessary; to a large extent, the current debate on waste reduction (as exemplified by the Committee discussions) gives at least the appearance of hinging on this issue.

However, I believe that a much more fundamental issue is involved. I feel that many of the Committee members, though perhaps not all admitted it, began to realize that if the objectives of waste reduction are to be taken seriously, we must start to question some of our basic values and attitudes, particularly as they relate to our view of material goods. Of course, the implications of doing this are awe-inspiring; it is one thing to accept as 'sensible' Boulding's suggestion that we minimize rather than maximize material throughput, but it is another to face up to the upheavals that would be necessary to move to a system that does this.

It is understandable, therefore that the Committee was unable to achieve unanimity on anything but the weakest of recommendations. The lack of information on effects was cited as a limitation on their ability to agree on preferred policies, but I share the feeling of one member who commented that attitudes were decisive, rather than knowledge. Even with a 'massive intrusion of hard data and information on the waste reduction topic' (he stated), policy makers would 'still have to decide among alternatives which force us to rethink our basic attitudes about the way we live our lives and the manner in which we consume vital resources'.

My own feeling is that policy makers are not about to face up to this fundamental issue; instead, like the Committee, they will probably continue to debate proposed waste reduction measures as if the issue did not exist and, as result, they may never get to grips with the real problem.

REFERENCES

1. California State Solid Waste Management Board, *Resource Recovery Program,* Draft, 1975.
2. California State Solid Waste Management Board, *Solid Waste Generation Factors in California,* Bulletin no. 2, Technical Information Series, 1974.
3. According to EPA's Office of Solid Waste Management Programs, local government expenditure on solid waste management is currently of the order of $2–4 billion per year.
4. The approach was formerly known as 'source reduction'.
5. The present author was retained by the Board as a Consultant to assist the Committee in the analysis of waste reduction methods and the preparation of its report.

6. Office of Solid State Waste Management Programs, *Third Report to Congress — Resource Recovery and Waste Reduction,* Environmental Protection Publication SW-161, US Environmental Protection Agency, 1975.

7. The discussion concerning the definition of waste reduction was based to a large extent on a memorandum to the Source Reduction and Packaging Committee by Thomas D. Clark, 1975.

8. N. Humber, 'Waste Reduction and Resource Recovery — There's Room For Both', *Waste Age,* 1975.

9. A separate committee has reported on the subject of litter management in California. See California State Solid Waste Management Board, *Report on Litter Management in California: Conclusions and Recommendations,* 1974.

10. Little attention was paid to the litter problem, for the reason mentioned.

11. K.E. Boulding, 'The Economics of the Coming Spaceship Earth', in *Environmental Quality in a Growing Economy* (H. Jarrett, ed., 1966).

12. K.E. Boulding, 'Income or Welfare', *Review of Economic Studies,* no. 79, 1949/50.

13. Minnesota Pollution Control Agency, *Regulations for Packaging Review,* 1974. A temporary injunction currently prevents the Agency from enforcing these regulations.

14. The codes are given in the US Department of Commerce Numerical List of Manufactured Products (New, 1972), SIC basis).

15. Unless consumers react to having longer-lived products by increasing their *stock* of goods.

16. MIT Center for Policy Alternatives, *The Productivity of Servicing Consumer Durable Products,* 1974.

17. This would be a so-called 'REPA' analysis of the kind reported in R.G. Hunt and W.E. Franklin (Midwest Research Institute), *Resource and Environmental Profile Analysis of Nine Beverage Container Alternatives,* Environmental Protection Publication SW-91c, US Environmental Protection Agency, 1974.

18. See, for example: Applied Decision Systems, *Study of the Effectiveness and Impact of the Oregon Minimum Deposit Law,* Final Report, Presented to Oregon Legislative Fiscal Officer and Department of Transportation, Oregon Division of Highways, 1974; T.H. Bingham and P.F. Mulligan (Research Triangle Institute), *The Beverage Container Problem; Analysis and Recommendations,* US Environmental Protection Agency, 1972; T.H. Bingham et al. (Research Triangle Institute), *An Evaluation of the Effectiveness and Costs of Regulatory and Fiscal Policy Instruments on Product Packaging,* Environmental Protection Publication SW-74c, US Environmental Protec-

tion Agency, 1974; G.M. Gudger and J.C. Bailes, *The Economic Impact of Oregon's 'Bottle Bill',* 1974; California Legislative Analyst, *The Economic Impact of a Proposed Mandatory Deposit on Beer and Soft Drink Containers in California,* 1975; E.F. Lowry, T.W. Fenner and R.M. Lowry, *Disposing of Non-Returnables — A Guide to Minimum Deposit Legislation,* Stanford Environmental Law Society, 1975; A.A. Marino and L.A. Burch, *The Oregon Bottle Bill in California,* Preliminary Draft, California State Solid Waste Management Board, 1975; Office of Solid Waste Management Programs, *Questions and Answers on Returnable Beverage Containers for Beer and Soft Drinks,* US Environmental Protection Agency, 1975; Senate Task Force on Critical Problems, *No Deposit, No Return . . . A Report on Beverage Containers,* New York State Senate, 1975; US Department of Commerce, Domestic and International Business Administration, Bureau of Domestic Commerce, *The Impacts of National Beverage Container Legislation,* Staff Study, 1975; G.L. Wagner, *Report to the US Department of Commerce on the Oregon 'Bottle Bill',* 1973; D. Waggoner, *Oregon's Bottle Bill — Two Years Later,* 1974.

19. There is some dispute as to the precise trippage rate necessary to ensure that a returnable system would be ecologically sound. One study (Hunt and Franklin, *op. cit.*) suggests that the number may be as low as 2, while representatives of the glass container industry on the Committee claimed that 6 or 7 is the appropriate number. Available evidence suggests that trippage rates for returnable bottles in practice are generally higher than 7.

20. Currently about 6% of the municipal solid waste stream (average).

21. Bingham et al., 1974, *op. cit.*

22. *Ibid.*

23. F.L. Smith Jr, 'National Solid Waste Disposal Charges: Illustrative Design II', Office of Solid Waste Management Programs, US Environmental Protection Agency, 1975.

24. Bingham et al., 1974, *op. cit.*

25. This tax would not be proposed for durable goods since it would tend to encourage the production of less expensive products, which would probably be less durable.

26. This is the method of charging currently used by some private contractors.

27. One reason is that the composition of the Committee, while not wholly arbitrary, had been subjectively determined by a staff member of the Solid Waste Management Board.

28. The representative of the plastics industry also supported option 7, disposal tax by weight (which would presumably favor his industry over one manufacturing heavier packaging).

1-6 Energy Conservation and Fuel Production by Processing Solid Wastes

Harvey Alter

Source: *Environmental Conservation,* Vol. 4, No. 1 (Spring 1977) pp. 11-19. Reprinted with Permission of The Foundation for Environmental Conservation.

INTRODUCTION

The current, and overdue, interest in energy conservation and new fuel sources dictates examination of alternatives in the conduct of our technological practices and their associated public policies. For example, so-called energy accounting systems may well determine the course of public and private choices among production alternatives. Indeed, Gilliland (1975) points out how some such alternatives may include, often unknowingly, an energy subsidy. A case in point, not included in her exposition, is the current practice of disposing of municipal wastes without regard for utilization of the fuel potential of the organic fraction or of the energy that may be conserved through utilization of recovered materials — which already contain an energy investment.

The environmental implications of energy recovery from solid wastes extend even beyond these arguments. Utilization of the wastes as a source of fuel, and recovery of usable materials, constitute a more environmentally acceptable alternative to disposal. Even controlled tipping (sanitary landfill) may be environmentally damaging and involve a needless consumption of valuable land.

Municipal solid waste in the United States, the United Kingdom, and many western European countries — from household, commercial, and some industrial, sources — has, as a major component, paper, cardboard, plastics, wood, and other combustible materials, and, as a minor component, metals, glass, and other non-combustible materials. The combustible portion, by definition, is a fuel — or could be a feedstock for conversion to some other form of fuel (Alter, 1976). Solid wastes are sometimes incinerated (burned as received); but they may be mechanically processed to separate, and hence concentrate, the combustible portion. The separation can be carried further to prepare metals and glass in a form, and to a specification, that is suitable for refuse (Alter & Horowitz, 1975).

It has been pointed out by several authors (cited below) that use of such secondary materials is energy-conservative. The amount of energy which can be conserved in this way, as well as the total energy available from the combustible portion, has been calculated by several government agencies and other groups. Their work is reviewed and discussed here from the point of view of increasing energy conservation and, at the same time, establishing solid waste as a new fuel source by increasing the rate of implementation of processes to convert municipal solid wastes to sources of fuel and also to recover the usable materials in the waste. The generally accepted term to describe such processing is *resource recovery.*

There are, perhaps, five general methods of converting solid wastes to energy: (1) use as a supplementary solid fuel in either suspension or stoker-fired boilers (National Center for Resource Recovery, 1975*a*); (2) burning of the as-received material in water-wall incinerators (McAdam, 1976); (3) gasification by pyrolysis

41

(Fisher *et al.,* 1976); (4) conversion to oil by pyrolysis (Mallan & Titlow, 1976); or (5) biological conversion to methane (Kispert *et al.,* 1975; Pfeffer & Liebman, 1976). For each method there will be energy losses when the result is compared with the input energy available; there will also be eventual losses due to changes in efficiency which may occur through use of the new form of fuel produced as compared with the conventional fuel which it replaces. These losses must be accounted for (Alter, 1975).

The amount of energy that is necessary to convert municipal wastes to fuel and recover usable materials (in this instance only paper, metals, and glass) has been computed in detail for at least one method of processing (Sheng & Alter, 1975). Considerably more power can be generated than is consumed (approximately 8 1/2 times as much) without consideration of possible energy savings from utilization of the recovered materials or loss through energy consumption in transportation to users. Only recently have detailed thermodynamic boundaries for such computations been established (Bailie & Doner, 1975*a*).

Previous attempts to analyze the magnitude of the contribution which municipal solid wastes can make to domestic energy reserves (Federal Energy Administration, 1974; Lowe, 1974; Franklin *et al.,* 1975; Poole, 1975) computed the higher heating-value of the combustible portion of the waste (namely the heat of combustion at constant volume) for the quantities of waste generated in the United States both currently and in prospect in the near future. To this scenario are often added several others, such as the effect or likelihood of certain changes in the composition of the waste-stream. While these are seemingly valid approaches, they must necessarily rely on interdependent assumptions about the future.

A somewhat different (and perhaps more conservative) approach is taken here. The energy potential of the waste-stream generated in the United States in 1971 (the last year for which reliable statistics are available) and 1974 (by extrapolation) are computed, including the energy conservation available from materials recovery. The analysis is then extended to the near-term future, based on likely conversion and substitution efficiencies (defined later) and on likely rates of

implementation of new resource-recovery plants. The approach is seemingly less sensitive to the usual assumptions of changes in waste quantity (*per caput* and total), composition, and population. The analysis based on rates of implementation of resource recovery must also rely on assumptions of future action, but can be easily adjusted — perhaps year-to-year — as new plants are constructed and the rates of implementation change.

Before proceeding, it is important to establish a few new terms in the field of alternative energy sources, whether these be from municipal wastes or from other materials or bases such as the sun, the wind, and the oceans.

DEFINITIONS

When solid wastes are processed to produce a solid, liquid, or gaseous, fuel, the heat of combustion of the product fuel is necessarily greater than that of the input waste (upgrading of fuel quality being the major reason for processing). The Law of Conservation of Mass–Energy thus dictates that there will be losses in mass of fuel delivered as compared with waste processed. These losses must be accounted for in estimating the energy potential of the waste-stream, although some previous analyses appear not to do so.

The usual measure of fuel value (or energy potential) of new fuel sources is the *heat of combustion* — the heat released during complete burning under specified laboratory conditions. The heat of combustion is an inherent property related to molecular structure. Frequently, the values for the heats of combustion of new and alternative fuel supplies (such as solid wastes) are multiplied by appropriate conversion factors to express the energy potentially available from the alternative sources in 'newspeak' units, such as 'barrels of oil equivalent'. But this ignores losses and inefficiences during processing, and implies that the waste could be thus converted to so many barrels of oil, or other unit — which is untrue. To avoid such errors and confusion, the following three new terms are suggested (cf. Alter, 1975):

The *arithmetic equivalence* is the heat of combustion, or higher heating value (HHV), of the waste or some processed form of the waste, multiplied by a conversion factor to express the HHV in units of barrels of oil, or some other convenient unit for discussion. The arithmetic equivalence has no meaning other than this.

The *conversion equivalence* accounts for the energy losses during the conversion of raw waste to produce fuel or energy. This would be the HHV of the wastes, multiplied by the efficiency of the conversion process but less the energy input to the conversion process. Another way of expressing it would be the energy output, as product, of a given process, less the energy required to operate the process, and less the losses resulting from unrecovered products as compared with the input waste.

The *substitution equivalence* allows for use of the new fuel as a substitute for a conventional fuel to produce the same energy-product (such as steam, electricity, heat, etc.). In a given application, the new fuel may perform with the same, greater, or lower, efficiency than the fuel which it is replacing.

A method of computing the substitution equivalence for production of a particular energy-product has been described (Bailie & Doner, 1975*b*). In its essence, the method computes the substitution equivalence (SE) as:

$$SE = \frac{\text{efficiency of use of conventional fuel}}{\text{efficiency of use of waste-derived fuel}}$$

to produce the same energy-product (e.g. steam or electric power). The efficiencies are the energy conversion efficiencies as usually measured — say, in a boiler to raise steam — and listed in standard reference sources (Babcock, & Wilcox, 1963; Fryling, 1966) at least for conventional fuels. It is the substitution equivalence that should be used as the basis for energy policy planning and not the arithmetic equivalence, as seemingly is done now.

WASTES AS AN ENERGY SOURCE

The several reported analyses of municipal solid waste as a new energy source (*see* above) are not completely independent in that the authors used one anothers' data freely. This is not so much a criticism as a reflection of the limited nature of the available data.

Energy conservation through resource recovery of municipal solid waste can be from two types of reuse: (1) utilization of the organic frac-

tion as a fuel or as a feedstock for conversion to fuels, or (2) utilization of recovered materials in the manufacture of 'new' materials, with consequent savings in the energy consumption during processing. Both forms of conservation have been analyzed and will be discussed later in this paper.

The Amount of Waste Available

The United States Environmental Protection Agency estimated that approximately 113 Mtons* of municipal solid wastes (MSW) were generated from residential and commercial sources in the U.S. in 1971 (Smith, 1975). This result may be combined with population figures for the country as a whole and in the Standard Metropolitan Statistical Areas (SMSAs) to compute the waste generation rates for 1971 and to estimate the rates for 1974 as indicated in Table 1. Further extrapolation to future years could be made, if warranted.

The materials in these wastes which potentially can be recovered in a form and to a specification that is suitable for reuse are, particularly, magnetic metals (usually termed ferrous metals), aluminum and other non-ferrous metals (usually reclaimed as a mixture), glass, and some paper**. The amount of recoverable paper in mixed wastes is questionable; so for purposes of this discussion, the paper is included in the fuel fraction.

One study has included reuse of recovered thermoplastics in calculation of energy savings (Federal Energy Administration, 1974). However, there is no known technology for recovering such material from mixed municipal wastes, and the small amount — 1.5 or 3.8%, according to National Center for Resource Recovery (1973) and Smith (1975), respectively — of plastics seems best included in the fuel fraction. (Much plastic waste from industrial sources is never discarded but recovered and reused, so such industrial wastes, together with others that are reused, are excluded from the present discussion.)

The composition of United States municipal solid waste has been reported (National Center

---

* = Megatons, each of a million tons. International (S.I.) units are used throughout this paper.
**This is more easily stated than achieved — *see* Alter & Reeves (1975).

Table 1. Municipal Solid Waste (MSW) Generation in the United States.

Statistic	1971	1974
U.S. Population[a]	207 millions	212 millions
Total MSW generated per year[b]	113.4 Mtons	125.2 Mtons
Per caput MSW generated per day (per 365 days year)	1.5 kg	1.6 kg
SMSA Population[c]	146 millions	151 millions
MSW generated in SMSAs	87.1 Mtons	97.1 Mtons
Per caput MSW generated in SMSAs per day[d] (per 365 days year).	1.6 kg	1.8 kg

Notes:

[a]Population for 1971 is from Statistical Abstract of the United States, U.S. Department of Commerce, Bureau of Census, Washington, DC., 1973, pp. 5-6, series E projections. Population for 1974 is an estimate based on these figures.

[b]U.S. Environmental Protection Agency, Second Report to Congress, Resource Recovery and Source Reduction, Washington, D.C., 1974, pp. 3-5.

[c]SMSA = Standard Metropolitan Statistical Area, for which this is Economic Projection 1990 (U.S. Department of Commerce, Social and Economic Statistics Administration, Bureau of Economic Analysis, Washington, D.C., 1974, p. 75). Figure for 1974 estimated by interpolation.

[d]Figure for 1971 from Lowe (1974), Appendix II, pp. II-2 and II-8, who suggests that residents of SMSAs generate more waste per person than their rural counterparts, and proposes a 1971 rate of 1.6 kg per person per day. Although the method of determining this amount is not indicated, it does represent an 8.8% increase over the national *per caput* rate given in the Table above. The rate of 1.8 kg was computed using this estimated 8.8% increase.

for Resource Recovery, 1973; Smith, 1975), with good agreement between the two sources. The composition figures from the former are used here; they are lower, so that energy savings derived from them provide a more conservative estimate than would be the case with the figures of Smith. The composition is: magnetic metals 7.0, aluminum 0.7, other non-ferrous metals 0.3, and glass 9.0%, of the weight of the waste (as received). (The aluminum content varies geographically across the country and the effect of this will be accounted for later in this paper as part of the variation in the amount of metal which may be recovered and reused.)

Energy Savings from Materials Recovery

The composition of the waste and the waste generation listed in Table 1 are combined to derive Table 2, which lists the amounts of recoverable materials in the municipal waste-stream (SMSAs only) for 1971 and the 1974 projection. The focus is on waste in these urban areas because it is much more likely that this material will be collected and processed in industrial-sized plants for resource recovery than that the corresponding materials in rural areas will be so treated.

The amounts of materials in the waste in the SMSAs are multiplied by the expected efficiency of recovery for each material (National Center for Resource Recovery, 1972; Michaels *et al.,* 1975) to derive the total amount of the materials listed which could have been recovered if such plants had been operating on all of the MSW collected in the SMSAs. This computed potential recovery is compared with the number reported similarly in two other studies, and it is found that agreement is reasonably close.

The amounts of materials that are potentially recoverable for the years listed, both as computed here and as reported by others, are combined to estimate what is termed Potential Recovery (Baseline Figure, *see* Table 2). Note that this is neither an exact figure nor the average of the several listed, but, rather, a rounded conservative judgemental estimate for purposes of policy analysis and strategy planning. Deviations from this baseline will be analysed later.

The computed baseline is entered in Table 3 and used to compute the energy savings which would have been realized if the amounts of materials listed in Table 2 had been recovered and reused in primary manufacturing operations. The energy savings from using each recovered material are listed in Table 3 from two sources. The large disagreement between the values given for the manufacture of steel from recovered scrap in the two referenced sources is not understood, the data from Franklin *et al.* (1975) being used to compute the energy savings, where possible, because more information is given as to their basis than in the other source. The computed energy savings may be compared with values given in the literature. Thus the values listed for reuse of scrap aluminum and copper may be compared with the similar values of 348 GJ/ton and 48.7

Table 2. Amounts of Recoverable Materials in the U.S. Municipal Waste-stream (SMSAs* only).

Material	Weight% in Waste	Amount Available, SMSAs 1971 (Mtons)	Amount Available, SMSAs 1974 (Mtons)	Estimated Recovery Efficiency[a,b] (%)	Estimated Recovery Efficiency[c] (%)	Potential Recovery (Mtons)				Potential Recovery Mtons/y. Baseline Figure (see text)
						1971	1974	(Note c)	(Note d)	
Magnetic Metals	7.0	6.10	6.80	94.5	85	5.77	6.43	6.26	4.3	5.8
Aluminium	0.7	0.61	0.68	70.0[b]	65	0.43	0.48	0.40	0.27	0.36
Other Non-ferrous Metals	0.3	0.26	0.29	80.0[b]	75	0.21	0.24	0.10[e]	NR	0.18
Glass	9.0	7.86	8.74	64.0	NR**	5.02	5.60	NR**	3.3	5.0

[a]National Center for Resource Recovery (1972).
[b]Michaels *et al.* (1975).
[c]Franklin *et al.* (1975).
[d]Federal Energy Administration [data for 1970] (1974).
[e]Reported as copper, *see also* Chapman (1974).
*SMSA = Standard Metropolitan Statistical Area (*see above*).
**NR = Not Reported.

Table 3. Baseline Figures and Computed Energy Savings which would have been Realized if Amounts of Materials Listed in Table II had been Recovered and Reused.

Material	Potential Recovery (Mtons/Year) = Baseline Figure	Energy Savings (GJ*/ton)		Energy Savings, 10^{17} J/Yr Per Material		
		Note c	Note d	Baseline Figure	Note c	Note d
Magnetic Metals	5.8	49.0	13.8	2.85	3.07	0.60[b]
Aluminium	0.36	280.7	232	1.02	1.11	0.63[b]
Other Non-ferrous Metals[a]	0.18	74.7	NR	0.14	0.72	NR
Glass	5.0	NR	2.91	0.15	NR	0.95[b]
				TOTAL 4.16		

[a]Determined for Copper.
[b]Values for a 'limited supply' scenario of less than total waste processing. Other scenarios are given with wide variation among the computed values. The limited supply scenario is not fully described, but it gives the closest match of energy saving from aluminum reuse to the other numbers.
[c]Franklin *et al.* (1975).
[d]Federal Energy Administration (1974).
*GJ = Gigajoules = 10^9 or one thousand million Joules (J).
NR = Not Reported.

GJ/ton, respectively, derived from metallurgical practices in the United Kingdom (Chapman, 1973, 1974).

The energy savings which are potentially realizable from materials recovery in the SMSAs, when based on the waste generation and composition of 1971 or 1974 as computed here, are in reasonably good agreement with the comparable values of Franklin *el al.* (1975), but are only in fair agreement with those of the Federal Energy Administration (1974). The discrepancies stem from differences in reported values for the energy savings per ton of recovered materials.

The total baseline energy savings listed in Table 3 are 4.16×10^{17} J/yr, which may be compared with total United States consumption in 1971 of 7.24×10^{19} J and in 1973 of 7.88×10^{19} J (Federal Energy Administration, 1974). The potential savings of energy from materials recovery and reuse in the SMSAs (Baseline Figure) is thus of the order of 0.5% of this consumption.

Energy Savings from Fuel Recovery

The magnitude of the contribution of the organic portion (i.e. the combustible portion) of MSW as a new energy or fuel source can be estimated in a manner similar to that used in Tables 2 and 3; the corresponding values are given in Table 4 for the arithmetic equivalence of the waste that would have been potentially collectible in the SMSAs in 1971 and 1974. The calculation is made for two likely but different values of the heat of combustion of the waste, to show the effect of the different values used by others. The maximum difference thus resulting is from 20 to 25% of the total estimated arithmetic equivalence; this difference will later be compared with the effect of variation in the values of the substitution equivalence. Several values for the heat of combustion or HHV have been reported, such as 9:30 MJ/kg (Kaiser, 1965), 10.5 MJ/kg (Institute for Solid Wastes, 1970; Lowe, 1974), and as low as 9.0 MJ/kg (Pope, Evans & Robbins [firm], 1972), all 'as-received'.

It may be argued that the HHV used in making the estimates in Table 4 should be the values for a refuse-derived fuel – whether solid, liquid, or gaseous – and not the HHV for MSW (as-received). Of course, this can be done only if the

Table 4. Estimation of Arithmetic Equivalence of MSW as a New Energy Source.

HHV* of MSW	1971 SMSAs	1974 SMSAs	Arithmetic Equivalence 10^{17} J/yr		Baseline Figure (see text)
MJ**/kg	Mtons	Mtons	1971	1974	10^{17} J/yr
9.30	87.3	97.2	8.12	9.04	
10.5	87.3	97.2	9.13	10.2	9.11

*HHV = Higher Heating Value = heat of combustion.
**MJ = Megajoule = 10^6 or 1,000,000 Joules (J).

total mass of waste generated is adjusted for the conversion equivalence resulting from the processing to make the refuse-derived fuels. The results of doing this would be the same as is indicated in Table 4.

In Table 4, again, a Baseline Figure is asserted and will be used in the discussion to follow. The Baseline Figures estimate of the arithmetic equivalence of the energy potential of MSW in the SMSAs is 9.11×10^{17} J/yr (1.26% of total United States energy consumption in 1971), which compares well with a previously computed value of 8.77×10^{17} J/yr in 1971 (Lowe, 1974).

EFFECT OF FLUCTUATIONS IN RECOVERY RATES

Materials

The Baseline Figure savings from materials recovery listed in Table 3, namely of 4.16×10^{17} J/yr, are of course realizable only if the quantities of materials listed in Table 2 are actually recovered and reused (with the energy savings listed in Table 3). The effects of fluctuation in the amounts of recovered and reused materials on the Baseline Energy saved are shown in Fig. 1.

In Fig. 1, the two diagonal axes represent the fraction of Baseline Energy that would be obtained from recovery of all materials conserved by recovery of steel or aluminum. The horizontal axis is the fraction of the total Baseline Energy recovered. The diagonal lines are labelled as to the percentage recovery of steel. The right-hand diagonal axis is labelled as to the percentage recovery of aluminum as well as by adding other non-ferrous metals and glass.

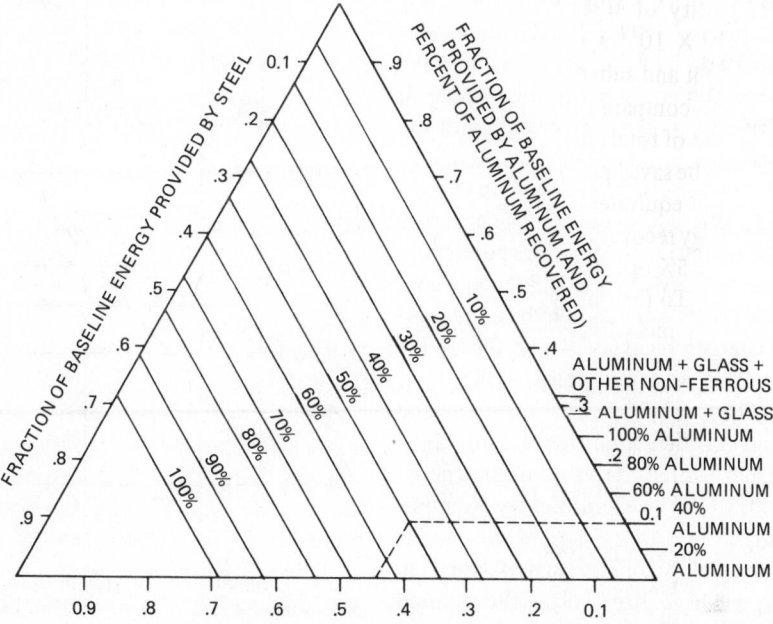

Fig. 1. Fraction of baseline energy conservation available from materials recovery and reuse.

As an example of how to read Fig. 1, a horizontal line is drawn from right to left to correspond to the recovery of some fraction of available aluminium. Where this line intersects a steel recovery line, the fraction of Baseline Energy conserved is read on the horizontal axis. A dashed line is drawn at an aluminium recovery of 40% to intersect the line for a steel recovery of 50%. The intersection is read on the horizontal axis as a recovery of 0.44 of the Baseline Energy available from all materials recovery and reuse.

Energy or Fuel

The amount of energy recovered is directly proportional to the amount of waste that is processed for energy recovery, corrected for the substitution equivalence for using the refuse-derived fuel instead of fossil fuel. Only a small fraction of the Baseline Figure of 9.11×10^{17} J/yr (see Table IV) is currently recovered. Obviously, this amount can be increased by increasing the quantity of waste that is processed, and may be further increased or decreased according to the value of the substitution equivalence for the particular use of the recovered energy. Values of the substitution equivalence may realistically range from 0.8 to 1.3 (Bailie & Doner, 1975b).

The net amount of energy recovered by a particular resource recovery process depends on the process conversion efficiency or some similar measure of losses sustained during the conversion process. There is a great deal of ambiguity over what is or may be called 'conversion efficiency' or some similar term (Bailie & Doner, 1975a). As an example of the magnitude of conversion losses, one author lists 'net conversion efficiency' for some nine energy-recovery processes and the values vary from 37 to 70% (Poole, 1975).

Applying these results to the Baseline Figure for energy savings of 9.11×10^{17} J/yr (arithmetic equivalence), the conversion reduces the savings by from 3.37 to 6.38×10^{17} J/yr. A minimum case, then, may be the lowest conversion equivalence multiplied by the minimum substitution equivalence. A maximum case may be raising the Baseline Figure arithmetic equivalence by a substitution equivalence that is less than unity (more efficient than the fossil fuel it replaces); a value of 0.8 is used for illustration. The result is new Baseline Figures of energy savings that may be possible from the minimum and maximum cases. The difference far exceeds the differences in estimates which may be caused by choosing one of the quoted values for the higher heating value of MSW, as discussed previously.

The possible energy savings from processing the baseline quantity of MSW may, then, vary from 2.70 to 10.9×10^{17} J/yr when corrected for both conversion and substitution effects. It is more realistic to compare this result with statistics such as those of total energy consumption or barrels of oil to be saved per day, than to compare the arithmetic equivalences. The comparison is that the energy recovery savings potentially vary from 0.3 to 1.5% of total U.S. energy consumption in 1971. To this should be added savings from materials recovery — say, 0.6 of the Baseline Figure — as a mid-point of Fig. 1, or 4.07×10^{17} J/yr. The potential materials and energy savings together total from 0.9 to 2.07% of the reported United States domestic energy consumption in 1971 (Federal Energy Administration, 1974).

The baseline savings for both materials and energy recovery will be realized only as the required amount of MSW is processed for resource recovery. The Baseline Figure will be exceeded as both recovery and the amount of waste available for processing increase. The latter amount cannot easily be projected, although some have tried (Federal Energy Administration, 1974; Lowe, 1974). However, the rate of increase of recovery can perhaps be predicted.

FUTURE ENERGY SAVINGS FROM MSW

Various studies of future energy savings from municipal solid wastes have started with estimates of arithmetic equivalences and have been extrapolated to future waste-generation rates. Related and alternative approaches are based on estimates of future conditions of the economy, availability of capital, changes in consumer preferences, government actions, and other effects that are difficult to predict and thus result in estimates of ranges of likely energy savings. A combination of these and other factors will still allow some sort of rate of implementation of resource recovery as an alternative to disposal, which rate may be predictable following a simple assumption or assertion.

It is reasonable to expect that, during any given year, the rate of establishment of new resource-recovery processing capacity will be proportional to the number of facilities existing at the time.

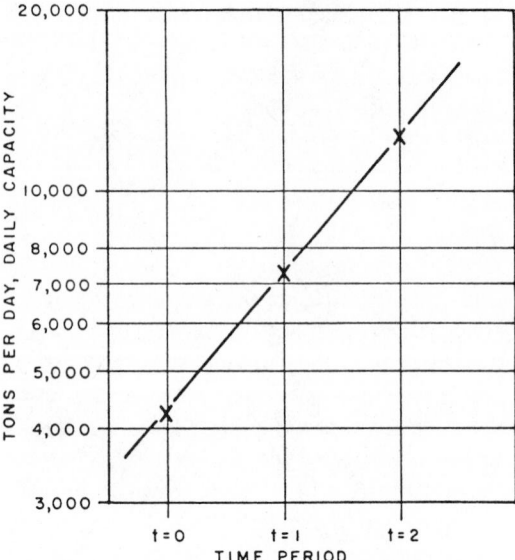

Fig. 2. Estimated rate of growth of resource recovery processing.

The reason for this is simply that municipal authorities are more likely to build a facility if there are other facilities to copy — at least in the United States. If this is indeed true, then the rate of increase in processing capacity in the country will be this proportionality, or:

rate of bringing new capacity on-line = c·n,

where c is a proportionality constant and n is the number of tons of MSW that are being processed at a given time. The number of tons that may be processed in the future, at time t, can then be computed by integration*. The result is:

$$n = n_0 \, e^{ct}$$

were n_0 is the number of tons that are being processed at $t = 0$.

The applicability, or reliability, of this expression as a predictor is tested graphically in Fig. 2, using published data (National Center for Resource Recovery, 1975b) with a good deal of judgment as to when certain plants, now in construction or planning stages, will be on-line. The operating period 1974-75 was arbitrarily chosen

---

*The derivation is based on a first-order process. The rate of change in number of plants is proportional to that number, or $dn/dt = cn$, which integrates to $\ln n = ct + c'$ (where c' is the constant of integration). If n $(t = 0) = n_0$, $c' = \ln n_0$, or $\ln n/n_0 = ct$; $n = n_0 \exp(ct)$.

as $t = 0$. The other operating periods are 1976-67 ($t = 1$) and 1978-79 ($t = 2$). The equation of the line in Fig. 2 is $n = 4237\ e^{0.54t}$, for $t = 1, 2, 3\ldots$ for units of n in tons per day. This relationship can be used to calculate the total expected daily tonnage of MSW to be processed in a future time-period, assuming the rate constant c does not change.

The predicting equation is, of course, derived from only three points and also involves considerable judgment about resource recovery plants that are now in the planning stage; consequently it is somewhat uncertain. However, the fit of the three points to the straight line encourages us to think that this type of relationship may be the proper predictor. Also, as resource recovery progresses and more plants come on-line, the predictor can be tested further and the coefficients up-dated.*

The equation for resource recovery implementation is easily used to predict when the Baseline Figure for energy recovery can be achieved in the near-term future. To do this, it is assumed that the values used for the rate constant apply only to energy recovery. (This seems reasonable because most of the resource-recovery plants that are planned or in construction for the time-periods indicated in Fig. 2 are primarily energy-recovery plants.) Also, it is assumed that the weighted average of the substitution equivalent for all plants is unity. This is likely to be nearly the case if the preponderance of plants prepare a solid refuse-derived fuel for burning with coal either in suspension or in stokers. Then,

$$\frac{[(n_0 e^{ct})\,(250\ days/yr)\,(9.3\ MJ/kg)\,(1000\ kg/ton)]}{\text{Baseline Figure for Energy Recovery}}$$

is the fraction of the Baseline Figure achieved at a future time. This expression reduces to:

$$(1.08 \times 10^{-2})\ e^{ct},$$

and is plotted in Fig. 3 for different values of the rate constant for implementation, c. The plotting shows that if the present rate of resource recovery implementation continues, the Baseline Figure energy savings will not be fully achieved

*Of course, there is an upper limit to the amount of waste that can be processed for energy recovery, which is the amount of waste generated. This limit is implicit in the discussion, although not explicit in the mathematical expression.

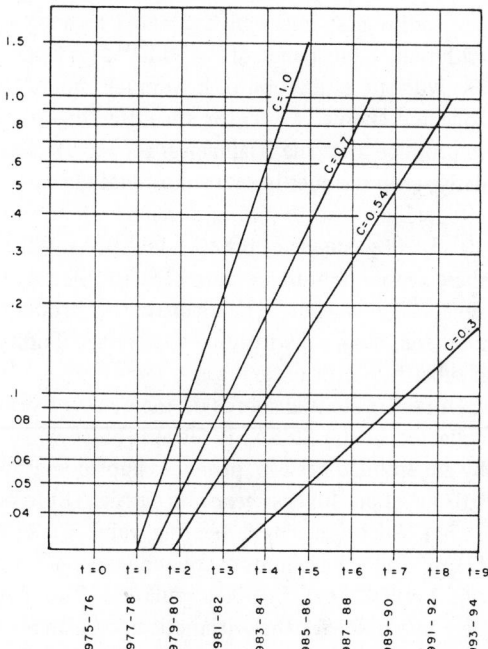

Fig. 3. Fraction of baseline energy likely to be recovered at different rates of resource recovery implementation.

in the U.S. until the time-period past 1991-92. If the rate is increased, say to $c = 1$, full Baseline Figure energy savings will be achieved before 1985-86, and maintenance of this rate could carry the savings higher — always presuming that the wastes are generated and processed.

OTHER SOURCES OF WASTES

So far, the discussion has dealt primarily with the household wastes collected in the SMSAs. But there are other sources which, at least in part, are accumulated in central locations, if not collected. Examples of such wastes that are suitable as sources of energy include certain industrial wastes (such as paint sludges), feedlot manures, and agricultural and crop residues.

The potential utilization of paint sludges for fuel, or as a feedstock for pyrolysis, has been discussed (Alter & Ingle, 1974), and it was estimated that paint sludges (United States only) have an arithmetic equivalence of $0.7 \times 10^{15}\ J/yr$. Undoubtedly, there are other combustible sludges from manufacturing operations which are similarly collected or accumalated — a sludge, by definition, being in fact accumulated.

Feedlot manures were estimated to have an arithmetic equivalence of 7.4×10^{17} J/yr (1972-73) without estimation of how much should be collected (Poole, 1975) for anaerobic digestion to produce methane (Halligan *et al.*, 1975). Similarly, crop residues have been estimated to have attained an arithmetic equivalence of 56.9×10^{17} J/yr by the year 2000 (Poole, 1975). All of these amounts must be corrected for their conversion equivalence. The ultimate fuel product, methane, has a substitution equivalence of unity if substituted for natural gas.

A large potential source of energy that is now collected in the SMSAs is sewage sludge which, by anaerobic digestion, produces approximately 0.03 m³ of product gas *per caput* per day (Brooks, 1974). Such gas has a heating value of 21.8 MJ/m³, which amounts to an annual generation of 2.1×10^{14} J per 100,000 population. This may be compared with the arithmetic equivalence of the solid waste generated per year per 100,000 population, which amounts to approximately 47.4×10^{14} J.

SUMMARY AND CONCLUSIONS

Disposal of municipal solid wastes may result in needless environmental damage and loss or degradation of land. In addition, the material and fuel resources contained in the wastes remain unused. The extents of these latter in the entire United States are estimated in this paper.

New terms are introduced to aid more precise estimation than hitherto of the amount of energy which can be conserved through processing and recovering the resources in municipal solid waste. Further, the likely rate of implementation of resource recovery in the U.S. is predicted on the basis of a simple model which relies on the assumption that the rate of implementation is proportional to the number of plants that are or will be actually on-line.

There is a great temptation to combine the rate of implementation with the sum of the energy potentially recoverable from the various sources of wastes, and to convert the answer to, for example, so many barrels of oil per day. As is indicated in the discussion, this exercise is not technically justified. Nonetheless, the energy that is potentially recoverable from solid wastes

has an arithmetic equivalence of the order of magnitude of 1 million barrels of oil per day (1.6×10^6 m³, or 158×10^6 liters) in the United States alone, and even more if a generous fraction of agricultural and crop residues could be garnered for processing. This order of magnitude, perhaps as much as substitution equivalence, should be compared with the stated U.S. goal of conservation of 2 million barrels of oil per day (presumably also an arithmetic equivalence) from all sources by the end of 1977 – not just from solid wastes (Ford, 1975).

The analogy of solid waste as an 'urban ore' has been used to the point of almost becoming trite. Nevertheless it may well be timely to extend the analogy to waste as an urban oil-well or coal-mine.

REFERENCES

1. Alter, H. (1975). Energy equivalents. *Science,* 189, p. 175.
2. Alter, H. (1976). [Huishoudelijk Afval als Grondstof voor de Chemische Industrie. – in Dutch.] *Chemisch Weekblad,* April, pp. 205-10.
3. Alter, H. & Horowitz, E. (Eds) (1975). *Resource Recovery and Utilization.* (STP 592.) American Society for Testing and Materials, Philadelphia, Pennsylvania: vi + 200 pp., illustr.
4. Alter, H. & Ingle, G. (1974). Coatings wastes as energy sources. *American Paint J.,* 58(54), pp. 58-63.
5. Alter, H. & Reeves, W.R. (1975). *Specifications for Materials Recovered from Municipal Refuse.* (EPA 670/2-75-034.) U.S. Environmental Protection Agency, Cincinnati, Ohio: ix + 110 pp.
6. Babcock & Wilcox [firm] (1963). *Steam: Its Generation and Use,* 37th edn. Babcock & Wilcox, New York, N.Y.: 582 pp., illustr.
7. Bailie, R.C. & Doner, D.M. (1975a). Evaluation of the efficiency of energy resource recovery systems. *Resource Recovery and Conservation,* 1(2), pp. 177-86.
8. Bailie, R.C. & Doner, D.M. (1975b). Evaluation of energy substitution equivalent. *Resource Recovery and Conservation,* 1(2) pp. 188-91.
9. Brooks, R.W. (1974). Conversion of sludge into utilizable gas. Pp. 55-74 in *Practical Waste Treatment and Disposal* (Ed. D. Dickinson). John Wiley, New York, N.Y.: xvi + 214 pp., illustr.
10. Chapman, P.F. (1973). *The Energy Costs of Producing Copper and Aluminum from Primary Sources.* (ERG 001.) The Open University, Milton Keynes, England: 78 pp.
11. Chapman, P.F. (1974). Energy conservation and recycling of copper and aluminum. *Metals and*

Materials, June, pp. 311-9; *see* also *The Energy Costs of Producing Copper and Aluminum from Secondary Sources*. (ERG 002). The Open University, Milton Keynes, England: 110 pp.

12. Federal Energy Administration (1974). *Energy Conservation Study*. Report to Congress, Office of Conservation and Environment, Washington, D.C., 182 pp.

13. Fisher, T.F., Kasbohn, M.L. & Rivero, J.R. (1976). The Purox System. *Proceedings Clean Fuel Symposium*. Institute of Gas Technology, Chicago, Illinois: 14 pp.

14. Ford, G.R. (1975). Presidential 'State of the Union' Address.

15. Franklin, W.E., Bendersky, D., Park, W.R. & Hunt, R.G. (1975). Pp. 171-218 in *The Energy Conservation Papers* (Ed. R.H. Williams). Ballinger, Cambridge, Massachusetts: xix + 377 pp., illustr.

16. Fryling, G.R. (Ed.) (1966). *Combustion Engineering*. Combustion Engineering, Inc., New York, N.Y.: 562 pp., illustr.

17. Gilliland, M.W. (1975). Energy analysis and public policy. *Science*, 189, pp. 1051-6.

18. Halligan, J.E., Herzog, K.L. & Parker, H.W. (1975). Synthesis gas from bovine wastes. *Industrial Engineering Process Design & Development*, 14, pp. 64-9.

19. Institute for Solid Wastes (1970). *Municipal Refuse Disposal*. Prepared by the Institute for Solid wastes of American Public Works Association, Public Administration Service, 1313 East 60th Street, Chicago, Illinois: xvii + 538 pp., illustr.

20. Kaiser, E.R. (1965). *Chemical Analyses of Refuse Components*. American Society of Mechanical Engineers, ASME Paper No. 66WA/PID-9, November: unnumbered.

21. Kispert, R.G., Sadek, S.E. & Wise, D.L. (1975). An economic analysis of fuel gas production from solid waste. *Resource Recovery and Conservation*, 1, pp. 95-109.

22. Lowe, R.A. (1974). *Energy Conservation Through Improved Solid Waste Management*. (Report SW-125.) U.S. Environmental Protection Agency, Washington, D.C.: 39 pp.

23. McAdam, W.K. (1976). Design and pollution control features of the Saugus, Massachusetts, Steam Generating Refuse-Energy Plant. *Resource Recovery and Conservation*, 1(3), pp. 235-44, 2 figs.

24. Mallan, G.M. & Titlow, E.I. (1976). Energy and resource recovery from solid waste. *Resource Recovery and Conservation*, 1(3), pp. 207-16, 3 figs.

25. Michaels, E.L., Woodruff, K.L., Freyberger, W.L. & Alter, H. (1975). Heavy media separation of aluminum from municipal solid waste. *Society of Mining Engineers, AIME Transactions*, 258, pp. 24-40.

26. National Center for Resource Recovery (1972). Pp. 3-21 in *Materials Recovery System*. Engineering Feasibility Study, National Center for Resource Recovery, Washington, D.C.: vi + 365 pp., illustr.

27. National Center for Resource Recovery (1973). Municipal solid waste: Its volume, composition, and value. *N.C.R.R. Bulletin*, 3(2), pp. 4-13.

28. National Center for Resource Recovery (1975a). Refuse-derived fuels: Application for utilities: *N.C.R.R. Bulletin*, 5(1), pp. 2-9.

29. National Center for Resource Recovery (1975b). Resource recovery systems: a review. *N.C.R.R. Bulletin*, 5(2), pp. 26-33.

30. Pfeffer, J.T. & Liebman, J.C. (1976). Energy from refuse by bioconversion, fermentation, and residue disposal processes. *Resource Recovery and Conservation*, 1(3), pp. 295-313, 6 figs.

31. Poole, A. (1975). The potential for energy recovery from organic wastes. Pp. 219-308 in *The Energy Conservation Papers* (Ed. R.H. Williams). Ballinger, Cambridge, Massachusetts: xix + 377 pp., illustr.

32. Pope, Evans & Robbins [firm] (1972). *Solid Waste Management Ten Year Plan*. Montgomery County, Maryland, p. 28.

33. Sheng, H.P. & Alter, H. (1975). Energy recovery from municipal solid waste and method of comparing refuse-derived fuels. *Resource Recovery and Conservation*, 1, pp. 85-93.

34. Smith, F.A. (1975). *Comparative Estimates of Post Consumer Solid Waste*. (Report SW-148.) U.S. Environmental Protection Agency, Washington, D.C.: 18 pp.

1-7 Notes on Changes in Energy Economics

Frank Austin Smith

Source: Adapted from a Paper in the *Proceedings* of the Mineral Economics Symposium, A Challenge for the Materials Industry: Changing Energy Economics. Washington, D.C. November 9, 1976, pp. 95–109. Printed with Permission of the Author.

The specific purpose of this paper is to explore possible impacts of recent changes in energy economics on resource recovery from post-consumer solid wastes. There are a number of interesting hypotheses that might be explored in this regard; but before doing so, it may prove useful to define the waste stream itself more clearly and to describe briefly the general features of the resource recovery sector that we will be dealing with.

I. THE POST-CONSUMER WASTE STREAM

The term "post-consumer" is used to distinguish waste flows associated with the use of final products by households and commercial sectors as opposed to wastes from industrial processing operations. In short, they are the wastes from "consuming" the physical through-put of the economy rather than the wastes from producing it. Table 1 provides a summary of the approximate current quantity and material composition of the municipal segment of this waste flow, including quantities currently recycled for subsequent productive reuse. (U.S. Environmental Protection Agency, 1975).

Of the 144 million tons per year generated by the household and commercial sectors, about 9 million tons are currently recycled, leaving 135 million net tons to be disposed of in landfills, incinerators, and by littering. The non-recycled material includes about 44 million tons of paper, 13 million tons of glass (mainly containers), 12 million tons of metals, 5 million tons of plastics, and lesser amounts of rubber, wood, and textile wastes. It is apparent that resource recovery from these municipal waste sources is not yet extensively practiced in most places or for most products and materials.

Excluded from the figures in Table 1 are a number of other post-consumer waste types such as junked autos (about 15 million tons per year), municipal sewage sludges (another 10 to 20 million tons per year) and demolition wastes (perhaps 30 million tons per year). Of these categories, only the metals in autos and other demolition sources are widely salvaged.

II. THE RESOURCE RECOVERY SYSTEM

The "resource recovery system," analogous to the virgin materials extraction and processing system, is composed of a very broad heterogeneous grouping of economic sectors and industries. It includes, to one degree or another:

- *Households and commercial establishments* that segregate ("source-separate") particular waste types like old newspapers for recycling.
- *Waste collectors,* usually private but sometimes city-run, that concentrate the materials from many small sources, sometimes in mixed-waste form and sometimes in segregated form.

Table 1. Post-Consumer Residential and Commercial Solid Waste Generated and Amounts Recycled, by Type of Material, 1973. (As-generated wet weight, in millions of tons)[a]

Material Category	Gross Discards	Material Recycled[b]		Net Waste Disposal of		
		Quantity	Percent	Quantity	% of total Waste	% of Nonfood Product Waste
Paper	53.0	8.7	16.5	44.2	32.8	51.8
Glass	13.5	0.3	2.1	13.2	9.9	15.5
Metals	12.7	0.20	1.6	12.5	9.3	14.6
Ferrous	11.2	0.2	1.4	11.0	8.2	12.9
Aluminum	1.0	0.04	4.0	1.0	0.7	1.2
Other Nonferrous	0.4	0.0	0.0	0.4	0.3	0.5
Plastics	5.0	0.0	0.0	5.0	3.7	5.9
Rubber	2.8	0.2	7.1	2.6	1.9	3.0
Leather	1.0	0.0	0.0	1.0	0.7	1.2
Textiles	1.9	0.0	0.0	1.9	1.4	2.2
Wood	4.9	0.0	0.0	4.9	3.6	5.7
Total of Nonfood Product Waste	94.2	9.4	9.9	85.4	63.4	100.0
Food Waste	22.4	0.0	0.0	22.4	16.6	26.2
Yard Waste	25.0	0.0	0.0	25.0	18.5	29.3
Misc. Inorganic Wastes	1.9	0.0	0.0	1.9	1.4	2.2
Total	144.0	9.4	6.5	134.8	100.0	157.8

[a]Estimates by the Resource Recovery Division, Office of Solid Waste Management Programs.

[b]Resource recovery in 1973 included only material recycling. Energy recovery accounted for negligible amounts.

- *Specialized secondary materials dealers* that sort, categorize, size reduce, and ship recovered materials to industrial users.
- *Waste disposal and transfer station operations* that sometimes perform hand sorting of special items or magnetic separation of ferrous metals from collected mixed refuse.
- *Large-scale mixed waste processing plants* — the newly developed technology designed to process the entire mixed-waste stream for material and energy recovery. Only a handful exist at present, but they will be operating at scales up to 2000 tons per day in a dozen or more cities within the next 3 or 4 years. Some will be operated by city governments, others by private companies.
- *Secondary materials processing industries* that operate plants to repulp waste paper into paper products, reduce secondary non-ferrous metals, process iron and steel

scrap into new metal, and the like. Some of these are independent firms that operate only in the secondary material field; others operate in both secondary and virgin materials. Some processes produce a 100-percent secondary product, while others blend recycled with virgin feedstock. Some firms in each field are vertically integrated back to their respective raw material sources while others are not.

In general, the secondary materials sectors have not been very extensively studied by economists, and the economics of resource recovery is not at all well developed or understood.

III. NOTES ON CHANGES IN ENERGY ECONOMICS

Assuming that the subject of changing energy economics refers to the recent period of rapidly

Table 2. Average Unit Cost of Fuels and Electric Energy
Purchased by U.S. Manufacturing Industries, 1962-74.

| | Annual Survey of Manufacturers[a] | | BLS/WPI[b] (1967=100) | |
	Total Dollars per Million Btu	Index 1967=100	Fuels & Electricity	Crude Fuels
1962	0.63	97	97	92
1967	0.65	100	100	100
1971	0.79	122	114	139
1974	1.46	224	208	219
1975			245	272
1976			265	306

[a]Bureau of the Census, U.S. Dept. of Commerce, M74 (AS)-4.1, p.5. Converted from dollars per 1000 kwh to dollars per million Btu.

[b]Wholesale Price Index from the Bureau of Labor Statistics, U.S. Department of Labor.

rising fossil-fuel prices, questions concerning the timing and extent of these price changes need to be considered in any discussion of possible impacts. Tables 2 and 3 thus represent an attempt to characterize and measure the relevant energy price changes.

The first column of Table 2 presents the nominal dollar cost per million Btu of energy, on the average, to U.S. manufacturing industries as reflected in the *Annual Survey of Manufacturers* by the U.S. Department of Commerce. The figures show a substantial increase, from 66 cents per million kJ (63 cents per million Btu) in 1962 up to 1.43 dollars per million kJ (1.36 dollars per million Btu) in 1974. With respect to 1967, taken here in column two as a point of comparison, the dollar cost on the average went up about 124 percent through 1974. For comparative purposes, the Bureau of Labor Statistics (BLS) wholesale price indices for fuels and electricity (essentially processed fuels) and crude fuel products complement the Annual Survey of Manufacturers figures and update the relative magnitude of the increase in the nominal price of fuel to 1976.

Business decisions are probably not made on the basis of nominal price increases alone, and in the period since 1971 or 1972, at least, the prices of most goods were increasing quite rapidly. This is shown in the first column of Table 3 as measured by the BLS wholesale price

Table 3. General Measures of Energy Price Changes, 1950-76.[a]

| | BLS Wholesale Price Indices (1967 = 100) | | | |
	All Commodities	Crude Fuels for Processing	Processed Fuels and Electricity	Processed Fuels Relative to All Commodities[b]
1950	81.8	77.9	87.1	1.06
1960	94.9	92.8	90.8	0.96
1970	110.4	122.3	106.2	0.96
1971	113.9	138.5	114.2	1.00
1972	119.1	148.7	118.6	1.00
1973	134.7	164.5	134.3	1.00
1974	160.1	219.4	208.3	1.30
1975	174.9	271.5	245.1	1.40
1976[c]	184.3	306.0	265.0	1.44

[a]Source: Bureau of Labor Statistics, U.S. Department of Labor.

[b]The index for processed fuels and electricity divided by (or "deflated" by) the index for all commodities.

[c]1976 prices are for the month of July.

index for all commodities. Other papers in these proceedings have indicated concern about how fast construction costs or the costs of capital were rising, or about how rapidly labor costs have been going up. The important point in Table 3 is indicated in the final column in which the processed fuels and electricity index is "deflated" by the all-commodities index to show how the relevant energy prices have behaved *relative* to other industrial goods prices. This shows that relative to all prices, processed fuel and electricity prices decreased slightly through 1970, and that even as late as 1973 they had not increased relative to other prices. In fact, only since 1973 have average fuel and electricity prices increased relative to other wholesale prices. Since 1973 they have risen about 44 percent faster through the middle of 1976.

There's a great deal of detail missed in this discussion especially in terms of individual fuel trends and regional variations. However, it does help to focus on the principal issue for the present discussion which is how energy costs have behaved *relative* to other costs. In this sense, for the industrial economy as a whole, the energy economics picture has changed significantly only since 1973, and even then considerably less than might have been supposed.

IV. SOME HYPOTHESES ABOUT ENERGY IMPACTS

There are at least two interesting hypotheses that might be explored concerning possible impacts of increased energy costs on post-consumer solid waste and resource recovery.

The first relates to how the quantity and composition of the post-consumer solid waste stream itself might be affected by changing energy economics. To the extent that different materials (cardboard vs. aluminum), or products (physical goods vs. personal services), or consumer "technologies" (refillable vs. throwaway beverage container systems) require significantly different purchased energy inputs, an increase in energy prices should cause a shift in consumer purchases to a less energy-intensive market basket through its differential impact on final product prices. This is a very broad and

a rather important subject, but it will not be explored further in this paper.

The other hypothesis is that resource recovery, unlike most of the materials sectors previously discussed in this volume, will generally tend to be favored by increasing energy prices. One reason for this is that as can be determined, materials recycling as a system or sequence of industrial processes is almost invariably less energy-intensive than virgin systems (Calspan Corporation, 1976; Gordian Associates, 1976, 1977; Hunt and Franklin, 1973). Therefore, the argument is that rising real costs of energy will have a greater effect on virgin materials systems than they will on secondary materials systems, thereby providing a competitive advantage to the secondary material.

Although a complete analysis is not possible, the remainder of this paper is an attempt to provide some quantitative perspective on this facet of resource recovery.

Impacts on Recycling

It is evident from the previous discussion about Tables 2 and 3 that energy cost factors have changed. A pivotal question for present purposes is how much the *differential* cost of products utilizing secondary (recycled) raw material may have changed relative to those using virgin raw material. An approximate answer for a number of products is presented in Table 4.

The top row on Table 4 (taken from Table 2) represents the average cost of purchased energy by U.S. manufacturers, in dollars per million Btu, from 1967 to 1976. The lefthand column lists several products. Beside each product, in parentheses, is the energy advantage, if any, for the secondary raw material. For example, the number 7 beside carbon steel indicates a saving of 7 million Btu per ton in comparison with a virgin steel supply system based on iron ore. For aluminum ingot there are two figures, 258 million Btu per ton and 164 million Btu per ton. The 258 figure represents the total energy differential for virgin aluminum produced from domestic bauxite using energy derived from fossil fuel. The 164-million-Btu figure is virgin aluminum reduced via hydropower from imported bauxite.

Table 4. Change in Secondary Raw Materials Energy Cost Advantages, 1967–76. (Dollars per ton of product)

	1967	1974	1976
Avg. U.S. Mfgr. Unit Energy Cost (dollars per million Btu)	$ 0.65	$ 1.46	$ 1.72
Products (and secondary material energy use advantage, million Btu per ton)			
Carbon Steel (7)	$ 4.55	$ 10.20	$ 12.06
Aluminum Ingot: a. (258)	168.00	376.00	445.00
b. (164)	107.00	239.00	282.00
Glass Containers (2.5)	1.63	3.65	4.31
Paper and Board Products			
Newsprint (9)	5.85	13.13	15.51
Printing and Writing (0)	0.0	0.0	0.0
Tissue (0 to 10)	6.50	14.60	17.23
Corrugated (0)	0.0	0.0	0.0

The numbers in the main body of Table 4 simply represent the product of multiplying the top row (say 65 cents for 1967), which is the unit cost of energy, times the energy saving from recycling (say, 7 million Btu for carbon steel). Thus, at 65 cents per million Btu in 1967 there was an energy cost advantage for the secondary material of 4.55 dollars per ton of carbon steel 1.63 dollars per ton for glass containers. In 1976 the energy cost advantage for secondary materials had increased proportionally with the increase in unit energy costs to about 12 dollars per ton for carbon steel, several hundred dollars per ton for secondary aluminum, and to over 4 dollars per ton for glass containers. For some paper products the *purchased* energy advantage is zero because the virgin product derives such a substantial source of its energy from by-product fuel.

Each row in the table thus indicates what the changing energy prices have done to the competitive position of secondary materials vis-a-vis virgin materials, *other things being equal,* which of course they have not been.

Table 5 carries the analysis one step further in terms of relative perspective. In part A, the energy cost differences from Table 4 are "deflated" by dividing through by the BLS wholesale price index for all commodities. This essentially converts the nominal dollar changes into so-called "real" changes relative to general inflation levels. In these terms the change between 1967 and 1976 in energy cost advantage of the secondary materials is reduced from a 165 percent increase to a 45 percent increase. In absolute dollar terms the change may or may not still look significant, but nothing like the first impressions.

Part B of Table 5 provides an alternative method in which the nominal dollar values from Table 4 are presented as percentages of the products' own selling prices. This indicates that, for example, in 1967 the energy advantage of recycled carbon steel was about 4 or 5 percent of the selling price of various types of carbon steel. By 1976, the energy factor had risen only slightly to about 5 to 6 percent of the selling price of these same type of carbon steel because the steel prices had risen almost as fast as energy prices. For both glass containers and newsprint the shift in differential energy cost relative to the price of the product has also been very small. For aluminum it has been significantly greater, as one would expect, since aluminum is an extremely energy-intensive product.

It may be interesting to note that, as far as the Environmental Protection Agency (EPA)

Table 5. Changes in Relative Energy Cost Advantage of Recovered Materials, 1967–76.

Products		1967	1974	1976
	A. Energy cost differences deflated by BLS wholesale price index (dollars per ton of product)			
Carbon Steel		$ 4.55	$ 6.38	$ 6.59
Aluminum Ingot				
(a)		168.00	235.00	243.00
(b)		107.00	149.00	154.00
Glass Containers		1.63	2.28	2.36
Newsprint		5.85	8.21	8.48
	B. Energy cost differences as percent of products' own selling prices			
Carbon Steel		4 to 5%	4 to 6%	5 to 6%
Aluminum Ingot				
(a)		34	55	51
(b)		21	35	32
Glass Containers		1	1.8	N.A.
Newsprint		4.1	7.1	5.3

can document, aluminum is the only product in the post-consumer solid waste stream that has shown a major increase in resource recovery during the last few years. It is unlikely that this is due solely to changing economics; however, the aluminum industry reports that can recycling has gone up from essentially zero in 1970 to about 25 percent or so of aluminum can shipments by 1975. This is a very significant increase and, compared with other products in the waste stream, a very high recycling rate. They said things like that couldn't be done. The aluminum and brewing companies basically are responsible for it.

The general conclusion from this preliminary analysis is that the increase in energy costs over the past few years has probably tended to favor recycling. However, with respect to the large-volume materials in the solid waste stream — namely, paper, glass, and ferrous metals — the economic stimulus cannot have been very great. This is because most of the relative cost advantage attributable to changes in energy cost factors was essentially neutralized by increases in other factor costs and general price inflation, and also because the energy *cost differential* for most materials is not a very large part of the total cost of the virgin material.

1-8 Resource Recovery as a Solid Waste Management Option

W.E. and M.A. Franklin and M.E. Weber

Source: Adapted from Chapter V of *Solid Waste Management* and the Paper Industry by Franklin Associates, Ltd. and International Research and Technology Corporation, 1979, pp. 64–83. Reprinted with Permission of The American Paper Institute, Inc., Washington, D.C.

INTRODUCTION

Resource recovery has become an important topic in the United States in recent years. Increasing costs for fossil fuels and the threat of shortages have spurred the search for alternate energy sources. Municipal solid waste is seen as a major energy source, along with wood and other biomass, sewage sludge, solar power, and others. Shortages of some natural resources and the need to recycle scarce materials also stimulate interest in resource recovery.

The potential of solid waste as a fuel may be illustrated by a simple calculation. The energy content of solid waste averages 4,500 Btu per pound, or 9 million Btu per ton. Thus one ton of solid waste is equivalent in Btu content to 1.55 barrels of crude oil, and the municipal solid waste generated in the United States in 1976 (135.5 million tons) is equivalent in Btu content to 210 million barrels of crude oil. This amount of energy, 1.2×10^{15} Btu, is about one percent of the nation's annual total energy needs. This is the gross recoverable energy unadjusted for process efficiency, which can range from 26 percent to 85 percent.

In addition to the organic fraction of solid waste which may be burned as fuel, other valuable components may be recovered and recycled. These include paper, ferrous metals, aluminum and other nonferrous metals, and glass. It is apparent that paper occupies a unique position in the resource recovery picture, since a part of it can be removed and recycled into paper products and the non-recyclable portion can be burned as fuel. In this chapter we address resource recovery as a solid waste management option that leads to resource conservation.

The first topic of this chapter is the current trends in resource recovery technology and capital costs. An economic analysis of resource recovery is given in which the internal rates of return of different recovery technologies are summarized. The geographic distribution of solid waste is summarized to show where MSW occurs in greatest concentration.

A baseline forecast of resource recovery is then developed. A forecast of the number of resource recovery plants by size and the annual processing of solid waste that is likely to take place assuming no stimulation is developed for this section. These data are then translated into capital cost data in terms of 1977 dollars. The next step in the resource recovery forecasts is to spread the implementation over the 1981 to 1990 period more or less uniformly. Here the 1981 base year was normalized to reflect actual known implementation that is more or less committed in 1978, and to carry forward that estimate in current dollars through 1990. The same is also done for an accelerated program of resource recovery implementation.

RESOURCE RECOVERY TECHNOLOGY TRENDS

Resource recovery may be broadly defined as recovery of energy and/or materials from the mixed municipal solid waste stream. In a true technical sense, energy recovery is a solid waste processing technique. A complete discussion of resource recovery technologies is included in Appendix I. Resource recovery may be practiced from industrial wastes, but that is not a subject for this report.

Materials Recovery

Materials which may be recovered from solid waste include paper, ferrous metals, aluminum and other nonferrous metals, and glass. Materials may be recovered from municipal solid waste either as a self-contained process, or in combination with energy recovery from solid waste. If the materials are recovered as a part of an energy recovery system, then the material recovery is generally referred to as "front-end" recovery (processed before the energy recovery).

Recovery of ferrous metals by magnetic separation from shredded refuse is frequently practiced without energy recovery. Materials might also be recovered from mixed municipal solid waste by the process of source separation. That is, valuable materials such as paper, aluminum, ferrous metals, and glass may be hand sorted from the waste and sold, although cost and quality considerations limit the practice today.

If energy recovery is being practiced, the solid waste may be preprocessed by such mechanical means as trommeling or shredding to produce a fuel. Front-end materials recovery might then be a part of the process. For instance, the ferrous metals would commonly be removed by magnetic separation. Methods are being developed to remove aluminum and glass from the processed solid waste, but these are still in demonstration stages and are currently undergoing testing. Some work is being done on recovery of paper from processed solid waste, but presently waste paper can best be recovered via source separation or separation at the processing plant. Plant design could allow for separation of paper at the front-end of a system to provide flexibility in directing paper to fiber use or energy recovery.

Energy Recovery

Energy may be recovered from solid waste as steam, electricity, or fuels. The fuels may be in solid form to be burned to produce steam or electricity, or may be in the form of oil or gas. Refuse-derived fuel, incineration, pyrolysis, and other techniques will be discussed here.

Refuse-derived Fuel. Refuse-derived fuel (RDF) is usually defined as a supplemental fuel for use in fossil fuel (coal)-fired steam generators. RDF may be produced in fluff, wet pulped, densified, or dust form. A list of RDF systems which are operational, under construction, or contracted for is included in Appendix M.

Fluff RDF. Fluff RDF is prepared by mechanical means such as shredding and air classifying, so that the mainly organic light fraction of the solid waste is used for burning. Generally some front-end processing is used to remove metals or other materials for sale, and to remove these noncombustibles to lower the ash content of the fuel. The RDF thus prepared is sent to a separate facility, such as a utility boiler, for burning in combination with fossil fuels. Some fluff RDF systems are relatively simple, involving one stage of shredding and one stage of air classification. Other systems may add trommeling, double shredding lines, additional classification, and sophisticated methods for the removal of aluminum and/or glass from the solid waste.

The first commercial demonstration of the use of fluff RDF was in St. Louis beginning in 1972. This plant was in operation until 1975, when it was closed. The same type of process was installed at Ames, Iowa, where the process is operating successfully, although the expected quantities of solid waste are not being received. A plant at Milwaukee, Wisconsin (Americology) was started up in 1977.

Wet Pulped RDF. A variation of the dry fluff RDF process described above is a wet process for obtaining RDF. This process, called Hydrasposal™, was evolved from paper industry technology. Such a system is currently being built at Hempstead, New York by Black Clawson/Parsons & Whittemore, Inc.

Densified RDF. A densified RDF (d-RDF) is undergoing development at the facility of the National Center for Resource Recovery in Washington, D.C. By increasing the density of the RDF, lower transportation costs and possibly improved handling could be attained. The d-RDF undergoes a process similar to that for fluff RDF, but the product is run through a pellet mill where it is formed into easily-handled pellets. This process is not commercial at this time.

Powdered RDF. Combustion Equipment Associates, Inc. is producing a fine RDF called Eco-Fuel™. Because this fuel is dust-like, it is easily burned in a coal-fired boiler. CEA also claims that their RDF can be used commercially in oil-fired boilers. The process uses a chemical treatment which has not been made public. CEA has an Eco-Fuel™ plant in East Bridgewater, Connecticut, but the plant experienced an explosion in 1977 which closed down its operation for a number of months. The Eco-Fuel™ has not been used commercially.

Summary. RDF fuel has an advantage in that it can be burned in an existing boiler, thereby saving the expense of building a new boiler, although the existing boiler may have to be modified to use RDF. The technology is not highly complex compared to pyrolysis, for example. In addition, industrial boilers requiring replacement could be designed to accept RDF, and electric power plants may decline as a market in the future.

Disadvantages of RDF include the cost of transportation from the processing facility to the burning facility and the fact that RDF has been viewed principally as a coal supplement for large-scale power plants. Industrial plants have not yet developed as a market. Because it is not economic to transport RDF very far, there must be a local market for the product. Densified RDF and dust RDF have the disadvantage of requiring more processing, which always adds expense. These have not been commercially tested, so no firm conclusions can be drawn.

Incineration. Incineration is a traditional, well-understood method of disposing of solid waste.

In the past, refractory-lined stoker-fired incinerators have been in common use, but in recent years these have been displaced by waterwall incinerators. A waterwall incinerator has a combustion zone which is surrounded by a welded steel tubing filled with water.

Mass Burning Incinerators. A mass burning incinerator receives unprocessed waste which is burned on a grate, producing steam. It is possible to recover metals from the residue of such an incinerator. Mass burning incinerators for resource recovery are listed in Appendix M.

The first United States waterwall incinerator with energy recovery was built by the Navy at Norfolk, Virginia and has operated successfully since 1967. Another well-known example is the incinerator in Nashville, Tennessee. Both of these produce steam for heating and cooling in the area. A 1,200 ton per day (TPD) waterwall incinerator is operating in Saugus, Massachusetts, where steam is produced for industrial use.

Semi-Suspension Waterwall. A more recent development is the semi-suspension waterwall incinerator, which burns coarsely shredded solid waste. The solid waste is fed by a spreader-stoker, and is burned in a semi-suspended condition. A semi-suspension incinerator is under construction in Hempstead, New York. It will burn the wet-pulped fuel produced by the Hydrasposal™ method described earlier. Semi-suspension incinerators are also under construction in Akron, Ohio and Niagara Falls, New York. A list of eight resource recovery semi-suspension waterwall incinerators under construction or contracted in the United States is included in Appendix M.

Fluidized Bed Incineration. A fluidized bed incinerator utilizes a heated bed of small particles such as sand. Hot air blown from underneath keeps the particles in motion and facilitates burning of material such as solid waste introduced into the incinerator. There is no commercial resource recovery fluidized bed incinerator in operation in the United States at this time, but one which will burn solid waste and sewage sludge in combination is being built in Duluth, Minnesota.

Modular Incineration. A modular incinerator may be defined as a unit having a capacity of less than 50 tons per day. These modular incinerators lend themselves to use in combination with one another to achieve a desired capacity. They are currently being manufactured by six or seven companies in the United States. Waste is partially burned in a primary combustion chamber in a starved atmosphere, and the gases produced are then burned to completion in a secondary combustion chamber under a steam boiler. Small modular incinerators of this type are operating in Blytheville, Siloam Springs, and North Little Rock, Arkansas and are being installed elsewhere to process MSW. These modular incinerators have the advantage of flexibility, small size, simplicity, and low capital cost.

Summary. Incineration of municipal solid waste to produce steam has the advantage of a very low requirement for fossil fuel. It is also often able to substitute for fuel oil or natural gas fuels. Also no processing of the municipal waste is required, at least for the mass burning incinerators. The size of the incinerators can be varied according to need. Some disadvantages are that the steam produced is at a lower temperature and pressure than that produced by a coal-fired boiler. Some boiler tube corrosion problems have been experienced, for example, at Nashville. Also, steam is a product which cannot be stored; therefore there must be a customer available to use the steam as it is produced.

Pyrolysis. A few years ago there was a great deal of excitement and interest in the process of pyrolysis to produce a combustible oil or gas from solid waste. Some recent difficulties and failures have dampened the interest in this process. Pyrolysis is a thermochemical reaction which takes place, in the strict definition, in an oxygen-free atmosphere. As the term is commonly used, the process may take place in an oxygen-free or an oxygen-starved atmosphere. The pyrolysis process can produce a gaseous product or an oil product, and the quantity of either depends on the temperature of the reaction.

Probably the best-known example of a pyrolysis reaction for converting solid waste to fuel is the Occidental Flash Pyrolysis™ system in San Diego, California. This pyrolysis process is designed to produce oil from an extensively processed solid waste. Recent reports have been received indicating that demonstration is having technical problems and the Oxy demonstration plant has been shut down. However, Oxy is expected to remain active in the field.

Another pyrolysis process which has experienced difficulty is the Monsanto Landgard process, which was demonstrated in Baltimore, Maryland. This plant is a 1,000 ton per day plant scaled up from a small pilot plant. Great difficulties were experienced in its early operation, including slagging problems and air pollution problems. The Monsanto Company, which developed the process, has withdrawn, but the City of Baltimore has committed to put the plant in operation.

The Union Carbide Corporation has developed a pyrolysis system called the Purox Converter in South Charleston, West Virginia. This system has worked well in tests, but it has not been developed commercially. The initial cost and operating costs appear to be higher than the other systems.

Summary. The advantage of the pyrolysis process which produces an oil or gas product is that the product supposedly could be used without modification of an existing boiler. The disadvantages have been outlined; the systems are unproven and require a great deal of processing, which is always expensive.

Other Techniques. Biological digestion of the organic fraction of solid waste to produce methane gas is an experimental process at the present time. The digestion may be anaerobic (in the absence of oxygen) or aerobic (in the presence of oxygen.)

Codisposal of Solid Waste and Sewage Sludge

Currently there is a considerable interest in the possibility of codisposal of municipal solid waste and sewage sludge solids. This process is seen as advantageous because it would reduce the volume of both wastes, thereby reducing requirements for landfill. Another advantage is that the energy obtained from burning solid waste could then be used to bring the sludge to the point where it can burn by itself. (This is called the autogenous point.)

Solid waste and sludge may be disposed of together by incineration, using methods which are already in use for disposal for sludge and/or solid waste alone. The most common method now used for disposal of sludge by incineration is the multiple hearth incinerator. In this type of incinerator, the waste cascades down a series of hearths so that it is combusted as it falls from level to level. A test has been made in Central Contra Costa County, California, where fluff RDF and sewage sludge were successfully incinerated together. A 1,000 ton per day multiple hearth incinerator is now being designed to codispose solid waste and sewage sludge.

Codisposal using a fluidized bed incinerator is being planned for Duluth, Minnesota, where such a plant is now under construction. There are also plans to codispose solid waste and sludge in Harrisburg, Pennsylvania, where an existing waterwall solid waste incinerator is to be used for codisposal in the future.

Theoretically, pyrolysis systems can be used for codisposal of solid waste and sludge, but this process is still in the experimental stage. Experiments are also being carried out on the biological application of codisposal of solid waste and sludge. An anaerobic test plant for codisposal is being built in Pompano Beach, Florida. Aerobic digestion for codisposal is planned in Wilmington, Delaware, where this process will be part of a much larger RDF plant.

While codisposal seems to be quite feasible, and is being tried in several localities, there are a number of barriers to its use. One of the outstanding barriers is the fact that the solid waste and the sewage sludge are often controlled by different political entities, and therefore there are institutional difficulties for a combined system.

COST OF ENERGY RECOVERY SYSTEMS

Accurate capital and operating cost information is difficult to acquire. Current energy recovery systems are too few in number and have oper-

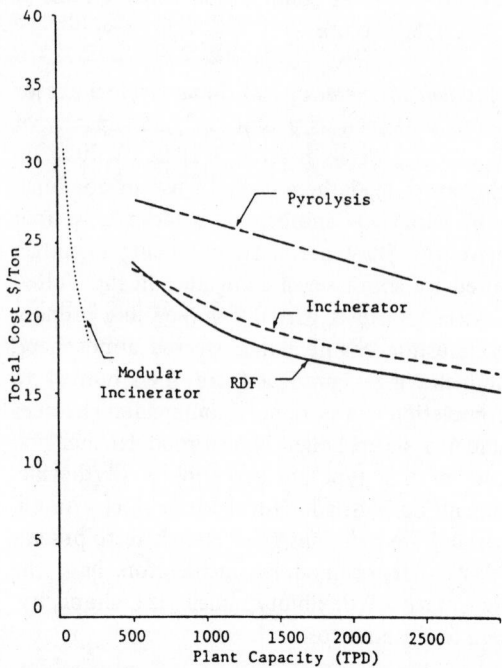

Figure 1. Cost per Ton of Energy Recovery Systems Versus Daily Capacity.

ated for too few years to provide a significant amount of reliable cost data. However, a compilation of average cost by system and tons per day (TPD) capacity* is shown in Table 1. A discussion of resource recovery economics is given in more detail in Appendix K. These data should be viewed in context with the specific assumptions and estimates on which they are based. Consequently they should be used as best estimates and not as absolutes.

Figure 1 is a graphical presentation of the data in Table 1. This shows rather dramatically the cost differences by system. Pyrolysis represents the highest cost, with RDF plants and incineration being in a lower range. However, incineration includes the boiler portion of the system. If the cost of a boiler were added to RDF costs, then the costs for RDF would be much higher for incineration. This reinforces the position that RDF is competitive when a coal-fired boiler already exists at a

---

*Capacity is a general measure of throughput potential, but there are seasonal fluctuations in the amount of MSW available at a given time as well as mechanical efficiency factors to consider in arriving at actual waste processing potential.

Table 1. Economics of Selected Resource Recovery Systems. (1977 Dollars)

Type of System	Products	Capacity TPD	Capacity TPY	No. of Employees	Capital Investment Thousand Dollars	Capital Investment Dollars/Daily Ton	Amortization Costs Thousand Dollars/Year	O&M Costs Thousand Dollars/Year	Total Costs Thousand Dollars/Year	Total Costs $/Ton
Refuse-derived Fuel	RDF, steel, aluminum	3,000	765,000	120	65,752	21,917	6,207	5,340	11,547	15.09
		2,000	510,000	90	47,683	23,841	4,501	3,959	8,460	16.59
		1,000	255,000	59	27,531	27,531	2,599	2,378	4,977	19.52
		500	127,500	41	16,098	32,196	1,520	1,490	3,010	23.61
Waterwall Incineration	Steam	3,000	819,000	107	101,000	33,667	9,534	5,136	14,670	17.91
		2,000	546,000	84	71,400	35,700	6,740	3,805	10,545	19.31
		1,000	273,000	55	41,100	41,000	3,880	2,278	6,158	22.56
		500	136,500	33	22,500	45,000	2,124	1,364	3,488	25.55
Pyrolysis (Andco-Torrax)	Steam	2,460	785,400	85	95,623	36,221	9,026	8,165	17,191	21.89
		1,980	589,050	72	75,964	38,366	7,170	6,600	13,770	23.38
		1,320	392,700	56	54,921	41,607	5,184	4,889	10,073	25.65
		660	196,350	38	28,802	43,639	2,719	2,646	5,365	27.32
Modular Incineration (continuous operation)	Steam	200	59,500	16	4,291	21,452	480.5	625.2	1,105.7	18.58
		100	29,750	12	2,394	23,937	273.8	404.1	677.9	22.79
		50	14,875	9	1,514	30,280	172.9	278.8	451.7	30.37
Modular Incineration (5 day/week operation)	Steam	200	47,500	9	4,281	21,404	479.5	517.4	996.9	20.99
		100	23,750	7	2,395	23,949	273.6	303.9	557.5	24.32
		50	11,875	5	1,501	30,025	171.5	191.4	362.9	30.55
Hydrasposal (wet pulping) Black Clawson	Electricity, color-sorted glass, aluminum, steel	3,000			112,000	37,333	10,572			
		2,000			81,000	40,500	7,646			
		1,000			46,500	46,500	4,389			
		500			26,700	53,400	2,520			

Source: Franklin Associates, Ltd.

location considering energy recovery, and is adapted to MSW as a supplementary fuel.

Modular incinerators have costs as low or lower than RDF or incineration at low capacities. However, the cost of a modular incinerator does not include any extensive materials handling system. If several modular units were combined to achieve, for example, a capacity of 500 or 1,000 tons per day, an extensive materials handling system (holding pit, overhead crane, ash removal, etc.) would be needed and this would increase costs.

ECONOMICS OF RESOURCE RECOVERY

Economic comparisons of alternative disposal techniques are necessary in a world where resources are limited and growing increasingly scarce and where it is espcially important that projects with the greatest return be selected.

The disposal techniques that are alternatives to traditional landfill disposal or incineration for which the most detailed financial analyses have been carried out are refuse-derived fuel (RDF) plants and waterwall incineration plants which produce steam. The methodology used in these analyses is a variant of benefit/cost analysis in which the internal rates of return (IRR) of alternative investment scenarios are calculated.* Using the IRR as a decision tool relieves the decision-maker from specifying a discount rate or borrowing cost of capital and instead solves the equations for the IRR. Thus the decision-maker is free to compare the IRRs of the best available opportunities and to determine for which investments IRRs

---

*The internal rate of return on an investment project is the discount rate which causes the present value of the net returns on a project to be zero. The IRR is a basis for ranking a group of potential investment projects. Thus, the internal rate of return can be thought of as the yield on total investment after time discounting cash flows – both costs and benefits – into present values. The IRR must be at least equivalent to the borrowing cost of capital to be acceptable. For example, a borrowing rate of 7 percent would imply indifference to investments with IRRs of 7 percent; rejection of those with IRRs below 7 percent; and a favorable view of those above 7 percent. However, the 7 plus percent IRR would only be necessary, not sufficient, to indicate the investment should be undertaken. The actual investment selected would be that one whose IRR is not only greater than the cost of money but also greater than the IRR for alternative investments to serve the same need.

exceed the borrowing rates by the greatest amount. For purposes of the resource recovery analysis, it may be assumed that the borrowing rate for resource recovery facilities would be close to that for state and local governments and that the public borrowing rate would constitute the cutoff point beyond which it would be uneconomic to undertake an investment.

The RDF and waterwall plant cost and revenue projections were based on engineering economics (developed by Franklin Associates in other studies) and on an estimate of current values of recoverable products. The relative prices of the inputs and outputs were not assumed to be affected by the building of the resource recovery plants but were assumed to be affected by general economic conditions continuing in the future.* The relative price assumptions underlying these forecasts were that labor, land, and most raw materials' costs would move with a general inflation rate of 5 percent per year. Energy, capital equipment, and construction expenditures would inflate by 2 percent more than general prices (at 7 percent); aluminum values at 6 percent; glass and ferrous metals at 4 percent (i.e., less than general inflation).

The sale of waste paper for fiber furnish has not been factored into the resource recovery calculations because it was assumed that waste paper source separation preceded the delivery of solid waste to the recovery facility, and that any remaining paper was so mixed in with other refuse as to be irretrievable except as energy. Care should be taken, however, in planning recovery facilities so as to fully assess source separation. In this way, an energy recovery plant can be designed to maximize the total anticipated benefits to the community and to allow for source separation and recycling to the extent competitive market conditions will support it.

Regardless of the resource recovery technique selected, a tipping fee is part of the revenue stream. In theory a tipping fee could be as high as the cheapest alternative net disposal costs but would not be higher because then it would be cheaper to continue using the traditional disposal methods. However, there

---

*That is, the amounts of resources supplied and demanded by the resource recovery plants would be sufficiently small in relation to the macroeconomy as to have no price effect.

Table 2. Summary Table: RDF Plant Financial Analysis. (In thousand current dollars)[1]

	1978[2]	1980	1981	1982	1983	1984	1985	1986	1987	1988	1989
1,000 TONS PER DAY											
CASE 1 ($6 Tip Fee)											
Net (Cost) or Benefit	(25,900)	(330)	(660)	(680)	(695)	(725)	(735)	(750)	(765)	(785)	(795)
Tipping Revenue	0	885	1,860	1,955	2,050	2,150	2,260	2,375	2,490	2,615	2,745
Total	(25,900)	555	1,200	1,275	1,355	1,425	1,525	1,625	1,725	1,830	1,950
CASE 2 ($14 Tip Fee)											
Net (Cost) or Benefit	(25,900)	(330)	(660)	(680)	(695)	(725)	(735)	(750)	(765)	(785)	(795)
Tipping Revenue	0	2,065	4,340	4,555	4,785	5,025	5,275	5,540	5,815	6,105	6,410
Total	(25,900)	1,735	3,680	3,875	4,090	4,300	4,540	4,790	5,050	5,320	5,615
2,000 TONS PER DAY											
CASE 1 ($6 Tip Fee)											
Net (Cost) or Benefit	(44,900)	(140)	(250)	(235)	(200)	(200)	(140)	(105)	(65)	(10)	35
Tipping Revenue	0	1,775	3,720	3,905	4,100	4,305	4,520	4,750	4,985	5,235	5,495
Total	(44,900)	1,635	3,470	3,670	3,900	4,105	4,380	4,645	4,920	5,225	5,530
CASE 2 ($14 Tip Fee)											
Net (Cost) or Benefit	(44,900)	(140)	(250)	(235)	(200)	(200)	(140)	(105)	(65)	(10)	35
Tipping Revenue	0	4,135	8,680	9,115	9,570	10,045	10,545	11,075	11,630	12,210	12,820
Total	(44,900)	3,995	8,430	8,880	9,370	9,845	10,405	10,970	11,565	12,200	12,855

	1990	1991	1992	1993	1994	1995	1996	1997	1998	1999
1,000 TONS PER DAY										
CASE 1 ($6 Tip Fee)										
Net (Cost) or Benefit	(805)	(815)	(830)	(840)	(845)	(850)	(845)	(850)	(845)	(840)
Tipping Revenue	2,855	3,030	3,180	3,340	3,505	3,680	3,865	4,060	4,260	4,475
Total	2,050	2,215	2,350	2,500	2,660	2,830	3,020	3,210	3,415	3,635
CASE 2 ($14 Tip Fee)										
Net (Cost) or Benefit	(805)	(815)	(830)	(840)	(845)	(850)	(845)	(850)	(845)	(840)
Tipping Revenue	6,730	7,070	7,420	7,795	8,185	8,590	9,020	9,475	9,945	10,440
Total	5,925	6,255	6,590	6,955	7,340	7,740	8,175	8,625	9,100	9,600
2,000 TONS PER DAY										
CASE 1 ($6 Tip Fee)										
Net (Cost) or Benefit	100	165	245	335	430	535	655	805	935	1,090
Tipping Revenue	5,770	6,060	6,360	6,680	7,015	7,365	7,730	8,120	8,520	8,950
Total	13,565	14,300	15,085	15,920	16,795	17,715	18,700	19,750	20,825	21,975
CASE 2 ($14 Tip Fee)										
Net (Cost) or Benefit	100	165	245	335	430	535	655	805	935	1,090
Tipping Revenue	13,465	14,135	14,840	15,585	16,365	17,180	18,045	18,945	19,890	20,885
Total	13,565	14,300	15,085	15,920	16,795	17,715	18,700	19,750	20,825	21,975

Note: Details may not add to totals due to rounding.

[1] Assumes tipping fee inflates at 5 percent per year.

[2] 1979 is zero and 1980 is the first year of operation, which are assumed to be at a 6-month rate.

Source: International Research and Technology Corporation and Franklin Associates, Ltd.

Table 3. Summary Table: Waterwall Plant Financial Analyses. (In thousand current dollars)[1]

	1978	1980	1981	1982	1983	1984	1985	1986	1987	1988	1989
1,000 TONS PER DAY											
CASE 1 ($6 Tip Fee)											
Net (Cost) or Benefit	(44,000)	1,405	3,055	3,325	3,615	3,920	4,250	4,625	5,010	5,425	5,890
Tipping Revenue	0	885	1,860	1,955	2,050	2,150	2,260	2,375	2,490	2,615	2,745
Total	(44,000)	2,290	4,915	5,280	5,665	6,070	6,510	7,000	7,500	8,040	8,635
CASE 2 ($14 Tip Fee)											
Net (Cost) or Benefit	(44,000)	1,405	3,055	3,325	3,615	3,920	4,250	4,625	5,010	5,425	5,890
Tipping Revenue	0	2,065	4,340	4,555	4,785	5,025	5,275	5,540	5,815	6,105	6,410
Total	(44,000)	3,470	7,395	7,880	8,400	8,945	9,525	10,165	10,825	11,530	12,300
2,000 TONS PER DAY											
CASE 1 ($6 Tip Fee)											
Net (Cost) or Benefit	(76,400)	2,885	6,256	6,783	7,350	7,961	8,615	9,322	10,091	10,917	11,801
Tipping Revenue	0	1,770	3,720	3,905	4,100	4,305	4,520	4,750	4,985	5,230	5,495
Total	(76,400)	4,655	9,976	10,688	11,450	12,266	13,135	14,072	15,076	16,147	17,296
CASE 2 ($14 Tip Fee)											
Net (Cost) or Benefit	(76,400)	2,885	6,256	6,783	7,350	7,961	8,615	9,322	10,091	10,917	11,801
Tipping Revenue	(76,400)	4,135	8,680	9,115	9,570	10,045	10,545	11,075	11,630	12,210	12,820
Total	(76,400)	7,020	14,936	15,898	16,920	18,006	19,160	20,397	21,721	23,127	24,621

	1990	1991	1992	1993	1994	1995	1996	1997	1998	1999
1,000 TONS PER DAY										
CASE 1 ($6 Tip Fee)										
Net (Cost) or Benefit	6,365	6,900	7,465	8,075	8,740	9,450	10,210	11,030	11,910	12,865
Tipping Revenue	2,885	3,030	3,180	3,340	3,505	3,680	3,865	4,060	4,260	4,475
Total	9,250	9,930	10,645	11,415	12,245	13,130	14,075	15,090	16,170	17,340
CASE 2 ($14 Tip Fee)										
Net (Cost) or Benefit	6,365	6,900	7,465	8,075	8,740	9,450	10,210	11,030	11,910	12,865
Tipping Revenue	6,730	7,070	7,420	7,795	8,185	8,590	9,020	9,475	9,945	10,440
Total	13,095	13,970	14,885	15,870	16,925	18,040	19,230	20,505	21,855	23,305
2,000 TONS PER DAY										
CASE 1 ($6 Tip Fee)										
Net (Cost) or Benefit	6,983	7,725	8,528	9,405	10,343	11,385	12,500	13,707	15,031	16,447
Tipping Revenue	5,770	6,060	6,360	6,680	7,015	7,365	7,730	8,120	8,520	8,950
Total	12,753	13,785	14,888	16,085	17,358	18,750	20,230	21,827	23,551	25,397
CASE 2 ($14 Tip Fee)										
Net (Cost) or Benefit	18,523	19,845	21,248	22,765	24,373	26,115	27,960	29,947	32,071	34,347
Tipping Revenue	13,465	14,135	14,840	15,585	16,365	17,180	18,045	18,945	19,890	20,885
Total	26,218	27,920	29,728	31,670	33,723	35,930	38,275	40,772	43,441	46,282

Note: Details may not add to totals due to rounding.

[1] Assumes tipping fee inflates at 5 percent per year.

Source: International Research and Technology Corporation and Franklin Associates, Ltd.

are circumstances where higher tipping fees in the early years of a recovery plant might be charged in exchange for lower fees in the later years, when the plant would have a greater cash flow. In addition, where resource recovery can be encouraged as a means of realizing benefits that accrue to society as a whole, but are difficult to assign specifically,* a public subsidy in the form of premium tipping fees, favorable tax treatment, or bond guarantees, could be justified. Also, the provisions of RCRA will lead to higher landfill costs in order to meet the standards of practice for proper disposal.

It is difficult to determine one appropriate tipping fee that includes all of the above considerations and yet can be generalized to suit a prototype test case. As a result, two tipping fee rates have been used in this analysis. The choices were $6 and $14 per ton (based on actual estimates of what appear to be the average and highest "normal" range landfill costs in the continental U.S.)**

The internal rates of return were calculated after the cost and revenue calculations were integrated with the tipping fee examples (Tables 2 and 3). These IRRs are summarized in Table 4, and should not be interpreted as representative of any specific area of the country. Also, the cost and revenue assumptions underlying this *analysis* are specific but should be examined carefully for any given local situation because they could be highly variable. Assuming appropriate cost and revenue assumptions are used, the relevant borrowing rates and opportunity costs of capital (i.e., next best available returns on investments) for a particular service should govern the decision to invest or not to invest. Naturally the availability of private investment

---

*An increasing awareness of the existence of social costs (e.g., pollution) and the need to allocate them has inspired public intervention in the economy. It is equally important, of course, to include social benefits (e.g., quality of life) in the decision-making process, but because they are sometimes even more difficult to quantify than social costs, social benefits have frequently been left out of policy analysis.

**Although some places claim higher or lower costs, the $6 and $14 range is representative of total landfill costs (including cost of land in the different parts of the country).

Table 4. Comparison of Internal Rate of Return Calculations for Waterfall Incineration Plants and Refuse-Derived Fuel Facilities.*
(Percent)

	IRR at Tipping Fee of	
	$6/ton	$14/ton
RDF		
1,000 TPD	3.83	14.47
2,000 TPD	8.23	18.14
WATERWALL		
1,000 TPD	13.00	17.46
2,000 TPD	14.67	19.46

*All calculations are based on current dollar cost and revenue estimates designed to reflect changing relative prices and 20-year operating periods.

Source: International Research and Technology Corporation and Franklin Associates, Ltd.

funds increases as the anticipated rate of return on capital rises. Where social benefits may be greater than purely financial measures would indicate, the decision criteria should be expanded accordingly. If the investment is socially desirable and adequate private sector funding is not forthcoming, then public funding should be investigated because tax exempt bonds have a lower cost to the borrower (but are subsidized by the general taxpayer because of their tax-exempt status).

POTENTIAL FOR RESOURCE RECOVERY IN THE U.S.A.

Solid waste is generated everywhere people live. However, to have sufficient waste to make resource recovery feasible, the waste must be generated in an area of concentrated population. Therefore, the potential resource recovery sites in the U.S.A. have a finite limit. Although resource recovery is potentially feasible in a community of any size, it is in the larger cities and population centers that the most emphasis on resource recovery has been placed to date. In addition, the principal resource recovery technologies (e.g., RDF and waterwall incineration) are designed to serve populations which can generate and deliver at least 500 tons per day of solid waste to a resource recovery facility. This is the minimum

Table 5. Regional Resource Recovery Potential in the 150
Largest SMSAs, 1990.

Region	Processable Waste* (000 TPY)	Potential Resource Recovery Plants (TPD)				
		50–300	500	1,000	2,000	3,000
New England	5,914	13	7	7	2	1
Middle Atlantic	20,155	27	13	15	10	7
East North Central	17,811	25	20	16	10	3
West North Central	4,831	8	7	5	3	–
South Atlantic	13,972	36	13	15	3	4
East South Central	3,370	11	7	2	2	–
West South Central	6,756	16	10	5	2	2
Mountain	3,244	6	5	2	1	1
Pacific	15,595	21	17	7	9	5
SMSA TOTAL	91,648	163	99	75	42	23

TPY = tons per year.
*Processable waste is defined as 75 percent of MSW generated in SMSAs with populations greater than 250,000 in 1990.
Source: Franklin Associates, Ltd.

quantity that would make most resource recovery technologies feasible.*

For each SMSA, the amount of processable waste available in 1990 was calculated. (Processable waste is estimated to be 75 percent of waste entering the solid waste stream. The actual quantity of source separated materials such as aluminum cans, newspapers, corrugated containers, etc., is excluded from this data base.) The resutls of these calculations are tabulated in Appendix H. The forecast quantities of processable waste for SMSAs by geographic region and nationally are summarized in Table 5. As may be seen in Table 5, the total processable waste in the 150 largest SMSAs will be about 92 million tons in 1990. A total of 402 resource recovery plants would be required to process this amount of solid waste, including 163 units below the size of 500 tons per day. A total of 239 resource recovery plants of 500 tons per day to 3,000 tons per day in capacity would also be required.

The tabulation of the national resource recovery potential in the largest SMSAs is not meant to be a description of actual resource recovery implementation. Rather it is simply an estimate of the total market for resource recovery in large SMSAs, without regard to

the practicalities of whether resource recovery could be implemented or not. In fact, it is most unlikely that resource recovery would be implemented nationwide in all of the locations summarized in Table 5 and in Appendix H. The practical potential for resource recovery is discussed in the section which follows.

To further demonstrate how waste generation varies within a given geographic region, a summary of municipal solid waste net generation for the Kansas City metropolitan area is given in Table 6. The rate of residential

Table 6. Municipal Solid Waste Net Discards —
Kansas City Metropolitan Area, 1974. (In
pounds/person/day and tons by source)

Category of Waste	lb/ person/ day	Tons/ Year
Residential: Urban	1.60	
Suburban	2.40	
Unincorporated	1.80	
Weighted Average	2.14	572,757
Commercial	1.18	316,941
Total	3.32	889,698

Population Base: 1,468,000

Source: Mid-American Regional Council, *Resource Recovery and Hazardous Waste Study*, Task 2.1, "Quantities and Characteristics," Black & Veatch, Consulting Engineers, and Franklin Associates, Ltd., 1977.

*There are small-scale recovery such as modular incineration available that can be used in communities of 250,000 or fewer people.

waste generation is dependent upon whether the urban core of the metropolitan area is involved, or the suburban and the unincorporated areas. Also, commercial waste is shown separately in the table. These waste generation factors are extremely important for resource recovery basic design parameters. (There is more than one instance where a waste generation rate was used based on some published national average that did not reflect the actual situation in the specific location. For example, if "average" municipal solid waste is the design parameter, 3.3 pounds per person per day would be expected to be delivered to a plant on average. However, if only residential waste were available to the plant, then the plant could be overdesigned by 36 percent if residential waste were equated with total municipal solid waste.)

A BASELINE FORECAST OF RESOURCE RECOVERY IN THE U.S.A. TO 1990

A forecast was made of the number of resource recovery plants that will be operational in 1990 unusual government intervention. The number of resource recovery plants which could be supported by the processable solid waste was calculated for each SMSA and aggregated into regions as discussed in the previous section.

A summary of baseline data on quantities of solid waste available for processing by resource recovery plants is presented in Table 7. These data are summarized for both the United States as a whole and for the 150 largest SMSAs.

The actual baseline forecast for resource recovery implementation is presented in Table 8, which summarizes the number of plants by size and the annual processing of solid waste for the baseline conditions. This forecast summarized in Table 8 was developed with a straightforward methodology. First, a careful review was made of the resource recovery plants that are in actual operation, or under construction, or which are committed to a construction program. These data as compiled gave a reasonably firm basis for resource recov-

Table 7. Baseline Resource Recovery Data, 1975 and 1990.

	1975	1990
TOTAL UNITED STATES		
Population (millions)	213.6	245.1
Total waste generated (million tons)	136.1	190.5
Source separation (million tons)	8.0	11.2
Waste paper source separation (million tons)	(6.9)	(9.7)(e)
Total Waste disposed (million tons)	128.1	179.3
150 LARGEST SMSAs		
Population (millions)	141.6	167.4
Total waste disposed (million tons)	85.0	122.2
Processable waste (million tons)	63.8	91.6

(e) = estimated

Source: Franklin Associates, Ltd.

ery implementation to the year 1981. Second, the average rate of activity and implementation was extended to 1990. This determined the baseline resource recovery implementation scenario.

As shown in Table 8, there will be an estimated 89 resource recovery plants of 500 tons per day or larger in place by 1990. These plants have the potential to process 30.7 million tons of municipal solid waste in that year, including the relatively small tonnage which would be processed through small plants of 100 tons per day or less. This tonnage would represent about 25 percent of the municipal solid waste generated in the 150 largest SMSAs in 1990, or about 17 percent of the total municipal solid waste generated in the U.S.A. in that year. However, it should be noted that the ability to process this quantity of municipal solid waste will not necessarily be translated into reality even if the plants are in place. The actual solid waste processed is much more likely to be in the range of 18 to 25 million tons in 1990, reflecting a composite of special

Table 8. Baseline Solid Waste Processing Estimates for Resource Recovery, 1990. (In tons)

Type of Technology	Plant Capacity (TPD)	Plant Throughput (TPY)	Number of Plants	Total Throughput (1,000 tons)
Modular Incineration	100	23,750	30	713
Modular Incineration	100	29,750	30	893
Refuse-derived Fuel[1]	500	127,500	15	1,913
Refuse-derived Fuel	1,000	255,000	16	4,080
Refuse-derived Fuel	2,000	510,000	9	4,590
Refuse-derive Fuel	3,000	765,000	4	3,060
Incineration for Energy[2]	500	136,500	15	2,048
Incineration for Energy	1,000	273,000	16	4,368
Incineration for Energy	2,000	546,000	9	4,914
Incineration for Energy	3,000	819,000	5	4,095
Totals	—	—	149	30,674

[1] Estimates for RDF include both fluff and powdered RDF plants.
[2] Estimates for incineration include waterwall incinerators, wet pulping, and codisposal with sewage sludge.
Source: Franklin Associates, Ltd.

situations including plants in startup, plants with insufficient solid waste to process, and plants which are unable to process their design capacities for various reasons. Nonetheless it is likely that somewhere in the order of 19 to 14 percent of the municipal solid waste generated in the United States in 1990 will be processed through various types of resource recovery systems that year. A graphic representation of solid waste generation and resource recovery is given in Figure 2 and illustrates the range in which actual resource recovery might take place.

The implementation summary of Table 8 is translated into capital cost data in Table 9 on the basis of 1977 dollars. (Backup detail is presented in Appendix L.) As can be noted, the capital required to achieve the baseline level of resource recovery will be 3.7 billion (constant 1977) dollars by 1990.

The final step in the baseline forecast was to spread the implementation over the 1981 to 1990 period more or less uniformly as was done in Table 10. The 1981 base year was normalized to reflect annual known implementation committed in 1978, and projects that estimate in 1977 dollars. In the baseline case, after the facilities are fully implemented the total capital requirement in *current* dollars is 5.5 billion dollars compared to 3.7 billion dollars (*constant* 1977).

There are two other scenarios that could develop in the 1980s which we felt are less probable. In one scenario we could foresee the "collapse" of energy recovery and curtailment of development of resource recovery. This

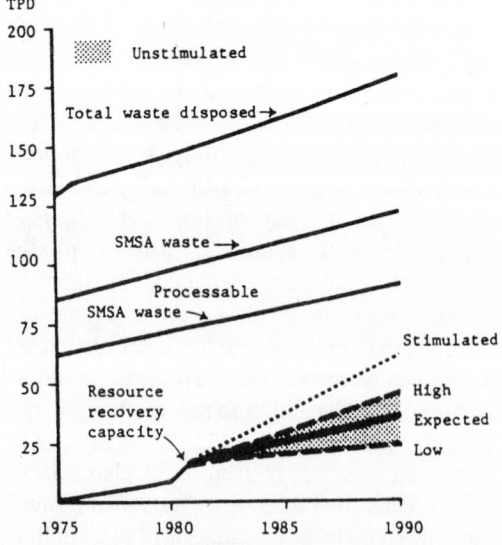

Figure 2. Solid Waste Disposed and Resource Recovery Capacity for the Baseline Case, 1975 and 1990.

Table 9. Total Baseline Capital Investment for Resource Recovery Implementation, 1981 to 1990. (In constant 1977 dollars)

Type of Technology	Plant Capacity (TPD)	Capital Investment ($1,000)	Number of Plants	Total Capital Required ($ million)
Modular Incineration	100	2,400	60	144.0
Refuse-derived Fuel[1]	500	16,100	15	241.5
Refuse-derived Fuel	1,000	27,500	16	440.0
Refuse-derived Fuel	2,000	47,700	9	429.3
Refuse-derived Fuel	3,000	65,750	4	263.0
Incineration for Energy[2]	500	22,500	15	337.5
Incineration for Energy	1,000	41,100	16	657.6
Incineration for Energy	2,000	71,400	9	642.6
Incineration for Energy	3,000	101,000	5	505.0
Totals	–	–	149	3,660.5

[1] Estimates for RDF include fluff, powdered and wet pulped RDF plants.

[2] Estimates for incineration include waterwall incinerators and codisposal with sewage sludge.

Source: Franklin Associate, Ltd.

scenario could be argued based on the following facts: (1) every energy recovery system in operation today is suffering one or more of three ills — (a) insufficient waste throughput; (b) product specification problems, (c) mechanical operating problems. Of course the economics become very unfavorable under these circumstances. (2) Technologies that have not been proven commercially successful may fail.

Thus, a bleak picture can be drawn for resource recovery today, but this view appears to be too pessimistic. At a minimum, energy recovery is in for more years of "shake down" and "working out the bugs." However, the pressure of decreasing landfill availability (mostly a political problem), intensified standards for land disposal, and rising energy costs leads us to believe that the momentum now established will be continued through the 1980s. The high disposal cost areas, primarily the Eastern Seaboard and industrialized Midwest, and the environmentally active regions — mostly the West Coast states — will continue to push toward "a better disposal alternative" called energy recovery. Thus, while we seen an arduous path ahead for resource recovery, by the same token we believe the pressures exist to keep the momentum going.

A scenario can also be built for a "boom" in resource recovery — the conversion of a nation of landfills into a nation of energy and material recovery systems. The arguments are persuasive — infant but rapidly developing recovery technologies, soaring energy costs, scarce materials, reindustrialization of stagnating areas, intolerable disposal costs, environmental problems. The optimist can argue just as convincingly as the pessimist. It would only take one or two things to accelerate implementation — a few unarguable successes among the systems now in operation or under construction; or a massive project such as is contemplated by the New York/New Jersey Port Authority. Alternatively, a big influx of Federal funds could create a boom. Our view is limited to the 1980s and we believe that at this time the stimulation of resource recovery will happen — but in 10 more years, not in three. Time is the ingredient needed now to let energy recovery develop, mature, and become more competitive in its own right. Add to this the slowness with which governments embrace and implement new technologies, and we believe the baseline we have drawn is realistic, and neither a "doomsday" nor a "utopian" concept.

Table 10. Baseline Resource Recovery Implementation for 1990. (Number of plants by type and capacity by year; capital investment by year in 1977 and current dollars)

	1981		1982		1983		1984		1985		1986		1987		1988		1989		1990		Totals	
	No.[2]	$ Mil.	No.[2]	$ Mil.	No.[2]	$ Mil.	No.[2]	$ Mil.	No.[2]	$ Mil.	No.[2]	$ Mil.	No.[2]	$ Mil.	No.[2]	$ Mil.	No.[2]	$ Mil.	No.[2]	$ Mil.	No.[2]	$ Mil.
Modular Incineration																						
100 TPD (continuous)	3	7.2	3	7.2	3	7.2	3	7.2	3	7.2	3	7.2	3	7.2	3	7.2	3	7.2	3	7.2	30	72.0
100 TPD (5 day/week)	3	7.2	3	7.2	3	7.2	3	7.2	3	7.2	3	7.2	3	7.2	3	7.2	3	7.2	3	7.2	30	72.0
	6	14.4	6	14.4	6	14.4	6	14.4	6	14.4	6	14.4	6	14.4	6	14.4	6	14.4	6	14.4	60	144.0
Refuse-derived Fuel																						
500 TPD	3	48.3	1	16.1	1	16.1	1	16.1	1	16.1	1	16.1	1	16.1	2	32.2	2	32.2	2	32.2	15	241.5
1,000 TPD	8	220.0	1	27.5	1	27.5	1	27.5	1	27.5	1	27.5	1	27.5	1	27.5	1	27.5	0	–	16	440.0
2,000 TPD	3	143.1	0	–	0	–	1	47.7	1	47.7	1	47.7	1	47.7	1	47.7	1	47.7	0	–	9	429.3
3,000 TPD	1	65.8	0	–	0	–	0	–	0	–	1	65.8	1	65.8	1	65.8	0	–	0	–	4	263.2
	15	477.2	2	43.6	2	43.6	3	91.3	3	91.3	4	157.1	4	157.1	5	173.2	4	107.4	2	32.2	44	1,374.0
Incineration for Energy[1]																						
500 TPD	6	135.0	1	22.5	1	22.5	1	22.5	1	22.5	1	22.5	1	22.5	1	22.5	1	22.5	1	22.5	15	337.5
1,000 TPD	6	246.6	1	41.1	1	41.1	1	41.1	1	41.1	1	41.1	1	41.1	1	41.1	1	41.1	2	82.2	16	657.6
2,000 TPD	4	285.6	0	–	0	–	1	71.4	1	71.4	1	71.4	1	71.4	1	71.4	0	–	0	–	9	642.6
3,000 TPD	4	404.0	0	–	0	–	0	0	0	–	1	101.0	0	–	0	–	0	–	0	–	5	505.0
	20	1,071.2	2	63.6	2	63.6	3	135.0	3	135.0	4	236.0	3	135.0	3	135.0	2	63.6	3	104.7	45	2,142.7
Total Plants and Capital (Constant 1977 Dollars)	41	1,562.8	10	121.6	10	121.6	12	240.7	12	240.7	14	407.5	13	306.5	14	322.6	12	185.4	11	151.3	149	3,660.7
Total Capital[3] (Current Dollars)		1,562.8[4]		170.6		182.5		386.5		413.6		749.2		602.9		679.0		417.6		364.6		5,529.3

[1] Incineration for energy is principally waterwall incinerators producing steam; but this category also includes wet pulping and codisposal of sewage sludge.
[2] Number of plants constructed that year.
[3] Construction cost escalation for current dollars was assumed to be 7% per year with a base year of 1977.
[4] The capital investment for 1981 represents the normalized 1977 cost of plants now actually operating, under construction, or under contract.

Source: Franklin Associates, Ltd.

ACCELERATED RESOURCE RECOVERY

This section evaluates the impacts and associated costs and benefits of a possible accelerated increase in resource recovery facilities. With such stimulation the solid waste disposal needs of 50 percent of the population in the 150 largest SMSAs in the United States (34 percent of the total U.S. population) could be met (plus the needs of numerous smaller jurisdictions via the use of modular incinerators).

It was assumed that the distribution of the new resource recovery facilities over the urban United States would be roughly even. In addition it was assumed that the technology of resource recovery facilities would be about evenly divided between RDF and waterwall incineration; that the additional plants would be constructed over a 9-year period; and that the markets and technology necessary for their efficient functioning would be there when needed. The year 1990 was used as the target for full implementation of the new plants.

Figure 2 compares the baseline resource recovery to a stimulated resource recovery pattern. Table 11 presents the basic data for the total number of plants and total solid waste throughput in 1990. It is estimated that 298 plants are required to process 61.3 million tons of solid waste annually. In Table 12 the data are translated to capital investment requirements in constant 1977 dollars. To fully implement resource recovery, the capital cost would be 7.3 billion dollars.

Finally, in the accelerated resource recovery scenario, the implementation was uniformly distributed over the 1981 to 1990 time frame. The capital costs are translated into current dollars in Table 13. It would require 12.7 billion (current) dollars to implement accelerated resource recovery compared to 7.3 billion (constant 1977) dollars. An additional 149 plants at an incremental capital cost of 3.6 billion (constant 1977) dollars or (7.2 billion current dollars) would be needed to guarantee that the solid waste disposal needs of 50 percent of the population of the 150 largest SMSAs would be serviced by 1990. If this much additional investment in resource recovery were to be stimulated, traditional landfill solid waste disposal requirements could be reduced by about 30 million tons in 1990 (over five times the solid waste impacts of a product charge on paper).

Table 11. Solid Waste Processing Estimates to Process 34 Percent of the Waste in the U.S.A. in 1990.[1] (For accelerated resource recovery)

Type of Technology	Plant Capacity (TPD)	Plant Throughput (TPY)	Number of Plants	Total Throughput (1,000 Tons)
Modular Incineration	100	23,750	60	1,425
Modular Incineration	100	29,750	60	1,785
Refuse-derived Fuel	500	127,500	30	3,825
Refuse-derived Fuel	1,000	255,000	32	8,160
Refuse-derived Fuel	2,000	510,000	18	9,180
Refuse-derived Fuel	3,000	765,000	9	6,885
Incineration for Energy	500	136,500	30	4,095
Incineration for Energy	1,000	273,000	32	8,736
Incineration for Energy	2,000	546,000	18	9,828
Incineration for Energy	3,000	819,000	9	7,371
Totals	–	–	298[2]	61,289

[1] Accelerated resource recovery in 1990 is defined as 50% of the waste in the 150 largest SMSAs or 61.2 million tons per year processed. This is 34% of total municipal waste generated for dispostal in 1990.

[2] 178 plants excluding modular incineration.

Source: Franklin Associates, Ltd.

Table 12. Capital Investment for Accelerated Resource Recovery Implementation, 1975 to 1990 (In constant 1977 dollars)

Type of Technology	Plant Capacity (TPD)	Capital Investment ($1,000)	Number of Plants	Total Capital Required ($ million)
Modular Incineration	100	2,400	120	288.0
Refuse-derived Fuel[1]	500	16,100	30	483.0
Refuse-derived Fuel	1,000	27,500	32	880.0
Refuse-derived Fuel	2,000	47,700	18	858.6
Refuse-derived Fuel	3,000	65,750	9	591.8
Incineration for Energy[2]	500	22,500	30	675.0
Incineration for Energy	1,000	41,100	32	1,315.2
Incineration for Energy	2,000	71,400	18	1,285.2
Incineration for Energy	3,000	101,000	9	909.0
Totals	–	–	298	7,285.8

[1] Estimates for RDF include fluff, powdered, and wet pulped RDF plants.

[2] Estimates for incineration include waterwall incinerators and codisposal of sewage sludge.

Source: Franklin Associates, Ltd.

Total solid waste processed would be increased by 16 percent, given the anticipated new plants by type, scale, and net benefits. The financial benefits to society of resource recovery implementation can be broken down into: (1) employment gains; (2) sales of aluminum, steel, glass, RDF, and steam; (3) reduction in tons of solid waste to be landfilled, and the resource conservation benefits implied by these sales; and (4) a downward pressure on prices to the extent that total output can be increased by more efficiently using scarce resources. These benefits must be weighed against the possibility that accelerated implementation could lead to improperly planned and designed facilities in the fast pace of construction.

RESOURCE RECOVERY AS AN MSW DISPOSAL POLICY

Acceleration of the implementation of resource recovery is a potential policy action which could result in solid waste disposal by increased recycling and energy recovery, both of which are resource conservation techniques that result in the disposal of solid waste. With a principal emphasis on selected recycling of materials, and conversion of residual combustible materials to energy, the issue of resource conservation is made more compatible with the reality of resource abundance of those materials in MSW.

The goal of stimulating resource recovery, however, is to increase the economic efficiency of municipal solid waste disposal by encouraging the least expensive non-inflationary solid waste management solution. Encouraging resource recovery *per se* does nothing directly to internalize full consumption costs, nor to discourage consumption, but it does reduce waste by recovering materials reusable as energy or raw materials.

By reducing waste, resource recovery has the effect of increasing the availability of resources. Economic efficiency is improved and society is better off if more goods can be produced with resource recovery than without it. But, capturing these benefits requires that resource recovery facilities be technologically feasible, their inputs available in the quantity and quality required, and their outputs actually demanded and used at prices that economically justify the facilities. Even if these criteria can be met, large increases in resource recovery may require initial public sponsorship of some sort because the size of investments, their amortization timing, and early risks may preclude private sector financing. However, there may be social objectives (social benefits)

Table 13. Accelerated Resource Recovery Implementation for 1990. (Number of plants by type and capacity by year; capital investment by year in 1977 and current dollars)

	1981		1982		1983		1984		1985		1986		1987		1988		1989		1990		Totals	
	No.[2]	$ Mil.	No.[2]	$ Mil.	No.[2]	$ Mil.	No.[2]	$ Mil.	No.[2]	$ Mil.	No.[2]	$ Mil.	No.[2]	$ Mil.	No.[2]	$ Mil.	No.[2]	$ Mil.	No.[2]	$ Mil.	No.[2]	$ Mil.
Modular Incineration																						
100 TPD (continuous)	3	7.2	6	14.4	6	14.4	6	14.4	6	14.4	6	14.4	6	14.4	7	16.8	7	16.8	7	16.8	60	144.0
100 TPD (5 day/week)	3	7.2	6	14.4	6	14.4	6	14.4	6	14.4	6	14.4	7	14.4	7	16.8	7	16.8	7	16.8	60	144.0
	6	14.4	12	28.8	12	28.8	12	28.8	12	28.8	12	28.8	14	28.8	14	33.6	14	33.6	14	33.6	120	288.0
Refuse-derived Fuel																						
500 TPD	3	48.3	3	48.3	3	48.3	3	48.3	3	48.3	3	48.3	3	48.3	3	48.3	3	48.3	3	48.3	30	483.0
1,000 TPD	8	220.0	2	55.0	2	55.0	2	55.0	2	55.0	3	55.0	3	82.5	4	82.5	4	110.0	4	110.0	32	880.0
2,000 TPD	3	143.1	1	47.7	1	47.7	1	47.7	2	95.4	2	95.4	2	95.4	2	95.4	2	95.4	2	95.4	18	858.6
3,000 TPD	1	65.8	0	0.0	1	65.8	1	65.8	1	65.8	1	65.8	1	65.8	1	65.8	1	65.8	1	65.8	9	592.2
	15	477.2	6	151.0	7	216.8	7	216.8	8	264.5	9	264.5	9	292.0	10	292.0	10	319.5	89	319.5	89	2,813.8
Incineration for Energy[1]																						
500 TPD	6	135.0	2	45.0	2	45.0	2	45.0	3	67.5	3	67.5	3	67.5	3	67.5	3	67.5	3	67.5	30	675.0
1,000 TPD	6	246.6	2	82.2	2	82.2	2	82.2	3	123.3	3	123.3	3	123.3	4	123.3	4	164.4	4	164.4	32	1,315.2
2,000 TPD	4	285.6	1	71.4	1	71.4	1	71.4	1	71.4	2	142.8	2	142.8	2	142.8	2	142.8	2	142.8	18	1,285.2
3,000 TPD	4	404.0	0	0.0	0	0.0	0	0.0	0	0.0	1	101.0	1	101.0	1	101.0	1	101.0	1	101.0	9	909.0
	20	1,071.2	5	198.6	5	198.6	5	198.6	7	262.2	9	434.6	9	434.6	9	434.6	10	475.7	10	475.7	89	4,184.4
Total Plants and Capital (Constant 1977 Dollars)	41	1,562.8	23	378.4	24	444.2	24	444.2	27	555.5	29	727.9	30	755.4	32	760.2	34	828.8	34	828.8	298	7,286.2
Total Capital[3] (Current Dollars)		1,562.8[4]		530.7		666.6		713.3		945.5		1,338.2		1,486.0		1,600.1		1,866.6		1,997.3		12,716.1

[1] Incineration for energy is principally waterwall incinerators producing steam; but this category also includes wet pulping and codisposal of sewage sludge.
[2] Number of plants constructed that year.
[3] Construction cost escalation for current dollars was assumed to be 7% per year with a base year of 1977.
[4] The capital investment for 1981 represents the normalized 1977 cost of plants now actually operating, under construction, or under contract.

Source: Franklin Associates, Ltd.

served in promoting resource recovery, e.g., reduction in imports of fuel or reduced need for landfill sites that would justify public sector participation at least in the beginning of a project.

THE ROLE OF THE PUBLIC SECTOR IN SOLID WASTE MANAGEMENT

Whenever significant externalities are present that make it impossible for a market mechanism to fully allocate costs and adequately charge for benefits, then a cautious suggestion of a role for government in the economy can be made.   If the market distortion is one where the social cost of an activity is greater than the financial cost, then there may be reason to argue overconsumption is taking place, and that a mechanism is needed to discourage consumption by bringing the financial costs closer to the true social costs.

The existence of positive externalities (i.e., social benefits) is also apparent in the solid waste management field. Where there are social benefits, the value to society of an activity is greater than its market price. For example, the value of reducing the need for conventional landfills should not be measured only by the accounting for the costs of landfills. The open market price for land does not reflect the social costs to the neighboring land of an undesirable disposal site.* The public hearing process will produce much less land available for disposal than the open market price for land would suggest. If the most desirable practical landfill standards, when fully implemented and accurately costed, would result in tipping fees higher than at present, then the social value of foregoing landfill operations is currently being understated in the market. At this time the "market price" of landfilling is relatively low. To the extent landfilling is underpriced, then the market values of alternatives to landfill will also be artificially low. Meeting the stan-

dards envisioned in RCRA will do much to bring the "market price" of landfill close to the social cost.

In the meantime, public intervention in the form of subsidizing the alternative to traditional landfill up to the difference between social and market values could be justified. In fact, one justification voiced in discussing public stimulation of resource recovery facilities construction is that these facilities provide an alternative to relying entirely on traditional landfill operations, especially where population density and land scarcity are important considerations.   In addition, these facilities can encourage recycling of recoverable products by providing a more stable supply of secondary materials, at more predictable costs than is frequently the situation now.

The operation of resource recovery facilities gives immediate and tangible values to society in the form of recovered materials and/or energy that otherwise would have been wasted, and an improvement in the environment vis-a-vis the effects of traditional landfills. MSW also typically has to be hauled further if landfill disposal is used, because people want landfills as far away from their own property as possible. Resource recovery facilities, on the other hand, can be built in industrial centers which are usually closer to the generation of MSW than landfill sites. Also, stimulating energy recovery can help reduce U.S. reliance on scarce fossil fuels and diminish the need to import petroleum products by making energy recovery a viable option for public utilities or private industries in many areas of the country.**

The economic track record of resource recovery in the United States has not been good because of four major reasons.   First, the technologies have not yet been fully proven in commercial use. The pace of technology development is increasing, however. Second, the steady volumes of MSW required for efficient system operations have not actually

---

*There are documented cases too where a landfill has increased the value of a piece of land because it made it usable for recreation, housing or other uses.

*Energy recovery from MSW does not "solve" the energy problem by any means. It makes a small contribution to meeting energy demands, but one which can be of significant value to the customer(s) of a resource recovery system.

been processed (either because the plant is over-designed or does not operate reliably). Finally, the markets for recovered materials have been uncertain (either because of the failure to meet specifications or because of the generally low quality of the recovered product). Finally land disposal sites have been readily available up to now.

The basic marketing problem has been that many of the recoverable materials, e.g., glass (made of sand) and ferrous metals, are among the earth's most abundant (and easy to transport) natural resources. Also, the market for recovered energy, where it is to be substituted for coal (which is relatively abundant), is not as strong as that for fuel oil or natural gas substitutes. Finally, vertically integrated firms have had little incentive to recycle; it is more economical for vertically integrated firms to produce value added onto their own virgin natural resources.

In addition, it has been very difficult to determine appropriate tipping fees, if "appropriate is taken to mean the cost of the next best alternative disposal techniques, i.e., sanitary landfill. Furthermore, adequate resource recovery may not be privately financed by relying solely on the market mechanism. Therefore, except in limited circumstances, it is unlikely that the private sector will be able, unassisted, to accelerate resource recovery significantly.

The questions then become whether the potential socio-economic benefits of accelerated resource recovery justify public support, and if so, in what form. Various forms of public support have been granted to private and quasi-private economic activities in the past, e.g., public utilities, railroads, and truckers via an effective, if not intentional, highway subsidy. The supports have taken the forms of tax relief, debt guarantees, monopoly franchising, public rate setting to assure a minimal return, and direct public investment. The common denominators to these public interventions have been that a socially valuable service is being provided, for which it is impossible to charge individual beneficiaries, and for which economies of scale are so great and important that the private sector cannot be

expected to assume the full burden of investment risks in order to provide the service. This is especially true where initial investments are very large, payout times are long, or technological risks and uncertainties are high. So, the crucial issue is deciding under what circumstances resource recovery facilities fall under the rubric of justifiable public or quasi-public projects. The actual selection of the public policy tool will have income and wealth distributional implications and, undoubtedly, will affect general prices and capital availability.

Whether materials and energy recovery benefits warrant greater public intervention than they now receive and, if so, what kinds of equity and distributional prices are to be paid, will ultimately be a political as well as an economic decision. It should be noted that nearly every resource recovery system in operation today, under construction, or planned has public funds (although usually backed only by the revenues of the facility, not taxpayer obligations) as the financing base. (Only a very small amount of Federal money has flowed into resource recovery to date.) Private capital has provided some of the "up front" risk to get systems into the marketplace.

RESOURCE RECOVERY FINANCING OPTIONS

If a case can be made for public support of resource recovery implementation, then the appropriate fiscal or monetary tool must be selected. Basically, the choice boils down to whether or not there can and should be a clearly identifiable relationship between the source of funds and their end use. For example, user fees are tied to specific public services when it is fairly easy to identify the beneficiary of particular services. In the case of resource recovery, if the beneficiaries are the communities and the users of the outputs of the facilities, they will be a cross section of the general population. It is also hard to narrow to a manageable few the generators of the inputs, i.e., MSW. Where it is difficult to precisely identify "gainers" and "losers" financing resource recovery, an ear-marked tax, such as a product charge, has no special justification, and it might be desirable to finance resource recovery from general revenues. On the other hand, if the price of MSW disposal, i.e., landfill charges, understates the true cost to society of disposing of solid waste, and a tax could be designed to make the price truly reflect social costs and be levied appropriately, then such a tax might reasonably be used to finance solid waste management, including resource recovery. Thus, if a product charge were to be implemented, investing its proceeds on research, development, and construction of resource recovery facilities could be a sound public finance mechanism.

Assuming the product charge is not ultimately adopted, then there are two ways to broadly distribute the public costs of resource recovery — debt or debt guarantee and general revenues or tax credits. Borrowing the total amount of capital needed to accelerate resource recovery would have little impact on national capital markets, but if the debt were incurred by individual states or local cities with constitutionally imposed public debt ceilings, then it could deter states or local governments from making other investments. The rules regarding debt guarantees vary from place to place and normally, industrial revenue bonds do not count against a state or local debt ceiling, but would be in competition for capital in the local and regional, as well as national markets. In a way, financing from general revenues could have the same impact as borrowing, since the money withdrawn from general revenues for solid waste management might have to be replaced by debt to cover other public expenditures. If this were the case then the socio-economic impact to be evaluated would be the income distributional implications of public borrowing to finance resource recovery. On the other hand, if the money were truly to be generated by a special appropriation from the general fund, then the real issue becomes one of whether taking money from society in the pattern established by the tax system and, in effect, returning it to the groups whose solid waste management needs are benefited, will result in an acceptable redistribution of income.

SUMMATION

The idea of accelerating the construction of resource recovery facilities so that 50 percent of the municipal solid waste of the 150 largest SMSAs could be processed by 1990, compared with 17 percent without stimulation, should be evaluated further. Resource recovery is an alternative to traditional landfill and will become increasingly profitable as landfill standards are tightened, and their costs and hence tipping fees rise. Resource recovery facilities generally result in low pollution, require less transporting of solid waste, and provide more employment than landfills. Also, they encourage recycling and energy recovery and, in time, could be a stabilizing force in the secondary materials markets.

The market economics of resource recovery today, however, do not warrant unaided private sector investments above the "baseline" case. This is partly due to weak recovered product markets, and partly to uneven or inadequate MSW supplies given the engineering specifications of most resource recovery plants. In addition, underpricing of landfill disposal places an artificially low ceiling on the tipping fees so that the social value of resource recovery may be greater than its financial profitability would suggest. Therefore, considerable thought should be given to evaluating the true benefits to society of resource recovery, and if these benefits are found to exceed their accounting prices, public support of resource recovery should be forthcoming.

Although a particular public financing mechanism is not advocated in this report, it is possible to suggest certain decision criteria. If services and beneficiaries can be linked, then user fees are indicated. Otherwise, the allocation of public funds should be made according to the priority ranking of society and, within that ranking in such a way as to get the most benefit possible per dollar. For example, if society has decided to allocate a certain amount of funds to waste management, the distribution of the waste management fund should be done so as to minimize the benefits of the last or marginal dollar spent. The determination of whether the marginal expenditures go for research and development or plant and equipment, for water, air, or land protection, for liquid or solid waste, etc., should be made on the basis of the greatest benefit per unit of cost. The choice of whether to use taxation or debt must take into account the overall monetary and fiscal policy goals of the decision-making entity, and the regional economic impacts of the choice needs to be evaluated. Because of the sizeable cost of waste disposal (about $4.5 billion per year for collection and disposal of MSW) matters, and given some of the problems of the product charge, it may be appropriate to look to existing funds for resource recovery support.

1-9 Resource Recovery as a Pollution-Control Device

Albert Klee and Judith Gordon

Source: Reprinted from *Waste Age,* Vol. 10, No. 4, (April 1979) pp. 49–52. Reprinted with Permission of National Solid Wastes Management Association.

Every type of refuse disposal — like nearly every activity of an industrial society — causes a certain amount of pollution. Now, with the country beginning a slow but inexorable shift from landfill to resource recovery for much of its refuse, it's time to wonder — how will new disposal systems affect the pollution from wastes? Will resource recovery help or hurt the environment?

The forms of pollution from conventional landfills and incinerators are familiar to waste control managers. All landfills produce some leachates (contaminated water). Well-engineered landfills contain that leachate, or attenuate it through soils isolated from drinking water sources; poorly run dumps let it seep all over the landscape. The stacks of conventional incinerators, unless carefully shielded with precipitators and other pollution-control devices, pump clouds of particles and fumes into the air. There are other miscellaneous forms of waste-related pollution. Methane seeps into the air from landfills; process water from incinerators becomes fouled; and so on. Generally, pollution from waste disposal is not among the chief environmental offenders. But with 173 million tons of municipal refuse generated in the United States in 1975 — an amount expected to rise to 197 million tons in 1990 — it's obvious that the ecological consequences of waste disposal cannot be ignored.

Faced with ever-increasing waste loads, many communities and private companies look to resource recovery systems. The attractions of these techniques are recycling refuse for re-sale (the most valuable commodity being energy from burned paper and plastics) and reducing the volume which must go to landfills. Naturally, companies that build resource recovery plants are most concerned with energy production, because that is where the builders make their money. But as important as new energy sources are, even under ideal conditions resource recovery will never satisfy more than a wisp of the country's power requirements. In the long run, the environmental impact of resource recovery could be its most significant accomplishment.

BURNING ISSUES

Burning anything produces potential pollutants. Since all refuse-to-power combinations involve combustion, many assume that resource recovery will lead to net increases in the pollution caused by refuse disposal. Proposed resource recovery projects have had difficulty winning air-emissions approval in some places, particularly California, where regulations are most stringent. Yet a study just completed, under EPA sponsorship, by the Mitre Corporation of McLean, Virginia, indicates that increased use of refuse-to-energy plants will cause a net *drop* in the amount of pollutants released into the environment.

In order to study the environmental impact of resource recovery, two scenarios were imagined. In the first scenario, it was supposed that little change in disposal practices takes place between now and 1990. Ninety-five per cent (by weight) of municipal refuse would continue to go to landfills; the rest would be burned in incinerators. The quantity of waste was assumed to escalate in proportion to projected population increases; the composition of waste was assumed to stay the same. The emissions from present disposal mechanisms were based on actual data or, in the case of landfill leachate, equilibrium modeling.

This no-change scenario formed a baseline against which to compare other possibilities. A second scenario supposed that, by 1990, only 80 percent of our wastes would go to landfills. Five per cent would still go to incinerators; 7.5 per cent would go to processing-type resource recovery that produces refuse-derived fuel (like those in Ames, Iowa, and Rochester, New York) and recovered materials; and 7.5 per cent would go to mass-burning systems which recover heat and residue materials (like the plant in Saugas, Massachusetts). Comparing these two scenarios made it possible to project whether more resource recovery would be good or bad for the environment.

CATCH IN THE NET

To make such a comparison complete, it's vital to consider the "net" effects of recycling. Recovered materials like ferrous metals will replace metals made from virgin ore — replace some of the pollution created during that process, like coal-fired generating stations, which have their own pollution problems. In special cases like recovery of aluminum — where recycled metals require only five per cent the energy consumed by virgin materials — some energy use would be eliminated altogether. In every case that recovered materials reduce or eliminate pollution from the manufacturing of virgin commodities, the social picture improves.

Two things must be remembered about these scenarios. First, they are based on assumptions, not predictions. No one can say for certain that 15 per cent of our wastes will be recycled by 1990, for instance. The actual figure may be far more, or far less. Fifteen per cent sounded like a reasonable assumption on which to base a study, but it should not pass for clairvoyance. Second, the study did not consider all pollutants

associated with municipal refuse — just the major ones. Refuse handling emits trace quantities of vanadium, for instance. Its effect is too slight to be worrisome.

CLEARING THE AIR

As can be seen in Table 1, the net impact of resource recovery is primarily favorable. Net emissions of all but three air pollutants would be reduced by the increased-recycling scenario. Emissions of carbon monoxide would drop by about 2.3 million tons per year in 1990. Emissions of carbon dioxide would drop by 310,000 tons. Nitrous oxide emissions would decrease 150,000, methane emissions 114,000 tons. Smaller reductions would occur for sulfur oxides (about 23,000 tons) and hydrocarbons (about 7200 tons). The total amount of particulates would increase slightly (by about 1000 tons). Aldehydes (an organic derived from alcohols) would increase about 2500 tons, and chloride emissions would move up more sharply, by 140,000 tons.

Remember these figures are net effects. A fundamental reservation about resource recovery plants is that they emit particulates. This is surely true. The "direct" effect of the 1990 increased-recovery scenario — taking into account only what happens at the recovery plants — is a 14,850-ton increase in annual particulate emissions. But when the particulate emissions avoided during virgin material and energy production are figured in — in other words, when the entire social picture is considered — the "net" effect is only a 1000-ton increase. In most air emission categories, the "direct" effect of increased recovery is increased pollution. But when all of resource recovery's secondary effects are recognized, the net effect is a cleaner society.

WATERED DOWN

The study found that, in the increased-recovery scenario, pollutants discharged to surface waters increased in almost every category. This is because more recycling plants mean more process waste water. Aluminum discharges would increase 918 tons per year; chlorides somewhere from 2000 to 15,000 tons; cyanide would not

Table 1. Clearing the Air — Effect of the "increased-recovery" scenario on air pollution.

POLLUTANT[a]	DIRECT EFFECTS[b]	SECONDARY EFFECTS[c]		NET EFFECTS[e]
	RESOURCE RECOVERY	MATERIALS PRODUCTION	ENERGY PRODUCTION[d]	
Particulates, total	+14,850	-10,654	+4,050	+1,046
SO$_x$ (as SO$_2$)	+40,050	-5,155	-32,800	-22,805
NO$_x$ (as NO$_2$)	+(17,200 to 34,400)	-51	-(156,980 to 174,800)	-(131,296 to 166,316)
CO	+(5,175 to 15,550)	-2,305,000	-(210 to 11,140)	-(2,289,660 to 2,310,965)
Hydrocarbons (as CH$_4$)	+1,500	-5,385	-3,340	-7,245
Aldehydes (as formaldehyde)	-(1,900 to 1,970)	NA	+2,470	+(2,525 to 2,595)
Chlorides (as HCl)	+(71,800 to 99,450)	NA	+(81,780 to 110,940)	+(109,630 to 166,440)
Particulate Fluorides	0	0	NA	0
Gaseous Fluorides	0	0	NA	0
NH$_3$	NA	-231	NA	-231
CO$_2$	-310,000	NA	NA	-310,000
CH$_4$	-114,000	NA	NA	-114,000

[a]Tons that will be emitted in 1990.

[b]Direct effects of resource recovery on municipal solid waste disposal. Includes emissions attributable to refuse-derived fuel (RDF).

[c]Indirect environmental effects of using recovered materials to replace virgin materials in materials and energy production. Does not include environmental effects of mining virgin materials, or transporting virgin and recovered materials.

[d]Includes pollutants from cofiring of coal and RDF. Credit is given for emissions from coal not burned.

[e]Sum of direct and indirect efforts of resource recovery, corrected to eliminate double counting of the emissions attributable to RDF (which are included in both direct and secondary effects). "Plus" indicates an increase in emissions, "minus" a decrease.

Table 2. Wilder Water — Effects of the
"increased-recovery" scenario
on water pollution.

	DIRECT EFFECTS[b]
POLLUTANT[a]	RESOURCE RECOVERY
Aluminum	+918
Barium	+394
Calcium	+3.310
Chloride	+(2,365 to 15,210)
Chromium	+10
Copper	+1
Cyanide	0
Iron	+14
Lead	+23
Magnesium	0
Manganese	+14
Phenols	0
Phosphate	+(158 to 709)
Sulfate	+(2,520 to 3,940)
Zinc	+45

[a]Net difference in tons of pollutants that will be discharged in 1990. "Plus" indicates an increase in pollutant discharge, "minus" a decrease.

[b]Pollutants in waste water from materials and energy production not included in study.

Table 3. Lighter on the Leachate —
Effect of the "increased-recovery" scenario
on landfill pollutants.

	DIRECT EFFECTS[b]
POLLUTANT[a]	RESOURCE RECOVERY
Cadmium	−3
Calcium	−(4,400 to 540,000)
Chloride	−(375 to 183,500)
Chromium	−89
Copper	−112
Iron, total	−69.500
Lead	−120
Magnesium	−(1,210 to 1,170,000)
Manganese	+5 to −9,400
Nickel	−103
Potassium	−(2,150 to 285,000)
Sodium	−(2,550 to 580,000)
Sulfate	−(25 to 285,000)
Zinc	−13,250

[a]Net difference in tons of pollutants that will be present in landfill leachate in 1990. "Plus" indicates an increase, "minus" a decrease.

[b]Solid wastes from mining of virgin materials and from materials and energy production not included in study.

change; and so on. This part of the study, however, considered only direct effects. There is no subtraction of savings in waste water pollution from the secondary effects of reduced virgin-material and energy production. (See Table 2.)

Finally, as expected, the study predicts that pollution potential of landfill leachate would be reduced by increased recovery. Annual leachate production would contain three tons less cadmium; 25 to 285 tons less sulfate; about 100 tons less each of the metals chromium, copper, lead, and nickel; and one million tons less of magnesium. Again, in this category (Table 3) no secondary effects were considered. Increased recycling, as it replaces certain virgin materials, would lead to reductions in mining and manufacturing wastes that end up in landfills. This should lead to further reductions in leachate, but such reductions were not calculated.

OVER EQUIVALENT BARRELS

Some miscellaneous calculations of the study included the prediction that the increased-recovery scenario would decrease landfill needs by 44,260 acre-feet yearly. This is about 85 per cent what would be needed in 1990 without increased recovery. This reflects the fact that all refuse combustion systems require landfill acreage to dispose of their residues or ash.

Energy produced by the hypothetical 1990 resource recovery network would be about 161,000 billion BTUs, or the equivalent of 28.8 million barrels of crude oil. The energy conserved by substituting recycled materials for virgin ones in steel, aluminum, and glass production would be 75,000 billion BTUs, or about 13.4 million barrels. This is a secondary energy saving of nearly half again the "visible" energy production of the plants.

Totaling the two leaves a net energy saving of 236,000 billion BTUs, or about 42 million barrels of crude. This is not an overpowering figure. Currently, the United States imports more than seven million barrels of crude per day. This makes the total saving scarcely a week's worth of imports, or maybe one per cent the nation's total annual oil consumption. Every saving of an energy resource is important, of course. But seeing resource recovery as a means to energy recycling only is a needlessly limited perspective. Resource recovery can guard the environment by reducing pollution. That must not be forgotten.

1-10 A Handbook on Scrap Futures Markets and Futures Trading

Roger Dower and Robert C. Anderson
Source: Adapted from a Report Prepared for the U.S. Environmental Protection Agency, Cincinnati, Ohio, 1979, 28 pp.

INTRODUCTION

The idea of futures trading in scrap materials is neither novel or untried. In 1955 futures trading in ferrous scrap was initiated on a Chicago commodity exchange, only to be withdrawn after one year. The concept was reviewed in recent years by the Department of Commerce in a series of presentations to ferrous scrap buyers and sellers on the mechanics of futures trading. Last year, a New York commodity exchange organized a ferrous scrap futures advisory committee, with the task of investigating the potential for renewed futures trading in ferrous scrap. More recently, after attending a symposium on the subject, the same exchange decided to develop a model ferrous scrap futures contract and propose it for trading.

The recurring interest in scrap futures trading has resulted from several conflicting motivations. The 1955 scrap futures contract was introduced at a time when the exchange was trying to generate trading interest. The Commerce Department presentations followed in the wake of the commodity shortages of 1973-74, in an apparent attempt to initiate a futures market in ferrous scrap as a forecasting tool. The current work of the Environmental Law Institute in scrap futures originated in an interest in futures markets as a device for stabilizing secondary materials markets and thus, perhaps, stimulating resource recovery.

Until recently, the scrap processing and consuming industry's interest in futures trading has beem minimal. Past discussions have rarely focused directly on the needs and concerns of scrap dealers or consumers. Many industry members view futures markets as outside their normal business transactions, offering few benefits to anyone but the speculators who take advantage of other market traders. Given this lack of understanding of futures markets, it is little wonder that broad industry support for the concept is just beginning to materialize.

The purpose of this report is to provide a foundation for informed discussion and debate on the merits of and potential for organized futures markets in wastepaper and ferrous scrap. To this end, it is our intention that the report serve as a primer on the structure of futures markets and the mechanics of futures trading, with emphasis on the economic benefits to industrial traders in the markets. Particular attention is paid to those characteristics of futures markets that may have a bearing on whether wastepaper and ferrous scrap can be successfully traded on a futures market.

In addition, incorporated into this discussion are relevant conclusions and comments made at a recent symposium on scrap futures trading. The desirability and feasibility of organized futures markets in ferrous scrap and wastepaper was the topic of a symposium sponsored by the U.S. Environmental Protection Agency and the

Environmental Law Institute on May 14th and 15th 1979.* The symposium provided a forum for preliminary industry discussion on the potential merits and barriers to futures trading in wastepaper and ferrous scrap. Commodity exchange officials and industry representatives spoke to audience of wastepaper and ferrous scrap consumers and dealer/processors on a number of different topics including the role of the commodity exchange in futures markets and the uses of futures markets for buyers and sellers.**

The design and implementation of a futures contract in wastepaper or ferrous scrap is a process requiring close interaction and cooperation among a commodity exchange and members of those industries. The purpose of the EPA grant under which this work was performed was to provide the initial step in this process. In a sense then by this report, presenting a mix of theoretical and practical issues that draw upon a larger research report prepared for EPA by the Environmental Law Institute and remarks made during the Scrap Futures Symposium, summarizes the progress which has been achieved.†

WHAT ARE FUTURES MARKETS?

Much of the mystery and distrust surrounding futures markets stems from attempts to distinguish futures trading from other sorts of market transactions. Strictly speaking, futures markets are organized market places for trading in future commitments, or futures contracts, for a commodity. While similar in concept to forward contracting, a common practice that enables both sides of a market to plan ahead of the current market period and to make good use of the resources under their control by smoothing out irregularities in demand and supply, futures markets are unique in several respects.

---

*From this point on the Scrap Futures Symposium will be referred to as the "Symposium".

**The Symposium speakers and the participants are listed in the Appendix.

†Anderson, R.C. and R.C. Dower, *An Analysis of Scrap Futures Markets for Stimulating Resource Recovery,* prepared for the Solid and Hazardous Waste Research Division of the U.S. E.P.A., EPA-600/8-78-018.

First, futures trading takes place on an organized exchange. Futures contracts in a commodity are bought and sold in one well-defined trading area or "pit" of a commodity exchange trading floor. In fact, trading outside this area is prohibited by law. Second, the futures contracts are standardized with respect to the quantity, quality, delivery terms, and so forth. The specifications of a futures contract are extremely detailed, covering the purity of the commodity to be delivered, the method of shipment, and the terms of payment, and the month during which delivery is to be made. The only aspect left unspecified is the day of the month in which delivery is to take place. In other forward contracts, the terms differ depending upon the specific needs of the buyer.

Futures contracts are usually traded up to a year in advance, with contracts designated for delivery in specific months throughout the year. For example, a copper futures contract traded on the Commodity Exchange, Inc. (Comex) in New York calls for delivery of 25,000 pounds of 99.9 percent pure copper cathodes. The delivery months are January, March, May, June, July, September, and December. Delivery can be made from any of the six Comex warehouses located across the country. Choice of the warehouse from which shipment will be made and the actual date of shipment within the delivery month are decided by the seller of the contract. While these last two points would seem to work to the disadvantage of the buyer, the market compensates for the uncertainty over delivery.

It is important to emphasize that futures markets are rarely used to make or take delivery of the physical commodity. Confusion over this point was expressed by many attending the Symposium, particularly members of the wastepaper industry. Of the hundreds of thousands of futures contracts traded on U.S. exchanges every year, only one or two percent is satisfied by the seller making delivery and the buyer accepting delivery. More often, a market trader who sells a futures contract will buy a similar offsetting futures contract before the contract reaches maturity (before the delivery month) and thus cancel his position in the market. For example, should a trader sell a May copper futures contract in January, he has two choices to follow with the contract. He can hold it until May, when he is legally bound to deliver 25,000 pounds of copper, or he can, at any time prior to May, buy a May contract. In the latter case, he has both bought and sold a May copper contract and has effectively cancelled any obligation to deliver or purchase copper. Although a futures contract is a legally binding contract to deliver or purchase a commodity at some future date, it does not transfer title to a commodity. This aspect of futures trading must be completely understood. The strict terms of futures contracts do not, generally, represent the most profitable transaction terms for a commercial buyer or seller of the commodity in the cash market.* It is this point as well as the other unique features of futures markets, such as the fact that actual buyers and sellers of futures contracts are unknown to each other, that allow futures trading to supplement, and in some instances, temporarily substitute for the forward trading that occurs in most markets. The commercial trader is usually better off negotiating his own contract in the cash market and using the futures market for other purposes. To view futures markets as delivery markets overlooks these more important functions which are outlined in the next section.

WHY FUTURES MARKETS?

This section addresses two questions raised in the last chapter: If futures markets are not for delivery what do they do and why would anyone want one? While there are several uses for futures markets, this report focuses on the two most important to commercial traders: risk shifting or risk management, and the financial aspects of futures trading.

Price Risk Shifting

Futures markets enable commercial buyers and sellers of a commodity to shift the risk of doing

---

*Throughout this report, the term "cash market" will refer to transactions that take place in the normal commercial channels and market place. These transactions may involve futurity, such as forward contracts, but are not organized in the sense of futures contracts.

business in an uncertain market environment by hedging against unfavorable movements in the price of inputs and outputs. Basically, risk shifting or the hedging function of futures markets involves taking an opposite position in the futures markets from one held in the cash market. A buyer in the cash market who wants to hedge against a price decline would sell in the futures market. If the price of the commodity does decline, he takes a loss in the cash market, but by buying back the futures contract at a lower price than he sold it for, his gains on the futures market transaction offset his losses in the cash market, and he is able to stabilize his profit margin and his income.

For a hedge to be successful, the price of the commodity in the cash market must be closely related to the futures price of the commodity for the nearest month of delivery. While this would almost certainly be true for market transactions involving the same commodity as described by the futures contract, it may also be the case for two less clearly related commodities. Buyers and sellers of copper scrap are able to hedge their purchase, sale, or inventory decisions against any of the copper futures contracts traded. As demonstrated in Figure 1, this is because the price of copper scrap moves closely with the price of primary copper which, in turn, is closely related to the futures price of copper.

During the Symposium several references were made to futures markets being price insurance markets. In other words, that by hedging on futures markets a buyer or seller could insure against price changes and therefore, income or profit margin changes. This analogy was described by a commodity exchange official as not being entirely accurate. Hedging on a futures market does not eliminate risk like an insurance market, but rather reduces risk and provides a mechanism for coping or managing risk. Futures prices and cash prices are only rarely perfectly correlated. To the extent that they diverge, a hedger on a futures market is still exposed to some risk.

In futures trading, price risks are shifted. Commercial buyers and sellers shift the risk of unfavorable movements in the cash price for a commodity to other traders in the futures market, particularly speculators, who are willing

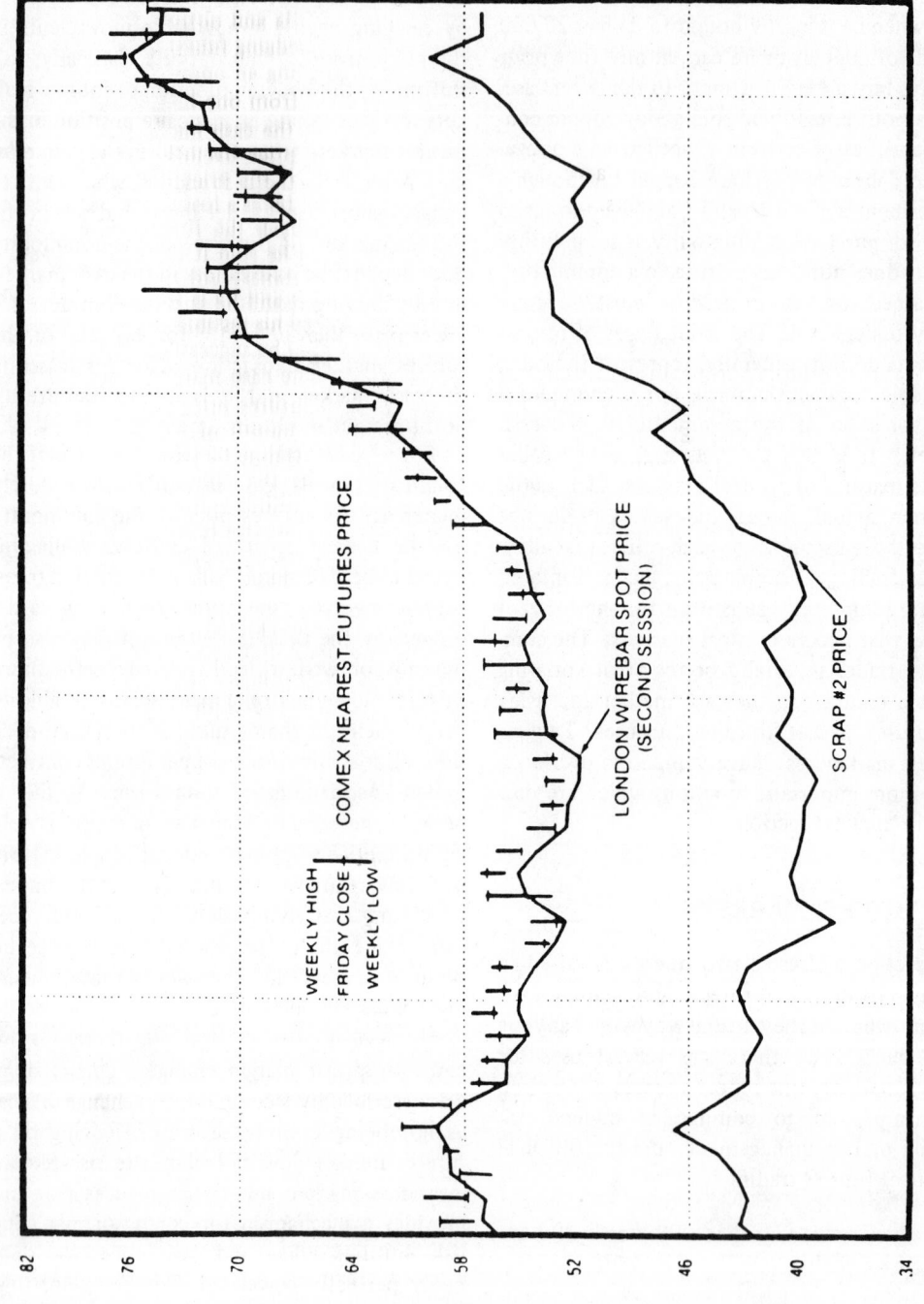

Figure 1. Copper prices: futures, wirebar, and #2 scrap.

to accept this risk in hope of financial gain. In Section 4, the extremely important role played by speculators in making a successful futures markets is described in some detail. At this point, suffice it to say that many of the benefits of futures trading to commercial users result from speculators' willingness to accept the price risks shifted to them by hedgers.

Financial Benefits

Futures markets can be thought of as financial institutions and futures contracts as financial instruments. As Professor Hieronymus states in his well regarded book, *The Economics of Futures Trading,* "It is not a financial institution in the sense of a bank in which money is received from one group of people and loaned to another. Rather, it is a means by which loans made by banks or operating money otherwise secured by businesses are guaranteed against loss." Holding inventories of any commodity, and particularly of scrap commodities, is expensive; if the value of these inventories can be protected from adverse price movements, financing will be more readily available. Futures markets allow commercial traders the opportunity to trade commodity obligations for equity or money obligations. Thus, loans for expansion and other purposes can be acquired at much more favorable terms, if the lending institution knows that its investment is protected from a major price-induced loss.

A simple example of one type of financial benefit from futures trading involves the use of equity capital for financial inventories. Imagine a firm with $1,000 of equity capital to be used to acquire inventory holdings of a commodity. If the firm promises to hedge that inventory, it might be able to obtain a loan rate of 90 percent from a lending institution. This would allow the firm to have $10,000 worth of commodity in inventory. Without hedging, the loan rate might be only 60 percent, which would control only $2,500 of the inventory given the initial $1,000 equity capital.

HOW FUTURES MARKETS WORK

In order to have even a cursory understanding of the mechanics of futures trading, one must understand the players and the rules of the market. In this section, we introduce the participants in futures markets and describe the structure in which futures trading takes place.

The Players

For the purposes of this report, the participants in futures trading are divided into three groups: hedgers; speculators; and the commodity exchange. It should be kept in mind that only for the third group is the definition clear enough to be consistently true.

Hedgers. Hedgers are the commercial participants in futures trading. These traders have, or plan to have, a commodity commitment in the cash market. They are the buyers, sellers, wholesalers and brokers of a commodity. The chances are that they are not trading in futures markets to accept or make delivery of a commodity, but to shift the risk of uncertain future price movements.

Without hedgers, or more properly, without the commercial demand for the hedging services of a futures market, the market is doomed to a short life, if it gets started al all. Evidence indicates that only a handful of futures contracts exist without strong hedging demand. This point was alluded to by a commodity exchange speaker at the Symposium, who identified the extent of industry participation in a futures market as one of the major determinants of a successful contract.

While the importance of hedging demand may seem obvious, it is extremely relevant to consideration of futures trading in ferrous scrap or wastepaper. The 1955 ferrous scrap contract, as mentioned earlier, failed due to a lack of trading interest. While the reasons for this are obscured by the passage of some 25 years, the failure of the market appears closely related to a lack of hedging interest. The exchange neglected to design a contract that appealed to scrap buyers and sellers or to bring scrap traders into the decision process. Feeling that the futures contract did not conform to their standard industry practices, and that it would not serve a useful purpose, commercial traders shunned the market.

Commercial or industrial participation in futures trading actually has a two pronged impact on trading volume. One, it determines hedging volume and at the same time determines speculative trading interest. As mentioned by one speaker at the Symposium, if adequate hedging demand is established in a futures market, speculative participation usually follows. This aspect of futures trading and the role of the speculator is discussed more fully below.

Speculators. Along with hedging demand, speculative trading provides the other necessary ingredient of a successful futures market. Speculators are traders with no stake in the commercial market for a particular commodity. Ostensibly, they trade solely for the purpose of profiting from favorable movements in the prices of futures contract. If they think prices for a commodity will rise over a particular period of time, speculators will buy futures contracts in hopes of selling them later at a higher price. The role of speculators in futures markets is actually more subtle and far-reaching than this. The misconceptions concerning speculators in futures markets, several questions on which were raised by industry participants in the Symposium, justify an explanation of their part in insuring a well-functioning futures market.

Trading activity on the major commodity exchanges suggests that speculators tend to enter markets in which there is heavy hedging activity. It is in this type of market that speculators find the best opportunity for profits. This also works to the advantage of the hedgers by enabling them to get in and out of the market quickly. Without the trading activity of the speculators, it would be difficult for hedgers to buy and sell when they want to. Speculators willingly accept the price risk the hedgers want to avoid. It was stated earlier that futures markets allow commercial traders to exchange commodity obligations for monetary ones. It is the speculator who provides the monetary obligation. In a sense, the speculator is the financier.

All too often, speculative trading on futures markets is assumed to have a destabilizing effect on prices and to downgrade the integrity of the marketplace. In fact, economic evidence suggests the opposite. By buying when they think prices will rise and selling when they think prices will fall, speculators help stabilize prices. This point of view was defended by several representatives from commodity exchanges at the Symposium. Of course, it cannot be said that speculators, or hedgers for that matter, never try to corner a market or take advantage of a thin (low trading volume) market. However, the incidence of market abuse in futures trading is amazingly low, for trading rules enforced by the exchange allow little opportunity for such behavior.

The Commodity Exchange. In the United States, commodity exchanges are nonprofit organizations formed to serve the needs of their members. Exchanges provide a location for futures trading as well as the rules for that trading. Besides setting the rules of trade and enforcing those rules, exchanges actively engage in research and publication. Membership is open to all individuals of good character and financial soundness. Although, on most large U.S. exchanges, the number of members is limited.

Adjunct to the exchange is the Clearing House, which in most cases is actually a separate corporation. Clearing House members must be members of the exchange, but not all exchange members belong to the Clearing House. The Clearing House is the watch dog of trading activity on the exchange floor, and more importantly, an active participant in the trading process. All trades are made through the Clearing House and one of its members. The Clearing House guarantees all trades and assures openness and honesty of the market. If a seller, for example, were to default on a contract, the Clearing House would be responsible for seeing that the buyer of that contract was satisfied and that the defaulting seller was properly chastized. At the Symposium, exchange officials pointed out that no buyer or seller of a futures contracts in the U.S. has ever suffered monetary loss due to a default.

Admittedly, this is a brief overview of the complex workings of a commodity exchange. We have only highlighted some of the more important functions. One other extremely important function or role of a commodity exchange is presented in Section 6. This involves the choice of commodities made by the exchange for futures trading. This is a decision made solely by the exchange and will have a direct bearing on the feasibility of futures trading in wastepaper and ferrous scrap.

With the participants in futures markets now identified, a few general points are in order. First, the characteristics of the players have been oversimplified. The actual distinction between hedgers and speculators is blurred. Whereas the earlier definition suggests that the primary interest of hedgers is risk shifting rather than speculative gain, very often hedgers have the same motivation as speculators. Second, for every buyer of a futures contract there is a seller, and for every winner a loser — even though the actual buyers and sellers may not be known to each other. There is no need to; the Clearing House guarantees that a delivery takes place, the terms of the contract will be met. Finally, all the players have significant roles in assuring that the futures markets operate properly and efficiently, and that the markets provide the services for which it is intended.

The Rules of the Game

Trading in futures markets is a procedure formalized by the commodity exchange and by law. Futures trading takes place in a specified area of the exchange floor during specific hours of the day. Only members of the exchange may be present on the floor and engage in trading. These members may trade for their own accounts, for the accounts of a brokerage house, or the latter's customers. To insure that all trades are public and competitive, offers to buy and sell must be made by "open outcry," which, because of the loud din on the exchange floor, is normally interpreted to include hand signals as well as shouts. Price moves for a particular contract on any given day are usually limited by the exchange; for example, copper futures are limited to price changes of 3 cents per pound. If the price change in any given day reaches the limit set by the exchange, trading is suspended for the day. Generally, price changes during trade in the current delivery month are not limited. In response to a question at the Symposium on this subject, an exchange representative stated that the price limits are set in response to guidelines from the Commodity Futures Trading Commission (CFTC), the regulatory agency charged with oversight of the futures trading industry, and that the limits were for speculators who would not be aware of large changes in the price of a contract.

Buying and Selling in a Futures Market. To understand futures trading, it is useful to follow, in a simplified fashion, the procedures by which futures contracts are bought and sold. Suppose, for illustrative purposes, that a commodity exchange offers a ferrous scrap futures contract for trading. Assume further that a ferrous scrap dealer or processor has accumulated in inventory a quantity of ferrous scrap similar in quality to the grade of scrap described by the futures contract. He wants to hedge that inventory against the risk of a decrease in the price of scrap. To do this, he could sell a futures contract. After checking the current futures price quotes, contained in most major newspapers, and evaluating all the available market information, he would call his commodity broker or commission merchant and instruct him to sell one ferrous scrap futures contract in the delivery month that is nearest to the month in which he thinks he will sell his inventory. (He would actually want to sell enough futures contracts to insure that the quantity called for in the futures contracts matched his inventory holdings as closely as possible.)

For the broker to execute the trade, the hedge must have a large enough account with the brokerage house to cover the margin requirement for the contract. The margin requirement represents "good faith" or performance money, for which a minimum level is set by the exchange. The brokerage house can set any margin requirement above the minimum. (Generally, it ranges from 5-10 percent of the contract's value.) An interesting distinction was made during the course of the Symposium between the margin requirement on futures contracts and the margins on securities or stocks. Payment of a stock margin gives the buyer title to the stock and, therefore, actual ownership or equity in the entity represented by the stock. Payment of a futures contract margin provides no title of ownership to the particular commodity. This would not happen until the buyer of the futures contract decides to take delivery on the contract and pays the full contract amount. Payment of the margin does give the right to accept delivery or make delivery.

With the financial issues settled, the broker would call his floor representative with instructions to sell one ferrous scrap contract for the delivery month named by the hedger. The floor representative will make his desire to sell a contract known to the other traders in the pit by hand signals or by calling out the order. If another floor trader wants to buy at that price, he responds in kind, and the trade is made. The floor traders have the responsibility to see that the floor observers, exchange employees keeping account of the trading activity, are aware of the price, quantity, and other aspects of the trade. These observers feed the information into a computer system that sends out the results of the trade across the world. The floor traders also fill out time-stamped forms giving the particulars of the trade. These forms are used by the Clearing House to settle the accounts at the end of the day. Finally, the brokerage house is notified of the trade and in turn informs the scrap dealer. The total time elapsed between the floor broker making the trade and the scrap dealer learning the results is only a matter of minutes.

The scrap dealer is now short -has sold-one futures contract. Had he purchased a contract, he would be considered long one contract. At the end of the trading day, the Clearing House reconciles all trades and computes the gains or losses accrued to each trading position. If the futures contract sold by the scrap dealer has risen in price, the dealer will have lost in that day's trading. To keep his equity at the required level, he may have to increase his account with the brokerage house. Should the price of the contract drop by the end of the day, he will have gained on the transaction, and the difference between the selling price and the closing price will be credited to his account.

The process of taking in and paying out based on changes in the daily price of the futures contract continues until the position is closed out. This is done in one of two ways. During the delivery month, the scrap dealer could decide to deliver under the terms of the contract or, more realistically, he could take an offsetting position in the market by buying a ferrous scrap contract at any time prior to the delivery month. He would take the latter course if he decided to sell his inventory position. A simple call to his broker is all he needs to close out his position with the Clearing House.

The scrap dealer's net gain or loss in holding the inventory of scrap and hedging in the futures market depends on how closely the futures price and the market price followed each other. Any gain or loss, however, will be greater if he does not hedge his cash market transaction. If the market price rises in the period during which he holds the futures contract, he will lose on the futures market but gain on his inventory position. Again, he could have greater revenues had he not hedged, but, on the other hand, he could have taken a loss if the market price fell.

Table 1 provides a numerical example of how a scrap dealer could enter into a selling hedge and protect his inventory holdings. In April, a scrap dealer buys in the cash market a certain quantity of ferrous scrap at $75.00 a ton to be processed and placed into inventory until the Fall. At the same time, he sells a September futures contract for $72.50 a ton. (The difference in the two prices results, in part, from the costs of holding scrap from April to September.) Throughout the summer the price of scrap falls, and in August the dealer decides to sell his inventory. He sells his stocks of processed scrap for the current market price of $73.00, taking a loss of $2.00 per ton in the cash market. Yet he buys back the futures, which has also dropped in price to $70.50, and thereby makes a profit

Table 1. Example of a Selling Hedge.

Activity	Cash Market	Futures Market
April:		
Buy	$75.00	–
Sell	–	September $72.50
August:		
Buy	–	September $70.50*
Sell	$73.00*	–

*Loss, $2.00; gain, $2.00; net loss, 0.

of $2.00 per ton on the futures market. The net loss or gain on the deal is zero. Although a simplistic demonstration — for example, commissions and processing costs are ignored — it does show how one can hedge against unfavorable price movements in the cash market.

Throughout the Symposium several other methods of hedging on futures markets were suggested by speakers and participants. One, of interest to consumers of scrap materials, is broadly called a buying hedge and is a means of protecting against rising raw material costs. Suppose that in April an electric furnace operator enters into a contract with a scrap dealer/processor for a certain quantity and quality of ferrous scrap to be delivered to the mill in August at the market price prevailing at that time. In April the market price for the scrap is $75.00 per ton but because the consumer is uncertain what the price will be in August he wants to protect himself from a rise in the price of scrap that would make it unprofitable to use the scrap in his furnace. He could hedge his forward contract in the cash market by buying a futures contract.

Using the hypothetical ferrous scrap futures contract introduced before, the mechanics of the buying hedge are outlined in Table 2. In April the electric furnace operator enters into the cash market contract for delivery in August and buys one September futures contract at $72.50 per ton. (This assumes, of course, that the consumer's cash market contract is covered by one futures contract and that the nearest delivery month to August is September.) The current market price for one ton of ferrous scrap is $75.00. Suppose now that by August

Table 2. Example of a Buying Hedge.

Activity	Cash Market	Futures Market
April:		
Buy	–	September $72.50
Sell	–	–
Market Price	$75.00	–
August:		
Buy	$77.00	–
Sell	–	September $74.50*

*Loss, $2.00; gain, $2.00; net loss, 0.

the price of ferrous scrap has risen by $2.00 to $77.00 per ton. He is forced to buy the scrap at a loss, relative to the April price, of $2.00. At the same time, the futures price has also risen by $2.00 and he sells his contract for $74.50 and makes $2.00. As in the case of the selling hedge, the furnace operator's net loss on both transactions was zero.

The procedures for making or taking delivery on a futures market have not been discussed because delivery does not often occur. Suppose, however, that the hypothetical scrap dealer does decide to deliver his scrap inventory to satisfy the futures contract. This question was raised several times at the Symposium and will be addressed below. First, though, it is necessary to introduce a few concepts.

Delivery on a Futures Contract. A futures contract spells out the procedures for delivery: delivery location; shipping mode; payment; etc. The instrument transferring title to the commodity is called a warehouse receipt or shipping certificate, depending on whether the commodity is delivered from inventory or current production, respectively. In the former case, the exchange will either own or have approved the warehouse or location of the inventory from which delivery can take place. Traders wishing to deliver on the futures market must own the commodity at the warehouse. In the latter case, where delivery takes place from current production, only those sellers classed as "regular" for delivery by the exchange can deliver on the market. To insure a standard of quality, the exchange requires a seller to demonstrate financial and moral integrity. The exchange guarantees that the commodity delivered on the market meets the strict requirements of the contract, and in some cases it also conducts inspections to this end. If the contract calls for the use of a shipping certificate, it will state whether the commodity is to be shipped by rail or truck. In general, the terms of delivery specified in a futures contract will follow the normal delivery and pricing procedures used in the cash market.

To return to the scrap dealer who wants to deliver on his ferrous scrap futures contract: on the first day of the delivery month, the

Clearing House notifies him that he must submit the appropriate delivery instrument or take an offsetting position in the market. At any time during that month, the scrap dealer must present a delivery notice to the Clearing House, which in turn passes it on to the contract buyer. Since the original contract sold by the scrap dealer may have changed hands any number of times, the Clearing House simply gives the delivery notice to the contract buyer who has held a buying, or long, position for the longest period. In essence, the delivery notice says to the buyer that the quantity and quality of ferrous scrap called for in the contract is ready and waiting for him. The buyer can, if trading in the contract has not ceased, close his position in the market by selling a ferrous scrap contract for the same delivery month. Or, he can accept delivery by paying the amount specified in his contract to the Clearing House, which then sends the payment to the seller. In most commodity markets for futures trading there is an active secondary market for delivery instruments; the buyer of a futures contract can pay for the delivery instrument and sell it later in the secondary market. Hardly ever does a buyer of a futures contract take delivery on a commodity for which he has no need.

A ferrous scrap contract has been used as an example here. A wastepaper contract could be used by industry members in exactly the same manner. The rules of futures trading vary, in small ways, from exchange to exchange and the uses of these markets differ from commodity to commodity. Nevertheless, the major points presented remain common to all future markets.

THE BENEFITS OF FUTURES TRADING

Having presented the basic concepts of futures trading in ferrous scrap or wastepaper, the report turns to the last two general areas of concern: if a futures market in either of these commodities was established, how would the futures trading affect the current market for secondary materials; and, what practical considerations are relevant to assessing the possibility of futures trading in wastepaper or ferrous scrap? The last two sections of this report treat these questions in turn.

The effects of futures trading on cash markets for those commodities with no present futures trading are, to some extent, conjectural. The nature and extent of such impacts will be a function of the type of commodity, the structure and performance of the industry, the success of the futures market, the number of commercial traders, and a host of other factors. Nevertheless, several probable impacts were discussed at the Symposium and will be presented here. It is important to restate that futures markets or futures trading does not change market operations or industry practices, rather they supplement these practices.

The provision of a mechanism for risk management or risk shifting is the most obvious and most important result of futures trading. As was stressed by a number of the speakers at the Symposium, this role of futures trading is particularly important for the wastepaper and ferrous scrap markets, which historically have been characterized by volatile prices. The usefulness of a risk-shifting market would be limited if other market mechanisms, such as forward contracting and vertical integration back to sources of raw material suppliers, were extensively used. Indeed, one commodity exchange speaker stated that a criteria for successful futures trading was a forward contracting system that was not operating properly. The consensus of the industry participants at the Symposium was that the current system for forward contracting in the wastepaper and ferrous scrap industries was not strong enough to stabilize the market and that a futures market would help buttress this mechanism.

A risk management market would have several indirect impacts on the cash markets for ferrous scrap and wastepaper. One, it would tend to stabilize producer and consumer revenue by allowing commercial users to assure themselves of fairly constant profit margins. A number of participants at the Symposium questioned this point, saying that they made their money off the highs and lows in the market. They were reminded by an exchange official that you would hedge only when you wanted the protection and stability. Two, because buyers and sellers of scrap could protect their investments that depend in some way on the price of scrap, financing for these investments would be more readily available and probably at more favorable terms. It should be added, that capital tied up in inventories could also be freed for use in other investments.

During the course of the Symposium other potential benefits of futures trading were identified, some of which were a result of risk shifting and others a result of the structure of futures markets. Generally, futures markets would aid in the dissemination of prices and other types of market information and provide for open and competitive price formation. An additional point, mentioned by an exchange representative, was that futures markets can reduce the possibility of contracts going soft. This was explained by the fact that when a forward cash market contract is hedged, there is less incentive or need for one side of the contract to attempt to modify that contract if the market moves in an unfavorable way.

Benefits more specific to the wastepaper and ferrous scrap industries were mentioned by some of the industry speakers. A ferrous scrap dealer/processor argued that a ferrous scrap futures contract could result in steel mills having more consistent participation in the cash market for scrap, steel mills being better able to cope with the world market for scrap, and steel mills having less need for government intervention in export market for scrap. A point on which there was some division of opinion concerned whether a futures market would aid in guaranteeing a constant supply of wastepaper or ferrous scrap to consuming mills (i.e., that a futures market could be used to cope with supply risk as well as price risk). Generally, the mill representatives saw this as a possibility while the dealer/processors did not. It should be remembered that futures markets are not delivery markets, and only occasionally would a consuming mill be in a position to take delivery or want to take delivery.

A strong argument, supported by statistical evidence, can be made that futures trading stabilizes the cash market prices for a commodity. With dissemination of more detailed information on future market conditions, consumption, production, and inventory planning decisions can be made in more organized fashion,

thus leading to more stable prices. Whether this would be the case if futures trading were initiated in ferrous scrap or wastepaper was not answered at the Symposium. However, it should be noted that as long as the demand for wastepaper and ferrous scrap is highly dependent upon swings in the business cycle — which remain relatively difficult to predict — prices for these materials will always fluctuate. Futures trading should, nonetheless, remove some of the uncertainty.

As stated earlier, the extent to which the benefits enumerated here would be realized if futures trading in ferrous scrap or wastepaper were initiated is, perforce, somewhat difficult to say. Furthermore, the impact of a scrap futures market on recycling rates is even more uncertain. Although not addressed in a formal way by the Symposium participants, the general consensus appeared to be that while a futures market would help decision makers cope with the uncertain nature of scrap material supply and demand, the existence of other technological and institutional constraints limited any potential increase in the consumption of scrap inputs.

DESIGNING A SCRAP FUTURES CONTRACT

A significant portion of the Symposium was devoted to discussions on what a futures contract in ferrous scrap or wastepaper would look like and whether such a contract would be successful. Before presenting the details of those discussions, it would be useful to briefly summarize the criteria used by an exchange to determine the feasibility of initiating futures trading in a commodity.

Exchange Criteria for Trading

Simply put, an exchange will list any commodity on a futures market that they feel will generate adequate trading volume. While no one industry characteristic will insure a successful market, the presentations and remarks made by the commodity exchange officials participating in the Symposium do provide some guidance to the general industry features that they evaluate to determine the potential for futures trading in a commodity.

- The market for the commodity must be characterized by a sufficient degree of price volatility such that there will be a demand for a market mechanism that limits exposure to the price risk. In other words, there must be a hedging demand for the futures contract. Furthermore, speculators are attracted to markets with highly fluctuating prices.
- There must be an active and competitive cash market for the commodity. The cash market price is a major input into the futures market price. Only rarely, if ever, is a futures market established in the absence of a strong cash market.
- The commodity in question and the cash market for the commodity must be homogeneous enough to allow for determination of a standard trading contract. This would include description of the commodity, size of the contract, delivery procedures, etc. The point here is that if a contract is designed such that it follows accepted industry practices and if a futures contract favors one side of the market over another, trading in that contract may be limited to the favored side.

The remainder of this section will be devoted to a more thorough analysis of this last criterion. Its importance cannot be overemphasized. This report has stressed the need for commercial demand to insure a successful futures market. Perhaps more than any other criterion, an exchange will look at the potential industry participation in futures trading to determine whether to trade that commodity. The level of hedging demand is heavily influenced by whether or not the futures contract follows industry practices. This is important for two reasons. First, the futures contract must be affected by the same market forces and information that affect the cash price for a commodity. If it is not, the cash price and the futures price would not move together and the futures contract would not be a useful hedging device. Second, the contract must be designed so that industry members will accept it and delivery on the market will occasionally take place.

The last point may seem trivial in light of the fact that futures markets are rarely delivery markets. Yet, while futures markets are not strictly intended as delivery markets, delivery on the markets, or more accurately the possibility of delivery, assures the primary, risk-shifting function of the markets by forcing the futures prices and cash prices together. If, for example, the futures price of a contract in the delivery month was extremely low relative to the current cash price for the commodity, buyers of futures contract would elect to take delivery on the contracts and thus force the futures price up. A poorly designed futures contract, that did not appeal to industry members, would never lead to delivery.

Contract Grade

There are many grades of wastepaper or ferrous scrap in commercial use. The first, and according to several speakers at the Symposium the most important issue in designing a standard ferrous scrap or wastepaper futures contract, is the choice of a grade of scrap for trading. According to commodity exchange speakers at the Symposium, this grade should account for a large volume of the commercial market transactions in the scrap commodity. Other criteria, mentioned during the course of the Symposium, include a relatively well-defined or homogeneous grade, and that the grade should be easy and inexpensive to inspect. Although a futures contract would probably call for delivery of only one grade, it should be designed so that other grades of scrap can be hedged against it; that is, the price of the futures contract grade should closely correspond to the prices of other grades of the commodity. In essence, the grade of wastepaper or ferrous scrap chosen for futures trading should be one for which at least some buyers of the contracts will want to take delivery and some sellers make delivery.

Several speakers at the Symposium made suggestions as to the appropriate grade for futures trading in ferrous scrap. Two grades of scrap were most often listed: No. 1 Heavy Melting scrap, and Shredded scrap. Other grades such as No. 2 Bundles were felt to be too difficult to inspect and did not constitute a large enough portion of the cash market. Of these, shredded scrap seemed to many to be the best choice. The quality of No. 1 Heavy Melting was said to vary from one source to another and thus there would be no way of assuring a constant quality. (One scrap consumer did prefer No. 1 scrap.) Shredded scrap, on the other hand, was said to be easy to inspect and to be relatively uniform across different production sources. At least one speaker did note, though, that while Shredded scrap made up approximately 30% of the export market it made up much less of total domestic consumption and therefore might not generate sufficient trading volume. The 1955 ferrous scrap contract was defined in terms of No. 1 Heavy Melting which some observers say was one of the reasons for its failure.

The discussions on wastepaper were not as specific in terms of possible contract specifications. This was mainly due to the fact that for many of the representatives from wastepaper consuming and supplying firms, the Symposium was their first introduction to the concept of futures trading. The references to a trading grade that were made suggested that a grade of corrugated containers or newsprint would be the best choice. Of the two, one speaker preferred corrugated because more of it is traded in the cash market and it is generated through a more easily influenced system. The bulk of newsprint comes from households, whereas corrugated containers are mostly retrieved from a smaller number of institutional sources.

The choice of the grade of scrap for futures trading will affect the quantity of the commodity called for delivery in the contract. The lot size defined in the futures contract should be comparable to the size of normal cash market shipments of a particular grade. One suggestion for a wastepaper contract called for 50 tons for each contract. For ferrous scrap, the estimates of the most useful contract size ranged from 100 to 200 tons. A model ferrous scrap contract designed in 1976 calls for delivery of 200 tons. The 1955 ferrous scrap contract called for 160 tons of No. 1 Heavy Melting scrap.

Pricing Scheme

The prices quoted for futures contract should be similar to the pricing system used in the cash market for a commodity. For example, the copper contract traded on Comex is quoted in cents per pound of copper delivered to the Comex warehouse. If a copper futures contract buyer accepted delivery on his futures contracts, he would have to pay the price called for in the contract, plus the transportation charges from the warehouse to the delivery point. If delivery on the contract comes from current production, prices are normally quoted F.O.B. as some base point.

Very few comments at the Symposium were directed at a specific pricing scheme for wastepaper and ferrous scrap, except that the scheme would have to follow the manner in which these commodities are priced in the cash market. In general, this would be dollars per ton delivered to the consuming mill. The finer points would depend on the specific delivery terms outlined in the contract. An example was provided by one speaker who mentioned that the model 1976 ferrous scrap contract called for price moves in multiples of 25 cents with a price move limit of $10 per day.

There was a significant amount of discussion on an issue closely related to design of a pricing scheme; that is, the impact of transportation costs on the feasibility of a scrap futures contract. The major point was that transportation costs make up a large portion of the price of scrap materials because of the bulky nature of these commodities. The question was raised whether the high ratio of transportation costs to total per ton scrap value relative to other commodities for which there is futures trading would, in some way, work against the success of the market. The Symposium discussion did not generate an entirely clear answer. It does not appear to be a problem, though, since both wastepaper and ferrous scrap are transported and traded through normal commercial channels. The high transportation costs would only serve to limit the distance the scrap would be shipped under futures trading. It would not affect the hedging use of the market. The question of high transportation costs does act to reinforce the need for a futures contract design that mimics standard industry practices.

Delivery Terms

Great concern was expressed by many of the industry representatives at the Symposium over the terms of delivery under a scrap futures contract. Most of the concerns came from scrap consumers who saw futures markets as delivery markets not as risk management markets. We have stated earlier that only a small portion, perhaps 1-2 percent, of all futures contract traded end up with delivery. At the same time, we have also stressed the need for a contract design that facilitates delivery for the few times delivery will take place. Here again, existing delivery practices in the industry are the guide for the definition of delivery terms in a futures contract.

On most futures contracts, delivery is made from inventories, or if inventories of the commodity are not held, from current production. If delivery is made from current production, a shipping certificate is used as the instrument transferring title to the commodity. In essence, it states that a contract lot of the commodity is ready for delivery in a railcar or truck and will be shipped to the buyer. When delivery is made from inventory, a warehouse receipt serves the same purpose. It describes the contract lot and the location of the warehouse or holding area in which the lot is stored.

The implicit consensus at the Symposium was that deliveries of wastepaper and ferrous scrap would be made from warehouses or storage lots. Questions were raised as to where these warehouses would come from. Several answers were provided. One, the market could provide the warehouses. Individuals might see an opportunity for making money by providing the service of warehousing. This is done for several agricultural commodities for which there is futures trading. Two, the exchange could provide warehousing facilities. Three, the exchange could designate a number of existing processing yards as points from which delivery can take place. Only those dealers/processors licensed by the exchange could make delivery on a futures contract.

If the commodity is to be delivered from current production or warehouses, the method of shipment to the buyer must be spelled out in the futures contract. There seemed to be general agreement that for ferrous scrap, transportation would undoubtedly be by rail. One speaker suggested that for wastepaper, the contract could be defined in terms of railcars, (for example, each contract involves one railcar lot of scrap), but delivery could also be made by truck with the same quantity being delivered. This would recognize the fact that most wastepaper is shipped by truck not rail.

To insure that the grade of the commodity called for in the futures contract is actually delivered, the futures contract must specify how the commodity will be inspected for delivery. In cash market scrap transactions, the buyer generally has the right to inspect and reject deliveries if they do not meet his requirements. On a futures markets, since the exchange guarantees all deliveries, the buyer does not have the same inspection prerogatives; he must accept delivery. Of course, if the grade of scrap delivered under the contract was not as described in the contract, the buyer would have recourse through the exchange.

Several Symposium participants expressed the opinion that because of their inability to reject shipments under the futures contract, no buyer would ever take delivery. Since they produce to order, and each different output requires a different grade or quality of scrap input, any uncertainty over the delivery grade would be detrimental to the success of the contract. While this point was debated back and forth at the Symposium there are ways for a commodity exchange to minimize the uncertainty. One, as mentioned before, the exchange should choose a grade of scrap that is as clean as possible and have a great deal of buyer confidence. Two, the contract could call for inspection of the commodity at the point of shipment, be that a warehouse or a scrap dealer's yard, by an independent third party. Three, only those scrap dealers with a sound reputation in the market, or those who post a bond guarantee, could be allowed to deliver on the futures market. The first and the last points would inevitably be taken into consideration by an exchange. The second point did not receive great support for those attending the Symposium and is probably not feasible.

While there are finer points to be resolved in outlining the inspection procedures and other features for a scrap futures contract, it should be noted that most commodity markets are characterized by long-term relationships between buyers and sellers. Raw materials users tend to deal with trusted suppliers. In this sense, the markets for scrap materials are no different. Futures markets do not impinge upon this process. If a scrap futures contract buyer cannot use the specified contract grade in his production processes, he does not need to take delivery, but he can still use the market for hedging purposes.

As an alternative to the delivery requirements reviewed here, one commodity exchange official introduced a concept that would greatly ease the design of a scrap futures contract. The idea involves settlement of a futures by cash transfers rather than physical delivery. The idea would require that all contracts are settled at some relation to the cash price for a commodity. While the cash settlement concept would eliminate the need for specification of a contract grade and delivery procedures in a futures contract, a well developed cash market for the commodity where prices are known must be present. If one of the benefits of a futures market, price discovery, is already being provided by the cash market, then a futures contract based on cash settlement might be feasible. If this were the case, the futures markets would be a purely hedging market. It is unclear whether cash settlements could be applied to wastepaper or ferrous scrap futures contracts. Doubts were expressed whether the cash markets for ferrous scrap or wastepaper fit the requirements noted above. Furthermore, the cash settlement concept still must be approved by the Commodity Futures Trading Commission, although modified forms of cash settlement are used in some current futures contracts.

Conclusions

Of all the points discussed in this section, the ability to define a standard grade for trading seems to be the most crucial as far as initiating a successful futures contract in wastepaper and ferrous scrap is concerned. However, while several speakers addressed this subject and reviewed the weaknesses of the current specifications for futures trading, most parties agreed that a grade of wastepaper or ferrous scrap

could be defined for futures trading with little adjustment to current practices. The guidelines suggested by industry participants were that the grade must be specified with enough flexibility so that scrap dealers and processors could meet delivery requirements and stringent enough that at least some scrap consumers would take delivery. As a general rule, this applies to all of the contract design considerations raised here.

SUMMARY AND CONCLUSIONS

The purpose of this report was to identify some of the important features and uses of futures markets and to outline some of the practical considerations that must be evaluated before such markets can be established in wastepaper or ferrous scrap. The risk management and financial functions of futures markets can provide large benefits to commercial users of the markets with little or no costs imposed on the industry itself. This point was well taken by those attending the Symposium, some of the discussions from which are summarized in this report. Although there were varying degrees of sophistication concerning futures markets among those participating in the Symposium, all but a few regarded futures trading in wastepaper or ferrous scrap as a potentially useful adjunct to their normal business transactions.

This is not to say that futures trading in ferrous scrap or wastepaper will become a reality in the near future. Several barriers, such as industry education and delineation of a standard contract for trading must be overcome before futures trading in these materials can be initiated. The Scrap Futures Symposium and this report are only the beginnings of this process. For wastepaper, a greater effort to demonstrate the usefulness of futures trading and the mechanics of futures trading to industry members must be made before a model contract can be devised or before a commodity exchange will take a strong interest. All of the wastepaper consumers and suppliers represented at the Symposium remarked that before more specific discussions on a wastepaper futures contract could take place, they would need further presentations on how futures markets work. With the support of an industry trade association and several of the Symposium participants, plans for such presentations are under way.

In the case of ferrous scrap, the deliberations are much further along. Based, in part, on the comments generated during the Symposium, and earlier reports on futures trading in ferrous scrap, Comex in New York has decided to develop a model ferrous scrap futures contract. The model will be presented to the Board of Comex and interested industry parties. If the reactions are favorable, the model contract, or a modified version of the contract depending on the industry comments, may be introduced for trading.

1-11 The Treatment of Resource Recovery in Solid Waste Plans

W. David Conn

Source: Resource Recovery and Conservation, Vol. 2, No. 4 (November 1977) pp. 365–372.
Reprinted with Permission of Elsevier Scientific Publishing Company.

The Resource Conservation and Recovery Act of 1976 [1] requires that States or regional authorities undertake comprehensive planning for solid waste management, with objectives that include maximizing the utilization of valuable resources and encouraging resource conservation. Prior to the passage of this legislation, California (among other States) already had its own requirements for solid waste planning, each county having being required to submit a plan, with the concurrence of the cities, to the State Solid Waste Management Board (SSWMB) by January 1, 1976. In the hope that lessons for the implementation of the new Federal Act could be learned from the experience in California, this author has reviewed plans obtained from about half of the State's 58 counties, focusing on their treatment of resource recovery*.

CALIFORNIA'S STATE POLICY ON RESOURCE RECOVERY

County solid waste management plans in California are required to be consistent with the State Policy for Solid Waste Management, as adopted by the SSWMB on December 20, 1974. This Policy lists as an objective:

*The number of plans available for review was limited due to the fact that many counties were late in preparing them; indeed, some have not yet been submitted to the SSWMB and others have so far failed to receive Board approval.

"To assure that county solid waste management plans include a resource recovery element which factually documents the quantity of solid waste that a county determines it will recover from its waste stream. The plan must include the review of regional or interjurisdictional feasibility of resource recovery systems and in the case of rural counties give special attention to at least source separation of wastes for recovery, all towards the goal of reducing the statewide annual tons per capita of residential and commercial wastes now disposed of in landfills by 25 percent between the years 1972 and 1980".

To meet this requirement, guidelines issued by the SSWMB specify that each plan must include a discussion of materials and/or energy recovery systems, as well as a factual analysis of resource recovery programs if they are not deemed feasible. The analysis must show that a regional resource recovery program was also considered. The establishment of source separation programs and/or deposit centers for recyclable materials must be considered where appropriate. Provision must be made for periodic review of "the state of the art." In addition, the economic feasibility of the entire plan must be analyzed, showing for the short-term the capital and operating costs of the handling, disposal, and resource recovery systems envisioned in the program. Economic analysis for the medium and long term periods of the plan may be general.

THE TREATMENT OF RESOURCE RECOVERY IN CALIFORNIA COUNTY PLANS

The plans that were reviewed vary considerably in their treatment of resource recovery. Some contain fairly detailed descriptions of available systems, while in others there are only brief outlines or no descriptions at all. Where systems are described, greatest emphasis is generally placed on "high technology" approaches, involving mechanized front-end separation of materials and fuel, and/or rear-end combustion or pyrolysis. Many of the descriptions appear to be based on reports published by the Council on Environmental Quality [2], the U.S. Environmental Protection Agency [3,4], and/or the SSWMB [5,6]; indeed, some plans quote extensive sections of these reports verbatim, either in their text or in an appendix. Descriptions of alternative "low technology" approaches are generally limited to a mention of either neighborhood recycling centers where individuals can voluntarily bring their separated materials or salvage operations at landfill sites where manual scavenging is permitted (sometimes as a means of supplementing the wages of landfill operator). Systematic approaches involving, for example, source separation with separate collection are rarely described in any detail.

The plans also vary considerably in their discussions of the economics of recovery systems. Some contain virtually no economic data at all, it being stated simply that the (high technology) systems are very expensive to build and operate. Others quote the actual or, more often, the estimated costs of systems currently in operation or under construction elsewhere, without attempting to adjust these figures according to the particular conditions prevailing in the county concerned. In only a few plans is there evidence of some attempt to explore in detail the likely economics of implementing a system locally.

Virtually all of the plans comment that resource recovery systems are still at an early stage of development and that tremendous uncertainties surround their actual performance and costs when operating at full scale. This is the reason given by some counties for not including any economic data in their plans; instead,

they undertake to observe developments and conduct studies in the future as and when these are deemed appropriate.

The availability of assured markets for recovered energy and materials is recognized in many plans as being one of the most critical factors affecting the feasibility of resource recovery systems, but very little detailed exploration of markets is reported. Again, many plans recommend further studies to be done in the future.

DISCUSSION

It is obvious from the plans reviewed (and information obtained from the SSWMB staff regarding other plans) that the State's goal of reducing the per capita residential and commercial solid wastes going to landfill by 25 percent between 1972 and 1980 will not be met. With only three years to go, most counties are still talking about resource recovery in generalities and have failed to do the detailed planning that is necessary before any kind of system can be implemented.

"High Technology" Resource Recovery

It is reasonable to expect a significant difference in the consideration given to high technology resource recovery facilities for residential and commercial wastes by rural counties compared with counties that are heavily urbanized. The former tend to have relatively small quantities of these wastes requiring disposal and in general they are more likely to be able to find suitable landfill sites. The latter are faced with much larger quantities of waste and may have considerable difficulty in locating sites that are technically, economically, and politically acceptable for use as landfills. Recognition of this difference is implied in the State Policy which requires that rural counties "give special attention to at least source separation of wastes for recovery." For many rural counties, a simple "back-of-the-envelope" calculation is sufficient to show that a high technology facility, with its very substantial capital and operating costs, is infeasible.

For the urbanized counties, the situation is somewhat different. It seems clear from the

State Policy and the guidelines that the SSWMB intended these counties to examine *in detail* the possibility of establishing resource recovery facilities before 1980. Instead, many counties have prepared documents that are at best described as "plans for plans." However, in fairness to the counties involved, it should be pointed out that even if they had more closely examined the available high technology options, it is likely that many would have reached conclusions no different from those in their present plans. Indeed, an unwillingness to make a commitment at this time to the construction of high technology facilities cannot be considered altogether unreasonable.

Despite the considerable optimism voiced in the past few years regarding the development of mechanized materials and energy recovery systems, it is true to say that the only process to have been fully proven in full-scale, continuous operation is waterwall incineration; however, this is very expensive (especially when very stringent emission control standards must be met) and it is likely to be uneconomic in most places. Front-end separation leading to the preparation of a refuse-derived fuel for combustion in an existing furnace (with appropriate modifications) appears to be a process with significant potential; full-scale plants have recently started up in Ames, Iowa, Chicago, Illinois, and Milwaukee, Wisconsin. The long-term technical and economic viability of the process has yet to be demonstrated.

The development of pyrolysis has been slower than originally anticipated; some unexpected technical problems have been encountered (such as the difficulties in meeting air emission standards, which largely contributed to Monsanto's withdrawal from the demonstration project in Baltimore) and costs have soared (for example, the total project cost of Occidental's 200 ton per day demonstration plant in San Diego, originally estimated at about $4 million, is now expected to be $14.4 million [7]*). Under these circumstances, and in view of the tight fiscal constraints within which nearly all local govern-

ments are currently operating (as well as the low priority generally afforded to solid waste projects) it is understandable that most counties would be unwilling to shoulder the risks involved in making a commitment to a single capital-intensive technology. They would prefer to wait and see first how the new generation of plants will fare elsewhere.

Source Separation

In view of the technical and economic uncertainties associated with high technology systems at the present time, increasing attention is being given to source separation as a means of resource recovery. As mentioned earlier, the State Policy in California requires that the rural counties at least consider this approach. Trials both in the United States and in Europe have shown that under the most favorable circumstances, systems involving source separation by households and separate collection of recovered materials can reduce the quantity of waste requiring disposal by other means by as much as 25–30 percent (by weight) [8,9]. Key ingredients of a successful system seem to include household motivation (almost invariably enhanced by extensive public relations efforts), the availability of compartmentalized collection vehicles, and (as in all resource recovery systems) assured markets for the products. The approach has the feature that it is labor rather than capital intensive, which may be a distinct advantage at a time of high unemployment [10]. However, it probably stands the greatest chance of success in smaller communities (up to 300,000 population, suggests one EPA source) where enthusiasm and a commitment to participate may be most readily generated.

The approach being discussed here is different from one that is limited to the establishment of neighborhood recycling centers where individuals can voluntarily bring their separated materials. Systems based on recycling centers have undoubtedly played an important role, not least in raising the public's consciousness about resource problems and providing individuals with an opportunity to make a tangible contribution to the cause of conservation, but they have not on the whole caused a significant

---

*The total project cost includes design, construction, start-up, and demonstration. Construction has accounted for much of the price escalation.

and sustained reduction in the remaining waste stream. In order to achieve this reduction, it is important to have most (rather than just a few) households participating on a regular basis; but this is only likely to happen if the occupants can count on regular collection of their separated materials. Regular and assured collection is also essential if long-term agreements are to be signed for the marketing of these materials.

With very few exceptions, counties have failed in their plans to examine in detail the potential for source separation with separate collection. If they were serious about considering this potential, they would at the very least have assessed their ability to deploy compartmentalized collection trucks to pick up the separated materials; in addition, they would have examined the availability of markets for separated materials. Failure to have performed these basic tasks indicates a lack of real commitment.

THE STATE POLICY RECONSIDERED

The poor performance of most counties in pursuing resource recovery options in their solid waste management plans highlights a basic problem: even though the SSWMB has set the goal of a 25 percent reduction in the statewide annual tons per capita of residential and commercial wastes going to landfill by 1980, it has provided no details of how this can or should be achieved and it has given no tangible incentive to the counties to take the necessary action. Simply urging the counties to give "high priority to the recovery of resources" and requiring them to plan for the establishment of recovery facilities if and when these are feasible has not proved sufficient.

It is important to remember that one of the reasons for the State setting an explicit goal is the belief that the present level of resource recovery, as determined by the actions of local solid waste agencies and the private sector, is (by some adopted criterion) "too low." This belief might be held for a variety of reasons: for example, it is widely felt that certain government policies (such as the favorable tax treatment given to the extractive sector and regulated freight tariffs that favor virgin over secondary materials) as well as the environmental

"subsidy" given to virgin materials* and the failure of product prices to reflect the costs of disposal, all tend to excessively encourage the extraction and use of virgin materials (and the generation of waste) while discouraging resource recovery [3,11]. In addition, many people feel that the actions of private individuals and firms in the marketplace in making provision for the future may not adequately reflect the preferences of society as a whole (and certainly cannot reflect the preferences of unborn generations); thus the social value of resource recovery as a means of conserving natural resources may not be fully realized [12].

There is no "uniquely correct" level of resource recovery; this is ultimately a matter of value-judgement. One of the roles of the SSWMB is to make such judgements, a role that the Board has performed by deciding on the 25 percent figure now contained in State Policy. However, setting the goal has not in itself removed existing economic and other biases against resource recovery; thus the counties have found themselves having to produce plans that can be shown to be economically feasible, while at the same time they have been asked to strive for a goal that is based at least partly on non-economic considerations**.

It follows that if the State seriously wishes to see its goal achieved, it should do more to make resource recovery an economically viable proposition for the counties. At the very least, the State should act rapidly to remove (or persuade the Federal government to remove) as many as possible of the present biases against recovery. Beyond this, the possibility of providing local agencies with some degree of financial assistance should also be considered. An outright subsidy might be difficult to justify, although it could be argued that this would be a way of paying for benefits of resource recovery accruing to the State (and nation) as a whole rather than to the individual counties. Such benefits would include, for example, a reduction

---

*This results from the uncompensated environmental costs of extraction, which are generally greater than those of recovering secondary materials.

**In this context, "economic" is effectively synonymous with "financial".

in the reliance placed on imported raw materials and/or the release of scarce natural resources for other uses.

However, a more acceptable method of assisting the counties might be to introduce a state-wide scheme of product charges and to return the revenues thus raised to the local communities for use in financing resource recovery and other solid waste services. The product charge concept has been discussed extensively elsewhere [3,13-17], and its possible application in California was recently considered by a committee of the SSWMB [18,19]; the approach could be used to make those responsible for designing and manufacturing the products that ultimately constitute the waste stream also responsible for the costs of handling/disposing of this stream (thus causing these costs to be reflected in the price of the products).

This is not to say that the counties themselves should rest content with their own efforts so far in promoting recovery. As pointed out earlier, most counties show little evidence in their plans of having seriously investigated all available options (particularly those involving low technology) that could prove economically viable even under existing conditions. Furthermore, there is some justification for local communities to consider paying a little more for "disposing" of their wastes by resource recovery than by landfill, since they would thus gain benefits that are not reflected in the economic accounts (for example, the benefits of a reduction in environmental impact).

CONCLUSIONS

In implementing the planning requirements of the new Federal solid waste legislation, particularly in the treatment given to resource recovery, at least two lessons can be learned from the experience in California.

First, it is important to try to ensure that the planning process represents more than a token response to the Act's requirements and intent. In California, most of the county plans discuss resource recovery only in generalities and there are too many promises of studies to be conducted in the future; rarely does it appear that the planning process has included (as it

should) a serious attempt to identify all possible options (including low as well as high technology approaches), a detailed evaluation based on pre-defined criteria of those options that might be applicable *within the local context,* and the development of a detailed program for implementation of the options that are selected*. Perhaps the most significant benefit to be gained so far from the consideration of resource recovery in the California county plans has been educational: elected officials, professional staffs, and citizens involved in the planning process now know at least a little more than most did previously about resource recovery options. However, whether this is enough to have made the whole process worthwhile is not at all certain.

Second, it is apparent that simply establishing as a goal the increased utilization of waste is unlikely to persuade local authorities to intensify their resource recovery efforts if these are judged to be uneconomic or only marginally economic. Not only must existing biases against resource recovery be removed to improve its economic attractiveness, but there must also be recognition that the goal is based at least partially on considerations that are not reflected in economic calculations. The question of who should pay for resource recovery ought to be explicitly addressed.

REFERENCES

1. Public Law 94-580.
2. Midwest Research Institute, 1973. Resource Recovery: The State of Technology. Council on Environmental Quality, Washington, D.C., 67 pp.
3. Environmental Protection Agency, 1974. Second Report to Congress: Resource Recovery and Source Reduction. Environmental Protection Agency, Washington, D.C., 112 pp.
4. Environmental Protection Agency, 1974. Decision-Makers Guide in Solid Waste Management. Environmental Protection Agency, Washington, D.C., 157 pp (2nd ed. published 1976).
5. California State Solid Waste Management Board, 1974. Bulletin No. 3: Resource Recovery Systems. State Solid Waste Management Board, Sacramento.

---

*Some unnecessary duplication of effort could have been avoided if the State had more thoroughly researched and evaluated alternative technologies and provided this information in common to all counties *before* they began their planning.

6. California State Solid Waste Management Board, 1975. Bulletin No. 5: Current Status of Resource Recovery Systems and Processes. State Solid Waste Management Board, Sacramento.

7. C.E. Kaufman, Solid Waste Program Manager, County of San Diego, personal communication, 1977.

8. Environmental Protection Agency, 1976. Source Separation – The Community Awareness Program in Somerville and Marblehead, Massachusetts. Environmental Protection Agency, Washington, D.C., 81 pp.

9. M. Tolstoy, Atervinnings System ASAB AB (Sweden), personal communication, 1976.

10. Seldman, N.N., 1976. Low Technology Versus High Technology Approaches to Resource Recovery, Second California Recycling Conference, Santa Barbara.

11. League of Women Voters, 1972. Recycle: In Search of New Policies for Resource Recovery. League of Women Voters Education Fund, Washington, D.C., 39 pp.

12. Page, T., 1973. Economics of Recycling. In: Congressional Research Service, Environmental Policy Division, Resource Conservation, Resource Recovery, and Solid Waste Disposal, Studies Prepared for the Committee on Public Works, U.S. Senate, Serial No. 93-12, pp. 8–43.

13. Ackoff, R.L., 1974. Redesigning the Future: A Systems Approach to Societal Problems. Wiley, New York, 187 pp.

14. Bingham, T., forthcoming. An Analysis of the Allocative and Distributive Effects of a Disposal Charge on Packaging. In: D.W. Pearce and I. Walter (Editors), Resource Conservation: Social and Economic Dimensions of Recycling, New York University Press.

15. Smith, F.L., forthcoming. Pollution Charges – The Practical Issues. In: D.W. Pearce and I. Walter (Editors), Resource Conservation: Social and Economic Dimensions of Recycling, New York University Press.

16. National Commission on Supplies and Shortages, 1976. Government and the Nation's Resources. U.S. Government Printing Office, Washington, D.C., 211 pp.

17. Environmental Protection Agency, 1977. Fourth Report to Congress: Resource Conservation and Recovery. Environmental Protection Agency, Washington, D.C.

18. Conn, W.D. (Editor), 1976. Proposed Policies for Waste Reduction in California. State Solid Waste Management Board, Sacramento, 88 pp.

19. Conn, W.D., 1977. Waste Reduction – Issues and Policies. Resources Policy, 3.

Part 2
Planning, Procurement, Marketing, Economics, and Finance

In this section the focus shifts from the national level to the local level. A large number of topics are covered. Each is essential to implementing a project at the local level where project implementation takes place. National policies affect relative prices as they are seen locally, but it is the local planning, procurement and marketing that actually cause a positive - or negative — decision to take place. For years there has seemed to be a widely held belief that communities should shift from traditional forms of disposal to resource recovery and, as an added bonus, make money from their heretofore unwanted refuse. In the first reading in this section, Franchot Buhler addresses this supposition under the title, "Is there Gold Among the Garbage?" The answer, "not likely," places the local level decision in perspective. The "gold in garbage" perspective is one with many pitfalls. As Richard W. Chase, former president of the Connecticut Resource Recovery Authority states, "Establishing a sound program to efficiently plan and implement resource recovery is, more often than not, a unique, challenging, and difficult experience." Problem areas abound; Chase's "Five Rules for Resource Recovery" highlight the more important points to consider.

In the next reading, some successes and, more often, failures are highlighted in Stephen Burks' and Clint Page's "Resource Recovery: Is It for Your City?" A good number of cities have invested in resource recovery. One might consider them the lead city group. Will the others follow? There is reason to believe that the progress made in the early years may not continue at the same accelerated rate. In fact, there may be a pause while the gains, such as they are, are consolidated and the risk-takers see whether the bets they made pay off. This is the subject of the next reading by James Abert entitled, "Resource Recovery: the Economics and the Risks."

Resource recovery is easy to talk about in concept, but there is ample evidence that it is not as easy to effect in practice. The subject of the next reading is, "Waste to Energy: Applying the Technology in the Real World." The authors, Glenn Swinehart and Whitney Sanders, are both professional engineers. Their article covers virtually every topic important to implementing a resource recovery project.

In the Abert and the Swinehart and Sanders readings, the subject of risk is highlighted. There are various risks associated with resource recovery. It is technically complex. Also because it is a production enterprise, it is different from most public works. "Resource Recovery: the Management of Technical and Economic Risks," is the title of the next reading. Elements of risk covered are: (1) quantity of waste, (2) composition of waste, (3) performance of separating and processing equipment, (4) recovery of products to market specifications, (5) continuity of markets for recovered products, (6) stability of prices paid, and (7) effect of future environmental control regulations as they concern obsolescence of equipment and, as one would suspect, the requirements for additional funding this generates.

What to do? "Overcoming Barriers to Resource Recovery" is the title of the next reading. This prescriptive article is authored by Susan J. Kinney and, in part, is a report on the proceedings of a MITRE Corporation sponsored symposium titled, "Actions to Increase Resource Recovery Implementation." This reading introduces the concept of waste stream control, a concern to be expanded in the next reading of this section. The issue of waste stream, or flow control, as it is called, came to the fore with the passage of an ordinance by the City of Akron which required all waste collected within the City limits, "whether by private or municipal haulers," to be taken to the Recycle Energy System where the waste is used as fuel to produce the steam which the city is obligated to supply by contract to various users. This ordinance has been challenged in the courts. The reading that reports on this litigation is authored by John Holcomb and Richard Cohen. Since waste can be 25 percent or more paper, as one would expect, the secondary paper industry is concerned about the Akron ordinance. Does it allow for source separation? In resource recovery circles this has become known as the "burning issue." Which is preferred, the recycling of paper for its fiber content or burning for its energy content? The goal of all parties, of course, is flow control legislation based on value, not simply regulation.

A recent Supreme Court ruling concerning state delegation of monopoly power to cities has cast a shadow over the ground underlying the lower courts decision in the Akron case. It is expected that when the Akron case is put to this new test, which requires specific delegation, the earlier ruling will be overturned.

Environmental impacts are a concern of any industrial facility. Resource recovery plants are no exception. The next reading urges the anticipation of the environmental impacts of resource recovery facilities. This is necessary if the facility is to produce a net positive environmental impact on the area it serves. Impacts that must be considered include: transportation, processing, combustion, and disposal of residuals.

What is recovered must be sold. Clearly, this is an axiom of resource recovery. And, as the next reading points out, "There is little to be gained from building a resource recovery facility if the recovered materials cannot be sold." Markets are the key ingredient, so states the author. The reading is entitled, "Marketing Recovered Materials, a Guide for Planners." A sample letter of intent is included.

What if you are the community considering implementing a recovery project? There are several standard approaches to "How to Buy Resource Recovery." This is the title of the next reading. The tips given by Stephen G. Lewis should help smooth what has been, for many communities, a rocky road. He presents options for ownership, operation, implementation, and procurement. These are combined into five basic approaches for acquisition: conventional, turn-key, full-service, full-survice with government ownership, and modified full-service. All are discussed in the reading.

Economics are an important ingredient to any resource recovery implementation decision. The subject of break-even economics is introduced in the next reading by Donald Mihelich. This is followed by a case study of a planning effort conducted by the Metropolitan Washington Waste Management Agency. The study was prepared for Washington, D.C., by the National Center for Resource Recovery. A summary of the three separate reports prepared for the Agency appears here. The titles of the three reports indicate the important elements of a planning effort. They are: Markets Study, Feasibility Study, and Network Study. The latter involves the forecast location of a series of facilities in the metropolitan area.

The final two readings in this section have to do with financing. One must raise money in order to build the plants. This is usually done by turning to the bond market. Jeffrey Clunie and Robert Taylor discuss "Elements of Financial Risk." Their reading identifies the major elements and describes how they should be evaluated in the financing of a solid waste resource recovery project.

The facility must generate the net revenues necessary to pay off the long-term financing. This ability is directly connected to the contracts for the sale of energy, the sale of recovered materials, waste control and possible competition in the local marketplace. More detail on how "real world" resource recovery projects are financed is given by Charles A. Ballard in the final reading of this section. Entitled "Resource Recovery Financing," the article relates how four cities met the financing needs for their resource recovery projects. Several of these arrangements are quite complex and indicate the innovative financial solutions necessary, and indeed appropriate, to investing in this new, risky, and emerging area. This area has some characteristics of a public work, but it is more akin to an entrepreneurial endeavor. It is not surprising then that several of the financing models developed evidence elements common to both private and public financing.

2-1 Is there Gold Among the Garbage?

Franchot Buhler

Source: *Sky* Magazine (April 1979), pp. 10–16. Reprinted with Permission of Halsey Publishing Company and the Author.

To a small group of people in this country the news of more hikes in the price of imported oil is not all bad. Now that may sound downright un-American, but it isn't. For this growing band of "waste watchers," the petroleum price increase means that the economic value of garbage and trash as an energy replacement for fossil fuels is also on the rise. And what could be more American than that — taking a liability like garbage and converting it into a timely asset.

After all, that's the way it was when that early American recycler, Paul Revere, made his famous ride. We had to recycle then, just as we had to during the four great wars of our nation's history. But in between, and since World War II, recycling has gone downhill.

Recycling advocates walked a long and lonely path for years, but now that the pressure's on to find new sources of energy, "resource recovery" is coming into its own. Since 1970, when Congress passed amendments to the federal solid waste act, "resource recovery" has become the new buzz word for salvaging what can be recycled and burning the rest to produce energy.

Although greeted with such fanfare in the early Seventies — over 100 congressional hearings have been published on the subject — resource recovery has had a rocky road since. Some of its supporters have overdramatized its development, and many of its critics have ignored its true accomplishments. So what is the truth about resource recovery? Is it a golden fantasy of the environmental imagination? A magic technological fix? Or a workable answer to our messy, multiplying waste disposal problems?

"RESOURCE RECOVERY IS FOR REAL . . ."

- If you stayed tonight in the 440-room Hyatt Regency Hotel in Nashville, Tennessee, the heat or air conditioning in your room would come from energy supplied by the city's garbage and trash.
- If you visit the General Electric plant in Saugus, Massachusetts, near Boston, you will find it using industrial process steam made from the refuse collected in 13 nearby towns and produced in an attractive facility owned and operated by Wheelabrator-Frye.
- If you lived in Milwaukee, Wisconsin, Ames, Iowa, or Hempstead, New York, you would know that a portion of your community's electricity comes from fuels made of urban waste materials and burned in specially-designed, or modified, power plants. A small portion, admittedly, but a significant portion because it is replacing expensive fossile fuels.
- If you checked out North Little Rock, Arkansas, you could see a small incinerator — taking only 50 tons of waste a day — which produces steam for sale to an industry located 1,000 yards away.
- If you lived in Boca Raton or Temple Terrace, Florida, or any of the numerous cities around the country sponsoring household separation programs, you would leave your bundled old newspapers at curbside for regularly scheduled pick up and recycling.

- Or, if you have the spunk of an 87-year-old woman in Alhambra, California, or the financial need of a college student in Tampa, you may collect aluminum beverage cans and sell them back for 17 cents a pound or better to Reynolds, Kaiser or Alcoa recycling centers, depending on where you live.

According to Dr. Rocco Petrone, director of the Washington, D.C., based National Center for Resource Recovery, there are now some 30 resource recovery plants on-line or committed. Some are fully operating, some are in the testing and shake-down phase, and some are under construction. These projects represent a variety of technologies, and they range in size up to a facility capable of processing 3,000 tons a day for energy and materials recovery. "All together," observes Dr. Petrone, "the capital investment for these facilities approaches $1 billion. Obviously, resource recovery is for real."

BUT NOT ALL IS WELL

Active professionals in the field, such as consulting engineers, project managers and company representatives, are the first to admit the problems we have faced along the way. Some systems using shredders to chop up the waste for better processing and combusting have had explosions. Most every new plant has had start-up problems of one kind or another and many technical questions remain which can only be answered, in most cases, through years of operating experience.

"We've had failures," says a leading consulting engineer in the field, "but none of them have been total losses. We've learned a lot that will make the systems built from now on much, much better."

"Sure, we've had setbacks," echoes the project manager of a major resource recovery corporation, "but they have been quite normal for technology demonstrations." A big factor, everyone agrees, is that most projects were planned with a limited track record to lean on and, therefore, there was little idea of the magnitude of problems to be encountered. The thorniest disappointments have been mostly due to scale-up problems, as systems tested very well on a pilot scale but turned up unexpected "bugs" when prototypes were built on a much larger scale. Demonstration plants sponsored by the U.S. Environmental Protection Agency (EPA) in the 1970's, such as the Baltimore/Monsanto project, demonstrated as much as anything else the unknowns that crop up unannounced when too big of a leap is made in size.

Perhaps the best example of the mixed reviews for resource recovery is the Nashville project. It got "front-page attention during a problem-plagued period of early operation," points out Dr. Petrone, but "now that Nashville is performing well, one reads very little about it." The Nashville system burns refuse and supplies heating/cooling service to a number of downtown government and private office buildings. "In September, 1978," reports Milton Kirkpatrick, the Executive Vice President and General Manager of the Nashville Thermal Transfer Corporation, "the Nashville plant completed processing one-half million tons of city waste, an energy savings of 32 million gallons of fuel oil. Had that same amount of solid waste been buried," says Kirkpatrick, "it would have covered 200 acres six feet deep."

SOME WORKING EXAMPLES

The most recent project to get underway, embarking on a preliminary trial and testing period, is in the Town of Hempstead, located on Long Island. With a population of 850,000, Hempstead would be the 11th largest city in the U.S. if it were ranked with the Chicagos and the L. A.s and wasn't overshadowed by New York City. During one recent week in January, the Hempstead plant turned 4,000 tons of garbage into two million kilowatts of electricity, equivalent to the weekly power needs of 14,300 homes. *The New York Times* called it "one of those small, unheralded steps by which a new technology comes of age." Eventually, the plant should provide 15 per cent of the area's electricity needs.

Furthermore, Hempstead illustrates a number of emerging trends in the resource recovery field. The $90 million plant was built and will be operated by Parsons & Wittemore, an international firm with 125 years experience in the pulp and paper industry. Capable of processing 2,000 tons a day, the plant incorporated equipment adapted from the pulp industry and tested at a 50-ton-per-day plant in Franklin, Ohio, and a 150-ton-per-day plant in Tokyo, Japan. Financing for the project was provided by a consortium of private insurance companies. The $17.50 per ton the town pays for the system represents a savings over the current $19 per ton disposal costs. The town's share of the revenues from recovered materials and energy sales is expected to reduce the cost another $4 per ton. The next project for Parsons & Wittemore, an even larger one, is already under construction in Dade County (Miami), Florida.

The building of resource recovery plants of this size and sophistication, however, cannot be accomplished overnight. The Monroe County (Rochester), New York, project, for example, started because landfill sites were running out of space in the late Sixties. An engineering study followed in 1970, supplemented later by voluntary work contributed by the Rochester Engineering Society and still more planning performed by Monroe County and its design engineer, Raytheon Service Company. Today the system is 95 per cent completed. Equipment trials are underway, and by mid-year the 2,000-ton-per-day plant should begin separating materials and preparing a boiler fuel — called "refuse derived fuel" — for sale to a local utility.

In some parts of the country where waste disposal is costly and recovery is too big for a single community to undertake, statewide authorities have been created to plan, build and operate resource recovery systems. The Connecticut Resources Recovery Authority, the nation's first, has just completed a facility serving the greater Bridgeport region that will convert 1,800 to 2,200 tons of refuse per day to energy.

Drawing heavily upon private enterprise, the Connecticut Authority has combined the proprietary technologies and corporate experience of two companies in its Bridgeport plant, with Combustion Equipment Associates providing its process for ECO-FUEL®II, a patented, powdery fuel for use in power plants, and the Occidental Petroleum Corporation its aluminum

and glass recovery methods. Handling the waste materials for nine municipalities, the $53 million Bridgeport project is a model of cooperation between state and local governments and private enterprise.

Delaware, Rhode Island, and Wisconsin have also passed laws establishing statewide authorities and all three are currently in the midst of planning major resource recovery facilities for their communities.

While governmental bodies are saddled with the responsibility of what to do with the garbage we produce, private companies have accepted the challenge of building systems that can recycle and convert our wastes into marketable resources. Signal Companies, through its UOP subsidiary, is a good example. UOP (formerly Universal Oil Products) several years ago acquired marketing rights for the Joseph Martin incineration system, developed and used successfully in Europe for decades. The UOP system, as well as others, uses a technology called water-wall incineration. The walls of the incinerator include water-filled tubes. The burning refuse heats the water tubes making steam for use in industry or to generate electricity. Water-wall boilers of this type are specialized units equipped with all the necessary air pollution control devices to meet state and federal environmental standards.

UOP built the Chicago Northwest plant in 1970 as a conventional waste disposal incinerator, with no recovery. Recently, the plant has been modified and it will soon begin selling steam to a nearby candy factory. Within the past year, UOP has been selected for negotiations as the prime contractor for a Massachusetts project that would eventually serve 50 communities, and for a countywide project in Pinellas County (St. Petersburg), Florida, that would take 624,000 tons of refuse annually and make electricity.

IN THE OLD WORLD, IT'S OLD HAT

One of the ironies of resource in the U.S. is its slow acceptance, compared to Europe. At Dusseldorf and Munich, at three different locations in Paris, near Rotterdam and in Switzerland, waste-burning plants have been common for years. The Dusseldorf plant, for instance, has been in service nearly 14 years, earning $21 million in steam sales and $22 million in fees from refuse collectors. A survey by Battelle Memorial Institute in Columbus, Ohio, found over 260 plants in the world making steam from burning waste materials — but only six were in the U.S.

Sixty-five years ago, in 1914, England had 200 incineration plants of various types, and 65 of them produced electricity from steam.

The West European communities had reason to get a head start, however. Limited land for dump sites, higher energy prices, and technical experience with lowgrade fuels spurred the development of European systems. It isn't that we've been so dumb about resource recovery in this country; rather, we were just spoiled for years by low-cost dumping and cheap energy. It was tried — in the 1920's Miami's refuse was burned for steam to power a turbine to drive a water pump — but it never caught on. In Norfolk, Virginia, a water-wall, refuse-combustion unit has been operating since 1967, but generally, it has been easier and cheaper just to dump our garbage and forget it.

That era is coming to an end. Under the Resource Conservation and Recovery Act passed by Congress in 1976, many of the disposal practices of the past and present are outlawed, as of 1983. Violators may face fines of $50,000 a day. Aside from federal law and similar state laws setting standards for all solid waste handling facilities, the public has gotten into the act, too.

A recent national survey of landfill space for waste disposal concluded that over 500,000 square miles are available within a 30-mile circle of the nation's 272 largest urban areas — enough for 4,000 years. But as every mayor and county commissioner knows, there is someone in every one of those available square miles who will say, "Don't put it here." Former Houston mayor Louie Welch summed up the classic local official's quandry when he explained: "Everyone wants us to pick up the garbage, but no one wants us to put it down."

Yet it has to go somewhere. Our annual production of residential, commercial and institutional garbage now exceeds our output of steel. We churn out enough of it, writes Robert Reno in *Newsday*, "to fill the New Orleans Superdome from floor to ceiling twice a day, including weekends and holidays."

The best answers seem to be (1) to reduce the waste stream as much as possible; (2) to recycle the marketable materials; (3) to convert the combustibles to energy; (4) and to dispose of remaining residues in an environmentally sound manner. In addition to the projects which recover energy, numerous communities are reducing their volume of wastes for final disposal by five to fifteen percent with newspaper recycling programs.

Three private companies, Media General, Knight-Ridder Newspapers, and Cox Enterprises, have created a joint venture called Southeast Paper Manufacturing Company in Dublin, Georgia. Using proven de-inking technology, this Georgia mill (now nearing completion and scheduled to open in mid-1979) will turn old newspapers into recycled newsprint at the rate of 157,000 tons per year. In the six southeastern states from which the plant will buy its waste paper supply, this new market is expected to double the demand for used newspapers. West Palm Beach, Florida, city manager, Richard Simmons, says his city could not have started its paper recycling program without this new market. "It costs us a little over $17 a ton to collect our newspapers, and the guarranteed floor price that Southeast Paper Company gives covers that. Anytime the price floats higher," says Simmons, "that's just gravy and a savings for our community."

Nevertheless, when all the marketable materials are removed from the waste stream, even under the most ideal conditions, 70 to 80 per cent of the volume remains, and most of this is burnable. Furthermore, the revenues which can be generated by resource recovery are far more attractive on the energy side. As an example, one project now operating expects about $1 million annually at the outset from the sale of recovered materials, mostly aluminum, but five times that much from the sale of energy.

As the economic value of garbage begins to climb, new legal questions rear their heads. The question of "Who owns the garbage?" is an issue of increasing litigation. If a government or a private firm builds a resource recovery plant without legal, legislative or contractual title to and control of the necessary volume of refuse, then the plant operator is left without a source and supply of raw materials to feed the system.

Getting approvals for plant locations are getting harder and more time consuming too. "Siting is the big question," says Russell Brenneman, based on his experience as President of the Connecticut Resources Recovery Authority. So big, in fact, that he is exploring a legislative proposal creating a special state commission for resolving these very difficult choices.

Two federal agencies are trying to help communities and industry with their resource recovery programs. The U.S. Department of Energy (DOE) has Congressional approval for demonstrations using several means of financial support. The interest here is in new energy sources and conservation; in accepting some of the financial risks of technology demonstration that will lead to the commercial viability of a number of systems. "The federal government is not going to solve this problem," says Charlotte Rines of DOE's Urban Waste Technology Branch, but it is offering limited aid. DOE selected 20 projects from among 87 applications last year for financial assistance. Since then, the U.S. Environmental Protection Agency has announced the availability of $15 million in federal resource recovery funds as part of President Carter's urban program. 194 applications were received — a strong indication of increasing widespread interest.

Which brings us back to the question of "gold in garbage." Professionals in the field object to the phrase as misleading. "There are some profits to be made and efficiencies that benefit the taxpayers," says Dr. George Mallan with Americology, American Can Company's resource recovery subsidiary, "but it's no gold mine." Others quickly point out that what really makes waste-to-energy systems financeable is the "tipping fee" or charge paid by the governmental or private entities bringing waste to the plant. The tipping fee is usually comparable to, or slightly less than, the current cost of other disposal options. One project now in operation expects to earn at the outset close to $5 million from energy sales and more than $8 million from tipping fees.

That exact ratio does not apply to every project, yet it clearly demonstrates that even the good projects face a net cost initially, even if they project a break-even or profit margin in the distant future.

Can this fledgling, still-costly technology for solving our waste disposal problems really be the wave of the future? What are the prospects?" "Very bullish," says Dr. Mallan.

"The future for energy and materials recovery from solid waste is very bright," comments Harvey Funk, Assistant Vice President with Henningson, Durham and Richardson of Omaha, Nebraska. "Eventually," says this nationally-known consultant, "every community of 50,000-plus population will be touched by some aspect of resource recovery." Dr. James Abert of the National Center for Resource Recovery agrees. He believes resource recovery is going to happen. The question in any given location, he says, is "when?"

Energy and economic trends seem to support that conclusion. The price of No. 6 residual oil used to generate electricity in Jacksonville, Florida, has risen 700 per cent since 1971, an increase typical of many areas. According to the best estimates available, the cost of refuse disposal for Florida's cities and counties went up about 25 per cent in 1977–1978. Similar trends are at work in all sections of the country. As a result of these impacts, as well as a better understanding of the risks associated with resource recovery, "There is a chance," says James Barker, President of the Boston-based DSI Resource System Group, "that people may stop studying the problem to death and get on with it. Resource recovery has a few key ingredients," says Barker, "and it doesn't take forever to determine its feasibility."

Those who study such things have pointed out that recycling levels in the U.S. reached their peak during the four great wars of our nation's history: the War for Independence, the War Between the States, World War I and World War II. Maybe we can use recycling and resource recovery to fight the battle of inflation.

Who knows? That revolutionary recycling ethic may yet become alive and well in these United States.

2-2 Five Rules for Resource Recovery

Richard W. Chase
Source: *NCRR Bulletin*, Vol. VI, No. 4 (Fall 1976) pp. 93-94. Reprinted with permission of National Center for Resource Recovery.

Our experience with resource recovery planning in Berlin, Bridgeport, New Britain and New Haven, Connecticut, proved clearly and forcefully that any organization or group — particularly from the public sector — should set forth a set of ground rules or operating rules before undertaking a resource recovery venture. Following are what I believe to be five of the more important points to consider.

1. *Acknowledge the existence of "Murphy's Law,"* which is in effect that *anything that can go wrong will go wrong.* Believe me, it's true. And you should be prepared to deal with it. You won't, of course, know *what* will go wrong, but you can be sure that out of 100 possible problem areas, 30 will materialize.

   Also, situations and conditions are going to change *after* planning decisions have been made. The Congress may change the tax law; your board of directors may change; the political leadership of the community may change, or the company's business fortunes may change. Without question, there will be unexpected changes, just as there will be wrathful misunderstandings and emotional problems — both real and imagined.

   I once started counting the number of lawyers that had spent more than one solid working week on the Bridgeport project. I stopped counting when I passed 50, because it was more than I could expect to have that many lawyers — counsel for the two companies involved, counsel for underwriters, counsel for all the towns involved, counsel for the utilities, our general counsel and bond counsel — to agree on anything, much less a major program to operate for the next 25 years.

2. *Make absolutely certain in the beginning that the decisions you are about to make and the program you are about to establish are in the best interest of all of the organizations and individuals it is to serve.* If your proposed program is not going to be a "good deal" for everyone involved — public, utility, municipality, state, private operator, etc. — you're going to find that the whole program will unravel and fall apart.

   If your fundamental objectives are in everyone's best interest, then you will have at the beginning eliminated a number of unpleasant and unnecessary problems, any one of which could have possibly scuttled your project.

   Whatever the various interests of the parties involved may be — political, economic, environmental or others — know that they will vary with each community. Once you have identified the primary interests of each group, *put yourself in their shoes* . . . and make your decisions accordingly.

3. *Adapt the technology to fit the problem — not the problem to fit the technology.* That may sound like an unnecessary statement to have to make, but it happens. We are all, I think, fascinated by technology, and a lot of companies are promoting very hard one form of

technology over another. This combination leads to the "technology initiated approach," which says: "We have the answer. Where is the problem?"

Despite its frequency of occurrence, this simply is the wrong way to go about solving any problem. No one technology is completely right. The amount of waste, fuel and materials markets, type of resource recovery system needed and availability of landfill space are just a few of the considerations that vary with each community. This can be a difficult problem, because there are companies which strongly prefer and promote certain technologies.

You must understand your own problem first, then select a number of companies with differing technologies to review your particular problem or needs. From these, select the system or combination of systems that best meet your requirements.

Remember, the key is to have the ability to identify and fit the right technology to your particular circumstances.

4. *Determine as early as possible the degree of financial risk each party should and will accept.* This is particularly important if you are dealing with a municipality. A municipality is hardly a concrete entity when you are conducting business with it. You may find yourself addressing a director of public works, a mayor, a local legislative body or other elected or appointed officials who may not be in office after the next year or two. So, recognize that with any city you're dealing with a *diffusion of decision-making responsibility* among people in relatively short-term positions.

Remember that it will be the local legislative body that will vote on your 25-year program — when it reaches that point — and not the administrative personnel with whom you worked on the planning . . . and who may not even be in office when it is voted upon. You will also find that the company people who are "out there selling" are much more willing to accept risk than their company's top management, executive committee and board of directors. Many times, and in good faith, the company representative will say: "Yes, we'll take that risk" or "sure, that's our responsibility." Yet, when you reach the point of signing contracts or agreements, you'll find their legal or financial people saying: "Are you out of your mind? You can't take that risk. What about our bank loan agreements, bond indentures or stockholder relations?"

Even when you clear these conditions with the company's top legal and financial people — which you should certainly do — there will still be those who will say when it comes time to sign legal documents, ". . . well, we didn't agree to that" or " . . . that wasn't our understanding at the time." And, without doubt, many of these are "good faith" mistakes. They're not attempts to mislead or deceive, but just the natural enthusiasm of people trying to sell or develop something and overstating their case.

5. *Finally, be sure that all parties involved in your resource recovery program planning understand ˆhat decision-making responsibility has ᴠᵉᵉᵑ assigned to whom, and the operational and procurement processes to be employed.* It's most important that everybody knows what his role is, the limits of his decision-making and the need to keep all other members of the venture apprised when important commitments are made and significant actions are taken.

In an *open* process there should be few "surprises" for anyone. All parties — municipalities, companies, utilities and state agencies — should be kept well-informed on exactly what is going on. Consequently, each party is confident that all business is being conducted in an open, responsible manner, and not through "back door" manipulations and political pressures.

One of the wisest decisions that any resource recovery project planner can make is to keep the design, procurement and development process as brief as possible. Begin by selecting the right administrative personnel and the right legal, financial and engineering advisors. You should, as a result, be able to make all major decisions within 60-to-90 days after receiving detailed proposals on any aspect of the project.

In summary, let me again stress that the pitfalls I have outlined are not necessarily unique to resource recovery projects, but can surface during any major joint venture between government agencies, institutions and private firms. And, they need not present insurmountable obstacles . . . as long as you can anticipate and be prepared to handle them.

2-3 Resource Recovery: Is It for Your City?

Stephen Burks and Clint Page

Source: *Nations Cities,* Vol. 15, No. 7 (July 1977) pp. 9–14. Reprinted with Permission of National League of Cities.

Nobody wants trash. Consumers put it out and hope it will be picked up. Municipal officials want to make it disappear as cheaply as possible. Environmentalists don't want it dumped in the open, buried so it pollutes land or water, or burned so it pollutes the air. In fact, environmentalists would like to see less of it.

About the only people that want trash are the resource recovery people — today's technologically sophisticated ragpickers — who think they can pull out of the virtually unending stream of municipal waste enough reusable materials, fuel, or energy to make it worth their while to build and pay for the equipment necessary to separate the treasure from the trash. And while this does seem to solve almost everybody's problems with trash, it's a relatively new approach and far from being perfected. So far, while there is great promise in the resource recovery business, all that glitters is not gold.

Nowhere has that been more apparent than in Baltimore, where a large pyrolysis plant that was designed to convert municipal waste into steam, scrap iron, and other usable materials at the rate of about 1,000 tons a day hasn't come anywhere close to doing what it was designed to do. Not only did the plant not start up on schedule, it hasn't yet run for any lengthy period of time. It has been plagued with mechanical breakdowns and rising costs. The private developer (Monsanto Enviro-Chem Systems) pulled out early this year, leaving the city understandably miffed. But Baltimore has soldiered on, largely because of the already sizable investment (some $22 million) it has in the plant.

The story got fairly good play in Baltimore and Washington, D.C., papers primarily because it was a good horror story: supertechnology fouls up. But that view of it is a little misleading. What's more accurate is to say that the project was an experiment: technology that had succeeded in a smaller pilot plant was being tried out at a much larger scale, and things didn't go the way they were expected to. Scaling up from 35 tons a day to 1,000 is the sort of giant step that only works out well in "Mother, May I?" As things started going wrong, more money was needed to try to put them right; eventually Monsanto got tired of spending money and time on the project, and they may have run out of ideas. Baltimore, with too much invested and too much to lose, couldn't pull out. Under city management the plant has been handling about half its designed amount of trash and selling steam to the city utility company: not a success, but not the failure the headlines suggested.

The Baltimore story is interesting because it involves all the characters and many of the conflicts that make up the resource recovery drama. There is a city with a solid waste problem, a private developer with a process, and a government agency (the Environmental Protection Agency) with money and a desire to try a new process.

It was from the combination of many cities, several private systems, and EPA that the resource recovery movement, particularly the high-technology side of it, got its real start in the early '70s, and so far results have been mixed. A $70 million project in St. Louis in which the utility company, Union Electric, was going to fuel its generators with refuse-derived fuel was scratched because of financial problems and regulatory difficulties. A recent Missouri law prohibits power companies from adding the cost of new facilities to customers' bills until the facilities are in operation; coupled with that problem was public objection to some of the transfer stations that would have been necessary to the project. Skyrocketing costs brought an end to a proposed energy recovery system in Westchester County, New York. From an original estimate of $54 million, costs for a Union Carbide solid waste and energy recovery system quickly climbed to $114 million, and the county canceled the contract.

Some other projects already operating aren't the financial successes they were expected to be. One, in Saugus, Massachusetts, is operating somewhat below capacity (850 tons a day compared to its 1,200 tons a day maximum), not because it can't handle the full amount but because it can't get it. The plant serves several communities, and some find it cheaper to dispose of their rash through landfill. A similar situation has hampered the 200-ton-per-day plant in Ames, Iowa. The plant is processing 150 tons a day, again because some of the communities it was built to serve are trucking their trash to a neighboring county's landfill.

SUCCESS STORIES

There are successes, too, and they shouldn't be ignored. A plant in Franklin, Ohio, has been processing an average of 35 tons of solid waste a day since 1971 to yield ferrous metal scrap and a low-grade fiber that is sold to a nearby manufacturer of roofing felt. The Nashville (Tennessee) Thermal Transfer Plant, which ran into immediate mechanical problems because of an attempt to reduce deficits by cutting back on equipment expenditures, has apparently overcome these probelms. Although the plant ended up costing more than anticipated, it is now working well. December, 1976, and January, 1977, were two of the plant's best months (and two of the coldest): during that time the plant operated on solid waste alone 93 percent of the time, providing steam to a number of downtown buildings, public and private. (During the summer it provides chilled water for cooling.)

From the successes and failures, it becomes apparent that there is more to success in resource recovery than just a lot of trash. That's where it starts, of course: Americans generate a lot of trash — about 3 1/2 pounds per person per day in 1973, some four pounds per person per day by 1980, according to EPA figures. What's more, we spend well over $6 billion a year to get rid of it.

Resource recovery promises to reverse that: it promises to take something with a negative price and from it extract materials or energy for which there is a demand and, therefore, a positive price. The numbers are impressive. Out of the total of 145 million tons of municipal trash that's collected each year, there are 44 million tons of recoverable paper, 11 million tons of recoverable ferrous metals, 1.3 million tons of aluminum, 13 million tons of glass, and the energy equivalent of 145 million barrels of oil.

That potential bonanza has attracted a lot of prospectors. More than 30 companies manufacture and sell resource recovery systems and eqiupment in this country. In 1976, an EPA-sponsored study by the Mitre Corp. showed that in 1973 the top 20 resource recovery companies had combined revenues of $23 billion and combined assets of $18 billion.

There is little argument that these firms have entered the resource recovery field for their own benefit. Manufacturers of pollution control equipment see resource recovery as a logical diversification. Can and bottle manufacturers find it preferable to change their production systems to conserve raw materials: beverage distributors find recycling the materials more attractive than dealing with reusable containers. Resource recovery does shift the burden of collection and sorting from the manufacturer to the public sector; legislation calling for reusable containers or for product charges that include the cost of recycling in the manufacturers' costs could reverse that shift.

Besides being a big and growing business, resource recovery is a complex business. It responds in large part to the same forces of supply and demand that affect any business, but it is made more complex because it often involves a troubled marriage of private enterprise and public interest, with neither partner being exactly sure of its role.

RISKY BUSINESS

The trouble centers on the risk inherent in a developing technology and an enterprise that depends on supply and demand for its success. The market-related risks are ones that municipal governments don't assume willingly or easily, even if the potential benefits are great. On the other hand, most city officials understand political risks, and the political risk of failure is great. The reason isn't hard to understand. The technology, to begin with, is highly complex and, at present, generally unproven. This leaves policy makers vulnerable to a variety of "vendors" with numerous possible combinations of equipment and numerous financing, purchasing, and operating arrangements, all of which promise, but cannot assure, that the proposed facility will be financially self-sufficient. Since making a profit usually requires large volumes of waste, many facilities must bring together a number of local jurisdictions. The possibility of jurisdictional conflicts, added to the general public controversy usually surrounding public facility-siting decisions, makes for additional political hazards.

The risks, however, begin and end with money — anywhere from $2 million to $3 million for plants like the one in Franklin, Ohio, or the one being built in Lane County, Oregon, to $18 million for the plant that recently went into operation in Milwaukee, and up to as much as $73 million (Hempstead, New York) and $82 million (Dade County, Florida). All of that money has to come from somewhere: from municipal bonds or other municipal sources for the city's share; from investment capital, dumping fees, and the revenues from the sale of materials or energy for the private share. In some cases, the Environmental Protection Agency has provided demonstration grants but not operating funds.

The way the risks are shared has a lot to do with the actual financial profile of a project and with the way the benefits are distributed. The more the project falls in the public sector, the more it will be run for the benefit of the city or locality. The more it falls into the private sector, the more it will be run like a profit-making business venture: dumping (also called tipping) fees

will be higher, and the emphasis on maximum revenues will be greater. That's all well and good when projects are strictly private or strictly public, but it makes things difficult when the two are combined as they so often are.

THE BALTIMORE CASE

The Baltimore plant is a case in point. Of the original $26 million kitty, the city put up $11 million, the state $4 million, Monsanto $4 million, and EPA $7 million as a demonstration grant. When problems began to crop up, the city, with the greatest share of the risk — to say nothing of a trash problem that won't go away — had no choice but to stay in the game. Monsanto, on the other hand, could, and probably wisely did, fold — at least for that hand.

In Baltimore, public investment greatly exceeded private investment, but that isn't always the case. In other plants, the private investment has been the greater one, and in Milwaukee, the recently opened resource recovery plant has been built entirely with private funds; it is owned and operated by Americology, the American Can Company's resource recovery subsidiary.

Private investment in resource recovery should increase in the future although there does seem to be a shortage of capital. Congress has indicated through the Resource Conservation and Recovery Act that it considers resource recovery a private enterprise. The only obstacle is that shortage of capital, and the private interests feel that seed money or other incentives should be available to make up for it.

While each locality, each plant, and each process is different, there are some general factors that affect the success of resource recovery projects. The starting point for any city government is its own solid waste disposal system. In many parts of the country, traditional landfill operations are still the most economical of the acceptable solutions if there is land available within reasonable distance. In other areas, particularly the more densely populated sections of the country, land suitable for landfill already has been used up, or its use has been blocked by environmental considerations, or it has been put to more profitable use. The closer a community is to running out of economical ways to dispose of waste, the better resource recovery looks.

Two other major factors a city should give close attention to are the nature of its municipal waste — what types of trash the city generates and what can be recovered from it — and what markets exist for the recovered materials. Resource recovery plants are designed to operate efficiently and economically at a given daily volume; changes in the flow can throw the economics out of kilter and turn a successful plant into a flop. To avoid that, many resource recovery contracts between private contractors and cities specify that the private developer is to be protected against changes in the type and amount of trash. Private developers usually want long-term contracts, and the protection can include provisions for higher dumping fees or other financial penalties. These clauses could make a city think twice about a bottle bill, for example, or any other ordinance that would change the waste stream — a point not overlooked by the environmentalists.

The other side of the supply and demand equation — demand — should be obvious. There is little point in recovering paper fiber if there is no readily accessible market for paper fiber; there's no reason to generate steam unless there is somewhere to use it.

The nature of the raw material and the existing markets also directly influence the type of process and equipment to be used. The processes are complicated (below), and they involve a variety of equipment. There are shredders and pulpers to reduce everything to small bits, air classifiers to separate paper and plastsics from metals and glass, magnets to remove ferrous metals; there are even devices that can electronically separate aluminum from the rest of the trash or optically sort glass by color although they aren't truly practical.

Getting overenthusiastic about the technological side of resource recovery can be almost as dangerous as recovering materials for which there is no market. There is little to be gained by having the most technologically advanced resource recovery plant if all that needs to be done, or is justified by the market, is to separate heavy items, such as metals and glass, from the lighter plastics and paper.

The equipment itself can be a problem. Some of the equipment on the market today does a good job of what it was designed to do, but because resource recovery is still a growing technology, there are processes that have yet to be perfected.

Aluminum, for example, is a key product for resource recovery; its price hasn't dropped below $200 a ton in years. Mechanical or electronic separation of aluminum, however, has a way to go. There hasn't been a successful, full-scale demonstration of a technology to recover aluminum from mixed waste, and the best device so far, the eddy current separator (or "aluminum magnet") has the disadvantage of separating zinc, tin, and brass at the same time, leaving further sorting of the materials — and further sorting out of the process — still to be done. Even with the good prices paid for recycled aluminum, electronic separation is too expensive to be practical today.

Glass separation is a little more advanced, but it's still not technically or economically practical. That's what the Environmental Protection Agency concluded after two years of testing in Franklin, Ohio. The problem is that glass must be sorted by color if it's to be marketable, and the best optical scanners can't do the job as consistently and as cheaply as the human eye.

There's another problem inherent in the machinery of resource recovery. Like all machinery, it wears out and breaks down. Hammers in hammermills wear out and need to be retipped; seals stop sealing and have to be replaced; kiln linings crack and have to be repaired. The more complicated the process and the machinery, the more parts there are to wear out, and repairs slow down the process and add to the costs.

SCALE IS A FACTOR

Another basic factor that seems to be at work in the resource recovery field is the matter of scale. The problems in Baltimore are a prime example. What had worked at 35 tons a day didn't work at 1,000. The jump was perhaps too big, too soon. Although the new plants in Chicago and Milwaukee may prove that the technical problems of large-scale facilities were only a temporary stage in the development of resource recovery hardware, other problems remain. Among these, the most important are the reliability of the markets for both garbage and the recovered products. The Ames and Saugus plants are operating at only three-quarter capacity, not because they don't work, but because they can't find enough garbage. Their prices are not competitive with nearby landfills. Columbus, Ohio, in contrast, has had to abandon temporarily a paper-recycling program because, in only four months, it collected more used paper than the contractor could sell, driving him into bankruptcy. These experiences highlight the importance of guaranteed long-term markets at both the input and output ends of the resource recovery system if they are to be successful. The Carter administration has, however, shown a growing interest in reducing the volume of trash production; the solid waste section of the 1977 Carter environmental message, for example, emphasizes the importance of "two principal causes of the solid waste problem: excessive packaging and inadequate use of recycled materials." Given the short-term uncertainty of the products market and the long-term uncertainty of the garbage market, avoiding the well-ingrained American penchant for "bigger and better" machinery may be well advised. Despite the dangers of "overscaling," high-technology resource recovery is inherently based on scale economies, and it is therefore likely to be limited for the foreseeable future to larger cities or groups of cities that can afford the costs and that can provide the necessary raw materials and markets.

For cities that cannot consider the high technology systems but need or want an alternative to landfilling, a number of medium- and low-technology approaches to resource recovery are available. Like high-tech systems, medium-tech systems mechanically separate recyclable material from mixed garbage, but they don't burn the light fraction (paper, plastics) as a supplemental fule. Several of these systems (in Leigh County, Pennsylvania, and Norman, Oklahoma) use a composting process that reduces the non-ferrous solid waste (often combined with sewage sludge) to a humus, which is then marketed as a soil conditioner. Although the composting techniques have proven reliable for small communities (generally under 50 tons per day), markets for the compost are sometimes hard to find. In addition, the process itself, particularly when the garbage is mixed with sewer sludge, produces an odor that can get both physically and politically unpleasant.

Medium-technology resource recovery, even if it only separates out the ferrous fraction and shreds and disposes of the reaminder, prolongs the life of landfills up to 50 percent, thus delaying the increasingly onerous task of locating new landfill sites. In addition, landfills using shredded waste have fewer maintenance problems and generally lower costs.

Local policy makers often have as much difficulty choosing medium-tech shredders and magnetic separation composting systems as they do high-tech ones. Cost and performance data is usually more readily available for the medium-tech equipment than for the newer, high-tech machinery. The cost, however, is usually great enough to justify an outside consultant (preferably one who does not have a stake in a potential bidder for the contract) to provide precise cost estimates of the alternatives.

LOW-TECH VS. HIGH-TECH

The low-technology approach relies on people rather than machines to recover resources. Usually referred to as either collection/recycling or source separation systems, some form of this approach is currently used in more than 90 cities. Essentially, low-tech systems involve the presorting of garbage into specific categories where it is generated (home, business, institutions, etc.). Usually, the categories are paper, metal, and glass although sometimes a leftover category is included and sometimes glass is not collected separately.

Source separation programs are obviously a less expensive way to recycle materials because they eliminate the need for fancy machinery. One estimate is that if individual households spend six minutes per week separating trash, a $100,000 facility could handle a city-wide resource recovery program that would cost millions of dollars if done mechanically. The question, however, is whether source separation works for any extended period in all communities. Where neatness, discipline, and thrift are longstanding traditions or where environmental awareness has recently developed source separation can and does work well. There are, however, communities in which physical decay, wasteful habits, or general recalcitrance probably would work against source separation. It also can be a political bombshell when the Los Angeles City Council passed specific requirements for the baling of garbage, sorting of bottles, and the like, public rejection of the idea made source separation an explosive political issue that may have helped elect Sam Yorty mayor.

The economics of recycling are improving. Reynolds Aluminum is expected to return more than $100 million to consumers in 1977 for recycled aluminum cans, and the Garden State Paper Company, which has organized separate newspaper collection programs in 43 cities, has increased its volume to 500,000 tons per year and expects to handle 700,000 tons per year by 1979. The Carter administration's plan to implement government-wide paper-recycling programs and to study seriously the feasibility of product charges (taxes on producers who use virgin materials in packaging) also point to a growing emphasis on recycling.

PEOPLE, NOT MACHINES

As might be expected, the low-tech and the high-tech advocates are not usually the best of friends. The low-tech people point to the high capital costs, the high energy costs, the unproven technology, the emissions problems, the loss of jobs, and the implied emphasis on a continuation of current waste generation patterns.

The high-tech advocates counter with the arguments that much has been learned in the demonstration projects to date; that additional financial commitments (preferably by the federal government; if not, by state and local government and private industry) are necessary to assure that these lessons are translated into a "second generation" technology that will recover materials and produce energy much more efficiently; and that these technologies can be proven and gain widespread adoption if such commitments are made. The current

chicken-and-egg situation of unproven technologies and government reluctance to commit resources must be broken, they argue, so that we can fully realize the recovery potential of garbage.

As with most things, the truth probably lies somewhere between the extremes. The high-tech approach surely has more potential than we have seen to date and probably deserves either more support or less fetters from government in developing new facilities. What is clear is that high-technology resource recovery systems must be done right or not at all. The Nashville experience, in particular, shows how cost cutting to save a project (equipment expenditures were cut in an attempt to deal with early cost overruns) ends up costing much more in the end. Communities considering these types of systems should therefore be ready to go considerably beyond their budget if necessary to produce a reliable facility.

LESS WASTE IN THE FUTURE?

The low-technology model, too, deserves additional attention. Much more could be done, at relatively little cost, to better determine what it takes to get people to play the sorting game. Changing our wasteful ways may not be as difficult as many people have assumed, particularly if there is something to be gained.

What of the future? For the short term, resource recovery probably will remain a secondary concern of most cities, either an expensive luxury or a personal nuisance, depending on what type of system is being used or considered. For the long term, however, the prospects are much better. Basic economics inevitably will increase the value of recovered materials as virgin materials and fossil fuels are depleted. Politically, resource recovery is likely to become more attractive as landfilling becomes more difficult and as local jurisdictions develop new approaches to solving common problems. Socially, public support for recovery will increase as energy and other material shortages become more widespread.

But that happy day is still some time off. Changing the basic values of a waste-oriented society so that they will sort their garbage and convincing local officials that they shoul invest

$20 million to $50 million in what often appears to be a Rube Goldberg "infernal machine" will take both patience and persistence. But the initial, most difficult steps have been taken, and 10 or 20 years hence we just may find that we have again "muddled through" to a balanced and effective national system of resource recovery. And there, silhouetted against the skyline, perhaps bronzed like baby booties as a tribute to its notoriety, will be the Baltimore Pyrolysis Plant.

2-4 Resource Recovery:
The Economics and the Risks

J.G. Abert

Source: *Professional Engineer,* Vol. 45, No. 11 (November 1975) pp. 29–31. Reprinted with Permission of National Society of Professional Engineers.

Municipal refuse, the throw-away of our consumption-oriented society, should represent a major target for the nation's resource conservation efforts. Actions must be taken that will permit the retrieval and reuse of depletable and even replenishable resources, along with the possible conversion of the balance of the organic materials in refuse into fuel sources that can help alleviate a portion of the national energy problem. What this means is maximizing, consistent with local economics, conversion-reclamation possibilities while minimizing the amount of solid waste going into landfill or simply destroyed with no useful byproduct.

There has been significant progress toward the accomplishment of this goal during the past few years. However, there is room for concern about what may be the non-events of the next few years. There is reason to believe that the nation may be entering a half-decade or so of pause while the gains of the recent past are consolidated and while the risk takers of this era, and the sideline-watchers of these risk takers, see whether the bets they made pay off or not. What are the underlying causes of this deceleration in the nation's progress toward incorporating resource recovery as a component of municipalities' solid waste management systems?

First, risk is not out of the venture. There are not at present more than one or two operating sites and even these are not buttressed by operating data. We are not at a point in time when prospective purchasers of recovery can visit sites, inspect operating data, look at independent evaluations and come to the conclusion that they want brand X but paint theirs green.

A second underlying cause of a possible slowdown in the rate of progress is that the potential users of the recovered materials, and this includes refuse fuel, have had little experience with the recovery product. Recently I had a call from a paper company — a user of coal to produce inplant steam. They had been considering a refuse fuel application. One purpose of the call was to tell me that their economics demanded a 70-plus percent refuse-to-coal proportion. Where could they get some data on this, they asked. I told them nowhere. As far as I know, it has not been done. They said, what should they do? My reply was, "Get a good deal on the fuel price and bite the bullet on the conversion cost and try it."

Unspoken is the fact that if they do not, someone else might and in their area there is not enough refuse fuel to go around. If it works, the returns are going to go to those who venture forth first. The incentive is clear. But even if they are amenable to taking the technological risk in order to attempt to obtain the benefits, the next reason underlying the prospects for a slowdown is not so easy to overcome.

A third cause for a possible slowdown is the difficulty of getting the refuse supply under long-term contract. Procurement regulations at the state and local level are simply not designed for relatively high capital, cost-risky ventures that require negotiation and long-term contracts.

The fourth reason for a slowdown is the shortage of risk-taking mechanisms. Money from the Federal government to which we generally look for risk bearing in the national interest, seems to be all but gone. Also, the states as third party risk takers have not developed institutions, approaches, and, most importantly, the perspective of being risk takers for prototype sites. More common behavior on the part of the states is to want to imitate a banking institution engaged in portfolio maximization. Also, political pressures at the state level work toward the diffusion of the available funds rather than planned programs systematically developing alternatives for later replication under less risky circumstances. The latter requires the political will to concentrate the resources available. This will is often lacking.

The fifth reason that progress in resource recovery may decelerate is that there is a private sector conflict to be resolved. The question is at which margin should the bulk of the economic activity called "resource recovery from municipal waste" fall. Should it be at the margin of public health which would lead one to conclude that resource recovery should be performed by the public sector or should it be viewed at the margin of the sale of the recovered materials or fuel values in competition with private enterprise? This implies private operation and ownership. Since these firms do not enjoy the "cheaper" capital of public activities or recourse to the tax base to cover shortfalls between costs and sales revenues, one might argue that a fairness doctrine would suggest that resource recovery should not be able to avail itself of quasi-public funding mechanisms. The debate over these issues which probably will not be resolved except on a case-by-case basis cannot help but slow the rate of progress of resource recovery.

The sixth and final reason for a likely pause in the rate of advance of resource recovery concerns the movement to change the composition of the waste stream, not by the normal process of changes in consumer taste, technology, or income distribution, the fundamental tenets of utility theory and the optimal allocation of resources, but rather through regulation and the changing of relative prices among various forms of packaging. Without making a value judgment about the desirability

of public policy actions to change the composition of the waste on a national scale, the impact at the community level is clear.

It simply offers the prospects of higher dumping fees for resource recovery. It is axiomatic that revenues for a plant, whether private or public, must cover cost. There are two sources of revenue: 1. returns from the sale of recovered products; and 2. the dumping fee which could be in the form of a line item budget appropriation. Together they must cover cost. Reducing the metals and glass in the waste stream cuts down on potential recovery revenues without significantly reducing costs. Hence, dumping fees go up.

Put differently, there is a risk of early obsolescence of capital outlays. This is an added element of risk. The price of resource recovery goes up as this is factored into the equation, and fewer cities look to recovery as a viable option in competition with their nonrecovery alternatives. This is another underlying cause which may bring about a pause in recovery progress.

Why do I view the prospects for such a pause with some alarm? Because I believe that a great deal of conservation can be accomplished through recovery. In fact, taking into account the realities of the political process, the discounted price impacts of investing in longer-lasting consumer durables, and the ever-increasing diseconomies of highly labor intensive repair versus highly capital intensive equipment, more conservation may occur during the next decade or so through recovery than through any other approach. This probably is true even if one could analytically show that on pure efficiency standards (these are certainly not the only standards to be used for public policy) recovery is second best.

My concern is not simply with the delay of a year or so in effecting prototype efforts covering institutional arrangements and technology. These, in themselves, involve relatively little in the way of either tons recycled or Btu's captured from what otherwise would have been buried or burnt to no productive end. Rather, my concern is with the delay the lack of a continued emergence of prototypes will have on broad-scale replication.

For example, in one city with which I am familiar, an agreement (already approved with the money appropriated by a potential refuse fuel user) may be delayed for at least a year and a half because there seems to be no way to find $200,000 for needed pneumatic transfer systems. Budget cycles do not accommodate readily to targets of opportunity.

The 200-to-300 tons per day the pilot plant would burn is of no great importance. Nor really is the fact that the city would recoup its investment in roughly three years. What is important is that this particular metropolitan area, at 3000 tons per day (or more), is going to be set back in time by a year or so because of the delay in the pilot project. That time represents a great many Btu's, money going for coal, and a higher disposal cost than there need be for the area's taxpayers. The potential savings could be used for other public purposes such as education, health, or welfare. It could also be left in the pockets of the householder.

Prototype facilities and institutional arrangements must continue to be effected. The economies are such that the benefits of earlier implementation rather than later appear to warrant the development of a network of prototype sites testing different approaches to recovery. Replication is the key to reducing disposal budgets.

The key to resource recovery seems to be size reduction. Some systems do not need it, but most do. What does it cost? For example, if a plant processes between 500 and 700 tons per day (this represents the refuse of between 300,000 and 500,000 people), the cost of shred and landfill would be between $6 and $8 per ton. It could be higher than this in the metropolitan Northeast. There is an assumption of public land available at no cost.

Add to this a materials recovery system which would attempt to recover some paper, ferrous metals, nonferrous metals and glass. In terms of costs, this would add another $6–$8 per input ton.

Not all of the processes for this recovery have been tested or operated on a production scale. But if they all worked, there would be available for sale: ferrous metals (mostly cans), aluminum (again, mostly cans), glass, other

nonferrous material as a mixture, and some relatively low-grade hand-picked, corrugated paper. The other separations would be done automatically.

What revenues are there likely to be for all of this? The answer is roughly $6–$10 per input ton with the bulk of the revenues coming from ferrous metals and aluminum. Net this against costs and if everything works, the dumping fee would be about $6 per ton minimum.

How much of this could be covered by the sale of refuse for its fuel value? In a utility burning situation where prepared refuse is used as a supplementary fuel, we understand that Chicago and Toledo are negotiating in the 40 cents per million Btu range. A ton of refuse fuel has around 10 million Btu's. Therefore, the price would be about $4 per ton of refuse fuel. What does this mean in terms of covering production costs?

Suppose there is a ten-mile haul distance from shredder and air classifier to the using power plant. Assume 12¢ per ton mile for the transportation costs. Assume also that 60 percent of the input waste is converted to refuse-derived fuel. In this case, the $4 per ton gross revenue from the sale of the fuel will cover about $2 of its cost of production. Therefore, even with materials recovery, a Chicago-like deal would still have a dumping fee, or its equivalent, of $4 per ton or more.

If one were just to make refuse fuel, my calculations are that the cost would be between $7–$10 per input ton of refuse. To cover this with a ten-mile haul distance would take a sales price of $1.35 a million Btu's.

This is not outside the realm of possibility, but it is probably not the kind of deal one is going to get from those who are among the first to use the material. They will want a relatively large potential benefit to cover what they see as the relatively large risk.

It can be shown that when the risk and uncertainty have been worked out, recovery will compete with landfill in almost all the major metropolitan areas of the country. Therefore, the cost of not continuing to develop prototype models from both the institutional side and the technology side is high, and actions are needed to continue the momentum of the past few years.

What are the actions needed? First and foremost is a better understanding of the public versus private issue. We must grapple with the financial impact on disposal budgets of the difference between the expected return on public capital and that expected from private capital, including a return for entrepreneurial risk. We must convey this to those who make the political and administrative decisions about refuse.

Next, I think we must strengthen our third party risk-sharing mechanisms. My preference would be to do this at the state and regional levels. For example, depending on how it is implemented, the New York State Environmental Bond Act could provide an excellent prototype.

Finally, we must come to grips with the need to develop more sophisticated procurement practices in the public sector at the local level. Resource recovery, which in large measure is an R&D venture, cannot be purchased like #2 soft lead pencils. In dealing with municipalities, resource recovery is in the proverbial chicken and egg situation. No one can build and operate full-scale plants without refuse. Cities have the refuse but do not have the mechanism to even give it away, or so it sometimes seems. Finally, cities will not buy the technology unless it has been proven in practice. This is the catch-22 of resource recovery.

In summary, a broad range of prototype systems in place and operating is the key to continued progress in resource recovery. Some states and some communities must resolve the chicken and egg problem. They must do more than their share.

2-5 Waste-to-Energy: Applying the Technology in the Real World

Glenn A. Swinhart and Whitney A. Sanders

Source: Adapted from two articles that appeared in *Solid Wastes Management*, entitled (1) Applying the Technology in the Read World, Vol. 22, No. 5 (May 1979), pp. 20-21, 24, 28, 88, and (2) Waste-to-Energy Contracts Cover A Host of Legal and Institutional Issues, Vol. 22, No. 6 (June 1979), pp. 56, 58, 60. Reprinted with Permission of. Communication Channels, Inc.

In today's economic climate, energy is by far the most valuable resource recoverable from municipal solid wastes, and bulk burning of unclassified wastes in an energy recovery plant is the most cost-effective means of extracting that energy.

A typical ton of solid wastes contains energy worth from $25 to $35 in terms of fuel oil cost for equivalent energy. Without a ready market, recoverable materials, which have a current value of $2 to $4 per ton of solid waste, are seldom worth the added capital expense and operating complexities of the separation equipment required.

Under present conditions, there are no short-cuts to a successful energy recovery facility; these facilities require specific, individualized engineering backed by equally specific management, legal and investment services. There are no catalogs from which an energy consumer can purchase an off-the-shelf package energy unit for standardized application.

Solid waste-to-energy facilities are necessarily complex and, regardless of size, are comparable to a large central power plant in automatic control sophistication, specialized design and construction. Materials handling, fuel feeding, ash removal, air pollution control, and overall operating procedures are more complicated than those of a similarly sized fossil fuel plant. A major obstacle to standardization is the variability of fuel quality. Municipal wastes, unlike fossil fuels, vary daily and seasonally in BTU and moisture content as well as in volume available at a specific site. Matching the varying waste stream to the energy customer's requirements is the most important technical aspect of a successful project.

Complexities extend far beyond the hardware. A typical facility requires the cooperation of the owner, usually a city, township, county, or authority which may or may not operate the facility itself; energy purchasers; and one or more governmental units, possibly in combination with private sources, to provide the continuous waste stream. With these complicated interrelationships, a clearly defined management approach and authority and a single responsible program manager representing the controlling organization are highly desirable to keep the project on time and within budget. Such management can ensure transmission of information to all parties concerned and can make prompt decisions on approvals or changes as studies, design, and construction progress.

Development of a waste stream to a point where its flow can be guaranteed is essential but cannot be assumed.

To the extent that a governmental unit collects and disposes of its own refuse with its own personnel, this waste stream can easily be diverted to the energy recovery facility and, in communities of the necessary size, can provide the bulk of fuel requirements. However, if the waste stream depends upon several smaller communities, each with its own system; upon private haulers under franchise; or upon haulers privately selected by the waste generators, the situation becomes more complex and time-consuming to organize. Control of the waste stream is crucial, and usually can be accomplished in a reasonable time. However, the greater the number of participants, the longer the time usually required to gain control of the waste stream.

FORM OF ENERGY

Once the fuel stream is developed, the waste-to-energy conversion system chosen must be capable of delivering energy to the consumer in a form readily usable by him. The primary and most efficient conversion is to steam or high temperature hot water generated directly in the boiler. If required by the consumer, secondary conversion can produce electricity or chilled water at reduced overall thermal efficiency and increased capital cost.

Electricity production costs must compete with larger and thermally more efficient public utility generation. This approach results in lower revenue per invested dollar.

These concepts are best illustrated by the relative value of one million BTUs (1 MMBTU) in each energy form, as shown in Table 1.

These relative values indicate that steam and hot water are equally desirable energy forms because of lowest equipment costs and greatest energy value ratio. Chilled water, though it requires the highest capital investment, provides the next best energy value ratio. Co-generation of steam and electricity, with sale of both, is next on the list. Electricity as a sole product, because of its price competition and lower overall efficiency, produces the lowest energy value ratio and income.

NEEDS OF ENERGY BUYER

The needs of the energy buyer (or buyers) are one main factor governing selection of the overall system. If his year-round hourly requirements for steam or high-temperature hot water equal or exceed the hourly output of the energy plant, he can use all the energy produced. Under such conditions, capital invested in an energy facility returns the maximum energy available and therefore maximizes potential revenue. Energy purchases at any rate less than total plant output, of course, tend to reduce revenue per invested dollar.

Conversion of energy to secondary forms requires additional capital for equipment, adds to maintenance costs because of increased system complexity, and reduces overall thermal efficiency; thus sale of secondary energy forms in a competitive energy market tends to return less per invested dollar.

In a period of continuing inflation, the cost of energy produced in a resource recovery plant will increase at a slower rate than the cost of that produced by a typical industrial fossil fuel plant, for the following reasons. In a conventional oil-fired package boiler system, most of the total annual cost is in fuel and labor; amortization of capital costs as a share of total annual costs is low because the energy system is relatively low in original cost. Furthermore, fuel costs are increasing at a rate higher than the general inflation rate and show no signs of abating.

Resource recovery plants, on the other hand, are much more capital intensive. In the studies we have performed, typically 50% of total annual costs are in debt service in the early years. As inflation continues, the other 50% of costs – operations, personnel, maintenance, etc. – will increase with the general inflation rate. However, since the annual debt service cost is a fixed dollar amount each year, this fixed cost acts as a brake on inflation of the total annual cost. The overall cost of a unit of energy produced, therefore, increases at a slower rate than the general inflation.

This slower rate of increase per energy unit cost gives the resource recovery facility a strong bargaining point in establishing contracts with energy buyers.

PLANT CONSIDERATIONS

Waste-to-energy plants are not the remedy for the solid waste disposal problems of every community; but when the proper combination of waste disposal costs and energy demand exists, the energy recovery plant can be an effective solution.

Table 1. Relative Value of One Million BTUs (1 MMBTU) in Each Energy Form.

Hypothetical Industrial Energy Costs

Steam $3.50 per 1,000 lb.
(#2 fuel cost @ 43 cents/gallon in 85% efficiency boiler exclusive of labor, operating and maintenance costs)

Electricity $0.025 per KWH
(Assumed industrial rate)

Chilled Water $0.050 per ton-hr.
(Assumed value of chilled water)

Value of 1 MMBTU Delivered from Waste Plant

Steam or Hot Water

$$\frac{1 \text{ MMBTU}}{1,040 \text{ BTU/Lb. Steam}} \quad \times \quad \frac{\$3.50}{1,000 \text{ Lb. Steam}} = \$3.37 \text{ per MMBTU}$$

Electricity (Turbine driven generator, 60% efficiency, 400 psig satuated steam at turbine inlet)

$$\frac{1 \text{ MMBTU}}{15,600 \text{ BTU/KWH}} \times \$0.025 \text{ per KWH} = \$1.60 \text{ per MMBTU}$$

Chilled Water (Turbine driven centrifugal chiller, 60% efficiency, 400 psig saturated steam at turbine inlet)

$$\frac{1 \text{ MMBTU}}{13,070 \text{ BTU/ton-hr.}} \times \$0.05 \text{ per ton-hr} = \$3.82 \text{ per MMBTU}$$

Total Project Costs – 150 TPD Waste, 40 MMBTU Net Output

(4500 BTU per lb. waste fuel, 80% thermal efficiency)

Steam or Hot Water	$6.5 million
Co-generation of Steam and Electricity	$7.0 million
Electric Generation	$7.5 million
Steam and Chilled Water	$8.0 million

Energy Value Ratio (Hourly Revenues/$ Million Invested)

Steam or Hot Water

$$\frac{\$3.37 \times 40 \text{ MMBTU}}{\$6.5 \text{ million}} = \$20.74$$

Chilled Water and Steam (50% of Each)

$$\frac{\$3.37 \times 20 \text{ MMBTU}) + (\$3.82 \times 20 \text{ MMBTU})}{\$8.0 \text{ million}} = \$17.98$$

Co-generation (60% Steam, 40% Electricity)

$$\frac{(\$3.37 \times 24) + (1.60 \times 16)}{\$7.0 \text{ million}} = \$15.21$$

Electricity

$$\frac{\$1.60 \times 40 \text{ MMBTU}}{\$7.5 \text{ million}} = \$ 8.53$$

In general terms, when landfill costs are high and/or landfills are scarce, and when energy customers are available near a suitable processing site, consideration of an energy recovery facility is warranted. Table 2 presents a number of factors which affect the overall feasibility of a given project.

The decision to construct an energy recovery plant is, in the authors' opinion, basically a business decision, subject, of course, to the limits of present technology. Such a plant requires long term commitments and substantial investment in capital and operating dollars. Therefore the preliminary analysis of feasibility is a critical step in the decision-making process. For these reasons, it is important that the analysis realistically appraise all of the factors which impact economic and technical feasibility. Several of the more common problems of energy recovery plant feasibility are discussed in the following paragraphs.

DATA GATHERING

Since accurate data are essential to a valid study, the initial survey and audit of the solid waste stream and the potential energy market is most important. Unfortunately, many communities do not maintain accurate records of the quantity and characteristics of their solid waste stream on a daily and seasonal basis; this is necessary information to match energy production to potential usage. Municipal wastes are bulky and do not store well; sheer bulk and odor problems make storage for more than three or four days impractical.

Wastes must be burned and energy sold at a rate consistent with the flow of the waste stream to achieve highest efficiency and revenues.

Potential customers must be evaluated on their use of energy hourly, daily and seasonally. Gathering this information on such a time-detailed basis may require development of infor-

Table 2. Factors Affecting Feasibility of a Project.

Item	Most Attractive	Least Attractive	Potential Solution	Possible Problems
Waste Stream	Municipal system going to municipal fill; stable waste flow.	Private haul to landfill owned by hauler; seasonal variation.	Require private hauler to use municipal system.	Confusion as to who ultimately maintains ownership of solid waste.
Fuel Quality	Low moisture content; good commercial waste proportion.	High moisture content; mostly agricultural waste.	Find good source of dry waste for mixing to improve energy content.	Difficulties in finding this alternate source of waste.
Energy User	Process steam load 7 day/week, 24 hours/day in excess of MSW plant output. Good backup from existing fossil fuel plant.	Seasonal heating requirement less than would be produced by proposed waste stream.	Co-generate electricity with excess steam.	Value of electricity is much lower. Capital costs increase.
Location	One central user.	Potential customers dispersed.	Provide major distribution system.	Increased capital cost. Increased thermal losses. Increased maintenance.
Energy Form	Steam or high temperature hot water.	Electricity	Co-generate, but maximize percentage of steam sales versus electricity sales.	Increased capital cost. Lower energy value ratio than 100% steam sales.

mation not readily available in the customer's records.

Ensuring an appropriate balance between waste stream input and energy output requires accurate production/demand profiles on an hourly, daily, and seasonal basis. Simple averaging of annual waste production and energy consumption to hourly and daily values could lead to an improperly sized plant producing insufficient revenue to offset capital and operating costs.

TECHNOLOGICAL CONSIDERATIONS

There is no question that municipal waste contains valuable energy. However, as a fuel, municipal waste presents many problems not normally encountered with fossil fuels. The solid wastes are bulky and may contain problem substances and incombustible material; these wastes are non-homogeneous, and vary unpredictably in their characteristics from day to day and season to season in terms of ultimate analysis. This situation is in direct contrast to the consistent standards of other boiler fuels. Furthermore, the quantity generated by a given community may vary from week to week and season to season.

For these reasons it is essential that the preliminary analysis of feasibility closely compare developed technologies and equipment in relation to the situation under study.

AVAILABLE TECHNOLOGIES

Developed technologies that can be considered for incineration of solid waste and generation of steam or high temperature hot water fall into five general categories, all of which are used in conjunction with waste heat boilers. Those categories, with typical ton-per-day capacity ranges, are given in Table 3.

The controlled air and rotary combustor systems, with their modular approach using relatively small units, adapt readily to the lower tonnage ranges of efficient solid waste combustion. The traveling grate systems operate effectively in the transition ranges between the smaller modular systems and the larger systems; many of these are in operation in Europe. The multiple-hearth furnaces and suspension-fired systems usually appear in the larger installations.

Table 3. Technologies and Ton-Per-Day Capacity Ranges.

System	TPD
Controlled air system with:	0-200
Refractory wall	
Water-cooled wall	
Air-cooled wall	
Water-cooled rotary combustor	30-900
Traveling grate system with:	
Refractory wall	100-500
Water wall	300+
Suspension-fired water wall incinerator	
using refuse derived fuel	300+
Multiple hearth furnace	300+

All of these systems, except for the suspension-fired systems, burn unclassified bulk waste. Suspension-fired systems usually require shredding and materials separation by air classification, which produces a shredded combustible fraction of the waste as fuel.

Each of these systems has advantages in certain situations. Parameters to be considered in evaluating the systems for specific applications include:

- First cost.
- Operating costs.
- Maintenance costs.
- Reliability.
- Thermal efficiency.
- Availability.
- Operating experience.

These variables must be weighed in each application to define the best choice of available technology for the particular situation.

EFFICIENT TRANSMISSION DISTANCE

Efficient transmission distances for forms of energy generated by an energy recovery plant are governed by economics rather than by technical limits. If the value of the delivered product — steam, high temperature hot water, chilled water or electricity — is high enough, the capital investment in transmission and distribution systems can be justified. Even superheated, high pressure steam required to drive turbines can be transmitted for several miles providing the steam entering the transmission system is at high enough pressures and temperatures. Steam for building heating and process uses can be economically distributed through distribution systems totalling many miles. Hot water and chilled water systems likewise can extend considerable distances. Electricity seldom requires its own transmission systems but usually ties into existing power grids at a point close to the generator. As a practical matter, one recently designed plant will co-generate electricity through an in-plant turbine-generator set and then pipe exhaust steam out to energy customers at pressures and temperatures still high enough for heating and process uses. In another instance, superheated steam will be transmitted nearly a mile to operate a turbine-generator set at the customer's sewage disposal plant, with turbine exhaust steam used to dry sludge.

Another characteristic of steam which affects its usefulness is its chemical cleanliness, which has nothing to do with the fact that "dirty" solid wastes are the fuel. In food processing plants, for instance, process steam cannot contain certain standard additives usually used to retard corrosion and scale formation in the boiler and distribution system and to reduce the concentration of oxygen in the condensate. Substitute additives are available and acceptable to the Federal Food and Drug Administration for use in food processing steam.

LIFE-CYCLE MAINTENANCE

The commitment to proceed with a waste-to-energy facility actually includes two commitments if the life-cycle performance and cost projections are to be met. The first is the decision to build the facility. The second, and one which system owners find easy to treat lightly, is the equally necessary commitment of operator and maintenance expenses to keep the systems in top condition and at full capability. These are complex systems and require fully competent operators and regular and thorough maintenance. Scrimping on such expenditures is shortsighted; the larger costs of eventual major equipment failure far outweigh the short-term savings resulting from less than adequate maintenance.

Thorough operator training, adherence to periodic maintenance schedules and dedication of necessary funds to spare parts and tools can be the most cost-effective investments made in a project. Maximum availability of equipment makes possible maximum revenues.

The fact that waste-to-energy conversion is fairly new in this country affects practically every aspect of development and operation of a facility, from early planning through design, construction and lifetime operation. There is not a large amount of literature on successful projects, nor are there standardized components such as those available for fossil fuel energy equipment. Furthermore, the work force experienced in the operation and maintenance of energy conversion facilities is limited.

This lack of a widely understood body of knowledge makes proper operator training, like thorough and detailed engineering design, particularly necessary. Versatile and thoughtful operators can, for instance, adapt to the variability of the solid waste fuel. An example of considerations to which operators must be constantly alert is the method used in one installation to reduce fluctuation in waste stream quality. Here, when rain is predicted, the crane operator who feeds the incinerators sets aside dry wastes already on the tipping floor, and requires haulers to drop the wet wastes in another area. He then mixes the wet and dry wastes one for one before charging the incinerator. This mixing reduces the impact of a rainstorm on the energy output of the facility.

COST ESTIMATING

Several problems are associated with the development of project cost estimates. Obviously, accurate project cost is critical since project feasibility is based in part on the project capital cost, and funding is arranged on the basis of this estimate. Overrun can be embarrassing and in some cases disastrous. Some of the considerations in the preparation of the project cost budget are:

- Resource recovery projects are historically slow in developing. Lead time from conception to project completion is frequently four to five years. The initial analysis must recognize this factor and adjust costs accordingly, allowing for inflation in *all* costs involved.

- Prices obtained from suppliers must be scrutinized carefully to ensure inclusion of *all* equipment which will be required in the final design.
- Allowances must be provided for:
  - Legal and underwriter costs.
  - Start-up and shakedown costs.
  - Management and administration costs.
  - Engineering and design costs.
  - Office supplies and spare parts costs.
  - Personnel training costs.

FUNDING CONSIDERATIONS

Selecting the right alternative or combination of alternatives for funding a waste-to-energy project is as important as selecting the right technology alternative. Among many options which may be available to a community are:

- Federal or state grants, loans, or loan guarantees.
- General obligation bonds, guaranteed by the taxing power of the issuing body.
- Revenue tax deficiency bonds repaid by revenues from the waste-to-energy facility but guaranteed by the full faith and credit of the taxing body to the extent of any shortfall in revenue.
- Revenue bonds guaranteed only by revenues from the facility.
- Revenue bonds guaranteed by the energy customer.
- Leaseback, in which an outside party finances and builds the facility to community specifications, then leases it to the community on an annual price basis; the community does not issue bonds or incur long-term debt.
- Private design/build/own/operate: community sets performance specifications and selects best bid; bidder designs, builds, owns and operates plant for set period of years, at the end of which title reverts to the community. Community pays a set tipping fee per ton, and receives a share of income from energy and materials sales.

Resource recovery projects are capital intensive and usually require long term financing.

However, in some instances, existing legislation does not permit a public body to enter into contracts which extend beyond the term of office of the elected officials comprising the public body. In such situations, corrective legislation may be required to permit such a long term commitment; or a separate authority may be created with the power to enter into long term contracts.

Another fairly common type of limit on bond issuance is a specific debt ceiling on total indebtedness of the governmental unit, whether in general obligation bonds or in revenue bonds. This situation may also call for a special vehicle to own, issue bonds for, and possibly operate the energy recovery plant.

The most common guarantee basis for acceptable bond issues is the projected revenue of the energy recovery plant, and for this reason the financial stability of the contracting energy buyer weighs heavily in the considerations. The energy consumer should be a substantial company or entity. In our experience, investment bankers rank energy customers as follows:

1. Federal government.
2. State government.
3. Local government.
4. Large diversified corporations.
5. Large single product corporations.
6. Others.

These criteria are important because the energy customers establish the salability of the bonds. Without tax-free bond sales, the feasibility of the project is reduced because interest rates become so high that it is difficult to support a project on the revenue from energy sales alone without prohibitive tipping fees.

Contractual relationships in establishing an energy recovery facility are so critical and complex that discussion of such contracts will appear as a separate article in the next issue.

An energy recovery project like those described in last month's article places a city, county or township in what is usually a new position in relation to the private sector; the local government unit becomes the supplier of a competitive commodity — energy — to purchasers who may have alternative sources for the same commodity.

Governments frequently supply a purchased service or commodity to the private sector and to other governmental units; e.g., water, electricity, gas, steam, sewerage and solid waste disposal. None of these, however, ordinarily competes with available alternative sources; the governmental supplier is almost invariably in a monopoly situation where rates are set by the supplier under a legally established rate-setting procedure.

The present expansion of governmentally owned or sponsored waste-to-energy facilities indicates that governments are beginning to compete in this new market.

Government bodies may have a two-edged advantage in the field. First is the governmental unit's frequent control of the waste disposal stream, since collection and disposal of urban solid wastes is traditionally a domain of government. The second edge is the capacity of financing through tax-exempt bonds of various sorts. The low interest rates of these bonds compared to financing available to a private entrepreneur are a real advantage.

In our experience, dependable, efficient waste-to-energy conversion technologies are available. However, voters, elected officials and investors have an understandable scepticism toward waste-to-energy feasibility, being abundantly aware that there have been some outright failures, some marginal successes and very few completely successful resource recovery installations in this country.

Two strong pressures favoring waste-to-energy conversion are the increasing environmental and cost problems in disposal of solid wastes and the rising costs of fossil fuel. Favorable situations exist today that would not have been so favorable a short time ago; and more situations will be successful candidates in the future because of these pressures.

Each situation, however, should be developed through careful advance analysis of technical, legal and financial feasibility before substantial commitments are made. Each project is unique, and the complex institutional and contractual arrangements required will vary with the situation.

PRIMARY CONTRACTING PARTIES

The primary contracting parties may include:

- The owner or sponsor of the resource recovery facility, usually a governmental entity — a city, township, county or authority.
- Energy customers, including industrial steam buyers, private or public owners of buildings to buy heating steam and chilled water for air conditioning and utility purchasers of electricity.
- Public refuse collection systems in addition to the energy facility owner (where several communities join efforts in a waste-to-energy project).
- Private contract haulers and collectors.
- Private purchasers of recovered materials such as glass and metals. (Such buyers will seldom contract on a long-term basis to buy these materials because the market demand and price fluctuate; they may, however, specify the types of materials they will buy when justified by market prices.)
- Construction contractors, subcontractors and suppliers.
- A private designer/builder/operator of the facility.

A secondary group of contracting parties are those associated with study, design, legal and financing aspects of a project. They normally include engineering/architectural consultants, general legal counsel, bond counsel and investment bankers.

Although this second group requires a comparatively small percentage of the total dollars invested in a resource recovery project, it is through their efforts that the feasibility of a project is established. Their projections, both technical and economic, are a highly important feature in the salability of the plan.

LIMITED EARLY COMMITMENTS

In the crucial early stages of a project, the potential owner of a resource recovery facility can, with a limited commitment, measure the feasibility of the project with the assistance of the types of consultants listed above.

The essentials of an energy recovery project are: a guaranteed solid waste stream, a facility for energy conversion and delivery of energy to customers and long-term energy customers.

Within those broad parameters there are innumerable possible combinations of technical, legal and financial arrangements. A well-executed preliminary study will:

- Define sources, volume and characteristics of the available waste stream.
- Study alternative technologies for conversion of wastes to energy and recommend a favored alternative.
- Locate potential customers and define their energy needs.
- Develop possibilities for siting the facility and distribution of the energy in various forms; steam, high temperature hot water, chilled water, or electricity.
- Obtain at least letters of intent from both waste suppliers and energy customers.
- Define existing legal constraints which will affect establishment of the facility and recommend legislative or other remedies to those constraints.
- Estimate project life-cycle costs including financing costs.
- Estimate life-cycle revenues.
- Make recommendations on management approach and organization, financial risk allocation, and types of capital funding.
- Define various approaches to construction that are compatible with the economic and institutional characteristics of the specific situation.

The results of such a study will give a potential owner or sponsor of a resource recovery facility a set of facts and figures on the basis of which that governmental entity and its elected officials can decide whether and how to proceed further with the project — all without major contractual commitments in advance of such a decision to proceed.

A thorough study of this nature will establish whether the project is feasible and will point out the problems which require solution before the project can be brought to fruition.

WASTE AND ENERGY ARRANGEMENTS

To be acceptable to financial underwriters, the contracts should be, at a minimum, for the same period (usually between 15 and 30 years and typically 20 years) as the duration of loan agreements or financing bonds.

A promising energy customer arrangement is one providing interruptible steam service in which the energy supplier is not bound to provide a constant supply of steam. Such a contract allows for variations in the supply of solid wastes and for down-time of the energy recovery facility, and eliminates the need for redundant mass burning equipment. This type of arrangement requires a customer who can use all the steam produced at the energy facility and can provide additional steam needed from his own boiler plant. Under these circumstances, the energy facility can profitably contract to provide steam at a price below the customer's cost to generate his own. The arrangement factors in the cost of fossil fuel, which is expected to continue to rise, providing constant percentage savings to the customer but also increasing waste facility income to compensate for inflation.

In a contrasting firm contract type of arrangement, the energy recovery facility contracts to be the sole supplier of steam for heating and chilled water for air conditioning to a group of buildings. This service must be constant. In one such instance, the energy facility has installed redundant waste-burning equipment and a fossil-fueled boiler as backup. Even though this redundant capability accounts for about one-third of the capital cost of the entire facility, the delivered price of the energy is still competitive with energy from other sources.

In another possible arrangement, steam production in the city's energy recovery facility might be remotely controlled by stationary engineers in the boiler plant of the customer. The customer would use the waste plant to satisfy a portion of the base load for his operation and would supplement that supply as required by his own existing fossil fuel boilers. Since fewer stationary engineers would be required at the city waste plant, labor cost at that plant and therefore the total cost of energy from the city plant would be lowered.

However, underwriters have raised questions about the selling of bonds for a facility that is not autonomous, and lawyers say that there are liability questions raised by such a remote control arrangement. The present outlook is that remote control may not be acceptable for these reasons.

Electricity sales contracts typically call for interruptible service to the electric utility at a specified rate per kilowatt hour which is, of course, considerably lower than the utility's selling rate. The utility's normal selling rate includes costs of fuel, capitalization and distribution. Waste-recovered energy sold to a utility displaces only the utility's fuel cost; other fixed costs remain the same. Since large utility generation is more efficient than that achievable in an energy recovery plant and since the addition of electric generation is an added capital cost to the recovery facility owner, electricity sales command such a low price that they are usually a secondary consideration, at best, to the energy facility.

There are exceptions, however. The first arises when a plant can distribute steam after electricity generation to a steam customer for whom the lowered steam temperatures and pressures are acceptable. In one instance, the energy facility boilers will produce steam at 400 psi saturated; the pressure will drop through the turbine-generator set to about 200 psi.

A second exception occurs when the steam customer's demand fluctuates, and he can use full steam flow only part of the time. In such instances, additional cost for generation equipment is often justified, and electricity is generated to sell to a utility when the steam customer's demand is down.

A third possibility may occur when no steam customer is available and the primary value of the facility is disposal of solid wastes in an area where landfill charges are very high. In these instances, uses of steam for electrical generation can be an added economic benefit, assuming a willing utility customer exists.

Energy user contracts may become complex, guaranteeing not only delivery and price, but quality standards as well. For instance, steam sold to a food processing plant must meet federal Food and Drug Administration standards. Chemical cleanliness is essential, and types of chemicals used to prevent boiler corrosion are tightly limited. FDA inspectors may check on steam quality at any time. Contracts for any steam sales should specify acceptable pressures, temperatures, percentages of moisture and chemical content.

WASTE SUPPLY AND ASH REMOVAL CONTRACTUAL ARRANGEMENTS

Waste supply and ash removal contracts can vary considerably. In a situation where the energy recovery facility is a not-for-profit corporation which never has ownership of the solid wastes, the supplying city delivers the wastes to the facility and removes the residue, maintaining ownership throughout the process. A more typical situation is one in which the city is both the collector of the solid wastes and the owner of the recovery facility, and therefore will deliver the wastes and remove the ash with no necessity for outside contracts.

In a situation where an authority owns and operates a recovery facility, it will contract with supplying communities for a continuous flow of solid wastes, frequently at a tipping fee considerably lower than current landfill fees. Energy sales revenue makes the lower fee possible. Since the major supplying communities are members of the authority, few problems generally arise in such waste supply contracts. The authority disposes of the ash residue.

Most private haulers are already contractors to local governments, which can specify disposal locations and terms in such contracts. Those private haulers who work under contracts with private parties can be controlled by legislation which specifies acceptable disposal sites.

Contracts for solid waste supply must, for funding purposes, be specific and binding as to both volume and flow. Municipal refuse does not store easily; it is bulky and can become malodorous. It is technically possible, of course, to provide odor-free storage facilities for solid wastes, but the added capital cost of such facilities may make them uneconomical. As a practical matter, from both an economic and a technical point of view, wastes should be burned at substantially the same rate at which they are delivered to the energy plant.

FUNDING ARRANGEMENTS

As can be seen from this discussion, institutional and legal aspects of a resource recovery project are two complicated and potentially difficult areas requiring careful consideration in the development of contracts.

It is also briefly noted here that the primary institutional concern, funding, presents another set of problems to a community interested in resource recovery. Funding methods affect the types of contractual arrangements developed.

One of these problems is a community's debt ceiling and its relationship to bond interest rates. Since resource recovery facilities are so capital intensive, a governmental entity is often eager to find a means of funding which does not unfavorably impact its bond credit rating. Many governmental units are restricted by law to a maximum debt ceiling, and even though a waste-to-energy project is planned to be self-retiring, the governmental entity may be liable for payment of the bonds, depending upon the type of funding used. For example: a $7 million energy facility liability out of a total debt ceiling of $35 million may have the effect of lowering the entity's rating and increasing the interest rates it will have to pay on any future financing.

CONSULTANT CONTRACTS

In the early phases of a project, the types of agreements with an AE consultant can be flexible and, in fact, do vary widely. However, the common thread tends to be that the interested governmental entity wants to limit its investment until some degree of potential feasibility is demonstrated. Contracts usually are limited to a fixed price for a well-defined scope of work, or to a "not-to-exceed" contract covering actual expenditures.

Such contracts are sometimes fairly simple letter-type contracts based on a consultant's proposal modified to meet the clients needs, or simple purchase orders. The parties to the contract may be one or several governmental entities; or they may be a local government and a potential energy customer in the private sector.

Our experience indicates the need for flexibility in planning for an energy recovery facility in the early stages. Technical, legal, economic and funding feasibility are so interdependent that data gathering and preliminary concepts in all these areas are often carried on simultaneously, with requirements defined as the studies progress. It may be found advisable to bring in other communities, to explore federal and state funding, or to tentatively line up energy customers before the feasibility report can be completed and followed by a package of contracts for final design and construction. Elements of capital costs, potential income, reliability of waste supply and energy sales, risks and who should assume them, and legal liabilities all must be carefully considered for the various alternatives presented in a thorough feasibility study. Alternatives can be technical, legal, institutional and financial in various combinations.

To sum up, in our experience the most prevalent and complicated problems met in establishing waste supply and energy sales contracts are institutional and legal, not technical.

2-6 Resource Recovery: The Management of Technical and Economic Risks

Harvey Alter
Source: NCRR *Bulletin,* Vol. 9, No. 4 (December 1979) pp. 80–84. Reprinted with Permission of National Center for Resource Recovery.

Resource recovery is probably the most technically involved, hence difficult, planning and implementation project a governmental body is likely to encounter. Unlike civil works or public service functions (such as police and fire protection or education), resource recovery is a production enterprise more akin to the business functions of the private sector. As such, there are technical and economic risks which must be addressed and assessed. Experience shows resource recovery must be planned and implemented *in spite* of technical, economic and institutional uncertainties. The new challenge to government officials is, then, how to implement what they view as public health and civil works projects in a way that manages inherent risks.

ELEMENTS OF RISK

The elements of risk perceived by planning officials are: **(1) quantity of waste; (2) composition of the waste; (3) performance of separating and processing equipment; (4) recovery of products to market specifications; (5) the continuity of the markets for the recovered products and the stability of the prices paid** and **(6) the effect of future environmental control regulations as concerns obsolescence of equipment or processes and need for additional funds.**

Quantity of Waste

Problem. A recovery facility should be planned and economics justified on receiving a set quantity of waste daily. Waste should be provided on a "put or pay" basis for the amortized life of the facility. For this reason, the future availability of waste must be known.

The responsibility for maintaining public health enables local governments to require that waste be delivered to a particular location. However, there is a trend toward contracting collection and disposal to the private sector, which cannot be required to deliver the waste if it denies them their livelihood. Some accommodations, therefore, will have to be made.

Further, the quantity of waste is usually estimated from determinations of some average per capita generation, population, and estimation of their growth. There is indication that past estimations are either wrong or have been misinterpreted. For example, retrospective analysis of domestic waste collection in two cities shows that the per capita generation has changed little (if at all) over the past ten years; this is in spite of U.S. Environmental Protection Agency (EPA) estimates to the contrary. Some U.S. recovery plants, notably Ames, Iowa, and Milwaukee, Wis., have experienced deliveries far below that expected from estimates based on national averages. Also, it is reported that in England the per capita generation increased only 10 percent (by mass and 50 percent by volume) over some 45 years. At the same time, early reports indicate that the generation has increased markedly in the Netherlands in recent years, but not in Germany. Rarely do planners allow for differences in generation rates due to differences in sizes of communities or differences in the activities of the population of the community.

Solution. *The quantity of waste presently available for processing should be determined* *well in advance of plant implementation by installing a truck scale as early as possible.* The time period for resource recovery planning, leading to a firm contract, is frequently three to five years, so a record of waste quantities can be accumulated. This retrospective record can be used for prospective estimation, especially when combined with estimates of population growth. Estimates should be conservative; additional plant capacity in future years can be secured by operating additional shifts or excess waste can be directed to landfill. The cost of the latter may well be less than operating a plant year after year far below its design capacity.

Composition of Waste

Problem. The composition of the waste varies with the time of the week, the season of the year, size of the community and, sometimes, region of the country. More importantly, the composition is likely to change over the life of a recovery plant as technology, consumer preferences and consumer affluence change. An example is the recent introduction and likely future growth of the use of the retortable plastic film-aluminum foil laminate pouch for the room temperature storage of food, as a replacement for the familiar "tin" can.

Solution. The composition of waste is difficult to determine with any great statistical certainty. Samples can be analyzed but this determines the composition only at that time and future changes cannot be estimated. *However, an analysis can be used for baseline economic estimates for initial planning and for later determining adjustment (up or down) in tipping fee according to later analysis and recovery experiences.* This is important if operation of the plant is contracted.

The composition of waste is widely variable in the sense of an ore assay for determining materials recovery and consequent economic projections. The composition is not widely variable in considering the design and performance of most unit operations, or for the preparation of refuse-derived fuel (RDF). For example, the content of magnetic metals may vary from three to six percent by weight, a two-fold increase for estimating revenues, but only a three percentage point change which does not affect design or operation of a magnetic separation system. Similarly, in considering the preparation of some form of RDF, the waste may be viewed as a mixture of mostly different kinds of paper products and some plastic film diluted by a mixture of non-combustible materials. The fluctuation of the total content of fuel components will not be as great as any of the individual paper products.

Equipment Performance

Problem. The operation of plant equipment to specification is often tenuous. Designers and manufacturers of the equipment are presently unable to offer firm guarantees of either performance or operating costs. While redundant equipment lines help offset this risk, they also increase costs. At issue is equipment and process reliability. Confusing the issue is the mistaken belief that a resource recovery plant must operate with the absolute reliability required of disposal facilities.

Solution. In the absence of guarantees from equipment vendors and designers, perhaps the only way to assure proper operation of the equipment (beside careful and competent design) is to establish a reserve fund for mechanical changes after commissioning and to allow for extra shifts for maintenance. Few plants have done either. Start-up and shakedown operations are intended to find and define shortcomings; too often, however, no capital is reserved to make the necessary changes.

There is an unfortunate tendency to duplicate an existing plant. As resource recovery is an emerging technology, there must be a willingness to incorporate new techniques and systems. Municipalities must, understandably, be prudent, which accounts for their seeking a "proven" technology already in operation.

A way of overcoming the perceived risk of equipment not working is to engage in what is termed "prudent innovation" by incorporating modest but new changes. This approach might be encouraged and financed by the federal or state governments through a program which, after review of plans prior to construction, provides a fund (perhaps a maximum percentage of total capital cost) for repairs and retrofits after construction and start-up to correct operating difficulties. After a given period of time, operating shortcomings can be documented and identified and a plan formulated and costed to effect necessary changes in order to make the plant fully operable. During the periods of problem identification and correction, the fund may also supplement the revenue shortfall from selling non-specification products at a discount. This feature will encourage continued operation of the plant.

Product Specifications

Problem. Standard specifications for recovered materials and fuels are just now emerging, principally as the result of the efforts of the American Society for Testing and Materials. Steam and electricity must also be sold to specification. Failure to meet required specifications, for which there is little experience, can result in rejection and economic loss. Sometimes the specification for delivered steam or electricity cannot be met without use of an auxiliary fuel. Alternatively, a waste-to-steam facility may have to reduce excess capacity during part of the year in order to dispose of the waste and have sufficient capacity for the remainder of the year.

Solution. *Markets for recovered materials and energy products must be secured early in the planning process.* Allowing market specifications to dictate the technology to be employed is the basis for choosing one type of plant over another. For example, there is healthy competition today among vendors of various heat recovery incinerators and of mechanical processing systems for RDF. A disadvantage of the competition is the present confusion over which system is "best," if indeed such a judgment can ever be made. The bases for picking a system are initially simple: they are cost and the ability to meet the market.

Markets can be secured through contingent letters of intent to purchase (or bid to purchase), delineating the amount, delivery schedule, spec-

ifications, terms and prices. The fluctuations in secondary materials prices can be avoided, or at least lessened, by incorporating a floor price (the minimum to be paid at any time during the contract). The exchange price can increase from the floor as some fraction of a published commodity quote (*e.g.*, a published scrap price), but the seller must realize that this fraction may be well less than one in return for the floor price. This is, in effect, selling at a discount; the floor price trades upside and downside risks between buyer and seller.

Related to the market, users of RDF are concerned whether the new form of fuel will damage or otherwise interfere with the efficient use of their boiler (or other recovered materials interfere with their production processes). These risks can be alleviated by the establishment of a new form of boiler insurance against the unknown risks of premature failure. Because private carriers could not now estimate these risks, governments may have to participate in the underwriting so as to bring the premiums within range of normal types of business or boiler insurance premiums.

Product Marketing

Problem. Secondary materials, including those recovered from municipal waste, are marginal sources of raw materials. Their demand and prices are subject to worldwide variations. Implementors of resource recovery plants cannot expect to enter the spot market for secondary materials in competition with traditional sources of scrap and find assured buyers. It has been suggested that there should be government intervention to assure that industry purchase the materials recovered from waste. This is a dangerous suggestion if there are no offsetting actions to make certain that the materials recovered from waste do not merely displace traditional sources of scrap which would then accumulate as wastes. *What is needed are actions which increase the total demand for scraps of several grades.*

Solution. The effect of fluctuating secondary materials prices on the economics of a recovery plant can be alleviated, to some extent, by market arrangements, especially the use of floor prices. Indeed, government planning officials may much prefer to obtain secure floor prices instead of maximum exchange prices, so as to predict the economics of a plant in case everything went wrong, so to speak.

It is important in the planning and economic projection of a new recovery plant to realize that with or without markets and specifications, the recovered products do not correspond exactly to existing markets for specific grades of scraps. For example, paper recovered from mixed wastes is not No. 1 News; recovered cans do not conform to No. 2 Scrap Steel Bundles. A buyer may refer to existing prices for conventional grades in setting prices but materials recovered from mixed wastes are not likely to either compete directly against traditional grades on quality or sell for the same price.

Management of the risk of fluctuating market prices, through advance market agreements and floor prices, may only be a short-term solution. The only long-term solution may be to increase the demand and use of all sorts of secondary materials through changes in industrial practices.

Environmental Considerations

Problem. Environmental regulations, such as those governing air emissions from combustion units, may change during the 10 or 20 years of amortized life of a resource recovery plant. These changes may well require additional investment for control technology in order for the plant to comply with the law. This ordinary business risk for the private sector (otherwise there would be little environmental improvement) may well be an unexpected and unwelcome expense for the public sector.

Solution. The risk of future changes in environmental regulations is real and may be more of a certainty than a risk. Public sector officials rarely set aside a reserve fund for later plant changes, optimistic that new funds could be secured from future tax income. This may be true and effective, as long as it is recognized that future investment in control technology will raise the future cost of disposal, whether the

plant is owned and operated by the public or private sectors. It is unrealistic to assume that society will exempt environmental control projects (such as resource recovery) from all future environmental control regulation. *Public sector managers should adopt some of the practices of the private sector and establish a reserve fund for future equipment changes and improvements.*

Economic Risks

The net cost of resource recovery is the tipping fee, as determined by the capital and operating costs of the recovery technique employed less the revenues from the recovered products. The tipping fee may be obtained either from the general tax-based or collected as a user charge. The net cost, compared to alternative forms of disposal (*e.g.,* landfill) will often determine whether a community will implement resource recovery. *A common mistake is to compare the future cost of recovery with the current cost of disposal.* The latter will increase with inflation, the increased difficulty of obtaining new sites, and the imposition of new environmental regulations.

For energy recovery systems, generally the more that is invested in the system, the higher the gross revenue from the energy product. Upgrading waste to a narrower specification RDF, or converting the RDF to steam or alternatively to electricity, all costs money. The question is if the additional cost of upgrading can be covered by the additional revenues.

Another point in making the economic decision to implement resource recovery is whether to consider the first or life-cycle costs. In all probability, the first cost of recovery is likely to be higher than landfill but after some period of time, a breakeven point is reached when the projected cost of recovery will be less than the projected cost of landfill. This is illustrated in **Figure 1**, which plots several costs as a function of time.

In Figure 1, the cost of alternative disposal is plotted as increasing at a rate of six percent per year. The operating cost of a recovery plant is shown increasing at the same rate. However, the amortization cost is constant over the life of the recovery plant and the revenue

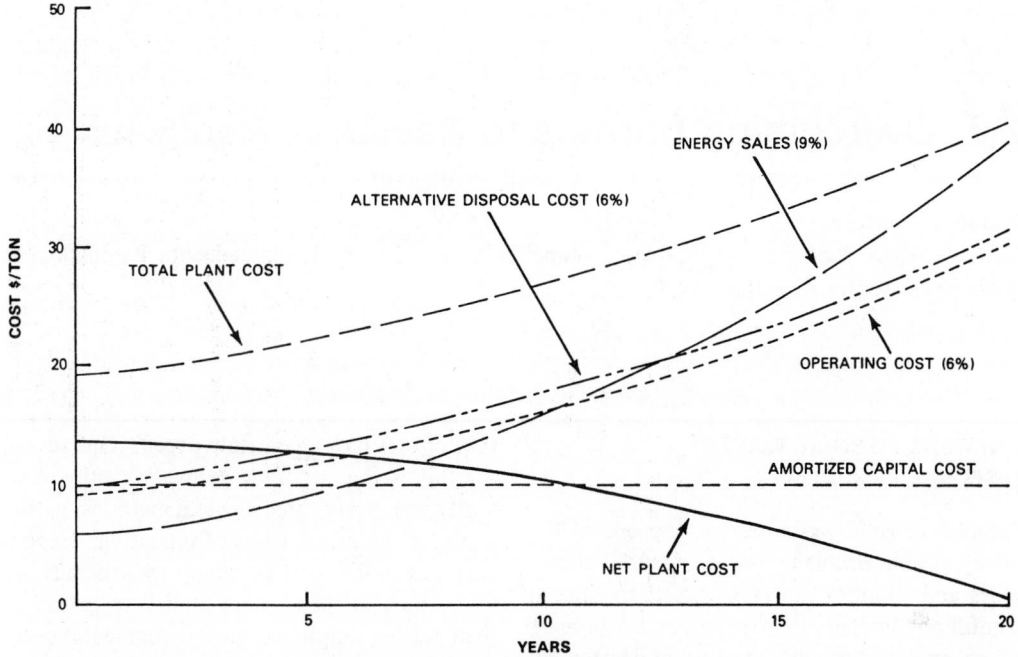

Figure 1. Economic readiness of urban waste.

from energy sales is shown increasing at a conservative rate of nine percent per year. As a result, net recovery plant costs decrease with time and are less than alternative disposal costs (the curves cross) at about the fifth year. The period to breakeven will depend, in part, on the differential in inflation rates between operating costs and energy prices.

A community has to decide if it will absorb a higher cost of recovery (compared to alternative disposal) for an initial period as an investment against breakeven and lower costs of recovery in future years. This type of economic decision is common in the private sector, but not the public, where elected officials are understandably more concerned about first costs than life-cycle costs.

Conclusions

In most public sector planning, the economic and technical aspects are analyzed, the sums tallied, and a decision made as to which way to proceed. In resource recovery, when the sums are tallied, the decision is still unclear because of the uncertainties remaining. Risk will still be present — a situation likely to continue for some years. Decisions must be made in spite of this risk, which is another way of saying that risk must be managed.

An important viewpoint for the public sector is that not every aspect of resource recovery can be optimized. Some balance and tradeoffs are required. Whereas the usual governmental conservatism can be maintained, there must still be some "prudent innovation." If not, there will not be resource recovery and the energy and material resources in our waste will merely be burned or buried. In short, the public sector must begin to incorporate some of the risk management techniques more familiar in the private sector or must be willing to contract resource recovery ownership and operation to the private sector and be willing to share the risks with them. It is unrealistic to expect the private sector to assume all of the risk if the public sector is unwilling to do so.

A conservative but optimistic projection is that within a few years this subject will be viewed as unnecessary. Both the private and public sectors will have gained experience in resource recovery and learned to manage what will be considered "trivial" risks. The challenge is how to hasten that day.

2-7 Overcoming Barriers to Resource Recovery

Susan J. Kinney

Source: *NCRR Bulletin*, Vol 9, No. 2 (June 1979) pp. 28–34. Reprinted with Permission of National Center for Resource Recovery.

ANSWERS TO SOLID WASTE DISPOSAL PROBLEMS

Disposal of solid waste has become one of the most pressing problems faced today by states, cities and counties. In many areas, traditional landfill and incineration operations are proving to be environmentally unsound and often inadequate to handle ever-increasing amounts of solid waste. State and local officials must undertake the difficult and time-consuming task of finding an alternative method of solid waste disposal that will provide a long-term answer to disposal needs in a manner that is both environmentally and economically acceptable.

Resource recovery is, in many areas, the best long-term disposal method presently available. First, it is a partial solution to a major environmental disgrace — extensive pollution of surface and ground water by inadequate land disposal of solid wastes, the pollution of air by uncontrolled or ineffectively controlled incineration, and the needless waste of significant land resources. Second, it is conceivable that waste-derived energy or fuel products could supply two to three percent of the nation's energy requirements. *Although it cannot be considered a major new energy source, resource recovery can provide for specific energy needs.*

WHY HAS RESOURCE RECOVERY IMPLEMENTATION BEEN SLOW PACED?

Despite the advantages of resource recovery over traditional disposal methods, implementation efforts have been slow paced. One reason for this is that resource recovery can be more costly than traditional disposal methods, particularly in the initial years of operation. Experience has shown that communities generally are not willing to spend more money to get rid of their wastes simply for the environmental benefits of resource recovery. Even where costs are essentially equal, however, resource recovery is usually chosen only after all other disposal alternatives are deemed unavailable. In other words, lack of a feasible alternative appears to be the key motivating force behind the selection of resource recovery.

Most obstacles to implementation can be traced back to the fact that resource recovery involves the utilization of new, often insufficiently proven, technologies and new institutional arrangements between government and industry. Most public sector problems (*e.g.*, public transportation and wastewater treatment) have traditionally been resolved by the establishment of public operating entities to operate the required systems or facilities. These systems and facilities are usually "off-the-shelf" purchases, and therefore their procurement is a straightforward matter using well-established procedures; communities know what they need to buy, they have bought the product before, and their normal procurement methods facilitate the purchase.

In contrast, there has been little experience in planning for and purchasing resource recovery facilities. Furthermore, the approach to resource recovery procurement differs from established approaches to public sector problems.

In handling solid waste management problems, the public sector has moved toward the use of the private sector not only to design and construct, but also to operate resource recovery facilities. A resource recovery project is essentially a business venture with the accompanying business risks and financial requirements that are an integral part of any business enterprise. Resource recovery involves the acquisition of a raw material (solid waste) and its conversion into products in the form of energy and materials. The parties involved in a resource recovery project must agree to long-term contracts for solid waste input and for the purchase of energy products as security for project financing. Because of the newness of resource recovery technology, it is not yet an "off-the-shelf" purchase, and therefore established procurement and financing approaches are often not suitable for or conducive to its purchase. MITRE is now working with the U.S. Environmental Protection Agency (EPA) to develop a resource recovery management model. The first version of the model contains more than 400 significant activities necessary to plan and procure a resource recovery system. Perhaps the sheer complexity and magnitude of this process itself is one of the significant barriers impeding implementation.

NUMEROUS UNCERTAINTIES AND RISKS

Experience has indeed shown that the resource recovery planning and procurement process is complex and unfamiliar to most of the participants. In addition, the numerous uncertainties and risks associated with resource recovery cause what is already a complex process to be even more difficult and time-consuming. Commitment on the part of public officials is required in order to overcome the risks and uncertainties that can stand in the way of implementation.

State and local governments must carry out a thorough investigation of their solid waste management problems and the feasibility of resource recovery. If resource recovery appears to be their best option, they still must decide whether an economically and politically defensible decision to proceed with resource recovery

implementation can be made, given the probable uncertainties in:

- The amount of waste available to the facility, at present and in the future;
- Markets for energy and materials and the projected income available from the sale of these products;
- The availability of landfill, environmental standards pertaining to landfill, and projected costs of landfill operations;
- The technical reliability of resource recovery processes; and
- The legality of the implementation plan and strategy.

In order to minimize the problems and issues that can arise because of these uncertainties, it is advisable that local officials complete a thorough front-end planning effort prior to system planning is often a lengthy and expensive process, but the investment is worthwhile, as it will ensure the later success of implementation efforts.

WASTE STREAM CONTROL

Controlling the waste stream is one of the most difficult and important problems to overcome in planning a resource recovery facility. A minimum tonnage of solid waste must be contractually committed for delivery to a facility in order to guarantee throughput and disposal fee revenue, as well as energy and materials products revenue. It is absolutely necessary to demonstrate a guarantee of these revenues in order to secure project financing.

Furthermore, the issue of waste stream control must be resolved in the early stages of system planning because the anticipated waste influx influences design considerations. It must be decided whether the facility will be designed only for those wastes for which long-term commitments exist or if allowances will be made for additional wastes, which would seek entry after alternative disposal sites close or become economically unattractive. For example, industrial wastes often do not lie within a community's collection responsibility and therefore cannot be guaranteed by a community. These wastes are usually handled under short-term contract with private haulers who prefer to haul to the least expensive disposal facility. Planners can choose to ignore industrial waste and force private haulers to seek increasingly scarce landfill space, or they can plan to accommodate the industrial waste and negotiate who will bear the risk of such waste not being brought to the facility.

Many existing and planned resource recovery facilities are large-scale systems which require regional service areas to achieve the necessary solid waste input. In order to acquire control of the waste stream in a region, individual long-term commitments must be received from many communities. This has proven to be a monumental task, particularly in states where there are no established authorities with waste disposal powers and where community participation in a resource recovery project is voluntary. Communities are apprehensive about entering long-term contracts for waste disposal with resource recovery projects because of the perceived risks involved. They wonder "How are we going to be sure that this plant is filled up with waste? Will others sign up and meet their commitments? What happens if I sign up first? Is there something in the contract that I have overlooked and will be sorry for later? If I do sign a long-term contract for this project, what assurance do I have that another technology will not cause it to become just another white elephant?" These concerns must be recognized and addressed by project leaders in order to encourage voluntary community participation.

States or cities can take action to control the waste stream through legislation, user charge systems, or the establishment of a franchise system. States can enact legislation to give cities the authority to control the waste or to give cities legal ownership of the waste. Experience has shown, however, that states are hesitant to use mandatory measures for waste control, even where the authority to do so has been established.

A user charge system is a method by which participating communities (households) and businesses are directly charged an amount which reflects the approximate cost to dispose of the waste volume collected from each source. With this system there is a zero tipping fee at the facility. Participants voluntarily give the local jurisdiction responsibility for disposal of their wastes, and thus control over the waste stream is obtained.

The establishment of a franchise system for solid waste disposal is another method through which the disposal of waste can be controlled. With this system, resource recovery facility operators are assigned a specific service area or waste shed. At present, an informal franchise system for collection is in use in some Michigan communities. Leadership for the institution of franchise systems would probably have to come from the federal level.

There is a question of equity associated with attempts to control the waste stream. Resource recovery facilities are competing with established disposal facilities for waste, usually with government backing. Private haulers and landfill operators, who are established in the waste disposal business, strongly object to having their waste supply diverted to a new resource recovery facility. This issue is present regardless of whether the waste is being controlled by ordinance (as in Akron, Ohio), through state legislation, or by seeking voluntary participation through waste supply contracts.

State and local governments are in need of information about the waste control issue and guidance in resolving the problem in their area. They should be able to anticipate the problems that they will face in obtaining control of the waste stream, such as legislation that forbids communities to enter long-term disposal contracts. Therefore, a study should be undertaken of state legislation affecting waste control and alternative approaches that have been used to resolve the problem. Compilation of a set of model state laws and reasonable standard approaches to the probem based on what is learned from successful experiences would be useful.

ENERGY MARKETS

In the experience of most resource recovery projects, another difficult problem to overcome in facility planning is securing a commitment for the long-term purchase of refuse-derived energy or fuel products at an equitable price.

Investor-owned electric utilities are promising long-term markets for electricity, steam, or refuse-derived fuel (RDF); unfortunately, they are reluctant to become involved in resource recovery projects.

The primary responsibility of an electric utility is to provide reliable electric service to its customers at the lowest possible cost, while providing an adequate rate of return to its shareholders. The lack of full-scale demonstration of resource recovery projects and the resultant uncertainties and risks that are associated with the industry are therefore major disincentives to utility participation, because they can have a nagative impact on the reliability and cost of electric service. Furthermore, an electric utility is required to pass any increase or decrease in fuel cost on to its ratepayers. For this reason it lacks any economic incentive to become involved in the use of an essentially minor new energy source. An electric utility would receive no economic compensation for its assumption of risk.

Regarding the purchase of electricity or steam, the utility's reluctance stems mainly from this lack of incentive to buy. The utility is relatively indifferent to this new energy source for two reasons: first, the amount of available refuse-derived steam or electricity is often insignificant in relation to a utility's total energy requirement; and, second, cost pass-through requirements prevent utilities from making a profit on the purchase. In the case of RDF, the lack of incentive is compounded by the technical risks associated with the use of this product. Utilities are concerned about the unpredictable and potentially damaging effects on their boilers of firing RDF.

Experience has shown that electric utilities will require the following assurances before making a commitment to purchase energy or fuel from a resource recovery facility:

- The reliability of service will not be impaired;
- The net cost of the ratepayer will not be increased;
- Capital investment risks will be minimized; and
- Environmental standards will still be met.

Futhermore, utilities are in need of a reliable data base on technical issues so that they can confidently assess the extent of the risks that are associated with the use of refuse-derived fuels. They also need clarification of economic and contractual issues, so that when entering projects they have full awareness of the risks they have contractually assumed.

Public utility and public service commissions should be made aware of the status and needs of the resource recovery programs in their states. The importance to these programs of utility participation and support should be stressed. Public utility and public service commissions should be encouraged to actively promote the concept of cooperation between resource recovery and public utilities, and should consider the enactment of regulatory change which would facilitate this cooperation. For instance, utilities might be more inclined to participate in resource recovery projects if any cost savings could be distributed between their ratepayers and their shareholders, therefore, a method for providing incentive would be to release utilities that purchase refuse-derived energy from cost pass-through requirements for that energy.

NONCOMPLYING ALTERNATIVES TO RESOURCE RECOVERY

The problem of competition from existing landfills and incinerators that are not in compliance with environmental regulations is yet another obstacle to resource recovery implementation. It is important for communities that are looking for a solution to a solid waste disposal problem to realize that, regardless of the method chosen, the true cost of solid waste disposal will be borne by the community. For this reason, there should be no inequities or hidden subsidies which make a currently operating facility appear attractive when it is not. Many disposal facilities that are now relatively low-priced, compared to resource recovery, are not in compliance with environmental standards or landfill regulations. Although disposal costs at these facilities are attractively low, the community will also eventually pay for cleanup of the environment.

It is widely recognized that if disposal facilities are properly designed, constructed, and operated, the cost will be higher than at substandard facilities. The evenhanded enforcement of environmental standards at all waste disposal facilities is, therefore, a widely endorsed method for helping to close the gap between the costs of resource recovery and landfills. More state pressure is needed, however, in order to bring existing facilities into compliance.

The uncertainty associated with the availability of landfill makes it difficult for both communities and resource recovery planners to anticipate the future need for resource recovery, and communities will often shy away from resource recovery as long as they believe that their landfill might be available for several more years. It is essential that undesirable disposal alternatives are eliminated so that sound planning for long-term waste disposal can be performed, whether or not the chosen disposal will be resource recovery.

TECHNOLOGICAL UNCERTAINTIES

At present there are few resource recovery technologies which have been satisfactorily proven or demonstrated, and every project now being undertaken has some degree of risk associated with its system performance. Furthermore, environmental standards that may be promulgated in the future may make resource recovery systems being implemented today technologically or economically obsolete. The high level of risk related to technology is a major deterrent to the implementation of even the most promising systems.

In order to increase the rate of demonstration of resource recovery technologies, federal financial assistance for support of innovative and soundly planned projects has been authorized and is presently being evaluated. This assistance would be available in three main forms; loan guarantees, loans, and price support. With a loan guarantee, the full faith and credit of the United States, would be placed behind a portion of the debt incurred in construction of a resource recovery facility. The financial consequences of project risks would thereby be shifted from project participants and bondholders to the federal government. A loan guarantee would be used to support the financing of a project that is worthy of demonstration, but that would not otherwise be built because of a high level of risk. Alternatively, federal loans would provide direct financial support of a project which would otherwise not be built because of the inability of the participating parties to obtain a loan at reasonable or at any cost. Price supports would be used to reduce the economic uncertainty of a project that stems from weak or unstable energy or material markets. With this mechanism, federal money would be used to support the price of recovered energy or materials, thereby reducing the burden on the tipping fee as the source of project revenue.

Federal financial assistance to support the demonstration of promising technologies must be accompanied by continued research and development efforts for both large and small scale technologies. With the continued improvement and demonstration of resource recovery technology, the level of project risk will be significantly reduced and resource recovery will become a disposal option that is chosen with confidence.

IMPLEMENTATION PLAN

In addition to the issues that are related to the technical and economic feasibility of resource recovery, there is a group of problems that are related to the legality of the implementation plan. Difficulties are often met in negotiating contracts and allocating risks, procuring the resource recovery system, and developing a financial package.

RISK ALLOCATION

The long-term contracts that are required in resource recovery projects lead to a very careful definition of risks and how they will be assumed. The assignment of some risks is reasonably obvious, such as the guarantee of system performance, but it is difficult to assign the risks related to the energy market, project financing, and waste input. A lack of precedent and inconsistency in state laws and practices has complicated the task of risk allocation.

Existing surveys of resource recovery contracts apparently do not adequately convey how or why final positions on risk allocation were reached.

Communities are anxious to learn the risk posture assumed in earlier projects as well as the basis for allocation in each case. This knowledge would help communities decide which risks they could appropriately assume and would provide examples for the way in which risk allocation is translated into a written contract. Thus, the contract negotiation experience of earlier resource recovery projects should be decumented, and based on this earlier experience, model contracts should be developed to serve as a framework in future projects.

PROCUREMENT APPROACH

Selection of a procurement method is an important determinant of how risks are allocated. At present, the preferred method for procuring resource recovery is the full-service approach with competitive negotiation. With this approach, a full-service contractor is selected through the evaluation of competitive industry proposals and negotiation of a contract with a single firm for facility design, construction, and operation. The full-service approach tends to carry with it the highest system cost, but has the lowest risk related to operation. Since a single firm is used for design, construction and operation, there is a signel point of responsibility and, thus, it is easy to fix responsibility if a problem occurs. The two important characteristics of the competitive negotiation process are that it removes lowest bid as the major criterion for selection and it allows the procuring agency to discuss the proposals with bidders before a selection is made. It therefore provides an opportunity for full consideration of the important technical, financial, marketing, environmental, and management interrelationships of a proposal.

The main problem with utilizing this preferred procurement approach is that many states have laws which prohibit its use. An inventory of state procurement processes and pertinent legislation should be undertaken for states that have or will be procuring resource recovery.

Potential obstacles to resource recovery procurement (such as restrictions on competitive negotiation, long-term contracting, or the use of revenue bond financing) should be identified so that timely efforts to initiate changes in legislation or to modify the procurement approaches can be made. The development of model procurement codes for various procurement approachs would provide a framework to be followed and would assist communities in foreseeing potential problem areas in their procurement efforts.

IRS REGULATIONS

The development of a financing package for a resource recovery project is complicated by International Revenue Service (IRS) regulations and rulings. The financing of resource recovery through general obligation bonds (which are backed by the full faith and credit of participating communities) is no longer recommended for most projects because of the large capital requirements associated with these facilities. Tax-exempt revenue bonds as part of relatively complex financing packages are now more common, as these financing packages require individual rulings by the IRS — rulings which often take as long as six months.

The extent to which the use of tax exempt revenue bonds has been allowed in the financing of resource recovery facilities and the utilization of investment tax credits and depreciation allowances has varied from project to project. Project financing is often tailored around obtaining these tax benefits since their presence can make several dollars per ton difference in the tipping fees. The uncertainty in the outcome of IRS rulings results in delay and legal costs to resource recovery projects. The IRS, therefore, should clarify guidelines for the use of financing mechanisms and should develop consistency in ruling procedures. The standardization of IRS rulings will make it possible to determine the tax status of project financing with more certainty and with less delay.

FRONT-END PLANNING

As previously stated, in order to address the uncertainties associated with resource recovery and thereby maximize the probability of successful project implementation, an extensive and costly front-end planning effort must be undertaken. The first step of the front-end planning stage consists of the delineation of system objectives and the identification of technology and design options. The appropriate choice of resource recovery technology and system design stems from a clear statement of what objectives the system is expected to meet coupled with the feasible range of options dictated by the local situation (markets, available waste quantity, etc.). The objectives must be clearly defined and the options accurately identified before a judgement can be made on which technology/design option most closely matches the objectives. The final selection of technology and design must take into account the relative importance or weight that local participants attach to net disposal cost per ton, environmental impacts, acceptable level of reliance on landfill, demonstrated history of system performance, degree of innovation, extent of recovery, and other factors.

Thorough front-end planning not only ensures sound decision-making, it also facilitates preparation of the Request for Proposals (RFP), a document that has a direct impact on the ultimate success of a project. Potential resource recovery contractors need reliable and complete information in order to prepare responsive and well thought-out proposals. The project parameters, objectives, and assumptions that are identified in the RFP serve as the basis for technical and management decisions by responding firms. Most resource recovery firms will spend the time and money to prepare a proposal only in response to a thorough and well-planned RFP, because such an RFP s an indication that a project has a good chance of success. Over the past few years, the credibility of the resource recovery industry has suffered because of flurries of planning activity at the local level without timely follow-through and implementation. This problem can often be traced back to inadequate RFP preparation and front-end planning.

The main problem with front-end planning is that local jurisdictions often do not have the money to hire consultants to assist in dealing with important financial, legal and technical issues. The high up-front costs of system planning can prevent communities from initiating planning and procurement efforts. The Environmental Protection Agency and the Department of Energy have recognized this need and have established responsive programs through which financial and technical assistance are made available. Nonetheless, there is a need for expansion and modification of these programs to make assistance more widely available and more specific to the needs of individual projects.

DIFFICULTIES CAN BE OVERCOME

It is clear that there are many easily identifiable obstacles to resource recovery implementation that delay what is an inherently complex implementation process. Nonetheless, resource recovery remains a widely pursued solid waste disposal option, and the extensive activity in the field is an indication of the abiding interest in this technology. Ongoing experiences in resource recovery implementation are leading to the improvement and standardization of planning and procurement methods, and technologies are continually being developed and perfected. We have learned quickly from past efforts, and have gained important insight into the problems that are encountered in implementation. It is essential that we continue to disseminate the knowledge gained in first-hand project experience in order to facilitate future efforts. Armed with this knowledge and the cooperation and dedication of leaders in the field of resource recovery, the difficulties in resource recovery implementation should rapidly be overcome.

The MITRE Corporation sponsored a symposium in October 1978 entitled "Actions to Increase Resource Recovery Implementation." One hundred and fifty participants, representing all levels of expertise and involvement in the field of resource recovery, gathered to identify barriers to implementation and to discuss methods by which they could be minimized. This article reflects the ideas that were generated at the meeting, and is based on the experiences and opinions of MITRE's resource recovery staff.

2-8 Flow Control Ordinance: City of Akron

John E. Holcomb and Richard Cohen
Source: The Authors. Reprinted with Permission of the Authors.

In December, 1976, the City of Akron, Ohio, Summit County and the Ohio Water Development Authority* (OWDA) entered into a cooperative agreement to enable the OWDA to sell $46,000,000 worth of revenue bonds to permit the City of Akron to construct a recycle energy system (RES). The RES was a plan whereby solid waste, currently being landfilled, would be used as fuel to fire boilers which would, in turn, generate steam to be distributed throughout the downtown business district. Numerous factors, including the current steam producer's (Ohio Edison Co.) desire to discontinue steam service and the chronic problems inherent in landfill operations caused the City to decide on the RES as the best alternative to solve its solid waste disposal problems.

To facilitate the marketing of the revenue bonds funded by the sale of steam, the City and OWDA concluded that all waste collected within the city limits, whether by municipal or private haulers, should be taken to the RES to insure an adequate supply of fuel. Accordingly, on October 4, 1976 the Akron City Council passed Ordinance Number 841-1976 which established this requirement (attached).

This ordinance and cooperative agreement were challenged in the United States District Court for the Northern District of Ohio, Eastern Division, before the Honorable Leroy Contie.** In their complaint the plaintiffs alleged that their right to due process of law under the

Fourteenth Amendment to the United States Constitution was violated; that their property was taken in violation of the Fifth Amendment to the United States Constitution as applied to the states through the Fourteenth Amendment; that the defendants restrained interstate commerce in violation of Article I, Section 8 of the Constitution; that the ordinance and cooperative agreement violated Article XVIII, Section 3 of the Ohio Constitution; and finally that they violated Sections 1 and 2 of the Sherman Act, 15 U.S.C., §§1-2. In its opinion upholding the validity of the cooperative agreement and the ordinance, the Court considered all of the above arguments, and the following is a review of the District Court's decision.

In reference to the antitrust argument the Court noted the Sherman Act's purpose is to render illegal any agreement in restraint of trade. In its analysis of possible antitrust violations, the Court cited various reasons to exempt the challenged activities from the operation of the Sherman Act. The Court assumed arguendo that if private parties had entered into the covenants contained in the cooperative agreement and had attempted to carry out the terms of the challenged ordinance, their actions would violate the Sherman Act. The court noted, however, in *Parker vs. Brown,* 317 U.S. 341 at 350 (1943) the United States Supreme Court stated:

"Nothing in the language of the Sherman Act or in its history suggests that its purpose was to restrain a state or its officers or agents from activities directed by its legislature. In a dual system of government in which, under the Constitution, the states are sovereign, save only as Congress may constitutionally

---

*The OWDA is an eight member board created by an act of the Ohio Legislature which is codified at Chapter 6123 of the Ohio Revised Code.

**Glenwillow Landfill, et al. vs. City of Akron, et al.,* Case Number C 78-65A (C 78-1733A a consolidated case).

subtract from their authority, an unexpressed purpose to nullify a state's control over its officers and agents is not lightly to be attributed to Congress."

Thus, in *Parker* the U.S. Supreme Court declared that actions which derive their force and effect from the legislative command of the state are exempt from the Sherman Act. The district court also relied on *Bates vs. State Bar of Arizona,* 433 U.S. 350 (1977) which exempted state action from the Sherman Act.

In an attempt to overcome *Parker* and its progeny, the plaintiffs relied upon the case of *City of Lafeyette vs. Louisiana Power and Light Company,* 435 U.S. 389 (1978) which was decided after the filing of the complaint in the instant action. *Lafeyette* involved a situation where a municipal light plant competed with other power companies in areas outside of the city limits. The Supreme Court held that the City of Lafeyette violated antitrust laws as all of their anticompetitive activities took place outside of the city limits. Thus, the City of Lafeyette could not invoke the shield provided by *Parker,* supra.

The District Court distinguished *Lafeyette* since the Akron ordinance is effective only within the city limits and was adopted to provide city residents with safe and sanitary waste disposal. Noting this difference Judge Contie relied upon the opinion of the plurality in *Lafeyette* which stated that municipalities may legitimately exercise their governmental powers by providing services on a monopoly basis.

By utilizing the *Parker vs. Brown* reasoning and distinguishing the *Lafeyette* case, the Court herein has found that the cooperative agreement and ordinance are exempt from the Sherman Act since the OWDA is a state agency and its power to determine state policy concerning the issuance of state revenue bonds for facilities like the RES is supreme. The Court held that the state has a legitimate interest in promoting safe and sanitary methods of solid waste disposal. The policy of the state in ensuring the health and safety of the people of Ohio is articulated in Section 6123.03 of the Ohio Revised Code which states in pertinent part:

"It is hereby declared to be the public policy of the state through the operations of the Ohio water development authority . . . to provide for the comfort, health, safety, and general welfare of all employees and other inhabitants of the state and for the conservation of the land, air and water resources of the state through efficient and proper methods of disposal salvage and reuse of or recovery of resources from solid wastes thereby eliminating or decreasing accident and health hazards including rodent and insect sectors of disease, public nuisance and the adverse effect on land values caused thereby and the scenic blight marring the landscape [and] to assist in the financing of solid waste facilities . . . In furtherance of such public policy, the Ohio water development authority . . . may make loans and grants to governmental agencies for the acquisition or construction of solid waste facilities by such governmental agencies . . . and may issue solid waste revenue bonds of this state payable solely from revenues, to pay the cost of such projects."

Thus, the OWDA's actions are exempt from the Sherman Act as its powers are derived from state legislative enactments.

In addition to the exemption from the Sherman Act provided by the involvement of a state agency the defendants relied on Article XVIII, Section 3 of the Ohio Constitution (Home Rule Provision) which permits chartered municipalities to formulate certain policies which control within their boundaries. Article XVIII, Section 3 states:

"Municipalities shall have authority to exercise all powers of local self-government and to adopt and enforce within their limits such local police, sanitary and other similar regulations, as are not in conflict with general laws."

The Ohio Courts in applying this constitutional provision recognized that local governments are responsible for regulating the collection and disposal of solid wastes, by monopoly if the City finds it appropriate. See *State ex rel. Mooch v. Cincinnati,* 120 Ohio St. 500 (1929); *City of Canton v. VanVoorhis,* 61 Ohio App. 419 (1939). Accordingly the instant Court found the ordinance to be a proper exercise of local governmental authority within the city limits. Thus, the Court held the contested activities exempt from the reach of the Sherman Act for two alternative reasons.

Another area of attack by the plaintiffs came under Article I, Section 8 of the United States Constitution as being in violation of the commerce clause. In evaluating an ordinance under the commerce clause, the Court stated that it must be asked:

"(1) whether the challenged statute regulates evenhandedly with only 'incidental' effects on interstate commerce, or discriminates against interstate commerce on its face or in practical effect; (2) whether the statute serves a legitimate local purpose; and if so, (3) whether alternative means could promote this local purpose without discriminating against interstate commerce *Hughes v. Oklahoma,* 99 S. Ct. 1727, 1736 (1979)."

The Court herein held that the ordinance directly affects intrastate commerce and any effect on interstate commerce would be indirect. This conclusion was reached as the ordinance acts only upon solid waste and any burden is indirect and incidental on the interstate movement of recyclable goods. Further, the Court concluded that the ordinance serves a legitimate local purpose as it was enacted to fulfill the RES plan; i.e. the safe and efficient disposal of solid waste materials generated within the City. Finally, the Court determined in its commerce clause analysis that the plaintiffs failed to show how the City's goals could be implemented by legislation imposing a lesser burden on interstate commerce. Therefore, the challenge to the ordinance under the commerce clause failed.

Additionally, the plaintiffs raised two arguments under the due process clause of the Fourteenth Amendment. The first was that the ordinance was not sufficiently related to legitimate governmental objectives to pass scrutiny under the Fourteenth Amendment's due process clause. Secondly, they allege the ordinance takes property without compensation as prohibited by the Fifth Amendment as applied to the states through the Fourteenth Amendment.

The Court concluded that the construction of RES and the ordinance serve to advance valid governmental concerns and public purposes, including the continued health, safety and welfare of City residents, by the regulation of solid waste disposal without the inherent ecological problems of landfills.

Finally, the plaintiffs contended that their property had been taken without just compensation. In its analysis, the Court noted that before any waste could be collected within the City, a license had to be obtained. By placing a condition on the licenses requiring the waste be disposed of at the RES, the waste collectors were analogized to a new owner of a home subject to a zoning ordinance; these individuals not being entitled to treatment under a nonconforming use theory.

The Court acknowledged that the transfer stations and the landfill operators had an expectation that the waste collectors would continue to dispose of waste at their facility. However, the Court held that the plaintiffs failed to demonstrate how this expectation rose to the level of a legitimate claim of entitlement or other property interest protected by the Fifth Amendment.

In concluding that the ordinance was not a compensable taking under the Fifth Amendment, the Court cited various U.S. Supreme Court cases* which held that reasonable restrictions imposed for the health, welfare and safety of the population are not unconstitutional deprivations of property, but a legitimate exercise of police power. These regulations involve the adjustment of rights for the public good which frequently curtail the use or exploitation of private property. Therefore, even if the ordinance infringed upon private property rights, it was not invalid under due process analysis.**

*Village of Euclid v. Ambler Realty, 272 U.S. 365 (1926) Goldblatt v. Town of Hempstead, 369 U.S. 590 (1962) Andreas v. Allard, 48 U.S.L.W. 4013 (Nov. 27, 1979)

**The decision in this case was issued on December 13, 1979. It should be noted that the plaintiffs have expressed their intention to appeal this decision to the United States Court of Appeals, Sixth Circuit in Cincinnati, Ohio.

Offered by ....

ORDINANCE NO. ....–1976 amending Sections 850.06, 1068.06 and 1068.14 of the Codified Ordinances of the City of Akron to revise licensing requirements and service charges with respect to the collection and disposal of garbage and rubbish within the City, and declaring an emergency.

WHEREAS, in connection with the financing of the City's recycle energy facility, it is necessary to provide for revised service charges for the collection and disposal of garbage and rubbish and to revise licensing provisions to require that garbage and rubbish collected by private haulers be disposed of at the new facility when completed.

NOW, THEREFORE, BE IT ENACTED by the Council of the City of Akron, Ohio:

Section 1. That Section 850.06 of the Codified Ordinances of the City of Akron, Ohio, is hereby amended so as to provide as follows:

"Section 850.06 PLACES OF DEPOSIT; CHARGES

"(a) Until such time as the City's recycle energy plant begins accepting rubbish for disposal, no rubbish shall be deposited by the holder of a rubbish hauler's license within the corporate limits of the City except at a place designated in writing by the Mayor. From and after the date on which such plant begins accepting rubbish for disposal, all rubbish collected within the corporate limits of the City by a holder of a rubbish hauler's license shall be deposited at such plant; provided that rubbish which is not acceptable for disposal by such plant shall not be deposited within the City except at a place designated in writing by the Mayor.

"(b) In the event that the Mayor designates to holders of rubbish haulers' licenses that rubbish hauled, and from and after the date referred to in paragraph (a) above, rubbish not acceptable for disposal at the City's recycle energy plant, shall be deposited at a sanitary landfill site operated by the City, or at a site being operated under agreement with the City, then such rubbish hauler shall pay to the City a fee for each load of rubbish so deposited, according to a schedule of charges

prescribed by the Mayor. The charges prescribed by the Mayor shall be of such amount as to reimburse the City for the cost incurred in disposing of the rubbish so deposited.

"(c) The Mayor is hereby authorized to promulgate such rules and regulations as may be required to carry out the intent of this section."

Section 2. That Section 1068.06 of the Codified Ordinances of the City of Akron, Ohio, is hereby amended so as to provide as follows:

"Section 1068.06 GARBAGE COLLECTED BY CITY OR PRIVATE HAULERS

"No person, except duly authorized collectors of the City or private haulers licensed pursuant to law, shall collect or remove any garbage or rubbish accumulating within the City or use the streets, avenues and alleys of the City for the purpose of collecting or transporting the same. All licenses granted to such private haulers and all contracts or other forms of authorization of duly authorized collectors shall require that all garbage or rubbish collected and transported under authority of such license, if acceptable for disposal by the City's recycle energy plant be disposed of at such plant from and after the date on which such plant begins accepting garbage and rubbish for disposal."

Section 3. That Section 1068.14 of the Codified Ordinances of the City of Akron, Ohio, is hereby amended so as to provide as follows:

"Section 1068.14 SERVICE CHARGE

"There is hereby established a fee, for combined curbside collection of garbage and rubbish of three dollars ($3.00) per quarter-year, beginning January 1, 1974, and continuing through December 31, 1977, and payable in advance. For so long as and provided the City Demonstration Agency or any other agency or entity pays the three dollar ($3.00) per quarter fee for service to residents of the Model Cities area, then the three dollar ($3.00) per quarter fee provided for herein shall be suspended for said Model Cities residents. The Director of Public Service is authorized to promulgate rules and regulations for the collection of said service charge, and he is further authorized with the consent of Council to adjust said charge upward or downward on January 1 of each of the years 1975 through 1977, inclusive, such adjustment to be made only to the extent that may be necessary to maintain the total cost of garbage and rubbish collection borne by the general revenue of the City of Akron at $830,000.00 per year. The said service charge shall be applicable only to households which participate in the collection program.

"Effective January 1, 1978, there is hereby established a fee for combined curbside collection of garbage and rubbish and for the disposal thereof of _____ dollars per month, payable in advance. The Director of Public Service is authorized to promulgate rules and regulations for the collection of said service charge and he is further authorized with the consent of Council to adjust said charge upward on January 1, 1979 or on January 1 of any year thereafter. The Director of Public Service is further authorized on January 1 of any year when there is on deposit on such date and appropriated by this Council a sum of money to pay costs of such collection and disposal to adjust said service charge downward to a charge which will produce funds which when added to the sum of money so on deposit and appropriated will be sufficient to pay all costs of such collection and disposal. The said service charge shall be applicable only to households which participate in the collection program."

Section 4. It is found and determined that all formal actions of this Council concerning and relating to the passage of this ordinance were passed in an open meeting of this Council, and that all deliberations of this Council and of any of its committees that resulted in such formal action, were in meetings open to the public, in compliance with all legal requirements including Section 121.22 of the Ohio Revised Code.

Section 5. That this ordinance is hereby declared to be an emergency measure for the reason that the provisions hereof should become effective at the earliest possible time in order to permit the financing of the recycle energy facility to be accomplished without undue delay, and provided that this ordinance receives the affirmative vote of two-thirds of the members elected or appointed to Council, it shall take effect and be in force immediately upon its passage and approval by the Mayor; otherwise, it shall take effect and be in force at the earliest time allowed by law.

Passed: OCT 4 1976   , 1976

Edward Davis   Ray Kapper
Clerk of Council   President of Council

Approved: OCT 5 1976   , 1976

William R. Burd   ,   Acting
Mayor

2-9 Environmental Impacts of Resource Recovery Facilities Should be Pre-determined

Allen Serper

Source: Adapted from two articles that appeared in *Solid Waste Management,* (1) Environmental Impacts of Resource Recovery Facilities Should be Pre-determined, Vol. 21, No. 2 (February 1978) pp. 20, 22, 46–47, and (2) Anticipation of Environmental Impacts of Facilities Urged, Vol. 21, No. 3 (March 1978) pp. 60, 62, 64, 88. Reprinted with Permission of Communication Channels, Inc.

Resource recovery from mixed municipal refuse involves the centralized processing of collected raw waste to separate recyclable materials and to convert the remaining mixed fractions into useful material(s) or energy forms. Because of the heterogeneous nature of mixed refuse and the economics of recovery, virtually all systems are designed as multiple-product operations. At minimum, ferrous metal is magnetically extracted for recycling and at least one major commodity is derived from the organic fraction — usually a fuel or converted energy (steam).

Depending on economic considerations, other inorganic materials are recycled, such as glass cullet (mixed or color sorted), aluminum, and other heavy nonferrous metals. Alternate approaches thermally convert various mixed inorganic fractions into a slag or frit material for use as a construction aggregate or in other building products. Energy recovery processes that are available or are under development include the direct firing of either raw or shredded wastes in heat recovery boilers or in water wall combustion units to produce steam, as well as the mechanical and thermal processing of wastes to produce various intermediate solid, liquid, or gaseous fuel products for onsite use or sale to commercial industries. As an alternative to energy recovery, a variety of other options for utilizing the organic components of solid waste are also in use or are under development.

Pyrolysis is a relative newcomer to the field of resource recovery, although the principle has been used for years in other industrial processes. It is often referred to as destructive distillation. In a pyrolysis system, the refuse, such as plastics and paper, is heated in a controlled atmosphere, decomposes, and is recovered by distillation as separate gaseous, liquid, and solid fractions. Typically included in the recovered products are such compounds as methane, methanol, fuel oils, and inorganic residue, such as glass and metal.

Four Basic Processes

Of the many competing and complementary systems, only four processes have been widely accepted. These include:

1. **Water wall combustion** (extensively employed in Europe)
2. **Separation** of ferrous scrap, glass, etc.
3. **Refuse derived fuel processes (RDF),** both wet and dry processes, including onsite combustion
4. **Pyrolysis system.** The high cost of pyrolysis systems has caused doubt as to their commercial feasibility.

Most of the mixed wastes processing systems to be considered involve complex capital-intensive technologies, requiring high initial capital costs. This factor, together with significant economies in capital and operating costs for larger sized plants, restricts most of these systems to large cities or county-wide applications. Thus far, the economics are favorable for cities and regions where disposal costs are high due to the unavailability of local landfill sites. Resource recovery facilities will be, and are being, established in urban and heavily populated suburban areas where the environmental problems are particularly critical.

Basic Impacts

The basic impacts to be considered can be classified under four broad categories:

1. **Atmospheric Emissions.** Atmospheric emissions are produced by the operation of the refuse recovery boilers. Vehicle emissions are produced when the refuse is transported to the point of processing. There are also emissions from the refuse processing equipment, such as air classifiers and shredders.

2. **Wastewater.** The discharge of wastewater is produced by the operation of the facility. These discharges include processing water wastes, wash waters, and waters associated with the combustion process, i.e., cooling tower and boiler blowdown.

3. **Landfill and Waste Disposal.** Processing the refuse generated bottom and fly ash that must be disposed of in some manner.

4. **Local and In-Plant Environmental Impacts.** Local and in-plant environmental impacts include: (1) the containment of the malodorous air within the plant; (2) maintenance of the carbon monoxide levels in the tipping area within OSHA limitations; (3) fogging and deposition of solids produced by the operation of the cooling tower; and (4) noise associated with the operation of the plant and the delivery of refuse to the facility.

AIR POLLUTION

Municipal Refuse As Fuel

The emissions produced by the combustion of municipal refuse fuel will depend on the composition of the refuse. Municipal refuse is far

Table 1. Chicago RDF Mass Balance for 1,000 Tons/Day Refuse Input.

High Heating Valve (Btu/lb)	Raw Refuse Component	As Rec'd (Wt. %)	Fuel Fraction T/D	%	Reject Fraction (T/D)
5,600	Corrugated box board	3.67	35	4.9	1.7
5,980	Newspaper	12.73	125	17.6	2.3
5,810	Magazines/books	3.74	35	5.0	2.4
5,193	Misc. paper	24.77	235	33.0	12.7
14,230	Plastics	4.09	38	5.3	2.9
6,670	Textiles	3.16	30	4.4	1.6
7,060	Wood	2.23	18	2.5	4.3
4,030	Leaves, shrubs, grass	2.06	17	2.4	3.6
4,420	Food waste	10.94	100	14.1	9.4
8,450	Rubber & leather	1.22	10	1.4	2.2
2,080	Fines (< 1 in.)	11.45	50	7.0	64.5
709	Metals	9.89		0.3	—
—	Steel	(9.07)	1.7	—	89.0
—	Aluminum	(0.50)	2.0	—	3.0
—	ONF	(0.32)	0.1	—	3.1
82	Glass, ceramics, stones	10.05	15	2.1	85.5
		100.00	711.8	100.0	288.2
	Moisture	(25%)	(225)	(31.6)	(25)

Table 2. Ultimate Analysis and Heating Value for Typical Mixed Municipal Solid Waste.

Component	Analysis (As Received) (% by Weight)	Analysis (As Received) (% by Weight)
Moisture	25.1	0.0
Carbon	25.2	33.5
Hydrogen	3.2	4.3
Oxygen	18.8	25.2
Nitrogen	0.4	0.5
Chlorine (organic 0.16, inorganic 0.14)	0.3	0.4
Sulfur	0.1	0.1
Metal	8.7	11.6
Glass, ceramics	12.2	16.3
Ash	6.0	8.1
Total	100.0	100.0
High heating value	4,400 Btu/lb	5,600 Btu/lb

from being an easily characterized homogeneous fuel. It varies widely depending upon geographical, seasonal, and weather-related factors. This variation will affect the emissions characteristic of stack gases.

Table 1 describes the constituents of refuse fed to and through the Chicago refuse derived fuel (RDF) plant.

Many estimates of the major chemical constituents of municipal solid wastes have been prepared. Table 2 is a typical compilation and can be considered valid for refuse found in the midwestern and northeastern parts of the country.

Little information is available concerning the existence of potentially hazardous trace materials that may be found in stack gases of facilities utilizing municipal solid wastes as a fuel. A compilation of expected trace materials in the combustible fraction of urban refuse is presented in Table 3. Most of the elements presented in Table 3 can be found in coal. Table 4 is a listing of elements that have been found to be in higher concentrations in RDF than in coal.

Particulate matter has been the primary concern of most waste-to-energy systems. It has been found that when RDF has been mixed with fossil fuel in a power plant boiler, higher particulate emissions have resulted. This is to be expected since the ash content of refuse is much higher than that of coal or oil.

Refuse is inherently a low sulfur fuel containing less than 1/10 the amount of sulfur found in typical low sulfur coals. Sulfur dioxide formation has not been a problem. By

Table 3. Trace Elements in Urban Refuse.

Major Elements Average Content (1,000–100,000 ppm)	Minor Elements Average Content (0.1–999 ppm)	
Aluminum	Antimony	Manganese
Calcium	Arsenic	Mercury
Chlorine	Barium	Molybdenum
Iron	Beryllium	Nickel
Magnesium	Bismuth	Niobium
Phosphorus	Boron	Platinum
Potassium	Cadmium	Rubidium
Silicon	Cesium	Selenium
Sodium	Chromium	Silver
Sulfur	Cobalt	Strontium
Titanium	Copper	Tantalum
Zinc	Germanium	Tin
	Gold	Tungsten
	Lead	Vanadium
	Lithium	Zirconium

Table 4. Trace Elements Found in Higher Concentrations in RDF Than in Coal.

Antimony	Lead	Sodium
Barium	Lithium	Tin
Bismuth	Mercury	Titanium
Cadmium	Nickel	Tungsten
Chromium	Phosphorus	Zinc
Copper	Silver	

**Table 5. Average Emission Factors for the Incineration
of One Ton of Municipal Solid Wastes.**

Particulates	1.5	Based upon meeting EPA standard of 0.08 grams/scf at 12% CO_2
Sulfur oxides	1.5	
Carbon monoxide	35	
Hydrocarbons	1.5	
Nitrogen oxides	2	
Hydrogen chloride (estimated)	0.6	Based upon 0.3% chlorine in light fraction of municipal solid waste

co-firing of RDF with coal, substantial reductions in sulfur oxides emissions have been noted.

The formation of nitrogen oxides from the combustion in resource recovery boilers has been substantially less than in utility boilers due to the relatively low temperature at which most refuse fired boilers operate.

The other criteria pollutants such as carbon monoxide and unburned hydrocarbons are not considered a problem in resource recovery boilers due to high flame turbulence and combustion time.

The chlorine contained in most municipal refuse is in the form of sodium chloride and chlorinated synthetics, which form hydrogen chloride when heated. Small quantities of hydrochloric acid are produced due to sodium chloride and chlorinated synthetics found in municipal refuse.

The average emission factors for the incineration of one ton of municipal solid wastes are presented in Table 5 in pounds.

If a well-designed electrostatic precipitator is utilized, 99.5% of the particulate matter can be removed, thus minimizing the facility's impact on the local air quality.

In light of recent EPA regulations concerning significant air quality deterioration, any resources recovery facility emitting more than 100 tons per year of particulate or sulfur dioxide matter will require an air quality impact analysis. This analysis determines the incremental increase in ambient pollutant concentrations due to operation of the facility. The incremental contribution of the facility must meet EPA limitations, which are based on local air quality.

In addition, if the facility is located in a non-attainment area (an area where the ambient pollution concentrations exceed the standards),

an emission offset analysis will have to be performed. This tradeoff study quantifies the beneficial aspects of the facility on the local air quality.

Vehicle Emissions

As part of the overall impact evaluation of a resources recovery plant, the pollutants emitted by motor vehicles associated with delivery of refuse to the plant must be analyzed to determine concentrations of carbon monoxide, hydrocarbons, and oxidants in the vicinity of the plant.

The evaluation of vehicular emissions and the resulting impact on air quality consists of documenting the existing traffic conditions (i.e., traffic volume, average vehicle speed, modal mix, etc.) in the area surrounding the plant and then defining the associated air quality levels.

Peak and average pollutant concentration patterns can be predicted from meteorological and background air quality data when available. Projected traffic volumes, including the proposed routes of the refuse trucks, are used as input to a diffusion model, which is used to calculate ambient concentrations of pollutants.

For comparative purposes, predicted pollutant concentration patterns are then calculated for traffic conditions with and without the vehicles associated with the recovery plant. An assessment of the impact of plant-associated vehicles relative to the projected traffic volume is then performed. The results of these evaluations are used to reach conclusions and recommendations concerning the impact of refuse delivery and existing traffic on air quality in the vicinity of the plant.

If existing traffic patterns and local ambient air quality data are not available, special tests must be conducted to determine the cause and effect relationships of vehicular emissions and ambient pollutant concentrations. In addition, the study must determine pollutant concentration patterns in the vicinity of major intersections near the proposed plant for a variety of meteorological and traffic conditions.

Processing Operations

With the exception of bulk incineration, all resources recovery plants employ some degree of front-end processing such as shredding, air classification, and separation. Inherent to these processing operations are air emissions of particulate matter.

The light combustible materials separated by air classifiers are carried by an air stream, usually discharging to a cyclone/fabric filter combination. Dust-laden air is often drawn off by hoods located over shredders and conveyors. This dusty air is usually vented to series of cyclones and fabric filters before being discharged to the atmosphere.

First-generation resources recovery plants did not employ adequate control equipment to remove the fine particulate dust from the air streams. However, the combination of cyclones and fabric filters now utilized at most resource recovery plants has significantly reduced the discharge of fine dust to the atmosphere. If the combination of cyclones and fabric filters is designed properly, the dust generated by front-end processing can be considered to have a negligible impact on local air quality.

The text so far has considered air pollution issues. In the paragraphs that follow other environmental impacts are considered including water pollution, landfill, and local and in-plant impacts.

Water is utilized to some extent in all resource recovery facilities. The most common use is in the cleaning of refuse pits and processing equipment. The wastewater that results from washing and cleaning will contain high levels of biochemical oxygen demand (BOD), chemical oxygen demand (COD), and total dissolved solids (TDS).

Water is also used in the glass recovery process. It is estimated that three to four thousand gallons of water will be used to recover glass from one ton of municipal wastes. This water will also be high in BOD, COD, and TDS. The water effluents from the waste pyrolysis process, if untreated, can pose a significant pollution problem due to the presence of fairly concentrated amounts of organic and inorganic compounds.

The EPA effluent guidelines and standards applicable to steam electric power generation plants require strict effluent standards for all new sources. Included under these guidelines are resource recovery plants that generate power.

The guidelines prohibit once-through cooling and require that cooling towers be employed. In addition, all wastewaters (blowdown of the cooling tower and boilers, etc.) that are discharged to the local water bodies must be treated prior to discharge. The guidelines specifically state that no detectable amounts of zinc, chromium, phosphorus, or other corrosion inhibitors are to be discharged.

Cooling tower blowdown is usually one of the largest volume wastewater streams requiring treatment. Other waste streams include boiler blowdown; demineralized regeneration; wastewater treatment filter backwashes; cleaning wastes; floor, roof and yard drains; and sanitary wastes.

The two basic waste types are conservative and nonconservative. The nonconservative wastes include heat, oxidizable or otherwise, unstable chemicals, and biodegradable materials (sewage). The conservative wastes of concern can be divided into suspended solids, dissolved solids, and oils. An unacceptably high or low pH may also be considered a conservative waste problem.

The basic treatment technique for nonconservative wastes is retention to allow dissipation. Retention time can be reduced, or even eliminated as an important element, by employing facilities or processes to speed up the dissipation rate. Thus, cooling ponds represent retention devices to allow the dissipation of waste heat before discharge. While not necessarily their immediate purpose, cooling towers speed up the evaporative process, the major process involved in the heat dissipation. Retention time in a recirculating system is the major element involved in dissipating residual chlorine; here, reducing agents, such as sulfur dioxide or bisulfite, are sometimes employed to speed up the process.

Where biodegradable materials are involved, biological treatment is employed to oxidize materials to less objectionable or nonobjectionable forms. Treatment ponds, with or without aeration, may be employed, but typically the processes are speeded up by the use of sewage treatment plants. Oxidation products include water, carbon dioxide, and nitrates. Phosphates are also present in the effluents from treatment plants. Because nitrates and phosphates are objectionable where algal blooms are a problem, they are sometimes removed. In some cases, dissolved carbon dioxide is thought to be the critical element in causing algal blooms, but generally it is not considered an objectionable form. Reducing agents are sometimes employed to reduce nitrogen compounds to ammonia (rather than or after oxidizing) and to allow stripping (volatilizing) the ammonia.

With respect to conservative wastes, taken from simplest to most difficult to handle, oil is separated from water in oil separators, in which the oil floats to the top of a containment or series of containments for separation.

The pH of a wastewater stream is adjusted as required to meet effluent standards by the addition of a base (usually lime but sometimes sodium hydroxide) to raise pH or the addition of an acid (usually sulfuric acid) to lower pH. Where some individual waste streams have a high pH and some a low pH, they are frequently mixed in a neutralizing basin. This mixing tends to reduce or eliminate the need for neutralizing chemicals.

The most frequently used method for removing suspended solids is sedimentation. Here again, retention time in a quiescent settling basin or clarifier is the important element. Coagulants may be used to speed up and augment the process. Other means of removing suspended solids are filtering and centrifuging.

With respect to dissolved solids removal, where the objective is to meet standards for discharging to a receiving stream, techniques are employed to remove the specific contaminants of concern. Methods used include ion exchange and chemical reduction, pH adjustment, and precipitation in sedimentation ponds.

Dissolved solids problems (as well as other problems) in meeting effluent standards can be avoided by not discharging to a receiving stream. Wastewater can be used for irrigation or can be reduced to a sludge or solid for disposal as a solid waste. The two basic processes for reduction of the wastewater to a sludge or a solid are evaporative processes and reverse osmosis.

The following methods are considered by the writer to be the most cost-effective methods of reducing the environmental impact of cooling system discharges.

1. Utilizing corrosion-resistant materials in cooling system construction, thus reducing the requirements for corrosion inhibitors.
2. Providing settling ponds for blowdown before discharge, thus reducing the suspended solids concentration, precipitating some dissolved solids, dissipating nonconservative wastes, and producing an effluent that may be suitable for reuse.
3. Utilizing mechanical means to control microbiological growth, thus reducing the amount of chemical biocide required.
4. Operating cooling systems at high pH in conjunction with organic dispersants, thus reducing corrosivity and corrosion inhibitor requirements.
5. Operating cooling systems at higher cycles of concentration (requiring the control of suspended solids and scale-forming substances through makeup or sidestream treatment by sedimentation and/or softening), thus reducing the quantity of blowdown for final treatment and discharge.

LANDFILL

The conversion of refuse to energy generally reduces the volume of municipal solid wastes by a factor of 10, thus reducing the need for landfill sites. The bottom ash and fly ash recovered from boilers utilizing refuse as a fuel have been found to contain trace elements such as beryllium, mercury, cadmium, and lead. However, this impact on the local environment is minimal when disposed of in a properly designed and operated landfill site.

LOCAL AND IN-PLANT ENVIRONMENTAL IMPACTS

Odor Control

Associated with every facility that receives or processes raw municipal wastes is the potential for producing malodorous air.

Most facilities prevent the malodorous air from escaping to the ambient by keeping the facility at a negative pressure compared to the ambient and by venting the air through the boilers where the malodorous substances are incinerated. For facilities that do not have boilers, or where the quantity of air vented to boilers is insufficient to provide adequate ventilation, an odor control system will be required, especially during the warm summer months.

Decaying refuse produces the following malodorous compounds: aldehydes, amines, organic acids (acetic, butyric), organic sulfur, and organic nitrogen compounds. The threshold value for all of these substances is below 0.001 parts per million (ppm), except for acetic acid, which is about 0.5 ppm. Thus, a high efficiency odor control system will be necessary.

The two types of system in use are adsorption with activated carbon and absorption in a scrubber using potassium permanganate. The activated carbon approach has been shown to be more effective than scrubbing with permanganate. The cost of replacing or regenerating the carbon is cheaper than the cost of make-up potassium permanganate.

Carbon Monoxide Levels

A resource recovery facility processing 2,000 tons per day of raw refuse will receive approximately 250 refuse trucks per day. The number of trucks that may be operating in the tipping area at any one time can vary from 6 to 12. These trucks, especially if gas powered (gas powered produces 100 times more carbon monoxide than diesel trucks), can produce concentrations of carbon monoxide in excess of 50 ppm if sufficient ventilating air is not provided.

In addition, it is necessary to provide adequate fresh ventilating air, on the order of six to eight air changes per hour. The return air ducts should be located so that exhaust gases from the refuse vehicles are removed from the work area in the most efficient way possible.

Impact of Cooling Towers Fogging Potential

During the colder months, the operation of cooling towers has the potential for producing adverse environmental impacts, such as increased local fogging and icing of adjacent structures.

Under most meteorological and operating conditions, at least a small portion of the effluent is nearly always visible above a cooling tower. This is the result of cooling of the moist effluent air to a super-saturated state as it is forced from the tower before significant mixing can take place within the plume of the tower. These supersaturated conditions can result in a visible plume, or cloud, near the orifice of the tower.

When supersaturation leads to the formation of a cloud or cooling tower plume, the condensed water vapor takes the form of very small water droplets. Clouds and fog (which is simply a cloud on ground level) are composed of tiny droplets of water ranging from two to 50 micrometers in diameter. Thus, the operation of the cooling tower creates a visible plume with characteristics that are equivalent to an elevated fog or cloud. It is, therefore, necessary to perform a fogging potential analysis in the vicinity of the cooling towers.

Fogging potential is created when sufficient excess water vapor is added to existing moisture in ambient air near the ground to induce saturation or supersaturation and the formation of fog. A measure of the quantity or concentration of water vapor in dry air is defined as the mixing ratio. The ambient mixing ratio is a function of the dry-bulb temperature at a particular wet-bulb temperature. The saturation mixing ratio is when the wet-bulb temperature is equal to the dry-bulb temperature. At a given dry-bulb temperature, the saturation vapor deficit is the difference between the saturation mixing ratio and the ambient mixing ratio.

Fogging potential is defined in terms of saturation vapor deficit. Large saturation vapor deficits are typically observed during the warmer months of the year, as well as warmer hours of the day, and minimize the frequency of occurrence of fogging potential. Small saturation vapor deficits usually occur during the cooler months of the year, as well as during the evening or early morning hours of the day. In general, the fogging potential is greatest in the winter months during the daylight hours.

The fogging potential analysis is performed by computing plume rise and plume length and estimating the frequency of occurrence of fogging downwind of the towers. Ground-level concentrations of water droplets are computed for the combinations of atmospheric stability and wind speed observed in the region and combined with statistics on temperature-humidity occurrence to determine the frequency of occurrence of concentrations sufficient to cause saturation of the atmosphere at ground level.

Plume Downwash

The previous section described plume behavior and the fogging potential during light to moderate wind conditions. When stronger winds are present, aerodynamic downwash can contribute to short-term "localized fogging" in the immediate vicinity of the cooling towers. This structure-induced fogging phenomenon can cause short-term reductions in horizontal visibility in areas adjacent to the towers.

Depending on the wind and its persistence in relationship to the orientation of the cooling tower bank, the wind creates pressure forces around the tower, which act to draw the plume toward ground level, even at moderate wind velocities. This effect will be greatest when the windflow is at an oblique angle to the longitudinal axis of the cooling tower cell and least when the winds are parallel to the tower axis.

Icing Potential Analysis

During downwash conditions, the plume will descend to ground level and may intersect man-made structures (e.g., transmission lines and supports). At temperatures below freezing with small saturation deficits (high relative humidities), icing may result. However, visual observations in the vicinity of wet mechanical drift towers have indicated that for towers with properly designed drift eliminators the potential for icing is virtually eliminated.

Salt Drift Losses

During the normal operation of cooling towers, circulating water flows through the fill section. The impact of the falling water on the splash bars creates small water droplets, some of which are forced through the tower by the mechanically induced air stream. When these entrained droplets, called drift, leave the cooling tower, the exit velocity and buoyancy of the warm exit air provide the energy necessary to carry the drift particles aloft in the cooling tower plume. The downward force on the particles is the force of gravity; however, its effect on particle trajectory depends on the mass of the drift droplets.

Some of the drift droplets exiting the tower are small, and therefore, gravitational forces on them are negligible and atmospheric turbulence dominates their movement. Other larger droplets are initially affected by gravity. These droplets, in time, partially evaporate and their subsequent trajectories also become affected by atmospheric turbulence. Ambient temperature and moisture content determine the reduction of particle size due to evaporation, and the particle terminal velocity is a function of the particle size and the air viscosity.

As the cooling tower plume rises, disperses, and cools, the buoyancy in the plume is dissipated, evaporation of the droplets begins, and a separation takes place between the larger drift particles that will eventually deposit dissolved salts (salt drift) on the ground and the small particles that will remain suspended.

To determine the salt deposition rates and to predict the downwind suspended particulate concentration levels associated with cooling tower salt drift losses, a mathematical model is used. Data and information pertaining to the orientation and physical dimensions of the tower as well as the tower performance characteristics and proposed operating configuration

**Table 6. Measurements of Peak Noise Levels
Near Resource Recovery Plants.**

Vehicle Noise	Location	Noise Level
Refuse vehicle starting	at 25 feet	85 dB(A)
Refuse vehicles on level ground at constant speed	at 25 feet	80 dB(A)
Refuse vehicle on slope constant speed	at 25 feet	83 dB(A)
Four vehicles discharging in tipping area at the same time	at 50 feet outside	62 dB(A)
External Noise Level Measurements		
General plant noise	at 150 feet	57 dB(A)
	at 300 feet	52–54 dB(A)
	at 1,000 feet	45–46 dB(A)
Cooling tower (mechanical draft)	at 95 feet	69 dB(A)
	at 400 feet	60 dB(A)
	at 800 feet	54 dB(A)
Internal Noise Levels		
General plant noise	Inside metal recovery area	90–92 dB(A)
	Boiler room	78–82 dB(A)
Turbines	Inside turbine room	88 dB(A)
Vehicles tipping	Tipping area	88–91 dB(A)

are required as input to the model. Of specific interest are the drift rate and droplet mass-size distribution. In addition, it is necessary to provide input data on either the annual average or monthly average total dissolved solid concentrations in the circulating water as well as one year of either onsite or other local hourly average meteorological data.

Noise

A refuse disposal plant will produce noises from numerous sources within the plant and will be responsible for some external noise sources. Noise levels at the boundary of a site depend upon many factors including the back noise level, the degree of isolation of individual components of the plant, the degree to which the whole plant is enclosed, and the type of construction of the building. Typical measurements of peak noise levels near and in resource recovery plants are presented in Table 6.

If the facility is located where refuse delivery vehicles pass through residential areas or other sensitive areas of the community, it may be necessary to perform a noise monitoring program to determine the impact of refuse delivery on the community noise levels. The noise levels and traffic counts should be obtained at locations near the major traffic routes traveled by the refuse trucks at the plant boundary and in nearby populated areas. The noise survey should determine statistical and weighted sound pressure levels (L_{90}, L_{50}, L_{10}) for each of the selected monitoring locations.

The increase in noise levels due to the refuse delivery can be determined by comparing the noise levels measured with projected noise levels due to the increase of trucks. The projected traffic-related noise, can be calculated by procedures outlined in the National Cooperative Highway Research Program Reports 117 and 114.

2-10 Marketing Recovered Materials

Harvey W. Gershman
Source: *NCRR Bulletin,* Vol. V, No. 4 (Fall 1975) pp. 74-83. Reprinted with Permission of National Center for Resource Recovery.

Resource recovery technology is steadily advancing the ease and efficiency with which materials may be reclaimed from municipal solid waste for sale and reuse. But there is little to be gained from building a resource recovery facility if the recovered materials cannot be sold. Therefore, it is mandatory that a municipality have reasonable assurances that markets for the materials exist before investing large amounts of capital in the building and/or operation of a recovery facility.

Municipalities generally are accustomed to buying, but not to selling; therefore, some simple guidelines to marketing are in order. This article considers the marketing of several materials recoverable from municipal solid waste; steel, paper, glass, aluminum and other non-ferrous metals. Of course, the key to the above statement is the definition of the word *reasonable.* As will be pointed out, vague promises certainly do not fit the definition. However, indefinite, spot-market-priced, iron-clad, "no out" agreements are equally unrealistic and to insist on them is a way to virtually ensure that substantive planning for a recovery facility will flounder.

MARKETS FIRST

The cost of recovering materials from municipal solid waste can be covered by revenue from two sources: (1) sale of recovered by-products, and (2) fees charged for tipping, or dumping. The latter is often a user service charge or a line item in the municipal budget. Management prudence and public demand seek to keep the tipping fee minimal and, if possible, unchanging over several years of operation. This fee can be approximated over the first few years of a resource recovery facility operation only to the extent that the sales revenue from recovered products can also be estimated for the same period. The financial forecasts of a facility are based, therefore, on market commitments for the sale of recovered products taken in conjunction with the capital and operating costs, with the dumping fee required being simply the amount necessary to ensure economic viability. Market assurances are indeed a first step in planning because the customers' specifications for the recovered products dictate what array of recovery processes are to be used and how they are to be operated to meet these specifications. The necessary steps in locating potential customers and concluding market commitments for the first several years of plant operation in advance of plant design have been accomplished in several cities around the country. This "marketing from a developmental approach" may be performed by a municipality, its consultant or a potential contractor.

In the general area of marketing recovered products, two basic approaches have evolved. The first relies on systems bidders to secure their own market agreements, and to offer the strength of their markets as a facet of their bids to build, own and/or operate a proposed facility. The second attempts to secure these commitments in advance of a system procurement. In the latter case, the developmental marketing is effected directly by the public sector or by consultants, with the markets being assigned to the systems winner if he is to operate the facility or simply used by the public sector if the facility is operated by a municipal, regional or state government or authority.

The Objective of the Advance Marketing

Regardless of who performs the marketing, a few essential steps must be followed if a sale is to be concluded for products recovered from solid waste. The marketing approach developed here is directed at obtaining binding letters of intent written with the objectives of eliminating — or greatly reducing — the risk of not selling the plant output, and of establishing a realistic forecast of sales income prior to budget authorizations, or at the very least, prior to plant construction. In this way, a degree of financial assurance for the public sector is obtained.

MARKETING AND SALES STRATEGIES

Sellers' and Buyers' Assurances

The poor reputation of materials recovered from waste stems from past experiences; in general, sufficient material of the required quality was not produced and delivered on schedule. To overcome this, the potential operator of a resource recovery plant must be prepared to make certain assurances prior to marketing. Potential customers must be assured of product quality, quantity and delivery as they are for any other raw material. The burden in this regard is clearly on the prospective producer.

The quality of the recovered product (its specifications) must assure utility in current manufacturing processes. Certainly, at the outset, an existing industry, accustomed to operating on particular raw materials, cannot be expected to alter in major ways its processes to accommodate a recovered material merely because it supports the desirable goal of increased resource recovery. Assured quality means that the resource recovery plant must be prepared to establish quality control, testing and measurement programs. Sale "to a specification" also means that failure to meet the specification will result in downgrading the material quality and price or, worse, rejection of shipments. Finally, sellers must be prepared to assure the quantity delivered over a period of time. Such contractual delivery schedules are commonplace and necessary. A plant manager must be assured that his raw material will arrive on schedule so that production can continue.

While these assurances may seem unduly restrictive, they are normal procedures in any production or raw material supply industry. As a production activity, resource recovery may be foreign to municipalities more accustomed to service functions. If, therefore, a municipality is unprepared to offer the necessary product assurances, this is one reason it should seriously consider delegating the resource recovery marketing and production to the private sector.

Sales Strategies

Before a municipal planning group embarks on a market survey for the use of recovered materials, the following six factors should be clearly understood:

Don't Try to Sell Garbage. You cannot give garbage away, let alone sell it. Products must be recovered clean and to a specification. Recovery by itself is not a reason for sale and appropriate recovery processes will have to be chosen to meet specifications. Of course, one has to be concerned about the types of testing employed to determine whether recovered materials meet specifications. It would be well to establish the tests as soon as possible in the marketing process.

Utility in Current Processes. Markets for recovered material will be more easily established when the material is to be used in an existing process than when it is for use in a product or process designed specifically for that recovered material. Also the demand for the product will be broader the more analogous it is to a current secondary material rather than a unique process which may in itself have only a narrow market.

Meet Local Markets. There are two reasons for this. First, the obvious one of reducing freight costs and second, the too often overlooked one, that a seller must offer customer services. There has to be contact between buyer and seller, and this is best done when transportation and communications distances are minimal. For example, one avoids long distance calls, personal travel and lost freight shipments. Combined, these are worth a consideration of discounting gross selling price when compared to what a more distant market may be offering.

Don't Overoptimize Recovery Processes. There is a natural tendency — especially by municipalities in the face of public pressure — to attempt to maximize revenues rather than return on an investment or other measure of investment success. Maximization of revenues means recovery followed by upgrading or conversion to a higher gross value product. There seems little sense in adding processing steps to the recovery plant if these can be or are being done by a scrap processor or other existing industry. Generally, there is a greater amount of material to be processed at these facilities which leads to more economical use of capital equipment. Of course, for some of the recovered products — such as glass — this option may not be available to the first group of recovery facilities.

Beware Price Optimism. There are several published listings of prices paid for secondary metal and paper materials. The prices refer to standard grades of secondary materials, not necessarily to products recovered in a resource recovery plant. Hence, do not expect to receive these prices. For example, the price paid for can scrap may be tied to No. 2 steel scrap bundles, but old cans are clearly not No. 2 bundles and may be worth less. Aluminum recovered from municipal solid waste is not the same as the standard scrap grade of "smelters' old sheet." Also, the quoted prices are for the "spot" market. Clearly, a *quid pro quo* for a long-term commitment is an exchange price at some discount from the spot prices. To "play" the spot market is to risk having large inventories.

Beware Market Penetration Costs. Some planners, perhaps in an attempt to maximize gross revenues, have considered adding product manufacturing facilities to the resource recovery plant, such as a wallboard plant utilizing recovered paper or a cinderblock plant utilizing recovered glass. Consider the cost, though, of also having to add a sales force, a distribution system and an advertising budget to sell a new, untried, unknown product. And consider the effect when the competitor's salesman tells a customer, "It's made from garbage." Overcoming the new product's lack of acceptance is a "market penetration cost" and may present an obstacle to the economic success of a recovery venture.

THE MARKET SURVEY

In planning resource recovery facilities, two types of market surveys are often conducted. The more usual and uncritical market survey is to locate everyone within a certain radius who uses steel, paper, glass, etc. The second is the start of the "developmental approach" recommended here. It is based on a combination of general familiarity with local industry, the ability of known resource recovery processes to produce materials to somewhat simple specifications and the marketing and sales strategies discussed above. Combining all of these, there are certain likely local markets for each material to be recovered. Matching these to local conditions, combined with negotiation of advance commitments, constitutes the "market survey."

In the developmental approach to marketing, the limited local survey is followed by obtaining Letters of Intent (LoI) for the purchase of materials likely to be recovered. These are intended to obtain an assured financial forecast for a proposed facility and one LoI per material can be sufficient. One signed LoI is worth a great many "maybes." This is a key element in this approach.

The prospective markets for the several materials recoverable from municipal solid waste are listed in Table 1. These listings offer a starting point in identifying which local or nearby businesses to contact. The trade-offs of selling products to dealers and scrap processors as opposed to primary producers — in price, terms and required product quality — will be discussed separately.

The Specification

After locating the prospective markets, the next step is to approach the potential buyer, remembering your plant is not built and there are no samples to show. With these limitations, a strong and binding advance commitment to purchase is sought. At this point, a specification — not a product — is being sold.

The specification is a designation of particulars of form and/or composition as the basis for acceptance or rejection, for sale or use, to be agreed upon by buyer and seller.

Chances are the prospective buyer is unfamiliar with specifications for products recovered

Table 1. Prospective Markets for Recovered Materials.

Material	Market and Use	Remarks
Old newspapers	De-inking for new news; as-is for chipboard	Most old news sold through dealers. Some can be sold directly to de-inking plants.
Separated corrugated	New corrugated, kraft paper or linerboard	To dealers or mill. Few mills in urban areas, hence function of dealer.
Old cans	Detinning Blast furnace (New iron) sell direct or to Steel mills scrap processor Foundry (Not yet commonplace) Ferroalloy Copper mines (Best through dealer)	Few detinning plants. New ones can be built locally if quantity sufficient. Ferroalloy industry only in few areas.
Other steel scrap	Scrap processor	Material a complex mixture of alloys and types. Need a scrap processor.
Aluminum cans	New can stock − to primary producers Secondary uses − to primary producers and dealers	Sold F.O.B. recovery plant.
Miscellaneous aluminum	Secondary uses	Salable to dealers and producers.
Mixed other non-ferrous metals	Scrap processors	Mixture must be processed.
Glass cullet	Glass container manufacturers	Must be ultra-clean. Better market if color sorted.
Glass sands	Brickyards − for use as a flux	Market not yet established. Great interest shown based on preliminary experience.

from refuse, although he has specifications for current virgin and secondary materials. It is the responsibility of the prospective seller to familiarize the buyer with available specifications for recovered materials as a starting point for negotiations. Table 2 lists sources of such specifications. Within the present state-of-the-art, the specifications offered in these articles can serve as the starting point for negotiations. Reasonable changes can be made, of course, to meet the particular needs of the buyer; for example, requiring the recovered material to be baled to a certain size and density.

At the same time, one constantly should be aware that there is a natural tendency on the part of the buyer to seek changes in a specification to bring the refuse-based secondary product closer in form and composition to the commonplace raw material or known secondary material. There are dangers that such changes may unreasonably add capital and operating costs to the recovery plant and may impose restrictions beyond the control of the operator of the plant. An example

of the latter is prohibiting all plastics and other nonmetallics in scrap cans. This is not within the control of the operator because some plastic materials are normally used in can construction.

Role of the Scrap Processor

The scrap processor (or paper dealer) generally buys to a lower specification and at a lower price than the eventual user of the secondary product. Matched against this potential for profit are two valuable services performed by the processor. One is the ability to spread the recovered material into several markets and/or to several customers within a market. This helps to balance economic demands and consequent price changes over a long period. The second service is upgrading low-value scrap; i.e., processing mixed paper or dirty cans to grades suitable for remanufacture, or processing old appliances or automobiles into salable commodities.

In return for these services, the scrap processor receives a fee, which results in a lower gross

Table 2. Sources of Specifications for Recovered Materials.

All materials	Glass
ASTM Committee E-38, Resource Recovery American Society for Testing & Materials 1916 Race St. Philadelphia, Pa. 19103 EPA Report 670/2-75-034, "Specifications for Materials Recovered from Municipal Refuse," H. Alter and W.R. Reeves, 1975	Glass Container Manufacturers Institute 1800 K St., N.W. Washington, D.C. 20006 **Non-ferrous metals** National Association of Recycling Industries, Inc. 330 Madison Ave. New York, N.Y. 10017
Steel American Iron and Steel Institute 1000 16th St., N.W. Washington, D.C. 20036	**Aluminum** The Aluminum Association 750 Third Ave. New York, N.Y. 10017
Paper American Paper Institute 260 Madison Ave. New York, N.Y. 10016 Paper Stock Institute of America 330 Madison Ave. New York, N.Y. 10017	National Association of Recycling Industries, Inc. 330 Madison Ave. New York, N.Y. 10017 Aluminum Recycling Association 1775 K St., N.W., Suite 215 Washington, D.C. 20006

price paid for the scrap to the resource recovery plant as compared to what may be paid by a paper mill, steel mill or another primary producer. However, the reduced purchase price must be evaluated by the municipal planner in light of the value of the services and the consequent reduced investment in resource recovery facilities and operation.

Until recently, and with rare exception, scrap processors and dealers have been unable (or unwilling) to offer municipalities or prospective recovery plant owners/operators certain terms in the advance commitments to purchase the recovered materials. These are the critical terms dealing with length of the commitment and guarantees of floor price. The reason is simple: scrap processors often do not have the financial resources of the primary materials producers, hence they cannot as easily offer the same type of binding Letters of Intent. Recently, however, there have been several cases of scrap processors offering assurances in these areas. This is an important breakthrough.

THE LETTER OF INTENT

The Letter of Intent is the instrument negotiated between the resource recovery planner and the potential purchaser of recovered materials. The LoI is the culmination of the market survey. It is the financial underpinning to the resource recovery plant, and the precursor to the buyers' purchase order.

Often in the past, planners were willing to accept weak and noncommittal expressions of interest offered by unsure, unconvinced or uninterested buyers. Some of these letters and telegrams are classic examples of committing nothing but adding large loopholes. The following texts of two typical, although hypothetical, letters illustrate the point:

"Per our telephone conversation, it is my understanding that your city will produce approximately 30,000 tons per year of incinerated ferrous metallics from its solid waste recovery system.

"Our corporation could accept 30,000 tons per year of incinerated ferrous metallics. The value of this material will depend on its chemical composition, density, and the market for scrap at the time of purchase. If and when this material is available, we will consider, assuming no changes in market conditions, the purchase of this material at competitive scrap prices in accordance with its metallurgical value. Response to this request

is not to be considered as a purchase order or a firm commitment on our part to make future purchases. It is simply an expression of the fact that markets do exist for this recycled material in the steel industry."

"While this is not to be construed as a commitment to buy, should the glass recovered in the production facility now being designed be as good for our purposes as that from the sample we referred to in our previous letter, we estimate that we would be interested in considering purchases of 8,000 to 12,000 tons per year at $13 per ton f.o.b. our plant.

"We wish to emphasize that color variation, etc., due to season and geographic origin affecting potential utility to us cannot be assessed in advance. A period of a year or longer of production trials prior to firm commitments to buy would, in our opinion, be mandatory even though the aforementioned tests are encouraging."

Obviously, such commitments are worthless; they cannot assure that the output of the resource recovery plant will be sold. Moreover, there are cases where properly binding commitments have been negotiated. Some aspects which must be considered in negotiating such advance commitments are given below.

Terms and Conditions

The fundamental terms and conditions of an advance commitment to be included in the LoI are *length of commitment, quantity of material, quality, delivery schedule, termination* and *price* (which will be discussed separately). The LoI may be worded as an intent to issue a purchase order to the resource recovery plant subject to the terms and conditions set forth in the advance commitment.

The *length of commitment* should be long enough to allow the recovery operation to start and gain momentum. For most materials it is unreasonable to expect the advance commitment to be for the full financing term, which is likely to be 10 or more years, unless the operator is prepared to accept a rather high discount on the selling price over the term. Because of the length of time needed to plan and construct a recovery plant, even a five operating year LoI may translate to eight or nine calendar years.

The LoI has to specify the quantity of material to be sold. The quantity, of course, cannot exceed the estimated amount of the material in the waste multiplied by the quantity of waste committed to the resource recovery plant multiplied by the estimated recovery efficiency. Because of the uncertainty as to the combined productivity of the process, the quantity of recovered material to be delivered may be expressed as a range for the first year, subject to adjustment within this range after the first operating year.

The *quality* of the material to be delivered is delineated by a specification which becomes part of the LoI. Furthermore, the LoI should address who will be responsible for the accompanying test and quality control program as well as the bases for rejection or downgrading.

Also, operators of facilities must guarantee *delivery* of a specified quantity and time schedule if they are to service the customers (buyers). The operator may not divert deliveries to "spot" markets, even at higher prices, except as this may be provided for in the Letter. This is discussed in more detail below.

The delivery schedule is based on quantity per day, week or month and method of delivery, stating form of transportation and minimum shipments. This is essential information for planning the storage facilities, shipping dock and railroad siding or truck unloading facilities at the user's plant.

Termination clauses must be fair. Obviously, the seller cannot expect the customer to continue if the plant closes. The buyer cannot reasonably terminate if the product is merely suspected of interfering with some operation or quality point. This is particularly true in the case of refuse-derived fuel. *Force majeure* should be given its usual narrow interpretation and should not be expanded to cover such types of risks as equipment failure.

There is another aspect of termination to consider. The contract price agreed upon in the LoI may be exceeded at times by the spot market price for that form of scrap. (This was particularly true during 1973.) There will be a natural temptation for the seller to want to take advantage of such situations, but doing so will deny the buyer assured quantities of material. A fair compromise which has been arrived at in some instances is that the LoI permits the seller to seek a higher price on an annual basis during years two through five, with the original buyer having the right to match that price and so continue as the buyer. If the seller deals with another buyer, it must be for a reasonable length of time (say a minimum of one year). In return for guarding the original buyer against the seller playing the spot market and so disrupting deliveries, the original buyer agrees to take back the seller, at the original terms, should there be a one or more year absence with another buyer. Obviously, this is very much a give-and-take arrangement to permit the seller to shop for a higher price while still protecting the original buyer in return for his other guarantees.

An important point about LoI's is that because some of the recovered material to be sold will substitute for, or be in addition to, standard scrap grades, the LoI means that the recovery plant is first in line to purchase as the buyer's scrap needs may be diminished — not last, as is often the case with new sources of supply.

Pricing Arrangements

There are several ways the exchange price — *i.e.,* the price paid for the recovered material — can be established and expressed in the LoI. If the price is not fixed throughout the term of the LoI, every effort should be made to obtain a floor price in addition to the exchange price relationship. The floor price is an essential element in the financial forecast so necessary to justify capital outlays in both private and public sectors.

When the price is fixed in the terms of the contract, it is obviously the floor price.

Alternatively, prices for some recovered products, steel and paper in particular, may be tied to scrap quotes. For example, scrap cans may be purchased for some percentage of a No. 1 or No. 2 scrap bundle price as quoted in a standard periodical for the steel scrap industry (Scrap quotes are for particular markets around the country).

A third pricing arrangement pegs the price the buyer pays to what is paid for a like grade to another supplier. This is a useful arrangement at times when the buyer has no historical pattern related to a commodity quote and/or the recovered product is a small amount of total raw material

purchased. This type of arrangement has been used for old newsprint when the purchasing mill and its largest supplier were not in an area covered by one of the standard quoting services. Presumably, it is the basis for determining market prices for glass cullet where the price paid for the cullet is determined by the cost of equivalent raw material (predominantly sand and ash).

A classic bargaining issue is whether to trade some of the upside benefits for a lessening of the potential downside risk — or vice versa. For example, the seller may have to choose between accepting a price of No. 2 bundles but a $10 per ton floor price or a fraction of No. 2 bundles (say 65 percent) with a $20 per ton floor price. The choice is judgmental but highly influenced by the need, in most planning and financial justification processes, to minimize downside risk. In the latter pricing arrangement, the argument is that the buyer is entitled to the 35 percent (or other) discount in exchange for offering a reasonably high guaranteed floor price. The floor price helps to control downside risk in terms of the producer. During times of high prices, therefore, the buyer benefits with a lower priced source of materials; during times of low prices, the seller benefits by having a guaranteed buyer even though the buyer may be suffering a loss.

These are suggested pricing mechanisms. All are subject to negotiation and all may benefit from an incentive discount when negotiations bog down. (An incentive discount might be, "Sign now — I'll drop the price $1/ton.")

Some of the standard periodicals which publish scrap quotations are listed in Table 3.

Private vs. Public Ownership

The discussion of terms, conditions and pricing is generally applicable whether the resource recovery facility is to be privately or publicly owned. An exception is that if privately owned, the potential owners have the right to negotiate their own arrangements and prices independent of any consideration other than the final price bid or charged to the municipality.

If the resource recovery plant is to be publicly owned, the dicta of fairness and open government generally require that all responsible and responsive bidders have an opportunity to bid for

Table 3. Published Scrap Quotations.

American Metals Market (ferrous and non-ferrous
    metals)
7 East 12th St.
New York, N.Y. 10003

Iron Age (Ferrous and non-ferrous metals)
Chilton Co.
Chilton Way
Radnor, Pa. 19089

Official Board Markets (Paper and paperboard
    products)
Magazines for Industry, Inc.
20 North Wacker Dr.
Chicago, Ill. 60606

Secondary Raw Materials (all secondary materials)
Market News Publishing Corp.
156 Fifth Ave.
New York, N.Y. 10010

the recovered material. The challenge, then, is how to secure the LoI as an advance commitment while still preserving public bidding rights. An innovative solution used recently by several agencies is a Letter of Intent to Bid (as distinguished from a Letter of Intent to Buy). A sample LoI to Bid accompanies this article.

In signing an LoI to Bid, the potential purchaser agrees in essence to submit a response to an invitation to bid for the purchase of recovered material at some time in the future. The LoI to Bid covers all of the necessary terms and conditions and the price structure. The potential bidder further agrees that the bid will not be less than a stated price. Generally, the floor price is specified in the request and the exchange price, or exchange price relationship, is the competitive aspect of the response. These prices can then be used for financial planning, just as with an LoI to Buy. Of course, they probably will be lower since it is clearly only a first round in the procurement for the products. The bidder may increase this price when responding to the final invitation to bid and the actual rights to the product are at stake.

There are two cautions in dealing with an LoI to Bid. One is that prior to final bid opening, an attempt should be made to keep the exact prices in the LoI's confidential because knowledge of any one firm's price could be used to advantage by a competitor. This confidentiality may be arranged through a consultant or other trustworthy third party. The second caution is that the legality of this approach has not been tested. However, it seems reasonable, fair and open, and, hence, at least within the spirit of public bid laws.

Cancelling the LoI

Municipal planning for resource recovery is a lengthy process, taking three years or longer in many communities. Even after this length of time, resource recovery is not always implemented. It is not fair to ask a potential buyer to maintain a commitment this long unless there is some reasonable chance that the plan will be implemented. A potential buyer's commitment is his plan to use a certain amount of recovered material, generally at the exclusion of making other commitments elsewhere.

A fair approach is to have a statement in the LoI (whether to Bid or Buy) terminating the commitment unless the municipality has demonstrated substantial progress toward implementation by a certain date, subject to renewal. Substantial progress may be completion of a planning document, issuance of a request for proposals, or similar event. Also the commitment may be nonexclusive but be based on which of several communities receiving commitments from a buyer finalizes its arrangements first.

WHO DOES THE MARKETING

Obtaining advance commitments for the purchase of recovered materials is the single most important step in resource recovery planning. The commitments provide some of the advance financial assurances municipal managers seek and the specifications accompanying the commitments determine major aspects of the type of plant to be built. Clearly, however, the advance commitments are not iron-clad. There is still some risk on the markets side. This is a fact of life unavoidably associated at this time with any venture of this sort.

The various steps leading to obtaining a set of Letters of Intent to Bid or Buy have to be done by technically knowledgeable and skillful negotiators. The process takes time, and it is unlikely that the municipal managers competent to conduct it have that time. The marketing, to be done properly, in all likelihood will have to be delegated by the municipality to someone else. This may be done in several ways.

The municipality may engage a consultant to conduct the marketing process and provide LoI to Bid. The municipality then completes the bid process and the price relationship and specifications of the winners are integrated into the planning/implementation process. This can be done whether the intent is for public or private ownership and operation.

Potential bidders of a resource recovery plant may provide LoI's in their bids. The municipality must delineate the minimum terms and conditions acceptable and possibly even provide the form of the LoI, or the bids will not be comparable. This arrangement more readily allows use of proprietary recovery processes than the former.

Finally, under plans for a privately owned resource recovery facility, the municipality may merely require bidders to provide a LoI to Buy, according to minimum terms and conditions, as part of the evidence of ability to perform. An alternative to the LoI here is self-insuring the market for some products, which can be done by some of the larger conglomerate companies.

Passing the burden of market attainment to the private sector has an intuitive appeal in that the municipality need only be concerned with the result of a well-constructed LoI and the net tipping fee and not the many steps in between. The private operator can be held to meeting product specifications; hence, he must produce a salable product, and the municipality is largely relieved of the risk of whether the "black boxes" really work. However, some cautions are in order. This approach goes hand in hand with a serious request for proposals to build and operate a facility.

Preparing a satisfactory request for proposals is not an inexpensive undertaking; considerable time and resources are required. Likewise, from the private sector's standpoint, preparing the response involves much more than just the market-ing effort. Therefore, unless there is a rather strong level of commitment from the public side, it is not likely that respondents will make a maximum effort in preparing their proposals and obtaining market assurances. This commitment generally means assurances that the community has the money to build a facility or has completed − or at least begun − the legislative processes necessary to pay a reasonable tipping fee. However, before this can be made to happen in most communities, the market work and the preliminary feasibility analysis must be completed. The reader will note that he has come full circle. While the transfer of responsibility for markets or for simply fixing the price as a method of establishing who bears the risk of failure is attractive in concept, it has not worked well in practice. This should be kept in mind when the decision as to "who does the marketing" is being made.

CONCLUSION

In summary, economic and market analysts have long attempted to predict the fluctuations of the secondary materials markets with limited success. Trends can be identified but, if nothing else, commodity price histories clearly illustrate the "up and down" nature of the secondary materials industry. These markets are well known to reflect the marginal supply and demand situation.

Properly worded Letters of Intent can avoid many of the difficulties associated with the fluctuation of secondary materials pricing.

The LoI represents a simple, easily understood arrangement and is particularly attuned to the public scrutiny that an investment in or commitment to resource recovery is bound to attract in a community. This not to say that the public is likely to take a negative position. On the contrary, interest undoubtedly will be positive and will be reinforced by carefully described, procedurally correct arrangements which demonstrate the potential for a financially sound project.

ADVANCE LETTER OF INTENT TO BID FOR THE PURCHASE OF RECOVERED PRODUCTS

This sample "Letter of Intent to Bid" is taken from: **Technical Manual for the Pennsylvania Solid Waste-Resource Recovery Development Act, 1975** *(Commonwealth of Pennsylvania, Department of Environmental Resources), a publication prepared by the National Center for Resource Recovery for Pennsylvania's Department of Environmental Resources.*

WHEREAS, the _____ Corporation (hereinafter called the CORPORATION) endorses resource recovery from municipal solid waste as a means toward a cleaner environment and preservation of natural resources, and

WHEREAS, the CORPORATION recognizes the need to develop firm expressions of intent to purchase materials or energy products recovered from waste within known financial parameters as part of the planning process for a new endeavor such as this, and

WHEREAS, _____ (hereinafter called the DEVELOPMENT AGENCY), is evaluating the prospects of substituting resource recovery for its traditional means of solid waste disposal, and

WHEREAS, the DEVELOPMENT AGENCY recognizes the need to establish financial underpinnings for the determination of the economic feasibility of processing up to _____ tons per day of municipal solid waste to produce up to _____ tons per day of _____ (hereinafter known as the PRODUCT) in a form usable and acceptable to the CORPORATION according to the Specifications attached to this *Agreement* and made part hereof,

THEREFORE, in consideration of the fact that the legal authority to sell recovered products may rest upon a requirement to advertise for the purchase of such products, it is mutually agreed between the CORPORATION and the DEVELOPMENT AGENCY that:

I. The CORPORATION, as an expression of its support of the municipal solid waste recovery program, agrees to:

(1) Offer herein a firm commitment to bid for the purchase of the recovered PRODUCT at prices not less than those entered here should the DEVELOPMENT AGENCY be required or decide to effect a competitive procurement, and

(2) Agrees that if public bidding is not necessary and not the course chosen by the DEVELOPMENT AGENCY then the conditions of this Letter of Intent may be considered as a bona fide offer to purchase the recovered product at prices not less than those entered here.

(3) Respond should a bid be required with a bona fide offer to purchase which will include the following:

(a) It will be a firm bid for five (5) years offering an Exchange Price either fixed or related to a commodity quote, and if the Exchange Price is not fixed, it will offer a Floor Price below which the Exchange Price will not fall during the term of the contract.

(b-1) If the Exchange Price to be paid by the CORPORATION is to be fixed dollar amount per unit of product, f.o.b. the recovery facility (or the CORPORATION'S plant - choose one), the bid shall not be less than_____per ton.

OR

(b-2) If the Exchange Price is to be based on a commodity quote, the monthly Exchange Price shall relate to the quotation at the close of that month for_____(the same or the appropriate analogous commodity and location) as published in the last issue of the month of_____ (fill in source of quote) using the (midrange or highside, or lowside—choose one) of the quote, f.o.b. the recovery facility (or the CORPORATION'S plant - choose one). If the Exchange Price is to be bid in terms of a percentage of the quoted price, the Exchange Price shall not be bid at less than _____ percentage of appropriate quote as defined above. (Fill in percentage)

(c) If the Exchange Price is not fixed, a Floor Price will be bid which will not be below $_____ per ton f.o.b. (fill in dollar amount) the recovery facility (or CORPORATION'S plant — choose one).

(d) The CORPORATION shall retain the right to reject any material delivered which does not meet Specifications. Such rejection will be at the expense of the resource recovery plant.

(e) The bid will be subject to *force majeure*.

(f) It will be noted the Additional Conditions of the CORPORATION covering general terms and conditions of purchase, acceptance, delivery, arbitration, weights, and downgrading not explicitly covered in this Letter of Intent or by reference, will be negotiated according to good business practices and include such Additional Conditions as are attached to this *Agreement* and made a part hereof.

(g) This Advance Letter of Intent to bid is null and void if during the period between its execution and the actual bid or negotiated contract the CORPORATION'S plant ceases operation or ceases use of this or equivalent grade of recovered PRODUCT. The JURISDICTION shall further recognize that a clause similar to this shall be incorporated in the actual bid when made or contract when signed.

(h) This Advance Letter of Intent may be assigned by the DEVELOPMENT AGENCY.

II. The DEVELOPMENT AGENCY agrees:

(1) To see that the recovery plant establishes specification assurance procedures for the recovered PRODUCT, using good industrial quality control practiced in recognition of the CORPORATION'S use technology as practiced in their_____ plant, so as to produce and offer the recovered PRODUCT for sale in a form and to the required Specification, usable in the plant with minimum alterations to present processing technology and business practices, and

(2) To require, should a contract be effected as a result of the Advance Letter of Intent, that the PRODUCT be delivered to the CORPORATION according to conditions and prices determined herein and not diverted to the spot market which may on occasion be higher than the Exchange Price determined by the pricing relationship set forth here or as modified by the contract.

(3) That should the CORPORATION'S plant, as specified herein, become saturated in its ability to handle the recovered PRODUCT as a result of other Letters of Intent issued by the CORPORATION being converted into firm contracts for delivery and purchase prior to effecting such arrangements as a result of this commitment, the provisions of this Advance Letter of Intent become null and void.

The CORPORATION will communicate to the DEVELOPMENT AGENCY that information about its use technology and business practices which the CORPORATION at its sole discretion shall consider necessary so as to assure receipt of the recovered material in form and cleanliness necessary for use by the CORPORATION. Such communication shall be on a nonconfidential basis, unless otherwise subject to a subsequent confidentiality agreement.

This Advance Letter of Intent shall become null and void on_____ unless effected into a contractual relationship or mutually extended by both the CORPORATION and DEVELOPMENT AGENCY.

Witnessed by:

_____

Witnessed by:

_____

DEVELOPMENT AGENCY

By:_____

CORPORATION

By:_____

2-11 How to Buy Resource Recovery

Stephen G. Lewis

Source: *American City & Country,* Vol. 90, (September 1975) pp. 91–93. Reprinted with Permission of Morgan-Grampian Publishing Company.

Planning and implementing a multimillion dollar refuse processing system contractually committed to operation for a period of over 20 years is serious business. Resource recovery systems are new, basically untried, inherently risky, and complicated.

Once the market for recovered materials or energy has been established, certain key decisions must be made. Early in the planning process, determine:

- Who will own the facility: the state, county, city, a public authority, or private industry?
- Who will actually operate the facility?
- What system, services, facilities, equipment or materials are to be purchased as a package?
- What procurement method will be used?

The basic decision to be made is whether the system will be owned publicly or privately. If it is to be owned publicly, then a second decision is whether it will be operated with government employees or under contract with a private firm.

Frequently, government ownership and operation is tried as a matter of tradition and policy, but there are important reasons why that may be inappropriate when dealing with resource recovery. The project, for example, may require flexible personnel or financial practices or special marketing skills. Thus, private ownership and operation may be important to consider. The ownership and operation decision can also be affected by unique features of the project.

The government unit itself may be the primary customer, such as a municipal power plant, for the energy product produced. In such a case, it may be institutionally simpler to choose government ownership. In some situations, it may not be possible to finance the system with public funds. Thus, private financing (and private ownership and operation) may become necessary. When the resource recovery process to be used is too risky or proprietary, private ownership and operation should also be considered.

There are two basic methods of procurement generally used by state and local governments. These are formal advertising and negotiated procurement. Formal advertising is always a competitive bid procedure. Negotiated procurement can either be competitive or sole source.

When the options for ownership, operation and implementation are combined with the two methods of procurement, five approaches for acquisition of resource recovery systems can be defined. They can be identified as:

- Conventional.
- Turnkey.
- Full service.
- Full service with government ownership.
- Modified full service.

No matter what procurement approach is used, it is important that it be tailored for a community's particular situation.

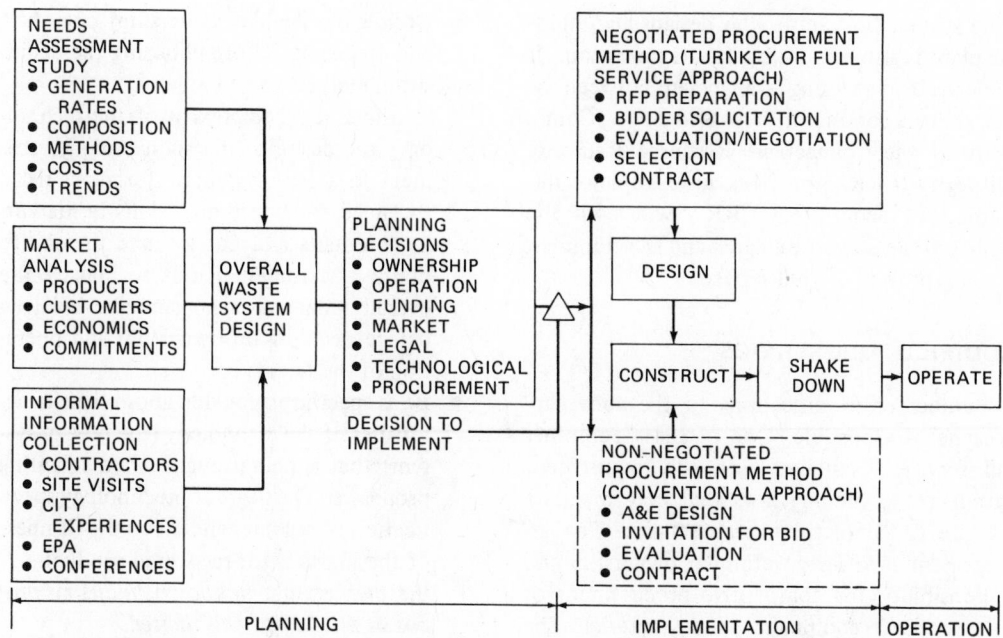

Comprehensive planning forms a strong foundation for effective implementation and operation.

CONVENTIONAL APPROACH

Traditionally the conventional approach is used by cities to procure public buildings, incinerators and wastewater treatment plants. It is almost always accompanied by government ownership and operation of the facility. Although it gives the city full control of the project, it also places the responsibility for system implementation, including initial process performance, on the city. It is often used where there is a firmly committed government market, such as in Ames, Iowa, where the fuel fraction of the city refuse will be used in a municipal power boiler, or where there is a proven process technology, such as in Akron, Ohio, where waterwall incineration will be used to produce enough steam for heating the downtown business area.

TURNKEY OR DESIGN/BUILD

When a system contractor is hired to design and implement the resource recovery system in one package, that is using the turnkey approach. It is always accompanied by city ownership and operation where the city does not want to have the responsibility for system implementation.

In addition to assigning sole responsibility for the project to a single party, turnkey provides the city with some assurance regarding initial process performance — if the plant does not operate as specified, the city does not have to accept it. An example of this type of approach is found in Baltimore, Md., where Monsanto Enviro-Chem Systems, Inc. has designed and constructed a 1000-tpd pyrolysis plant.

A third acquisition approach commonly used is called full service. It adds the elements of private ownership and operation to the turnkey method. The systems contractor has full responsibility for financing, design, implementation, continued operation and ownership. The full service contractor is offering the city a service instead of a facility, and will usually charge the city a disposal fee for delivered solid waste. Hempstead, N.Y., is an example of this approach with Black Clawson Co. providing the full service.

ADD GOVERNMENT OWNERSHIP

A fourth approach is a variation of the full service approach where the facility is owned by the government rather than private industry. The advantage over the turnkey approach is that the same system contractor who designs and builds the plant is also responsible for its operation. It lends itself to a leasing arrangement between the city and the contractor. The Bridgeport, Conn., plant of the Connecticut Resource Recovery Authority (CRRA) provides an example of this method of acquisition. CRRA will own the facility while Garrett Research and Development Co. will provide the full service.

MODIFIED FULL SERVICE

A number of modifications to the above approaches are possible. One of these combines full service advantages with the requirement to adhere to bidding laws that may mandate the use of competitive procurement. The arrangement involves government ownership and responsibility for competitive procurement of construction, equipment and material. The private responsibilities include design, supervision of construction, shakedown and operation as a package.

Monroe County (Rochester), N.Y., used a competitive method to select Raytheon Service Corp. as overall systems contractor for its resource recovery facility. Raytheon, in turn, provides the county with bid packages to allow competitive procurement of construction, equipment and installation. Raytheon will then be responsible for overall management during construction and plant shakedown and will operate the resource recovery facility for a five-year period.

The key issues that must be considered in planning and implementing resource recovery are quite complex and very interrelated. Some points to remember include:

- **Don't "purchase"** a resource recovery system in the same way as other less risky capital facilities. One alternative is to award a "franchise" to a private company using a "full service" acquisition approach. Others may also be developed.

- **Decide on facility** ownership, operation and financing before choosing the acquisition method to be used.

- **Consider the complexity** of the technology, the desire of the sponsoring government to accept system performance risks, the need for continuing skills in marketing products and energy, and the ability of the governmental unit to manage the overall financial arrangements involved before deciding on ownership and operation of the facility.

- **Be as specific as possible** about the characteristics of the technology (the type of system) that is being sought when soliciting proposals. The degree of technology specification is most dependent on the firmness of the markets for recovered products. *If the markets are unknown, industry proposals should not be solicited.*

- **Use the "request-for-proposal"** package to communicate the requirements of the sponsor to the potential bidder. A lack of specifics about the form, level and dependability of service required will lead to industry proposals difficult to evaluate.

- **Evaluate industry proposals** with a highly qualified team experienced in resource recovery technologies, economics, marketing, and system management, as well as the requirements and politics of the local area.

With states and cities in various stages of resource recovery facility planning and implementation and private industry advertising its capability to design, construct and operate the "right" facility for a particular area, new techniques and procedures, different from those traditionally used to acquire conventional public works, will be needed. States and cities must not only understand their own needs and capabilities, but also have the technical, management and financial flexibility to respond to changing technologies and provide the "business opportunities" necessary for an industry response.

2-12 Breakeven Economics of Resource Recovery Systems

Donald L. Mihelich

Source: *Proceedings* of the Fifth Mineral Waste Utilization Symposium, Chicago, Illinois, April 13-14, 1976, pp. 53-57. Reprinted with Permission of None Needed.

INTRODUCTION

At the rate that resource recovery studies and projects are proliferating around the country, it may soon become unpatriotic for a community not to have an energy and metals recovery plant instead of a landfill.

Although the EPA[1] suggests 200 to 250 short tons of Municipal Solid Waste (MSW) per day as the lower limit for such recovery plants, and suggests a minimum population of 175,000, Ames, Iowa, with a population of 40,000, is installing a $5.5 million facility, while the community of Siloam Springs, Arkansas – population 8,000 – is installing a $450,000 incinerator to generate and sell steam.[2]

This apparent anomaly leads to the question "What really is the economic breakeven volume for my city for a resource recovery plant?" or stated in other terms "We are currently landfilling; can we afford to install a resource recovery facility without raising present or planned collection fees, disposal fees or taxes?" or stated still another way, "Are we a candidate for an economic feasibility study for a resource recovery plant?"

The objective of this paper is to provide a simplified methodology so that municipal planners and decision makers will have a rough order of magnitude of the amount of capital their project or community can afford to spend (affordable capital at breakeven) on a resource recovery facility to have it at least break even.

Specifically omitted are the many other factors necessary to successfully place such a facility in service. Some of these factors are markets, political considerations, institutional factors, financing, ownership, operation, engineering and contingency plans. These items are properly part of the Phase I Feasibility Analysis which most experts agree is mandatory for any resource recovery project to avoid false starts, painful delays and unworkable contracts and systems.

APPROACH

The approach visualizes the construction of the resource recovery facilities as a capital investment which msut be justified economically. Thus the operation of these facilities must at least pay the cost of the capital investment (breakeven). In order to properly begin, a few major assumptions are in order.

Process System Assumptions

These are four major resource recovery approaches currently underway in the United States.[3] These are 1) Incineration with heat recovery, 2) Materials Recovery, 3) Pyrolysis and 4) Refuse Derived Fuel (RDF).

A recent article[4] comparing ten systems selected the RDF system (as exemplified by the Union Electric, St. Louis experiment) as being the most cost effective when an existing boiler could be easily modified to accept the RDF. The RDF system was selected for the purposes of this study because of the increasing trend nationwide to coal-fired boilers for larger steam and power generation plants. Thus, the chosen model assumes that a suitable boiler already exists or will be justified by other needs, and the application of the capital will be for the RDF plant, transfer stations and modest boiler modifications. If a more expensive system is contemplated, it is obvious that the amount of affordable capital will purchase less capacity.

Financing Assumptions

Of the many ways to finance a capital project, the method known as Solid Waste Disposal Revenue Bonds was chosen because of the easier marketability (7.5% average rate in mid 1975). These bonds are secured by revenues from the operations and a mortgage on the facility.

If other financing is chosen, the cost of capital will probably be higher, and the net effect will be that the project will be able to support less capital than that shown in order to break even.

Suffice to say, that the cost of capital is a very dominant and sensitive variable, and the financing mechanism must be one of the early decision points.

PRO FORMA OPERATING STATEMENT

With these premises, a pro-forma operating statement was constructed for a typical year of operation for a baseline plant, and plants of varying sizes (Table 1), and the amount of capital which could be supported by these operations was determined. The development of this operating statement required further assumptions.

As mentioned, the primary objective of this paper is to describe a methodology for determining the initial economic feasibility of a resource recovery plant. The assumptions and rationale used herein are based on late 1975 data and must be considered as generalized and subject to change. Specific site information should always be used when available. The pro forma analysis assumes a level operating capacity as shown for the project life. The facility is assumed to operate at this annual tonnage for 20 years.

The following rationale was used to convert tons of MSW to population.[5] Of the three criteria for MSW (generated, collected and deliverable), the primary concern is deliverable. For a mixed urban-suburban-rural area one person generates four pounds of MSW per day, or 1460 pounds per year. In a mixed-urban-suburban-rural area, only 80% of that generated is considered deliverable. Thus, although 100,000 people may generate 73,000 tons per year, only 58,400 tons are deliverable. This equates to 1.72 people per ton. Thus, 100,000 tons delivered is equivalent to 172,000 people.

Revenues from the disposal of refuse are projected at $5.00 per ton in order to reasonably approximate the majority of expected fees paid to dump at new landfills and/or transfer stations. It must be understood that this fee is dominant and sensitive variable and must be adjusted for local conditions in order to be competitive in the local situation. The disposal or dump fee varies from $1.50 per ton is some areas of the West to over $19.00 per ton in New England.

This analysis assumes a constant material balance as follows:[6] one ton of MSW contains 80% RDF, 8% ferrous metal, 1% nonferrous metal, 10% glass and 1% tailings.

The incoming MSW contains an average of 5000 BTU/lb (10,000,000 BTU/ton). When 80% of the incoming material is upgraded into RDF by removal of the non-combustibles, each pound of RDF is assumed to contain 6,250 BTU. (12,500,000 BTU/ton of RDF). The fuel will be sold at $1.50 per million BTU ($18.75 per ton of RDF) to reflect a competitive price to coal in 1980. This, of course, represents the most significant revenue source. Total revenues will actually include interest income from the Bond Reserve Fund. The interest income will average approximately 1% of the value of the bonds. For simplification it is omitted from these calculations.

Expenses are segregated into variable operating costs and fixed operating costs. Variable operating costs are those expenses that vary with volume (sometimes called direct costs or "out of pocket" (OOP) costs). In the model all operating costs are considered variable, although by the strictest interpretation some of them are fixed. Fixed operating costs are those expenses which do not vary with volume (sometimes called time costs or standby costs — the cost of just keeping

Table 1. Resource Recovery Plant Pro Forma Operating Statement for a Typical Year of Operations. Dollars in Thousands

	Unit Price Per Ton	Material Balance(4)	30,000 / 50,000	50,000 / 86,000	100,000 / 172,000	200,000 / 344,000	330,000 / 567,000
Revenues							
Disposal Service Fees	$5.00	100%	$150.0	$250.0	$500.0	$1,000.0	$1,650.0
Sales of Refuse Derived Fuel	18.75	80%	450.0	750.0	1,500.0	3,000.0	4,950.0
Sales of Ferrous Metals	30.00	8%	72.0	120.0	240.0	480.0	792.0
Sales of Non Ferrous Metals	120.00	1%	36.0	60.0	120.0	240.0	396.0
Sales of Glass (as mixed cullet)	5.00	10%	15.0	25.0	50.0	100.0	165.0
Total Revenues			$723.0	$1,205.0	$2,410.0	$4,820.0	$7,953.0
Expenses	Cost Per Ton						
Variable Operating Costs							
Labor & Supervision	$2.59		$200.9	$242.6	$374.1	$595.8	$854.7
Power	1.62		121.9	150.6	232.9	370.8	534.6
Other Utilities & Supplies	0.08		5.3	7.4	11.7	18.6	26.4
Maintenance	0.85		60.6	79.0	124.1	197.2	280.5
Miscellaneous Expense	0.32		21.3	29.7	46.7	74.2	105.6
Disposal Costs	0.90	1%	60.8	83.7	131.4	208.8	297.0
Total Variable Operating Costs			$470.8	$593.0	$920.9	$1,465.4	$2,098.8
Fixed Operating Costs							
Debt Service Coverage			$252.2	$612.0	$1,489.1	$3,354.6	$5,854.2
Total Expenses			$723.0	$1,205.0	$2,410.0	$4,820.0	$7,953.0
Profit or Loss			0	0	0	0	0
Affordable Capital at Breakeven			$1,260.0	$3,060.0	$7,445.0	$16,773.0	$29,270.0

Plant Capacity	Straight Line Factor	NCRR Economy Of Scale Factor	"In House" Economy Of Scale Factor	Economy of Scale Factor Used in This Model
330,000 TPY Baseline	1.0	1.0	1.0	1.0
200,000 "	0.60	0.68	0.71	0.70
100,000 "	0.30	0.41	0.47	0.44
50,000 "	0.15	0.24	0.33	0.28
30,000 "	0.09	0.15	0.25	0.20

the doors open). In the model this is considered Debt Service Coverage. The sum of the fixed operating costs and the variable operating costs equals the revenues at the breakeven.

Variable operating costs were chosen to conform to the format and numbers used by the National Science Foundation, the Urban Technology Center of Columbia University.[4] These costs were assumed to be the baseline variable operating costs, and the other costs were derived from this baseline using an economy of scale factor derived from the average of the results of the curve described in the NCRR work[7] and in-house private estimating practices.

A comparison of these approaches and the factor used in the model above. This means that if an item of operating cost for the 330,000 TPY baseline plant were $100,000, then the same item of cost for a plant of 50,000 TPY capacity, instead of costing $15,000 (straight line proportion), would cost $28,000 because of the economy of scale factor.

No allowance for transportation costs has been made. Transportation costs may be more or less, depending on the location of the power plant. In many smaller communities, the chances are that the power plant will be closer to the centroid of generation than the existing or planned landfill, so the transportation costs may be the same or slightly less (e.g., Ames). In larger cities or regions, the chances are that the power plant will be located further away from the centroid and transfer stations and added transportation costs may be required (e.g., St. Louis).

Fixed operating costs were identified as being the cost of debt service coverage. The debt service coverage is the ratio of funds available for debt service to the total debt service requirement. It is assumed to be approximately 2 to 1 as a minimum to satisfy the requirements of the bond holders. Thus, this debt service coverage ratio becomes a dominant and sensitive fixed expense variable and must be used to determine how much capital the project is capable of supporting. The debt service interest is assumed to be 7.5% per year on the unpaid balance. The principal repayment will be in 20 equal payments.

To calculate debt service coverage and affordable capital at breakeven, for example:

1. Calculate revenues $7,953.0
2. Calculate total variable operating costs $2,098.8
3. Subtract total variable operating costs from total revenues

$7,953.0 - $2,098.8 = $5,854.2

This is the allowable fixed costs available for debt service coverage.

4. Divide the debt service coverage by 2 to account for the 2 to 1 debt service ratio demanded by the bond holders.

$$\frac{\$5,854.2}{2} = \$2,927.1$$

5. Divide this number by 2 to account for approximately equal principal and interest over the 20 year life of the bond. This number is equivalent to the annual principal payment.

$$\frac{\$2,927.1}{2} = \$1,463.5$$

6. Multiply the annual principal payment number by 20 years to get the approximate value of the affordable bonds to supply the capital.

$1,463.5 \times 20 = $29,270.0

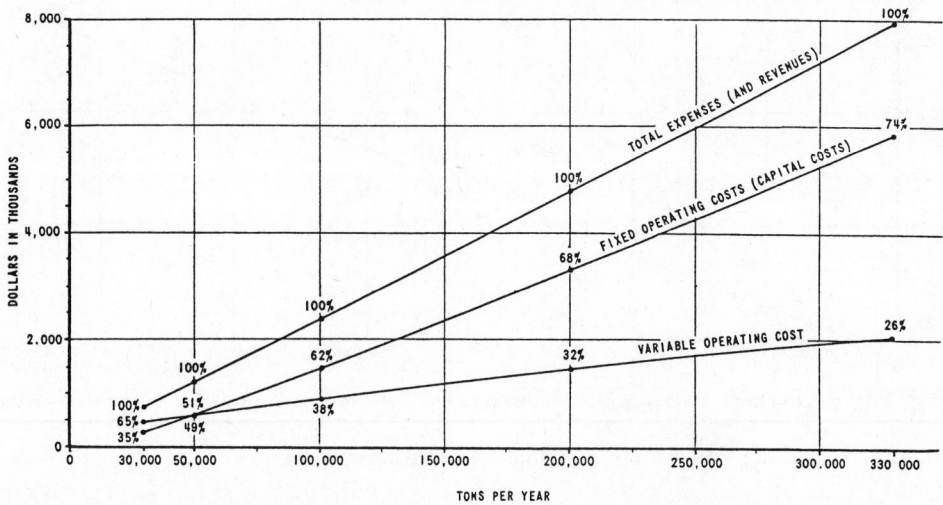

Figure 1. Relationship of fixed operating and variable operating costs.

RESULTS AND CONCLUSIONS

The cost data developed in Table 1 has been graphically displayed as a set of curves in Figure 1. Of particular interest in this display is the behavior of the variable operating cost over the range of plant sizes. The baseline plant, sized to process 330,000 tons per year, has variable operating costs of 26% revenues. For the plant sized to process 30,000 tons per year, the variable operating costs rise to 65% of the revenues.

This, of course, reflects the so-called "economy of scale factor" used in this model, and the fact that revenues decrease faster than variable operating costs.

The effect is to pinch off the amount of affordable capital at the lower end to keep total costs in line with total revenues. The pie charts shown in Figure 2 also depict this relationship.

A curve of affordable capital at breakeven derived from Table 1 is shown in Figure 3. It

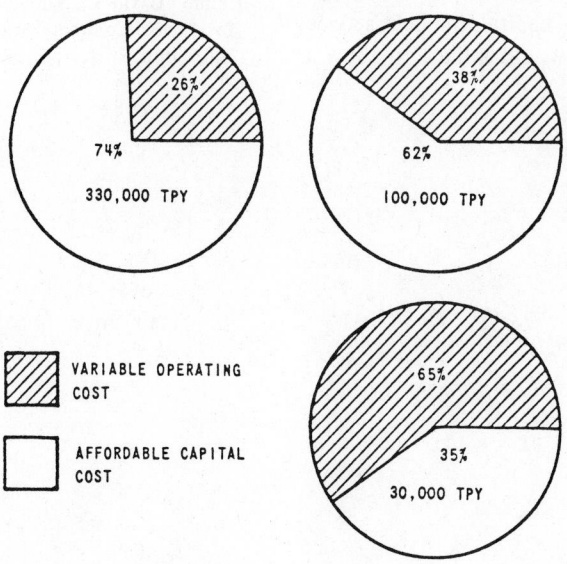

Figure 2. Relationship of operating cost and affordable capital.

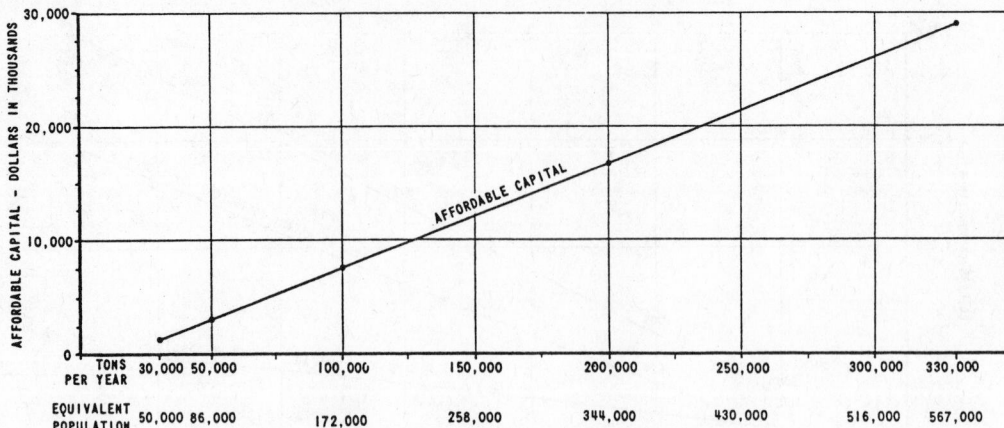

Figure 3. Affordable capital at breakeven.

shows the amount of capital a population range of 50,000 to 567,000 could support.

Thus, from this curve, an area with a population of 50,000 could afford a resource recovery plant with total capital costs of $1 1/4 million and still have the facility pay for itself.

For 100,000 people, the affordable capital jumps to $4 million, and at 200,000 people, approximately $9 million becomes the upper capital target.

Note that the affordable capital curve is the amount one can afford to spend for a plant and break even. It is not intended to indicate what a plant of that size should or will cost.

Pratically speaking, if the project did not require all the affordable capital, the debt service coverage requirement would reduce to allow a profit or a reduction of disposal service fees or other revenues.

REFERENCES

1. Lowe, Robert A., Energy Recovery from Waste, U.S.E.P.A. 1973.
2. Siloam Springs Plant Turns Garbage to Needed Energy — Tulsa World, Oct. 3, 1975.
3. Greco, James R., Alternate Technologies for Resource Recovery, NSWMA Technical Bulletin June/July 1975.
4. Schulz, Dr. Helmut W., P.E., Energy from Municipal Refuse: A Comparison of Ten Processes, Professional Engineer Nov. 1975.
5. Hollander, Herbert, I. Gilbert & Assoc., Reading, Pa. Private Communication.
6. Klumb, David E., Union Electric Co., St. Louis, Mo. Private Communication.
7. NCRR Bulletin Spring 1975, page 43 Figure 2.

2-13 Steps to Resource Recovery for the I-95 Complex

Source: Adapted from a National Center for Resource Recovery report of the same title, April 1976, 28 pp. Reprinted with Permission of National Center for Resource Recovery.

There are important differences between planning for resource recovery and planning for the more traditional municipal public works and service projects. For this reason, a somewhat different planning process is described here.

This reading summarizes the background of the project and the specific analyses which were performed. Part of the background was identification of resource recovery goals by the participating jurisdictions. It was realized that the type of resource recovery plant that seemed appropriate for this area was one that would process the waste to extract saleable materials and prepare a refuse-derived fuel (RDF) for burning as a supplemental fuel at a local utility power station. Following this identification, the detailed planning process began. It consisted of three activities which are described in the separate reports: *Markets Study, Feasibility Study,* and *Network Study.*

The *Markets Study* was the first step in securing advance commitments and minimum prices for the purchase of materials (for the first five operating years) to be recovered from solid waste. The accompanying specifications, which determine how a plant has to perform, led to the *Feasibility Study.* This step examined the design and associated costs of the plant, and compared potential costs to potential revenues. It examined the questions of whether such a plant would be technologically and economically feasible. This led to the third step, or the *Network Study,* which examined whether the location of the first recource recovery plant was

satisfactory, considering the area's long-term solid waste management needs.

One step in the planning process is to secure an advance commitment for the acceptance and sale of the fuel. This has not been concluded, since a secure, long-term commitment has not yet been obtained. This summary report describes why the sale of the fuel may not be concluded with as secure a commitment as the materials, and examines the consequences. The accompanying analysis shows that the absence of such a commitment need not interfere with implementation of the plant, as recommended.

This reading summarizes considerations which led to the recommendation that the D.C. City Council underwrite the financing of a resource recovery plant in Lorton, Virginia, to process a small portion of the solid waste of the District of Columbia, the City of Alexandria, and Arlington and Fairfax Counties.

Our everyday solid waste discards contain potentially valuable fuel and materials. Their extraction and processing in a useable and saleable form is called *resource recovery.* It is a relatively new activity for municipalities and, unfortunately, there are few examples to follow in applying resource recovery as an alternative to the more traditional forms of disposal — burying and burning.

But, resource recovery is a production activity (extraction and processing to customer's specifications) and hence, different in scope, planning and implementation than the usual municipal public works and service projects. The economic success of resource recovery relies on the sale of the recovered products. Assuring these sales, especially in advance of design and construction, adds to the difficulties in municipal planning.

The relationship among recovery technology, market possibilities and overall economic projections — even in the current time-frame — is rather complex. This summary attempts to explain this complexity so that the responsible municipal officials and the citizens can decide if resource recovery will be a prudent investment for the metropolitan Washington area.

The final recommendation is for a 650 ton per day resource recovery plant which is small relative to the 4000 tons per day of municipal waste which may soon be received at the I-95 landfill. The recommendation is also to produce a wide variety of products for sale so as to assure continued revenues as secondary materials markets vary with the economy. This conservative approach is intended to minimize capital investment at this time while having an opportunity to "debug" the technology for the local governments, establish the necessary institutional arrangements for resource recovery, and develop reliability in the view of the purchasers of the fuel and materials produced by the I-95 Complex.

The success of other municipalities in planning and implementing resource recovery has varied. The planning process summarized here is cautious and step-wise, with identification of pitfalls — and means of avoiding them.

As will be seen later, the solid waste in the metropolitan Washington area, like the waste in most other parts of the country has as a minor fraction metals, glass, and other noncombustibles; and, as a major portion, paper and other combustibles. This encourages investigating the possibilities for recovering reusable steel, glass, aluminum, and other nonferrous metals and processing the majority of the combustible material to some form of refuse-derived fuel (RDF) or other energy product.

"THE I-95 COMPLEX"

The District of Columbia has been a principal force in developing the I-95 Complex. In March 1971, the District faced a severe solid waste disposal problem. The District's Department of Environmental Services (DES) recommended, and Mayor Walter Washington proposed, the creation of a regional solid waste processing and disposal center on property within the District of Columbia's Correctional Center at Lorton, Virginia. The name, I-95 Complex, derived from the location's access to Interstate Route 95.

The Nothern Virginia jurisdictions were receptive to such a proposal, as many of their solid waste disposal facilities are either approaching capacity or facing closure. Together, these facilities dispose of more than 1600 tons of Northern Virginia's solid waste daily. The development of the I-95 Complex at Lorton, both for sanitary landfill and eventual resource recovery processing, was seen as the solution to this common problem.

An Agreement. In November 1971, the District reached an agreement with Fairfax County, clearing the way for an interim sanitary landfill to be established on a 22-acre site at Lorton. This was seen as a temporary solution to the District's and the other participating jurisdictions' immediate disposal problems.

Twenty-two acres will not last long for such quantities of solid waste. In conjunction with the opening of the interim landfill, DES conducted an initial study to lay the groundwork for the implementation of a more extensive regional land reclamation, resource recovery and recreation complex at Lorton.

The Memorandum of Understanding. On February 15, 1973, the District, Fairfax County and the Council of Governments' Waste Management Agency (representing the City of Alexandria, the Alexandria Sanitation Authority and Arlington County) signed a *Memorandum of Understanding* after a public hearing in Fairfax County on this subject. This agreement called for the development of a Resource Recovery, Land Reclamation and Recreation Complex at I-95. It was also an expansion of the interim agreement between these jurisdictions on the joint usage of the potential landfill acreage at this site. The *Memorandum* committed the participants at the I-95 landfill to implement resource recovery at the Lorton site. Furthermore, the District was to pay for the engineering of the recovery facility and to provide the capital funding for its construction. However, all would share in capital "pay-back" as well as operating costs and revenues.

During the summer of 1973, the I-95 Policy Committee was formed. This committee is composed of representatives from the District, Fairfax County and the Waste Management Agency.

CHOOSING A RECOVERY PROCESS FOR I-95

The Refuse-Derived Fuel Option. At its initial meetings the I-95 Policy Committee began to search for suitable resource recovery options.* It was soon clear that one such alternative was being demonstrated at a federally assisted project in St. Louis, involving the City of St. Louis and the Union Electric Co. Started in 1972, this energy recovery pilot project was developing data on the feasibility of burning processed solid waste in power plant boilers as a supplement to the boilers' conventional fossil fuel. It appeared that properly prepared refuse could be substituted for as much as 20 percent (by heat value) of the boilers' coal without at least any short-term adverse effects. An advantage of this approach lies in the economies of power production in large facilities.

There was sufficient interest in this approach for Potomac Electric Power Co. (PEPCO) and the District to fund a joint study to determine the feasibility of PEPCO using this type of refuse-derived fuel. The final report deals with the various facets of energy production from municipal refuse and the facilities that would be needed.** The study indicated that such a program would have economic benefits to both

*On March 19 and 20, 1973, officials from the participating jurisdictions and Citizens' Advisory Committee members met for two days of presentations on recovery technology, economics and institutional relationships supplemented by discussions of the local situation. The presentations were given by the National Center for Resource Recovery, Inc.

**Feasibility Study for Resource Recovery for Municipal Refuse.* Burns and Roe, Inc. (Oradel, New Jersey) November 30, 1973, 86 pages.

parties and recommended that they proceed to implement a resource recovery program similar to that being demonstrated in St. Louis.

Refuse-derived fuel has generated increasing interest. Fairfax County officials and citizens had contacted the Virginia Electric and Power Co. (VEPCO) as to their interest in utilizing RDF in their boilers at Possum Point, and had been encouraged by VEPCO's apparent willingness to consider this option. In November 1973, the Fairfax County Board of Supervisors' Solid Waste Advisory Committee recommended this approach. However, VEPCO has re-evaluated RDF for use in their total system, which they saw primarily as being based upon nuclear power. Because of expected low boiler utilization rates, VEPCO's analyses showed that the I-95 Complex would have to "pay" for VEPCO to utilize RDF at the Possum Point Station.*

Highlighting the Reasons. The rationale behind the decision to place primary emphasis on a refuse-derived fuel (RDF) should be understood. Energy utilization takes place in an existing plant; i.e., the boiler of the power company. Consequently, the need for a large capital outlay for a boiler is eliminated. Second, there is a ready market for the electricity to be generated. Third, it is possible to take advantage of the economies of scale associated with large utility boiler complexes in contrast to other systems where refuse is the primary fuel. Even then, RDF would make up only a small portion of the total fuel consumed at most medium-to-large power stations.

The preference for investigating further the new approach was based in part on the District's experience in soliciting a resource recovery program. In October 1972, DES met with some 21 solid waste management firms to discuss implementing a resource recovery program. Subsequent to the meeting, some nine companies responded to a general request for proposals issued by the District. After detailed review, the consensus was that none of the offers met

*According to information supplied by VEPCO, this amount would be $48 per ton in 1975 and increasing substantially in future years.

the needs of the District.* It was concluded that the technology was too speculative and that the necessary agreements for marketing the energy could not be reached.

Independent Support. Recent literature studies also support the relative desirability of the RDF option.** One example is a study by the Bechtel Corp. for the Electric Power Research Inst. released in March 1972. This report analyzed the available processes for energy recovery from municipal solid waste. These included: preparation of a solid fuel; pyrolysis to produce a fuel oil; anarobic digestion of landfilled refuse to produce methane gas; electric power generation using hot gases from a fluidized bed incinerator to drive a turbine; and incineration of refuse with heat recovery. The Bechtel report† states that:

> "The case of most interest is supplemental firing of prepared MSW (municipal solid waste) fuel in a coal-fired boiler."

Since PEPCO fires coal at Potomac River and Benning Road, as well as at several other plants, this is an important conclusion.

Since the above information supports the position of the I-95 Policy Committee, it refers only to the preliminary selection of RDF as a basic strategy. Later reports support this selection.

---

*The proposals were reviewed by the District's Department of Environmental Services, the Department of Defense, the Environmental Protection Agency, and the National Center for Resource Recovery.

**See: *Fuels From Municipal Refuse For Utilities: Technology Assessment.* Final Report to Electric Power Research Inst. Bechtel Corp. (March 1975); *Energy Recovery from Solid Waste* (Vol. 1: Summary Report and Vol. II: Technical Report). See also: NASA/ASEE Systems Design Institute, University of Houston (September 1974); *Resource Recovery: A State of Technology.* Prepared for the Council on Environmental Quality by the Midwest Research Inst. (February 1973); E.B. Berman and E.A. Couruhan, *n Economic Approach to Solid Waste Management Planning,* Mitre Corp. (March 1975); F.A. Ferguson, Park L. Morse, and Katherine A. Miller, *Refuse As a Fuel For Utilities.* Prepared for Pacific Gas and Electric Company (San Francisco, California) by Stanford Research Institute SRI No. 2869 (March 1974).

† Bechtel report, *op. cit.* pp. iv and v.

The various independent studies are summarized in *Table 1*, as a status summary of resource recovery systems. Most of the various systems are proprietary and are in the first stages of construction or operation. It is noteworthy that almost all of the processes for preparation of combustibles gaseous or liquid fuels start with either shredded waste or, more often, RDF. Thus, a resource recovery plant for the preparation of RDF is a potential supplier of material for later conversion to gaseous or liquid fuel, should such conversions later prove practical and economical.

Next Steps. In addition to continuing negotiations with the potential fuel user, the next step is to appraise the feasibility of materials recovery as a means of complementing production of the RDF energy product. The main candidates for materials recovery are paper, magnetic metals, glass, aluminum and other nonferrous (nonmagnetic) metals such as brass. This can be seen in *Figure 1* which is a simplified schematic representation of the process. RDF is the principal product of the initial processing steps. In essence, it comes out first, leaving a fraction of the waste for materials recovery processing.

What Is In the Waste. *Table 2* presents two different perspectives of "what is in the waste?" The first might be called "materials composition," in that it notes the potentially recoverable targets of paper, ferrous, aluminum, other nonferrous and glass. The second looks at the waste from the perspective of what is combustible and what is not. Clearly, most of the waste can be burned. The noncombustible potential materials recovery targets make up roughly one-fifth of the waste.

THE THREE STUDIES

Influencing the decision to proceed with a budget request for a 650 ton per day full-scope recovery facility at Lorton were the results of three successive studies performed by the National Center for Resource Recovery, Inc., under contract to the Metropolitan Washington

Table 1. Energy Recovery Systems Status Summary.

Process Type	Vendor	Output	Status
Solid Fuel Preparation	Generally, non-proprietary, although some proprietary process steps.	Solid Fuel for co-firing in existing facilities, or as 100 percent in especially designed RDF combustors.	Has gained some acceptance by both private and public sector operators.
Pyrolysis to Fuel Gas	Proprietary: Union Carbide, Inc.; Monsanto Enviro-Chem Systems Inc.; many others.	Burnable low BTU gas (125–350 BTU/scf) for on-site or nearby combustion/utilization.	Pilot and some full-scale prototype plants being developed privately and under sponsorship.
Pyrolysis to Fuel Oil	Proprietary: Occidental Research and Development (formerly Garrett).	Burnable oil (75 percent BTU of F.O. No. 6) for firing in existing facilities.	200 ton per day plant under construction in San Diego County, with EPA sponsorship.
Anaerobic Digestion for Methane	NRG: Dynatech R/D, Inc.; others.	Burnable gas (1000 BTU/scf) can be pipelined and burned in existing facilities.	50–100 ton per day demonstration plant being built in Pompano Beach, FL, with ERDA sponsorship. Landfill gas recovery being demonstrated in Palos Verdes, CA.
Electric Power Generation with Gas Turbine	Proprietary: Combustion Power Co. (but with EPA sponsorship).	Electricity.	Difficulty experienced in gas clean-up unresolved at present time.
Raw Refuse Incineration with Heat Recovery	Proprietary: various; can be designed by A & E component – procured.	Low-pressure steam for district heating, cooling or industrial use. Also steam to drive turbine for electricity generation.	Commercially available. Practiced in Europe in various forms.

Table 2. Estimated Refuse Composition of the I-95 Complex.

Combustible Components	% (By Weight)	Noncombustible Components		% (By Weight)
Paper and Plastics	43.6*	Ferrous Metals		10.2
Yard Waste	9.7	Light	9.2	
		Heavy	1.0	
Food Waste	9.9	Aluminum		0.7
Rags and Wood	5.1	Other Nonferrous		0.3
Total, Combustibles	68.3	Glass		10.5
		Flint (clear)	4.5	
		Colored	6.0	
		Other Noncombustibles		10.0
		Total, Noncombustibles		31.7

*Newspaper is estimated to be about 15 percent of the waste input.

Source: Compositional data for the I-95 Complex refuse was derived from sampling by the U.S. Bureau of Mines (1973) and NCRR (1974). Both sets of samples are of waste received at the District of Columbia Solid Waste Reduction Center No. 1, on Benning Road. For comparison with national averages, see F.A. Smith, Comparative Estimates of Post-Consumer Solid Waste. U.S. Environmental Protection Agency. Report 530/SW-148 (Washington, 1975).

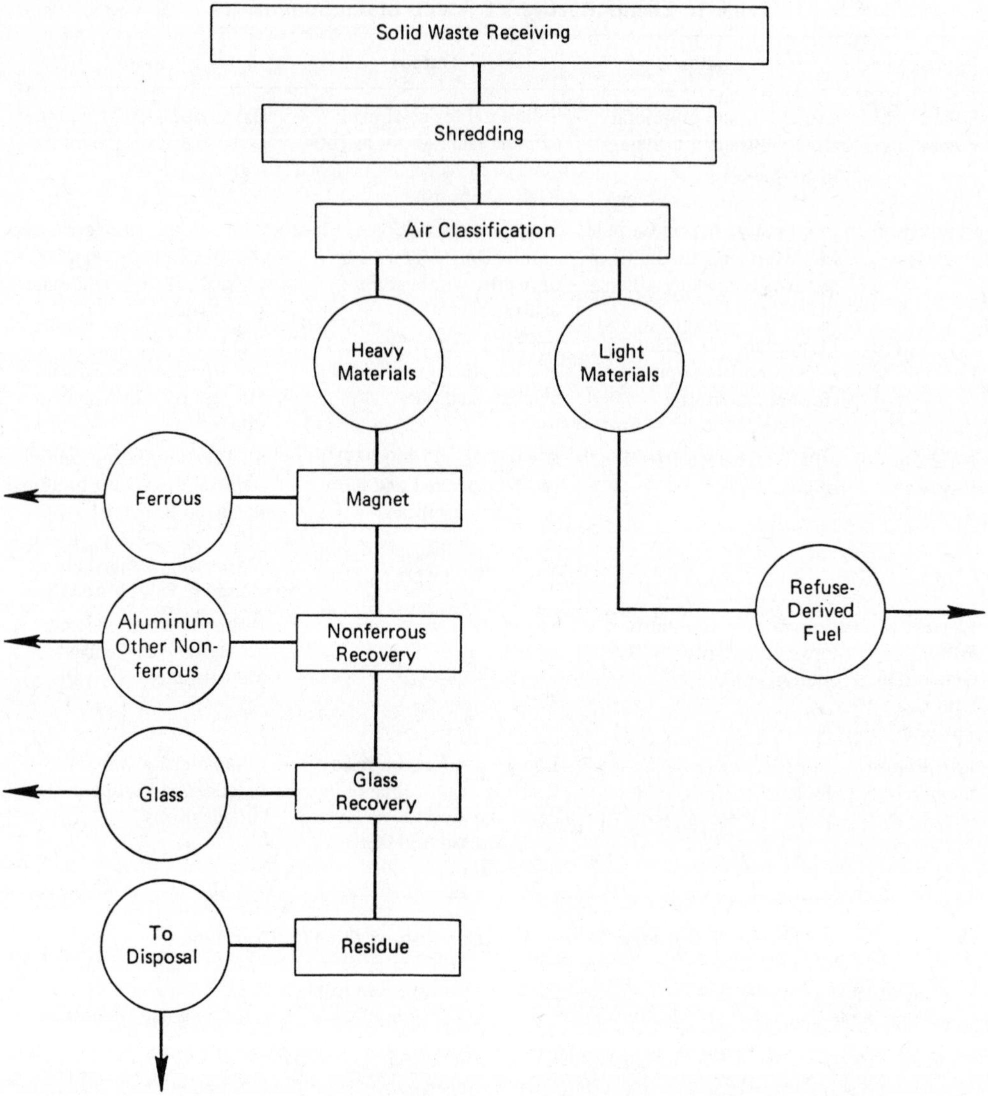

Figure 1. Simplified Diagram I-95 Resource Recovery Program.

Waste Management Agency.* These studies are entitled:

Markets for Recoverable Resources From Mixed Municipal Solid Waste, (1974); *Engineering and Economic Feasibility Study For the I-95 Complex*, (1975); and

---

*The *Markets Study* was not printed in volume. Copies were delivered to the I-95 participating jurisdictions and to the Metropolitan Washington Waste Management Agency. The report can be read at the latter location as can the *Feasibility Study* and *Network Study*.

Solid Waste Management Network Analysis For the I-95 Complex, (1975).

Markets Study. The *Markets Study* was the first step in this sequential planning effort. Through this study, it was possible to define in advance markets for those materials which might be set as recovery targets for the Lorton facility. The market commitments obtained as a result of the *Markets Study* effort represent an extensive series of assurances that customers will purchase the recovered materials for the first five operating years of the resource recovery plant, for the most part, for at least a guaranteed floor price. The commitments obtained were contingent upon the I-95 Complex proceeding with plans toward implementation of a facility within a reasonable time, as an unqualified advance market commitment can only be secured for a short period of time.

The *Markets Study* produced reasonably assured markets, subject to certain specifications. By knowing the targeted markets, it was possible to proceed further with a conceptual engineering design, as well as cost and revenue comparisons. The value of the recovered products and the specifications required by the users are key inputs to the next step in the planning process.

Feasibility Study. The task of the feasibility step was to: (1) determine the most appropriate technology and evaluate its chance of achieving projected output rates and market specifications; and (2) compare proposed facility costs with the revenue estimates as a basis for its economic feasibility. (The marketable products to be recovered were RDF and those materials covered by the *Markets Study*.) This is even more complicated than it would appear. In this case, a particular complication was the situation with the refuse-derived fuel market, — while logically bound to PEPCO — was specifically undefined. How this was handled in the *Feasibility Study* is explained later.

Because the advanced commitments secured the revenue projections for the materials but not the fuel, the *Feasibility Study* has to answer two questions: (1) "what is the minimum bargain that must be struck for the RDF to achieve financial comparability with landfilling," and, (2) "is it reasonable to expect that this can be achieved?"

The Indifference Value. The minimum RDF price which could be accepted to achieve financial comparability with landfilling is referred to as the "Indifference Value" (IV) and is expressed in dollars per million BTU's of heat content of the RDF delivered to users. This is how energy users normally buy fuel. In the present context and suppose, as an illustra-

tion, the IV is determined to be $0.31 per million BTU's, a price resulting in resource recovery being less expensive to the participating jurisdictions than the conventional landfill at Lorton. A bargain struck below $0.31 per million BTU's makes resource recovery "cost-increasing," when compared to simply continuing to landfill at the I-95 Complex. The key to understanding the indifference concept is to realize that IV represents the swing point. Recovering a lower value than that computed is cost-increasing while receiving higher value leads to savings and a *"disposal dividend."*

Network Study. The third study focused on the economically optimum locations for resource recovery plants. It is important not to lose sight of the fact that plant location is important. For the four jurisdictions, there was more to be considered than needs. Long-range questions needed to be answered before selecting the initial facility. Considerations of size, site, location, compatibility with other plants and other locations, extent of processing, transportation costs and landfill consumption had to be addressed in order to determine the proper solid waste management network.

Findings of the *Network Analysis* indicated that decentralized, full-scope processing would be the preferred network. That is, multiple sites at different locations closer to the generation areas are preferable to one processing plant sited at Lorton handling all of the 4000-plus tons of waste generated per day. A 650 ton per day facility is compatible with this decentralized approach. While the Lorton I-95 Complex is an excellent location in some respects (closeness to landfill, availability of utilities, zoning, etc.), it would appear that it is not the ideal site for a plant beyond roughly 1,300 tons per day capacity.

THE RDF BARGAIN

Before looking at the *Markets Study* in detail, it is essential to point out some of the intricacies of "bargaining" over the sale of the energy product. Several utilities around this country (including PEPCO) have agreed in principle to accept RDF and burn it. However, none of the agreements are as "ironclad" as has been reached in the purchase of recovered materials. The reasons for this are due to the understandable reluctance of a utility to accept a fuel which requires new investment for handling and burning, and which *might* interfere with the reliable production of power.

Also, it must be clearly understood that the *Markets Study* was not intended to establish an advance Letter of Intent for the energy product. By instruction of the I-95 Policy Committee, the negotiation was reserved for the participating jurisdictions through a negotiating committee chaired by a member of the Policy Committee.

Economic Rules Govern. The laws of economics state that when something that has a negative value suddenly appears to have a positive value when viewed from a different perspective, one automatically and without fail generates a bargaining, negotiation and conflict situation. And, when this occurs, there is no right answer to the question of "how much is it worth?" Understanding this point is perhaps the most important single input to an overall understanding of the proposed resource recovery project. It is certainly the most important point in developing an understanding as to why the final RDF "bargain" is being approached cautiously and purposefully by the Policy Committee.

There is no "right" value for the waste energy because it is just that, *waste-energy*. To the energy user the optimal position is the lowest possible price, even if less than the cost to dispose of the waste by other means. It is waste, and the user sees himself providing a disposal service. To the provider of the waste, he is selling "energy," and his optimal position is to demand a price just slightly less than the energy user has to pay for an alternative fuel. At this point, a bargain must be struck that will be "mutually beneficial."*

The terminology "mutually beneficial" is carefully selected to indicate that it is highly unlikely that the user will enter into an arrangement where the contract represents a real commitment unless there is some benefit to him. It is also unlikely that the I-95 Policy Committee would approve such a project unless there is some financial benefit. Measures must be sought to overcome this dilemma.

It should be clear that there is no "right" way to mathematically identify the "correct" exchange price.

The "correct exchange (or selling) price" must be considered in relation to the "Indifference Value" of the fuel to the participating jurisdictions. The Indifference Value is the price at which the jurisdictions are indifferent (i.e., don't care, economically) whether the fuel is sold or landfilled. At a selling price less than the Indifference Value (IV), the jurisdictions are better off economically to landfill; at a higher price, the converse is true.

The Incentive. The utility cannot expect to strike a bargain at the participating jurisdictions' Indifference Value. At this IV exchange price, the jurisdictions obviously have no financial incentive to undertake the project. For the same reason, it is unlikely that the user will agree to a bargain at his indifference point. The indifference value of the user is essentially the cost of an equivalent amount of fossil fuel, minus the incremental costs of firing RDF.* Some expect that this will, or can, be made to happen.

Repeating the theme of this section, the agreement must be reached. This is always the case when the nature of a business transaction is such that both parties can benefit regardless of where the negotiated price falls, so long as it is not at either side's indifference point.

Technology of Production and Use. The technology of RDF production and use is rather straightforward. One can make a simple RDF through shredding and air classification. Work underway at several locations in the U.S. and abroad is aimed at improving the quality of the

---

*In theory, the same argument applies to the materials recovery side. However, in the materials case, there are markets developed, as there are many buyers.

*Some of the factors affecting this cost are: the capital costs of ancillary equipment for storing, handling and firing RDF, operating and maintenance costs, the way a utility prices power production, etc.

fuel. There are similar efforts to increase the quantity of the useable fuel product yield. Appropriate improvements could, therefore, be incorporated into the final design of the facility.

This technology picture is not as clear on the user's side as there has been only limited operating experience with RDF. The St. Louis project — the only one with operating experience to date — has burned less than 50,000 tons. In terms of the proposed I-95 project, (which will burn roughly 400 tons per day), this would account for only 125 days. Obviously, little has been determined about long-term effects with such low tonnages, although the operator, the Union Electric Co., is confident enough to proceed with a $70 million investment for additional RDF production and burning facilities based on their experience.*

The RDF Bargain Elsewhere. Several communities around the country are preparing to burn RDF. It is interesting to review how they are approaching the "RDF bargain."

In Ames, Iowa, where the plant came on-line in late 1975, the City operates a resource recovery facility, and "sells" the RDF to the municipally-owned and operated power plant. In Chicago, where a resource recovery plant is well under construction, the City takes the risk in that the utility will accept the RDF only when the plant scheduled to burn it is operating at a prescribed level of capacity. It is, of course, the utility which determines the capacity. (The price paid is approximately 30 percent of the alternative fuel cost.) In Milwaukee, the contractor has assumed part of the risk for a plant under construction. The utility has agreed to accept the fuel for a trial period after which it can terminate the agreement or set a price favorable to it based on operating experience. Interestingly, the basic tipping fee to be paid by the City to the contractor (Americology) is $9.75/ton of waste, which is high compared to the present disposal fee at I-95.

In each case, there are "special circumstances" compared to the kind of RDF bargain

which would suit the I-95 project. Ideally, the latter would be an advance purchase agreement as firm as that obtained for the recovered materials. As noted, there is little reason to expect that such an agreement could be achieved.

The Advantages of Going Slowly. The strategy of the I-95 Policy Committee in marketing RDF has been not to rush to a premature bargain. Hopefully, the future will bring with it increased confidence in the technology and, therefore, the chances for a favorable contract.

THE MARKETS STUDY

The cost of processing municipal solid waste for resource recovery is offset by the sale of recovered by-products and from a tipping (or dumping) fee. The latter is either a per ton service charge or a simple fixed charge appearing as a line item in the municipal budget. In either case, management prudence and public demand seek to keep the tipping fee minimal. The financial estimates and projections for a recovery facility, therefore, are based on obtaining market commitments for the sale of recovered products during the first few years of operation.

Obtaining such commitments is, then, a first step in planning. Moreover, the potential customers' specifications for the recovered products dictate what array of recovery processes would be used and how they would be operated to meet these specifications.

The Letter of Intent Approach. The approach of the *Markets Study* was to obtain binding Letters of Intent written with the objectives of eliminating — or greatly reducing — the risk of not selling the plant output and also to establish a realistic forecast of potential sales income prior to budget authorizations. In this way, the financial assurances the public sector seeks are obtained before construction of a resource recovery facility is undertaken.

Traditionally, market studies have listed all possible markets that might accept outputs from a processed solid waste stream. Such identifications have been made regardless of the industry's present technology as it would relate to the use of a new type of raw material.

---

*It is important to point out that, in effect, the Union Electric Co. will be both producer and user of the RDF and hence, there is no issue of selling the fuel.

In contrast, the principal objective of the *Markets Study* was to obtain Letters of Intent from as many materials markets as possible. The letter of Intent is negotiated between the resource recovery planner and the potential purchaser of recovered materials. It brings the market survey to culmination. It is the financial underpinning of the resource recovery plant and the precursor to the buyers' purchase orders. Anything weaker, or less comprehensive, can not assure that the output of the resource recovery plant, produced to specifications, will be sold.

A Perspective of the Effort. Basically, the type of effort described here might be called "contingency planning." This is a technique to help overcome market and institutional barriers to the development of a resource recovery industry. On the local level, joint action is required which involves municipalities, markets and owner/operators. Action on the part of any of the parties acknowledges that uncertainties can be reduced by allowing each party to make its commitment or participation contingent upon the similar cooperation of all other parties. In this way, no individual is required to act unilaterally because each is assured of general cooperation before his commitment takes effect. By allowing parties to make their decision contingent upon the participation of others, the uncertainty due to interdependence is reduced. Individual risk is diffused into group risk.

Without this approach, there is a temptation for parties to attempt to improve their bargaining position by "voting last," or by adopting an inflated viewpoint of the potential for profit. The output of the *Markets Study* is a conditional estimate of potential revenues. The condition is meeting the specifications. Of course, the materials must be present in the refuse in the first place and extracted from it in the projected tonnages as well.

The Letters Are Not Open Ended. THE OFFER EXPIRES UNLESS THE PROJECT PROGRESSES. Planning for resource recovery is a lengthy process, having taken three years or longer in many communities. And, then it has not always been implemented. Knowing that

such potential users have been involved in such efforts, it was not considered fair to ask them to maintain commitments without some demonstration that the project would come to fruition. A potential buyer's commitment is his plan to use a certain amount of recovered material to the exclusion of making other commitments.

The approach adopted in the *Markets Study* was to place a statement in the Letter of Intent terminating the commitment unless the jurisdictions demonstrated substantial "progress" toward implementation by a certain date. Specifically, the term "progress" was left vague in the Letters of Intent and had to be defined and agreed upon by the offerers. Substantial progress could be completion of a planning document, issuance of a request for proposals, or a similar event. The judgment of what constitutes substantial progress is difficult to make. For example, a few Letters of Intent were withdrawn during the downturn in secondary raw material prices in 1975. Of course, this was not the reason given. For example, one buyer judged that submission of the budget for the resource recovery project was not "substantial progress."

To Bid or to Buy. If the resource recovery plant is to be publicly owned, as is contemplated here, open government and fairness generally require that all responsive bidders have an opportunity to bid for the recovered material. The challenge, then, is how to secure the Letter of Intent as an advance commitment while still preserving public bidding rights. The answer was a *Letter of Intent to Bid.*

In signing a Letter of Intent to Bid, as distinguished from a Letter of Intent to Buy, the potential purchaser agrees to submit a response to a public invitation to bid for the purchase of recovered materials at some future time. The Letter of Intent to Bid covers all of the necessary terms and conditions and the price structure. The potential bidder further agrees that the bid will not be less than a stated price. This minimum stated price can then be used for financial planning, as with a Letter of Intent to Buy. When responding to the final invitation to bid, the bidder may increase this price at his option.

In the contacts with potential buyers, it was assumed that the commodities would eventually go out for bid. Approaching users from this standpoint creates a hesitation on their part to offer their best price; the signed Letter of Intent will become public information and may serve as a minimum target for other bidders. Their hesitancy can well be understood and appreciated.* With respect to obtaining quotations for the Letter of Intent, users can be expected to withhold their highest bid, knowing that they probably will have to make a better offer at the time of bidding in order to purchase the material. The Letter of Intent, however, does assure that they will at least bid and that the price will not be lower than what is shown in the Letter. In this respect, the Letter of Intent is a bid, and can be assumed binding.

Terms and Conditions. The conditions of an advance commitment to be included in the Letter of Intent are length of commitment, quantity of material, quality, delivery schedule, termination and price.

Period of Commitment. The length of commitment should be related to the financing terms of the resource recovery plant or, at the very least, long enough to allow the recovery operation to get off the ground and gain momentum. It is highly unlikely — and unreasonable — to expect the advance commitment to include the full financing term, which will be 10 or more years. Each of the letters obtained as a result of the *Markets Study* are for five *operating years.* Because of the time needed to plan and construct a recovery plant, this will translate to eight or nine calendar years, which is a rather long advance commitment.

Specifications. The quality of the material to be delivered is delineated by a specification which becomes part of the Letter of Intent. Futhermore, the Letter identifies who will be

responsible for the accompanying quality control program, as well as what the basis will be for rejection or downgrading.

Letters of Intent requiring materials specifications so tight that they cannot be met are meaningless. Hence, this Markets Study and the Letters of Intent contain what are considered to be reasonable specifications which can be met by current and developing technology.*

Delivery. The operator of the facility must guarantee delivery of specified quantities on a prescribed schedule if he is to properly service the customers (buyers). This means that the participants in the I-95 Complex guarantee that those recovered materials which they will offer for sale will be delivered to the selected buyer in the bidding process.

The delivery schedule is based on quantities per day, week or month, and methods of delivery stating the form of transportation and minimum shipments allowed. This is essential information for planning and pricing the storage facilities, shipping dock and the user's facilities.

Termination. Termination clauses must be fair. Obviously, the seller cannot expect the customer to continue if the plant closes. And, the buyer cannot terminate the purchase agreement if the product is merely suspected of interfering with some operation or quality point.

---

*The Center, in performing the *Markets Study*, attempted to limit access to the actual bids and to disguise them. (Copies of the Letters of Intent and the exact bid price were made available to the Metropolitan Waste Management Agency.) Also, some amount has been subtracted from each offer whose exchange price was related to a commodity quote. This is the reason for the term "in excess of," which appears in some of the tables.

*The determination of specifications and quality control procedures for recovery from municipal waste of both energy and materials products have been the center of attention among a number of interested groups during the last four years. An early effort, sponsored by the Environmental Protection Agency and accomplished by the National Center, produced *Specifications for Materials Recovered From Municipal Refuse.* Environmental Protection Technology Series (EPA-670/2-75-034, May 1975), 109 pages. National Environmental Research Center, Office of Research and Development, U.S. Environmental Protection Agency, Cincinnati, Ohio 45268. (Two companion articles have appeared in the quarterly, *NCRR Bulletin:* "Specifications for Recovered Materials . . . A Prerequisite to Marketing." (Fall, 1975), Vol. V, No. 4, pp. 86–99; and Part II, (Winter, 1976) Vol. VI, No. 1, pp. 13–22.

In addition, note should be taken of the American Society for Testing and Materials and their Committee E-38 and its subcommittees structure which, along with the various secondary materials organizations, develop consensus specifications for recovered materials and fuel products.

Prices — "Exchange" and "Floor". In most cases, price appears at two places in each Letter of Intent. The first is called the *exchange price.* In some cases, it is fixed; in others it is a certain percentage of a published commodity price. For example, in the case of the light ferrous fraction (magnetic metals, mostly steel cans), Number 2 Dealer Bundles (a standard scrap commodity quote) is used. The fixed price may be an initial fixed amount. Aluminum, for example, may be subject to some escalation which is defined in advance and not tied to a commodity price series.

Letters of Intent were obtained for all of the materials except glass fines, commingled waste newspaper and commingled waste corrugated.* The letters obtained cover some 86 percent of the estimated value of the recovered materials in the waste (exclusive of the RDF fraction), as based on December 2, 1974 prices. This calculation is exclusive of the *exchange price* to be determined during the negotiation process (i.e., when final public bids are received which can be for more, but not less than the prices quoted in the letters).

The second price mentioned in most of the Letters of Intent is called the *floor price.* The *floor price* becomes applicable if the exchange relationship produces a price below the figure stated as the *floor price.* In terms of the established markets, the *floor price* should yield the lowest revenue for that particular commodity during the time the Letters of Intent are in effect. Of course, the material must still be produced according to the specifications.

Since the letters cover five operating years (starting around 1978), the potential user firms will have presumably hedged somewhat against future uncertainty in offering both *exchange prices* and *floor prices.*

The letters obtained varied somewhat in approach and language, because the initial goal was for signed documents as a substitute for vague promises. While desirable, the objective was not to standardize legal and purchasing

arrangements among various industries and firms. Because of the difficulty in sorting out the best bidder when there are two "floating" variables, it appears best to assert one in advance and, in this case, the *floor price* seems to be the appropriate choice. The current letters provide a basis for specifying these *floor prices.* It will then be left for the winning bid to be determined simply on the basis of the proposed *exchange price.*

Market Continuity and Variability. It is important to understand the difference between economics and technology as they relate to the *Markets Study.* If the materials are produced to specifications, then a market exists for five operating years. This covers *market continuity,* which poses a problem in the case of RDF. *Market variability* is another matter. If the *exchange price* is fixed, there is no concern. If it is tied to a commodity, there is a variability and a precise forecast is impossible. A *floor price* will allow for a minimum projection of revenues for the product in question.*

Establishing the Viability of the Market for Recovered Materials. *Table 3* shows the companies that have offered the advanced commitments.** *Table 4* shows the dollar amounts. "In excess" means that the actual dollar amount is greater but is not given exactly as a courtesy to the bidders. Advance markets were obtained for an estimated 86 percent of the materials recovery revenue potential (exclusive of RDF) using December 2, 1974 *exchange prices* or the appropriate fixed price. These cover light

---

*While secondary materials markets exhibit continuity (there generally is a demand), there is some variability. Listed below are prices for five commodities with quotations taken at six-month intervals beginning December of 1971. No. 1 News: $22, $20, $20, $18, $50, $35 per ton. Corrugated: $22, $22, $24, $33, $55, $45 per ton. No. 1 Heavy Melting Scrap: $27, $34, $41, $51, $85, $99 and No. 2 Dealer Bundles: $22, $27, $29, $40, $46, $49 per long ton. Old sheet and cast aluminum: 5 1/4¢, 5 1/2¢, 8 1/2¢, 10¢, 14 1/2¢ per pound.

**The Letters of Intent (see *Table 3*) remained in force after the July 1974 "statement of adequate progress" was released by the Metropolitan Washington Waste Management Agency. Two Letters were not continued at that time by the Alexandria (Va.) Scrap Corp., and the Garden State Paper Co.

---

*This is in contrast to source separated newspapers and corrugated. The plan for the facility is to handpick some news and corrugated from the mixed waste. This is a rather common practice for some commercial wastes when the markets are good for these products.

Table 3. Advance Commitments Obtained in the Markets Study.

Company	Material
Alexandria Scrap Corp.	– Heavy Ferrous and other Nonferrous
Aluminum Co. of America	– Aluminum
Anchor Hocking Corp.	– Glass
Bethlehem Steel Corp.	– Light Ferrous
Garden State Paper Co.	– Source Separated Newspapers
M & T Chemicals, Inc.	– Light Ferrous
Reynolds Metals Co.	– Aluminum
Vulcan Materials Co.	– Light Ferrous

Table 4. Materials Revenues.

Materials	Exchange Price	Floor Price
Ferrous		
Light	In excess of $55/long ton[1]	$20/long ton
Heavy	In excess of $72/long ton[1]	Not obtained
Nonferrous		
Aluminum	$300/ton[2]	$250 plus
Other Nonferrous	In excess of $350/ton[1]	Not obtained
Glass		
Flint	$16/ton - fixed	Same as
Color-Mixed	$15/ton - fixed	Exchange
Color-Mixed Fines	$15/ton[3]	Price
Commingled Paper		
Waste Corrugated	$20/ton[3]	$20/ton[3]
Waste News	$10/ton[3]	$10/ton[3]

[1] Based on quotations taken from the commodities market on December 2, 1974.
[2] One of the aluminum bid prices contains an escalator clause for the second through the fifth plant operating years.
[3] Prices for glass fines, waste corrugated and waste news are estimates, and are not covered by advance Letters of Intent. (See text for a discussion of the situation with glass fines and of the alternative to using the corrugated and news as RDF).

ferrous, heavy ferrous, aluminum, other nonferrous, flint glass cullet and some color-mixed cullet. Commingled waste corrugated, commingled waste newspapers and color-mixed glass fines are not covered by formal advanced commitments.

In the case of the waste news and waste corrugated, the lack of an advance commitment is not considered serious, since these combustible materials have revenue potential as RDF. At an RDF bargain of approximately $.60 per million BTU's, it would take an average $15.00 per ton *exchange price* to make it worthwhile to handpick the material. More detail is given on this in a later discussion of the *Feasibility Study*. It is only important, at this point, to note that recovered paper has a revenue potential, either as a fiber or as a supplementary fuel.

In the case of glass fines, the situation has improved. It now appears that properly prepared glass can be sold to the glass container manufacturing market. However, it may be more beneficial to pursue a local market which may have less stringent specifications. Two firms have expressed interest in using glass fines in their brick-making process. Because this is a new use for glass, however, they wish to sample it before signing a Letter of Intent. It is expected that tonnage samples of material could be supplied to them from a pilot plant (not that planned for Lorton) sometime early 1977. Letters of Intent could then be in hand before the design of the proposed plant is finalized.

Summary. A number of significant breakthroughs were made in the *Markets Study* by obtaining corporate commitments to purchase. In most cases, multiple advance commitments to bid were obtained, thereby setting up a truly competitive situation for the actual offering of the recovered products to the marketplace. The *Markets Study* set the stage for the *Feasibility Study,* the design and cost examination of a plant capable of producing materials to the specifications contained in the Letters of Intent.

THE FEASIBILITY STUDY

Resource recovery, as a concept, represents a systematic, long-range approach to solid waste management. As the pressures of waste disposal and the scarcity of materials and energy values mount, resource recovery will increase in appeal and application.

A Private Sector Analogy of the Economics.
While the I-95 project is contemplated for the public sector, it does have a revenue component. In this respect, the I-95 project is more like a private investment decision.* First, there are two distinct types of revenues to be considered: those from the recovered products, and those from dumping fees charged by the I-95 Complex for the disposal of MSW at the site.

The second aspect is that there is always some uncertainty as to the revenue. This is simply because the producer never has complete control over all forces affecting the market.

The final point is that if recovery cannot compete economically with landfill, then a recovery based disposal concept should probably not be adopted. The decreasing amount of landfill space will, however, raise the *current* costs considerably.

Technical Feasibility. Engineering and economic feasibility studies also help determine technical feasibility which is more subjective and less contingent on analysis.

Risk avoidance, rather than risk tolerance, guides the technical side of the feasibility evaluation. In this *Feasibility Study,* there is a greater, but certainly not total tolerance for risk than accepted usually in public works decisions. An objective of the study was for the jurisdictions to be in a position to take advantage of technology emerging during the long budget process without having to develop another submission for this project.

RDF Progress. Economics and technical feasibility depends on the RDF product. As the *Feasibility Study* was getting under way, there was a possibility of an eventual market with PEPCO. The I-95 Policy Committee became aware that PEPCO had signed a *Memorandum of Understanding* with Montgomery County, Md. and the Washington Suburban Sanitary Commission (WSSC) to use RDF mixed with sewage sludge in a planned generating boiler at Dickerson Station. Even though this project

would not begin operating before 1978, the I-95 Policy Committee was encouraged by PEPCO's cooperation with another jurisdiction on a similar project.

In the spring of 1975, a PEPCO position paper noted that it was "prudent" to consider substituting some portion of the fossil fuel currently being burned for refuse-derived fuel where possible. This paper said that, "the company considers that the burning of refuse-derived fuel is currently technically feasible and environmentally and socially extremely sensible." In the position paper, PEPCO reaffirmed its intention to "cooperate with area jurisdictions on the formulation of projects ... to develop meaningful refuse burning programs." Then, in August 1975, PEPCO committed to spend $55 million to purchase new electrostatic precipitators for its Potomac River Plant. These air pollution control devices are designed for coal and RDF emissions.

The need for the multijurisdictional approach of the I-95 Complex was also reinforced. In the position paper, PEPCO stated that "it is the responsibility of the many political subdivisions in the company's service area to implement a uniformity in approach and specification with respect to refuse-derived fuel." PEPCO also called attention to the need for "impersonal garbage." Jurisdictional boundaries are not to stand in the way of the provision of the RDF to a plant. PEPCO's concern was that local ordinances might be passed limiting the jurisdictional source of the fuel. This is within the spirit of the present *Memorandum of Understanding.*

Future Recovery Revenues. Long-term price trends also seem to favor resource recovery. Most expect that energy prices will increase faster than other commodities. However, the demand for and, hence, the price of secondary materials should also follow a long-term upward trend relative to other prices. This belief is underscored in the report to the President by the National Materials Commission.* From the standpoint of recycling waste, this is encouraging and is another factor underlying the decision to

---

*The classical distinctions between private and public sector activities are discussed in: R. Dorfman, *Measuring Benefits of Government Investment* (Brookings Institution, Washington, 1965).

*Material Needs and the Environment Today and Tomorrow. Final Report of the National Commission on Materials Policy (Washington, 1973).

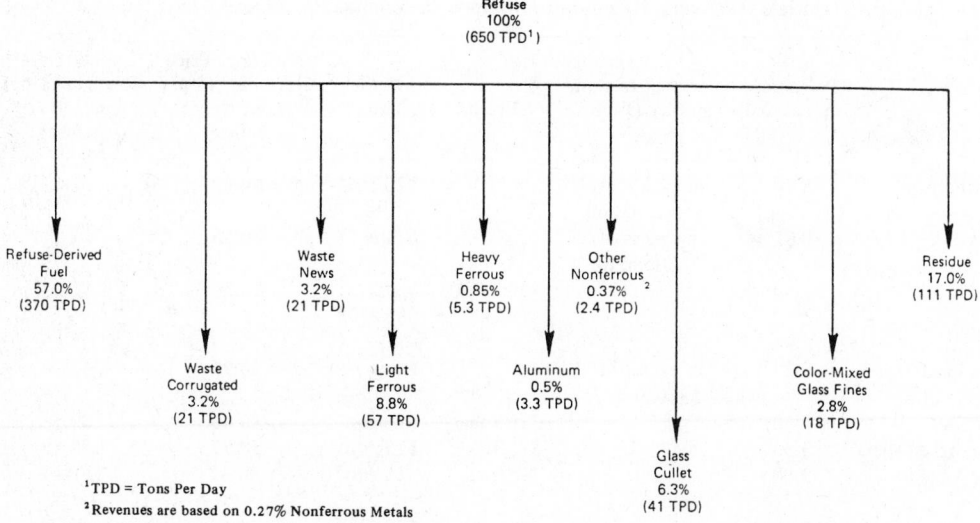

Figure 2. Disposition and Output of Products from the I-95 Complex Resource Recovery Processing.

look somewhat differently at risk and risk aversion during the conduct of the *Feasibility Study*.

The Feasibility Approach. Based on (1) the market commitments, (2) the presumption that a contract would be obtained for a refuse-derived fuel product, and (3) the fact that the RDF approach has the minimum capital costs of the various energy options, it was decided to evaluate the technological and economic feasibility of resource recovery processing. This included RDF as well as all of the materials reviewed in the *Markets Study*.

The Study. The *Feasibility Study* started with a set of recovery targets. *Figure 2* shows the targets in terms of projected recovery percentages for the facility which in turn depends on the estimates of the composition of the waste, *Table 5. Figure 2* also lists the targets as tonnages to be produced.

Using the exchange price relationships at their value on December 2, 1974, a revenue in excess of $9.67 per input ton could be expected.* This is detailed in *Table 5,* which also shows how a floor price value of $5.17 is developed. The floor price, again, is the minimum

that would be obtained during the contract period, subject to the same caveats as before about recovery rates and the ability to meet specifications.

In the *Feasibility Study,* facilities of 650 and 1,300 tons per day were investigated.* Six different product transportation approaches were compared for each. Only one facility size (650 TPD) and one transportation approach (the least costly) is presented here. The other options are detailed in the *Feasibility Study.* This transportation approach was to have the same trucks delivering raw refuse to Lorton take the RDF to PEPCO's Potomac River Station in Alexandria on the way back. No additional capital cost for new trucks is involved. However, there is an operating cost assigned, since the tonnage going to PEPCO is relatively small compared to the amount of raw waste delivered to the Lorton site. However, interjurisdictional pricing arrangements must be worked out in order to preserve the I-95 Complex cost center concept. This general issue is introduced again in the section in the *Network Study.* Appropriate cost accounting and allocation is important to the future implementation of recovery at Lorton.

---

*The in-excess number results from an attempt to preserve some confidentiality as far as the actual offers are concerned.

---

*These size plants were chosen for analysis in order to build on a previous work for a 650 TPD facility.

Table 5. Materials Recovery Revenue Estimates: Exchange Prices and Floor Prices.[1]

Materials	Percentage Recovered	Exchange Price Related to Commodity Quotes	Fixed	Floor Price	Exchange Price Revenue[4] ($ per input ton of refuse)	Floor Price Revenue ($ per input ton of refuse)
Light Ferrous	8.80	in excess of $55/long ton[4]		$20/long ton	$4.32	$1.57
Heavy Ferrous	0.85	in excess of $72/long ton[4]		None	$0.55	---
Aluminum	0.50		$300/ton[2]	in excess of $250/ ton	$1.50	$1.25
Other nonferrous	0.27[5]	in excess of $350/ton		None	$0.95	---
Flint Glass	2.50		$16/ton	$16/ton	$0.40	$0.40
Color-Mixed Glass	3.80		$15/ton	$15/ton	$0.57	$0.57
Color-Mixed Glass Fines	2.80		$15/ton[3]	$15/ton[3]	$0.42	$0.42
Waste Corrugated	3.20			$20/ton[3]	$0.64	$0.64
Waste News	3.20			$10/ton[3]	$0.32	$0.32
Total Revenue					$9.67	$5.17

[1] These are gross revenues. They do not include transportation, which will be added as a *cost* in the overall economic analysis.
[2] The aluminum bid price increases each year from more than $300/ton in year one to more than $400/ton in year five.
[3] Prices for glass fines, waste corrugated and waste news are estimated, and are not covered by advance Letter of Intent.
[4] Based on December 2, 1974 commodity market prices where appropriate.
[5] Basis for revenue only. Actual output of 0.37% includes non-metallics for which no revenue is received.

It should be understood that the cost figures presented in the *Feasibility Study* cannot be interpreted as exact point estimates in spite of being quoted to the nearest cent, because of the sources from which it drew its basic data. Because of the lack of precise knowledge concerning the composition of the refuse, efficiency of the separation process, and calculations of costs and revenues, it is necessary to assume an uncertainty range of plus or minus 15 percent for each summary number that actually appears in the study.

Feasibility Determined in the 1974 Period. Note that the costs for the feasibility question are separate from the forecasting necessary to prepare actual budgets. The feasibility discussion is in 1974 dollars. This is appropriate for an initial determination of feasibility. However, because discussion is based on 1974 dollars, caution must be exercised *not* to interpret the numbers in the *Feasibility Study* as a projected budget. Costs quoted cannot be used for bud-

getary purposes without time-phasing and the application of inflation factors.

Handling the RDF Market Gap. As stated, the RDF market has not yet been secured through any agreement (p. 192). The Indifference Value for RDF is defined as the minimum value for the exchange price, in order for the net operating cost of a Lorton-sited facility to be equivalent to simply landfilling an equivalent amount of refuse where the cost of the latter is assumed to be the same as Lorton's projected operating landfill cost for 1975. This is $3.79 per ton.* This same figure is used for the projected cost of landfilling the unrecovered residue from the facility. Recall that 17 percent of the input is not recovered and must be landfilled.

Figure 3 illustrates the IV concept for the 650 TPD resource recovery facility. The left

---

*The actual charge budgeted for FY 75 was $5.93 per ton. The additional $2.14 per ton was attributable to the one-year expensing of what would normally be amortized capital outlays.

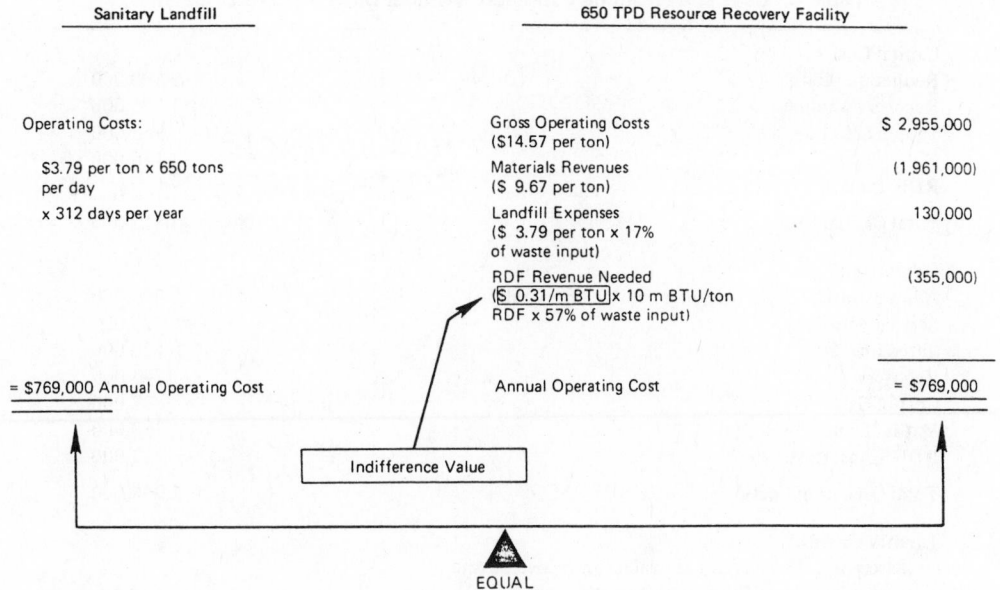

Sanitary Landfill		650 TPD Resource Recovery Facility	
Operating Costs:		Gross Operating Costs ($14.57 per ton)	$ 2,955,000
$3.79 per ton x 650 tons per day		Materials Revenues ($ 9.67 per ton)	(1,961,000)
x 312 days per year		Landfill Expenses ($ 3.79 per ton x 17% of waste input)	130,000
		RDF Revenue Needed ($ 0.31/m BTU x 10 m BTU/ton RDF x 57% of waste input)	(355,000)
= $769,000 Annual Operating Cost		Annual Operating Cost	= $769,000

Indifference Value

EQUAL

Figure 3. The Indifference Principle.

side shows the cost of continuing to landfill 650 TPD. The assumption is that no resource recovery facility is built. It can be seen that the operating budget for this would be $769,000. The right side is made to balance out at the same annual operating cost; but, in this case, the recovery facility is assumed to be built and processes the 650 tons of waste. The approach of balancing costs and revenues as illustrated by *Figure 3* is used to determine the Indifference Value that must be obtained in order for the plant to "break even."

Cost and revenue figures come from the *Feasibility Study*. *Table 6* shows the least costly of those options evaluated. Other transportation alternatives considered were rail, the purchase of additional trucks, and the elimination of the backhaul feature from the trucks employed.

On the right side of *Figure 3*, gross operating costs of the facility are shown as $14.57 per ton, or $2,955,000 annually. December 2, 1974 prices are assumed for the sale of recovered materials. This is $9.67 per ton, or $1,961,000 annually. The analysis assumes that 57 percent (by weight) of the refuse emerges as RDF. The RDF is assumed to have a heat value of 5000 BTU's per pound, at a moisture content of 27.5

percent, as delivered.* The recovery facility must bear the cost of its residue disposal (17 percent of the input), in addition to selling its RDF. In order to obtain the desired net operating cost of $769,000, simple subtraction shows that RDF has to account for $355,000 annually in revenues. The required IV easily can be determined by multiplying 650 tons per day X 312 days per year X 57 percent X 10 million BTU's per ton RDF X the unknown IV and setting this product equal to $355,000 per year. Solving for the unknown IV then produces a figure of $0.31 per million BTU's, which is far less than 1975 coal prices in the Washington area.

*Based on 380 samples taken November 9, 1973 through December 10, 1974 at the Union Electric Meramec Plant.

	As-Fired Basis		
	Moisture	Ash	BTU/Pound
Average	27.5	18.5	5,006
Maximum	63.0	53.8	7,593
Minimum	3.0	7.6	2,293

. . . D.L. Klumb, *Union Electric Company's Solid Waste Utilization System.* Paper presented to Energy Recovery from Solid Wastes Symposium, College Park, Maryland (March 1975); *Resource Recovery and Conservation.* (1976) *1* (3), p. 225.

Table 6. Cost and Revenue Estimates (Annual Basis — 1974 Dollars).

Capital Cost	
Reduction Module	2,590,000
Recovery Module	3,106,000
Support Module	963,000
Mat'ls. Trans.	156,000
RDF Trans.	− 0 −*
Total Capital Costs	6,815,000
Operating Costs	
Administration Costs (includes capital amortization)	1,099,000
Service Area	222,000
Shredding Area	490,000
Recovery Area	746,000
Cost of Sales	27,000
Mat'ls. Trans. Costs	358,000
RDF Trans. Costs	13,000
Total Operating Costs	2,955,000
Landfill Credit	
(Based on a $3.79 credit for each ton recovered and	
therefore not landfilled − 83% of the input.)	639,000
Exchange Price	
Estimated Mat'ls. Revenue (Based on a sales price of $9.67 per input ton	1,961,000
at an average daily input of 650 tons of waste.)	
RDF Revenues Needed ($)	355,000
RDF Indifference Value ($/MBTU)	0.31
Floor Price	
Estimated Mat'ls. Revenue (Based on a sales price of $5.17 per input ton	1,048,000
at an average daily input of 650 tons of waste.)	
RDF Revenues needed ($)	1,268,000
RDF Indifference Value ($/MBTU)	1.10

*Trucks hauling refuse to the Lorton site from the District will return via the Potomac River station in Alexandria. These trucks are part of the collection system and no costs were assigned to the project for their purchase.

The Disposal Dividend. The disposal dividend potential can be explained in this example. Suppose the RDF bargain is struck at $.65 per million BTU's in 1974 prices rather than $.31. This generates an additional $390,000 of income over or above the $355,000 RDF "revenues needed" figure. This amounts to a cost reduction of more than $.50 per input ton of waste.

A somewhat uncertain area in determining net costs is the landfill credit. A figure of $3.79 was assigned for every ton of refuse diverted from landfill operations. It was not possible to make an exact estimate of the savings attributed to not having to landfill the recovered materials simply because data are not available upon which to base this calculation. The proposed operating cost of the I-95 landfill for FY 75, was, therefore, utilized.* There are two problems with this estimator: (1) it is an average rather than a marginal number, and from this standpoint it may be biased upward; i.e., it could be too high; and (2) it is not a total cost number that private accounting practices would amortize. This introduces a downward bias. Because of the actual accounting procedures followed, it did not seem to be possible to develop an accurate marginal cost estimate. At the level of detail of this analysis and considering other uncertainties, this appears to be satisfactory. If

*V.L. Stanhope, *Proposed I-95 Capital and Operating Budget for FY 75.* (D.C. Department of Environmental Services), June 3, 1974.

marginal landfill costs are higher than $3.79 per ton, the IV value would be lower and recovery would be competitive with landfill at a lesser RDF bargain.

Is the IV in the Bargaining Range?   The application of ordinary algebra to solve for the IV value, which results in the energy value being treated as a residual, does not mean that energy recovery is being downplayed. To the contrary, the IV values are simply the minimum values which allow resource recovery to be competitive with sanitary landfill at the Lorton site, under either *exchange price* or *floor price* conditions.

Whether these IV values can be obtained is speculative, because market assurances for RDF have not yet been obtained (this also accounts for the analysis methodology). Therefore, the ultimate question of overall economic feasibility is a matter of future consideration. However, December 1974 coal prices in the D.C. area were at the $1.65 per million BTU's level. When materials revenues reach the December 1974 exchange price level, the target Indifference Values will be well below the current price of coal. The latter, after subtracting estimated costs of possible problems in RDF handling and combustion, must be regarded as the upper limit, or Indifference Value, from the perspective of the coal burning user.

When materials revenues are at the floor price level, the RDF IV is raised to $1.10 per million BTU's. Here, the RDF IV may be outside the "bargaining" range. However, these materials revenues do not take into account heavy ferrous and nonferrous metals for which it was not possible to obtain a *floor price*. Therefore, these materials were given a zero value in the *floor price* calculation even though there should always be a market at some price.

Sensitivity Analysis.   Finally, one should ask the question of how sensitive the IV value is to less than full realization of the materials recovery revenue expectations (and vice versa), and the sensitivity of the facility's economics to a poor RDF bargain. *Figure 4* illustrates this trade-off. Illustrated in the upper left intercept is the level that materials recovery revenues must reach

in order for the IV to become zero. At materials recovery revenues of $11.20 per input ton, recovery would be competitive with landfill even if RDF were delivered to the users at a zero RDF bargain. Conversely, the right intercept on the horizontal axis illustrates the IV price which would enable materials products to be delivered to their markets at a zero *exchange price*. This figure is an IV of $2.02 per million BTU's (around the current price of oil). Note that at the *floor price* calculation produces a required IV figure of $1.10 per million BTU's.* This illustrates that the 1974 analysis, an RDF exchange value of about this figure would be economically sound. If ferrous recovery alone succeeds, the IV will be $1.20 per million BTU's.**

Can and Bottle Legislation.   What would be the impact of can and bottle legislation on the economics of the facility once it was built? An analysis was prepared which assumed losses in revenues of 9 percent for ferrous metals, 36 percent for aluminum and 42 percent for glass. (These estimates are difficult to make with precision. However, they were reviewed by the Environmental Protection Agency, among others, and judged to be a reasonable starting point.) Based on the December 1974 *exchange prices*, this would mean a new materials recovery revenue estimate of $8.23 per input ton. Additionally, less tonnage would be available for processing. This would translate into a new IV of $.61 per million BTU's.

The initial Lorton facility landfill will be receiving up to 4,000 TPD, of which only 650 would be processed for recovery. It should be noted that the waste, after container legislation will have less metals and glass and more combustibles. This adjustment changes the IV value. Because there is more RDF per input ton of

---

*Remembering this does not take into account the sale of heavy ferrous or other nonferrous metals, and uses assumed figures for color-mixed glass fines, corrugated and waste newspapers.

**All of this is in 1974 costs and prices. The actual bargain has to be higher because it will not be realized until sometime after 1978.

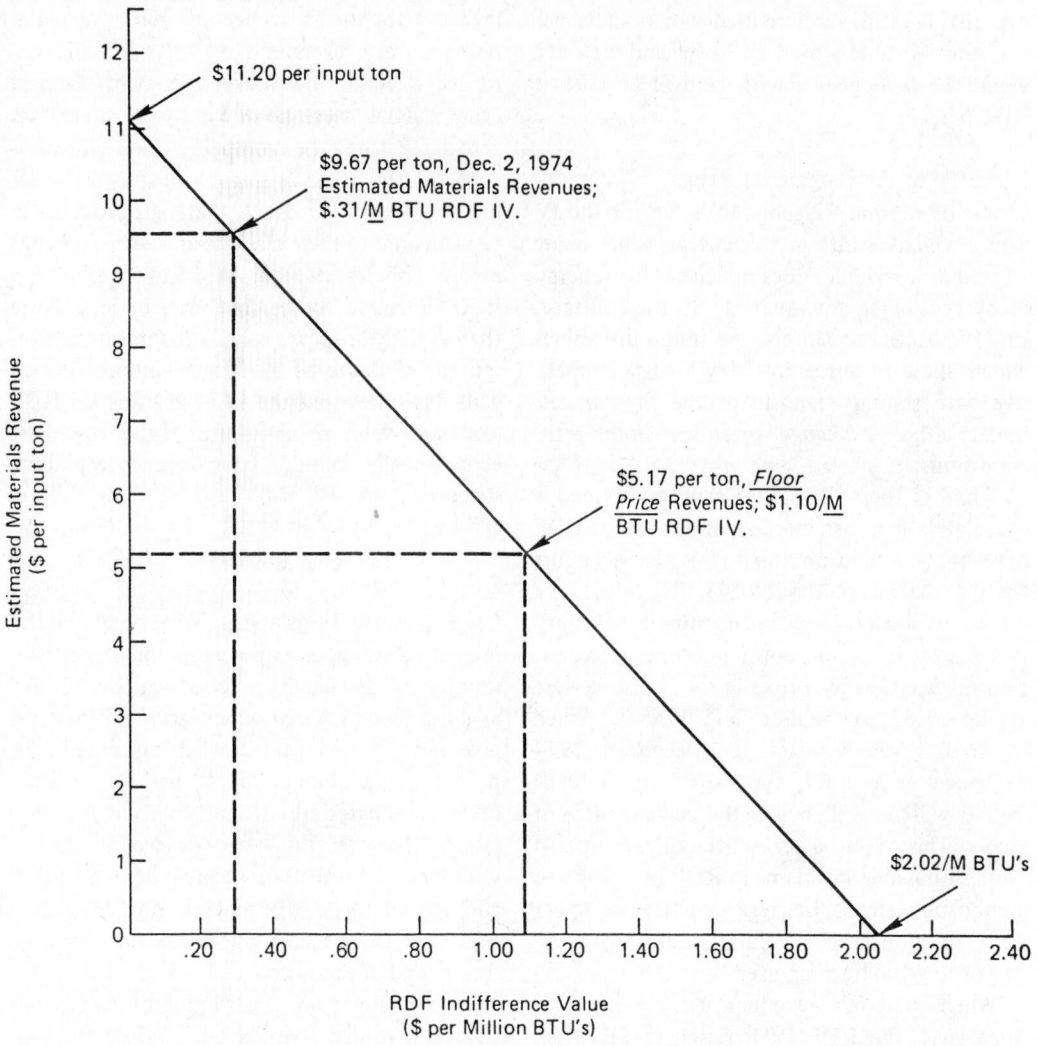

Figure 4. Trade-off Between Estimated Materials Revenue and RDF Indifference Value for 650 TPD Facility.

waste, the initially impacted IV of $0.61 *decreases* to $0.47 per million BTU's.*

Handpicked Commingled News and Corrugated.
Two of the materials recovery revenues are derived from handpicking commingled waste newspapers ($10 per ton) and waste corrugated (20 per ton). If commitments for the handpicked material cannot be obtained (and they have not been to date), the estimated materials revenues would be reduced by $.96 per input ton. With-

out a market, there would be no handpicking, and the output of RDF would be increased 6.4 percent, or 128 pounds of RDF per input ton of refuse. At a 6800 BTU's/pound heat value for paper, 0.87 million BTU's per input ton would be added to the RDF output. Further, operating costs could be reduced, and if no handpicking is contemplated at the start, the baling equipment would not be procured.

A calculation made in the *Feasibility Study* showed that at an RDF bargain of $.60 per million BTU's, one would be as well off using the paper and corrugated as RDF rather than handpicking it when the latter yields a price of $10 and $20, respectively. Since the RDF bargain

*When additional waste is available for processing, the RDF quantity produced by a 650 ton per day facility increases from 371 to 393 tons per day.

may be in this range, the lack of advanced market commitments for handpicked waste newspaper and corrugated is not considered serious.

A Relatively Small Facility First. To proceed with large-scale resource recovery (thousands of tons per day) without first establishing a small-scale facility (hundreds of tons per day), would be less than prudent. If RDF markets are actually obtained, higher capital outlays for scaling-up the capacity of the initial facility may be warranted. Expansion could be accomplished by enlarging the receiving area of the facility and adding a third operating shift for greater throughput. This would require further investment.

Summary. The *Feasibility Study* and the *Markets Study* represented several steps in a systematic development plan to evaluate the potential for resource recovery by the participating jurisdictions. Contained therein are perhaps the strongest set of market commitments yet developed in *advance* of either approved funding or a signed contract. It should be noted that the RDF "bargain" has not been finalized. This, however, is the case nationwide and perhaps is not a cause for delay.

Communities that have moved to the "commitment" stage in advance of a firm energy market appear to have done so as a result of evaluating the rather large benefits of earlier success in such an endeavor. Presumably, they believe that their users will not terminate the contracts they have signed, even though in all cases they have the right to do so. While the communities face the potential of such a decision outdating their processing facilities and

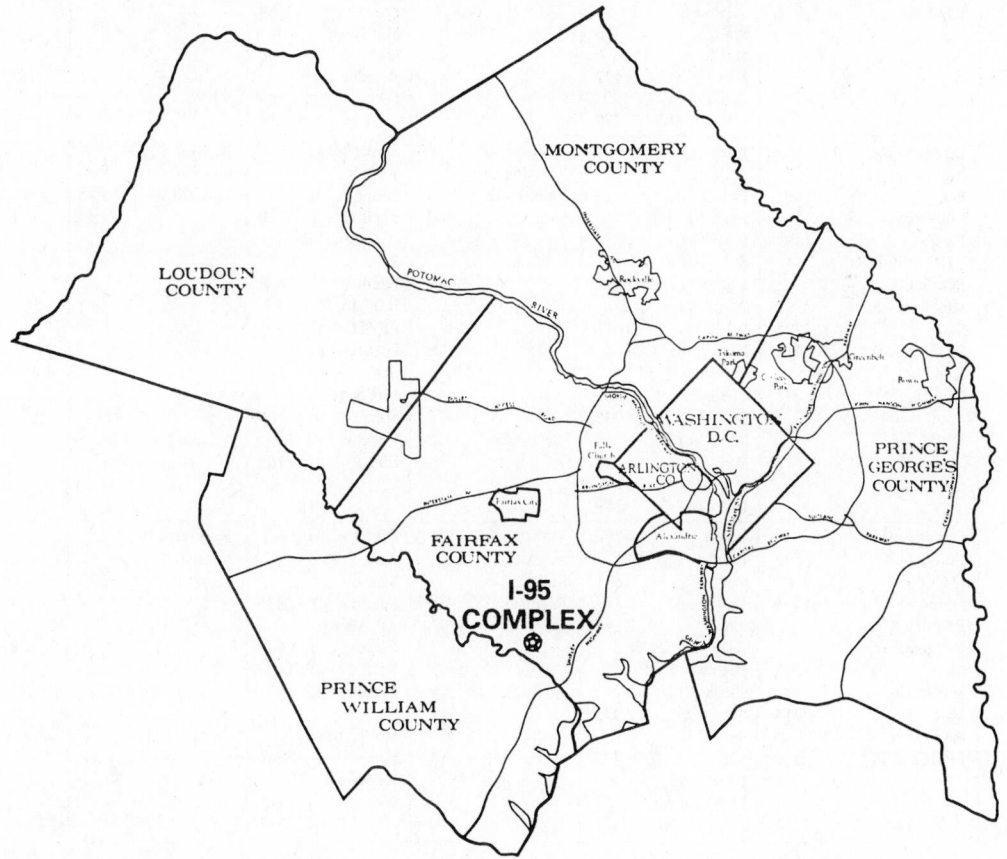

Illustration: Metropolitan Washington area showing location of I-95 Complex in Lorton, Virginia. Participating I-95 jurisdictions are shown shaded.

Table 7. Alternative Solid Waste Management Networks.

Network Scenario	District of Columbia Trans/Disp Mode	TPD	Fairfax County Trans/Disp Mode	TPD	Arlington County Trans/Disp Mode	TPD	City of Alexandria Trans/Disp Mode	TPD	I-95 Complex Trans/Disp Mode	TPD	Possible Operational Timeframe
H	Transfer to I-95	1593	Transfer to I-95 Direct to I-95	500 1141	Transfer to I-95	400	Transfer to I-95	239	Full Scope Facility at I-95 RDF to PEPCO Potomac R. & Morgantown Sta. Mat'ls. to Mkt. Residue Land-fill at I-95	3873 2208 1007 658	1985
I	Direct to D.C. Full-Scope Facility Full-Scope Facility RDF to PEPCO Benning & Morgantown Mat'ls. to Mkt. Residue to I-95 Landfill	1593 1593 908 414 271	Direct (1141) and transfer (500) to Fair-fax County Full-Scope Fac. Full-Scope Fac. RDF to PEPCO Potomac R. & Chalk Pt. Sta. Mat'ls. to Mkt. Residue to I-95 Landfill	1641 1641 935 427 279	Transfer to Arl-Alex Full-Scope Facility	400	Direct to Arl-Alex Full-Scope Facility Arl-Alex Full-Scope Facil-ity RDF to PEPCO Potomac R. Sta. Mat'ls. to Mkt. Residue to I-95	239 639 364 166 109	Residue Disposal at Landfill	659	1985
J	Direct to D.C. Full-Scope Fac. Full-Scope Fac. RDF to PEPCO Benning & Morgantown Sta. Mat'ls. to Mkt. Residue to I-95 Landfill	1593 1593 908 414 271	Direct to Fair-fax County Full-Scope Fac., 1 at I-95 (650 TPD) & 1 at I-66 area (991) 2 Full-Scope Facilities RDF to PEPCO Potomac R. & Chalk Point Sta. Mat'ls. to Mkt. Residue to I-95 Landfill	1641 1641 935 427 279	Transfer to Arl-Alex Full-Scope Facility	400	Direct to Arl-Alex Full-Scope Facility Arl-Alex Full-Scope Facility RDF to PEPCO Potomac R. Sta. Mat'ls. to Mkt. Residue to I-95	239 639 364 166 109	Residue Dis-posal at Landfill	659	1985
K	Direct to D.C. Full-Scope D.C. Full-Scope Benning & Morgantown Sta. Mat'ls. to Mkt. Residue to I-95 Landfill	1593 1593 908 414 271	Direct to Fairfax County Full-Scope Fac. RDF to PEPCO Potomac R. & Chalk Pt. Sta. Mat'ls. to Mkt. Residue to I-95 Landfill	1641 1641 935 427 279	Transfer to Arl-Alex Full-Scope Facility	400	Direct to Arl-Alex Full-Scope Facility Arl-Alex Facility RDF to PEPCO Potomac R. Sta. Mat'ls. to Mkt. Residue to I-95	239 639 364 166 109	Residue Dis-posal at Landfill	659	1985

causing loss of the capital invested, they have decided to move ahead. In one sense, the materials recovery targets of the facility proposed for Lorton provide a hedge against this. However, only the future will tell whether these other jurisdictions as well as this metropolitan area have made a correct evaluation of recovery's promises and pitfalls.

THE NETWORK STUDY

The purpose of the *Network Study* was to test the validity of a resource recovery plant proposed as a result of the *Feasibility Study*.

The *Network Study* is an attempt to optimize the regional management of solid waste in the future. There are distinct advantages to a regional approach: risks can be spread, and economies of scale may result in lower capital and operating costs for the overall system. There is also a larger base of support for financing such high capital cost efforts as resource recovery. Arrangements for sale of energy and materials products can be performed for all, rather than for each jurisdiction separately. An approach based on multijurisdictional criteria, once adopted, will centralize the decision-making process to the benefit of the multiple participants. Regional planning reduces the "critical" nature of the problem on an individual jurisdictional basis, and eliminates haphazard solutions.

It is obvious that the proposed 650 TPD facility is not sufficient to handle all the waste generated by the participating jurisdictions. Granted, the *Memorandum of Understanding* located the facility at Lorton. At that time, most expected that a very large plant would be built at Lorton.

Is Lorton the Best Location? It was possible to generalize by going back to the initial presumption of a large scale *centralized* plant at Lorton and to contrast this with a series of *decentralized* systems each with plants at multiple locations throughout the area. In doing so, it quickly became evident that transportation costs were the prime driving force in determining the preferred solid waste management network. In this regard, a large centralized

facility at Lorton suffers. It is simply not strategically located with reference to the waste generation areas and the potential RDF user locations. The reader will recall that the "ground rules" of the *Feasibility Study* were to assure that the refuse was already at Lorton. The cost of transporting it to Lorton was not considered. The cost center for the *Feasibility Study* consisted of processing at Lorton, including the cost to dispose of the residue, and the cost of transporting to market each of the recovered products — RDF and the materials. The *Network Study* adds to this the cost estimates for transporting the refuse from generation centers to a processing facility — Lorton or another plant in the system depending upon which of the eleven alternative networks are being evaluated. The *Network Study* is, therefore, a complete analysis and a check on the results of the *Feasibility Study*.

While complete in the sense that it accounts for all relevant costs, the *Network Study* is only a preliminary analysis. Even then, it turns out to be a rather formidable document. This is because the question asked really is a rather difficult one. See, for example, *Table 7* which shows waste and product flows for only four of the alternatives considered.

Minimum System Cost. The *Network Study* was to evaluate alternative networks in terms of systems costs. *Table 8* reflects an analysis of the four selected resource recovery networks. Given are gross costs annual, gross costs per ton, revenues per year, net costs annual and net costs per ton of waste processed. It should be noted that there is a difference between minimum system's costs and average costs to each jurisdiction. This is illustrated for selected networks in *Table 9*.

From this table one can see the fragile nature of any coalition. All systems provide differential benefits and impose differential penalties. This tends to be destabilizing. Therefore, the second point is to optimize within the coalition, a path that might break up the cooperative endeavor and thereby sacrifice the opportunity of achieving the merit of any of the more desirable networks.

Table 8. Selected Network Costs and Revenue Estimates (1974 Dollars).

Network	Gross Costs ($/Year)	Gross Costs ($/Ton)	Revenues ($/Year)		Net Costs ($/Year)	Net ($/Ton)
H	25,265,500	20.90	RDF	5,166,720	9,827,580	8.13
			MAT'LS	10,271,200		
				15,437,920		
I	20,395,100	16.88	RDF	5,164,380	4,959,520	4.10
			MAT'LS	10,271,200		
				15,435,580		
J	20,942,700	17.33	RDF	5,164,380	5,507,120	4.56
			MAT'LS	10,271,200		
				15,435,580		
K	20,024,500	16.57	RDF	5,164,380	4,588,920	3.80
			MAT'LS	10,271,200		
				15,435,580		

RDF revenues assumed to be at $0.75 per million BTU's and *materials revenues* at $8.50 per input ton for full facilities.

Table 9. Gross Cost Per Ton by Individual Participating Jurisdiction and for I-95 Complex as a Whole.

Network	District of Columbia Gross Cost per Input Ton	Fairfax County Gross Cost per Input Ton	Arlington County Gross Cost per Input Ton	City of Alexandria Gross Cost per Input Ton	I-95 Complex as a Whole Gross Cost per Input Ton
Centralized					
H	$27.09	$14.30	$25.09	$18.09	$20.90
Decentralized					
I	$15.00	$17.38	$21.77	$17.77	$16.88
J	$15.00	$18.45	$21.77	$17.77	$17.43
K	$15.00	$16.66	$21.77	$17.77	$16.57

The *Network Study* found that such an initial 650 TPD facility at the I-95 site is compatible with each of the preferred networks. However, to go beyond 1,300 TPD at the Lorton site would not be warranted unless better site locations are not available.

THE CURRENT STATUS

The recommendations resulting from the three studies is that construction of the first resource recovery facility be undertaken. The Feasibility Study shows that a facility to process 650 TPD of the area's solid waste is a prudent first step. It offers an opportunity for the participating jurisdictions to become familiar with the technology and to open markets. The economic projections show that the cost (in terms of tipping fee, and including capital amortization) can be competitive with continued landfilling at Lorton.

Implementation of the resource recovery facility according to the 1973 Memorandum means that the District of Columbia underwrites the bonds for facility design and construction, and all of the participating jurisdictions contribute to the payback of the construction portion of the bonds through payment of their portion of the tipping fee.

The recommendation was put before the District of Columbia City Council as part of the Department of Environmental Services' Fiscal year 1976 Capital Improvements Program. The request was for $9.651 million for the design, procurement of equipment and construction of the 650 TPD facility.

At the time this report was written, the budget request was undergoing Congressional review. Assuming Congressional approval, the City Council could then consider passage of bond authorization acts on each part of the Capital Improvements Program. However, at a later date the U.S. Senate deleted this item from the budget and effectively "killed" the project.

2-14 Elements of Financial Risk

Jeffrey F. Clunie and Robert G. Taylor
Source: *Proceedings* of the National Waste Processing Conference, Chicago, Illinois, May 7–10, 1978, pp. 287–293. Reprinted with Permission of The American Society of Mechanical Engineers.

ABSTRACT

Generally engineers concern themselves with the mechanical operating aspects of a solid waste resource recovery facility. However, the prospective investor who is asked to finance such a facility is often more concerned with the non-mechanical aspects involved. These aspects affect the ability of the facility to generate the net revenues necessary to pay off the long-term financing required to construct the facility and therefore investors may be more interested in the contracts for the sale of energy, the sale of recovered materials, the availability and guaranteed delivery of the solid waste and the possibility of a loss in revenue because of the future installation of a more advanced type of facility within the service area. This paper identifies how the major elements that affect the flow of revenues and financial risk must be evaluated in the financing of a solid waste resource recovery project.

INTRODUCTION

In 1972, revenue bonds of the Nashville Thermal Transfer Corporation, the country's first large-scale solid waste resource recovery facility, were offered for sale to investors accompanied by newspaper stories proclaiming the dawning of a golden age of a new technology, "Cash from Trash" and "Solid Gold from Solid Waste". The bonds received a provisional A rating and the investment community eargerly awaited the operation of a new system which helped solve the dual problem of disposing of solid waste and recovering the energy which existed within that solid waste. However, in the years that have followed, various operating problems have been experienced at Nashville and at several other solid waste resource recovery facilities and the once ebullient investor has tended to become wary and cautious and is now much better informed concerning the various elements of risk which inherently exist in any such proposed facility. Accordingly, any community, authority or organization desirous of financing the cost of a solid waste resource recovery facility through the sale of some form of long-term debt to the investment community must be prepared to clearly identify all potential areas of financial risks and explain the steps taken to reduce the potential loss of revenue due to such risks.

The five major areas affecting the net earning capability of a facility are: (1) the technical soundness of the proposed solid waste resource recovery facility; (2) the availability and quantity of solid waste to be disposed of; (3) the revenue-producing contracts; (4) the cost of construction of the facility; and (5) the cost of operation of the facility. Each one of these matters will be given very careful consideration by any and all potential investors.

It should be pointed out that in the context of this paper, the term "investor" is generally used in a financial sense to denote those individuals or institutions who purchase the long-term debt issued to pay for the cost of constructing the facility. However, when reviewing financial risk, the "investors" who are concerned with such matters include not only financial institutions, but also the municipality or company constructing and operating the facility, the engineers designing the facility, the customers purchasing the recovered steam energy and recyclable material and the taxpayers located within the service area of the facility. All of the above are making an investment of one form or another.

It should further be noted that the term "solid waste resource recovery facility" can cover a broad spectrum of technologies ranging from composting and recycling centers, through bulk burners with no front-end separation to pyrolytic converters and refuse derived fuel (RDF) facilities with front-end separation and material processing. The type of technology ultimately chosen for use by a community may vary depending upon the amount of land available for solid waste disposal, the size of the community, the amount of capital expenditure which can be supported and the availability of suitable customers for the sale of the recovered energy and recyclable materials. This paper generally limits its scope to a discussion of those solid waste resource recovery facilities which include the generation of some form of steam energy and the recovery of recyclable materials.

TECHNICAL FEASIBILITY
OF THE FACILITY

Obviously, one of the most basic concerns any investor would have centers on whether or not the facility, as designed, is mechanically sound and technically feasible. During the past several years, stories of billowing black smoke, superheater failures, boiler tube corrosion and explosions within shredders have altered investors that serious potential problems exist with the operation of any facility using a combustible fuel.

Investors want to be assured that the facility, as designed, is sound from an engineering point of view. Care and consideration must show that the components of the facility have been suitably sized and compliment one another. There is little to be gained in having an incinerator boiler capable of disposing of 2000 tons of solid waste per day if the front end feeding system is capable of handling only 500 tons of solid waste per day, particularly if the economics have been based on an assumed operating level of 2000 tons of solid waste per day. It is

also important that adequate redundancy and bypasses have been included within the design of the facility so that solid waste can continue to be used as the principal source of fuel in the incinerator boilers in the event a problem should develop in the front end material handling process.

The facility must also be designed to meet increasingly stringent environmental standards. Investors want to be assured that the facility as designed will be capable of meeting federal, state and local criteria for site requirements, noise and traffic standards, watershed requirements and air emission control levels and that it is unlikely that the operation of the facility (and the generation of revenues) will be either halted completely or seriously curtailed pending the issuance of a Compliance Order by the Environmental Protection Agency. Air quality is of particular concern and care must be taken that the proper type of air quality control equipment is being installed, that tests indicate it has successfully met the air quality standards for the particular site where the facility is to be located, and that it is properly sized in relation to the other components of the facility.

There is also concern that the design of the facility assures that the incinerator boilers are capable of generating the quantity of steam energy and at the conditions and quality standards which are required in the service contract(s) negotiated with the steam energy customer(s). The inability of the facility to supply the quantity or quality of steam required by a contract will affect not only the amount of revenues derived but may also, dependent upon the terms stated therein, negate the service contract.

A similar question of plant design relates to the facility's ability to recover ferrous and nonferrous metals, glass, corrugated cardboard and other recyclable materials in the quantities required by service contracts and which have been projected in the proforma operating results showing financial feasibility. The ability of the facility to recover recyclable materials is a function of both the technical design of the facility (magnetic separators, air classifiers, etc.) and the composition of the solid waste being disposed of at the facility. Because of the possibility of passage of "bottle-bills" which could seriously affect the amount of aluminum beverage containers and glass bottles within the solid waste stream, it is generally more desirable to be able to show the financial feasibility of a particular facility without relying upon potential revenues from any recyclable materials other than ferrous metals. Furthermore, the state of the art for much of the equipment being utilized in the recovery of other recyclable materials is still relatively new and continued changes and improvements are probable.

The anticipated availability of the incinerator boilers can also have a significant impact upon the financial feasibility of a facility as it can affect both the amount of operating revenues received in the form of tipping fees as well as the operating expense related to the amount of supplementary fossil fuel which must be burned to supply steam energy during those times the incinerator boilers are unable to utilize solid waste as a fuel. For example, should the proforma operating results indicate financial feasibility on the basis of the incinerator boilers being able to fire solid waste as a fuel for 85 percent of the time and if actual operating experience prove that incinerator boiler availability is actually only 60 percent, then tipping fee revenues would be approximately 30 percent lower than projected and fossil fuel expense could increase by approximately 167 percent. Such an occurrence could impair the ability of the facility to meet its debt service requirements. Investors have become wary of overly optimistic claims concerning boiler availability and prefer to see that financial feasibility can be shown on the basis of proforma operating results prepared using relatively conservative assumptions.

The expected useful life of the facility also represents an area of concern to any investor, particularly if the facility is to be financed by means of the issuance of revenue bonds. If debt service requirements are to be paid exclusively from operating revenues, it is essential that the expected useful life of the facility is equal to or greater than the amortization period of the bonds.

SUPPLY OF SOLID WASTE

Since a solid waste resource recovery facility's primary source of raw material, and a portion of its operating revenues, are dependent upon the amount of solid waste disposed of, investors have become increasingly concerned that there is an adequate supply of solid waste available and that provisions have been made which assure its delivery to the facility.

Any review of the supply of solid waste must begin with a determination as to the amount and composition of the solid waste being generated within the service area of the facility. A review of the quantity of solid waste can be made on the basis of any one of the following: (1) historical records which have been kept by either existing landfills and incinerators within the service area or by municipal and private haulers of solid waste; (2) a composite average based upon analyses of the quantity and composition of solid waste prepared in other parts of the country; and (3) performing an actual study for a twelve-month period of the quantity and composition of all of the solid waste within the proposed service area of the facility. Performing an actual study as part of the financing analysis is not normally considered a viable alternative due to the length of time required to perform a study and the prohibitive expense associated with performing such a study. Therefore information available from other studies of the solid waste in the general area of the proposed facility is used when available. An estimate of the quantity of solid waste which is prepared on the basis of historical tipping records is generally acceptable, particularly if the results approximate those averages for the nation as a whole. Should the review indicate major differences between available historical records and national averages, then an analysis and explanation as to the reason for such differences would be required. This entire matter of the amount of solid waste becomes increasingly critical depending upon the size of the facility and the amount of solid waste in the service area. For example, the amount of solid waste will be of smaller concern to a facility with a daily capacity of 1000 tons located in a service area where a total average of 4000 tons per day are available to the facility for disposal than it will be to a facility with a daily capacity of 1200 tons located in a service area where a total average of 1250 tons per day are available to the facility for disposal. In the latter example, a much more careful review of the availability of the solid waste should be made, particularly if financial feasibility is predicted upon processing 1200 tons per day.

In conjunction with the quantity review, the composition of the solid waste and the seasonal fluctuations in the rate at which it is generated must also be considered. The composition of the solid waste is important in two respects: (1) the composition will determine the amount of recyclable materials which may be recovered from the solid waste which in turn will affect the operating revenues; (2) the composition will determine the heating content of the solid waste, a facet which can affect both the operating revenues from the sale of steam energy and the operating expenses associated with supplementary fossil fuel. The composition of the solid waste can vary from region to region depending upon the commercial and industrial activities of an area, the density of the population, the average income level and consumption habits of the population and the climate of an area. To cite an extreme example, the solid waste generated in a region where the principal industry is the manufacture of rubber and plastic goods, which is very heavily populated by an upper middle class population purchasing a lot of disposable products packaged in paper and plastic, and which is located in an area where there is very little precipitation in the form of either rain or snow, will have a much higher heating content than the solid waste which is generated in a region where the principal industry is the harvesting of watermelons, which is sparsely populated by a low income population who spend the majority of their earnings on food, housing and clothing and which is located in an area which experiences a large amount of precipitation throughout the year.

The composition of the solid waste can also be affected by the passage of "bottle bills" which would require the payment of a deposit for returnable glass, aluminum and metal containers. The institution of a bottle bill could significantly decrease the amount of aluminum in the waste stream and could also decrease the amount of glass. The impact of a bottle bill must be considered if the financial feasibility of a facility is predicted upon the solid waste having

the national average quantities of glass and aluminum which are to be recovered and sold as recyclable materials.

Seasonal fluctuations in the generation of solid waste must also be taken into account when reviewing the economics of a proposed facility. Past studies which have been made on the generation of solid waste indicate that monthly variations in the generation of solid waste may fluctuate between 15 and 20 percent above and below the average rate for the year. During the spring and early summer the quantity of residential solid waste can be higher due to an increased amount of yard clippings, old leaves and dead branches as well as the disposal of "antiques" which had been stored in attics, cellars and garages. However, during the winter months immediately following the New Year, the generation of solid waste can be lower as consumer purchases decrease following the gluttony of the Christmas holidays. Because it is impractical to stockpile solid waste for much more than a week, such seasonal fluctuations must be taken into account both when projecting the operating revenues and expenses of the facility and when negotiating the quantities of steam energy required to be delivered in accordance with the provisions of steam energy sale contract(s). This is particularly important because those winter months in which the smallest amount of solid waste is being generated are often the same months in which there is the greatest steam energy demand due to the cold weather.

Similarly, provision should be made in the form of some type of sanitary landfill to dispose of that solid waste generated during those months in the spring which may exceed the disposal capability of the facility. As cited above, the impact and importance of seasonal fluctuations is dependent upon the size of the facility as it relates to the amount of solid waste available for disposal being generated within the service area.

Investors are concerned that there is not only an adequate supply of solid waste but also that there is a guarantee that such solid waste will be delivered to the facility. Municipal ordinances requiring the delivery of either all the solid waste collected within a service area, or a guaranteed minimum quantity during the amortization period of the long-term debt, offer the greatest assurance to investors that a continued supply of solid waste will be made available. A review of those locations available for the disposal of solid waste which represent a possible alternative to the facility may also be desirable as there may be either privately owned and operated sanitary landfills, incinerators or similar solid waste resource recovery facilities within the service area. A determination should be made as to the possible impact such alternative locations may have upon the operation of the facility and it may prove necessary to secure the passage of further municipal ordinances which prohibit the construction of competing solid waste resource recovery facilities within the coporation limits of the municipality(s).

Municipal ordinances may also be necessary with regard to the collection of the solid waste. An investor wants to be sure that there is a continual and steady supply of solid waste being delivered to the facility in the quantities and at the times it is needed for the resource recovery operations. If solid waste is to be collected and delivered to the facility only five days per week, there must be enough of a supply of solid waste on hand and adequate storage facilities be made available to assure that the plant operation will be continued throughout the weekend or a holiday period if such operation is required to fulfill the provisions of the service contracts. Failure to do so, in the case of a steam energy system, may result in the necessity of using fossil fuels during periods when such solid waste is not available.

Requirements concerning the pickup and collection of residential and commercial solid waste may also be subject to municipal ordinances. If the local governing authority requires that all residential and commercial solid waste shall be put out for collection only in waterproof plastic bags and containers and that the vehicles collecting such solid waste must also be waterproof, the heating value of such solid waste will not be decreased due to the increased moisture content from rain or snow. This may increase operating revenues due to the increased commodity of steam energy available for sale, and decrease operating expenses by requiring

less supplementary fossil fuel to be burned in order to incinerate moisture-laden solid waste.

Municipal ordinances may also govern the types of solid waste which are allowed to be delivered to the facility for disposal. Large quantities of liquids, dangerous chemicals, dead animals, automobile bodies and explosives are not desirable items to process at a facility and a municipal ordinance prohibiting the delivery of such solid waste should both facilitate the operation and increase the expected useful life of the facility.

REVENUE-PRODUCING CONTRACTS

Once an investor has been assured that the facility as designed is technically sound and that an adequate supply of solid waste is available, the next concern to be dealt with is a determination that the operating revenues of the facility are sufficient to meet future debt service obligations. This will require a careful review of the terms and conditions of all revenue-producing contracts.

Generally, the single most important revenue-producing contract is for the sale of steam energy and the provisions of this contract will generally receive the most scrutiny from investors. They will be concerned as to how the steam energy will be utilized and to whom it is to be sold. If steam is being privided for a central heating district in a metropolitan area, a review will be made of the relative economic well-being of the major heating customers. If the steam is to be sold to one or two major users for some type of manufacturing process, then a review will be required not only of the individual steam customers, but also of the industry as a whole in which such customers are engaged. It will provide little comfort to an investor to discover that the major steam customers manufacture a product which may shortly become obsolete or for which there is little future demand. Additional information on major steam customers should include how long they have been in business, their position within their own market, the likelihood that they will continue their operation in their present location, how integral steam is to the manufacturing process and whether or not it is likely to continue to be required in similar quantities.

An electric utility represents another possible customer for the facility's steam energy, and again investors will be interested in the economic well-being of the service area for which such a utility provides electric service, as well as the financial status of the electric utility itself.

The provisions which should be considered when negotiating contract(s) for the sale of the steam energy include the following:

1. Length of term of contract should be equal to the amortization period of the long-term debt which was issued to finance the cost of the facility.
2. Identification of maximum and minimum demands and quantities of steam energy.
3. Determination of whether or not steam quality provisions must be met to include consideration of the temperature, pressure and purity of the steam.
4. If steam condensate is to be returned to the facility, the method of determining the credit to be given for such condensate return.
5. The method to be employed in escalating customers' rates for steam energy service. Are such increases to be a function of the increase in the cost of alternative fuels, increases in total operating expenses, or increases in the Consumer Price Index or an alternative index?
6. A determination of whether the contract is to provide a guarantee that service rates can be increased in order to meet debt service coverage on certain bond covenants.
7. In the event of the inability of the facility to provide steam energy by means of solid waste as a fuel, is it necessary to provide service by using some type of fossil fuel and for how long a period of time must such service be provided?

Revenues from tipping fees also represent an important portion of most facility's operating revenues and the contracts associated with said tipping fees will be carefully reviewed by investors. Their concerns will include the following:

1. Whether the cost for disposing at the facility is competitive with alternative methods, such as sanitary landfills, incinerators or other resource recovery facilities.
2. The present status of those sanitary landfills and incinerators which are located within the service area of the facility. Do they meet environmental criteria? What is their useful remaining life under current operating conditions?
3. Those provisions within the contract which deal with the method for escalating the tipping fee during the ensuing years.
4. The length of the term of the contract.
5. Provisions dealing with the delivery of a guaranteed minimum and/or maximum amount of solid waste within a given time period.

To a lesser extent, operating revenues will also be available from the sale of recovered materials. Such materials may include ferrous and nonferrous metals, glass, corrugated cardboard and the sterile residue ash. Generally, the sale of each type of recyclable material will require the negotiation of a separate contract. Such negotiations should include consideration of the length of term of the contract, the establishment of minimum and/or maximum amounts of recovered materials which must be supplied or purchased and the criteria concerning the quality of the recovered products. It is generally desirable to be able to show financial feasibility is not jeopardized by the loss of the operating revenues from the sale of recovered materials, the quantity of which could be reduced due to legislative action such as a bottle bill.

CONSTRUCTION OF THE FACILITY

Investors also want assurance that the facility is going to be built as proposed, within the scheduled time period and for the estimated construction cost. Accordingly, a careful review of the construction aspects of the facility will generally be undertaken.

Questions concerning the qualifications and capabilities of the design engineer are likely to include inquiries as to the engineer's previous experience in the design and construction of facilities including the same basic components. Information may also be requested concerning the history of similarly designed facilities and a description of any operating problems such facilities have encountered. The description should also include mention of how such operating problems have been corrected and what remedial measures have been taken in the design of the currently planned facility to assure there will not be a recurrence of such problems.

One can also anticipate that investors will show considerable interest in the estimated total construction cost of the facility. They will want to know: what percentage, if any, of the cost of construction is already under firm contract; what escalation factors and clauses have been included within the construction contracts; how much of a contingency for escalation and overruns has been allowed in the estimated construction cost; what recourse is available if failure to have the facility constructed in time will result in the cancellation of contracts for the sale of steam energy; and the method by which any major construction cost overruns will be financed. It may be desirable during the construction period to have an Independent Consulting Engineer and/or Project Supervisor monitor the construction. Such an overview by a third party gives assurance to the investor that only required changes and necessary additional costs are included. This overview may take the form of quarterly operating reports to bondholders, approval of any additions in the design of the facility costing in excess of some stated amount, or approval of any deletion to the design of the facility which may in any way reduce the capability of the facility to produce the quantity of steam energy upon which the financial feasibility of the facility was based.

OPERATION OF THE FACILITY

Assuming that the facility is sound from an engineering point of view, that there is an adequate supply of solid waste, that the revenue-producing contracts assure sufficient operating revenues and that the facility is constructed on time and within the estimated budget, the investor's final area of concern is the actual day-to-day operation of the facility and the assurances that the facility will be operated in such a manner as to protect the investment which has been made in the facility.

If the facility is to be privately owned and operated, investors will be interested in the previous experience, if any, the owner has had in operating a solid waste resource recovery plant and whether or not the facility has operated properly and profitably. If the facility is to be municipally owned, investors may find additional comfort if the municipality hires a Project Supervisor who has had previous experience in the solid waste resource recovery industry to operate the facility. The hiring of a Project Supervisor may provide a municipality with experience and expertise in the processing of solid waste which it might not otherwise be able to obtain. It may prove desirable to include performance and incentive provisions within any service contract between the municipality and a Project Supervisor.

Investors will also be interested in any additional controls which have been provided to help protect their investment while the facility is being operated. Such controls may well include the hiring of an Independent Consulting Engineer to report to bondholders on the following matters:

1. The preparation of an annual report to the bondholders on the operations of the facility and recommendations as to the operating and capital budgets, the operation and maintenance of the facility and the schedule of rates and charges.
2. The preparation of a quarterly operating report on whether the relationship of revenues from the products and services of the facility are adequate to perform the obligations and covenants required in the bond indenture.
3. Preparation of a feasibility study for any modification, addition or improvement

to the facility which will cost more than some stated amount.

4. A review of the qualifications of those individuals proposed to be employed at the facility in a management or supervisory capacity.

5. A review of those personnel and duties required to operate the facility.

SUMMARY

The decision to proceed with the construction and operation of a solid waste resource recovery facility is one which requires a very careful review of a large number of variables, both technical and financial. However, it is imperative to keep in mind that if such a facility is to be financed through the issuance of some form of long-term debt, the prospective investors may be provided with all the information associated with developing the financial feasibility of the project. Therefore, the design of the facility, the negotiation of contracts, the procurement of a supply of solid waste and the planned operation of the facility should be done in such a manner as to reduce the perceived risk of investing in the facility.

The extra care and effort expended in the planning and design during the formative stages of the project should be more than compensated for by the fact that long-term financing has indeed been obtained and at an interest rate which continues to make the facility financially feasible. It should be remembered that the investment market place is a competitive situation in which different projects are competing against one another in an effort to attract investors' money. In this particular market, the lower the perceived risk is to the investor, then the greater the desirability of investing in the facility. This will enhance the ability of the facility to obtain the necessary long-term financing and at a lower interest rate than other projects in the investment market which have a higher perceived risk. A difference of 1 percent on the interest rate for a $50,000,000 bond issue with a level debt service amortized over 20 years is in excess of $360,000 per year or more than $7,000,000 for the 20 years. This type of saving points out the importance of identifying and reducing major elements of risk in a solid waste resource recovery facility.

2-15 Resource Recovery Financing

Charles A. Ballard

Source: *NCRR Bulletin,* Vol. VII, No. 3 (Summer 1977) pp. 73–80. **Reprinted with Permission of National Center for Resource Recovery.**

Any discussion concerning financing options for solid waste disposal/resource recovery systems must be viewed objectively. We are, after all, discussing a new industry — one, in fact, so new that the historical lack of meaningful investment, by definition, precludes widely accepted financial precedents. Nevertheless, some patterns are beginning to emerge, albeit far more slowly than might be considered in the nation's best interest.

The financing of solid waste disposal/resource recovery systems should not be viewed as unique. Financial alternatives must address operating objectives, which may be subjective and result from preconceived bias, past experience or local circumstance.

Before exploring these objectives, one might ask how financial institutions view solid waste projects. Financial institutions are generally receptive to investment in solid waste disposal/resource recovery systems, provided that the principal risks of a guaranteed waste stream, system reliability, technological and mechanical obsolescence, economic viability and product marketability are assumed by a responsible party or parties. Also, a rate of return commensurate with other risks should be reasonably assured. In this regard, the resource recovery area should not be viewed as unique, as such protections would be prudent, if not legally required, in all fiduciary lending.

The concept of "risk sharing" is being more broadly discussed, though not yet fully accepted. Under such a concept, the risks earlier discussed (a guaranteed waste stream, system reliability, product marketability, etc.) would be analyzed, dissected and ultimately assumed by the interested party exercising the greatest direct control over each particular risk area. Unfortunately, some exposures, such as *force majeure*, legislative change, etc., fall beyond the control of any individual participant, or that of all participants collectively. Further, it is impossible to anticipate, with any degree of assurance, all possible "risks" which might arise during a prolonged operating period. Often it is in the latter two areas that financial negotiations for private investment stall or become abortive.

RECURRING PROBLEMS

As with anything new, there are problems which must be addressed. And, as with most problems, there are also solutions. Let's look at the two separately. First, the problems. While an array of specific problems exists on an individual, case-by-case basis, there are several which recur with regularity and without regard to specific geographic location:

Municipal Inexperience. While municipalities may be generally aware that private investment sources are available, specifics of implementation, particular investment parameters and associated legal requirements are often foreign to traditional municipal financing practices. Accordingly, municipalities are often improperly equipped to avail themselves of such sources even if they were generally aware of the sources' existence.

Legislative Restrictions. Municipalities, unlike members of the private sector, are generally permitted only to take action or perform services, or contract for the performance thereof, as may be authorized by specific affirmative legislation. Often such legislation permitting direct or indirect employment of private investment capital either does not exist or may be unduly restrictive in practical application. In the case of the Town of Hempstead, N.Y., for example, efforts by the Town to employ private capital for resource recovery were substantially delayed until state laws could be changed to permit the Town's execution of a long-term contract for solid waste disposal.

Further, many municipalities are statutorily required to employ competitive bids in letting contracts for services with the private sector. Such a requirement is often prohibitive in the resource recovery area due to the complexities of proprietary technology, capital requirements, marketing agreements and systems application.

Questions as to the enforceability of municipal obligations have recently surfaced as an additional obstacle. Actions taken by the City of New York, affirmed by judicial review, as well as those taken by Congress have appeared to serve to relieve a municipality of contractual performance if such relief is deemed to be in a municipality's best interest. Recent court decisions indicate that the contrary is true, but the proliferation of such action could serve as an effective bar to the flow of private investment capital into the municipal sector for resource recovery applications or for other purposes.

Other general legislative restrictions and interpretive questions related thereto — exist, but are not viewed as insurmountable.

System Reliability. With few exceptions, the lack of operating resource recovery systems in the U.S. precludes factual demonstration of continued on-line reliability. Such reliability is of particular importance to a municipality which, once committed to a solid waste system, has no readily available alternative for disposal. Reliability is of equal importance to a project's overall economic viability to the extent that its revenue is dependent upon material input and recovered products. Technological considera-

tions, often beyond a municipality's scope, may be involved in assessing reliability including such independent variables as the changing composition of solid waste, environmental regulations, water availability and other factors.

Revenue and Cost Control. Established price indices (*i.e.,* the Consumer Price Index), often suggested as the independent basis for revenue adjustment in municipal contracts, may not reflect actual cost increases or efficiencies of a particular resource recovery system. This can give rise over a period of years to the possibility of either unjust gain or financial disaster for the system operator. Further, "turnkey" construction agreements are often either unavailable or available only at prohibitive cost. Included as considerations in construction costs are such factors as strikes, material unavailability and supplier delays. All are beyond the scope of direct control.

Long-term Markets for Recovered Products. Resource recovery systems generally involve one or more reclaimed products: energy or energy equivalents, ferrous metals, nonferrous metals, paper or glass. The availability of each product is a function of solid waste composition. To the extent that changes in composition occur, either by legislative, voluntary or evolutionary process, intended product availability would be either adversely or favorably affected. Further, even without composition changes in the solid waste stream, demand (and therefore value) of a particular product may fluctuate radically, rendering contractual risks difficult for both seller and purchaser to evaluate.

FOUR CITIES' SOLUTIONS

Now that we have discussed some of the problems, it may be helpful to review the solutions that four cities are employing to finance solid waste disposal facilities. Each of these cities has embraced one of a series of options. Reviewing each option briefly:

- **General Obligation Bonds** commit the full faith and credit of a municipality to the repayment of the principal of and interest on borrowed funds.

- **Special Revenue Bonds** may take numerous forms, but essentially, a stream of revenues is pledged to secure the repayment of bonds issued. These revenues may be from a special taxation district, an unrelated revenue district, the financed project, or from some other source.
- **Industrial Development Revenue Bonds** may be employed to the extent that the financed project meets certain requisite conditions of the Internal Revenue Code.

These first three options generally involve tax exempt financing; i.e., the interest payable to bondholders is exempt from federal income tax under the appropriate provisions of the Internal Revenue Code.

- **Private Sector Financing** involves, directly or indirectly, a pledge of the credit of a participating corporation.

Additionally, each of the preceding four options may be combined to obtain necessary funding.

Perhaps the case-by-case review of four examples may bring into better focus the application of the financing options described. As may be expected, the subject cities have varying populations, characteristics, and objectives.

City A has a service area population of approximately 250,000. Under the stated characteristics regarding its solid waste disposal/resource recovery facility, City A:

- desires no ownership of the subject facility;
- desires no direct management responsibility for the operation of the facility;
- has no credit support that it could offer to the facility's financing; and,
- desires no participation in facility profits.

Simply, City A's facility objectives include the dependable and environmentally sound disposal of solid wastes and partial recovery of these solid wastes.

City B has a service area population of approximately 850,000. It desires no direct facility ownership or management responsibility for a 20-year period. It has no credit support to offer, but does desire a meaningful profit participation. As with City A, City B desires dependable and environmentally sound disposal of solid wastes but it has as an additional objective, total resource recovery.

City C has a service area population of approximately 550,000. City C desires immediate ownership of the facility, and a limited management responsibility. It is able to afford limited credit support, and is interested in a profit participation. Its facility objectives are otherwise similar to those of City B.

City D, with a service area population of approximately 1,300,000, desires ownership of the facility upon its completion, and limited management responsibility. Through state bonding, it has strong available credit support. Its profit participation desires and other facility objectives are similar to those of Cities B and C.

City A

City A's solution (See Figure 1) is not an overly complex one, but often simplicity rules the day in meeting objectives. City A may enter into a disposal contract with a private sector operator for the disposal of its solid wastes. The contract will provide hauling and disposal services. Through powers granted under state law, the City is authorized to issue Industrial Development Revenue Bonds for the acquisition or construction of facilities which inure to the benefit of the City, the state, or its citizens. The City may issue such bonds, limiting bondholders' recourse to those revenues pledged to secure the bonds.

To generate such revenues, the City will enter into a 20-year lease with the operator for the use of the facility, and issue its limited recourse bonds in an amount sufficient to construct the facility. These bonds will be secured by the pledge and assignment of the lease payments receivable from the project operator. The proceeds of the bond issue will be placed in trust and construction contractors will be paid as delivery progresses. The

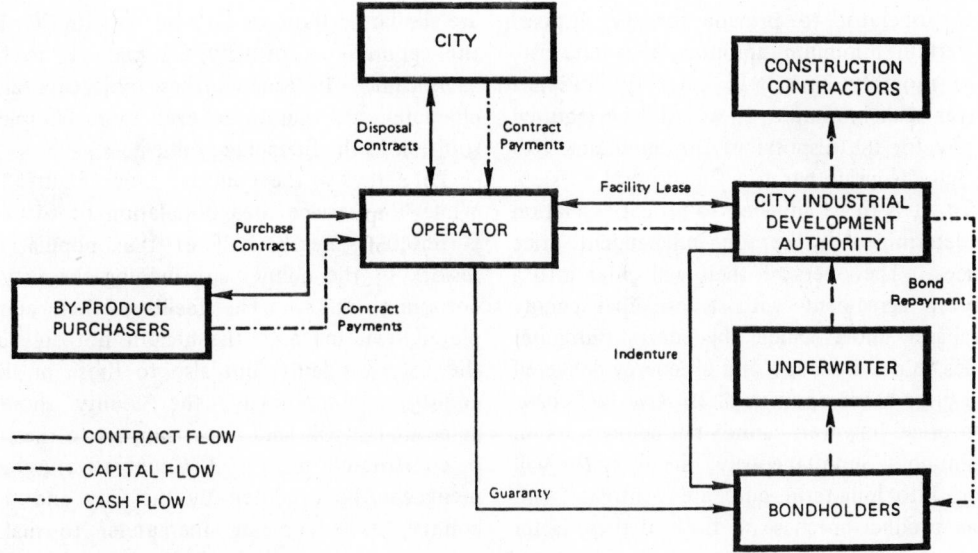

Figure 1. City A.

operator will give its guarantee of lease payments to bondholders and, further, will enter into contracts with certain purchasers of recovered items. Through the City's auspices, the operator is able to receive lower-cost, tax-exempt financing, but will be required to pledge its direct credit to secure such financing. In this example, the credit of a private sector corporation is combined with a city's authority to issue tax-exempt industrial development bonds to finance the solid waste disposal facility.

City B

City B has a more complex problem (Figure 2). The cost of a full resource recovery operation servicing the needs of 850,000 people will be substantially in excess of that experienced by City A. Few corporations are either able or desirous of employing their credit in such a manner. Nevertheless, the funding problem can be solved by the structure shown.

Tracing first the contract flow, City B enters into a 20-year contract with a private

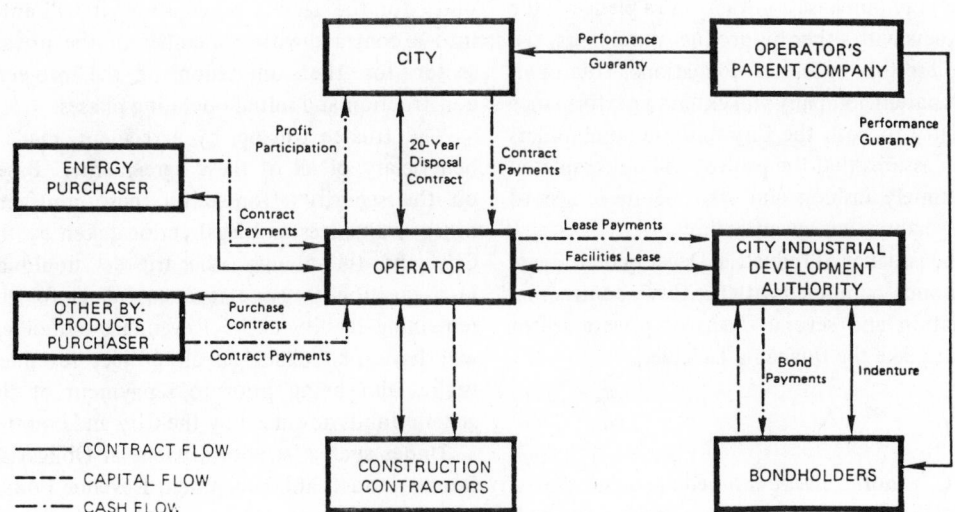

Figure 2. City B.

sector operator to provide for the disposal of certain minimum amounts of solid waste on a monthly basis. If the City does not deliver such minimum, it will still be required to pay for the disposal of the minimum. Although the price per ton for disposal is established, it is to be adjusted to reflect escalation as determined by certain independent price indices. The operator then will enter into a 20-year agreement with a principal energy purchaser under which the energy purchaser agrees to purchase any and all energy delivered at a price based upon its alternative fuel costs; such price, however, cannot fall below a stated minimum. Simultaneously, the operator will enter into long-term purchase contracts with other product purchasers. Each of these latter contracts will contain minimum "take or pay provisions," providing that products will be purchased at prices based upon market conditions, but in no event will such prices be below stated minimums.

As with City A, City B has authority under its state laws to issue, through an industrial development authority, Industrial Development Revenue Bonds. The operator may enter into an agreement with the industrial development authority to lease the completed facility for 20 years at annual payments sufficient to amortize the debt issued. The operator will secure its obligation to make lease payments with a pledge of the disposal contract with the City, a pledge of the energy purchase contract, and a pledge of the contracts with other by-product purchasers. To complete this "circle of obligations," the operator's parent company will extend a performance guaranty to both the City and the bondholders which assures that the project will be completed in a timely fashion and will operate in accord with performance specifications.

The issuance of Industrial Development Revenue Bonds, combined with the City's contractual obligation and several forms of private sector credit, make the financing feasible.

City C

City C, as noted, desires immediate ownership of the facility and has limited credit support available, but its other objectives and characteristics are similar to those of City B. As with City B, the capital cost of City C's plant is to be significant. In general, these objectives and characteristics dictate an even more complex solution to the financing problem.

Let's review the contract flow (Figure 3). While the service area population of City C is 550,000, nearly half of that population resides in the county surrounding the City's corporate limits. The facility, when completed, will inure to the benefit not only of the City residents, but also to those of the county. Accordingly, the county should agree that it will lend direct support to the to-be-constructed plant. A Cooperative Agreement can be executed by the City and the county, each agreeing thereunder to make available its general funds in the cumulative amount of approximately 30 percent of the facility's installed cost. A bond trustee acting on behalf of the bondholders, will be made a beneficiary of this agreement.

City C then will enter into numerous 25-year agreements with energy purchasers, providing for the long-term purchase of energy at prices to be adjusted to reflect the plant's actual operating and capital costs. No profit margins will be included. The City further will enter into contracts with independent construction companies for the construction of the subject facility.

Because City C desires only limited responsibility for the facility's operation, it will enter into a contract with a member of the private sector for the supervision of the project's construction and initial operating phases.

The trustee will be, by agreement, made a beneficiary of all of these agreements. Based on the security afforded by these contracts, other ordinances and legal action taken by the City and the county, the trustee should be in a position to issue revenue bonds for the remaining facility cost. Revenue bondholders will have first claim on all project revenues, such claim being prior to repayment of the general funds advanced by the City and county.

Under such a structure, General Obligation Bonds, Industrial Development Revenue Bonds, and Private Sector financing, through the assignment of "take or pay" energy contracts,

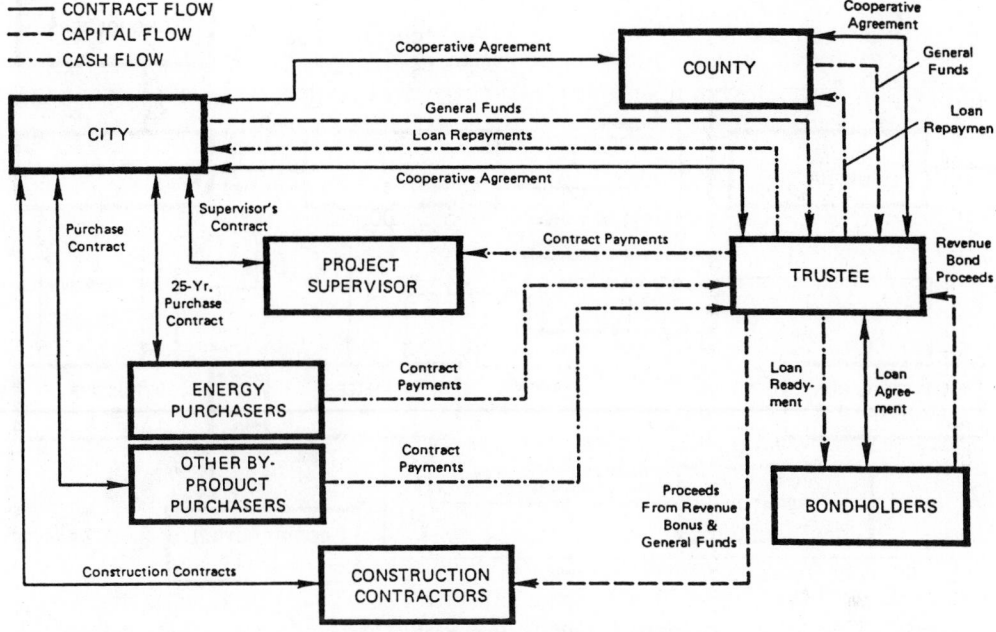

Figure 3. City C.

may be combined to accomplish the project's funding.

City D

City D's objectives are similar to those of City C except in one particular regard. Strong credit support is available, through state auspices, once the project is constructed and in operation.

Accordingly, City D has two stages to its financing plan: one during the construction stage, the second during the operating state.

First, the construction phase (Figure 4), and again, let's follow the contract flow. Because the county government has direct responsibility for the disposal of solid wastes, that political subdivision is to be employed in preference to the City. The county will enter into an agreement with the state to provide for the facility's permanent funding on completion. The county further will enter into agreements with a private sector member for the construction and operation of the subject facility. The construction phase includes a "turnkey" price. The major energy purchaser will agree to purchase the facility's energy products for

a 20-year period. Because the private sector operator will be involved during the operating period, it also will be party to this agreement.

Based upon this agreement with the county and the energy user, the contractor may enter into the contracts for the facility's construction.

To finance the construction phase, several additional agreements are required. The funding agreement between the county and the state provides that the state will make its funds available prior to the commencement of construction. These funds will be held in escrow by Trustee B until completion of construction. Such agreement addresses the concerns of a changing state legislature, administration, etc. Trustee B, having funds on deposit, may then enter into a funding agreement with Trustee A, providing that upon "completion" such funds will be transferred to Trustee A. Trustee A, armed with Trustee B's agreement, a construction loan agreement with the operator, and an agreement with the operator's parent company guaranteeing timely completion, may issue notes — secured by such agreement — to short-term lenders to fund construction requirements.

When construction is completed and operations commence, the structure changes slightly

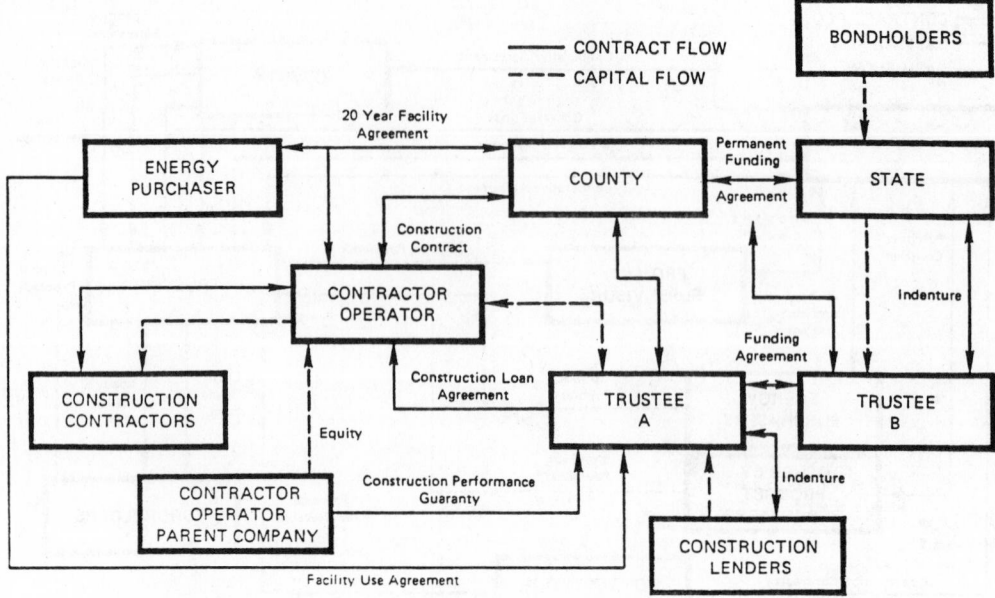

Figure 4. City D – Construction Phase.

(Fgure 5). Instead of a construction performance guarantee, the contractor's parent company will have a continuing operating performance guarantee, assuring both the county and
the energy purchaser that the facility will per-

form in accordance with design specifications.
The state funds, heretofore held by Trustee B,
will be transferred to Trustee A, who will then
repay construction lenders and other contract
funds advanced by the contractor on behalf of

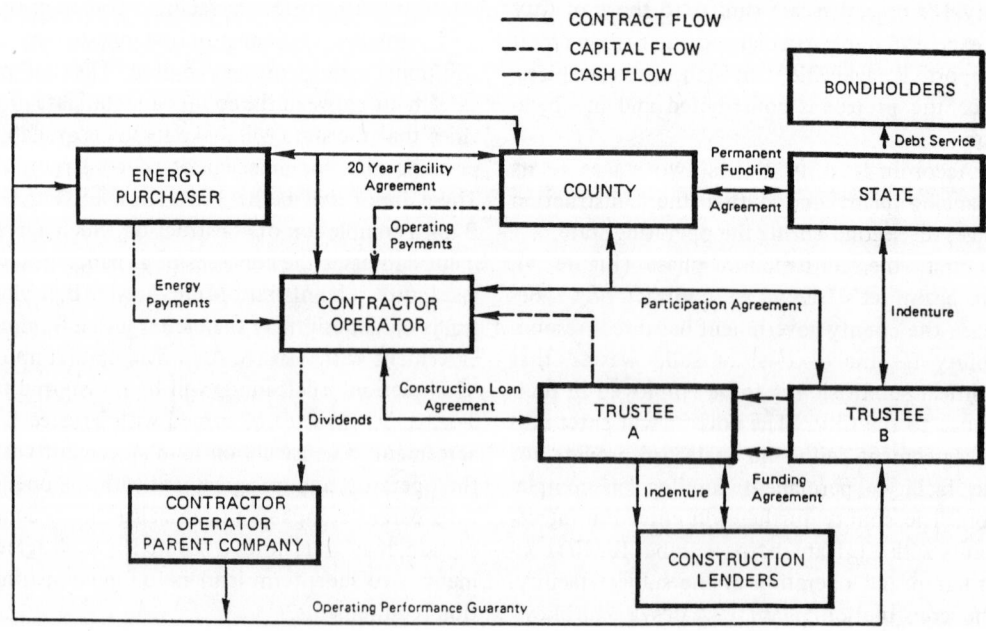

Figure 5. City D – Completion & Operating Phase.

the county. Energy payments from the energy purchaser and operating payments from the county will be sufficient to pay operating and maintenance expenses of the contract and, it is to be hoped, allow some cash flow to accrue to the county's benefit. Under this structure, General Obligation Bonds and Private Sector capital will be jointly employed to fund the project's completion and capital costs.

The four solutions discussed have varying degrees of complexity. The complexities are necessary, however, to address the earlier discussed obstacles, many of which have been self-made by existing municipal structures.

SIMPLIFICATION POSSIBILITIES

In my opinion, there are ways of simplifying the problems to facilitate financing of resource recovery projects. Each possibility requires some change:

- Municipalities should objectively examine their current cost of solid waste disposal, employing generally accepted accounting practices in such appraisals. Again, while there are notable exceptions in this area, many municipalities have employed either outdated techniques of cost accounting or no cost accounting at all in such determinations, often having ignored landfill acquisition costs, depreciation expenses, administrative and overhead costs, etc. Without such knowledge, the comparative cost of resource recovery cannot be properly evaluated. Such an examination should also be conducted regarding environmental "costs" related to current disposal techniques. This latter examination should be given reasonable priority in an overall analysis.

- In multi-jurisdictional projects, conscious efforts should be made by municipal participants to minimize interterritorial rivalries. In some instances, such political considerations have delayed, perhaps indefinitely, the development of meaningful regional resource recovery programs.

- Municipalities should be disabused of the mistaken belief that solid waste, through resource recovery, becomes a valuable asset in the hands of private enterprise. Claims to the contrary notwithstanding, even the most advanced resource recovery technology does not today generate sufficient revenue from materials or energy recovery to cover the operating and capital costs related thereto. Garbage, therefore, must be recognized as a municipal problem, and municipalities should be willing to shoulder a substantial portion of the risk — and the rewards — of resource recovery.

- Interested states should review, in conjunction with qualified legal and financial consultants, existing legislation governing municipal contracts, solid waste revenue (or industrial revenue), bond financing and related statutes, amending such legislation where necessary to accommodate the reasonable requirements of private investment capital. Where advisable, necessary or appropriate, the possibility of establishing statewide or regional agencies or authorities, or of redirecting certain state revenues to the resource recovery area for collateral purposes, should be examined.

- Both the federal and state governments can best facilitate the development of resource recovery by instituting meaningful and strict enforcement on a local level of environmental regulations affecting solid waste. Simple raw landfilling is still the most widely employed method of municipal waste disposal due to the low direct cost associated therewith; disregard of long-term environmental costs and public policy is the rule rather than the exception.

Part 3
Waste as a Source of Raw Materials

Earlier readings, presented in Part 2, indicated that recycling the materials found in municipal waste could have a small but beneficial impact on the annual supply of such materials as paper, steel, aluminum, glass, copper, tin, etc. The readings in this part examine materials recycling more explicitly. Most look at mechanical separation from mixed, usually called co-mingled, waste. However, the first reading, by Elizabeth Johnson, looks at source separation under the title, "Source Separation: A Resource Recovery Option." Indeed, at present, by far the largest amount of materials recycling occurs as a result of source separation. Also, as Johnson points out, "large, capital-intensive mechanical resource recovery systems are not always economically feasible — especially in smaller communities . . . ." Source separation depends on the participation of the individuals who do the separating. The question is, what prompts persons to participate? In the reading by J.F. Witmer and E.S. Geller, an interesting attempt to influence behavior and promote paper recycling in a university setting is described.

Newspaper recycling is a special case. Reference has already been made to the so-called burning issue. Should one recycle paper for its fiber content or burn it for its energy value? Robert Davis and Bruce MacDonald examine this issue. The title is indicative of the contents: "What's to be Done with Used Newspapers? Debate Rages On." A number of cases are developed to illustrate the trade-off that occurs with changes in energy prices and the price of old newspapers. As one would expect, landfill costs also play an important role.

Over the last few years there has been some effort to mechanically separate paper fiber from co-mingled waste. While there are many articles on the source separation of paper readily available elsewhere in the literature, those that concern mechanical separation are not as easily obtained. Therefore, a decision was made to present a fairly complete set of readings on mechanical separation of fiber in this volume. Marc Renard sets the stage in his paper, "Technical Barriers to the Recovery of Secondary Fibers from Municipal Solid Waste." This is followed by a description of work conducted at the University of California, Berkeley, where fiber was recovered using a combination of dry processing (shredding, air classification, and screening), and wet processing (hydropulping and pulp cleaning). The authors conclude that the mechanical properties of the refuse-derived pulp are comparable to those of typical commercial pulp furnishes containing virgin or ground wood. Reports on two European systems appear next. The first is the Flakt system. The second is the R-80 Krauss-Maffei approach. The Flakt paper describes a pilot plant built in Stockholm. A full scale plant has been built in the Netherlands which has exhibited the "scale up" operational difficulties seen in most first generation prototype full sized resource recovery plants throughout the world. A pilot R-80 plant exists in Munich. In the final reading, on the subject of mechanical separation of paper fiber, Marc Renard describes a series of three tests using differently separated paper-rich feedstocks from three resource recovery plants. As with the other authors, he too is optimistic as to the potential for mechanical separation.

The next reading considers the recovery of ferrous scrap from municipal solid waste. Various markets, both current and potential, are described: detinning, copper precipitation, blast furnace, steel-making furnaces, iron foundries and ferroalloys. Rocco A. Petrone is the author of this state-of-the-art summary. Aluminum recovery is discussed in the reading that follows. At present, most aluminum is returned for reuse through consumer-based source separation programs. This is described briefly, followed by a narrative covering the several attempts to remove aluminum, primarily aluminum beverage cans, through electromechanical means. The concept of eddy-current separation is introduced and described. This reading is followed by another that looks more closely at separation based on density rather than conductivity. This is an application that has been used by automobile scrap processors for a number of years. The reading reports on a specific configuration of density separation, i.e., a cyclone separator.

Glass recycling is not yet as advanced in the United States as paper, steel, and aluminum recycling. There are voluntary programs relying on household separation and, of course, beverage container deposits cause the return of tonnage quantities of glass, both refillable and non-refillable. The next three readings discuss two approaches to mechanically separating glass from mixed municipal waste. The first of these is through the use of electro-optical sorters. The target is color-sorted glass suitable for use in making new beverage containers. Two readings describe this approach. The first is by John P. Cummings and discusses United States experience at a pilot operation in Franklin, Ohio. The second describes a parallel effort underway in Great Britain. A different approach to recovering glass relies on froth flotation. Aggregates containing 85% to 90% glass are ground to a sandlike consistency, and this material is selectively floated to recover the glass, in this case, color mixed, but otherwise meeting industry raw material specifications. J.H. Higinbotham tells how it is done in his reading, "Recovery of Glass from Urban Waste by Froth Flotation." Glass container industry specifications are quite tight. Therefore, attention has been given to alternative uses for recovered glass-rich concentrates. One of these is lightweight structural concrete as described in the next reading.

The final two readings in this section look at the potential for recycling plastics and rubber. Neither is as far along as the materials already discussed. A.G. Buekens offers "Some Observations on the Recycling of Plastics and Rubber" in the first reading, and Arthur Purcell looks at "Tire Recycling: Research Trends and Needs" in the second. The reader will see that mixed plastic, called polymer "alloys" by Buekens, are difficult to use. In his view, the future of plastics recycling depends on the development of new markets for plastics with inferior properties and the development of processes to improve on the mixed plastics likely to be the product of municipal waste recycling. Purcell views positively the future of tire recycling and calls for research on what he calls the four R's of tire recycling: reduction, reuse, reclaiming and recovery.

3-1 Source Separation: A Resource Recovery Option

Elizabeth Johnson

Source: *NCRR Bulletin*, Vol. VII, No. 1 (Winter 1977) pp. 3-10 Reprinted with Permission of National Center for Resource Recovery.

A growing interest in resource recovery in the United States has been fostered by a number of factors. These include the need to conserve the nation's limited natural resources, and provide environmentally acceptable methods of disposing of our solid waste. Another consideration is the growing shortage of available sites for use as sanitary landfills in densely populated areas.

Large, capital-intensive, mechanical resource recovery systems are not always economically feasible – especially in smaller communities with correspondingly smaller volumes of waste. In such cases, the most practical means of resource recovery may be source separation, *whereby the householder separates recyclable materials from the refuse for separate collection and subsequent recycling.*

A recent study showed that about 30 percent by weight – or 40 percent by volume – of the solid waste from the average household is recyclable. This represents about 80 pounds of recyclable paper, cans and glass per month from each household.[1] The time required to separate these recyclables from mixed refuse in each household was reported to be about 69 minutes per month. Table 1 summarizes the separation time requirements for a specific quantity of generated recyclables. As seen, the separation of newspapers is the easiest step for a householder because less time is required for peper per unit weight than other materials.

The most familiar approach to household source separation has been for residents to deliver their separate recyclable materials to "recycling" or collection centers. The main drawback to this method is that it obligates householders to be both willing and able to transport their wastes to a receiving center. And, recent experience has shown that few householders are willing to do this. For these reasons, the separate collection method is stressed here.

ECONOMICS

The factors determining the net cost of separate collection are:

- The costs of the vehicles and the manpower involved in the collection;
- The number of homes serviced within a collection area;
- The fraction of households in the collection area;
- The fraction of households in the collection area willing to participate;
- The amount of refuse generated per family;
- The market price of the separated materials;[2] and
- The savings in terms of materials diverted from the regular disposal system.

The first step in community planning for source separation is to acquire reasonable assurance that markets exist for the recovered materials. Market outlets should be judged as to:

- Ability to handle all materials from the municipality;
- Minimal administration requirements;
- Tolerance of fluctuations in quantity and quality of materials;

Table 1. Householder Separation Time Requirements vs.
Quantity of Recyclable Material Generated.

Material	Householder Preparation (% of total time)	Quantity Separated (% of total weight)	Time to Weight Ratio
Glass	29	24	1.2
Tin/Bi-Metal	43	9	4.8
Aluminum	9	1	9.0
Newspaper	19	66	0.3

Note: As the above findings were derived from samples too small to be deemed representative of any specific municipality or region, they are presented here for general interest only.
Source: R. Sterns, "The Economics of Separate Refuse Collection," *Waste Age,* 5, No. 3, (May/June 1974), pp. 6-15. SCS Engineers, *Analysis of Source Separation of Solid Wastes, Separate Collection Studies,* April 1974, prepared for U.S. Environmental Protection Agency. p. 9.

- Tolerance in wide variation of moisture content; and
- Commitment to work with the municipality, including long term agreements.[3]

An advance letter of intent from potential buyers to the municipality (or other directors of the source eparation program) is often the instrument used to guarantee sale of the recovered materials and to evaluate the financial feasibility of the program. The community is thus assured of the length of commitment to purchase, quantity of materials to be purchased and the agreed upon price.[4] The advance letter of intent – which can be contractually binding – should be negotiated to determine a *floor price* for the recovered materials. This floor price is the minimum the buyer must pay for the materials, regardless of fluctuations in market prices.

The cost of separate collection is reduced by the revenue from the sale of the separated materials, as well as by savings from not having to dispose of the waste. When predicting savings from having less waste for disposal, the method of disposal is the principal factor. In communities where the collector pays a second party for disposal, separate collection reduces costs in direct proportion to the quantity of waste diverted for recycling.* However, where the collector is also the disposer, there are fixed costs of operating the disposal system so that the annual cost of either incineration or landfilling may not be decreased in direct proportion to a reduced load even though the facilities' life may be extended.

When evaluating a source separation program, disposal savings should be given serious consideration. The amount of waste diverted from "conventional" disposal by means of recycling is directly related to the portion of the population participating. Figure 1 is a diagram which enables an estimation of the disposal savings resulting from a recycling program. By drawing a line from a particular population level on the left axis through a point on the center line, which indicates a level of participation, the amount of solid waste diverted from the "conventional" waste stream, by means of a recycling program, can be read from the right axis. For example, a community of 80,000 residents, realizing a participation rate of 50 percent in a multi-materials program, will have approximately 7300 tons less of solid waste to dispose of each year.

Caution must be taken, however, when using this figure. The composition of waste varies greatly by community, with seasons and even days of the week. The figures derived from Figure 1 are based on national averages; hence, they serve only as a general guide or first estimate of the amount of material a community may be able to divert from disposal to recycling.

Adding separate collection, then, may decrease a community's waste collection and disposal costs if it now pays per-ton delivered to the

---

*At least in the short run. Large diversion can be expected to be followed by a price increase as the fixed or variable cost situation is not significantly different for the private operator in comparision to the publicly owned or operated disposal site. Even so, the private operator may have more options for the use of the fixed equipment.

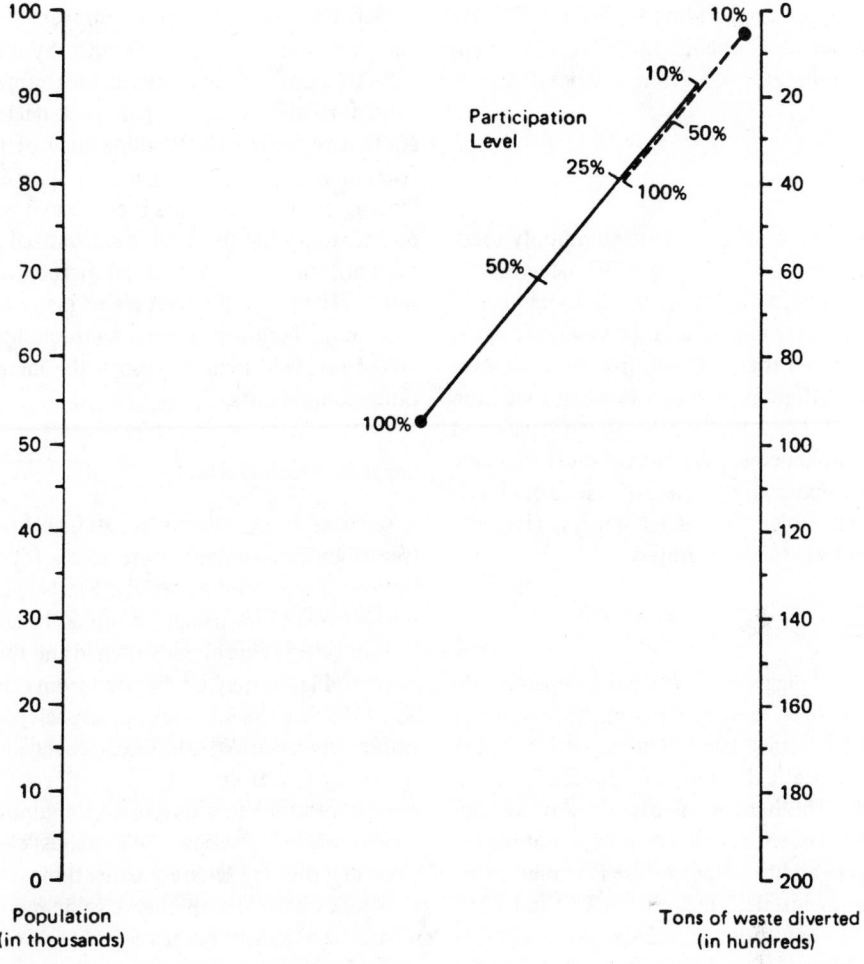

Solid line ——— represents recycling program recovering glass, metal and newspaper. Upper broken line ---- represents recycling program recovering only newspaper.

Assumptions: 3.5 lbs. of waste per person per day,
containing: 8.4% newspaper
10.0% glass
10.0% metal
28.4% x 3.5 lbs. = .99 lbs. or
approximately 1 pound of recyclables
per person per day.

Figure 1. Estimation of Disposal Savings from Recycling Program.

disposal site. Adding separate collection may increase unit costs of disposal if the fixed costs of operating an incinerator or landfill are high and the amount of waste delivered is reduced.

Finally, re-routing of collection vehicles (or otherwise using them more efficiently) may reduce costs. It is difficult to generalize how these various factors may affect a particular community's collection and disposal costs if separate collection is added. In 1974, a survey of 11 communities with separate newspaper collection revealed that, for the average price of $31 received for the newspaper, adding separate collection reduced collection and disposal costs by an average of about seven percent.[5] At some lower price for the recovered newspaper, perhaps in the range of

$10 to $20 per ton, adding separate collection may only be a break-even proposition, or perhaps even a losing situation from a strict financial standpoint.

METHODS

Two methods of collection are commonly used, especially when collecting separated newspapers. In one method, a rack is mounted on regular refuse collection trucks to hold the separated newspapers; in the other, collection of recyclables is made by a different truck, on a special collection schedule. A third method has been developed for the simultaneous collection of more than one recyclable material; this method uses a compartmentalized vehicle to collect papers, glass and cans, and keep them separated.

Piggyback Collection[1]

The rack, or "piggyback," system of separate collection has been used by a private contractor in San Francisco since 1962. One or two racks are installed beneath the body of a standard "packer" truck. The bundles of paper are picked up on regular residential collection days and placed in the racks and the other refuse is loaded as usual. Cost of installed racks were $80 and $250 in 1974 for capacities of 1/2 cu. yd. and 1-1/4 cu. yd., respectively. This system allows mixed refuse and separated newspapers to be collected simultaneously, and crew size may remain the same as before the source separation program. These benefits may be more than offset by the incremental time required to onload and offload the paper.

In San Francisco, the average incremental time required per collection stop, where newspapers were placed out for pickup, was 14 seconds. If a collection route consists of 500 stops and there is 80 percent participation, this results in an incremental time increase of 1-2/3 hours to the collection crew. Moreover, if the racks fill with paper before the trucks fill with refuse, then the newspaper must be offloaded into lugger boxes. In Madison, Wis., the newspaper was offloaded into lugger boxes or dump trucks prepositioned in collection areas. Each truck spent more than 15 minutes off its normal route per truckload (driving time and rack unloading time).

San Francisco tried to circumvent the problem of trucks leaving their routes by unloading full racks onto other trucks at prearranged locations for delivery to a paper stock dealer. This alternative reduced offloading time of racks to five minutes. When the incremental time for offloading at transfer points is combined with that of onloading the material, a substantial amount of work time is diverted from the collection route. The cost effectiveness of many rack systems may, therefore, depend on the ability of the mixed refuse system to absorb the incremental time requirements.

Separate Truck Method

A separate truck — usually a standard packer — travels an independent route solely for the collection of separated materials. Start-up costs for this approach are usually minimal because collection vehicles are already owned and the equipment and labor may be diverted from other public works functions or standby capacity. For example, when Fort Wroth, Texas, changed the collection system from backyard service to curb service, it resulted in a cutback in equipment for regular refuse collection. This enabled two crews to be diverted for separate collection.

Studies have shown that a vehicle collecting separated news can cover from three to five normal collection routes each day, because:

- There are fewer items to handle at each stop;
- There is usually less than 100 percent participation;
- No time is required to return containers to curb; and
- Participating householders may not place the materials out every collection day.

To maximize the benefits from the faster collection procedure, a separate collection program should permit only curbside collection and minimize crew size to perhaps two workers per truck.

An alternative approach is the multi-materials collection system which utilizes a specially designed compartmentalized vehicle for the simultaneous collection of several different recyclables. This approach will be discussed in more detail below.

PARTICIPATION

The primary goal of a source separation program is to turn the public's interest into action. The amount of recyclable materials generated from any community depends on how many people accept and are involved in the program. Stimulating motivation within the community may be a difficult task. Some considerations which may initiate participation are group pressures, frequency of interaction and attractiveness of program.

PUBLIC EDUCATION[3]

Public education is needed to overcome the psychological problem of asking people to separate what they no longer want. Sorting may appear as a step back in time, have a stigma of poverty or economic depression, and may be viewed as a demand on leisure time.[6] Public education has to teach that some form of separate collections need not require the hand separation of mixed wastes.

Citizens can be informed through:

- Use of a *Recycling Program Logotype* — to make the program more readily identifiable;
- *Newspapers, Radio and Television* — to reach a majority of people at planned intervals;
- *Community Letters* — a personal means of communications, and an official commitment of the city to the program;
- *Posters and Graphic Displays* — for schools and retail establishments;
- *Community "Hot Line"* — to provide residents with a means for direct communication about the program;
- *Complimentary Calendar* — to be a continuous reminder of the program;
- *Intensive School Programs* — to educate students as to the benefits of, and need for, recycling; and
- *Inserts with Utility Bills* — to take the message into all homes and businesses.

Public education should be continued for a number of years, or until source separation becomes a habit. The importance of ongoing publicity was tested in one sanitation district in New York City. At the beginning of the program, with extensive publicity, 22 tons of separated newspaper were collected the first month. By the sixth month, when all publicity had stopped, the quantity of paper collected had dropped to three tons.

IMPORTANT PROGRAM CHARACTERISTICS

The simplicity and convenience of a separate collection program, with advance notices of schedules, frequency of pick-ups, and regularity, will substantially determine the number of participants. For example, a householder may be given the option of setting out the recyclables on every collection day, rather than having to remember a separate collection schedule. Also, a program may begin modestly, with one or a few recyclables (*e.g.*, newspaper only) and then grow by increasing the number of recyclables. This could help the citizens to adapt to a multi-materials separation process. Householders also seem to separate a larger portion of their waste when storage requirements are minimal. Consequently, the frequency of pick-up is an important factor in planning a separate collection program.[5]

SOCIO-ECONOMIC STATUS

The extent of participation by householders has been observed to increase with a rise in their socio-economic status. The wastepaper generation in a high income neighborhood may be two to three times that of a medium to low income neighborhood in the same community; as income increases, so does the likelihood of a family subscribing to a newspaper or using more convenience packaging.[7] Education has the same effect on participation mainly because higher education usually leads to higher income and greater environmental awareness. Table 2 summarizes participation in a separate collection program divided by socio-economic range. It is apparent that the most favorable group for future recycling programs, using these results as an example, would be in the "over $10,000 per year income" (1970 base) category.

Other findings are consistent with those for Delaware County. Rockville, Md., a city of approximately 50,000 population, collects separat-

Table 2. Participation in Separate Collection Program Delaware County, Pa.

Family Income Range	Percent Participation Newspaper	Glass
Up to $10,000/year	4.8	6.8
$10,000 to $15,000/year	16.6	14.1
Over $15,000/year	18.9	17.5

Source: The Delaware County Solid Waste Test Report, prepared for the Delaware County Commissioners, November 1975.

Table 3. Participation in Newspaper Separate Collection Program Rockville, Md.

October 1974 to November 1976
Based on 1970 Census Data

Average Participation	Median Income (1969)	Median Education	High School Graduates in Population
62%	$18,844	15.7 yrs.	90.1%
46	13,170	11.9	60.0
44	12,992	12.7	75.7
33	14,834	12.5	70.9

Source: C.R. Bostater, "Case Report, Newspaper Source Separation; A Survey of the City of Rockville, Maryland." Unpublished paper prepared for course E.M. 55.684, The American University, Washington, D.C., December 1976.

ed newspaper monthly in four collection districts of private homes. The participation of households was related to a 1970 census[8] showing again a correlation between participation in the source separation program and socio-economic status. The latter is measured as median family income and the years of education of the adult family members. The results are summarized in Table 3.

SCAVENGING

Scavenging is the collecting of separated material from curbside by unauthorized persons, resulting in loss of income to the separate collection program. The extent of scavenging fluctuates with market conditions; as the price of recyclable material increases, so does the probability of scavenging. Hempstead, N.Y., provides a good example of the effect price increases have on scavenging, and the positive effect of an ordinance to prevent it. When the city was receiving $9 per ton for newspaper, there was no evidence of scavenging; but as paper prices reached $17 per ton, Hempstead realized a loss of approximately 40 percent of the paper on the curbs. The hardest hit areas were patrolled and six summonses were issued during the month. This action caused a significant drop in the amount of scavenging. A community considering source separation should formulate an anti-scavenger ordinance to provide a legal basis for control of unauthorized collectors. Program officials, however, should consider the costs of enforcing such an ordinance, and ensure that it will not interfere with newspaper drives traditionally conducted by charitable organizations.

EPA DEMONSTRATION PROGRAMS

Many smaller communities desire to recover paper, steel and glass, but cannot afford large mechanized plants. The challenge is to combine the best features of separate collection programs with the ability to process some waste fractions on a limited scale.

An experimental program of this nature was established in Sweden about five years ago.[9] Paper was collected separately; cans and bottles were collected as a mixed fraction and separated at modestly-sized, centrally-located centers. This program formed the basis for a "multi-materials source separation" program now being conducted in Marblehead and Somerville, Mass., with assistance from the U.S. Environmental Protection Agency (EPA).[10] The objective of these programs is to demonstrate the extent to which materials can be *economically* recovered from the waste stream through source separation. It is anticipated that the results of the programs will be of considerable benefit to other municipalities across the country, and that the techniques developed can be directly transferred to other source separation programs.[11]

Somerville is an urban, "blue collar" community with one of the highest population densities in the country. In Somerville, 65 percent of the families rent their homes or apartments, the median income is $9600 per year (1970 base) and the median education level is 11.6 years.[3] Somerville had not had a recycling program prior to the EPA grant.

By comparison, Marblehead is a more affluent suburban community with a population density about half that of Somerville. The program has been in effect since January 1976 without interruption. While 15 percent of the families rent their homes or apartments, 85 percent own their residences. The median income is $14,300 per year (1970 base), and the median education level is 13.3 years.[3] A curbside, multi-materials recycling program had been practiced for several years, but had met with comparatively little success.

Marblehead has as its goal a 25 percent reduction (by weight) in municipal solid waste through the recycling program. Somerville's goal is a 15 percent reduction.[3]

Both programs are designed to maximize the recovery of separated materials from the conventional waste stream by:

- Establishing a favorable long-term market for recovered materials;
- Minimizing collection costs; and
- Maximizing the participation rate of their citizens.

A favorable, long-term market was found for recovered materials from both cities and advertising for competitive bids, requiring a guaranteed floor price contract (described in Table 4), and assuring a stable supply of materials.

The programs involve weekly collection of newspaper and mixed cans and glass on the regular collection day by a specially built (noncompacting and top loading with a partitioned bucket) compartmentalized truck. The concept of combining glass and cans is being tested to help reduce the inconvenience to households and improve collection. The mixture is processed through a mechanical system for size sorting, magnetic separation, cleaning and shredding. Aluminum cans are separated by hand from a conveyor carrying large nonmagnetic items.

Collection costs are kept to a minimum by using the compartmentalized trucks, collectors from the available labor pool and increased efficiency of collection routes. Table 5 summarizes the costs and revenue of Marblehead's mixed waste (conventional) collection system formerly used, and the source separation-mixed waste system currently used. In reviewing the table, it is important to note that disposal savings and materials revenues are sufficient to decrease the net cost of Marblehead's disposal system.

To keep the operation simple and maximize public participation, the communities ask that the householders divide their waste into only three fractions: paper; cans and glass; and all other materials. No preparation procedures, such as removing metal rings from bottles or flattening of cans, are required. Also, there are frequent,

Table 4. Materials Prices (dollars per ton).

	FOB Somerville			Marblehead (FOB Plant) in Salem, Mass.		
Material	Floor	Current as of Dec. 1976	Year's Average	Floor	Current as of Dec. 1976	Year's Average
Paper	2	11	14	5	17	21
Clear or Colored Glass	10	10	10	12	12	12
Cans	5	5	17	10	10	20
Average Mix*	4.75	9.25	11.25	8.80	13.60	17.20

*In dollars per ton and assuming one ton of materials is 50 percent paper, 25 percent cans, 25 percent glass in Somerville; and 40 percent paper, 20 percent cans, 40 percent glass in Marblehead.
Source: H. Vaccaro and H. Baily, Source Separtion: A Cost Effective Low Technology Resource Recovery Option (Cambridge, Mass.: Resource Planning Associates, Inc., 1976); Somerville and Marblehead Recycling Program Monthly Progress Report (Cambridge, Mass.: Resource Planning Associates, Inc., November 1976).

Table 5. Marblehead Annual Costs & Revenues (Dollars).

	Collection without source separation	Collection with multi-materials source separation
Refuse Collection Labor	$131,000	$131,000
Recycling Collection Labor	–	65,500
Recycling Equipment (operation & depreciation)	–	10,500
Refuse Equipment (operation & depreciation)	21,000	21,000
Disposal	189,500	142,100
Recycling Bins (leased)	–	5,900
Materials Revenue*	–	33,540
Net Cost	341,500	342,460

*Assuming the 1976 average price of $17/ton of recycled materials.
Source: H. Vaccaro and H. Bailly, *Source Separation: A Cost Effective Low Technology Resource Recovery Option* (Cambridge, Mass.: Resource Planning Associates, Inc., 1976).

simultaneous curbside collections of all materials. An intensive public education campaign has been conducted to publicize the success of the programs in order to encourage interest. Both communities have enacted ordinances requiring separation of recyclables from refuse.

To date, Marblehead's program has proved to be more successful than Somerville's in that from 60-to-80 percent of the Marblehead residents participate weekly in the current program (which currently recovers approximately 25 percent of the town's residential waste, compared with approximately seven percent in Somerville). Marblehead was able to utilize spare labor capacity already on the payroll, provide jobs for several additional men, improve its public image, and still reduce overall waste disposal costs by $28,140 in an eight-month period.* On a normal day, about nine tons of recyclables are collected and delivered by three-man crews in an average of 5 1/2 hours. After eight months of program operations, the 24,000 residents of Marblehead have recycled more than 1,480 tons, or about 124 pounds per resident.[3]

Recycling in Somerville has not yet reached a breakeven level. Still, the high residential density may eventually be responsible for an even more efficient collection operation than in Marblehead. In the first eight months the program was

*The "eight month" period referred to here is actually a little less – from program startup on Jan. 12, 1976, through Aug. 31, 1976.

in progress, 1,548 tons of glass, cans and paper were recovered. From this recovered material, Somerville realized a disposal savings of $22,921 and revenue of $20,550.

OTHER METHODS OF SOURCE SEPARATION

In communities such as West Orange, N.J., and in towns surrounding Dayville, Conn., householders separate all of their glass containers for separate collection. In Connecticut, the glass is collected by private dealers for delivery to a local glass container plant. Money from the sale of the glass is returned to the various town treasuries.

There is also a so-called "neighborhood concept" of source separation, where materials are collected in small vehicles, rather than large compactor trucks, and delivered either to centrally located bins or directly to processing plants.[11,12] It is reported that these plants have been operating for more than three years and cost approximately $100,000 per 300 ton daily capacity. The plants simply crush materials and convey them to rail cars or trucks for shipment to markets.[12] Several operating examples, particularly the so-called "ORE Plan," have been described. In at least one community, residents pay a reduced monthly fee to a private collector for having separated their refuse into various fractions.[13,14,15]

The experience of some neighborhood or small town source separation programs has been described. In Nottingham, N.H. (1200 population plus several thousand during the summer), residents bring their household wastes to the site of the old town dump. There, they deposit separated components (newspapers, corrugated, clean mixed paper, metals, glass and others) in a receiving building. The glass and metals are crushed prior to shipping to customers. A survey of 150 year-round residents indicated general satisfaction with the system. Apparently, the revenues from the program exceed the costs.[16]

Source separation is also practiced in Europe. In France, for example, there is separate collection of some 1 1/2 liter plastic mineral water bottles by dealers who bale the plastic and sell it for re-use. In Huddersfield, England, Oxfam Activities Ltd., and overseas relief charity, has been operating a source separation program for two years. Collection is made once a month at 5500 homes. There are four levels of recyclables — glass and cans, textiles, paper and aluminum — which are segregated into four, differently colored plastic bags. Cans are further separated from the glass by magnets and the glass is then hand-sorted by color. Sales agreements were signed for all separated material and any inconvenience to the householders is reduced through the use of the colored bags.

CONCLUSION

A successful source separation program can be an excellent low-technology means of retrieving valuable materials from the municipal solid waste stream, thus conserving materials and reducing the amount of waste to be burned or buried. Experimental programs have demonstrated that as much as 20-to-30 percent of a community's waste may be recovered by such a program.

To initiate and maintain a successful program requires careful municipal planning and administration, as well as continuing cooperation on the part of the citizens. In large, densely-populated metropolitan areas, source separation is probably not as practical as a large mechanical resource recovery facility; however, in areas where such a mechanical system is not viable, source separation deserves serious consideration as an alternative to merely disposing of solid waste.

REFERENCES

1. SCS Engineers, *Analysis of Source Separation of Solid Wastes, Separate Collection Studies.* April 1974. Prepared for the U.S. Environmental Protection Agency.
2. "Source Separation Residential Collection." National Solid Wastes Management Association, *Technical Bulletin,* 5, No. 6 (July 1974).
3. Vaccaro, Henry S., and Henri-Claude Bailly, *Source Separation: A Cost Effective Low Technology Resource Recovery Option* (Cambridge, Mass.: Resource Planning Associates, Inc., 1976).
4. "Marketing Recovered Materials . . . A Guide for Planners," *NCRR Bulletin,* 5, No. 4 (Fall 1975): 75-83.
5. Sterns, R., "The Economics of Separate Refuse Collection," *Waste Age,* 5, No. 3 (May/June 1974): 6-15.
6. Caldwell, Lynton K., "Responsiveness and Responsibility: The Anomalous Problem of the Environment," in *People vs. Government: The Responsiveness of American Institutions,* Leroy N. Rieselback ed. (Bloomington: Indiana University Press, 1975).
7. Hansen, Penelope, *Residential Paper Recovery: A Municipal Implementation Guide.* U.S. Environmental Protection Agency, 1975.
8. Bostater, C.R., "Case Report, Newspaper Source Separation: A Survey of the City of Rockville, Maryland." Unpublished paper prepared for course EM 55.684, The American University, Washington, D.C., December 1976.
9. *Households Contributing to Resource Recovery.* Survey published by the Swedish Institute for Resource Recovery, Malmo, 1975.
10. Hansen, Penelope, "Resource Recovery through Multi-Materials Source Separation," *Waste Age,* 7, No. 10 (October 1976): 30-34, 44.
11. Michaels, A., "Source Separation — A Test Program," *Public Works, 107,* No. 4 (April 1976): 62-65.
12. Seldman, N.N., "High technology Recycling: Costly and Still Wasteful," *Compost Science, 17,* No. 2 (March/April 1976): 28-29. *Environmental Action Bulletin,* Oct. 16, 1976, and Dec. 25, 1976.
13. Duncan, R.C., "The 'ORE Plan' for Recycling Household Solid Waste: An Alternative Garbage Collection System," *Compost Science, 16,* No. 1 (January/February 1975): 24-32.
14. Duncan, R.C., "The Role of the ORE Plan in Developing a Nationwide Recycling Network," *Compost Science,* 17, No. 3 (Summer 1976): 25-32.
15. Duncan, R.C., "Developing a Northwest Recycling Network," *Seriatim Journal of Ecotopia,* Fall 1976, pp. 87-92.
16. Tichenor, R., "The Nottingham System for Resource Recovery," *Compost Science,* 17, No. 1 (January/February 1976): 20-25.

3-2 Facilitating Paper Recycling

J.F. Witmer and E.S. Geller

Source: Reprinted from the Journal of Applied Behavior Analysis, Vol. 9, pp. 315–322. Reprinted with Permission of The Society for the Experimental Analysis of Behavior, Inc.

Ecological imbalance from the accumulation of waste materials has grown slowly and undesirable consequences remain remote for most people (Pirages, 1973). Even simple programs for handling environmental problems rarely get widespread support. For example, voluntary recycling programs have been set up in many communities, but even the most effective projects reduce solid waste by less than 1% (Hall and Ackoff, 1972). In 1973, 130 million tons of refuse were collected in the United States ("U.S. Finds A Rich Resource: The Nation's Trash Pile," 1974). Although much of this material could have been reused, recylcing requires a "reverse-distribution process," whereby the consumer becomes the first rather than the last link in the distribution process (Margulies, 1970). The present study was designed to study applications of behavior technology to initiate a paper-recycling process. Since paper makes up about 50% of environmental litter (Finnie, 1973), paper-recycling programs both reuse waste paper and reduce litter.

In an earlier application of reinforcement contingencies to promote paper recycling, residents of university dormitories were given a lottery coupon for delivering at least one sheet of paper to a collection room during a raffle contingency (Geller, Chaffee, and Ingram, 1975). For a contest condition, two dormitories were paired and the dormitory residents who collected the most paper in a week won $15 for their treasury. The amount of paper collected during the raffle and contest contingencies was equivalent and markedly greater than that collected during baseline conditions.

Given apparent widespread concern for ecology among college students, prompting alone might significantly increase paper recycling. Geller et al. (1975) announced each contingency by means of posters displayed on the bulletin boards of each dorm floor. Thus, results of low participation in that study may have been due to ineffective prompting; perhaps few residents attended to bulletin-board announcements and therefore, most were not aware of the recycling program. Hence, the low participation was possibly due to a lack of contingency awareness, rather than a lack of contingency effectiveness. A more comprehensive prompting procedure was implemented in the present study by delivering written announcements of the recycling program to every dormitory room.

In addition to comparing paper-recycling behaviors following prompting with those due to a procedure combining both prompting and reinforcement techniques, the present research also compared the behavior effects of two reinforcement methods: an individual contingency that provided a raffle coupon for each pound of paper delivered and a group contingency that provided $15 for the treasury of one of two dorms whose residents collected the most paper in a week. In the raffle condition of the Geller et al. study, a raffle ticket was given for each paper delivery, regardless of the amount of paper delivered. This resulted in individuals making numerous, repeated deliveries each day with small amounts of paper. The raffle contingency of the present study emphasized the quantity of paper delivered by offering the dorm resident one raffle coupon per pound of paper delivered. Thus, greater amounts of delivered paper fewer deliveries were expected in the present study than were observed in the prior program. The present research examined proximity effects by recording the room numbers of residents making paper deliveries and comparing distances to the collection site.

METHOD

Subjects and Setting

The residents of four male and two female dormitories on the campus of Virginia Polytechnic Institute and State University served as subjects. A room on the first floor of each dorm had been designated as a paper collection center by the Campus Committee for Ecological Rebalance (REBAL). REBAL collected the paper every two weeks and sold it to a paper mill for $15 a ton.

REBAL had promoted paper recycling in all campus dormitories for more than 16 months before the start of this study by maintaining one 76 by 86 cm recycling poster on the bulletin board of each dorm floor. The posters indicated the location of the collection room and the times that the room would be open (i.e., 5:30 to 7:30 p.m. Monday through Friday).

Contingencies

All dorms began the experiment with a two-week Baseline condition. For the next three weeks, two dorms received a Prompt condition, two received a Raffle contingency, and two received a Contest contingency. During the last three weeks, the prompting and reinforcement procedures designed to facilitate paper deliveries were removed from all six dorms in a Follow-up condition equivalent to Baseline. The dorms were paired as follows: (a) one male and one female dorm, each having a capacity of 333 students, received the Prompt condition; (b) one male and one female dorm, each having a capacity of 180 students, received the Raffle contingency;[2] (c) one R.O.T.C. male dorm

and one civilian male dorm, each having a capacity of 333 students, received the Contest contingency. All dorms were filled approximately to capacity.

For the Baseline and Follow-up recordings the situation was exactly as it had been, except that a REBAL poster appeared on the collection-room door and a data recorder sat in the collection room from 5:30 to 7:30 p.m. Monday through Friday, recording the amount of paper delivered by each person. In addition, the data recorders kept track of the amount of paper brought to the collection room and left in front of the door at times other than the prescribed collection period (i.e., from 7:30 p.m. on a given day until 5:30 p.m. the next day).

On three consecutive Sundays, following two weeks of Baseline recording, identically designed flyers describing the appropriate contingency for the week were distributed under the door of each dorm room. The message for the Prompt condition read:[3]

RECYCLE PAPER
YOU CAN HELP TO:
  PRESERVE OUR NATIONAL RESOURCES
  PROTECT THE ENVIRONMENT
  SAVE TREES
  ALLEVIATE THE PAPER SHORTAGE
  BRING ALL RECYCLABLE PAPER
    (INCLUDING THIS SHEET)
TO COLLECTION ROOM ON FIRST FLOOR
    MONDAY – FRIDAY
    5:30 – 7:30 p.m.

During the raffle contingency the written message was:

RAFFLE
WIN PRIZES EACH WEEK!!
1 COUPON PER POUND OF PAPER
BRING ALL RECYCLABLE PAPER
    (INCLUDING THIS SHEET)
TO COLLECTION ROOM ON FIRST FLOOR
    MONDAY – FRIDAY
    5:30 – 7:30 p.m.
A LIST OF PRIZES AND RULES IS
POSTED ON COLLECTION ROOM DOOR

---

[2] A coin was flipped to determined which dorm-pair would receive the raffle contingency (the pair with 333 students per dorm or the pair with 180 students per dorm) and which would receive only a prompt.

[3] Illustrations of the actual flyers will be furnished on request to E. Scott Geller.

The Raffle rules explained that residents would receive one coupon for every pound of recyclable paper brought to the collection room on weekdays from 5:30 to 7:30 p.m. The 10 prizes raffled off each week had been donated by 24 local merchants and ranged in value from $3 to $20. The prizes were grouped so that each week's total value was approximately $80.[4]

For the contest flyers the message was:

CONTEST
BETWEEN BRODIE HALL
AND VAWTER HALL
THE MOST RECYCLABLE PAPER
EACH WEEK
WILL WIN $1500
BRING ALL RECYCLABLE PAPER
INCLUDING THIS SHEET)
TO COLLECTION ROOM ON FIRST FLOOR
MONDAY – FRIDAY
5:30 – 7:30 p.m.
DETAILS ARE POSTED ON
COLLECTION ROOM DOOR

The contest rules, an expansion of the information given in the flyer, were posted on the collection room door of the two dorms involved.[5]

Personnel and Procedure

The data recorders were undergraduate students fulfilling a requirement in a behavior modification course taught by the second author. Advanced undergraduate psychology majors were collection-center managers and supervised the data recorders' daily procedures as partial fulfillment of an undergraduate research course. All paper was weighed at the end of the 2-hr period by both individuals. To ensure reliability of measurement, weekly weighings were taken by the authors. The discrepancy between the daily and weekly totals ranged from zero to six pounds, with the largest discrepancy being 0.8% of the total weekly poundage.

---

[4] An illustration of the raffle announcement that listed the prizes is available from the second author on request.
[5] An illustration of the poster that described the contest rules is available from E. Scott Geller on request.

When arriving at the collection room at 5:30 p.m., the collection-center manager and data recorder immediately weighed any extraneous paper (i.e., any paper that had been left at the collection site since the previous collection period) and recorded the results. The data recorder collected all paper brought to the room, obtained the room number of each person delivering paper, and kept the day's paper separate from other paper in the room. For the Raffle condition, the data recorder weighed each student's paper in his presence and then gave the participant one raffle coupon for each pound of paper delivered. One half of each raffle ticket, containing the name and room number of the resident, was deposited in a raffle box; the other half of the coupon was retained by the resident.

RESULTS

Pounds of Paper

The largest amount of paper delivered on any day was 188 pounds by the female dorm during the Raffle; this dorm's largest Baseline value was 86 pounds. The largest poundage for males in the Raffle condition was 193 pounds, as contrasted with this dorm's largest Baseline quantity of 18 pounds. In the Contest contingency, the male civilians delivered a high of 482 pounds on the ninth day of Contest, whereas the high for the R.O.T.C. dorm was only 71 pounds delivered on the eleventh day of Contest. The contest dorms had almost identical Baseline levels, the civilian dorm reaching a high of 23 pounds and the R.O.T.C. dorm reaching a high of 15 pounds. The Prompt condition appeared to have relatively little influence; the quantity of paper delivered increased from a Baseline high of 20 pounds to only 21 pounds on the ninth day of prompting for females and from a high of three pounds in Baseline to a peak of 15 pounds during prompting for males.

The three-week follow-up period resulted in an immediate and marked drop in pounds of paper delivered during the critical hours by residents of the female raffle dorm (i.e., from 488 pounds on the last day of Raffle to 31 pounds for the first day of Follow-up). For the male raffle dorm, daily pounds of paper delivered from 5:30 to 7:30 p.m. decreased at a more gradual rate, increasing from a daily high of 52 pounds in the third week of Raffle to 80 pounds on the first day to Follow-up, and then dropping to zero pounds by the third day of Follow-up.

After the Contest weeks, paper delivered from 5:30 to 7:30 p.m. decreased for both contest dorms (i.e., for civilians the poundage changed from a high of 60 pounds in the third Contest week to 30 pounds on the first day of Follow-up week, and for the cadets from 71 pounds to one pound). The amount of paper delivered during the critical hours in the two prompt dorms increased slightly during Follow-up, reaching a daily high of 50 pounds for females and 35 pounds for males.

Some relatively consistent-sex differences can be observed in the results from the two pairs of male/female dorms. For the dorm-pair given the Prompt treatment, females delivered more paper than males in all but one week of the study. Similarly, for the raffle dorm-pair, females were consistently higher during Baseline and Raffle, although males delivered more paper than females during Follow-up.

During the Contest contingency, there were pronounced between-dorm differences in amounts of paper delivered. The civilians delivered more paper than the cadets during all three weeks of the contest, although the weekly totals for the civilian residents decreased over the three contest weeks (i.e., Week 1 = 742 pounds, Week 2 = 637, Week 3 = 144). It is noteworthy that several civilians verbalized to the data recorder that they were determined to win each contest in order to help finance weekend dorm parties. Indeed, the males described the parties that took place after each contest and each party was attended by an estimated 100 dorm residents. Such parties are not permitted in the military-style R.O.T.C. dorm.

The total quantities of paper delivered during the critical hours was 117 pounds for the Prompt condition, 2159 pounds for the Raffle contingency, and 1633 pounds for the Contest contingency. Extraneous paper (i.e., paper delivered at times other than between 5:30 and 7:30 p.m.) totalled 193 pounds for the Prompt condition, four pounds for the Raffle contingency, and 293 pounds for the Contest contingency. Thus, the

Raffle and Contest conditions promoted delivery of markedly greater amounts of paper during the critical collection hours than did the Prompt condition.

Participation

A paper delivery was defined as a dorm resident delivering at least one 21.6 by 28 cm sheet of paper to the collection room between 5:30 and 7:30 p.m. Monday through Friday. For each dorm, the average number of deliveries was lower during Baseline than during the contingency of the next three weeks. In the Prompt dorms, the males had peaks of one delivery during the third day of Baseline and three deliveries in the first day of Prompt; females had peaks of two deliveries on the eighth and tenth days of Baseline and five deliveries on three occasions in the third week of Prompt. Both raffle dorms showed marked increases in participation as a result of the Raffle contingency; males increased from a daily high of five deliveries on the seventh day of Baseline to eight on two occasions during Raffle, and the number of female deliveries increased from four to 10 across the same period. For the contest dorms, the civilians showed a substantial increase in participation during the Contest (i.e., from a peak of three on the ninth day of Baseline to a peak of 18 on the fourth day of Contest). In the R.O.T.C. dorm, however, participation for these same weeks decreased from three to four deliveries.

A weekly proportion of resident participation was found by dividing the number of individuals from a given dorm who made paper deliveries by the total number of residents in that dorm. The highest proportion of participation occurred for the Raffle condition, reaching peaks of 0.141 during the second Raffle week for females and during the third Raffle week for males. The highest participation proportions for the Prompt dorms were 0.054 in the third week of prompting for females and 0.018 in the first week of prompting for males. Per cent participation by the cadets exceeded the civilians only during Baseline (i.e., weekly highs of 0.022 versus 0.018); during the Contest, participation in the civilian dorm increased to a weekly high of 0.099 for the second contest, compared with the highest proportion of 0.039 for the cadets during the first contest.

Proximity

The room numbers of the agents of the paper deliveries were an indication of the distance travelled to reach the collection site. For this analysis of proximity effects, divisions were determined by floor, and proportion of participants per dorm floor was determined for each condition.[6] During Baseline, the majority of participants in every dorm were first-floor residents. In addition, for each dorm the relative number of first-floor participants decreased as a function of each treatment condition and remained below the Baseline proportions during Follow-up. An increase in participants from dorm floors other than the first floor was particularly apparent during the Raffle contingency for females and during the Contest contingency for civilians. As a result, a chi square test of homogeneity was significant in both of these cases ($ps < 0.02$). The residents of these particular dorms consistently collected the largest quantities of weekly paper during treatment. It is noteworthy that for all but one dorm (i.e., prompt/male) the participation distributions during Follow-up were more similar to the Baseline distributions than were the distributions during treatment conditions.[7]

DISCUSSION

The positive reinforcement contingencies (i.e., the raffle and contest) prominently increased quantities of paper delivered to dormitory collection rooms above Baseline levels and above the levels observed subsequent to distributions of flyers urging paper-recycling behaviors for the improvement of ecology (i.e., the Prompt condition). However, the percentage of dormitory residents who participated in the recycling program was disappointingly low (i.e.,

[6] Preliminary analyses divided each dorm floor into specific sections based on relative walking distance from the collection room, but no consistent within-floor variations were observed.

[7] A table of the proximity data is available on request to the second author.

less than 15%). Since every resident was informed of the reinforcement contingency by means of a flyer delivered to his or her room, it is reasonable to assume that most dorm residents were aware of the treatment condition. Thus, low participation in the paper drive was not due to a lack of contingency awareness as speculated by Geller et al. (1975), but rather to a lack of contingency effectiveness.

For the Raffle contingency, virtually all paper was delivered to the collection room between 5:30 and 7:30 p.m. when the coupon reinforcers were available, indicating that the Raffle was the motivating factor for those few individuals who did make paper deliveries. As expected, the contingency of giving one coupon per pound of paper resulted in a greater volume of paper per visit, and virtually eliminated the repeated visits observed by Geller et al. (1975). A substantially greater amount of paper was collected during the raffle of the present study than during the raffle of the previous study. However, the percentage of resident participation during raffle contingencies was similar for both studies, indicating that the larger paper quantities in the present study were due to greater individual effort. The increased numbers of prizes per raffle in the present study (i.e., 10 versus four) probably influenced the differences.

The Contest contingency produced results directly opposite to the investigators' hypothesis that a group contingency would be more effective in an R.O.T.C. dorm, whose residents frequently act as a unit, than in a civilian dorm with no obvious group structure or unity. Perhaps the Contest contingency was more effective in the civilian dorm because certain residents of this dorm specified a method for spending the contest winnings that implied a common group reward. Specifically, the money from each contest was used to procure beer for weekend parties in the dorm. Such parties are not permitted in the R.O.T.C. dorm and, therefore, the between-dorm comparisons were biased by the fact that the $15 was translated into a group reinforcer for the civilians but not for the cadets. Perhaps the decreasing amounts of paper collected by the civilians over the three contest weeks was due to an increasing realization that the cadets were not providing competition.

Prompting alone was clearly the least effective intervention technique. Although most dorm residents should have become aware of a worthwhile ecology program through the prompting procedure, few individuals took the trouble to participate. Whereas there was some increase in both participation and amount of paper delivered during prompting, the changes were not substantial. Hence, the present study indicates that community ecology programs should at least offer individuals the possibility of receiving a tangible reward in return for their ecology-improving behaviors.

The relative convenience of the desired behavior is certainly an important factor determining the efficacy of ecology-promoting procedures. For example, prompting procedures alone were sufficient to augment the probability of an ecology-improving response when the response merely required the selection of drinks in returnable rather than throwaway containers (Geller, Farris, and Post, 1973; Geller, Wylie, and Farris, 1971) or the disposal of a handbill in a convenient location (Geller, 1973, 1975; Geller, Witmer, and Orebaugh, in press). In the present study, prompting not only had little influence on the relatively inconvenient behavior patterns of carrying recyclable paper to a collection room, but the probability of making paper deliveries was usually highest when the response was most convenient (i.e., when the resident's room and the collection room were on the same floor).[8]

In conclusion, the procedures and results of the present investigation illustrate practical and effective procedures for promoting a reverse-distribution process that could be easily refined for community-wide application. For example, community collection centers could offer raffle coupons for particular quantities of recyclable commodities: and, as a result of the present study (and that by Geller et al., 1975), the authors predict that community merchants would donate raffle prizes in return for the

"good will" and publicity accompanying their support of a community ecology project. In addition, recycling contests between civic and/or church groups could be organized, and prize money could be procured from the sale of collected paper of aluminum to recycling plants. However, voluntary programs such as these are by no means sufficient Mandatory programs such as municipal ordinances requiring the separate collection of paper and incentives for industry to use recycled paper are possible long-range solutions to the recycling problem. Whatever programs are implemented, individual cooperation is important and projects such as those presented here could help to initiate and maintain the appropriate behaviors. Although the market for recycled paper is at present low, aluminum is in great demand for recycling and the procedures outlined here are easily generalizable to that and other commodities.[9]

REFERENCES

1. Cash in trash? maybe. Forbes, January 15, 1970, p. 20.
2. Finnie, W. C. Field experiments in litter control. Environment and Behavior, 1973, 5, 123–144.
3. Geller, E.S. Increasing desired waste disposals with instructions. Man-Environment Systems, 1975, 5, 125–128.
4. Geller, E.S. Prompting anit-litter behavior. Proceedings of the 81st Annual Convention of the American Psychological Association, 1973, 8, 901–902 (Summary).
5. Geller, E.S., Chaffee, J.L., and Ingram, R.E. Promoting paper-recycling on a university campus. Journal of Environmental Systems. 1975, 5, 39–57.
6. Geller, E.S., Farris, J.C. and Post, D.S. Prompting a consumer behavior for pollution control. Journal of Applied Behavior Analysis. 1973, 6, 367–376.
7. Geller, E.S., Witmer, J.F., and Orebaugh, A.L. Instructions as a determinant of paper-disposal behaviors. Environment and Behavior, (in press).
8. Geller, E.S., Wylie, R.C., and Farris, J.C. An attempt at applying prompting and reinforcement toward pollution control. Proceedings of the 79th Annual Convention of the American Psychological Association, 1971, 6, 701–702 (Summary).

---

[8] Since residents with rooms on the same floor as the collection room were more likely to pass by the collection room with a REBAL poster on its door, the observed proximity effects may have been due in part to systematic prompting differences among dorm residents.

---

[9] By the end of the present study, the return for recyclable paper had dropped from $15 to $12.50 per ton, and at the time of preparing the revision of this manuscript there was no market for recyclable paper in Southwest Virginia.

9. Hall, J.R. and Ackoff, R.L. A systems approach to the problems of solid waste and litter. *Journal of Environmental Systems*, 1972, **2**, 351–364.

10. Margulies, W.P. Steel and paper industries look at recycling as an answer to pollution. *Advertising Age*, 1970, **41**, 63.

11. Pirages, D.C. Behavioral technology and institutional transformation. In H. Wheeler (Ed.), *Beyond the punitive society*. San Francisco: W.H. Freeman and Company, 1973, Pp. 57–70.

12. U.S. finds a rich resource: The nation's trash pile. *U.S. News and World Report*, May 13, 1974, p. 24.

3-3 What's to be Done with Used Newspapers?

Robert Davis and Bruce MacDonald

Source: Adapted from Article with the Same Title Published in *Waste Age,* Vol. 8, No. 7 (July 1977) pp. 50–66 Reprinted with Permission of The National Solid Wastes Management Association.

Under the two-fold stimulus of public concern for the environment and rising solid waste collection and disposal costs, responsible state and local officials must carefully assess three available options for effective solid waste management: materials recovery, energy recovery and landfill.

One proven method of confronting the burgeoning solid waste problem has been source separation programs to divert used newspapers from disposal. This popular approach stems from recognition that newspaper extraction from residential areas can be accomplished with relative ease. Further, properly implemented programs can be both practicable and economically attractive, and can conserve natural resources.

Concurrent with the influx of separate newspaper collection programs in the early 1970's, the concept of recovering energy from municipal solid wastes through incineration, pyrolysis or other means became the subject of renewed interest. The dramatic increase in energy prices since 1973 has drawn even greater attention to energy recovery as an attractive concept. Accordingly, the existence of technically sound and economically attractive choices other than direct disposal via landfilling poses a dilemma for the municipality considering new measures to deal with solid waste.

In this context, how should used newspaper be managed? Should it be recovered and recycled for material value? Should it be left in the solid waste stream for conversion to energy? Should all intrinsic values be ignored and newspaper be disposed via landfill?

This article seeks to heighten general awareness of the recovery/disposal dilemma that communities face. Important issues that need to be assessed and factors that affect trade-offs among possible recovery/disposal options are highlighted. There are no easy answers although the ultimate decision should be based on a solution with the highest economic value to the municipality.

SOURCE SEPARATION

Newspaper recovery via source separation is practiced in over 120 cities and town across the country. Including San Diego, San Francisco, Salt Lake City, El Paso, Madison, and Ridgewood, N.J. This resource recovery option requires voluntary or mandatory separation of newspapers from residential refuse by citizens. Separated newspapers are bundled or bagged and placed at the curb at scheduled intervals. The newspapers are collected either by trucks devoted solely to this purpose, or integrated as part of the regular solid waste collection. In the latter case, separated newspaper is usually placed in receptacles attached to the regular collection vehicle; compartmentalized vehicles have also been tested. Current experience shows the

integrated approaches are preferred when participation rates are low, while separate truck collection is preferred at high participation rates.
Whichever method is used, separately collected
newspaper is delivered to or picked up by a local
paper dealer and thus diverted from disposal. Because of fluctuating paper prices, municipalities
should obtain a long-term contract with a guaranteed floor price. In this manner, a municipality is protected from down-side risk in the paper
market while a revenue is returned.

WASTE-TO-ENERGY

There are many approaches to recycling solid
waste for energy; some are in the experimental
stage, while others have been rejected as impractical or uneconomical. There are, however, three
generic classes of currently operating energy recovery systems: waterwall incinerators, refuse-
derived fuel facilities and pyrolysis systems.
Each approach operates at a cost which is recovered by a combination of tipping fees, sale
of recoverable materials and sale of the derived
product.

Regardless of the resource recovery approach
adopted, sanitary landfill is and will be required
to dispose of residual waste, demolition-type
waste which is normally not amenable to recovery and certain "hard-to-handle" industrial
solid wastes. (These sources can account for
more than 50 per cent of total urban waste.)

EITHER OR?

Solid waste management approaches are sometimes discussed as if they were mutually exclusive, i.e., choosing either source separation,
capital/technology intensive processing or direct
disposal via landfill automatically eliminates
the others from consideration. Fortunately, this
is not the case. The approaches can be mixed
and matched as follows:

- landfill only
- source separation and landfill
- energy recovery and landfill
- source separation and energy recovery and
  landfill.

What are the trade-offs with regard to handling used newspaper? Should newspaper be recovered and recycled as a resource thus freeing
virgin resources for other use? Should the newspaper fraction be converted to energy to assist
in achieving a greater measure of energy independence? Or should newspaper be landfilled?

As a recyclable material, used newspaper has
many applications. Direct recycling into fresh
newsprint provides a market with consistent demand. Other major consumers of used newspaper
include manufacturers of boxboard, insulation,
roofing felt, molded products and wallboard.

PROS & CONS OF RECYCLING

Recycling newspaper as newsprint has widespread appeal from the standpoint of environmental benefits. The U.S. Environmental Protection Agency (EPA) has found that the manufacture of low grade paper from used paper saves
water and energy and creates less air and water
pollution and solid waste.

Recycling used newspaper lessens demands
on forest resources and conserves energy. A
pound of newspaper produced in a virgin mill
requires about 12,000 BTUs while a recycling
mill can produce the same pound of newspaper
for 9,000 BTUs so energy is also saved.

Recent reports from EPA, the Department
of Commerce, and the United Nations state that
despite improved forest management, spiraling
paper demands will exceed pulpwood supply by
the 1990's.

Source separated newspapers save tipping fees
and also provide cities/private haulers with a
sales opportunity. Revenue and diverted disposal savings from such programs reduced overall collection costs by an average of six per cent
in 17 cities studied.

Unlike energy-based options newspaper recovery through source separation and separate
collection involves minimal capital investment.
Most communities are able to implement a program without addditional investment in labor
or vehicles. EPA studies suggest. Should a separate newspaper collection program be discontinued, no large investment would be sacrificed.

To be successful, source separation programs
require municipal endorsement and extensive

publicity to reeducate citizenry and induce an effective change in refuse set-out habits. Improperly promoted and hastily planned programs will not flourish.

In the past few years, prices paid to municipalities for used newspapers have varied from as little as $5 per ton to as much as $50 per ton. The low end is generally not adequate to support a separate collection program. To circumvent market fluctuations cities/private haulers should enter into long-term contracts with guaranteed floor prices.

While newspaper recovery is an attractive option for cities and towns, source separation does not provide a total solid waste management solution. Energy recovery is another approach. At about 7600 BTUs per pound, newspaper approaches the energy content of low grade coal. This raises the possibility that newspaper, along with the rest of the combustible solid waste, can be converted to energy.

PROS AND CONS OF ENERGY RECOVERY

With diminishing domestic energy sources, municipal solid waste could be a useful source of energy. No citizen cooperation is required (newspaper is included with other solid waste). Also, energy supply contracts traditionally have long durations, thereby causing less revenue uncertainty.

Used paper is a renewable energy source, whereas fossil fuels cannot be replaced once the current supply is consumed. With unfavorable pulpwood supply/demand forecasts, however, the fiber content of municipal solid waste should not be relied on for future planning.

Once newspaper is consumed for energy value it cannot be recycled again, either as paper or as energy.

Capital costs for energy recovery systems are high. Depending on the approach, a jurisdiction of 250,000–500,000 people could pay $20–$50 million or more for an energy recovery system. This is many times the investment cost of either source separation or landfill options. With the energy recovery approach, investment (and hence commitment) is so high that program discontinuance is economically and politically difficult. Further, energy recovery facilities

generally operate at a "loss" which is subsidized via increased tipping fees and/or increased municipal taxes.

Steam- or gas-based energy recovery systems must be located within one or two miles of the customer. This can impose severe siting constraints on such facilities. An energy facility can be confronted with a sales loss if a major buyer goes out of business. Finding a new buyer within the same one to two mile radius could be difficult. Prospective customers would have the municipality "over a barrel."

Although preliminary results from the Ames, 1A energy recovery facility indicate that there may be potential for "low-tonnage" systems, energy systems heretofore have been deemed feasible only in large metropolitan areas. Unit operating costs can become excessively high in a jurisdiction of fewer than 250,000 people.

Recovering the energy value of paper fiber independent of the other municipal solid waste components is not feasible. The capital costs would be exorbitantly high in relation to the energy produced since paper represents only a fraction of the total solid waste stream. Conversely, EPA estimates that newspaper can be extracted from the solid waste stream with a nominal BTU loss of five per cent at typical citizen participation rates (30 to 50 per cent). Wheelabrator-Frye, operators of the Saugus, MA energy recovery facility, estimate the BTU loss for newspaper extraction to be only 2-3 per cent.

Where markets do not exist for used paper and/or energy cannot reasonably be recovered from solid waste, newspaper is landfilled with the attendant loss of material and energy value (unless methane is recovered).

PROS AND CONS OF LANDFILLING

With paper dealers often distant from rural communities, nominal newspaper recovery efforts and associated transportation costs become an expensive proposition. Under these circumstances, sanitary landfill of the newspaper may be the only option. Consolidation of rural county disposal sites to a single sanitary landfill serviced by a network of transfer stations, however, may present a transportation system in which a paper recovery program could be piggy-backed.

Newspaper is cellulosic and, consequently, yields carbon upon decomposing in a landfill. This is necessary for methane production. Although the material value of newspaper is substantially greater than its contribution to production of this low grade gas, there is nonetheless an energy value if newspaper markets are unavailable.

Properly conducted sanitary landfill can assist in reclaiming unusuable land for moderate development.

Although unsanitary land disposal sites are diminishing in favor of well-managed, environmentally acceptable sites, loose newspaper can result in litter and visual blight.

Landfilling municipal solid wastes has generally been a relatively inexpensive disposal option. As landfill replacement becomes necessary, sites are located further from metropolitan areas resulting in (1) less collection productivity due to increased haul distances, or (2) transfer stations to maintain collection productivity with attendant transfer costs. A source separation program can preserve existing landfill space in the near term, and reduce transportation/interim handling in the future.

Source separation of newspaper does not have to result in a "deficit" to an energy system. The deficit produced by removing newspaper from the solid waste stream can be filled by accepting solid waste from municipal private haulers outside the immediate jurisdiction. These peripheral sources generally dispose of solid waste with energy content equal to or greater than the amount of newspaper removed through a source separation program. In addition, the municipality is able to collect additional revenue from tipping fees charged to the peripheral haulers.

THE WEIGHT-FOR-HEAT TRICK

For energy recovery systems based on steam operation, there is yet another benefit from newspaper recycling. Almost all waterwall incinerators built over the last few years are heat-limited. That is, most steam recovery systems are limited in their capability to handle solid waste. Since newspaper has a higher heat value

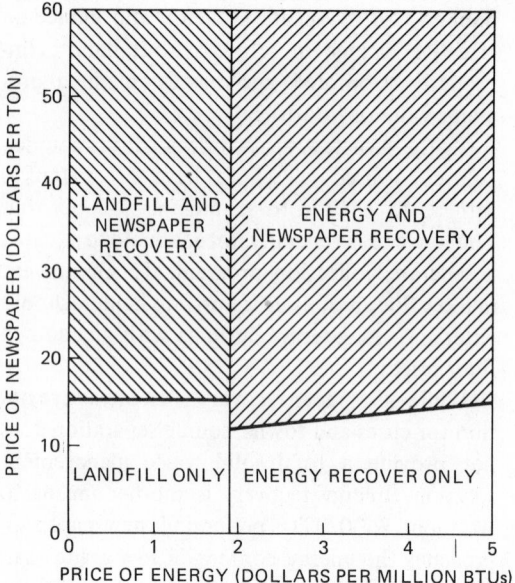

Graph of the "baseline case."

than mixed municipal solid waste, it takes more than one ton of solid waste to produce the same heat as one ton of newspaper. Theoretically, as much as 1 1/2 tons of solid waste with heat value of about 5,500 BTUs per pound could be substituted for each ton of newspaper (at 7,600 BTUs per pound) that is recovered prior to incineration, thereby increasing system capacity. Thus, newspaper recycling and energy recovery are actually compatible alternatives.

With these relationships in mind, the following paragraphs take a closer look at economic factors that influence recovery/disposal decision-making.

A multitude of variables need be examined when considering resource recovery/disposal options. Consideration must be given to such factors as composition of the local solid waste stream; existing recovery/disposal practices and associated physical/economical/technological life; prevailing prices for newspaper and energy; and so on. Acknowledging the dilemmas confronting decision makers regarding potential options, a generalized mathematical model is offered to analyze the economic compatibility of newspaper recovery with energy recovery/disposal options.

For the sake of consistency, the model is constrained to a hypothetical jurisdiction generating municipal refuse at a rate of 1,200 tons per day (TPD). Newspaper extracted via source separation/separate collection programs is assumed to have been replaced by waste from peripheral municipal or private haulers at the rate of 90 per cent of the extracted newspaper quantities.

Variable parameters and numerical values used reflect "expected," "newspaper favorable," and "newspaper unfavorable" conditions. "Expected" values are derived from sources found in public literature and generally reflect nationwide averages. "Favorable" values are indicative of local conditions wherein used newspaper is ideal (e.g., newspaper of greater content in the solid waste stream than a nationwide average, high disposal costs, high energy recovery costs, and so on). Conversely, the "unfavorable" values reflect a jurisdiction where local conditions are outwardly discouraging to newspaper recovery.

Using the generalized data referenced above, the model was exercised to illustrate nine varying conditions:

CONDITION #1 – "BASELINE CASE"

The accompanying chart represents nationwide average conditions and can be analyzed by simply reading up from the horizontal axis the price that is currently paid for energy, expressed in dollars per million BTUs, (One barrel of oil = 6 million BTUs; one ton of coal = 26 million BTUs. Thus, an energy price can be obtained by dividing coal prices per ton by 26, or oil prices per barrel by six) and across from the vertical axis the price that is currently paid for newspaper, expressed in dollars per ton. The point at which the two lines across predicts the economically favorable approach under local conditions for recovering newspaper. For example, at $25 per ton for newspaper and $2 per million BTUs for energy, the combination of newspaper recovery and energy recovery is preferred over energy recovery alone, landfill alone, or landfill plus newspaper recovery.

The graph displays one reason why energy recovery has only recently become economically attractive. Until the last few years, energy prices were between 40 cents and $1 per mil-

lion BTUs, well away from the chart sector where energy recovery is preferred. The recent surge in energy prices, chiefly attributable to the OPEC oil cartel, has now inflated energy prices to about $2 per million BTUs ($12 per barrel of oil), whereupon energy recovery begins to become economically attractive.

The line between "energy and newspaper recovery" and "energy recovery only" is sloped because the baseline condition assumed that not all of the newspaper which is recovered can be replaced by solid waste from other sources – only 90 per cent of it. If all the newspaper could be replaced, the line between "energy only" and "energy and newspaper" would be flat.

The ensuing six charts, Figures 1-6 represent conditions where one or more baseline conditions have been changed to assess sensitivity.

CONDITIONS #2 AND 3: ENERGY RECOVERY LOSS SENSITIVITY

Figure 1 represents the case where energy recovery costs are 50 per cent higher than expected – either through cost overruns, interest rate increases, or other factors. By comparing Figure 1 with the master graph, it can be seen that higher energy recovery costs shift the "landfill/energy" line to the right. Energy prices would have to be at the equivalent of just over $20 per barrel of oil to economically justify energy recovery under these circumstances.

Figure 2 portrays the case where energy recovery costs are 50 per cent lower than expected (this case is a proxy for the cost of the refuse-derived fuel concept). If the RDF concept proves technically viable, Figure 2 shows that energy recovery becomes increasingly attractive relative to landfill, with insignificant change in the desirability of newspaper recovery through source separation/separate collection.

CONDITIONS #4 AND 5: NEWSPAPER RECOVERY SENSITIVITY

In Figure 3, nationwide average conditions are assumed, except that the cost of separately col-

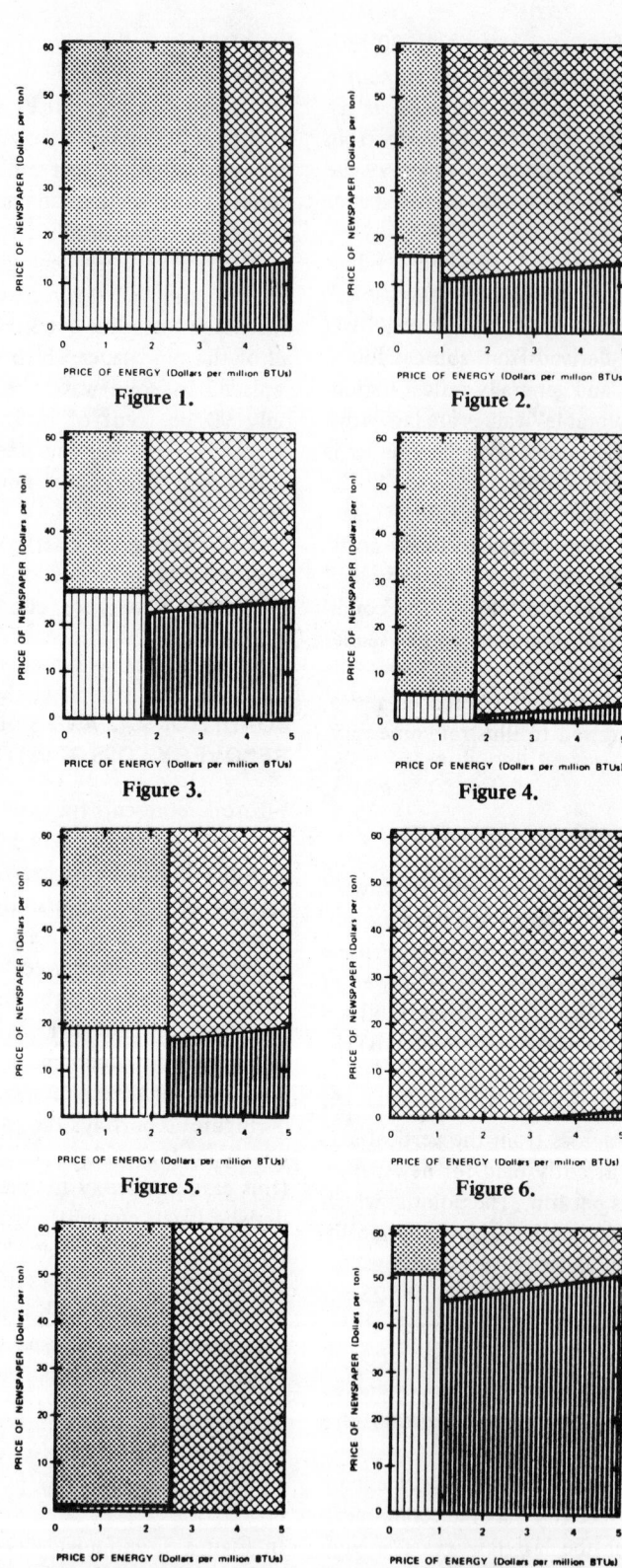

Figure 1.

Figure 2.

Figure 3.

Figure 4.

Figure 5.

Figure 6.

Figure 7.

Figure 8.

lecting newspaper is assumed to be 50 per cent higher than average. This results in an upward shift of the line between energy recovery and energy and newspaper recovery. Again using an example of $25 per ton for newspaper and $2 per million BTUs for energy, the combination of energy and newspaper recovery is still preferred — though just barely. For this particular case, uncertainty in the applicability of the nationwide average conditions to any particular community makes the other options almost equally likely. In this situation a community should probably opt for the material value on the basis that "it will be there to use again."

Figure 4 portrays the impact on baseline conditions if twice the newspaper is collected over what average conditions would suggest. This situation could occur where a particularly effective publicity campaign has been undertaken and the residents are highly motivated. In this circumstance, newspaper recovery is desirable at all but the lowest prices paid for newspaper. The trade-off between energy recovery and landfill for the balance of the solid waste is unchanged when compared to the result displayed in Figure 3.

CONDITIONS #6 AND 7: LANDFILL COST SENSITIVITY

Figures 5 and 6 indicate the impact of rising landfill costs. The range of $2 to $15 per ton for landfill costs encompasses disposal rates charged in most metropolitan areas. Low rates are certain to rise in the near future as available space and environmental controls become more stringent. As might be expected, landfill disappears as an economically attractive disposal option as disposal costs rise, assuming the validity of baseline energy recovery costs.

CONDITIONS #8 AND 9 OVERALL SENSITIVITY

Figures 7 and 8 depict the trade-off under two general sets of circumstances. Figure 7 represents the case where all the parameters have been assigned values that are favorable toward the newspaper recovery option. Figure 8 represents the case where all the parameters are unfavorable. In the first case, newspaper recovery is always preferred except when landfill is virtually free. In the second case, newspaper recovery is economically preferred only when used newspaper prices are at the historically high levels of $50 per ton.

The models presented are by no means the final word on whether or not a newspaper or energy recovery program should be undertaken. They do, however, provide a first look at the economic realities of the material versus energy recovery situation.

3-4 Technological Barriers to the Recovery of Secondary Fibers from Municipal Solid Waste

Marc L. Renard

Source: *Proceedings* of the 1978 Pulping Conference, New Orleans, Louisiana, November 5–8, 1978, pp. 333–345. Reprinted with Permission of The Technical Association of the Pulp and Paper Industry and the Author.

OUTLINE OF THE STUDY

The present paper discusses the main technological barriers to the recovery of secondary fibers from urban waste; in other words, from *selected* fractions of mixed commercial, office or household waste containing a high percentage of potentially recoverable paper fibers.

The National Center for Resource Recovery Inc. (NCRR), a not-for-profit organization, sponsored by industry and labor, has been, since its creation in 1971, devoting a substantial part of its resources and effort to research and developments projects in energy and materials recovery from municipal solid waste. As part of this endeavor, NCRR undertook, under a National Science Foundation grant, a study of the *technological* barriers impeding increased recovery of secondary fibers from this source. In the proposal, it was stressed that only technological barriers would be addressed, and that besides "each topic will be free of institutional considerations, such as marketing disadvantage of secondary materials, freight rate structures, or governmental intervention in a legislative, taxation or subsidization manner." Thus, given a set of present or potential suppliers, purchasers and users of secondary fibers from urban waste, only the constraints imposed by technology (whether actual or not) will be

assessed. Many of those limitations are directly tied to the capabilities of existing wastepaper processing equipment. Therefore, criteria or guidelines should appear from the analysis leading to a *selective* processing of refuse at a recovery plant designed to recover secondary fibers as a feedstock acceptable by industry.

The study will review the contaminents present in urban wastepaper and the main techniques available for their removal. Technological limitations, as they could be inferred from the technical or commercial literature, or from consultations with manufacturers, will be reviewed. In view of these limitations, what contribution could the resource recoverer make to alleviate the problem of contaminants? Using a "selective wasteprocessing" approach, several possible feedstocks will be described, and their suitability for manufacturing into new paper products will be assessed.

Finally, based on preliminary data, a brief account of recent tests performed in May and June 1978, as part of this project, at the Western Michigan University Paper Recycling Pilot Plant, will be given. In these experiments, selected feestocks from municipal solid waste from three major metropolitan centers were supplied by the National Center, decontaminated and made into paper rolls on the WMU 25-inch Fourdrinier machine.

PRESENT RATE OF RECYCLING FROM URBAN WASTE

In the U.S., a 15.5 percent figure for paper and paperboard recovery (6.8 million tons per year) from gross paper and board discards (23.1 million tons per year) in post-consumer municipal waste is given by the Environmental Protection Agency (EPA), for the year 1975, in its Fourth Report to Congress (August 1977).[1] It is also pointed out, in the same document, that "wastepaper recycling dominates the recovery statistics, comprising about 88 percent of total recovered tonnage . . ."[2]

Worldwide, as sketched in Figure 1, wastepaper recovery data from the FAO (Food and Agriculture Organization) of the United Nations,[3] for the year 1977, were obtained after surveying 57 countries. Complete or partly complete returns were obtained from 37 countries, representing some 85 percent of the total 1977 world paper and paperboard capacity. The "wastepaper recovery rate" was defined as

W.R.R. = 100 × (Wastepaper collected for reuse)/(Apparent consumption of paper or paper board ± net trade in converted paper and paperboard products, excluding printed materials)

It is plotted in Figure 1, for the 25 respondent countries having the highest recovery rates. An increase of 1.9 points is registered in the U.S. recovery rate, compared to the 1975 figure.[4]

Despite this favorable trend, there remains that at the date of this writing, the tonnage of paper fibers recovered from *mixed* municipal waste is for all practical purposes negligible, in spite of isolated exceptions, such as the recovery of a fiber product at Franklin, Ohio,[5] (wet pulping process) or bundled newspapers on the tipping floor at Milwaukee, Wisconsin[6] (dry process). Based on conservative estimates of 100 million tons of waste per year generated in the Standard Metropolitan Statistical Areas (SMSA's), a 35 percent paper content by weight, and a 40 percent efficiency in recovering the fibers, there exists a potential source of 14 million tons of material per year, a staggering amount by any standards. As municipalities negotiate long-term contracts for the supply of

waste-derived energy with users, much of the fiber material present in mixed municipal waste might be sent in mixed municipal waste might be "earmarked" for combustion, and lost for use as a feedstock by the paper industry.

This being kept in mind, it appeared worthwhile to investigate how, in specific instances, the resource recovery process, which is now oriented towards the production of a fuel, can be designed for recovery of secondary fibers from mixed MSW. Information or comments from a cross section of the industry (paper- and equipment-manufacturers), trade associations, wastepaper dealers, researchers or governmental organizations were solicited and gethered during a working session organized by the Center on November 10, 1978, after the 1978 TAPPI Secondary Fibers in Washington, D.C. Remarks or suggestions from these individuals or organizations were most helpful to guide the course of this study.

TECHNICAL OBJECTIONS TO THE USE OF SECONDARY FIBERS FROM MSW

The two main classes of technological problems associated with the reuse of secondary fibers from urban waste are:

1. *contamination*[7], either in the original consumer product, and/or during commingling with the remainder of the refuse, and/or during the waste processing operations themselves (such as shredding, air classification, pneumatic conveying, etc.)
2. *degradation* of the physical or esthetic properties of the product with one or more reuses of the fiber[8] (shortening of the fibers, specks, etc.)

The approach most generally taken is to consider these aspects one at a time, namely by developing a "cleaned" fiber furnish, the functional properties of which are then analyzed and compared to standard reference products, for better or worse.[5,9] The question of contaminants in recovered secondary fibers is therefore of paramount importance.

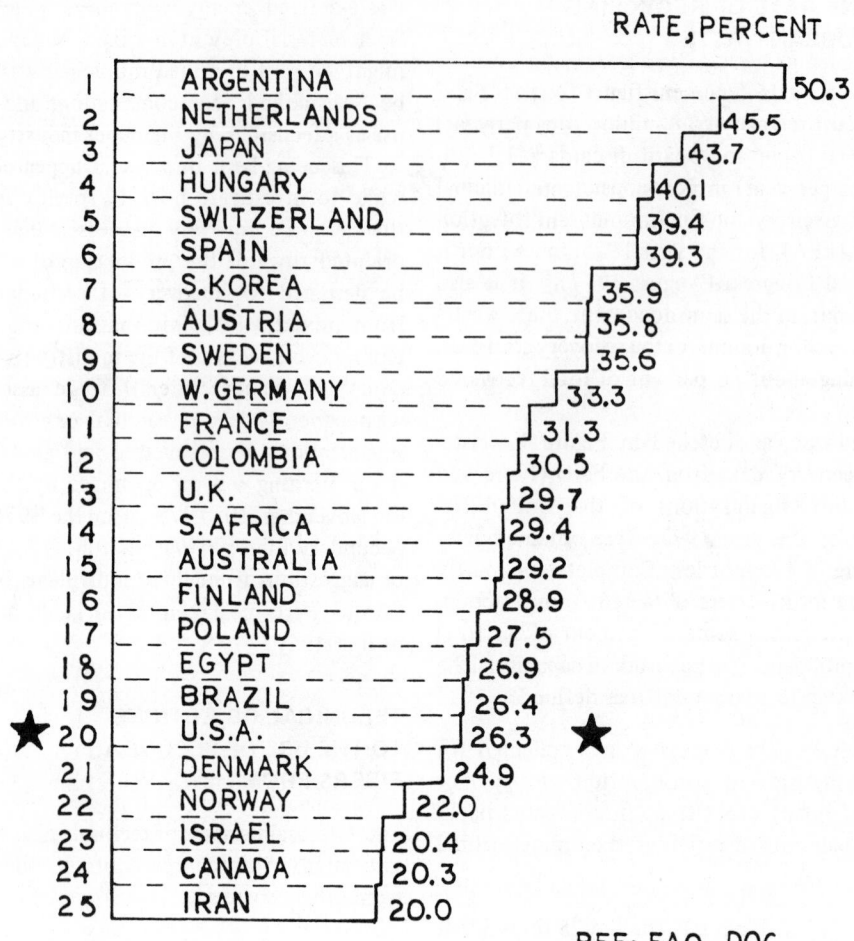

Figure 1. 1977 Wastepaper recovery rate.

CONTAMINENTS IN URBAN WASTE PAPER: CLASSIFICATION AND CHARACTERISTICS

Contaminants have been defined as "any material that has a deleterious effect on a product or the usability of a waste material."[10]

Any classification of contaminants is to some extent arbitrary. The following list of eight "groups" which were selected follows the pattern of both earlier A.P.I. classifications and the results of the 1973 Midwest Research Institute (MRI) survey of approximately 100 mills:[11]

C1. Plastic films, foams and papers
C2. Cynthetic, hot melt adhesives

C3. Metal foils
C4. Inks (particularly rubber or latex based, ultra-violet (UV) or magnetic)
C5. Wet-strength, waxed papers
C6. Asphalt, tar-laminated papers
C7. "Junk": wire, wood, metal chips, synthetic and natural fibers, human or animal hair.
C8. Pressure-sensitive adhesives
C9. Miscellaneous food and yard wastes

Of these various contaminatns, the so-called "stickies" are of particular concern because they may create adhesive spots on the equipment or product, at the risk of damaging the machines, hampering mill operations or lowering product quality. These adhesives typically would appear under C2 (hot melts), C4 (latex), and C8 (pressure-sensitive adhesives), although, as pointed out by W.E. Franklin in the MRI study,[12] a number of other contaminants might appear as "stickies" given the appropriate temeratures.

A short discussion of the characteristics of each contaminant potentially present in urban waste paper will indicate the degree of difficulty associated with removing the contaminats from the fibers during the cleaning process.

- Plastic films, foams and papers: many of the plastics have densities close to that of water, i.e. specific gravities in the range of 0.9 to 1.2. Others have density ranges straddling that of cellulose (1.54).[13] Polystyrene particles will become stickies given the right temperature.[14]
- Metal foils: in this case, the large difference in density between the metal (aluminum, mostly) and the fibers should allow screening and/or centrifugation out of the fiber stock.[15]
- Inks: chemical washing or flotation deinking regputedly have only limited efficiency to remove "special inks" (rubber, UV, magnetic, etc.)
- Wet strength compounds and waxes: different ranges of pH and temeratures are required, depending on the nature of the resins (polyamides or formaldehydes), to break the bond with the fiber.[16] Wax globules, initially molten in suspension, might reappear downstream as solid particles having a low temperature melting point.
- Asphalt: asphalt is effectively dispersed, either under pressure[17] or at ambient pressure in other processes.[18] Dispersion is combined with appropriate screening and cleaning. Removal techniques appear effective.
- Junk, synthetic and natural fibers: dirt solids (stones, glass, specs), metal clips, twines, if course, are removed at the junk box or by the ragger. Finer particles of density significantly different from one are removed by direct or reverse[19] centrifugal cleaning. Small shreds of non-pulping natural fibers, such as sisal, or synthetic fibers, weaken the product if not previously screened out of the stock.[20] Some manufacturers of waste paper cleaning equipment told us that, in their view, short lengths of human or animal hair are a significant problem in urban waste paper. In our own test runs, described below, this particular contaminant although in very small concentrations, indeed appeared to be ubiquitous.
- Pressure-sensitive adhesives: due to their polymer components, these contaminants are possibly the most troublesome of the stickies, since they behave like a highly viscous liquid at moderate temperature.[21] Also, the tackifier, softening at an intermediate range of temperatures (80°F–280°F) might pass through the successive stages of screening and reappear as a solid particle downstream.
- Miscellaneous food and yard wastes: obviously, this contaminant is germane to wastepaper extracted from urban refuse. According to some National Center (NCRR) studies, it might typically represent 26 percent of the total weight of the raw refuse, as received.[22] More than half (from 55 to 60 percent) of these 26 percent, or about 15 percent of the total weight of the waste as received, is moisture. The solids would thus represent approximately 11 percent by weight, of the unsegregated refuse. Removal of these contaminants do not appear to be of much concern. In a 1973 paper, D.R. Raymond (St. Regis Paper Co.) reported on an evaluation of the raw material from the Black-Clawson Fiber Claim plant at Franklin, Ohio, and mentioned that "one major contaminant was grass and yard wastes which appeared to be eliminated by mild chemical treatment or air flotation."[23]

POSSIBLE STRATEGIES FOR URBAN WASTE PAPER

In the case of selected furnishes, such as OCC (old corrugated containers), oversize news, computer printout sheets, it is possible to narrow down the main contaminants to a small number, maybe two or three, of the long list given above.

The wastepaper treatment will be tailored to both the source of the raw material and nature of the contaminants, and to the expected quality and grade of the final product. For example, non-paper fibers are perceived as more of a contaminant in old newspapers used in newsprint than if they are the raw material for making boxboard.

The paper fraction of urban waste, however, by its very nature, will contain plastics, asphalt, "stickies" of various kinds, wet strength cardboard, fabrics, hair and various metals. In this situation, contaminants removal would be aimed at the whole spectrum on contraries, and even setting aside economic constraints, appears as a tough technical assignment.

Two approaches might be contemplated to deal with the problem:

1. the *"minimum grade"* strategy: this means getting rid of only just enough of those contaminants that would defintely prevent use of the recycled fibers in the manufacture of the most easily "attainable" existing product, such as boxboard, construction paper, hardboard.

   As an example, such was the approach taken at the Black-Clawson, Franklin, Ohio, resource recovery plant. The ultimate fiber product was a felt-paper to be used in construction.

   A variation on this theme is to aim at less conventional or "hybrid" applications, where the partially decontaminated or cleaned furnish could be used, alone or in combination with other materials. A 1972 study by Battelle Institute listed, among many other possibilities: insulation materials, paving materials, door cores, concrete forms, concrete underlayers, structural members, land stabilizers, etc.[24]

2. The "selective furnish" strategy: It is obvious that a manufacturer producing high quality printing paper from secondary fibers is quite selective in his choice of recycled material. In a similar way, resource recovery plants will enhance the prospects for secondary fibers reuse by "selective wasteprocessing." An ex-

ample is to "skim off" corrugated sheets of bundled newspapers on the tipping floor or from a conveyor belt, prior to shredding, and recover a "commingled" product at a lower collection cost.[25,26]

Needless to say, practical considerations, particularly the economics of reuse, might require that both approaches be combined, the result being a "low grade" secondary fiber product in spite of all the fairly sophisticated steps taken by the urban waste processor to avoid further contamination is intimately tied to the techniques and equipment available for processing the feedstock: the latter are now examined in the same detail.

TECHNIQUES FOR CONTAMINANTS REMOVAL: CAPABILITIES AND LIMITATIONS

Survey of the Literature on Existing Processes. Using the classification of contaminants given previously, and two bibliographical reports from the Institute of Paper Chemistry[27,29] as a point of departure, we proceeded to list, classify and count methods for removal of contraries, by class of contaminants. Since some of the "processes" are little more than patent disclosures without further R & D follow-up, or are only partly successful, the figures below should be treated with some caution.

Contaminant (See 4)	Number of Removal Processes
C1 (plastics)	21
C2 (hot metals)	3
C3 (metal foils)	3 (special purpose)
C4 (inks)	34
C5 (wet strength)	8
C6 (asphalt)	7
C7 (synthetic fibers)	6
C8 (pressure-sensitive adhesive	1

On this basis alone, it is clear that de-inking, for example, has reached the status of a "classical" operation (at least on common inks), whereas only partial, somewhat satisfactory solutions exist for hot melts or pressure sensitive adhesives removal.

Survey of Equipment Manufacturers. Over a period of more than six months, consultations took place with vendors or manufacturers of wastepaper processing and cleaning euqipment. We contacted directly, by telephone and by mail, vendors or manufacturers representing some 15 companies. These were U.S. manufacturers, U.S. licensees of foreign technology, or European manufacturers. Commercial or technical literature was requested and reviewed to assess the capabilities and limitations of the equipment or process. If some names of responding manufacturers are given in the references, it is merely for the sake of illustration, without any attempt to give complete lists or alternatives, and with no implied recommendation.

Basic Unit Operations in the Decontamination Process. Depending on the nature of the feedstock and its contaminants, the final product to be manufactured and the equipment manufacturer, there will be wide variations in the type and number of unit operations, and in the way these are combined in a process flow chart.

In fact, to label processes, some equipment manufacturers use a system of coding,[29,30] based on a number or code letter, such as

$$x_1 \quad x_2 \quad x_3$$

$x_1 = (x_1)_0$ means "secondary fibers"

$x_2 = \ldots$ refers to the type of defibering process, such as: pulper; deflaker; disintegrator; hot disintegrator...

$x_3 = \ldots$ labels the method of screening, such as: low or high consistency; flotation; combination screening...

One code word, for instance, indicates a combination of unit operations suitable for the "regeneration of high-grade fibers from plastic- or metal-laminated paper"; another one is designed for the "regeneration of high-grade bitumenized paper."[29]

Although it might be potentially applicable, the method of chemical solvent extraction[31] shall not be discussed, since it appears to be more suited to separate one specific contaminant from the secondary fibers. The emphasis here is placed on mechanical and thermal methods reaching the wider variety of contaminants present in mixed waste.

The main unit operations to be reviewed are: pulping; deflaking and refining; screening; centrifugal cleaning (direct or reverse); washing; flotation; asphalt or general dispersion systems.

Pulping. The pulper, as a unit, defibers the wastepaper feedstock in water. A paper fiber slurry is produced which, when pumpable, is withdrawn from the pulper and after cleaning, is sent to refiners, deflakers, separators, etc.

From our previously mentioned survey of commercially available equipment for wastepaper pulping, the following features emerge:

- Most domestic pulpers have a vertical axis of rotation, whereas most of the systems adapted from originally European designs have their axis horizontal.
- Among industry and equipment specialists whom we consulted, a wide consensus was registered that, in the pulping process, any cutting of the fibers and size-reduction of the plastic or film-like contaminants should be avoided.[32] This will allow easier removal of the contaminants, either by the ragger, in the pulper or further downstream, as the case may be.
- Low-consistency systems (1 percent to 2 percent) have extraction plates under the rotor, with small holes of 1/8 inch (min.) diameter. Lightweight trash is picked up by the ragger, or floats. Periodic removal of the floating debris can be replaced advantageously by double-hole extraction, namely by adding a 30° to 60° sector with holes of up to one inch in diameter as part of the pulper. The "big hole" stock is cleaned by centrifugation. The light accepts are deflaked, screened on a vibrating screen of which the accepts are sent back to the pulper or taken downstream.[33]
- High-consistency systems (3 percent to 7 percent) extract the pulp through large holes (1/2″ to 1″ diameter).[32,34,39] In a number of such systems, a secondary pulper, separator or deflaker, follows with a small hole (4mm to 8mm) extraction plate.[34,36] Removal of lightweight

impurities is intermittent, generally. Another method uses the pulper as a "slusher," the stock being extracted through large holes (up to 1.5" diameter) prior to centrifugal cleaning and defibering at 30–35 percent consistency.[37]

- One very-high consistency system has two consistency zones: 15 to 20 percent initially, with no extraction; 3 percent in the next zone, extraction through small holes (6mm).[38,39]
- Horsepower requirements per ton per day are lower for the high-consistency systems than for the low-consistency ones,[39] possibly at a penalty in stock quality.

Deflakers, Refiners, Separators. These pieces of equipment are located downstream of the pulper (and possibly a stage of centrifugal cleaning.) Their role is to: break up or disentangle flakes and fiber fundles; condition the material by a "brushing" action in order to fibrillate its surface; make the fiber flexible and pliable and obtain a speck-free product. Some, such as the Turboseparator, are viewed more as predeflakers and contaminant removing devices.[40]

Geometries vary widely: double disc configuration, horizontal vortex chamber, one or two conical or cylindrical screws.[31,37,40–43]

The trends would appear to be towards higher consistency refining (up to 30–35 percent) and fiber treatment with minimal cutting.

Screening. Screening in the wastepaper processing system often, but not always, follows centrifugal cleaning devices (high pressure drop) discussed below. Both pressure screens and open vibrating screens with circular perforations or slots are used.[44–47] Fine screening is also obtained by rotating vibrating slotted screens,[48] or foil rotors rotating in front of one or two stationery screens.[44–46,49] Some systems combine centrifugal cleaning and pressure screening in one single device, and may be used to protect deflakers, refiners and screens, and increase their efficiency.

The shape and dimension of the perforations or slots have to be selected carefully as a function of the desired throughput, consistency of the stock and shape of the debris or contaminant to be screened out (long, thin shives or flat particles; round or cubical particles).[45]

Consistency affects the efficiency of the screening process in a way that is best determined experimentally. Correction factors on throughput for a given device, slot or perforation dimension, and stock consistency have been developed depending on the nature of the furnish. (For example: multiply throughput by 1.0 to 1.8 for 100 percent mixed wastepaper; 0.7 to 0.8 for roofing felts; 2.0 to 3.0 for woodfree and wood containing writing and printing papers, etc.[44])

From available technical documentation, it appears that pressure screening is effected at 0.2 to 1.2mm (0.008" to 0.05").[50,51] Open vibrating screens have plate perforations from 1.2mm to 10.0mm (0.5" to 0.40") at consistencies in the range of 0.5 to 4 percent.

Centrifugal Cleaning. The fiber suspension is injected tangentially into a cylindrical chamber, under which a long conical selection is located. "Heavy" materials are centrifuged to the outer wall (in direct cleaning). The cleaned stock leaves through an outlet at the top of the core. In reverse cleaning, the cleaned stock leaves at the bottom and the rejects (light materials) exist through one (at the top center) or two (top center and top periphery) outlets.

High efficiency units for fine cleaning operate at a 30 to 50 psi pressure drop and consistencies between 0.5 and 1.5 percent. Units removing large prticles of density sufficiently different from the stock work on smaller pressure drops (10 to 20 psi) at consistencies up to 6 percent. Coarse particles cleaning units have pressure drops of about 0.1 psi and operate at consistencies around 1 percent.[52–56]

Washing. Once screened and cleaned, the stock might have to be washed to remove chemicals, dispersed inks, etc. Flotation is treated below. The other methods commonly used involve a drainage of water and chemicals by passage of the stock over open surfaces:[49] vacuum, disc-type, Lancaster, sidehill, pressure washing can be mentioned.

Flotation. Inks attach to air bubbles in a solution containing flotation agents. The ink-containing froth is then skimmed off. Yields are high, in the 80 to 95 percent range. Water and specific power consumptions are low.[57-59]

Asphalt or General Dispersion System. In one of the systems examined, the stock, after pulping, cleaning and pressure screening is thickened to 6-8 percent consistency, fed into a screw press, which brings the consistency to 35-45 percent, then into a continuous digestor. Steam is introduced into the pressure vessel at about 75 psi. The asphalt softens and melts, and is distributed over all fibers. Specific power consumption is said to be about 1 hp/TPD. Steam consumption is 0.9 lbs steam/lbs fiber.[60]

Another process operates at atmospheric pressure, to avoid the high cost of pressure vessels. The bitumen, which melts around 145°C, is dispersed, by purely mechanical means, at high energy input into a modified deflaker, using a stock at 30 percent consistency. Preheating of the stock by steam to 85°-95°C produces a free stock, for the same specific energy intput, than a purely mechanical energy transmission method. In a typical example (mixed wastepaper containing 10 percent bituminous paper), the first 15 KWH/100 KG input were found to disperse the bitumen effectively, with a less spectacular added improvement for an additional 15 KWH/100 KG input.[41]

SUMMARY OF TECHNOLOGICAL LIMITATIONS OF WASTEPAPER PROCESSING EQUIPMENT

From this survey of available wastepaper processing equipment, a general profile of limitations can be drawn:

- Metal foils: are only effectively screened or centrifuged, if they have not been cut down to a size comparable to the smallest dimension of the extraction plate holes, or pressure screens (0.2 to 0.3mm, approximately).
- Junk; sunthetic or natural, nonpulpable fibers: see metal foils.
- Plastic films, foams and papers: see metal foils.

- Asphalt: effectively dispersed at high pressure and temeprature, or at ambient pressure with preheating of the stock and high specific mechanical energy input in a modified deflaker.[41]
- Inks: both washing and flotation methods are effective on "normal" inks. UV inks, with an acrylate-based component in the binder, prove hard to de-ink by standard methods. A manufacturer reports good success in treating papers with UV inks with chemical solutions containing sodium sulfite and sodium hyposulfite, which decompose the products of polymerization.[61] The pigment particles are removed by flotation. A pH of 8-8.5 and temperatures of 45°-60°C are required. Apparently, such secondary fibers would have to be processed separately. Other types of newspaper printing inks, acrylate based, are said to form such a strong bond with the fibers that often de-inking, many mottled fibers remain. Slow speed kneading at 25 percent consistency still results in a homogeneous, somewhat less bright product.
- Wet strength compounds: if the wet-strength producing agent is considered as a contrary, rather than a stock to be reclaimed by chemical treatment, the key is to avoid cutting the material to a size preventing later screening by slotted or perforated screens: see metal foils.
- Waxes: the waxes can be dispersed to some extent, but their percentage by weight in the feedstock should be low.
- Hot melts, synthetic adhesives: would be screened out, except if particles of these substances are of size comparable to 0.2 to 0.5 mm.
- Pressure-sensitive adhesives: again, these particles should be of a size quite larger than 0.2 to 0.5 mm, and "solid-like" at screening temperature, to be removed from the suspension.

Therefore, the most serious technological obstacles to the processing of urban wastepaper are caused by the presence of pressure-sensitive adhesives; hot melts and synthetic adhesives breaking up in particles 500 microns and under; special inks, particularly of the polymerizing type; and waxes if not at very low concentrations.

GUIDELINES FOR SELECTIVE WASTEPROCESSING

After this brief overview of the problems associated with the removal of contaminants, what should the waste processor do — or refrain from doing — to enhance the recovery and quality of secondary fibers from mixed urban waste?

- To be avoided:
  - *Mixing* of paper furnishes still identifiable at the tipping floor of the recovery plant.
  - *Imbedding* of contaminants into the paper fraction by impact, shearing, compression. It is well known, for example, that glass, metal or other fines are "hammered" into the paper flakes after hammermilling.
  - *Further Cutting or Shredding* on a coarse (–4″ to –5″) paper rich fraction already obtained by waste processing. Any treatment to separate paper from plastics should be based on differential properties and should not result in an increased generation of fines. For example:
    * difference in ballistic coefficients, possibly with thermally induced changes in shape for the various fractions[62,63]
    * difference in dielectric constants[64]
    * difference in melting or softening temperatures[65]
    * difference in sinking times.[66]
- Recommended are the following approaches:
  - Picking at the tipping floor of commingled bundled newspapers and corrugated material.
  - Trommeling with large holes (4″ and up) of the raw product. Prior to any shredding or size reduction by other means, the material is "loosened" and screened by successive falls in a rotary screen (trommel). The fraction of paper

in the oversize material is significantly larger than in the input material by a factor of the order of 2.
  - Further enrichment of the paper-rich fraction. (Aerodynamic, flash drying, thermal, electrostatic methods)
  - Dry screening prior to pulping, for example trommeling following air classification as recently described by G. Savage, L. Diaz and G. Trezek.[67] The goal is to eliminate as many small (.2 to .6mm) fines of pernicious contraries (hot melts, pressure sensitive adhesives, styrofoam etc.) as possible.

A SAMPLE OF MODEL FURNISHES FROM URBAN WASTE

A "model furnish" is taken to mean here one of the feedstocks which might result from careful, selective processing of mixed urban waste. Three such "models" are briefly considered. After discussing their likely composition and the nature of contaminants, processing steps are examined.

Model Furnish "A": Air classified light fraction of coarsely shredded (–4 in.) municipal solid waste (MSW).

This feedstock results from a process of air classification of coarsely shredded MSW (–4 in.). A dry screening step preceeds them trommeled in a rotary screen having holes of diameter 3/4 in., which removes much of the grit and fines generated by the shredding. Based on a normal split (around 50/50) by weight of "light" to "heavies" in the air classifier, it is expected that about 30 percent of the light fraction prior to trommeling will not be paper. The main "other than paper" items are generally plastic and fabrics, accounting for some 15 percent of the light fraction. After trommeling, the paper fraction increases its percentage in the oversize material.

Since the main contraries appear to be light plastics, shredded styrofoam, pressure-sensitive adhesives, synthetic or non-pulpable fibers, hair, and special inks, the steps recommended for better fibers recovery are:

- no further mechanical size reduction
- gentle, "non-cutting" pulping

- screening out of fines (done by trommeling)
- stages of pressurized screening with small perforations or slots for contaminant removal.

Again, note that furnish "A" is very similar to the one processed by G. Trezek, et. al.,[67] but the shredding is coarser here (4 in. instead of 2 in.) and air classification follows a step of dry screening on the shredded material.

Model Furnish "B": Unshredded trommel overs from large holes rotary screen.

For large (meaning 8 in., approximately), circular or rectangular holes in the trommel, the oversize material consists of large pieces of kraftpaper, corrugated material, newspaper; large pieces of plastic film fabrics, wood, metal bars; but relatively little glass, food wastes, aluminum or styrofoam. The addition of a moving "ragger cable" in the trommel allows the removal of filament-like debris (twines, cables, plastic tape).[68]

For this 8 in. trommeling scheme, a pneumatic pick-up of the lights from the oversize conveyor belt apparently results in a decent, paper-rich fraction containing few contaminats. For example, preliminary data from such a system at Warren Spring, U.K., indicate that the feedstock obtained has only one main contaminant, plastics, for about 5 percent by weight.

At the NCRR "Recovery I" full-scale recovery plant (650 TPD), in New Orleans, trommeling is through a 4 in. hole, and the paper content of a similar furnish "B" is significantly smaller than in Warren Spring.

The guidelines for processing should be to avoid any cutting before or during pulping, to allow mechanical removal of plastic films and fabrics. Centrifugal cleaning should eliminate metal or glass fines.

Corrugated from Mixed Commercial Waste. From 1974 to 1976, experiments on separating secondary corrugated paper materials from mixed commercial wastes were conducted by NCRR at its Washington pilot plant (ETEF).[69] 4-1/2 in. nominal shredded commercial waste was run through an air classifier with a main updraft (125 hp fan) and possible use of an air knife (15 hp), as in Fig. 2. A typical flow sheet

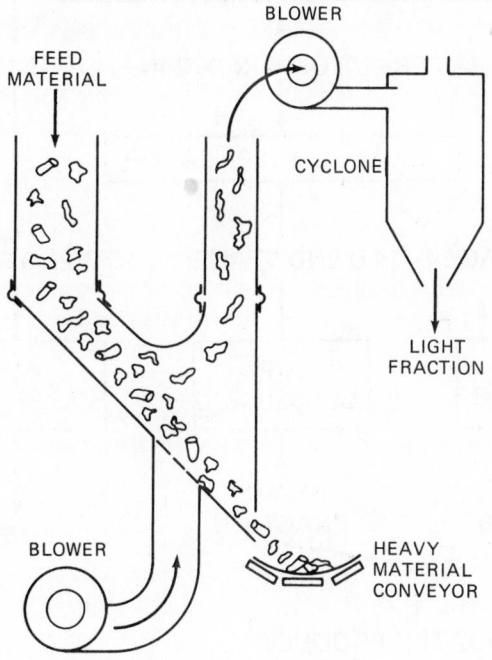

Figure 2. Air classifier.

is given in Fig. 3. It is seen that a "corrugated product" results from two successive stages of air classification, after the removal of magnetic materials, aluminum and two 2 in. fractions. Yields of 74 to 98 percent (of corrugated) and purities of 66 to 93 percent were obtained. If the corrugated paper is dropped with the heavies, contamination by light plastic should be minimal. This furnish should be relatively easy to decontaminate, and overall not extremely far away from a target such as "no more than 5 percent outthrows..."

PRELIMINARY DATA ON DECONTAMINATION AND PAPERMAKING EXPERIMENTS

The feedstocks described as furnishes A and B in the preceding section, for example, are not, at the present time, actually produced at any of

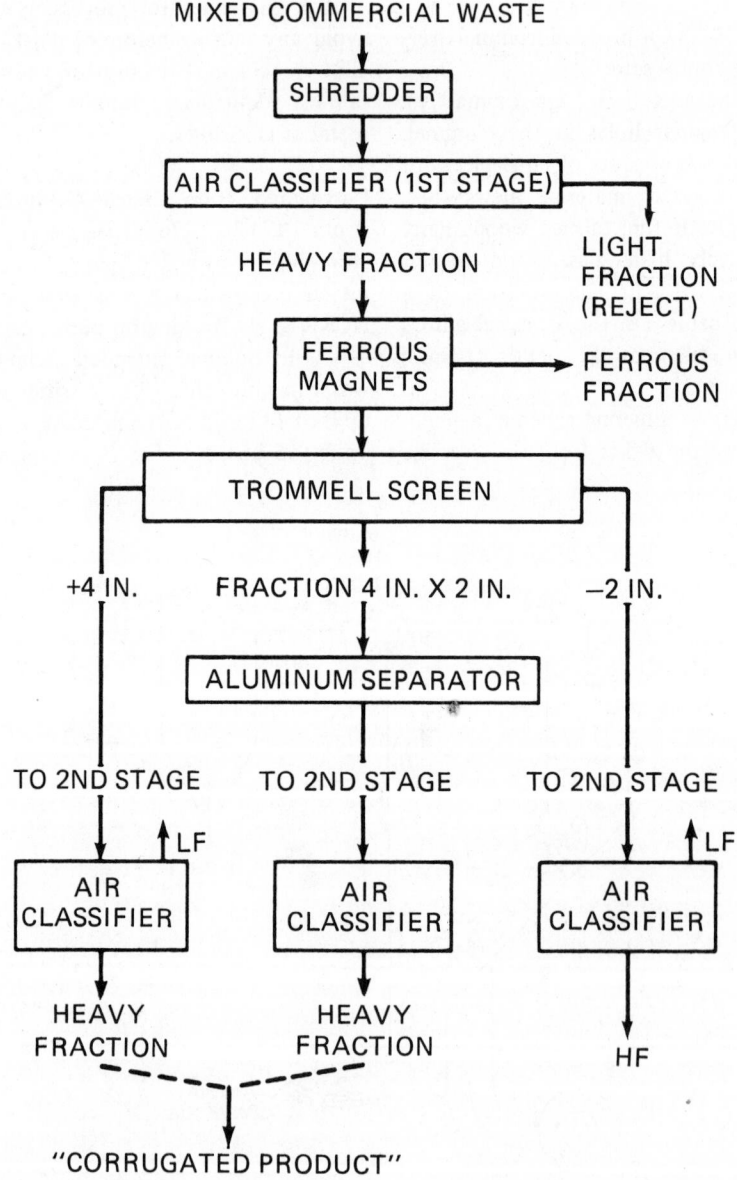

Figure 3. Flow sheet (No. 3)

the existing recovery plants but could easily be by adding only one or two relatively inexpensive processing steps: trommeling with small holes in the first case, flail milling and light air-classification in the second case.

To go from the realm of speculation to real-life experimentation, we decided to run tests on materials obtained from existing resource recovery plants handling mixed municipal solid waste, with the small amount of additional processing on the dry material required by the nature of the furnish.

We dealt with three "real furnishes" from major metropolitan areas: Washington, D.C., New Orleans, Louisiana, and Milwaukee, Wisconsin. Two were obtained and processed by NCRR, with the cooperation of the Bureau of Mines (Washington, New Orleans). One was picked up at Milwaukee, at the Americology plant. These feedstocks were then processed at the Western Michigan University, Kalamazoo, Paper Recycling Plant, as a joint effort of NCRR and WMU. Handsheets (at various stages of cleaning) and full paper rolls were made from all three feedstocks.

Data at the data of this writing are still partial and preliminary, and we shall limit ourselves to the main qualitative results.

- Samples of 150 to 200 lbs of three furnishes from urban waste were processed.
- The three furnishes were: furnish A of section 9 (Washington, D.C.); furnish B of section 9, with 4 in. trommel holes (New Orleans, Louisiana), subsequently flail milled and "light air classified" (hood classifier) at the U.S. Bureau of Mines pilot plant in College Park, Maryland; furnish C was commingled newspapers from Milwaukee, Wisconsin (Americology plant).
- In all three cases, a very satisfactory degree of cleanliness in the final pulp was obtained after a small number of purely mechanical operations, involving pulping, separating, vibratory screening, pressurized screening and centrifugal cleaning. The resulting paper products appeared to be a potentially good feedstock for box-board filler or backliner material, pending a more thorough evaluation.
- All three cleaned stocks were used on the WMU 25-inch Louis Calder Fourdrinier papermachine, and large rolls of paper were produced without incidents, web breaks or "stickies."

After completing this investigation, we would welcome the opportunity to report, in full, our findings to this association, at one of its forthcoming meetings.

CONCLUSIONS

Careful and selective front-end processing of mixed municipal waste permits the recovery of various types of paper rich fractions containing fewer contaminants. These are, for the most part, of a size and type that allow existing waste-paper cleaning equipment to operate efficiently. Preliminary results confirm this conclusion, based on three furnishes from major metropolitan areas which were decontaminated and made into paper rolls on the Fourdrinier machine at the Western Michigan University Paper Recycling Plant, Kalamazoo, Michigan.

ACKNOWLEDGMENTS

This work was supported by a grant from the National Science Foundation, under grant No. APR6513864; Ritchie Coryell, Project Officer. Many thanks are due to the Bureau of Mines, Edmonston, Maryland, especially P.M. Sullivan, Supervisory Chemical Engineer, for the use of their laboratory facilities and the cooperation of the staff.

REFERENCES

1. U.S. Environmental Protection Agency, *Fourth Report to Congress. Resource Recovery and Waste Reduction.* SW-600, Aug. 1, 1977., p., 19.
2. Ibid., p. 17.
3. Food and Agricultural Organization (FAO) of the United Nations, Advisory Committee on Pulp and Paper, 19th Session, Rome, May 31–June 2, 1978. "Waste Paper Data 1976–1977." Document FO: PAP/78/5. April 1978.

4. Food and Agricultural Organization (FAO) of the United Nations, "Waste Paper Data 1975-1976." Document FO: MISC. 77/8, May 1977.

5. Paul G. Marsh, "Paper from Garbage." Presented at 57th Annual Meeting sponsored by the Canadian Pulp and Paper Association, Technical Section, Montreal, Canada, Jan. 26-29, 1977.

6. J.E. Duckett, "Reclaiming Materials and Energy in Milwaukee," *NCRR Bulletin,* Fall 1977, Vol. VII, No. 4.

7. W.E. Franklin, R.G. Hunt, *Paper Recycling: The Impact of Contaminants. 1973-1985,* Midwest Research Institute and Franklin Associates for the Solid Waste Council of the Paper Industry, October 1975.

8. A.J. Felton, "Secondary Fiber," in *Handbook of Pulp and Paper Technology,* K.W. Britt, Ed. Van Nostrand Reinhold Co., NY, 1970, pp. 75-87.

9. H.W. Kindler, "Research into the Hygienic Qualities of Paper Recovered by Mechanical Sorting of Municipal Waste," Babcock-Krauss-Maffei, W. Germany. Paper presented at 1st World Recycling Conference, Basel, Switzerland, March 1978.

10. Ref. (7), p. 172.

11. W.E. Franklin, *Paper Recycling: The Art of the Possible.* 1970-1985. Midwest Research Institute, Kansas City, 1973, 181 pp.

12. Ref. (7), p. 31.

13. Machine Design Magazine, *Materials Reference Issue,* Penton, Inc. Cleveland, Ohio 1976, pp. 120-169.

14. Ref. (7), p. 45.

15. Ref. (8), p. 77.

16. Ref. (8), p. 86.

17. Ref. (8), p. 87.

18. W.H. Siewert, "The Preparation of Waste Paper Containing Bitumen by the Escher Wyss Process," *Wochenblatt Für Papierfabrikation,* No. 8, 1968.

19. B. Morse, H.J. Brown, "Secondary Fiber Usage: Contaminants and Their Removal," TAPPI Papermakers Conference, Atlanta, Georgia, pp. 239-247. June 5-8, 1972.

20. Ref. (7), p. 79.

21. Ref. (7), p. 69.

22. D.N. Fan, "On the Air Classified Light Fraction of Shredded Municipal Solid Waste. 1. Composition and Physical Characteristics." *Resource Recovery and Conservation,* 1 (1975), pp. 141-150.

23. D.R. Raymond, "Raw Material for Papermaking Fibers" *AICHE Symposium Series. Processing and Utilization of Forest Products,* No. 139, Vol. 70, pp. 93-98.

24. Battelle Columbus Laboratories, *A Study to Identify Opportunities for Increased Solid Waste Utilization: Paper Report, Vol. 3,* Battelle Columbus Laboratories, June 1972, 163 pp.

25. National Center for Resource Recovery, Inc. *Materials Recovery System, Engineering Feasibility Study,* Washington D.C., 1972.

26. A. Alter, K.L. Woodruff, A. Fookson, B. Rogers, "Analysis of Newsprint Recovered from Mixed Municipal Waste." *Resource Recovery and Conservation,* 2 (1976), pp. 79-84.

27. J. Weiner, V. Pollock, *Reclaimed Fibers,* Bibliographic Series, No. 248, The Institute for Paper Chemistry, Appleton, Wisconsin, 1971, 259 pp.

28. J. Weiner, V. Pollock, *Reclaimed Fibers,* Bibliographic Series, No. 248, Supplement I, The Institute for Paper Chemistry, Appleton, Wisconsin, 1975, 171 pp.

29. Voith-Morden, Inc., *Secondary Fiber Regeneration Brochure,* Portland, Or., and Heidenheim, FRG.

30. G.G. Cianci, "The Modular Approach to Waste Paper Systems Based on Contraries Classification," Beloit Italia, Pinerolo, Italy, November 1977.

31. R.D. Good, "Solvent Extraction of Secondary Fibers," TAPPI Alkaline Pulping/Secondary Fibers Conference Papers, Washington, D.C., November 7-9, 1977, pp. 285-291.

32. T. Bähr, W. Musselmann "Voith-ATS-N System, A New Approach to the Preparation and Screening of Secondary Fibers" Wochenblatt für Papierfabrikation, No. 20 (1975), 7 pp.

33. Ref. (8), pp. 84-85.

34. L.E. Clark "BELCOR. The Combination Coarse Screen, Repulper and Centrifugal Separator" Presented at the TAPPI Secondary Fibers Conference, Boston, Massachusetts, 1974.

35. Voith-Morden, Inc. ATS-N *Wastepaper Pulping System Brochure #1217,* Voith-Morden, Inc. Portland, Oregon.

36. IMPCO-ESCHER WYSS. *Stock Preparation Machines Brochure,* The Ingersoll-Rand Company, Nashua, New Hampshire.

37. MODOMEKAN AB, *Pulp Machinery Brochure,* Modemekan, Inc., Atlanta, Georgia.

38. Ahlstrom Trading, Inc., *Fibreflow Brochure,* Machinery and Equipment Division, Glens Falls, New York, 1977.

39. S. Rutquist, F. Sundman, J. Venho, "Fibreflow," *Pulp and Paper International,* March 1977.

40. L. Göttsching, W.F. H 11, W. Otto, "The Turbo Separator: A New Element for Waste Paper Stock Preparation," *Paper Technology,* June/August 1973, pp. T129-T134.

41. W.H. Siewert, "The Preparation of Waste Paper Containing Bitumen by the Escher-Wyss Process," Wochenblatt für Papierfabrikation, No. 8, 1968.

42. Beloit-Jones, *DD 4000 Refiners and Dispersalls Brochures,* Dalton, Massachusetts.

43. Black-Clawson, *Celluclone & Hydraflaker Brochures,* Middletown, Ohio.

44. Bird Machine Co., *Bird-Grubbers Labyrint & Deflaker Brochure,* S. Walpole, Massachusetts.

45. Bolton-Emerson Co., *Finckh Vertical and Jonsson Screen Systems Brochure,* Lawrence, Massachusetts.

46. Bird Machine Co., *Centrisorter Pressure Screen Brochure,* S. Walpole, Massachusetts.
47. Black-Clawson Co., B.C. *Wandel Vibrating Screen & Selectifier Screens Brochures,* Middletown, Ohio.
48. Voith GMBH, *Stock Preparation, Data, Dimensions and Tables,* Heidenheim, Germany, 1971.
49. Ref. (7), p. 78.
50. H. Hutzler, "A New Screen for Wastepaper Systems," *TAPPI,* Vol, 58, No. 11, Nov. 1975.
51. J.W. Michael, "Pressure Screens: Comparison of Systems and Experiences Gained with the Finckh Verticle Screen" *Wochenblatt für Papierfabrikation, 95,* No. 23/24, pp. 913–920.;
52. Bird Machine Co., *Centrifugal Cleaners Brochure,* S. Walpole, Massachusetts.
53. Beloit Jones Co., *Centrifugal Cleaners Brochure,* Dalton, Massachusetts.
54. Voith GMBH, *Centrifugal Cleaners Brochure,* Heidenheim, Germany.
55. Black Clawson Co., *Liquid Cycline Brochure,* Middletown, Ohio.
56. Ref. (36), pp. 6–10.
57. IMPCO-Escher Wyss, *De-inking Brochure,* Nashua, New Hampshire.
58. Voith GMBH, *De-inking of Secondary Fiber by Flotation,* Heidenheim, Germany.
59. R.P. Cruea, "De-inking. Laboratory Evaluations and Total System Concepts" Black-Clawson Co., TAPPI 1977 Alkaline Pulping/Secondary Fibers Conf., Washington, D.C.
60. Ref., (7), pp. 86–87.
61. H. Ortner, R.F. Wood, H. Gartemann, "De-inking. Its Present Stage and Development" *Wochenblatt für Papierfabrikation,* No. 16, 1975.
62. J.F. Laundrie, "Recovery and Reuse of Wastepaper from Shredded Household Trash" Forest Product Labs Report 252, Madison, Wisconsin, 1975.
63. C. Cederholm, "Paper Fiber Recovery System," *Flakt Engineering,* Vol, 2, No. 2, April 1978.
64. P.M. Sullivan, M.H. Stanckzyk, M.J. Spendlove, "Resource Recovery from Raw Urban Refuse," Bureau of Mines, RI 7760, College Park, Maryland, 1973.
65. J.F. Laundrie, J.H. Klungness, "Effective Dry Methods of Separating Thermoplastic Films from Wastepapers," Forest Products Labs FPL 200, Madison, Wisconsin, 1973.
66. G. Welshans, J. Liskowitz, M. Perez, "Recovery of Various Paper Grades by Selective Wettability," *TAPPI,* 59, No. 8, August 1976.
67. G.M. Savage, L.F. Diaz, G.J. Trezek, "Fiber from Urgan Solid Waste: Recovery Procedures and Pulp Characteristics," *TAPPI,* Vol. 61, No. 6, June 1978.
68. A. Alter, "European Materials Recovery Systems," Environmental Science & Technology, American Chemical Society, Vol. 11, No. 5, pp. 444–448.
69. National Center for Resource Recovery, Inc., "Experiments Separating Useable Secondary Corrugated Paper Materials from Mixed Commercial Solid Wastes," Report to the API Paperstock Conservation Committee, Washington, D.C., July 1976.

3-5 Fiber Recovery from Municipal Solid Waste

G.M. Savage, L.F. Diaz, and G.J. Trezek
Source: Reprinted From *Proceedings* of the Sixth Mineral Waste Utilization Symposium, May 2–3, 1978, Chicago, Illinois, pp. 222–228.

INTRODUCTION

Depletion of our national forest reserves coupled with an increasing public reluctance to allow the opening of new timber areas to harvesting have resulted in a decrease in the basic raw material for pulp and paper production, namely wood. One consequence of this dwindling supply is rising prices for lumber as well as for paper products. In addition to the poor economic consequences, the harvesting of vast regions of timber may pose serious climatological consequences. Evidence is available that supports the contention that destruction of forests has a deleterious effect on the carbon dioxide balance of the atmosphere with the net effect being the possibility of altering the world climate (1).

As an alternative to the use of forest lands for securing the raw material for pulp and paper production, the possibility exists for exploiting a heretofore untapped source of cellulosic fiber, that is the paper fiber present in solid waste presently being landfilled. Here the means of recovering paper fiber from refuse will be explained. At the same time the properties of handsheets formed from fiber recovered from solid waste will be presented as well as compared to those of other types of wastepaper. Successful and efficient recovery of fiber from the municipal solid waste stream requires an encompassing management plan ranging from solid waste processing to pulp mill technology. We have examined fiber recovery from the standpoints of refuse collection, mechanical pre-processing, hydropulping, cleaning, water treatment, and determination of recovered pulp properties.

As previously reported by Trezek and Golueke (2), experiments conducted at the Richmond Field Station of the University of California (Berkeley) have shown that fiber recovery from municipal solid waste is technologically feasible provided that a certain processing sequence is followed. Here we wish to: 1) discuss some of the most important considerations involved in pre-processing solid waste for extraction of a fraction rich in fiber for eventual hydropulping, 2) evaluate the effect of the source of the waste (i.e., residential and commercial) on the properties of the fiber, 3) compare the properties of fiber recovered from refuse with those of other secondary fibers, and 4) examine the water quality aspects of pulping and cleaning operations.

In the processing system to be described fiber recovery from both residential and commercial solid waste has been evaluated. The former category refers to refuse collected from residential neighborhoods while the latter pertains to waste collected from businesses, shopping centers, and institutional sources. Commercial solid waste tends to contain more paper than residential solid waste. Fiber recovered from commercial sources also generally exhibits superior strength properties than that recovered from residential sources.

Refuse was supplied to the laboratory through the courtesy of the Richmond Sanitary Service. Inasmuch as some packer trucks normally service commercial areas, it was possible to randomly select one of these trucks for the experiments. Similarly, trucks that service residential areas delivered their contents to the laboratory whenever experiments were conducted on processing residential waste. Several truck loads were processed over a one-year period for each waste category. Consequently, any effects on the results caused by seasonal variations in the composition of the refuse should be accounted for in the data.

In order to minimize the water quality problems in the pulping of refuse derived fiber and to maximize the strength properties of the recovered pulp, a significant degree of dry processing precedes the hydropulping (or wet processing) operation. In the dry processing system, mechanical separation techniques are employed to obtain a fiber-rich fraction from solid waste. The fiber-rich fraction is subsequently hydropulped and cleaned in the wet processing system. Handsheets formed from recovered fiber were tested for freeness and strength properties in accordance with the applicable TAPPI standards. Finally, in order to assess the water treatment aspects of processing refuse derived pulp, the water quality of the pulping effluent was determined using standard wastewater analyses.

THE FIBER RECOVERY SYSTEM

The overall system consists of a dry process and a process which includes water or wet process.

The main components of the dry processing system are: 1) a hammermill grinder (rated at ten tons per hour), 2) a vertical air classifier, 3) a cyclone and air-lock feeder, and 4) a rotary cylindrical screen (trommel). The system is capable of processing up to four tons of refuse per hour and typically produces a wastepaper fraction in the range of 40% to 60% (by weight) of the input total. The wastepaper serves as feedstock for the wet processing system. The percentage of the raw waste which is recovered as wastepaper fraction is dependent upon the type of waste being processed, i.e., residential or commercial.

The wastepaper fraction is extracted from the incoming waste stream through the following processing sequence. First, raw refuse is size-reduced in the hammermill grinder to a nominal

size of 90% passing a two-inch screen. The size reduced material is then conveyed to the air classifier where it is separated into a light fraction (mainly paper, plastic, fines, etc.), and a heavy fraction, comprised primarily of metals, glass, aggregates, etc. This separation is accomplished using air suction through the air classifier to extract the light fraction from the shredded refuse.

The light fraction is subsequently de-entrained from the air stream using a cyclone. The "lights" are removed from the cyclone by an air-lock feeder and are deposited on a conveyor. The conveyor feeds the trommel screen. The trommel serves the purpose of removing the fine materials (both organic and inorganic), which have a low fiber content, from the larger materials which have a high paper content. The oversized material from the screen, termed "screened lights", is the fraction that is subsequently used as the input to the wet processing facility. The removal of the "fines" at this stage of the process not only improves the quality of the wastepaper but also, as will be discussed later, reduces the extent of water treatment in the wet process.

For a more detailed description of the dry processing system the reader is referred to references 3, 4, and 5.

The wet processing facility receives the screened light fraction from the dry plant. This part of the system consists of: 1) a hydropulper, 2) a plastics removal screen, and 3) a bank of centrifugal cleaners. The wet phase of the process is initiated by pulping the light fraction at consistencies ranging from 1.5% to 3.0%. Pulping is carried out in such a manner so that only the fiber is slurried while the plastics retain their relatively large particle size. The latter effect is important in the plastic removal operation. After the material is pulped, it is transported to the plastic removal screen. The plastic removal operation was specifically designed to remove most of the plastics and at the same time dilute the slurry to approximately 0.5% solids. A consistency of 0.5% is compatible with centrifugal cleaning.

Centrifugal cleaning is accomplished with two banks of high-efficiency liquid cyclones ("tricleaners"). The cleaners remove dirt, grit, fine plastics, hot melt and other contaminants from the slurry.

Table 1. Composition of Screened Light Fraction.

	Corrugated (a)	Newsprint (b)	Other Paper (c)	Total Total (d)[3]	Plastic (e)	Other Contamination (f)
Wastepaper Mill Feedstock[1]	75.3%	—	—	75.3%	14.1%	10.6%
Average Commercial[2]	44.7%	3.0%	42.2%	89.9%	5.7%	4.4%
Average Residential[2]	25.6%	52.9		78.5%	7.7%	13.8%

[1]Sample from wastepaper mill hydropulper located in the San Francisco Bay Area.
[2]Average of samples taken over one year.
[3](d) = (a) + (b) + (c); (d) + (e) + (f) = 100% of sample.

Pulping and cleaning operations at the laboratory were performed on a batch-basis. For a thorough description of the wet phase the reader is directed to reference 1.

The water treatment requirements for the wet plant were evaluated by building a laboratory scale wastewater treatment plant and processing through it the water used for cleaning the fiber. The plant was of the activated sludge type and included: 1) a reservoir, 2) a metering pump, 3) an aeration chamber, and 4) a settling chamber. Several experiments were conducted: each time the B.O.D. (biological oxygen demand) and C.O.D. (chemical oxygen demand) of the effluent were measured as well as the amount of sludge produced.

RESULTS OF STUDY

In order to assess the feasibility of using fiber recovered from solid waste, the composition of screened lights was determined. Samples from both commercial and residential dry processing runs were hand picked to determine fiber, plastic, and "other contamination" content. Furthermore, in two instances the total fiber content was differentiated into corrugated, newsprint, and "other" paper fractions for a commercial and a residential batch.

The results of the composition analysis are presented in Table 1. As the data in the table show, samples removed from the screened light fraction of commercial refuse furnished fiber contents averaging 89.9%. The remaining 10.1% of the screened lights was composed of 5.7% plastic and 4.4% other contaminants. On the other hand, residential solid waste yielded a screened light fraction averaging 78.5% fiber, 7.7% plastics, and 13.8% other contaminants. On the average commercial wastes yielded approximately 15% more identifiable fiber than residential waste.

To determine the potential of using wastepaper recovered from solid waste as a feedstock for a wastepaper mill, a stock sample was obtained from a hydropulper of a local wastepaper mill, analyzed, and compared to screened light fraction. The feedstock for the wastepaper mill consisted mainly of recycled corrugated containers and packaging materials collected from various commercial industries and businesses in the area. The results in the table show that the stock sample contained 75.3% corrugated, 14.1% plastics, and 10.6% other contaminants. A comparison of the composition of the mill sample with that of both commercial and residential screened light fraction shows that refuse derived wastepaper can equal or exceed the fiber content of typical wastepaper mill furnish.

Differentiation among fiber categories, namely corrugated, newsprint, and "other paper," in both commercial and residential screened lights provides information that has a direct bearing on sheet properties. As expected, commercial screened lights were high in corrugated (roughly 50% of the total fiber content) while in residential screened lights corrugated comprised approximately 33% of the total fiber content. The higher percentage of corrugated in commercial screened lights provides a higher percentage of long fibers in the pulp than that contributed from residential screened lights. Dissimilarities between the mechanical properties of handsheets formed from pulp derived from commercial and residential screened lights are largely attributable to the higher amount of corrugated and the correspondingly lower quantities of groundwood fibers found in commercial solid waste.

In order to ascertain the functional dependence of mechanical properties on fiber source, commercial and residential solid wastes were processed separately in both the dry and wet processing facilities. Samples of clean fiber collected in the wet plant were used to form handsheets. The results of the tests performed on the handsheets are given in Table 2. The data show that handsheets formed from fiber recovered from commercial sources had an average freeness of 580, burst factor of 17.9, and a tear factor of 138. The freeness varied from 485 to 650 while the burst factor remained approximately constant ranging from 16.5 to 19.2. The maximum and minimum tear factors were 114 and 182, respectively. The tensile factors for handsheets from commercial sources spanned 2,495 to 3,170 meters.

For handsheets made from residential sources the freeness varied between 275 and 350. The average CSF was 330. The burst factor averaged

Table 2. Properties of Handsheets Formed From Fiber Recovered From Solid Waste.

COMMERCIAL SOURCE

Experiment Number	CSF (mℓ)	Burst Factor	Tear Factor	Tensile Factor
1	535	16.5	182.0	2,495
2	650	17.9	114.0	2,520
3	650	18.0	134.0	3,170
4	485	19.2	120.0	2,870
Average	580	17.9	138.0	2,765

RESIDENTIAL SOURCE

Experiment Number	CSF (mℓ)	Burst Factor	Tear Factor	Tensile Factor
1	345	15.5	123.0	2,280
2	275	18.1	98.0	2,510
3	340	13.9	163.0	2,080
4	350	15.9	176.0	2,260
5	350	14.7	102.0	2,500
Average	330	15.6	132.0	2,325

15.6 while ranging from 13.9 to 18.1. Similarly, the tear factor averaged 132 varying from 98 to 176. Finally, the breaking length averaged 2,325 meters with maximum and minimum values of 2,510 meters and 2,080 meters, respectively.

Comparison of the average sheet properties of commercial and residential-derived pulp show greater strength properties for sheets formed from commercial, as opposed to residential, screened light fraction. The high proportion of kraft fiber found in commercial waste provides the long, flexible fibers conducive to good strength properties. The most noticeable effect of the higher percentage of kraft fibers is in the significant increase in the average tensile strength of commercial and residential recovered fiber, namely 2,765 versus 2,325 meters, respectively.

Comparisons and conclusions regarding pulp freeness of wastepaper recovered at our laboratory from the two solid waste sources are difficult because of the lack of proper equipment for mechanically treating the stock after hydropulping, namely deflaking, beating, and refining. In our laboratory an extended duration of hydropulping was used to compensate for the lack of this equipment.

This is at best, however, a poor substitute for beating, and consequently the difference in average freeness values are of interest only to indicate that commercial stock differs from residential stock — a fact which is further amplified by the results of analyses carried out on the composition of the screened lights. Fiber recovered from residential sources tends to contain less chemical fibers and more brittle groundwood fibers than fiber recovered from commercial sources. The short groundwood fibers contribute to the lower average freeness of pulp recovered from residential waste, and their high lignin content results in diminution of the strength properties of the formed sheets.

It should be mentioned here that the absence of refining equipment to properly treat the pulp stock may have reduced the strength properties obtainable in the sheets. For this reason the properties reported herein should be considered on the conservative side in that proper refining would probably have resulted in greater strength properties. However, the degree of improvement cannot be estimated at this time.

Table 3. Properties of Wastepaper Pulps.

Wastepaper Category	CSF (mℓ)	Burst Factor	Tear Factor	Tensile Factor
Newsprint[1]	220	12.5	69.1	2,465
"Super mixed"[1]	245	15.4	81.6	2,630
Groundwood Shavings[1]	255	17.9	94.8	2,920
Magazines and Books[1]	265	14.7	86.2	2,870
Residential Source	330	15.6	132.0	2,325
Telephone Books[1]	385	17.6	103.5	2,640
Commercial Source	580	17.9	138.0	2,765
Cupstock[1]	630	26.6	186.0	4,150
Colored Tabulating Cards[1]	640	31.3	147.3	5,400
Corrugated Boxes[1]	630	50.7	158.0	5,420

1) From reference 13

Possible improvements in the mechanical properties of paper produced from paper fiber recovered from solid waste could result from the addition of high freeness pulp containing a large quantity of long fibers. A number of studies have examined the dependence of paper strength upon fiber length, including those conducted by Clark (6), Arlov (7), Forgacs (8), and Morton and Alexander (9). Research conducted by Brecht and Klemm (10), Antonsen (11), and Law and Garceau (12) has shown that certain combinations of long and short fibers exist for optimization of paper properties. There is no reason why the results of these investigations could not be applied to improving the properties of refuse derived pulp. In time further research regarding improvement in the properties of fiber recovered from solid waste may be warranted.

In order to establish comparisons for commercially and residentially derived pulps, previous results on wastepaper pulp properties reported in the literature are of interest. The freeness and strength properties of a number of wastepaper categories tested by Klungness (13) are shown in Table 3. In addition both commercial and residential source categories have been added to the table. The properties of pulp obtained from residential sources fall between those of magazines and books and telephone books. On the other hand, commercial source pulps fall between cupstock and colored tabulating cards.

The strength properties of pulps recovered from residential and commercial refuse are compared to those of selected pulps, Table 4.

This comparison aids in determining the feasibility of using refuse-derived pulp as a potential pulp mill furnish. The data in the table show that fiber recovered from residential solid waste is similar to that of 100% deinked newspapers and spruce groundwood. Although both burst and tear properties tend to be greater than those for 100% deinked newspapers and spruce groundwood, the tensile strength of pulp derived from residential sources tends to be somewhat lower. Pulp reclaimed from commercial solid waste is similar to newsprint furnish and the 66%/34% mixture of commercial wet broke and deinked newspapers.

In order to assess the full significance of fiber reclamation from solid waste, some water treatment problems associated with the pulping and

Table 4. Properties of Selected Pulps.

	Burst Factor	Tear Factor	Tensile Factor
100% Deinked[3] Newspapers	9.3	38.3	2,861
Spruce Groundwood	10.7	44.2	2,610
Residential Source	15.6	132.0	2,325
66% Commercial Wet Broke[1] & 34% Deinked Newspapers[3]	15.5	51.4	3,175
Commercial Source	17.9	138.0	2,765
Newsprint Furnish[2,3]	15.4	82.4	3,300

[1]70% groundwood, 30% bleached softwood kraft
[2]A mixture of groundwood and chemical pulp used in the manufacture of newspaper.
[3]From reference 13

cleaning processes were investigated. The ramifications of screening the air-classified light fraction to remove fines and organic material before wet processing were documented through separate pulpings of screen oversize and undersize materials and subsequent BOD and COD determinations of the water used for pulping each screen fraction.

The effluent from the pulping operation (minus pulp and other solids) exhibited the following BOD and COD characteristics:

	BOD (mg/ℓ)	COD (mg/ℓ)
Screen oversize (screen lights)	362	1,630
Screen undersize (reject material)	998	2,880

These results indicate that the BOD and COD of the water were reduced considerably through screening of the air-classified lights.

Pertaining to waste water treatment of the effluent from the hydropulper, the reduction in both BOD and COD and the production of sludge as a consequence of activated sludge wastewater treatment were investigated. A laboratory scale wastewater treatment was constructed for these investigations. The experimental program called for pulping of the screened lights, de-watering the pulp slurry, and pumping of the effluent to the water treatment plant. In the first series of tests a four hour per day pumping period and a detention time of 3.5 days were observed. The amount of sludge produced during these experiments fluctuated between 0.625 and 1.000 grams per hour on a dry weight basis. The treated effluent was clear, odorless, and the BOD and COD were 10 mg/ℓ and 31 mg/ℓ, respectively.

A second series of tests was conducted in which wastewater from the hydropulper was pumped continuously to the wastewater treatment plant. A twenty-four-hour timer was used to cycle the feed-water pump every fifteen minutes. The detention time for this series of tests was 2.1 days. The treated effluent under these conditions of continuous operation was odorless, was slightly turbid, and the BOD was 9 mg/ℓ.

The final series of tests involved the re-use of the treated effluent from the wastewater treatment plant in the pulping operation. Wastewater from the hydropulper was pumped into the treatment plant, treated, and recycled into the pulping process. This sequence was repeated several times, and the appearance and quality of the treatment plant effluent was the same as in the second series of tests, that is, odorless, slightly turbid, and having a BOD of 9 mg/ℓ.

The results of these experiments appear to indicate that conventional activated sludge treatment can successfully be used to treat wastewater from pulping operations which use screened light fraction. Moreover, the recycling of process wastewater treated in this manner did not pose any problems with regard to water quality.

DISCUSSION

This research has reported on a processing technology for recovering fiber from solid waste. The processing sequence has succeeded in reducing the water quality problems associated with the pulping of refuse derived pulp such that conventional wastewater treatment can be employed. Fiber recovered from residential solid waste exhibits strength characteristics similar to those of 100% deinked newspapers and virgin groundwood. On the other hand, fiber recovered from commercial solid waste possesses slightly greater strength properties similar to those of a typical newsprint furnish of groundwood and chemical pulp.

The cellulosic content of urban solid waste is considerable. Presently, some two million tons of paper per year are landfilled in the San Francisco Bay Area alone (14). Given the technical means as described here for fiber recovery, the solid waste stream can be viewed as a resource to be exploited. It is hoped that as a consequence of this research stimulation will be provided for the recovery and utilization of fiber from solid waste. Not only would fiber recovery reduce energy and raw material expenditures within the pulp and paper industry, but the present disposal problem of post-consumer fiber would be greatly reduced or eliminated.

REFERENCES

1. Woodwell, G.M., The Carbon Dioxide Question, Scientific American, 238 (1):34 (1978).
2. Trezek, G.J., and C.G. Golueke, "Availability of Cellulosic Wastes for Chemical or Bio-Chemical Processing"; AIChE Symposium Series 158, Bio-Chemical Engineering-Energy, Renewable Resources and New Foods, Vol. 72, 1976.
3. Savage, G.M., L.F. Diaz, and G.J. Trezek, "The Cal Recovery System"; *Compost Science,* Vol. 16, No. 5, Autumn, 1975.
4. Savage, G.M. and G.J. Trezek, "Screening Shredded Municipal Solid Waste", *Compost Science,* Vol. 17, No. 1, January/February, 1976.
5. Trezek, G.J. and G.M. Savage, "MSW Component Size Distribution Obtained from the Cal Resource Recovery System"; *Resource Recovery and Conservation,* 2 (1976).
6. Clark, J. d'A., *Tech. Assoc. Papers.* 25:556 (1942).
7. Arlov, A.P., *Norsk Skogind.* 10:342 (1959).
8. Forgacs, O.L., *Pulp & Paper Can.* 64 (c):T89 (1963).
9. Marton, R., and Alexander, S.D., *Tappi* 46 (2): 65 (1963).
10. Brecht, W., and Klemm, K.H., *Pulp & Paper Can.* 54 (1):72 (1953).
11. Antonsen, O., *Norsk Skogind.* 14 (8):353 (1966).
12. Law, K.N. and Garceau, J.J., *Pulp & Paper Can.* 77 (2):63 (1976).
13. Klungness, J.H., "Secondary Fiber Research at the Forest Products Laboratory"; *Tappi* Vol. 58, No. 10, Oct. 1975.
14. Diaz, L.F., G.M. Savage, R.P. Goebel, C.G. Golueke and G.J. Trezek, *Market Potential of Material and Energy Recovered from Bay Area Solid Wastes;* Report prepared for State of California Solid Waste Management Board, March 1976.

3-6 Recovery of Paper from Municipal Solid Waste

Curt Cederholm and Jorgen G. Hedenhag

Source: *Proceedings* of the 1979 Pulping Conference, Seattle, Washington, September 24–26, 1979, pp. 275–280. Reprinted with Permission of The Technical Association of the Pulp and Paper Industry.

INTRODUCTION

The recent energy crisis has vividly demonstrated the necessity of finding alternate sources of fuel, and has focused worldwide attention on energy conservation and on recovery of energy and usable materials from solid waste.

The disposal of municipal solid waste has become a monumental problem in the U.S. and in other countries with high standards of living. Landfill is the most common method of municipal solid waste disposal today. It is, however, rapidly being replaced by other methods for reasons of hygiene, environment and aesthetics. Incineration will most likely gain more acceptance in the years to come. While this disposal method has for many years been commonplace in Europe, it has its problems. It appears, however, that the industry has now developed effective and reliable air pollution control devices, one of the items that in the past has caused the incineration method many problems.

In search of alternate sources of energy, it becomes apparent that an enormous energy potential is available in municipal solid waste. The heat developed during incineration can be used for production of steam for heating or cooling purposes or for generation of electricity. We can therefore expect incineration, in conjunction with some sort of energy recovery, to become a more common means of solid waste disposal.

Another method for recovery of energy is converting solid waste to a fuel (Refuse Derived Fuel or RDF). The advantages of this method are obvious: RDF can be transported and stored more economically than steam and electricity.

Several other methods of extracting energy from municipal solid waste are in various stages of development.

The Flakt Group has taken a somewhat different route and has developed a system for recovery of recyclable materials from solid waste. This is without any doubt the most energy conserving way of all recovery processes. Although variations in composition are great depending on seasonal changes and geographic location, common U.S. municipal solid waste contains approximately 35–45% paper, 8% steel and 10% glass.

The economical benefits of recycling glass are doubtful, but recycling of steel and paper is in most cases quite attractive. The problems connected with reuse of postconsumed materials are always contamination of foreign material and the presence of impurities. The Flakt system, however, yields a paper so free from impurities that it can be used directly in the paper mill without causing problems to subsequent processing equipment.

This paper describes the Flakt system for recovery of paper from municipal solid waste and its ability to segregate paper made from mechanical pulp from that made from chemical pulp. It also discusses qualities and potential usage of Flakt paper as raw material for paper manufacturing and it outlines space requirements and cost figures.

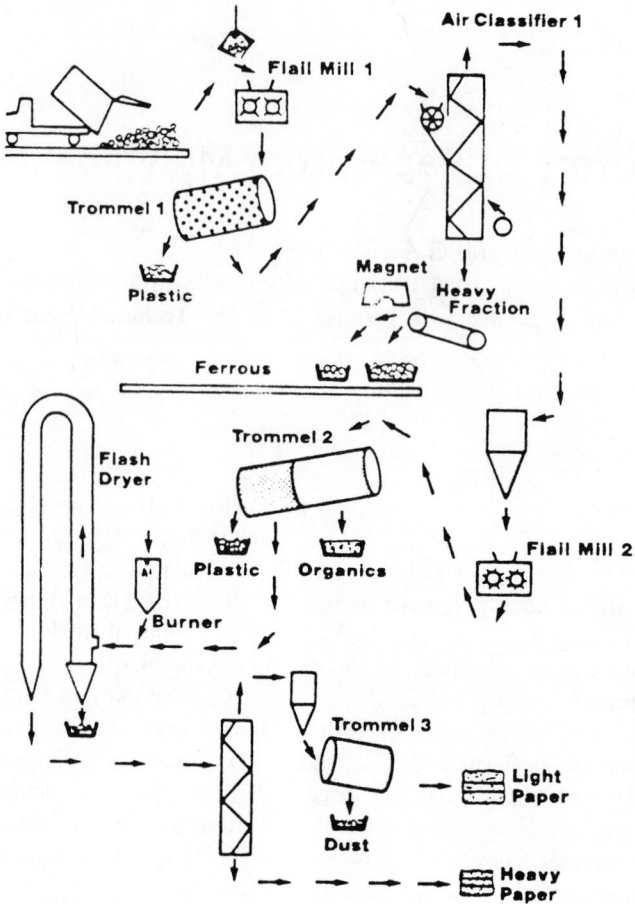

Figure 1. Flow-sheet of Flakt demonstration plant in Stockholm, Sweden.

In 1975, Flakt started a demonstration plant in Stockholm, Sweden, with a processing capacity of 5.5 tons of solid waste per hour. This plant has been the design base for the commercial plants now under construction.

THE FLAKT RRR SYSTEM

Figure No. 1 shows a flow sheet of the demonstration plant in Stockholm. It is somewhat simplified, but describes adequately the principle of operation of the Flakt RRR system (RRR stands for resource recovery from refuse). The demonstration plant was installed on the tipping floor of one of the two municipal incineration plants in the city of Stockholm, Sweden. This plant has since been dismantled because the city required the space for other purposes.

Any truck delivering refuse to the incinerator could be selected at random and its cargo could be processed in the Flakt plant. No manual sorting and picking were made.

The system works as follows:

The refuse is fed directly into Flail Mill #1. The purpose of this mill is to break open plastic bags and to liberate enclosed material for further processing. It is important to understand that this is not an ordinary shredder. A Hammermill type shredder, for example, would do irreparable damage to the end product. It would pulverize glass and organic matter and impact them on the paper. Subsequent processing in the Flakt plant could not remove all of these impurities, but they would end up in the final product. It is noteworthy that a Flail mill uses approximately 1/10 of the electric power

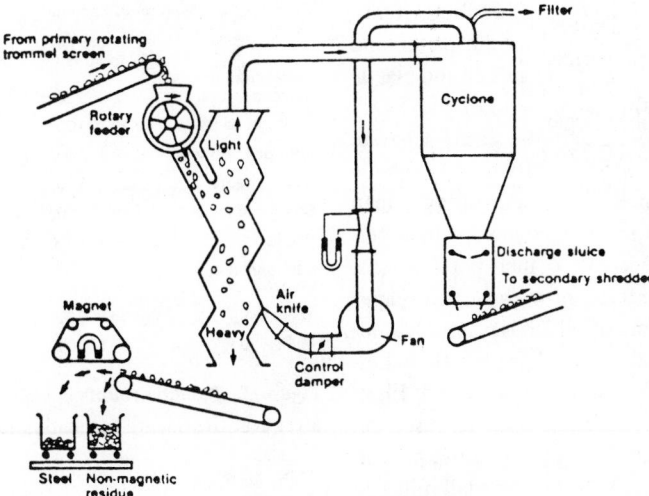

Figure 2. Air classifier.

consumption of a Hammermill for the same capacity. A steel beam or a 4x4 wooden beam that would jam a Hammermill goes through the Flail mill in one piece, nicked only in a few places by the flails.

The material passes through rotating Trommel #1. It has a low RPM and 8″ round holes. In this trommel, large objects and plastic sheets are rejected from the system while the accept is conveyed to the Air Classifier #1.

A lot of literature has been written on air classifiers, most all of it dealing with classification of relatively homogeneous materials. It is, however, difficult to think of a more heterogeneous material than municipal solid waste. Consequently, a classifier designed according to textbook principles does not work very well if at all on refuse.

Years of research and laboratory testing lie behind the Flakt air classifier. At first glance, it may look like any conventional zig-zag classifier, but the air is introduced not through the bottom, but through several air knifes giving the turbulence necessary for good classification. Another important item is the feeder for the air classifier. It is specifically designed to avoid pulsations in the feed. (See Figure #2.)

The heavy fraction falls to the bottom of the classifier onto a conveyor belt and passes under a magnet separator. The heavy fraction consists of steel, aluminum, glass and heavy organic matter. The magnet separator extracts the ferrous

material. If the reject happens to contain a high percentage of aluminum, this stream could be passed over an eddy-current separator for recovery of aluminum. Otherwise, this stream normally goes to landfill.

The light fraction exits through the top of the air classifier and the material is conveyed by air to a cyclone, where it is separated from the air stream. The air is then returned to the classifier in a closed loop. This has several advantages: In passing through the air knife fans, the air is heated and performs a certain amount of drying of the material. The closed loop, further, provides a constant flow of air of known density and moisture content, which is necessary for the proper performance of the air classifier and will result in a low power consumption. The bleed-off air stream necessary to remove evaporated moisture is minute compared to the air flow through the classifier. This bleed-off air has to be filtered before being exhausted to the atmosphere, and the air filter surface required is, consequently, very small.

The material collected in the cyclone goes to Flail Mill #2. This mill is somewhat similar in design to Flail Mill #1, but will yield a material that in appearance is similar to fine shredded refuse. It is very important, however, that this fine shredding takes place after the refuse has passed the primary mill and air classifier #1, where the main portion of the impurities has been removed. The material exiting from Mill

#2 shows a different degree of shredding. Thus, organic matter is pulverized, while paper and paperboard are about 2 inches in size and plastic sheets are considerably larger.

Rotating Trommel 2 can now easily separate the paper fraction from plastics and organic matter. The trommel is a slow rotating screen drum with the first section having 3/4 inch perforations and the second, 4 inch perforations.

The accepted material now consists of paper and paperboard, some of which is plastic coated, some textile fibers and some light plastic flakes. This material is fed into the so-called Flash Dryer. This piece of equipment is based on Flakt's experience in drying of cellulose pulp in suspension. The Flash Dryer, the Flail mill and the air classifier represent most of the research and development spent on the Flakt RRR system.

The purpose of the Flash Dryer is threefold:

1. In the first stage, the material is dried to approximately 95% dryness.
2. In the second stage, the material is exposed to an air temperature of approximately 300°F for 5 seconds. The purpose of this shock treatment, which will not deteriorate the quality of the paper, is to de-activate the bacteria and prevent further bacteria growth. This process is called sanitizing and is not to be confused with sterilizing. The reduction in bacteria count is, however, significant, and tests have shown that after years of storage, this treatment has prevented further bacteria growth.
3. The third purpose of the Flash Dryer is to shrivel up thermo plastic pieces, and to give them different free fall characteristics as compared to those of paper. The Flash Dryer acts as a classifier and the plastics fall to the bottom of the dryer. Still, another advantage of drying is that sticky elements become brittle, and breakdown in the passage through the fan and are separated in Trommel 3.

The heat source for the Flash Dryer is a gas or oil fired combustion chamber. Reject from the Flash Dryer contains mostly plastics and textile material.

Tests	Number of bacteria/g of paper		Reduction
	Before heat treatment	After heat treatment	
Heterotrophic bacteria , total	72,000,000	3,100,000	96
Coliform bacteria	12,000,000	340,000	97
Enterobacteriaceae	8,900,000	520,000	94
Acinetobacter	23,000,000	1,900,000	92
Staphylococcus	5,500,000	790,000	86
Bacillus	650,000	51,000	92
Salmonella or Shigella	0	0	
Yeast fungi	1,900,000	81,000	96
Mildew fungi	560,000	22,000	96

Figure 3. Bacteria counts in paper samples before and after heat treatment. Incubation temperature: 35°C.

The dried material is pneumatically conveyed to Air Classifier 2, which is basically of the same design as Classifier 1, but operates with different air velocities. Here the paper is separated into so-called light and heavy fractions. The light fraction, which consists mostly of newsprint and paper made from mechanical pulp and thermomechanical pulp with some elements of tissue, shows a very high degree of purity and can be used directly in paper manufacturing. Before being baled, the paper passes Trommel #3 where dust, fine sand and some organic matter are removed.

The heavy paper fraction exiting from the bottom of the Air Classifier consists of predominantly Kraft paper, linerboard and corrugated qualities. This fraction has a higher degree of impurities, but can, nevertheless, also be used directly in paper manufacturing of certain grades.

PAPER QUALITIES AND POTENTIAL USAGE

The light and heavy fractions as derived from the Flakt RRR system have been thoroughly tested in a great number of paper mill laboratories.

Actual production trials have also been conducted, where several tons of light and also heavy fraction have been run on a regular paper machine. The tests show that by and large the light fraction is quite acceptable as feed stock or additive for center layer of linerboard. The bending stiffness and tensile strength are in the same range as for virgin mechanical pulp. If

Property	Flakt Paper		Source Separated Newsprint	Virgin Mechanical Pulp
	Mixed Fraction	Light Fraction		
Screening residue %	11.5	2.5	2-5	—
° SR	37	46	62	51
Basis weight (g/m³)	80	80	80	80
Density (kg/m³)	506	469	564	450
Tensile strength (Nm/kg)	22.7	21.1	36.2	19.1
Module of elasticity (GN/m²)	1.74	1.53	2.06	1.33
Bending stiffness (Nm/kgm²)	1.12	1.24	0.96	1.22
Brightness (% Eirepho)	42	42	40	—

Figure 4.

high tensile strength is required, perhaps only a portion of the feed stock can be RRR paper. Separate tests have shown, however, that the heavy fraction is quite acceptable as an extender to corrugated medium.

Figure #4 shows the properties of the Flakt grades as compared to virgin pulp and source-separated newsprint. It has been claimed that newsprint source-separated in households is of the highest attainable quality. Tests show however, that consistent high quality can be maintained far better in a recovery plant than at source separation or through manual sorting.

It is a well known fact that the municipal solid waste varies in composition with geographic locale and over different seasons. Hundreds of tons of refuse from different places in Europe have been tested in the Flakt demonstration plant in Stockholm.

Several tons of refuse from Middlesex County, New Jersey were air freighted over to Stockholm and tested. Figure #5 shows a comparison of different municipal waste tested. The most

striking conclusion of the tests is that although the input may vary drastically, the amount and the quality of the paper yielded in the RRR plant is amazingly uniform and consistent.

One problem experienced during most of the tests in making paper from the fiber attained from the RRR plant was in the area of defibration and screening. It became obvious that the conventional equipment for defibration used in paper mills is not particularly suited for recycled fibers. To illustrate this point, it is worthwhile mentioning that two identical paper samples were tested in a high speed refiner and in a Valley beater. The screening residue attained was 15% and 3% respectively. The high speed agitation seems to break up the impurities into small fragments which will cause problems in the screening process. A more gentle defibration is attained in a so-called "Fibreflow" unit which, in essence, is a rotating screen trommel. No difficulties were experienced in the screening when a "Fibreflow" drum was used. RRR paper was added as an extender to paperboard stock at different mills constituting from 15%

MSW Composition %	Sweden Stockholm	Holland Wijster	USA Middlesex County
Paper	50	23	28
Ferrous	5	3	5
Plastics	8	6	5
Food Waste	20	37	40
Other	17	31	22
Total	100	100	100
Water Content	22	37	18

Figure 5.

to 50% of the total furnish. No detrimental effects could be detected in the final product. It is, therefore, safe to say that RRR paper can be used as an extender in the manufacturing of certain grades of paperboard, corrugated medium, and industrial towelling. Coupled with a more gentle defibration, it is also possible that the light fraction can be used in manufacturing of newsprint, where, traditionally, there is a great demand for recycled fibers.

SPACE REQUIREMENTS AND COST OF A RRR PLANT

The Flakt RRR plants are constructed in a modular system. The size of a module is determined by the total processing capacity of refuse. The plant size is normally described in tons per day (TPD). The operating time is usually two shifts, i.e. 16 hours per day. The modules are 250 TPD and 500 TPD.

We will here review a 500 TPD module. The size of the building including tipping floor and space for one week of paper storage is about 30,000 sq. ft. The Flash Dryer is located outdoors, and the residue is disposed of in an adjacent landfill.

Figure #6 shows a cost estimate for the plant. It is assumed that the RRR plant and the landfill can be run by 6 operators and one foreman per shift. Cost for electric energy and oil for the Flash Dryer are estimated at 3 cent/kWh and 75 cent/gallon. The disposal cost computes to $4.47 per ton of refuse. Including the cost of disposing of the residue, the total cost will be in the order of $5-6 per ton. By the shredding, the volume of the residue handled at the landfill will be reduced. This decreases the operating cost and increases the lifetime of the landfill.

Compared to today's disposal costs in Metropolitan areas of $7-20 per ton, these cost figures seem quite attractive. Private operators, charging tipping fees of $7-20 per ton, ought to realize a good return on investment for a RRR plant operated in conjunction with a landfill.

With an incinerator plant, it will be even more attractive.

CONCLUSION

In conclusion, we would like to emphasize that recycling of usable materials in solid waste is by far the most energy conserving of all resource recovery methods.

The Flakt RRR system yields a paper, that is of such a quality, that it can successfully be used as furnish or extender for various paper and paperboard qualities. With the exponential cost increases in energy that we are presently experiencing, the RRR system can provide a valuable alternative for economical resource recovery.

EQUIPMENT COST	$5,600,000
BUILDING, LAND ETC	1,400,000
	$7,000,000
CAPITAL COST	
Equipment (10 years life)	$ 560,000
Building (20 years life)	70,000
Interest & Taxes	570,000
Total Capital Cost	**$1,200,000**
OPERATING COST	
Personnel cost	$ 270,000
Electric power	18,000
Oil or gas for Flash Dryer	45,000
Miscellaneous	12,000
Equipment maintenance	30,000
Total Operating Cost	**$ 375,000**
Total Cost Per Year	$1,575,000
REVENUE FROM RECOVERED MATERIAL	
Light fraction paper @ $25/ton	$ 506.250
Heavy fraction paper @ $10/ton	169,500
Ferrous material @ $35/ton	278,250
Gross Revenue	**$ 954,000**
Freight & storage	(50,000)
Net Revenue	**$ 904,000**
Total Cost Per Year	$1,575,000
Net Revenue	$ 904,000
Net Cost Of Disposal	$ 671,000
Disposal Cost Per Ton	$4.47

Figure 6. Cost estimate for a 500 TPD Flakt RRR plant.

3-7 Research into the Hygienic Qualities of Paper Recovered by Mechanical Sorting of Municipal Waste

Hubert W. Kindler

Source: *Conservation and Recycling,* Vol. 2, No. 3/4, 1979, pp. 263–267. Reprinted with Permission of Pergamon Press, Ltd.

OBJECTIVE OF THE RESEARCH AND TESTS PROGRAMME

The Bavarian ministry for environmental protection and state development subsidized, as early as 1973, the development of a recycling pilot plant by the German company Krauss – Maffei AG, Munich. The process for the recovery of valuable materials from municipal waste was designated "R 80" and has since reached such a degree of maturity that sorting plants of its type can be erected and operated on a commercial scale.

Both paper and cardboard have a proportion of 20 – 40 wt-% (equivalent to 30 – 60 vol-%) of municipal waste. The qualities and properties of these components which can be sorted by an existing recycling plant are of economic importance to both plant designers and paper mills. Therefore, a research programme was applied for by Badcock Krauss – Maffei-Industrieanlagen GmbH in order to test the hygienic and physical properties of the waste paper with the official subject:

Research of the hygienic qualities, processing and applications of papers produced on the basis of waste paper which was recovered by mechanical sorting.

This application was approved by the German Federal Board of Environmental Protection (Umweltbundesamt), Berlin, on 3 December 1976. The test programme which was carried out in the only existing waste sorting pilot plant of this scale in Germany, the R 80-Plant in Munich and in two conventional paper mills, is described in the following.

DESCRIPTION OF THE 5 TONS/H R 80-PLANT OF BKMI IN MUNICH

Refuse from towns and cities is delivered to the plant by truck. It is conveyed from a hopper to a magnetic separator, which extracts magnetic scrap, i.e., ferrous materials. This scrap is delivered to the scrap market. The refuse is subsequently directed to a crushing unit, where it is subjected to coarse crushing. At the same time, bundles and bags of waste are torn open so that their contents can be sorted. The particular advantage of this system is that the refuse is crushed only as far as is absolutely necessary for operation of the plant. In this way, the refuse remains in its original shape for as long as possible; the re-cyclable materials can thus be re-used more easily and more economically and the energy consumption of the plant is kept low.

After the coarse-crushing stage, a second magnetic separator extracts the ferrous scrap-metal contained in the opened waste bags and bundles. In the subsequent sieving stage compostable matter, such as garden and vegetable refuse, is separated from other re-usable materials. The compostable materials can then be conveyed to a composting plant. The refuse remaining after the sieving process, which contains a high proportion of re-cyclable materials, undergoes further separation in a ballistic separator. In this equipment the refuse in constantly aerated to optimise the sifting effect.

Three separate fractions emerge from the air-separation stage: the light fraction, which includes paper, plastic sheets, light textiles; the medium fraction, which includes cardboard, compressed paper, some plastics and textiles etc. and the heavy fraction, which includes heavy plastics, non-ferrous metals, bones, wood, stones, etc.

These fractions are now exposed to further treatment, according to how the re-cyclable material is to be re-utilized. In the case of the light and medium fractions, impurities in the paper and cardboard content can be extracted by re-sieving; the materials are then conveyed to the paper-technological plant.

During paper-technological treatment, the pre-cleaned fraction is fed into a pulper, in which the re-usable fibres are pulped in water. Items which cannot be pulped, such as plastic sheets, etc., are continuously discharged by a ragger. The process produces a fibrous raw material which, depending on the requirements of the paper mill for which it is destined, can be sorted, cleaned, and have specks removed via the power vibrator and centric cleaner. At this stage, the plastic sheets accumulate automatically. These are treated on the Krauss – Maffei Auto-Dissector which converts them into granules. These sheets are shredded, agglomerated, cooled and subsequently dyed. The agglomerates can be conveyed directly to machines such as extruders, injection moulding machines etc. and simple industrial parts can be produced. A pre-sorting between thermoplastic and polymeric materials is not necessary.

The heavy fraction can be converted to energy via a waste incineration plant, or disposed of in some other way. Under certain conditions, the heavy fraction can be retreated in order, for example, to recover the broken glass and non-ferrous metals.

EXECUTION OF THE RESEARCH PROGRAMME

BKMI; sorting out waste paper

From 14 February until 18 February 1977, the following quantities of municipal waste from the city of Munich were delivered and sorted out by the BKMI-R 80-pilot plant: 291 dustbins of 1.1 m^3 each were emptied, which was equivalent to 31.3 tons of waste. The sources of this waste were both purely residential areas and regions with commercial industrial structure. The R 80-plant of 5 tons/h capacity was operated in the conventional order:

dosing hopper
magnet 1
cusher
sieve 1
air separator 1
sieve 2
air separator 2

This means that magnet 2 and sieve 3, which are provided for large capacity plants, were omitted. The spread of paper and cardboard content of the waste was between 15 and 32% by wt, the mean value being 26.4% by wt. The plant gave trouble-free service for the full period of 5 days, with 3 operators per shift.

The 31.3 tons of waste contained 8.3 tons waste paper, of which 5.1 tons (61%) could be sorted by the mechanical R 80-plant. Since the other fractions were not the object of this programme, they were delivered to the municipal waste incinerators at Munich-North.

The waste paper was baled to bales of 500 kg, stored for a period of 7 days and shipped to the Escher Wyss factory, Ravensburg, for further processing.

Escher Wyss, Production of Fibres

The 10 bales of 500 kg each of waste paper were dissolved in the Escher Wyss dispersion plant in a pulper of 6 m^3 capacity. The dissolving agent was fresh water for the first 4 bales and sieve-press effluent (white water) for the other six bales. The suspension had a consistency of 4–5% bone dry matter. A total of 1890 kg non-paper wastes was accumulated in the pulper as large foils, textiles, wires, wet strength papers and other components with high water content.

Now the fibres flowed from the intermediate chest via high density cleaner, fiberizer and centric cleaner to the vibrating screen. In these units some 382 kg of undesirable ingredients were removed.

After this, the suspension was dewatered in a double wire press to 25 – 30% dry matter and the fibre felt disintegrated in a screw. This "crumpy material" was heated up to 90°C by injection of 162°C-steam in a heating screw, in order to plasticize dirt particles and to reduce the bacteria content.

In the subsequent disperser the fibres were screened and the crumb materials loaded on a lorry for shipment to the Herzberg paper mill. The total batch was 10.3 tons dispersed waste paper with 31.8% = 3.3 tons dry matter, the balance being handling loss. To distinguish this paper from the usual waste paper, we will call it "recycled waste paper".

During the preparation, samples taken from wire press, disperser and white water were deep-frozen and sent to Herzberg for an investigation of the bacteriological load during the single process stages. The processing of waste paper was trouble free, the physical properties were good and the appearance uniform.

Herzberger Papierfabrik; Production of Cardboard and Bacteriological Tests.

The paper recovered from the R 80-plant had a non-fibre portion of 6.6% and was specified as grade A 00. Its proportion of corrugated board was high, that of cardboard surprisingly low. A disadvantage was that sanitary papers were not completely sorted out. With respect to properties such as moisture and ask content, tensile strength, elongation and burst resistance, no significant deviations could be found from the values of grade B 12 which is normally used as waste paper feedstock in the Herzberg factory. The crumpy material delivered from Ravensburg had a temperature of 45°C and had lost its bad odour of residuals. It was graded as B 12 (max. 1% of dirty components).

	% R 80-paper	% B 12 waste paper
Sample 1	10	90
2	20	80
3	30	70
4	50	50
5	0	100

It is normal practice to blend different waste paper qualities. In this programme the R 80-paper (A 00) was mixed with waste paper grade B 12 in 4 variations: A total of 13.5 tons raw material was charged to the board machine for a production of grey board having 600 g/m^2. The crumpy matter could be processed with blended waste paper on a conventional stock preparation. All other operations were also trouble-free.

The white water was tested and the results indicated increased COD- and 5 day BOD-values and higher concentrations of both settling and dissolved components. The dimensions of COD and 5 day BOD are equivalent to CSB and BSB$_5$ in the German language. This implies a higher load for the mechanical, chemical and biological purification systems.

The determination of bacterial yeast and mould fungus indicated high loads for the recycled waste paper. The germ number of the white water was also considerably increased, whereas yeast and mould fungus remained unchanged. The cardboard had doubled germ numbers with an addition of 50% recycled waste paper, but this would still be acceptable even for food packing purposes.

The physical, chemical and sensory tests showed no significant deviations between cardboards from waste paper and mixed waste paper, except a small decrease in bending rigidity and tensile strength, when the proportion of recycled waste paper was increased. Also the properties for further processing such as punching printing, grooving, glueing and coating with paper appeared equivalent to those of waste paper of grade B 12. All these results were confirmed by a series of parallel tests carried out in the Institute of Food Technology of the Munich Technical University.

DISCUSSION OF TEST RESULTS AND CONSEQUENCES FOR THE APPLICATION

It was no surprise to find higher loads of bacterial and mould fungus in recycled waste paper, because of the contamination by other residues during collection, storage and transport is obvious. The thermal treatments of the fibres from recycled waste paper in the dispersion plant and on the board machine were sufficient to reduce the bacteriological values so that there is no objection to the use of such cardboard as packing material, except for food packing and as toys and other consumer goods. The physical, mechanical and chemical properties are equivalent to those of commercial waste paper, grade B 12.

Paper plants equipped with a hot dispersion plant and effluent purification can be employed for the production of a mixture of both waste papers. It is advisable, however, to have additional heating stages in the process in order to reduce the bacteria: a drying process of 10 min at 100°C would pasteurize the recycled waste paper. On the other hand the cellulose fibres tend to form a horny skin at 72°C, with a subsequent loss of quality. The additional fuel costs of drying would increase the sorting costs by 25%. Therefore, the availability of waste heat from existing plants, for instance, from incineration or pyrolysis plants, would be a great advantage.

An alternative would be the use of bacteriocides in the concentration of 1 kg per ton of

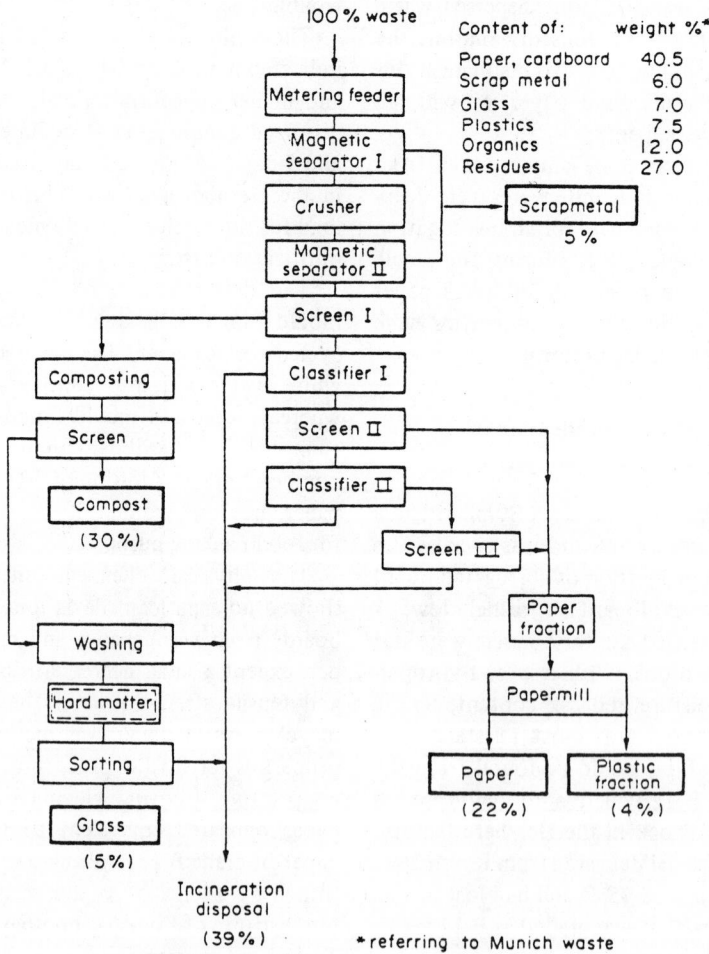

Figure 1. Waste sorting plant – system R 80 from BABCOCK K.

recycled waste paper. This could be accomplished by spraying an aqueous solution over the surface of the papers during the sorting process. Since this would increase the water content in the waste paper, direct processing to fibre stock would be required, without transportation to a remote paper mill.

A third possibility, with sorting and paper plants adjacent to each other, would be to add the bacteriocides directly to the pulper of the dispersion plant with permanent control of their concentration. The insoluble components of the waste paper could be removed and blended with the residual fraction of the R 80-plant which is supposed to be incinerated. The heat involved for the fibre making process could in this combination be derived from waste heat from the incinerator plant.

3-8 Selective Dry Processing, Pulp Cleaning and Paper Making Tests on Three Feed-stocks from Municipal Solid Wastes

Marc L. Renard

Source: *Proceedings* of the 1979 Pulping Conference, Seattle, Washington, September 24-26, 1979, pp. 247-258. Reprinted with Permission of The Technical Association of the Pulp and Paper Industry and the Author.

INTRODUCTION

The first paper in this series[1] examined the technological barriers to the recovery of secondary fibers from selected fractions of mixed municipal waste. After a survey of processes and equipment available for the removal of contaminants and an identification of their limitations, it was possible to formulate guidelines for selective waste processing with the objective to enhance fiber recovery.

Within the time and financial limitations of this investigation, it appeared of interest to gain some "hands on" experience by mechanically processing, in the dry state, a number of waste fractions to convert them to potential feedstocks for paper making. These feedstocks were subsequently pulped and decontaminated at the Paper Recycling Pilot Plant of Western Michigan University, Kalamazoo, MI. Paper rolls were produced, their properties measured and potential uses were examined. Finally, a small number of bacteriological measurements were performed on the finished paper rolls.

The previous paper[1] summarized guidelines for enhanced recovery of secondary fibers from mixed municipal waste. Important points are:

— avoid mixing of identifiable furnishes at the tipping floor of the recovery plant
— prevent imbedding of contaminants into the paper fraction (particularly by high impact shredding)
— avoid unnecessary cutting or shredding of the paper fraction
— resort to "enrichment" processes, in particular for the separation of paper and plastics by aerodynamic, thermal, electric or other means[6,7]

A sequence of operations, in the dry state, and prior to the pulping process, in accordance with these guidelines, is described here as "selective waste processing."

OBJECTIVES OF THE TESTS

Obviously, most secondary fiber mills asked to "try" a refuse-derived fiber material on their production lines might be reluctant. Contaminants or contraries, even if no higher than a few percent, might be different or more variable than in usual furnishes. Thus, problems of various kinds are perceived and anticipated; operating troubles, lower production rates, bacteriological hazards, wastewater contamination, etc.

At the industrial scale, these barriers to recovery cannot be dismissed lightly. However, it seems possible to prepare useful feedstocks from some waste streams so that the mill operator might be handling a paper "concentrate" having little in common with the image conjured by the expression "garbage paper."

Obvious questions exist regarding the capability of relatively standard or readily available machinery, at wastepaper mills, to handle such feedstocks, decontaminate them and produce a cleaned pulp. The behavior of this pulp on the paper machine has to be evaluated critically. After which, a determination could be made of the grade of products for which, by itself or more likely in combination with other sources of fiber, this recovered material could qualify. As one step, it would appear that pilot plant runs, on full scale machinery, at realistic flow rates, are likely to indicate trends and problems requiring immediate attention, thereby leading to ultimate long-term trials by industrial operators.

Accordingly, a number of trial tests were conducted in decontaminating and cleaning several feedstocks from mixed municipal waste. Paper rolls were obtained, of which the properties, yields and speculated use were determined.

The rationale behind these tests is illustrated in Fig. 1. Starting with raw waste "W_i", the approach was to:

- select a method "A_i" of dry-processing W_i, resulting in a feedstock "F_i", which
- wet-processed by the set of devices "B_i", tailored to the nature and size of contaminants in F_i, would
- result in a reasonably clean pulp P_i", which
- could be handled by paper-machine "C" and made into paper roll "Z_i".

PROCESSING OF THREE MUNICIPAL SOLID WASTES INTO THREE FEEDSTOCKS

General

Municipal waste composition by component is quite variable with the location and time of year[8]. Under the headings "paper," "cardboard," are grouped a wide variety of paper products, fiber types and lengths, finishes, fillers, laminates, etc. For example, the content of paper products was found to range between 35%[9,10] to 42%[11] or 48%[10]. So, based on such reports, it is possible to define a range of 35 to 45 wt.% of the as-received raw waste as "paper products." Of this quantity, a fraction might be identifiable at the tipping floor, such as bundled, commingled (i.e., post packer truck) newspapers or large pieces of clean corrugated material.

Various wastepaper cleaning devices can remove many contaminants from the secondary fibers. This is provided that these particles are not of such small dimensions (0.2 to 0.5 mm, typically) that they will pass through pressurized screens or be part of the accepts after centrifugal cleaning. Hence a strong technological incentive exists to keep at their original size contaminants such as plastics, foamed polystyrene, non-pulpable fibers, wet-strength compounds, and non-water soluble adhesives. If, however, some coarse size-reduction has been effected

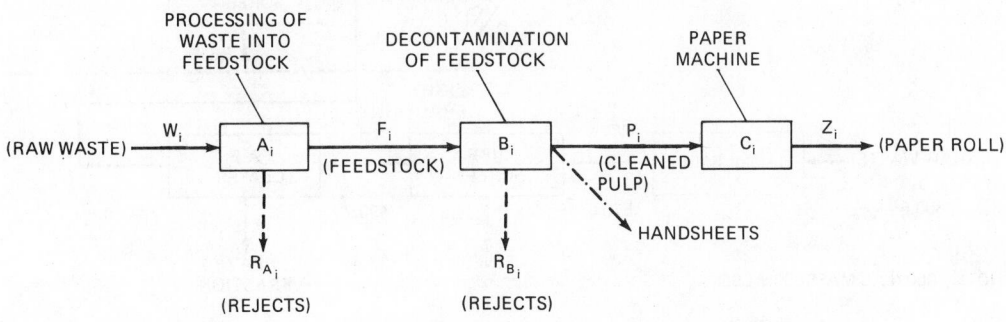

Figure 1. Schematic process flow.

(as required, for example, by air classification), some step of dry screening is called for, with a size of the openings much larger than the minimum dimension of wet screen holes or slits.

The three feedstocks described below were selected to provide some insight on the coupling between these aspects of dry processing and the wet pulping and cleaning operations.

Feedstock F_1: Washington, D.C.

This feedstock resulted from a sequence of dry processing steps represented in Fig. 2. W_1 (raw waste) came from residential neighborhoods in the Northeastern section of Washington, D.C. From a paper making viewpoint, its approximate composition is (ercent by weight)[12]: paper: 73%; Rejects: 27% (plastics: 7.5%; textiles: 7.7%; other: 11.8%).

Of the original 343.5 lbs of light fraction trommeled, F_1 represented 68.4 wt.%. In other words, 31.6 wt.% had been screened out, mostly as small size materials − including both paper particles and contraries, and paper fiber was concentrated in the oversize. For example, after trommeling light fraction (3/8 in. (9.5 mm) diameter screen holes), Trezek[15] established that a 60.2 wt.% paper content, prior to screening, resulted in an oversize fraction containing approximately: paper fiber 79, plastics 8 and "others" 13 wt.% and an undersize product with only: paper 20. and plastics 1.4 wt.%.

It is reasonable to state that the loss in potentially recoverable fibers will be small, as part of the screen rejects.

Feedstock F_2: New Orleans, LA

An interesting feature of this feedstock is that no coarse size-reduction in a hammermill was used, but instead a mere loosening or low energy cutting of a feed product already much richer in fibers than the original raw waste. This is illustrated in Fig. 3, showing that trommeling of the raw waste (without prior shredding) was followed by inspection and manual removal of oversize, bulky objects. These "trommel-overs" were shipped to the U.S. Bureau of Mines, Edmonston, MD, pilot plant for the further processing shown in Fig. 3.

W_2, raw waste, came from households in New Orleans, LA, to a full scale resource recovery facility (RECOVERY I). The composition of the input waste is, typically[17]: paper products 37.0, plastics 3.4, yard waste 8.4, others 51.2 wt.%. It is screened in a trommel, with 4 3/4 inches diameter holes, which has been described elsewhere[17]. This device functions as an effective remover of potential contraries[18,19]. The average composition of the oversize product is found to be[17]: paper products 58.5, plastics 4.9, yard waste 4.9, others 31.7 wt.%. Note that 43.6 wt.% of the input waste reports to the oversize fraction.

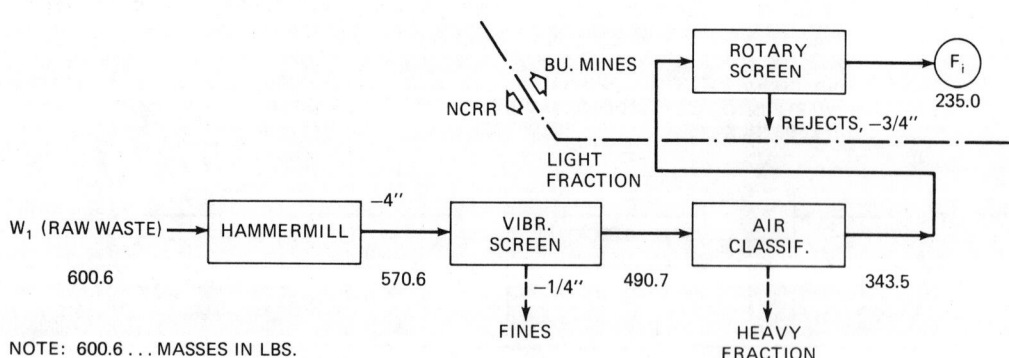

Figure 2. Processing of raw waste into Feedstock F_1 (Washington, D.C.).

Flail-milling by swinging bars attached to counterrotating hubs[20] results in a "loosening up" of the material, after which the "suction hood" picks up the lighter pieces of paper, plastics and fabrics. The mass balance is shown in Fig. 3 (masses in lbs). The hood classifier heavies, incidentally, were described by the operator as "grit, dirt, heavy plastics, metal and corrugated board"[21].

Although the detailed particle-size distribution of, and nature and percentage of the components in, feedstock F_2 was not measured, the composition could be estimated based on previous observations on the size of trommel overs at New Orleans, assuming: (1) the flail mill is adjusted so as to reduce to a critical size (~4 inch) 90% of the paper fraction; and (2) 20% of the plastics and 80% of the natural or synthetic textiles remain in the heaviest stream. The estimated composition is: paper products 78.3, plastics 5.8, yard waste 7.3, others 8.6 wt.%. Based on this, feedstock F_2 would have 21.7% contraries, consisting in the main of yard waste (grass clippings, other vegetable matter), plastics, fabrics and food waste, in this order.

Yard and food wastes, described by Raymond[21] as "floatables," do not seem to be "problem contaminants." According to Raymond's experience with material from the Black-Clawson Fibreclaim plant (Franklin, OH), ".. ; grass and yard wastes . . . appeared to be eliminated by mild chemical treatment or air flotation"[21]

The present prediction of content of contraries was found to be in good agreement with the value measured during wet processing tests, namely 24 wt.% rejects (which included some trapped paper fiber)

Feedstock F_3: Milwaukee, WI

The 1500 ton per day resource recovery facility at Milwaukee, WI, is owned and operated by the AMERICOLOGY Division of American Can Company. A detailed description and discussion of this plant has appeared[22]. As part of the front end processing, bundles newspapers collected commingled with the waste in the packer truck were picked out of the raw refuse, manually or using a long fork, by a worker located along the conveyor feeding the primary shredder. The newspapers were sent down a chute towards a container, for sale as wastepaper to an industrial manufacturer.

In 1975, NCRR published a study comparing the contamination of commingled and separately collected newspaper bundles in a residential section of the greater Washington metropolitan area[23]. The authors concluded, subject to caveats relating to bundling or packing, moisture levels, etc., that " . . . seemingly, commingled bundled newspaper can be recovered as clean

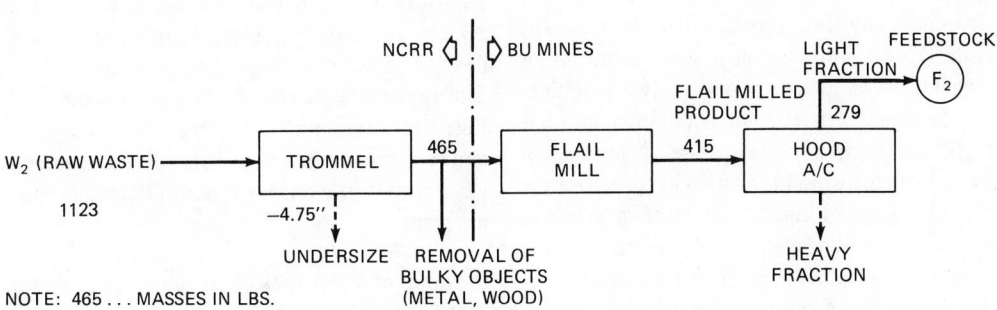

Figure 3. Processing of raw waste into Feedstock F_2 (New Orleans, La.).

(or nearly so) as separately collected." The need to test in production the suitability for reuse of the recovered paper was recognized, although no degradation of the cellulose had been detected.

Accordingly, in the present investigation, it was decided to use as a third feedstock F_3, a sample of commingled newspaper from Milwaukee. This sample, weighing 171 lbs, was grabbed from the shipping container, bagged in plastic and processed within two days at the pilot plant of Western Michigan University. The material, upon visual inspection, appeared to be all news, somewhat soiled and containing a few possible contraries, in the form of surface wetting or refuse "inserts" (food, plastic wrappings) between the stacked and bundled newspapers. On a quantitative basis, it is expected that contraries should not exceed one percent, consisting mostly of thin polyethylene sheets (plastic bags), twine, metal clips and food wastes.

DECONTAMINATION OF THE WASTEPAPER PULP

Equipment Used

The pulping, cleaning and papermaking tests using the three feedstocks were run at the Pilot Paper Recycling Plant of Western Michigan University, Kalamazoo, MI, under the direction of Mr. Robert E. Kinsey. It is described elsewhere.[24]

Basically, it consists of a variety of full-scale wastepaper cleaning and processing machines, which can be connected quickly and simply into almost any flow configuration desired. The system operates in a discontinuous – continuous manner ("burp" mode): one or two machines operations are carried out at commercial rates of 100 gallons per minute. The accepts or rejects are then stored in several chests before the next operation. Finally, the cleaned stock is used to make handsheets or paper rolls on the 25-inch Louis Calder Fourdrinier machine.

In Appendix A, an item by item description of the main pieces of equipment used in the pulping and cleaning phases is given. Operating conditions (consistency, HP, etc.) are also listed. Physical parameters quoted were used for all three feedstocks, unless otherwise indicated.

Flow Diagrams

General. In view of the limited scope and duration of these tests, no systematic attempt was made to optimize yield or quality for a given yield, by empirically trying a large number of equipment combinations in various process flows. Rather, an experimental procedure was selected by the WMU staff, based on the nature and appearance of the contaminants. Some operating conditions, such as flow rates in pressurized screens, were determined by trial and error.

In some cases, it was determined that the "minimum set" of machines (such as was used for feedstock F_1) did not clean to a degree judged sufficient by visual inspection of handsheets. Centrifugal cleaning was then added, resulting in the "maximum set."

Cleaning of Feedstock F_1: "Minimum Set". The flow diagram for the wet processing of F_1, the processed material from Washington, is shown in Fig. 4 ("Minimum" set). Based on the handsheets made from stock at the exit of the last stage (pressurized screen), the quality was judged good enough by the WMU specialist not to require additional, centrifugal cleaning. Operating conditions are given in Table 1.

Cleaning of Feedstock F_2: "Maximum Set". After the processing steps used for F_1, the handsheet obtained still contained an unsatisfactory amount of small-size light contraries (hair, plastics, foamed plastic) and heavy ones (glass, grit, sand). Another stage of cleaning was added, i.e., a battery of contrifugal cleaners (see Appendix A) for F_2 and F_3. Accepts, light rejects and heavy rejects were sampled to make handsheets. The applicable process flow diagram is shown in Fig. 4 ("Maximum" set). Operating parameters and test data are listed in Table 1. Final accepts were stored in a chest for use in the paper making tests.

Cleaning of Feedstock F_3 (Commingled News): "Maximum Set". At the pulping stage, it was readily apparent that the feedstock was practically all newsprint. The total mass of rejects after all cleaning operations was found to be very small indeed, namely 1.13 lbs for an input of 151 lbs (dry basis) and would likely not require

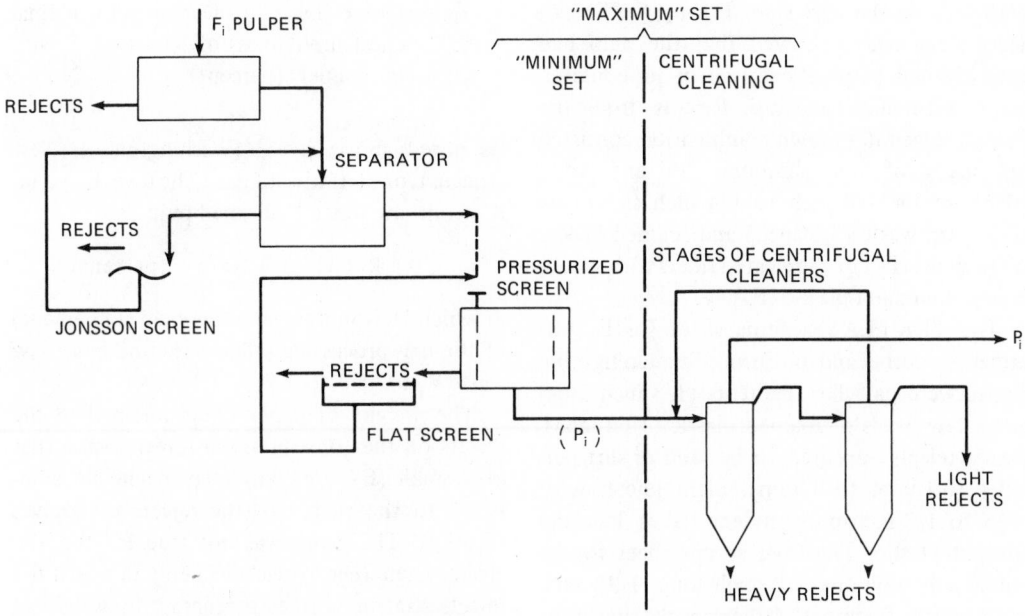

Figure 4. Wet processing sequence ("minimum" and "maximum" sets).

additional processing past the "minimum set" to be usable as a filler stock, or for most core stocks (paper tubes). These experiments, however, attempted to reach the highest quality achievable by simple, mechanical means, so it was decided to use the "maximum set" for F_3 also. The process flow is again as in Fig. 4 ("Maximum" set). Test data and parameters are also listed in Table 1.

Table 1. Test Data and Operating Conditions.

	Feedstock		
	F_1	F_2	F_3
Net mass (lbs)	235	279	171
Pulper consistency (%)	6	6	6
Pulping, duration (min)	20	25	20
Pulping temperature (°F)	160	160	160
Separator-Deflaker:			
a) Consistency (%)	2.5	2.5	2.5
b) Pressure drop (PSI)	8	8	8
Pressurized screen:			
a) Consistency (%)	0.7	0.7	0.7
b) Pressure drop (PSI)	2	2	2
Centrifugal cleaner:			
a) Consistency (%)	–	0.6	0.6
b) Pressure drop (PSI)	–	40	40

Handsheets and Rejects

Handsheets (8 inch x 8 inch) made from pulper stock (end of the cycle) were: light grayish blue (F_1), grey-brown (F_2) and grey (F_3), respectively. They included the following main contraries: large (up to 1-1/2 inch) shreds of polyethylene bags (F_1), strips of plastic films (up to 3-1/2 inch long) and pieces of plastic straw (F_2), filament-like (3/8 inch) pieces of plastic film (F_3). The pulper rejects were collected and a grab sample dried. Upon inspection, they were found to consist of mostly large (up to 4 inch) pieces of polyethelyne film, water-resistant paper, plastic tape and foamed plastic (F_1 and F_2). No pulper rejects were observed for F_3.

After the separator (BELCOR), the quality of the handsheet improved markedly. Remaining contaminants were: flakes of plastic film, from 1/8 to 1/4 inch in size (F_1, F_2) and fragments of hair (1/4 inch) (F_2). The Belcor-Jonsson rejects were mostly strips of polyethylene and formed plastic beads (F_1, F_2).

The handsheet made from the Finckh screen accepts was the last one made from F_1, and was considered "sufficiently clean" by the WMU specialist. The sheet, of much smoother texture than previously, had less than ten specks of size

1/16 inch on the wire side. For F_2, the Finckh accepts handsheet showed that the pulp had been cleaned of practically all of its contaminants 1/16 inch and up. Rejects from the Finckh screen-flat screen combination consisted principally of hair, aluminum foil and wood sticks, in the 1/8 inch to 1/4 inch size range (F_1); yard waste (3/8 inch) and foamed plastic (1/16 inch) (F_2) or aggregated fibers with specks of aluminum and plastic (F_3).

The TRICLEAN accepts sheet for F_2 was rather smoothe and uniform. Remaining contraries were hair-like filaments (1/8 inch long) and a few beads of foamed plastic (3/64 inch). Heavy rejects appeared to be sand or dirt particles (0.1 mm to 1 mm). Light rejects were 1/16 to 1/8 inch polyethylene flakes, hair and foamed plastic. The final accept sheet for F_3 contained only one 1/8 inch long, 1/32 inch wide plastic fragment. Other specks and dots, about 1/64 inch in size, appeared with a density of at most 1 per square inch.

MASS BALANCE AND YIELDS

Estimates are derived for the yield of cleaned pulp, *per unit mass of feedstock F_i into the pulper.* This yield, Y_i, is accordingly defined as

Y_i = 100 x (mass of cleaned pulp in final chest/input mass of feedstock F_i into the pulper) (percent)

As noted above, i = 1 (Washington, 2 (New Orleans) or 3 (Milwaukee). The overall yield, K_i, from raw waste to cleaned pulp, is:

$$K_i = (D_i Y_i)/100 \quad \text{(percent)}$$

in which D_i is in each case the yield (in percent) of the dry processing scheme leading from raw waste W_i to feedstock F_i.

The weight of paper fibers retained in the rejects on the Jonsson or flat screens was either very small (F_3) or completely negligible compared to the weight of the rejects themselves (F_1, F_2). The same was not true for the Triclean system (centrifugal cleaners), in which the rejects streams, a fixed percentage by weight of the input stream, are a mixture of fibers and contraries. The fiber yield is computed by a loss method, as detailed in Table 2. Estimates for the moisture content, m, of the three feedstocks at the time of pulping was placed by the WMU operators at: 10% (F_1); 10% (F_2); 12% (F_3); all wet basis. Note that the figure for F_2 is within a close range of the moisture level (8%) measured

Table 2. Estimated Yields Per Input Feedstock Ton (Y_i) or Input Waste (K_i).

Rejects at	F_1 (Washington) mass, lbs, bone-dry	% Total	F_2 (New Orleans) mass, lbs, bone-dry	% Total	F_3 (Milwaukee) mass, lbs, bone-dry	% Total
Pulper	39.2	18.5	53.8	21.4	0	0.00
Jonsson (from Belcor)	6.13	2.9	4.24	1.7	0.060	0.24
Flat screen (from Finckh)	0.80	0.4	1.09	0.4	0.076	0.24
Triclean*	–	–	1.12	0.5	0.991	0.58
Total rejects	46.13	21.8	60.25	24.0	1.127	0.66
Input mass	211.5		251.1		150.5	
Yield Y_i,% (input F to cleaned pulp)	78.2		76.0		99.3	
Overall yield K_i (input waste to cleaned pulp)	30.6		18.9[†]		99.3[††]	

*Estimated for primary centrifugal cleaning set at 18% reject rate of the entering material. Includes fiber and dirt.

[†]Assumes 5% oversize bulky material removed prior to flail-milling.

[††]Input waste: commingled newspapers.

for a mixture of the three cyclone products in the Bureau of Mines process.[25]

From the results in Table 2, it is seen that yields, referred to the input feedstock mass, are in the middle to upper seventies for Washington and New Orleans and practically 100% for Milwaukee. They are comparable to, or higher than, those expected from mixed waste-paper used by board mills, where 25% contraries is said to be relatively common. Subject to evaluation in an actual industrial environment, and to some improvements in the dry processing phase, it seems that the range of these fiber yields might be acceptable in a relatively wide range of potential applications.

PAPER MAKING EXPERIMENTS ON WMU 25-INCH FOURDRINIER

The cleaned pulp from each of the three feedstocks was run on the Western Michigan University 25-inch Louis Calder Fourdrinier machine, described elsewhere[27]. In these trials, the stock "P_i" was pumped from the chest to the paper machine at 0.5% consistency. The speed was 80 FPM. The stock formed up readily on the Fourdrinier. It acted like a relatively slow stock, indicative of a somewhat low standard freeness. No attempt was made in these tests to see how fast the stock could be run. Rather, the intent was to concentrate on obtaining a good, even formation which would give reproducible physical properties.

The runs, about 15 minutes in duration each, were described as normal for a relatively slow stock. Three paper rolls were produced with a width of 20 3/4 inch. From these rolls, samples were taken for the determination of the various paper properties; including a bacteriological assay of limited scope.

With all three feedstocks, the sheet behaved well on the machine. It had enough strength to transfer from the belts to the drying section, through the various draws, with no difficulty of any kind and without breaks or holes. These observations on the Fourdrinier are a good omen for the running characteristics of the stocks on a cylinder machine, better suited for slower stock and operating at lower speeds.

The drying proceeded satisfactorily at normal operating temperatures. Although the moisture levels at the output were not recorded, it was the machine operator's experienced judgment that the product had adequately dried before leaving the machine. In all cases, the run was terminated when the chest was depleted.

PROPERTIES OF PAPER SHEETS

Samples from the paper rolls manufactured on the Fourdrinier were used to determine properties. These measurements are bound to be more realistic than those obtained from handsheets, and might be significantly different due to the different characteristics of the draining process in both cases. Accordingly, caution should be used when attempting to compare the results given below with those describing the properties of handsheets of somewhat similar furnishes.

Two types of tests for properties were run: a) mechanical-physical tests (at WMU pilot plant), and b) bacteriological assay at Gillette Research Laboratories, Rockville, MD).

Mechanical-Physical Tests

These tests were performed at the WMU pilot plant laboratory, in accordance to TAPPI: T 227-58, T 403-OS-74, T 233-05-75, T 411-OS-68, T 410-OS-68, T 452-58, T 494-OS-70, T 414-ts-65. The results are given in Tables 3 and 4. Under the specific feedstock, besides the average reading, the range is indicated between parentheses, where relevant.

DISCUSSION

From the fiber length analysis given in Table 4, it is seen that the sample obtained from Washington has a lower percentage of larger fibers (2%) than either from the New Orleans or Milwaukee sources (4%). However, in *breaking length* as well as in *bursting factor*, it does not significantly differ from the Milwaukee sample. The tear factor (49) for Washington is somewhat higher than for New Orleans or Milwaukee (42), possibly indicating a better inter-fiber bonding.

Table 3. Properties of Roll Samples.

Pulp from		F_1 (Washington)	F_2 (New Orleans)	F_3 (Milwaukee)
Property (units)				
Canadian Standard Freeness (milliliter)		225	415	255
Bursting Strength and Range (PSI)		8.5 (6.4 – 11)	7.3 (6.5 – 8)	12.1 (10 – 15.2)
Weight per Unit Area (g/m²), Dry Basis		53.0	72.5	69.2
Bursting Factor, BF (m²/cm²)		11.3	7.1	12.3
Brightness*		50.5	40.5	41
Tensile Strength (kgf/m)	MD** CMD**	170.3 103.9	MD 180.0 CMD 99.3	MD 217.7 CMD 155.7
Breaking Length (m)[†]	MD CMD AV.	3023 1844 2434	MD 2332 CMD 1287 AV. 1809	MD 2955 CMD 2113 AV. 2534
Tear Resistance (grams/ply)	MD CMD AV.	28 24 26	MD 30 CMD 31 AV. 30.5	MD 28 CMD 30 AV. 29
Tear Factor (m²)[††]		49	42	42
Caliper (inch)		0.00424	0.00571	0.00595

*From handsheets
**MD = machine direction: CMD = cross machine direction
[†]W_c = air-dry basis
[††]Only applies to handsheets (T 220-OS-71). However, data reported were measured on roll samples.

Table 4. Fiber Classification (by length) of Roll Samples.

Pulp from	F_1 (Wash.)	F_2 (N.O.)	F_3 (Mil.)
Retained on Tyler Screens Size*			
14 (1.19 mm)	2	4	4
28 (.595 mm)	27	35	30
48 (.297 mm)	22	27	23
100 (.149 mm)	22	20	20
Short Fibers (Balance)**	27	14	23

*Standard T233 OS-75 (Medium-fibered pulps)
**By Difference

In spite of its higher content in long fibers, the New Orleans sample (F_3) fared worst of the three in *bursting factor* and *breaking length*. Its *tear factor* was 42, the same as Milwaukee's. It is conjectured at this stage that the lower strength properties of F_3 could be explained by the relatively larger size "defects" or "impurities" in the sheet (particles of glass, sand, dirt, small plastic flakes). An added step of dry screening with small holes (3/4 inch) prior to pulping might be of help.

Freeness is to a large extent determined by the percentage of fines. The CSF reading was highest for New Orleans (415) due to its much lower percentage of fines (14%), as expected. The freenesses for Washington (225) and Milwaukee (255) were comparable, and in the range expected for waste newsprint.

Brightness measurements were made only for the sake of completeness. Alone among the three samples examined, the Washington roll had a rather pronounced bluish grey color, attributed to the inclusion of carbon paper from office waste. This color explains the higher brightness reading (50.5) compared to New Orleans (40.5) and Milwaukee (41).

The specific masses of the sheets, in g/cm^3 (dry basis) were 0.492 (F_1), 0.500 (F_2) and 0.458 (F_3).

Klungness[26] and Savage et al.[27] reported values for properties of selected pulps or pulps processed from residential wastes. Comparisons are difficult; the results from (27) are for handsheets only. For residential waste, their average figures were: burst factor = 15.6 (m^2/cm^2), tear factor = 13.2 (m^2), breaking length = 2325 m, CSF = 330 ml. However, the average furnish (which was screened light fraction, previously shredded to 90% minus 2 inch) contained 25.6% corrugated and 52.9% newspaper and others, out of a total fiber content of 78.5%. The three feedstocks described here were either all news or mostly news with little corrugated in their fiber content, which, added to the quite different drainage and formation of handsheets, would explain the lower burst factor and much lower tear strength observed. The observations obreaking length are within the same range as those reported[27].

Comparison with (26) for waste paper pulps from newsprint, super mixed, deinked news and spruce groundwood, would indicate that the pulps produced here are quite similar in freeness, burst and tear to 100% deinked newspaper or spruce groundwood (but with lower strength for sample F_2). Addition of a corrugated fraction (handpicked or otherwise recovered) would likely bring the above properties to levels comparable to those of super mixed.

BACTERIOLOGICAL TESTING*

The objective was to evaluate, in a preliminary way, the extent of microbiological contamination of the paper rolls from the mixed waste feedstocks. As controls, an unopened package of ordinary office legal pads was also tested.

For each sample, four 5 cm x 5 cm squares from three locations 15%, 30% and 50% across the width of the roll were cut and placed into a sterile bottle, to which 100 ml Neutralizing Buffer (DIFCO) were added. Culture tests were performed on this Neutralizing Buffer. (The tests performed are briefly described in Appendix B). The results are summarized in Table 5. As could

*Performed by Gillette Research Institute, Rockville, Md.

Table 5. Results From Bacteriological Analysis.

	From edge	Total bacteria	Spore-formers	Cellulolytic bacteria	Molds	Coliforms	Fecal Strep.
				Number of Organisms/cm^2 Paper			
F_1: Washington	− 5 cm	482	57	425	<1	<1	<1
"	− 15 cm	170	111	59	<1	<1	<1
"	− 25 cm	454	318	136	<1	<1	<1
F_2: New Orleans	− 5 cm	1788	1788	<1	<1	<1	<1
"	− 15 cm	2356	2440	<1	1	<1	<1
"	− 25 cm	1873	2214	<1	<1	<1	<1
F_3: Milwaukee	− 5 cm	482	312	170	1	<1	<1
"	− 15 cm	397	397	<1	1	<1	<1
"	− 25 cm	482	454	26	3	<1	<1
Blank: Legal greyboard pad	− 2 cm	15	14	1	<1	−	−
"	− 9 cm	23	7	16	<1	−	−
"	− 16 cm	8	<1	8	<1	−	−

Source: Gillette Research Institute, Rockville, MD (Test Report 09/22/78)

be expected, the "blank" or control contained fewer organisms than any of the samples from mixed waste origin. There was a significant difference between total level for the New Orleans sheet, on one hand, and the Washington and Milwaukee paper, on the other hand. The latter two samples were not significantly different. However, it should be stressed that all of the bacteria in the New Orleans sample were spore-formers.

Molds were absent (New Orleans, Washington) or present in small numbers (Milwaukee). More significantly, no coliform or fecal *Streptococcus* were found in any of the samples.

Alter *et al.* (28) examined the microbiological contamination of post-consumer newsprint. Separately collected paper (A, B) was, among others, compared to commingled dry (C) and commingled wet (E) samples. Whereas E was almost sterile, C had a total count of 520 organisms/cm^2 comparable to the figures given here for Washington (F_1) and Milwaukee (F_3). Nearly all these were cellulolytic organisms (510) with few bacterial spores (6.75).

It is not felt that the presence of bacteria as spore-formers should be a matter of concern in a product which has not undergone any bleaching or cooking at high pH and temperature, or to which no slimicides have been added. On the other hand, bacteriological contamination could be a potential technological barrier in the industrial paper mill environment and the seriousness of this barrier would have to be tested in full scale industrial experiments. At this stage, however, the total absence of fecal *Streptococcus* or coliforms in the product can be construed as an encouraging indication of lack of contamination hazards from this kind of furnish.

POSSIBLE USES IN PAPER MILLS

The present investigation is limited only to the technological barriers to paper recovery. Some of these were evaluated, to a degree, through this limited number of experiments at the pilot scale. Others, such as the logistics of rejects disposal and wastewater treatment become more clearly apparent at the pilot stage. Therefore, the proposed possible uses for the various cleaned pulps are only tentative at this stage.

Further investigation should be at the small-size industrial scale, with proper emphasis put on the various technological constraints, such as power and water consumption, wastes disposal water effluents and biological decontamination. With these reservations in mind, some possible uses for the pulps produced can be proposed.

Regarding all three feedstocks, it can be stated that the decontaminated stocks can be cleaned to the point of being useable for higher grade applications than roofing or flooring felts.

In the case of Washington (F_1), the presence of some carbon paper gave the sheet a blue color. The possibility of staining and/or color changes was mentioned as a drawback. A suggested use is as filler in boxboard type of items (see list under F_2).

As regards New Orleans (F_2), whether or not this material can be considered for liner material in boxboard materials will, to a large extent, depend on whether or not the furnish is contaminated with asphalt and like materials. If the cleaned pulp is reliably asphalt-free, suggested uses would include: liner material or ordinary chipboard for boxboard items (table backs, game boards, record album cases, small hardware boxes, etc.); core stock; grey backing of gypsum or wallboard. If this is not the case, use would be possible as a filler material in boxboard items.

The sample from Milwaukee (F_3), as such, did not meet the quite stringent specifications of recycled news. In addition to possible recycling as news (after upgrading and deinking), other possible uses would be: tissue manufacturing, news portion of back liner on ordinary chip board, core stock, face side of wallboard.

CONCLUSIONS

Based on the technological capabilities and limitations of wet processing equipment, and on selective dry processing approaches designed to be compatible with this equipment, a set of trial experiments was conducted to better understand the complementary aspects of the processes, and evaluate the products obtained.

In these tests, it has been shown — although on a small number of feedstocks and in a pilot plant situation — that most contaminants from a variety of selective "paper fiber concentrates" could be removed by a small number of mechanical steps performed on the fiber suspension. These steps were carried out by machines or devices in actual size, working at realistic industrial through-put rates, and of rather wide availability in paper mills handling mixed wastepaper.

The product cleaned pulps were used to make paper rolls on a pilot scale Fourdrinier machine. Roll sample showed mechanical and physical properties comparable to deinked news and relatively close to a super mixed furnish. Bacteriological assays showed few celluloytic bacteria and no evidence of potentially hazardous microorganisms.

In conclusion, indications are that technological barriers to the reuse of secondary fibers from municipal waste can be surmounted by a judicious blend of dry, front-end processing and wet pulp cleaning, in a feedback mode by which the handling of dry solid waste to extract a paper fraction is to a large extent a function of the availability and capabilities of wastepaper cleaning machinery at the user's plant. Whether this approach is fully successful technologically on a production line, and justified economically at a given location, will only be determined in each particular case by a careful assessment of the feedstock, its source and the potential user, culminating in full scale trial production runs over long periods of time.

ACKNOWLEDGEMENTS

This research was supported by a grant from the National Science Foundation, under Grant No. APR 7513864; Ritchie Coryell, Project Officer. The author wishes to express his thanks for the cooperation of P.M. Sullivan, Supervisory Chemical Engineer (U.S. Bureau of Mines), W. Young (Americology) and M. Stradal (Reed Paper Co.). In running the tests, generating the data and interpreting the results, the contribution of the WMU Pilot Plant staff, especially R.E. Kinsey, was essential and is appreciated.

REFERENCES

1. Renard, M.L. Proc. TAPPI 1978 Pulping/Secondary Fibers Conf., New Orleans, LA, Nov. 5-8, 1978:333-345.
2. Laundrie, J.F., Forest Prod. Lab. Rept. 252, Madison, WI, 1975.
3. Laundrie, J.F., and Klungness, J.H., Forest Prod. Lab. Rept. 200, Madison, WI, 1973.
4. Cederholm, C., Flakt Engineering, 2:2, April 1975.
5. Sullivan, P.M., Stanckzyk, M.H. and Spendlove, J.J., U.S. Bureau of Mines, RI 7760, College Park, MD, 1973.
6. Trezek, G., U.S. EPA Rept. EPA 600/2-77-131, July 1977.
7. Savage, G.M., Diaz, L.F., and Trezek, G., *TAPPI*, 61 (6):15-18, August 1977.
8. Wilson, David G. (Ed.), Handbook of Solid Waste Management, Van Nostrand Reinhold Co., NY, 1977:17.
9. U.S. Environmental Protection Agency, Fourth Report to Congress, Resource Recovery and Waste Reduction, SW-600, Aug. 1, 1977:14.
10. Winkler, P.F. and Wilson, D.C., Compost Sc,: 6-11, Sept.–Oct. 1973.
11. Edison Electric Institute, Solid Waste Task Force, A Compliation of Case Studies of Solid Waste Utilization Projects Involving Investor-Owned Electric Utilities 19, August 1977.
12. Stradal, M., (private communication), November 16, 1977.
13. Alter, H. and Arnold J., Nat. Center for Resource Recovery, Tech, Rept. TR-5, Washington, D.C., July 1978.
14. Alter, H., U.S. EPA Report Grant R80391, Nat. Center for Resource Recovery, Washington, D.C.:12-47, May 1979.
15. Op. cit. (6):71.
16. Bernheisel, F., Bagalman, P. and Parker, W., Proc. 6th Min. Waste Utilities Symposium, U.S. Bureau of Mines, IITRI, Chicago, IL:254-260, May 1978.
17. Warren, J.L., Resource Rec. and Conserv., 3:97-111, 1978.
18. Woodruff, K.L. and Bates, E.P., ASME Proc. 1978, Nat. Waste Proc. Conf:249-261, May 1978.
19. Op. cit. (9):3.
20. Sullivan, P., Test Rept., April 25, 1978.
21. Raymond, D.R., AIChE Sympos. Series, Proc. and Utilization of Forest Products, Nc. 139, Vol. 70:93-98.
22. Duckett, E.J., NCRR Bulletin, Fall 1977, VII, 4.
23. Alter, H., Woodruff, K.L., Fookson, A., Rogers, B., Resource Rec. and Conserv., 2:79-84, 1976.
24. Western Michigan University, Paper Recycling Brochure, Dept. of Paper Sc, and Engrg., Kalamazoo, MI, 1977.
25. Western Michigan University, Pilot Plant Series for Industry Brochure, Dept. of Paper Sc. and Engrg., Kalamazoo, MI, 1977.
26. Klungness, J.H., TAPPI *58* (10):128, 1975.
27. Op. cit. (7):16-17.
28. Op. cit. (23):82.

APPENDIX A
EQUIPMENT USED IN PULPING AND
CLEANING PHASES (WMU)

Pulper: Black-Clawson Hydrapulper, 6 feet diameter, Vokes rotor, 5/8 inch extraction holes, 60 HP drive, 510 RPM

Separator: Jones-Beloit, Belcor, 24 inch diameter, 1/8" extraction holes, 50 HP drive, 900 RPM

Open screen
(vibrating): Bird, Jonsson Model 8, 1/8 inch holes

Pressurized
screen: Bolton-Emerson, Finckh AG, Model 01, 12/1000 inch slits, air foil speed 700–800 RPM

Centrifugal
cleaners: Bird, Triclean, 4 inch diameter, 4 feet high

Flat screen
(vibrating): Make not available, 0.020 inch slots (transverse direction)

APPENDIX B
TASKS PERFORMED
IN BIOLOGICAL ASSAY

a. Total number of bacteria:
Method used: A.O.A.C. spiral plate method (#46.C.10) on Trypticase Soy Agar (BBL) with single TSA four plate count conducted simultaneously for counts between 1 and 300 in the extract. Incubation of plates was at 34°C for 48 hours.

b. Spore-forming bacteria number was determined by heating a portion of the neutralizing buffer extract at 75°C for 15 minutes, then determining the number of viable organisms as above.

c. It is assumed that all bacteria, except spore formers, are capable of degrading cellulose, and the number of celluloytic bacteria is calculated by subtracting the number of spore formers from the total number of bacteria. Mold count is determined as for the total number of bacteria except that Mycophil Agar (BBL) is used instead of TSA. Incubation was at 24°C for 5 days.

d. Testing of the papers was made for coliforms, using Lauryl Sulfate Broth (BBL). Incubation was at 34°C for 48 hours.

e. The papers were also tested for fecal *Streptococcus* using KF Streptococcal Agar (BBL). Incubation was at 34°C for 48 hours.

3-9 Recovery of Ferrous Scrap from Municipal Solid Waste

Rocco A. Petrone

Adapted from a presentation to the International Iron and Steel Institute, XI Annual Conference, Rome, Italy, October 12, 1977. 39 pp. Reprinted with Permission of National Center for Resource Recovery.

INTRODUCTION

This paper discusses the recovery of ferrous scrap, principally metal containers, from municipal solid waste (MSW). For the purpose of this paper, MSW ferrous scrap is defined as the magnetically recoverable fraction of mainly household refuse. Most of this fraction is from steel-based food and beverage cans. MSW ferrous scrap defined in this manner has been found to contain about 80 percent cans (and other light ferrous such as wire, nails, etc.) and 20 percent heavy ferrous (brake shoes, bicycle frames, pipe, etc.) Although both incinerated and unincinerated metals may be considered recoverable, the discussion in this paper primarily concerns the higher quality, unincinerated, MSW ferrous scrap.

As the largest single component of MSW ferrous scrap, metal cans are easily recovered and the technology exists to increase considerably the present recycling rate.

Historical Background. There are several interesting historical facts about the recycling of iron and steel — some dating back to biblical times. In Joel 3:10 there is this admonition, "Cut your ploughshares into swords, and your spades into spears." And one of the greatest prophets of the Old Testament, Isaiah 2:4 said, ". . . and they shall turn their swords into ploughshares and their spears into sickles." In Micah 4:3 ". . . and they shall beat their swords into ploughshares, and their spears into spades." Implicit in these three passages is the universal need to reuse or recycle materials. There is no better example than these to impress upon us the necessity to recycle and reuse as much materials as possible.

While the history of recycling dates back to biblical times, the origin of the steel can dates back less than 200 years. Initially, the utilization of the can grew slowly. With improvements in the technology of metals and metal forming, usage of steel cans increased greatly. This development gave mankind a sanitary, efficient, and economical distribution system that increased the standard of living around the world.

Production of Metal Cans in U.S. Figure 1 shows the growth in the annual production of metal cans produced in the United States since 1950.[1] The table also shows the corresponding number of steel cans produced. The production of metal cans more than doubled between 1950 and 1970 with an eight billion can increase from 1970 to 1975. According to the U. S. Can Manufacturers Institute, steel can production in the U. S. has averaged more than 65 billion each year since 1970. This equates to approximately 5 million tons of steel that are discarded in the municipal solid waste stream each year.

COMPOSITION OF MUNICIPAL SOLID WASTE

According to the United States Environmental Protection Agency (EPA), U. S. households and light commercial sources currently generate about 136 million tons of municipal solid waste annually.[2] Excluded are data on mining, agricultural, industrial processing, demolition and construction wastes, sewage sludge and junked autos. At this time, less than six percent of this post-consumer municipal waste is recovered for productive uses, the remaining 128 million tons being disposed of in the nation's landfills and incinerators.

What is the composition of this waste and what does it contain? It contains food wastes, leaves and lawn clippings . . . old newspapers, magazines and assorted papers . . . food and beverage cans and bottles . . . old clothes and wrappings . . . broken small appliances and toys . . .

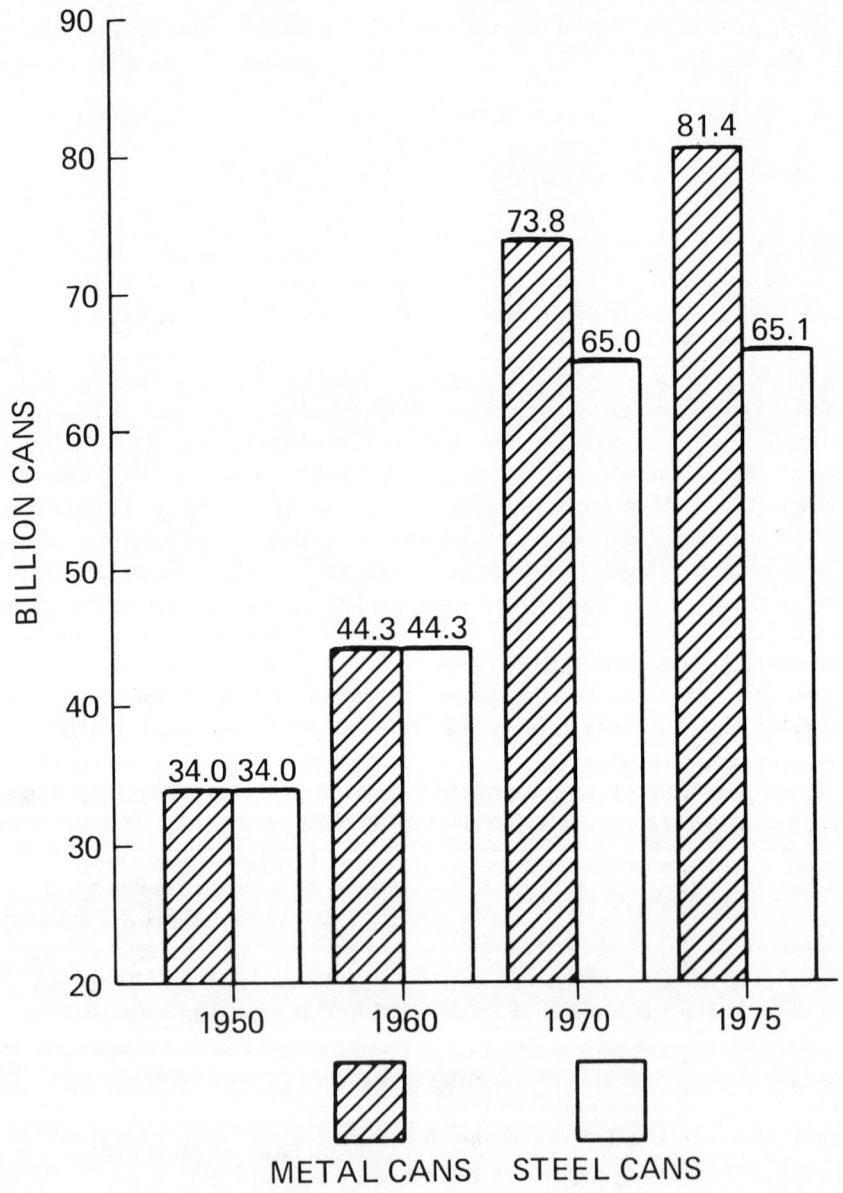

Figure 1. Growth in the annual production of metal cans produced in the U.S. since 1950.

paint cans, cosmetic jars and tubes . . . the residuals of modern-day living.

Figure 2 shows the average composition of municipal solid waste. Metals make up about 10 percent, of which 9 percent are ferrous metals and 1 percent nonferrous.

MSW Ferrous Scrap in Solid Waste. Gross discards of ferrous metals in 1975 were 11 million tons.[3] There were 2 million tons of major household appliances disposed of in 1975. These are usually collected and disposed of or recovered separately, and, as such, do not become part of the normal municipal solid waste stream. This leaves approximately 9 million tons in the municipal solid waste stream which consists of 5.5 million tons of steel cans and 3.5 million tons of

other light and heavy ferrous products. The separation of these ferrous products from the municipal waste stream is the goal of resource recovery through magnetic separation.[4,5,6]

MARKETS

The recovery of ferrous metals from refuse is futile unless someone is willing and able to use what is recovered. This introduces the subject of markets.

In the U. S., the American Iron and Steel Institute (AISI) has identified six major markets or uses for MSW ferrous scrap.[7] These are detinning, copper precipitation, blast furnaces, steelmaking furnaces, iron foundries and ferroally production. These markets and their approxi-

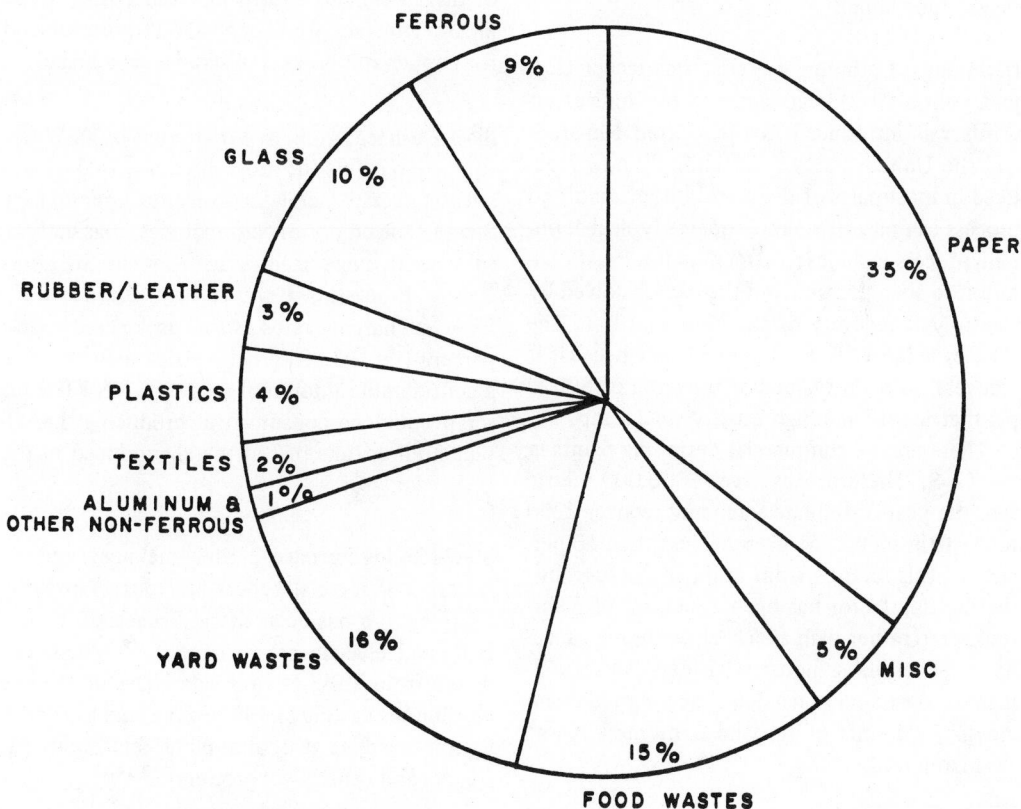

Source: EPA *Fourth Report to Congress,* 1977.

Figure 2. Composition of municipal solid waste (1975).

Table 1. U.S. Markets for Ferrous Scrap.

	Approximate 1975 Consumption (Thousands of Metric Tons)
Detinning	725
Copper Precipitation	450
Blast Furnaces	3,500
Steel-Making Furnaces (purchased scrap only)	24,000
Iron Foundries (purchased scrap only)	6,500
Ferroalloys (includes ferrosilicon only)	270

Source: U. S. Bureau of Mines, Washington, D. C. 1977.

mate use of all forms of purchased ferrous scrap are shown in Table 1. Each market can be reviewed individually.

Detinning. Detinning was first practiced in Germany almost 100 years ago and not long afterwards was introduced in the United Kingdom and the United States.[8] Detinning is now practiced in most parts of the world but primarily to process can-makers scrap. Today's typical detinning process includes treatment in hot caustic solution to strip the tin from the can, followed by electrolytic recovery of tin from solution. The process is ideal for resource recovery because it recovers both tin (valued at upwards of $9000 per metric ton) and high quality steel scrap.

There are 14 commercial detinning plants in the U. S. These process over 7000,000 metric tons per year of tinplate scrap and recover 2200 tons of tin metal. At present, less than 10 percent of this scrap is from municipal refuse, but the limiting factor has been a lack of MSW ferrous scrap rather than a lack of detinning capacity. The detinning industry has expressed a willingness to expand as needed to accommodate increasing amounts of tinplate containers recovered from refuse.*

---

*Note: It has been estimated that it would require a supply of 50,000 tons/year of tinplate scrap (roughly the output from processing 2000 tons/day of municipal solid waste) to justify investment in a new detinning plant.

Copper Precipitation.[9] The copper industry uses light gauge ferrous scrap in the recovery of copper from mining wastes. Overburden and tailings containing as little as 0.1 percent copper are treated with sulfuric acid to form copper sulfate solution. This solution reacts with ferrous scrap causing copper to precipitate. Steel cans provide an excellent source of light gauge iron for copper precipitation. Before the cans are used in the process, however, they must be cleaned of organic contaminants. This is accomplished either in detinning plants or in special plants designed to burn to organics under carefully controlled conditions. Approximately 450,000 metric tons of ferrous scrap are used for copper precipitation each year in the U. S., but only 10 percent of this scrap now comes from municipal refuse. The copper recovered by this method amounts to about 140,000 tons per year or 10 percent of total U. S. copper mine production. The ability of this market to absorb increasing amounts of MSW ferrous scrap will depend on future demand for copper and on overall scrap steel demand.

Blast Furnace.[10] Blast furnace use of MSW ferrous scrap offers the most direct method of substituting scrap metal for iron ore. Granite City Steel (a subsidiary of National Steel) has successfully used nuggetized scrap from the St. Louis Refuse Processing Plant as blast furnace feed. Even at charging rates as low as 1 percent or 2 percent (i.e., 10-20 kg/net metric ton hot metal), a considerable amount of recovered MSW ferrous scrap could be consumed in producing the 90-plus million tons of hot metal produced in the U. S. each year.

Steel-Making Furnaces. Steel-making is still the largest market for all types of ferrous scrap. MSW ferrous scrap has been charged successfully into BOF and electric arc furnaces.[11,12] Steels produced from MSW ferrous scrap have undergone continuous casting and hot rolling and have been used to produce structural plate, reinforcing bar (rebar) and other steel products.[13,14,15]

Iron Foundries.[16,17] Iron foundries appear to be another excellent market for MSW ferrous scrap. Foundries are widely distributed geographically in the U. S. MSW ferrous scrap has been successfully used to produce gray and ductile iron castings. There are more than 2000 foundries in the U. S. consuming about 6.5 million metric tons per year of purchased scrap, but almost none of this comes from municipal waste at this time.

Ferroalloys. One market worthy of mention for the sake of completeness is ferroalloy production, especially the production of ferrosilicon. Although this market is a relatively small scrap consumer (about 270,000 metric tons per year), it has been estimated that up to 75,000 tons per year of MSW ferrous scrap could be consumed in ferroalloy production.[18]

CHARACTERISTICS OF MSW FERROUS SCRAP

Although it is easy to identify potential markets, the far more difficult and important task is to match the needs of these markets with the characteristics of MSW ferrous scrap. The first step in this process is to review the characteristics of MSW ferrous scrap.

As shown in Table 2, the iron yield, metallurgical contaminants and organic contamination of MSW ferrous scrap can be compared with other types of scrap. Naturally, the exact composition of any type of scrap will vary from lot to lot just as the composition or iron ore varies, but the figures shown in Table 2 are reasonable, in our judgment, for the purpose of this discussion.

Iron Yield. The iron yield (i.e., iron content) after melting) for MSW ferrous scrap has generally been reported to be around 90 percent. This

compares favorably with shredded auto scrap (currently the highest priced steel scrap in the U. S.) and is considerably higher than yield figures reported for incinerator residue scrap. High iron yield makes MSW ferrous scrap more useful than incinerator residue scrap for iron- or steelmaking purposes.

Metallurgical Contaminants. Contaminants are of great concern to purchasers of steel scrap. The effects of the major contaminants of MSW ferrous scrap are discussed later in this paper, but the levels of contaminants are shown in Table 2.

Tin content is generally higher for MSW ferrous than for other forms of scrap. The actual tin content of MSW ferrous scrap will vary with the proportion of tinplate cans found in the local refuse. Mechanical recovery processes have little effect on tin content.

Copper content of MSW ferrous scrap is generally low.

Aluminum from the easy-open tops of bimetallic beverage cans is found attached to MSW ferrous scrap but, to some extent, aluminum content is affected by mechanical recovery processes. In general, the finer the shredding before final magnetic recovery, the lower the aluminum content.

Organic Contaminants. Organic contaminants (sometimes called combustibles) include both loose organics (labels, food scraps, etc.) and lacquers applied as part of can construction.

Lacquers represent about 2 percent (by weight) of canstock and are not affected by the usual resource recovery processes. Loose

Table 2. Comparison Among Three Types of Ferrous Scrap (all amounts shown as percent by weight).

	MSW Ferrous Scrap	Incinerator Residue Scrap	Shredded Auto
Iron Yield	90+	60	90+
Metallurgical Contaminants			
Tin	0.3	0.2	0.03
Copper	0.1	0.25	0.01
Aluminum	2	–	0.01
Organic Contaminants			
(loose and lacquers)	4	–	–

Source: National Center for Resource Recovery, Inc., unpublished review of several reported analyses. 1977

organics, however, can be controlled by variations in shredding, air classification and/or magnetic recovery. Research conducted at the NCRR pilot plant in Washington, D. C. indicates that a goal of 2 percent loose organic contamination can be achieved realistically.

To summarize Table 2, the major characteristics of MSW ferrous scrap are that: its iron yield is quite high relative to incinerator residue scrap; its copper content is less than incinerator residue or auto scrap; and its tin and aluminum content are notably higher than other forms of scrap. Organic contamination is dependent on the degree of processing during recovery but is generally higher for MSW ferrous scrap than for the other forms of scrap. The high iron content is a definite plus for this scrap as a competitive source of iron units; the low copper content provides an advantage over auto scrap; but the tin, aluminum, and organic contaminants merit special discussion.

Effect of Contaminants. The NCRR has recently published a series of reports on the problems of tin, aluminum and organic materials as contaminants of MSW ferrous scrap.[19,20,21] In preparing these reports, the Center reviewed the metallurgical literature and consulted with experienced persons from steel companies, iron foundries, scrap processors, detinners and governmental agencies such as the U. S. Bureau of Mines and the U. S. National Bureau of Standards. After searching the literature and listening to the review comments of those in the industry, several conclusions can be drawn about the effects of tin, aluminum and organic contaminants on the reuse of MSW ferrous scrap.

Tin is known to affect the properties of iron and steel products.[19] Tin has been shown to reduce ductility and impact toughness and, in combination with copper, to induce hot shortness (or edge cracking) during hot rolling. The NCRR report on tin concludes that although some cast iron (e.g., malleable iron) and some steels (e.g., rotor steels) can tolerate almost no tin, there are large tonnages of other iron and steel products (e.g., gray iron castings or structural steels) which can tolerate tin in the amounts likely to result from use of MSW ferrous scrap.

Table 3. Tolerances for Tin Among Potential Uses for MSW Ferrous Scrap.

Potential Use	% Tin Limit*
Iron	
Gray	.1
Ductile (Pearlitic)	.06
Malleable	.02
(fully annealed)	(.08)
Steel	
Concrete Reinforcing Bar	.1
Structural	.1
Sheet	.02
Rotor	.02

*Sources: See Reference No. 19.

Table 3 lists tolerances for tin among some major iron and steel products. The level shown for gray iron (0.1 percent) has actually been shown to be beneficial for this type of castings. The tin levels shown for structural steel and for reinforcing bar are based on successful production of these types of steel with upwards of 0.1 percent tin content.[22,23]

Actual tin residuals in iron and steel products will vary with scrap charging rates, tin content of the scrap and so forth. To give some idea of the magnitude of tin residuals, national scrap statistics from the U. S. can be cited. In 1975, total U. S. ferrous scrap purchases for steel production were about 28 million metric tons. If all the tinplate and tin-free steel used for packaging that year (4.2 million metric tons) had been recovered and used in steel-making without detinning, MSW ferrous scrap would have accounted for only 15 percent of purchased scrap. A 15 percent charge of MSW ferrous scrap (0.3 percent tin) and an 85 percent charge of other purchased scrap (reported average tin content of 0.03 percent) into an electric furnace would yield a steel product with at most 0.07 percent tin — which is below the listed limits for structural steel or rebar. This analysis is extremely conservative because complete recovery of the steel discarded in MSW is unrealistic, and much, if not most, MSW ferrous scrap will be detinned prior to use in steel-making.

At this point, one might agree that MSW ferrous scrap would work well for gray iron foundries or rebar producing mini-mills but wonder how the scrap can be used in an integrated mill which may produce products ranging from rotor steels to rebar. In an integrated mill the scrap specifications are understandably aimed at the most sensitive mill product (in this case, rotor steel) in order to assure that contaminants like tin do not find their way into the specialty products. A solution to the integrated mill problem is different techniques of scrap management, that is, improved methods for keeping track of residuals in both purchased scrap and revert scrap. Better scrap management will be a major challenge to the iron and steel industry as it attempts to make use of MSW ferrous and other less expensive grades of scrap without sacrificing product quality.

Another contaminant of recovered MSW ferrous scrap is aluminum, but aluminum poses different problems than tin.[20] In detinning, aluminum is quite reactive with the caustic solution, thus consuming chemicals, causing foam, and adding to processing costs. Detinners have developed techniques for coping with aluminum, and thus aluminum is not a barrier to the detinning of MSW ferrous scrap, although detinners may apply price reductions based on aluminum content.

When MSW ferrous scrap is used without detinning, steel mills may experience minor changes in slag chemistry al aluminum oxidizes and reports to the slag. The oxidation of aluminum in steel-making furnaces effectively eliminates the aluminum contribution from MSW ferrous scrap as a metallurgical contaminant in the finished steel.

There has been some concern in the literature about the pinholing that could occur in iron castings if aluminum were not completely oxidized in the cupola. It has been shown that at least 85 percent of the aluminum will oxidize during normal cupola operation, and that scrap preheating or increased scrap/coke ratios can increase this oxidation percentage.[24] Also, changes in mold materials have been shown to reduce pinholing among iron castings made from MSW ferrous scrap.[25]

Organic contaminants including loose organics and lacquers used as can coatings may have some minor effects on the reuse of MSW ferrous scrap.[21] Organic contaminants lower the yield of available metal per ton of scrap and can also consume caustic chemicals during detinning. The consensus among potential users seems to be that these problems are not major limitations on the use of MSW ferrous scrap.

Specifications. Probably the best evidence that contaminant problems can be overcome is the development of consensus specificstions for MSW ferrous scrap (and other recovered materials) that is taking place within the American Society for Testing and Materials (ASTM) Technical Committee E-38 on Resource Recovery. This committee includes 180 members representing producers, users, researchers and regulators of recovered materials and fuels. Participation on the committee is entirely voluntary as is the use of any specifications produced. ASTM specifications are well regarded both within and outside of American industry.

The ASTM specifications for MSW ferrous scrap proposed by the Ferrous Metals Subcommittee are currently undergoing balloting within the committee so it would be premature to review any specific compositional limits. It can be reported that separate specifications have been prepared for each of the various markets. That is, there are specifications for detinning, copper precipitation, iron foundries, ferroalloy production and a combination specification for blast furnace and steel-making use. Hopefully, these will be published as tentative ASTM specifications by the end of the year.

SUMMARY

Although much remains to be done to increase the amount of ferrous scrap recovered from MSW, there is ample cause for optimism about the future of resource recovery in general and ferrous metals recovery in particular.

The costs of solid waste disposal in an environmentally sound manner are increasing. This factor, along with the potential revenue from material and energy recovery, is serving to stimulate additional resource recovery plant capacity in the United States.

The iron units available from MSW ferrous scrap are being recognized as a valuable resource for iron- and steel-making. Steel-making from ferrous scrap consumes only 15 to 25 percent of the energy needed to make steel from virgin ore.[26]

Specifications for potential markets for MSW ferrous scrap are being developed through the voluntary consensus process under the ASTM auspices.

Perhaps the best reason for optimism is that resource recovery seems to be maturing as an industry. The industry has begun to make the transfer from theory to practice and in the process is developing confidence in its ability to recover energy and reusable materials from refuse. In the long run, resource recovery not only makes good environmental sense but good business sense as well.

REFERENCES

1. Can Manufacturers Institute, "Metal Cans Shipments Report 1976," Washington, D. C., 1977. 8 p.

2. U. S. Environmental Protection Agency, Office of Solid Waste, "Resource Recovery and Waste Reduction; Fourth Report to Congress." Environmental Protection Publication SW-600, Washington, D. C., U. S. Government Printing Office, 1977. (In press.)

3. U. S. Environmental Protection Agency, Office of Solid Waste, "Resource Recovery and Waste Reduction; Fourth Report to Congress," Chapter 2, Table 4. Environmental Protection Publication SW-600, Washington, D. C., U. S. Government Printing Office, 1977. (In press.)

4. Alter, Harvey; Natof, Stuart L.; Woodruff, Kenneth L.; and Hagen, Ronald D., "The Recovery of Magnetic Metals from Municipal Solid Waste," National Center for Resource Recovery, Inc., Washington, D. C., July 1977. 64 p.

5. National Center for Resource Recovery, Inc., "Resource Recovery Activities . . . A Status Report," *Resource Recovery Briefs,* Washington, D. C., May 1977. 4p.

6. National Center for Resource Recovery, Inc., "Steps to Resource Recovery for the I-95 Complex," Washington, D. C., April 1976. Prepared for the Metropolitan Washington Waste Management Agency (A Subsidiary of Metropolitan Washington Council of Governments). 28 p.

7. American Iron and Steel Institute, Committee of Tin Mill Products Producers, "Progress Report on Recycling," Washington, D. C., 1975. 8 p.

8. Linley, B.D., "Tinplate Recycling," *Resource Recovery and Conservation,* Vol. 3, No. 2, pp. 225-226, 1977.

9. Schroeder, H. J., U. S. Bureau of Mines, Washington, D. C. Personal communication, June 16, 1977.

10. Ostrowski, E.J., "The Bright Outlook for Recycling Ferrous Scrap From Solid Waste." Presented at the American Institute of Chemical Engineers meeting, Boston, Mass., April 1975.

11. Ostrowski, E.J., "Recycling of Tin Free Steel Cans, Tin Cans and Scrap From Municipal Incinerator Residue." Presented at the 79th General Meeting of the American Iron and Steel Institute, New York, N. Y., May 26, 1971.

12. Ostrowski, E.J., "Evaluation of Municipal Solid Waste Ferrous Scrap From St. Louis Resource Recovery System in the Florida Steel Tampa Works Electric Furnace." Unpublished Internal Report, National Steel Corp., Weirton, W. Va., 1975. 27 p.

13. Copeland, M.I.; Howe, J.S.; and Sarvis, J.C., "Effect of Copper and Tin on Mechanical Properties of Hot-Rolled 0.2 Wt-Pct Carbon Steels." Report of Investigations No. 8183, U. S. Bureau of Mines, Washington, D. C., 1976.

14. Hunter, W.L., "Steel From Urban Waste." Report of Investigations No. 8147, U. S. Bureau of Mines, Washington, D. C., 1976.

15. Makar, H.V.; Kaplan, R.S.; and Janowski, L.; "Evaluation of Steel Made With Ferrous Fractions From Urban Refuse." Report of Investigations No. 8037, U. S. Bureau of Mines, Washington, D. C., 1975.

16. Helmink, R.C.; Ruff, G.F.; and Wallace, J.F., "Ferrous Metal From Municipal Wastes As Charge Material for Cast Iron." American Foundrymen's Society Transactions, Vol. 82, pp. 525-534, 1974.

17. Helmink, R.C.; Ruff, G.F.; and Wallace, J.F., "Further Studies on Ferrous Metal From Municipal Waste As a Charge Material For Cast Iron." American Foundrymen's Society Transactions, 1975.

18. American Iron and Steel Institute, Committee of Tin Mill Products Producers, "Progress Report on Recycling," Washington, D. C., 1975. 8 p.

19. Duckett, E. Joseph, "The Influence of Tin Content on the Reuse of Magnetic Metals Recovered From Municipal Solid Waste," *Resource Recovery and Conservation,* Vol. 3, 1977. (In press.)

20. Duckett, E. Joseph, "The Influence of Aluminum Content on the Reuse of Magnetic Metals Recovered From Municipal Solid Waste," National Center for Resource Recovery, Inc., Washington, D. C., 1977.

21. Duckett, E. Joseph, "The Influence of Organic Content on the Reuse of Magnetic Metals Recovered From Municipal Solid Waste," National Center for Resource Recovery, Inc., Washington, D. C., 1977.

22. Copeland, M.I.; Howe, J.S.; and Sarvis, J.C., "Effect of Copper and Tin on Mechanical Properties

of Hot-Rolled 0.2 Wt-Pct Carbon Steels." Report of Investigations No. 8183, U. S. Bureau of Mines, Washington, D. C. 1976.

23. Hunter, W.L., "Steel From Urban Waste." Report of Investigations No. 8147, U. S. Bureau of Mines, Washington, D. C. 1976.

24. Daellenbach, C.B.; Lindeke, R.R.; and Mahan, W.M., "Utilization of Refuse Scrap in Cupola Gray Iron Production." Proceedings of the Fifth Mineral Waste Utilization Symposium, cosponsored by the U. S. Bureau of Mines and IIT Research Institute, Chicago, Ill., April 13, 14, 1976.

25. Helmink, R.C.; Ruff, G.F.; and Wallace, J.F., "Ferrous Metal From Municipal Wastes As Charge Material for Cast Iron." American Foundrymen's Society Transactions, 1974.

26. Franklin, W.E., et al; "Potential Energy Conservation From Recycling Metals in Urban Solid Waste," in The Energy Conservation Papers. R.H. Williams, editor, Ballinger Publishing Co., Cambridge, Mass. pp. 171-217, 1975.

3-10 Aluminum Recovery: A Status Report

James Abert

Source: *NCRR Bulletin,* Part 1, Vol. VII, No. 2 (Spring 1977), pp. 37–45; Part 2, Vol. VII, No. 3 (Summer 1977), pp. 68–72. Reprinted with Permission of National Center for Resource Recovery.

Aluminum is the most abundant metal and the third most abundant element in the earth's crust. It was actually one of the first materials used by man, though not in its metallic form. When pottery began to be used by the ancient civilizations in northern Iraq around 5300 B.C., clay consisting largely of hydrated silicate of aluminum was used to produce the finest wares. Certain other aluminum compounds such as the "alums" were widely used by the Egyptians and Babylonians as early as 2000 B.C. in chemical processes, vegetable dyes and medicines.

Despite this long association with man, it took 7000 years before this metal could be separated from the clay, because of the tenacious bond between aluminum and oxygen. It was not until the 1850's that aluminum was isolated in any measurable quantities. The process developed by SainteClair Peville produced aluminum by heating sodium and aluminum chloride, but this approach proved too expensive for the widespread use of the metal. Aluminum's true versatility could not be exploited until 1886 when Charles Martin Hall and Paul T. Heroult, working independently in the United States and France, discovered an electrolytic process to separate aluminum from its bonded oxygen. This basic process, which is still used today, is the foundation of all aluminum refining.

The aluminum industry is the youngest of the major nonferrous metal industries. It has had one of the fastest growth rates of any industry. In 1939, the U.S. primary aluminum industry consisted of only one firm, which turned out less than 164,000 tons of metal that year. Today, 12 domestic producers ship approximately 6.4 million tons per year.[1] This amounts to a 40-fold increase in a span of 37 years, or an average annual growth in excess of 100 percent per year in relation to the base year amount.

Aluminum products discarded after use are one component of what has been called "urban ore," or the materials used and then discarded by consumers as waste. Economic considerations both encourage and discourage the recycling of these discards. One aspect of this is the differential between the cost of producing a finished product from virgin material and its cost if recycled material is used. This is particularly true in the case of aluminum. Although aluminum is only a small (about one percent) proportion of post-consumer waste, the economic incentives to recycle it are large — in fact, according to the Aluminum Association, it takes only five percent as much energy to provide a pound of aluminum from scrap as it takes to produce it from virgin sources.[2] In 1975, an amount equivalent to approximately eight percent of domestic primary aluminum production was recycled with the scrap being reclaimed from post-consumer sources and an additional 22 percent from new scrap sources.[3] With rapidly increasing costs of plants and equipment, energy and raw materials providing increased incentives for recycling aluminum, a rapid increase in recycling is predicted. This article looks at the methods by which present day aluminum recycling is accomplished and looks at prospects for the future. The technologies range from household separation, which might be called presorting, to eddy current classification followed by air knife cleanup.[4]

ALUMINUM IN REFUSE

Although small in absolute amount, aluminum is still the principal nonferrous metal found in municipal solid waste. In some instances, it accounts for as much as 90 percent of the total nonmagnetic metal content. The remainder is a diverse mixture of red and white metals, principally copper and zinc alloys. However, the amount of aluminum in the refuse varies widely from a low of around 0.5 percent to slightly more than 1.0 percent by weight. The other nonmagnetic metals constitute about 0.2 to 0.4 percent. The amount of aluminum is dependent on the extent to which aluminum cans are used for metal beverage packages in a community. If this were the case, for 50 percent of the overall market, the aluminum percentage would be close to 1.0 percent; *i.e.,* it would be on the high side of the range and the predominant nonmagnetic metal would be aluminum.[5] In addition to beverage cans, discarded aluminum comes from such sources as light foil, rigid foil items like frozen dinner trays, packaging (other than beverage containers), lawn furniture and various kinds of castings, including automobile parts. In addition, there may also be turnings and trimmings from small manufacturing facilities and even discarded siding, storm doors and windows.

While there are more than 200 recognized and registered aluminum alloys, the various products fall into two general classifications: *wrought* and *cast.* Unfortunately from a recycling standpoint, there are sharp differences in the chemical composition of the wrought and the casting alloys. Aluminum targeted for reuse in wrought products must have originally been used for that purpose. The metallurgy of the cast alloys makes them unsuitable for wrought and to a large extent the reverse is true, although a principal penalty paid for using wrought metal for castings is in the economic return. A high-quality wrought scrap generally is worth more than a casting scrap, although it is a mistake to portray casting alloys as "off-spec" wrought. They have specifications which are "tight" in their own right; some are even more costly to produce. Off-specification wrought is more like a junk ingot to be used for de-ox metal or blending in wrought or cast metals.[6] Because of this, the objective of aluminum recycling is to recover aluminum in two separate forms. The first consists principally of packaging, such as beverage containers and rigid foil, for reuse in wrought products which, as one might suspect, is the product classification of the original beverage cans. The second recovery target is the remainder of the aluminum principally for blending, as previously described.[7]

For several reasons, the aluminum must be in a form with a low surface-to-volume ratio (a high bulk density); hence, it must be either baled, briquetted or shredded. One concern is to reduce transportation costs. Unless it is compact, truck and railcar load capacities can not be effectively utilized. A second reason, and this depends on the technology of the melt process, is to avoid melt loss during remelting. The more modern techniques, such as exterior well, salt immersion, can utilize shredded material. A shredded product reduces the potential for trapped moisture. Older style open hearths perform a more efficient remelt if the material is baled or briquetted. However, if the material is very small (less than 12 mesh, for example), there will simply be excessive losses in the remelting regardless of approach. Hence, there is little reason to pay to ship fines in this size range to the remelt facility. The processing steps used to effect the recovery of the metal should seek to avoid the production of large quantities of fines; those that are produced should be screened out prior to shipment.

Organic materials in the recovered scrap also present a problem, because carbon does not alloy with aluminum and hence will burn off in the remelt furnace. This either (1) creates an additional load on the air pollution control equipment, or (2) finds its way into the dross, which is the industry term for slag. In both cases, organic materials are contaminants and add to processing costs.

Sand, grit and glass also cause problems. They also result in an increase in the dross and the larger pieces end up in the bottom of the melt, causing both an increase in fuel consumption and a decrease in furnace capacity. Iron and copper will alloy at the melt temperature, possibly causing the end product to be off specification. Therefore, such contamination must be kept low. The next section discusses target specifications for recovered aluminum.

SPECIFICATIONS

Previously, the distinction was made between wrought or cast reuse prospects. In general, because the wrought material is more costly to make, it brings the highest prices in the scrap market. As one would expect, it is also the more difficult specification to which to produce the recovered material. Although most scrap specifications are based on the source of the metal — i.e., industrial process rather than municipal refuse — a report prepared by NCRR for the U.S. Environmental Protection Agency (EPA) sets forth a target cast and secondary alloy product specification given in chemical composition limits.[8] This is reproduced in Table 1. The reader can contrast this specification with the three grades of recovered aluminum given in Table 2. The first of these is a wrought product; the second is a slightly off-grade wrought material that would require significant

Table 1. Chemical Composition Limits for Recovered Aluminum: Target Specification for Possible Reuse in Cast and Secondary Alloy Products.

	Maximum Weight
Si	1.00%
Fe	1.00
Cu	2.00
Mn	1.50
Mg	2.00
Cr	0.30
Zn	2.00
Pb	0.30
Sn	0.50
Others	0.12*
Fines	3.00
Aluminum	remainder

*Less than 0.04% each.

Source: U.S. Environmental Protection Agency, *Specifications for Materials Recovered from Municipal Refuse*, No. 670/2-75-034 (May 1975), p. 51.

dilution with new metal in the remelt process; and the third moves even further from the wrought target.[9] In terms of revenue, failing to meet the first specifications but meeting the third results in a 33 1/3 percent reduction in the price paid for the recovered material.

Table 2. Chemical Composition Limits for Recovered Aluminum: Target Specifications for Possible Reuse in Wrought Products.

	Maximum Weight		
	No. 1	No. 2	No. 3
Si	0.30%	0.65%	1.00%
Fe	0.70	0.85	1.00
Cu	0.25	0.65	1.00
Mn	1.50	1.50	1.50
Mg	2.00	2.00	2.00
Cr	0.10	0.10	0.30
Ni	0.05	0.10	0.30
Zn	0.25	0.65	1.00
Ti	0.05	0.05	0.05
Bi	0.02	0.03	0.30
Pb	0.02	0.03	0.30
Sn	0.02	0.03	0.30
Others — each	0.04	0.04	0.05
Others — total	0.12%	0.15%	0.15%
Aluminum	remainder	remainder	remainder

Source: Letter of Intent for Recovery 1, New Orleans, La., from Reynolds Metals Co. Other buyers of recovered aluminum may have varying specifications and pricing formulas.

For the target specifications given in Table 2, there are also some other conditions: (1) fines (under 12 mesh) must not exceed three percent of the gross weight of a shipment or else there will be a reduction in the price paid; (2) if the finished product is baled, it must have a minimum density of 30 lbs./cu. ft., or if shipped in a shredded condition, the material must have a density of 15-to-25 lbs./cu. ft.; (3) organics and other nonmetals must be controlled so that the melt will yield a net weight figure of at least 85 percent of the original shipment sampled and measured on an assay basis. "Deduct" clauses apply if this target is not met. For specifications of this type, typically this is about one-half cent a pound for melt yields in the 80-to-85 percent range, and two cents a pound for yields from 75-to-80 percent. The chemical analysis in the table applies to the material after the melt. For household separated aluminum packaging, on average, about 87 percent by weight of each shipment is realized as metal ready for reuse. The weight loss is either inherent in the remelt process itself or incurred because some material was not metal to begin with, but rather lacquer and sealant on the cans or organics or other non-aluminum contaminants. There is also loss caused by adherent moisture. It is clear, then, that free organics have to be kept low — two percent is the target figure and this is included in some specifications for the recycled material — in order to meet the aftermelt target given here of a minimum of 85 percent metal. Also, the proportion of fines is directly and exponentially correlated with higher process losses. The same sort of increasing direct correlation exists as organics rise. Therefore, as with fines, lower levels of organics are more desirable and this discussion should be seen as encouragement to decrease organics and fines when it can be accomplished in order to achieve the most favorable pricing structure.[10]

SOURCE SEPARATION

Source separation or consumer recycling depends on the setting aside of recyclable waste materials at the source of generation by the generator, after which these discards must be transported either directly to the end user or to some intermediate collection point. While initial transportation is usually provided by the generator (householder), public or private collection vehicles may be used. The standard intermediate point is a collection or "recycling center." This is often a point of assemblage for several materials — paper, glass, steel cans and aluminum. In the case of aluminum, that industry operates or sponsors more than 2100 collection centers, some of which are mobile, truck-mounted facilities.[11] As a result of this effort, it is estimated that *one out of every four* aluminum beverage cans sold in 1975 was recycled.[12]

A variant on the householder delivery approach, which is the mainstay of the pre-sorting approach, is multi-material separation at the source with a common, but compart-mentalized, pickup. These multi-material household separation systems, such as the two being tested in Somerville and Marble-head, Mass., require some processing. The basic plan is that the ferrous metals, aluminum and glass are collected in one container and taken to a processing point. There, the ferrous is magnetically separated. The remaining glass and aluminum is then subjected to an impacting device. The glass, being friable, is broken into small pieces; the aluminum, being malleable, is simply dented or bent, but not broken. The glass, which then is in small particles, is screened out and delivered to a centralized processing facility for further cleanup. The aluminum, mostly can scrap, is delivered for remelt.[13]

MECHANICAL PROCESSING FOR ALUMINUM RECOVERY

Initial Classification and Concentration

For the most part, technology-based aluminum recovery systems require an initial size-reduction step followed by several unit processes designed to produce an aluminum — or, more accurately, a non-ferrous — concentrate. The latter generally is a mixture free of magnetic materials although it contains such heavy organics as wood, rubber, rags, etc. Most of the light organics — paper, food wastes, yard trimmings and film plastic — will have been removed in one or more air classification steps after initial size reduction. The key to air classifier efficiency is sensitivity or, put differently, the ability to distinguish between aluminum and other contaminating materials with similar characteristics. The purpose of air classification is to separate the light organics from the metals and glass. In air classifier terminology, the lights "fly" and the heavies "drop." The difficulty with aluminum, from an air classification perspective, is that it is light. Also, some of the shapes of the aluminum in the waste tend to have airfoil characteristics which cause them to fly. As a result, there is a very real trade-off in the air classifier operation. High air velocities blow out the lights more efficiently and reduce the organic concentration of the heavy fraction, making the later recovery of aluminum, that correctly reports to the heavies, easier. However, increased air velocity also flies more aluminum, which is then lost to the aluminum processing equipment. Air classifier manufacturers have produced classifiers of different shapes with various types of baffling and residence times within the separation area in an attempt to better separate organics (combustibles) and inorganics (noncombustibles), while reducing aluminum (and glass) carry-over to the light fraction. The combustible/noncombustible terminology is used here to highlight what is perhaps the dominant influence in the design of most air-classification systems: to improve the characteristics of the lights as fuel. Metal and glass in the light fraction are clearly undesirable, as both raise the ash content of the fuel.[14]

Either after or before air classification, the magnetic materials are removed. Often there are several stages of magnetic separation. There are two reasons for this: (1) in general, the aluminum separation equipment cannot tolerate magnetic metals to any large degree; and (2) even small traces of ferrous metal in the final product is a contaminant in terms of meeting the higher value product specifications. For example, the highest valued specification discussed previously only allows for 0.70 percent by weight of ferrous.

Since there is bound to be some ferrous in the chemical composition of the recovered aluminum mix, every effort should be made to remove free ferrous, or that which is uncombined either physically or chemically. Therefore, the concentrate entering the aluminum recovery unit processing segment of the recovery facility is composed of refuse heavy enough to fall in the air classifier and essentially is free of magnetics. There will not be much light aluminum foil because most of this material will have flown in the air classifier along with most of the pull tabs. There will be some rigid foil containers and balled household foil in the heavies. Aluminum ends of bimetal cans — unless they were separated from the steel body of the can in the initial size-reduction step — will have been removed by the ferrous magnet. As separation of the steel can body from the aluminum can lid generally does not occur unless the shredding

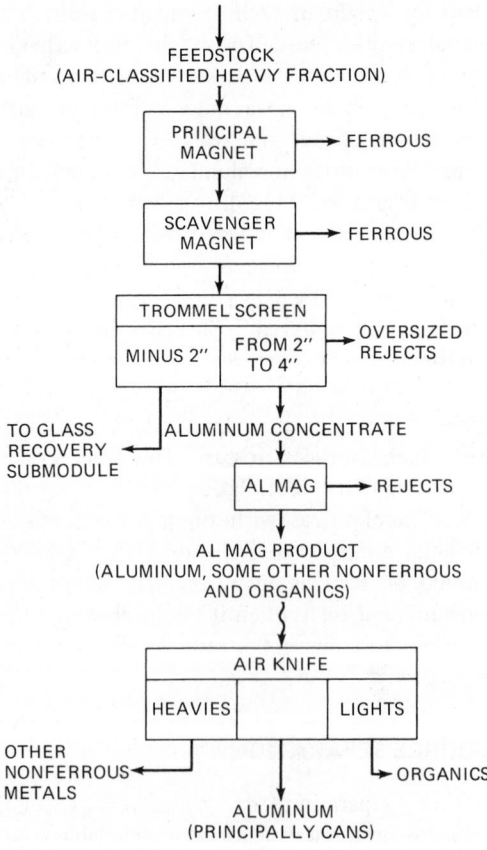

Figure 1. Aluminum recovery submodule at NCRR equipment test and evaluation facility, Washington, D.C.

is to small particle sizes (which is costly), the bulk of the aluminum ends of steel cans are not available for recovery as aluminum; rather, they are a contaminant of sorts in the steel. When the initial size-reduction step is accomplished through hydrapulping, the aluminum recovery operates somewhat differently, as there is no air-classification step. This is discussed later.

"Al Mag" Separator with Air Knife Cleanup

The "aluminum magnet" or "Al Mag" system, manufactured by Combustion Power Co., is a dry method of separation based on the principle that metals passing through an electromagnetic field generate an electric current in each piece of metal. These "eddy currents" have a magnetic moment, or force, which can be phased to repel the magnetic moment of the applied field. Separation occurs because of the repulsion and the nonferrous materials in the concentrate are expelled from the waste. The target is aluminum cans, with the objective of recovering a product which will conform to the highest grade wrought specification. Unfortunately, the device, like all the machines discussed here, is not sufficiently sensitive to completely differentiate among aluminum cans and other nonferrous shapes. The eddy current generated — for example in a smaller but more dense piece of die cast — may be the same as that developed by the movement in the field of a less dense but larger aluminum shape, i.e., a twisted three-quarter inch piece of an aluminum can. The physical laws governing the operation of the device will repel both, or neither, but will not distinguish between the two. Later processing and different principles must be used. Also, when thrown — the nonferrous metals are literally thrust out of the waste stream — certain organics, such as pieces of textiles caught on the aluminum, tend to get carried along. These too must be later separated as the amount is greater than the organics allowed for by the specification.

There are two installations currently piloting the Combustion Power Co. Al Mag and a third in New Orleans (Recovery 1) is due to come on line shortly. The two aluminum recovery pilot plants presently in operation are Ames, Iowa,

and the National Center's Equipment Test and Evaluation Facility (ETEF) in Washington, D.C. Figure 1 shows the flow for the aluminum recovery submodule at ETEF. At ETEF, the heavy fraction of the air classifier (between 30 and 40 percent of the input waste by weight) is targeted to contain roughly 60-to-70 percent of the original aluminum in the stream. This is because the Washington area is high in aluminum cans. Hence, the bulk of the aluminum in the heavies would be aluminum cans. The other 30-to-40 percent of the initial aluminum content of the waste would be lost to the light fraction. A portion of this could be cans as well, particularly pieces of cans that have been torn apart in the initial shredding step.[15] From the air classifier, the heavy fraction passes by a magnet, which removes more than 90 percent of the magnetic material. The remaining material enters the aluminum recovery subsystem.

The first operation in the Al Mag system is the removal of the additional ferrous material, i.e., that which escaped the earlier magnets. The remainder of the material then passes into a two-stage trommel screen. The trommel screen is a rotating drum three feet in diameter and eight feet in length, operating at 11 rpm. The first four feet of the screen consists of holes two inches in diameter and the second four feet consists of holes four inches in diameter. The minus-two is a glass-rich fraction, which at ETEF is directed to the glass recovery subsystem. The two-to-four-inch material is the initial aluminum concentrate, containing aluminum cans and other heavy material in this size range, along with some organics. The plus-four-inch material goes through the drum and exits as a reject. It generally consists of magazines and damp balled paper as well as plastic bottles and wood and rubber products which have escaped the tearing and crushing action of the shredder.

The Al Mag is fed with the two-to-four-inch fraction and attempts the split between aluminum and the other materials as described earlier. The Al Mag residue is made up of paper, heavy plastics, some wood, pieces of shoes and generally other items which are not recyclable. This is about three percent of the waste as originally fed to the shredder. The Al Mag utilizes four pairs of water-cooled electromagnets arranged about a 24-inch-wide conveyor. Magnets are arranged so that two pairs of magnets cover each half of the belt (see Figure 2). The first two pairs remove material from one-half of the belt, while the other two pairs are located adjacent, but downstream to the first pair, and remove material from the other half of the belt. The air gap between the top and bottom portion of the magnets can be varied. Most of the ETEF test work has been with either a 3 1/2 inch or 4 1/2 inch gap distance.

The magnets utilize three-phase, 460-volt power. Power consumption is about 22 kilowatts. The magnets are sequentially switched off at 45 second intervals for about five seconds each to prevent any tramp magnetic metals, which escaped the earlier separation steps, from becoming entrapped and constricting the flow of material on the belt. The electromagnets are water cooled, using a water flow of about 160 gallons per hour. At this flow, the water gains about 70°F in cooling the magnets.

The conveyor belt speed is variable up to 400 feet per minute. Most of the test work has utilized belt speeds in the 170-to-300 range. The belt is a slider-type configuration of 0.04-inch-thick nylon with a stainless steel splice.

Efficiency and product contamination are important. Al Mag efficiency has been measured as high as 99 percent at a 0.07-ton-per-hour feedrate of the two-to-four-inch fraction and 150-feet-per-minute belt speed to 66 percent at a 1.9-ton-per-hour feedrate and a 320-feet-per-minute belt speed. These measurements were taken on native aluminum actually in the waste stream. In this case, the cans are — because of the shredding — substantially deformed; most are actually in pieces (halves and thirds). The design rate of the Al Mag is approximately one ton per hour of input material consisting of roughly 40 percent nonferrous metal.[16] Other test work performed with standardized aluminum shapes seeded into the stream, a process which greatly facilitates measurement, showed excellent performance — well over 90 percent recovery on whole cans at feedrates as high as four tons per hour.

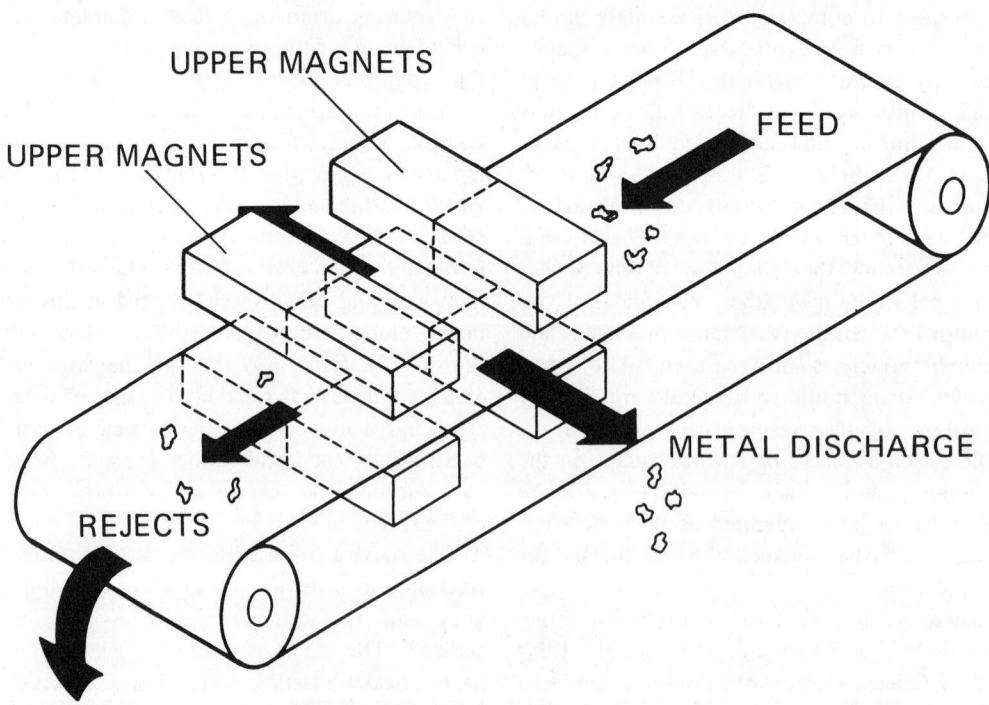

Figure 2. Combustion Power Co. "Al Mag."

Organic carry-over has been a problem on a number of test runs. The goal is to produce material from the submodule as a whole, including the air knife to be described, with a loose organic content of less than two percent. Test runs show the loose organics of the Al Mag recovered product to be in the 20-to-25 percent range with, it appears, little direct relation to the feedrate. This is contrary to expectations and is being investigated.

In addition to organics, chemical analysis of the Al Mag product clearly shows that some other nonferrous is being separated along with the can stock. This confirms visual observation of the material. Table 3 shows the weighted average of a number of test runs. This is the unseeded refuse of Washington, D.C., which contains about one percent aluminum overall and about 0.6 percent aluminum cans. In the tests, much of this can-aluminum was lost prior to the Al Mag step; first by reporting to the light fraction during air classification and, second, being lost either in the minus-two-inch fraction or to the over-four-inch fraction. The latter was due to blinding of the four-inch trommel holes during the higher throughput runs. If Al Mag efficiency were held constant, an increase in the ability of the prior steps to add to the number of aluminum can recovery opportunities for the Al Mag would effect a dilution of the impurities caused by the other nonferrous. This is simply because there would be more cans available for recovery, i.e., those now lost in air classification and trommeling. Nevertheless, it would probably not be sufficient to bring the copper and zinc composition down to the best wrought scrap specification (See Table 2). This is why the air knife is needed in the system.

Air Knife

The Aluminum Co. of America (ALCOA), which owns the Al Mag in place at ETEF, developed a laboratory-scale, two-stage air knife to reduce the organics in the Al Mag product and separate the cast aluminum, copper-based and zinc-based metals from the can stock. The air knife blows off the light organics and, using the same principle of relative density, blows the light aluminum can stock away from the heavier and generally more compact shapes of the red metals. On a "batch" basis, the results have been good. Organics have been reduced to five percent, which approaches the two percent goal. The numbers in the third and fourth columns of Table 3 show the results in terms of the chemical composition of the can stock product. The zinc level has been brought within specification, while copper is still a bit high. A larger air knife device, based on the laboratory model, has been built by the Center

Table 3. Chemical Analyses of Aluminum Products.

	Al Mag Product		Air Knife Product	
	Range (%)	Weighted Average (%)	Range (%)	Weighted Average (%)
Si	.1 − .6	.2	.1 − .2	.2
Fe	.4 − .7	.5	.4 − .6	.5
Cu	.1 − 1.8	.9	.1 − 1.2	.5
Mn	.7 − .9	.8	.8 − .9	.9
Mg	.6 − .9	.8	.6 − .8	.7
Cr	.02	.02	.01 − .02	.02
Zn	.05 − 6.7	1.5	.05 − .2	.1
Ti	.02	.02	.02	.02
Pb	.00 − .09	.01	.00 − .01	.00
Sn	.00 − .03	.00	.00	.00

Source: Lee C. Blayden, "Aluminum Recovery with Eddy Currents," paper presented to Society of Mining Engineers of AIME, Las Vegas, Feb. 23, 1976.

and is in operation at ETEF, although still on a batch basis. Reynolds Metals is also conducting air knife development work and a third type of air knife, designed by an air classifier manufacturer, has been purchased and is being installed at Recovery 1 in New Orleans. It is hoped that this "multi" approach will produce beneficial results.

Recyc-Al

Occidental Research Corp.,[17] a subsidiary of Occidental Petroleum Co., has developed an eddy current separation system to recover nonferrous metals, primarily aluminum, from the waste stream. The system, called "Recyc-Al," has gone through several steps of development and testing. For some time, a device designed for small particle size was located at the EPA-sponsored recovery facility in Franklin, Ohio. There, it was operated on feedstock from the fiber, aluminum and glass recovery demonstration plant. However, the principal development work on a larger particle size machine (for 1 1/2 to 3-inch material) was performed at Occidental's La Verne, Calif., research facility.

A full-size system is being installed at El Cajon, Calif., in San Diego County, as part of an EPA recovery demonstration project. Another system will be installed in Bridgeport, Conn., as part of the Occidental and Combustion Equipment Assoc. joint venture to build and operate a recovery facility for the Connecticut Resources Recovery Authority.[18] The flow of material through the San Diego County facility is as follows (see Figure 3):

After primary shredding, the material is air classified. The heavy fraction is passed through a trommel screen which effects separation with the plus-one-half-inch, minus-four-inch fraction directed to the Recyc-Al system. Primary magnetic separation has already taken place. It is expected that the material as it arrives at the Recyc-Al system will be about 7-to-10 percent nonferrous metals mixed primarily with plastics, wood, rags, paper and cardboard. A second magnet scans for tramp ferrous after which the material is conveyed through the eddy current separator. The nonferrous metals are repelled by the linear induction motors upward and off the edge of the nonmetallic belt. Early models employed

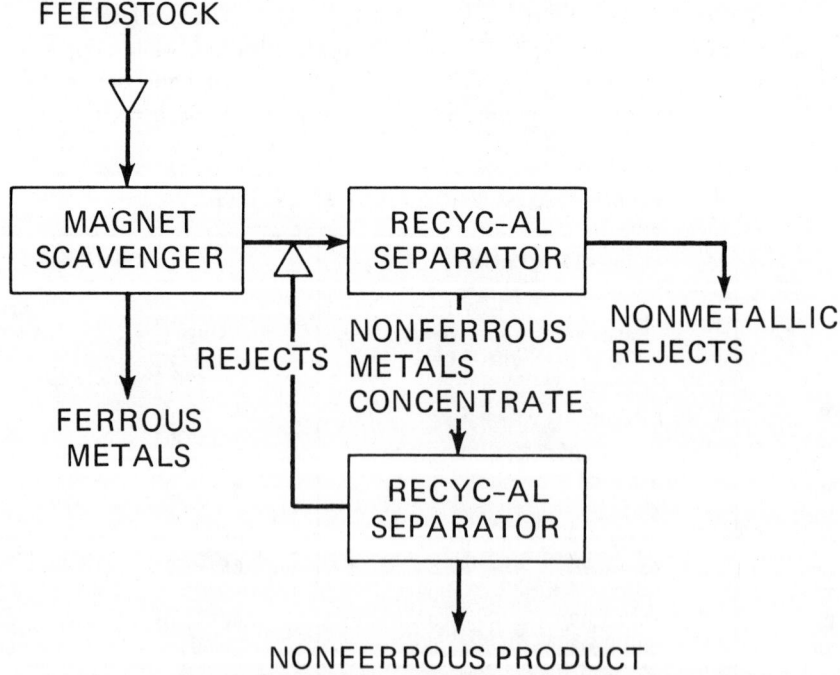

Figure 3. Recyc-Al System, San Diego County.

stainless steel belts. The use of the nonmetallic belt has made the separator more tolerant of tramp materials; in fact, it has been found that virtually all of the tramp iron rides down the belt as if it were nonconductive. This was an important finding and reduces the concern about tramp metals being entrapped on the belt in the separation area and blocking the feed.

There are two stages of separation. The first is expected to produce a concentrate which is about 83 percent metallic. This material is passed through a second eddy current separator for further cleaning. This eddy current is targeted to reduce the nonmetal content of the concentrate to between two and three percent. The system in Bridgeport will be extended by an additional step to attempt a separation among aluminum and the other nonferrous metals as a mixed product. The plan is to use an air classifier for this separation.

As a system, Recyc-Al should recover most of the nonferrous metals with the exception of certain poorly conductive alloys like lead and nonmagnetic stainless steel. Tangled wires will be missed, as will foil-backed paper. The target is an overall efficiency of 80 percent recovery of the metals that enter the system after the trommeling step.

The nonferrous metals recovered by the Recyc-Al separation system, as it is installed in San Diego, include materials in addition to aluminum can stock, rigid foil and other wrought products. The output, therefore, is best suited for sale to a nonferrous metals processor who may either attempt to separate out the aluminum or simply blend the aluminum and other nonferrous concentrate with scrap aluminum from other sources to achieve a composition suitable for his intended use. The degree to which the mixed metal approaches the wrought specification is principally a function of the number of aluminum cans in the initial waste stream per ton of waste delivered to the plant. The higher the aluminum can concentration — all else being equal — the higher the potential for achieving the wrought aluminum specification. Table 4 shows the composition of the Recyc-Al nonferrous metal product.

Pulse-Sort

In the late 1960's, there was early developmental work on eddy current separation at Vanderbilt University, some of which was supported by federal sources and some privately. In part, this work has led to the construction of an aluminum can separator called "Pulse-Sort." Pulse-Sort is a joint venture of Magnetic Separation Systems, Inc., of Nashville, Tenn., and Carpco, Inc., of Jacksonville, Fla. Carpco is the manufacturer. The installation of Pulse-Sort separators is currently underway at the Baltimore County and Milwaukee resource recovery facilities. Pulse-Sort differs from the Combustion Power Co. Al Mag and Occidental's Recyc-Al in that separation takes place during a vertical fall of the metals concentrate rather than on a horizontal belt. It is expected that the machine will recover 85 percent of the aluminum cans in the feed with not more than a five percent organic contamination. The preseparation of ferrous metals is said not to be necessary.

Inclined Ramp

Sometimes referred to as the "sliding board," the "inclined ramp" approach to separating nonferrous metals from preprocessed nonferrous concentrate was developed by the

Table 4. Recyc-Al System Performance on San Diego Refuse.

Element	Weight
Si	.58%
Fe	.41
Cu	.70
Mn	.74
Mg	.26
Cr	.01
Ni	.05
Zn	2.63
Ti	.01
Pb	.02
Sn	.01
Others	—
Aluminum	Balance

Source: Booker Morey, Occidental Research, telephone conversation, April 1977. Separator used was at the La Verne research facility.

Raytheon Co. It is partially based on experimental tests conducted by Raytheon in conjunction with the U.S. Bureau of Mines. In particular, the Bureau of Mines research facility in College Park, Md., was utilized for portions of the developmental work. It is expected that this approach, which involves permanent magnets and no moving parts in the separation device itself, will be used in the resource recovery facility being built in Monroe County, N.Y.

After several stages of size and density separation — shredding, screening and air classification — the nonferrous concentrate is made to slide down an inclined ramp (see Figure 4). Particle size is about two inches. Permanent magnet strips of alternating polarity are embedded into the surface of the ramp, with the strips being inclined themselves at an angle of approximately 45° to the ramp axis. The nonferrous concentrate is fed in at one corner of the top of the ramp (at the point labeled chute) and allowed to slide down. The organic, or nonmetallic, particles are not affected by the magnetic field at the ramp surface; hence, they slide straight down the incline. However, an eddy current is set up in the metallic particles because their slide moves them through the magnetic field. The current is, in effect, a "force" and its direction is approximately perpendicular to the magnet strips. This causes the metallic particles to veer from a straight downward slide and effects a separation. The metallics and the nonmetallics are collected in separate containers.

Pilot testing has shown an ability to separate between 70 and 80 percent of the nonferrous metals in the chute feedstream with a metallic metals purity of 90-to-98 percent.[19] The device to accomplish this separation consists of two sequential ramps (a two-pass device as far as the material is concerned). After this, further processing is accomplished to separate the mixed nonferrous into two products: one that is primarily light aluminum, and one consisting of heavy aluminum and the remaining non-magnetic metals. The latter is called the copper-zinc product. The separation is produced by a heavy media device which floats the light aluminum and sinks the heavier metals.

Heavy Media

There are at least a dozen heavy media (also called dense media) systems in operation today producing separate streams of aluminum and other nonferrous metals from the mixed nonferrous concentrate of automobile-shredding operations. Dense media is an appropriate name for the system because it relies on distinguishing metals by their differences in density. Aluminum will float on a liquid with a specific gravity greater than 2.6 while the stainless steel and the red metals will sink. The medium is generally finely ground ferro-silicon or magnetite suspended in water. The density of the liquid is controlled by the amount of the finely ground material introduced.

Various tests have been conducted using this approach to recover the aluminum fraction from mixed municipal refuse. Some of the work was at laboratory scale as reported by Reynolds Metals Co., beginning as early as 1972. Other work of a similar nature, but using full-size equipment, was conducted by the National Center for Resource Recovery.[20] The results of these tests led the Center to specify a heavy media approach to the initial design of the facility that has become Recovery 1 in New Orleans. However, at small scale, the initial

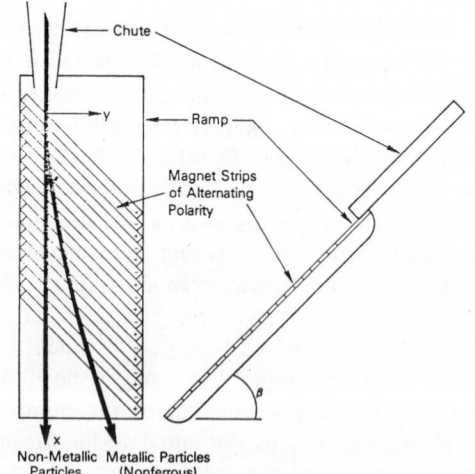

Source: David B. Spencer and Ernest Scholmann, "Recovery of Nonferrous Metals by Means of Permanent Magnets," *Resource Recovery and Conservation, 1,* No. 2 (1975): 153.

Figure 4. Schematic diagram of metal separator in frontal view (left) and side view (right).

cost of a heavy media system is rather high. Even a recovery facility in the 1000 ton per day range does not produce the amount of non-ferrous concentrate of a small automobile-shredding facility. As a result, and with the advent of the eddy current separation technique tested by the Center at ETEF, a design change was made for Recovery 1 substituting the eddy current approach for heavy media. Nevertheless, as more recovery facilities come on line, principally located to best realize the energy potential of the waste as a fuel, it may be that the most effective nonferrous metals recovery approach will be the production of only a nonferrous concentrate at each individual recovery plant. The separation of the concentrate into its principal components can take place at a centrally located, heavy media facility. This clearly is a future development which must take place in parallel with, or as a slightly lagged function of, the planning for and construction of energy recovery plants.

Black Clawson

The Black Clawson approach was originally developed and demonstrated at the EPA/Glass Packaging Institute-sponsored recovery plant at Franklin, Ohio. The Black Clawson Co., which also supported the demonstration, will

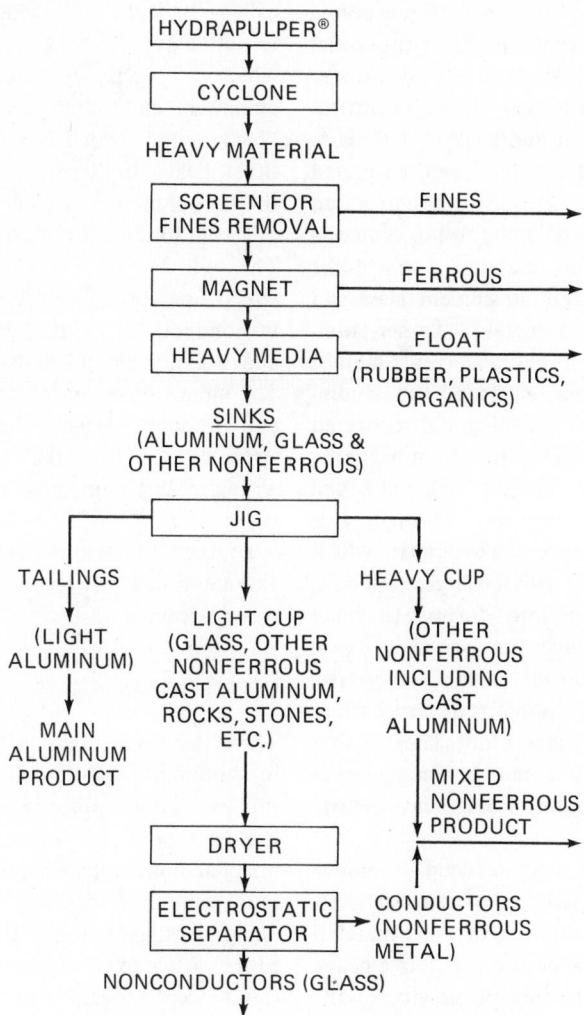

Figure 5. Aluminum recovery in Black Clawson System.

install similar but refined systems in its facilities soon to be constructed in Hempstead, N.Y., and Dade County, Fla. All of these facilities will accomplish the initial solid waste size reduction step by using a Hydrapulper.® This essentially is a rotary hammermill immersed in water in which the refuse is converted into a slurry. In Franklin, the principal product to be recovered is fiber used in the manufacture of roofing felt. In Hempstead and Dade County, the slurry that remains after the bulk of the metals, glass and stones have been removed will be dewatered to reduce the moisture level to about 50 percent and used as boiler fuel. Metals and glass recovery is included in all three plants.

Aluminum recovery occurs at three points in the process (see Figure 5). After the initial hydrapulping step, the slurry is passed through a cyclone which distinguishes, through centrifugal force, between light and heavy fractions.[21] The heavier material, having been extracted from the Hydrapulper through a perforated plate with relatively small holes, is less than one inch in size. The material has a gravel-like appearance and is about 80 percent glass and 10 percent nonferrous metals. Larger, non-pulpable materials, primarily ferrous metals, have already been ejected from the Hydrapulper through another opening and recovered separately. At Franklin, the nonmagnetic, oversized heavies were brought back and added to the Hydrapulper infeed. Through this recycling, aluminum cans, for example, which initially may have gone with the larger materials, eventually were torn into fragments small enough to pass through the one-inch holes. Small particles of ferrous metals, of course, remain in the glass and nonferrous concentrate and are separated magnetically later. The remainder of the concentrate is, among other items, rubber, tile, roofing, rock, heavy plastic and wood.

This concentrate is next screened to remove fine, unrecoverable particles of broken glass, sand, stone, etc. The larger particle-size material is magnetically scalped before it enters a heavy media separator. The specific gravity of the media is adjusted in the range of 1.6-to-2.0. At this specific gravity, the organic matter

floats and the inorganic sinks. The former — consisting of rubber, plastics and bone — is discharged. The sink fraction is a fairly clean concentrate of nonferrous metals and glass. The principal contaminants are rocks, stones and ceramics. The next step is jigging, to separate the light fraction composed of wrought aluminum (in this case, particles of beverage cans, frozen dinner trays, etc.) from the heavy fraction composed mainly of mixed nonferrous metals such as brass, zinc, copper and lead. Separation is accomplished by pulsating the water in the jig; light materials are carried to the top while heavier particles remain near the bottom. Actually, three separations are made: (1) the wrought aluminum product, here called "tailings" following mineral processing terminology; (2) the so-called "light cup," which is a glass concentrate including some aluminum and other nonferrous; and (3) the "heavy cup," which is the cast aluminum and other heavy nonferrous metals. Recovery of the final aluminum product occurs as a necessary precondition to the glass recovery operation. The unit process is electrostatic separation which operates, after drying, on the difference in conductivity of the glass and the metallic and nonmetallic portions of the concentrate. The metals so separated are added to the heavy cup product. Hence, there are two product streams. The first, the tailings, is targeted for wrought aluminum specifications. The second, the heavy cup and the electrostatic discharge, is a mixed nonferrous fraction. The amount of aluminum depends on the characteristics of the waste stream.

CONCLUSION

There has been much progress in the recovery of aluminum from household discards. Clearly, the presorting approaches currently hold the lead in terms of tonnage recycled. Multi-material household separation, a variant of the more common recycling center approach, is being investigated under the sponsorship of the EPA. As a relatively low capital investment, this concept appears to have merit. Other, more capital-intensive methods, designed for larger-scale recovery plants, are now passing out of the pilot stage and into prototype operation. If successful, they hold promise of further increasing the aluminum recycling rate.

REFERENCES AND NOTES

1. Aluminum Association,*Annual Statistical Review,* 1975 (preliminary 1976 data), p. 6.

2. Aluminum Association Publication T-12, *Use of Aluminum in Automobiles: Effect on the Energy Dilemma* (February 1977); see also P.R. Atkins, "Recycling Can Cut Energy Demands Dramatically," *Engineering and Mining Journal, 174,* No. 5 (May 1973): 6971; and J.C. Bravard, H.B. Flora and Charles Portal, *Energy Expenditures Associated with the Production and Recycling of Metals,* (Oak Ridge, Tenn: Oak Ridge National Laboratory, November 1972), 91 pp.

   The National Commission on Supplies and Shortages gives a figure of 1/12 for the relationship between energy conserved by producing aluminum from scrap versus virgin; *Government and the Nation's Resources: Report of the National Commission on Supplies and Shortages,* No. 052-003-00271-0 (Washington, D.C.: U.S. Government Printing Office, December 1976, $2.00). The figure cited appears on p. 156.

3. For 1975, new ingot production was 3,880,000 tons. Recycled material amounted to 1,182,000 tons, of which 863,000 tons was so-called "new scrap," which is in-plant production scrap and 319,000 tons of "old scrap," which is postconsumer recycled metal. The eight percent figure cited in the text is 319,000 divided by 3,880,000.

4. For an excellent discussion of aluminum and other nonferrous metals recovery of all kinds, including shredded automobiles, see: Robert F. Testin, *Recovery of Nonferrous Metals from Solid Waste,* paper presented at the American Institute of Chemical Engineers Symposium on Recycling, Atlantic City, N.J., Aug. 24-Sept. 1, 1976; 49 pp.

5. Across the nation (1976), aluminum containers made up approximately 60 percent of the malt beverage can market and about 23 percent of that for soft drinks.

6. The principal use of aluminum scrap coming from traditional sources has been the secondary aluminum industry to make casting alloys. However, the widely-used die casting alloy 380 has an upper limit of 0.1 percent on magnesium and 0.5 percent on manganese. Wrought products, such as beverage cans, have higher magnesium and manganese contents. For example, can bodies are composed of 3004 alloy with a magnesium content of 0.8-to-1.3 percent and a manganese content of 1.0-to-1.5 percent. The alloys used for can ends have a 4.0-to-5.0 percent magnesium content and 0.2-to-0.5 percent manganese range. For secondary smelters to use this material would require it to be "demagged" (which is wasteful of magnesium) and diluted with low manganese materials. However, it can be used to make new can stock. There are magnesium losses in the smelting operation which are sufficient to bring the mix of ends and body alloys (the ends are 28 percent of the total can weight) very near the original 3004 can body alloy specification.

7. The reason for including rigid foil with cans is that foil is 8079, 1235 or 3003 series alloy, depending upon the application. These alloys are generally compatible in the amounts found in waste with the 3004 alloy used for aluminum can bodies and 5182 alloy which is the principal one used for can ends. As stated in the prior footnote, alloys 3004 and 5182 melted together in the proportions found in the can yield a composition sufficiently similar to 3004 that a mixed metal of the two can be used to produce new 3004. 5182 is higher in magnesium but some of this is lost in remelting the recovered material.

8. The report is entitled *Specifications for Materials Recovered from Municipal Refuse,* Environmental Protection Technology Series, EPA 670/2-75-034, prepared for the National Environmental Research Center, Office of Research and Development (Cincinnati: U.S. Environmental Protection Agency, May 1975), 109 pp. Available from National Technical Information Service, PB 242 540/35. The document discusses specifications for the principal candidates for materials to be recovered from waste. There are several specification sources for aluminum recycled from more traditional scrap operations, such as in-plant trimming, construction demolition, etc. These include the National Association of Recycling Industries, 330 Madison Ave., New York, N.Y. 10017; The Aluminum Association, 818 Connecticut Ave., N.W., Washington, D.C. 20006; and the Aluminum Recycling Association, 1775 K St., N.W., Suite 205, Washington, D.C., 20006. Typical grades for aluminum scrap are: new aluminum can stock, old can stock, mixed aluminum castings, old aluminum foil, aluminum grindings and segregated new aluminum alloy clippings, (from National Association of Recycling Industries, *Standard Classification for Nonferrous Scrap Metals,* Circular NF-73).

9. These specifications are taken from the Reynolds Metals Letter of Intent to Purchase the aluminum recovered at Recovery 1 in New Orleans, as is the price reduction. In addition, Committee E-38, Resource Recovery, of the American Society for Testing and Materials, 1916 Race St., Philadelphia, Pa. 19103, has been working on grade specifications and test methods for aluminum recovered

from the municipal waste stream. The Nonferrous Metals subcommittee, E-38.03, handles the aluminum area. H.V. Makar, U.S. Bureau of Mines, is chairman of this subcommittee.

10. In plant melting operations when the organic coating on can stock burns off, a nearly equivalent amount of aluminum is burned up in addition to the normal melt loss. Additional losses of aluminum through entrainment in the salt flux will further reduce recovery. Samples of shredded clean cans, after screening for fines, have been sent under the auspices of ASTM Committee E-38.03 to three primary aluminum producers and four secondary smelters for assay evaluation. Results from these tests indicated a recovery around 90 percent on a laboratory assay basis. In general, scrap having reduced percentages of organics and fines and having a density range of 14-to-17 lbs. per cu. ft. could have a favorable effect on pricing.

11. Aluminum Association, *Aluminum Can Recycling Information* (Aluminum Association, 1977), 4 pp. For a survey article on source separation, see: "Source Separation . . . A Resource Recovery Option," *NCRR Bulletin,* 7, No. 1 (Winter 1977): 3-10.

12. In 1975, 90,000 tons of cans were recycled, which was 26 percent of the weight of the number of cans produced (source: Aluminum Association Statistical Committee). It is expected that the 1976 figures will be even higher.

13. The impactor step is not present in the plant processing the Somerville and Marblehead, Mass., mixed glass and can fraction. There is very little aluminum in this geographic area. Those cans which appear in the recovered material are handpicked.

14. A number of *NCRR Bulletin* articles have discussed methods to realize the energy potential in waste: "Municipal Solid Waste . . . A Source of Energy," Vol. 3, No. 3 (Summer 1973), pp. 3-14; "Densified Refuse-Derived Fuel," Vol. 6, No. 1 (Winter 1976), pp. 4-9; and "Air Pollution from Burning Refuse Fuels," Vol. 3, No. 1 (Winter 1977), pp. 15-27. A forthcoming issue will contain an article on air classification.

15. Unfortunately, air classifier performance to date has not consistently achieved this objective. The proportion of whole or partially crushed cans in the heavy fraction has often been about 60 percent rather than the 90-plus percent needed to achieve the target figures.

16. Testin, Robert F., *Recovery of Nonferrous Metals,* previously cited, p. 36.

17. Formerly Garrett Research and Development Corp.

18. For further discussion of these projects, see: B. Morey, T.D. Griffin, A.K. Gupta and I.V.T. Hopkins, "Resource Recovery from Refuse," *Proceedings* of the Fifth Mineral Waste Utilization Symposium (Chicago, April 13-14, 1976), pp. 184-194; and G.T. Preston, "Resource Recovery and Flash Pyrolysis of Municipal Refuse," *Waste Age, 7,* No. 5 (May 1976): 83-98.

19. Spencer, David B., "Solid Waste Resource Recovery Facility, Monroe County, New York," *Proceedings* of 1976 National Waste Processing Conference (Boston, May 23-26, 1976), p. 419. The *Proceedings* has 585 pages plus a supplement and is available from ASME United Engineering Center, 345 East 47th St., New York, N.Y. 10017. See also: Michael R. Grubbs and Bela M. Fabuss, "Nonferrous Separation – A New Unit Operation," paper presented at the 1976 AIME Meeting, Las Vegas, Nev., February 22-26, 1976.

20. See Robert F. Testin, "Recovery of Aluminum from Solid Waste," paper presented at Stanford Research Institute Symposium on Solid Wastes, Oct. 23-24, 1974. 27 pp. Also see H. Alter, S.L. Natof, K.L. Woodruff, W.L. Freyberger and E.L. Michaels, "Classification and Concentration of Municipal Solid Waste," *Proceedings* of Fourth Mineral Waste Utilization Symposium, E. Aleshin, ed. Bureau of Mines and IIT Research Institute, Chicago, May 7-8, 1974, pp. 70-76; and E.L. Michaels, K.L. Woodruff, W.L. Freyberger and H. Alter, "Heavy Media Separation of Aluminum from Municipal Solid Waste," *Transactions of SME, 258* (March 1975): 34-39.

21. The description of the process followed in developing the text for this article is from a brochure available from Black Clawson. The title is *Hydrasposal – Fibreclaim: Solid Waste Recycling and Resource Recovery Plant/Franklin, Ohio, USA* (available from Black Clawson Fibreclaim, Inc., 200 Park Ave., New York, N.Y. 10017).

3-11 Resource Recovery from Solid Wastes by Water Only Cyclone Process and Heavy Medium Cyclone Process

P.C. Reeves, J.H. Absil, H.H. Dreissen, and A.T. Basten

Source: Adapted from an article with the same title in *Conservation and Recycling*, Vol. 2, No. 3/4, 1979, pp. 233–254. Reprinted with Permission of Pergamon Press, Ltd.

INTRODUCTION [1,2]

In 1946 Dutch State Mines developed a technique known as cyclone separation. Two processes, heavy medium cyclone separation and water only cyclone separation, ensued. These techniques are basically gravity separations, but gravity is a relatively weak force and an extended time may be required to effect a gravity separation. In the cyclone process, the force of gravity may be exceeded several hundred times by the centrifugal force; but since all particles are affected by the same force, an efficient gravity separation is still made, but it is efficient down to a much smaller size. This technique has been applied to commercial plants for the last 25 yr for the separation of coal, ore and other minerals, in size ranges from 50 to 0.5 mm, or in some cases, even finer.

Since 1975 Stamicarbon has executed intensive text programs on the application of this technique for the recovery of aluminum and other non-ferrous metals from several types of solid wastes such as: automotive scrap, municipal solid waste, car batteries and incinerator residue.

Before dealing with the results of these test programs and the actual results of the first commercial plant for automotive scrap, which has been operating since January 1977, a description of the separation equipment applied will be given.

HEAVY MEDIUM CYCLONE [3,4]

The heavy medium consists of an aqueous suspension of very fine e.g. — $50\mu m$, magnetite or ferrosilicon particles or a mixture of these two types. (Media Solids)

Figure 1 shows the heavy medium cyclone. The feed, an aqueous suspension of product particles and separating medium, is forced

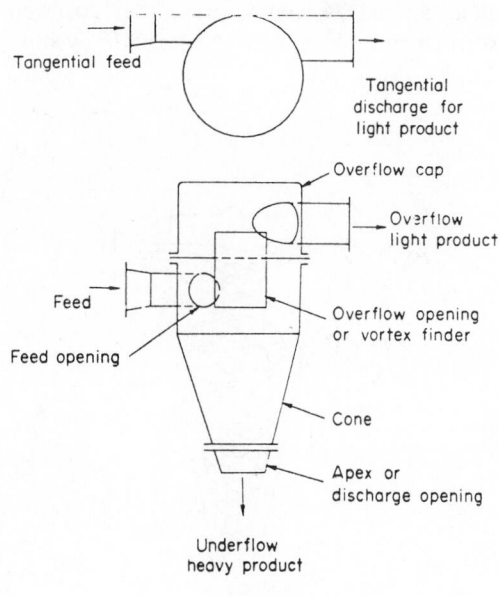

Figure 1.

tangentially into the cyclone. The specific gravity of the separating medium is adapted to the required specific gravity of separation. Being fed in tangentially, the suspension will adopt a fast rotational motion in the cyclone body (see Fig. 2). In the core of the cyclone a very fast rotary flow moves towards the overflow opening.

Since the suspension leaves the cyclone on a radius smaller than that on which it is introduced, the tangential flow velocity will increase towards the cyclone center. In theory the rotation of a particle in a cyclone is subject to the rule $V \times r$ = constant, with V being the tangential velocity and r the radius on which the particle is rotating. However, owing to friction, viscosity effects, etc. this ideal condition will not be reached completely. From our investigations we arrived at the formula $V \times r^n$ = constant, in which $n = 0.5$. This shows that in any case the tangential velocity, and hence the centrifugal acceleration, increases when a rotating liquid or solid particle moves towards a smaller radius. The velocity gradient thus set up in a cyclone results in considerable shearing forces being created, which is of importance for separations that have to be effected in rather viscous media.

The formula for centrifugal acceleration, $a = \dfrac{V^2}{r}$, indicates that the centrifugal acceleration, a, and in consequence the separating force, is strongest near the center of the cyclone. In the heavy medium cyclone, the medium as well as the particle to be separated are subjected to the centrifugal forces. Since these forces act also on the very fine medium solids, the specific gravity of the medium will increase towards the spex discharge opening. Therefore, the specific gravity of separation in a heavy medium cyclone is always higher than the specific gravity of the medium in the feed.

Particles having a specific gravity higher than the specific gravity of separation move towards the wall of the cyclone and next follow a non-tangential path along this wall, to be discharged through the apex opening. Particles having a lower specific gravity are forced towards the cyclone center and sent to the overflow opening by the strong non-tangential current. If the right kind of feed of the right specific gravity is applied, any specific gravity of separation between 1.3 and 3.8 can be reached. Some particles arriving in the core leave this core again under the influence of the centrifugal acceleration imparted to them, to move to the apex discharge opening along the wall. At the point where, near the apex opening, the non-tangential current is directed upwards into the core, the particles can again be selected for discharge through either the apex or the overflow opening. Internal recirculation thus effects a good separation even between particles having specific gravities near the specific gravity of separation. Particles much below the specific gravity of separation will, immediately after entering the cyclone, move rapidly towards the center and issue through the overflow opening without first being circulated. Very heavy particles, on the other hand, will immediately after getting into the cyclone move rapidly along the wall, and issue through the apex opening. The separating medium leaves the cyclone together with the light product and the heavy product. It will be clear that the medium will next have to be recovered from the product to be cleaned. The manner in which this is done will be dealt with afterwards. The heavy medium cyclone separates only according to the specific gravity of the particles and, in principle, operates independently of particle size and shape.

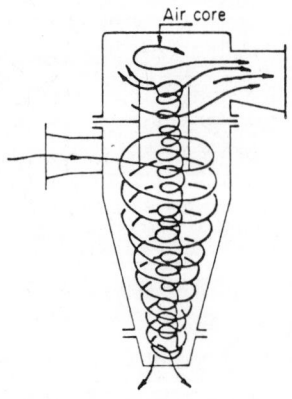

Figure 2.

WATER ONLY CYCLONE [3,4]

The water only cyclone differs from the heavy medium type in that it has a different geometric shape and operates with water instead of with a heavy medium. It separates less efficiently than the heavy medium cyclone and can be used only for cuts between specific gravities of 1.0 and 2.0.

Figure 3 is a sketch of a water only cyclone. When the light and heavy particles are introduced into this cyclone together with water, both types will be flung against the wall. The particles are then conveyed to the apex opening by the strong non-tangential current along the cone wall. Consider, for example, the case in which a mixture of coal (specific gravity 1.3) and shale (specific gravity 2.0) suspended in water is fed into a hydrocyclone. On arriving in the apex, the coal and shale particles are concentrated and part of them will be seized by the central upward current along the air-filled core and be conveyed towards the overflow opening. Many of these particles will, on their way to the overflow opening, be centrifuged out again and be recycled to the apex opening. At the beginning of their travels in the current along the hollow core, the solid particles have no velocity in the direction away from the axis of the cyclone nor in the direction of the vortex finder. In order to get them out of the central current, an acceleration must be imparted to these particles in the direction away from the axis. They need only cover a very small distance to get out of the central current, so that their radial velocity in leaving this current is low and the resistance to their acceleration is, at first, negligible. Consequently,

the distance covered, in a radial sense, is approximately proportional to the acceleration experienced by a particle. Whether or not a particle can leave the cyclone through the overflow opening depends only on the magnitude of the centrifugal acceleration acting upon that particle in the central current and on the distance between the end of the vortex finder and the conical wall. The centrifugal acceleration depends on the specific gravity of the particle. By means of a simplified formula, it can be calculated that for a coal particle in water this acceleration

$$A_c = C \left(1 - \frac{1}{1.3} \right) = 0.20\,C,$$

and for shale in water

$$A_s = C \left(1 - \frac{1}{2.0} \right) = 0.50\,C.$$

Consequently, the time needed for the shale to leave the central current is much shorter than that needed by the coal. In this way, a separation between the coal and shale can be effected, provided the cyclone parameters are properly chosen. The coal leaves the cyclone through the overflow opening, whereas the shale, which can escape from the central current fairly quickly, is returned to the apex opening, through which it is finally discharged. Several secondary effects may occur, of course. However, it is chiefly the mechanism described here that accounts for the separation in a cyclone designed to give an increased separating density.

Nowadays water only cyclones are applied not only in many coal washeries, but also in plants for the separation of palm nut kernels from broken palm nut shells (specific gravity 1.07 and 1.25). One of the main factors influencing the specific gravity of separation is the length of the vortex finder (L).

From the foregoing it will have become clear that a cyclone of this type can be applied for the separation of light product, such as rubber and plastic particles, from metal fragments.

SIEVE BEND [3,4]

In plants employing the heavy medium or water only cyclone process, an important part is played

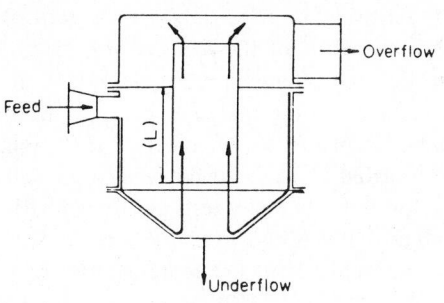

Figure 3.

also by the sieve bend. In the former type of plant, it is used for removing the medium suspension from the products and in the latter for dewatering the products. Therefore, a somewhat more detailed description of this device is given. The sieve bend installation, Fig. 4, consists of a feed box, a feed spout and a curved screen. The feed box distributes the feed material over the full width of the screen. In the feed spout, the material is given in tangential velocity prior to being fed onto the curved slotted screen deck, the bars of which are arranged normal to the feed stream. As a characteristic feature of the sieve bend, a thin layer is now peeled from the stream each time this traverses a bar. Since the thickness of this layer is substantially smaller than the distance between the bars and the size of the particles contained in it cannot normally be greater than half the slot width, screening on a sieve bend is to a much finer size than the slot width would suggest. There being no particles of a size near the slot width reporting to the underflow, no clogging can occur, which gives this device an advantage over other types of screen. The screening action is performed very fast, at a high feed rate, so that the capacity per unit of screen area is very high. This is exemplified by the fact that, in screening at a size of 0.5 mm, a sieve bend area of 1 m^2 suffices for handling no less than 130 m^3/h of suspension.

APPLICATION OF THE CYCLONE TECHNIQUE ON SHREDDED AUTOMOTIVE SCRAP

Shredded automotive scrap has used heavy medium separation for some time in a conventional heavy medium vessel. However, using the float and sink method, there is significant correlation between efficiency and the size of the particles being separated in a gravity type vessel. The finer the product, the more influence the viscosity of the medium has on the efficiencies.

The conflict between gravity and viscosity prevent any efficient separation below 6 mm size in a gravity type vessel. But, it is also necessary to recycle − 6 mm products,

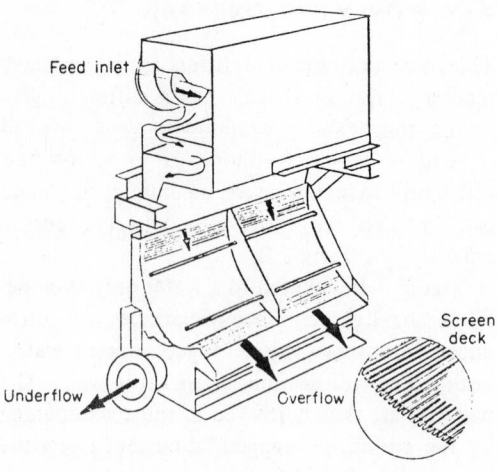

Figure 4.

if true recycle economies are to be achieved [5].

Test Work

In 1975 Stamicarbon started an extensive test program on the application of the cyclone technique for the separation of shredded automotive scrap in the 50 × 1 mm size range. This test program was executed at the pilot plant of Stamicarbon, with materials obtained from Dutch shredder plants.

Pilot Plant. The pilot plant consists essentially of a tank with a pump, a 350 mm diameter cyclone for the separation and two sieve bends for dewatering the cyclone overflow and underflow. For the recovery of rubber, plastic, etc., use was made of a water only cyclone, with the pump tank containing water only. For separating out the metals, the pilot plant was equipped with an aqueous suspension of ferrosilicon or a mixture of ferrosilicon and magnetite, of the required specific gravity. In the tests done in this pilot plant, it was necessary for the materials obtained from the shredder plants to be screened at 30 mm, so as to avoid blockage of the feed to the 350 mm cyclone. From many tests performed with ores and coal, it was known that the results obtained in this pilot plant are representative of those to be obtained with a commercial cyclone with a diamater of 600 mm (24 in.). This latter cyclone can handle fragments up to 50 mm without getting blocked. The sieve bends applied in the pilot plant had 1.5 mm slots, so that all product parts larger than 0.8 mm were recovered in the overflow. The sample materials received from the shredder plants were first passed through magnetic drums, so that the pilot plant cyclone had only to handle the non-ferrous fraction.

Feed Products. The feed samples proved to contain a wide variety of materials, which indicated that the commercial plant should be made suitable for handling feeds of fluctuating composition. A typical specific gravity distribution for a shredded non-ferrous product is shown in Fig. 5. Because of removal of dust (-1 mm) by air classifying near the shredder, the samples received mainly had particle sizes from 1 mm to 64 mm.

Tests on the Recovery of Rubber and Plastic by Means of a Water Only Cyclone. A sample of shredded non-ferrous scrap was used in a series of tests conducted to find the optimum dimensions. In order to obtain different specific gravities of separation, different vortex finder lengths were applied. The main requirement was the separation of all +1 mm rubber and plastic particles from the metal fraction. All products obtained in the cyclone tests were subjected to analysis by means of heavy liquid in the laboratory. It appeared that with the theoretical cut adjusted to a specific gravity of 1.8, not a single rubber or plastic particle was contained in the heavy +1.8 mm product. The 350 mm diameter water only cyclone was found capable of handling easily 5 ton/h of non-ferrous scrap. The table given as Fig. 6 summarizes the results of one of

Specific Gravity	% By Weight	Components
-1.8	25	Rubber and plastic
1.8-2.6	15	Glass, other non-metals and light alloys
2.6-2.8	20	Mainly aluminum
2.8-3.3	5	Some alloys
+3.3	35	Heavy metals, e.g. zinc and copper
Total	100	

Figure 5. Specific gravity composition of the shredded non-ferrous product.

these tests. The results are clearly satisfactory. Even from this feed sample, which contained 32% dirt (rubber and plastic), a fairly clean metal product with only 4.5% dirt could be recovered. Hardly any metal is lost in the dirt fraction − only 1% of the +3.0 specific gravity product and 2% of the +1.8 specific gravity product.

Tests Conducted with the Heavy Medium Cyclone. The feed samples used for these tests had been taken from the underflow of a water only cyclone, which means that they contained hardly any rubber or plastic fragments. The investigations were carried out for the purpose of obtaining the following two products:

1. a heavy product, containing the metals having a specific gravity of +3.0 and
2. a light product, containing all aluminum, light alloy and non-metal fractions having a specific gravity of -3.0.

For recovery of these products, the cutting point should lie at a specific gravity of about 3.0. On the basis of our experience and know-how in the field of mineral separation by

Specific Gravity	Components	Composition in % by Weight			Recovery in %	
		Feed	Overflow	Underflow	In Overflow	In Underflow
-1.8	Rubber plastics	32	97	4.5	91	
+1.8	Non-metals metals	68	3	95.5		98
Total		100	100	100.0		
+3.0	Heavy metals					99

Figure 6. Results of water-only cyclone test.

means of heavy medium cyclones, it was decided to use a cyclone of this type having a 60° cone angle for handling a feed with a specific gravity of, for instance, 2.4. The first series of tests with the 60° cone cyclone was carried out with a separating medium consisting of ground ferrosilicon 85% of which was sized below 50 μm. Figure 7 is a table of typical test results, showing that the cyclone underflow contained heavy metals only and was free of aluminum which was highly acceptable. The overflow, on the other hand, has a somewhat high heavy metal content (specific gravity +2.9) — viz. 5%. From mineral separation it is known that the finer the size of a medium the sharper and, thus, the more efficient the cut will be. A new series of tests was therefore conducted with a medium consisting of a mixture of atomized ferrosilicon (95% -40 μm) and ground magnetite (95% -50 μm). The results of these tests are also tabulated in Fig. 7. This table shows that the results are clearly better than those obtained in the first series, the amounts of +2.9 and +3.0 heavy metals decreasing to 3.9% and 3.0% respectively. With the aid of these yields and the distribution of the +3.1 and -2.9 specific gravity fractions, we could then calculate the recoveries, which amounted to 96% for the +3.1 heavy metals, while the loss of -2.9 specific gravity aluminum contained in the heavy metals was only 1%.

The overflow of this heavy medium cyclone, i.e., the light product, with specific gravities ranging from 1.8 to 2.9, consisted largely of aluminum and to a minor proportion of such impurities as glass and light metal alloy fragments. There are various possibilities for further upgrading of the aluminum fraction, if necessary. For instance, a second heavy medium cyclone might be installed for treatment at a specific gravity of 2.7, fine glass particles might be removed by screening or a crushing followed by a screening treatment might be applied. In consultation with the operators of a Dutch shredder plant, it was decided not to start test work on this upgrading for the time being and to keep the first commercial plant as simple as possible. Further efforts, therefore, were aimed at developing a suitable flow-

sheet for a plant which was first to remove rubber and plastic and next to separate aluminum from the heavy metals. This plant should be capable of handling 7 ton/h of non-ferrous product from a shredder.

FIRST COMMERCIAL PLANT FOR SEPARATION OF SHREDDED REJECTS FROM SCRAP AUTOMOBILES

In January 1977 the first commercial plant for the separation of shredded automotive scrap, following the developed flowsheet, was put into operation at Dalmeyer Metalen B.V., Nieuwerkerk ann de Ijssel, near Rotterdam, The Netherlands.

This plant is used to separate aluminum and other heavy metals such as brass, bronze, zinc and copper.

Shredding and Air Classifying Operation

The scrap cars are shredded in a Lindemann Shredder. A preliminary air classification of the shredded products takes place at the discharge of the shredder. The main air classifying takes place in a horizontal rotating drum air classifier. The air classified heavies are introduced to a magnetic drum for the removal of ferrous scrap from the non-ferrous metals and coarse non-metallic impurities.

Since the top size of the feed to the cyclone plant is limited to about 50 mm (2 in.), the mixture of non-ferrous metals and non-metallics is collected in batches and re-run through the shredder before being introduced into the heavy medium plant. When the material is re-run, due to the absence of organics and ferrous material, the shredder is capable of more than twice its normal capacity. The reshredded rejects are screened at 50 mm to protect the cyclone plant against oversized particles.

Cyclone Separation Plant

The flow sheet is indicated in Fig. 8. The plant consists of two circuits — the water only cyclone circuit and the heavy medium circuit. The product 50 mm × 0 is introduced first into the water only cyclone circuit

Product	First series			Second series		
	Feed	Overflow	Underflow	Feed	Overflow	Underflow
Specific gravity of heavy medium	2.44	2.43	3.29	2.40	2.39	3.1
Yield in % of wt.	100	70	30	100	70	30
Composition	% By weight	% By weight	% By weight	% By weight	% By weight	% By weight
Specific gravity						
−2.65	13.5	19.3	0			
2.65−2.79	50.6	72.1	0.6	67.4	96.1	0.5
2.79−2.90	2.7	3.8	0			
2.90−3.0	0.8	1.1	0	0.6	0.9	0
3.0−3.1				0.8	1.1	0
3.1−3.3	0.5	0.6	0.2			
+3.3	31.9	3.1	99.2	31.2	1.9	99.5
Total	100.0	100.0	100.0	100.0	100.0	100.0
Visual appraisal		Aluminum non-metals and small amount of heavy metals	Only heavy metals as zinc, copper free of aluminum		Aluminum non-metals and small amount of heavy metals	Only heavy metals e.g. zinc, copper free of aluminium
Recovery of heavy metals + 3.1 Sp. Gr. in %		—			96	
Loss of aluminum − 2.9 Sp. Gr. in %		—			1	

Figure 7. Results of series of tests with the heavy medium cyclone with 60° cone.

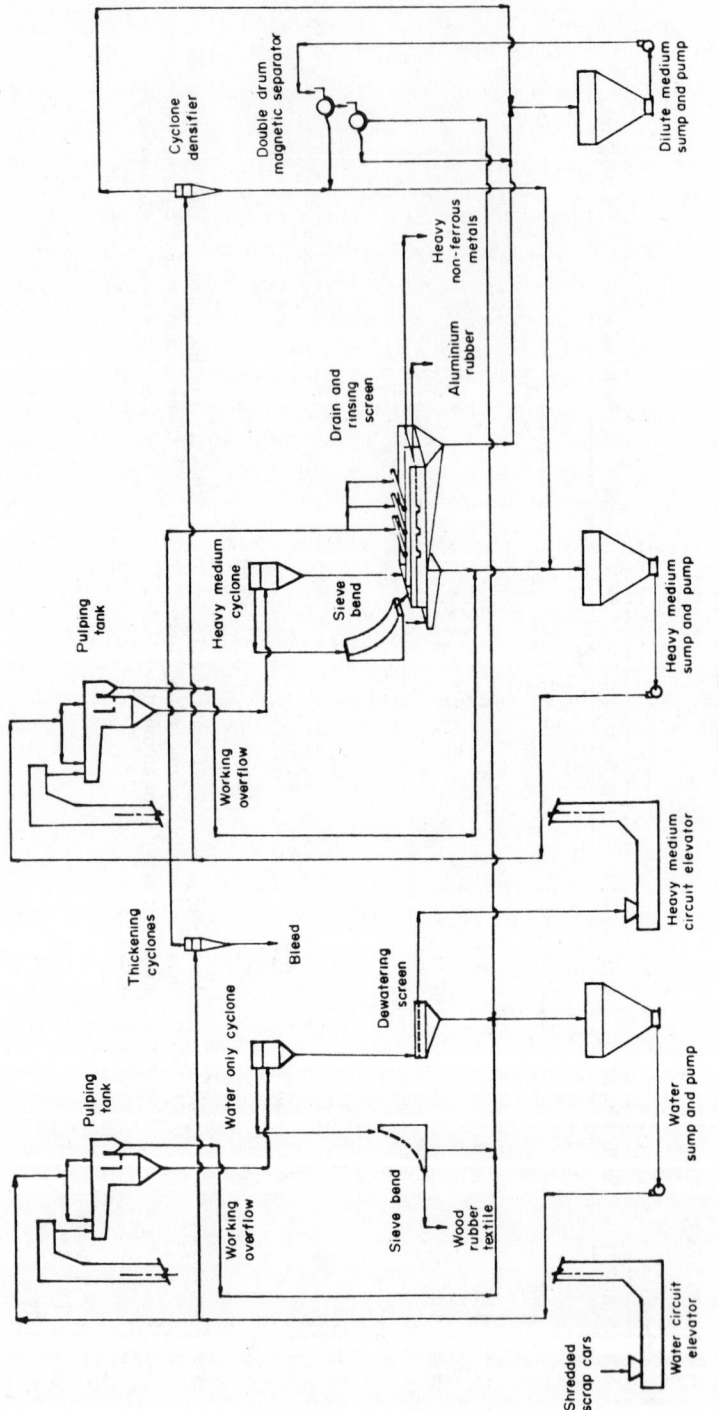

Figure 8.

by a feeder, a bucket elevator and the pulping tank. In the pulping tank, the feed product is mixed with water from the water sump and the mixture is fed by gravity to the 600 mm diameter water only cyclone. In this cyclone most of the non-metallic impurities, having a relatively low specific gravity, are separated from the non-ferrous metals and are discharged through the vortex finder and overflow to a reversible sieve bend for dewatering. The overflow from the sieve bend, which is primarily non-metallic, is collected in a container and the udnerflow water and –1 mm particles are recycled to the water sump.

The underflow from the water only cyclone, containing the non-ferrous and some non-metallic impurities, is discharged through the apex opening and dewatered on a vibrating screen at about 1 mm.

The underflow of the screen is returned to the water sump. The overflow of the screen is the feed product to the heavy medium cyclone circuit and is discharged into a second bucket elevator for transportation to the heavy medium cyclone circuit pulping tank.

To avoid the possible concentration of fine particles in the water only cyclone circuit reaching a level which is too high, a small portion of the water from the pulping tank is pumped to 250 mm diameter thickening cyclones. The underflow of these cyclones is the bleed from the water only cyclone circuit and the overflow is directed to the heavy medium circuit for use as rinsing water.

The mixture of non-ferrous metals and non-metallics is mixed in the second pulping tank with heavy medium pumped from the heavy medium sump. The heavy medium used is an aqueous suspension of magnetite and atomized ferrosilicon in order to maintain the relatively high specific gravity required for this separation.

The mixture of product and heavy medium from the pulping tank is fed by gravity into the 600 mm diameter heavy medium cyclone. In the heavy medium cyclone, the non-metallics and the light non-ferrous metal (aluminum) are separated from the heavy non-ferrous metals (copper, zinc, brass and lead). The lighter fraction is discharged through the vortex

finder the overflow to a sieve bend and further on to half of a vibrating screen. The heavy fraction from the apex of the cyclone is discharged directly onto the other half of the vibrating screen. The heavy medium which is discharged from the underflow of the sieve bend and from the first section of the vibrating screen is returned to the heavy medium sump. The medium which adheres to the product is rinsed off on the final portion of the screen and is directed to the dilute medium sump. The diluted medium is pumped from the dilute medium sump to a double drum magnetic separator. The concentrate of this separator is fed to the heavy medium sump as make-up medium. The tailings from the heavy medium separator are returned to the water sump in the water only cyclone circuit as make-up water.

In order to keep the water adhering to the feed particles from decreasing the specific gravity of the heavy medium by dilution, a small part of the heavy medium from the medium sump is fed to a 250 mm diameter cyclone densifier. The concentrated underflow from this densifier is fed to the heavy medium sump and the overflow is directed to the dilute medium sump.

APPLICATION OF THE CYCLONE TECHNIQUE TO SHREDDED MUNICIPAL SOLID WASTE

In 1975 Roberts and Schaefer Co. was approached by Reynolds Metals Co.* for a process to recover aluminum, specifically can aluminum from municipal solid waste.

In the application of the cyclone separating process to shredded municipal solid waste, it was necessary to recognize the difference in the composition between the shredded automobile scrap and the pre-treated municipal solid waste. The primary difference between the two products is in the shape of the aluminum component. In the municipal solid waste, the aluminum content is crumpled, shredded pieces of cans. It was considered of primary

---

*Richmond, Virginia, U.S.A. – major aluminum producer.

importance to run tests to determine the effect of shape factor on the separation results.

Test Work

A 50 mm product lot was composed by Reynolds Metals Co., representative of shredded municipal solid waste, which had been treated by air classifying (air classifier and VIP) and by magnetic removal of ferrous materials. The composition of the product was as shown in Fig. 9.

Since the test unit was equipped with a 36 cm diameter cyclone allowing a maximum feed particle of 25 mm (1 in.), the product was screened to 25 mm and 39% was found to be +25 mm with 61% –25 mm. The composition of the –25 mm fraction used in the test is shown in Fig. 10.

The goal of this text was to produce an aluminum fraction free of wood, rubber and heavy metal with a recovery of at least 85% of available aluminum. A 2-stage system was originally planned, the first stage using a water only cyclone with a 75° cone to remove all non-metals of 1.7 specific gravity or less such as wood and rubber. The heavy fraction, consisting of the underflow of the water only cyclone, which contains all the metal and heavier non-metals such as glass and stone, was to be separated in a second stage heavy medium cyclone with a 60° cone. It was anticipated that the heavy medium circuit would produce a light fraction containing aluminum, rock and glass, and a heavy fraction containing all the heavier metals. Several short test runs were made in the water only cyclone

to determine the setting at which the best results could be obtained, based primarily on the visually acceptable metal losses.

After having achieved the satisfactory setting a prolonged test was run, which was carried out to obtain a suitable amount of light product and heavy fractions of the water cyclone which would enable the completion of the experimental program with the heavy medium cyclone to produce final product for analyses. Detailed analyses of these products were run.

The results of the prolonged experiment with the water only cyclone are shown in Fig. 11.

The lost aluminum in the light fraction was 3%. This was considered acceptable. The wood was totally removed from the heavy fraction; however, the heavy fraction did contain some red rubber and, as expected, most of the glass and rock.

The heavy fraction from the water only cyclone underflow produced with this prolonged test was used as feed material for the heavy medium cyclone separation.

Previous work for automobile scrap separation established that the light fraction from the 60° heavy medium cyclone will contain all particles having a specific gravity lower than about 3.0 specific gravity, and the heavy fraction will contain all of the particles above a 3.0 specific gravity. Therefore a few short tests were run to achieve the specific gravity of the medium for the prolonged heavy medium test.

The results of the prolonged heavy medium test are shown in Fig. 12.

The aluminum content of the heavy fraction was 2.4%. In addition to this aluminum, the heavy fraction contained about 6% non-metallics.

Component	% By Weight
Wood	29.2
Rubber	23.4
Glass	7.3
Rock	10.9
Al (Cans)	14.6
Zn	7.3
Cu	7.3
Total	100.0

Figure 9. Composition of 50 mm shredded municipal waste after air classification (air classifier and VIP) and magnetic removal of ferrous materials.

Component	% By Weight
Wood	34.4
Rubber	10.5
Glass	12.3
Rock	20.2
Aluminum	12.7
Heavy non-ferrous	9.9
Total	100.0

Figure 10. Composition of the 25 mm – 1 in. fraction used in the test.

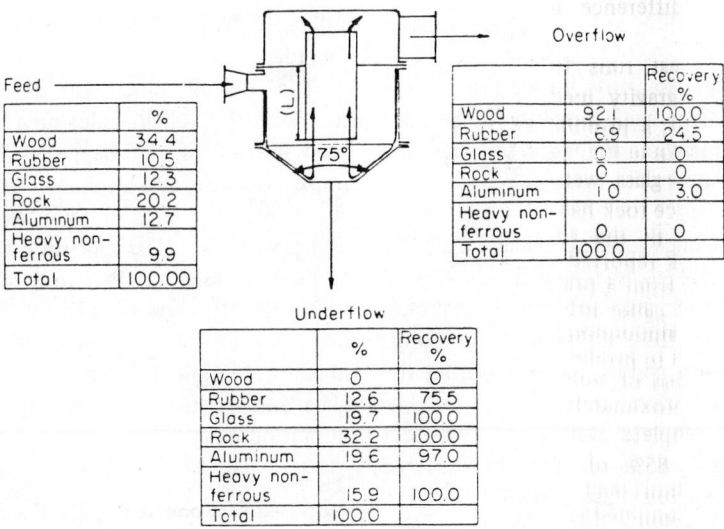

Feed

	%
Wood	34.4
Rubber	10.5
Glass	12.3
Rock	20.2
Aluminum	12.7
Heavy non-ferrous	9.9
Total	100.00

Overflow

		Recovery %
Wood	92.1	100.0
Rubber	6.9	24.5
Glass	0	0
Rock	0	0
Aluminum	1.0	3.0
Heavy non-ferrous	0	0
Total	100.0	

Underflow

	%	Recovery %
Wood	0	0
Rubber	12.6	75.5
Glass	19.7	100.0
Rock	32.2	100.0
Aluminum	19.6	97.0
Heavy non-ferrous	15.9	100.0
Total	100.0	

Figure 11.

This percentage can be reduced by a small increase in the specific gravity of separation. This would also result in a lower loss of aluminum without any significant decrease in the recovery of heavy non-ferrous metal. Of the aluminum in the feed product to the heavy medium cyclone, approximately 97% was recovered. This calculates to about 94% of the aluminum in the original –25 mm feed product to the combined circuits.

Unfortunately, the aluminum still contained a considerable percentage of rubber. Rubber is especially unacceptable in the re-melt process of aluminum, since it contributes a significant amount to the air pollution problems. It was, therefore, decided to supplement the original experimental program by an additional test separating the light fraction from the 60° heavy medium cyclone in a 20° heavy medium cyclone. This decision was reached based on the many years of experience in heavy medium separation in the minerals industry, where minerals are separated successfully in a 20° cyclone even though they

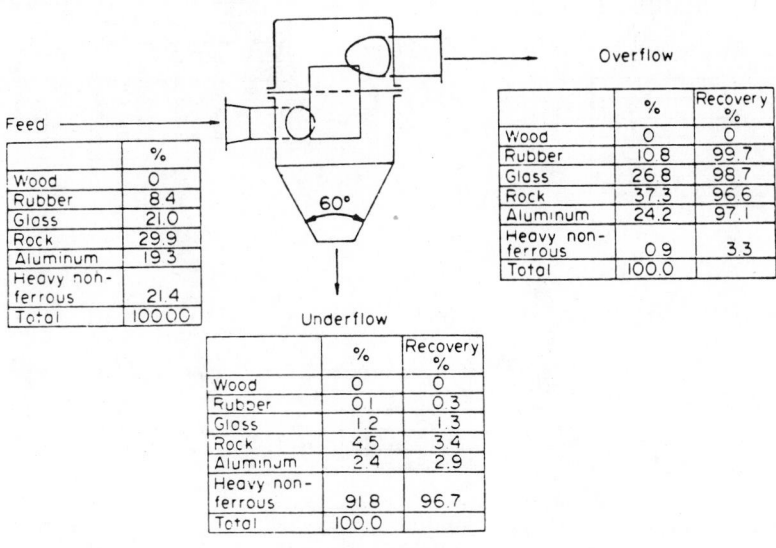

Feed

	%
Wood	0
Rubber	8.4
Glass	21.0
Rock	29.9
Aluminum	19.3
Heavy non-ferrous	21.4
Total	100.00

Overflow

	%	Recovery %
Wood	0	0
Rubber	10.8	99.7
Glass	26.8	98.7
Rock	37.3	96.6
Aluminum	24.2	97.1
Heavy non-ferrous	0.9	3.3
Total	100.0	

Underflow

	%	Recovery %
Wood	0	0
Rubber	0.1	0.3
Glass	1.2	1.3
Rock	4.5	3.4
Aluminum	2.4	2.9
Heavy non-ferrous	91.8	96.7
Total	100.0	

Figure 12.

have very little difference in specific gravity.

After a few test runs to determine the optimum specific gravity medium to be used for this experiment, a prolonged test was run. The results are shown in Fig. 13.

All rubber and glass were removed from the aluminum. Since rock has a specific gravity close to or equal to the specific gravity of aluminum, this rock reported to the aluminum fraction; however, from a practical standpoint, this rock does not cause problems during the re-melt process for aluminum.

This further step to produce clean aluminum did result in the loss of some of the available aluminum — approximately 10%, but the result of this complete system is a recovery of approximately 85% of the aluminum in the original -25 mm feed stock. As mentioned earlier, the compiled sample was screened at 25 mm. The +25 mm was not included in the test work. From experience, the separation of coarse particles is normally more efficient than the separation of small particles. Therefore, the overall recovery for the aluminum as well as for the heavy non-ferrous metals in a

full scale plant will be higher, if the +25 mm is included.

The overall aluminum recovery can be increased by small adjustments in the specific gravity of the heavy medium to maximize quantity of rubber free aluminum. As a practical matter, the clean aluminum along with the glass and rock should be sent through a small impact mill which will pulverize the glass and rock but will have virtually no effect on the aluminum. This then would make it feasible to screen out the rock and glass and produce a clean, top quality aluminum product.

Proposed Cyclone Separation Plant for Shredded Municipal Solid Waste

Before the flow sheet of the cyclone plant is discussed, a typical municipal solid waste plant similar to those existing in several cities in the United States will be discussed.

At this time the primary reason for a municipal solid waste plant is to reduce the amount of material which is going to landfill, since mass landfill is very expensive and is

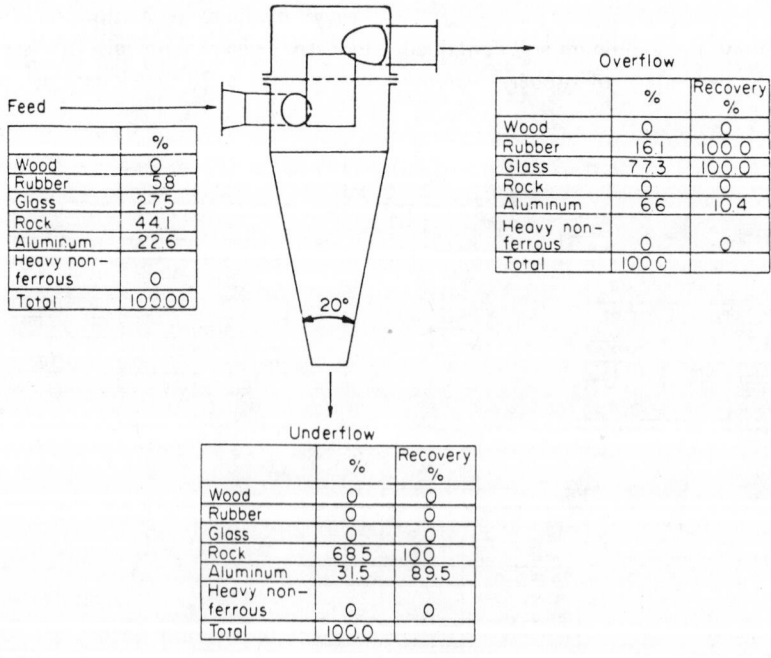

Feed

	%
Wood	0
Rubber	5.8
Glass	27.5
Rock	44.1
Aluminum	22.6
Heavy non-ferrous	0
Total	100.00

20°

Overflow

	%	Recovery %
Wood	0	0
Rubber	16.1	100.0
Glass	77.3	100.0
Rock	0	0
Aluminum	6.6	10.4
Heavy non-ferrous	0	0
Total	100.0	

Underflow

	%	Recovery %
Wood	0	0
Rubber	0	0
Glass	0	0
Rock	68.5	100
Aluminum	31.5	89.5
Heavy non-ferrous	0	0
Total	100.0	

Figure 13.

environmentally unsound. Most current treatment plants consist of a shredder and air classifier to produce a burnable product, which is used as fuel or supplemental fuel in power generation plants. Approximately 60-80% of the municipal solid waste is suitable for use as a refuse derived fuel, or "RDF" as it is called. The remaining portion is passed over a magnet for the recovery of ferrous metals and the balance consisting of heavy fabrics, rubber, glass, rock, aluminum, zinc, brass, copper, etc. is commonly sent to a landfill operation or a resource recovery section. This last product is the product to which the cyclone separation process would be applied. If this product also happens to have a maximum top size of about 50 mm, it can go directly to a cyclone separation plant; however, if the top size is larger, a secondary shredder should be installed. The secondary shredder would produce a top size of about 38 mm. The reason for this is that the specifications of the major aluminum producers in the United States for can aluminum require a shipping density of 15 lb. per cubic ft, which just happens to work out to a particle size of 38 mm.

Between the secondary shredder and the cyclone plant would be a screen to eliminate the +38 mm from the feed, which could be recycled back to the shredder and to eliminate the -12 mesh aluminum which is not acceptable, in the final aluminum product. Once the material has been through the secondary shredder, it is strongly suspicioned that the -12 mesh will contain most of the glass and rock which would otherwise enter the plant.

Cyclone Plant Flow Sheet

There are several options in applying the cyclone cleaning to municipal solid waste available to the prospective buyer. First, the water only cyclone process can be applied by itself to produce a metal rich concentrate in several different small communities. These concentrates can be shipped to a central plant which can apply heavy medium final separation to the total conglomerate. This idea can be used in an area with a dispersed population, where the economics of building a complete plant in each community may not be justified. The water cyclone circuit can easily remove 75% or more of the non-metallics in the feed, with the remainder to be treated in heavy medium cyclones.

A second method would be to build a plant which is composed of a water only cyclone circuit and one heavy medium cyclone circuit from which a product would be assimilated for batch type re-cleaning in heavy medium to produce the final products. This type of plant would be visualized for a medium size community of 200,000-400,000 population. In the larger metropolitan areas, it should be economically feasible to build a plant which is composed of a water only circuit and two heavy medium circuits. It is this type of flow sheet that will be discussed and is shown in Fig. 14.

In this flow sheet, both heavy medium cyclones are fed from their respective sumps which combine heavy medium and the products to be separated. The feed to the water only cyclone will be fed by gravity if the top size of the material is larger than 25 mm. This is done to avoid trouble and avoid plugging of the pump by the material being fed. Wood is especially a problem for a pump-fed operation. There is also a very strong possibility that the chunky heavy metals may settle out in horizontal runs of the piping, since the medium in only water. When feeding a cyclone with heavy medium, the problem is eliminated for the most part because the specific gravity of the medium itself tends to keep the particles in suspension.

The water only cyclone circuit is completely separated from the heavy medium circuit insofar as the water is concerned. The reason for this is that municipal solid waste contains organic material which can dissolve in water. To avoid contamination of the heavy medium, the overflow of the thickening cyclones in the water only circuit is not used for the rinsing water in the heavy medium circuit but is returned to the water sump. Further, since most of the fine particles -12 mesh are removed by the screens ahead of the plant, the underflow of the thickening cyclones would be minimal.

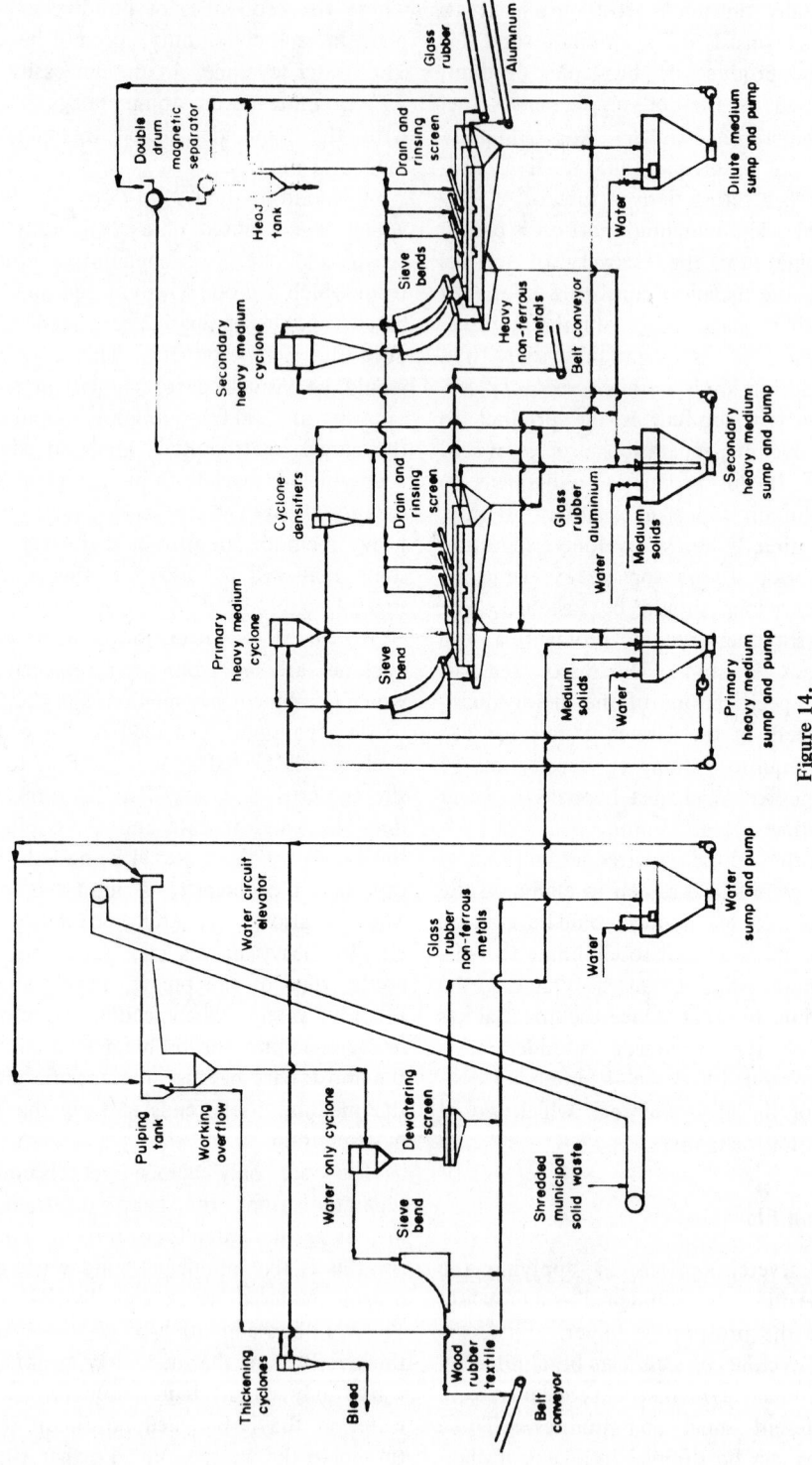

Figure 14.

Recovered metal from automotive scrap	Aluminum from municipal solid waste	Aluminum from auto. scrap and municipal solid waste	Heavy non-ferrous
Recovery in % of weight of metal in feed to cyclone plant	$\geqslant 90$	$\geqslant 85$	$\geqslant 95$
Composition in % of wt.			
Organics, including rubber	Traces to free	Traces to free	$\leqslant 1$
Aluminum	99	99	2
Heavy non-ferrous metals	1	1	97

$\geqslant$: Equal or larger.

Figure 15. Guarantees for recovery and composition of the recovered metals.

The heavy medium cyclone circuit itself is a closed circuit. The tailings are used as rinsing water. This also affords the opportunity for operating the three circuits independently, in case one is shut down for any reason. Since each circuit is independent, this also affords the opportunity to operate the heavy medium cyclone's stages in reverse if necessary or advantageous.

The operation of this plant is basically the same as the operation of the first commercial plant for automotive scrap, which is previously described in this paper, and it is not necessary to reiterate that description.

This brings out an interesting feature envisioned for the application of this type of plant. It is entirely feasible to operate this plant on municipal solid waste for one shift in a day and then by simple specific gravity adjustments, use the same plant for the second shift for shredded auto scrap or other wastes. The only prerequisite for these other materials is that they have no longer top size than that which is designed into the solid waste stream.

APPLICATION OF THE CYCLONE TECHNIQUE ON INCINERATOR RESIDUE FROM MUNICIPAL SOLID WASTE

Stamicarbon has already executed an intensive test program on incinerator residue from a Dutch incinerator.

This work was done at the Stamicarbon Pilot Plant under contract for the Institute for Waste Disposal, a Dutch Governmental Institute.

The results of this test work are not available for publication at this moment. However, we can mention that the preliminary results indicate a promising application for heavy medium cyclones.

The municipal solid waste in the Netherlands does not contain as much aluminum as that in the United States. Therefore, a test program has been scheduled with incinerator residue which will be obtained from an incineration test in the United States.

GUARANTEES

The guarantees for the recovery and the composition of the aluminum and the mixture of heavy non-ferrous metals produced as end products with a recovery system, composed of a water only cyclone circuit, a primary heavy medium cyclone circuit and a secondary heavy medium cyclone circuit are given in Fig. 15.

The guarantees for the total losses of media solids are given in Fig. 16.

These guarantees are valid for any recovery plant, as long as the plant is operated in accordance with the instructions and with the correct composition of the heavy medium solids.

FURTHER INVESTIGATIONS

The following investigations are still under study.

1. The separation of aluminum into two grades differing in specific gravity for which the heavy medium cyclone is a suitable instrument. It is capable of effectively separating two components,

Free product to cyclone plant	Total losses in kg per tonne of feed to heavy medium cyclone plant	Total loss in lbs. per short ton feed to heavy medium
Automotive scrap	0.8	1.6
Municipal solid waste	1.5	3.0

Figure 16. Guarantees for losses of heavy media solids.

whose specific gravities differ only marginally. For instance, two plants are already in operation, where +1 mm KCl particles with a specific gravity of 1.97 are separated quite efficiently from +1 mm NaCl particles having a specific gravity of 2.25.

2. The separation of rubber and several kinds of plastics from each other. For instance, the specific gravity of polyvinyl chloride is higher than that of polypropylene. This is all the more important since there is a distinct trend towards building lighter cars in which use more plastics nd aluminum. Recycling of rubber and plastics will become necessary.

3. The separation of wire from insulation after cryopulverization or other methods of liberation of the metal from the insulation.

CONCLUSION

The economic success of the first cyclone cleaning plant for shredded automotive scrap is conclusive proof that this is a viable application for the water only cyclone and heavy medium cyclone principle.

The test work performed on the shredded municipal solid waste, the crushed car batteries and incinerator residue has a very strong correlation with the first commercial plant for automotive scrap. The cyclone process is a very profitable method for recovery of aluminum and other non-ferrous metals because of the high efficiency and the continuous production of saleable products.

The applications of the cyclone technique on the resource recovery from the different types of solid wastes are patented by Stamicarbon in Europe, United States and other countries.

Roberts and Shaefer Resource Service, exclusive licensee of Stamicarbon b.v., for the United States, is building a large scale plant for the demonstration and further research of applications.

REFERENCES

1. H.H. Dreissen and A.T. Basten, Reclaiming products from shredded junked cars by the water only and heavy medium cyclone processes, Proceedings of the Fifth Mineral Waste Utilization Symposium, Chicago, (U.S.A.) p. 378 (1976).

2. P.C. Reeves, J.H. Absil, H.H. Dreissen and A.T. Basten, Resource recovery from shredded scrap cars and shredded municipal solid waste by water only cyclone processes and heavy medium cyclone processes, Proceedings of the First World Recycling Congress, Basle (Switzerland). Part II, 1/13/i (1978).

3. H.H. Dreissen, The contribution of Stamicarbon/DSM to the technology of the concentration of minerals and coal, De Ingenieur Mijnbouw, 27 October (1972).

4. H. Dreissen and F. Fontein, Application of hydrocyclones and sieve bends in the wet treatment of coal, minerals, and mineral products, Annual Meeting AIME, Dallas, Texas, Paper No. 63FB18. February (1963).

5. L.R. Mahoney and J.J. Harwood, The automobile as a renewable resource, *Resourcer Policy* I (5), September (1975).

3-12 The Recovery of Waste Glass Cullet for Recycling Purposes by Means of Electro-Optical Sorters

H. Stirling

Source: Adapted from an article with the same title in *Conservation and Recycling,* V976, 1976, pp. 209–219. Reprinted with Permission of Pergamon Press, Ltd.

INTRODUCTION

This paper is concerned with recovery of glass, which normally constitutes 10% of Municipal Solid Waste (MSW). In Britain, it is estimated that nearly a million tons of glass are discarded annually [1] and it is encouraging that the Department of the Environment has recently allocated £1 million for the construction of two MSW recovery plants in the North of England.

Glass container manufacturers have traditionally used between 10–20% cullet in glassmaking because it melts at a lower temperature than the basic raw materials, aids their mixing, saves energy, and reduces furnace wear [2]. However, for optimum utilization and value, waste glass should be color sorted, since cullet of mixed colors impairs the purity of the final glass product. Similarly, waste glass must be free from all contaminants such as ceramics and bottle tops, since these cause flaws in the glassware and damage the furnace linings. The main market requirement is for flint (clear) cullet, but green and amber are also of value, each type having to conform to strict specifications.

The principal method employed for color sorting is an electro-optical technique. This method is also applicable to the removal of opaque impurities, although other techniques such as electrostatic separation, and froth flotation are in use. However, these are outside the scope of this paper which is to electro-optical separation only.

HOW AN ELECTRO-OPTICAL SORTER WORKS

An electronic sorter consists of four basic parts, shown in Fig. 1.

1. *A Feeding system* to provide a controlled feed to the inspection area.
2. *An Inspection system* to measure the optical properties of the particles.
3. *An Evaluation system* to electronically translate the optical measurement into an accept/reject signal.
4. *A Separation system* to remove reject particles by means of a precisely timed air blast [3].

Feed

The feed system meters the appropriate number of particles per unit time by means of a vibrating tray. From this, the particles drop on to an inclined chute down which they accelerate under gravity to speeds as high as 4 m/sec. The chute also aligns the product stream into the optical center of the inspection area.

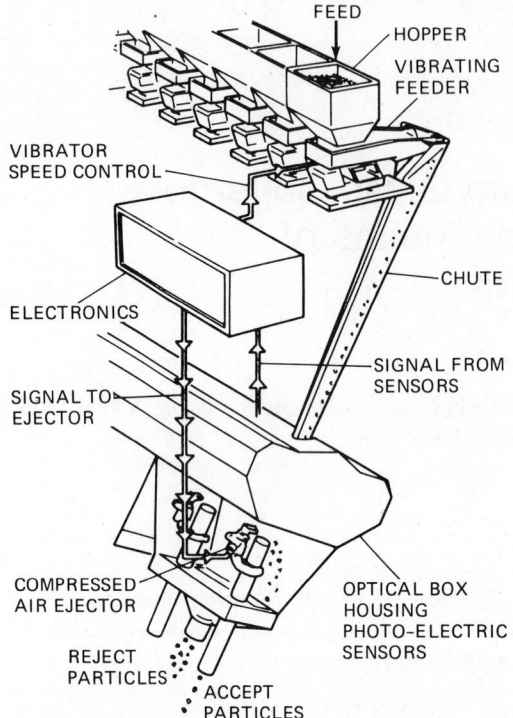

Figure 1. Schematic Diagram of Electronic Separator

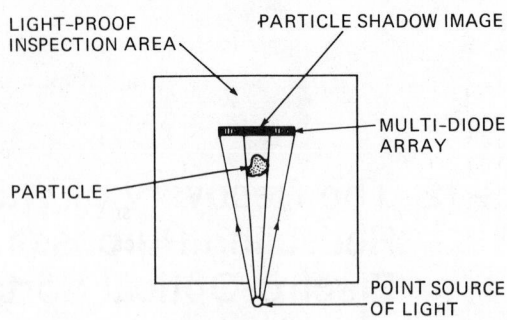

Figure 2. Optical box – transparency sorter (plan).

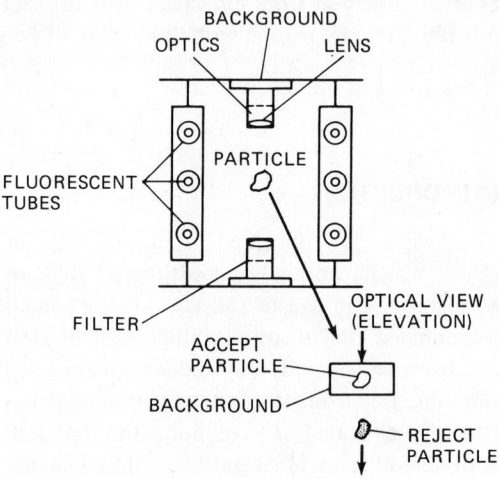

Figure 3. Optical box – color sorter (plan).

Inspection

The Transparency and Color Inspection techniques differ, and must therefore be considered separately.

Transparency (see Fig. 2). This system measures the amount of light transmitted through the particles. The inspection area, or 'Optical Box', is dark; a bright point source of light on one side of the optical box shines across the particle flow stream on to a high resolution multi-diode array, mounted horizontally on the other side of the box. Any opaque pieces block out the light source, causing a sharp shadow image to fall on the array; this is sufficient to produce a signal.

Color (see Fig. 3). The color technique is more complicated, and is based on the measurement of reflected light and, to a lesser extent, transmitted light. The sort depends on the fact that different colored glass particles have, at certain wavelengths, different reflectivity and absorption values. In this case, the optical box is evenly illuminated by fluorescent tubes on two sides. Photocell detectors view the particle stream from the two other sides of the box, filters being incorporated in the viewing aperture to select the optimum waveband over which the measurement should be made. The particles are viewed by the detector as they fall in front of an illuminated background. The color of this is chosen so that it appears to have brightness between that of the accept and reject particles. In practice, this means that a dark particle will give a decrease in signal whereas a light particle will give an increase, and an unambiguous decision can easily be made by the electronics.

Evaluation System

The signal from the solid state detectors has first to be amplified. This is done by a low noise, low level current amplifier placed close to the detector to avoid interference problems. The amplified signal can then be passed on to the decision-making circuits. These take the form of a level discriminator which classifies all signals of a certain polarity and exceeding a certain noise threshold as reject signals, and the corresponding particles as reject particles. When several detectors are used, as with the photodiode array in the transparency sorter, it is necessary to take all the decision signals from the various detectors and apply a logic function to arrive at a single final decision.

The final link in the chain is the ejector drive circuit which couples the decision output signal to the separation system.

Separation System (see Fig. 4).

The separation system or ejector consists of a high speed solenoid valve which releases short blasts of compressed air through a nozzle. This ejection device exhibits the essential features of rapid action, reliability and mechanical strength. The separation process takes place while the particles are in free fall. Accept particles are allowed to continue along their normal trajectory into an accept receptacle while the carefully controlled air blast deflects the reject particles out of this trajectory and into a reject receptacle.

The whole process is extremely fast, the ejector being capable of removing 300 pieces of glass of an average size of 15 mm every second.

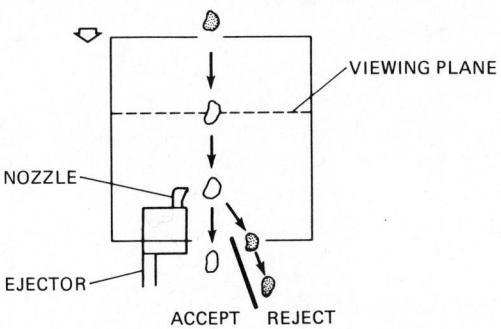

Figure 4. Optical box – separation system (side elevation).

THE PERFORMANCE OF CULLET SORTERS

Glass may be recovered from a mixture containing glass, ceramics, bottle tops and similar materials, and the first stage in the recovery process is to present it to the machine in convenient size fractions. Suitable ranges are 15–20 mm and 20–40 mm, although it is now possible to sort smaller sizes, of less than 5 mm. The product must be clean and dry. Cullet of this type can derive from glass works, general glass industry scrap or from MSW recycling plants; MSW glass is mostly in the form of no-deposit containers.

Having discussed the principles of operation of an electronic sorter, the actual performance of cullet sorters under plant conditions must now be examined.

Transparency

The separation of mixed glass from opaques is shown in Fig. 5, and it can be seen that, as the throughput increases, the glass recovery falls. Consequently, for any given installation there will be a break-even point for the optimum number of machines against the amount of glass recovered. Under plant conditions, the percentage of opaques in mixed glass would meet a specification of 0.5% in a single pass, but in

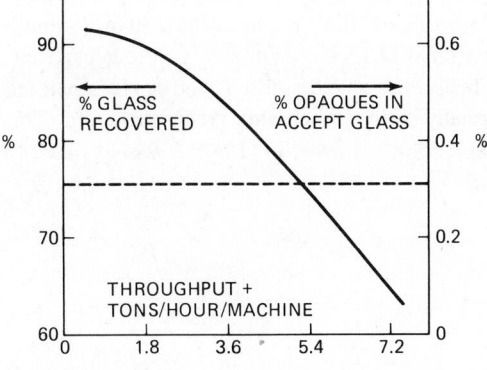

PERFORMANCE AT CONSTANT SENSITIVITY AND VARIABLE THROUGHPUT
AVERAGE CONCENTRATION OF OPAQUES IN INPUT = 6.12%   SENSITIVITY = 400

Figure 5. Transparency sorter (cullet) separation of opaques from glass.

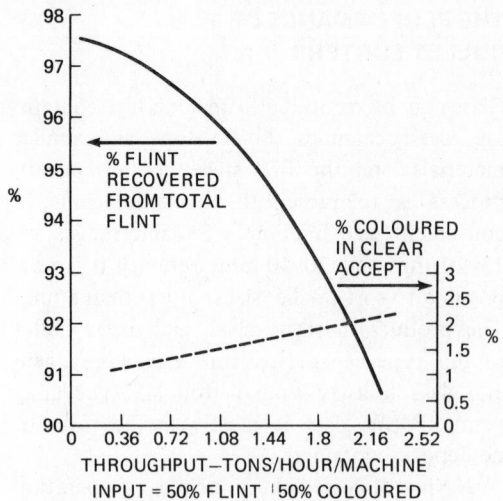

Figure 6. Color sorter (cullet) separation of flint from colored.

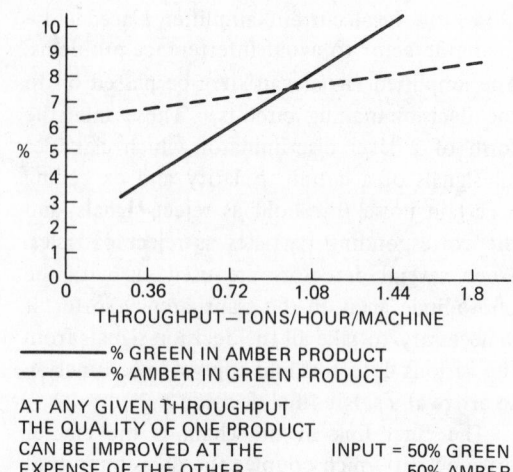

Figure 7.

applications where a tighter specification than this is required, a second pass through the sorter is recommended. It should also be noted that in MSW plants the concentration of refractories in opaques may only be of the order of 10% (true refractory being the most deleterious material in a glass remelt product).

Color Sorting

Flint glass can be separated from mixed colored glass as illustrated in Fig. 6. At throughputs of up to 1.5 tons/h, it could be expected that 95% of the flint is recoverable at a contamination of 1.5% of mixed colored particles. Finally, the mixed colored glass can be separated usually into amber and green products. This separation, shown in Fig. 7 would meet a specification of 10% contamination of one color in the other on both products.

Note: (i) All percentages are on a dry weight basis.

(ii) All the graphs are based on Laboratory trials, substantiated by plant results, for size range 5-20 mm (+1/4-3/4).

REFERENCES

1. E. Douglas and P.R. Birch, Recovery of potentially re-usable materials from domestic by physical sorting. *Resource Recovery and Conservation* 1, 4 (April 1976).
2. J. Milgrom, Recovery of glass from municipal wastes. *Resource Recovery and Energy Review*, pp. 10-13. (March/April, 1975).
3. W.S. Maughan, The use of automatic optical sorting equipment for industrial quality control. *Proc. Soc. Photo-optical Instrument Engineers*, 60, pp. 99-107 (1975).

3-13 Glass and Non-Ferrous Metal Recovery Subsystem at Franklin, Ohio

John P. Cummings

Source: Adapted from a Paper Published in the *Proceedings* of the Fifth Mineral Waste Utilization Symposium, Chicago, Illinois, April 13–14, 1976, pp. 175–183.

INTRODUCTION

At this time, with energy, material and land shortage, the recycling of any and all materials appears to be the best answer for Solid Waste Management. The Glass Container Manufacturers Institute has announced that approximately 3% of the glass containers manufactured each year have been recovered at their, over 100, glass plant reclamation centers. The container glass has been shown to be one of the most recyclable of all packaging products. Cullet, broken glass, is used as part of the match material needed for glass container manufacturing. In most cases, the amount of cullet used in the normal batch is between 15 and 20% of the total weight of glass made. The cullet which has been recovered from outside sources is used at the same time the glass plant's offware is used. Some work has been done on sand sized, non-color sorted cullet recovered from solid wastes by froth flotation.[1] However, the use of this cullet is limited because it is not color sorted. Aluminum is also recovered at ecology recycling stations, which have been supported by beverage manufacturers, retail stores and the aluminum manufacturing industry.

The Franklin, Ohio project was funded by the City of Franklin and Black Clawson with moneys from within Solid Waste Division of the Public Health Service, U.S. Government, in 1968, as a demonstration unit to show an innovative solid waste disposal technique.[2] The principal concept at the Franklin, Ohio site was the recovery of usable materials, principally the recycling of ferrous metals and paper fiber from municipal solid waste. The remaining organic material was burned and the remaining inorganic fraction placed in a sanitary landfill. The concept was to take raw waste or trash from packer trucks and put it into a rotating hammer-mill and break the material up under water so that the solid waste was converted into a pulpable water slurry of a 3 to 4% consistency. Some objects, specifically brick, stone, shoes, the bottom of a champagne bottle and crushed cans, are ejected through the bottom of this rotating hammer-mill. These materials are recovered, the magnetic portion scalped away, the remaining portion is put back onto the tipping floor to be rerun through the system. The remaining material is now less than one inch in diameter and it is carried in a slurry to a liquid cyclone which segregates the inorganic fraction from the organic fraction. The inorganic fraction is truly a glass-rich fraction and that is the material which is conveyed over to the glass and aluminum recovery system. The remaining material continues on through the Black Clawson system where the paper fiber may be recovered, or the entire organic material may be used as an energy source, i.e. a fuel.

The Environmental Protection Agency has a number of projects involved in research efforts designed to project the major components of post consumer waste over the next 15 to 20 years as a base line for various policy decisions. A great deal of this effort has been toward municipal wastes, which is approximately 80% organic, 20% inorganic material, with 9.7% being glass, 9.5% metal, and 1.4% miscellaneous inorganics.[3] Packaging waste has increased very substantially in per capita terms and its composition has also shifted considerably over the past several years. The estimated growth rate of post consumer solid waste is expected to be approximately 4.5% per year. Because this growth is expected to continue, and because a fairly significant amount of this growth is in recoverable materials with the value of the recovered materials increasing as our availability of virgin materials decreases, and with the effect that energy savings can be expected in most cases, then continued resource recovery will become a main direction for waste disposal in the years to come.

THE PROCESS

The original design and engineering for the Franklin Subsystem has been discussed in the previous paper given at the 4th Mineral Waste Utilization Symposium back in 1974.[4] The system at that time was designed to clean and color sort the glass into three colors and recover aluminum for reuse in container or other manufacturing processes. Since that time, there have been several changes or modifications to the system. Several of the components from the original system are still included within the overall processing system, but there have been substantial changes to get more efficient and better results. Because the facility is a demonstration site, the various experiments or design changes were set up based upon what knowledge had been learned in previous and from other experimental operations. The way the system is now set up, material from the liquid cyclone is conveyed across into the subsystem and is magnetically scalped. From the magnetic scalping device, the material is placed on a vibrating screen, which is a Sweeco screen,

and the fines and some dirt with organic residue is washed off, the fines being arbitrarily defined as anything less than 1/4 inch. This undersized material will not be color sorted or recovered in any way, and it is sent to the landfill.

The vibrating wet screening device has improved the cleanliness of the inorganic fraction by much better elutriation process than in the prior screening device. The screen which had been set up to remove oversized material, that is, greater than one inch, has been deleted. Through experimentation, no reason was found to reject the so-called larger or oversized pieces of material.

After the screening, a conveyor carries the material across to the heavy media separation unit. The heavy media separation system is held at a specific gravity of 2.0. This removes the heavier organic materials, specifically plastics, that have slipped through the liquid cyclone in the main system. All the floated material is returned to the main plant to be burned, and it would be used as a fuel in a larger system. The sink material, that is the material that has specific gravity greater than 2.0, is sent on to the jigging operation. Previous work has shown that the use of a dense media system can be an extremely useful unit process in order to get rid of superfluous materials in waste glass stream. The difficulty with a dense media system is that aluminum has approximately the same specific gravity as does container glass material, and the aluminum is one of the materials which has to be removed from the cullet in order for the waste glass to be a useful ingredient in glass container manufacturing.

The jigging operation is one which is well known to most mining operations and mineral beneficiation systems. It is an old and well-proven unit process. Jigging, for all practical purposes, is a pulsating water media elutriation and segregation machine, such that a lightweight or an apparent lightweight material, is floated off, leaving the heavier material at the base of the jig. The operation, as set up at the Franklin site, has three streams — the lightweight, mostly aluminum can-type stock; the medium fraction, which is mostly glass; and a very heavy fraction, composed generally of cast metals, such as brass keys, coins, cast aluminum, cast zinc, or lead-form material. The jigging operation is an extremely effective and efficient process. It is a very rugged piece of equipment and with the feed material held for the proper residence time within the jigging operation, a very clean aluminum, glass and heavy metal fraction can be obtained from this process. The composition of the aluminum coming off of this particular unit at Franklin is discussed in a later section. The heavy metal fraction composition, which is a cup fraction from the base of the jigging operation, is discussed in the later section as well. The glass fraction now remaining is conveyed from the jigging operation to the rotary kiln dryer. The rotary kiln dryer gets rid of the excess water which is on the surface of the glass material, and the material coming from the rotary kiln is now in discreet, warm particles.

The glass fraction is carried by a conveyor to the high tension electrostatic separation unit. This process is well known for the segregation of material and has been used for many years in the mining industry and other mineral beneficiation industries. The principal upon which the high tension electrostatic separator works has been discussed in other papers.[4] However, in all reported cases in past history, the use of electrostatic separation has been for materials that were less than 8 mesh in size. The use of this particular device for the segregation of material from plus 1/4 inch to minus 1 inch in size has proved to be an excellent operation for the recovery subsystem where it separates out natural stone and the remaining cast metal materials, as well as residual aluminum can stock, which remains in the glass fraction. This segregation of cyrstalline, i.e., conductor, materials by static charge displacement, is similar to that electric potential which builds up on metal when an electrical field charge is imposed upon it. When the charge has been transferred to the rock or crystalline material, including what metals are left in the system, the charge effect makes it possible to segregate non-conductive material, such as glass, ceramics, and clay products from metallic and natural rock materials. The application of the electrostatic high tension unit process was first proven at the Carpco Laboratories. However, this high tension electrostatic unit is an extremely valuable tool for segregating out materials, and when the materials are dry and warm it is an extremely efficient process.

The glass fraction coming from the high tension electrostatic device is conveyed by bucket elevators into hoppers which feed v-shaped belts for the separation of ceramics from the glass fraction by use of a transparency device. The transparency device is a relatively new addition to the processing line at Franklin and is based on the need to remove an extremely high incidence of ceramic or refractory materials found in the glass fraction. These refractory materials are detrimental to the manufacture of glass containers. They cause imperfections in the glass container which destroys the integrity of the jar or bottle. The transparency device is quite similar to the color sorting device. The feed rate from the hoppers is controlled by a vibrating device controlled by the flow and material level. The material is dropped from the v-shaped belt in a known projectory, so it passes with a known pathway through an optical box which has a photo cell assembly in it. By various design characteristics there can be as many as three optical devices or three photo cells within one optical box. However, at Franklin we are utilizing only one photo cell per channel, or one photo cell per optical box. For the separation of the opaque materials causes a null signal within the electronic logic and that particular particle is blown away by a high pressure air ejection device. The material, once it has been transparency sorted, is then passed on to a color sorting operation which works quite similarly to the opacity or transparency sorter.

In a previous study at Franklin, the glass composition was segregated into flint, amber and green glass. However, experimentation within the industry found that there was no need to make a triple color sort of glass fraction, and that a fling, non-flint, i.e., colored glass, fraction would be sufficient, so that the devices at Franklin are set up to only do one selection, that is to segregate the flint glass from the colored glass. For the separation of flint from colored glass, the darker or colored glass causes a deviation in the null signal, and then a device for the ejection of the dark or colored particle is triggered and that piece of material is blown away. The electronic logic of this system is such that there is a sufficient time lag from the time the target particle is observed in the optical box, until it has reached the selection point where it is falling freely through the ejection envelope. The selection time, which is controlled by the electronic logic, actuates the pneumatic valve and blows the free-falling particle from the stream.

At Franklin the opacity/transparency segregation unit and the color separation unit are composed each of six channels which can easily segregate approximately 200 lb per channel per hour, or nominally 0.6 tons per hour. Two new units with six channels each, which have better feed and electronic logic systems, are placed in Franklin at this time. These devices are far more efficient than the previous or older devices and both of these instruments are able to handle up to 300 lb per hour per channel, or 0.9 ton per hour per device.

CHARACTERISTICS OF RECOVERED GLASS

The primary purpose at the Franklin, Ohio demonstration project was to recover materials from solid waste which could be reused. In accordance with this purpose, the recovery of clean color sorted glass as well as nonmagnetic metals was the reason the glass and non-ferrous metal recovery subsystem was put together. Previous studies have given the compositions of various materials left in the solid waste inorganic fraction. At Franklin, the solid waste fraction which comes over to the subsystem from the main plant is approximately 10% on a dried weight basis. Of the total fraction received at the glass/metal plant, magnetic metals make up 6% of the total. Natural rock, stone and ceramics make up approximately 10%. Nonmagnetic metals, 4%, organic and other miscellaneous, 2%, and the glass, approximately 78%. With the limitations on the color sorting device, that is materials less than 1/4 in. cannot be segregated into color, approximately 2/3 of the glass is recoverable.

The glass recovery system has gone through three progressive stages. The original material

which was color sorted was examined and characterized as to composition and how it could be utilized within the glass container manufacturing. Samples were taken over a long period of time and close physical and optical examination of the three colored glass fractions showed a very high incidence of refractory material within all three fractions. Color sorting of itself was highly efficient and did an effective job of separating the glass into three different color components. The high refractory count of individual pieces, mainly clay ceramics, within the glass fractions caused great dismay among many of the glass companies because the material which had been recovered would be unsuitable for use in a glass furnace. White clay or refractory particles amounted to between 1 and 4% by weight within the flint fraction, and from 4 to 8% in the amber and green fractions. The first concept utilized to segregate out the opaque, i.e., refractory materials, from glass was a single channel device of experimental design produced by the Sortex Company to eliminate opaque objects from the other transparent material. The results of this single channel laboratory style opacity sorter on a flint glass were reported elsewhere.[5] The refractory content after the transparency segregation was approximately 5.5% of glass cullet by weight, whereas the Glass Container Manufacturers Institute guideline for Franklin cullet required 0.05%. The flint cullet had more green glass remaining in it, approximately 3.25%, which was higher than the GCMI standard of 1% maximum green glass in the flint cullet fraction. With these results, the transparency device and the color sorting device were examined much more closely and modifications were made in the systems.

A six-channel device for opacity sorting based upon the experience from the single channel experimental unit at Franklin was manufactured and placed at Franklin. The device had several drawbacks, among which were the blow-down or cleaning arrangement for the lens area within the optical box, and the feeding operation which was not as efficient as in the prior instrument. The results of the flint and color glass fractions based upon the interim sorting installation over a two-month period of time is shown in Table 1.

Table 1. Original Sorters Recovered Cullet.

	Flint	Colored
Glass	98.1	92.3
Flint	87.2	36.8
Colored	10.9	55.5
Stones & Ceramics	1.8	7.0
Metal	Trace	Trace

Table 2. New Sorters Recovered Cullet.

	Flint	Colored
Glass	99.8	99.7
Flint	98.6	27.8
Colored	1.2	71.9
Stones & Ceramics	0.1	0.3
Metal	Trace	Trace

Table 3. Composition of Aluminum Factors.

	Air Classified	Electrostatic	Linear Induction
Aluminum and Metal	39.6%	73.8%	96.4%
Glass	1.6%	1.7%	–
Trash	55.7%	24.3%	3.5%
–20 Mesh	3.1%	0.2%	Trace

Based upon the studies of this area and because a new feeding device and ejection operation had been devised, two new optical sorting devices were placed at Franklin. The results from these new sorters, that is the third stage operation, are shown in Table 2. The most noteworthy achievement of this glass and metal recovery subsystem is the fact that the equipment has been able to reduce the ceramic content over a period of time by making various adjustments and developments in the optical sorting devices found through experimentation.

The glass container manufacturing companies found that it was not necessary to color sort glass into the flint, amber and green fractions, but a single color separation, that is flint from non-flint, would suffice for the industry needs.[6] The present subsystem segregates the glass into a colored fraction and a flint fraction based upon the needs of the glass container industry. The present refractory level is not acceptable under the new GCMI standards; however, progress has been made and continued endeavors should remove refractory contamination to, or below, the required standard.

NON-FERROUS METAL CHARACTERISTICS

Experimentation at the subsystem within the Franklin complex has given several non-ferrous fractions, most aluminum; however, there has been some copper, copper alloy, lead base metal and some zinc in our basic recovered metals. As noted in the previous discussion, several changes were made within the system to improve the recovered glass. The same thing has been true of the recovered non-ferrous metal fraction. The original system had an air classifying unit wherein the equipment recovered a fair amount of can stock. An analysis of this particular fraction is given in Table 3. Also shown in Table 3 is a composition of the electrostatic high tension metal composition which we were able to get out of the air classified bottom's fraction. However, that same fraction run through the linear induction device gives a 93.2% aluminum, 3.0% other metal, and about 3.5% nonmetal. There was minus 20 mesh material. It can be seen that the potential for aluminum scrap recovery is to utilize the linear induction device to segregate out a rich aluminum fraction. Table 4 gives a chemical analysis of aluminum against a standard can stock, cast scrap, and the

Table 4. Chemical Assay of Aluminum.

Element	Can Stock	Cast Scrap	Franklin
Si	0.15	Any Level to 15.0	0.13
Fe	0.40	1.0	0.40
Cu	0.12	Any Level to 10.0	0.09
Mn	0.9 to 1.0	<1.25	0.64
Mg	1.1 to 1.3*	Any Level to 5.0	0.70
Cr	0.01	0.5	<0.03
Zn	0.04	1.0 to 3.0	0.85
Ti	0.02	–	<0.05
Pb	0.00	0.5	<0.05
Sn	0.00	0.5	<0.01
Ni	0.00	0.5	<0.01

*Melting loss not included.

Franklin recovered aluminum assay. This particular scrap was assayed by using the molten salt method. Scrap was mixed in and collected in a pool beneath the salt and the results of these tests give a comparison of the acceptable grades of container alloy or cast alloy. It should be noted that the material is unacceptable for container use. Therefore, it is possible that this scrap material would be best suited for cast or form alloys because the specifications for these particular alloys of aluminum are less stringent than those for can stock. The linear induction/eddy current device is discussed in detail elsewhere; however, this type of subsystem does an efficient job of non-ferrous metal recovery.

With the new changes in the system, that is the incorporation of the dense media and jigging operation, metal recovery has increased with the heavy metal as well as platey metal fractions from the jigging operation. The bottom of the jig has a very heavy metal fraction composed mostly of cast and form metals. Table 5 shows the metal content of this cup fraction which is an extremely heavy material composed mostly

Table 5. Cup Metal Recovery.

Pot Metals	49.4%
Copper/Alloys	33.5%
Lead	7.0%
Aluminum	0.6%
Stone/Ceramics	3.8%
Miscellaneous	5.7%

of coins, keys, poured or formed metal materials. From the very top of the jig a different metal fraction, that is the can or form stock fraction, which amounts to 86% aluminum alloy, 5% other metals including foil of various kinds, and 9% of miscellaneous materials. It can be seen that were the eddy current device used to upgrade this aluminum fraction it would be a very clean and useful fraction for foil or can stock utilization.

COSTS AND REVENUES

The operating and capital costs for that portion of a Raw Refuse Plant with an input of 2,000

Table 6. Glass and Metal Recovery Based on 2000 TPD Raw Refuse Input.

Capital Cost		
Process Equipment	$2,000,000	
Installation & Building[1]	500,000	
		$2,500,000
Operating Cost		
Personnel @ $25,000/Year[2]	$ 300,000	
9 Operating		
3 Maintenance		
Maintenance Supplies	$ 100,000	
5% Base Installation Costs		
Utilities[3]	$ 50,000	
Amortization[4]	$ 430,000	
Miscellaneous[5]	$ 10,000	
		$ 890,000
Income		
Glass — 25,000 Tons @ $20/Ton —	$ 500,000	
Mag. Metal — 5,000 Tons @ $25/Ton —	$ 125,000	
Non-Ferrous Metal — 2,500 Tons @ $200/Ton —	$ 500,000	
		$1,125,000

[1] No land price.
[2] With benefits.
[3] Electricity, water, sewage, etc.
[4] Based upon 15 years.
[5] Includes phone, office supplies, etc.

tons per day, in order to recover reusable glass, ferrous and non-ferrous metals from an inorganic fraction are shown in Table 6. These costs, while based on the experience taken from the experiment at Franklin, also include new design and improved equipment, specifically designed for solid waste recovery, and with the economy size incorporated, the plant operation would be a basic continuous 24 hour per day, with a total or 12 personnel including supervisory people. The building, to contain the process line, would be approximately 4,000 sq ft and about 60 ft in height. The height advantage would enable the total process to be tiered such that a gravity feed would replace many elevators and conveyors, the concept being that the gravity feed would allow all products to be directed to outside bins for railroad or trailer truck removal.

The operating and amortization costs are based on the suspected maintenance requirements as well as the personnel salaries. The income estimates are based on either contracts in being at the present time for the material, or the price which can be expected based on present day prices for the recovered materials. The estimates of recovered material value are based on the least price which can be anticipated within the near future. The costs of the recovery subsystem are based upon the fact that this subsystem would be contiguous to a normal recovery plant wherein the organic fraction would have been removed. No transportation costs are anticipated between the main system and the subsystem in this analysis. The income is based on delivered price.

SUMMARY

The Franklin, Ohio subsystem has proven that production color sorting of a glass rich fraction taken from municipal solid waste is technically feasible. This experiment has also shown that in order to have an economically viable system of recovering any inorganic fraction the recovery of all materials, i.e., glass, nonferrous, and magnetic metals must be segregated and used as a portion of the valued materials. The production style opacity device has come a long way. It still does not meet the present GCMI specifications, but perhaps other methods of getting rid of ceramic materials are available and should be tried. It should also be noted that through changes in the system utilizing a linear induction device or the jigging operation there has been an upgrading of the nonferrous fraction into two or possibly three different fractions, one of which is a can stock salvage material which may be used in containers manufacturing. The addition of these various unit processes has enhanced the economics and increased the efficiency of this recovery process. Future work, especially for the removal of opaque or refractory materials from the remaining glass material should be worked on, as well as more efficient machine size and design for economy of size.

REFERENCES

1. Morey, Booker, and J.P. Cummings, Proc. Third Mineral Waste Utilization Symposium, IIT Research Inst., 311 (1972).
2. Herbert, William, Ibid., 306.
3. Resource Recovery and Source Reduction; Second Report to Congress, U.S. E.P.A., O.S.W.M.P., E.P.A. SW-118, U.S. Govt. Printing Office, Washington, DC, (1974).
4. Cummings, John P., Proc. Fourth Mineral Waste Utilization Symposium, IIT Research Inst., 106 (1974).
5. Stewart, Michael W., Report to GCMI, Franklin Cullet Furnace Trial (1974).
6. Cummings, John P., Cullet Market Needs and Specifications, Presented to Tenth Meeting Amer. Inst. Mining, Metallurgical and Petroleum Engineers, New York, NY (1975).
7. Morey, Booker, J.P. Cummings and T.D. Griffin, Recovery of Small Metal Particles from Non-Metals Using an Eddy Current Separator (1975).

3-14 Recovery of Glass from Urban Refuse by Froth Flotation

J.H. Heginbotham

Source: Reprinted From *Proceedings* of the Sixth Mineral Waste Utilization Symposium, Chicago, Illinois, May 2–3, 1978, pp. 230–240.

INTRODUCTION

As part of its research program, the Bureau of Mines, U.S. Department of the Interior, investigates new or improved metallurgical technologies that are needed to help maintain adequate mineral and metal supplies while conserving natural resources through the recovery of values from secondary resources such as urban refuse. Early in this work a process was devised and a pilot plant was constructed to reclaim valuable materials from the residues of municipal incinerators.[3] Products from the primary section of the pilot plant include clean ferrous scrap, mixed nonferrous metals, and glass aggregates. A major portion of the current flowsheet is shown in figure 1.

Following development of the incinerator residue system, a companion process was developed and a pilot plant constructed to recover materials from unburned urban refuse.[4] Products reclaimed in this pilot plant include ferrous scrap, aluminum, mixed heavy nonferrous metals, glass aggregates, and combustibles for use as fuel.[5] A major portion of the raw refuse flowsheet is shown in figure 2.

Glass aggregates recovered in both systems contain approximately 10 percent nonglass materials (principally ceramics, brick, and stones), making the products unsuitable for use as cullet in the manufacture of glass containers. To be acceptable for use as cullet, glass recovered from urban waste must meet a rigid set of specifications that has been imposed by the glass container industry.[2] The most critical requirement involves the permissible number of refractory particles that can be tolerated in a specified quantity of cullet. The minus 20-plus 40-mesh fraction of a 1-pound sample of cullet (minus 20- plus 150-mesh), in which there are an estimated 600,000 particles, cannot contain more than 2 refractory particles, and the minus 40-plus 60-mesh fraction cannot contain more than 20 particles.

The specifications include the statement, "For the purpose of evaluating cullet coming from a municipal resource recovery system, these particles will be considered refractory until the glass container manufacturer can certify otherwise." The particles referred to are foreign particles in a 1-pound sample of cullet that are separated from the glass by heavy liquid at 2.65 specific gravity. Corundum, mullite, zircon, chromite, spinel, sillimanite, andalusite, kyanite, and cassiterite are listed as being refractory in sizes larger than 60 mesh. Ceramic ware, vitreous clay, chinaware, bricks, tile, gravel, and concrete fragments are objectionable since they can result in partially fused inclusions in the finished glass. Metallic aluminum, radio tube parts, spark plug porcelain, chrome ore, or chrome refractory in any amounts are the most objectionable cullet contaminants.

Even though these specifications were not available during the early years of research on incinerator residues, it was evident at that time that the minus 20-mesh glass aggregate remaining from nonferrous metal recovery operations would not be suitable for use as cullet. Pioneering

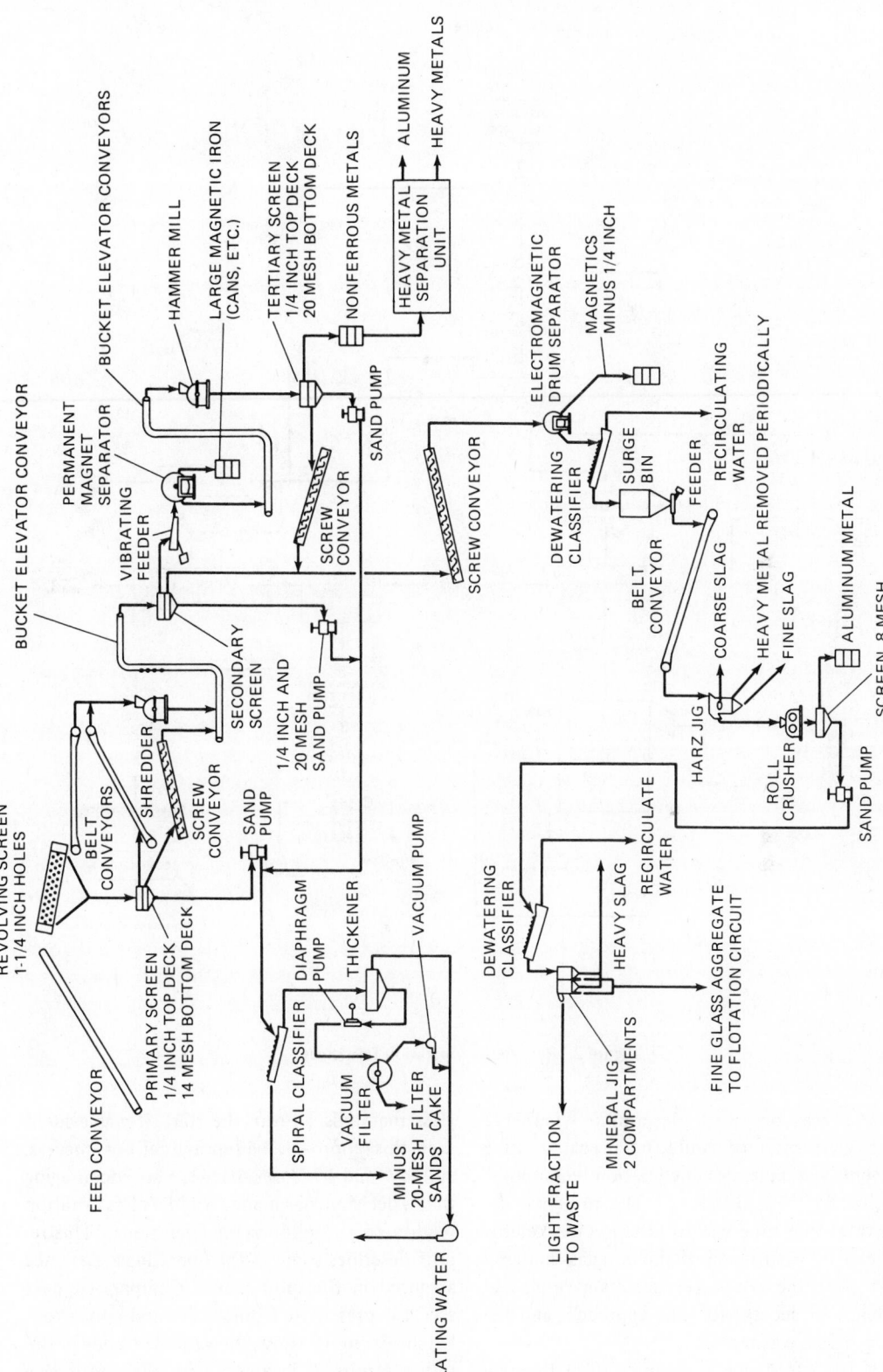

Figure 1. Municipal incinerator residue recovery flowsheet.

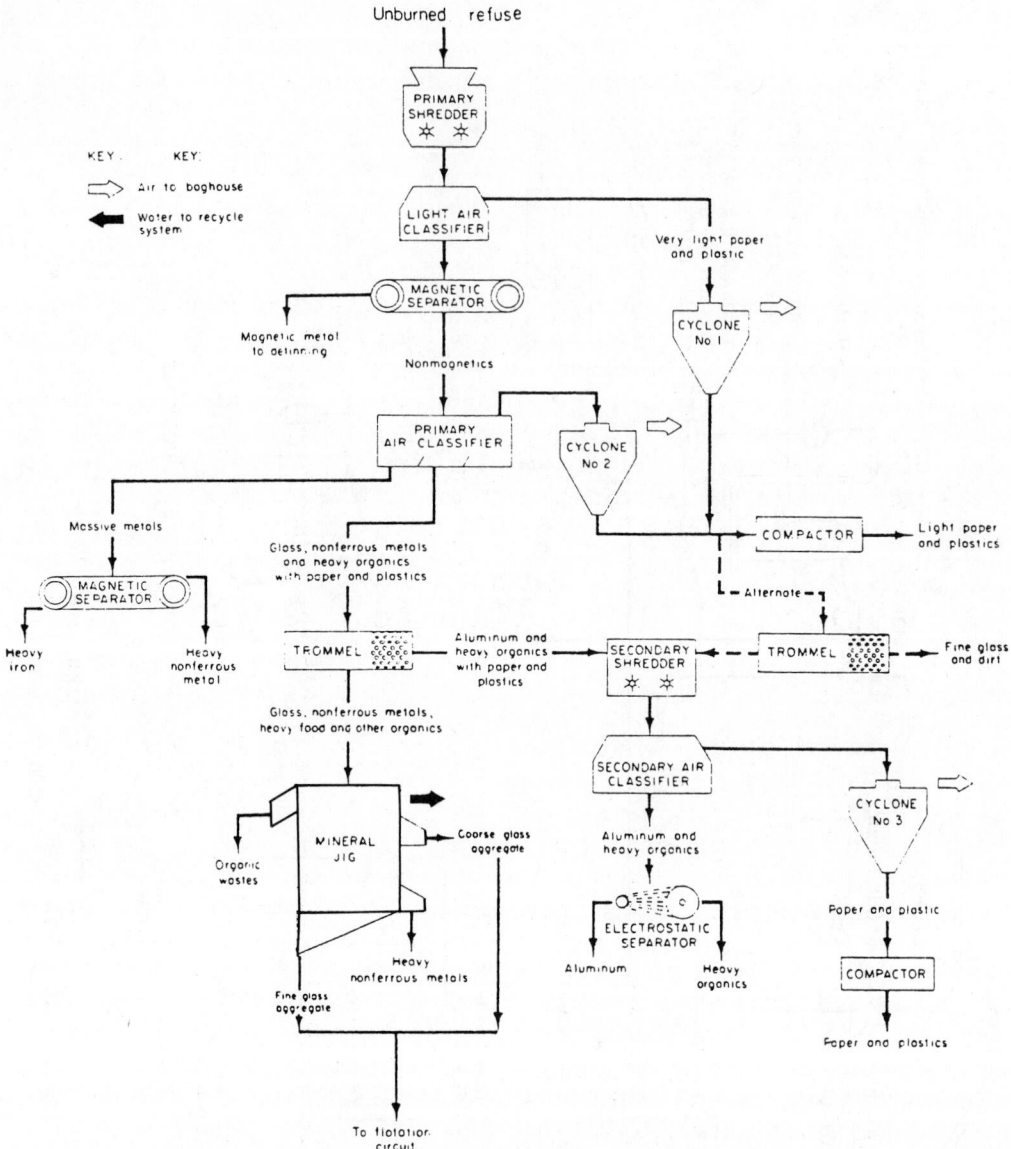

Figure 2. Raw refuse separation flowsheet.

research was begun to determine whether a clean glass product could be prepared using conventional minerals beneficiation technology, specifically froth flotation. The principal objective at that time was to obtain a marketable product by floating all of the nonglass material away from the glass. Test results gave no real evidence of success for this approach, and the test program was recessed.

In 1970 testing was resumed with the new objective of floating glass away from all non-glass materials. From the start, it was evident that this approach had potential for success, and by mid-1972 results were so encouraging that a decision was made to add a glass flotation section to the pilot plant operations. This report describes some of the operating experience acquired in the pilot plant. Comparative data are also presented from earlier and concurrent batch testing to show the variable trends in flotation results as influenced by the controlling parameters.

FROTH FLOTATION

Although "froth flotation" is a well-known term to people in the mining and minerals industry, it may be totally unfamiliar to those who are far removed from mining yet who may be deeply involved in resource recovery from urban waste. For them, a brief explanation of the process and some companion terms may add meaning to the discussions that follow.

Froth flotation is a process for separating, in aqueous suspension, finely divided particles that have different surface characteristics. In the mining industry it is the most widely used method of separating the valuable and waste constituents of ores. In the solid waste processing industry it will be used as part of a system to separate glass particles from waste materials consisting mainly of ceramic and rock fragments.

In bench-scale tests finely divided particles to be separated are mixed with water in the approximate ratio of 3 parts water to 1 of solids, and this mixture is added to the cell in an amount that will fill the cell to within 3/4 inch of the overflow lip. When activated, the impeller (agitator) keeps the solids moving around in suspension and at the same time draws in a controlled amount of air that is dispersed throughout the mixture in the form of small bubbles.

A small amount of chemical, commonly known as a collector reagent, is added to the mixture to coat the glass particles and make their surfaces water-repellent or hydrophobic. The coated glass particles buoyed to the surface of the pulp. They become part of a froth that overflows the lip of the cell. At this point they become known as concentrates. When a properly selected collector reagent is used, the nonglass particles in the pulp are unaffected and remain in the main body of the pulp which, in commercial-size units, is continuously discharged over an adjustable weir at the tail end of the cell that controls the pulp level within the cell. Upon discharge from the cell the nonglass particles are called tailings.

Cationic collectors are used for the flotation of glass. These can be, for example, aliphatic amine acetates derived from either tallow or coconut oil fatty acids. According to one supplier of these chemicals,[1] "Cationic chemicals consist of molecules which, on ionizing in an aqueous pulp, liberate a long-chain ion carrying a positive charge. This fatty cation will attach to those particles in the pulp that have a high concentration of negative surface charges to provide a hydrophobic (water-repellent) surface favorable to bubble attachment and flotation." Glass particles are negatively charged and are affected in this manner.

Both tallow and coco amines have very limited solubility in water. By neutralizing the amines with an acid, such as acetic, an acetate salt is formed which is readily soluble in water. Modified amine derivatives include diamines, which possess both primary and secondary amine groupings and therefore have greater cationic activity than the corresponding amines.[1] Diamines are readily neutralized to form water-soluble diacetates. The acetates are commercially available, and both amine and diamine acetates have been used in Bureau of Mines investigations.

BATCH FLOTATION TESTS

For batch flotation tests, most of which preceded continuous operations, three types of material were used. One type represented feed to the flotation section of the incinerator residue processing plant; another represented feed to the flotation section of the raw refuse plant; and the third was made up entirely of bottles that were collected before reaching the trash can. They were carefully washed and crushed to provide uncontaminated glass samples for many of the comparative tests.

Batch testing, besides showing the way for continuous operations, greatly facilitated the acquisition of comparative data to show variable trends in flotation results as influenced by the following —

1. Kinds and quantities of chemical additions.
2. Desliming of flotation feed.
3. Particle size of solids in flotation feed.
4. Flotation feed pulp pH level.
5. Conditioning of flotation feed with reagents.
6. Retention time of pulp in flotation cells.

Table 1. Comparison of Cationic Collectors for Flotation of Glass.

Collector	Quantity, pound per ton	Weight-percent of glass floated		
		First test	Second test	Average
Amine acetate T	0.05	52.2	53.8	53.0
Amine acetate C	.05	41.7	47.1	44.4
Diamine acetate T	.05	97.9	97.7	97.8
Diamine acetate C	.05	96.7	96.7	96.7
Diamine acetate T	.034	85.3	78.6	81.9
Diamine acetate C	.034	70.6	62.9	66.7

C — coco derivative. T — tallow derivative.

7. Ratio of water to solids in flotation feed.
8. Concentrate cleaning operations.

Chemical Additions

Reagents (chemicals) used experimentally in glass flotation tests were of four types: frothers, collectors, depressants, and regulators.

Frothers are used to produce the froth by means of which glass particles are collected at the surface of the pulp and then overflowed from the cell.

Collectors form a film on the surface of glass particles in the pulp to make them water-repellent and thus aid in their attachment to air bubbles that carry them to the surface of the pulp.

Depressants are used with the intention of preventing the flotation of nonglass particles without interfering with the flotation of glass particles.

Regulators are used primarily to modify the alkalinity or acidity of flotation pulp.

Collectors. Coconut and tallow amine and diamine acetates were the collectors used throughout the test program. To minimize the number of variables in batch-test series conducted to compare such other factors as pH levels and the effect of particle size in flotation feed, coco diamine acetate was used almost exclusively. The amines serve as both collectors and frothers. The tallow derivatives gave a more lively and selective froth than the coconut oil derivatives, but when the two were mixed in equal parts the froth resembled that of the tallow amines. The tallow amines appear to have somewhat better collecting capabilities.

In Table 1 the relative collecting strengths of coco and tallow amines and diamine acetates are compared. The sample used for this series of tests was one of all glass that had been crushed to pass a 20-mesh screen and then hand-screened to remove the minus 150-mesh portion. All tests were run in duplicate.

The sensitivity of cationic collectors to slight variations in test conditions favors duplicate tests when making critical comparisons. For the diamine acetate comparison, the tests were made using different amounts of reagent. Glass recoveries were quite similar when using 0.05 pound of reagent per ton* of glass in the feed, and to offer a more convincing reagent comparison, additional tests were made using 0.034 pound of reagent per ton of glass. All results are included in Table 1.

Other comparisons of cationic collectors for flotation of glass were made in two series of tests designed primarily to show the effect of different quantity additions on the percentage of glass recovered in the flotation concentrates. Tallow and coco diamine acetates are again compared in Table 2, and in Table 3 tallow amine and diamine acetates are compared.

Different lots of material were used for the tests in each series. In the Table 2 series, a portion of glass aggregate recovered from raw refuse was crushed to minus 20 mesh, and the minus 150-mesh portion was then removed by screening. This lot contained approximately 8.0 percent nonglass material such as ceramic and rock fragments; therefore a weight recovery of 91 to 92 percent in the flotation concentrate represents a glass recovery of approximately 100

*Ton, as used throughout this report, refers to the short ton of 2,000 pounds.

Table 2. Comparison of Diamines T (Tallow) and C (Coco).

| Collector | Quantity | | Weight-percent of rougher flotation concentrates |
	Milliliters	Pound per ton	
Diamine acetate T	3.0	0.10	59.7
Diamine acetate C	3.0	.10	58.8
Diamine acetate T	4.0	.13	85.6
Diamine acetate C	4.0	.13	74.8

percent in a product that is essentially 100 percent glass.

For the Table 3 series, glass was handpicked from a different lot of raw refuse aggregate. This was crushed to minus 20 mesh, and the minus 150-mesh portion was screened out before individual test portions were split out by riffling. As the sample contained only glass, a weight recovery of 100 percent in the flotation concentrates was possible.

In both tables reagent additions are shown in two ways: in milliliters of a 1-percent solution per test sample of 600 grams, and the equivalent in pound per ton of dry solids in the flotation feed. The latter way of reporting reagent additions is customary.

The high glass recoveries obtained in many tests in which less than 0.10 pound of reagent was used per ton of solids in the feed can be attributed in large part to the careful preparation of test samples that was essential to obtain reproducible results when using less than optimum amounts of reagents. In continuous operations reagent amounts between 0.15 and 0.2 pound per ton of feed were usual requirements for good flotation, probably because of less efficient desliming of flotation feed. When using these higher amounts, the sensitivity of the reagents to feed variations was not as great as

that experienced in batch testing when using less than optimum amounts.

The collecting strengths of the diamine acetates are shown by test results to be superior to those of the amine acetates. Microscopic appraisals of the test products indicate that tallow derivatives are only slightly more selective in separating glass from nonglass particles than the coconut oil derivatives.

Test results alone do not indicate an unequivocal superiority of one reagent over the others. More pronounced than in other respects is the apparent advantage in using the tallow derivatives because of their lower cost per ton of glass floated. Prices in effect as of May 1977 for amine and diamine acetates in 30-drum lots (390 pounds per drum) were quoted by one supplier as follows:

Ta low amine acetate . . . . $0.67 per pound
Coco amine acetate . . . . . $1.02 per pound
Tallow diamine acetate . . . $0.80 per pound
Coco diamine acetate . . . .   NA (but probably about $1.02 per pound)

Using the glass recovery figures in table 3, 0.12 pound of tallow amine acetate is used to recover 96.5 percent of the glass, whereas 97.4 percent of the glass is recovered with 0.08 pound of

Table 3. Tallow (T) Amine and Diamine Acetate Additions and Corresponding Glass Recoveries.

| Collector | Quantity | | Weight-percent of glass floated |
	Milliliters	Pound per ton	
Amine acetate T	2.5	0.08	44.4
Amine acetate T	3.0	.10	87.9
Amine acetate T	3.5	.12	96.5
Amine acetate T	4.0	.13	98.5
Diamine acetate T	1.5	.05	14.8
Diamine acetate T	2.0	.07	72.0
Diamine acetate T	2.5	.08	97.4

tallow diamine per ton of solids in the feed. Therefore, in terms of reagent cost per ton of glass floated, the comparison is 8.06 cents for the tallow amine and 6.82 cents for the tallow diamine. This reagent cost analysis shows a definite advantage in using diamine acetate T for the flotation of glass.

Frothers. The frothing capabilities of cationic reagents were mentioned earlier. In pilot plant operations particularly, they provided plenty of froth with good characteristics for glass flotation, and no other frothing reagent was used. In some batch tests, pine oil, methyl isobutyl carbinol (MIBC), and an alcohol frother were tried in amounts of 0.0 pound per ton of solids in the feed and found to be compatible with all cationic collectors with which they were used. Test results shown in table 4 favor the use of a frothing reagent, and its possible use industrially is worth further investigation.

Samples used for the testing of frothers were cut from a batch of glass aggregate from raw refuse that had been crushed to minus 20 mesh and deslimed. Diamine acetate C was the collector in all tests shown in Table 4. It was added in the amount of 0.07 pound per ton, and 0.05 pound of frother per ton of feed was added in each case.

Depressants. Cullet-quality glass concentrates can be produced by froth flotation without the use of depressants. Results of a few exploratory tests did not show any benefit from their use.

Table 4. Tests to Compare the Use of Frothers.

Frother	Float product, wt-pct
None	72.9
MIBC	87.8
Pine oil	89.3
Alcohol frother	87.2

Regulators. Measured in terms of glass recovery, best flotation results were obtained when the natural pH of the flotation pulp was unchanged by chemical additions (regulators). This is shown in Table 5, which includes glass recovery data of tests in which pH values were varied from 4.1 to 10.5. Soda ash (Na_2CO_3), caustic soda (NaOH), and sulfuric acid (H_2SO_4) were used for pH adjustments. Tapwater having a pH value of 7.8 was used in all tests. When mixed with ground glass or ground glass aggregate in the ratio of 3.67 parts water to 1 of solids, which was usual for these tests, the pH value of the water was raised to 9.2. During a typical test this value dropped to 8.7. In all tests there was a significant change in pH measurements taken at the beginning and end of flotation. These were averaged and are shown in the table under the heading "Mean pH range." In acid pulps (below pH 7.0) the second reading was invariably higher than the first; in alkaline pulps (above pH 7.0) the reverse was true.

Test conditions included 600-gram test samples; 2,200 milliliters tap water — pH 7.8; addition of 0.10 pound of diamine acetate C per ton of solids in feed; conditioning pulp 1/2

Table 5. Glass Recoveries at Different pH Levels.

Additive, lb/ton	Mean pH range	Weight-percent of concentrates		
		All glass from clean glass bottles	Glass aggregate recovered from raw refuse	Glass aggregate recovered from incinerator residues
0.66 H_2SO_4	4.1– 6.6	49.6	59.6	—
0.33 H_2SO_4	5.6– 7.4	94.1	79.4	85.8
—	9.2– 8.7	97.9	84.6	95.6
0.5 Na_2CO_3	9.6– 9.2	95.5	81.9	93.9
0.167 NaOH	9.7– 9.4	93.6	81.0	96.5
0.334 NaOH	10.2–10.0	81.6	68.3	90.1
0.50 NaOH	10.5–10.2	55.2	59.6	82.4

minute with reagents; flotation time — 3 minutes. Although glass recoveries were slightly less in tests made with additions of soda ash or sulfuric acid in small amounts, a lighter, more selective froth resulted. This effect was particularly noticeable in continuous pilot plant operations, and small amounts of either soda ash or acid were frequently used to regulate the character and volume of froth. To offset the small drop in glass recovery, the collector addition was increased slightly in these operations.

Desliming of Flotation Feed

Successful cationic flotation of glass requires that the flotation feed be essentially free of slimes (minus 150-mesh particles). Batch test results show that glass recoveries drop off sharply as the quantity of slime in the feed increases, when a fixed amount of reagent is used. Slimes also have an adverse effect on the sharpness of separation between glass and nonglass particles.

The slime fraction of the glass-rich portion from incinerator residue contains carbonaceous material and fly ash in sufficient quantities to completely inhibit glass flotation. In many cases adequate removal of this slime requires a two-stage desliming operation. The glass-rich aggregate obtained as an intermediate product in processing raw refuse contains some slime-making materials which, after the crushing step before flotation, have a pronounced detrimental effect on reagent performance if allowed to remain in the flotation feed.

A further requirement in preparing feed for flotation is that the surfaces of all particles be clean and, in particular, free from fatty substances. It frequently happens that in aggregates from raw refuse there are nonglass particles coated with what is probably kitchen grease of some kind. This condition promotes their flotation, and unless corrective measures are taken, these particles can end up as contaminants in the glass concentrates. Corrective measures used in batch testing and continuous operations include (1) adding detergents to the pulp before desliming and (2) removing the grease-coated particles by flotation before the cationic collector is added. The material thus removed can be cleaned and returned to the flotation circuit.

Flotation Feed — Particle Size

Glass particles 10 mesh in size have been successfully floated, but there is a strong preference for a flotation feed in which the particle size range is between 20 and 150 mesh. This preference takes into account its compatibility with other requirements for good flotation and cullet specifications.

When treating ores to separate valuable minerals from barren rock or to separate two or more minerals from each other, the size reduction of flotation feed particles by grinding must take into account the mesh size necessary to free each from the other. This holds true also in the treatment of incinerator residue aggregate for the recovery of a cullet-grade glass product. Partial fusion of some glass in the incinerator results in the formation of conglomerates that must be crushed or ground fine enough to separate the glass and slag constituents. In glass-rich aggregates from raw refuse, the glass and nonglass contents are in the form of discrete particles so that size reduction is not a determining factor in the quality of the glass product recovered and it is only necessary to reduce all feed particles to floatable size. A typical size analysis of aggregate from raw refuse, showing the glass content of each size fraction, is presented in Table 6. The plus 10-mesh portion of the aggregate in Table 6 contained 90 percent glass.

Samples crushed to minus 14 mesh were used in some tests, but in most tests minus 20-mesh samples were used. Table 7 is included to show particle size distribution for test samples that were roll-crushed in stages to minus 14 and minus 20 mesh. Similar data are included for a minus 20-mesh sample with most of the minus 150-mesh material screened out.

Minus 150-mesh material is partially removed from flotation feed for two reasons: it adds to reagent costs, and the allowable extent of its presence in cullet is limited by specifications.

Test results show a preferential coating of the fine-size particles in flotation feeds by cationic collectors. To quantify this effect, a series of tests was made using test portions cut from a newly crushed batch of washed bottle glass from which the minus 150-mesh size fraction had been removed by screening. Starting with the minus

Table 6. Size Analysis of Glass-rich Aggregate.

Screen fractions		Wt-pct	Wt-pct	
Inch	Mesh		Glass	Nonglass
Plus 0.371	—	6.3	91.7	8.3
0.371 x 0.263	—	18.9	86.8	13.2
.263 x .185	3 x 4	23.0	91.2	8.8
.185 x .131	4 x 6	19.5	92.2	7.8
.131 x .093	6 x 8	15.7	90.5	9.5
.093 x .065	8 x 10	10.1	87.4	12.6
Minus 0.065	—	6.5	ND[1]	ND[1]

[1] Not determined.

Table 7. Size Distribution of Test Samples.

Screen size, mesh	Wt-pct		
	Minus 14 mesh	Minus 20 mesh	Minus 20 plus 150 mesh
14 x 20	13.4	—	—
20 x 28	18.7	19.2	20.2
28 x 35	16.0	20.9	22.0
35 x 48	14.1	16.9	20.5
48 x 65	12.2	14.7	15.8
65 x 100	8.0	9.7	11.8
100 x 150	5.6	6.5	7.0
150 x 200	4.9	5.6	1.9
Minus 200	6.1	6.3	.7

Table 8. Effect of Fine-size Particles on
Flotation Reagent Consumption.

Minus 150 mesh in sample, pct	Wt-pct of float		
	First test	Second test	Average
0.00	98.4	96.8	97.6
2.50	96.7	96.7	96.7
5.00	97.2	95.6	96.4
7.50	90.8	86.9	88.8
10.00	73.9	84.3	79.1
15.00	66.8	72.6	69.7

Table 9. Effect of Particle Size on Glass
Recovery with Fixed Amounts of Reagent.

Size fraction mesh	Float product, wt-pct
14 x 20	91.4
20 x 28	97.8
28 x 35	98.9
35 x 48	98.7
48 x 65	98.1
65 x 100	97.0
100 x 150	60.8
150 x 200	49.2

20- plus 150-mesh glass, test portions were prepared with different amounts of minus 150-
mesh glass added. Batch tests using these samples were run in duplicate with the addition in
all tests of 0.05 pound of coco diamine acetate
per ton of solids in the feed. Results of these
tests are shown in Table 8.

To further compare the relationship of particle size and reagent requirement, a series of tests
was made on different size fractions of an all-
glass sample that had been crushed to minus 14
mesh. The size fractions listed in Table 9 were
screened out, and a representative portion of
each was coated with the same amount of
reagent used in all tests. Results show a sharp
decline in glass recoveries on sizes below 100
mesh. This corresponds to a higher reagent requirement for these sizes.

Partial removal of the minus 150-mesh material from flotation feed as a waste product requires that the crushing of glass-rich products before flotation be done in such a manner as to produce a minimum amount of that size material.

Conditioning Flotation Feed With Reagents

Conditioning pulp with reagents before flotation, which is customary in ore treatment plants,
is not necessary when cationic reagents are used
for glass flotation. Contact between reagent
and glass surfaces requires but a few seconds,
and in continuous pilot plant operations the best
flotation results were obtained when the reagents were fed to the feed box of the No. 1
rougher cell.

Flotation Feed Pulp Density

Except for the purpose of calculating cell volume requirements, the pulp density of flotation
feed is of little importance. it can be 30 or 35
percent solids of which 85 or 90 percent are
glass particles. Most of them will report to the
froth layer in a matter of seconds, leaving only
a few percent solids in the main body of pulp.
Approximately 90 percent of the solids in the
feed are removed from the cell in the froth, and
the pulp removed from the cell as tailings will
contain only about 3 percent solids.

In continuous operations the pulp density of
flotation feed was normally held at 25 percent
solids, but when a buildup of slime in the pulp
caused some deterioration in reagent effectiveness, the ratio of water to solids was temporarily increased as an effective way of purging
the circuit.

Residence Time of Pulp in Flotation Cells

A relatively short residence time is required for
glass flotation. This will vary, but under normal
conditions 3 to 4 minutes should be allowed for
rougher flotation and 2 to 2-1/2 minutes for
each cleaning stage. In most batch tests all of
the enriched froth was removed in 2 minutes or
less, but the quality of concentrates was generally better when froth formation and removal
were retarded by using a controlled amount of
air.

In a reagentized pulp large flocs of glass particles form quickly at the commencement of
aeration. The rapidity of their formation can
be controlled by the amount of air admitted;
with lesser amounts of air flocculation is less
pronounced and the entrapment of nonglass
particles in the flocs is less likely to occur.

Cleaning of Rougher Concentrates

Specifications of a glass concentrate acceptable
for use in making container glass place greater
importance on the quality of the final product
than on glass recovery. In this respect it was
found worthwhile to clean the rougher concentrates three times by refloating them. In pilot

plant operations a small amount of reagent is added to the second and third cleaning stages to control the amount of recleaner tailings. These usually contain less than 5 percent nonglass material in the form of discrete particles and are returned to the rougher circuit via the desliming classifier. The only tailing discard is that from the rougher circuit.

Magnetic cleaning of flotation concentrates helps to ensure their meeting cullet specifications. Batch and pilot plant tests show that from most concentrates a significant quantity of nonglass material can be removed by high-intensity magnetic separation. This accounts for an improvement in the quality of concentrates from incinerator residues by the reduction of the iron content from a typical 0.4 to 0.6 percent FE_2O_3 to under the acceptable level of 0.2 percent.

Flotation concentrates from raw refuse are cleaned magnetically to remove refractory particles, all of which are classified by glassmakers as having specific gravities greater than 2.65. In an illustrative test, 0.15 percent of a 1-pound sample of flotation concentrates was removed magnetically. When parted with heavy liquid at 2.65 gravity, the sink fraction of the magnetic product amounted to 0.04 percent of the initial sample. It is estimated by grain count that this fraction can contain upwards of 600 particles; if more than 2 of these in the minus 20- plus 40-mesh portion and more than 20 in the minus 40 plus 60-mesh portion are determined to be refractory, the concentrates before magnetic separation would not have met specifications. Because it is possible that in many cases the sink fraction will contain refractory particles, magnetic separation is suggested as a possible means for their removal.

PILOT PLANT OPERATIONS

In late 1976, approximately 4-1/2 tons of coarse glass-rich aggregate recovered from processing of urban refuse was processed in the pilot plant. It contained 90 percent glass and 10 percent nonglass materials consisting mostly of ceramic and rock fragments. The glass fragments, all of which were less than one-half inch in size, were present in the following colors:

Clear glass	73.0 pct
Amber glass	17.0 pct
Green glass	9.0 pct
Blue glass	.2 pct

Preliminary batch testing showed that 75 to 80 percent of the glass in the aggregate could be recovered in a high-grade flotation concentrate which, after the removal of a small quantity of weakly magnetic material, proved to be of cullet quality. The principal loss of glass in these tests was in desliming the flotation feed.

Continuous operations illustrated in figure 3 include –

1. Stage-crushing the dry aggregate in a hammer mill, followed by screening and roll crushing to minus 20 mesh.
2. Desliming the minus 20-mesh material in two stages before flotation using spiral classifiers adjusted to overflow minus 150-mesh solids.

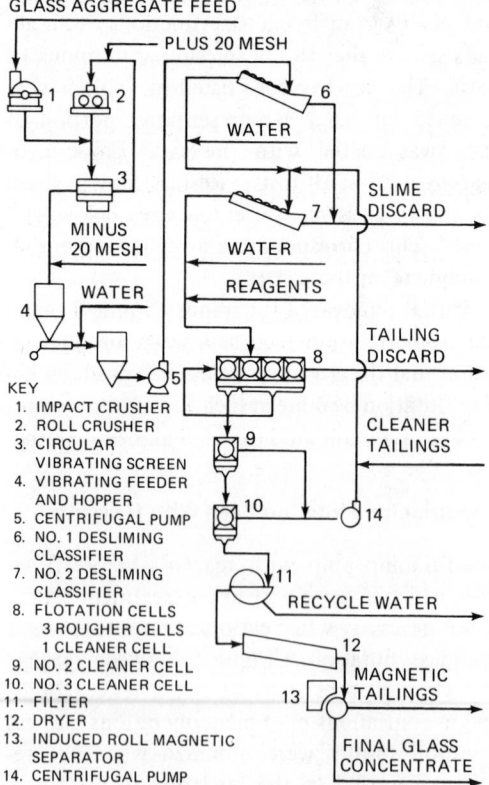

KEY
1. IMPACT CRUSHER
2. ROLL CRUSHER
3. CIRCULAR VIBRATING SCREEN
4. VIBRATING FEEDER AND HOPPER
5. CENTRIFUGAL PUMP
6. NO. 1 DESLIMING CLASSIFIER
7. NO. 2 DESLIMING CLASSIFIER
8. FLOTATION CELLS 3 ROUGHER CELLS 1 CLEANER CELL
9. NO. 2 CLEANER CELL
10. NO. 3 CLEANER CELL
11. FILTER
12. DRYER
13. INDUCED ROLL MAGNETIC SEPARATOR
14. CENTRIFUGAL PUMP

Figure 3. Flowsheet of continuous glass flotation section.

Table 10. Summary of Pilot Plant Operation.

Product	Wt-pct	Glass, pct[1]	Glass distribution, pct
Slime discard	11.3	90.0	13.7
Flotation tailings	16.2	40.0	7.3
Flotation concentrates	70.3	99.9	79.0
Composite	100.0	88.9	100.0

[1] Glass content of all products was either estimated or calculated.

3. Rougher flotation of glass at natural pH with the addition of 0.2 pound of diamine acetate per ton of solids in the flotation feed.
4. Cleaning rougher concentrates by refloating three times.
5. Magnetic cleaning of final flotation concentrates.

The pilot plant units were operated 6 to 7 hours per day on consecutive workdays. After some minor adjustments, the operation was stabilized with a feed rate of 350 pounds of material per hour. Froth characteristics were varied from time to time by adding small amounts of sulfuric acid to lower the pH of the flotation pulp to between 7.2 and 7.5 or by feeding a mixture of coco and tallow diamine acetates. No apparent advantage resulted from these changes. The quantity of tailings from the cleaner cells was another variable controlled by changing reagent additions. There are four-cell rougher section of the pilot plant flotation circuit and two single-compartment reagent feeders.

The flotation feed was deslimed in spiral classifiers with flared sides. The use of wet cyclones for this purpose would have had some advantages because of their greater flexibility.

Operating results are summarized briefly in Table 10. Manpower limitations precluded the recording of data necessary for a mass balance table to show details such as circulating loads; in its absence, Table 11 is included to show the amount of cleaner and recleaner tailings that are usual in batch testing.

Experience gained from pilot plant operations makes it unsafe to say that the day-in and day-out production of flotation concentrates will meet the stringent cullet specifications in continuous operations; this is due to the existing lack of precise quality-control methods, the human fallibility of operators, and the inaccuracies that are possible with current methods of product evaluation.

Representative portions of the magnetically cleaned flotation concentrates were sent to five glass companies for evaluation. None of the reports received was in agreement regarding the number of refractory particles in the samples, but there was general agreement that the product could be used for making container glass. One company did not determine the number

Table 11. Summary of Typical Batch Flotation Test.

Product	Wt-pct	Glass, pct[1]	Glass distribution, pct
Slime discard	7.6	70.0	5.8
Rougher tailings	10.2	40.0	4.5
Cleaner tailings	4.5	90.0	4.7
Recleaner tailings	2.3	95.0	2.4
Recleaner concentrates	75.4	99.9	82.6
Composite	100.0	91.2	100.0

[1] Glass content of all products was either estimated or calculated.

Table 12. Refractory Particles Reported in Evaluations of Froth-floated Glass by Container Manufacturers.

	Refractory particles	
	Minus 20 plus 40 mesh	Minus 40 plus 60 mesh
A company	0	40.0
B company	5.0	12.0
C company	0	38.0
D company	5.0	23.0
Average	2.5	28.3

of refractory particles in the sample but made fusion tests and reported the sample to be of better quality than much of the cullet now used. Refractory particles reported to be in samples evaluated by four of the companies are shown in Table 12. The number of refractory particles reported is those found in a 1-pound sample. The minus 20- plus 40-mesh fraction represents 42 percent, and the minus 40- plus 60-mesh fraction represents 32 percent of the sample. Specifications allow 2 refractory particles in the minus 20- plus 40-mesh fraction and 20 refractory particles in the minus 40- plus 60-mesh fraction. The average numbers in the table provide a more acceptable evaluation than any of the individual sample evaluations, and although these show excessive numbers of refractory particles in the product, it is reported to be of usable quality for container manufacture. The froth-floated product contains glass of several colors; it is known as mixed-color cullet and can be used in making green and amber container glass.

CONCLUSIONS

It has been demonstrated by batch and continuous testing that cullet-quality glass products can be recovered from solid waste streams by froth flotation. The technology and equipment involved have been highly developed in the minerals industry. The glass product of this technology is untried commercially, but three resource recovery plants now under construction that will use froth flotation in glass recovery systems demonstrate confidence in the emerging resource recovery industry that this product can be used to make new glass containers.

REFERENCES

1. Armour Chemical Company. Mineral Flotation With Armour Cationic Chemicals. Chicago, Ill., 1955.
2. Glass Packaging Institute. GCMI Specifications for Glass From Resource Recovery Systems. Suite 400, 1800 K St., NW, Washington, DC 20006, Jan. 14, 1976.
3. Henn, John J. Updated Cost Evaluation of a Metal and Mineral Recovery Process for Treating Municipal Incinerator Residues. BuMines IC 8691, 1975, 44 pp.
4. Sullivan, P.M., and H.V. Makar. Bureau of Mines Process for Recovering Resources From Raw Refuse. Proc. 4th Miner. Waste Utilization Symp., cosponsored by the Bureau of Mines and IIT Research Institute, Chicago, Ill., May 7-8, 1974, pp. 128-141.
5. _____. Quality of Products From Bureau of Mines Resource Recovery Systems and Suitability for Recycling. Proc. 5th Miner. Waste Utilization Symp., cosponsored by the Bureau of Mines and IIT Research Institute, Chicago, Ill., Apr. 13-14, 1976, pp. 223-233.

3-15 Lightweight Structural Concrete Aggregate from Municipal Waste Glass

K.J. Liles

Source: Reprinted From *Proceedings* of the Fifth Mineral Waste Utilization Symposium, Chicago, Illinois, April 13–14, 1976, pp. 219–222.

INTRODUCTION

The Federal Bureau of Mines has been active in the recovery of byproducts from mineral and metallurgical processes for over 60 years.[1] Since 1968, the Tuscaloosa Metallurgy Research Laboratory has conducted waste utilization research concerned with the development of building products from the metal-free glass constituents separated from municipal incinerator residues. The glass fraction obtained from the Bureau's incinerator residue separation process[2] represents about 48 weight-percent of the total residue.[3]

The first phase of the research was directed toward producing building brick.[4] The second phase of the investigation was concerned with the production of glass wool thermal insulation.[5] The third phase was undertaken to determine the fluxing properties of waste glass and how those properties might be utilized to decrease the required firing temperature and/or the firing time of structural clay products made from common clays.[6] This report describes the utilization of waste glass as a major component of a lightweight aggregate suitable for use in structural concrete.

RAW MATERIALS

Waste Glass

The glass used in the aggregate tests was a sample of mixed glass, slag, ceramics, and stone reclaimed from incinerator residues at the Bureau's incinerator residue processing plant.[7] A chemical analysis of the product is given in Table 1.

Clay

The clay used in the study was a coal measure underclay from Walker County, Ala. This clay is a texture of kaolinite, illite, a small amount of montmorillonite, and about 50 percent free quartz. Clay was added to the lightweight aggregate mix to provide the following: (1) a plasticizer for the pelletizing process, (2) a stabilizer for the soda content of the waste glass, and (3) a source of added strength for the fired pellets.

Sodium Silicate

Mixtures containing viscous silicates are subject to swelling when subjected to sudden heating.[8] The sodium silicate used in the testing program has a dry powder with a $Na_2O:SiO_2$ weight ratio of 1:3.22. Although liquid sodium silicate

Table 1. Chemical Analysis of Waste Glass Used in Lightweight Aggregate Tests.

Constituent	Weight-percent
SiO_2	66.9
Al_2O_3	3.9
Fe_2O_3	.9
B_2O_3	1.5
Na_2O	11.4
K_2O	1.0
CaO	8.3
MgO	2.1
S	.2
Loss on ignition	2.6
Trace elements[1]	.5

[1] Trace elements include Cu, Mn, Pb, and Zn.

Table 2. Compressive Strength of Dry
Pellets Made with Various
Percentages of Clay Additions.

Composition, percent clay added	Compressive strength, lb/sq in.
5	29.5
10	58.5
15	147
20	288
25	163

could be utilized, the powdered form was used in these tests to facilitate ease of handling and accuracy of measurement.

EXPERIMENTAL WORK

Grinding

The waste glass used in the studies was a minus 20-mesh glass obtained from the Bureau of Mines continuous processing plant for reclaiming and recycling municipal incinerator residues. Cellular formation in the lightweight aggregate was evident only when the waste glass was milled to minus 200 mesh. This approximates the standard size acknowledged for fluxing materials in the ceramics industry.* A series of tests was conducted to determine the minimum time required to grind the glass to greater than 95 percent minus 200 mesh. A porcelain mill was used for the tests with porcelain balls for grinding media. The tests showed that a minimum of 8 hours was required to provide a material containing 95 percent minus 200-mesh particles.

Aggregate Formulation

A 20 percent clay to 80 percent glass ratio was selected for pellet formulation based on tests made to determine dry compressive strength. In these tests the weight-percent ratios of clay to waste glass ranged from 5:95 to 25:75. The 20-percent addition showed a high dry compressive strength and was chosen as being the most suitable for pellet formation. The results of the dry compressive strength tests are shown in Table 2.

*Previous studies using waste glass as a flux in brick composition indicated that minus 200-mesh glass was the most effective flux.[9]

Sintering Tests

The results of a series of tests made to determine the optimum sintering time-temperature relationship when using various quantities of sodium silicate are shown in Table 3. The objective of the sintering tests was to achieve a structurally sound pellet weighing 45 to 50 lb/cu ft, and for economic reasons, using as little sodium silicate as possible. The pellets used for these tests were made on an 18 inch, variable-speed, disc pelletizer.

From the results shown in Table 3, the optimum conditions for the most suitable lightweight material appeared to be a mix containing 2 percent sodium silicate that was fired at 1,550° F for 15 minutes. Under these conditions a pellet with a bulk density of 48 lb/cu ft with very good pore structure was produced.

As a result of these preliminary tests a quantity of pellets was then formed on a 36-inch-diameter continuous-feed disc pelletizer. These pellets were fired in the box-type laboratory kiln for 15 minutes at 1,550° F. As specified by ASTM procedure,[10] the loose pour weight of the expanded pellets was 38 lb/cu ft. The loose pour weight is determined by filling a 0.1-cubic-foot container to overflowing, leveling the surface of the aggregate with the top edge of the container with a straightedge, and weighing.

Concrete Tests

For use in concrete tests, the glass aggregate produced was crushed by a roll crusher and screened to provide a material that fell within American Society for Testing and Materials (ASTM) grading requirements for 1/2-inch to No. 4 sieve coarse aggregate.[11] A screen analysis of the crushed glass aggregate compared with ASTM requirements shown in Table 4 indicates that the crushed aggregate closely approached the ASTM specifications.

To evaluate the crushed aggregate as a basic ingredient in concrete, 3-inch diameter by 6-inch long concrete test cylinders were prepared using the following basic field mix: Type I cement, 6 sacks (564 pounds); coarse aggregate, 20.0 cu ft (700 pounds); river sand, 12.5 cu ft (1,256 pounds); water, 6 gallons per sack of cement (325 pounds).

Table 3. Bulk Density[1] of Expanded Glass Aggregate as a Function
of Time, Temperature, and Sodium Silicate Content.

Temp.,	Firing time, minutes			
	5	10	15	20
1.0 percent sodium silicate				
1,450	109.2	111.1	113.6	115.4
1,500	108.6	108.6	106.1	104.8
1,550	84.2	83.0	76.1	72.4
1.5 percent sodium silicate				
1,450	108.6	103.0	105.5	98.6
1,500	104.8	98.6	91.1	87.4
1,550	78.6	65.5	65.5	64.3
2.0 percent sodium silicate				
1,450	97.3	86.7	83.6	78.0
1,500	88.6	79.2	68.0	65.5
1,550	59.9	51.2	48.0	soft
2.5 percent sodium silicate				
1,450	78.6	67.4	62.4	59.3
1,500	66.1	56.8	53.0	49.9
1,550	46.8	39.3	soft	soft
3.0 percent sodium silicate				
1,450	78.6	62.4	48.7	43.1
1,500	46.8	38.1	38.1	soft
1,550	29.3	soft	soft	soft

[1] In lb/cu ft (suspended weight method).

Table 4. Size Analysis of Crushed Glass Aggregate
Compared with ASTM Requirements.

	Wt-pct passing indicated screen size				
	3/4-in	1/2-in	3/8-in	No. 4	No. 8
ASTM C 330	100	90–100	4–80	0–20	0–10
Glass aggregate	100	100	86.2	16.3	6.2

After steam-curing 28 days, the cylinders were tested for compressive strength and unit weight. Test data from six concrete cylinders are shown in Table 5. For comparative purposes the ASTM[12] specification data also are shown. These data show that the expanded glass aggregate produced lightweight concrete meeting ASTM compressive strength-unit weight specifications.

A test cylinder from the above group was exposed to weathering for a 1-year period before testing. After being exposed to weather

Table 5. Concrete Test Data.

Cylinder No.	Unit weight, lb/cu ft	Crushing strength, lb/sq in
1	105	2,700
2	103	2,575
3	102	2,275
4	105	2,425
5	104	2,875
6	105	2,450
Average	104	2,550
ASTM[1]	105	2,500

[1] ASTM specification C 330-69 after 28-day steam cure.

conditions at Tuscaloosa, Ala., for 1 year, the cylinder had a unit weight of 102 lb/cu ft and a crushing strength of 3025 lb/sq in., which indicates no deleterious effects from weathering.

Specimens of expanded glass aggregate also were tested for potential alkali reactivity using the ASTM mortar-bar and chemical procedures. The mortar-bar method measured an expansion of 0.025 percent after 6 months' storage at 100°F. Normally cement-aggregate combinations are considered to have harmful alkali reactivity if expansion is greater than 0.05 percent at 3 months or 0.1 percent at 6 months.

The chemical method[14] analyzed 307 mM/l of dissolved silica and a reduction in alkalinity (R_c) of 553 mM/l. This coordinate on the ASTM curve[15] is in the zone termed "aggregate considered innocuous."

CONCLUSIONS

The results of this investigation indicate that lightweight aggregate suitable for use in structural concrete can be produced utilizing waste glass as the principal raw material.

When fired at 1,550° F for 15 minutes, a mixture of 78 percent waste glass, 20 percent underclay, and 2 percent dry sodium silicate produced aggregate having a bulk density of 38 lb/cu ft. Glass aggregate concrete with an average unit weight of 104 lb/cu ft had an average compressive strength of 2,550 psi after steam curing for 28 days. After 1 year of exposure to weather conditions, the unit weight was 102 lb/cu ft and the compressive strength was 3,025

psi. To meet ASTM specification C-330-69, concrete having a unit weight of 105 lb/cu ft must have a minimum compressive strength of 2,500 psi.

As the ASTM indicates that the chemical method cannot be used as the sole factor in determining alkali reactivity, no definite conclusions on alkali reactivity can be reached until the mortar bars have been stored at temperature for at least   months. However, preliminary results indicate that the glass aggregate has no deleterious effects when used in making concrete.

REFERENCES

1. Kenahan, C.B., R.S. Kaplan, J.T. Dunham, and D.G. Linnehan, "Bureau of Mines Research Programs on Recycling and Disposal of Mineral-, Metal-, and Energy-Based Solid Wastes." BuMines IC 8595, 1973, 54 pp.
2. Sullivan, P.M., and M.H. Stanczyk, "Economics of Recycling Metals and Minerals From Urban Refuse." BuMines TPR 33, 1971, 19 pp.
3. Johnson, P.W., and J.A. Barclay, "Economic Studies of Uses of the Glass Fractions From Municipal Incinerator Residues." BuMines IC 8567, 1973, 44 pp.
4. Tyrrell, M.E., I.L. Feld, and J.A. Barclay, "Fabrication and Cost Evaluation of Experimental Building Brick from Waste Glass." BuMines RI 7605, 1972, 33 pp.
5. Goode, A.H., M.E. Tyrrell, and I.L. Feld, "Glass Wool From Waste Glass." BuMines RI 7708, 1972, 16 pp.
6. Tyrrell, M.E., and A.H. Goode, "Waste Glass As A Flux for Brick Clays." BuMines RI 7701, 1972, 9 pp.
7. Work cited in footnote 1.
8. Vail, J.G., "Soluble Silicates in Industry." Am. Chem. Soc. Monograph Series, No. 46, The Chemical Catalog Co., Inc., New York, 1928, pp. 185–186.
9. Work cited in footnote 4.
10. American Society for Testing and Materials. Standard Method of Test for Unit Weight of Aggregate. C 29-71 in 1974 Annual Book of ATTM Standards: Part 14, Concrete and Mineral Aggregates; Manual of Concrete Testing. Philadelphia, Pa., 1974, pp. 4–5.
11. _____ . Standard Specifications for Lightweight Aggregates for Structural Concrete. C 330-69 in 1974 Annual Book of ASTM Standards: Part 14, Concrete and Mineral Aggregates; Manual of Concrete Testing. Philadelphia, Pa., 1974, pp. 229–232.
12. Work cited in footnote 11.

13. American Society for Testing and Materials. Standard Method of Test for Potential Alkali Reactivity of Cement-Aggregate Combinations (Mortar-Bar Method). C 227-71 in 1974 Annual Book of ASTM Standards: Part 14, Concrete and Mineral Aggregates; Manual of Concrete Testing. Philadelphia, Pa., 1974, pp. 142–147.

14. ———. Standard Method of Test for Potential Reactivity of Aggregates (Chemical Method). C 289-71 in 1974 Annual Book of ASTM Standards: Part 14, Concrete and Mineral Aggregates; Manual of Concrete Testing. Philadelphia, Pa., 1974, pp. 186–195.

15. Work cited in footnote 14.

3-16 Some Observations on the Recycling of Plastics and Rubber

A.G. Buekens

Source: *Conservation and Recycling,* Vol. 1, No. 3/4, 1977, pp. 247-271. Reprinted with Permission of Pergamon Press, Ltd.

INTRODUCTION

For some time now, the recycling of plastics and rubber has been given considerable attention, and is closely connected with other contemporary problems such as the protection of the environment, the treatment of waste, the saving of energy and the maintenance of a favorable balance of payments by industrial countries.

Unit quite recently there was little public interest in the recycling of raw materials. Yet, it is one of man's oldest activities. The trading of ferrous and non-ferrous scrap, old paper, rags, glass, old cars and machines is well-known[1]. Long before the publication of the report of the Club of Rome, such traders were usually prosperous, although very dependent upon the state of the market. More recent is the interest of the recycling industry in synthetic materials; these have been recycled in Belgium for the last twenty years[1].

Little is gained by discussion of the conservation of raw materials or energy balances. Further developments must be supported by an increase in the price of raw materials, a renewal of collection, grading and processing techniques, a change in our social patterns of behavior and, as a last resort, by government aid. This could take the form of investment in, or financially backing investments in, research and development activities, or giving concessions for collecting, grading and transporting of used materials, or setting aside a number of outlets for selling recycled products. Government intervention, however, may disturb the market and often results in subsidizing economically non-viable projects.

THE SIZE OF THE PROBLEM

At the moment, the world production of thermosetting plastics is 40-45 million tons per annum[2], if one includes some base materials for the paints, adhesives and paper industry. So far, this figure has doubled about every five years.

In addition, the intrinsic properties of plastic products have improved in a remarkable way, but the extraordinary resistance of some plastics to atmospheric conditions in general and to biodegradation in particular is sometimes regarded as a disadvantage for products with a short service life. However, there is no danger of infiltration of food chains by plastics, in contrast to heavy metals or chlorinated pesticides.

A significant percentage of plastics is used as packaging materials, which soon become domestic waste. Toys, clothes and toilet articles have an intermediate length of service life, while cable-sheathing, machine parts and domestic appliances last for a considerable time. Unless these synthetic materials are recycled, they eventually enter the refuse stream. At present, in Western Europe and the U.S.A. 2-6% by weight of domestic waste comprises plastics and resins.

In Japan the corresponding figure is 7-12% by weight, but it seems to be inflated by insufficient cleaning of the plastic after sorting and by the presence of plastic-containing composites[52].

Table 1. Use of Plastic Materials (tons/p.a.).

	Belgium, 1970[3]	The Netherlands, 1975[4]
Thermoplastics		
Polyethylene, LDPE		108 000
Polyethylene, HDPE	111 500	39 000
Polypropylene, PP		20 000
Polyvinylchloride, PVC	65 000	161 000
Polystyrene, PS	36 000	43 000
Others	3 000	n.sp.
Thermosets		
Phenoplasts	40 000	n.sp.
Aminoplasts		38 000
Polyurethanes	26 000	n.sp.
Polyesters	11 000	15 000
Polyacrylates	24 000	n.sp.
Alkyd resins	n.sp.	23 000

n.sp. = not specified.

Table 1 gives data on the use of plastic materials in Belgium (1970) and in the Netherlands (1974).

From a national point of view, household refuse is one of the most important potential sources of synthetics. Selective collection could yield a significant tonnage of useful materials. However, collectors generally have not been able to obtain more than a low percentage of the total consumption of paper or glass.

So far, plastic waste coming from the user has not been recycled consistently on a commercial basis, but only in a few cases involving demonstration projects.

A second important source of raw materials is the plastics industry itself. According to Lawrence[5], the processing of thermoplastics involves wastage of 5-15% scrap; for thermosets this figure increases to 10-30%. This waste consists of trimmings, runners, torn or badly formed products, production surpluses, etc. Thermoplastic waste that is not soiled or mixed with other materials, is cut up by the producers and reprocessed, supplemented, if necessary, with virgin raw materials. This internal recycling process is important also in the paper, glass and metal industries, and considerably reduces the amount of waste produced.

However, plastic waste is not recoverable if it is soiled or mixed up with another material.

Tufted carpets, coated paper, and other composite products also enter this category.

A third kind of waste is formed during the actual production of polymers. Lawrence[5] suggests that 13% of the total output of plastics does not reach a first class specification. A particular product may not conform with the usual specifications: often, however, it still has very reasonable properties. Instead of putting such a product onto the market under their own trade name, many producers prefer to sell it to a recycling company at about half its normal market price.

In some production departments, e.g., packaging departments, considerable wastage can occur. Here the recycling company sweeps up, washes and purifies the product. The new product, being a conglomeration of various types of the same polymer, does not reach the usual specifications, but by mixing it before use and during the processing, its properties become more homogeneous.

The last type of waste plastic can be found in the recycling industry itself. Copper from electricity cable was formerly reclaimed by burning off the plastic or rubber cable-coating. This led to air pollution, apart from the additional loss of some of the copper. Modern mechanical separation methods produce not only the desired copper but also recycled plastic.

Of these different types of waste plastics, at present only pure unmixed waste is recycled. The size of the recycling industry (excluding internal recycling) is not known. Figures for recycled raw materials in the U.S.A. range from 150,000 tons/p.a.[5], to a more likely figure of "a few" hundred thousand tons[9]. Kucera[9] suggests 100 000 tons p.a. for the United Kingdom.

These figures seem very low, since a leading Belgian recycling company recycles ca. 40 000 tons/p.a., a second ca. 10 000 tons/p.a., whereas a third recycles an unknown, but large quantity in the form of floor tiles.

Mack[6] divides waste synthetic materials that are not recycled internally, into three categories (see Table 2). Type A is good well-defined waste which can be re-used in less demanding applications. Type B is obtained in industries producing household or electrical appliances, cars etc. Such waste is easy to collect but mostly difficult to re-assimilate. Type C incorporates all the synthetic material which enters the domestic waste stream.

The transport of plastic waste is very expensive on account of the low bulk density of this material. Hence, the waste is often compacted or ground up before transportation, especially when it arises in the form of films, foams or fibers.

Rubber holds a special position among synthetic wastes. The world production of rubber attains ca. 10×100 tons/p.a. to which a somewhat larger quantity of additives (carbon black, oil, chemicals, textiles, etc.) is added. Half of the production of rubber is used in tire manufacturing and another 15% in other applications inside the automotive industry[10]. Each year ca. 250 $\times 10^6$ old tires are discarded in the U.S.A. alone, and some 40×10^6 in W. Germany. Old tires generally reach commercial enterprises such as tire dealers, petrol stations, carcass dealers, recapping and expediting firms[10]. These enter-

prises number ca. 50 000 in W. Germany. The flow of new and old tires to and from manufacturers and importers, tire dealers, carcass dealers, recappers, service and petrol stations, and tire users has been analyzed in the Netherlands by S.V.A.[11].

VARIOUS VIEWPOINTS ABOUT RECYCLING

In relevant literature, one can find widely diverging data about waste plastics and rubber and what should be done with them. Before reading a survey it is worth having a close look at possible connections between the authors and their subject.

The plastic producers and their associations are usually of the opinion that it is impossible to produce a reasonable product with sufficient sales potential from soiled or inter-mixed materials. However, they will encourage recycling if it improves the economic position of plastics versus paper, glass, and other packaging materials[52].

They concentrate their attention on the effect that synthetic waste has on destroying domestic waste (by incineration, burial, composting) come to the conclusion that any such influence is completely acceptable. References [2] and [12] are publications of this kind.

The few authors from synthetics-producing companies view with regret the loss of part of their raw materials. They have great interest in internal recycling schemes and, indeed, actually implement them. In Belgium, they are also studying the recycling of soiled and inter-mixed waste through their association Fabriplast[13].

A third interested party comprises the recycling companies. There are few of them and they are notably discreet. Over the years they have gained experience in locating, purchasing, purifying and processing unmixed, industrial synthetic waste. The main difficulty is buying it from a known and reliable source at the lowest possible

Table 2. Production of Waste Plastics (U.S.A.).

	Type A	Type B	Type C	Total (millions tons)
1971	0.2	0.3	1.5	2
1975	0.3	0.7	3	4
1980	0.6	1.4	6	8

price. They have no interest at all in waste that is inter-mixed or of doubtful composition. Their production program consists of making second grade granulates and semi-manufactured and cheap mass products such as drainage pipes, board, tiles, buckets, combs, toys etc.[9] .

An important category of writers pleads for the conservation of raw materials and in particular of plastics. Often they ask for an end to the use of plastics as packaging materials. Moreover, they want as much plastic as possible to be recycled in its original form (i.e. not as calories, binders or fillers).

Finally, a large group of writers from public or private research institutes is involved in developing processes or machines that help recycle plastics in one way or another.

A reader can get the impression, especially from the last two groups of authors, that there are no obstacles to recycling even the strangest types of waste plastics. However, such a conclusion is premature as most of the processing, sorting and pyrolysis processes have not yet passed the pilot stage and the re-use of the more difficult types of wastes is not yet economically justified.

POSSIBILITIES IN RECYCLING

The best way to recycle waste synthetic materials is to re-use them in their original form, if necessary in less demanding applications.

If, however, the raw materials concerned are soiled, mixed with another material or of unknown composition, such a process produces sub-standard and possibly unmarketable products. Washing and purification of synthetic waste is a feasible proposition, but contemporary sorting methods cannot deal with the very low tolerances for impurities compresing other types of plastics. More elaborate methods, on the other hand, are not (yet) justified economically.

Plastic materials are available in a large number of grades, which vary in molecular weight, molecular weight distribution and structure. Prior to processing, a number of additives, such as stabilizers, antioxidants, plasticizers, lubricants, pigments or dyes, antistatic additives, flame retardants, reinforcing agents and fillers are added. At the end, almost every product has a different composition.

The chemical identification of plastics waste is a slow process involving considerable instrumentation, such as i.r. spectroscopy, thermogravimetry, differential thermal analysis, mass spectrometry, pyrolysis-gas chromatography and selective dissolution. In practice, men go by the look, feel, sound and behavior on burning as a basis for judgment. Moreover, reprocessors have a large experience of handling plastics and a good knowledge about the type and grade of plastics and additives used in each application. They have developed the art of mixing different grades of the same plastic and produce a blend with the right melt index. When color sorting is impractical they recycle the material after addition of carbon black or a master-batch with a dark dominant color. Similar plastics still may contain incompatible additives; when a lead based PVC-stabilizer comes into contact with a mercapto-based stabilizer, black dots of PbS appear[29] .

A certain amount of reclaimed material is often compounded into new rubber. The recovery of rubber forms a separate field of research, as indicated by a series of 67 patents gathered by Szilard[14] concerning aspects of technology, applications and additives.

The recycling of phenol-, urea- or melamine-formaldehyde resins seems to be particularly unusual. After being ground to powder, they can be used as, e.g., fillers or fertilizers. With un-crosslinked virgin resins these fillers can be turned into a new product.

Polyester, polyurethanes and, in general, the polycondensation and polyaddition polymers can be hydrolized or re-esterified into a monomer or a useful product, if sufficiently homogeneous.

Pyrolysis of synthetic materials is an interesting development. The end-products are mostly inflammable gases, oils, carbon and in a few cases also petrochemical raw materials.

Incineration offers the single immediate benefit of producing heat. At the moment more than 90% of crude oil is directly burned, whereas synthetic materials, which could be initiated by u.v. radiation or some other method. However, disposing of synthetic waste in this way is of no benefit at all to society and might be a danger to the environment.

In this survey, the accent lies above all on processing methods, which are of course only one aspect of a problem that includes collection, transport and marketing possibilities. The latter area in particular opens up many questions.

RECYCLING OF UNMIXED, WELL-DEFINED WASTE

Purified, unmixed, thermoplastic waste of known origin and composition can almost always be recycled by its producer or a company specializing in reprocessing.

Some well-defined, industrial wastes can also be recycled after use: such is the case with plastic bottles, shrink foil, wrapping foil, bags, shockproof packaging, etc.

The various types of waste are carefully kept apart and if necessary, sorted by hand into type and color, or just washed and dried. After a grinding process, the waste can be regranulated. A relatively small amount of this new raw material is mixed with a large amount of fresh material or with comparable recycled materials until homogeneous constant properties are gained. The resulting material is frequently made into mass products (garden hoses, buckets) with a wide market, which have a relatively heavy weight and large tolerances concerning size and properties.

The rate of waste generation depends on a number of factors, such as the kind of processing method, the length of individual runs, the quality of the feed material, the skill of the operators, etc. Table 3 gives some data on the types and quantities of waste, generated in various processing methods.

Home or purchased scrap can be recycled more easily in one processing method than in another, depending on its sensitivity to a homogeneous and variable melting behavior, foreign contamination, or a loss in mechanical properties of the material. This loss occurs by aging, oxidation and in each processing or finishing step.

Polyolefines tend to oxidize with time and thermal treatment. The melt index of polypropylene increases, due to a decrease in molecular weight. The influence upon the melt behavior of polyethylene is more complex, the decrease in molecular weight being accompanied by crosslinking. During reprocessing, color changes may also occur: PVC turns brown by thermal decomposition, PP by oxidation. Transparent PS can become opaque. The different processing methods and their ability to absorb wastes have been reviewed in the literature[15].

Local recycling cannot always be justified economically. In the *extrusion* of tubes, rods and profiles, for example, the rate of scrap generation is small. *Injection molding* is quite sensitive to the presence of foreign scrap and of contaminants, since they can clog the injection nozzle and other narrow channels inside the mold's cavity. In addition various types of flow marks and other defects may occur. The molten state of the resin, the relatively high pressure and compacting action of the machine, on the other hand, are favorable factors in the reprocessing of contaminated resin[15].

The "Remaker" from Werner and Pfleiderer is an inexpensive machine designed specifically for this sort of work. Its low working pressure allows more rapidly cooling aluminum molds for rapid heat abstraction to be used. Waste can, without much preparation (washing, purifying), be manufactured into thick-walled articles such as shoe soles, bicycle saddles, toys etc.[5]. The "Reverzer" of Mitsubishi is also a well-known injection machine.

With some machines, a number of impurities such as pieces of rubber or metal can be removed during the actual processing by using a strainer; in some models the sieve is automatically replaced when it gets blocked.

Film scrap is recycled by fabricators, either after chopping and pelletizing, or, less frequently, by direct feeding with an auger feeder. No contamination or variation in melt viscosity can be tolerated. Scrap plastic can be accepted for reuse in heavy constructional or agricultural *film* and *sheet,* provided foreign material is eliminated by straining.

Film, fibers and *cellular plastics* are very light and must be densified to a free flowing, granular material. The bulk density of the granules should be the same as for regular feed.

Film and fiber scrap can be compacted using the "plastcompactor" of Condux-Werk. The scrap is fed to a cutter mill with fixed and rotating cutter blades. The resulting fluff is sintered between a rotating and a water-cooled fixed disc.

Table 3. Type and Generation Quota of Waste in Various Processing Methods. After [15].

Origin	Type and quantity of waste

Dry blending
  Banbury mixer
	Powder agglomerates, removed by screening
	    drippings, aborted runs.

Extrusion compounding	Chunks and strands from extruder purging. Wastes generated during faulty operation (overheating, impure feed). Custom compounding: 1-2% of throughput. In line compounding: 0.2% of throughput.

Injection
  molding
	Sprues and runners. Normally reground and reprocessed in amounts ranging from 1-15%
	of total feed.
	About 1% dirty grindings, floor sweepings, chunks from purging and contaminated
	  moldings.

Extrusion of pipe,
  rod, tubing and
  profiles
	2-3% scrap for common extrusion processes. Up to 40-50% scrap for items machined
	  from rod stock.

Film blowing	Start up, tail and reject film. Extruder purgings.
Sheet extrusion	Scrap generation: 15% in PE, 25% in PVC, 40% in oriented PP-film.
Extrusion coating	6% loss in extrusion coating on paperboard, 5-6% in wire and cable coatings.
Coextrusion	9-10% scrap (sometimes 20%), generally sold to convertors.
Injection blow molding	Practically no scrap.
Extrusion blow molding	Amount of pinch-off, depending upon excess length of parison. Minimized by good design.
Rotational molding	Removal of open sections and small amounts of trim flash.

Dip and slush
  molding
	No cut-off arises, since the material forms a solid solution on the mold. There is, how-
	  ever, a great potential for contamination of the plastisol or the fluidized solids-bath,
	  resulting in rejected parts.

Casting	3-5% loss.
Calendering	Drippings from mixer and calender rolls (less than 1%). Trim, front and strip and tails (6-7%).
Thermoforming	Trimmings arise in significant quantities.
Laminating	8% in high pressure lamination. Side trimmings or scrap cuttings when forming labels, bags, etc. from laminates.
Spreader coating	6-10% scrap, little of which can be recycled.
Cellular plastics	5-10% in expanded PS.
Compression and transfer molding	2-5% Flash (excess) material.

Sintering occurs in a matter of seconds at below the melting point, under the combined action of friction heat and pressure. Thermal degradation is low, since temperature and residence time are restricted to a minimum. The densified material leaves the sintering zone by centrifugal force, in lengths of *ca.* 3-4 cm. After cooling with air, it is cut to the desired size. The feed rate and the distance between the two discs can be varied, and the rotating disc can also be water-cooled, according to the type of material to be recovered[16,17].

Packaging Industries (Hyannis, Maine) recycles film from PE, PP and PS and from hard or plasticized PVC without pelletizing it. The film is fed into a plasticizing cyclinder and heated by friction from rotating and stationary cutting bars. It adheres to the outer wall because of centrifugal force. As soon as the material begins to melt and agglomerate, it is cooled by water. When processing nylon or polyester thread, part of the production is of inferior grade. In view of the sensitivity of spinning processes, internal recycling is not to be recommended here.

Free-Flow Packaging Corp., (Calif.) now produces foamed PS from recycled foam and virgin PS. The proprietary method of densifying the foam involves size reduction, removal of blowing agents, densification and rapid feeding of a pelletizing extruder.

Foreign scrap cannot be recycled in *extrusion coating*, since melt viscosity specifications are critical. Moreover, the electrical performance of wire and cable coatings must be excellent.

In *cable extrusion* the scrap is formed during starting, calibrating and halting of the extruder, and changing of a cable drum. The Swedish Maskin AB Rapid has developed a hot granulator for immediate recycling of plastic. The melt flows into a cutter, is air-cooled, chopped and recirculated. The same machine is suitable for recycling melts from calendering and extrusion compounding.

Co-extrusion is a very difficult processing method and yields composite materials, which cannot directly be recycled.

Melt viscosity control and color consistency are very critical in *blow molding*. Preferred materials are high molecular weight HDPE or PVC, after addition of a high temperature stabilizer. Even recycling of home scrap is difficult: contaminations, variations in resin molecular weight, moisture or volatile hydrocarbons can all cause fracture of the parison during the blow cycle[15].

In *rotational molding* a narrow distribution of molecular weight is required, to avoid early or incomplete melting. The scrap should be reusable in other processing methods[15].

Casting of thermoplastics, e.g. of PMMA, involves an irreversible polymerization reaction. Hence, direct re-use is impossible. Waste is reused in injection or compression molding. Thermosets are not yet re-usable[15].

Trim, front end and tails can be recycled in *calendering,* unless the material is composite. Contaminated sheet and calender drippings are undesirable. In the manufacture of floor tiles many types of PVC-waste can be recycled. Particulate contaminations should be thoroughly eliminated, to avoid damaging the expensive, chromium-plated calender rolls[15].

Thermoforming trimmings cannot be recycled directly, but can be incorporated in thermoforming sheet. Many sheet producing operations use an average of 40% regrind. Proper housekeeping and a good process layout are paramount in scrap recovery[15]. Recycling is more difficult when the sheet is a laminated composite, as in the case of motor oil containers. In a patent of Phillips Petroleum Co., the PVC-coating is applied in a specific geometric pattern, so that the trimmings consist of PE only[15].

Laminated scrap and coated products have a multilayer structure and often contain thermosets. They are hardly recoverable, except by special methods.

Floor sweepings and soiled plastics can be recycled only after thorough cleaning. Burned plastics are, of course, no longer suitable for recycling, except in undemanding applications, e.g. PVC floor tiles.

RECYCLING OF MIXED WASTES

Survey

Recycling of mixed wastes is difficult for technical and commercial reasons:

1. Each component has a different melting behavior, rheology and thermal stability. At a given processing temperature some components may be melted, others remain solid, and others still decompose thermally.
2. Polymer mixtures are generally mutually insoluble. Even after thorough mixing they still consist of discrete phases, dispersed in a continuous phase. Unless there is sufficient adherence between the different phases, the mechanical properties of such mixture are quite poor. They lack both toughness and rigidity, and have a low sales potential. Even if new markets could be developed for such materials, it is highly questionable whether they will be of sufficient a size and whether the material will command an economic price.

Different strategies can be followed in recycling mixed wastes:

1. Segregation of the various components, type by type.
2. Addition of compatibilizers, which improve the adherence between the polymer phases.
3. Use of suitable processing methods, which take into account the differences in melt behavior and stability of the various components.
4. Use of very simple processing methods which make few demands on the melt

behavior of the raw material, (melting in a salt bath, compression molding).

5. Use of the waste in second grade applications such as fillers, binders, etc.

Sorting and Purification of Mixed Plastic Waste

A plastics concentrate can be separated from household refuse, using integrated sorting systems, such as the one operated by the City of Rome, the T.N.O. separation system[18], or one of the systems developed by the U.S. Bureau of Mines[19].

Often, this plastics concentrate is obtained by moistening the mixture: the paper absorbs moisture, becomes denser and can be separated by a second air classification step. Conversely, thermoplastic film can be removed from the mixture, by contracting it in a hot air stream. The U.S. Bureau of Mines has developed an electrostatic drum separator, which uses an electric high-voltage field. The mixture is fed onto an electrically grounded, rotating drum. The damp paper attains the potential of the drum, is attracted by the active electrode and is removed. Plastics remain pinned to the drum, until they are removed by a wiper blade[20].

M.I.T. developed a highly sophisticated sorting system, in which components are scanned individually and identified by means of their i.r. reflection spectrum or the damping characteristics of an impact[21]. Plastics can also be separated from paper by wet pulping, using either a conventional or an ultrasonic pulper.

In all but the simplest processing methods, the mixed plastics should be freed from contaminants, such as dust, labels and metal particles. After being chopped, the plastics can be cleaned with hot water, separated from the slurry, and dried. Labels can be removed by attrition scrubbing with sand.

Metal particles must always be sorted out carefully, mainly to prevent the processing machines getting damaged. The particles come from aluminum bottle tops, aluminum foil and electrical or mechanical parts. Steel can be removed magnetically, while other metals can be located by an inductive metal detector attached to and controlling an ejection apparatus. If the metal content is of the order of a few per cent, this method rejects an important fraction of the raw material.

Sink/float methods allow a mixture of plastics, extracted from municipal refuse, to be sorted in to PP (specific gravity = 0.90), LDPE (0.92), HDPE (0.94-0.96), PS (1.05-1.06) and PVC (1.22-1.38). Water, water-alcohol mixtures, and a $CaCl_2$-solution are suitable separation media. Elutriation with pure water also allows PS and PVC to be separated[19].

In practice these methods are rarely used. The apparent density of pieces of plastic material is affected too much by encapsulation and adhering air bubbles and, furthermore, by all the possible additives, plasticizers and fillers which might have been used in the processing.

Mitsui Kinsoko Engineering Service Co. (Tokyo) has developed a flotation process, in which the wetting characteristics of some plastics are altered, selectively, by means of proprietary wetting agents. The process can separate PVC from mixed plastics, PP for PE, HDPE from LDPE, polyesters from cellulose triacetate and numerous plastics from non-plastics[26].

A few polymers dissolve in water or other solvents, but the solutions formed are extremely viscous and the solvents cannot be completely removed from the recovered plastics[52]. Other polymers swell in a solvent and this can be used to separate electric cable from its sheathing.

Normally, additives cannot be removed from plastic materials. Flexible PVC, however, contains large amounts of valuable plasticizer. Vinyl Recovery Ltd. has developed a steam extractor unit to separate the plasticizer from the PVC. The value of the residual PVC is doubtful, since PVC recycling often requires addition of supplemental plasticizer.

Hafner Industries, Inc. patented the reclamation of both PVC and plasticizer from mixed plastics by extraction of these components with a solvent, such as methylethylketone, dimethylformamide or ethylenedichloride. The PVC is then precipitated from the extracted liquor by means of a nonsolvent (a lower alcohol). Solvent and plasticizer are recovered from the filtered liquor by distillation.

Huge quantities of PVC-coated fabric waste are available from car-upholstery manufacture. Gerwain Chemical Corp. (Frackville, Penn.) operates a commercial plant with a capacity of more than 1 000 tons/p.a. The process was invented by Horizons Research and entails chopping the scrap, dissolving non-fibrous material, filtering off the fibers, evaporating and drying[26].

Large amounts of waste are generated in the manufacture of photographic film. Depending on the production stage at which the waste arises, the film underlayer is covered with one or more layers of other material. The PETP-underlayer can be recovered after removal of the soil and the other layers of the film structure. S.A.Agfa-Gevaert (Mortsel, Belgium) demonstrated the recovery using batch equipment, and operates a pilot-plant, consisting of washing and rinsing equipment, and of filtering centrifuges. It should be emphasized that sorting and purification of plastic wastes are still in a stage of development, and that commercial applications are almost non-existent, especially in the field of mixed municipal wastes.

The recovery of PTFE must be put into a separate category on account of its high price. Cleaning it can involve a long physical and chemical process: treatment with perchloric acid or ozone is not without danger. The product recovered is re-sintered. Its loss of mechanical properties is not unimportant but is not a problem in many applications.[33]

Adherence in Polymer Mixtures

A blend of two or more polymers, such as PE, PS, PVC, has a heterogeneous structure, the minor constituents forming dispersed phases, the major constituent the continuous phase. Often, two different polymers are incompatible, i.e., the different phases show little or no adherence. Stress concentrations arise around the dispersed polymer particles, and the mechanical properties show a dramatic decrease[22]. This happens when even the smallest amount of PVC is added to polyolefins. The tolerance of PS to PVC is somewhat greater. Small amounts of low molecular weight polyolefins in PVC behave as a lubricant and they are therefore, not unacceptable.

The compatibility is much better when the two polymers have a similar constitution. Small additions of LDPE are acceptable in PP and even increase the tensile strength by *ca.* 10%[29].

LDPE and HDPE have a different melting point and difficulties may arise, even though they are miscible.

In cases where the mixed polymer phases show adherence, the resulting polymer alloy often combines desirable properties of both polymers[23].

Selected additives may increase the adherence between two polymer phases. Addition of sequentially chlorinated polyethylene (CPS) acts as a plasticizer, but has been considered, erroneously, to be a compatibilizer. Copolymers, such as ethylene vinylacetate (EVA) improve the adherence. Graft copolymers, prepared by Friedel-Crafts alkylation of the aromatic rings in PS with the olefinic groups in LDPE, act as emulsifiers in mechanical blends of these two components. The copolymer concentrates at the interface and adheres to both polymers. The tensile strength of the ternary mixture increases with the amount of copolymer[24].

For several years the "Centre de Récherches Scientifiques et Techniques de l'Industrie des Fabrications Métalliques" (C.R.I.F., Liege, Belgium) has been studying the mechanical properties of binary alloys, such as PS/PE, plasticized PVC/PS plasticized PVC/PE, ABS/PE, EVA/PC, using a Patfoort short-screw plastificator, which is claimed to show the advantages of both the disc plastificator and the extruder.

The phase distribution was influenced by addition of various fillers, which could act as nucleating agents for the dispersed phase, of compatibilizing agents, which improve the adherence between different phases, and of curing agents, which could act as a cross-linking agent between the two phases. In PE/PS mixtures most fillers were found to decrease the mechanical properties; only an addition of calcined alumina was slightly beneficial. Addition of a peroxide curing agent hardened the PE-phase, but failed to induce the desired interphase cross-linking[13].

The Sidac-division (Ghent, Belgium) of U.C.B. was capable of making agricultural film and refuse bags from a mixture of virgin resin with up to 40% of mixed plastics, sorted from the Ghent composting plant. Commercial application is being considered, but the cost and complexity of preliminary cleaning still act as a deterrent[25].

Initiatives in Recycling

Several recycling initiatives have received ample publicity even though in many cases they are dealing only with the conventional recycling of purified, unmixed synthetic materials. The "Golden Arrow" dairy farm (San Diego, Calif.) collected used PE milk containers; after being ground they were used as drainage pipes. This idea got into difficulties over specifications which prevented the use of recycled raw materials in this application. Gold Plastics Service Inc. (LA) and the Dow-Alta-Dena program also recycle PE milk containers. Gulf Oil replaces its metal motor-oil cans by high density PE containers that can be recycled.

Recycled Plastic Product Corp. (New York) makes racks for wine bottles out of PS from plastic beakers. Mobil Plastics recycles foam egg cartons in their original form.

Western Electric is studying the recycling of ABS parts of telephone equipment[7]. Chem. Tac Specialities (Detroit) has found a method of using PE, PP and PS in powders, coatings and emulsions.

Homogenizing processing methods have been applied by Werner and Pfleiderer (Remaker), Mitsubishi (Reverzer), C.R.I.F., Japan Steel Works (after processing to a powder and mixing with fresh plastic material), Kobe Steel Works (after melting at 180-250°C), U.C.B.-Sidac and others.

In England, Kabor Ltd. produces items such as window boxes, pallets and partitions for pigsties from reclaimed polymers, including plasticized paper.

Regal Packaging also make large articles from waste, which may contain some copper, wood or textiles. The synthetic waste is softened in an oven and pressed into a mold. One should realize that the pressing has a longer cycle than the injection molding, so that the production rate is not very high. The mixing also leaves much to be desired. The plant costs £25 000, and has a capacity of 5000 pallets/month.

In Nuneaton, England a type of board is made from plastics waste: it is said to cost less than multiplex. Moreover, the material is good for screwing, nailing or glueing.

Menges and Hoffmann discuss the processing of mixed waste with 0, 5, 10 or 15% of bitumen as a binder. After mixing for 3, 5 or 7 min, a homogeneous mass is obtained in which metal and thermosets are incorporated. After cooling, this can be granulated. The manufacturing cost, including energy, is estimated at ca. 0.1$/kg[30].

The same authors propose that synthetic waste should be processed with a foaming agent and thus produce insulation sheeting. This could be done on the dock side.

Farukawa Electric Co. make foam products from mixed waste. The Satenaizo Co. use these in road construction, whereas Japan Synthetic Paper makes them into an aggregate board.

In the Netherlands, a new material called "Restaplast" has been developed, in which separated synthetic waste acts as a binder. Applicational possibilities include, among other things, complete roof coverings with roof tile motif, and the "do it yourself" market.

One of the more popular ideas in waste treatment is to let the wastes be consumed in construction materials. Hoffmann Plastics Co. (Chicago) and also the Cement and Concrete Research Institute are studying the use of reclaimed plastics in concrete. Resistance to crack formation would be improved by such an addition, and the adhesion and elastic properties, the hydration rate and the coefficient of thermal expansion are also modified.

Obviously, most of the low-grade applications save nothing but some low quality wood, or some other, still more plentiful, material[52].

The above list of experiments in recycling is of course, by no means complete. Many of these applications will never capture a place in the market. In addition, they must be carefully labelled: obviously the user has the right to know the extent of possible safeguards offered by the material he is getting. If this is not done, the image of plastics throughout the world could be jeopardized.

Thermosets and Rubbers

The direct re-use of thermosets and rubbers is almost impossible on account of the crosslinks between the various chains. It can be contemplated only after thermal, chemical, mechanical or photochemical degradation.

The recovery of petrochemical raw materials by hydrolysis of polyurethanes, polyesters and polyamides is discussed in the previous section. The solid waste problem originating from the fabrication of rubber products has been analyzed elsewhere[31]. Consumer rubber wastes can be recycled, or disposed of by tipping, incineration or thermal decomposition.

Recapping (retreading) extends the lifetime of a tire, but sooner or later it gets damaged beyond repair. Recapping of car tires continues to lose ground, but recapping of large tires is still economic, as can be seen from a typical cost structure (1976):

Carcass (truck tire	1500 B.F.
New rubber	550 B.F.
Rubber solution	30 B.F.
Utilities (steam, air, electricity, . . .)	130 B.F.
Wages and production cost	540 B.F.
Depreciation of equipment and financing cost	300 B.F.
Commercial and overhead cost	1200 B.F.
Total cost	4250 B.F. (36 B.F. = $\overline{1 \text{ U.S.\$}}$)

The final cost compares favorably with the selling price of a new truck tire (6000–7000 B.F.).

Traditional recapping involves a long series of operations. After thorough inspection of the interior of the tire, *ca.* 20–25% of tires are rejected. Deep scars on the outer surface are repaired by cleaning the scar, application of a suitable sheet of rubber and vulcanization. The old tire surface is now eliminated by means of cutters and rotating metal brushes. Rubber solution is squirted over the resulting round and rough surface. The tire is fixed on a rim, and a flat extruded profile of unvulcanized rubber is glued on top and sides. Then the tire is loaded into a steam-heated mold and vulcanized for *ca.* 2h. The tire surface is pressed into the mold by inflating the inner tire. After unloading and inspection, the recapped tire is returned to its owner, or sold.

In the *"cold sole" recapping* method only the top of the tire is roughened. After application of the rubber solution, the "cold sole", i.e. a vulcanized road surface, is glued to the tire by means of an unvulcanized rubber foil. Any entrapped air is carefully squeezed out and the layer between the cold sole and the tire is vulcanized in an autoclave. The unchanged side of the tire is painted black and, after inspection, the tire is ready.

Production cost can be controlled only in well-organized and efficient recapping shops. In Belgium the number of tire recappers declined from 40 in 1965 to *ca.* 10 at present.

Tires can further be re-used as a buffer in docks, harbors and along roads. Artificial reefs have been constructed from tires in Australia, Florida and other countries. After a while these reefs become covered with corals, and become a breeding place for fish. Extraction tests have shown that no contamination of the seàwater is likely[10].

Tire cuttings can be re-used in a number of applications, such as knee-caps, soles, gaskets, etc. The presence of steel cord causes additional difficulties in cutting the tire and in finding outlets for the cuttings.

Tires can be cut by shears or pulverized by cryogenic methods. Cryogenic Recycling Intern., Inc. (La Crosse, Wis.) operates a mobile cryogenic unit in which rubber and also plastic can be ground up. Ets. George (Lièqe, Belgium) shredded rubber tires in a cryogenic shredder plant for baled cars.

A series of possible outlets for rubber meal has been studied. Addition of rubber meal to the soil would improve its porosity, accelerate the growth of plants and selectively destroy a number of undesirable insects[10].

Vulcanized rubber lacks solubility in and adherence to asphalt. Hence, rubber meal is no suitable additive to asphalt concrete. Mixtures of asphalt, powdered rubber and mineral fillers could be used as an elastic, thermal insulating, intermediate road layer. Cost limitations make this an impractical solution to the problem of rubber waste disposal[10].

Bayer AG has developed the use of pulverized rubber in sports ground and other elastic surfaces. Pulverized tires can be mixed with reactive PU-resin and molded, or directly applied on a suitable undersoil. Reticulation follows in a matter of minutes or hours, depending on resin and activator types, temperature, air humidity, etc. Foaming is also possible[10].

Table 4.

	Price paid by processor ($/ton)	Market price of virgin plastic ($/ton)
clear PE	10 - 20	225 - 400
clear PS	40 - 60	310 - 350
clear PVC	90 - 110	240 - 400
clear cellulose acetate	120 - 160	1,240

Rubber meal can be used for its absorptive power, e.g. as a partition material in chromatographic columns, or as an ion exchanger. It seems unlikely, however, that these outlets will use more than extremely small amounts of rubber waste.

Regenerated natural rubber no longer has the properties of virgin material. Limited amounts can be re-used as an additive, since it makes extrusion easier and it improves the stability of extruded goods[10].

Cost Factors

For some time now it has been dangerous to mention investment and cost factors without making a long series of reservations. Published cost factors tend to be unreliable and are almost never comparable, since they are often accounted for on differing bases (depreciation, rate of interest, distribution of general costs). Such problems occur in all industries, but are especially marked in the recycling business.

The buying price of plastic waste is mostly between zero and 0.155/kg, depending on the degree of pollution, the homogeneity, the partial degradation etc. Off-specification products command, generally, more than half the market price for high-grade products.

In most cases the direct processing cost of the reprocessor are in the range $0.08–0.25/kg.

The selling price of the reworked synthetic waste, in the form of granulate for example, must be sufficiently below the normal market price for its purchase to be attractive to the less demanding buyer. A 15–40% reduction of the normal price is usual. Kucera[9] gives a number of prices for reprocessed plastics, as for 1970. Sittig cites the following prices[15].

In some cases the scrap of expensive polymer can only be re-used in common grade applications. MBS-impact modifier is a valuable ($200/ton) additive in the manufacture of PVC-bottles. During the production of MBS, part of the material arises in the form of coarse granules, which are useless as an additive. This coarse material can still be blended with ABS, but the lower rank of this application is of course reflected in the price paid by the reprocessor (*ca.* $50/ton).

Care should be taken with cost factors cited in literature, especially when considering unproven processes for the recycling of mixed or soiled plastics. Investment cost is often based on machinery only, disregarding other items of plant cost, such as buildings, or investment in auxiliary and administrative services. When all commercial and overhead costs, together with the lower productivity, are taken into account, the cost advantage of processing mixed vs virgin plastics becomes much lower than generally expected. Furthermore, the technical specifications that can be guaranteed using these low grade materials, are not comparable to the established specifications for plastic materials.

CONCLUSIONS

Recycling of well-defined plastic wastes is no longer a problem. Recycling of mixed, soiled or ill-defined wastes is, however, still in its infancy, and a number of deterrents exist against recycling[15]:

1. No proven techniques exist for separating mixed plastics.
2. Identification of unknown plastics is very difficult.
3. Aging and reprocessing decrease the mechanical properties and performance of plastics. A drastic loss occurs in the presence of even small amounts of impurities.

4. Upgrading techniques are almost non-existent.
5. Collecting and shipping costs are high, because of the low bulk density, especially of film, foam and fiber.
6. Trade channels for reclaimed plastics are not well established.
7. Standard grades and specifications do not exist for reclaimed plastics.

Commercial outlets for reprocessed mixed waste are hence restricted to large mass, low-quality products.

Rubber and thermosets can be recycled only after mechanical, thermal or chemical degradation.

Pyrolysis of Plastics and Rubber

Survey. The pyrolysis or thermal decomposition of polymers yields gases, distillate fractions and char, which can be recycled in the form of fuels or as petrochemical raw materials and products. Pyrolysis can be conducted at various temperatures, reaction times, pressures, and in the presence or absence of reactive gases or liquids, and of catalysts.

Temperature is the most important operating variable, since it determines the stability of feedstock and reaction products and the rate of thermal decomposition. High temperatures favor the production of simple gaseous products, low temperatures that of liquid products.

Pyrolysis, for most plastics, begins at 300–400°C. The pyrolysis reaction is somewhat influenced by the presence of additives such as stabilizers, plasticizers and pigments. In most processes a relatively low temperature (400–500°C) is selected.

The required reaction time is determined principally by the reaction temperature. At a given temperature the formation of primary products, e.g. monomers, is favored by short residence times, the formation of thermodynamically stable products (H_2, CH_4, aromatics, carbon) by long residence times. Low pressures (under vacuum, in the presence of an inert diluent) favor the production of monomer, high pressure that of complex, liquid fractions.

The reactor type is mainly determined by heat transfer and feed and residue handling considerations. In many proposed processes the polymer is dissolved in a bath of molten polymer or wax, or dispersed in a salt bath. Other processes suggest the use of the excellent heat transfer and mixing properties of a fluidized bed.

The required heat of reaction is generally supplied by external heating of the reaction vessel. Some processes use an external heat carrier, e.g. superheated steam or circulating molten salts, sands or pebbles, to heat the charge. One process (Sanyo) uses the dielectric losses, arising by the high frequency oscillation of electrically polarizable molecules. The problem of heat transfer can be eliminated by partial oxidation of the reactor contents. In this case, the product stream is diluted by combustion products. This makes the recovery of useful products more difficult and reduces the calorific value of the pyrolysis gas.

The pyrolysis of plastics. In the pyrolysis of plastics the thermal decomposition may follow different reaction patterns[36]:

1. Decomposition into the monomer (PMMA, PTFE).
2. Fragmentation of the principle chains into lengths of variable size (PE, PP).
3. Decomposition according to both previous schemes (PS, PIB).
4. Elimination of simple components, leaving a charred residue (PVC yields HCl, PVAc yields (HAc).
5. Elimination of side-chains, followed by cross-linking.

Polymethylmetacrylate can be decomposed thermally into the monomer with a very high yield. The monomer is either re-polymerized, or used as an additive in lubricating oil. At very high temperatures (500-700°C), PTFE can be turned into the monomer in the presence of superheated steam[33].

Polyethylene and polypropylene can be thermally decomposed into a broad range of hydrocarbons. At 400°C the products consist mainly of C_7 to C_{22} paraffins and olefins[37]. At lower temperatures the molecular weight of the fragments is higher and cross-linking also occurs[38]. At high temperatures, a mixture is formed of gaseous products, such as H_2, CH_4, C_2H_4, C_3H_6, and others.

PVC loses HCl when the temperature reaches about $200°C$. When processing PVC-containing wastes, the formation of corrosive gases must be taken into account; this inflates plant construction cost. The gaseous effluent must also be purified in a scrubber.

Thermosets, such as phenolic and ureaic resins, show a complex degradation reaction over a wide temperature range.

Current research initiatives in the pyrolysis of polymers are summarized in Table 5.

Union Carbide has succeeded in turning thermoplastic materials into waxes, fats or oils, depending on the pyrolysis temperature and contact time used. As a starting material the following materials are used: PE, PP, PS, PVC, PETP, PA and multi-component mixes. The equipment consists of an extruder screw, a pyrolysis tube and a cooler. A de-volatilizing extruder is used in the presence of easily decomposing polymer (PVC).

The pyrolysis products of HDPE can be used as polish, printing ink, release agent or as a lubricant for polymers. The viscosity of the melted wax falls as the "cracking severity" increases, whereas the number of vinyl and vinylidene bonds increases. The presence of these bonds make it possible, chemically, to give the waxes emulsifying and adhesive qualities[48].

Multi-component mixes give at increasing "cracking severity" a brittle resin, tar, grease, fluid and gases. The tar can be used in asphalt concrete or for agricultural purposes where the absence of carcinogenic polynuclear aromatics is considered to be an advantage[48].

Japan Steel Works has developed the analogous NIKKO-process, in which not only the melting but also the pyrolysis is carried out in the body of the extruder. The products are separated by fractional condensation[36]. Japan Gasoline Co. has used a conventional tube furnace for heating ground-up plastic waste, which is previously dissolved or suspended in oil. After separating the cracked products, a medium oil fraction is recycled to act as a carrier for the plastic waste[36].

Tsutsumi has studied the pyrolysis of foam PS in a tubular reactor, using superheated steam as a heat carrier. The steam is superheated to $650°C$ by an internal combustion-type superheater, requiring 40 l oil/ton of steam. Linear velocities of 15–25m/s prevent carbon deposition in the reactor[45].

Nichimen and Toyo Engineering Corp. have studied catalytic decomposition, respectively, in a solid catalyst-bed (Fig. 1) and in a fluidized bed. The feed preferably does not include char-forming polymers[36]. Little is known about the operation of these catalytic reactors. Possibly, carbon formation is a serious problem.

A number of processes make use of a tank reactor, containing a bath of molten products or molten salts. The bath is heated indirectly. Stirring or circulation of the bath is necessary, to obtain homogeneous reaction conditions, improve the heat transfer, and prevent

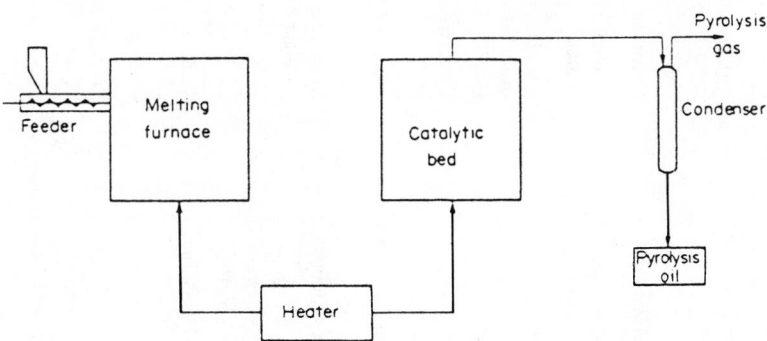

Figure 1. Fixed bed catalytic cracking (Nichimen).

Table 5.   Thermal Decomposition of Polymers.

Process developed by	Reactor type & heating method	Reaction temperature, °C	Plant capacity, tons/day	Feedstock	Products	References
Union Carbide	Extruder, followed by annular pyrol. tube, electrically heated	420-600	0.035-0.07	PE, PP, PS, PVC, PETP, PA, mixes	Waxes	[48]
Japan Steel Works	Extruder					[36]
Japan Gasoline Co.	Tubular reactor, externally heated			Dissolved or suspended in recycle-oil	Heavy-oil	[36]
Prof. Tsutsumi	Tubular reactor, super-heated steam as a heat carrier	500-650	1	PS-foam		[45]
Nichimen*	Catalytic fixed bed reactor			Mixed plast., no char-forming polymers		[36]
Toyo Engineering Corp.	Fluidized bed catalytic reactor		0.5	Mixed plast., no char-forming polymers		[36, 50]
Mitsui Shipbuilding & Engineering Co.	Stirred tank reactor, polymer bath	420-455	24-30	Low mol. w. polymers (PE, APP)	Fuel-oil	[43, 50]
Mitsui Petrochemical Industries Co. (Chiba Works)						
Mitsubishi Heavy Ind. (Mihara Works)	Tank reactor with circulation pump and reflux cooling	400-500	0.7/2.4	Polyolefins	Naphtha kerosene fuel-oil	[42, 50]
Kawasaki Heavy Ind.	Polymer bath, formed by PE and PS	400-450	5	Mixed plast. PE + PS content 55%	Gas-oil HC1	[36, 50]
Ruhrchemie AG, Oberhausen	Stirred tank reactor, salt bath	380-450	1.2	PE	Oil, wax	[37]
Japan Gasoline Co.	Fluidized bed	450	0.2	PS-waste	see [28]	[28] Fig. 16
Prof. Sinn, Univ. of Hamburg	Fluidized bed Molten salt bath	640-840 600-800	Laboratory scale Laboratory scale	PE, PS, PVC type rubber		See [28]

Table 5. Continued

Process developed by	Reactor type & heating method	Reaction temperature, °C	Plant capacity, tons/day	Feedstock	Products	References
Sanyo Electric Co.§	Tubular reactor with a screw for carbon removal, dielectric heating	260 (PVC), followed by 500-550	0.3 (pilot) 3 (Gifu) 5 (Kusatsu)	Foam PS, mixed plast. (select. collect.) asphalt with 6% S	Monomer Fuel-oil HC1	[28. 45. 50]
Sumitomo Shipbuild. & Machinery Co. (Hiratsuka Lab.)	Fluidized bed, partial oxidation	450-470 600 (28)	3-5	Mixed plastics incl. PVC	Heavy oil HC1	[28, 50] HC1
Government Industrial Research Institute	Fluidized bed, partial oxidation	400-510 550	Bed diameter: 3.5/ 15/30/50 & 120 cm	PS-chips	Monomer and dimer Gasific. prod.	[39]
Nippon Zeon, Japan Gasoline Co. (Tokuyama)	Fluidized bed, partial oxidation	350-600 (400-500 mostly)	24 pre-commercial plant	Sheared tires	Gas, oil, char	[47]
Kobe Steel	Externally heated, rotatory kiln	600-800	5 (pilot)	Crushed tires	Gas, oil, char	[28, 41]
Bureau of Mines/Firestone	Electrically heated retort	500/900	Laboratory scale	Tire cuttings	Gas, oil, char	[49]
Hydrocarbon Research Inc.	Autoclave	350-450		Tires		[28]
Zeplichal	Conveyor band, vacuum			Tires		[28]
Herbold, W. Germ.			6	Tires		[32]

*With Osaka City Industrial Research Institute, Shinko Precision Instruments [50].
With the Plastic Waste Management Institute.
§With the Government Industrial Devt. Laborat., and Prof. Endo (Hokkaido Univ.).
In collaboration with Prof. Tsutsumi (Osaka Univ.).
In collaboration with Prof. Yoshida (Tokyo Univ.).
In collaboration with Prof. Schnecko, Dunlop, Hanau (W. Germany).

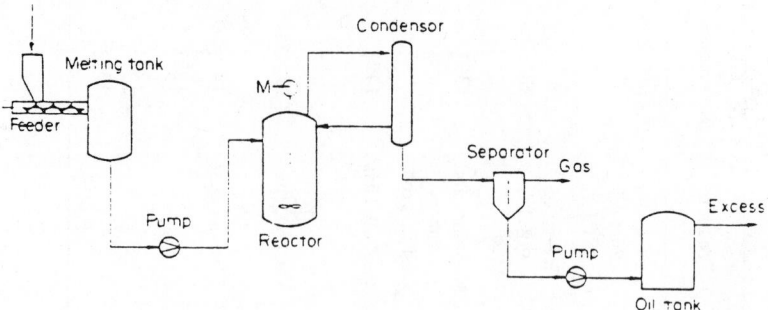

Figure 2. Pyrolysis of plastic refuse in a stirred tank.

accumulation of charred residue on the heat transfer surfaces. The following problems were encountered [37, 43]:

1. The accumulation of charred polymer causes fouling of the heat transfer surfaces. This can be prevented only by continuous or periodic bleeding of part of the reactor content.
2. Entrained droplets and waxy materials can clog the outlet lines, and build up a layer on the product condenser.
3. Level control is difficult, since no gauge can be introduced into the charge. The level can be determined by means of the apparent temperature difference between the liquid and the vapor phase [43].

In the Mitsui Shipbuilding and Engineering process[43] low molecular weight PE and atactic PP are melted and pumped into a stirred tank reactor. The cracking products are distilled off: part of the entrained mist and some relatively high molecular weight products are condensed and return to the reactor. At bench scale the yields were: 4–5% gas, 90% oil and 5–6% residue. The oil fraction consists of n-paraffins, 1-olefins and isomers in the range C_5–C_{28}. The gas fraction consists primarily of C_1–C_4 hydrocarbons (Fig. 2).

The Ruhrchemie-process differs from the Mitsui process in that the polymer bath is replaced by a bath of molten salts, heated in a separate vessel[37].

Mitsubishi Heavy Industries has developed a two-step process for the pyrolysis of plastics.

In a first melting vessel the temperature is kept at 300°C, resulting in a rapid decomposition of PVC. The vapors are scrubbed in an absorption tower. The molten material is fed into the pyrolysis vessel, operated at 400–500°C. The boiling range of the product oil can be varied and the problem of clogging by waxy compounds avoided by a suitable selection of the temperature (170–300°C) in a cooled reflux zone on top of the reactor (Fig. 3). The process is still at the pilot-stage[42].

Kawaski Heavy Industries has developed an analogous technique. A polymer bath is obtained by melting PE and PS. A mixed feed, containing, PVC and even thermosets, is pyrolyzed at 400–500°C in this bath. These contents have to be continually replenished with fresh PE and PS from the feed; a combined ratio of these plastics of more than 55% is required. After the separation of the fluid products, the HCl that has been formed is removed in a scrubber. Having been washed a second time with alkali the gas, together with part of the liquid fraction, is burnt. Charred products must be removed from the bath; they contain, *inter alia,* heavy metals from the stabilizers, pigments, etc.[36].

The Japan Gasoline Co. uses a fluidized bed reactor for the pyrolysis of shredded PS-waste. An unusual feature is the presence of a stirrer inside the bed [28, 36].

The work of Sinn *et al.* was covered extensively in this journal [28], as was the Sanyo microwave process.[28, 36, 45].

Sumitomo Shipbuilding and Machinery Co. converts shredded plastic waste by partial oxidation in a fluidized sand-bed. The purification chain of the pyrolysis gases consists of:

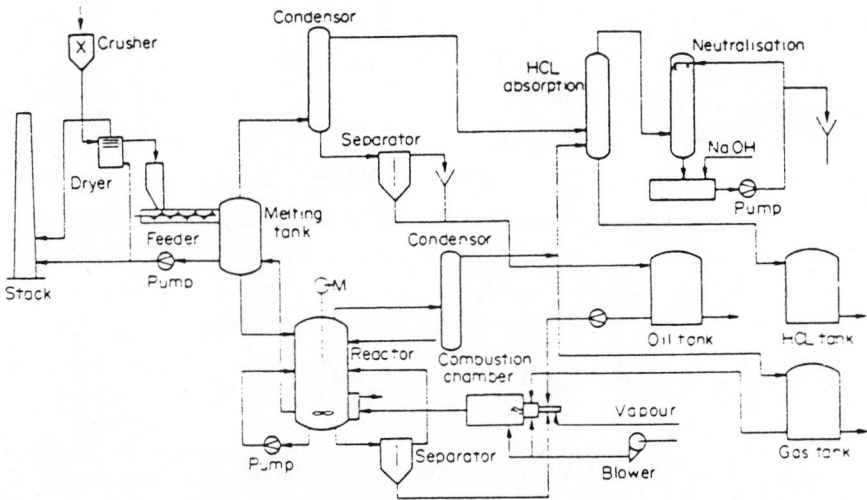

Figure 3. Pyrolysis of plastic refuse in a melting bath.

1. A cyclone for removing entrained sand and char particles.
2. A distillation column yielding a non-condensable gas, a light, and a heavy oil fraction.
3. A combustion chamber for disposal of the pyrolysis gas and the light oil.
4. A water scrubber, followed by a caustic scrubber.

Yoshida *et al.* [39] have studied the pyrolysis of PS-chips in a fluidized bed, heated by partial combustion. Monomer and dimer were recovered in good yielder up to 510°C. At 550°C extensive gasification occurred.

Gasification and pyrolysis have been hailed as the future disposal methods for domestic wastes. When applied to petrochemical or polymer wastes, these methods are still more promising, since the products obtained (monomers, waxes, fuel-oil) are valuable. As a rule, pyrolysis processes have been operated only at bench or pilot scale and for limited periods of time.

Only the Mitsui process has been applied continuously for a prolonged period (since 1971) and at a relatively large scale (24 tons/day). In spite of the smooth, automatic operation and the high quality of the feedstock, the plant has operated at a slight financial loss[43].

Hence, it seems that plastic pyrolysis processes have to be operated at a scale of at least 100 tons/day to be economically viable. Such quantities of plastic waste can hardly be recovered from refuse without excessive collection and transportation cost. Tsutsumi reports that selective collection at Kusatsu yields only *ca.* 0.3 tons/day.[45]

The position of rubber waste is slightly more favorable, since old tires are available at a smaller number of commercial enterprises.

The Pyrolysis of Rubber

The pyrolysis of rubber has been studied under an inert atmosphere, under vacuum, and in both a reducing (H_2, CO) and an oxidizing atmosphere).

Pyrolysis under vacuum allows a high yield of monomers and dimers and a better quality of char to be obtained. Pyrolysis under hydrogen pressure lowers the yield of dienes, and all liquid fractions are less unsaturated[32]. Oxidative pyrolysis also yields oxygenated compounds, such as methanol and phenol[10].

The U.S. Bureau of Mines conducted a research program, wholly funded by Firestone, on rubber tire pyrolysis. The apparatus consisted of an externally heated, sealed, bench-scale retort, which was normally used for studying the coking of coal. The volatile products passed through a series of condensors, an electrostatic precipitator, and acid and caustic

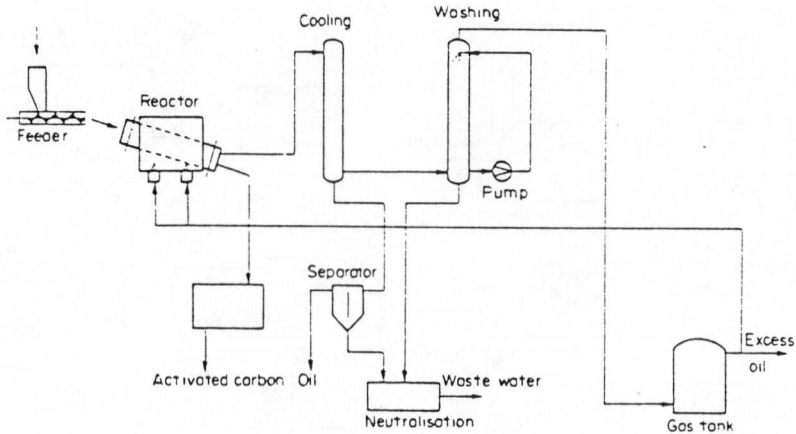

Figure 4. Pyrolysis of tires in a rotary kiln furnace.

scrubbers. Runs were made at 500 and 900°C, using different types and sizes of tire cuttings. The following results were obtained:

1. High temperatures (900°C) increase the yield of gas and char, and decrease the yield of oil.
2. At 500°C the calorific value of the gas is much higher, due to the presence of C_3 and C_4-hydrocarbons, which are rapidly cracked to H_2, CH_4 and C_2H_4 at 900°C.
3. At 900°C the oil was more viscous, contained less low-boiling components and had a higher aromatic content. The aromatic content was somewhat lower with truck tires (containing natural rubber) than with butadiene-styrene rubber.
4. At 900°C the yield and the specific surface area of the char were higher[49].

The increased yield of char is in disagreement with other data, and can be explained either by the higher cracking severity or by secondary cracking of primary gaseous and liquid products.

In the Kobe Steel process, crushed tires are continuously fed into an externally heated rotary kiln, and decomposed into volatile and charred material. The residence time in the reactor is about 15 minutes. The volatile material enters a cooling tower and is separated into oil and a gas; this contains H_2S and, after caustic scrubbing, it is used for heating the kiln (Fig. 4).

At 850°C the following yields (by weight) were obtained: 51.3% of oil, 15.2% of gas, 33.5% of char. The oil can be used as a fuel oil, or as a process oil for rubber compounding. After crushing, the char can be used as carbon black for reinforcing rubber, or as activated charcoal for wastewater treatment. Most of the ZnO contained in the tires remains in the char as ZnS[41].

The Nippon Zeon Co. has developed a fluidized bed partial oxidation process for converting shredded tires into gas, oil and char. The process gases are purified by means of a cyclone separator, an oil quench using pyrolysis oil, an oil separator, an H_2S-scrubber and an afterburner (Fig. 5).

The tires are pretreated in a two-stage shearing breaker. The bead wires and steel cords can then be stripped off and removed by a magnetic separator.

A maximum oil yield of 52.0% (by wt) is attained at 450°C. The lean gas and the char yield are, respectively, 14.4 and 33.6%. The oil has a density of 0.95 and a sulphur content of 1.0–1.4%. The char has an ash content of 8–12%, 5% of which is zinc.

Unpulverized and pulverized char show, respectively, medium and good rubber-reinforcing properties. Steam activation at 850°C yields an activated carbon equivalent or even superior to commercial grades.

Schnecko, on the other hand, is cautious in evaluating the potential re-use of pyrolytic carbon black in rubber tires[32].

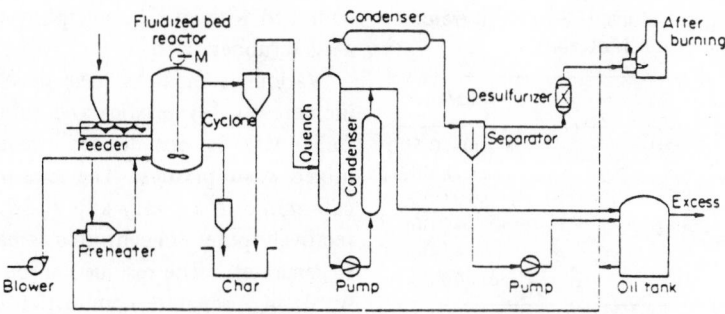

Figure 5. Pyrolysis of tires in a fluidized bed reactor.

Zeplichal obtained a low-boiling (160°C) fraction, a viscous oil (160–180°C) and a high-boiling (180–220°C) fraction by heating powdered rubber under vacuum on a band conveyor. The low boiling fraction represented 50% by weight and contained butadiene, isoprene, isopentenes and styrene. The unsaturated viscous oil could be epoxydated to yield a rubber plasticizer, and the asphaltic oil could possibly be used in road construction[10].

Fiber remnants could be used in acoustic insulation elements, for stabilization of dunes, etc. The penetrating smell remains, however, a problem[10].

Hydrolysis and Other Chemical Methods

Polycondensation and polyaddition polymers can, in principle, be depolymerized by hydrolysis. Different companies have developed processes on this basis which appear still to be at the laboratory or pilot stage.

Large amounts of wastes are generated during the transformation of foams, an appreciable part of the material being cut away to arrive at the desired form. Waste generation in flexible foams (mattresses, cushions, sponges, . . .) represents 20% of the raw material. Only a small part of these wastes can be recovered, e.g. as carpet underlay, foam agglomerate, etc. Also, the head and the sides of the polyurethane casting constitute a source of waste material, which can at present only be incinerated.

In the U.S. automotive industry the annual consumption of flexible PU-foams amounts to 135 000 tons. In Belgium the rate of PU-waste generation amounts to 14 000 tons/year or a value of about $14,000,000 of raw materials.

The economic importance of these losses prompted several major companies (Ford Motor Co., General Motors Corp., Bayer AG, S.A.P.R.B.) to study the recycling of these wastes.

In the G.M.-process and PU-waste is hydrolyzed by superheated steam at 300°C and atmospheric pressure. Hydrolysis yields a waterfree polyol, which can be re-used after cooling and filtering, and the diamine corresponding to the original di-isocyanate. The diamine is condensed and purified by decantation, extraction, azeotropic and normal distillation[26]. The P.R.B.-company is investigating the optimum conditions of hydrolysis and the possible markets for the recovered products. The toluene diamine can be re-used in the manufacture of di-isocyanate. The polyols consist of a variable mixture of unknown polyol compounds, depending on the type of foam hydrolyzed.

Both consumption and specific rate of waste generation are smaller in the field of rigid foams. Upjohn[26] has developed a recovery process, which is based on an ester inter-change with an aliphatic diol.

Bayer AG has studied not only the hydrolysis of flexible foams, but also of polyesters and polyamides. Very pure Nylon-6 waste is used for caprolactum production by Dutch State Mines[52].

Chlorinated wastes can probably be recovered by methods such as chlorolysis and oxychlorination, together with liquid and tarry wastes from petrochemical processes.

Table 6. Heating Values of Some Polyreice and Other Materials.

	kJ/kg
Household refuse	4 200–10 500
Paper, wood (dry)	*ca.* 18 000
PVC	21 000
PS	42 000
PE	46 000
Fuel oil	*ca.* 46 000

INCINERATION

The incineration of plastic waste along with domestic waste is regarded favorably by the plastics producers. They point to the possibility of releasing a considerable amount of heat, which can be used for the production of steam or even electrical energy.

The various types of plastics do indeed have a high calorific value (see Table 6), but are not an ideal fuel. They cannot be pumped, they melt during incineration, and they could drip off the grid bars and continue their combustion in the ash compartment. In practice, however, these problems become serious only when the plastics content of refuse exceeds 10%[53].

Some plastics (PS, PVAc, polyesters, epoxy resins, etc.) and rubber burn with a sooty flame, necessitating a good afterburner. Moreover, the incinerator plant (induced-draught fans, electrostatic precipitator, furnace lining) can be damaged by the almost explosive combustion of a large heap of highly combustible material. This can occur when an inexperienced crane operator omits to mix deliveries of household and industrial waste.

Some HCl arises in municipal incinerators during the combustion of chlorine-containing polymers and by the high temperature chemical reaction between kitchen salt and water vapor. The flue gases typically contain 500–2000 mg/m^3 (s.t.p.), to be compared with *ca.* 150 mg/m^3 (s.t.p.), specified by current air pollution codes.

It has been proved that HCl plays an important part in the corrosion of boiler pipes, by synergy with the sulphates present. Moreover it contributes somewhat to the air pollution, since most incinerators in Western Europe are equipped with an E.S.-precipitator but not with a gas scrubber.

Various companies have developed specific incinerators for plastics and rubber. Takuma Boiler Mfg. Co. has devised a plant for burning mixed waste plastics. The feed material is first carbonized in a rotary kiln at 300°C, so that a relatively pure, concentrated stream of HCl gas is generated. The residue can be burned afterwards in a separate combustion chamber[44]. Mitsui Shipbuilding and Engineering Co. have built an incinerator for atactic polypropylene[51], and Lucas has developed a circular hearth for the incineration of tires, where a mechanical device pushes the tires from the peripheral feeding point to the discharge point in the middle of the hearth.

The presence of nitrogen in the polymer molecule can also cause additional air pollution (NO*x*). Monsanto has studied this aspect experimentally, by evaluating a new packaging material containing nitrogen[8].

PVC stabilizers are responsible for the emission of minute particles, containing heavy metal-oxides (Pb, Cd, Zn), which cannot be removed completely by dust arresting equipment. Fortunately, the stabilizer content of PVC decreased from several per cent a number of years ago, to *ca.* 1–2% at present. The combustion of rubber causes the emission of sizeable quantities of ZnO-particles.

Biodegradation

Some plastics, because of their applications in packaging, contribute considerably to the litter problem. This problem can be alleviated only by better education of the public and by providing adequate facilities for getting rid of wastes in a controlled fashion. Littered plastics break down quite slowly.

The biodegradability of plastics can be enhanced by:

1. Introduction of u.v.-sensitive polymers, such as α-carbonylvinylcompounds, into the polymer chain.
2. Addition of initiators, which form chain initiating free radicals under the influence of u.v.-light.

3. Addition of an u.v.-sensitive complex of an oxidation catalyzing metal to the polymer.

Soluble polymers, such as PVA and isopropylcellulose are also biodegradable.

Scott (Aston, England), and Guillet (Toronto, Canada) have developed polymers which break down relatively quickly in sunlight [34, 35], and other organizations have also carried out research in this area.

Some biodegradable packaging materials are being marketed at present in Scandinavian countries, in Japan and in France.

As a rule, however, industrial circles are not convinced of the real possibilities of these types of packaging material. New polymers or compounds must be able to stand up to a comparison with the properties, processing capabilities, and price of the established polymers. Every fault in the timing of the breakdown can have disastrous results. Moreover, little is known about the nature and the properties of the degradation products.

CONCLUSION

If the sorting of domestic waste gradually became accepted in the coming decade, then large amounts of soiled or mixed synthetic waste would become available. Selective collection of household or commercial waste could also produce substantial amounts of mixed polymer.

At the moment, however, not a single processing method is technically or economically able to make use of this opportunity. One has either to find applications for plastic materials with inferior properties, or to develop methods of making different plastics compatible so that a material with reasonable properties and a higher monetary value can be obtained.

The separation of polymer mixtures into a number of types of plastic materials is a real possibility. With the techniques currently available, however, the number of "mistakes" is still too great. Hence, the materials obtained are not marketable.

The pyrolysis of plastics and rubber, possibly together with household waste, is a relatively uncomplicated way of recovering part of their potential energy. Straightforward incineration or biodegradation cannot be considered a fully satisfactory way of processing these wastes.

ABBREVIATIONS USED

ABS	acrylonitrile-butadiene-styrene copolymer
APP	atactic polypropylene
CPE	sequentially chlorinated polyethylene
EVA	ethylene vinyl acetate copolymer
HDPE	high density polyethylene
LDPE	low density polyethylene
MBS	metacrylate butadiene styrene copolymer
PA	polyamide
PE	polyethylene
PIB	polyisobutene
PMMA	polymethylmetracrylate
PP	polypropylene
PS	polystyrene
PTFE	polytetrafluorethylene
PU	polyurethane
PVA	poly vinylalcohol
PVAc	polyvinylacetate
PVC	polyvinylchloride

REFERENCES

1. A.G. Buekens, Recycling in Belgium, International Congress on the Recycling of Materials, Rotterdam, 26–27 November (1974).
2. Belgian Plastics association, Report of the Commission on Plastics and the Environment, Brussels, December, (1972).
3. Industrial Association for the Protection of the Environment, L'emballage plastique dans les ordures ménagères, Brussels December (1971).
4. The Dutch plastics industry, *Plastica* 28 (1975).
5. J.R. Lawrence, Status report on plastics recycling, ASTM Special Publication 533, 50 (1973).
6. W.A. Mack, Recycling plastics: the problems and the potential solutions, *ibid.,* 3 (1973).
7. L.A. Squitieri, Use of old telephone plastic – a feasibility study, *ibid.,* 40 (1973).
8. E.J. Temple, Incineration of refuse with LOPAC containers, added *ibid.,* 28 (1973).
9. K. Kucera, Plastmassenabfalle, theoretische und praktische Moglichkeiten der Verarbeitung, B.I.R., Brussels (1971).
10. W. Hoffmann, *Gummi Asbest Kunststoffe* 28, (1), 38 (1975).
11. Stichting Verwijdering Afvalstoffen (S.V.A.), Old tires (in Dutch), S.V.A./1569.
12. A.J. Warner, C.H. Parker and B. Baum, Solid waste management of plastics, Research Study prepared by De Bell & Richardson, Inc. for the Manufacturing Chemists Association.

13. C.R.I.F., Le recyclage des déchets de matières plastiques par la formation d'alliages polymériques, (November 1974); Brussels Étude de la Formation d'Alliages Polymériques en vue de la Réutilisation des Déchets de Matière Plastique, Brussels, June (1975).

14. J.A. Szilard, *Reclaiming Rubber and Other Polymers,* Noyes Data Corp., Park Ridge, N.J. (1973).

15. M. Sittig, *Pollution Control in the Plastics and Rubber Industry,* Noyes Data Corp., Park Ridge, N.J. pp. 134–163 (1975).

16. H. Samans, *Kunststoffe* **62** (4), 221 (1972).

17. H. Samans, Technische Tagung des Verbandes Kunststoff verarbeitender Industriebetriebe der Schweiz (VKI), (28th May 1974, and 3rd September 1974).

18. F.J. Colon, Recycling of paper, *Conservation & Recycling* **1**, (1), 129 (1976).

19. J.L. Holman, J.B. Stephenson and J.W. Jensen, Processing the plastics from urban refuse, T.P.R. 50, U.S. Dept. of the Interior, February (1972). E.G. Valdez, K.C. Dean and J.H. Bilbrey, Recovering PU-foam and other plastics from autoshredder reject. USBM 8091 (1975).

20. M.R. Grubbs and K.H. Ivey, Recovering plastics from urban refuse by electrodynamic techniques, T.P.R. 63, U.S. Dept. of the Interior, December (1972).

21. D.G. Wilson and S.D. Senturia, Design and performance of the M.I.T. process for separating mixed municipal refuse *Proc. 4th Mineral Waste Utilisation Symposium,* Chicago, p. 117., 7–8 May (1974).

22. W.M. Batentsen and D. Heikens, *Z. Wekstofftechnik* **1**, 49 (1970).

23. Anon. *Gummi Asbest Kunststoffe* **27**, (2) 463 (1974).

24. W.M. Barenisen, D. Heikens and P. Piet, *Polymer* **15**, 119 (1974).

25. J. Bontinck, personal communication.

26. N.R. Iammartino, New routes tackle tough plastics-recycling jobs, *Chem. Engng* **83**, (4), 54 (1976).

27. H. Sinn, Recycling der Kunststoffe, *Chemie-Ing.-Techn.* **46**, (14), 579 (1974).

28. W. Kaminsky, J. Menzel and H. Sinn, Recycling of plastics, *Conservation and Recycling* **1**, (1), 91 (1976).

29. G. Herten, personal communication.

30. G. Menges and W.I. Hoffman, Moglichkeiten und Grenzen des Recyclings von Kunststoffabfällen, *Müll and Abfall* **4**, 114 (1974).

31. R.J. Pettigrew and F.H. Roninger, Rubber re-use and solid waste management, Publication SW-22c, E.P.A., Washington D.C. (1971).

32. H.W. Schnecko, Zur Pyrolyse von Altreifen, *Chem. Ing. Tech.* **48** (5), 443 (1976).

33. B. Arkles, Recycling PTFE, in, *Polymers and Ecological Problems.* Plenum Press, New York (1973).

34. J.E. Guillet, Polymers with controlled lifetimes, *ibid.,* p. 1.

35. G. Scott, Delayed action photo-activator for the degradation of packaging polymers, *ibid.,* p. 27.

36. M. Endo, Techniques for pyrolysing plastics Waste, *Japan Plastics Q.* 29, October (1973).

37. S. Speth, Aufarbeitung von Polyathylen-Ruckstanden zu Niedermolekularen Destillaten, *Chemie Ing. Tech.* **45**, (8), 526 (1973).

38. A.G. Buekens and M.H. Vanheule, unpublished results (1975).

39. S. Mitsui, H. Nishizaki and K. Yoshida, Communication at ACHEMA, Frankfurt (1976).

40. Conference Papers of the First International Conference, Conversion of refuse to energy, Montreux (Switzerland), 4 November (1975).

41. A. Takamura, K. Inque and T. Sakai, Resources recovery by pyrolysis of waste tyres, *ibid.,* p. 532.

42. K. Matsumoto, S. Kurisu and T. Oyamoto, Development of process of fuel recovery by thermal decomposition of waste plastics, *ibid.,* p. 538.

43. Y. Kitaoka and H. Sueyoshi, Conversion of waste polymer to fuel oil, *ibid.,* p. 555.

44. T. Oda, K. Chiba and H. Hosokawa, Thermal-decomposition of plastic waste containing PVC, *ibid.,* p. 561.

45. S. Tsutsumi, Thermal and steam cracking of waste plastics, *ibid.,* p. 567.

46. T. Oda, Plastics waste disposal, *Chem. Economy Engng Rev.* p. 29, December (1970).

47. Y. Saeki and G. Suzuki, Fluidized thermal cracking process for waste tires, *Rubber Age,* February (1976).

48. J.E. Potts, Reclamation of plastic waste by pyrolysis, *Am. Chem. Soc., Div. Water, Air, and Waste Chemistry,* Chicago, p. 229, 13–18 September (1970).

49. J.A. Beckman, D.J. Bennett, A.G. Altenau and J.R. Laman, Yields and analyses of the products from the destructive distillation of scrap tyres, *ibid.,* p. 195.

50. Staff Writers, Trends in development of plastic waste disposal techniques, *Chem. Econ. Engng. Rev.* **4**, (10), 29 (1972).

51. Y. Kitaoka and H. Mineshima, Utilization of waste atactic polymer as a boiler fuel, Ref. [40], p. 544.

52. G. Schuur, private communication.

53. R. Rasch, Kunststoffe und Umweltprobleme, *Neue Verpackung,* 1421 (1975).

3-17 Tire Recycling: Research Trends and Needs

Arthur H. Purcell
Source: **Conservation and Recycling, Vol. 2, No. 2, 1978, pp. 137–143. Reprinted with Permission of Pergamon Press, Ltd.**

INTRODUCTION

In the U.S.A. there are approximately as many waste tires generated annually as there are people. This relationship holds roughly in other developed countries, although *per capita* tire disposal patterns vary between nations. This means, however, that every year billions of gallons of fuel oil equivalent are being discarded through tire disposal; only a fraction of this is being recovered or conserved through recycling or waste reduction processes.

Clearly, tires pose an important challenge to energy and materials conservation. Tires, which are essential to our transportation systems, are highly energy intensive. Production of SBR rubber for new tires entails energy expenditures on the order of 156 MJ/kg (67 000 Btu/lb).

The energy required to make a retreaded tire, however, is less than a third of this. Similarly the energy used to produce reclaimed rubber from waste tires, recover carbon black from waste tires, or to perform any of a number of recycling operations on waste tires is considerably less than the energy required for comparable virgin material operations.

A growing number of researchers are concerned with the energy conservation potential of reducing and recycling rubber tire wastes. Research can be conducted in four distinct areas, which we have called the 'Four R's' [1] : *Reduction, Reuse, Reclaiming* and *Recovery*. *Reduction*, the first option, involves finding ways to (a) use less rubber per tire and/or (b) make longer-lasting tires. *Reuse* of chemically unaltered tire material, in whole tire or other form, provides the second research area. Improving long-practiced rubber *reclaiming* technology is the third research option. *Recovery,* the fourth 'R', encompasses developing and improving techniques for recovering heat value, constituent materials, and chemicals from waste tires.

TRENDS

A recent study for the U.S. Department of Energy (for which the author served as a principal team member) coupled with independent work, has looked critically at these 'four R' options as well as selected proposed waste rubber research projects. These efforts indicate that:

1. The options of *energy recovery* and carbon black recovery from waste tires are of the greatest interest to researchers both inside and outside the rubber tire industry. Significant research efforts are still needed, however, to bring down the cost of such recovery, particularly energy recovery.

2. The direct *reuse* of waste tires provides the greatest materials and energy conservation potential. This area continues to stimulate innovative thinking but only limited research.

3. *Retreading,* the most widely practiced form of reuse, can greatly increase its contribution to tire recycling efforts if certain institutional and technological factors are overcome.

---

*This paper was presented at the First World Recycling Congress, Basle, Switzerland, 6–9 March 1978.

4. Innovative research is needed to improve the *reclaiming* picture; little, however, seems to be forthcoming.
5. *Reduction* of waste rubber at the source through (a) use of high-mileage tires and (b) decreasing tire rolling resistance are of substantive interest. High mileage tires continue to be controversial. The subject is generally thought of as too complex for non-industry researchers; little new research appears to be forthcoming within the industry, however, on high-mileage tires.

REDUCTION

There are 6 major options for the reduction of the use of rubber in making tires.

1. Substituting natural rubber for synthetic rubber.
2. Substituting other less energy-intensive materials for rubber in tires.
3. Using less rubber per tire (smaller, lighter).
4. Increasing tire durability.
5. Using fewer tires per vehicle (by eliminating the need for a spare tire).
6. Using automobiles less.

The potential for reduction of rubber waste through these options varies considerably. Option (1) has a potential of reducing the use of synthetic rubber, replacing it with the renewable resource of natural rubber, by 35% beyond today's current usage patterns. Natural rubber tires use about 40% less energy, even if the potential fuel value of natural rubber is included. Options (2) and (3) probably have no near-term or intermediate term potential. Option (4), which embodies the 160 000 km (100 000 mile) tire concept, could cut energy use for tire production by up to 75%. Option (5) is under development in the U.S. and abroad. Option (6) is a reasonable possibility.

The substitution of natural rubber (NR), which is a low-energy renewable resource, for synthetic rubber (SR) is a proven technology; NR is actually superior to synthetic rubber in most instances. Currently, about 25% of all rubber used in tire manufacture is NR, chiefly for heavy duty off-road vehicles. The Malaysian Rubber Bureau, principal research and public relations arm of the NR industry, claims that NR could comprise up to 60% of all applications without significant technological problems [12] : it is further claimed that NR will eventually be cheaper than SR. While SR is generally used for tread material, there are no major technical problems with NR – SR substitution.

The substitution of other less energy-intensive materials for rubber in tires poses a greater technical challenge. It has been argued that, since many portions of a tire are not subject to heavy wear, they might be made out of a less durable (and less energy-intensive) material than rubber. While this theory is sound, it appears unlikely that, in the short or intermediate term, such substitution will be practicable. (It should be pointed out that the moon lander vehicle did not use rubber for its tires.)

The technological feasibilities of using less rubber per tire (for given performance standards) or, alternatively, of making tires of greater durability (options 3 and 4) are not certain. It appears that technological considerations have been optimized in producing tires, and that it would be very difficult to maintain present performance standards if less rubber were used in otherwise equivalent tires. More durable tires, most notably the 160 000 km (100 000 mile) tire, are feasible from a technical standpoint. Increasing tread thickness and material hardness, as well as augmenting belting, are the major improvements needed.

Little substitution research or experimentation is being done or contemplated. The natural rubber industry, of course, is pushing to increase its share of the market and has had some success, moving from about 20 to 25% in the past 2 years. The status of the 160 000 km tire is unclear. Michelin reportedly has produced prototypes. The American tire industry acknowledges that it currently produces some 160 000 km truck tires, apparently with success. Dunlop in the U.K., is marketing tires reportedly so resistant to punctures and blowouts that spare tires can be eliminated.

An important waste reduction research area under serious consideration by at least one major tire manufacturer is that of decreasing tire rolling resistance, as well as tire weight [2] . If tire rolling resistance can be decreased such that automobile gasoline mileage is increased by as little as 5%, an oil equivalent of approximately two radial tires could be saved annually (based on U.S. average driving mileage).

REUSE

The greatest energy, material, and environmental savings in tire recycling accrue through direct reuse of waste tire rubber, without chemical alteration of it. Waste tires can be reused in three main ways: (1) for making retreaded tires, which puts them back into the service for which they were originally designed; (2) for alternative uses in whole form; (3) as substitute materials, in generally altered form.

By definition, reuse involves generally low-technology approaches, thus minimizing research and development needs.

The tire retreading industry is the greatest reuser of waste tires. The retreading industry, contrary to popular belief, is actually a growth industry. Growth has been limited in the U.S. industry to about 3%, however [3]. A major limiting factor has been the double-edged problem of (a) lack of tire carcasses suitable for retreading and (b) lack of economically viable means for disposing non-retreadable tires accumulated by retreading businesses. Improper tire care by vehicle drivers prevents millions of tires from maintaining retreading quality. Centralized waste tire collection systems — which would reach the maximum amount of waste tire sources — generally do not exist.

Tire retreaders face significant economic problems of how to dispose of non-retreadable tires. Only about 20 − 25% of the tires that enter retreading shops are retreadable.

Research indicates that the 'logjam' created by accumulation of rejected tires is a significant barrier to retreading. A 'closed loop' system of tire recycling is clearly needed, in which (a) the maximum amount of waste tires would first be inspected for retreading and (b) a continuous demand for non-retreadable tires for other recycling purposes would exist. The Tire Retreading Institute has endorsed such a system, feeling that it could greatly increase retreading[4].

Contributing to this 'logjam' is the important problem of inspection of tires for retreadability. Because visual inspection is slow and unreliable, a number of sophisticated technologies have been developed. These include: holography, X-ray, infrared and ultrasonics.

Inspection through any of these methods is expensive, entailing as much as 10% of the total cost of retreading a tire. None of these methods is totally reliable. The area of tire casing inspection is an important one for tire recycling research, in need of much more refinement.

Several rubber manufacturers have promoted the reuse of whole waste tires for fish reefs; experimental reefs in coastal waters in the U.S.A. appear to indicate that fish breeding can be encouraged, with no apparent water pollution effects, by building reefs of waste tires. One area in need of further investigation is the use of waste tires in soil erosion prevention. By interlinking whole waste tires with clamps or cables, large 'nets' can be made which can be placed on erodable areas. There is some indication that the use potential for this option is high[2].

Several tire reuse options are possible through mechanically altering waste tires. These fall into two main categories: (a) reuse of large chunks or pieces of tires and (b) reuse of finely-ground tires. The first category includes use of tire chunks for such diverse uses as soil conditioner and shock cushioning pads. The technology of these applications is straightforward, with little need for research.

Reuse of finely-ground rubber entails more significant technological considerations. Recent research, such as at Gould, Inc. (Chicago, Ill.) indicates that if waste rubber can be ground finely enough, it may be reusable as a direct substitute (up to about 30% mix) for virgin rubber in rubber manufacturing processes. Gould has announced a mechanical process which reduces 0.6 cm (0.25 in.) dia pieces of scrap rubber to a powder whose ultimate size is 90% below 20 μm, with retention of the rubber-like qualities of the original material. The process is conducted at room temperature or slightly higher, thus involving no thermal degradation[6]. Little additional information is available on the Gould process, or on a recently reported British process[7], due to proprietary considerations; it appears, however, that it could represent a major research breakthrough in efforts to directly reuse vulcanized rubber in manufacturing processes.

Rubberized asphalt paving material, utilizing finely-ground tires, has been demonstrated as a viable rubber reuse option[8]. This option is of particular interest because it appears to create a product superior to aggregate-based asphalt. At the present time, however, economics of this material are generally quite unfavorable.

RECLAIMING

Reclaiming is the only 'true' form of rubber recycling; in reclaiming, waste rubber is ground up, devulcanized, and put back in a batch from which new rubber products are made. The demand for reclaimed rubber has fallen drastically over the past several years[9]. This has been primarily due to the technological limitations of reclaimed rubber ('reclaim'). Reclaim has significantly poorer mechanical properties than comparable virgin rubber due, primarily, to the uncontrollable carbon black distribution in it. Since well over half of all rubber applications are for tires, this means that reclaim has very limited applicability for the major share of the tire market. Its energy attractiveness nonetheless, is significant. Reclaim production requires only about 20% of the energy of virgin rubber production[10]. Hence, reclaim should be playing a greater role in lower-grade rubber products. Little research and development has gone into reclaiming, however, with the result that the reclaiming industry is generally running on antiquated systems and equipment. As noted in a recent Firestone Tire and Rubber Company report:

"What is required in the reclaim industry is a new reclaim process which would be amenable to continuous operation with significantly reduced labor and energy requirements. A very low-cost reclaim could be used to advantage in mechanical goods in which dynamic physical requirements are not very demanding or in other non-rubber uses, such as in asphalt, where definite beneficial effects can be realized[2].

RECOVERY

The urgent need to develop new energy sources and reduce use of fossil fuels for non-fuel uses has resulted in strong emphasis on energy and carbon black recovery from waste tires. Energy can be recovered from waste rubber as heat or fuel through direct combustion, and pyrolytic decomposition, as well as other chemical and biological methods. Carbon black can be recovered through all these processes except direct combustion.

Direct combustion of waste tires has successfully been demonstrated for both whole tires and shredded tires. Tire furnaces have, however, posed significant air emission problems and additional research is needed in this area. Use of shredded tires as a supplement to coal furnaces [heat value of rubber: 32 MJ/kg (14 000 Btu/lb] has been demonstrated at a number of installations, with few problems encountered in charges on the level of $10 - 20\%$.

Pyrolysis of waste tires continues to be of strong interest in the tire recycling research and development community. Discouraging economic aspects of pyrolysis served to damp the initial interest of the early part of the decade. The steep price rises of energy of the past few years, coupled with continuing forecasts of shortages, have served to reawaken interests in pyrolysis.

A number of pyrolysis techniques have been developed. These include: inert atmosphere, oxidative, steam atmosphere, and molten salt processes. None of these has yet been shown to produce high-quality carbon black, although inert atmosphere pyrolysis appears to come closest. The oxidative, steam and molten salt methods are exothermic, which makes them more attractive from the energy recovery standpoint. All four systems produce oil, gas and char. Gas production is favored at higher temperature, while oil is favored at lower temperatures.

There are important advantages and disadvantages of each pyrolysis option. It is clear that a comprehensive testing, standardization, and analysis effort must be made to determine whether one or two systems deserve priority in application of limited research and development dollars. Goodyear Tire and Rubber Company, conjunction with The Oil Shale Corporation, is currently developing a full-scale pyrolysis plant in Colorado, using ceremic ball heat transfer technology; this project will, hopefully, serve to answer some of these questions.

A promising, though not well developed, method of chemically recovering carbon black from scrap tires is that of depolymerized scrap rubber (DSR). In this process, waste rubber is heated in an aromatic processing oil to effect dissolution of the hydrocarbon portion of the rubber. The resulting product is a dispersion of recovered carbon black in a heavy oil. Initial investigations show that the carbon black is approximately of standard quality. The DSR oil (after removal of the aromatic portion) can be used as a supplement to No. 2 fuel oil.

Another undeveloped method for carbon black recovery from waste tires entails mixing and heating ground rubber scrap and conventional carbon black feed stock oil and reacting in a standard carbon black furnace. While little actual research in this area appears to have been performed, it is important to note that U.S. pat. on the process have been issued.

OBSERVATIONS

A large number of options for waste rubber and tire recycling exist. A good number of them particularly in the energy and carbon black recovery areas, are in need of further research and development. For several processes the technology appears to be in place, but the economics are unfavorable. This raises the question of the interrelationship between tire recycling technology and economics. In most cases, technological refinements, even on so-called proven processes, could probably make positive contributions to recycling economics. A good case in point is retreading. While retreading is a proven technology, its economic situation can greatly be strengthened through (a) development of cost-effective technologies to recycle non-retreadable reject tires and (b) improve the ratio of retreadable to reject tires. This latter point brings into focus the question of *design for recyclability*. As tires become more sophisticated and more durable, they are becoming less recyclable. Rethinking tire design could

reverse this trend, however. Development of methods to better protect the tire bead from bending forces would aid retreading. Similarly, returning to the use of chafers which protect the bead toe would reduce the tendency of the tire bead toe rubber to tear during mounting or demounting. Limited tire sizes and strengthening sidewalls are other design-for-recyclability options.

The steel-belted tire poses significant obstacles for nearly all tire recycling processes where size reduction is necessary. While steel belts were instituted as an improved performance measure, further research may find belting material economically and technologically equal, or superior to steel, but more compatible with recycling.

In regard to size reduction, one area of growing research interest is that of improving waste tire processing economics through increasing efficiency of shredding. Efforts ranging from intricate sequencing and modifying of standard shredding hardware to cryogenic reduction systems are being developed. The U.S. government has recognized the importance of shredding problems in tire recycling, and has, through the Resource Conservation and Recovery Act, provided some economic incentives for shredding research.

There are a number of information and communication barriers that must be overcome if waste tire research efforts are to be optimized. These include the following:

1. Lack of standard data base on recycling trade-offs. While it is recognized that rubber recycling has energy and environmental benefits, there is insufficient information on (a) the quantitative nature of these benefits and (b) methods for resolving trade-off questions.
2. Inadequate understanding by researchers of the total waste rubber picture. Many researchers have innovative ideas on some aspects of tire recycling, but seem to pay little attention to others that are intimately connected; e.g., a researcher proposes an innovative system to produce certain grades of shredded rubber for given applications but appears to have

little idea for which markets exist for the product. Or a researcher seeks to develop a process for producing large amount of marginal quality carbon black without ascertaining that the black will have widespread use.

3. Lack of on-going formalized communication between rubber tire manufacturers, outside researchers, government agencies, and waste tire dealers and processors. The meshing of needs and available resources in the waste tire area is made much more difficult by the lack of such inter-institutional communication.

The lack of standard data bases on recycling trade-offs is an important barrier to improving rubber recycling's contribution to energy and materials conservation efforts. Data exist on energy and environmental impacts of waste rubber alternatives. The data vary, however, and it is not clear which best reflect relative impacts. In addition, no uniform method exists for resolving trade-off questions between tire recycling alternatives. Consequently, a party interested in waste tire research may inadvertently start out on the wrong direction in terms of long-term value of a project.

The problem of trade-off resolution in recycling has been addressed scientifically for the beverage container area. The Midwest Research Institute has developed what it calls the 'Resource and Environmental Profile Analysis' (REPA) system. Through REPA, a quantitative evaluation can be made of beverage container recycling alternatives. Development of a REPA-type system for waste tires could be of great potential in helping set research priorities.

Waste tire researchers need to coordinate with each other in order to maximize their limited resources and thus minimize the second barrier. The need for coordination and communication between technically-oriented and economically-oriented researchers is particularly acture for the waste tire area. Such cooperation would not only increase the practicality of research efforts but could facilitate strengthening of research team competence. In the example given for the shredding research, a coupling with

waste rubber markets would be an obvious action.

The lack of formalized inter-institutional communication on waste tire matters — a third barrier area — aggravates the first two areas. All parties in the waste tire and rubber area need vehicles through which they can share ideas and information, ideally on a regular basis.

TIRE RECYCLING: WHAT LIES AHEAD

It is generally agreed that within 5 or 10 years very few tires will be discarded without being subjected to some kind of recycling process. At this time it is not clear what kind, or kinds, of processes will predominate. It will probably be a mixture of them, forming a closed network. Research in the near future will play a crucial role in determining how best to recycle tires.

Retreading should continue to be a reliable, and very efficient method of recycling tires. Improved tire design is possible, and will aid retreading. Similarly, the high energy value of waste tires and other rubber, and the relatively minor technological problems associated with burning this material, would seem to indicate that using waste rubber as a fuel supplement will become an important part of rubber recycling. The role of pyrolysis is still unclear; future research and development efforts may, however, bring this option to the forefront. A number of other methods, in strong need of research and development, should also be filling in the tire recycling picture in the years to come.

REFERENCES

1. A.H. Purcell, Research trends and information needs of tire recycling workers, *Proc. Nat. Tire Disposal Symp. Natn. Tire Dealers and Retreaders Ass.*, 14–15 June, Washington, D.C.
2. J.A. Beckman *et al.*, Scrap tire disposal procedures, *Rubber Manufacturers Ass. Conf. and Workshop*, 13–15 September 1977, Cincinnati.
3. Tire Retreading Institute, Private communication.
4. Tire Retreading Institute, Testimony before the U.S. Resource Conservation Committee, 17 November 1977, Washington, D.C.
5. Smithers Scientific Services, *A Study of the Feasibility of Requiring the Federal Government to Use Retreaded Tires.* U.S. Environmental Protection Agency Contract No. 68-01-2906 (1975).

6. *Chem. Eng. News* 55 (25), 6 (1977).

7. G. Cheater *et al, A Study of the Reclamation and Reuse of Waste Tires.* Rubber and Plastics Research Association of Great Britain (1976).

8. H. Goddard, *Non-Waste Technology: The Case of Tires in the United States Proceedings,* U.N. ECE Seminar on Non-Waste Technology and Production. Pergamon Press, Oxford (1977).

9. A.H. Purcell, Waste rubber: an emerging resource, *Nat. Center Resource Recovery, Winter Bull.* (1974).

10. Resource Plan Associates, *Energy Conservation Through More Efficient Use of Waste Tires.* U.S. Dept. of Energy (May 1977).

11. G.O. Wyatt, U.S. 3674433 (4 July, 1972); C.E. Scott, U.S. 3700615 (24 Oct, 1972); A.R. Pelofsky, U.S. 3725314 (3 April, 1973).

12. Malaysian Rubber Bureau, Private communication.

Part 4
Waste as an Energy Source

It is clear that municipal waste has an energy value. How much and the appropriate method by which to realize this value are matters about which there are some differences of opinion. The readings in this section specifically address issues at the heart of the controversy. Not that there is any real question that it would be beneficial to combust or convert refuse to obtain a usable form of energy. Not in this age of an almost frantic search for alternative domestic energy sources. After all, as pointed out earlier, what is more domestic than household discards? Rather the questions concern the choice of the best technology and this involves trade-offs among various types of risk, including markets, process efficiency, and environmental impacts.

The first reading is adapted from a working document of the U.S. Department of Energy. The subject is the commercialization of energy from waste systems. The report, prepared in late 1979, takes a fairly optimistic tone. For many technologies and for the economic circumstances surrounding waste disposal in many communities, the adoption of an energy-from-waste disposal option is seen as having the characteristics of a commercial endeavor. But differently, there are commercially ready technologies that can meet the price and performance demands of these communities.

The report points out that there are some unknowns and, likewise, there are beneficial ways that government, at the federal level, can speed the rate of advance of the commercialization process, including providing additional options through research and development. This reading not only covers the subject matter of this volume, but should be of added interest in that it offers an example, and a fairly good one, of the thought process that underlies the formulation of a federal government program. Many of the ideas offered in this document become embodied in the charter for DOE's Office of Energy from Municipal Waste, legislatively mandated about a year later with the passage of the Energy Security Act.

The most commercial of the technologies advanced for converting waste into energy is the European mass burning approach. The next four readings are concerned with this method. The first, by Thomas J. Cunningham, Jr., summarizes a longer report prepared by the Battelle Columbus Laboratories for the U.S. Environmental Protection Agency. The second is a shortened version of an article by L. Barniske reporting on the mass burning of waste in the Federal Republic of Germany. This reading adds detail to Cunningham's summary. The third reading examines a number of the problems that have been encountered by U.S. importers of the European mass burning energy recovery technology. The problems — high-temperature corrosion, tube erosion, and excessive particulate emissions — have also occurred in Europe. The author of this reading is Charles O. Velzy. He concludes that "tube wastage should not be a problem with effective use of overfire air, judicious use of protective coatings, conservative volume and velocity in the furnace and convection bank, and limitation of steam temperatures." Also, "a properly sized two-field electrostatic precipitator following a well-operated furnace and boiler appears to be more than adequate to comply with present Federal regulations related to dry particulates." The final reading directed uniquely to the mass burning technology is a report on the Saugus, Massachusetts, refuse-to-energy plant, perhaps the most successful and publicized U.S. facility of this type.

An overview describing the potential for air pollution arising from the burning of waste as a fuel, either through mass burning or after processing — to be burnt singularly or as a supplemental fuel — appears next. The reading that follows looks in more depth at the question of metals emissions and serves as an introduction to the readings on processing waste with the objective of improving its characteristics as a fuel. This is in contrast to mass burning. Processing is also a subject of some controversy as indicated by the title of the next reading, "Prepared vs. Unprepared Refuse Fired Steam Generators." The authors come down on the side of the prepared fuel.

As indicated above, processed fuel is burnt either singularly in a boiler dedicated solely to its use or as a supplemental fuel along with coal and, in one instance, oil. The City of Akron has recently brought on the line a dedicated boiler, burning processed waste (RDF). This program is described in the next reading. Currently the facility is undergoing major modifications to rectify problems encountered during the initial burning period. This is followed by two early, and brief, readings on supplemental fuel projects. Both were R&D efforts supported by the U.S. Environmental Protection Agency. The first fired what has come to be called "coarse" RDF in a small spreader stoker-traveling grate type boiler in Columbus, Ohio, and the second developed experimental data concerning the co-firing, with coal, of a pelletized RDF, called d-RDF, at an Air Force base, also in Ohio. The "d" stands for densified. The data gathered and reported is typical of that associated with these early R&D efforts. This d-RDF project was followed by several other d-RDF R&D efforts. One, a burn at the State of Maryland Correctional Institute for Men near Hagerstown, Maryland, was followed by a more extensive burn at a General Electric plant in Erie, Pennsylvania. As yet, there has been no commercial project. Jay Campbell summarizes the d-RDF situation in his reading, "Waste Fuel Densification: Review of the Technology and Applications."

Much of the literature pertaining to co-firing focuses on large electric utility boilers. The Environmental Protection Agency's St. Louis demonstration, frequently referred to in the readings included in this volume, was of this type. A great many considerations must be taken into account. Some are mentioned in L. Barniske's reading, which appeared earlier, describing waste-to-energy programs in the Federal Republic of Germany. John L. Rose, in his reading, "Economic Factors in Refuse-Derived Fuel Utilization," reprinted from the 1979 *Proceedings* of the National Waste Processing Conference, develops them in some detail. Over the years an area of controversy has centered on whether the utility should value the energy derived from the use of waste as a fuel at its base load cost of conventional fuel or at a value equivalent to its marginal cost fuel, sometimes diesel or gas used to drive peak-load generators. In the first instance waste competes with the utilities most efficient equipment. In the second instance, its least efficient. In the latter case, the waste has a higher fuel substitution value. Recently, principally as a matter of public policy favoring the use of alternative fuels, the Federal Energy Regulatory Commission has ruled against the base-loading fuel-cost avoidance argument. It has adopted the principle of "full avoided cost," which is much broader and more favorably prices the energy produced by an alternative fuels project.

The longest operating RDF co-fired project, where the final energy product is electricity, is the program at Ames, Iowa. The next reading reports on this project, which began processing waste in November of 1975. The article gives a description of the equipment suit, the costs and the revenues. It is as complete a description as any appearing in the open literature. For most projects, often because such information is proprietary, the "net income" picture is a matter of conjecture.

Over the years various refinements have been suggested for improving the quality of RDF in order to make refuse, processed for co-firing or for use in a dedicated boiler, a more usable fuel and, hence, to increase its economic value. The assertion that a trommel stage (a rotary screen) can help achieve this goal is the subject of the next reading, "RDF: Quality Must Precede Quantity." Following this is a report on one of two major plants employing what are considered unique and proprietary processing approaches. These are the Combustion Equipment Associates, Bridgeport,

Connecticut, and the Hempstead, New York, and more recently, the Dade County (Miami), Florida, plant of Parsons-Whittemore.

Most RDF plants are simply a collection of what is generally off-the-shelf technology and do not in themselves represent a proprietary system. The Parsons-Whittemore process employs wet size reduction, i.e., Hydrapulping^{TM}. The Combustion Equipment Associates process uses heat and chemicals to reduce the RDF to a dustlike consistency called ECO Fuel^R II. No detailed description of the operation of the Hempstead plant is available. However, a fine article on the shakedown of Bridgeport has recently been published and is reprinted here. At the time this set of readings is being assembled, both the Parsons-Whittemore Hempstead plant and the Combustion Equipment Associates Bridgeport plant are in serious trouble. The Hempstead plant has been closed for several months over a dispute with the town concerning the payment of fees and a dispute with the U.S. Environmental Protection Agency over stack emissions. Combustion Equipment Associates ran out of money and, consequently, the necessary time to bring the Bridgeport project to its design operating conditions. Although Bridgeport's fuel quality had been excellent, the rate of production was not sufficient to cover the cost of the project. The Bridgeport facility has been taken over by Combustion Equipment Associates' joint venture partner, Occidental Petroleum. At present, the plant is closed awaiting Occidental Petroleum's decision as to whether or not to proceed, and if so, in what fashion.

A final RDF use is described in the next reading. This is the use of RDF as a kiln fuel. The author is E. Joseph Duckett. It is a carefully done report on the merits, problems and uncertainties associated with this possibility. There have been a number of R&D projects associated with RDF as a fuel for cement kilns, but as yet no commercial application. This reading completes the subject of direct combustion of waste — either mass burned or processed. The remaining readings in this section look at variations on the energy recovery theme, where the goal of the energy-from-waste process is to convert the waste into a more readily usable fuel, generally burnable gas. The first reading introduces the PTGL concept. PTGL stands for pyrolysis, thermal gasification or liquefaction. This article, by Jerry Jones, is reprinted from *Chemical Engineering*. It illustrates the extremely broad range of possibilities that exist in this area. An early application of a quasi-pyrolysis system was the Landgard process constructed as a U.S. Environmental Protection Agency demonstration at Baltimore, Maryland. To put it bluntly, this project has had its "ups and downs," as described in the reading. Not described in the Article is the fact that the plant is now "down for the count." The decision has been taken to scrap the facility and replace it with a conventional mass burning energy recovery plant.

The decomposition of landfill refuse produces methane, whether you want it to or not. Attempts are being made to tap this production as an economic resource. Not every landfill is a good candidate, as pointed out in the next reading. Some that are, are described. If landfills produce methane from the decomposition of the refuse, one should certainly be able to do so under controlled circumstances. How, and how well, is the subject of the next reading, which reports on the Department of Energy's proof-of-concept project at Pompano Beach, Florida. The project's feedstocks are municipal refuse and sewage sludge.

The final reading has to do with co-disposal, meaning the joint disposal of household refuse and waste water treatment (sewage) sludges. There is considerable interest in this, partially motivated by the availability of funding under the federal government's massive waste water treatment program. This dwarfs monies available at the federal level for solid waste management, resource recovery, and even energy from waste.

4-1 Draft Report of a Commercialization Strategy for Energy from Urban Wastes

Donald Walter, Steve Levy, and Charlotte Rines

Source: Adapted from U.S. Department of Energy Commercialization Strategy Report for Energy from Urban Wastes. (TID-28852) 26 pp.

ENERGY FROM URBAN WASTES

INTRODUCTION

According to federal estimates, 200 million tons of urban solid wastes and 14 million tons of sewage solids (dry basis) will be discarded annually in the U.S. by 1985. The combustible portion of these wastes represent a total available Btu content of 2.0 quads. The inorganic components in solid waste represent an additional quad if recovered and used to replace virgin ores. About 65% of the above potential of 3.0 quads is considered available for use in emerging waste-to-energy technologies today. Currently, less than 1% of the nation's total waste stream is processed into energy or energy-intensive materials.

Three broad technologies are potentially available to recover energy and energy-intensive materials from urban wastes: mechanical, thermal and biological. Mechanical processing separates wastes into various components, including metals, glass, and a refuse derived fuel (RDF). Generally, a mechanical process is a preliminary step to the thermal and biological technologies.

Combustion and pyrolysis are two thermal technologies. The former uses excess oxygen to complete oxidation and recovers that energy as steam or hot water. The latter limits oxygen so that the reaction is one of volatilization. The recovered products are combustible gases, liquids or solids which can be used as fuel or for chemical feedstocks.

Biological technologies use living organisms or their products to convert wastes to useful products. A large number and variety of such systems are under development. One system employing anaerobic digestion of solid and liquid wastes is being studied in a proof-of-concept facility at Pompano Beach, Florida. Another bioconversion process, the recovery of methane from sanitary landfills is at or near the commercialization stage of development.

DEVELOPMENT HISTORY

The recovery of energy from wastes probably originated about the beginning of the 20th century with combustion plants mass burning waste to recover steam. Further development largely involved incineration, without heat recovery, solely to reduce waste volume. In the 1950's in Europe, heat recovery and the use of waterwall furnaces in place of refractory lined furnaces began. However, to date most development was directed towards incineration for volume reduction rather than a heat recovery rationale. The open questions revolve around process optimization and control from a recovery of energy standpoint.

Materials recovery has been practiced throughout history in wartime by some form of source separation. Attempts to apply machines to mixed municipal refuse date from the late 1960's. These attempts, to date, generally have been through adaptation of equipment developed for other industry. Some success has been achieved. Generally the products recovered are metals, glass, paper fiber, and refuse derived fuel (RDF). RDF is then used in another energy recovery process. Other energy recovery technologies are at lesser stages of development.

Worldwide experience indicates that commercialization is feasible although there are a number of technical, economic and institutional barriers that currently limit the use of wastes.

From a technical standpoint the daily variability of urban waste makes control and optimization of any process difficult. Further development and optimization of equipment is necessary to improve efficiency and reduce capital costs although there are no foreseen technological barriers and basic breakthroughs are not needed.

Waste to energy plants to be economically viable depend on two major sources of income: the sale of the energy product and a fee to dispose of waste in the plant (tipping fee). Additional income can be realized from the sale of recovered materials. Where landfill or energy costs (tipping fees) are high, waste based systems can compete with fossil fuels. Of the plants in operation, only one is enjoying economic success.

There are currently several market constraints. Many of the recovered products such as RDF and steam cannot be stored for long periods or transported economically long distances.

Institutional issues are many and complex. Perhaps the principal issue is that cities are conservative, risk avoiders, and more concerned politically that their urban wastes disappear than with resource recovery. Additional problems involve waste stream control, difficulty of regionalizing waste processing, and to this point lack of control on land disposal of wastes although regulations are now mandated and in development. The difficulty of obtaining new landfill sites, however, is exerting a positive influence particularly in more populous areas.

Because of the high front-end costs and the risks associated with using a new technology, financing these facilities may be a problem, particularly for local government units. Marketing the energy and materials is essential for the economic viability of these technologies. However, many local governments do not have marketing expertise. Often governments cannot legally enter into the long-term contracts that are essential for using these capital-intensive technologies. In addition, electric utilities, which potentially represent a large market for refuse derived fuel, do not have an economic incentive to use this fuel because of fuel cost pass through provisions and contracted long-term fuel supplies.

COMMERCIALIZATION READINESS ASSESSMENT FOR ENERGY FROM URBAN WASTE

TECHNICAL READINESS

Operational Status

Mechanical Separation. These techniques separate wastes into various components to effect their recovery. The metallic components, glass and paper fibers are recycled to displace virgin ores. The reported energy savings for recycling materials range from 25% to 95% of the energy of production from virgin materials.

The general process involves homogenization by size reduction and separation by size, weight, shape, density and other physical properties. A typical processing line would utilize shredding for size reduction of raw refuse, followed by some form of air classification to separate the particles into a light (organics) and a heavy (inorganics) materials stream. The light fraction, without further processing, has generally come to be known as "RDF" (for refuse derived fuel).

A demonstration unit to produce RDF at St. Louis proved the basic feasibility of the mechanical separation processes, transport and storage techniques, and the combustion of fluff RDF to replace 5 to 27 percent of the pulverized coal used in suspension-fired utility boilers. A great deal of work remains on the refinement of equipment components and the technical and economic optimization of the basic technology.

The preparation of densified RDF by pelletizing, briquetting, or extruding is now being explored and evaluated and is particularly adapted for stoker and spreader-stoker furnaces. However, it has not been demonstrated commercially, and the costs, handling characteristics, and firing characteristics must yet be evaluated. The advantages of densified RDF are greatly improved storage and transportation characteristics.

There is one operating facility recovering and using RDF on a daily basis. This facility has encountered a series of economic and technical problems. A second facility is entering its first year of production evaluation prior to finalization of fuel sales contracts. Several facilities are in shakedown phase or under construction.

The production of dust RDF (particles smaller than 0.15 millimeter) is being developed in a proprietary pilot-plant process. After adding an embrittling chemical, coarsely shredded waste is pulverized to a dust-like consistency. The resulting dust RDF has a higher Btu content than fluff RDF (7,500 to 8,000 Btu/pound versus 5,000 Btu/pound); greater density and homogeneity and decreased moisture content. In addition, it may be capable of direct co-firing with fuel oils. However, the dust-like composition necessitates special handling to minimize the danger of an explosion. A full scale facility is under construction.

The "wet" mechanical separation process utilizes hydropulping technology adapted from the pulp and paper industry to reduce the raw waste to more uniform size and consistency, followed by a centrifugal, liquid cyclone process for separating the pulped mass into light and heavy fractions. The original pilot plant at Franklin, Ohio, is still operating although it no longer produces a low grade fiber for a roofing felt plant as originally intended. After successful test burns of a 50% organics, 50% moisture pulp, a full scale facility designed to burn the pulp to recover steam is now under construction.

Combustion. These techniques burn waste for the recovery of heat energy. They are the most technically developed systems and employ special grates in a waterwall furnace to burn as received urban waste and recover steam either at saturated or superheated conditions. Over 250 plants are operating in Europe and Japan. There are 7 plants operating in the United States, although 3 of these were originally constructed as incinerators and are still fully marketing the steam they produce. Worldwide, there have been a number of technical problems with corrosion/erosion process control being the most serious. The most recent European designs have solved these problems but an increased capital cost.

The more popular U.S. development seems to be the recovery of RDF for sale to coal-using facilities. With modifications existing boilers can use RDF as a supplemental fuel. Most development has aimed at the large suspension fired utility boiler and, while test burns have been encouraging, technical problems have developed. These are related to burning characteristics, slagging and environmental control equipment performance. All except the latter can be solved. The degradation of control measures such as electrostatic precipitators will require significant capital cost to solve.

Another version being demonstrated is the combustion of RDF in a dedicated boiler as a principal fuel. Normally the boiler is of spreader-stoker design and some consideration is being given to the use of fossil fuels, such as high sulfur coal, as a load leveler and steam production stabilizer.

Finally, the only available small scale system is a packaged two chamber incinerator with waste heat recovery. This technique is practical at the 25 to 100 TPD scale. In these units partial oxidation occurs in the first section of the unit and causes a portion of the waste material to degrade and give off combustible gases. These gases, as well as products of combustion and particulate from the first chamber, flow to a second chamber where they are combusted with excess air and a natural gas or oil pilot flame. The combustion products then flow through appropriate heat transfer equipment to produce steam, hot water or hot air. Four small cities and over 60 industrial plants use the technique with heat recovery equipment today.

Pyrolysis. Thermal gasification and pyrolysis systems are under development. Several systems are approaching the full scale demonstration stage. Specific discussion is not included on individual techniques since they are still in the developmental stages. However, in the future they will enter the same market place and broaden the range of options and market/waste stream interfaces available for commercialization activities.

Bioconversion. These techniques use living organisms or their products to convert organics into useful energy forms. Wastes placed in sanitary landfills ultimately degrade into methane which poses environmental and safety hazards. An emerging technology is to recover and utilize that methane for energy purposes. Other processes are in the developmental stages. DOE is sponsoring a process that converts the organics in urban waste to methane under controlled conditions. This process is at the proof-of-concept stage and is not expected to be commercialized until the late 1980's.

One bioconversion process to recover methane gas from existing landfills is at or near commercialization. Because of the explosive nature of the gas increasing attention has been paid to controlling the migration of the gas. Subsequently the use of the gas for energy purposes developed. Today there is one operational site, two sites in development, one site in construction and 10 sites in an advanced planning stage to utilize the recovered gas. It is estimated that 1 trillion cubic feet of methane is potentially recoverable from existing landfills with 55 billion cubic feet of pipeline quality available yearly just from the 100 largest landfills.

Capital and Operating Cost Experience

The costs presented in this section are estimated from reported expenditures in the literature. Because detailed breakdowns and the basis for reporting these costs are not provided, these estimates must be reviewed as preliminary. We feel the costs for a new facility would be somewhat higher than those reported here.

The production of a refuse derived fuel requires two distinct expenditures: (1) to process the waste and (2) to utilize the RDF. Capital costs for the RDF plant are expected to range between $10,000 and $20,000 (1978) per ton of daily capacity. A typical 1,000 TPD RDF facility is expected to cost $15,000,000 to construct. The O&M cost for the RDF plant are expected to be $5.40 to $9.80 per ton of waste processed. This is exclusive of revenues from tipping fees to dispose of the waste and the sale of energy and materials. The cost of firing refuse as a supplementary fuel depends on the method of firing, and the ash disposal methods employed. A typical capital cost to modify existing boilers to use the RDF from a 1,000 TPD plant is estimated to be $5,000,000 (1978) while the O&M costs are estimated to be $3.80/ton.

Waterwall furnace capital costs, expressed in 1978 dollars, range between $25,000 and $50,000 per ton of daily capacity. For example, the Chicago Northwest Incinerator cost $23,000,000 in 1970. This is equivalent to $25,000 per ton of daily capacity in 1978. The cost of land and energy product utilization facilities are not included. The construction of a typical 1,000 TPD waterwall combustor is estimated at $35,000,000. Operating and maintenance costs have been reported (adjusted to 1978 dollars) between $5 and $12 per ton exclusive of tipping fees and sales of materials and steam. Estimates of O&M cost for a waterwall combustor are $10/ton.

The capital costs for a two chamber packaged furnace at North Little Rock, Arkansas were reported to be $1,500,000 for a 100 TPD facility. Operating and maintenance costs (exclusive of steam sales) for a period January 1, 1978 to March 31, 1978 were reported to be $8/ton.

Current Development, Tests, or Demonstrations Underway

All three waste-to-energy technologies considered here have been demonstrated on a commercial scale. Longer operating histories, and demonstrations under varying economic and institutional situations, are needed before the technologies can be considered proven. A comprehensive RD&D program is underway to develop and test further the various technological options.

MARKET/ECONOMIC READINESS

Market Description

Energy produced from solid waste competes directly with fossil fuels in the residential, commercial, institutional, industrial and utility fuel markets. The metals, glass, paper, and other materials recovered from waste will compete with virgin materials used to produce these respective products. Competition for the waste by landfill owners can significantly affect the economic viability of these waste-to-energy technologies. As environmental controls and regulations become more stringent, landfill costs will increase and the economic competitiveness of waste-to-energy plants will improve.

Energy used for space heating and cooling, hot or chilled water, steam or electricity in the residential, commercial and institutional markets can be supplied, in part, from solid waste using district or community energy systems. Many institutions such as hospitals and universities can use self-generated waste to supplement their energy needs. Approximately 40% of the fossil fuels consumed in the industrial and utility markets are used to produce steam. These sectors represent a major market opportunity for steam produced from waste.

Energy or fuel produced from solid waste is marginally competitive with fossil fuels. As markets for its use become established and the cost of disposal at competing landfill facilities increase due to the increased costs of land acquisition and environmental compliance.

Potential Competing Technologies

Emerging technologies (such as coal gasification, or oil shale, which provide a substitute for, increase the supply of or reduce the demand for fossil fuels) are potential competing technologies. However, the proposed urban waste techniques appear fully competitive with the reported economics of emerging technologies. The most significant competition to RDF facilities and waterwall and multichamber combustors may well come from other urban waste conversion techniques such as pyrolysis and biological processes. These latter techniques have the advantage of converting waste into a competitive priced, more transportable and storable fuel gas or oil. The products recovered could also be used as chemical feedstocks.

Life Cycle Cost Comparison

Waste to energy, systems unlike conventional energy conversion systems, are paid to accept fuel. As a result a more expensive energy conversion technology can still deliver competitively priced steam. If the cost of alternative urban waste disposal methods rises, as expected at a faster rate than the GNP due to costs of site acquisition and environmental compliance, waste to energy technologies could deliver steam cheaper than systems using oil or LNG. This assumes, however, that disposal charges are increased allowing steam prices to fall. An aggregate cost reduction for waste disposal and steam generation is expected under this scenario.

Typical cost factors for RDF and waterwall and controlled air incinerator technologies result in cost competitive energy systems. If steam remains competitive with the reference energy costs and savings revert to the community, then increased disposal costs to the community will be approximately $4/ton today, there will be no extra cost in 5 years, and disposal costs will be completely eliminated in 20 years.

Market Barriers

The principal market barriers are institutional constraints which are discussed in detail in a later section. Specifically, the inability to control waste, to raise money for risk ventures or to market the energy produced will limit commercialization of these technologies. The development of model codes, research, development and demonstration and the provision of financial support in the form of price supports, loan guarantees, cooperative agreements and the like can help to overcome these barriers.

ENVIRONMENTAL READINESS

There are no foreseeable environmental barriers facing the urban waste conversion technologies. The environmental requirements have been identified and the R&D can be conducted in a time frame consistent with the technology development.

Although waste-to-energy processes are considered environmentally beneficial in that they reduce the volume of waste requiring landfill disposal and produce useful energy and recoverable materials, care must be exercised to ensure that the processes do not cause significant environmental pollution or adverse impacts on health or safety. There are regulatory aspects facing commercial expansion of urban waste conversion but these are not "show stoppers" although they do require parallel environmental R&D to ensure that adequate characterization, control development, and testing are performed to meet the existing and projected standards.

All of the urban waste conversion processes must comply with federal and state ambient air and water quality and solid waste disposal standards. For the combustion process, demonstrated commercial controls (electrostatic precipitators and baghouses) are available to meet existing standards for particulates and no major compliance obstacles are foreseen. For the combustion process, EPA has proposed *NSPS* standards for particulates and sulfur dioxide. Using the available controls, the particulate standards should not present any problem. Urban solid wastes, when burned as the principal fuel, tend to produce higher concentrations of hydrogen chloride (HCl) than other fuels. Possible future regulation in the U.S. can be anticipated. Control can be achieved through wet scrubbers. The pyrolysis processes have

no specific standards. Stack emissions, such as particulates, will have to be controlled. For the bioconversion processes, little environmental date on air emissions, water pollutants, and solid wastes are available and no process specific standards have been drafted.

Waste waters will have to be treated to meet local standards if discharged into municipal sanitary sewers; state-enforced *FWPCS* permit regulations must be complied with if discharged into waterways. Spraying waste waters on landfill areas may add to the buildup of undesirable inorganic and organic substances in aquifers. On-site treatment and recirculation can be an effective control for these conversion processes. No major obstacles are foreseen for meeting water standards if Best Available Control Technology (BACT) is applied. For pyrolysis and bioconversion processes, characterization R&D is needed with emphasis given to determining quantity and quality of waste water streams as they are suspected to be high in both organic and inorganic materials. Much of the water-related controls needed at incineration and RDF plants involve improved practices and designs to handle waste water streams and thus present no barriers.

Solid residuals for landfill disposal from urban waste plants will need to be characterized and controls developed as necessary to meet EPA regulations being formulated under the Resource Conservation and Recovery Act of 1976. Whether these wastes are classified hazardous or nonhazardous will determine how they are managed. EPA criteria guidelines for determining if a waste is hazardous are in draft form. The extent of the waste control impact cannot be assessed until the solid waste streams are characterized and assessed against the EPA criteria. The extent of the hazardous nature of the wastes could impact resource recovery of materials and conventional landfill disposal operations.

Continuing health and safety assessments are required to characterize and evaluate streams for unregulated pollutants such as organics, microbiological constituents, acids, and trace metals to determine the impact of these pollutants on the environment and human health. Related safety and operating-hazard studies are needed to improve the working conditions to decrease the accident rates, among the highest in the country.

INSTITUTIONAL READINESS

Institutional Barriers

There are a number of institutional barriers to implementation of waste-to-energy plants. These barriers may be more restrictive than technological and market concerns noted previously; however, they are amendable to solutions.

One critical barrier is the perception that municipal officials have of solid waste, viewing it as a disposal problem and not as under-utilized resources.

Another critical barrier is the control and quantification of the waste stream. To be viable any plant must be ensured of an adequate supply of waste. In the past, the local government was normally viewed as owning the waste and responsible for its collection and disposal. This view is being challenged in courts in Ohio, and it is likely that private sector refuse haulers will continue to challenge this view in other states as well.

Waste quantification is a serious barrier. Past practice indicates a universal trend towards seriously overestimating the available quantity of waste normally. This situation, in large extent, is responsible for economic problems of the Ames, Iowa plant.

Another institutional barrier is traditional municipal and state public-bidding practices that require municipalities to accept the lowest bidder, based on detailed item-by-item engineering specifications. This is incompatible with the evolving "innovative" technologies that characterize resource recovery as well as innovative contracting procedures such as full service contracting. The federal government should encourage states and localities to amend their procurement statutes to permit more flexible evaluative or negotiated bidding. This will provide adequately for competition and for protection of the public interest at the same time removing a major obstacle to resource recovery implementation.

The substantial front-end time (3–7 years) and money required for municipal project planning development constitutes a major obstacle to resource recovery implementation. Contracts, grants or loans to reduce these front-end costs are ways in which the federal government can help mitigate this problem.

Manufacturer Status

There are a number of private sector manufacturers, engineer design firms and risk venture firms with interests in the waste-to-energy field. Most are attempting to match the desires of the locality. Some firms prefer full service contracts where they are responsible for ownership and construction and operation of a facility. Some risk venture groups propose to develop a full service contract but have no proprietary or licensee position in the specific technology they are using. At the other end of the spectrum is the manufacturer selling his product as a portion of the plant to be owned and operated by others.

BENEFITS ANALYSIS

Energy Impacts

By 1985 an estimated .27 quads of energy could be recovered directly from urban waste. Another .08 quads could be recovered in the form of energy intensive materials. The aggregate energy recovery in the form of steam, electricity, fuel or materials could exceed 2.0 quads by the year 2000.

Because there are several technologies vying for market acceptance it is difficult to predict whether the energy or fuel recovered will be in the form of RDF, steam, or electricity and which materials will actually be recovered. Consequently, there are no estimates as to which fuels will be replaced by the respective waste to energy technologies.

Recipients of Benefits

The benefits will largely accrue to the respective communities served by an energy recovery system through stabilized wasted disposal costs, reduced waste collection costs and increased revenues from the sale of recovered materials and energy. Benefits will also accrue to the buyers of the materials and energy produced, because these products will be sold at prices competitive with other forms of energy produced. Since desirable sitings are close to the source of waste production, many plants will be located in or near urban centers, thus proving competitively priced recovered materials and energy and serving as a catalyst for urban development.

Cost Impacts

The direct costs of commercialization of these technologies will be largely borne by the respective communities and industry. These costs should be more than compensated for by the benefits received. Indirectly, producers and distributors of fossil fuels and virgin materials as used to produce ferrous and non-ferrous metals, glass, paper and other materials recovered from waste may incur some losses of business. These losses are not expected to be detectable. In addition, some landfill owners may incur loss of business.

Other National Benefits

In addition to the fossil fuels displaced by the use of urban waste and the energy conserved from recovered energy intensive materials, energy may be conserved through reductions in the distances traveled by waste collection trucks. Other benefits include reduced operating and maintenance costs for waste collection trucks and conservation of limited virgin materials used to produce ferrous and non-ferrous metals, paper, glass and other products recovered from the waste.

Environmental benefits can occur because the sulfur content of urban waste is less than coal or oil. Also the land requirements for landfill and the associate environmental damage will be reduced through the commercialization of these technologies.

READINESS ASSESSMENT CONCLUSIONS

The various technologies indicate high potential for technical sources. However, further development and optimization for equipment is necessary to improve efficiency and reduce capital costs although there are no foreseen technological barriers.

Energy or fuel produced from solid waste can be cost competitive with fossil fuels as markets for its uses become established and the cost of disposal at competing landfill facilities rise due to increased costs of land acquisition and environmental compliance.

Waste-to-energy processes are considered environmentally beneficial in that they reduce the volume of waste requiring landfill disposal and produce useful energy and recoverable materials. However, care must be exercised to ensure that processes do not cause significant adverse impacts on health, safety, or the environment.

The perceptions of solid waste held by municipal officials, the difficulty of controlling and acquiring sufficient waste to support resource recovery facility and public procurement regulations pose the most formidable institutional barriers to the implementation of waste to energy systems.

COMMERCIALIZATION STRATEGY FOR URBAN WASTE

ACTIONS

The Commercialization of waste to energy systems will be achieved in a timely manner if several impediments to energy recovery are reduced. For example:

- project risks
- demanding, time consuming, and costly project implementation
- competition from waste disposal alternatives

- aggregation and control of wastes
- stringent and costly project financing procedures

These impediments mitigate the ability of municipalities, industry, and the financial community to implement waste to energy projects.

Actions which the Federal government can take include clarifying existing tax regulations, thereby fostering private sector investment in waste to energy systems; offering limited price supports to help establish markets for energy recovered from Urban Waste; and strictly enforcing environmental regulations to ensure that competing landfill disposal facilities comply with existing environmental standards.

State and local governments can take action to modify existing public procurement regulations to ensure the timely, cost-effective and reliable completion and operation of energy recovery facilities.

COMMERCIALIZATION PROFILE

Energy produced from waste competes with fossil fuels in the residential, commercial, institutional, industrial, and utility fuel markets. With few exceptions the barriers to commercialization of waste-to-energy systems are applicable to all market sectors. For this reason, only one commercialization profile is presented.

RECOMMENDED STRATEGY

Immediate commercialization of Refuse Derived Fuel (RDF), mass-burning of waste in waterwall furnaces and multichamber furnaces, and methane extraction from some existing landfills is feasible. A concerted effort is planned to eliminate the remaining barriers to widespread commercialization of these techniques. This effort focuses on four areas of federal involvement:

Research, Development and Demonstration

Because some of the more important impediments to the widespread use of waste-to-energy systems stem from limited experience by municipalities and private industry with energy recovery technologies, an important goal of the commercialization strategy is to demonstrate promising energy recovery technologies at a commercial scale in a variety of institutional settings.

A research and development effort can be supportive of a specific demonstration project by making available the latest technical and operational characteristics. Additionally, an R&D program can contribute to the ultimate commercialization of waste-to-energy by bringing new promising technologies to the attention of industry and other concerned parties.

Training and Technical Assistance

The DOE program is intended to augment EPA's Resource Conservation and Recovery Panels program in situations where demonstration program support, under Titles II or IV of PL 95–238, is anticipated. This assistance program will provide meaningful support in accomplishing technological innovations in waste-to-energy systems, and in accelerating national commercialization.

The DOE training and technical assistance program will have three primary thrusts. First, projects which receive financial support under Titles II or IV of PL 95–238 may require the support of a pool of highly skilled and experienced professionals for advice on how to implement their projects. Second, the technical assistants will have some responsibility to see that DOE demonstration program funds are being effectively utilized, that project milestones are developed and met, and that the project has assembled the right mix of resources to carry out the implementation. Third, participants in resource recovery projects will be able to attend DOE-sponsored training programs which focus on how to deal with the numerous issues involved in implementing an energy recovery project.

Financial Incentives

A wide range of financial incentives could be utilized to foster the commercialization of waste to energy systems. Feasibility study and engineering design front-end costs will be partially supported through contracts and cooperative agreements. These mechanisms are intended to provide the incentive for organizations to consider the use of waste-to-energy technologies. A revolving loan fund can help reduce the capital cost of capital-intensive waste-to-energy systems. In some circumstances, price supports and government purchases of products can stabilize revenues to the facility and reduce the financial risks. In a limited number of circumstances high risk waste-to-energy projects could be supported by a loan guarantee mechanism.

These financial incentives are designed to encourage the use of waste-to-energy technologies by eliminating some of the initial development and economic barriers. At the same time, they use efficiently available federal funds. For example, a revolving loan can help support a number of facilities. Since revenues from these facilities will be used to repay the loan, additional facilities can be supported with the same federal financial commitment.

Coordination

A concerted effort to coordinate DOE's Urban Waste Technology Program with congressional, other federal agency, other DOE program, regulatory commission, and state and local government actions is being made. Congressional activities such as tax credits, energy pricing policies, and required fuel conversion can profoundly affect the commercialization efforts for waste-to-energy facilities. Actions currently being considered are largely complimentary. Similarly, many actions taken by the U.S. EPA on air, water and land pollution issues can affect commercialization efforts. Through an inter-agency agreement, we are working with the EPA to ensure that the goals of both agencies are properly addressed when policies and decisions are made.

The Urban Waste Technology Program should work closely with utility and other regulatory commissions to work out solutions to conflicting goals and it is hoped this will eliminate some barriers to commercialization.

Finally, DOE will work with state and local governments to develop procurement and financing approaches to ensure that waste-to-energy facilities are properly planned and installed, and that they are operated in conformance with local codes.

The Urban Waste Technology Branch's waste-to-energy commercialization strategy reflects the belief that the private sector is best able to marshal the necessary resources to overcome the technical, institutional, legal and financial complexities of waste-to-energy systems. At the same time, it recognizes that the public sector – as waste generator, possible project sponsor, and potential market for recovered energy – has to play a significant role.

Because the impediments to the commercialization of waste-to-energy systems are diverse, and to some extent unique to particular project settings, the program elements are necessarily diverse. The commercialization strategy also provides for flexibility of the federal response to individual project opportunities. To that end the proposed commercialization for Urban Waste focuses on several major program activities. In order of potential impact they follow:

- implementing a revolving loan fund and other financial incentives
- continuing a Research, Development and Demonstration Program
- providing a training and technical assistance program
- resolving coordination issues with federal, private industry, and state and local governmental units.

GOALS

The objectives of the Urban Waste Technology program are (1) to promote the use of urban waste as a source of energy and materials, and (2) to conserve energy through improved waste processing technologies. An active federal program to develop, demonstrate, and commercialize waste-to-energy technologies can accelerate the use of waste as an energy source and the conservation of energy through materials recovery and improved waste processing.

As indicated previously, 13.5% of the energy available from the municipal refuse that will be generated in 1985 can be recovered with a commercialization program, while only 5% is likely to be recovered without DOE involvement. These comparisons correspond to .27 and .10 quads recovered in 1985 from waste with and without a DOE program, respectively. An additional .08 quads can also be saved in 1985 in the form of recovered materials. By the year 2000, federal programs could be responsible for a 2.27 quad increase in energy recovered from urban waste.

The potential recoverable methane gas from existing landfills has been conservatively estimated at one trillion (10^{12}) cubic feet suggesting that 55 billion (10^9) cubic feet could be recovered annually by the year 2000. This translates to .05 quads of energy per year generated from a limited number of large landfills. Improvements in recovery techniques and expanded markets for low grade gases could increase this potential drastically.

Energy conservation activities directed to waste treatment facilities and the collection of municipal waste are also anticipated. The potential savings from conservation are not known at this time, but a 25% reduction in current energy consumption, of these activities, may be a realizable goal.

These goals are realistic because techniques like the mass-burning of waste in waterwall furnaces and small multichamber furnaces and the combustion of refuse derived fuel are ready for immediate commercialization. Federal activities can accelerate the commercialization process through a comprehensive program consisting of financial incentives; research, development and demonstration projects; expanded training and technical assistance and coordination with federal entities, private industry and other interested parties.

ACTIVITIES

Revolving Loan and Other Financial Incentives

The most effective federal role for the commercialization of urban waste is to reduce the economic, initial deployment and institutional barriers of waste-to-energy facilities, through the use of financial incentives. The types of financial incentives vary and include revolving loan funds, loan guarantees, insurance programs, cooperative agreements, contracts, price supports, government product purchases, tax credits, penalties and grants. Currently, the Urban Waste Technology Program has limited authority to use loan guarantees, cooperative agreements, contracts, price supports and grants to support the commercialization effort, through its demonstration program. Additional investment tax credits suggested by the National Energy Act may saturate the industry and, as a consequence, would have little effect on commercialization. Similarly, penalties are envisioned to have little value for commercialization. A grant program, similar to the one set up for wastewater treatment facilities under PL 92-500, is not necessary for waste-to-energy facilities that generate revenues and can eventually support themselves.

For the reasons stated above, tax credits, penalties and grants are not included in the commercialization plan. Rather an innovative revolving loan fund to reduce the costs and risks of waste-to-energy projects and to increase the likelihood that waste-to-energy technologies will be seriously considered by the public and private sectors, will be used as the cornerstone of the commercialization plan. Authority for loan guarantees, insurance programs, cooperative agreements, contracts, price supports and government product purchases will be sought or extended to supplement the revolving loan fund and thus provide the flexibility needed to encourage commercialization of waste-to-energy facilities.

The economic attractiveness of a waste-to-energy facility should be the primary incentive for its construction. However, initial deployment and planning costs that occur prior to construction often deter the public sector from considering these technologies.

If authority to implement a revolving loan fund is granted this could be used to help finance the planning, design and construction of commercial facilities where the risks are too high or return too low for commercial bankers, private industry, or local government to invest in the project. Revenues from the project or bond issues for construction will be used to pay back the loan, making funds available for additional projects. Once a particular technology has been shown to be economically viable in a commercial setting, the owner will be required to refinance the project through normal channels, thus freeing funds to support the commercialization of additional technologies which pose higher risks. This effort will also reduce the 20–40% financing cost of large projects.

A second innovative element of our approach is a federally sponsored insurance program to eliminate or reduce project risks. This insurance program would take several forms. One form would be to cover risks from situations beyond the control of the project sponsor such as changes in federal regulations or the loss of a project's energy markets or waste supplies. Another broad approach is to insure equipment that uses refuse derived fuel. Although short-term tests have indicated little effect from cofiring urban waste with coal upon boilers and other equipment, a considerable risk exists in the long-term effects of such actions. The possible adverse impacts of RDF upon its boilers is the major reason utilities have not exploited this concept.

Lastly, means must be developed to permit the economic integration of urban waste produced energy into large markets such as electricity. Private utilities need economic incentives to complement their public affairs motivation for the purchase and distribution of waste based energy.

Research, Development and Demonstration Programs

A number of on-going RD&D programs are being conducted through the Urban Waste Technology Branch. Through these programs progress is being made to eliminate technical and other barriers to commercialization. Continuation and some expansion of the R&D program in the environmental, technical and institutional areas is essential to commercialization

effort. The direction of the research and development effort is reviewed periodically to ensure that the research priorities reflect recent technological advances and DOE's current objectives.

Congress has authorized DOE to conduct a municipal demonstration program for urban waste (P.L. 95-238). Although our preferred approach is to encourage private commercialization ventures, the municipal demonstration program will play a significant role in the commercialization plan. The demonstration program will provide direct support for a number of commercial facilities involving various technologies and institutional arrangements. A successful demonstration will then help to eliminate some of the barriers to commercialization for all similar facilities.

A program announcement soliciting proposals for the demonstration program was released in June. Support for about 15 demonstration programs will begin in late FY 78 and carry over to FY 79. For the more promising projects, support will continue beyond FY 79. Funding under the municipal demonstration program will occur on a continuing basis.

Training and Technical Assistance

The primary purpose of this effort will be to increase private and public organizations' ability to plan and implement waste-to-energy techniques and consolidate the available information. Assistance must be provided to increase the size and quality of the technical community that designs, constructs, and operates urban waste facilities. Currently, there are very few technical experts in this field. Increased competition and improved quality within the technical community will enhance commercialization.

Information must also be provided to financial institutions, governmental units, and other non-technical organizations to increase their understanding of the waste-to-energy options available to them. This comprehensive program will reduce some of the uncertainties associated with using urban waste technologies.

Documents describing various technologies will be prepared. DOE has already published a series of reports describing the European experiences with waste-to-energy technologies. Additional publications are planned in a continuing program. Separate publications will be prepared for technical and non-technical audiences.

One of the barriers to commercialization is the lack of reliable economic data for waste-to-energy facilities. A group of studies may be conducted to summarize the cost of existing facilities in a consistent fashion. Other analyses will identify potential markets for the energy produced from UWT facilities. Benefit/cost studies of waste-to-energy systems will evaluate externalities (such as environmental damage, balance of payments, and price regulations); these studies will attempt to evaluate the total social value of waste-to-energy facilities. This will be a continuing effort with some studies being completed in FY 79.

The decision to build a waste-to-energy facility requires the evaluation of alternative options, including detailed economic and marketing studies. Many of the tasks involved in the evaluation process can be automated. For example, economic assessments of different waste-to-energy plants require the same generic steps and therefore, economic evaluation models can be formulated. Using region-specific information concerning a facility, economic information useful to decision-makers can then be generated. Models of this type can significantly reduce front-end costs while improving the quality of many studies. As part of the commercialization plan, such a model will be developed in FY 79. If this is successful, additional models may be developed later.

Workshops similar to the one conducted earlier this year by Johns Hopkins Applied Physics Laboratory are being planned as an integral part of the T&TA process. Workshops are an excellent mechanism for bringing together the various parties involved in the commercialization process for face-to-face discussions. This active mode of information dissemination has an advantage over passive modes in that information is transferred between all interested parties. A series of workshops will be held to broaden public understanding of resource recovery and DOE programs.

The use of gaming techniques is an effective way to educate individuals interested in waste-to-energy facilities and to make them aware of the problems and concerns of all individuals involved in a resource recovery project. Over a period of a few days, the participants play roles during the planning of a hypothetical waste-to-energy facility. As part of the commercialization plan we will develop a game in FY 79 and conduct a number of trial simulations throughout the country; the concept will be fully implemented during FY 80.

One of the barriers to commercialization is the lack of trained experts in the field of energy and resource recovery from waste. Few colleges and universities have programs devoted to this discipline. To help eliminate this barrier, a university work/cooperative program will be initiated. In a number of selected educational institutions a curriculum for resource recovery will be prepared. This curriculum should include a range of interdisciplinary courses covering the technical, economic, financial and environmental concerns associated with resource recovery. In addition to course work, students will be required to work during their educational programs in an area associated with energy and resource recovery. Federal involvement will include providing financial support for the preparation for the course work, providing grants to students within the program, and helping to organize the work program within the private and public sectors. The preparation of the curriculum is planned in FY 79 with student support beginning in FY 80.

A number of short courses in energy and resource recovery will also be prepared. These courses are useful in supplementing the education of persons who have completed their schooling and are in a position to participate in an energy and resource recovery project. We anticipate that these courses will be assembled with limited federal assistance, but will be offered through the private sector. One or two courses could be made available by FY 80. If they are successful, others will be developed.

Coordination

A concerted effort is being made to coordinate DOE's Urban Waste Technology Program with the actions of Congress, other federal agencies, other DOE branches, regulatory commissions, state and local government, and the private sector. A concerted effort will be made to modify PL 95–238 to include authorities for commercialization activities. These changes will affect Title II, Loan Guarantees and Title IV, Municipal Demonstration.

Many actions taken by the U.S. EPA can affect commercialization efforts. A joint plan for resource recovery RD&D will be completed with the EPA in FY 79. Other joint ventures are planned.

A number of the institutional and economic barriers to urban waste technology commercialization are associated with public/private sector interfaces. The planning, construction, and operation of a commercial waste-to-energy facility involves a number of participants. The major participants are the owner, operator, financier, supplier of waste, purchaser of energy, and a broker who helps coordinate the project. As the number of individuals and organizations increase, barriers to commercialization also increase.

A program to encourage the interaction of the private and public sectors is being developed. The private sector can take this lead role in a number of forms, either as the project financier, system operator, or energy product consumer. Still another approach is to have an independent party coordinate the activities of the myriad of participants. These independent brokers could be supported directly by the federal government or receive a commission from the parties involved in the project. A strategy for involving the private sector will be formulated in FY 79 and if the concept is favorably received it will be implemented in the following year.

4-2 Energy from Waste: A Report on Mass Burning in Europe

Thomas Cunningham

Source: *NCRR Bulletin*, Vol. 10, No. 1 (March 1980) pp. 14–16. Reprinted with Permission of National Center for Resource Recovery.

"Mass burning," or the use of raw, *unprocessed* refuse as a fuel in waterwall combustion or refractory chambers to produce steam and hot water is finding increased application in the U.S. The growing number of American cities now employing this heat recovery technique include Chicago, Ill.; Harrisburg, Pa.; Nashville, Tenn.; and Saugus, Mass. Other cities, including Akron, Ohio; Ames, Iowa; Bridgeport, Conn.; Milwaukee, Wisc.; and Monroe County, N.Y., have gone a step further by *processing* incoming solid waste; *i.e.,* removing the inorganic or non-combustible materials. The remaining organics can then be burned directly as a fuel supplement in conventional boilers.

The use of refuse as a source of fuel to produce heat and energy, however, originated in Europe in the late 1800's. Over the years, its popularity has grown throughout most of Europe, with major technological advances taking place in the 1950's. Today, more than 500 localities throughout the world are recovering useful energy products from previously discarded solid waste.

This reading summarizes a study prepared by the Battelle Columbus Laboratories for the U.S. Environmental Protection Agency on "Refuse-Fired Energy Systems in Europe: An Evaluation of Design Practices."

This study, published in late 1979, reviews 30 refuse-fired steam and hot water generators in eight European countries. Its principal objective was to gather information about European waste-to-energy practices and systems and to interpret this data as it may be commercially practicable in the U.S.

Included in the report is an analysis of European technical economic environmental and social experiences in the application of the water-tube wall (or waterwall) integrated furnace/boiler, and the refractory wall furnace with waste heat boiler. The water-tube furnace normally produces steam for electrical production, industrial uses and steam or hot water for district heating, while the refractory wall furnace primarily produces hot water for district heating.

The earliest account of refuse-to-energy conversion in Europe is an 1896 refuse-to-electricity and industrial steam plant in Hamburg, Germany. Early systems were sophisticated enough to produce electricity even though many of the systems were batch operated, with manual refuse feeding and ash removal. As these units were refractory walled, the steam quality (temperature and pressure) was limited. During the years between 1910 and 1945 there were many developments in refuse handling and major improvements in the refractory wall furnaces and the separate waste heat boilers. Many of the systems, however, were destroyed during World War II. This led to the development and evolution of the modern day water-tube wall integrated furnace/boiler. In the late 1940's and 1950's, vendors (led by Von Roll of Switzerland) began to develop methods to take more energy out of combustion gases. Basically, what had been learned about coal combustion in water-tube wall units was applied to refuse combustion.

The world's first integrated water-tube wall furnace/boiler began operation at Berne, Switzerland, in 1954. Two 100 ton-per-day (TPD) units produced steam for electricity, hot water

— through heat exchangers — and for direct industrial use. This original Von Roll plant is still operating today.

Since the mid-1950's, the use of water-tube walls as the furnace enclosure has increased dramatically. Also, the remarkable increase in refuse heating value has exerted substantial influence on furnace wall design. Many integrated furnace/boiler designs result in one-half of the energy removed going into the wall tubes while the other half goes into the convection banks. Water-tube wall furnace/boilers producing high temperature steam usually are chosen for high temperature steam systems producing electricity efficiently. Refractory wall furnaces with waste heat boilers, which are less expensive, are often appropriate for hot water or low-temperature steam applications.

Thus, the central European countries of West Germany, France and Switzerland have concentrated on high temperature steam systems for electrical production and district heating, while Scandinavian countries use more refractory wall furnaces with waste heat boilers to produce hot water for district heating.

What were some of the reasons that led many European cities to the alternative of refuse burning for the disposal of solid waste? There was a growing concern about the wastefulness of using valuable land for unsightly landfills and the effects of landfill leachate on ground water contamination. Too, European citizens and government officials were becoming more aware of the implications and long-term effects of landfills. Another major influence was the finding that it was possible to control air pollution from the burning of wastes by cooling the dirty exhaust gases. Despite the fact that refuse burning is two-to-four times more expensive than landfilling, many cities are still willing to pay the difference rather than landfill.

Prompted by concern for leachate and the scarcity of land, many European countries and cities undertook refuse burning construction programs between 1960 and 1973. Actually, by the time of the Arab oil embargo in 1973, some of the countries were "nearly saturated" with refuse burning plants.

The Battelle observers reached the conclusion that energy considerations have never been, and are not now, the driving force leading to the construction of most energy refuse systems. Cities build refuse-fired energy systems because they fear the long-term effects of landfill leachate; they perceive a shortage of land and officials are frustrated by the prospect of having to locate landfill sites every several years.

ECONOMICS AND FINANCE

Each of the 30 systems visited in Europe was owned by either the local municipality or a not-for-profit authority. Of the 15 plants studied in detail, cities own eight, authorities own six, and a nationalized electric company owns one. To the best of Batelle's knowledge, private enterprise does not own any daily operating resource recovery systems in Europe that use municipal solid waste.

It should be noted here that the 1976 "Solid Waste Management Guidelines" published by the U.S. Environmental Protection Agency states: "It is EPA's firm belief that attempts to predict (and compare) costs of various types of plants in a general way, apart from local circumstances, is more likely to mislead than inform. The range of assumptions regarding specific design, reliability, markets and other factors is too great to make such an analysis meaningful."

Capital investment costs per daily ton capacity have increased dramatically in Europe during the past 10 years. The 1960–1968 "capital cost per daily ton" ranged from $13,000 to $15,000 at three surveyed plants. The average for all 15 plants was about $35,000. The three plants built in 1975 and 1976 averaged about $70,000. Plants built in the early 1980's could initially cost more than $100,000 per daily ton capacity.

There are seven reasons contributing to this dramatic rise: inflation (land, capital equipment purchases, construction service fees, construction labor and materials cost); interest rates during construction; exchange rate devaluation; corrosion protective equipment designs; architecture and landscaping for neighborhood acceptance; more complex energy use systems; and the need for additional or more costly air pollution equipment.

American systems, during the same time frame, were usually less expensive than European systems. The American buyer often concentrates more on the lowest bid while the European buyer prefers a reliable system. Also, with the wealth of systems in Europe — some 275 — there are enough options to attract and hold qualified employees.

DISPOSAL COSTS

The net disposal cost, or tipping fee, is the cost borne by the citizens, taxpayers and/or generators of waste. This is the figure used to compare the technical alternatives for solid waste disposal (compost, landfilling, materials recovery, waste-to-energy, etc.). This ranges upward from a low of $6.27 per ton in Paris to a high of $48.25 per ton in Werdenberg, Switzerland. The Paris figure is not truly a comparable one because there is no depreciation expense included. Since the plant is owned by the City of Paris, depreciation does not appear in the operator's financial statement. Had normal depreciation and interest been included, the net disposal cost would be well in excess of $10 per ton. On the other hand, the Werdenberg community did not want to mar its scenic beauty with another landfill and knew that disposal costs would be high, especially since the cost must be divided by only 120 tons per day. This was the only plant surveyed that suffers from diseconomies of scale. The plants averaged $27 per ton for most expenses.

One surprising conclusion reached by Battelle is that over a wide range of plant sizes — from 120 to 1600 tons per day — there appears to be little significant economy of scale. The data suggests that the net operating and owning costs for plants within these size ranges and with the same plant configurations normalized for inflation, exchange rates, site costs, etc., fall in the range of $6 to $36 per ton, for the most part. While this range appears to be significant, the factors that cause the variation are not size-related as much as previously thought.

REVENUES

As a general rule, American refuse (household, commercial, and light industry waste) will produce a net salable 5000 pounds of steam per ton of refuse, while European refuse produces, perhaps, 4000 pounds of steam per ton of refuse. The typical European revenue for sale of energy averaged in 1976 about $7.50 per ton throughput, equivalent to about $1.88 per million BTU. It is felt that one reason that the Europeans have developed their refuse-energy systems is that over the years the price of energy has been higher than in the U.S.

All five of the 15 systems receiving the highest revenue per refuse input ton are providing energy for district heating. Their average revenue is $9.76 per ton. Steam is a most salable energy recovered commodity. District heating commercialization varies extensively by country. The world's largest district heating country is Russia. Commercialization is faster with more centralized planning and control where there is less pressure on immediate economic returns. In western Europe, West German systems deliver the most energy; Scandinavia, however, has the highest per capita rate.

The American district heating systems are mostly steam, while in recent years many European district heating systems use only hot water. It was suggested by many Europeans that the lackluster district heating situation in America during the past 20 years was partially the fault of using steam and not hot water. The typical European assessment is the energy losses are greater with steam, maintenance is higher, and steam can only be transported one-third as far as hot water.

An excellent example of district heating in the U.S. is the Nashville Thermal Transfer Corp. facility in Nashville, Tenn. It takes the process one step further with a cooling system. No district cooling system was observed in Europe. It would appear that certain economic benefits would accrue if district cooling could be provided in the summer. While the technology flow in the area of refuse to energy has been, for the most part, from Europe to the U.S., those Europeans who desire to increase summer loads and overall financial results might do well to look at the district heating and cooling system in Nashville.

Some key energy functions of the European systems visited are: 93 percent produce energy for internal use; 60 percent for district heating; 53 percent export electricity to a network; and 33 percent process steam for industrial use. Five of the 15 systems receiving the lowest revenue per refuse input ton are adversely affected by very competitive fossil fuel or nuclear electrical power stations. Their revenue averaged $5.30 per ton. As the price of conventional fossil fuel rises higher than the average inflation rate, there is a potential for the revenue from energy sale to rise, resulting in declining net disposal costs and tipping fees.

The Battelle group also visited seven "co-disposal" systems in Europe. Codisposal, or the simultaneous disposal of solid waste and waste-water treatment sludges, eliminates the need for two separate disposal activities. Five of the facilities have wastewater treatment plants located with the refuse burning plant. Sanitary services in Europe are often centralized and well coordinated. In four of the 15 plants, the energy value in refuse is utilized to drive off moisture in the sludge. Three of these plants then burn the dried sludge.

In 1977, the Europeans were well advanced in the combined destruction of refuse and sewage sludge within the same system. Of note is that each of the six major European manufacturers visited during this project has a codisposal system in operation. Most processes involve several stages of drying. Typically, a unit operation will convert incoming raw sewage sludge at 94-to-96 percent moisture to a 70-to-80 percent moisture. At this moisture level, the sludge has a thick consistency that can lead to dramatic moisture reductions down to 5-to-20 percent. The third stage of several processes is to combust where, by definition, the moisture content of the sludge goes to zero. From a reliability standpoint, each of the processes works a great part of the time. Unfortunately, data were not available on enough systems to perform an economic analysis.

SUMMARY AND CONCLUSIONS

One major conclusion reached by the study is that the mass burning of unprocessed municipal solid waste in heat recovery boilers is well established and can be a technically reliable, environmentally acceptable and economically sound solution to the problem of solid waste disposal.

The central European countries of West Germany, France and Switzerland have concentrated on high temperature steam systems for electrical production and district heating. Scandinavian countries use more refractory wall furnaces with waste heat boilers to produce hot water or low pressure steam for district heating. In fact, the continent's leading refractory wall furnace, hot water generator vendors are in Denmark.

U.S. municipal solid waste produces a net salable 5000 pounds of steam per ton of refuse, while European refuse produces 4000 pounds of steam per ton. The typical revenue for the sale of energy in Europe per ton of refuse in 1976 was $7.50, which is equivalent to about $1.88 per million BTU.

All the 30 systems visited in Europe were either owned by the local municipality or a not-for-profit authority. There is no doubt about the capital intensive nature of refuse-fired steam and hot water separators. The European attitude is that landfills are not the answer to their solid waste disposal problems; that the American type front-end resource recovery approach has a high processing cost, low materials revenue and the energy plant does not need the uniform fuel; that refuse-fired mass burning and energy production is the answer, even if ultimate disposal costs are higher.

The study also concluded that the lessons learned in 80 years of refuse-fired energy plant experience in Europe can be effectively utilized today by many U.S. communities.

Copies of the two-volume report, an Executive Summary and 15 trip reports are available from the National Technical Information Service, Springfield, Va. 22161.

4-3 Energy from Waste Utilization in the Federal Republic of Germany

L. Barniske

Source: Adapted from an Article by the Same Title in *Solid Wastes*, Vol. LXVIII, No. 2 (February 1978) pp. 64–82. Reprinted with Permission of The Institute of Solid Waste Management.

INTRODUCTION

This report describes the situation in the field of energy-from-waste-utilization in the Federal Republic of Germany.

Extensive experience in the field of refuse incineration has been acquired with currently operating facilities.

A description is given of four refuse incineration plants which are of interest on account of their respective type. Development trends are described.

Under the subject of "New Techniques for the Thermal Treatment of Waste" laboratory and technical tests and a research programme initiated by the Federal Government are described.

SURVEY OF REFUSE INCINERATION PLANTS

Historical Review

Nearly one hundred years ago, the idea of refuse incineration was given effect, and that was in 1876 in England.

In 1881 this new technique of refuse treatment came to be used in the U.S.A., too. At that time refuse incineration was principally practised for the purpose of hygienic disposal of potential bacteria nutrient medium.

The first recorded units in Germany date from 1893, when the City of Hamburg constructed an incinerator plant as a defence against epidemics. Further plants followed, for example in Berlin, Cologne, Frankfurt/Main, Kiel, Barmen, Fürth, Beuthen, Altona and Aachen. Most of these plants soon had to stop operation on account of structural defects and non-sufficient economy. At first it was expected that the total costs of incineration could be redeemed by selling steam or electricity and by reclamation of bricks from the solid residues. But it didn't succeed at all.

After the Second World War, the rapid economic recovery and progress in the standard of living involved a continual increase in the amount of refuse with an increase of combustibility. Under the pressure of new environmental protection laws a growing number of cities decided to introduce refuse incineration in order to alleviate their waste disposal problems.

Composition and Calorific Value of the Refuse

The household waste which makes up the main part (60 to 80 per cent) of the total refuse largely determines the calorific value, and that is the most important characteristic for combustion.

The high increase of packing material in connection with the decrease of the fine materials like ashes and sand involved a considerable growth of refuse volume and an adequate rise in calorific value. Both have effects on the operation of incineration plants.

At present the lower calorific value of the refuse amounts to 6,000 to 8,400 kJ./kg.

Table 1.

Fuel	Lower calorific value (kJ./kg.)	Steam generator efficiency (%)
Pit coal	29,000–32,000	78–82
Fuel oil	42,000	80–84
Natural gas	32,000	86
Sewer gas	15,000	85
Brown coal	8,000–16,000	76–80
Household waste	6,000– 8,400	65–75

(1,500 to 2,000 kcal./kg.). Estimates for the future had assumed an annual increase of about 400 kJ./kg. in calorific value, but this estimate appears now to be too high, at least for the near future.

In spite of the rather small portion of plastics in household waste, they have an essential importance for the process of incineration. Conglomerations of fusing plastics disturb the course of combustion. Due to the high calorific value of plastics and to the heterogeneity of the refuse superhigh temperatures can occur in some parts of the furnace which are able to damage the grates and the brickwork.

Hydrogen chloride in the flue gases of incinertion plants, which mainly originates from the burning of polyvinylchloride (P.V.C.), has often damaged the boiler tubes by corrosion. However, the risks of fireside corrosion could be diminished by constructional, operational, and organizational measures. Experiments showed that up to 10 per cent (by weight) of plastics in the refuse can be burned without difficulties on the conventional grates, provided that the refuse is evenly distributed and that the shape of the furnace guarantees a sufficiently well directed and increased injection of overfire air.

At present the household waste contains 2·5 to 3·5 per cent of plastics. About 0·5 to 0·7 per cent of that is P.V.C. waste. It is estimated that the portion of plastics will increase to 5 to 6 per cent, including 0·8 to 1·0 per cent of P.V.C.

Steam Production and Generation of Potential Energy

On the supposition that the lower calorific value of the refuse amounts to 8,400 kJ./kg. (2,000 kcal./kg.), and that the steam generator efficiency runs up to 70 per cent about 2·3 tons (Mg.) of steam can be produced out of 1 ton (Mg.) of refuse. From this steam quantity a potential energy of up to 500 kWh. can be generated by a condensing turbo-alternator set.

If the steam is to be applied to industrial or heating purposes, next to the tension of the steam will be released by a back-pressure turbine to a special heating (steam) pressure. The complete exhaust steam of the back pressure turbine then can be utilized profitably. In this way the thermal energy of the steam is economized at a high efficiency.

The quality of the refuse influences decisively the steam generator efficiency. High portions of ash and water in the refuse cause a lower efficiency. If the portion of cellulose preponderates the carbon content, in general the efficiency is higher than at converse relation. A comparison of the efficiencies of different steam generators (Table 1) shows that the values of incineration plants are the lowest.

The efficiencies of the incineration plants vary either more or less. Increasing sediments of flue dust upon the boiler tubes involve increasing flue gas temperatures and decreasing efficiencies.

Therefore, as to an effective utilization of the heat, the cycles of cleaning are kept short.

Existing and Planned Plants

The survey is restricted to facilities which are used predominantly for burning domestic refuse and similar waste. 43 refuse incineration plants are in operation.

Within the framework of refuse disposal planning, the refuse incineration facilities of *Eutin* and *Glückstadt* are to be closed down by 1980. The refuse incineration plant of *Munster* (District of Soltau) is in a similar situation. For the sake of completeness, the small facility of *Helgoland,* which is not included in the 43, is mentioned as well; it went into operation in 1962 with a capacity of 0·3 to 0·4 Mg./h. and is to be replaced by a larger unit (2 Mg./h.) by 1978.

In addition to the 43 refuse incineration plants mentioned earlier new plants are planned or under construction for the cities of *Bamberg* (3×6 Mg./h.), *Eschenlohe* (2×3 Mg./h.), *Hamburg* (2×6 Mg./h.), as well as at *Herten* for the central Ruhr region (5×20 Mg./h. for domestic refuse and 3×8 Mg./h. for industrial refuse), and at *Ingolstadt* (2×7 Mg./h.).

The development of refuse incineration in the Federal Republic of Germany since 1958 is shown in Tables 2 and 3. The greatest increase in number of refuse incineration plants occurred between 1965 and 1970. This trend slackened in the following years. While during the above period of time, about eight incineration units with an average capacity of 12 Mg./h. went into operation every year, this figure went down to an average of five units annually between 1970 and 1975 with a mean capacity of approximately 13 Mg./h. The discussion which has been going on for quite some time in public on whether refuse incineration plants are well enough adapted to the needs of the environment may have contributed to delaying the development originally envisaged, particularly between 1970 and 1975.

At the moment, incinerator plants serve about 15·6 million people. 25·3 per cent of the population of the Federal Republic of Germany.

For economic and ecological reasons, the main emphasis of refuse incineration is on large scale facilities for connurbations. A breakdown of the refuse incineration facilities according to the size of the communities they cater for shows that a major percentage of the population served by refuse incineration facilities lives in communities with more than 100,000 inhabitants. Approximately 76 per cent of the population in those areas are served by such facilities.

Table 4 clearly indicates the trend towards large-scale facilities with a throughput of more than 10 Mg./h., catering for a total of at least 100,000 inhabitants. In fact, almost two-thirds of the large-scale facilities have capacities of over 30 Mg./h., i.e. they cater for at least 300,000 inhabitants.

For large scale facilities the four types of mechanical grates shown below predominate. All have proved to be good.

Forward feeding grate:	14 facilities
Roller grate:	14 facilities
Reciprocating grate:	7 facilities
Travelling grate:	3 facilities

In such large-scale facilities, the heat released by burning the refuse is used for steam generation. In 22 out of 29 facilities, steam is used for electricity generation, sometimes in combination with district heating. In the remaining 7 facilities, steam is utilized directly for heating or industrial purposes.

The possible energy yield of the refuse currently being burned corresponds to approximately 3 to 4 per cent of the electricity generated from pitcoal in the Federal Republic of Germany.

Table 4 furthermore shows that large-scale facilities provide particularly favourable conditions both in technical feasibility and economic efficiency for scrap iron selection from incineration residues and for slag utilization.

Following the trend prevailing in the last few years, developments in the field of refuse will, in future too, concentrate on facilities with throughputs of at least 10 Mg./h. Here, the combined incineration of refuse and sewage sludge will become increasingly important. The experience to be gained with the *Krefeld* facility will show the line to be followed in this respect.

According to Table 3, out of all the communities of more than 100,000 inhabitants, areas with approximately another 5 million inhabitants could be served by refuse incineration plants. A realistic background for the realization of this objective is provided by the plans made by the Länder to build a total of between 18 and 20 new refuse incineration

Table 2. Development of Refuse Incineration.

	Number of plants		Number of incineration units		Refuse throughput in 1,000 Mg./a.		No. of inhabitants in hundreds in areas served by such plants	
	Increase	Total	Increase	Total	Increase	Total	Increase	Total
Up to 1960	1	1	2	2	80	80	200	200
Up to 1965	6	7	14	16	638	718	2,250	2,450
Up to 1970	i7	24	42	58	2,111	2,829	6,140	8,590
Up to 1975	9	33	28	86	1,753	4,582	5,000	13,590
Up to 1977	10	43	19	105	857	5,439	2,043	15,633

Table 3. Number of Inhabitants in Areas Served by Refuse Incineration Plants, in Relation to the Different Sizes of Communities.

No. of inhabitants in thousands	Number of inhabitants in the Federal Republic of Germany, classified according to size of community				Number of inhabitants in areas served by refuse incineration plants									
	No. of inhabitants in thousands		% of total population		Up to 1960[3]		Up to 1965[3]		Up to 1970[3]		Up to 1975[4]		Up to 1977[4]	
	1966[1]	1972[2]	1966[1]	1972[2]	Inhabs. in thousands	% of Category	Inhabs. in thousands	% of Category	Inhabs. in thousands	% of Category	Inhabs. in thousands	% of Category	Inhabs. in thousands	% of Category
Category I: up to 10	25,387·7	22,525·7	42·5	36·5	—		—		—		—		—	
Category II: 10–50	10,943·6	14,562·6	18·4	23·6	—		40	0·4	90	0·8	68	0·5	88	0·6
Category III: 50–100	3,758·6	4,843·5	6·3	7·9	—		130	3·5	130	3·5	515	10·6	575	11·9
Category IV: 100–500	8,912·8	9,345·7	14·9	15·1					1,995		2,818		4,231	
Category V: over 500	10,673·1	10,394·7	17·9	16·9	200	1·0	2,280	11·6	6,375	42·7	10,189	65·9	10,739	75·8
Total	59,675·8	61,672·2	100·0	100·0	200	0·3	2,450	4·1	8,590	14·4	13,590	22·0	15,633	25·3

[1] Statistical Yearbook 1967 } Verlag W. Kohlhammer GmbH,
[2] Statistical Yearbook 1973 } Stuttgart und Mainz.
[3] Based on figures for 1966.
[4] Based on figures for 1972.

Table 4. Classification of Refuse Incineration Plants According to Size and to Heat Utilization, Scrap Selection and Slag Reclamation.

Size of plant throughput in Mg./h.	Plants not utilizing heat	Plants utilizing heat			Plants selecting scrap-iron	Plants reclaiming slag
		Use of steam for heating and/or industrial purposes	Use of steam for power generation	Use of steam for power generation and heating purposes		
1–3	1	2*	—	—	—	—
3–10	4	5*	2	—	1	1
10–30	—	5	2	4	5	3
Over 30	—	2	9	7	9	12
Total	5	14	13	11	15	16

43

* Plants at Böbingen, Heidelberg, Marktoberdorf.
No steam generation.
Heat utilization for drying sewage sludge respectively for drying compost.

facilities under their long-term waste disposal programs which extend well into the nineteen eighties. This would mean that an average of between 250,000 to 280,000 inhabitants would be catered for by every new facility.

On the basis of the assumption that for areas with less than 100,000 inhabitants the importance of refuse incineration will continue to diminish because, among other things, other technologies have recently been developed for waste disposal (e.g. pyrolytic techniques), it can be said that the increased use of refuse incineration will probably have to be limited to a maximum of 20 million inhabitants, i.e. approximately 32 to 33 per cent of the total population.

Detailed Description of the Plants in Krefeld, Wuppertal, Oberhausen and Munich

Combined Refuse and Sewage Sludge Incineration Plant at Krefeld. Refuse incineration facilities for destroying domestic and industrial wastes as well as waste oil have already been built in several places. An advanced type of refuse incineration facility, which will be used not only for the above-mentioned types of waste but also for the incineration of both raw and biological sewage sludges, has been erected by the city of Krefeld. This refuse and sewage sludge incineration facility, called M.K.V.A., consists of three incineration units, one of which is intended as reserve unit. Together with the municipal sewage treatment facility, which is on the same premises, it forms an integral system from the point of view of power economy as well as of organization.

Via the vehicle weighing bridge, where weight and origin are registered, the refuse is taken to the dumping holes or the shears for bulky waste, located at the opening of the refuse bunker; from there it is filled into the bunker. By means of remotely operated cranes, the refuse is passed on from the refuse bunker to the feeding hoppers of the separate furnaces where it is burnt on roller grates.

The sludge produced in the sewage treatment plant is transferred to one of the day bins of the M.K.V.A. with a water content of 94 to 96 per cent, and its water content is subsequently reduced to approximately 74 to 76 per cent by means of a centrifugal separating machine. In beater mills, into which hot flue gases are admitted, this dehydrated sludge is dried and ground. The dust and water vapour is blown in directly above the refuse combustion chamber. Here, the dust is burnt while in suspension.

Waste oil to be disposed of is burnt by means of burners, after appropriate treatment. The slag produced during the waste incineration process including the flue dusts is quenched, the liquid and solid components are separated, and the solids are then transferred to the slag pit. From there, the slag is loaded on to trucks by means of a remotely operated crane and then transported away.

In order to make full use of the heat released during combustion, the furnaces are in a subsequent stage followed by steam generators. The super heated steam thus generated is transformed into electrical energy by means of back pressure turbines. This energy suffices for supplying the whole plant, including the sewage treatment plant. The steam behind the turbines is used for district heating.

Before the flue gases are released into the atmosphere via the stack, the dust contained in the gases is removed in a first cleaning stage except for a residual amount of approximately 2 percent, while noxious gases such as hydrogen chloride, sulphur dioxide and hydrogen fluoride are mostly washed out in a second stage.

Wuppertal Incineration Plant. The incineration service started in 1975. At first four firing units with roller grates each of 15 Mg./h. output at lower calorific values between 900 and 2,600 kcal./kg. were built. The plant is built on the site of a former quarry in Wuppertal-Kozert.

Each firing unit is equipped with six grate cylinders with a length of 3·5 metres and a diameter of 1·5 metres in step fashion; the speed can be controlled continuously.

Each steam boiler generates up to 50 Mg. of vapour at a maximum pressure of 32 bar, which is utilized for electricity generation by 20 megawatt turbine. The exhaust vapour condensed in the air condenser can again be fed to the feed water cycle of the boiler. The concept of later extension provides a fifth steam generator unit and a further 20 mega-watt turbine set.

The waste trucks of Wuppertal and Remscheid are unloaded in the storage bunker of the incineration plant, which has a capacity of 18,000 cubic metres. To this end, the trucks will enter a hall of approximately 26×70 metres of basal surface and of 9 metres in height. The furnaces are fed from the bunker by means of two grab cranes each with a capacity of 6 cubic metres. Two bulk-waste shears are built in for crushing bulky wastes. The output of each is 150 cubic metres per hour.

In the waste-water discharge line from the plant — approximately $9 \cdot 1$ m.^{3}/h. at the time of service of four furnaces — measures will be taken to prevent the temperature of the admitted water exceeding 40°C. when entering the draining ditch. A collecting pool is built for cooling water of excessive temperatures.

A flue gas scrubber for extensive precipitation of chlorine contents is part of the facilities of the incineration plant Wuppertal GmbH. Thus air pollution from exhaust gas can be kept as low as possible. The dust contents can be reduced to 100 mg./m.^{2} by means of electrostatic filters.

The Niederrhein Joint Refuse Incineration Plant at Oberhausen. In spring 1969, the Concordia Bergbau AG in Oberhausen was closed down. Not only the mine Concordia was to be closed down but also a mine power plant situated on the Rhine-Herne-Kanal.

After carefully studying all the details, after examining the possibilities for re-using materials, existing plant components and the need to acquire new installations, it was established that it would make technical as well as economic sense to convert the existing pitcoal mine Concordia into a refuse incineration plant.

The calculated maximum possible refuse throughput is 22 Mg./h. per unit, with a total of three units available. The facility was designed for a lower calorific value of 800 to 2,500 kcal./kg. This design data results in air and flue gas amounts which roughly correspond to the conditions previously found in the boilers

operated on pitcoal; the previous maximum steam output is reduced to approximately 50 per cent (50 Mg./h. per unit). The converted boilers, the boiler-house, the engine-house, the pumping plant and the workshops with the switching system were taken over from the existing power station. The coal bunker, part of the boiler house, the filter and the stack were demolished and replaced by up-to-date facilities. The generated steam is converted into electricity in two 16 megawatt back pressure turbines. The back-pressure steam is passed on to neighboring industrial firms or is used to meet the demand of the plant itself. The surplus steam is condensed by means of an air condenser.

The resulting condensate is then re-cycled.

The flue gases are released from the steam generator with a temperature of 220°C. and cleaned in electrostatic filters with an efficiency of 99·5 per cent. The maximum concentration of the dust emissions was limited to 100 mg./m.^{2} at a temperature of 0°C. and with a CO_2 content of 7 per cent. The maximum SO_2 content was fixed at $2 \cdot 5$ g./m.^{2}. For the first time, limits for HC1 ($1 \cdot 5$ g./m.^{3}) and for fluorine (10 mg./m.^{2}) were fixed. A site has been reserved for the possible later installation of a gas scrubber.

Refuse Power Station at South Munich. A power plant built between 1925 and 1928 was altered and equipped with a new high-pressure plant. Unlike other power stations, it not only supplies municipal electricity and district heat, but also provides for refuse incineration.

The boiler plant is divided into a refuse-heated boiler and a main boiler; their feed-water supplies are connected in series and their gas stacks in parallel, that is to say, the refuse-heated boiler is merely used to preheat the feedwater.

Natural gas is used as the main fuel, and heavy oil as reserve fuel. Municipal refuse is used as additional fuel.

In the case of a failure of the refuse boiler, the full steam output is generated by the main boiler. If there is a failure of the main boiler or of the turbogenerator, heat generation for district heating is ensured by the refuse-heated boiler.

According to the operators of the facility in Munich, the concept of a close linkage between electricity generation and refuse incineration will probably not become generally accepted in future, because electricity generation and refuse incineration facilities respectively are developing more and more in different directions in a big city in terms of demand, site and licensing procedure.

This becomes clear when one takes a look at the different importance attributed to municipal tasks, i.e. steam generation, district heating and refuse incineration.

The tasks of the power stations are as follows:

1. Electricity generation, which must be safeguarded.
2. District heating, which must be safe-guarded.
3. Refuse incineration.

The concept of refuse incineration, on the other hand, is the following:

1. Refuse incineration must be ensured throughout the year.
2. District heating only if there is enough demand.
3. Electricity generation as a byproduct.

DEVELOPMENT TRENDS IN THE FIELD OF INCINERATION

The improvement of conventional waste inciner-ation methods is aimed at substantially under three aspects:

1. Reduction or avoidance of emission of harmful gases, particularly hydrogen chloride and hydrogen fluoride. To this end the known dry and liquid method for elimination of harmful gases must be improved.
2. Improvement of availability of incinera-tion plants, reduction of failures and corrosive attack of certain parts of the plants.
3. Utilization of incineration residues (slags and flue ash) or economic preparation for controlled tipping.

In addition, the residues from refuse incinera-tion plants confront us with ever increasing problems. In 1973, we had about 1·5 million tons of slag and flue ash, and in 1976 about 2 million tons of residues were yielded.

At present, incineration residues are mostly brought to dumping places. The iron elements are separated by means of magnets and then re-cycled to the blast-furnace.

Incineration residues are partly used for land-fill at former sand and gravel pits; in doing so, we have to see to it that any possible damage to the ground water by the soluble salt elements of slag and cinder is avoided. Furthermore, the resi-dues could possibly be used for the construction of unclassified roads and for providing a firm foundation for sports grounds. They cannot be used, however, for the building of better roads.

In principal, slag and fly ash could, by means of high-temperature techniques, be converted into building materials such as sintered pumice; this is, however, not very attractive from the economic point of view.

The development of high-temperature tech-niques for the treatment of slag and fly ash offers the opportunity of converting the residues into insoluble materials so that they can be used for landscape modelling without any risk to the ground water. In its support for research and development in this field the Federal Govern-ment will take account of these other techniques for using refuse slag.

4-4 30 Years of Refuse Fired Boiler Experience

Charles O. Velzy

Source: Adapted from an Article in *Resource Recovery and Conservation*, Vol. 4, No. 1 (May 1979) pp. 83–98. Reprinted with Permission of Elsevier Scientific Publishing Company.

INTRODUCTION

The town of Hempstead has been operating energy from refuse plants since 1950. This paper presents the experience gained from the operation of the Town's two heat recovery plants specifically in the areas of boiler tube metal wastage, boiler fouling, particulate emission control, and maintenance and availability experience.

MERRICK PLANT

The four furnaces at Merrick are circular batch-fed units. The gases from two circular units discharge through flues to vertical combustion chambers from which they flow horizontally over a wet bottom to a common flue and then to a boiler. A three-drum natural circulation waste heat boiler serves each of the two pairs of batch-fed furnaces. The gases were originally discharged from the boilers through cyclones and an induced fan and out the stack. Recently the cyclones were replaced by electrostatic precipitators.

The Merrick plant experienced some tube failures in the 1950's which led to a boiler retubing in 1960. At that time, approximately 10% of the total of 1,224 tubes in each boiler had failed. The only analysis available cited as a reason for some failures the unexplained presence of copper deposits on the inside walls of the boiler tubes. Other tubes failed where stationary sootblowers had been attached to the tubes by welded brackets. No special precautions were taken to control future tube failures, since it was felt that the initial failures were the

result of unusual conditions. However, the stationary sootblowers were replaced with retractable blowers with bracket supports outside the boiler.

In the 1960's, additional tube failures were experienced resulting in a second retubing in 1966–67. At that time, a total of 118 tubes had failed and were out of service in boiler number 1, and 124 tubes had failed in boiler number 2. In retubing these boilers, approximately 25% of the tube surface was removed, reducing the total heating surface from 1,008 m² (10,883 ft²) to 771 m² (8,300 ft²) and reducing the gas velocity entering the boiler by 3.5 m/s (11 ft/s) (Table 1). Since this second retubing in 1966–67, one tube failure has been experienced — a distinct improvement from the previous 7 to 8 years required between major retubing. Plain carbon steel was used in both retubings.

The tube failures described above, and similar failures experienced at other plants incorporating waste heat boiler convection surfaces in the downstream flues of mass fired refuse burning plants, indicates that corrosion or metal wastage is a matter of concern in the design and operation of this type of plant.

ORIGINAL OCEANSIDE PLANT

The original Oceanside plant (designed by this firm in 1962) consisted of two units with single-drum controlled circulation boilers at the furnace

---

*Paper presented at the Engineering Foundation Conference, Unit Operations in Resource Recovery Engineering, Franklin Pierce College, July, 1978.

Table 1. Boiler Design Parameters.

	Merrick incinerator		Oceanside incinerator	
	Original boilers	Revised boilers	Original controlled circulation boilers	New natural circulation boilers
Design period	1949–50	1965–66	1962–63	1971
Average furnace burning rate, kg/h (lb/h)	12,700 (28,000)	11,300 (25,000)	11,300 (25,000)	13,200 (29,170)
Grate loading, kg/m²/h (lb/ft²/h)	390 (80)	250 (71)	300 (61)	350 (71)
Refuse heat content, MJ/kg (Btu/lb)	7.0 (3,000)	10.5 (4,500)	11.6 (5,000)	11.6 (5,000)
Flue gas:				
Unit volume, kg gas/kg refuse (lb/lb)	7 (7)		8 (8)	8.5 (8.5)
Boiler inlet temp., °C (°F)	980 (1,800)	980 (1,800)	980 (1,800)	1,080 (1,980)
Boiler outlet temp., °C (°F)	370 (700)	430 (800 est.)	330 (620)	315 (600)
Excess air (%)	100		128	150
Boiler pressure, gauge, kPa (psi)	1,700 (250)	1,700 (250)	3,200 (460)	3,200 (460)
Steam temp., °C (°F)	208 (406)	208 (406)	240 (462)	240 (462)
Total heat surface, m² (ft²)	1,010 (10,883)	770 (8,300)	1,250 (13,470)	1,890 (20,350)
Steaming rate:				
Av., kg/h (lbs/lh)	26,200 (57,800)	15,900 (35,000*)	31,400 (69,300)	45,800 (101,000)
Max., kg/h (lbs/lh)		18,100 (40,000*)	38,600 (85,000)	
Max. velocity at boiler entrance, m/s (f/s)	16 (52)	12 (41)	15 (48)	8 (27)
Av. draft loss through boiler, mm (in) water	38 (1.5)		46 (1.8)	22 (0.85)
Tube size, NPS	2½	2½	2	3¼, 2½
Tube wall thickness mm (in)	2.8 (0.110)	3.4 (0.135)	3.8 (0.150)	4.6, 3.4 (0.180, 0.135)

*Actual.

exit followed by large diameter cyclones for air pollution control. These boilers had previously been successfully applied to industrial applications where rapid swings in heat generation and high particulate grain loadings were experienced. This plant was designed prior to the availability of operating experience obtained from first-generation (early 1960's) modern European mass-fired water-wall boilers. The Oceanside plant is one of the few in the U.S. where heat energy from municipal solid waste is used to generate steam and, in turn, electricity. A unique feature of this plant is that the steam is condensed in desalinization units so that fresh water for in-plant process use can be generated from adjacent salt water. The furnace/boiler design parameters for this plant are listed in Table 1.

The original boilers in this plant suffered catastrophic tube failures. With the exception of two failures which resulted from wear by a sootblower. For both boilers, the operating time from initial operation to failure due to the typical metal wastage pattern was approximately six months.

The metal loss was most severe in the bottom of the boilers but gradually worked up through the entire convection surface. Once the first tube failed, additional tubes failed in rapid succession. An average of 3.3 days between failures was experienced during the latter months of 1967. In later years, by limiting the burning rate to about two-thirds of the design capacity and reducing steam pressure from 3200 kPa (460 psi) gauge to approximately 1,700 kPa (250 psi) gauge, the average operating time between progressive tube failures was extended to about 17 days. As the damage progressed, however, the average time between failures dropped off to about 10 days.

Consideration of the numerous attempts at explanations received during the early plant operation at Oceanside, reports of European experience appearing in the literature subsequent to 1966, discussions with metallurgists, and first-hand investigation of European installations in Paris, Stuttgart, Mannheim, Duesseldorf, and Munich, led to the conclusion that the metal wastage at Oceanside resulted from a combination of corrosion and erosion. It has been demonstrated that "high-temperature" corrosion

can proceed quite rapidly in the presence of chlorides adjacent to the affected metal surface, and with the proper composition and thickness of tube deposits, at temperatures as low as $260°C$ ($500°F$) [1-3]. Reducing conditions apparently increase the rate of attack. As surface deposits build up, the corrosion rate drops off rapidly. However, if gas velocities and particulate content are high enough, the external tube corrosion deposits will be eroded away, exposing bare metal to the rapid "high-temperature" corrosion. Several more detailed discussions of corrosion in refuse incinerators are contained in refs. [4-6].

MODIFIED OCEANSIDE PLANT

During the initial period of tube failures at Oceanside (1966-67), a number of articles appeared in the technical literature describing severe corrosion problems being experienced in several of the new European refuse fired boilers [3, 7-10]. By 1968, since no satisfactory explanation had been developed for the boiler metal wastage problem at Oceanside, members of this firm travelled to and compared first-hand our observations with experiences of plant operators in Europe. The valuable information obtained during this trip was then evaluated in light of observations at the Oceanside plant and modifications which had been made to improve tube life at the Merrick power generating incinerator plant.

Based on the information collected, a study and design program was initiated to establish overall design parameters for water-wall boiler units and for rebuilding the furnaces at the Oceanside plant to achieve improved operating and maintenance experience. As a result, in 1972, the Town contracted for a natural circulation water-wall boiler for one of the two 270 t/d (300 U.S. t/d) furnaces based on general design parameters developed during the study and listed in Table 1. The new boiler was designed to fit within the existing plant and thus is a unique product of a joint design effort between the boiler manufacturer and the design firm. The first unit was placed in successful operation in 1974; the second unit came on-line in 1977.

The grate, charging chute, induced draft fan, underfire air fan, and portions of the refractory construction at the furnace inlet are all that re-main of the original "chute-to-stack" system. A number of considerations guided the overall design of the new system. Furnace volume was maximized, within the constraint of the space available in the existing building, to assure that burnout of the combustion products would be complete prior to entering the boiler convection bank. The furnace envelope was to be, to the extent practical, a cooled surface, thereby re-ducing the temperature of gases entering the convection bank. Quantity, velocity and point of introduction of overfire air were also impor-tant design considerations. Horizontal tubes were to be avoided.

Three-dimensional scale model tests were conducted, per requirements of the construc-tion specifications, to finalize the size and shape of the furnace as well as the location and arrange-ment of overfire air nozzles. The configuration selected resulted in an average gas velocity through the furnace of 5 m/s (15 ft/s) and a furnace exit temperature of 850°C (1550°F) when firing at the design rate with 100% excess air. Overfire air can be introduced through 2 NPS pipe nozzles at two levels in each side wall, as well as at a single level through the front and rear wall, at a maximum pressure of 75 kPa (25 inches) water gauge.

Air-cooled silicon carbide walls were installed along the grate line to inhibit slag accumulation. Bottom supported waterwalls extend from the top of the silicon carbide walls to the furnace outlet. The waterwalls were coated to a level approximately 9 m (30 ft) above the grate with a relatively thin silicon carbide coating held in place by closely spaced 19 mm (3/4 inch) studs. This protects the tubes from metal wastage due to flame impingement and attack by constituents in the products of combustion without unduly inhibiting heat transfer. Tube thickness was also selected to be twice the thickness required by the ASME Boiler and Pressure Vessel Code. Thus, 3-1/4 NPS wall tubes, having a mini-mum thickness of 4.6 mm (0.180 in) were installed.

A multiple pass convection bank, formed of essentially vertical tubes, was chosen which was of sufficient size to preclude the need for an economizer. Boiler design exit gas temperature was 315°C (600°F). The gas velocity in the

initial downpass of the convection section where the gas passes between 2-1/2 NPS tubes on 150 mm (6 in) center spacing, is less than 10 m/s (30 ft/s). Tube thickness is twice that required by the Code, with minimum thickness of 3.4 mm (0.135 in). Seven sootblower locations were selected each with two half-width, retractable steamblowing sootblowers.

As indicated above, when designing a refuse-fired boiler plant burning as-received solid waste, one should incorporate certain design concepts to decrease maintenance and increase service life of the boiler. The most important of these concepts are: coating of the lower water-wall surfaces with silicon carbide and increased boiler size and tube spacings to decrease gas velocities. Thermal efficiency, which is a function of the difference between the boiler entering and exit temperatures, need not suffer as a result of in-corporating these concepts in the design of a new plant. However, one should expect to pay an estimated 10-20% more for such a boiler versus a unit designed to meet less conservative criteria.

Electrostatic precipitators, which replaced the original large diameter cyclones, were se-lected to operate at temperatures in excess of 300°C (570°F). The units included two fields in series with rigid-frame discharge electrodes installed between collection plates on 250 mm (10 in) centers. Average gas velocity through the precipitator was to be 1.5 m/s (4.5 ft/s). Collected flyash may be discharged either to the residue conveyors or directly to the flyash lagoons.

OPERATING EXPERIENCE AT OCEANSIDE

Three incidents of boiler tube failure have been experienced at the modified plant since its start-up in 1974. The first tube failure, discovered during the first firing, was attributable to a torch cut apparently made during boiler erection but after the hydrostatic test. In the second inci-dent, two tubes failed after more than 14,000 hours of operation. These failures were attrib-utable to cutting from water which had con-densed in the sootblower system. The failure occurred near the sidewall in the cavity between the screen tubes and the convection bank where the first sootblower in the blowing sequence enters the boiler. The problem was corrected by maintaining the sootblower system under full steam pressure at all times, realigning the sootblower piping to eliminate a point where condensate could accumulate reducing sootblower blowing pressure to 515 kPa (75 psi) gauge, and installing metal shields on the tubes where metal loss had been detected.

The third incident of tube failure occurred after more than 17,000 hours of operation. The failed tube was on the exterior of the furnace where a casing plate was welded to the tubes. Failure apparently was due to a stress concentration at this point. An attempt has been made to relieve such stress concentrations at similar points on the other unit.

Because of the problems with metal wastage in the original plant, arrangements were made in conjunction with the construction contract for remodeling of Unit no. 2 for retention of a testing company to periodically monitor tube wall thickness ultrasonically. Readings from the furnace side of a selected 3-1/4 NPS screen tube in the center of the furnace outlet are:

Date	Thickness measured	
3 July 1974	4.70 mm	(0.185 inches)
23 April 1975	4.83	(0.190)
5 Nov. 1975	4.83	(0.190)
12 March 1977	4.70	(0.185)
12 April 1977	4.70	(0.185)

Thus, to date, little or no metal wastage has been observed in the furnace screen area or the convection banks of these boilers.

No tube wastage has been detected under the silicon carbide coating on the waterwalls. However, some wastage [11] was detected on the furnace sidewalls of Unit no. 2 immediately above the silicon carbide coating during the early stages of operation of this unit. Two steps were taken to correct this situation: plant operation was modified to assure more effective use of overfire air and the level of silicon carbide coating was raised 1.8 m (6 ft, 3 in). No further wastage has been discovered during subsequent tube thickness measurements. The silicon carbide coating has held up well.

No problems have been experienced with fouling of the furnace screen tube section or the convection bank in the new boilers. Sootblowers are operated once per day and, even with the reduced blowing pressure, ash has not accumulated on the tubes. It has never been necessary in the more than 3 years since the startup of the new Unit no. 2 to hand clean or lance the boiler convection surface.

The original unit required a full or partial shutdown every few days to shed slag from the lower furnace walls. The modified units have never been shut down to remove slag from the furnace walls. However, there were structural problems with the silicon carbide air-cooled walls originally installed in the modified plant. These walls have been replaced with walls incorporating improvements by the original wall designer and are now performing satisfactorily.

The electrostatic precipitators, which were selected to meet Federal new source emission standards rather than the less stringent applicable New York State emission regulations, have been successfully tested. The results of compliance tests are as follows:

Unit no.	2		3	
Test date	11 Mar. 1975		22 June 1977	
Firing rate, kg/h (lb/h)	14,400	(31,800)	5,700	(12,600)
Emissions, stack				
N.Y.S. Part 222				
Allowed, kg/h (lb/h)	15.4	(34.0)	7.4	(17.5)
Actual, kg/h (lb/h)	6.0	(13.2)	1.7	(3.7)
U.S.E.P.A.				
Allowed, g/Nm^3 (gr/scf corr. to 12% CO_2)	0.18	(0.08)	0.18	(0.08)
Actual, g/Nm^3 (gr/scf corr. to 12% CO_2)	0.10	(0.045)	0.07	(0.03)
Emissions, precipitator				
entrance kg/h (lb/h)			26.8	(63.4)
g/Nm^3 (gr/scf, corr.)	no infor.		1.2	(0.55)

The manner in which the furnace is operated has been determined to have a noticeable effect on stack particulate emission rate. Findings in this regard have been published [12]. The precipitator entrance particulate loadings noted above provide a gross indication of the efficiency of the electrostatic precipitators. Since the particulate sampling conditions are poor at the precipitator entrance, as is usually the case in this type of plant, the reliability of these data is lower than the stack emission data.

FUTURE IMPROVEMENTS IN OPERATION

The modified Unit no. 2 has experienced three extended periods (4-6 weeks) of down-time since it was placed in operation in June of 1974. Two of these periods were due to mechanical problems with the boiler feedwater pumps while the third extended shutdown period was due to mechanical problems with the induced draft fan. The pumps and fan were originally installed in 1965.

Several observations regarding plant availability, and the effect of older equipment on plant availability, may be made from the information presented in Table 2. Thus, from the time of startup of Unit no. 2, total availability ranged from a low of 57% in 1974 to 72.8% in 1977. Availability, exclusive of unplanned shutdowns, ranged from 65% in 1974 to 74% in 1977. All of this unplanned shutdown was due to problems with the original equipment installed in 1965 with the exception of the tube failures cited earlier and a breakdown of the conveyors under the electrostatic precipitators, all of which occurred in 1977 and accounted for 6.4% of lost time during that year. Of the total time available, unplanned shutdowns caused by the original plant equipment ranged from 31% to 19.3%. The majority of this unplanned or emergency down-time was caused by specific items of equipment. Thus, in 1974, 70% of the emergency down-time was caused by boiler feed pump problems; in 1975, again, 50% by boiler feed pump problems and 25% by grate problems; in 1976, 72% by induced draft fan problems; and, in 1977, 60% by plugging of the siftings hoppers. On January 26, 1978, Unit no. 2 was officially turned over to the Contractor by the Town for installation of a new siftings conveyor system as a part of the originally planned plant improvements. If these major problems with original equipment could be overcome, availability for Unit no. 2 would range between 83 and 88%. Perhaps more time spent in planned shutdowns for preventive maintenance would pay significant dividends in additional Unit availability.

A second area of possible improvement in furnace operation is control of refuse feed to maintain control of furnace heat release as indicated by furnace temperature. Nowak [13] described a furnace feed control system developed at a plant in Stuttgart. Table 3 was developed from information contained in that paper and furnace temperature charts selected at random from the Oceanside plant. Thus, it may be observed that, prior to furnace feed control, the Stuttgart plant experienced half-hour temperature fluctuations of up to 100°C (180°F) and averaging about 55°C (100°F) with an overall change in temperature of 200°C (360°F) ocurring in 1-1/2 hours. Boiler inlet temperature readings in the Oceanside unit no. 2 plant over similar time periods indicate temperatures normally ranging, over half-hour periods, up to 122°C (220°F) and averaging about 65°C (117°F), with overall changes in temperature of 172°C (310°F) in 1-1/2 hours and 122°C (220°F) in 20 minutes.

In contrast, the control system on the Stuttgart plant limited temperature ranges to 66°C (122°F) and averaged about 28°C (51°F), with an overall change in temperature of 66°C (120°F) occurring in 30 minutes. An advantage noted for this method of control is a reduced tendency for tube metal wastage due to improved combustion conditions (decreased tendency for areas of reducing conditions to occur in the boiler). There was also an increase in refuse throughput capability in the plant since, with the reduction in heat release surges in the furnace, the plant units could normally be operated closer to their design conditions.

CONCLUSIONS

Several years of operation of the modified boilers in the Oceanside plant in the Town of Hempstead, New York have provided a long-term test

Table 2. Unit No. 2 Availability. Oceanside Plant, Hempstead, N.Y.

Year	Availability (%)		Lost time (%)			Ratio of major problems with original equipment to total problems (%)	Availability without major problems with original equipment (%)
	Total	Excluding planned shutdown	Planned	Problems with original equipment	Problems with new equipment		
1974	57	65	12.6 (incl. startup)	30.4	—	70 (Boiler feed pumps)	86
1975	68	71	4.4	27.6	—	50 (Boiler feed pumps)	83
1976	66	68	3.0	31.0	—	72 (Induced draft fan)	88
1977	72.8	74	1.5	19.3	6.4	60 (Plugging of siftings hoppers)	84

Table 3. Furnace Temperature/Feed Control.

	Max. temp. ranges in 1/2-hour periods, °C (°F)		Ave. temp. ranges in 1/2-hour periods, °C (°F)		Overall changes in temp.		
					Temp. °C (°F)		Time period
Oceanside plant (5 random seven-hour periods)							
	82	(180)	41	(105)	132	(270)	1 h 25 min
	82	(180)	49	(121)	154	(310)	1 h 30 min
	71	(160)	46	(115)	160	(320)	2 h 45 min
	104	(220)	43	(109)	104	(220)	20 min
	82	(180)	49	(120)	104	(220)	20 min
Stuttgart							
Without refuse feed control. 1 random seven-hour period	82	(180)	38	(100)	182	(360)	1 h 30 min
With refuse feed control 1.random seven-hour period	49	(120)	11	(51)	49	(120)	30 min

of the original design concepts. It has been shown that, with effective use of overfire air, judicious use of protective coatings, conservative volume and velocity in the furnace and convection bank, and limitation of steam temperatures, tube wastage need not be a problem in mass-fired water-wall furnaces burning refuse. The potential for tube wastage remains, however, if the unit is not operated carefully.

Careful selection of tube configuration and spacing to achieve conservative gas velocities along with proper location of sootblowers can eliminate convection bank tube fouling in incinerator boilers.

Properly cooled walls along the grate line shed slag effectively. However, design of these walls is critical to their operation and maintenance experience.

A properly sized two-field electrostatic precipitator following a well-operated furnace and boiler appears to be more than adequate to comply with present Federal regulations related to dry particulates.

Further improvements in furnace feed and temperature control is possible and is desirable.

REFERENCES

1. Nowak, F., April, 1970. Corrosion phenomena in refuse firing boilers and preventive measure, paper presented at the International Symposium on Corrosion in Refuse Incineration Plants, Dusseldorf, West Germany.

2. Kautz, K., 1978. Boiler metal wastage in the Stadwerke, Dusseldorf incinerator plant, in R.W. Bryers (Ed.), Ash Deposits and Corrosion Due to Impurities in Combustion Gases, Hemisphere, Washington, D.C.

3. Vogel, W., May 1967. Refuse disposal by incineration, Aufbereit. Tech., 283–285 (in German).

4. Rasch, R., Sept. 1969. Contribution to the thermodynamics of high temperature corrosion in refuse incineration plants, ISWA Information Bulletin, I: 12–17.

5. Miller, P.D., Boyd, W.K., Engdahl, R.B., Fischer, R.D., Krause, H.H., Reid, W.T., Reinoehl, J.E., Schulz, E.J., Vaughan, D.A., Webb, P.R. and Zupan, J., April 28 1972. Final report on fireside metal wastage in municipal incinerators, (Research grants EP-00325 and EP-00325-S1) to Solid Waste Research Division, National Environmental Research Center, EPA, by Battelle Columbus Laboratories, Columbus, Ohio.

6. Velzy, C.O., March 1974. Corrosion experiences in incineration, Paper No. 133, Corrosion 74, National Association of Corrosion Engineers, Houston, Texas.

7. Perl, K., Aug. 1966. Corrosion damage in boilers of refuse incineration plants, Energie, 353–354 (in German).

8. Rasch, R., April 1967. Present state of refuse incineration, Energie, 143–144 (in German).

9. Eberhardt, H., and Mayor, W., 1968. Experiences with refuse incineration in Europe. Prevention of air and water pollution, operation of refuse

incineration plants combined with steam boilers, design and planning, Proceedings of 1968 National Incinerator Conference, ASME, New York, pp. 73–86.

10. Fichtner, W., and Martin, F., 1968. Service requirements of a modern large refuse incineration plant, Proceedings of 1968 National Incinerator Conference, ASME, New York, pp. 117–122.

11. Hecklinger, R.S., Velzy, C.O., and Kempisty, J.C., 1978. Three years of operating experience with a waterwall boiler at the Oceanside Disposal Plant, in R.W. Bryers (Ed.), Ash Deposits and

Corrosion Due to Impurities in Combustion Gases, Hemisphere, Washington, D.C., pp. 207–215.

12. Hecklinger, R.S., 1977. Correlation of furnace operation and test results, in R.A. Matula (Ed.), Present Status and Research Needs in Energy Recovery from Wastes – Proceedings of the 1976 Conference, ASME, New York, pp. 56–67.

13. Nowak, F., 1978. Corrosion in refuse incinerating steam generators and preventive measures, in R.W. Bryers (Ed.), Ash Deposits and Corrosion Due to Impurities in Combustion Gases, Hemisphere, Washington, D.C.

4-5 Energy from Waste: Saugus, Massachusetts

E. Joseph Duckett

Source: *NCRR BULLETIN,* Vol. VII, No. 2 (Spring 1977) pp. 46–52. Reprinted with Permission of National Center for Resource Recovery.

A Wheelabrator is a rust-removing machine that works by bombarding steel with abrasive, shot-like pellets, developed 40 years ago by the company known as Wheelabrator-Frye, Inc.[1] The major characteristics of the Wheelabrator are that it is effective in removing rust, contains its own air pollution controls, uses less energy than alternative steel cleaning methods and is capital intensive rather than labor intensive.

Although aimed at a different problem and based on different technology, Wheelabrator-Frye's refuse-to-energy plant, constructed and now operating in Saugus, Mass., has attributes parallel to those of the original Wheelabrator machine. The Saugus plant is effective in disposing of solid waste, controls air emissions, recovers energy and is a capital intensive approach to waste disposal. Unlike the Wheelabrator machine, however, the development of the Saugus plant is significant as an institutional arrangement.

The formal title of the Saugus plant is the "Boston North Shore Resources from Refuse Facility." Although it is popularly known as a Wheelabrator-Frye facility, the actual name of the operating entity is the Refuse Energy Systems Co. (RESCO), a joint venture of Wheelabrator Energy Systems, Inc., a wholly-owned subsidiary of Wheelabrator-Frye, and the M. DeMatteo Construction Co.

The purpose of this article is to review the most prominent features of the Saugus plant. This solid waste facility was developed in response to the dual pressures of limited landfill space and rising energy costs. The plant utilizes waterwall incineration, an approach to recovering energy from the combustion of solid wastes. To date, it is the largest privately-financed refuse-to-energy plant in the U.S. See Table 1: Fact Summary.

BACKGROUND AND HISTORY

The primary motivation for the development of the Saugus plant was a disposal crisis in the Boston North Shore area.[2] Eleven North Shore municipalities relied on the DeMatteo landfill, located in the tidelands area of Saugus, for disposal of their solid wastes. After a brief closure of the landfill in 1967 and subsequent reopening, ordered by the governor of Massachusetts, the landfill was continually under pressure to close because it could not meet state environmental regulations. This pressure, culminating in a court order to close the landfill, led to a series of discussions among community and state officials, the DeMatteo Construction Co. and the General Electric Co. (G.E.).

General Electric operates a large manufacturing plant in Lynn, Mass., just across the Saugus River from the DeMatteo landfill. The G.E. plant uses large amounts of steam for electricity and for testing turbines and jet engines. At the time of the disposal crisis, G.E. was considering the replacement of two oil-fired steam generating units due for retirement.

In 1972, a proposed joint venture (called Thermal Energy Systems Co.) between DeMatteo

Table 1. Fact Summary, Saugus Refuse-to-Energy Plant.

Full title:	Boston North Shore Resources from Refuse Facility; Saugus, Mass.
Began operation:	November 1975
Principals:	RESCO (a joint venture of Wheelabrator Energy Systems, Inc., and M. DeMatteo Construction Co.) – developed and operate the plant
	General Electric Co., Lynn, Mass. – purchases steam under a 14-year contract with RESCO
	Eleven municipalities and two districts of Boston – deliver solid waste to the plant under 20-year contracts (Boston is on short-term contracts)
Volume:	Capacity is 1200 TPD; currently operating at 1000 TPD
Technology:	Von Roll waterwall incineration; Wheelabrator–Lurgi electrostatic precipitation; magnetic separation of ferrous metals from residue
Products:	Steam (625 psig; 785–825°F), 300,000 lbs./hr.; price tied to oil
	Magnetic metals (post-incineration), 60–90 TPD; estimated price $10/ton
	Residue landfilled
Cost:	Total cost of plant: $40 million
	Estimated costs and revenues per input ton (based on 1975 Bond Prospectus figures for 10th year of operation):

Costs		Revenues	
Debt service	$ 7.50	Tipping fee	$18.00
Operating	13.50	Steam	10.20
	21.00	Ferrous metals	.70
		Interest on	
		bond fund	.77
			$29.67

and Combustion Engineering, Inc., failed to materialize when Combustion Engineering withdrew.[3] Not long afterwards, DeMatteo and Wheelabrator-Frye formed RESCO and agreements were signed to begin construction of the project and to sell steam to G.E. Together, Wheelabrator and DeMatteo provided $10 million of initial capital for RESCO through equity contributions. General Electric signed a 14.5-year contract to purchase steam from the plant on an uninterruptible basis (24 hours per day) at specified minimum and maximum rates, and at a price tied to the cost of oil. At the time of these initial agreements (April 1973), no municipal commitments for delivery of solid waste to the plant had been made.

Construction required approximately two years. System design and construction management were performed by Rust Engineering, a subsidiary of Wheelabrator-Frye. The two major equipment purchases were the Von Roll waterwall furnaces (Wheelabrator-Frye is the U.S. licensee for Von Roll, Ltd. of Zurick,

Switzerland) and the Wheelabrator-Lurgi electrostatic precipitators. The construction contractor was the DeMatteo Construction Co.

The arrangement for financing construction of the plant was somewhat complex. In addition to the $10 million of initial equity capital contributed by the RESCO partners, $30 million was provided through the August 1975 sale of industrial development bonds. Under provisions of Massachusetts law,[4] bonds were issued by the Industrial Development Financing Authority of the Town of Saugus, but were not general obligations of the Town. Rather, the bonds were backed solely by the revenues (steam sales and disposal fees) to be derived from the plant and by a mortgage on the facility. Technically, Saugus owns the plant and leases it to RESCO; but, as a practical matter, the Town is merely a vehicle through which tax-exempt financing was secured. RESCO is responsible for operation of the plant and payment of both property taxes and the bonds. Under the lease, RESCO automatically becomes owner of the plant at the end of the 20-year bond payment period.

Although the project was constructed without direct use of public funds, the financing of the plant was designed to take advantage of two types of indirect public support.[5] The use of Industrial Revenue Bonds (for pollution control purposes) rendered the bonds tax-exempt, thus reducing the bond interest rate. The bonds bore an A rating and were sold at an effective interest rate of 7.6 percent, well below the 9.5 percent rate that would have applied to comparably rated corporate bonds. This difference of two percentage points represents approximately $450,000 per year, or roughly $1 per ton on a 1200 ton-per-day (TPD) plant. As a result of its legal status as "tax-owner" of the plant,[6] RESCO is able to take accelerated depreciation and investment tax credits in computing its federal taxes. It is difficult to quantify the benefits of these tax advantages, but their potential impact on the required tipping (disposal) fee charged to the participating communities should not be overlooked.[7]

While construction was underway, negotiations took place between RESCO and a consortium of nine municipalities to determine the conditions of the waste disposal contracts. The Mitre Corp. was consulted (with costs shared by RESCO and the communities) as an independent factfinder to prepare contract provisions that would be acceptable to both parties.[8] To date, 11 communities including the nine consortium members have signed 20-year contracts to deliver refuse to RESCO. The contracts require RESCO to accept the municipalities' solid wastes (with such exceptions as hazardous wastes and construction materials) for a tipping fee of +13 per ton with annual adjustment based on one-half the change in the area wage index and one-fifth the change in local tax rates. Municipalities must pay a premium (penalty) if they deliver more than 110 percent or less than 90 percent of the waste defined as their base tonnage (usually the tonnage from the preceding year).

See Figure 1 for a summary of the institutional relationships that attend the Saugus plant.

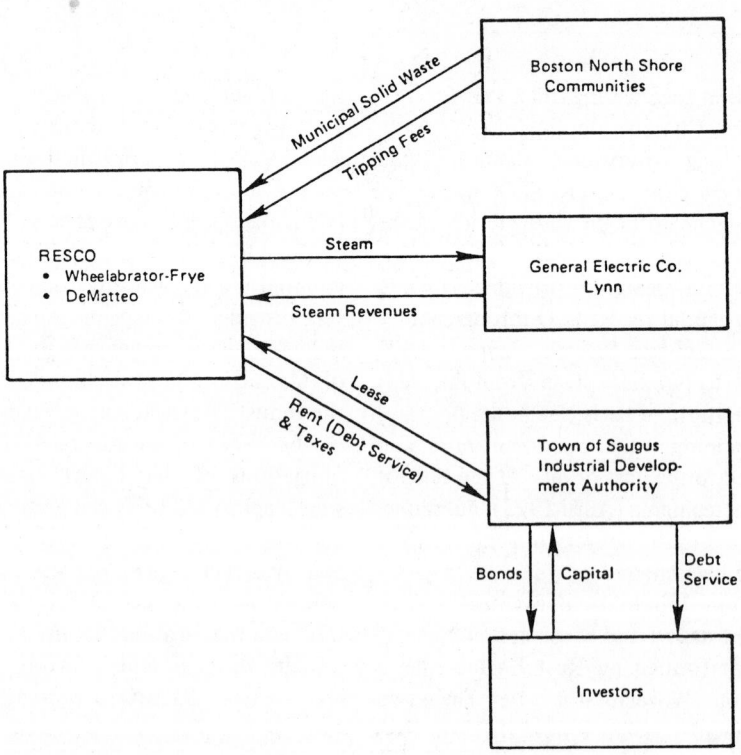

Figure 1. Institutional relationships for Saugus refuse-to-energy plant.

The figure lists the major participants in the Saugus operation, and indicates their interactions in financing and operating the plant.

The plant was completed in the fall of 1975 at a total cost of approximately $0 million, including land, financing costs and startup costs. The first 200 tons of refuse arrived in October 1975, with initial steam delivery in November. Since it opened, the plant has never turned away a truck.[9] Although it was designed to service 16 communities and to handle 1200 TPD, as of April 1977 it was processing about 1000 TPD from 11 surrounding communities and two waste collection districts of the City of Boston.[10] The Boston solid waste is handled under short term (competitive bidding) contracts at a rate of $14.20 per ton.[11] In July 1977, the tipping fee for the other 11 communities will increase to $13.56 based on the adjustment clauses in the long-term contract. Tipping fees at other disposal facilities in the Boston area have been reported to be as high as $18.95 per ton.[12] RESCO plans to pursue additional refuse "supplies" in the near future to bring volume up to 1200 TPD.

BASIC TECHNOLOGY AND PROCESS

The technological foundation for the Saugus plant is the Von Roll proprietary process for waterwall incineration.[13] Von Roll is an experienced designer and operator of refuse-to-energy plants with installations primarily in Europe and Japan. The Saugus facility is the first plant in the U.S. based on the Von Roll process. (Montreal has had a 200 TPD Von Roll plant in operation for seven years and Quebec City opened a Von Roll plant in 1974.)

There are two identical waterwall furnaces in the Saugus plant. Each is rated at a maximum capacity of 750 TPD to produce 185,000 lbs./hr. of steam at 690 psig, 875°F. These furnaces were approximately twice the size of the largest Von Roll furnaces in service at the time the Saugus plant was built.[14]

The process flow through the plant is relatively straightforward. The process steps can be described as follows:

1. Refuse is delivered in trucks, which pass over a weighing scale, back up to the tipping area and discharge into a deep indorr storage pit, capable of storing up to 6700 tons of waste (about five days of solid waste).

2. Refuse is lifted from the storage pit by one of two overhead cranes and transferred to the feeder hoppers serving the two gravity-fed furnaces.

3. Within the furnace, refuse descends along a series of three reciprocating grates separated by steps. The reciprocating action and the steps provide tumbling of the refuse to improve combustion. The uppermost grate is designed to dry the refuse; the middle grate is for initial combustion and the third grate is to complete combustion. No auxiliary fuel is required, although oil burners are available for use in cases of extremely wet refuse. Combustion temperatures are maintained in the range of 1000–1800°F. Under-fire and over-fire air volumes are controlled semiautomatically, as are grate movement speeds. Combustion air is drawn through the tipping area, thus maintaining negative pressure at the tipping entrance and drawing odors into the furnace atmosphere to be destroyed.

4. Heated gases and radiant heat of combustion produce steam in the waterwalls of the incinerator. The gases then pass through the three-stage (superheater, steam generator and economizer) pendant-type boiler tubes to produce more steam.

5. Steam arrives at the G.E. Lynn plant across the Saugus River at 625 psig and 785 - 825°F. The steam, conveyed through a one-half mile piping system, must be delivered 24 hours a day, and seven days a week, at a minimum rate of 65,000 lbs./hr. and a maximum rate of 350,000 lbs./hr.

The steam contract with G.E. calls for minimum delivery of two billion pounds of steam per year (an average of 228,000 lbs./hr.) at 970.3 BTU per pound.[15] At a reported "energy recovery" rate of 67 percent, it would require 885 TPD of solid waste to assure the minimum annual steam delivery rate. At full capacity (1200 TPD), the plant should supply 300,000 lbs./hr. of steam, or a maximum of approximately 2.6 billion pounds of steam per year. During its first year of operation, the Saugus plant processed 250,000 tons of solid waste and produced more than one billion pounds of steam.[16] (Note: Although the plant consists of two furnaces, each rated at a maximum capacity of 750 TPD, the average capacity of the plant itself is 1200 TPD, considering downtime for normal maintenance and repair.)

6. After passing through the boiler sections, combustion gases pass through two-field electrostatic precipatators which remove particulates. These precipitators have been reported to reduce particulate emissions to 0.04 grains per standard cubic foot (gr./scf).[17] This level of emission is below the 0.05 gr./scf standard of the Metropolitan Boston Air Pollution Control District and the 0.08 gr./scf federal standard for new source emissions.[18] Cleaned gases are discharged from a 178-foot-high stack.

7. The bottom ash from the furnace and the collected fly ash are combined, water-quenched and passed through a system to remove ferrous metals. The ash first moves through a trommel with 2 1/2-inch holes. The +2 1/2-inch fraction (approximately 60 percent ferrous metals) proceeds directly from the trommel to a truck reportedly for delivery to a local scrap dealer. The −2 1/2-inch fraction drops through the trommel onto a conveyor which passes under a magnet to remove fine magnetics, which also are delivered to the scrap dealer. The remaining aggregate is landfilled.

SPECIAL FEATURES

Several aspects of the Saugus plant merit special mention.

- Constructed on a landfill, the plant is supported by more than 600 pilings, some driven as far as 80 feet below ground to reach bedrock.
- The plant is equipped with a shredder for bulky wastes, but since a shredder fire in 1976, all wastes have been fed into the furnace without shredding. The furnace has a 22 x 4 foot opening and can accept bulky items.[19] Whenever possible, white goods (refrigerators, stoves, etc.) are kept separate from the other wastes and are sold to a local scrap dealer.[20]

- To assure uninterrupted steam supply, the plant includes standby oil jets in the refuse-fired boilers and two auxiliary oil-fired boilers capable of meeting minimum steam demand in the event of a main furnace shutdown.
- To transfer steam from Saugus to G.E., and condensate, oil and electricity from G.E. to Saugus, a utility bridge was constructed across the Saugus River at a cost of approximately $2 million.
- To reduce corrosion of the boiler tubes, a special rapping mechanism was designed to remove dust and scale from the tubes. After one year of operation, Wheelabrator reports that the rapping has helped reduce corrosion, but no quantitative data are available.[21]
- The plant uses public water supply and discharges any waste water into the public sewerage system. No water is drawn from or discharged into the Saugus River.[22]
- Materials recovery plays a minor role in the Saugus plant. The economics of the plant are based almost entirely on disposal fees and steam charges. At present, bulky and ferro-magnetic metals are recovered from incinerator residue in two metal-rich concentrates. Together, they represent approximately eight percent (by weight) of each incoming ton of waste, and are sold to a local scrap dealer under a short-term contract. Wheelabrator valued the concentrate at $10 per ton in its 1975 Bond Prospectus,[23] suggesting a low quality scrap product. Recovery of aluminum has been investigated but, at present, Wheelabrator reports that aluminum recovery would be uneconomical.[24] The nonmetallic residue has been mentioned as a possible aggregate material for use in Portland cement concrete, bituminous concrete or roadbase;[25] but at present, the material is being landfilled on a portion of the DeMatteo site.
- Under the provisions of the long-term disposal contracts, communities where waste decreases or who wish to institute source separation programs to recover salable materials (newspapers, bottles and cans)

may reduce their base tonnage by as much as five percent per year and may deliver as little as 90 percent of the base tonnage without penalty. For example, if a community delivered 100,000 tons to RESCO during year one of the contract, its base tonnage for year two would be 100,000 tons. If, during the second year, the community started a source separation program, it could deliver as little as 90,000 tons without penalty and could establish 95,000 as the base tonnage for year three. Then, in year three, it could deliver as little as 85,500 tons without penalty. This downward ratcheting of the base tonnage coupled with the 90 percent minimum delivery provision should accommodate a reasonably successful source separation program. In the example, delivery of 85,500 tons during the third year would represent about a 15 percent reduction in disposal tonnage from year one; this is sufficient to accommodate participation rates in the 50 percent range for multimaterial source separation and even higher for newspaper source separation only. There are few examples of source separation programs with participation rates as high as 50 percent.[26]

• One final feature of interest is the status of the Saugus plant as a tax-paying entity. The plant pays approximately $1 million per year in property taxes to the Town of Saugus. This equates to approximately $2.30 per ton at full (1200 TPD) plant capacity. It is interesting to note that for the Town of Saugus, this tax revenue will be more than three times the amount of its disposal payments to RESCO.

CONCLUSION

Against the variety of resource recovery options, the principal characteristics of the Wheelabrator approach, as demonstrated at Saugus, are its reliability and its cost. The Von Roll waterwall incinerator and the Lurgi electrostatic precipitator are proven technologies. As shown during the first year of operation, the Saugus approach is successful at disposing of solid waste, generating steam and meeting financial and environmental commitments.

To understand the success of the project, however, it is also necessary to review the economics of the Saugus facility. As presented in the Bond Prospectus feasibility report,[27] the profitibility of the plant is dependent, to a large extent, on disposal charges (tipping fees). Over the 20 year life of the plant, disposal charges are projected to account for 60 percent of total revenues, while steam sales are to contribute 35 percent, ferrous metals two percent and interest on the Bond Reserve Fund three percent. (It should be noted, however, that the Bond Prospectus appears to be quite conservative in its estimate of steam sale revenues. In the Prospectus, steam price is kept virtually constant throughout the life of the plant, even though the price of steam is tied to the price of oil. Most observers would predict increasing oil prices over the next 20 years). Despite dependency on disposal revenues, the 1976 Saugus tipping fee of $13.00 per ton is very competitive in the Boston area.

In conclusion, it appears that the Saugus plant is ideally suited, both technologically and institutionally, to the problems of the Boston North Shore area. The plant provides disposal at competitive prices for that area. It also provides a reasonably priced and reliable steam supply for the G.E. plant at Lynn. It represents one of the options available for consideration by municipalities in search of a "better way" to dispose of solid waste while tapping a new source of energy.

REFERENCES AND NOTES

1. White, Weld & Co., Inc., *Official Statement: Town of Saugus, Mass. Solid Waste Disposal Revenue Bonds, 1975 Series* (New York: White, Weld & Co., Aug. 7, 1975).

2. Kelliher, W.J., *et al.,* "The Boston North Shore System — A Case Study of a Multi-Community, Privately Financed Refuse Disposal and Energy Recovery System," *Proceedings,* First International Conference on the Conversion of Refuse to Energy, Montreaux, Switzerland, 1975 (New York: Institute of Electrical and Electronics Engineers), pp. 513–524.

3. "Wheelabrator Joins G.E., DeMatteo in $27 Million Refuse-to-Energy Plant," *Solid Waste Report 4*, No. 8 (April 16, 1973): 77.

4. U.S. Congress, House of Representatives Committee on Government Operations, *Solid Waste — Materials and Energy Recovery,* House Report 94-1319, 94th Congress, 2d Session, 1976, P. 11.

5. Stephens, W.C., and R.I. Simon, "An Economic and Financing Model for Implementing Solid Waste Management/Resource Recovery Projects," *Proceedings,* First International Conference on the Conversion of Refuse to Energy, previously cited, pp. 422–427.

6. Ballard, C.A., and R.D. Bain, "Financing Municipal Resource Recovery Systems," *Waste Age, 5,* No. 7 (October 1974): 6–7.

7. For a more detailed discussion of financing alternatives, see: C. Ballard, "Financing Resource and Energy Recovery: A Case Study Approach," *Waste Age, 8,* No. 3 (March 1977): 58, 60, 62, 63, 65.

8. Keliher, previously cited, p. 516.

9. Kehoe, J.M., personal communication, March 28, 1977.

10. *Ibid.*

11. Ahlstrom, T., personal communication, Nov. 3, 1976.

12. Hansen, P.M., "Resource Recovery Through Multi-Materials Source Separation," *Waste Age, 7,* (Oct. 1976): 34.

13. MacAdam, W.K., "Design and Pollution Control Features of the Saugus, Mass Stream Generating Refuse-Energy Plant," *Resource Recovery and Conservation, 1* (1976): 235–243.

14. White, Weld, previously cited, p. B-2.

15. *Ibid,* p. A-10.

16. This 67 percent energy recovery rate is taken from: H.W. Schulz, *et al., Resource Recovery Technology for Urban Decision-Makers* (New York: Columbia University Urban Technology Center, 1976), p. 17. This rate assumes that the energy content of the steam produced is 75 percent of the energy content of the wastes and that 10 percent of the energy in the steam is consumed during "processing." It is not certain that this 10 percent processing loss accurately reflects losses that may occur during transport through the half mile pipeline system at Saugus.

This reported 67 percent energy recovery rate is, however, consistent with steam output projections reported by Wheelabrator-Frye in a paper by W.K. MacAdam (cited previously).

17. Ahlstrom, personal communication, previously cites.

18. For a further discussion of air pollution and resource recovery, see: "Air Pollution from Burning Refuse Fuels," *NCRR Bulletin, 7,* No. 1 (Winter 1977): 15–27.

19. Kehoe, J.M., "RESCO — First Year of Operations," presented at the Fifth National Congress on Waste Management Technology and Resource and Energy Recovery, Dallas, Texas, Dec. 7-9, 1976 (J.M. Kehoe, Jr., Energy Systems Div., Wheelabrator-Frye, Inc.), p. 1.

20. Kehoe, personal communication, previously cited.

21. Ahlstrom, personal communication, previously cited.

22. Papamarcos, J., "Power From Solid Waste," *Power Engineering, 78* (September 1974).

23. White, Weld, previously cited, p. A-23.

24. Kehoe, personal communication, previously cited.

25. Wheelabrator-Frye, Inc., "Spec-Data" sheets for: Refuse Fired Boiler Residue Base and Sub-base Aggregates; Refuse Fired Boiler Residue Aggregate for Portland Cement Concrete; and Refuse Fired Boiler Residue Bituminous Concrete Aggregate; based on test residue from the Von Roll Incinerator in Montreal.

26. The 50 percent participation rate by residents referred to in the test is based on national averages and several assumptions that may not apply in all communities. The following illustration, however, suggests that a 15 percent reduction from 50 percent participation is not unreasonable.

National statistics (EPA's *Third Report to Congress: Resource Recovery and Waste Reduction,* 1975), indicate that household wastes contain 8 percent newspaper, 10 percent glass and 10 percent metal (primarily cans). To accomplish a 15 percent reduction in disposal tonnages through source separation and recovery of these materials would thus require about a 50 percent participation rate. For a further discussion of source separation programs, see, "Source Separation . . . A Resource Recovery Option," *NCRR Bulletin, 7,* No. 1 (Winter 1977): 3–10.

27. White, Weld, previously cited, pp. A.22, 23.

4-6 Air Pollution from Burning Refuse Fuels

James Abert

Source: *NCRR Bulletin,* Vol. VII, No. 1 (Winter 1977) pp. 15–27. Reprinted with Permission of National Center for Resource Recovery.

Combustion is the generally prescribed form for realizing the energy potential in waste. Mass burning incinerators with heat exchangers have performed this function for many years, particularly in Europe.[1] More recently, waste has been preprocessed with the objective of improving its characteristics as a fuel. This processed material — known as refuse-derived fuel (RDF) — has been burned in 100 percent refuse fuel suspension-fired boilers, and as a supplementary fuel in coal-fired utility boilers.[2] There are also plans to burn RDF as a supplemental fuel with oil which, if successful, could broaden the number of applications where the supplemental fuel approach could be realized.[3] RDF has also been further processed to produce a densified, refuse-derived fuel (d-RDF) in pellet or cubette form with characteristics similar to the coal used in stoker boilers. There has only been limited demonstration of this approach to date.[4]

Refuse has even been pulped, converted to a slurry from which the bulk of the inerts have been removed, then dewatered to produce a relatively homogeneous, although high-moisture content, fuel. This material would be combusted in the same manner that the wet bark from the wood products industry is burned for its energy value. The Hempstead, N.Y., project is the principal example of the intended use of this form of refuse fuel.[5] Various conversion processes have been developed to produce from municipal refuse hot gases, as well as gas or oil combustible in its own right.[6] Projects in Baltimore, Md., and South Charleston, W.Va. are two examples of this approach.

This article is concerned with air emissions and control for those applications which involve the direct burning of refuse as a solid fuel, with or without processing, and the use of the hot gases to produce steam. A later article will treat processes for converting refuse to liquid or gaseous fuel.

ASH AND EMISSIONS

Solid waste intrinsically has an ash content; that is, some of the waste is noncombustible. Even the waste that will burn will not combust completely. Paper, for example, is about eight percent ash. During burning, part of the ash component of refuse rises with the hot gases from combustion ("fly ash") and part falls to the bottom of the combustion chamber ("bottom ash"). The completeness of combustion, and hence the amount of ash, is also a function of the type and efficiency of the combustion process. Poor operation, such as running at higher ratios of air to waste than envisioned by the designers, results in both incomplete combustion and greater than anticipated volumes of air going through the air cleaning equipment and up the stack.

That part of the emissions resulting from the burning of waste that is carried along in the hot gases and has a measureable mass is known as *particulate matter,* or fly ash. The amount of particulate matter is, to some extent, sensitive to the temperature of gases. For example, at

500°F there are potential particulates in gaseous form that do not have a measurable mass. They condense to droplets, however, and react chemically to form particulate matter when cooled.

Unprocessed waste, dried and then burned in the laboratory, produces about 29 percent ash, some three-fourths of which is metal and glass. Table 1 identifies 21.34 lbs. per 100 of this material as coming from the metal and glass which, for all practical purposes, are not combustible. Most of the particulate matter comes from the remaining 7.65 lbs. — the "fine ash." This is on a dry weight basis. Using the 28.3 percent moisture figure given, 7.65 lbs. per 100 (dry) becomes 5.48 lbs. per 100 (moist). Hence, for every ton of waste fired — including its moisture — one can expect to generate 109 lbs. of fine ash. This compares to an overall ash content, including the metals and glass, of 416 lbs.[7]

Five factors are the chief determinants of the gross amount of particulates emitted: (1) the refuse composition; (2) the completeness of combustion; (3) the burning rate; (4) the grate system, and (5) the underfire air rate. A rule of thumb of 10–20 percent of the fine ash has been advanced for mass burning incinerators.[8] This would yield 11 to 22 lbs.

of particulate matter issuing from the furnace in the exhaust gas stream for each ton of refuse burned. It is the gas-suspended particulate matter that is the main target for air pollution control. The emission standards that apply for old sources and new facilities burning refuse are discussed in a later section of this article.

Poor combustion of the waste can also result in emission of carbon monoxide and several organic gases as well as particulates; e.g., hydrocarbons, oxygenated hydrocarbons and other complex compounds. No specific point source emission regulations exist for these pollutants. Good operating procedures should minimize their production. Various quantities of inorganic gases such as sulfur oxides and ammonia are also emitted. In addition, the emission of nitrogen oxides may result both from the nitrogen content of the waste and the oxidation of nitrogen in the combustion air. However, no specific federal emission regulations set point source standards for waste incineration in terms of these gases, although nitrogen oxide and sulfur oxides emissions from power plants burning conventional fuel are regulated (see Table 2) and ambient air quality standards exist for most of these gaseous emissions.

Table 1. Refuse Composition (100 lbs. of Dry Solids).

	% Moisture As Received	Wt. Lbs. Dry Basis	Lbs. Ash Dry Basis
Metal	6.6	11.19	10.13
Paper	24.3	45.59	2.74
Plastics	13.8	1.50	0.17
Leather and rubber	13.8	2.05	0.24
Textiles	23.8	2.38	0.08
Wood	15.4	2.96	0.09
Food waste	63.6	9.90	2.17
Yard waste	37.9	10.79	0.54
Glass	3.0	11.32	11.21
Miscellaneous	3.0	2.32	1.62
TOTAL	28.3 average overall	100.00	28.29

Source: Moisture column: W.R. Niessen and S.H. Chansky, "The Nature of Refuse," *Proceedings* of the 1970 National Incinerator Conference (ASME United Engineering Center, New York, N.Y., May 17-20, 1970), p. 8. Weight pounds and pounds ash from: W.R. Niessen and A.F. Sarofim, "Incinerator Air Pollution Facts and Speculation," *Proceedings* of the 1968 National Incinerator Conference (ASME United Engineering Center, New York, N.Y., May 5-8, 1968), p. 168.

Table 2. Federal Point Source Performance Standards for Fossil Fuel-Fired Boilers.

	SO$_2$ lb./10^6 BTU	ppm	NO$_x$ lb./10^6 BTU	ppm	Particulate lb./10^6 BTU
Coal	1.20	520	0.70	525	0.10
Oil	0.80	550	0.30	227	0.10
Gas			0.20	165	

Source: A Bogot and R.C. Sherrill, "Principal Aspects of Converting Steam Generators Back to Coal Firing," *Combustion, 47*, No. 9 (March 1976): 14.

Table 2 also gives the particulate standards. In terms of particulates, for the suspension type boiler 0.10 lb./10^6 BTU is approximately the same as 0.06 grains per standard cubic foot of gas emitted in the exhaust stream.[9] Presumably, the same point source standards would apply to power plants burning RDF along with regular fuel. However, there has been some discussion of relaxing the particulate standards for combined firing of RDF and conventional fuel and an exception governing whether a modification to burn RDF as a supplementary fuel reclassifies an old boiler as a "new source" has already been made. This is discussed in more detail later in this article.

Both nitrogen oxide and sulfur oxide emissions occur in solid waste burning, as shown below.[10] These figures are for refractory incineration, at the furnace exit, and are given in parts per million per volume:

Nitrogen oxides   23 − 25
Sulfur oxides   33 − 40
Hydrogen chloride   455 − 732

However, the amounts per ton of fuel burned are several orders of magnitude below those involved in the combustion of fossil fuel. Solid waste is a "clean fuel" from the standpoint of sulfur content, with a value of about 0.16 percent by weight. Most coals and residual oils used today range from about one-to-three percent sulfur.[11] Further, the alkaline nature of incineration ash causes one to suspect that most of the sulfur is retained in the ash rather than released as oxides in the stack. Thus, sulfur oxide emissions from solid waste burning generally are well below even the most stringent restrictions present or anticipated for heat exchanges of all types.

Restrictions on nitrogen oxide emissions from fossil fuel combustion have been formulated. Nitrogen oxide emissions per ton of fossil fuel are more than 10 times greater than those from burning wastes. It appears unlikely, then, that this contaminant will pose a problem in burning solid waste, either for 100 percent waste or RDF with fossil fuel.

Some concern has been expressed about emissions of hydrogen chloride (HCl) that might occur when waste is burned as a result of the presence of certain plastics, aerosols and food wastes. Hydrogen chloride is toxic to the eyes and respiratory system and if the amounts released during burning were great enough, a health problem would exist. There is also the possibility of corrosion of metal tube surfaces. If HCl emissions become a problem, control will be necessary, but since this gas is highly soluble in water, it can probably be effectively removed by water scrubbers. Also, some of the HCl reacts with particulate matter and can be removed by dry type particulate control systems. In the case of wet control systems, it probably will be necessary to add caustic or other alkaline material to reduce the acidic condition which would otherwise exist.

COLLECTION EQUIPMENT

The oldest and most simple form of particulate collection equipment is the settling chamber, with either a dry or wet bottom. These were the only types of air cleaning equipment used in incinerator plants in the U.S. before 1953 or 1954. Some few plants were also equipped with sprays or baffling within the settling chamber. Beginning in the mid-1950's, incinerators were equipped with batteries of parallel cyclones, which removed some 60-to-65 percent of particulate matter.

About one-fifth of the incinerators built since 1957 use wet scrubbers. In the scrubber, the particulate matter comes into contact with the water spray; the water may be atomized into the gas stream or the gas stream forced through the liquid. The efficiency is said to be in the 94-to-96 percent range. Under certain weather conditions, high water vapor concentrations provide a visible plume at the stack exit. Water vapor plumes are not regulated, but there is the psychological reaction of the public to the visible emission even though it may meet standards. There are also practical considerations, such as icing or fogging of nearby roads and buildings which mitigate against the use of this air cleaning approach in some places.

Most newer incinerators and coal-fired boilers use electrostatic precipitators as the principal means of emission control. Efficiencies in the range of 96-to-99.6 percent have been obtained on coal and oil. Design efficiencies for solid waste incinerators go as high as 98.5 percent. Electrostatic precipitators operate on the principle of electrically charging the suspended particulates and depositing the charged particulates on the surface of a collecting electrode. A high difference of electric potential is maintained between the electrodes in the precipitator, thus establishing a current flow. Potential differences of $12,000 - 30,000$ volts are involved. As particle-laden air passes through the field, suspended particles in the flue gas air stream collide with the charged ions and assume a charge themselves. The force exerted on the charged particles by the electric field causes them to be transported to the collecting electrode, where the charge is neutralized. To remove the particles from the collecting electrode, the collecting surface is vibrated.

Finally, fabric filters, or baghouses, offer a possibility for emission control when solid waste burning is involved. Although they are used extensively in industrial applications, only a few have been used on refuse-burning installations. Fabric filters operate on the same principle as the vacuum cleaner. The predominant filter is the dust cake which forms on the fabric. Cleaning is accomplished by mechanical or air shaking.

CONTROL REGULATIONS

Since 1960, the public has become acutely aware of the effects of pollution on the environment. Prior to 1960 few regulations existed concerning air pollution. Since that time, there has been a succession of regulations regarding the level of allowable emissions, each generally being more stringent than the previous one.

In the absence of other requirements prior to 1960, the guidelines used by combustion engineers and plant operators were those established by the American Society of Mechanical Engineers (ASME). These limited particulate emission to 0.85 lbs. per 100 lbs. of gas at 50 percent excess air. Various state and local codes were passed during the early 1960's. In May 1966, the Secretary of Health, Education and Welfare (HEW) was charged with the prevention, control and abatement of air pollution from federal government activities. These duties were transferred and expanded to the country as a whole with the passage of the Clean Air Act of 1970. The administrator of the U.S. Environmental Protection Agency (EPA) was given the task of promulgating standards for national air quality. A series of standards followed during 1971, the final two differing primarily in what was to be measured and how it was to be measured.[12] The important point is the marked decrease in allowable particulate emissions that took place in approximately one decade. This can be seen in Table 3, where each standard has been developed in common units of measurement. The most recent standards are expressed in the units of column three of the table: grains per standard cubic foot converted to 12 percent CO_2 by volume. Table 4 shows the conversion factors.

As one would expect, the tightening of standards imposed new equipment requirements on facility designers. The 1960 ASME requirements generally could be met with the

Table 3. A Decade of Tightening Emission Standards.

	Lbs./100 Lbs. Flue Gas at 50% Excess Air	Gr./std. Ft.³ at 50% Excess Air	Gr./Std. ft.³ at 12% CO_2	Lbs./Ton of Refuse Charged
1960 ASTM	0.850*	0.442	0.497	9.58
1966 Federal HEW	0.342	0.178	0.200*	3.77
1971 Federal EPA	0.362	0.188	0.212	4.00*
1971 Federal EPA	0.171	0.089	0.100*	1.88
1971 Federal EPA	0.136	0.071	0.080*	1.50

*Standard given in code

Source: Adapted from Greenleaf/Telesca, *Detail Engineering and Economic Report, Solid Waste Collection and Disposal, Metropolitan Dade County, Florida.* (May 1972) Vol. 2, p. V-38.

subsidence chamber baffles and sprays, provided that adequate operating attention was given to the plant. For example, if particulate matter issuing from a refuse-burning furnace averages 11-to-22 lbs. per ton of refuse charged — as was stated earlier — and the conversion factors presented in Table 4 hold, one needs an air cleaning efficiency of 13-to-56 percent to meet the 1960 standard. However, when this standard was in effect quartered, the required efficiency for the final set of 1971 standards rises dramatically to a new range of 86-to-93 percent. This requires the selection of the much more expensive equipment: electrostatic precipitators, baghouse filters or scrubbers.

MASS BURNING

It is not necessary to devote a great deal of space to the question of controlling emissions in the mass burning case. There are a number of installations where this is successfully accomplished, both here and abroad. There are some examples where the initial attempt has not been successful and where the retrofit of more effective equipment has been necessary. There is extensive literature on the subject of controlling emissions in the mass burning case. It will not be discussed here in favor of a more extensive description of the state of knowledge related to combined firing of RDF and conventional fossil fuels (coal and oil).

Table 4. Conversion Factors.

	Lb./ton Refuse	Lbs./100 lbs. Flue Gas at 50% Excess Air	Gr./Std. Ft.³ at 50% Excess Air	Gr./Std. Ft.³ at 12% CO_2
lb./ton Refuse	1.000	0.089	0.047	0.053
lb./100 lb. Flue gas at 50% excess air	11.270	1.000	0.520	0.585
Fr./std. ft.³ at 50% Excess air	21.310	1.930	1.000	1.120
Gr./std. ft.³ at 12% CO_2	18.850	1.710	0.890	1.000

Source: W.R. Niessen and A.F. Sarofim, "Incinerator Air Pollution: Tests and Speculation," *Proceedings* of the 1968 National Incinerator Conference (ASME United Engineering Center, New York, N.Y., (May 5–8, 1968). p. 169.

SUSPENSION FIRING OF RDF WITH COAL

The purpose of this section is to look at the co-firing of refuse-derived fuel with coal or oil in suspension-fired boilers. Data on this subject are quite limited. Burning the refuse fuel on grates is not considered here.

Several characteristics of RDF affect its quality as a fuel. RDF is produced by a size reduction step, generally a large shredder followed by air classification. Often a magnet is introduced between the size reduction step and the air classifier to remove the magnetic metals. The air classifier itself also serves as a metals remover in that its function is to separate the heavy materials from the lights. Almost all lights (paper, film, plastics, yard waste, etc.) are burnable. The heavies, consisting of glass, rock, etc., are more likely to be noncombustible; even if combustible, they would require a longer residence time in the boiler than the configuration of the boiler and its method of operation generally allows. This is because the boiler was designed for its primary fuel and not RDF.

One objective of RDF preparation is *quantity* enhancement; i.e., maximizing the proportion of the burnables in the raw refuse that, after processing, "reports" (in the terminology of air classification) to the fuel fraction. High velocity air classification can increase the amount of the burnable heavies — food wastes, wood, leather and rubber, plastics and textiles that report to the light fraction (fuel). Fine shredding is advocated as a means of reducing the bulk density of these combustibles. However, this approach also increases the proportion of the glass, procelain, pottery and rock which is shattered into particles sufficiently small to likewise report to the light fraction. Therefore, the reader should note that finer shredding and higher velocity air classification — while increasing the proportion of the heating value going to the RDF — increases the probability of ash production. This results from greater amounts of potentially combustible material in the light fraction with a bulk density that is too great to be burned in the particular heat exchange being used, and the likelihood of a greater proportion of nonburnable fines in the fuel fraction.

The alternative is to operate the combined size reduction and air classification steps so as to enhance the *quality* of the RDF. There is a penalty, in that fewer pounds per input ton of waste are delivered as fuel; hence, higher proportions of the waste and, consequently, the waste energy ends up in the landfill. If the production of RDF is seen as a means of alleviating a disposal problem, this concept will have a certain lack of appeal to public works officials.

It should be clear that the quality/quantity trade-off will have to take into account not only the production possibilities for the RDF and the ability of the user to handle increased bottom ash, but also the ability of his air cleaning equipment to control particulate emissions. In respect to the latter, data reported by EPA on the St. Louis demonstration project showed that at rated capacity of the particular boiler used, particulate emissions measured prior to the air cleaning equipment were essentially the same with the combined firing of RDF as when coal was burned alone, even though the ash content of the RDF was 19 percent compared to 7.8 percent for the coal (see Table 5).[13] Characteristics and composition of St. Louis RDF are shown in Tables 6 and 7.

Table 5. Composition of Refuse-Derived Fuel (St. Louis Experience).

Product	As Received % by Weight
Paper	58.9
Plastic	5.4
Wood	2.6
Glass	1.6
Magnetic metal	0.2
Other metal	0.6
Organics	2.9
Miscellaneous	26.2

Source: D. Bendersky, et. al., "St. Louis Refuse Fuel Demonstration Plant — Technical and Economic Performance," *Conference Papers: Conversion of Refuse to Energy*, First International Conference and Technical Exhibition, Montreux, Switzerland, Nov. 3–5, 1975. p.5.

Table 6. St. Louis Coal and RDF Characteristics (As Received).

	Per Pound of Fuel		Per Million BTU	
	Coal	RDF	Coal	RDF
Heat Value (BTU/lb.)	11,000	4900		
Moisture	13%	27%	12 lb.	55 lb.
Ash	7.8%	19%	7.1 lb.	39 lb.
Sulfur	1.2%	0.14%	1.1 lb.	0.29 lb.
Chlorides	0.38%	0.33%	0.34 lb.	0.67 lb.

Source: J.R. Holloway, "EPA Resource Recovery Demonstration: Summary of Air Emission Analyses," *Waste Age*, 7, No. 8 (August 1976): 51.

Table 7. Average Characteristics of Refuse-Derived Fuel (St. Louis Experience).

Heating Value	4900 BTU/lb.
Bulk Density	5.93 lb./ft.^{3}
Shred Size (%)	
Larger than 2 1/2 in.	2.5
Less than 2 1/2 in.	97.5
Less than 1 1/2 in.	94.0
Less than 3/4 in.	73.5
Less than 3/8 in.	49.0

Source: D. Bendersky, et. al., "St. Louis Refuse Fuel Demonstration Plant," p. 5. (See Table V.)

Most observers would agree that the St. Louis fuel fraction was produced with a view toward sending the maximum amount of the received refuse off in the fuel fraction. The overall bulk density and the size distribution of the St. Louis RDF is known (see Table 7). Unfortunately, no measure of the bulk density distribution of the individual particles appears in the literature on the project. However, there must have been a significant proportion of lights with bulk densities which did not permit their combustion during the period they were in suspension because bottom ash, with the combined firing, averaged seven times higher than when coal was fired alone. The data showed that only 87 percent of the potential energy in the RDF was released as heat in the boiler.[14]

The measurements taken prior to the air cleaning equipment for the combined firing show particulate matter emitted ranged from a low of approximately 3.2 lbs. per million BTU to a high of 4.4 lbs. per million BTU. The midpoint is 3.8, the same as the observed value for coal alone. Therefore, the ash emitted by the RDF substituted for coal must be essentially the same absolute amount as that of the coal it replaces. Clearly, since the total ash content of the RDF is much higher than the coal, a much smaller portion of the potential RDF ash must "fly" than the coal it replaced. If like proportions fly, the results could not be as observed. Alternatively, the coal may behave differently in combined firing; for example, some of the ash that would normally fly when coal alone is burned may combine with the uncombusted RDF mentioned earlier and fall with the bottom ash. However, the important point is to estimate the amount of particulate matter likely to be generated as the result of the substitution of RDF for the primary fuel regardless of the phenomenon that might explain it like the combustion theory just advanced.[15]

If all of the heat value of the RDF were used in the boiler, it would take 204 lbs. of RDF to substitute for a million BTU of coal. However, if the 87 percent figure is brought into play, only 4263 BTU per lb. of RDF fired are realized. This means that 235 lbs. of RDF are required to substitute for a million BTU of coal. At 19 percent ash, 44.65 lbs. of potential fly ash are injected into the boiler to realize a million BTU. The basic figures used here are shown in Tables 6 and 7. If, then, one uses the midpoint observed value of 3.8 lbs. of fly ash per million BTU, he will find that 8.5 percent of the total ash in the substituted RDF flies. The range using the upper observed value of 4.4 lbs. and the lower value of 3.2 would be plus or minus 15 percent or from a low of 7.2 percent to a high of 9.8 percent. Intermediate figures of interest are .01617 pounds of fly ash per lb. of RDF charged and 32.34 lbs. of fly ash per ton of RDF charged.

While this derivation appears to be rather straightforward, other methods of calculation produce different figures, generally higher. For example, one source shows a figure of 16 percent for the fraction of refuse ash which becomes fly ash when computed on the basis of a particular estimating equation.[16] The fact that this value is higher than the percent figure developed here is partially explained by the difference in base. The lower figure takes into account the noncombustion of 13 percent of the waste. Nevertheless, the state of the practice is accurately summed up in the following quote from the same source as the 16 percent figure:

There is no accepted design method for calculating particulate fly ash from combined suspension firing of refuse and conventional fuels. Control device sizing and performance valuation is, therefore, somewhat a stochastic procedure. Estimates for the fraction of refuse ash which ultimately becomes fly ash range from about .13 up to .50, according to various sources. Estimates determined from the analysis of actual test data range from .13 to .35.

Air Cleaner Impact

Because of the degree of air cleaning necessary for all coal and even most oil-fired boilers to meet air pollution standards, one can expect boilers with the capacity to burn significant amounts of RDF to be equipped with electrostatic precipitators (ESP). ESP collection efficiency is a function of (1) fly ash particle size; (2) ESP power input; (3) the individual particles' resistance to being electrically charged, and (4) the exhaust gas flow rate. According to the data developed at St. Louis, when RDF was fired with coal, each of these parameters except ash size changed so as to decrease the effectiveness of the installed ESP system. However, at rated boiler capacity, the ESP outlet (i.e., controlled) particulate emissions were approximately 0.15 lbs. per million BTU for combined firing, which was the same as for coal fired alone. This is an ESP efficiency of approximately 96 percent. Put differently, using the figure of 3.8 lbs. of particulate gen-

erated and arriving at the air cleaner inlet per million BTU — the average figure used earlier in the text — all but 0.15 lbs. were removed by the air cleaning system.[17]

The EPA requirement for "new source" coal or oil burning power plants is a maximum particulate emission of 0.10 lbs. per million BTU fired. As stated earlier, this is approximately the equivalent of 0.06 grains per standard cubic foot. If it had to meet the new source standard, the St. Louis plant would have needed air cleaning equipment capable of 97.4 percent efficiency, using the average figure of 3.8 lbs. of particulates generated per million BTU. For 4.4 lbs., the needed efficiency is 97.8 percent and for 3.2 lbs. it is 96.9 percent. This describes the range. However, as a result of an EPA ruling discussed later, the St. Louis plant — and others making similar conversions — are not reclassified as new sources as a result of the modifications to burn RDF. A "new source" is defined as one where construction or modification commenced after August 17, 1971. Old or "existing" sources are boilers which were built before that date. Even if, subsequent to August 17, 1971, they are modified to burn RDF, they will not need to meet the federal point source standards.

RDF, d-RDF AND STOKER FIRING WITH COAL

The previous section has discussed the burning of RDF in suspension. An alternative to this is the burning of the material principally on grates, in RDF form or densified so as to form a cube or pellet similar to lump coal.[18] The former approach has been demonstrated in Columbus, Ohio. The Ames, Iowa, project is multi-purposed in that it includes both burning RDF on grates and in suspension fired boilers. Finally, the National Center is participating in an extensive project researching the preparation and burning of d-RDF under EPA sponsorship. Burning investigations began in December 1976.

In the Columbus project, the material was blown into the boiler rather than being mechanically fed in with the coal as is sometimes the case. Ames follows the Columbus format. There is some data available on particulate and other discharges from the combined firing in Columbus. A point of this project was to look at the impact of firing low-sulfur refuse with various sulfur content coal to dilute and reduce overall SO_2 emissions; this was accomplished to some extent. Combined firing was effected with as high as 45 percent RDF by weight (30 percent by heat value). Unfortunately, in terms of particulate emissions, the base line data for coal alone is not comparable to the data taken on combined firing. However, the reports show the particulate from combined firing with only cyclones as emission control equipment to have been 0.65, 0.45 and 0.52 grains per standard cubic foot, depending on the percent of refuse fired and the type of coal being used. In pounds per million BTU, the measurements were 1.41, 0.90 and 1.09 respectively. To bring the 1.41 figure down to the 0.10 new source standard for boilers firing coal, additional air pollution control equipment with an efficiency of 93 percent would have to be added.[19] No data is available yet from the Ames boiler.[20]

RDF AND OIL

Although RDF has not been burned with oil, it is possible to estimate the potential impact on particulate matter. The text below develops an example using a 10 percent RDF heat contribution. The BTU rating of the boiler is 970×10^6 BTU/hr. Using the St. Louis numbers, RDF is assumed to have a heating value of 4900 BTU/lb. The heating value of the oil is given at 143,369 BTU/gal. The example illustrates how to estimate the emissions expected from the combined firing and hence to made a judgment as to whether or not the installed pollution control equipment could be expected to handle the discharge. From a financial standpoint, the answer to this question is one of the most significant factors in determining whether to adopt an RDF option.[21]

Steps in the Calculation of Required Air Pollution Control Efficiency:

1. 10 percent RDF burned = 97×10^6 BTU/hr.

2. At 4900 BTU/lb. RDF, there are 9.8 million (9.8×10^6) BTU/ton. If all of the combustibles burned, 9.9 tons of RDF per hour would be needed to meet the 97×10^6 BTU/hr. requirement. However, if the combustion follows the St. Louis experience, only 87 percent of the available energy is utilized. Therefore, 11.4 tons of RDF per hour must be charged to the boiler to meet the heat release requirement.

3. 90 percent oil = 873×10^6 BTU/hr. from oil.

4. At 143,369 BTU/gal., 6089 gallons are necessary.

5. Pre-aircleaner particulate emissions from 100 percent oil burning were measured as 0.093 lbs./million BTU.

6. Oil emissions in the 90 percent case are 0.093 lbs./10^6 BTU $\times 873 \times 10^6$ BTU/hr. = 81.2 lbs./hr.

7. According to St. Louis data, there are 32.34 lbs. of fly ash per ton of refuse charged.

8. RDF emissions (uncontrolled) then are 32.34 lbs./ton $\times$ 11.4 tons/hr. = 368.7 lbs./hr.

9. Total emissions are 81.2 lbs./hr. from the oil + 368.7 lbs./hr. from RDF = 449.9 lbs./hr.

10. Converting to lbs./million BTU, 449.9 lbs./hr. ÷ 970 million BTU/hr. gives an estimate of 0.464 lbs. of particulate/million BTU emitted

11. To bring this to the new source standard of 0.10 lbs./million BTU involves solving the equation: lbs./million BTU generated $\times$ (1.00 − efficiency) = lbs./million BTU emitted from the stack.

12. This yields a required efficiency of 78.4 percent.

It should be clear that using higher figures for the proportion of ash flying from the combustion of the RDF and higher RDF proportions will bring about the necessity for higher air pollution control efficiencies. Also, it should be pointed out that oil-fired units do not generally have very efficient control equipment simply because they do not need them to meet standards. This is because of the low particulate generation rate of the basic fuel. There are many boilers that burn both oil and coal where the air pollution equipment is designed to meet standards when the boiler is on coal.

It is known that units designed with efciencies of 95-to-98 percent on coal fly ash only achieve 60-to-70 percent when oil is fired. The estimate for oil and RDF is 70-to-85 percent.[22] This brackets the efficiency required to meet the 0.10 lbs. per million BTU figure developed in the example. It is important to place the example in a context which reflects a great many of the real world opportunities for combined oil and RDF burning. The efficiency of presently installed oil-firing air pollution control systems, while sufficient for oil, probably will not be capable of handling the RDF. However, if the air pollution controls are designed for coal firing, they may be sufficient to handle RDF as either a partial coal replacement or as a mixture of RDF and oil.

STANDARDS FOR COMBINED FIRING

As the text has illustrated, there are standards for conventional incinerators, i.e., those which fire 100 percent solid waste with only occasional use of auxiliary fuel for startup or to aid combustion when the refuse is wet. As described earlier, there are separate and different standards for conventional fossil fuel boilers. The reader should note that the modification of an old boiler has generally meant that it would then fall under new source standards. Therefore, early on, there was the question as to whether this would be the case when old boilers — defined as those constructed or modified prior to August 17, 1971 — were modified to burn a combination of solid waste and conventional fuel.

In 1974, EPA decided that the modification of boilers to burn waste in combination with fossil fuel would not mean a reclassification; therefore, the boilers do not have to comply with the new federal source standards. They would, however, remain regulated by the State Implementation Plans, and continue to be subject to standards promulgated by local authorities. The latter have been developed to allow communities to meet ambient air standards. In this regard, maximum allocations for each point source are set with respect to ambient conditions rather than in terms of a national standard for a particular type of emitter. In many cases, point source standards set at the local or state level are somewhat more liberal than the new source figure.

In addition, EPA's Office of Solid Waste Management Programs (now the Office of Solid Waste) and the Emissions Standards and Engineering Division of EPA's Office of Air Quality Planning and Standards took up the question of emissions standards for combined firing of coal and solid waste in boilers that are classified as new sources and which were either originally designed or subsequently modified to burn waste in combination with fossil fuels. A target date for formal proposal of these standards was early 1976. As of this writing, they have not been published.[23]

Current thinking has particulate standards based on a linear sliding scale for combined firing at various percentages of coal and solid waste. At one end of the scale, for 100 percent coal and zero solid waste, the standard would be 0.10 lbs. per million BTU of heat input. That represents the same point at EPA's new source performance standards for fossil fuel-fired steam generators. At the other end of the scale — for zero coal and 100 percent solid waste — the standard would be 0.18 lbs. per million BTU, or about the same as incinerator standards of 0.08 grains per standard cubic foot, corrected to 12 percent CO_2 assuming the solid waste being burned has 5000 BTU per lb. and is burned with approximately 50 percent excess air. For oxides of sulfur and nitrogen, the standard for combined firing would be the same as EPA new source performance standards for fossil fuel-fired generators, held constant for any solid waste percentage.

COST IMPLICATIONS OF AIR POLLUTION CONTROL

Many candidate boilers for supplemental firing of RDF or d-RDF will require modifications in terms of feeding systems, bottom ash handling equipment and more efficient air pollution control devices. The latter is particularly true for those boilers which were initially constructed solely for coal burning, but were later shifted from coal to oil (which produces less particulate and sulfur) when it appeared that this was more economical than having to add air pollution control equipment capable of meeting the ever-tightening emission standards. With the increased price of oil, many boiler owners are re-evaluating these decisions. Some are shifting back to coal, making the necessary capital investment to add air pollution control devices and rehabilitating their bottom ash handling capability. In fact, some boilers which were designed specifically for oil or gas are being given a coal burning capability.[24]

There is an opportunity to consider the supplemental burning of RDF or d-RDF in instances such as those described above. The purpose of this section is to develop some of the economic factors bearing in such a decision. The prime focus of the section is on the trade-off between RDF cost – both positive and negative – and the cost of the required boiler modifications, where the principal modification is assumed to be the outlay on air pollution control equipment. The terminology *positive* and *negative* refers to the fact that a user may pay for or be paid for burning refuse-derived fuel. One would expect that to pay for fuel would be the general case; however, there appear to be situations where the location of the fuel user's facility is such that a community may determine that the cost of paying a fuel user is less than the cost of transporting the refuse to a disposal site. If, as one might expect, the cost of gasoline and diesel oil continues to rise more rapidly than other prices, greater numbers of cities whose disposal sites are remote from the center of refuse generation

could find themselves in such a situation. Even now, it appears that if a community were paying more than $15/ton for disposal, it could afford to produce RDF at, say, $8/input ton of waste and with 60 percent of the waste by weight converted to fuel, pay the power company on the order of $1/input ton rather than dispose of the raw waste at a distant landfill site. This is $1.67 per ton of RDF – in round numbers, 17¢ per million BTU. This is where the power company has a facility downtown with adjacent land available where the refuse fuel could be produced. Hence, there is the possibility of a negatively priced fuel.

One should ask, when evaluating a situation such as this, what investment will fuel cost savings of different magnitudes support? Table 8 shows the capitalized value factors for varying combinations of internal rate of return and number of years amortized. The purpose of the table is to provide a means of evaluating in a generalized sense the worth in capital outlay terms of fuel cost savings. The use of the factors is developed in the example below.

With the factors from Table 8 in hand, assume further that RDF or d-RDF yields 10 million BTU per ton of fuel delivered. Hence, in a situation where 200 tons of refuse fuel were burned per day, 365 days per year, this would mean 73,000 tons per year or 730,000 million BTU per year. If, for illustrative purposes, the fuel cost savings were $1.00 per million BTU, then there is $730,000 available annually to offset capital outlays. To illustrate the magnitude of the capital outlay on air pollution equipment this could support, choose, for example, the 10 percent internal rate return, 15 years factor from Table 8. Multiplying this by $730,000 gives a figure of $5,552,380. (The reader should note that no allowance was made for covering operating costs which might be associated with the use of the RDF or

Table 8. Capitalized Value Factors.

Internal Rate of Return	Amortized Over		
	10 yrs.	15 yrs.	20 yrs.
5%	7.722	10.380	12.462
10%	6.145	7.606	8.514
15%	5.019	5.847	6.259
20%	4.192	4.675	4.870

d-RDF. This would, of course, have to be taken into account.)

Cost of Burning RDF

A recent study performed by Arthur D. Little Co. for EPA investigated the cost of burning RDF as a supplemental fuel.[25] While the cost estimating relationship presented there is not specific to any one installation, it serves for general feasibility calculations. According to the A.D. Little study, the capital cost of an electrostatic precipitator for a boiler which does not already have such a device is 61.3 times the design hourly steam ouput measured in pounds after the latter is raised to the .72 power. Annual maintenance costs are two percent of capital costs while power is one cent per 1000 lbs. of steam generated. Therefore, a 100,000 lb./hr. boiler run 8000 hours per year that did not currently have air pollution control equipment could expect a capital cost outlay of $244,000. However, the A.D. Little figures represent costs about seven years ago. Escalating the $244,000 for seven years at seven percent would bring it to slightly under $400,000. Amortized at 15 years at eight percent, this is roughly $42,700 per year. Adding $8000 for maintenance and $8000 for power, total annual costs would be $58,700.

If 1000 BTU is one lb. of steam at 100 percent efficiency, and if one assumes that a typical boiler has a 70 percent efficiency, then a 100,000 lb./hr. boiler producing 800 million lbs. of steam per year would use 1,144,000 million BTU per year. Assume, then, that 20 percent of this is derived by burning RDF; i.e., 228,800 million BTU. At 10 million BTU per ton of RDF, this is 22,800 tons of RDF, provided that all of the potential energy were realized. If RDF must bear the entire costs, the figures are approximately $2.56 per input ton of RDF of 26¢ per million BTU. Thus, in this example, RDF would have to be priced at least 26¢ per million BTU below competing fuels in order to offset the added costs of pollution controls.

Returning to the basic theme of this section, an important point is that shifting a portion of a user's fuel needs from his regular fuel to refuse fuel can generate savings. How much, of course, depends on the price of the refuse fuel and the price of the regular fuel. If the regular fuel is $1.00 per million BTU and refuse fuel is priced at zero, then after paying for the air pollution control, one achieves a dollar savings of $1 minus $0.26 or $0.74 per million BTU. Alternatively, a regular fuel price of $0.09 per million BTU and a refuse disposal fee paid by the community to the user equivalent to the $0.17 per million BTU mentioned previously would amount to a break-even situation for the community and exactly compensate the user for the air pollution controls. Of course, there are other costs involved in RDF firing and ash disposal.[26]

Paying for Equipment

A question that arises here is to what extent should the refuse fuel be expected to pay for the air pollution control equipment. This would depend on whether the added equipment is solely for refuse burning or whether the modification is being made in conjunction with a shift in basic fuel type or a simple upgrade of a facility that is not in compliance with regulations. Perhaps the optimum circumstances for refuse fuel is when a basic fuel shift is being made; then, refuse would only be expected to support the investment in air pollution control equipment in proportion to its share of the particulate matter generated. Of course, one must take into account any degradation of equipment performance brought about by the use of refuse as a fuel. The same rationale would apply to feed and storage systems as well as to bottom ash handling equipment.

Investments

The "Internal Rate of Return" term refers to private sector investment decision-making, including public utilities where the rate is regulated with the maximum set at somewhere between 15 and 20 percent. A point to be made here involves the value of funding capital outlays through public or quasi-public financial mechanisms, where the rate is lower. The investment usually is tax-free to actual pro-viders of funds so they are willing to invest their savings at lower interest rates than if they had to pay taxes on their earnings. Further, the security behind the investment is often the taxing power of the public sector which also generally serves to reduce the interest rate that must be paid to induce investors to offer their savings for use in a project. As can be seen from the table, the lower the interest rate, the greater the amount of initial capital outlay that can be supported by a given annual stream of savings.

It should be noted that the application of fuel savings to the support of capital outlays, which has been the principal thesis of the above discussion, runs counter to the way fuel cost changes are handled in most states where fuel cost increases and decreases are passed through directly to the consumer. The re-quirement to "pass through" diminishes the attractiveness of using refuse fuel. In other words, there is no direct incentive for the management of a utility to take whatever risk might be associated with this new fuel source. The approach described here may have more appeal.

SUMMARY

Clearly, refuse has energy potential, with a significant portion of any given ton being combustible. However, burning waste, like the burning of traditional fossil fuels, involves the generation and emission of various gases and particulate matter, which by law must be controlled. There is little mystery to control-ling emissions from 100 percent waste-burning installations built exclusively for the purpose of energy recovery from waste. The extent of the emissions and the degree of effectiveness of currently installed air pollution control equipment are key elements in any decision to substitute refuse for traditional fuels in an existing boiler. Precise knowledge is lacking in each of these areas, particularly where the feasibility of the combined firing of oil and RDF is the issue. To some extent, this also applied to the design of new air pollution control equipment either to be added to old

fossil fuel boilers to enable them to burn a combination of RDF and traditional fuel or to develop a new plant for this purpose. Future articles in the *NCRR Bulletin* will report on the progress made in resolving these issues.

REFERENCES AND NOTES

1. For the U.S. experience, see: "Can Nashville Thermal Live Up to Its Original Promise?" *Resource Recovery and Energy Review, 3,* No. 2 (March/April 1976): 10–12.

    Kelliher, W.J., et. al., "The Boston North Shore System – A Case Study of a Multi-Com-munity, Privately Financed Refuse Disposal and Energy Recovery System," conference paper: *Conversion of Refuse to Energy,* First Interna-tional Conference and Technical Exhibition, Montreux, Switzerland, Nov. 3–5, 1975 (hereafter cited as *Conversion of Refuse to Energy.)*

    MacAdam, W.K., "Design and Pollution Con-trol Features of the Saugus, Massachusetts Steam Generating Refuse-Energy Plant," *Resource Re-covery and Conservation, 1,* No. 3 (April 1976): 235–244.

    McEwen, Laurence B., and Steven J. Levy, "Can Nashville's Story be Placed in Perspective?" *Solid Wastes Management, 19,* No. 8 (August 1976): 24.

    Schulz, Helmut W., et. al., *Resource Recovery Technology for Urban Decision-Makers* (New York: Columbia University, Urban Technology Center, for the National Science Foundation, January 1976). 118 pp.

    Engdahl, R.B., *Identification of Technical and Operating Problems of Nashville Thermal Transfer Corporation Waste-to-Energy Plant.* U.S. Energy Research and Development Administration and Battelle Columbus Laboratories, Feb. 25, 1976. 28 pp.

    For Ontario, which preprocesses the waste, see: "The East Hamilton Solid Waste Reduction Unit – SWARU," *Waste Age, 6,* No. 3 (March 1975): 22–27.
2. See: "Ames, Iowa, Brings Resource Recovery to Small Town America," *Solid Wastes Man-agement, 18,* No. 11 (November 1975): 20.

    Chantland, Arnold O., and Harvey Funk, "Ames, Iowa, Opens Recovery System: Refuse Derived Fuel to be Used by City," *Waste Age, 6,* No. 10 (October 1975): 24–30.

    Funk, Harvey D., and Arnold O. Chantland, "Solid Waste for Power Generation Fuel in a Small City," in *Conversion of Refuse to Energy, op cit.,* pp. 268–273.

    Klumb, David, "Union Electric Company's Solid Waste Utilization System," *Resource Re-covery and Conservation, 1,* No. 3 (April 1976): 225–234.

Lacke, Jay C., "The Americology Approach to Resource Recovery," presented at a Steel Can Recycling Seminar, Hunt Valley, Md., Sept. 23, 1975.

Solid Waste Management and Disposal System for the City of Milwaukee, Wisconsin. Final report, De Leuw, Cather and Co., Chicago, April 1975. 338 pp.

"Solid Waste Recycling Program . . . A Report from Wisconsin," *NCRR Bulletin, 4,* No. 4 (Fall 1974): 7-11.

3. For further information, see: Canzano, Pasquale S., "The Delaware Reclamation Project," presented at the Second Annual Conference, Solid Waste Management, Worcester Polytechnic Institute, Jan. 11, 1973.

Lingle, Stephen A., "Demonstrating Resource Recovery," *Waste Age, 7,* No. 6 (June 1976): 45.

4. "Densified Refuse-Derived Fuel," *NCRR Bulletin, 6,* No. 1 (Winter 1976): 4-9.

Elo, Heikki K., and F. Robert Rhodes, "Solid Waste Fuel Pellets Provide Fuel Supplement," *Pollution Engineering, 8,* No. 2 (February 1976): 32-33.

Rigo, H.G., *Technical Evaluation of the Feasibility of Burning Eco-Fuel at Philadelphia Naval Shipyard.* Naval Facilities Engineering Command and the Army Construction Engineering Research Laboratory, Champaign, Ill., January 1974. 55 pp.

Rigo, H.G., and S.A. Hathaway, *Technical Evaluation Study: Energy-Recovery Solid Waste Incineration at Naval Station Mayport, Florida.* Army Construction Engineering Research Laboratory, Champaign, Ill., February 1975. 61 pp.

Rigo, H.G., *et al., Technical Evaluation Study: Solid Waste Heat Reclamation at Naval Air Test Center Patuxent, Maryland.* Army Construction Engineering Research Laboratory, Champaign, Ill., November 1974. 45 pp.

5. Arella, David G., *Recovering Resources from Solid Waste Using Wet Processing. A Summary Report.* U.S. Environmental Protection Agency and the City of Franklin, Ohio, 1974.

Landman, W.J., and W.J. Darmstadt, "Energy Recovery from Solid Waste," in *Conversion of Refuse to Energy, op cit.,* pp. 589-595.

For wood waste, see: Brown, Owen D., "Energy Generation from Wood Waste," *District Heating Magazine, 59,* No. 1, (July/August 1973): 109-122.

6. For further information see: Weinstein, Norman J., and Charanjit Rai, "Pyrolysis/State of the Art," *Public Works, 106,* No. 4 (April 1975): 83-86.

Fisher, T.G., M.L. Kasbohm and J.R. Rivero, "Purox System" in *Clean Fuels from Biomass Sewage, Urban Refuse, Agricultural Wastes.* Symposium Papers presented in Jan. 27-30, 1976, Institute of Gas Technology, Chicago, pp. 447-459.

Flanagan, B.J., "Pryolysis of Domestic Refuse with Mineral Recovery," in *Conversion of Refuse to Energy, op cit.,* pp. 220-225.

Levy, Steven J., "The Conversion of Municipal Solid Waste to a Liquid Fuel by Pyrolysis," in *Conversion of Refuse to Energy, op cit.,* pp. 226-231.

Zulver, Elliot, and Edsel D. Stewart, "A Full Scale Refuse Pyrolysis System for Baltimore, Maryland," in *Conversion of Refuse to Energy, op cit.,* pp. 238-243.

Levy, Steven J., *San Diego County Demonstrates Pyrolysis of Solid Waste.* U.S. Environmental Protection Agency, Environmental Grant No. S-80158, Washington, D.C., 1975.

Lingle, Stephen A., "Baltimore Pyrolysis and Waste-Fired Steam Generator Emissions," *Waste Age, 7,* No. 7 (July 1976): 6-9, 77.

Sussman, David B., *Baltimore Demonstrates Gas Pyrolysis,* U.S. Environmental Protection Agency, Grant No. S-801533, Washington, D.C., 1975.

7. The listed value is 20.8, which times 2000 produces the 416 lb. figure. W.R. Niessen and S.H. Chansky, "The Nature of Refuse," *Proceedings* of the 1970 National Incinerator Conference (ASME United Engineering Center, New York, N.Y., May 17-20, 1970). p. 8.

8. Niessen, W.R., and A.F. Sarofim, "Incinerator Air Pollution Facts and Speculation," *Proceedings* of the 1968 National Incinerator Conference (ASME United Engineering Center, New York, N.Y., May 5-8, 1968), p. 174.

9. Bogot, A., and R.C. Sherrill, "Principal Aspects of Converting Steam Generators Back to Coal Firing," *Combustion, 47,* No. 9 (March 1976): 13. Hence 1.67 times the particulate discharge measured in grains gives an estimate in pounds per million BTU. For stoker-fired units engineers generally multiply the grain loading by 2.2 to obtain an estimate of the particulate discharge in pounds per million BTU (for 12,000 BTU coal and 50 percent excess air). From conversation with H.H. Krause of Battelle Columbus Laboratories.

10. Kaiser, E.R., and A.A. Carotti, *Municipal Incineration of Refuse with 2% and 4% Additions of Four Plastics.* As presented here, the data are taken from Norman J. Weinstein and Richard F. Toro, *Thermal Processing of Municipal Solid Waste for Resource and Energy Recovery* (Ann Arbor, Mich.: Ann Arbor Science, 1976), p. 151.

11. U.S. Environmental Protection Agency, *Municipal Scale Incinerator Design and Operation* (formerly titled *Incinerator Guidelines – 1969*), 1973, p. 57.

12. The 0.080 standard does not include those materials which are in a gaseous state at the temperature at which they would be discharged from the furnace, but would condense to a liquid when cooled to normal temperatures. According to Greenleaf/

Telesca, "these generally amount to but a small part of the allowable particulate emission." Presumably, this accounts for the difference between 0.100 when these are controlled and the 0.08 when they are not. See E.F. Gilardi and H.F. Schiff, "Comparative Results of Sampling Procedures Used During Testing of Prototype Air Pollution Control Devices at New York City Municipal Incinerators," in *Proceedings* of the 1972 National Incinerator Conference (ASME United Engineering Center, New York, N.Y., 1972), p. 109.

13. Holloway, J.R., "EPA Resource Recovery Demonstration: Summary of Air Emission Analyses," *Waste Age, 7,* No. 8 (August 1976): 52. See also: Kilgroe, J.D., L.J. Shannon, and P.G. Gorman, "Emission and Energy Conversion from Refuse Processing and Mixed Fuel Boiler Firing," in *Conversion of Refuse to Energy, op cit.,* pp. 190–196. Shannon, L.J. and P.G. Gorman, *Union Electric Coal-Refuse Firing Boiler: Compilation of Environmental Test Results, October 1974 to July 1975.* (Kansas City, Mo.: Midwest Research Institute, July 1975).

14. See: *St. Louis Demonstration Project, Final Report* (Draft), Vol. II: "Power Plant Equipment Facilities and Environmental Evaluations"(Kansas City, Mo.: Midwest Research Institute, July 1976), p. 6. See also: Fiscus, D.E., P.G. Gorman and J.D. Kilgroe, *Bottom Ash Generation in a Coal-Fired Power Plant When Refuse-Derived Fuel is Used.* Paper presented at the ASME Solid Waste Processing Conference, Boston, Mass., May 23–26, 1976. 13 pp. (mimeographed). Available from D.E. Fiscus, Midwest Research Institute,425 Volker Blvd., Kansas City, Mo. 64110.

15. If the boiler is operated above rated capacity as is often the case, the test results measured prior to the air cleaning equipment are scattered. Four of the six combined firing observations show less particulate than the single base line coal observations. Two combined firings show more.

16. U.S. Environmental Protection Agency, *Performance of Emission Control Devices on Boilers Firing Municipal Solid Waste and Oil.* Environmental Protection Technology Series, Publication No. EPA 600/2-76-209. (Research Triangle Park, N.C. 27711: Industrial Environmental Research Laboratory, Office of Research and Development, July 1976), pp. 16–17.

17. Above rated capacity all six observations of the combined firing discharge were greater than the coal alone discharge base observation. Two were almost twice as large.

18. The Black Clawson wet pulping system approach is not discussed in this article.

19. Battelle Laboratories, *Environmental Effects of Utilizing Solid Waste as a Supplementary Power Plant Fuel.* Report to EPA Industrial Environmental Research Laboratory, Cincinnati. (Columbus, Ohio: Battelle Laboratories, 505 King Ave., Columbus 43201), p. 27. The grains per standard cubic foot figures came from the reference cited. The pounds per million figures were provided by H.H. Krause of Battelle. The conversion factor here averages 2.085 which is lower than the 2.2 suggested in reference 9.

20. A limited burning test of d-RDF and gas has been accomplished by the Wisconsin Solid Waste Recycling Authority. Emissions were well within the 0.3 lbs. per million BTU limit which pertains to the boiler used. (For information contact Warren Porter, Director of Engineering and Operations, Wisconsin Solid Waste Recycling Authority, 3321 West Beltline Highway, Madison, Wis. 53713.)

21. For approaches different from the one presented here, indeed different answers, see: *Performance of Emission Control Devices on Boilers Firing Municipal Solid Waste and Oil,* cited in reference 16.

22. *Performance of Emission Control Devices on Boilers Firing Municipal Solid Waste and Oil, op cit.,* p. 3.

23. Recently, new regulations have been promulgated to encourage the burning of wood waste in power plants burning conventional fuels. Previously, the heat contribution of the supplementary fuel was not counted in terms of determining whether the boilers met standards. The point at issue is blending wood residue with high sulfur fossil fuel to obtain a fuel mixture low enough in sulfur to comply with the sulfur dioxide standard. The overall particulate standard per million BTU has not been relaxed, however.

24. Bogot, A., and R.C. Sherrill, "Principal Aspects of Converting Steam Generators Back to Coal Firing," *Combustion, 47,* No. 9 (March 1976): 10–17.

25. Arthur D. Little Co., *Study of the Feasibility of Federal Procurement of Fuel Produced from Solid Waste* (July 1975), 255 pp. Available from the U.S. Department of Commerce, National Technical Information Service, PB-255-695. The A.D. Little study also provides data on the estimated costs of refuse receiving and preparation systems and storage and firing costs for several approaches to refuse burning for stoker-fired boilers. The study looks in less detail at suspension-fired, utility-type boilers.

26. According to Figure 3.1.1.5.3-1, page 3.27 of the A.D. Little study previously cited, a 63.5 ton-per-day system such as is illustrated here could expect to incur a cost of approximately $0.50 per million BTU for receiving, preparation, storage and firing. This covers capital cost and operating costs. It should be noted that costs increase rapidly as tons per day are decreased. For example, at 200 tons per day the estimate is $0.23 per million BTU.

4-7 Pre-Burn Separation Should Limit Metal Emissions

Stephen Law, Benjamin Haynes, and William J. Campbell

Source: *Waste Age,* Vol. 9, No. 9 (September 1978) pp. 51–59. Reprinted with Permission of National Solid Wastes Management Association.

If God had wanted metal to fly, He would have made parakeets eat ore instead of gravel. But traces of metal sometimes waft into the atmosphere anyway, from facilities that burn RDF or raw refuse. Pre-burn separation of certain waste elements should reduce this pollution.

In their familiar forms, metals are massive. If you punch a block of zinc, you hurt your hand, but the zinc goes nowhere (unless it falls on your foot so you also hurt your toes), Thus, its often difficult to sympathize with the environmentalist's worry that metals from waste processing will escape into the ecosphere. How could the block of zinc "escape" anything, unless propelled by a cannon?

But metals manifest themselves in forms other than bars and ingots. They form salts, powders, and other trace-carriers that can easily sift into ash or residues, or even waft up a chimney. Once free, trace metals can damage the environment, or pose a health hazard by slipping into the food chain. Unfortunately, one potential means for releasing trace metals is the combustion of municipal refuse in incinerators or refused-derived fuel (RDF) boilers.

The U.S. Bureau of Mines (a division of the Department of the Interior) has studied this, and other questions of waste processing and recovery, at its test plant in Edmonston, Md. A bureau of "mines" is involved in recycling research because re-use of wastes holds the potential for enhancing the nation's "mineral supply," something Congress ordered the Bureau of Mines to do.

An attractive re-use for municipal waste is its burning in heat-recovery incinerators, or processing into RDF. But if local authorities or businessmen will not burn refuse or its fuel derivitives for fear that it will pump trace metals into the air, this avenue of recycling will be stymied.

Along these lines, the Bureau of Mines studied the metals found in municipal waste and incinerator residues. Could some sources of trace metal emissions be eliminated from resource-recovery combustion? Particularly, how much of the problem metals come from the noncombustible or heavy segments of the waste stream, which might just as well be eliminated from an RDF anyway?

In brief, the study found that several metals – cadmium, chromium, lead, maganese, silver, tin, and zinc, and perhaps antimony, cobalt, mercury, and nickel – are released from all components of refuse during incineration. It found that the heavy metals, like cadmium and copper, are concentrated in the heavy-combustible portion of refuse (things like heavy-gauge plastics). Thus, it seems that separating the non-combustible and heavy-combustible items away from the light-combustible segment to be used as a fuel should lower the combustion system's metal release.

INTENTION COMBUSTION

The combustible fraction is approximately 70 per cent (by weight) of MSW, and is composed of paper, plastics, yard wastes, putrescibles, wood, fabric, and similar minor components that are separated from the metals, glass, and other non-combustibles during the operation of the pilot plant. This fraction can be a valuable supplement to coal in the generation of heat and electricity. Although the combustibles are a valuable source of energy, as demonstrated by a Bureau of Mines evaluation, some fuel users resist the advent of RDF as a fuel supplement because of speculation about trace-metal emissions to the atmosphere when RDF is burned with coal. It should be noted that the limited date available on combustion of refuse were derived from municipal incinerators where the waste was not separated into combustible and noncombustible fractions (that is, not processed into an RDF) prior to incineration.

If the total refuse feed is burned, as in common incinerators, the emitted metals may come from one or both of the two major components of input – the combustibles (paper, plastics, etc.) or the noncombustibles (metals, glass, ceramics, etc.). Will separation of the combustibles from the raw refuse result in lower concentrations in RDF of elements that are ecologically objectionable?

TESTING THE METAL

The average concentrations of metals in the combustible fraction of refuse were determined in earlier Bureau of Mines studies. Using a local incinerator processing an average of 920 metric tons (dry weight) of refuse per week as a model, the total input of 20 metals in combustibles were calculated (see Table 1). The light combustibles listed in table 1 are the products collected in the three cyclones of the Bureau of Mines pilot plant, and consist primarily of light paper and packaging materials, with plastic film and light fabrics. Based on pilot plant data, the following percentages of the combustibles report in the cyclone fraction: paper (93 per cent), plastics (70 per cent), fabrics (92 per cent), cardboard (46 per cent), leather and rubber (15 per cent), wood (14 per cent), and a negligible amount of food wastes. The heavier combustibles such as wood, leather, rubber, and heavy-gauge plastics are concentrated in the heavy organic product from a

secondary air classifier. Most of the food and yard wastes are concentrated in the organic wastes separated out by a mineral jig. The column in Table 1 showing input from the total combustible refuse consists of a weighted average of all the separate fractions.

HIGHER IN HEAVIES

Some metals are present in the heavier combustibles in significantly higher concentrations than in the light combustibles. For example, cadmium (as a stabilizer) was found in high concentrations in a majority of heavy-gauge plastics – 400 ppm in one instance – making heavy-gauge plastics a primary source of cadmium in combustibles. Copper has an average of 2,300 ppm in the heavy organic fraction of the total combustibles, as compared with 170 ppm in the light combustibles; possibly because of bits of copper screen, wire, and electronic components in the heavy organics. Iron, nickel, and other metals are also higher in the heavier organics, possibly for similar reasons.

The metals in the incinerator's fine bottom ash (excluding bulk scrap, cans, bottles, etc.), atmospheric particles, and aqueous effluents, are also listed in Table 1. The total combustible fraction of refuse shwon in Table 1 contains sullifient amounts of aluminum, antimony, calcium, copper, iron, lithium, magnesium, mercury, and sodium to account for the concentrations of these metals found in the incinerator residue. The metals not completely accounted for by the total combustibles are chromium, cobalt, lead, manganese, nickel, silver, tin, zinc, barium, cadmium, and lithium. However, the range of concentrations in combustibles for the latter three elements could account for the residue concentrations. The source of the eight to 11 additional metal quantities is concluded to be the non-combustible fraction of MSW.

The Ca, Cu, and Na in the table show an average input from all combustibles that is at least twice as high as the output observed in the ash residues. These elements may be leaving the incinerator with either bulk scrap or the slag. (Residues which do not come from noncombustibles were not included in the analyses shown in Table 1).

Table 1. Elemental Input from Combustible MSW and Output During 1 Week's Operation Of a Model Municipal Incinerator.

Element	Quantity, kg			Fraction remaining, %	
	Input from light combustibles a/	Input from total combustible MSW a/	Output in incinerator residues b/	Not accounted for by light combustibles, %	Not accounted for by total combustibles, %
Ag	1	2	6	83	67
Al	4,700	5,800	5,500	(15) c/	—
Ba	80	110	120	33	(8) c/
Ca	2,900	6,300	3,200	(9) c/	—
Cd	2	6	8	75	(25) c/
Co	1	2	6	83	67
Cr	25	35	60	58	42
Cu	80	230	50	—	—
Fe	880	1,500	1,500	41	—
Hg	0.5	1	1	(50) c/	—
K	410	840	720	43	—
Li	1	1	2	(50) c/	(50) c/
Mg	640	1,000	1,000	36	65
Mn	60	80	230	74	—
Na	1,900	2,900	1,500	—	—
Ni	7	10	50	86	80
Pb	130	210	620	79	66
Sb	20	20	20	—	—
Sn	10	10	90	89	89
Zn	370	500	1,000	63	50

a/ Based on 920 metric tons (dry weight) MSW per week, 53% light combustibles, 70% total combustibles

b/ Based on 62 metric tons fine bottom ash (bulk scrap, cans, bottles, etc., excluded), 20 metric tons fly ash, 3.8 metric tons atmospheric particles, and 133,000 liters c/ recycled water per week

c/ Could be accounted for by ranges in the original data

PULLING A MERCURY SWITCH

Although the mercury in the incinerator residues in Table 1 is apparently balanced by the mercury in the total combustibles going into the incinerators, no accounting has been made for the possibility of mercury escaping the incinerator as a vapor. Mercury may be volatilized from the noncombustible components of refuse, and not observed in the incinerator residues. For example, a local municipal incinerator (different from the model used in this study) was reported by the *Washington Star* to be losing "six pounds of mercury per day" to the atmosphere. The maximum capacity of that incinerator is about 1,360 metric tons of refuse daily. Assuming that 70 per cent of the total weight of urban refuse is composed of combustible materials and that it has a mercury content of 2 ppm, the maximum mercury output from the combustible fraction would be about 1.8 kg/day. More realistically, the actual operating capacity is about 1,000 metric tons per day and the average mercury concentration in total combustibles is only 1 ppm, corresponding to a calculated mercury output from combustibles of approximately 0.68 kg/day.

Based on these calculations, the separation of the combustible materials from the noncombustibles before incineration could result in a fourfold decrease in mercury emission. Further evidence that mercury emissions become insignificant when only the combustible fraction of refuse is burned can be seen in preliminary data from Department of Energy research. Its studies show that mercury emissions from a coal-fired power plant actually may decrease when an RDF supplement is used.

METALS LOST IN INCINERATION

After studying the analyses of the aggregate heavy nonferrous metal from both raw refuse and municipal incinerator bulk scrap residues, Sullivan and Makar said, "The raw refuse product contains at least three times the amount of lead found in the incinerated product. A significant part of the lead apparently is oxidized during the incineration and reports in the fine ash of the residues and the fly ash. Another difference is noted in the ratio of copper to zinc in materials from the two sources. In all probability, during incineration some of the lead apparently is oxidized during the incineration and reports in the fine ash of the residues and the fly ash. Another difference is noted in the ratio of copper to zinc in materials from the two sources. In all probability, during incineration some pf the zinc volatilizes and oxidizes, resulting in a significantly higher ratio of copper to zinc in the metal from incinerator residues." The incinerator residues studied by Sullivan and Makar are the bulk metal scrap that can be mechanically separated from the ash materials. Metals are apparently being lost from the noncombustible fractions of refuse during incineration.

ENTER ENF

Another approach for the identification of metals being introduced to incinerator effluents by both noncombustible and combustible sources is to look at the ratios of the metal concentrations before and after combustion. The absolute concentrations of incinerator residues will obviously be different from the concentrations in the unburned refuse, but the ratios of metal concentrations will often remain similar. If the ratio of one metal to another in the combustible fraction of MSW is observed to be significantly increased in every portion of the residues after combustion, the increase may be the result of additions of one metal from the noncombustible components of the waste. This is especially true if the metal used for the normalized comparison is relatively unaffected by the combustion process, e.g., iron or aluminum. A similar technique has been in use for several years by scientists attempting to determine the sources of particulates in the atmosphere.

Calling this ratio of normalized metal concentrations an Enrichment by Noncombustibles Factor (ENF), the ratio can be described by the following expression:

$$ \text{ENF} = \frac{(C_x/C_{Fe})\,i}{(C_x/C_{Fe})\,\text{combustibles}} $$

C represents the concentration of element x and iron in the combustion product i (bottom ash, fly ash, particles emitted to the atmosphere) and in the average combustibles prior to incineration.

The concentration of each element in the fine bottom ash, the fly ash, and the atmospheric particles, was divided by the corresponding concentration of iron in each residue. The same normalization to iron was made with the data for the combustible fraction of refuse. The results show the ratios of the two iron-normalized concentrations and the magnitude of the differences between the unburned combustiles and the resulting residues from combustion. Where all of the ratios are close to or less than unity, (e.g., aluminum, barium, calcium, copper, lithium, magnesium, and potassium) the contribution from noncombustible components is probably not significant. Although the ratios for mercury are quite low in the bottom ash and the fly ash, no appropriate data for mercury emissions to the atmosphere were available but the ENF is probably much greater than unity in atmospheric emissions.

Where the ratios are high in all incinerator products, (e.g., chromium, manganese, nickel, silver, tin, and zinc) the additional amount required to increase the ratio must come from the noncombustible components of the refuse. Some of the more volatile elements, (antimony, cadmium, lead, and sodium) show a slight depletion of concentration in the fine bottom ash and fly ash (except for lead), but a very marked increase in the atmospheric particles. These elements may also be partially — or in the case of lead, significantly — derived from the noncombustibles. A decision regarding the contribution of noncombustibles to the concentration of the element showing ENF values both above and below unity must be made by examining the ENF values for all incineration residues and the relative amounts of each residue. For example, the ratio of cadmium entering in the combustibles can be assumed to approximately equal the computed ENF values. The ENF value of 31 for cadmium in the atmospheric particles (representing only 4 per cent of the total residues) is high enough to bring the overall cadmium estimated output-to-input ratio to almost two, even though the ENF is 0.7 for the fine bottom ash (72 per cent of the total residues), and 0.7 for the fly ash (23 per cent). Performing

Table 2. Composition of Typical Refuse, Dry Basis.

Product	Percent
Ferrous metal	7.6
Aluminum	1.1
Heavy nonferrous metal	0.2
Plastics	5.0
Leather and rubber	.7
Fabrics	1.8
Wood	2.6
Corrugated board	3.5
Paper	51.7
Putrescibles	4.4
Glass	10.5
Miscellaneous	.9
Fine glass, grit, dirt, and ceramics	10.0

Source: Bureau of Mines

the same operations for other elements, lead is found to come from noncombustibles, with an overall output-to-input ratio of 4. Antimony must remain undecided, with a ratio of 1, and sodium has an overall ratio of only 0.5. (Actual input-output numbers are given in Table 1.)

OTHER LOSSES

Although volatility can be used to explain the depletion of some elements, (like antimony, cadmium, and especially mercury) from the fine bottom ash and in the fly ash, solubility in the quench waters and in the fly-ash scrubber waters may explain the low ratios for other elements such as calcium, potassium, and sodium. Copper may be lost to the bulk slag not included in the fine bottom ash analyses.

Cobalt shows some addition from noncombustibles in the fine bottom ash and in the fly ash, but not in the atmospheric particles. A comparison of aluminum-normalized data gave results similar to those for the iron-normalized data, except that cobalt was also enriched (2.3) in the atmospheric particles.

DECREASED CONCENTRATION

It is obvious that metals are being lost from bulk scrap metals, and perhaps from glass and

Table 3. Bulk Metal Sources In Municipal Solid Waste.

Refuse fraction	Composition	Pct of each fraction
Ferrous a/		
	Tin-plated cans	54
	Bimetallic tin-plated cans	14
	Bimetallic tin-free cans	8
	Bottle and jar caps	3
	Ends of paperboard containers	1
	Miscellaneous ferrous objects	16
	Paper and plastics	4
Aluminum		
	Cans	67
	Flexible foil	11
	Rigid foil	6
	Ends of bimetallic cans	7
	Miscellaneous aluminum	9
Heavy nonferrous b/		
	Wide variety of miscellaneous materials including keys, coins, light bulb sockets, plumbing, wires, etc.	
	Cu	39
	Zn	40
	Pb	17
	Sn	2
	Other (Ag, Ni, Sb, etc.)	2

a/ Magnetically separated materials with associated nonferrous components (tin, paper, plastics, etc.)

b/ Does not include the nonferrous metals associated with the ferrous and aluminum fractions, e.g., the tin-plated steel cans are a major source of tin in the noncombustible fraction.

ceramics, during incineration. Table 2 shows the percentage of each type of noncombustible and combustible in refuse. The most apparent contributors of metal emissions from noncombustibles are the scrap metals comprising the ferrous fraction (7.6 per cent), the aluminum fraction (1.1 per cent) and the heavy nonferrous metals (0.2 per cent). A breakdown of each of these fractions is given in Table 3.

Many of the metals coming at least partially from noncombustibles (antimony, cadmium, chromium, cobalt, lead, manganese, nickel, silver, tin, and zinc) are associated with the products in Table 3 as surface coating of galvanizing agents, solders, pigments, and similar surface applications, or as thin foils or wires, where high temperatures could cause flaking and volatilization from the bulk metal scrap. The separation of the noncombustibles from the combustibles prior to using refuse as a source of energy will, therefore, result in lower concentrations of several metals in the residues from combustion.

ANSWER TO THE BURNING QUESTION

Cadmium, chromium, lead, manganese, silver, tin, and zinc apparently come from the noncombustible components of refuse as well as from the combustibles. The removal of the noncombustible components of municipal solid waste by some recycling operation prior to use of the remainder for fuel will reduce concentrations of these seven metals. Also, concentrations of antimony, cobalt, mercury, nickle, and possible other metals may be reduced by separating the combustibles from the noncombustibles prior to burning. A further reduction of cadmium, copper, and other heavy metals possibly can be realized by not including the heavy combustibles — especially the heavy-gauge plastics — in the RDF supplement.

4-8 Prepared vs Unprepared Refuse Fired Steam Generators

L.J. Cohan, J.H. Fernandes, M.E. Maguire, and R.C. Shenk

Source: First International *Conference* on Conversion of Refuse to Energy. Montreux, Switzerland, November 3-5, 1975, pp. 407-415. Reprinted with Permission of IEEE, from Conference Papers on CRE Conversion of Refuse to Energy (First International Conference and Technical Exhibition, Nov. 3-5, Montreux, Switzerland.)

INTRODUCTION

Refuse has been converted into energy for many years. One of the first power plants in the United States to use municipal waste started operation in 1906. In Europe, its use has been more widespread, but it is obvious that refuse was not competitive economically with fossil fuels when viewed as fuel along. It could be justified only when the benefit of waste disposal was included in the evaluation.

A recent U.S. forecast projects that 1980 wastes could provide the energy equivalent of about 6 million tons of coal or 27 million barrels of low sulfur crude oil annually.

To date, most of the experience in burning refuse has been by mass burning, *i.e.*, taking the refuse as received with no preparation and burning it in a furnace. Currently, however, attention is being focused on preparing refuse by sizing it, separating the noncombustibles, and firing the remaining combustibles in suspension.

This paper compares prepared versus unprepared refuse firing. Combustion Engineering has experience in both methods.

COMBUSTION CALCULATIONS

Physically, mixed municipal refuse contains large quantities of paper, crates, and similar dry combustible materials, with a density that varies from 120 to 300 kg/m³ (200 to 500 lb/yd³).

While highly variable in appearance and density, chemical analysis is quite uniform, consistent with cellulose. Major variables are moisture, ash, and other solid inerts. Preparation can remove a major portion of the latter.

A certain amount of premixing is required to ensure a mixture capable of supporting combustion. Once mixing has been accomplished, the material must be dried and its temperature raised to the ignition point. Drying affects furnace temperature and proper burnout and is accomplished by convective heat transfer from air or gas flows and radiant heat transfer from the flame or furnace surfaces. The furnace can be designed so that drying is accomplished within the enclosure. Most incinerators incorporate furnace drying rather than predrying ahead of the furnace.

The effectiveness of the drying process is governed by four factors:

1. Moisture dispersion within the refuse mass, allowing maximum surface exposure.
2. Large temperature differentials — high gas temperatures are required for rapid drying (high rate of heat transfer).
3. Maximum refuse agitation to increase rate of heat transfer.
4. Particle size must be reduced to a size where the surface area is significantly increased thus permitting more rapid moisture loss.

This last requirement necessitates some form of preparation if maximum efficiency is to be obtained in both the drying and burning operations.

The heart of the reduction system is the burning of the material, accomplished by mass or suspension burning. Mass burning takes unprepared refuse and burns it with a minimum of mixing on a fuel-supporting and air-admitting surface called a stoker. Stoker firing is mechanical firing that provides continuous or intermittent feed, drying ignition, and burning of combustibles and discharge of noncombustibles. Stokers are classified as underfeed, crossfeed, or overfeed, based on the method by which fuel and air are introduced and their relative direction. Stokers for refuse burning may incorporate more than one of these basic classifications.

Evaluations of the mass and suspension burning systems will be based on all the applicable parameters for the total plant of three sizes; *i.e.,* 800, 1,200 and 1,600 ton/day two furnace plants. Each evaluation will include all of the ramifications involved in both mass burning unprepared refuse on a grate-type firing system and the necessary solid waste preparation to allow suspension burning of the refuse. The latter could also be supplied as supplemental boiler fuel in a conventional coal or oil furnace if that option was available. In the mass burning unit, recycling will be from the residue. In a prepared refuse system, all recycling will be from the more dense noncombustible portion separated from the incoming stream. All burning systems discussed here are of the newer type, in which the heat of combustion in the furnace as well as in the convective passes is absorbed by water-filled tubes.

Resource recycling considers, in addition to the fuel produced, ferrous and aluminum materials. The assumption is made that a secondary system will take other heavy materials from the prepared refuse and further process it outside the plant. This removal is assumed at no cost to the system. On the other hand, the ferrous and aluminum fraction will be credited to the system at prices equivalent to the U.S. average for last year.

The "front end" unburned ferrous material, with its predominance of metal cans, is a higher valued product than the oxidized material that is available in the residue from the mass burning unit. Therefore, the light ferrous fraction going to a metal recovery plant is priced higher than that recovered from the residue of a mass burning unit. At an American Iron and Steel Institute Seminar (Ref. 1 & 2), the recycling industry was warned that highly oxidized ferrous material from a mass burning incinerator was of no value to a detinner and it was of reduced value to the foundry industry because, as an oxide, it is more readily absorbed in the slag and a portion of it is lost.

The ferrous fraction makes up approximately 8% by weight of the raw refuse, with 60% of the ferrous fraction consisting of light ferrous (tin cans). The value of this light ferrous material is in a range of $25 to $60 per ton. The heavy ferrous is removed separately and comprises about 40% of the ferrous stream, with a value of $30 to $90 per ton. Provisions were included to densify each ferrous fraction as necessary. Based on the above data, the ferrous fraction from the residue was valued at $2.40 per input ton, while that from the prepared stream was valued at $4.00 per input ton.

Assuming it is economically viable to recover aluminum, several different separating concepts may be used. An aluminum magnet was the device included here. We assumed 0.6% aluminum in the raw refuse valued at $250 per ton with only 50% of the aluminum recoverable, or $0.75 input ton.

With prepared refuse, suspension firing is possible, permitting lower excess air operation and minimum corrosion because of the removal of some trace metals such as copper, zinc, aluminum, etc. These materials may not directly enter into the corrosion reaction, but they can act as catalyst and create a corrosive situation.

Environmental compatibility is a major concern in any modern system. Refuse burning is not feasible unless the applicable environmental regulations are met. With low excess air suspension firing systems, there is a substantial reduction in the gas quantities to be cleaned and this is reflected in the cost of air pollution control equipment.

These units generate steam and the assumption is made that the price of steam is tied to the value of oil. The figure used here to establish the value of steam is the 1975 price of oil in Eastern U.S., *i.e.,* $6.05 per thousand kilograms ($2.75 per thousand pounds) of steam delivered to the plant's stop valve.

The capital and operating costs for the proposed systems are presented in Table 1 where cost comparisons between the various sizes and different types of steam generating-incineration systems are compared.

The basis for the comparisons and conclusions drawn between the different types of incineration systems are:

1. Land costs were estimated at $300,000 for the 40,500 m² (10 acre) site.

2. Site preparation included fencing, roadways, utilities, drainage, landscaping, etc. at $700,000 for the 40,500 m² (10 acre) site.

3. Building costs were assumed to be $2.70 per square meter ($25/ft²). This includes heating, plumbing, air conditioning, ventilating, normal foundations, insulation, sprinkler systems, lighting, etc.

4. Capital costs included land, site development, the necessary building, construction, equipment investment, A&E fees and construction financing cost.

5. The equipment investment for the incinerator system includes feed conveyors, shredders, storage hoppers, firing and

Table 1.

	Mass Burning			Suspension Firing		
	800	1200	1600	800	1200	1600
I. Operation						
Days/Week....................................	5	5	5	5	5	5
Days/Year.....................................	250	250	250	250	250	250
Tons/Day......................................	800	1,200	1,600	800	1,200	1,600
Tons/Year (× 10³).............................	200	300	400	200	300	400
No. of Units...................................	2	2	2	2	2	2
II. Capital Cost (× $1000)						
Land (10 Acres)...............................	300	300	300	300	300	300
Site Work.....................................	700	700	700	700	700	700
Building, Structures—Erected............................	3,900	4,750	5,575	3,200	3,400	3,750
Equipment.....................................	8,250	10,165	13,398	13,200	16,250	20,150
Equipment Erection............................	4,950	5,794	7,235	7,920	9,263	10,881
Total Construction Cost........................	18,100	21,709	27,208	25,320	29,913	35,781
A&E Fee.......................................	905	1,085	1,360	1,266	1,496	1,789
Construction Financing.........................	2,281	2,735	3,428	3,190	3,769	4,508
Total Project Cost.............................	21,286	25,529	31,996	29,776	35,178	42,078
Total Installed Cost (T/D) (× 1000).............	26.6	21.3	20.0	37.2	29.3	26.3
III. Operating Costs (× $1000)						
Labor (44 men)................................	660	660	660	660	660	660
Utilities—$/Yr.................................	157	224	295	144	209	266
Maintenance (3% Total Project Cost).....................	639	766	960	893	1,055	1,262
Residue Disposal ($1.00/Ton)...........................	1,200	1,800	2,400	480	720	960
Administration (7½% Total Project Cost)................	1,596	1,915	2,400	2,233	2,638	3,156
Total Operating Cost...........................	4,252	5,365	6,715	4,410	5,280	6,304
Total Operating Cost/Ton......................	21.26	17.88	16.78	22.05	17.60	15.76
Total Project Cost (× $1000)...................	21,286	25,529	31,996	29,776	35,178	42,078
Steam Sale—$/Year (× $1000)...................	3,135	4,700	6,270	3,663	5,500	7,359
—$/Ton.....................................	15.68	15.67	15.67	18.32	18.32	18.32
Metal Salvage—$/Year (× $1000)................	480	720	960	950	1,425	1,900
—$/Ton.....................................	2.40	2.40	2.40	4.75	4.75	4.75
Sub Total—$/Ton...............................	3.18	−0.19	−1.29	−1.02	−5.47	−7.31
Debt Service (× $1000) (8%—25 Years).................	1,972	2,365	2,964	2,758	3,258	3,898
Debt Service—$/Ton............................	9.86	7.88	7.41	13.79	10.86	9.75
Net $/Ton.....................................	13.04	7.69	6.12	12.77	5.39	2.44

boiler system and flue gas cleaning equipment.

6. Construction financing was figured at 8% for the 3-year construction period.
7. Financing was 8% for a 25-year capital investment loan.
8. Operating costs included labor, utilities, maintenance, and administration. Loan amortization is presented separately.
9. Operating costs included:
   − power at 2 1/2 ¢ kilowatt
   − fuel oil at $2.37 per billion joules ($2.25 per million Btu)
   − water at 13.2 ¢ per cubic meter (50¢ per thousand gallons)
10. Administration costs were 7 1/2% of the total capital costs.
11. Operation was assumed as 5 days per week, 250 days per year with reduced steam demand arranged for unit outages.
12. Each system was assumed to have a 2-day refuse storage capacity.
13. All incineration systems included complete controls and remote control panels.
14. Residue and ash handling systems consisted of conveyors, silos, and related equipment.
15. No return on investment was computed because a systems comparison is what authors were determining.

The results are presented on a dollars per ton basis, as well as a capital cost basis.

The systems to fire the prepared and unprepared refuse were designed for steam condition of 750 F, 800 psig with a 225 F feedwater temperature. No redundancy in boiler capacity was incorporated in the design. The design assumed that when there was a unit outage, the excess material would be landfilled. No. 6 oil was available for stabilization, as well as auxiliary firing if there was an interruption in the refuse supply. It is assumed that the steam is for process use and delivered to an adjacent header.

UNPREPARED REFUSE BOILER DESIGN

There are many types of grate designs which have been used for burning municipal wastes. All of these grate systems require approximately 100 to 150% excess air to assure burnout. Usually, the lower 15 to 20 feet of the furnace is protected with refractory to limit corrosion due to a fluctuating furnace atmosphere. Since the cost of the grate is a relatively small percentage of the total cost, the type of grate is not considered critical to this economic analysis.

The system shown in Fig. 1 is considered typical of U.S. mass burning systems. It is considered reasonable to design for single furnaces capable of burning 400, 600, or 800 tons in a 24-hour period since there has been some experience with units up to 1000 tons/day.

The pit and crane format, with two cranes and a raw refuse pit sized for two days storage or 1,600, 2,400 and 3,200 tons was considered.

PREPARED REFUSE BOILER DESIGN

There are at least two concepts for burning prepared refuse. One is a spreader stoker fired system which has been widely used in the past for burning hogged wood waste, bagasse and other waste fuels. The second type is the suspension fired system (Fig. 2). Both of these systems burn a large portion of the refuse in suspension above the grate. The larger, more dense particles fall to the grate where burnout is completed.

The raw refuse receiving area will have a slab capable of one-day storage. There will be a second day of storage in silos located downstream of the preparation step. The concept considered in the evaluation is a suspension fired system.

Suspension Fired System

This design requires fuel preparation to approximately 1 1/4-inch top size. This sizing is possible with two stages of shredding and the material is small enough to be air classified to remove the more dense material. The advantage of this design is that the fuel can be conveyed with a high pressure pneumatic system to ports high in the furnace. These ports are aimed tangential to an imaginary circle in the center of the furnace.

Air aimed in a similar manner assists the suspension burning. The firing system and the fuel particle size help promote burning. The bottom

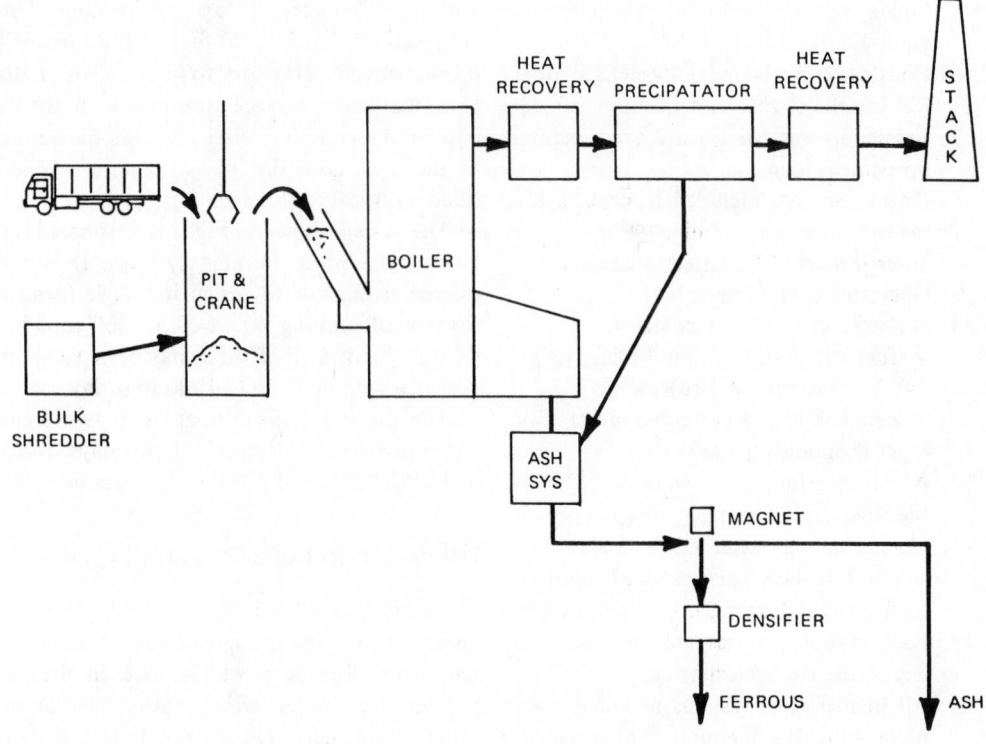

Figure 1. System for mass burning.

PREPARATION OF REFUSE

Unprepared Refuse System

For mass burning, the majority of the refuse coming to the facility does not require any preparation. However, approximately 15 to 20% of the material does require shredding to permit charging into the furnace. This shredder has to be oversizes to accept this material. For the purpose of the evaluation, we assumed a machine with a 80-inch wide x 60-inch diameter rotor of the horizontal-shaft hammer mill design equipped with a 1000-hp motor. Only one shredder was used (Fig. 1).

Prepared Refuse System

The preparation system for the suspension firing system included the following processing equipment (Fig. 2).

of the furnace has a small grate to permit burn-out of larger, more dense materials.

1. Two primary shredders and two secondary shredders.
2. Two air classifiers.
3. Two magnetic separators that recover light (tin stock) and heavy ferrous from the dense stream, plus the densifiers.
4. One aluminum magnet separator.

Conveyors are supplied to move material from the various processing stations. There is a 100% redundancy in the preparation systems, *i.e.*, there are two parallel lines each capable of shredding the total refuse quantity in 24 hours.

GAS WEIGHT AS A FUNCTION OF FIRING SYSTEM

The excess air for the mass burning system was assumed at 150% as opposed to 30% for the prepared refuse firing system. This means that the gas passing through the boiler, air heater, and electrostatic precipitator in the unprepared system is nearly double that of the prepared refuse firing systems.

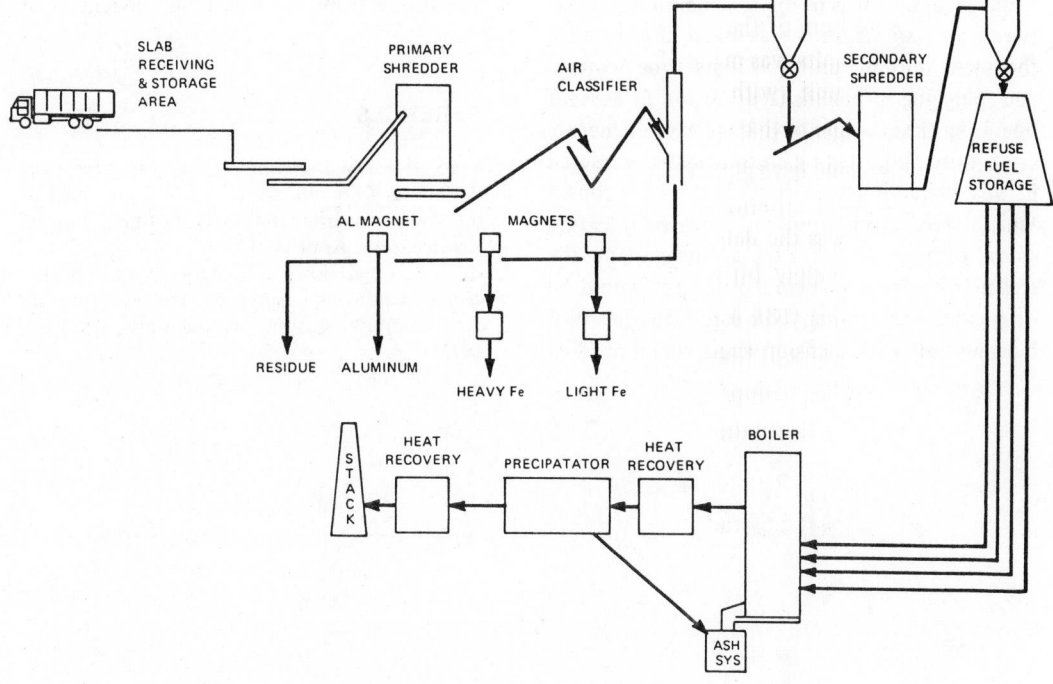

Figure 2. System for suspension firing.

ELECTROSTATIC PRECIPITATOR

The gas clean-up device used will be an electro-static precipitator. As described above, the precipitator to clean the gases from a mass burning boiler is larger because of the increased gas weight. A hot precipitator will be used with a design temperature of about 600 F. The outlet loading requirements are assumed to be 0.183 grams/dry cubic meter (0.08 grains/dry SCF). The required precipitator efficiencies were 98.4% for mass burning and 98.6% for prepared refuse firing. For the purpose of this study, the European type precipitator design was used.

EXIT GAS TEMPERATURE

Since a hot electrostatic precipitator is used, the air preheaters will be located after the precipitator and will be of the Ljungstrom® type. Therefore, the flue gas entering the air heater will be very clean and fouling is not expected to be a problem.

CONCLUSION

Table 1 computes the cost of disposal of municipal solid waste by each of the different steam generating incineration systems. On a net ton basis (the bottom line – the most significant figure), the mass burning unprepared refuse unit is highest cost in each category. It is the least expensive of the two systems on a total installed cost basis, but over the life of the unit, the income derived from marketing of recycled materials and the greater steam sales from the more efficient boilers justifies the added investment. This reduces the per ton cost to dispose of the refuse, therefore, the suspension fired system appears to have the best economics. If final separation had taken place after the second shredder of the suspension fired system, a more accurate density cut could be made by the air classifier and a cleaner fuel would be delivered to the boiler with added resources recovered from the waste stream. The complexities this would have introduced were not evaluated in this study. In a similar manner, if an accurate measure of the maintenance between the various units was made, the costs for the mass burning unit (with its tube wastage and plugging problems that result in loss of operating time) would have gone even higher.

A third important criterion not considered in this evaluation was the delivery of a consistent, stable steam supply for uses such as in a steam turbine. If this were a requirement, the steam from the suspension fired unit would be of greater value when compared to the mass burning unit with its fluctuating steam production resulting from the lack of homogeneity of the fuel.

REFERENCES

1. Read, D. "*The Detinning Market for Scrap Cans Recovered from Municipal Waste*," presented at the American Iron and Steel Institute, Boston, Massachusetts, April 30, 1975.
2. Ruff, G., Unpublished presentation given at the Recycling Seminar sponsored by American Iron and Steel Institute, Boston, Massachusetts, April 30, 1975.

4-9 The City of Akron's Waste-to-Steam Facility

Ronald W. Musselwhite

Source: Recycle Energy System: The City of Akron's Waste-to-Steam Facility, *NCRR Bulletin,* Vol. 10, No. 2, (June 1980), pp. 36–42. Reprinted with Permission of National Center for Resource Recovery, Inc.

More than a decade ago, Akron, Ohio, anticipated a landfill problem. Its only municipal landfill had been established in 1969 with a life expectancy of 10 years, and no new site was available after that.

That landfill problem — plus a few other factors — was instrumental in development of the City's new Recycle Energy System, a 1000 ton-per-day plant to produce steam from municipal, commercial and some industrial solid waste.

The idea of a waste-to-energy system for Akron was conceived in 1968 — three years before the pioneer Franklin, Ohio, resource recovery demonstration plant began operating and four years before the St. Louis Union Electric refuse-derived fuel demonstration program began. In 1979 — 11 years later, including two periods of inactivity because of waning interest — the first truckload of municipal refuse was processed and burned for steam.

The recycle Energy System (RES) is now more than halfway through its shakedown period, burning increasing amounts of refuse each week. In April 1980, 2000-to-3000 tons per week were being processed and steam supplied to more than 200 customers, including B.F. Goodrich Co., two hospitals, state and local office buildings, and many smaller customers on a downtown steam loop. The University of Akron and another hospital soon will be added. Full-capacity, continuous operation is expected this summer.

HISTORY

The first official steps toward RES were made by the Akron Department of Planning and Urban Renewal in 1969, when it commissioned a feasibility study. A few months later, the project was temporarily shelved due to lack of interest on the part of potential steam users and in the landfill situation as well. The project was reactivated and the study completed in 1971, only to be shelved again because of a combined lack of motivation and concern over the technological alternatives. During this time personnel from the City and from the architectural and engineering firm for the project, Glaus, Pyle, Schomer, Burns & DeHaven, Inc., visited various other projects.

Glaus, Pyle has been involved in the RES project from its inception. The Akron-based firm has been involved in thermal power plant projects throughout Ohio, and had performed engineering services for other Akron city projects. (Glaus, Pyle is also the A&E firm for the Hooker Chemicals and Plastics Corp. waste-to-energy plant starting up in Niagara Falls, N.Y.)

In 1973, the City Council decided to proceed with the project — spurred on by the Ohio Edison Co. (OE) announcement that it wished to abandon the steam plant serving about 250 businesses in downtown Akron. The plant was old, and renovations and emission control equipment would be prohibitively expensive, the company said. Also about this time, the first "energy crunch" appeared, providing evidence of fossil fuel shortages and higher energy prices in coming years.

Plant design proceeded. Construction and equipment bids were originally let in February 1975, but construction could not proceed until the financial package was put together and bonds issued almost two years later.

A major obstacle was a lack of committed steam buyers; the businesses on OE's steam loop were not sufficient to justify the planned facility. The City then found three additional large steam users: The University of Akron, City Hospital, and B.F. Goodrich Co.

The Markets were all committed before bonds were issued in 1976; and construction officially began with the awarding of contracts on Dec. 7, 1976, and groundbreaking the following day.

The City had a preference for hiring a contract operator rather than operating the facility itself, but had not implemented this preference. The underwriters insisted that a contract operator be hired before the bonds were issued if the City did not intend to operate the facility.

The City, the A&E and the operator all agree: there's a better way. If you're going to hire an operator, they say, bring him on board early in the project so that he can have input into the design and so that differences concerning the best unit processes for given applications, etc., can be worked out.

The first refuse was processed in July 1979 — a small amount for a test, as the plant was not then complete. Because of the increased amount of refuse processed and steam produced throughout the startup period, Ohio Edison is expected to shut down its steam plant in late summer, with RES providing all of its customers' steam.

PROCESS FLOW

Incoming packer and transfer trucks are weighed on a scale at the entrance to the tipping floor. The scales are automated for credit card operations and billing; the weight of each truck is recorded at an initial, empty visit, so that the trucks do not have to be weighed on the way out. After weighing, the trucks dump into one of the 14 dumping stations. Total time a truck spends on the tipping floor, including weigh-ins, is normally about five minutes.

At the dumping stations, the trucks dump directly into a 1785-ton capacity pit. Waste is moved from the pit onto the shredder infeed lines by means of two hydraulic multi-ram positive displacement unloading lines. Each line has a capacity of more than 100 tons per hour (tph).

The rams discharge into a surge bin, and flight conveyors feed the waste from the bin into the two, 1500 hp American Pulverizer horizontal hammermills. A grapple, operated remotely from the control room above the shredding lines, removes bulky, hazardous or other undesirable objects before they enter the shredders. The refuse is shreded to a minus four-inch particle size.

Fact Summary
Recycle Energy System — Akron, Ohio

Opening: First refuse processed July 1979; now in start-up with full operation scheduled for Summer 1980

Principals: City of Akron — owner

Glaus, Pyle, Schomer, Burns & DeHaven — designer

Teledyne National — construction supervisor and plant operator

Volume: 1000 tpd on a 3-shift, 5- or 6-day week when at full capacity (current operating level is about 2000- to-3000 tons per week)

Technology: Shredding; air classification; magnetic separation; RDF fired to produce steam in semi-suspension, spreader stoker-fired boilers

Product: Steam — 378,000 lbs./hr. saturated at 560 psig; ferrous metals

Costs & Revenues: Capital costs approximately $56 million. Financed by bonds from Ohio Water Development Authority, City of Akron and Summit County.

Tipping fee is $3.50 per ton; steam rates vary from about $1.80 to about $4.80 per 1000 lbs. (rates to increase by about 50% later this year)

Facility received funds under Oil Entitlements Program.

From each shredder, the material goes to a Triple/S Dynamics Vibrolutriator™ air classifier, which produces a split of about 70 percent lights and 30 percent heavies, depending upon moisture content. The heavy fraction passes under a drum magnetic separator for removal of ferrous metals. The ferrous is conveyed to a waiting trailer for transport to the buyer, a scrapyard in Wooster, Ohio. The heavy residue goes to another trailer for transport to the City's landfill, about five miles north of town. Ferrous recovery is presently about five-to-seven percent of the incoming refuse.

The air-classified light fraction is the refuse-derived fuel (RDF). It is conveyed pneumatically to a 2100-ton, double-sided Miller-Hofft storage bin. Two paris of augers at the bottom of the bin feed the RDF to a surge bin, from which it is fed into the boilers by flight conveyors and pneumatic transport lines.

There are three Babcock & Wilcox semi-suspension, spreader stoker-fired boilers, nominally rated at 126,000 lbs./hr. each. About 28-to-40 percent of the RDF burns in suspension; the remaining materials fall onto the grate for additional burning. Flue gases are cleaned by electrostatic precipitation. A waste heat economizer provides hot water and heat for the building and reduces the gas temperature leaving the stack to about 250°F.

The plant has two, 2000 KW turbine generators to furnish about one-third of the plant's power requirements.

Saturated steam at 560 psi is distributed through pre-insulated pipe to the existing Ohio Edison system at a pressure reducing station about one-half mile from the RES plant. New distribution lines carry steam to the B.F. Goodrich complex adjacent to RES, to the University of Akron 1 1/2 miles away, and to Akron City Hospital about two miles away. Condensate is returned to the RES plant for recovery.

PLANT DESIGN/CONSTRUCTION

The RES plant, designed by Glaus, Pyle, is located on an eight-acre plot near the center of the City's business district, allowing easy access for collection trucks and relatively short travel times from most Akron neighborhoods.

The facility's three boilers are expected to produce a total of 378,000 lbs./hr. of steam at full operating capacity. With boiler efficiency at 78.2 percent, about 3.9 pounds of usable steam can be produced from each pound of as-received refuse. Tests thus far have shown the RDF to have a heating value of between 5900 and 6300 Btu per pound.

The three boilers easily meet current steam demands — in fact, only two boilers are required to meet the demands of the noninterruptable customers. However, space has been provided for a fourth boiler should steam demand increase.

Space also is available in the plant for the addition of equipment for further materials recovery. Teledyne's Jerry Temple, the plant manager, sees a good possibility for aluminum recovery. Also, he added, there may be good value in reshredding the air classified heavies and oversize particles so that more can be used as fuel instead of being landfilled. This secondary processing might also give a sand-and-glass mixture; the glass could be recovered and the sand and inert material used as filler in construction projects.

(Temple recently left RES; the new plant manager is Ralph Iacono.)

David Chapman, deputy director of Akron's Department of Public Service, agreed that further recovery might lie ahead, but said that no such plans have been made at present. He emphasized that the first priority is to get the plant working efficiently at full capacity. Then, he said, other items like additional recovery processes can be considered.

Plant design includes several fire and explosion safety features. Besides the grapple mentioned earlier, which can remove hazardous articles before they enter the shredders, there is a Fenwall explosion suppression system and one side of each shredder has a vent to the outside. Also, some flue gas is vented into each shredder to cut down the oxygen content inside the shredders, lessening fire and explosion danger.

After air classification, the light fraction is blown into a cyclone at the storage bin for de-entrainment. The air is returned from the cyclone, with about one-third going back to the air classifier and two-thirds going to the boilers for use as combustion air. However, dust and fine

Akron Recycle Energy System
Simplified Process Flow Diagram

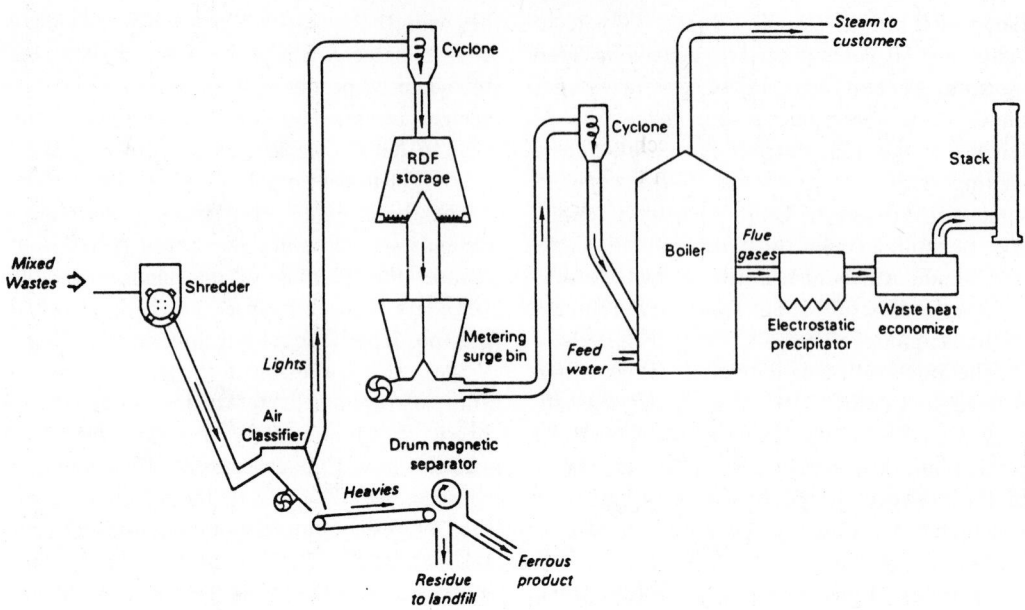

Fig. 1.

particulates suspended in this air tended to plug the preheaters; when this happened, the boilers had to be shut down and the preheaters cleaned. Also, the air being fed back into the air classifier created undesirable air currents that disrupted the separation of the material. A baghouse has been installed as a temporary solution to the dust problem, and the recycled air is not presently being reused in the plant. The situation is being studied for a more permanent solution.

After being de-entrained, the RDF is spread evenly into the storage bin by a shuttle conveyor. The 170-foot-long bin is split into two sides by a wedge-shaped section that directs the material downward to the screw augers that meter it out of the bin and onto a belt conveyor to the metering surge bin.

There have been some difficulties with attaining an even feedrate from the two-ton surge bin to the boilers; air cannons, installed to break up and aerate the refuse, have helped alleviate the problem. There are plans to sectionalize the surge bin and use a common distribution point to evenly distrubute the material into the different sections.

RDF is fed to each boiler through four air swept spouts. Rotary air dampers distribute the fuel from front to back and side to side. The furnaces, which use No. 2 fuel oil as an alternate fuel to produce steam when refuse is not available, soon will be modified to accept natural gas as a fuel also. Temple said that rubber (tires) is also being considered as a possible fourth fuel, though no decision is expected on that for at least several months. The combination of fuel flexibility and redundancy is intended to make Recycle Energy System a totally reliable source of steam for its customers.

Reports indicate that virtually all of the combustibles burn before leaving the grate. No appreciable slag accumulations are reported.

As of early this year, no data had been prepared on emissions from the plant. Full load adjustments to the electrostatic precipitator had not been made, although emissions problems are not anticipated.

As might be expected, the plant has had its share of problems. Some have been normal start-up difficulties, and some have resulted from using the nonhomogeneous and still largely untried feedstock of mixed wastes. None, however, appears insurmountable.

Bruce Pyle, of Glaus, Pyle, Schomer, Burns & DeHaven, noted that the plant still has some material handling problems . . . some operations that could be improved. The handling problems are shared with other feedstocks. "Bark, wood chips — all the cellulose fuels are not easy to handle," he said. "The problem is basically that there is not — and will not be for a time — proven, completely reliable, off-the-shelf technology for these materials. You cannot, with confidence, buy a piece of hardware that's going to do the job. You have to look at other plants and make the best judgment you can as to what will perform best; if it doesn't come up to your expectations, and you see some need for improvement, then you have to experiment or conduct trial-and-error tests to make those improvements."

Problems with return air and the surge bin have already been mentioned; some other materials handling problems are worth noting.

- "Bridging" of the raw solid waste in the receiving pit has been experienced due to the configuration of the bin. Material can roll to the outside or center of the bin, with the multi-ram feeders moving through without pushing the refuse. The bridging is broken up by means of a beam extended from the tipping floor above.
- Material was falling out of the shredders onto the shredder infeed flight conveyors, damaging the pans on the conveyors. This was corrected by installing deflector plates inside the shredders.
- Such items as plastic milk cartons, not being shredded into small enough pieces, were plugging the pneumatic lines. This problem was solved by welding extra bars onto the shredder grates to reduce the size of the holes and thus the size of the particles that pass through. Additional plugging in the elbows was eliminated by changing the transition pieces in the pneumatic lines.
- In the Miller-Hofft RDF storage bins, rags often become entangled in the screw augers, reducing the amount of material the augers can convey. A way to resolve this problem has not yet been found.

Everyone concerned seems to have confidence that the problems all will be solved in a matter of time.

Chapman emphasized the need for a long start-up period in which to solve such problems, particularly with untried equipment and uncommon feedstock: "I think one of the significant things we've learned here is to plan on taking a year to make the adjustments that are necessary to make the plant more functional and properly train all the plant operation personnel. When we talk to industrial plant managers," he added, "they tell us it takes up to a year to start a plant, and that's off-the-shelf technology."

FINANCING

The Recycle Energy System was financed by $46 million in tax-exempt bonds issued by the Ohio Water Development Authority, plus $5 million each in general obligation bonds issued by the City of Akron and Summit County. The County's involvement in the plant is largely limited to issuance of the bonds; it is not involved in refuse collection or disposal, and Akron's solid waste disposal facilities serve the entire metropolitan area.

Tipping fee at the plant is $3.50 per ton, but will increase about 50 percent when the plant is certified, probably at the end of the summer. This will still be lower than the $6 per ton charged at the City landfill.

Steam rates, negotiated in 1975–76, vary from about $1.80 to about $4.80 per 1000 pounds, with the average for large customers about $3.15, according to Chapman. Steam rates, too, are expected to increase about 50 percent upon certification, but they will still be about 25 percent lower than Ohio Edison is presently charging for steam from its plant.

(Certification is a procedure borrowed from the power industry — in the case of RES, it essentially means that the plant has demonstrated its ability to meet the minimum design requirements of 1000 tpd of refuse and 375,000 lbs./hr. of steam for an extended period.)

Total cost of the project to date is about $56 million, about $50 million of which are for direct and indirect construction costs. Total cost estimated at the time of the bond issue in 1976 was $46 million.

The steam contract with B.F. Goodrich Co. has been called "the real key" to the RES project. The Goodrich manufacturing plant and international headquarters office complex, the RES facility's next-door neighbor, uses steam for heating and cooling as well as industrial processes. Goodrich agreed to buy, on an interruptable basis, all the steam in excess of the other users' requirements, up to the full needs of the complex. Goodrich will use RES steam in preference to its own, but will maintain its own steam-generating facilities on a standby basis. Steam to the University of Akron and City Hospital also is interruptable, but on a difference basis. Steam contracts will all customers are for 25 years.

Teledyne National handled the marketing for the ferrous metals. Proceeds from the sale of the ferrous up to an established minimum go to the City; after that they are divided equally between the City and the operator.

The plant has an additional source of revenue — a relatively new one for resource recovery facilities. It is eligible for oil entitlement funds under a ruling last November by the Department of Energy's Economic Regulatory Administration (ERA). Thus far, the RES plant has received four oil entitlements payments totalling about $180,000.

The Oil Entitlements Program, administered by the ERA, is designed to equalize the cost of acquiring crude oil among U.S. refiners. Basically, it requires that refiners who purchase price-controlled crude oil must transfer funds, according to a formula, to refiners who must purchase imported oil at world market prices. In 1979, ERA extended to program to several alternate fuels, including those derived from municipal wastes.)

WASTE FLOW ORDINANCE

To ensure an adequate amount of refuse feedstock for the facility, thereby encouraging bond sales, the City passed an ordinance in October 1976 requiring that all waste collected in the City be taken to the Recycle Energy System plant when it opened. The ordinance was challenged in federal district court in 1978 by several private haulers and landfill operators in one of the more widely reported suits in the solid waste management industry.

The ordinance was part of an agreement with Summit County and the Ohio Water Develop-

ment Authority, and all three were named as defendants. The combined cases of *Glenwillow Landfill, et al. vs. City of Akron, et al.* and *Hybud Equipment Corp. vs. City of Akron* maintained that the ordinance deprived the plaintiffs of their property without due process of law, restrained interstate commerce and violated the Sherman Anti-Trust Act.

U.S. District Court Judge Leroy J. Contie, Jr., ruled in favor of the defendants on all counts. He ruled that the Ohio Water Development Authority is a state agency and thus immune to the Sherman Act; and that the state delegated its authority to the City in the area of solid waste disposal, and thus the anti-trust immunity extends to the City. He said the ordinance does not take property away from the collectors, but "the expectation that they would always be able to take the waste . . . to a disposal site of their choice," which is not a property right.

Judge Contie said that the waste does not move in interstate commerce, even though some recyclable materials taken from it might do so; therefore any restraint of interstate commerce is indirect and incidental and could be justified under a city's police powers. The court said the law is a "reasonable means" to achieve a legitimate local goal, and that it amounts to a regulation to control a nuisance, which only incidentally impacts on some solid waste collectors who separate recyclables from the collected wastes.

The court's ruling was issued in December 1979. The plaintiffs have filed an appeal with the U.S. Sixth Circuit Court of Appeals.

Meanwhile, the City and Teledyne report that private haulers appear to be more than satisfied to deliver their collected wastes to the RES plant for several reasons. The plant's paved roads and concrete tipping floor eliminate chances for trucks to get stuck in mud or have flat tires as in a landfill; a short turnaround time on deliveries; a central, downtown location; and a low tipping fee.

Over the past several months, there has been a gradual transition in steam supply, as RES supplied more and more steam to the Ohio Edison loop. Only one OE boiler is now operating, and it will be shut down when the RES facility is certified. The City will purchase the OE plant, steam lines, etc.; the plant will be maintained as a standby system for a time.

RES is processing refuse five or six days a week, three shifts a day, and is generating steam seven days a week.

The facility employs about 70 people, well above the originally projected level of 35-to-40. Chapman said it is expected that the highest number of people will be needed during the first year of operation, fewer the second year, and down near final manning levels by the third or fourth year. The final level is likely to be near 55.

The plant, designed to process 1000 tpd, could handle perhaps as much as 1400-to-1500 tpd, Temple estimated. Metropolitan Akron's trash generation is about the same as the plant's design capacity; in 1979 the City landfill accepted 365,000 tons of solid waste.

During the course of several conversations, the representatives of the City, the A&E firm and the operator were asked what advice they might offer to a community considering resource recovery. They emphasized different points according to each individual's perspective. Some have already been noted; others are listed below.

- *Marketing* — It is very important to identify and contract for markets early.
- *Look carefully before committing to the "full-service" approach.* (Pyle commented that the full-service approach will be around for a while, but it is a very expensive way for a city to put a project together, and its record of success "is not all that good.")
- *Decide on the appropriate system and get the project underway as quickly as possible.* Long delays for studies, etc., can mean as much as a 20 percent cost increase even before groundbreaking.
- *If there is to be an operating firm, hire the firm in the early stages of the project,* so it can have input into the design.
- *Be sure the system is economical and will meet the community's needs.*
- *Design the plant for ease of maintenance.* (As an example, Temple said he would have preferred to use front-end loaders to move incoming refuse to the shredder in-feed conveyor instead of the multi-ram system. It's simpler, he said, and if one loader breaks down you can always bring in another one.)
- *Allow plenty of time and funds for start-up* — at least a year. And avoid making up for construction delays by shaving time off the start-up period.

Despite occasional setbacks and difficulties, the City of Akron and its contractors appear to have developed and implemented a near-ideal solution to the City's dual need for (1) a means of solid waste disposal and (2) a source of energy for the business district. It will be instructive to watch the Recycle Energy System as it reaches full capacity, assumes total steam production responsibilities, and considers expansion to further materials recovery.

4-10 Processed Municipal Refuse: A Fuel for Small Power Plant Boilers

Donald A. Oberacker

Source: *News* of Environmental Research in Cincinnati, U.S. Environmental Protection Agency. Municipal Environmental Research Laboratory, (November 15, 1976) 4pp.

BACKGROUND

The current public energy awareness has sparked interest in the disposing of combustible municipal solid waste in various kinds of steam boilers. The rationale is one of recovering a fuel value of some 4000 to 7000 Btu's per pound of refuse, rather than simply discarding this energy as by incineration.

Research studies toward this goal have considered the use of several existing boiler designs and facilities including heat recovery incinerators, industrial or institutional boilers, municipal heating or light plant boilers, and large electric utility-power plant boilers. Currently, the U.S. Environmental Protection Agency (EPA) is supporting experiments in refuse firing of boilers in St. Louis, Ames, Iowa, and Columbus, Ohio.

This report summarizes EPA's brief but successful tests of co-firing mixtures of refuse and crushed-coal fuel in a small, 150,000 lb steam/hr, 12.5 megawatt municipal light plant boiler of the spreader stoker-traveling grate type at Columbus. Iniated in mid-1974, this project has performed a series of 8-hour instrumented research burns wherein the refuse provided from 15 to 35 percent of the steam generating energy with the balance supplied by crushed coal of 1, 3, and 5 percent sulfur content. Shorter term tests actually approached 50 percent from the refuse, and, optimistically, 70 percent may be feasible with proper refuse feeding and combustion control. Furthermore,

the less costly high sulfur coals burned without excessive SO_x emissions, due apparently to a synergistic effect between refuse and coal. The Columbus studies emphasized the determination of fireside boiler tube corrosion rates and environmental impact evaluation, primarily. Also included were insights into economic feasibilities, refuse processing requirements, and refuse handling and feeding techniques. EPA's research effort to date appears to have answered many initial questions concerning boiler tube life and the environmental feasibility of the concept. It therefore is planned to advance the Columbus project toward more detailed economic evaluations, longer term tests, and eventual full-time implementation of this procedure in the test boiler or in similar boilers.

SYSTEM DESCRIPTION

The refuse portion of the system is similar to that in ordinary incineration, except it involves first shredding then air blowing the refuse into the boiler combustion zone. In design, a spreader stoker-coal fired boiler is similar to a water wall incinerator. A revolving paddle wheel-like stoker is used for feeding coal. Interestingly enough, combustion is often started by manually feeding solid wastes such as cardboard and sections of railroad ties. After these materials produce a hot fire bed, the coal stokers are started.

Course shredding of the refuse to 4- to 10-nominal size pieces by a 5- by 8-inch grate

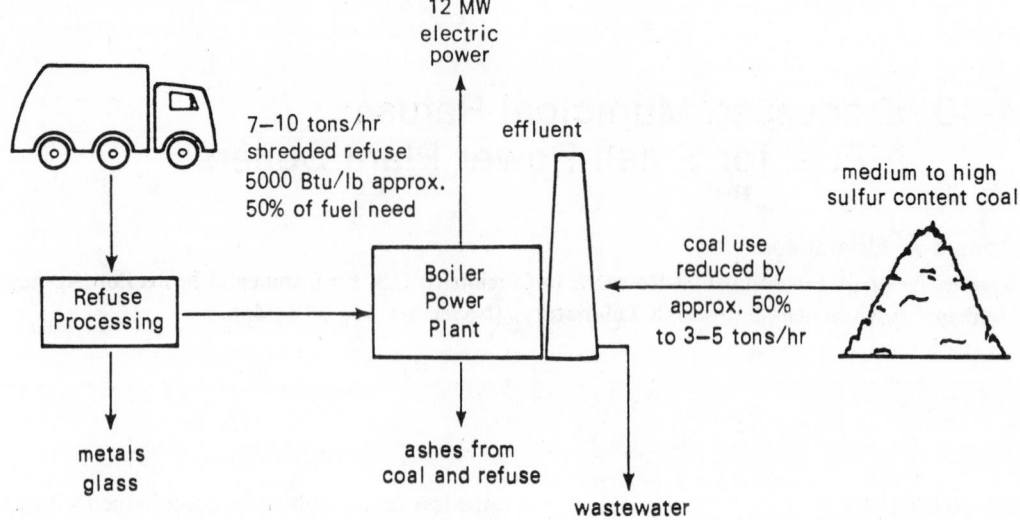

Figure 1.

hammermill facilitates air blowing the material into a convenient entry port in the boiler refractory wall, about 6 feet above the burning coal bed. The coal used is not pulverized; rather, it is fed in as purchased in "crushed" form. Crushed coal particle sizes range from fine dust to pieces about 2 or 3 inches across.

Processed municipal refuse is mostly dry paper or film-like matter, and these were observed to burn quickly in suspension as does some of the finer coal. The larger refuse pieces fall to the fire bed and finish burning on the grate. The normal burning coal bed depth of 4 to 12 inches did not appear to build up noticeably, even at the highest refuse feeding rates of nearly 50 percent on a Btu basis. Residence times on the order of 10 to 12 minutes on the grate provided for well burned-out refuse and coal ash. Although the refuse used had usually been postshredder magnetically separated and air classified, the boiler itself could operate on refuse which was shredded only. However, the recovery of metals and other resources lessens the materials handling problems at the boiler and should produce substantial economic benefits overall.

This project benefited by having shredded refuse delivered to the boiler site free of charge from one of three city-owned shredder installations in Columbus. Due to budget and time limitations, the refuse handling and feeding equipment was light-duty and temporary in

nature. The equipment used initially was agricultural machinery intended for handling farm forage or fodder and consisted of two forage hauler boxes, several farm conveyors, and a 10 horsepower silo blower. This temporary equipment was suitable for a series of 8-hour test burns; it also demonstrated that refuse storage and handling could be accomplished within some rather awkward and crowded working spaces in older boiler plants. Medium-duty industrial equipment is now being readied for some 800- to 1500-hour runs. For a permanent installation for refuse feeding, probably a still stronger all-weather system would be needed.

BOILER TUBE CORROSION MEASUREMENTS

Several 8-hour experiments (see Table 1) were conducted on this program. During these runs, the corrosivity of the combustion products was evaluated by inserting specially designed corrosion probe speciments in the furnace near the superheat tubes. At this location the gas temperature varied from 1100 F (593 C) to 1400 F (750 C). The specimen temperatures were maintained at 500 F to 950 F (260 to 510 C) as measured by thermocouples inserted in the specimens. Individual specimens were tube section 1 inch ID x 1.25 inches OD x 1.5 inches long (2.54 x 3.17 x 3.81 cm) consisting

Table 1. Data for 8-hour Experiments.

Experiment Date	Coal wt% Sulfur	Refuse wt%	Refuse Btu%	Average Steam Flow lb/hr
7/29/74	3.3	0	—	120,000
10/11/74	0.9	9	—	94,000
12/19/74	2.6	50	30	100,000
12/26/74	2.6	28	17	104,000
7/24/75	5.2	27	17	118,000
8/21/75	5.2	0	—	118,000
9/30/75	3.8	36	23	74,000
11/13/75	3.3	42	28	93,000

of the alloys A106, T11, P5, 405, 446, 316, 310, and JS700. Corrosion rates were determined by weight loss measurement procedures. Measured corrosion rates for some of the alloys tested are shown in Table 2 for various temperatures and conditions. These data show that the replacement of coal with up to 42 weight percent (28 Btu percent) refuse has little effect upon the corrosion rates for any of the alloys investigated. In contrast, the last column shows that burning only solid wastes results in an order of magnitude increase in corrosion rates for all of the alloys. Additional details of this corrosion research are available from Reference 7.

During exposure the specimens become coated with fly ash and particulates. The deposit-to-metal interface reactions are of primary importance in understanding the mechanism of metal wastage. Reactions between these deposits and the substrate depend upon the type of oxide scale on the metal substrates, the composition of the deposit, the thermal conductivity and stability of the deposit, and the duration of the exposure. This scale layer is usually quite thin and consists of several compounds which form at specific locations in the scale layer. The compounds in the scale layer on the corrosion specimens were analyzed by optical emission spectroscopy and wet chemical analysis. A detailed presentation of these findings together with an analysis of the probable chemical reactions which take place within these layers is presented in Reference 7.

STACK EMISSION ANALYSES

The stack emissions were measured by standard EPA techniques. The results are shown in Table 3. The analysis included measurements of sulfur oxides, nitrogen oxides, particulates, HC1, O_2, CO_2, CO, vinyl chloride and polycyclic organic materials. It should be noted that with 3 percent sulfur coal, and 36 weight percent (w/o) refuse, the SO_2, was reduced to 46 percent of the amount with coal only. However, in a similar run with 42 w/o refuse, the SO_2 was 86 percent of that with coal alone. In another run with the 3 percent sulfur coal, the SO_2, emissions were reduced to 41 percent of the baseline amount when using 56 w/o refuse. Thus the results to date show promise of lowered SO_2 emissions when firing refuse. More tests are needed to determine the amount of SO_2 reduction.

Table 2. Eight-hour Corrosion Rates Determined for Various Alloys (mils/hr).

Alloy	Metal Temp. F	Coal Only 1% S Coal	Coal Only 3% S Coal	Coal Only 5% S Coal	Coal Plus Refuse 3% S Coal 28 w/o Refuse	Coal Plus Refuse 5% S Coal 27 w/o Refuse	Coal Plus Refuse 3% S Coal 36 w/o Refuse	Coal Plus Refuse 3% S Coal 42 w/o Refuse	100% Refuse
A106	500	0.004	0.0005	0.002	0.002	0.002	0.003	0.001	0.16
	700	0.008	0.007	0.020	0.010	0.021	0.008	0.012	0.18
	900	0.022	0.027	0.063	0.030	0.068	0.031	0.035	0.020
T11	500	0.005	0.005	0.002	0.004	0.003	0.002	0.002	0.10
	700	0.006	0.007	0.013	0.005	0.018	0.006	0.005	0.12
	900	0.013	0.022	0.034	0.022	0.037	0.020	0.020	0.18
316	600	0.003	Nil	Nil	Nil	Nil	Nil	Nil	Nil
	700	0.005	Nil	0.001	0.001	0.001	Nil	Nil	0.056
	900	0.006	0.001	0.002	0.001	0.002	0.004	0.002	0.056

Table 3. Stack Emissions.

Item	3.2 w/o S Coal	36 w/o Refuse + 3.2 w/o S Coal
SO_2, ppm	2340	1190
SO_3, ppm	12	20
HCl, ppm	14	36
NO_x, ppm	210	127
O_2, %	10.4	9.1
CO_2, %	9.6	10.5
CO, %	0.1	0.022
H_2O, %	9.4	8.6
CH_4, ppm	Nil	2
C_2H_4, ppm	Nil	0.2
Polynuclear aromatic hydrocarbons, ng/m^3	7070	—
Vinyl chloride, ppm	Nil	Nil
Particulate, gr/scf	1.20	0.52

Another class of pollutants is the polycyclic organic material (POM). These are emitted from the stack during firing with and without refuse. A wide range of values has been obtained in the experiments to date. While those runs in which coal alone was burned generally showed the lowest amounts of POM, it is felt that poor combustion conditions are primarily responsible for the production of POM. Occasionally POM's of the carcinogen type were detected. No firm conclusions can be reached yet about relative POM amounts and types with combined firing until more baseline data are obtained.

Of the other gaseous components in the stack gases, none were present in amounts that would seem to constitute a problem. Small increases in the amount of HCl were found, i.e., 26 to 45 ppm, compared with 14 ppm from the coal alone. Incineration produced some 250 to 400 ppm of HCl by comparison. Nitrogen oxide concentrations appeared to reflect combustion temperatures rather than any direct effect of refuse burning. Other gaseous organic compounds were not present in significant amounts.

The solid particulate situation also requires more testing. The initial tests are difficult to evaluate in that two of the baseline runs were made before a major cyclone separator repair occurred. Judging from the amount of particulates found in some runs, it appears that refuse causes an increase in the amount of particulates.

CONCLUSIONS

Based on these initial studies, EPA plans to expand this research testing program toward longer, more meaningful runs. It is hoped that by mid-1977, the results of several 800- to 1500-hour runs will be available to the public.

REFERENCES

1. Battelle Columbus Ohio Laboratories, D.A. Vaughan and Associates, Report of First Year Research on Environmental Effects of Utilizing Solid Waste as a Supplementary Power Plant Fuel, report on EPA Research Grant R-804008, June 1975.
2. Thermo-Electron Corp., S.E. Nydick and J.R. Hurley, Study Program to Investigate Use of Solid Waste as a Supplementary Fuel in Industrial Boilers, report on EPA Contract No. 68-03-0355, January 1976.
3. Riley, B.T., Preliminary Assessment of the Feasibility of Utilizing Densified Refuse Derived Fuel (DRDF) as a Supplementary Fuel for Stoker Fired Boilers, report to EPA (unpubl.), 1975.
4. Midwest Research Institute, St. Louis/Union Electric Refuse Firing Demonstration Air Pollution Test Report, EPA-650/2-74-073, Contract No. 68-03-1324 task 2.
5. Midwest Research Institute, St. Refuse Processing Plant: Equipment, Facility, and Environmental Evaluations, EPA-650/2-75-044, Contract No. 68-03-1324 task 4.
6. PEDCO-Environmental Specialists, Inc., Ridgewood Army Weapons Plant Evaluation and Resource Recovery Feasibility Study, prepared for Hamilton County Ohio Board of Commissioners, April 1975.
7. Vaughan, D.A., H.H. Krause, J.F. Hunt, P.W. Cover, J.D. Dickson, and W.K. Boyd, Environmental Effects of Utilizing Solid Waste as a Supplementary Power Plant Fuel, Seventh Quarterly Progress Report on EPA Research Grant 804008-02-1, 1975.

4-11 District Heating with Refuse Derived Fuel at Wright-Patterson Air Force Base

A.J. Buonicone and J.P. Waltz

Source: *Mechanical Engineering,* Vol. 24, No. 11 (December 1977) pp. 35-38. Reprinted with Permission of The American Society of Mechanical Engineers.

INTRODUCTION

Current concern about energy supply and environmental quality has focused attention on how resources are utilized and the effects of resource use on the environment.[1] Escalating growth in materials consumption and waste generation, with its attendant effect on the nation's resource base is neither inevitable nor necessary. Energy can be conserved by improving upon current materials use and waste management practices. Converting municipal solid waste into energy is a solid waste management option that is becoming attractive, both environmentally and economically. The use of solid waste as such, offers several distinct benefits:

1. It reduces the consumption of virgin natural resources — the materials and energy.
2. It minimizes the amount of solid waste that ultimately must be disposed of — with the attendant reduction in the land required for disposal sites and the environmental damages that may result from improper disposal practices.
3. It reduces the atmospheric emissions, waterborn wastes, and industrial and mining wastes when a recycled material is substituted for a virgin material in production processes.[2]
4. It results in decreased sulfur oxide emissions due to the lower sulfur content of solid waste.

5. It is a readily available, growing — rather than depleting — domestic source of energy.

The utilization of solid waste as a supplemental fuel in utility power plants and district heating plants takes advantage of an established system for producing, distributing, and marketing energy through use of an existing boiler or a new one designed for this purpose. Consequently, the energy recovered from solid waste has an assured market.

In light of these considerations, Wright-Patterson Air Force Base (WPAFB) made arrangements with The Black Clawson Company to test in the base coal-fired boilers a refuse derived fuel (RDF) produced at the Franklin, Ohio resource recovery plant. The purpose of this test was to investigate the feasibility of utilizing RDF to supplement base coal supplies.

The RDF test was conducted during the week of 21-25 July 1975 on #1 boiler at the WPAFB Central Heating Plant, Building 770. Data was gathered during 34 hours of firing a 1:1 by volume coal/RDF mix, 6 hours of firing a 2:1 by volume mix, and 24 hours of firing coal (for comparison purposes).

RDF PREPARATION

The RDF pellets utilized in the Phase I test were prepared by the Black Clawson Company at the Franklin, Ohio resource recovery plant which has been in operation since June 1971. Although

485

the plant is relatively small, it uses commercial-scale equipment and operates on a daily basis as the sole solid waste disposal facility for the City of Franklin and surrounding townships. The system operation has been described elsewhere.[3,4]

In order to minimize any modifications to the existing coal-fired stoker-fed boilers, it was decided that the optimum RDF fuel should be pelletized and the moisture content controlled to a relatively constant level. This necessitated certain modifications to the Franklin operation which was already geared toward the production of a pulped product with a high and variable moisture content. Typical properties of the pulped organic fraction discharged from the cone press are presented in Table 1.

To provide the desirable RDF fuel, this pulped organic fraction was trucked to Oregon, Ohio, near Toledo and dried to approximately a 20% moisture level. Drying was accomplished in a triple pass model 125 Heil Rotary Dryer, owned by Toledo Alfalfa Company. As the name implies, this unit is normally used in the drying of alfalfa hay. Although the Oregon plant has a pelletizer and cooler following the dryer, the feed arrangement while perfect in pelletizing alfalfa, was entirely unsatisfactory for the Franklin dried material. Consequently, a temporary pelletizing system was set up at the Black Clawson Company, Middletown Laboratory, using a California "Century" pellet mill. A number of different diameter pellets were tried and the 3/8-inch diameter was chosen for the RDF tests at Wright-Patterson AFB.

Typical properties of the dried and pelletized RDF are presented in Table 2.

HEATING PLANT AND PREPARATIONS

Heating Plant Description

The central base heating system is composed of five large central heating plants, each with its own distribution system. The plant sizes range from 140,000 #/hr to approximately 500,000 #/hr. There is a total of approximately 60 miles of heating distribution piping on the base.

The site of the RDF test was Central Heating Plant, Bldg 770, which is one of two plants serving that part of the Base referred to as Area B. The distribution systems for these two plants are interconnected and the total summer load in the area is 50-60,000 #/hr.

Bldg 770 is equipped with two identical Edge Moor Iron Works boilers, of 60,000 #/hr capacity each, producing 125 psig saturated steam. These boilers, installed in 1956, are fired by "Detroit Rotograte" continuously forward traveling grate stokers. The stoker mechanism consists of a reciprocating feeder supplying fuel to an overthrow rotor which distributed fuel across the traveling chain grates. These grates constantly move toward the front of the boiler where the ashes are dumped into a pit below. Pollution abatement equipment at the plant includes cyclone separators (multi-clones) and an electrostatic precipitator on each boiler. The precipitators have been inoperable for some time.

The fuel handling system at the plant involves open coal storage in a large yard adjacent

Table 1. Typical Properties of the Pulped Organic Fraction Discharged from the Cone Press.

Property	Basis As Received	Dry
Energy, BTU/lb	3300	7400
Moisture, %	55.5	—
Ash, %	6.2	34.0
Chloride, %	0.07	0.17
Sodium, %	0.03	0.07
Softening Temperature, °F	—	2310
Density, lb/ft³	35.3	33.58

Table 2. Typical Properties of RDF Pellets Used in the Test Program.

Property	Basis As Received	Dry
Energy, BTU/lb	5800	7400
Moisture, %	21.5	—
Ash, %	11.2	14.3
Sulfur, %	0.32	0.16
Volatile, %	60.20	76.74
Fixed Carbon, %	10.46	13.32
Density, lb/ft³	36.3	29.9

to the plant. Coal shipments are received by rail, off loaded by a clamshell crane (rail type) and the fuel distributed throughout the yard by a bulldozer. Reclaiming fuel from the yard is also accomplished by the bulldozer and crane reloading fuel into a hopper car. The hopper car is placed over a track hopper to dump the coal. From the hopper the fuel is transferred on a short conveyor to the bucket elevator/flight conveyor which lifts the coal to the top of the plant depositing it in the 250-ton storage bunker. When the plant is in operation, the fuel falls out of the bunker into an automatic scale, weighing fuel in 200-pound increments with a counterbalanced bucket. From there, the fuel travels through a chute to the stokers which feed the fuel into the boiler.

As the stoker spreads fuel out on the grates, fresh air for combustion is forced up through the grates by the underfire air or forced draft fan. Additional combustion air is provided above the grates by the overfire air fan. Combustion gases exit the rear of the boiler and pass through the cyclone separator where most of the particulate matter in the gas stream is removed. The induced draft fan creates a negative pressure on the cyclone separator and the boiler and forces the exhaust gases out the stack into the atmosphere.

The ashes falling off the end of the traveling grates are collected in the bottom ash pit. The ashes removed by the cyclone separator are collected in the fly ash hopper. Both the bottom ash and fly ash are removed each shift by a vacuum ash conveying system and transferred to an ash storage silo. The ash silo is emptied periodically into dump trucks and the ashes taken to landfill.

Fuel Preparation

Due to the temporary operation setup by the Black Clawson Company to produce the RDF pellets, the pellets had to be made up in batches well in advance of the scheduled operating test. The pellets were placed in open top steel storage containers, covered with a tarp and polyethylene sheet and placed in storage. The initial run of pellets remained in storage for approximately one week, at which time they were delivered to the heating plant.

Two RDF-to-coal mixtures were chosen for testing. In addition to demonstrating and confirming the feasibility in the base boilers of a 20% energy substitution with RDF (testing elsewhere has indicated that 20% substitution would not be detrimental to operation of the boiler,[5] it was also decided to investigate the upper limits of energy substitution with RDF in an unmodified stoker-fired boiler. The two fuel ratios are summarized below:

Burn Date:	23 Jul	24 Jul
Volume Ratio (RDF: Coal)	1:1	2:1
Weight Ratio (RDF: Coal)	40/60	58/42
Energy Ratio (RDF: Coal)	23/77	37/63

Enough of the 1:1 mix (by volume) was made to provide a minimum of 24 hours operation. The quantity of 2:1 mix prepared was sufficient for a 6-hour test.

When the pellets arrived at the plant they were weighed on a nearby truck scale and then dumped in the coal storage yard. In order to determine the effectiveness of allowing the coal and RDF to mix as it passed through the fuel handling equipment in the plant, the RDF and coal mixing was handled by two different methods. The first was to form a pile of mixed fuel in the coal yard by taking alternate scoops, with the clamshell crane, of RDF and coal and then picking up and dropping this mixture a number of times to insure homogeneity. The mixture was then loaded into a hopper car. The second mixing procedure simply involved dumping alternate scoops of RDF and coal directly into the hopper car.

The storage bunker in the plant was not partitioned to allow segregated storage of coal and mixed fuel; hence, the bulk of the mixed fuel has to be stored outside in hopper cars. To protect the mixed fuel from inclement weather, pre-fabricated wood frames were placed on top of the cars and polyethylene sheeting nailed and taped to the frames to provide a weather protective cover. Some RDF pellets remained in the coal yard after mixing and it was noted that anything more than a small amount of rainfall would cause the pellets to break down to their original shredded form.

While running the mixed fuel through the fuel handling equipment in the plant it was observed that the final condition of the fuel as it arrived in the bunker was the same regardless of the mixing method used in loading the hopper cars. Exceptionally good mixing occurred during the transfer of the fuel from the transfer conveyor to the bucket elevator. This was attributed to the side-by-side location of the transfer conveyor and the coal elevator forcing the fuel to make a 90° turn while dropping off the conveyor into the elevator all resulting in excellent fuel mixing.

Stack Scaffolding

A special requirement of the test was to monitor boiler stack emissions. To provide complete and convenient access to the stack gases, two test ports were installed in the boiler stack and steel frame scaffolding was added to the induced draft fan decking to provide access to the ports and room for setting up test equipment.

FIRING SCHEDULE

To provide a valid comparison of coal-fired operation and mixed fuel operation, the test boiler was brought on line approximately 1 day prior to commencement of stack tests.

PLANNED TESTS AND DATA

Stack Emission Tests

Plans were made to conduct side-by-side comparison of the boiler stack emissions while firing 1:1, RDF: Coal Mix; Additional tests were planned for the 2:1 mix firing tests. However, due to the short duration of the 2:1 firing it was not expected that sufficient tests could be conducted to compare all emissions. Among the emission tests planned were the following:

    a. Particulates, EPA Method 5.
    b. Sulfur Dioxide, EPA Method 6.
    c. Nitrogen Oxide, EPA Method 7.
    d. Particle Size Distribution, University of Washington Mark III. Impactor and sieves (multiclone catch).

    e. Heavy Metals, atomic absorption.
    f. Halides, specific ion electrodes.
    g. Total Hydrocarbons, activated charcoal absorption.

Fuel Samples

While the boiler was in operation, samples were taken of the fuel as it was being weighed by the automatic scale. During all stack emission tests, samples were taken every 30 minutes and combined into 2-hour composites for analysis. During the remaining time operating on mixed fuel, samples were also taken every 30 minutes but assembled into 4-hour composites for analysis.

Boiler Logs

As a part of the normal operation of the plant, detailed operating logs are maintained including all the normal boiler operating parameters; fuel and steam flow, CO_2 of the stack gas, etc. In addition to the normal data recorded, the logs were modified to include additional information on the fuel and ash handling equipment.

    Stoker operation was monitored by measuring the speed of reciprocating feed mechanism using a hand tachometer and by measuring the length of the stroke of the mechanism. Fuel feed through the chutes to the stokers were observed by the boiler operator and the observations recorded on the logs.

    The traveling grates were monitored by measuring the depth of the ash bed with a calibrated probe and by measuring the speed of the drive mechanism with a hand tachometer. Operator comments on the condition of the grates and ashes were also recorded.

Ash Evaluation

Preliminary investigation of the properties of RDF revealed that a prime area of concern in the test should be the quality and quantity of ashes produced. Analysis of the RDF pellets prior to testing indicated high ash content and low ash fusion temperature. Unusual amounts of clinkering and a large increase in ashes to be hauled could have a significant impact on manpower and plant operation.

A visual examination of the bottom ashes was performed, providing side-by-side comparison of the ashes formed on the traveling grates by coal, 1:1 mix, and 2:1 mix.

A total ash weight and volume comparison was performed on coal and 1:1 mix ashes. This was accomplished by emptying the ash storage silo prior to commencement of the 24 hour run on coal, emptying all ash collection hoppers into the silo at the end of the run, and then emptying the silo again to weigh and measure the volume of ashes collected during the 24-hour period. This procedure was repeated for the 24-hour run on 1:1 mix. All ashes were measured and weighed dry, although a wet rotary dustless unloader is normally used in emptying the silo.

Firebox Inspection

Based on previous use of municipal waste as fuel,[6] a very serious concern in the performance of this test was the expectation that some corrosion/scaling of the fireside surfaces would occur. To provide a valid evaluation of the effects of firing RDF, the interior or firebox of the boiler was closely examined and photographed both before and after the test firing.

RESULTS

Fuel Analysis

Laboratory Analysis of the fuel samples taken every 30 minutes resulted in the average fuel properties given in Table 3.

Stack Emission Tests

A comparative study of the boiler stack emissions while firing coal, 1:1 RDF/coal mix and 2:1 RDF/coal mix was conducted by personnel from the Environmental Health Laboratory, McClellan AFB, California. The final report is not available at this time, however, the preliminary results are very favorable and are shown in Table 4. Notable areas of improvement are in SO_2 and HC emissions. Sulfur emissions are

Table 3. Average Properties of Fuels Utilized During Phase I Test.

Properties		Fuel		
		Coal	1:1 Mix	2:1 Mix
Energy BTU/LB	Dry	13562	12276	11069
	As Fired	12900	11327	9515
% Moisture	As Fired	4.88	7.73	14.01
% Ash	Dry	7.89	9.86	10.3
	As Fired	7.50	9.09	8.86
% Sulfur	Dry	0.71	0.58	0.50
	As Fired	0.67	0.53	0.43
% Chlorine	Dry	0.10	0.15	0.16
	As Fired	0.09	0.14	0.14
% Fixed Carbon	Dry	58.5	47.5	42.5
	As Fired	55.6	43.8	36.5
% Volatiles	Dry	33.6	42.6	47.2
	As Fired	31.9	39.3	40.6
% Hydrogen	Dry	5.16	5.52	5.71
	As Fired	4.90	5.09	4.91
% Carbon	Dry	77.1	65.8	65.7
	As Fired	73.3	63.5	56.5

Table 4. Stack Emissions (Comparison to Coal).

Emissions	1:1 Mix	2:1 Mix
Particulates	Unchanged	Highly variable. On the average unchanged
SO_2	Reduced by Approximately 50%	Reduced by Approximately 60%
NO_x	Unchanged	Highly Erratic. Generally Increased
HC (Gaseous − 350°)	Drastically Reduced − by approximately 20%	Drastically Reduced − by 95+%

reduced primarily as a result of the low sulfur content of the refuse derived fuel. The tremendous reduction of HC emissions is attributed to the combustion of the RDF (mostly cellulose) in the solid state as opposed to the combustion of off gasses as occurs in the burning of coal. This is a significant result in that it could have a considerable impact on smog formation in highly congested areas.

Halide and heavy metal emission test results will be available at a later date.

Stoker and Grates

Analysis of the data gathered on the stoker and the traveling grate mechanisms indicated that no unusual variations in equipment operation occurred while firing the 1:1 mix. However, during the 2:1 mix test considerable problems did occur which were revealed primarily through the operators observations and comments. The primary difficulty encountered in 2:1 firing was a general loss of control over fuel distribution. While it was possible to feed sufficient fuel to maintain the desired load on the boiler, the operator was unable to maintain an even distribution of fuel on the grates which resulted in a concentration of the fire in the rear of the firebox. Compounding this problem was the occurrence of fuel segregation in the automatic scale operation which carried over into the stoker feed chutes and ultimately resulted in a high concentration of RDF pellets in the fuel feeding one of the three stokers. An additional undesirable result during the 2:1 firing was

severe clinkering or fusion of the ashes on the traveling grate. This required "breaking-up" by the operator to maintain air flow through the grates and may very well have been a direct result of the high temperatures in the heavy concentration of fire at the rear of the boiler.

Ashes

A side-by-side visual comparison of the bottom ash collected gave the following results:

a. Coal − ashes very loose with a few small clinkers approx. 4 inches in maximum dimension.

b. 1:1 Mix − ashes very loose with a few small clinkers approx. 5 inches in maximum dimension.

c. 2:1 Mix − ashes mostly fused in large clinkers with a maximum dimension of approx. 24 inches.

The total weight and volume of the ashes collected in the silo are shown in Table 5.

Firebox Deposits

Comparison of the fire side surfaces before and after the firing test discerned at least three different instances in which material deposition occurred.

The first and perhaps most obvious of these instances was that of clinker formation on the refractory surfaces of the rear wall and rearward side walls of the firebox. The deposits on the

Table 5. Silo Ash Summary.

Fuel	Total Weight	Total Volume
Coal	4.97 tons	11.88 yd³
1:1 Mix	6.48 tons	14.13 yd³
% Change	+30%	+19%
% Change (On an equivalent energy output basis)	+17%	+ 7%

rear wall were continuous from just above the grate surface to about 6 feet above the grates (just below the upper overfire air nozzle). At the top, the deposits were granular and very loosely adhered. Moving towards the bottom, the deposits were progressively more fused together and more tightly adhered to the wall. At the bottom, the deposits were very smooth, shiny and glass-like in appearance, and were evidently in a fluid state as small stalactites were formed. The deposits on the rearward, lower portions of the sidewalls were identical to the uppermost deposits on the rear wall (loose and granular), with considerably more deposits found on the boiler tube surfaces. The majority of these deposits are attributed to firing the 2:1 mix, during which a heavy turbulent concentration of fire occurred at the rear of the grates and also during which the RDF migrated to the left stoker — it is believed that these occurrences created both the conditions for deposition (high localized temperatures) and the pattern of deposition (heavier concentration on left side). These deposits do not present a serious hazard to boiler operation and would probably not occur to any great extent during continuous 1:1 mix firing.

The second and perhaps most serious of the instances of deposition was that of the formation of flake-like deposits on the forward side wall boiler tubes. These deposits were generally most concentrated in the front portion of the side walls above the stoker ports, and appeared to be heavier on the left side of the boiler. While some flakes were formed on the front side of the tubes, the heaviest deposits were found on the back side of the tubes between the refractory and the tube, where the tube surface is the coolest. In appearance, the flakes were a pale yellow-to-tan with maroon edges, and had a very stretchy, sticky, consistency. The flakes evidently had a much greater coefficient of thermal expansion than the steel tubes as the flakes curled and fell off the tubes once the boiler cooled. Due to the heavier concentration on the left side, it is suspected that these deposits are also related to the 2:1 mix firing. The deposits present a possible hazard to boiler operation due to their location on the tubes and the unknown potential for corrosion and/or efficiency reduction over a long period.

An additional deposition phenomenon was the occurrence of "staining" of the sections of the chain grates. After the boiler was cooled and swept out, it was observed that instead of the normal overall rusty appearance, the grate sections appeared black and slightly polished in certain areas. Scraping the surface with a tool had no effect on the stained areas. The general appearance of this stain was quite similar to the shiny deposits on the rear wall, and appeared to be temperature related due to the lack of stain immediately around the air holes in the grates. Due to the small build-up and the possible relationship to the 2:1 firing, these deposits do not present a hazard to boiler operation over a long period.

CONCLUSIONS

The following conclusions can be drawn from the RDF test program:

1. Firing the 1:1 RDF/coal mix (by volume) caused no significant problems.

2. Firing the 2:1 RDF/coal mix (by volume) did cause certain operational problems which might require boiler modification for extended operation.

3. For use in stoker-fired boilers, a larger and more dense pellet would be desirable and could solve the control problems at higher RDF/coal ratios.

4. The RDF odor can be reduced to an acceptable level by drying, pelletizing, and air cooling immediately after dewatering in the cone press at the Franklin facility.

5. The potential scaling/corrosion problem caused by the scattered flake-like deposits found on the boiler tubes needs to be evaluated further.

6. The refractory deposits formed during the test are considered controllable and are not expected to be harmful to boiler operation.

7. Stack emission tests generally showed a beneficial effect on the environment. The decrease in hydrocarbon is especially encouraging in light of the potential for smog reduction.

8. Firing the 1:1 mix resulted in a nominal effect on total ash handling and hauling.

9. Utilizing RDF as a fuel conservation measure during the short duration test, approximately 19 tons of coal were conserved.

10. In the long term, utilizing RDF as a fuel supplement will complement solid waste management. After delivering the RDF pellets to the boiler plant, solid waste can be picked up and hauled back to the resource recovery facility.

REFERENCES

1. Rolinski, E.F., Buonicore, A.J., and Theodore L., "Evaluating Energy Policy Alternatives in Light of Environmental Considerations," Paper No. 75-08.2, 68th Annual Meeting of the Air Pollution Control Association, Boston, Massachusetts, June 15–20, 1975.

2. Office of Solid Waste Management Programs, First Report to Congress, "Resource Recovery and Source Reduction," EPA Publication SW-118, 3rd Ed, Washington, D.C., U.S. Government Printing Office, 1974.

3. Arella, David G., "Recovering Resources from Solid Waste Using Wet-Processing," EPA Report SW-47d, 1974.

4. Environmental Science and Technology, "Reclaiming Municipal Garbage," Vol. 5, No. 10, 998-999, October 1971.

5. Lowe, Robert A., "Energy Recovery from Waste," EPA Publication SW-36.ii, Second Interim Report, Washington, D.C., U.S. Government Printing Office, 1973.

6. Miller, P.D. ET AL. "Corrosion Studies in Municipal Incinerators," EPA Publication SW-72-3-3, Washington, D.C. U.S. Government Printing Office, 1972.

4-12 Waste Fuel Densification: Review of the Technology and Applications

Jay A. Campbell

Source: Paper Presented at the International Conference on Prepared Fuels and Resource Recovery Technology, Nashville, Tennessee, February 10–13, 1981, 19 pp.

INTRODUCTION

The emphasis of early waste-to-energy demonstration and commercial projects in the United States was on the preparation and firing of refuse-derived fuel (RDF) in suspension-fired boilers burning pulverized coal. These types of boilers, which are typically large with steam-generating capacitites generally over 180 Mg/hr steam, offer a potential for combustion of large quantities of waste. However, the plants tend to be concentrated near larger cities and, due to economies of scale and the nature of utility rate structuring, their cost of primary fuel tends to be lower. The pressures to minimize fuel costs is also less than that for industrial boiler operators.

The industrial and institutional boiler population, including those with steam-generating capacities of 30 Mg/hr to 110 Mg/hr steam includes some 8,500 units[1]. These boilers are widely dispersed in both large and small communities; and, because of their small size, they cannot benefit from discounts for quantity, purchases and deliveries of the coal. Regulations on sulphur dioxide emissions are also forcing these operators to either buy expensive low-sulphur coal or invest in costly air pollution control equipment.

For these reasons of location, size and fuel specifications and costs of this smaller power boiler market, there appears to be a good match to the availability, locations and fuel characteristics of waste-derived fuel. To minimize the modifications to the existing feed and combustion systems, densified form of refuse-derived fuel (d-RDF) rather than fluff RDF burned in suspension-fired boilers is desirable. The goal then is to produce a d-RDF with physical and combustion properties comparable to the "lump" or stoker coal normally burned in these industrial-scale boilers.

Production and test work on d-RDF accomplished by the National Center for Resource Recovery from 1976 to 1979 for the U.S. Environmental Protection Agency and Department of Energy has been reported both in final project reports[2,3,4] and on specific topics or in abbreviated versions in other papers[5,6,7]. This paper will include results and observations from each of these NCRR projects, as well as summaries of other activities in production, handling and combustion of d-RDF both in the United States and abroad.

PRODUCTION TECHNOLOGY STATUS

Densified refuse-derived fuel is obtained by compacting the light organic fraction of solid waste, which has been processed to remove noncombustibles into particles. The term d-RDF as used here refers to mixed residential or commercial wastes densified in pelletizing, cubing, extrusion or briquetting devices. Densification of biomass feedstocks, although of growing interest, is not considered here.

Densification Equipment

Pelletizing of RDF is accomplished with a hard steel die perforated with a dense array of holes

Table 1. Selected Densifier Equipment Suppliers.

Firm	Address
California Pellet Mill	1114 E. Wabash Ave. Crawfordsville, IN 47933
Agnew Environmental Products	P.O. Box 1168 Grants Pass, OR 97526
Papakube Corporation	1211 Rockhurst Dr. San Diego, CA 92120
Ferro-Tech	467 Eureka Rd. Wyandotte, MI 48192
Sprout-Waldron	Koppers Co., Inc. Muncie, PA 17756
Bühler-Miag	4515 Willard Ave. Chevy Chase, MD 20015
Trans Energy Systems	1605 116th Ave., N.E. Bellevue, WA 98004

from 6 mm to 32 mm in diameter. As the die and an inner set of pressure rollers rotate against each other, the feedstock is forced through holes, and the pellets broken off at random lengths up to 38 mm. Cubetting is a modification of pelletizing in which the d-RDF is produced in the form of cubes, generally 32 mm square.

Extrusion as a means of producing d-RDF employs a screw or reciprocating plunger to force the feedstock under pressure through a die. Large diameter cylinders (50 to 200 mm) are produced, and binding agents such as pitch or paraffin are typically added to increase integrity. (Artificial fireplace logs, for example, are manufactured by an extrusion process.) The larger cylinders place the products outside the size range acceptable for stoker-fired boilers.

Briquetting involves the compaction of feedstock in cavities between two rollers. A material is produced similar in size and shape to charcoal briquettes. Although some experimental work has been conducted in the briquetting of refuse, problems with feeding and binding have been experienced. Briquetting of d-RDF is not practiced commercially at this time.

The mechanism that bonds compacted refuse-derived fuel is not fully understood. With wood and agricultural feedstocks, natural binders in the form of lignin are present. For other materials and in most briquetting operations, binders

such as paraffin, lignins or bettonite (clay) are added. For densification of residential waste feedstocks, there has been no reported need or use of binders. Apparently the presence of moisture and lignin, waxes and greases in the waste combine to bind the particles.

A densification system is typically made up of several component parts: (1) a feeder, typically a screw bottom bin, to meter the feed to the system; (2) a conditioner or mixer, usually a screw conveyor where binders or other additives may be mixed with the feedstock; (3) the densifier with associated dies, rollers, drive system and base structure; and (4) a cooler, usually a conveyor carrying a thin bed of d-RDF through which air is drawn to remove excess heat or moisture and thereby harden the product.

Table 1 provides a partial listing of densification equipment manufacturers. A summary of some of the larger currently operating and notable older d-RDF production facilities in the U.S. and U.K. are noted in Table 2.

Densification Equipment Performance and Problems

As in many instances where equipment from other industries has been applied to solid waste, the performance of the densification equipment has not equalled performance on traditional agricultural and forest product residue feedstocks. The following discussion of solid waste densification will be viewed from the perspective of the differences in feedstock and application. Lacking extensive operational experience, such a viewpoint provides a good base for understanding observed performance or identifying needs for improved feed preparation and delivery systems.

Note that while nearly all of the densification efforts to date have been with pilot and experimental plants, most of the densifiers have been full size. Thus, the observations and data on throughput, reliability and feedstock/product relationships are valid for assessing commercial-scale performances, capabilities and limitations. Also note that these data and relationships should apply to most types of densifiers although experience has been exclusively with pelleting and cubetting-type machines.

Table 2. Summary of Selected d-RDF Production Facilities.

Operator/ Location	Operating Period	Plant Type/ Capacity	Front-end Processing	Densified Product	Report Ref.
Vista Chemical Co., Los Gatos, CA	1974–	Prototype, 5–7 Mg/hr	Trommel, shred, air classify, trommel	Ring extrusion, 6 mm to 38 mm dia.	–
Leigh Forming Co., Easton, PA	1977–	Prototype, 9 Mg/h	Shred, air classify	Ring extrusion, 16 mm dia.	–
NCRR, Washington, D.C.	1974–79	Pilot plant, 9 Mg/hr	Shred, screen air classify, shred	Ring extrusion, 13 mm and 25 mm dia.	2, 3, 4
National Recycling, Ft. Wayne, IN	1971–73	Prototype, 5–13 Mg/hr	Shred, air classify, screen	Cuber, 32 mm dia.	8
Maryland Environmental Service, Cockeysville, MD	1976–	Commercial, 9 Mg/hr	Shred, air classify, trommel, shred	Ring extrusion (2), 13 mm dia.	9
U.S. Navy, Jacksonville, FL	1980–	Prototype, 5 Mg/hr	Flail, trommel, classify	Ring extrusion, 19 mm dia.	10
Doncaster, U.K. (municipal)	1980–	Commercial, 10 Mg/hr	Trommel, air classify, shred, dry	Ring extrusion, 16 mm dia.	–
Bühler Miag, Inc., Eastborne, U.K.	1980–	Commercial, 9 Mg/hr	Shred, trommel, air classify, shred, dry	Ring extrusion, 20 mm dia.	–
Byker, U.K. (municipal)	1980–	Commercial, 30 Mg/hr	Shred, trommel, air classify, shred	Ring extrusion, 16 mm dia.	–

Throughput. Processing capacities of 8 to 12 tons per hour are common for pelleting traditional feedstocks with the equipment size and configurations utilized at NCRR, and several other waste densification plants. However, maximum capacities of only 5 tons per hour and sustained feedrates of only 2 to 4 tons per hour have been achievable with RDF feedstocks without frequent blockages or deterioration of d-RDF quality[2]. Rather than a single explanation for the shortfall, there seen to be several interrelated factors, including equipment configuration and condition, feedrate stability, and feedstock properties including moisture, density and particle size. The impact of these factors will be discussed below.

Equipment Configuration and Condition. Densifier capacity and product characteristics are affected by the die and roller configuration (die hole diameter, taper and thickness and roller diameter and surface covering). Lacking experience with waste feedstock, for the first generation plants these components have been selected based on the manufacturer's intuition. Today there is still insufficient documented operating experience with a variety of hardware configurations or feedstocks to improve much on such a selection process.

The impact of the condition of the dies and rolls on throughput was evident at NCRR in changes in throughput rate and the frequency of jams on the densifier with increasing wear on dies and rolls. When a new die with sharp corners at the hole inlet or new rolls with unworn corrugations were first installed, the feedrate could be increased by 40%; blockages and stalls of the machine were also reduced. After processing less than 100 Mg, the abrasive feed blunted the die and roll surfaces; again, only lower throughputs could be maintained without jams.

Feedstock Size. In traditional densification applications, the feedstock is reduced to a top size, equal or smaller than the diameter of the die hole opening. In all waste densification applications to date, the particle size has been larger than the die aperture. This would lead to greater power consumption and, thus, reduced capacity, as material must be sheared by the die and rolls as it is forced into the holes. In addition, materials particularly resistant to size reduction such as plastics and textiles have been observed to wind on augers and impellers and jam the rolls, stopping the machine.

In exploring sizing approaches at both NCRR and Warren Spring Laboratory (WSL), it was found that the product from hammermill and knife shredders varied both in the proportion of top size materials as well as particle and bulk properties[2]. Conclusions from the investigations suggested two or more stages of hammermilling necessary to achieve the same size control as could be obtained with a single pass through a knife shredder. In addition, the knife mill product tended to be flatter, crumpled less and have a higher bulk density than the hammermill product. Recognized limitations of a knife mill applied to solid wastes are suceptible to damage from tramp metals and wear from abrasive fines.

Moisture. The moisture content of most traditional pelletizer feedstocks is controlled by steam conditioning or drying to a level of 12 to 15%. NCRR experience suggests a comparable range of moisture of 12 to 20%; also, results in formation of pellets of good quality; moisture content between 20 and 30% resulted in generally acceptable but fluctuating pellet quality; with moisture content over 30%, pellets are difficult to form and have little sustained integrity. In all cases, it was noted the hardness and durability improved with cooling.

The first use of dryers to lower and control moisture content of the solid waste feedstock has been in commercial plants in Doncaster and Eastborne, U.K., which began operating in 1980. Results are not yet available.

Bulk Density. Agricultural and forest product feedstocks tend to have fairly consistent bulk densities in the range of 8 to 12 pounds per cubic foot. This compares to densities ranging from 2 to 5 pounds per cubic foot for waste fuels. Such lower and more variable densities lead to difficulty in introducing shredded waste into the working area of the densifier at a uniform rate. The feed augers tend to fluff or compress the feed or, at lower densities, the feed tends to temporarily bridge in the inlet section to the die. Both conditions lead to feed surging, a condition apparent in the fluctuating densifier

power consumption noted in making power measurements.

Power Consumption. The power consumption of the densifier is a function of the die and roller size and condition, feedstock properties (particle size, composition and moisture) and throughput rates (average and surges). With a 2.5 ton per hour feedrate, nominal wear on a 1/2 die and for a typical MSW waste feedstock, the measured power requirement was 82 kw or 36 kw/Mg/hr[2]. For an office waste (high paper) feedstock of similar size and moisture, power consumption over the same ranges of throughput was 55 kw/Mg/hr[4]. The reason for this difference is not known.

Both of these figures are higher by a factor of 2 to 3 than estimated of 16.4 kw/Mg/hr made by the densification equipment supplier based on experiences with other feedstocks[11].

Maintenance. Wear on the die and press roller is the most significant component of maintenance. While the wear patterns are similar to those observed for traditional feedstocks, they occur at a much faster rate with RDF. This is due both to the abrasive characteristics of cellulosic materials and the presence of abrasive inorganic fines (glass and grit) in the feed. Projections based on experience by NCRR suggest that a die life of 3500 Mg and roller life of 1700 Mg could be expected for a low-ash content (10–12%) waste feedstock. Measurement of wear on a variety of densifiers and components, over a long duration and for a range of feedstock characteristics, is required to develop reliable wear rates and maintenance costs for waste fuels densification.

d-RDF Properties and Characteristics

For utilization of d-RDF as a supplemental fuel in stoker boilers, there are several physical characteristics that have a bearing on handling, transport, storage, feeding and combustion. These include d-RDF size, particle density, bulk density, fines content and integrity. Typical values for these characteristics for d-RDF sampled at several production and boiler facilities are summarized in Table 3 and are discussed below. Data

Table 3. Summary of d-RDF Properties Results on Dry Wt Basis.

d-RDF Sample Source & Description	NCRR – As-Produced from MSW Ref. 2	NCRR – As-Produced from MSW Ref. 2	NCRR – As-Produced from Office Wastes Ref. 3	NCRR – Post Storage Ref. 13	Teledyne – Post Storage Ref. 13	PLM – As-Produced Ref. 14
No. samples	>25	>10	>10	4	13	Unknown
Diameter – mm	13	25	13	13	13	32 x 32 x 30
Length – mm	15.9	–	20	–	–	–
Pellet density	1.01	0.76	1.13	–	–	–
Bulk density – kg/m³	575	432	687	538	522	450
Fines content – % (–9 mm)	14.9	9.6	2.6	46.7 (–6 mm)	27.9 (–6 mm)	–
Moisture content – %	22.9	22.8	21.5	29	31.4	15
Ash content – %	23.4	22.8	9.6	30.7	13.8	10
Heating value – MJ/g	17.4	–	18.0	15.7	18.9	16.3
Carbon – %	42.6	–	46.0	40.6	45.7	–
Nitrogen – %	0.77	–	0.17	0.59	0.37	–
Sulphur – %	0.48	–	0.13	0.43	0.23	0.29
Chlorine – %	0.57	–	0.16	0.31	0.38	–

ash content, chemical composition and heat content are also shown. Care should be taken in comparing or interpreting these data since the sampling and analysis procedures may not have been consistent.

d-RDF Size. The d-RDF dimensions (cross-section and length) have an impact on handling through relation to packing density and to burning rate in the boiler. Most past and current commercial and test production has been with particles from 13 to 20 mm diameter or 32 mm square. Lengths are random, and range from 1 to 2 times the diameter. Difficulty with particles larger than these dimensions result from reduced bulk density and an increased tendency to bridge.

d-RDF Particle Density. More dense particles indicate higher mechanical strength and resistance to abuse. With denser particles flow is improved in and out of storage, and the ballistic behavior through the stoker system would more closely approximate particles of coal. Particle density of coal is on the order of 1.3 gm/cm³. Table 3 indicates pellet densities 10 to 20% below that for coal.

d-RDF Bulk Density. Due to the lower calorific value for d-RDF (typically 1/2 to 2/3 that of coal), a larger mass and volume of d-RDF must be fired to maintain the same boiler loading compared with coal alone. A higher bulk density is therefore desired in order to minimize the effects of increased fuel volume on the stoker feeder's capacity and combustion bed thickness. Higher bulk density will also alleviate possible problems in material flow during storage, retrieval and firing. The bulk density ranges in Table 3 reflect variation in d-RDF size and particle density as well as density variations related to the feed composition.

d-RDF Fines Content. For coal, fines are specified as screened, minus 6 mm material. The definition of fines for d-RDF has not been standardized, but in the cases where it is reported in Table 3, it has generally been defined as 3 mm less than the pellet diameter. Fines can accentuate material flow or segregation and result in dusting in handling and feed systems. While some fines may be desirable for obtaining a mix of suspension and grate burning (for coal a 30% fines level is often specified), higher levels of d-RDF fines could increase slagging on the boiler tubes and could overload air pollution control equipment. The tolerable level of fines will vary with the boiler fuel, equipment and operations at a specific site. It should be noted that fines content of the d-RDF product can be controlled by screening after production.

Integrity. The integrity of d-RDF product is defined as its ability to sustain handling without breaking or losing mechanical strength. Fracture planes are created in production of the pellets by pieces of plastic or textile that bond poorly to adjacent materials. Observations during storage and handling by NCRR[2] and Systec[13] further suggest the susceptibility to breakage is a function of moisture and temperature. Neither test methods nor units expressing relative integrity are as yet refined and defined for d-RDF, although they have been and are being explored[2,12]. The d-RDF particle density property is probably the best interim indicator of integrity.

Care in handling and storage after production is important to prevent delamination and disintegration leading to increases in fines content and reduced particle and bulk density. Such a loss in integrity can be seen in Table 3 in comparing the properties for d-RDF as-produced at NCRR and after handling and storage as-fired in the test burn in Erie, PA.

d-RDF Ultimate Analysis. The moisture, ash and chemical contents and heating values reported in Table 3 for the various d-RDF products are a function of the composition and preparation of the waste feedstock and are not properties directly affected by the densification process (although the reverse is not true as was seen in discussions on the densification process and equipment). From the standpoint of combustion, it is clearly desirable to produce a d-RDF with the highest possible heating value by minimizing moisture and ash to levels consistent with that required for densification.

Storage and Handling

The experience accumulated thus far with densified fuels has shown, as expected, that in addition to being easily handled and transported,

they alleviate the problems of material spillages, dusting and bridging, common with fluff forms of RDF.

However, NCRR experience with storage of more than 1000 tons of d-RDF from mixed municipal waste indicated that problems with degradation, composting and oxidation can occur over a longer term. After 10 months in a covered, 2 to 4 m high pile, several seams of smoldering pellets surfaced at the edges of the pile and ignited plastic sheet covers. The pellets themselves did not ignite, although the seams of pyrolyzed, charred pellets ran deep into the pile. Excavations revealed both very wet (>130% moisture) and dry areas (<4% moisture), interspersed with material of average, as-produced (20%) moisture contents. Such conditions indicated that significant moisture transfers had also been occurring. Both the wet and oxidized materials exhibited significant pellet degradation (increased fines).

The reasons and mechanisms for formation of the oxidized seams are not clear. It is felt that inadequate cooling of the pellets after production, use of an unventilated cover, the long storage period and interim movement of the stored material all contributed to the problems. Similar problems with oxidation of d-RDF in storage have apparently not been observed elsewhere, and it is felt that with proper storage conditions and/or for reasonable periods, the problem of oxidation would be eliminated and degradation held to a lower, more tolerable level.

Densification Costs

As part of the investigations of densification technology supported by EPA, the economics of d-RDF systems for small communities (100–200 tons per day) were explored.[2] In the study, the capital and operating cost for a densification module were estimated and used to back calculate what feed system preparation costs (plant and equipment) could be afforded, given a range of fuel values and landfill cost avoidance.

The reader is directed to the EPA report for detailed discussion of the approach and result of this analysis. For the purpose of the discussion here, only the costs developed for the densification module are cited.

Table 4 provides a list of equipment and costs for a 7.2 Mg/hr capacity densification module (2 each ring extrusion pelletizers with nominal 25 mm holes). Such a system operated two shifts per day (14 hr) and 250 days per year would produce 25,000 tons annually. Table 5 provides the operating and maintenance costs for a two-shift operation. Table 6 summarizes these costs yielding a total capital and operating cost of $9.68/Mg. Processing of the feedstock is presumed to include sizing to less than one inch, and controlling ash content to less than 12% (reflecting removal of most inorganic fines). Drying of feedstock is not suggested unless the average moisture content of the feedstock is above 25%.

DENSIFIED REFUSE-DERIVED FUEL COMBUSTION EXPERIENCE

Table 7 provides information on six test firings of d-RDF in the U.S. from the earliest reported tests at the Fort Wayne Municipal Power Co. in 1972.[8] Several are noteworthy for their duration or more detailed documentation of results.

More than 20 other tests (not shown) have been conducted (listed in Ref. 2,15). Most were of short duration (several hours) and generally yielded only observations of performance of the fuel handling system, and indications of significant changes in boiler responses, burnout and stack emissions.

In December of 1977, the EPA sponsored combustion trials using d-RDF at the Maryland Correctional Institute in Hagerstown. During the tests, 285 tons were burned over 230 hours at various blends of d-RDF and coal. No particular problems in material handling were observed.[16]

Stack opacity, along with SO_2, were found to decrease while chloride emissions increased. The Hagerstown program served as a feasibility field test to the larger scale test burn sponsored by EPA in a 150,000 lb/hr spreader stoker-fired boiler in Erie, PA, in early 1979.

Just over 1700 tons of d-RDF from the National Center and Teledyne National production facilities were burned at Erie in volumetric blends of coal to d-RDF of 1:1, 1:2 and 1:4. A full set of measurements and data was made

Table 4. Densification Module Equipment Cost Detail (Ref. 2). Two Densifiers — 1979 Costs

Item	Cost
Equipment	
Conveyors (4) — feed and product	$ 32,700
Densifiers (2) — w/surge bin, spare die and rolls, motor	184,600
Pellet cooler	14,500
Pellet screener	6,200
Motor control center	5,000
Freight and taxes	17,000
Installation	65,000
Building allocation — 75 sq m	20,000
Engineering	27,600
Contingency	17,300
Total Capital Cost	$389,900

Table 5. Densification Module Operating and Maintenance Cost Detail (Ref. 2). Two Densifiers — 14 hr/day — 250 day/yr; 7.2 Mg/hr Nominal Throughput — 25,200 Mg/yr.

	Annual	Unit Throughput
Labor (annual basis)	$ 30,000	$1.19
Materials, supplies	12,000	0.48
Utilities	32,250	1.28
Maintenance		
Dies	50,400	2.00
Rollers	32,250	1.28
Miscellaneous (densifier, conveyors, cooler, screen)	15,900	0.63
	$172,800	$7.34/Mg

Table 6. Densification Module Capital and Operating Cost Summary (Ref. 2).

Item	Annual
Capital Costs	
Total cost	$389,900
Annual 10%, 10 years	58,485
Unit cost	2.34/Mg
Operating Costs	
Labor	1.19
Materials, supplies	0.48
Utilities	1.28
Maintenance	3.91
Total Operating Costs	7.34/Mg
Total Capital and Operating Costs	$9.68/Mg

Table 7. Summary of Selected d-RDF Combustion Tests.

Location	Date	Boiler Type/Size	d-RDF Description/Blend	Report Ref.
Ft. Wayne, IN	1972	Underfeed stoker; 40,000 kW	36 Mg 38 mm x 38 mm cubes; 3:1 coal:d-RDF by volume	8
Chanute, A.F.B., IL	1975	Traveling chain grate, gravity overfeed; 16 Mg/hr steam	135 Mg 28 mm pellets; 1:1, 0:1 coal:d-RDF by volume	–
Hagerstown, MD	1977	Traveling grate, spreader stokers (2); 27 Mg/hr, 33 Mg/hr steam	252 Mg 13 mm pellets; 1:1, 1:2, 0:1 coal:d-RDF by volume	16
Washington, D.C.	1979	Underfeed multiple retort; 32 Mg/hr steam	113 Mg 13 mm pellets (office waste); 4:1, 3:2, 2:3 coal: d-RDF by volume	3
Erie, PA	1979	Traveling grate spreader stoker; 68 Mg/hr steam	1,260 Mg 13 mm pellets; 1:1, 1:2, 1:4 coal:d-RDF by volume	13
Wright-Patterson, A.F.B.	1980–81	Traveling grate, spreader stoker; 36 Mg/hr steam	Contracted for 7,200 Mg/y 13 mm pellets; 1:1 variable coal:d-RDF by volume	–

by Systems Technology on material handling, boiler performance and environmental control.[13]

The results of the Erie tests demonstrated that co-firing of coal and d-RDF had minimum impact in the performance of the power plant test boiler. Weathering and subsequent deterioration of the d-RDF from multiple handlings, transportation and storage (for periods of 5 to 18 months) were significant. Nearly 500 tons of the d-RDF fired to the boiler contained 50% unpelletized material (fines) with the other 1200 tons of d-RDF having an average of 30% fines. These material conditions led to some problems of channeling, erratic flow and bridging of the coal/d-RDF blends in the fuel bunkers, but had no noticeable influence in the operation of the stokers or fuel distribution in the furnace.

Boiler performance as measured by efficiency was reduced only 2 to 3% at the 1:2 coal to d-RDF blend. Derating of the boiler was not experienced with substitution of the d-RDF for coal (in part due to excess capacity in the design). While higher ash pellets (20–30% ash) tended to form ash clinkers, lower ash pellets (12–15%) did not exhibit this tendency. There was increased slag in the lower walls of the furnace but it was easily removed during scheduled maintenance. Fouling of the tubes was not observed. Testing on samples of slag and ash showed no corrosion problem.

Fom an environmental performance standpoint, the particulate emissions rate and precipitator performance was unchanged from firing coal only. Comparing gaseous emissions from combustion of coal alone to gaseous emissions from combustion of the blends, increases were noted in lead, cadmium, zinc and chromium; while hydrocarbons and carbon monoxide remained constant and sulphur dioxide decreased.

Several short-duration test burns were conducted in early 1979 at the Pentagon power plant near Washington utilizing pellets prepared from office wastes.[3] Firing trials were conducted with baseline coal, and blends of 20, 40 and 60% d-RDF by volume. Unfortunately, the tests were run with a reduced (40–50% of rated capacity) and fluctuating boiler load. Although bridging and channeling were again evident in the fuel bunker, they were less than that observed at Erie; this was probably due to the condition of the coal rather than that of the pellets. Segregation of the d-RDF and coal, which occurred during loading of the bunker, resulted in uncontrolled fluctuations in the ratio of d-RDF and coal fed to the boiler. At the 60% volumetric blend, this segregation resulted in higher volume feeds, which exceeded the stoker capacity and caused hot spots in the fuel bed in areas of high d-RDF concentration. These problems were not evident with the 20 and 40% blends.

The amount and handling of bottom ash was no different than with coal. Particulate emissions actually decreased, while the gaseous emissions displayed the same trends evident in the Erie tests.

Short-term, low-tonnage firings have been tested to date in the U.K. with small industrial boilers using reciprocating stokers.[17] The conclusions were that with newer modifications, d-RDF could be used in existing combustion systems and conform with environmental regulations. Significant data are expected over the next several years from the commercial d-RDF firing programs in Doncaster, Byker and Eastborne.

In Sweden, the PLM Company has test fired up to several hundred tons in several one to five day tests.[14] The results of these tests are yet to be reported.

REFERENCES

1. T. Divitt, P. Spaite and L. Gibbs, "Population and Characteristics of Industrial/Commercial Boilers in the U.S.," a report by PEDCO Environmental under Contract 68-02-2603 to the EPA Office of Research and Development, Research Triangle Park, NC, (1979).

2. J.A. Campbell and M.L. Renard, "Densification of Refuse-Derived Fuels: Preparation, Properties and Systems for Small Communities," final report EPA Grant 804150, National Center for Resource Recovery, Inc., Washington, D.C., December (1980).

3. J.A. Campbell, Final Test Report – "Demonstration d-RDF Burn at the GSA Pentagon Power Plant," Contract DOE-ES-76-C-01-3851, Task 8, October (1979).

4. Z. Khan and M.L. Renard, "The Use of Waste Oils to Improve Densified Refuse-Derived Fuels," Contract DOE-ES-76-C-01, 3851, Task 5, Washington, D.C., October (1979).

5. H. Alter and J.A. Campbell, "The Preparation and Properties of Densified Refuse-Derived Fuel" in Thermal Conversion of Solid Waste and Biomass Symposium Proceedings, American Chemical Society, Washington, D.C., September (1979).

6. J.M. Arnold and D.C. Hendrix, "Initial Mass Balance for Production of Densified Refuse-Derived Fuel, Technical Report RR77-3, National Center for Resource Recovery, Inc., Washington, D.C., December (1977), 6 pp.

7. C.C. Wiles, "The Production and Use of Densified Refuse-Derived Fuel," Proceedings, Fifth Annual Research Symposium, Land Disposal and Resource Recovery, Orlando, Florida, March (1979).

8. H.I. Hollander and N.F. Cunningham, "Beneficiated Solid Waste Cubettes as Salvage Fuel for Steam Generation," Proceedings, 1972 National Incinerator Conference, American Society of Mechanical Engineers, New York (1972), pp. 75–86.

9. K.R. Sheppard, "Fuels in a Waste-to-Energy System: The Teledyne Experience," presented at the International Conference on Prepared Fuels and Resource Recovery Technology, Nashville Tennessee, February 12, 1981. In press.

10. F.C. Hildebrand, "Navy Experience in the Conversion of Solid Wastes into Energy," Naval Facilities Engineering Command, Alexandria, Virginia, June (1979).

11. T. Reed and B. Bryant, "Densified Biomass: A New Form of Solid Fuel," SERI-35, Solar Energy Research Institute, Golden, Colorado (1978), 30 pp.

12. P.A. Vesilind, Duke University, Private Communication regarding research project on d-RDF properties and test procedures funded by EPA through ASTM Committee E-38 to begin at Duke in January 1981 (1980).

13. M. Kleinhenz, "Coal: d-RDF Demonstration Test in an Industrial Spreader-Stoker Boiler," Final Report EPA 68-03-2426 by Systems Technology, Zenia, Ohio, July (1980).

14. B. Hansen, "Process for the Recovery from Household Waste of Solid Fuel (d-RDF) Alternatively Secondary Paper and Their Reuse," Recycling Berlin '79, Vol. 2, K.K. Thome-Kozmiensky, ed., Springer-Verlag, Berlin (1979), pp. 937–941.

15. Proposed draft document for GSA Office Waste Removal and Procurement of d-RDF for Use as Supplemental Fuel in GSA Operated Boilers, Final Report DOE-ES-76-C-01-3851, Task 8A (1980).

16. H.G. Rigo, G. Degler and B.T. Riley, "A Field Test Using Coal: d-RDF Blends in Spreader Stoker-Fired Boilers, "Draft Interim Report EPA-68-03-2426 by Systems Technology Corporation, Xenia, Ohio (to be issued).

17. P.R. Birch, "Pilot-Scale Production and Firing of Densified RDF, Warren Spring Laboratory Report for The British Department of the Environment (1979), 7 pp.

4-13 Economic Factors in Refuse Derived Fuel Utilization

John L. Rose

Source: *Proceedings* of the 1978 National Waste Processing Conference, Chicago, Illinois, May 7–10, 1978, pp. 277–284. Reprinted with Permission of The American Society of Mechanical Engineers.

INTRODUCTION

Resource recovery is the processing of municipal solid wastes (MSW) to extract useful materials and/or energy. There are several basic approaches to resource recovery. One involves the combustion of unsegregated solid wastes with the recovery of energy from the combustion gases and of materials from the residues. Another approach involves the segregation of the solid wastes into various gravitational fractions and the use of the light fraction as a fuel supplement to recover its energy value.

Combustion with energy recovery is being utilized widely in Europe and to a lesser extent in the United States. The technology is considered to be available commercially, but its economic viability depends on the availability of a suitable market for the steam produced. Projects in Saugus, Massachusetts, Nashville, Tennessee, and Chicago (Northwest), Illinois, are examples of this approach in the United States.

The technology for the second approach is still somewhat developmental. St. Louis was the site of the first major demonstration of the burning of a refuse derived fuel (RDF) in a utility boiler. Since then, Ames, Iowa, Chicago, Illinois, and Milwaukee, Wisconsin, have completed plants producing RDF for co-combustion with fossil fuels. Several other plants are under construction. The technical problems associated with this process seem to be within the reach of our capabilities, but institutional problems have contributed to major delays on several of the proposed RDF projects. Data on the financial aspects of operating facilities is very limited.

One of the major institutional problems revolves around the pricing of the RDF. The RDF producers, agencies trying to dispose of their solid wastes, need an assured source of revenue in order to finance the construction of the processing facilities. Therefore, they are seeking long term commitments from their potential customers, who are primarily the privately owned public utilities.

The utilities, however, have little economic incentive to participate in a solid-waste-to-fuel project. In many cases any fuel costs saved must be passed on to the utility's customers. The utilities have had difficulties raising funds for their own capital needs, and any additional operating and maintenance expenses can only be recovered through a long process of rate setting by regulatory agencies. The utilities are unsure of what their future fuel requirements will be and how the product they are being asked to contract for will affect their generating facilities.

They are, therefore, reluctant to make long term commitments to buy RDF unless such commitments contain protective clauses in case their needs or costs change. Such clauses are often unacceptable to the solid waste agency or its bond buyers, or the private entrepreneurs.

In this situation of conflicting needs and interests, this paper will suggest a methodology for determining a value of RDF that takes into account some of the factors that create uncertainty for the buyer of RDF. It is hoped that,

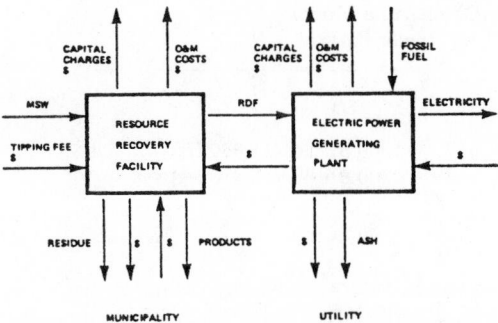

Figure 1. Resource recovery power generation system.

once these factors are recognized and evaluated, the municipal seller and the utility buyer of RDF will be able to arrive at contractual terms responsive to both their needs.

DESCRIPTION OF A RESOURCE RECOVERY/POWER GENERATION SYSTEM

One system for the recovery of the energy contained in MSW consists of a solid waste processing facility producing RDF and a power generating plant using the RDF in conjunction with conventional fuels. This system interfaces with the community solid waste management system at one limit and the power generating system at the other limit. The objective of the solid waste management system is to dispose of the community's solid waste in an environmentally acceptable manner and at the lowest possible cost. One objective of the power generation system is to produce electricity at the lowest possible cost. A resource recovery system will be economically viable if it reduces both the cost of solid waste management and the cost of power generation. This condition will be met if the savings by the power generating system exceed the costs of constructing and operating the resource recovery system, including any increases in the community's collection and hauling costs.

A schematic flow diagram for this system is shown in Fig. 1. Municipal solid wastes (MSW) are delivered to the Resource Recovery Facility, where they are processed into RDF, other recovered material products, and residues. There is a flow of funds corresponding to the flow of

materials. Revenues of the resource recovery agency consist of the tipping fees for disposal of the solid wastes accepted at the resource recovery facility and receipts for the sale of RDF and other recovered products. Expenditures consist of capital charges, operating and maintenance costs, and disposal costs for unmarketable residues.

On the power generation side, revenues are received for the sale of electric energy regardless of what fuel is used. The utility must therefore balance the savings resulting from the purchase of RDF against the capital cost for facilities required to allow the utility to burn RDF and any change in operating costs resulting from the burning of RDF.

For the resource recovery/power generation system to be feasible, there must be inducements to both the solid waste agency and the power generating utility.

As far as the municipality is concerned, this means minimizing their solid waste management costs. For the utility, it means, as a minimum, no additional costs over normal operating cost. The key element in bringing together the municipality and the utility is the price or value of the RDF.

To illustrate a method for determining the value of RDF to a potential utility buyer, a conceptual model of a resource recovery/power generation project has been developed and analyzed. The project consists of a 4,000 ton (3,636 t) per day MSW resource recovery facility and a 600 MW power plant which has been retrofitted to burn RDF in conjunction with conventional fuel. Data on these two facilities is contained in Table 1. The objective of this study was to determine the system operating characteristics and price structure that will result in the lowest overall solid waste disposal costs while accounting for all costs associated with generating power from RDF.

The model involves a number of assumptions, but it does represent the basic principles of resource recovery and power generation engineering and economics. These assumptions are:

1. The supply of solid waste and RDF is not a limiting factor.

**Table 1. Basic Data for Conceptual Model
of Utilization of RDF by Power Plant.**

Resource Recovery Facility Data	
RDF/MSW Ratio	50%
Heat Value, MSW	5000 Btu/lb. (11,630 J/g)
RDF	7200 Btu/lb. (16,750 J/g)
Overall energy recovery	
efficiency	72%
Power Plant Data	
Capacity	600 MW
Overall Efficiency	34%
Equivalent Heat Rate	10,200 Btu/kWh (10,760 kJ/kWh)
Input from RDF	20%
Utilization of RDF	
Fuel Requirements of Power	
Plant at Full Load	14.7×10^{10} Btu/day (1.55×10^{14} J/day)
Input from RDF at 20%	2.94×10^{10} Btu/day (3.10×10^{13} J/day)
Required RDF Production	
at 7200 Btu/lb.	
(14.4×10^{6} Btu/ton)	2040 t/day (1854 Mg/day)
Required MSW at 50% RDF/MSW	4080 t/day (3708 Mg/day)

2. The resource recovery facility will produce as much RDF as can be used by the power plant.
3. The optimum price will be the price at which the total revenues obtained for RDF are a maximum.
4. RDF represents the only major source of revenue of the resource recovery facility and other revenues will not affect the economics of the system.
5. The power generating station is part of an interconnected system of generating stations, so that there is a market for all the power that can be produced at that station.

COST OF PRODUCING RDF

Cost data for resource recovery plants producing RDF are slowly becoming available. The Third Report to Congress, Resource Recovery and Waste Reduction (USEPA-1975), presents normalized capital cost estimates for five plant designs of shredded fuel-type resource recovery plants. The plants employ a standard process consisting of some manual separation of paper, tires and oversized items, two-stage shredding,

one-stage air classification and magnetic separation of ferrous metals. The report indicates that capital costs for a 1000 ton (907 t) per day plant are of the order of $20,000 per ton of daily capacity, and that economics of scale would be minimal for plants with capacities in excess of 1000 tons per day. The report also gives estimates of operating and maintenance and total costs for such plants ranging from $11.60 to $22.50 per ton ($12.75 to $24.75 per t) of MSW processed, exclusive of the cost of residue disposal. These costs are reduced by the revenues received from the sale of recovered products. The maximum total revenues therefore result in a minimum disposal cost to the community.

Under some conditions, revenues from recovered resource products other than RDF may affect the overall economics of resource recovery. However, it has been assumed in this paper that revenues from the sale of RDF are the only revenues of the resource recovery facility.

COSTS OF PRODUCING ELECTRICITY

The principal variable cost element for generating electric power is the cost of fuel. For any specific boiler-turbine combination within a

Table 2. Schedule of Economic Dispatch Capacities
and Heat Rates for System Generating Units.

| Unit No. | Generating Capacity, MW | | Heat Rate, Btu/kWh* | |
	Unit	Cumulative Unit	Unit	Cumulative
1	1,000	1,000	9,000	9,000
2	800	1,800	9,600	9,200
3	600	2,400	10,200	9,500
4	400	2,800	11,000	9,700
5	400	3,200	12,000	10,000
6	360	3,560	12,500	10,250
7	240	3,800	14,000	10,500

*Multiply by 1055 to obtain kJ/kWh

a range of outputs, fuel cost is a direct function of the amount of electricity produced and the efficiency of the unit. Efficiency is the ratio of the thermal equivalent of the electric power produced to the heating value in the fuel required to produce that power. It is generally expressed as a heat rate, the number of Btu (kJ) required to produce one kilowatt hour of electricity. However, the efficiency of a unit varies as the load on (output of) a unit varies and for each unit there is a certain range, beyond which the efficiency declines rapidly. Also, different generating units have different efficiencies and, therefore, different fuel costs.

In order to evaluate the interaction between the resource recovery system and the power generating system, certain assumptions had to be made regarding the characteristics of the power generating network, of which the generating station described in Table 1 was a part. Data for the other stations in this network are contained in Table 2.

In this network, Units 1 and 2 represent relatively modern oil fired plants that do not have facilities for handling large amounts of ash. They are therefore not suitable for retrofitting to burn RDF. Units 3 and 4 represent former coal fired plants that have been converted to oil, but still have operable ash handling facilities. Unit 3 appears to be more favorably located in relation to the MSW processing facility and was therefore selected for retrofitting to burn RDF.

The heat rates shown in Table 2 reflect the efficiency of each unit in converting fuel to electricity. Since thermodynamically 1 kWh is equivalent to 3413 Btu (3600 kJ), these units

vary in efficiency from 37.9 percent to 24.4 percent.

Utilities will generally attempt to meet any given demand for electricity by operating the most efficient combination of generating units available at any given time. This is known as the principle of economic dispatch. It covers not only the operations of the generating units of a single utility, but those of a group of adjacent utilities. Utility "A" will buy electric power from an adjacent interconnected Utility "B" when that utility "B" can generate the power at a lower incremental cost than Utility "A."

The variation of fuel costs between different generating units is reflected in their position on the schedule of economic dispatch. This schedule tells the operator of the system which unit should be operated at any given time to meet an existing demand at the lowest total fuel cost.

It has further been assumed that the average load for this system is 2000 MW, that the peak load is 3500 MW, and that these loads are met by operating each unit as shown in Table 3.

Table 3. Summary of Operating Hours
for Each Generating Unit.

Unit No.	Hr/Year	Capacity Factor*
1	7,000	0.80
2	7,200	0.83
3	4,400	0.50
4	3,200	0.36
5	1,300	0.15
6	875	0.10
7	875	0.10

*Capacity Factor = Energy actually produced divided by rated capacity over period.

As indicated in Table 3, Unit 3 is currently being operated 4400 hr per year, representing a capacity factor of 0.50. This means that although the system has the capacity to utilize 2000 tons (1818 t) per day of RDF at a fuel ratio of 20 percent (20 percent of the heat input being supplied by RDF), it would actually average only 1000 (909 t) tons of RDF per day because of the operating characteristics of the generating plant.

Most of the power plants suitable for adaptation to co-combustion of RDF are older plants, less efficient than the more modern plants in the system or any new plants that might be added to the system during the life of the project. As new plants are added, the rate of utilization of the older plants decreases. In the model, it has been assumed that the utility is planning to add a nuclear plant to the system five years after the resource recovery project becomes operational and at that time, Unit 3 will only be required to operate 3600 hr per year. In year 10, another fossil plant will be added and at that time Unit 3 will be cut back to 2800 hr per year. The overall time frame for evaluation of the project is 20 years.

Under these assumptions, Unit No. 3 would therefore be operated for a total of 68,000 hr over the projected life of the resource recovery facility, or an average of 3400 hr per year. The impact of operating at less than full capacity on the economics of co-combustion will be discussed later in this paper.

COSTS OF RETROFITTING POWER PLANT TO ACCOMMODATE BURNING RDF

Costs to retrofit an existing power plant to accommodate the burning of RDF will vary widely from plant to plant. Table 4 shows an example of a preliminary cost estimate prepared by an eastern utility company for retrofitting a 600 MW plant which was originally designed as a dual-fueled (coal and oil) plant.

IMPACT OF RETROFIT COSTS ON VALUE OF RDF

There are two methods by which the costs incurred by a utility in order to retrofit an existing

Table 4. Capital Cost Estimate Retrofit of Power Plant to Accommodate RDF.

Description	Estimated Cost
Receiving building, main storage silo pneumatic transport	$ 3,500,000
Day silos and related piping	6,000,000
Blowers, burner controls, boiler modifications	7,000,000
Modifications to ash handling system	2,000,000
Owner costs – engineering, financing, construction supervision, outages	4,000,000
Contingencies	1,500,000
	$24,000,000

power plant can be assessed against the cost of the resource recovery project. One way would be for the utility to demand instant reimbursement. In this case, the retrofit costs become part of capital costs of the project. It is then up to the solid waste management agency to recover these costs through tipping fees and revenues from the sale of recovered products.

Alternatively, the utility can recover the retrofit costs through savings in fuel costs over what it would have had to pay if it had to rely only on conventional fuel. These savings could be expressed as a percentage of the price of an equivalent heating value of fossil fuel, or as a discount adjustment to the price the utility is willing to pay for the RDF. In this paper, this alternate method is used to illustrate the value of RDF, recognizing that:

1. Many utilities will insist on prepayment of retrofit costs because they cannot or do not want to assume the risks associated with resource recovery.
2. In some states, utilities would have problems recovering capital cost through a fuel price discount arrangement because they would be required to pass reduced fuel costs through to their customers.

If the latter approach is taken, the magnitude of this adjustment becomes a function of the total amount of RDF that will be used over the life of the system. It is then important to consider not only the capacity of the solid waste

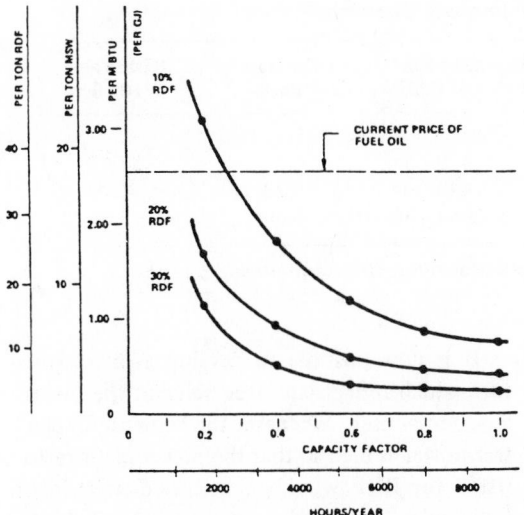

Figure 2. Unit charges required to recover capital costs.

burn as high a percentage of RDF as possible. For the conditions of this study, operations at a capacity factor of 0.30 and a fuel ratio of 10 percent would result in a capital charge for retrofitting cost equal to the cost of fossil fuel, thus indicating a zero net value for the RDF. Similarly, for a capacity factor of 0.40 and a fuel ratio of 30 percent the graph indicates a capital charge of approximately 20 percent of the cost of fossil fuel, thus indicating a net value of RDF equal to 80 percent of the cost of fossil fuel.

The number of annual operating hours to be used in determining the unit charge is the average number of hours over the life of the project. In the model system used in this paper, the average capacity factor over a 20-year project life is 0.39, although the initial capacity factor is 0.50. For a more rigorous analysis, the future year's capacity factors should be discounted by the present worth factor for the interest rate used in the study.

INCREASING THE USE OF RDF BY REDUCING THE PRICE

In the typical case, power plants suitable for retrofitting to accommodate RDF do not operate at high capacity factors. In the model used in this study, Unit 3 operates at a capacity factor of 0.50, representing 4400 hr of operation per year. Unit 2 operates 7000 hr per year at a heat rate of 9600 Btu (10,125 kJ) per kWh. If the fuel costs for Unit 3 were reduced so that they would be equal to those of Unit 2, Unit 3 could be operated whenever the schedule of economic dispatch called for Unit 2 to be operated. In this manner, an additional 2600 hr of operation could be obtained. Since the heat rate of Unit No. 3 is 10,200 Btu (10,760 kJ) Btu per kWh, the RDF equivalent to 600 Btu (635 kJ) per kWh generated would have to be furnished "free" in order to equalize the fuel costs of the two units. Only after the fuel costs of the two units have been equalized would the RDF have a value to the utility on par with its other fuels.

Table 5 shows the discount ratios necessary in order to "upgrade" Unit 3 to the level of Unit 2 in terms of fuel costs. Obviously, the discount ratio depends on the difference in heat rates between the generating unit using the RDF

processing plant to produce RDF, but also the capacity of the power plant to utilize the RDF. If the power plant operates at a low capacity factor now, and may operate at an even lower capacity factor in the future, the overall utilization of the system may be much less than would be indicated by the design capacities.

The impact of capital costs on the value of RDF is presented in Fig. 2. This figure shows the unit charges which must be assessed in order to recover capital costs given in Table 4 for various fuel ratios and annual hours of operation of the system. Unit charges are shown in terms of dollars per ton of raw waste processed (MSW), per ton of refuse derived fuel (RDF) used by the power plant, and heat content of the RDF (Btu or MJ). For comparison, the average current cost of fossil fuel of $2.50 per M Btu ($2.37 per GJ) is also shown. This graph is based on annual charges of $3,600,000 or 15 percent of the capital costs shown in Table 4. Similar graphs can be developed for other rates of annualizing capital costs.

It is apparent from Fig. 2 that in order to minimize the impact of capital charges, it is desirable to have a power plant that operates at as high a capacity factor as possible and that can

Table 5. Value of RDF to Improve Operating Ratio.

% of Heat from RDF	Btu*/kWh from RDF	Btu*/kWh from Fossil	Equivalent Btu* Value of RDF	Discount Ratio	RDF Value $/10⁶ Btu
0	—	10,200			
10	1,020	9,180	420	0.41	$1.02
20	2,040	8,160	1,440	0.706	1.76
30	3,060	7,140	2,460	0.804	2.01

Note: This table assumes no change in heat rate (efficiency) for RDF substitution.
*Multiply by 1.055 to obtain kJ.

and the more efficient unit operating at the higher capacity factor. In the model, it has been assumed that this difference is 600 Btu/kWh, representing about 6 percent of the total heat rate. Under these conditions, if only 10 percent of the heat input is obtained from RDF, the value of the RDF must be discounted about 60 percent, resulting in a value of the RDF equal to 40 percent of the fossil fuel cost for the additional 2600 hr of operation. If 20 percent of the heat input can be obtained from RDF, the required discount is about 30 percent, or the value 70 percent of the fossil fuel cost.

These discounts must be applied to the amortized value of the RDF — that is, the value after deductions have been made for capital charges. Thus, in the example used herein, if Unit 3 operates 4400 hr at 20 percent, the amortized value of the RDF will be $1.70/MBtu. If Unit 3 operates 7000 hr at 20 percent, the value will be $2.07 per MBtu for 4400 hr plus $1.44 per MBtu for 2600 hr, for an average value of $1.84. The effect of this discounting is to increase the value of RDF, the revenue obtained per ton of MSW processed, and the total revenue from sale of RDF by the percentages shown in Table 6.

Table 6. Effects of Discounting RDF.

PARAMETER	Heat Input From RDF 10%	20%	30%
INCREASE IN:			
Hours of Power Plant Operations	59%	59%	59%
Value of RDF	47%	15%	8%
Revenue per Ton MSW	15%	2%	1%
Total Revenue from Sale of RDF	83%	62%	60%

It is now possible to develop a price structure which reflects the true value of the fuel to a potential user. Whenever the demand for electric power is high so that the power plant retrofitted for RDF would be operated with fossil fuel under the schedule of economic dispatch, the value of the RDF to the utility is equivalent to the value of the fossil fuel it displaces, less amortization costs of the retrofit. However, during periods when the demand for electric power is such that the retrofitted power plant would not be operated under the schedule of economic dispatch, it would still be desirable — from the solid waste management point of view — to operate the resource recovery system. During these periods the price of the RDF is discounted, so that the cost of producing electricity by the public utility is not increased.

How much more revenue can be obtained by discounting will depend on the relative heat rates of the retrofitted plant and the plant it would have to replace in the schedule of economic dispatch, and on the ratio of RDF to fossil fuel. There may be periods when it would reduce overall solid waste disposal costs if the solid waste agency paid the power generation utility to accept RDF — that is, the RDF would have negative value to the utility, but this would still represent the lowest cost method of disposal.

THE IMPACT OF INCREASED OPERATING COSTS ON THE VALUE OF RDF

The most difficult to determine aspect of the co-combustion of RDF is its impact on operating and maintenance costs, other than direct fuel cost. For some of these costs it is possible to estimate upper and lower limits. Others can only be determined from actual operating experience after the project has been in operation long enough to yield representative and significant data.

Operating and maintenance costs that could be affected by the co-combustion of RDF include the following:

1. Changes in efficiency of the boiler. Since utility boilers are designed for a specific fuel, the addition of a different fuel may result in changes in flame characteristics and temperature which will affect the overall efficiency of the boiler. It may be necessary to add tubes or remove tubes. There have also been problems with incomplete burnout of the RDF because of the short residence time in the combustion zone. These changes be reflected directly in changes in boiler efficiency and therefore in fuel usage.

2. Ash handling. RDF appears to result in greater quantities of both bottom ash and fly ash. As a result, bottom and fly ash may have to be removed more frequently. Bottom ash removal generally presents no technical problem, but does result in increased materials handling costs. An increased amount of fly ash may require modification of the air pollution control equipment.

3. Boiler cleaning. Boilers must be cleaned at certain intervals to maintain the heat transfer efficiency of the tube surfaces. Firing RDF may result in more deposits on heat transfer surfaces and units burning RDF may therefore have to be cleaned more often than units burning other fossil fuel.

4. Corrosion or erosion. This factor is related to boiler cleaning. As much as five to ten years operating experience may be required to assess the impact of RDF on boiler component service life.

5. Loss of capacity during outages — modifications of the boiler, boiler cleaning, and major maintenance of the boiler all require that the unit be taken out of service while the work is being performed. Any increase in frequency of these procedures, therefore, reflects itself in the reduced availability of the unit and a reduced capacity factor. In addition, the need to purchase outside power or to operate less efficient units adds to the cost of producing electric power.

All operating costs can be expressed in terms of their effect on the overall plant heat rate. Any increase in operating costs will therefore require further discounting of the RDF, so that the overall operating costs are not increased.

SUMMARY

The market value of RDF is the value of its energy content less any costs associated with the recovery of that energy content. For a resource recovery system consisting of a solid waste processing facility and a power generating plant retrofitted to burn RDF with fossil fuel, the value of the RDF has been shown to be a function of the operating characteristics of the generating plant. The two most significant operating factors are the thermal efficiency of the plant as reflected in the fuel energy input required to produce a unit of electric energy, and the utilization of the generating plant as reflected in its capacity factor or number of hours of operation per year. In considering the utilization of the generating plant, it is important to consider not only current utilization but projected utilization over the life of the project.

Resource recovery/power generation systems are highly capital intensive, and capital charges therefore have a major impact on the value of RDF. Power plants selected for retrofitting should have good overall thermal efficiencies, be capable of accepting a high percentage of energy input from RDF without adversely affecting that efficiency, and operate at high capacity factors both on a current and a projected basis.

If the RDF-using generating plant is operated as part of a network of plants under a schedule of economic dispatch, under which only the most efficient combination of generating plants is used to meet a given demand for power, it may be possible by discounting the price of the RDF to increase the number of hours the plant operates, and thereby increase the total revenues to the solid waste management system.

The maximum unit price obtainable for RDF is not necessarily the price that results in the maximum revenue to the solid waste management agency, and the maximum revenue from the sale of RDF may not necessarily result in the lowest overall costs for solid waste disposal. Under certain conditions, it may be necessary to furnish RDF to a utility at no cost or even pay the utility for accepting RDF so as to minimize overall disposal costs.

At this point in time, the state-of-the-art of resource recovery/power generation by means of RDF is such that it is not possible to totally eliminate risk. Major questions remain concerning long range impacts of burning RDF with fossil fuels on operating and maintenance costs. There are too few projects with meaningful experience records. Evaluations of resource recovery projects currently being conducted by the U.S. Environmental Protection Agency should supply some of this data.

The best that can be done at this time is to identify some of the factors that have the greatest impact on the value of the RDF product, and thus permit an evaluation of the viability of a proposed project. It is hoped that the methodology suggested in this paper will be helpful in this evaluation process.

4-14 Economic and Flow Stream Analyses of the Ames Solid Waste Recovery System

S. Keith Adams, John C. Even, Jr., Petras Gheresus, and Robert A. Olexsey

Source: **PAPER PRESENTED AT THE 1979 AIIE ANNUAL CONFERENCE**, San Francisco, California, May 22-25, 1979, 9pp. **Reprinted with Permission of AIIE**

PLANT AND SYSTEM OPERATION

The Ames Solid Waste Recovery System was conceived in 1971 and completed in 1975. The processing of solid waste on a regular basis began in November 1975. The system is designed to shred municipal and commercial refuse and to separate light, combustible material from heavy material. The former, primarily paper, cardboard, fiber, and organics, is transported pneumatically to an Atlas storage bin and subsequently to the electric power plant to be burned with coal in boilers supplying steam to operate turbo-generators. In summary, the Ames Solid Waste Recovery System consists of three major subsystems: the process plant, the Atlas storage bin and the coal-refuse fired generators of the Ames electric power plant. The heavy material, consisting of ferrous and nonferrous metals, sand, glass, rubber, plastic, and wood, can be separated into several metallic components, plus rejects which are taken to the municipal landfill. Metallic classifications include ferrous, aluminum, and heavy, non-ferrous metal (primarily copper and brass). To date, the ferrous systems are the only metallic separation processes conducted on a continuous basis [1].

An overall process chart depicting recovery system operations, is given in Figure 1.

This system serves Ames and the surrounding county for a total population of 65,000.

At present time, the major systems of the process plant from an economic standpoint include:

1. Shredding (primary and secondary).
2. Magnetic removal of ferrous metals.
3. Air density classification to remove heavy, noncombustible material.
4. Transfer, storage, and retrieval of refuse-derived fuel (RDF) for the power plant.

COST AND REVENUES

Capital Investment

The initial cost estimated for the complete Ames Solid Waste Recovery System, including all processing, transfer, storage and retrieval facilities, was approximately $5.6 million. The actual cost was $6.3 million.

The total annual and monthly costs of capital recovery plus return are $428,426 and $35,702, respectively [2]. These figures are important not only because they indicate the total initial cost of the overall system, but also because they enable depreciation and capital recovery to be shown in relation to other operating costs. It can be seen that solid waste resource recovery is a capital intensive operation.

Operating Expenses

Gross operating expenses for the two-year period are classified in Figure 2. Principal and interest account for nearly half the total costs.

Major contractual expenses include utilities, freight, rented equipment, insurance, and all specialized maintenance and repair work

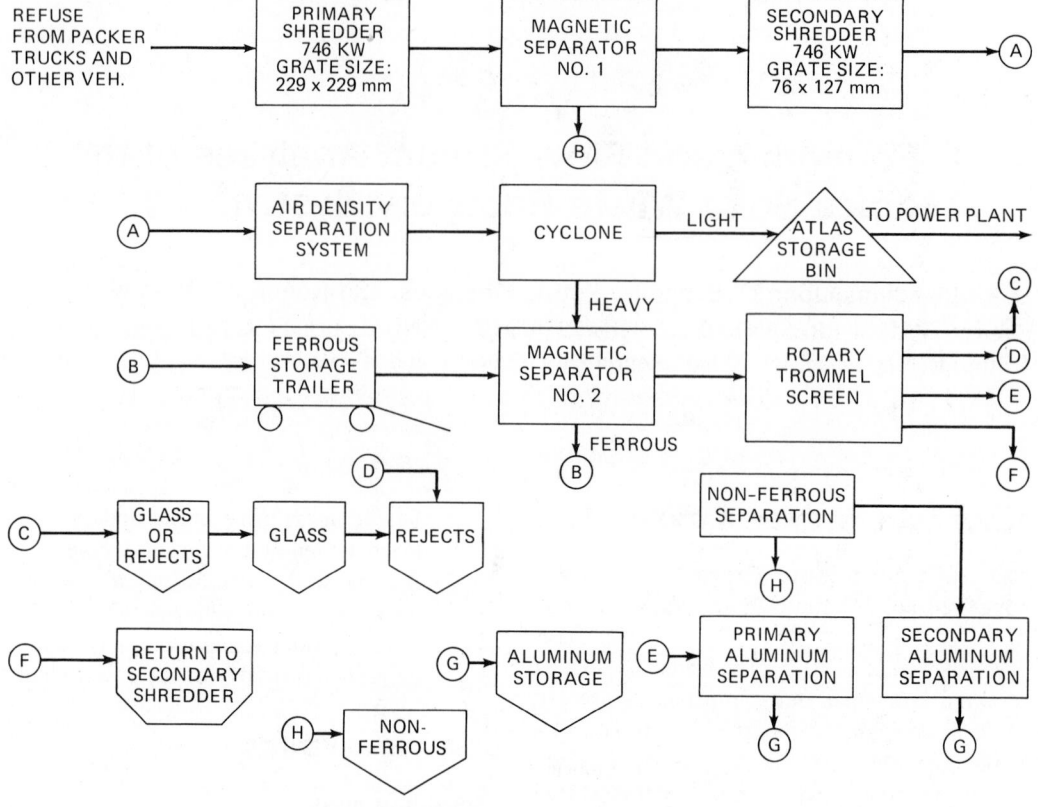

Figure 1. Process plant flow diagram.

performed by private contractors. Monthly expenses averaged $84,437 for the period. Major operating costs are shown in Table 1 on the basis of cost per Mg processed. The average overall processing cost includes transfer, storage and retrieval, and totals $24.93/Mg.

Labor

Total labor hours include operations, maintenance and overtime. Labor hours per month and per Mg of refuse processed for 1976 and 1977 are given in Table 2 [2]. Hours per Mg are nearly constant at 0.62. Labor hours allocated to major subsystem operations and to overall maintenance functions for 1976-77 are illustrated graphically on a percentage basis in Figure 3.

The operations category includes monitoring conveyor lines and processing equipment from within the process plant and making adjustments in material flow as needed. This category and

operation of the end loader which feeds refuse to the infeed conveyor each account for an additional 11 percent of labor time.

Overtime hours have averaged approximately 10 percent of regular hours. In terms of a general trend, labor hours vary somewhat with the total mass of refuse processed. Significant monthly variations occur because of random fluctuations in downtime and maintenance activity.

Table 1. Summary of Gross Operating Costs (1976-1977).

Processing	2 yr. costs	Cost per input (Mg)	(Ton)
Principle and interest	$ 992,592	12.21	11.11
Contractual	543,633	6.69	6.09
Salaries and wages	331,650	4.08	3.71
Commodities (supplies)	158,613	1.95	1.78
Total	$2,026,488	24.93	22.69

Table 2. Total Labor Hours Worked.

Operating period (year)	Total (hrs)	Labor hours Monthly avg (hrs/mo)	Per Mg of refuse (hrs/MG)
1976	13,110	1,873	0.61
1977	27,249	2,271	0.62
1976–1977	40,359	2,124	0.62

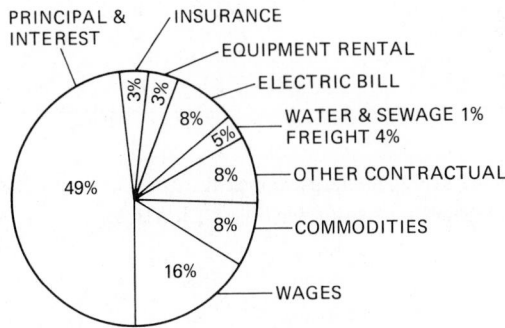

Figure 2. Operation expenses distribution.

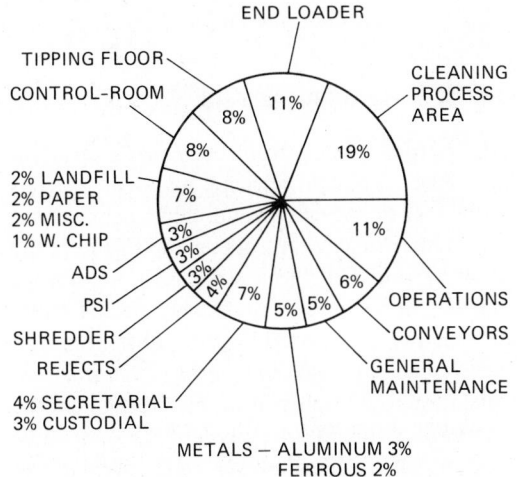

Figure 3. Labor hours distribution in percent.

Revenues from Reclaimed Materials

Revenues produced from the sale of recovered materials totaled $937,537, $11.55 for every Mg of refuse processed in 1976 and 1977. Primary sources of revenue were RDF and metals, which accounted for 72% and 21%, respectively, of total revenues received for materials. The price received during 1976 and 1977 averaged $37.53/Mg ($34.05/ton), and ranged from $34.42/Mg to $46.97/Mg. The average price was derived by combining weighted averages of revenues received for processed and nonprocessed metal.

The price received per Mg of RDF delivered to the municipal power plant has also varied. This variation is caused by several factors which include variation in heating value, the higher moisture content, and higher excess air required for combustion. These factors tend to reduce the boiler efficiency, and affect the fuel credit allowed which is based on the equivalent amount of coal replaced.

Revenues from Delivering Customers

Customers delivering refuse to the process plant are classified as private customers or credit card customers. The amount of refuse delivered by private customers is less than 10% of the total, but they generate over 47% of the customer tipping fee revenue. Credit card customers provided $25,769 in revenues during 1976 and 1977. Fees from other customers totaled $23,277.

Revenues received from process plant operations, including sales and fees, are summarized for 1976 and 1977 in Table 3 [3].

ELECTRICAL ENERGY

Consumption

Processing energy per Mg varies sharply from month to month because of large seasonal fluctuations in plant heating requirements. The overall trend is shown graphically in Figure 4. Increases during the summer occur for several reasons, including air conditioning of the control room and office areas. Table 4 gives seasonal

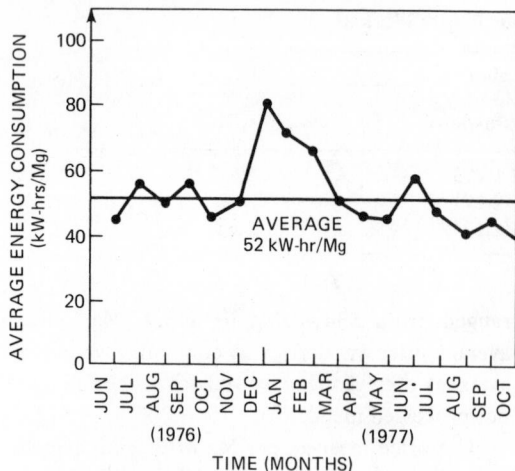

Figure 4. Average processing energy consumption.

averages for the five seasons covered during the two-year study period.   Standard deviations are calculated using monthly data.

Coal Savings by Burning RDF

The usage rate of coal without any RDF is 0.72 Kg Coal/KWH generated.   When burning coal plus RDF the rate drops to 0.46 Kg Coal/KWH generated, firing an equal amount of coal and RDF by weight.   The resulting contribution of RDF is one half that of coal. During 1977, 37,000 Mg of RDF was produced and burned which saved 18,500 Mg of coal.

Electrical Energy Balance

The average energy consumed in processing a megagram of refuse is 52 kWH which yields 0.84 Mg of RDF.   Based on the coal consumption rate from the previous section:

$$1 \text{ Mg coal} \quad \frac{1000}{.72} = 1390 \text{ KWH}$$

Using the conservative value of one half for the RDF to coal effective energy replacement:

$$1 \text{ Mg RDF} \quad \frac{1}{2} \times 1390 = 695 \text{ KWH}$$

One megagram of solid waste produces 0.84 Mg of RDF, therefore:

$$1 \text{ Mg solid waste} \quad .84 \times 695 = 583 \text{ KWH}$$

Table 3. Summary of Operating Revenue (1976-1977).

Sources of Revenue	2 yr. Revenues	Rev. per input (Mg)	(Ton)
Refuse-derived fuel	$672,278	8.28	7.53
Ferrous metals	198,345	2.44	2.22
Commercial haulers	25,769	0.32	0.29
Non-commercial haulers	23,277	0.29	0.26
Baled paper	9,528	0.12	0.11
Wood chips	4,992	0.06	0.06
Aluminum	2,848	0.04	0.03
Total	$937,537	11.55	10.50

The average energy consumption to process a megagram of solid waste is 52 KWH, so:

$$\frac{\text{Generation}}{\text{Consumption}} = \frac{583}{52} = 11.2$$

The electrical energy ratio for the RDF is 11.2 considering kilowatt hours generated relative to kilowatt hours consumed in processing.

FLOW STREAM ANALYSIS

The output streams from the Ames system are the RDF product, rejected materials, ferrous metals, glass and grit, wood chips, baled paper, and nonferrous metals. As seen in Figure 5, the flow in some of these streams − nonferrous metals, for example − is relatively low. The nonferrous metals separation system has been in a developmental stage and during 1977 was not operational. Outputs from this substem are the nonferrous metals and glass/grit. During three months of 1977, however, aluminum metal, which was handpicked from the reject stream, amount to 8 megagrams. The major plant outputs are the RDF, ferrous metal, and reject materials. Table 5 gives the total refuse processed by the system for 1976 and 1977 together with monthly average and standard deviation values [4].

Refuse Derived Fuel

Table 6 gives the heating value, mineral ash, moisture, and density for the RDF obtained over six months of weekly composite process

Table 4. Average Energy Consumption by Season.

Season	Season Average kW-hr/Mg	Standard Deviation kW-hr/Mg
1976		
Summer	49.92	4.74
Fall	50.76	4.41
1977		
Winter	73.16	6.16
Spring	48.10	2.59
Summer	47.56	6.90

Table 5. Total Refuse Processed.

Operating period (Year)	Refuse Processed Total (Mg)	Refuse Processed Monthly avg (Mg/month)	Average monthly deviation (mg/month)
1976	37,252	3,104	537
1977	44,027	3,669	742
1976–1977	81,279	3,387	696

Table 6. Comparison of Refuse-Derived Fuel and Iowa Coal.

	RDF	Typical Iowa coal
Heating value (kilogoules/kilogram)	12,000	21,000
Ash	18%	20%
Moisture	25%	13%
Density (kilograms/cubic meter)	98	–

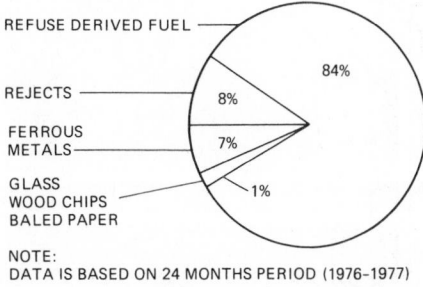

Figure 5. Reclaimed resources as percent of total refuse processed.

The sizing distribution by fraction of RDF flow entering the storage bin, is shown in Figure 7. The largest fraction of material is classified as less than 2 millimeters and represents 27% of the total; about 85% of the material is smaller than 38 millimeters.

Ferrous Metal

The processed ferrous metal output composition is shown in Figure 8 to be 97% of the stream. The rest of the constituents are each 1% or less by weight, representing small amounts of contaminants that must be dealt with by the ferrous product user.

The sizing distribution is shown in Figure 9. Here it is seen that material larger than 38 millimeters represents 78% of the flow. Note that the ferrous sizing is relatively large compared to the RDF sizing distribution (Figure 7). The bulk density of the ferrous output was found to be 307 kilograms per cubic meter.

Rejects

The characterization of the process reject material is shown in Figure 10; at 28%, the miscellaneous category for nonclassifiable material is the largest. Of the identifiable material, glass and wood are the largest fractions at 20% and 17%, respectively. This distribution represents the flow of material types going to the landfill.

Figure 11 gives the sizing distribution of the reject material with the greatest amount falling in the 19 to 38 millimeter range. An important characteristic of the reject material

plant flow stream sampling during 1977. The same average characteristics for typical Iowa coal are given for comparison. It is seen that the RDF has a lower heating value and a higher moisture content which represents a higher stack heat loss. The design of systems to use this fuel must take these characteristics into account.

The composition of the RDF for the same sample period, as shown in Figure 6, is 33% paper and 19% cardboard. The miscellaneous category, including nonclassifiable materials such as sand, grit, stone, dust, etc., represents 22% of the material.

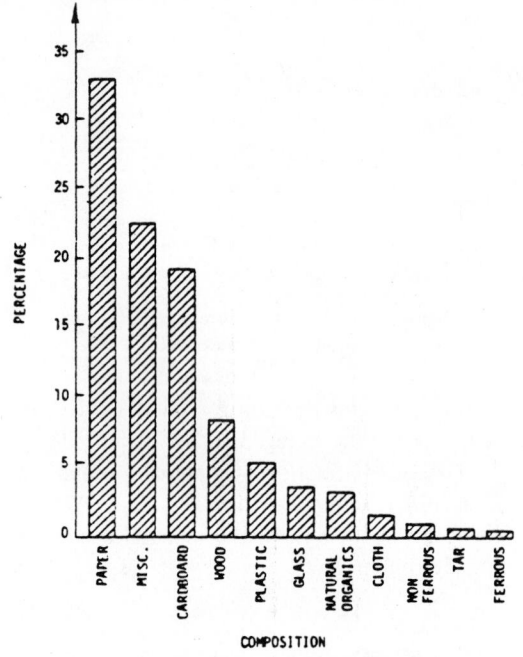

Figure 6. Average percent distribution by weight for composition of refuse derived fuel.

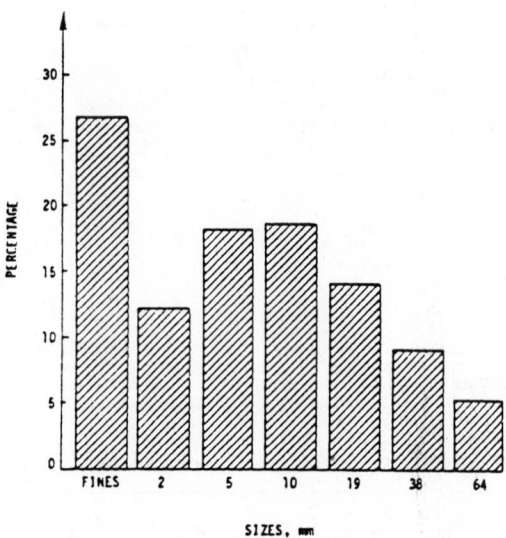

Figure 7. Average percent distribution by weight for sizing of refuse derived fuel.

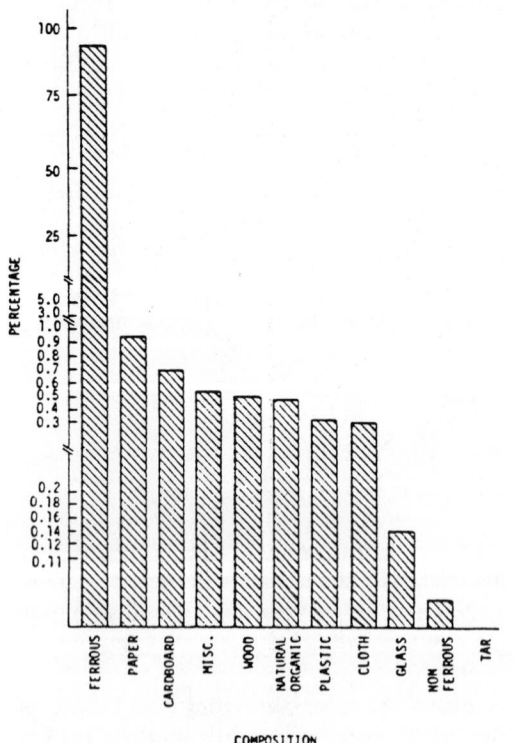

Figure 8. Average percent distribution by weight for composition of ferrous metals.

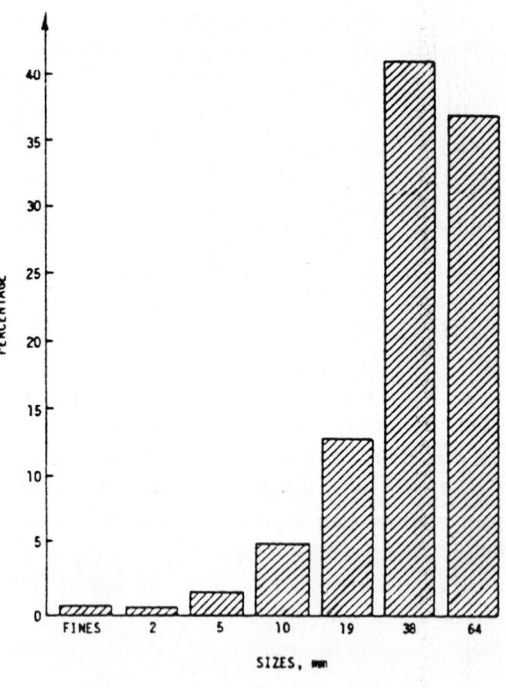

Figure 9. Average percent distribution by weight for sizing of ferrous metals.

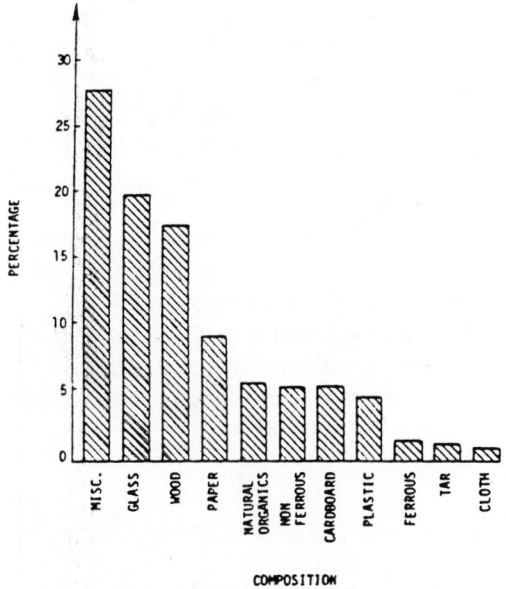

Figure 10. Average percent distribution by weight
for composition of rejects.

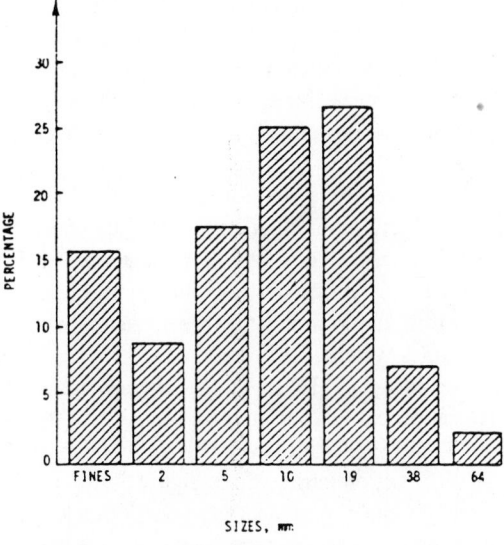

Figure 11. Average percent distribution by weight
for sizing of rejects.

is its lack of need for a soil cover; it can be stockpiled and left without any additional material handling. Part of the reason for this stability is the relatively high bulk density of 345 kilograms per cubic meter.

BREAK-EVEN ANALYSIS

The plant's sources of revenue are: RDF, ferrous and nonferrous metals, recyclable paper, wood chips, and tipping fees. During the 1976 and 1977 operations the RDF and ferrous metals accounted for 72% and 21%, respectively,

of the total revenue earned. The remaining income of 7% is relatively small by comparison. Therefore, the sales prices received for RDF and ferrous metals are critical in determining the break-even point of the Ames system.

Using the actual highest, average, and lowest sales figures for these two resources, a break-even analysis is summarized in Table 7 [4]. The actual prices received per Mg of ferrous metals were: $34.42 (lowest), $37.53 (average), $46.97 (highest); for RDF the prices were $7.32 (lowest), $9.84 (average), $14.68 (highest). These are shown in combinations assuming both

Table 7. Summary of Break-even Points (1976-1977).

| Sales price | | | | Break-even point | |
| Refuse derived fuel | | Metals | | | |
(S/Mg)	(S/Ton)	(S/Mg)	(S/Ton)	(Mg/Mo)	(Tons/Mo)
7.32	6.64	37.53	34.05	13,638	14,987
9.84	8.93	37.53	34.05	12,017	13,206
14.68	13.32	37.53	34.05	6,337	6,964
9.84	8.93	34.42	31.23	9,722	10,683
14.68	13.32	46.97	42.61	5,586	6,139
22.05	20.00	37.53	34.05	4,086	4,490
27.56	25.00	37.53	34.05	3,210	3,528
33.07	30.00	37.53	34.05	2,633	2,894

the average and maximum price received for each material. In addition, the sales price of RDF is hypothetically increased while keeping the other prices fixed in order to study the impact of RDF revenue on the break-even analysis.

Table 7 indicates that the break-even analysis is more sensitive to the refuse-derived fuel price fluctuation than it is to the ferrous metals prices. Thus, the revenue earned from the sales of refuse-derived fuel is the critical factor in determining the break-even point in the Ames system.

Referring to Table 5, the average mass of refuse processed per month was 3669 Mg in 1977 and 3387 Mg over the two-year period 1976-77. Comparing these figures with those given in Table 7 as necessary for a break-even to occur, it can be seen that fuel credits of approximately $22.00/Mg and a ferrous price of $37.00/Mg would be needed to achieve this. The ferrous price is equal to what is currently being paid. The RDF price corresponds to a coal price of $44.00/Mg ($50/ton) based on currently calculated coal/RDF heating equivalence ratio. Coal prices are now averaging $30.86/Mg ($28/ton). Between 1974 and 1979, prices for Iowa coal have risen from $11.35 to $26.20 per Mg (delivered). During the same period, prices for Wyoming and Colorado coal have risen from $17.05 to $39.47 per Mg (delivered). If only non-Iowa coal were being used in the electric power plant, a break-even point could be realized as early as 1980, the break-even point being defined as selling RDF at a value equalling its production cost. Total reliance on Iowa coal would result in a break-even point in 1985. It is common practice to mix the two types of coal to reduce sulfur emissions from Iowa coal. Actual ratios depend upon the quality of Iowa coal determined from emission and heating quality tests performed in coal samples. Ratios employed in recent years suggest a break-even point between two and four years from now. This break-even analysis assumes no increase in the price received for ferrous metal or changes in plant operating costs.

The aluminum separation system presents another interesting case for break-even analysis. This system originally cost $250,000. With repairs and modifications, the total investment in it is now approximately $300,000. Aluminum has been averaging about 0.5 percent of the total mass of refuse processed, and has a current scrap value of $331 per Mg. At the current annual refuse processing rate of 45,000 Mg, this would mean 225 Mg of aluminum per year or more than $74,000 in revenue. Such figures make this process potentially attractive. They have not been realized because of technical problems in debugging and maintaining the aluminum separation system. It is likely that these problems will be solved in time to make the investment worthwhile.

RECYCLING VERSUS ALTERNATIVES

The desirability of mechanized, capital intensive solid waste recovery should be studied with the same objectivity that any major industrial equipment proposal would deserve. Currently, the major challenger to solid waste recovery is landfill. Thus, it is desirable to compare both costs and benefits for these two alternatives, covering as many aspects of anticipated results as possible. A preliminary analysis of this kind has been done for the Ames system. Listed in order of decreasing importance, the three major dimensions of benefit and cost to those using the system were defined as:

1. Health
2. Economic
3. Legal and Social.

The solid waste recovery system benefits to health include:

1. Elimination of blowing dust, dirt, paper.
2. Elimination of odors.
3. Control of rodents.
4. Prevention of ground water leachates.
5. Prevention of methane gas generation.
6. Personnel not exposed to severe weather conditions.

The economic advantages for recovery plant are:

1. Refuse haulers are not required to operate in dirt, mud or snow.
2. Hauling travel time is reduced, including elimination of problem of getting stuck in mud or snow.
3. Plant can be located in town for easy access.
4. Value is recovered from resources, not buried and lost.
5. Extended life (10X) for landfill since rejects are only 10 percent of refuse.

The economic disadvantages of landfill are:

1. Loss of land value for sale or taxation.
2. Low utility of filled land for construction: special foundation construction and pilings are needed.

The legal and social benefits from a solid waste recovery system includes:

1. No legal problems over where to haul refuse; fees are paid and a location is established.
2. Personal involvement of individual citizens in delivering refuse; people are encouraged to bring in what ought to be thrown away.
3. Pride in the community and in knowing that proper, safe and permanent disposal has been made.

Obviously, these are interrelated; advantages and disadvantages associated with one dimension of improvement can impose limits or generate problems on another dimension. This paper has concentrated on economic aspects of solid waste recovery, but the most basic problems imposed by solid waste (or any waste) are in the realm of public health. Health costs are not always known or even predictable. It has been shown that potentially a solid waste recovery system can operate on a trade-off basis when the principle recovered product is refuse-derived fuel. The high cost of plant and equipment to produce RDF certainly cannot be ignored. Break-even is not automatic or guaranteed.

On the other hand, if sanitary landfill is selected, other costs must be met. These include;

1. Purchase of valuable land
2. Costs of the filling and burying operation, including construction of walls and "flooring" to prevent or reduce seepage of leachates
3. Facilities for operating personnel, including a building with restrooms, lockers and showers (Iowa Department of Environmental Quality requirement)

Cost of Operating a Landfill

The ever-growing magnitude of solid waste generation continues to demand more land that otherwise could be used for productive functions. The scarcity of land for landfill is very acute in the heavily populated urban areas of the United States. The land in the City of Ames and its vicinity is considered prime agricultural land. Thus, using this land for landfill competes with residential needs as well as agricultural products.

The costs of operating landfills are also increasing. Many communities prefer that their landfill be located far from their residences. The distance of the disposal site from the inhabitants who generate the waste can have a major influence on the cost of operating it. In view of the increasing cost of fuel, the cost of hauling refuse may become a major economic consideration in operating or implementing a landfill.

Today, landfill operating costs have increased threefold to fourfold in a matter of ten years. Currently charges of $11 to $17 per Mg ($10 to $15 per ton) are universal. In New York City, fees in excess of $22 per Mg ($20 per ton) are considered a bargain [5]. The City of Ames landfill is still being used to dispose of demolition and rejected materials, and diverted refuse if the Ames Solid Waste Recovery System is inoperable for more than three days. Currently the Ames landfill costs $8 per Mg ($7 per ton) to operate [3].

Indiscriminate disposal of any type of waste on land is known to contaminate drinking water. The U.S. Environmental Protection Agency discovered that leachate damage occurred in nine wells in Rockford, Illinois. The Peoples Avenue Landfill in Rockford was an unlined sand and gravel pit in operation from 1947 to 1972. It served about 125,000 people and accepted commercial, industrial and residential wastes. During its operation nine wells were contaminated. In 1966 four Quaker Oats Company wells, in 1970 four residential wells, and in 1972 one supply were abandoned. Damage was assessed at $205,000, which covered only the cost of drilling new wells [6]. It does not include some of the long-range environmental costs that are difficult to quantify and assign dollar values.

Landfill may be a short-term solution to the waste disposal problems. However, in view of the mentioned difficulties with landfills, long-range solutions are urgent. Disposal methods that are environmentally sound as well as economically feasible are needed. The resource recovery concept is a step toward this goal.

Currently, the total annual cost of operating the Ames Solid Waste Recovery System, less all sales and revenues derived from operating the system, amounts to about $11 per Mg ($10/ton) as a net cost. On an individual basis, $10 also equals approximately the cost per person per year for residents of Story County. This means that in comparing resource recovery with landfill, the health aspect as well as legal and social aspects must favor solid waste recovery to the extent of being worth $10 per year per person.

SUMMARY AND CONCLUSIONS

The Ames Solid Waste Recovery System has been discussed in terms of its operational economics using data for the past two years. Realization of the breakdown point has previously been shown to be achievable by the plant [4]. Now, on the basis of recent trends in coal prices and the heating value of RDF, breakeven appears likely to occur, in terms of balancing annual costs and revenues, within four years. Of course, no one can know the future, but the engineering economics of solid waste recovery are improving with time for this particular system.

It does not appear possible to consider all economic, health, environmental and social/legal aspects of solid waste recovery on a common quantitative basis. The most reasonable approach to dealing collectively with these problems appears to be first to examine the annual revenue − cost balance for plant operations, then to express any negative differences (costs > revenues) in terms of annual costs per individual served by the system, and finally, to evaluate this difference subjectively ("Is it worth it?") in terms of affected health and legal/social parameters and risks.

ACKNOWLEDGMENTS

This research was supported by the Engineering Research Institute of Iowa State University through funds provided by the U.S. Environmental Protection Agency, Municipal Environmental Research Laboratory, Cincinnati, Ohio, Grant No. R803903010. Gratitude is extended to this agency for its continued support of this work. In particular, thanks are due to Carlton Wiles for his encouragement.

The authors wish to thank their colleague Al Joensen and the following research and laboratory assistants whose effort and dedication in obtaining data, conducting numerical analyses, handling computer programs and writing reports made this paper possible: Terry Mc-Keighan, Mike Kosolcharoen, Habib Ataei, Marlin Eiben, Lari Hurlbut, Debbie Ross, Mesfin Yohannes, Dawit Gheresus, Tom Neal, Susan Even, Dave Joensen, and Greg Kelsay.

The authors also wish to acknowledge the generous assistance of public works city officials, including Arnold Chantland, Paul Hinderaker, and Kenny Moravetz. In addition, the support of municipal electric utility city officials, including Merlin Hove, Carl Baker, and Don Riggs, is appreciated.

The support provided by staff members of Midwest Research Institute is gratefully acknowledged. Individuals to be thanked include Doug Fiscus and Bob White.

REFERENCES

1. Adams, S.K. and Even, J.C., Jr. "The Economics of Municipal Solid Waste Recovery: Introduction through Application," *Proceedings, 1977 Spring Annual Conference, AIIE*, Dallas, Texas, pp. 53–58.

2. Gheresus, P., Adams, S.K. and Even, J.C., Jr. "Municipal Solid Waste Processing: A Look at Subsystem Economics," *Proceedings, 1978 Spring Annual Conference, AIIE,* Toronto, Ontario, Canada, pp. 55-63.

3. Hinderaker, P. (City of Ames, Iowa), city records and personal communication.

4. Adams, S.K., Even, J.C. Jr., Gheresus, P., and Joensen, A.W. "Using Solid Waste as an Industrial Fuel," *Proceedings, 1978 Fall Industrial Engineering Conference, AIIE,* Atlanta, Georgia, p. 83-90.

5. Cambourelis, J.P. "Resource Recovery for Municipal Solid Waste Disposal – An Overview," *Proceedings of the Sixth Mineral Waste Utilization Symposium, IITRI,* May 2-3, 1978, Chicago, Illinois, 151.

6. Shuster, A.K. "Leachate Damage Assessment, Case Study of the Peoples Avenue Solid Waste Disposal Site in Rockford, Illinois," U.S. Environmental Protection Agency, 1976, pp. 1-2.

4-15 RDF: Quality Must Precede Quanitiy. A Trommel Stage Can Help

G.M. Savage, L.F. Diaz, and G.J. Trezek

Source: *WASTE AGE*, VOL. 9, NO. 4 (April 1978) pp. 100-106. Reprinted with Permission of National Solid Wastes Management Association.

If a significant share of this country's waste stream is ever to be recovered, the final destination for millions of tons of refuse must be energy production. Energy is the only refuse-based product for which demand is assured. But before more than a few percent of the waste stream can be turned to power, ways must be found to make refuse-derived fuel (RDF) a more reliable product — a product useful in many kinds of boilers.

The most irksome drawbacks to RDF in combustion are its low heating value relative to fossil fuels, its high moisture content, and the large amount of ash it leaves. Associated with these specific problems is the more general RDF weakness — the substance varies in composition, sometimes containing elements which damage steam-making equipment.

These problems with RDF are deep enough that most potential customers for the fuel — utilities and factories with large furnaces or process-steam requirements — won't buy it. Utilities and industries are reluctant to buy RDF even though it is less expensive than the fossil fuel it replaces.

It should be possible to raise the combustion qualities of RDF to the point where it is usable in many existing boilers, and attractive to customers. This article describes some laboratory work done on this subject. This work was sponsored, in part, by grants from the EPA.

The article describes why, from a technical standpoint, RDF is inferior to fossil fuels — and what can be done about it. A productive avenue of attack, the research suggests, is adding a screening stage to the processing of the light fractions from which RDF is usually created. That screening is accomplished via a cylindrical rotary screen called a trommel.

THE FACTS OF LIGHTS

The RDF fuel receiving most attention at present is the fraction reclaimed through primary size reduction and subsequent air classification. Typically, such a fuel could be used either in a suspension burner or a moving-gate furnace. Suspension burning would probably require primary or secondary size reduction of light fractions to a usual size of 1.5 to one inch or less to assure complete combustion. On the other hand, a traveling-grate furnace could accommodate either the light fraction "as is," or in a pelletized form.

Although the light fraction contains an abundance of paper and plastic (usually 17,400 J/g and 37,100 J/g, respectively), it also contains materials that produce ash, and substances that are damaging to burner and boiler structures and the purity of the exhaust gases. The hydrogen chloride formulation resulting from the reaction of chlorides present in the light fraction as vinyl chloride and sodium chloride, for instance, may corrode the internal surfaces of the burner and boiler sections. These vinyl chlorides are formed during the thermal decomposition of polyvinyl chloride plastics (PVC). Chlorides may also be present due to the thermal decomposition of common table salt. These chlorides can combine with hydrogen from water present in the light fraction and form corrosive hydrochloric acid.

Further burner and boiler contamination problems result from traces of aluminum or glass fines (less than 1.5 mm) in the light fraction. Carryover of these fines during air classification is practically unavoidable because of their high drag-to-weight ratios. Although contamination may be considerably less than one per cent, a gradual buildup of silicon dioxide, aluminum oxide, or aluminum silicate deposits on heat transfer surfaces may occur. Such fouling can ruin that heat transfer characteristics of the surface of heat transfer components. In extreme cases, it can cause shutdown and overhaul of the boilers.

Even though light fraction is a much more homogeneous material than raw refuse, it cannot be considered a pure material from the standpoint of combustion. Because the light fraction is a mixture of materials, it is difficult to maintain an efficient combustion process. Material and moisture content variations in the light fraction result in daily fluctuations of as much as plus 15 per cent in its energy content, according to studies of the St. Louis plant. Because of the variability of its heat content, RDF probably is best used as a supplemental fuel.

Another reason for restricting the use of the light fraction to that of supplemental fuel is that, used as such, its detrimental effects are substantially lessened through dilution by the principal fuel. If RDF represents only a small percentage of the total fuel supply, the cumulative effects (surface fouling and corrosion) of the objectionable components may not seriously exceed the normal deterioration of burners, furnaces, boilers, and so on. Conventional cleaning equipment (steam cleaners, soot blowers, etc.) probably could cope with the additional fouling and corrosion contributed by the use of RDF as a supplement. Moreover, combined firing of RDF and fossil fuel would serve to attenuate the air pollution emissions (particulates, unburned hydrocarbons, etc.) associated with burning RDF.

AMONG THE ASHES

Since the light fraction is a solid fuel which leaves ash residue after combustion, provisions

Table 1.

	heating value, joules/gram (Btu/lb) as received	moisture	ash
RDF	12,018 (5,178)	23.1%	20.9%
Orient Coal	26,875 (11,579)	12.5%	7.6%

must be made for ash removal. Coal-burning furnaces have ash handling equipment and therefore could be used to burn light fractions. (Since coal and the light fraction of refuse require similar burning equipment, comparisons between the two are made throughout this article).

Several characteristics of the light fraction must be changed before its fuel qualities can be improved in terms of combustion, efficiency, and material handling. Briefly summarized the troublesome characteristics are: 1) low heating value as compared to coal, natural gas, or fuel oil; 2) a relatively high moisture content and 3) a relatively high ash content as compared to coal. The data presented in Table 1, in which comparison is made between properties of coal and refuse-derived fuel as fired at St. Louis, illustrates the point.

The inferiority of the RDF is readily apparent in the table. The heating value of Orient coal is 223 per cent that of the refuse-derived fuel. Its moisture and ash content are but 54.1 per cent and 36.4 per cent that of RDF.

Clearly the RDF leaves much to be desired with respect to its burning properties. Because of the great disparity in heating values, the weight requirement of RDF would be about 2.2 times that of coal to yield a given amount of energy. The ash production from an energy-equivalent amount of RDF would be more than six times that of Orient coal. A consequence of these differences is the storage and handling problem that could accompany a switch from coal to RDF in existing furnaces or boilers. The problem would be even greater if the RDF were to replace natural gas or fuel oil. Gas and oil have heating values in the 44,100 joules per gram (19,000 BTUs per pound) range with only slight moisture and ash contents.

The high moisture content of RDF is detrimental for three reasons. First, since water has no heating value, it is essentially an inert compound, acting to reduce the potency of a fuel. Second, upon evaporation during combustion, moisture acts as an energy absorber. In effect, it "steals" useable heat. Lastly, the moisture may recondense after combustion on cool surfaces of the burner or heat-exchanging equipment. This condensed water can then react with various gaseous emissions from the combustion, forming corrosive chemicals.

AN EXCLUSIVE SCREENING

Research at our laboratory indicates that through further processing, an RDF can be produced that lacks the undesirable qualities described in the preceding sections, and instead has reasonable heating value, low moisture content, and low ash content. The additional processing involves screening of the light fraction by a rotary cylindrical screen (commonly referred to as a trommel). Through a judicious selection of certain parameters (screen opening size, rotational speed, etc.) most of the fine materials in the light fraction can be removed. These fines typically are inert materials with little or no heating value. Hence, the removal of these materials serves to increase the overall heating value of the RDF by concentrating the combustibles remaining in the light fraction. Our experiments have shown that more than 90 per cent of the low-heating-value materials present in the light fraction can be removed with a trommel screen. By so doing, the paper content of the screened light fraction is increased to roughly 85 per cent (as compared to 60 per cent prior to screening). In general, the combustible fraction, which is the oversize material retained by the screen, represents from 40 per cent to 60 per cent of the refuse received by a resource recovery plant.

Our calorimetric data show that the average high heating value of the trommel-screened light fraction is approximately 18,568 joules per gram (8,000 BTUs per pound) of dry solids. This value is almost 19 per cent greater than that of the RDF used in the St. Louis demonstration. (Its average heating value was 15,627 joules per gram, or 6,733 BTU per pound.)

According to our research, the light fraction can be classified into two fractions on the basis of heating value: a high-heat fraction consisting mainly of paper and plastic, 18,568 joules per gram (8,000 BTUs per pound) dry; and a low-heat fraction composed of fines and organic materials, 10,830 joules per gram (4,666 BTUs per pound) dry.

A further benefit of screening the light fraction is manifested by a lowering of the moisture content. In our three years of processing municipal solid waste, we have found the average moisture content of the unscreened light fraction to be approximately 22 per cent, which is comparable to the average of 23 per cent noted in the St. Louis study. On the other hand, the moisture content of screened light fraction is only 16 per cent. The lower moisture content of the screened fuel is explained by the fact that the fraction of the lights which passes through the screen ("screen undersize") has a higher moisture content than that of the material retained by the screen, (i.e., the screened fuel). In terms of energy production, an unscreened light fraction, because of its 22 per cent to 23 per cent moisture content, suffers a corresponding decrease in heating value. The heating value of the screened fuel is reduced only 16 per cent because of moisture content. These points are illustrated in Table 2.

Moisture in RDF leads to a decrease in the overall energy recovery in another way. If the RDF were burned in a typical solid-fuel-fired steam generation unit, the inherent moisture would be heated, evaporated, superheated, and subsequently exhausted as water vapor

Table 2.

	unscreened light fraction	screened light fraction
heating value, joules/gram (BTU/lb) dry solids	15,627 (6,733)	18,568 (8,000)
moisture content	22.5%	16.3%
heating value, joules/gram (BTU/lb) as received	12,111 (5,218)	15,541 (6,696)
decrease	22.5%	16.3%

along with the other combustion gases. The energy thus absorbed by the water normally would not be recoverable since the exhaust gas temperatures are usually kept above the dew point to prevent condensation within the boiler section.

The enthalpy function (the heat flow into a closed system) can be used as a convenient quantity for determining the energy absorbed by water or water vapor. If heat is added to a substance at constant pressure, as is the case in a furnace, no external work is done by the system, and all heat is used to increase the enthalpy of the substance. Consequently, the change in enthalpy represents the heat absorbed at constant pressure. The discussion which follows deals solely with the water (or water vapor) derived from the moisture contained in the refuse-derived fuel. Since we are only concerned with energy loss resulting from the difference in moisture content, we need not consider the additional water created in the combustion reaction. Likewise, the heat transfer efficiency of the boiler (commonly about 80 per cent) is assumed constant for each type of fuel and consequently is neglected in this analysis.

WATER TAKES THE HEAT

For the purpose of illustration the temperature of the screened or unscreened light fraction is assumed to be 21°C (70°F), and the furnace is operating at atmospheric pressure. Hence, the moisture also enters the burner at 21°C (70°F) and 1×10^5 n/m² (1.0 atm). The moisture in the RDF absorbs energy as it is heated from 21°C (70°F) to 100°C (212°F). Upon reaching 100°C (212°F), the moisture evaporates and the water vapor is subsequently superheated to the equilibrium temperature of the combustion gases. At this point another assumption is made, namely that the gases (including the water vapor) are cooled 121°C (250°F) after passing through the boiler where heat from the combustion gases is transferred to the water flowing through the boiler tubes.

The heat lost, i.e., that portion not recovered in the boiler, in the exhausted water vapor can be expressed on the basis of energy per unit weight of water. The unrecovered heat is in the

form of: (1.) the energy required to heat the water from 21°C (70°F) to 100°C (212°F) at 1×10^5 N/m², namely, 330 joules per gram (142 BTUs per pound) water; (2.) the heat of vaporization at 100°C (212°F) and 1.0 atm, i.e., 2251 joules per gram (970 BTUs per pound); and (3.) the energy required to superheat the water vapor (assuming a constant pressure of 1×10^5 N/m² [1.0 atm] from 100°C (212°F) to 121°C (250°F), which amounts to 44 joules per gram (19 BTUs per pound). The total heat loss is the sum of these three quantities, or 2625 joules per gram (1131 BTUs per pound) of water.

When that heat loss is expressed in the terms of unrecovered energy per unit weight of dry solids, the following comparisons can be drawn. For unscreened refuse-derived fuel with a moisture content of 22.5 per cent, the water-solids ratio is 0.290. Therefore, the heat lost in the exhaust due to the moisture in the fuel is 2625 joules per gram (1131 BTUs per pound) water $\times$ 0.29, or 761 joules per gram (328 BTUs per pound) of solids. On other other hand, with screened light fraction at its usual moisture content of 16.3 per cent (water/solids = 0.195), the energy lost in the exhaust due to moisture content is 513 joules per gram (221 BTUs per pound) of solids.

A further comparison leads to the expression of the energy lost in the exhaust due to the moisture in the RDF as a per cent of the as-received heating value of the fuel. In the case of the unscreened light fraction, 12,111 joules per gram (5,218 BTUs per pound), the percentage of unrecovered energy is 4.9. For the screened light fraction, 15,541 joules per gram (6,696 BTUs per pound), the percentage of unrecovered energy is 2.8.

A breakdown of the heating values for unscreened and screened fuels provides some insight into the relative effects of the factors that reduce the amount of energy recovered from the two refuse-derived fuels. The greatest reduction in heating value for both fuels is due to the inherent moisture content. The net recoverable energy on an as-received weight basis from unscreened light fraction is 11,521 joules per gram (4,964 BTUs per pound), and that from screened RDF is 15,114 joules per gram (6,512 BTUs per pound). On the basis of these values screened light fraction has a 31.2 per cent higher heating value than that of unscreened light fraction.

If a screened refuse-derived fuel having a heating value of 18,568 joules per gram (8,000 BTUs per pound) dry is taken as the practical upper limit for a homogeneous fuel derived from solid waste, then the following conclusion is justified: The low heating value of the undesirable materials removable by screening the light fraction effectively reduces the potential heating value of refuse-derived fuel from 18,568 joules per gram (8,000 BTUs per pound) to 15,627 joules per gram (6,733 BTUs per pound) on a dry weight basis, or from 15,541 joules per gram (6,696 BTUs per pound) to 12,111 joules per gram (5,218 BTUs per pound) on an as-received basis.

Although a solid fuel with a high heating value is desirable, equally important is its possession of a low ash content. As previously mentioned, the unscreened light fraction, 12,111 joules per gram (5,218 BTUs per pound) as-received, has an ash content of 20.9 per cent. Expressed on the basis of grams of ash per million joules (MJ) of energy, or alternatively as pounds of ash per million BTU (MMBTU), unscreened light fraction yields 17.3 grams per MJ and 40.0 pounds per MMBTU. For comparison with the coal used in the St. Louis demonstration, 26,875 joules per gram (11,579 BTUs per pound), 2.8 grams of ash per MJ or 6.6 pounds per MMBTU are produced. Because the undesirable materials in the unscreened light fraction have been removed through screening, the ash content of the screened light fraction as measured in our laboratory is 12.1 per cent. In terms of an as-received heating value of 15,541 joules per gram (6,696 BTU per pound) for screened fuel, ash production from it would be 7.8 grams per MJ or 18.1 pounds per MMBTU.

The results of experiments conducted in St. Louis with regard to commercial use of a refuse-derived fuel and of studies conducted at the University of California (Richmond Field Station) on processing solid waste point to a method of producing a fuel from municipal waste that more closely approximates an "ideal" fuel than is presently the case with existing methods.

The hope of upgrading the presently unfavorable properties of refuse-derived fuel became the subject of extensive investigation at our laboratory. The study culminated in the development of processing scheme which can produce an RDF of superior quality. This improved fuel is obtained by screening the air-classified light fraction of municipal waste. Screening removes the fines and other materials having relatively low heating value, and thereby leaves a product characterized by an overall heating value higher than that prior to screening. Typically, the screened fuel has an as-received boating value of 15,541 joules/gram (6,696 BTUs per pound).

The improvement in fuel properties exceeds that of solely raising the heating value in that the moisture content is lowered to 16.3 per cent and the ash content to 12.1 per cent. The significance of the reduction in moisture content is the heat loss associated with the vaporization of the water.

INSTEAD OF COAL

The production of an RDF compatible with existing equipment in coal-burning facilities would represent a significant step in dealing with both the energy shortage and solid waste control. To obtain optimum performance from coal-fired boilers, the properties of RDF ideally should match those of coal. It is doubtful that the ideal condition can ever be met. Nevertheless, fuel characteristics of the unscreened light fraction can be improved through further processing.

Other problems remaining to be solved deal with the air pollution aspects of burning RDF. It is true that the extent of the emission of oxides of sulfur is not expected to be a problem because the sulfur content of raw refuse is so low — less than 0.15 per cent. This certainly does not extend to particulates, unburned hydrocarbons, oxides of nitrogen, carbon monoxide, and hydrogen chloride emissions resulting from combustion of RDF whether screened or unscreened. The gap in information about air emissions along with and the use of abatement equipment such as electrostatic precipitators, needs to be filled before the full potential of RDF as an energy source can be evaluated.

4-16 Eco-Fuel®II: The Third Generation

F. Hasselriis, H. Master, C. Konheim, H. Betzig

Source: Paper presented at the International Conference on Prepared Fuels and Resource Recovery Technology, Nashville, Tennessee, February 10–13, 1981, 19 pp.

BACKGROUND

Combustion Equipment Associates, Inc. (CEA) is an international company engaged in manufacturing of pollution controls, agricultural equipment, energy conservation and combustion systems, and design and operation of resource recovery facilities. These capabilities were used in developing a process to produce fuels from municipal solid wastes and biomass.

CEA's attention to resource recovery began a decade ago when residual oil was selling for under ten cents a gallon. Having just acquired International Boiler Works, a licensee of a major European water wall incineration technology, CEA could have pursued the direction of mass burning of municipal wastes. However, to a company in the forefront of designing pollution control systems, this appeared to be inconsistent with the thrust of national environmental policy. CEA sought an innovative method of extracting energy from refuse.

In the early 1970's CEA set up a facility to process municipal solid waste (MSW) and produce refuse-derived-fuel (RDF) at East Bridgewater, MA, where CEA was under contract to dispose of MSW using a more conventional incineration system. In association with Arthur D. Little (ADL), CEA produced a fluff RDF (ECO-FUEL®I). It was found that reduction of fuel moisture content to 15% or less would arrest microbiological activity, improving storage life, classification efficiency and the ash content of the fuel.

While this was a breakthrough in refuse-to-energy technology, ECO-FUEL®I shared some of the commercial disadvantages present in fluff RDF. Large particle size and low bulk density adversely affected storability, transportability and efficient combustion of this fuel.

In an effort to overcome these disadvantages, CEA and ADL began an intensive research and development program to design an advanced process for recovering energy and materials from MSW with these basic objectives:

- Reliability – the process should use proven equipment with high on-stream availability.
- Flexibility – it should be possible to modify the process to take advantage of future technology.
- Compatibility – the process should be compatible with other recycling programs such as source separation and source reduction.
- Recovery and Marketability – the process should strive for high recoveries of marketable by-products.
- Energy Efficiency – the process should maximize energy recovery and minimize use of fossil fuels and electric power in the overall process of converting MSW to energy.
- Mobility – the product should be a fuel which is readily and indefinitely storable, and which could be transported and metered using conventional industrial techniques.

Further laboratory development work suggested that use of a combination of selected, readily available, inexpensive chemicals, in combination with heat, embrittled the cellulosic fraction of MSW, essentially eliminating its troublesome fibrous nature, reducing it to a free-flowing powder with a dramatic reduction in grinding power requirements.

During most of 1973, laboratory investigations were continued to define more accurately the optimum conditions (i.e., the most effective chemicals, ratios of chemical to MSW and temperature ranges), for production of the dry powdered fuel (designated as RDF-4 by ASTM E-38) and named ECO-FUEL®II (ECO-FUEL). From January 1974 to September 1975, a pilot plant was operated to develop the design parameters for a commercial facility and to produce sufficient quantities of ECO-FUEL for evaluation and combustion testing. During this period about 18 tonnes of ECO-FUEL were produced.

Using the results of the three-year development program, a commercial-size prototype plant was built in the East Bridgewater and operation started in February, 1977. The plant could convert 20–25 tonnes per hour of MSW to 8–10 tonnes per hour of ECO-FUEL. Production was suspended in July, 1980 in order to concentrate manpower and resources on the startup of the new facility in Bridgeport, Connecticut.

ECO-FUEL FIRING

The first commercial demonstration of ECO-FUEL firing took place at Fitchburg, Massachusetts, in an industrial power boiler generating 9 tonnes per hour of steam. The boiler was equipped with a combination pulverized-coal/residual oil-firing burner, then burning oil only. A portable feed hopper, blower and duct, connected to the burner, permitted test-firing of the boiler at various ratios, including self-sustained firing without oil. CEA confirmed that ECO-FUEL could be stored, retrieved, metered and transported pneumatically to the burner, and that it burned better than pulverized coal. When firing ECO-FUEL in combination with No. 6 residual oil, the flame envelope became shorter and more luminous. When ECO-FUEL was fired alone, the flame was stable, clean and intense. The demonstration justified a larger, full-scale industrial application.

CEA acquired a steam and electric power-generating boiler plant in Waterbury, Connecticut and installed a permanent ECO-FUEL storage and firing system. The plant had two boilers, designed for coal firing (then burning oil), with most of the burner system for coal-firing intact. Unit #1, with a steam capacity of 125 tonnes per hour and Unit #2, with a 62 tonnes per hour steam capacity, were equipped with ECO-FUEL storage, metering and pneumatic fuel transport lines. After burning for over a year, performance confirmed the favorable observations at Fitchburg and provided the design criteria for commercial application of the ECO-FUEL burning system at a major electrical generating station.

THE BRIDGEPORT/RESOURCE RECOVERY FACILITY (1)

In 1976 CEA joined with Occidental Petroleum Company to form CEA/OXY Resource Recovery Associates, to design, construct, and operate a resource recovery system for the Connecticut Resource Recovery Authority (CRRA) in Bridgeport, Connecticut. Previous to this, CRRA had contracted with the United Illuminating Company (UI) to use all fuel produced at a Bridgeport Resource Recovery Facility in its Bridgeport Harbor Station.

CEA, performing as general contractor, broke ground in Bridgeport in June, 1976. Final engineering was conducted parallel with construction in order to expedite completion. Extensive midpoint modifications were under-taken following an explosion in the East Bridgewater facility in November, 1977. Strikes and severe weather created delays in 1978. The facility began to receive refuse in May, 1979.

During the startup phase it was decided to concentrate on startup of only one of the two parallel lines, so that the second line could be modified later with whatever revisions were found necessary. By the spring of 1980, the single line was up to half its design capacity, with an on-stream reliability of approximately 33%. In May, 1980, a task force of CEA personnel was assigned to accelerate the startup by eliminating choke points and areas of low operating reliability. This team addressed numerous areas which required optimization and heavy investment by CEA. During this period, high-quality ECO-FUEL was produced and fired at increasing rates, reaching a maximum of 600 tonnes per day of MSW processed with an on-stream reliability of 65%, and 51% firing at United Illuminating with excellent performance.

BURNING ECO-FUEL AT UNITED ILLUMINATING (2)

The 86 MW B&W boiler which generates 6.9 MPa (1500 psi) steam at 538 C (1000 f), has a high power cycle efficiency of 34%, requiring only 10.55 MJ per kWhr. It was equipped with three cyclone burners, originally burning coal or oil. Coal had not been burned for over 15 years, and much of the coal handling equipment was removed or inoperable. ECO-FUEL feeding systems were installed for each of the three burners, consisting of a fuel storage silo, Acrison weigh-feeder, rotary airlock, blower, and 200 mm pneumatic feeding lines discharging the fuel into the primary air duct of the cyclone furnace. Each burner system can feed up to 11 tonnes per hour, representing 200 GJ (189 million Btu) per hour. The three burners can replace 93 bbl per hour of residual oil, which is 65% of unit capacity.

A new ash-removal system was installed to remove the slag drained from the furnaces (mostly frit), transport it with sluicing water to a screen and thence to a container body for disposal. The fines are accumulated by a thickener and discharged to the waste water treatment system of the entire power plant.

Over a three-month period firing was tested up to 2.3 tonnes per hour through each burner, then advanced to 3.5 tonnes per hour. At this point slag was seen flowing into the slag tank, and a boiler inspection conducted to asses slag and flyash distribution throughout the boiler. The inspection team, composed of representatives of Babcock & Wilcox, UI and CEA found the cyclone walls were evenly coated with protective slag. The superheater-reheater tubes had soft brownish ash deposits on the leading edges which were loosely bonded and were easily removed by sootblowing. No bridging of tubes was observed. The hoppers below the superheater and economizer contained a granular ash and the Ljungstrom air preheater was clean. The precipitator catch was tan, as compared with the gray color with oil firing.

The conclusion of the inspection team was that "nothing was evident in the boiler that would indicate any immediate adverse affects in the boiler from firing ECO-FUEL." Subsequent inspections did not reveal essentially different conditions as the firing rates were increased to 20% and over. After each inspection samples of slag and flyash were taken for analysis. Utility officials have reported that the fuel has been proven to be entirely satisfactory and has caused no problems with the boilers; they only regretted that the supply was limited.

FUEL CHARACTERISTICS

Although it is refuse-derived, ECO-FUEL is, in the true sense of the word, a specification fuel since it has the required characteristics: a high heating value compared with many coals and wood; can be burned readily in burners and boilers designed for fossil fuels without changes to the burner; produces essentially the same furnace temperatures as fossil fuels; does not require more combustion air per unit of heat released than fossil fuels, nor are more gases released to the stack.

Actually, cellulosic materials in MSW and biomass crops and wastes require about 7% less oxygen for combustion and produce substantially higher flame temperatures than fossil fuels. Combined with their high volatile content and the low temperatures at which they are released, these materials can be made into fuels which improve the combustion of fossil fuels, provided that they are dried and reduced to small particles.

A good fuel should have these characteristics:

- Low moisture for rapid combustion; low excess air; high combustion temperatures and minimum boiler stack losses; and complete combustion of all components especially chlorinated ones.
- Low ash, reducing transport weight, boiler deposits and slagging, and minimizing ash-handling equipment.

- Small particle size to accelerate and assure complete combustion.
- Free-flowing characteristics to facilitate fuel handling, storage and feeding to the burner.
- High density to reduce storage and transport volumes and the size of feeding devices.
- Low variability of its properties to minimize upsets and unbalances of fuels/air ratios in combustion, pressure fluctuations in the furnace, and consequent requirements for excess air and generation of products of incomplete combustion.

ECO-FUEL meets the above requirements better than less-processed, refuse-derived fuels mainly due to its low moisture and powder consistency.

The original specifications of ECO-FUEL are listed in Table 1. The fuel produced actually improves on these specifications in moisture, ash and heating value, as shown in Tables 2 to 4.

The value of a fuel depends upon its chemical composition which determines its dry, ash-free heating value and, secondarily, upon its moisture and ash content, which subtract and detract from its use-value.

Table 2 compares the proximate and ultimate analyses of several coals, ECO-FUEL, Agrifuel and residual oil for comparison on a dry basis. Pine bark and ECO-FUEL have high volatile contents: 73 and 74%, as compared with coals, which range around 40%. On an ash-free basis, ECO-FUEL and AGRI-FUEL have 85% volatiles.

Table 1. CEA Specifications for ECO-FUEL®II.

Higher Heating Value	17,400–18,600 kJ/kg (7500–8000 BTU/lb)
Particle Size	less than 50% less than 200 mesh
Moisture Content	less than 5%
Sulfur Content	less than 1%
Ash Content	less than 15%
Specific Heat	0.45 BTU/(lb) (°F)
Density	0.3–0.6 g/cm³ (20–40 lb/cu ft)

Table 2. Comparison of Cellulosic with Fossil Fuels (Dry) (3).

	Pine Bark	Coals Western Penn.		ECO-FUEL	AGRI-FUEL*	No. 6 Oil
PROXIMATE ANALYSIS						
Volatile	72.9	43.4	37.7	74.0	83.0	99.5
Fixed Carbon	24.2	51.7	52.2	13.0	15.0	
Ash	2.9	4.9	10.1	12.0	1.1	0.5
ULTIMATE ANALYSIS						
Hydrogen	5.6	6.4	5.0	5.7	5.0	11
Carbon	53.4	54.6	74.2	42.0	43.9	88
Sulfur	.1	.4	2.1	.7	.2	1
Nitrogen	.1	1.0	1.5	.6	.5	
Oxygen	37.9	33.8	7.1	29.0	48.8	
HIGHER HEATING VALUE						
Dry MJ/kg	21.0	21.9	31.0	19.1	18.9	41.9
BTU/lb	9030	9420	13310	8200	8130	18000
Dry, Ash Free						
MJ/kg	21.6	23.0	34.5	21.7	19.1	42.0
BTU/lb	9300	9900	14800	9318	8220	18090

*AGRI-FUEL is produced by a CEA process for embrittlement and grinding of crop wastes such as bagasse and energy crops.

The dry, ash-free heating value of bark and ECO-FUEL is about the same, 21.7 MJ/kg, as compared with 23 for western coal, two thirds that of Pennsylvania coal and half that of the oil.

The heating value of undried RDF suffers severely from its high moisture and associated high ash. The thermal value of the fuel must be evaluated using as-received moisture. The moisture in the fuel contributes to the water vapor released in the combustion process, and also affects the excess air required for combustion, thus reducing the boiler efficiency.

Table 3 compares moisture, ash and higher heating values (HHV) of ECO-FUEL and two typical RDF-3 types. The moisture content of ECO-FUEL is 2.6 with a percent standard deviation (PSD) of 31%, whereas the St. Louis RDF is 26.6% with 27% PSD. The Ames RDF has about the same moisture but a smaller PSD, possibly because there is less food waste or the processing removes more of the variable-moisture materials. Ash content shows a PSD of about 22% for the RDF and 14% for the ECO-FUEL.

On an as-received basis the heating values vary substantially, ranging from 10.6 to 18.3 MJ/kg. On a moisture-and-ash-free basis the mean HHV ranges only from 21.2 to 22.2 kJ/kg, with percent standard deviations ranging from 2.6 to 6.2% of the mean. The as-received HHV ranges from 10.6 to 18.3 with a PSD range of 4.3 for the ECO-FUEL to 12.9 for the St. Louis RDF.

From the standpoint of combustion in a boiler, it is more appropriate to consider the fuel properties as related to a unit of heat released by the fuel, such as per GJ or Million BTU, as listed in Table 4.

Table 3. Comparative Properties of RDF-3 and RDF-4.

Property	ECO-FUEL (RDF-4) Mean %	SD	St. Louis (4) (RDF-3) Mean %	SD	Ames, Iowa (5) (RDF-3) Mean %	SD
Moisture	2.6	31.0	26.6	27.4	24.5	7.0
Ash	12.5	14.0	21.7	21.2	18.0	22.2
HHV, MJ/kg						
As Received:	18.31	4.3	10.62	12.9	11.98	4.2
Dry Ash Free:	21.69	3.5	22.19	6.2	21.16	2.6
HHV, BTU/lb						
As Received:	7870	4.3	4565	12.9	5150	4.2
Dry Ash free:	9324	3.5	9540	6.2	9096	2.6
Density, g/cc	0.48	12.6	0.07	22.0	0.17	14.1
Sample Period:	80 trucks		97 daily		22 weeks	

Table 4. Weight of Constituents of RDF per MJ of Heating Value.

	ECO-FUEL Mean %	SD	St. Louis (4) Mean %	SD	Ames (5) Mean %	SD
WEIGHTS, kg/GJ						
Fuel	54.6	4.3	94.2	6.4	83.5	7.8
Moisture	1.4	31	25.0	12	20.5	29
Ash	6.8	14	20.4	11	15.0	18
Sulphur	.38	13	.17	15	.36	25
Chloride	.33	13	.43	28	.20	45
Stack Gas	403		460		441	
Cubic Meters of Fuel	0.11	13	1.35	13	0.49	24

As-received properties are important from a transport standpoint, but weights per unit heat release are more important from the boiler standpoint. The sulfur content on this basis, eliminating the diluting effects of moisture and ash, will surprise many who are more familiar with data on an as-received basis. The sulfur content of refuse has a wide variability due to the variability of the constituents, such as food and rubber, which contribute to sulfur. There is close agreement on Moisture and Ash-Free Heating value (MAF HHV). Normal MSW, containing food and plastics, has a MAF HHV close to 9500 to 9600 BTU/lb. A relative lack of plastics and oils may account for the substantially lower MAF heating values reported for Ames.

The percent standard deviation (PSD) of the mean values of fuel shipment samples (collected as noted at Bridgeport, St. Louis and Ames), indicates the amount of variability of properties. The ECO-FUEL is much less variable than the fluff RDF-3 in most cases. The 31% variation in ECO-FUEL moisture represents 1% fuel moisture variation, as compared with 27.4% of 26.6 or 7.3% and 7% of 24.5 or 7.3% variation for the other RDFs, at one standard deviation. Translating standard deviation into confidence level, the weight of moisture in the fuel for 95% of the samples will vary within a range of +1-1.4%, 13% and 3% of the fuel weight for the ECO-FUEL, St. Louis, and Ames fuels, respectively.

Considering heat content, the difference is striking. One GJ is contained in 55 kg of ECO-FUEL, occupying 0.11 cubic meter. A GJ of RDF-3, on the other hand, would occupy 4 to 12 times the volume and would weight about 1.5 times more.

Handling characteristics include ease of removal from storage, transport weighing, and precise feeding to burners. ECO-FUEL stores and handles like other relatively free-flowing powders such as pulverized coal. Based on tests and observations at United Illuminating, it can be fed to burners with less than +1-2% variation in feed and about 1% weight precision. ECO-FUEL can be controlled fully automatically as a prime fuel.

Since ECO-FUEL is as combustible as paper and has the combustible characteristics of Pittsburgh pulverized coal, it is contained in vessels able to withstand at least 5 psi pressures. At UI, the design rating in the feeding system was increased to 40 psi, well within the range readily withstood by the pneumatic conveying blower and piping.

COMBUSTION CHARACTERISTICS OF ECO-FUEL, RDF-3 AND FOSSIL FUELS

Burning Profiles of distillate oil, ECO-FUEL powder and briquets, residual oil, and a typical coal published by Babcock and Wilcox (7) and Hecht (8), show the rate of weight loss versus furnace temperature, and thus the rate at which volatiles are released during combustion. Distillate (No. 2) oil starts to release volatiles directly above ambient temperature, and peaks at about 150 C. ECO-FUEL also has a small peak at this temperature, indicating, perhaps, the presence of oils. When the distillate oil is completely burned out, the ECO-FUEL peak starts, topping out at 300 C, and is burned out at 380 C. A small peak develops over 400 C.

Residual oil, being a blend, will show various peaks according to its composition. The curves shown are typical. The first peak coincides with the ECO-FUEL peak at 300 C. Additional peaks in the 400 to 500 C range represent the more carbonaceous oil fractions which are prone to cause soot or cenosphere formation since these particles do not all burn out within the furnace envelope.

The profile for ECO-FUEL briquets starts just as sharply as the powder, and at the same temperature, but is wider, and is sustained in the 400 to 500 C range due to the delayed combustion of the briquet. The volatiles are driven off quickly and the char which remains, although porous due to the loss of volatiles, burns more slowly, like residual oil.

Coal starts to burn at 300 C, peaks at 500 C, and continues to burn up to 800 C as the char remaining after devolatilization is burned. Since it has less volatile matter, the char is less porous and takes more time to burn. It is also nearly pure carbon, which requires a very high temperature to burn. This explains why coal is more prone to create black smoke and produces so much carbon in the flyash. Pulverized coal is faster burning, of course, but this material burns much more slowly than powdered ECO-FUEL.

In a comparison of ECO-FUEL with oil and coal, then, it can be described as slower-burning than distillate #2 oil, similar to the light fractions of residual oil, such as #4 oil, and much faster-burning than residual #6 oil, and pulverized and lump coals. We note that the low ignition temperature and high volatile content causes a rapid heat release, without the troublesome char phase which plagues residual oil and coals.

It is not surprising, then, that the use of ECO-FUEL with either residual oil or coal improves the combustion of these fossil fuels by the early release of gaseous fuel which accelerates the combustion of the slower-burning fuels, helping them to attain complete combustion within the furnace.

For the same reason that oil has to be atomized and coal pulverized, RDF must be size-reduced to achieve efficient combustion. The particle size has a significant effect on the time required to burn a particle. The combustion of pulverized fuels, such as ECO-FUEL and coal requires 0.1 to 1 second. The time required to burn RDF-3 is an order of magnitude greater, around 10 seconds. When relying on suspension firing of RDF-3, many combustion chambers cannot provide this much time, resulting in incomplete combustion and char.

Particle thickness is obviously important and affects combustion as does the length of a flake, since oxygen is not able to reach the burning material while water vapor and the products of combustion are leaving. Actual burning times of large particles of RDF-3 have been observed to range from 10 to 30 seconds, including time to heat up to ignition temperature, devolatilize and burn the char. (9)

Although drying the fuel requires additional capital and operating expense, these costs are more than compensated for by improved combustion efficiency and net energy recovery. In addition, variations in moisture content in the fuel create storage, transport and metering problems.

Poor combustion caused by variations in fuel moisture, rates of feed to combustion chambers and in particle size and shape results in boiler tube corrosion. Products of incomplete combustion can result due to such variations. These can present especially serious problems in the case of chlorinated dioxins and furans which can be formed under some combustion conditions.

EMISSION CHARACTERISTICS OF COFIRING WITH OIL

Figures 1, 2 and 3 show the SOx, particulate, and NOx emissions of the UI boiler at various firing rates up to 20% of heat input. The particulate data show the wide range of fluctuation characteristic of precipitator performance. All points are well under the state code of 85 ng/J (0.2 lb per million BTU), and are consistent with the assumed precipitator efficiency of 94% or better. The SOx increased as ECO-FUEL firing was increased, but stayed under the variance limit of 425 ng/J (1.0 pound per million BTU). NOx emissions show a clear reduction from 170 to about 100 ng/J (0.4 to 0.24 lb/million BTU) as ECO-FUEL firing was increased above 10% of total heat input to the boiler.

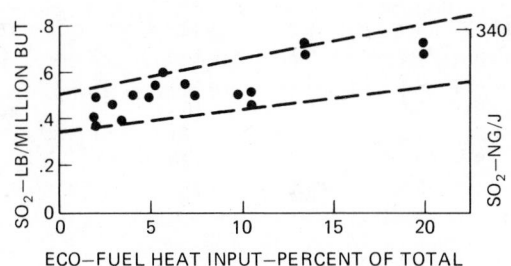

Figure 1. Emissions of sulfur dioxide vs percent ECO-FUEL input.

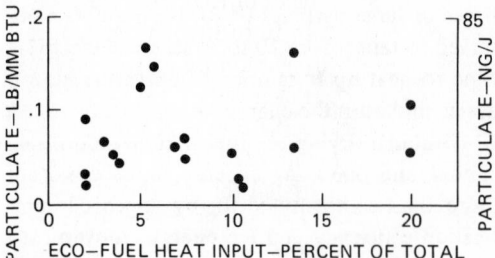

Figure 2. Particulate emissions vs percent ECO-FUEL heat input.

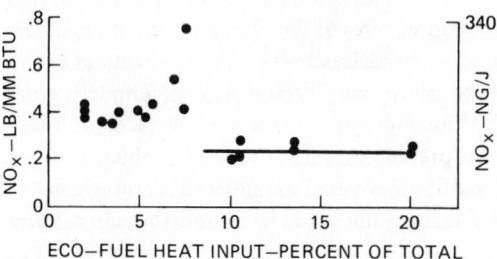

Figure 3. Emissions of nitrogen oxides vs percent ECO-FUEL heat input.

FUEL ASH, SLAG AND FLYASH CHARACTERISTICS

Table 5 shows analyses of fuel ash, slag, tube deposits, hopper ash and flyash samples taken after firing 2000 tons of ECO-FUEL in the UI boiler, in an effort to obtain a profile of ash chemistry throughout the boiler. The precipitator catch sample obtained during co-firing is compared with a sample taken for a period of oil firing.

THE ECO-FUEL PROCESS — THIRD GENERATION

The design of the Bridgport Facility was evolved from the East Bridgewater Facility. Many improvements resulted from operating experience and research and development both inside and outside CEA. Experience was obtained at East Bridgewater with a flail mill, primary trommel and air classifier/dryer and a secondary trommel to remove fine inerts. The high ash in the product showed that glass should be removed before shredding to avoid irreversible entrainment. The decision was made to use this arrangement at Bridgeport based on extensive testing, done by CEA's R&D department, of the Primary Trommel prior to shredding and supported by full-scale experience at Recovery One. This arrangement, combined with partial drying, produced a low-ash fluff RDF feed to the embrittling and grinding process and an ECO-FUEL product having an ash content which could be adjusted within the range of from 10 to 15%.

The third generation system was developed based on further R&D studies and in-plant testing and operation of the East Bridgewater and Bridgeport plants, which provided more complete understanding of the relationship between the unit operations, the amount of rejected materials and the product ash content.

Comprehensive project design data has been prepared for the third generation plant, including flowsheets, material and energy balances,

Table 5. Ash and Slag Profiles from ECO-FUEL/Oil Firing (2).

Analysis	Fuel Ash	Slag Bottom	Slag Furn	Superhtr Deposits	Air Htr Hopper	Precipitator Catch Oil/ECO-FUEL	Oil
SiO_2	50.7	15.1	13.9	26.2	32.2	27.6	19.3
Al_2O_3	11.3	40.0	41.9	6.1	16.5	12.8	10.5
MgO	1.2	3.3	9.0	3.2	4.8	5.9	5.5
CaO	8.0	5.2	1.4	5.5	10.4	8.8	5.9
Na_2O_3	5.8	1.5	1.0	4.7	7.6	7.2	7.0
Fe_2O_3	18.6	30.9	29.7	.4	12.1	12.1	11.5
SO_3	2.2	0.1	0.5	44.2	13.7	16.8	· 23.9
Ash Fusion Temperatures, Of:							
Soften	2200	1990	2105	1600			
Fluid	2400	2200	2200	1950			
Loss on Ignition, %				4.5			21.6

P&ID's and layouts. A plant model, major equipment specifications and detailed cost estimates have also been completed.

The third generation was designed to meet these objectives:

- Simplify the process as much as possible.
- Maximize equipment reliability and safety.
- Use straight-line arrangement of the main process equipment.
- Minimize the number of conveyors and material transfer points.
- Provide adequate access to equipment for maintenance.
- Improve dust and odor control.
- Isolate equipment with explosion potential.
- Provide means for diverting process flow streams during operation to permit minor maintenance.
- Provide flexibility in the process to permit tailoring the recovery streams to suit market conditions.
- Design the process for high energy efficiency and yield, consistent with economic considerations.
- Keep operating costs to a minimum.

Any actual facility must, of course, be tailored to suit the nature and amount of the MSW available and site-specific conditions. For the City of Newark and surrounding communities, the process was designed for a capacity of 2700 tonnes per day, with initial requirements far lower. Smaller plants and other conditions would dictate a slightly different process configuration and different equipment selection. However, this design illustrates some of the simplifications which would characterize this generation.

Figure 4 shows a simplified flow diagram of this process. The air classifier and secondary trommel, and the ducts, rotary airlocks and conveyors associated with them, have been omitted since their functions have been taken over by the primary trommels.

Major features of the third generation ECO-FUEL process:

- The system consists of two parallel processing lines to provide redundancy and capacity steps with practical equipment sizes.

- After weighing, the refuse trucks enter the closed trucking module and dump onto the tipping floor. MSW is processed on first-in, first-out basis, with daily floor cleaning to minimize odors.
- A trucking floor traffic controller coordinates the activities of the front loader operators who handle the MSW on the floor with the scale house and approaching trucks.
- Bulky waste is removed from the tipping area by front loaders. Other unwanted and hazardous materials are picked from the waste stream on the tipping floor.
- The front loaders deliver material to the conveyors which feed the Primary Trommels.
- Primary Trommels, with improved screening and classification, remove undesireable inert materials, primarily glass, from the stream which feeds the size-reduction unit, and thus eliminate the need for air classification and second-stage screening of fine inert materials. The removed materials may be further processed or landfilled to the extent determined by numerous technical, site-specific and economic conditions.
- Size reduction is performed by a cascade mill which has discharge grates to control the maximum particle size. This machine is a slow-speed, low-maintenance, reliable and safe device offering advantages, confirmed by CEA tests, for large-capacity plants. The mill discharge is diverted to one or both of two lines to for further processing.
- Magnets remove ferrous metal from the size-reduced streams, which are now essentially RDF-3 (fluff RDF). The degree of further processing of the ferrous fraction depends on market conditions.
- Embrittling agents are applied in rotating spray drums to the fluff before discharging it to the grinding mills.
- Ball mills, using circulating hot balls, grind the fluff RDF into ball mill product.
- Ball mill product is separated in a steam atmosphere from the circulating balls and discharged from a collecting cyclone into a separating screen.

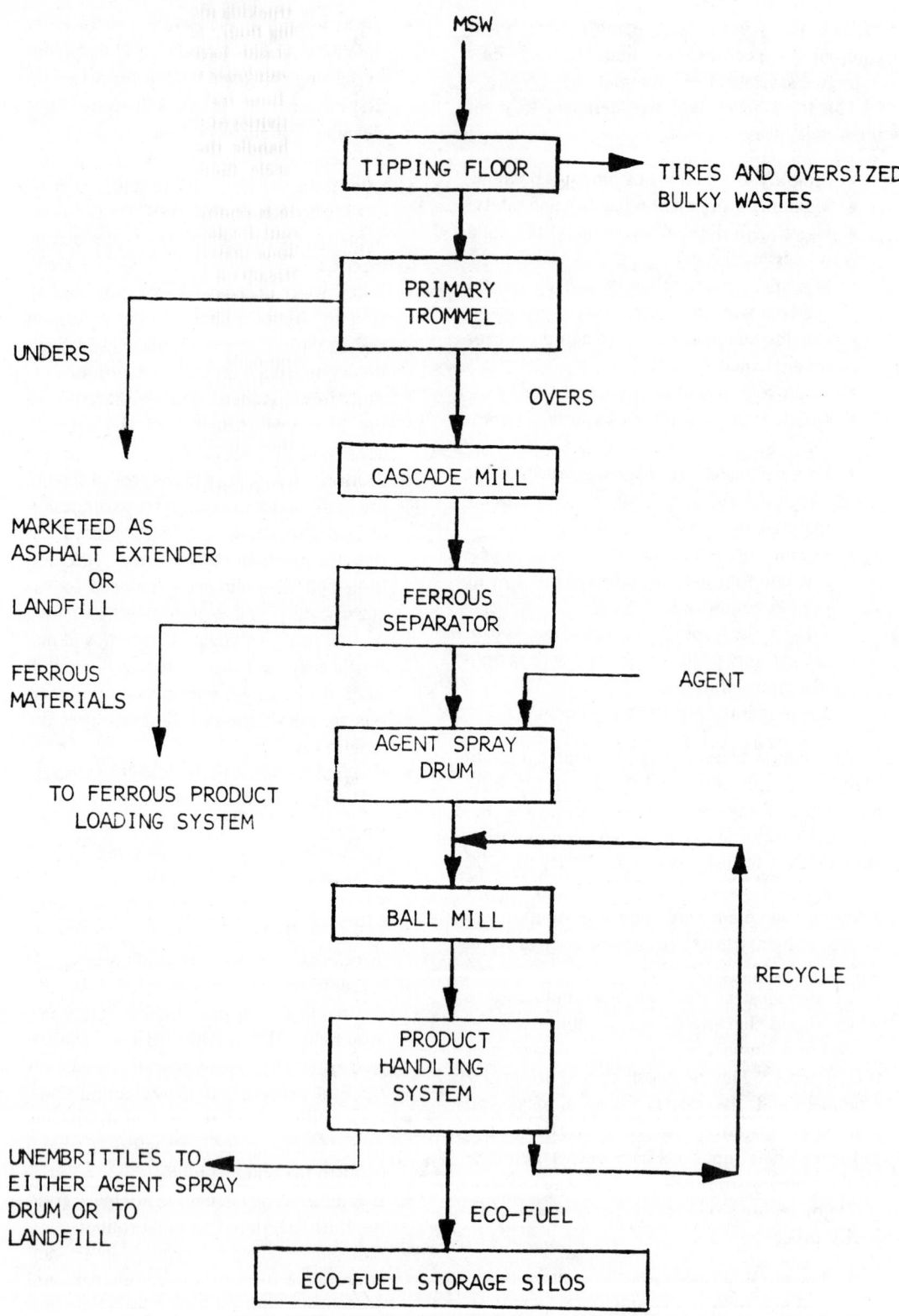

Figure 4. Flow diagram of third generation ECO-FUEL plant.

- Rotating screens are used in preference to flat deck screens for effective recovery of ground material from ball mill product. Oversized material is recycled or rejected.
- The ground material (ECO-FUEL) is cooled and conveyed to storage silos from which it is discharged to trucks for shipment to final users.
- Heat for the drying and milling process is provided by a process heater, capable of burning a variety of fuels including wastes, and which also serves as a thermal oxidizer for process odors.

This process is greatly simplified compared with the Bridgeport facility, yet provides flexibility to control the ash content of the fuel product to suit end-user requirements and adjust the quality of ferrous scrap.

It should be noted that the 'front end' process described delivers a material which is essentially RDF-3 (fluff) of minus 100 mm particle size, to the embrittlement/grinding portion of the process. Other front-end designs may be used to prepare suitable fluff for conversion to ECO-FUEL, including existing or contemplated plants.

ENERGY BALANCE AND YIELD OF THIRD GENERATION PROCESS

About 80–85% of the energy in the incoming solid waste (MSW) can be converted into ECO-FUEL. A portion of the residues can also be recovered and used to generate heat. The yield of energy depends upon the character of the highly variable MSW and the desired or required ash content of the product.

The energy required for milling the MSW is estimated to be about 72 kWH per Mg (65 kWh per ton). To generate this power at 10.55 MJ/kWh (10,000 BTU/kWh) requires heat energy of 756 MJ/Mg (0.65 million BTU per ton). A major portion of the milling energy is actually used to dry the MSW.

Drying the MSW requires the heat equivalent of about 23.8 liters of fuel oil per tonne (5.7 gallons per ton) of MSW. This represents a heat input of 927 MJ/Mg (0.8 million BTU/ton).

The energy invested in processing is thus 1683 MJ/Mg. If the fuel is not pre-dried, most of this

energy would have to be provided within the combustion chamber of the boiler to dry the fuel, taking time and space, and adversely affecting the combustion and the boiler efficiency by increasing the water vapor and excess air losses of the boiler.

The MSW is normally assumed to contain 10,932 MJ/Mg (4700 BTU/lb or 9,400,000 BTU per ton). The ECO-FUEL, we have seen, contains 18,258 MJ/Mg (7870 BTU/lb or 15,740,000 BTU/ton). If we recover 50% of the MSW weight as ECO-FUEL, the gross energy recovered in the fuel product is 18,258 × 0.5 or 9130 MJ/Mg of MSW, which is 83.5% of the available energy. If we subtract the energy invested in drying, we get the net energy recovered.

Gross energy recovered in ECO-FUEL = 18,258 × 0.5 = 9,130 MJ/Mg

Energy used in processing:

Power: 72 kWh/Mg @ 10.55 MJ/Mg = −756
Fuel: = 23.8 1/Mg at 39 MJ/1   = −927
Net energy recovered in ECO-FUEL = 7,447 MJ/Mg

The gross energy efficiency is the energy in the product as a fraction of the energy in the MSW, not considering the energy used for processing. To obtain the net energy efficiency we deduct the energy used in processing from product energy:

$$\text{Gross Energy Efficiency} = \frac{\text{energy in product}}{\text{energy in MSW}}$$

$$= \frac{9,130}{10,932} = 84\%$$

$$\text{Net Energy Efficiency} = \frac{\text{net energy in product}}{\text{energy in MSW}}$$

$$= \frac{7,447}{10,932} = 68\%$$

To make a valid comparison of RDF having various moisture contents with ECO-FUEL, a detailed analysis must be made to include the energy 'borrowed' in drying the MSW, the actual energy used in processing, and the actual boiler and power cycle efficiencies which result.

MARKETS FOR ECO-FUEL PRODUCTS

Resource Recovery has evolved into Waste-to-energy. The major focus of CEA has been to produce a high value refuse-derived fuel which replaces imported oil and can be burned in existing boilers. Each tonne of ECO-FUEL is equivalent to 2.82 barrels of residual oil, and can generate 1731 Kw of electric power when fueling an efficient generating system such as UI Units 1, 2, and 3.

As the price of coal increases, aided by price supports, the market is developing for ECO-FUEL briquets for firing in stoker and pulverized coal-fired boilers.

Firing of ECO-FUEL/oil slurries has a potential similar to that of coal/oil mixtures. Both require development of reliable methods of storage, pumping and controlling feed to the burners. It has been confirmed by Hecht (7) that ECO-FUEL/oil slurries can be atomized satisfactorily and burn well, due to the low ignition temperature and high volatile content of cellulosic materials.

ECO-FUEL has also been converted in laboratory scale and in pilot plant investigations to gas, methane, oil and gasoline, (10) and has been found to be a synergistic binder in coal gasification (Simplex process). Work remains to be done to determine where and to what extent these processes have economic application, and to what degree the feedstock must be prepared to suit these processes.

CONCLUSION

The choices for the future of the waste-to-energy industry are more clear as the result of the experience gained in the production and firing of ECO-FUEL. The alternatives of burning refuse without preparation or with minimum preparation in dedicated or remote boilers can be compared with the process which can convert MSW into a highly satisfactory storable, transportable, controllable alternate fuel, suitable for use in efficient power cycles, commanding maximum price and thus justifying this more complex, environmentally sound method of waste disposal.

REFERENCES

1. F. Hasselriis, "The Greater Bridgeport Waste to Energy System," ASME Ninth National Solid Waste Processing Conference, Washington, D.C., March, 1980.
2. F. Hasselriis, J. Lyons, C. Konheim, "Startup Considerations in Utility Use of Refuse Derived Fuel," Proceedings of the 15th Intersociety Energy Conversion Engineering Conference, Seattle, Washington, Aug., 1980.
3. F. Hasselriis, "Utilization of Biomass/oil Fuels in Petroleum-Fired Boilers," Symposium of Fuels and Feedstocks from Tropical Biomass, CEER, University of Puerto Rico, Nov., 1980.
4. D.E. Fiscus et al, "St. Louis Demonstration Final Report," EPA 600/2-77-155a, MERL/ORD/USEPA, Cincinnati, Ohio.
5. S.K. Adams, et al, "Flow Stream Characterization, The City of Ames, Iowa Solid Waste Recovery System," ERI/Iowa State University, Ames Iowa, March, 1979.
6. N.J. Stevens and J.C. Guillaumin, "Evaluation of Densified Refuse Derived Fuels for Use in Pulverized Coal-fired Steam Generators," Proceedings of the 1978 ASME National Waste Processing Conference, Chicago, Ill., May, 1978.
7. N. Hecht, work in progress under EPA funding.
8. J.B. Howard, "Combustion of Solid Refuse," Incinerator and Solid Waste Technology, ASME, New York, 1975.
9. F. Hasselriis, "Unit Operations in Waste to Energy," Ann Arbor Science, Ann Arbor, MI (in preparation).
10. T.C. Frankiewicz, "Energy from Waste," Ann Arbor Science, 1980.

4-17 RDF as a Klin Fuel

E. Joseph Duckett and David Weiss

Source: *Proceedings* of 1980 National Waste Processing Conference, Washington, D.C., May 11–14, 1980, pp. 387–400. Reprinted with Permission of The American Society of Mechanical Engineers.

INTRODUCTION

One approach to recovering energy from municipal solid wastes is the production of a refuse derived fuel (RDF). Such fuels can take a variety of forms which have been proposed for use in several types of combustion units, including boilers to raise steam and rotary kilns to produce cement and other construction materials. The types and potential uses of RDF have been reviewed. [1]

As mentioned, one of the potential uses for RDF is as a kiln fuel. Three of the major types of construction materials produced in rotary kilns are portland cement, quicklime and expanded shale (lightweight) aggregate. Each of these requires substantial amounts of energy for production and there is understandable interest among kiln operators in finding new sources of inexpensive fuels. Trial burns of RDF have been conducted in several kilns with promising results.

The purpose of this report is to investigate the potential for the use of RDF as a kiln fuel. The report reviews the results of trials and discusses the major research issues that need to be resolved en route to commercial use of RDF in kilns.

REFUSE DERIVED FUEL

Refuse derived fuel (RDF) is produced by the mechanical processing of municipal solid waste. For use in a kiln, a typical processing scheme for production of RDF might include shredding, screening and air classification of the wastes.

The fuel properties of RDF vary somewhat among plants and processing schemes but in comparison with typical coal properties, refuse derived fuels are generally lower in calorific value and sulfur content but higher in chlorine content. [2-6] The low sulfur content of RDF is a desirable feature because sulfur dioxide emissions from kilns are subject to air pollution regulations and the use of a low sulfur fuel facilitates meeting these regulations. Also, sulfur is considered a contaminant of some products made in kilns (e.g., lime) and kiln operators prefer to minimize the addition of sulfur to their kilns.

In addition to the chemical composition of the RDF itself, the chemical composition of the ash resulting from combustion of RDF is also important. RDF and coal ash are similar in silica (SiO_2) and alumina (Al_2O_3) content. RDF ash is generally lower in sulfur (SO_3) and iron oxide (Fe_2O_3) but higher in the alkaline oxides (Na_2O, K_2O) than coal ash. The importance of alkali content is discussed later in this report as a concern when using RDF in cement kilns.

PORTLAND CEMENT

Portland cement is an inorganic powder which, when mixed with water and an aggregate, forms the construction material, concrete. On the average, the production of cement* has been reported to require 6.3 million Btu of energy per ton of product (i.e., 7.3 GJ/t cement) [7,8].

---

*Although there are several types of cement other than portland cement, for the purposes of this report, the terms "cement" and portland cement are used interchangeably.

The Cement Making Process

The principal chemical elements required as feed for cement making are calcium, silicon, aluminum, and iron [7,9]. Calcium is supplied as calcium carbonate ($CaCO_3$) usually in the form of limestone. Silicon and aluminum are usually added either as oxides (e.g., silica sands) or as silicates (e.g., from clays and shales). Iron, as iron oxide, may be introduced as iron ore or, in some cases, steel mill scale [10].

The thermal processing of the mixed raw materials may be viewed in three stages: drying, calcining and clinkering. The first stage, drying, requires temperatures in the neighborhood of 212F (100C). The second stage, calcining, is the controlled heating of the mixture in order to dehydrate the materials and to drive off carbon dioxide from the limestone. Calcining temperatures are in the range 1000-1800F (550-1000C). Clinkering (sometimes called "burning") is the term for the chemical reactions that convert the raw materials into hardened granular masses (typically up to 1 in. or 25 mm in diameter) of calcium silicates, calcium aluminates and calcium ferrites. The clinkering reactions take place at temperatures in the range of 1800-2700F (1000-1500C). The resulting clinker is then air-cooled and ground to a fine powder (90 percent < 200 mesh) for use as portland cement.

For most (about 80 percent) cement production in the U.S., all three stages of thermal processing take place in rotary kilns. The wet or dry mixture of raw materials enters the rotating cylinder at the upper (or back) end of the kiln and proceeds through zones of drying, calcining and clinkering until it reaches the lower (front) end of the kiln where it exits as clinker. Heat for the operation of the kiln is supplied by suspension firing of fuels through burners located at the lower end of the kiln. The flow of the heated gases in the kiln is countercurrent to the flow of the raw materials.

Approximately 80 percent of the energy required for cement production is used in fueling the kiln [11]. Among the fuels used in cement production in 1978, pulverized coal accounted for 63 percent, natural gas for 20 percent, oil for 9 percent, electric power 7.8 percent and other fuels such as petroleum coke for 0.2 percent. In recent years, there has been increasing conversion of cement plants from the use of gas and oil to the use of solid fuels, primarily coal.

There are two features of cement kilns that make them unusual as furnaces for the combustion of coal. First is the fact that much of the ash from combustion of coal becomes incorporated into the clinker. It is a standard practice in the cement industry to adjust the raw material feed to account for the incorporation of coal ash into the clinker [12]. Second is the fact that the kiln itself acts somewhat as a scrubber for sulfur oxides, thus removing some potential pollutants from the exhaust gases. This scrubbing effect is partially present in the calcining zone of the kiln where calcium carbonate is converted to calcium oxide (lime) which can react with the sulfur oxides to form calcium sulfite and sulfate. This scrubbing effect permits the kilns to use relatively high sulfur fuels (reportedly up to 3-4 percent suflur) without exceeding air pollution codes [11]. Generally speaking, high sulfur coal can be purchased at prices below those paid for low sulfur (1 percent or less) fuels.

Despite the incorporation of much of the coal ash and sulfur dioxide into the clinker, the exhaust stream leaving the upper end of the kiln must undergo air cleaning before discharge to the atmosphere. Most modern cement plants employ electrostatic precipitation or baghouses, often with mechanical collection, to remove particulates (perhaps 90 percent) are fine particles of cement or raw materials rather than particles of fly ash from the fuel [13]. In some cases, the collected dusts are recycled through the kiln but in other instances — for reasons discussed later in this report — the dusts are considered detrimental to the chemistry of the process and are, therefore, discarded as wastes.

PROPERTIES OF CEMENT

The important properties of portland cement can be classed either as physical or chemical. These properties are summarized in Table 1 and are discussed below.

Table 1. Specified Limits for Selected Physical and Chemical Properties of Cement.*

Physical Properties	Specified Limit
Min. Compressive Strength	
3 day	1800 psi (12.8 MPa)
7	2600 psi (18.5 MPa)
28	3800 psi (27.0 MPa)
Time of Set (Vicat)	
Initial (min.)	0.75 hr.
Final (max.)	8 hr.
False set, final penetration (min.)	50%
Autoclave Expansion (max.)	0.80%
Chemical Properties	**Max. Allowable Weight Percent**
Alkalies	0.6
Chloride	2.0
Lead Oxide (PbO)	0.001
Magnesium Oxide (MgO)	5
Sulfate (SO$_3$)	3

*Source: Reference 14.

Physical Properties. A number of physical parameters are used as indicators of the strength and durability of the cement. The compressive strength of the cement is the most important physical parameter [14]. It is a measure of the force that can be applied to the cement before failure occurs. The time of setting is important because a cement that sets too quickly will stiffen before it can be placed. Air content of concrete up to 5 percent increases resistance to frost and to sulfates and improves the workability of the concrete mix. Higher air content can lead to increased thermal expansion and drying shrinkage of the concrete.

Chemical Properties. Among the chemical requirements for cement, three which merit discussion in this report are sulfur compounds, alkalies (Na$_2$O, K$_2$O), and chlorides.

Although the ability of cement kilns to remove sulfur dioxides (SO$_2$) from exhaust gases permits cement plants to use relatively high sulfur coals, there are limits on the amounts of sulfur which can be acceptably incorporated into the clinker. Excessive sulfate levels in cement have been associated with a condition known as "efflorescence"* during service. The incorporation of sulfur compounds into the clinker effectively limits the cement manufacturer's ability to add calcium sulfate (e.g., as gypsum) to control the setting time of the cement product. The formation of deposits (known as "rings") in the middle of the kiln is sometimes attributed to cake inducing salts such as calcium sulfate and/or alkalies [15].

The principal reason for limiting the alkali content of cement is prevention of the so-called "alkali-aggregate" reactions. It has been reported that certain aggregates, especially silicious aggregates such as opal-bearing rocks, chert and quartz, can react with alkalies in cement [16]. The reaction leads to formation of an alkali silicate gel which creates expansive forces within the concrete and has been associated with cracking and failure of concrete sections. In order for the reaction to occur, both a

*Efflorescence is the loss of water of hydration from a soluble salt which has migrated to the surface of concrete; efflorescence results in a white coating on the surface of concrete [15].

relatively high alkali content in the cement and the presence of sufficiently reactive constituents in the aggregate are necessary [17]. Despite this fact, it is common for cement users to specify "low alkali" cement whether reactive aggregates are used or not. ASTM Standard C-150 limits the alkali content of "low alkali" cements to 0.6 percent by weight.

Concern for chloride levels in cements is particularly important for cements to be used with steel reinforcing bars because of the effects of chlorides on the corrosion of steel. Small quantities of chlorides are acceptable in concrete and a chloride level of 2 percent or less in cement is often specified.

Major Research Issues

When considering the use of RDF in cement plants, there are several major research issues of interest. These include:

1. Handling properties of the fuel.
2. Ability to control temperature in the kiln (or precalcining furnace).
3. Effect of RDF combustion products on kiln coatings.
4. Effect of RDF combustion products on clinker chemistry.
5. Changes in physical properties of clinker and cement.
6. Effect of using RDF on air emissions. These issues are discussed in the following paragraphs.

Handling Properties of the RDF. Refuse derived fuels are different in form and appearance than fuels commonly used in cement plants. RDF's are primarily composed of fibrous materials and are in the form of thin plate-like particles (e.g., shredded newspaper), unlike coal which is primarily crystalline and in the form of spherical (or nearly spherical) particles. Generally speaking, cement kiln fuels are fed pneumatically, hence the need to design the RDF feeding system for pneumatic firing.

The pneumatic firing of RDF is not unique to the use of RDF in kilns. Refuse derived fuels have been pneumatically fed to both suspension and semi-suspension fired boilers [2, 3,

18-21]. In some cases, RDF has been used as the only boiler fuel but in others, RDF has been cofired with coal.

Ability to Control Temperature. Temperatures in the clinkering zone of a cement kiln are controlled to within ± 100F (55C) [22]. The sensitivity of the clinkering reactions to variations in kiln temperature makes temperature control an important requirement for proper kiln operation. Variation in the amount and composition of fuels fed to the kiln can affect temperature and these effects need to be controlled.

Effect on Kiln Coatings. Cement kiln operators maintain a coating or layer of deposits along the inside lining of the kiln. The coating layer serves to insulate the shell of the kiln from the high temperatures maintained within. The coating is primarily composed of silicates and is similar in composition to clinker [12]. For proper furnace operation it is important that this coating layer neither be built up excessively nor sloughed off. Although there is no specific feature of RDF which suggests any particular effect on the coating layer, there is a need to establish whether the use of RDF is likely to affect the kiln coating.

Effect of RDF on Clinker Chemistry. Because of the interaction among fuels and raw materials that takes place within a kiln, the chemical properties of the cement clinker are affected by the chemical composition of the fuel, especially the composition of the ash. As discussed previously, RDF is typically higher in ash and chlorine content but lower in sulfur content than most coals. The elemental composition of RDF ash is quite similar to reported compositions for coal ash, but combustion of RDF produces more ash per unit of energy supplied than does coal. Thus, RDF may contribute a disproportionately high amount of ash to the cement clinker.

Of particular interest are the potential effects of using RDF on the alkali and chloride content of the clinker. Estimates of the alkali contribution from RDF ash can be made based on reported deposition rates for fuel ash in the kiln and on the following assumptions. An average energy consumption of 6 million Btu/ton (6.9

GJ/t) of clinker produced is assumed. A coal with a calorific value of 12,000 Btu/lb (28 MJ/kg) [23] is used as well as a refuse derived fuel with a calorific value of 5500 Btu/lb (13 MJ/kg). Midrange reported values for alkali content (predominantly K_2O) of cement-making lime-stone and clay are 0.12 and 1.4 percent respectively [24]. A typical coal ash has an alkali content of 2.3 percent. Based on the results of RDF trials conducted at cement plants (without dust recycling), it is estimated that 90 percent of the total available Na_2O and 50 percent of the total available K_2O in the raw materials and fuel is incorporated into the clinker [25].

Given these simplifying assumptions, the alkali content of clinker produced by replacing 30-40 percent of the fuel with RDF, ranges between 0.45 and 0.64 percent as shown in Table 2. Except for the worst case assumptions, it can be seen in Table 2 that alkali levels in the clinker do not exceed the ASTM specification of 0.6 percent. The assumptions made are judged to be conservative, and, indeed, in actual RDF trials, the reported alkali content of the clinker has been consistently lower in alkalies than might be anticipated based on calculations such as those reflected in Table 2. Of course, the actual raw material contribution of alkalies is site specific and, where local clays contain high concentrations of alkali, cements may well exceed the 0.6 percent level — with or without using RDF as a kiln feed.

From the calculation shown above, it can be concluded that the RDF itself (at up to 40 percent of the energy input to the kiln) is not likely to contribute alkalies in excess of specified limits. For cements already approaching or at the alkali limit, however, the use of RDF could theoretically contribute sufficient alkalies to exceed the limit.

In assessing the effects of using RDF on alkali content, it is important to note that there are methods of controlling alkali build-up through modifications in kiln operations. The bypassing of some of the exhaust gas stream, for example, removes some of the entrained fuel ash particles from the kiln and thus lessens the opportunity for ash to become incorporated into the clinker. The discarding of collected cement dusts, which are rich in alkalies, is another approach to reducing the buildup of alkalies.

The relatively high chlorine content of RDF, as compared with most coals, raises concerns for the potential effect of using RDF on chloride levels of the clinker. Sodium and potassium chlorides (NaCl, KCl), either present in the RDF or formed by reactions between the fuel and the clinker can become volatilized at clinkering temperatures and then redeposited in molten form in the lower temperature zones of the kiln. Such deposition would tend to increase the chloride content of the clinker and can also create so called "sticky" conditions within the kiln coating layer. This "sticky" condition can lead to formation of rings within the kiln — an undesirable disruption of kiln operation.

Changes in Physical Properties of Clinker or Cement. Although there is no specific reason to suspect that RDF may adversely affect any of the physical properties of clinker or cement, there are at least two physical properties of

Table 2. Calculated Effect of Using RDF on Alkali Content of Cement Clinker.*

RDF Properties		Calculated Alkali Content of Clinker	
Ash Content	Alkali Content of Ash	RDF as 30% of Kiln Fuel	RDF as 40% of Kiln Fuel
15%	6%	0.45%	0.50%
15%	8%	0.49%	0.54%
20%	6%	0.49%	0.60%
20%	8%	0.54%	0.64%

*Note: See text for discussion of the assumptions.

research interest. First is the grindability of the clinker. Any decrease in grindability would increase the energy needed to grind the clinker and would, therefore, offset a portion of the energy savings due to the use of RDF. Second is the strength (1 day, 7 day and 28 day strength) of the cement. Strength is an important property of cement and one which cement manufacturers are understandably hesitant to jeopardize.

Effect on Air Emissions. As mentioned, the ash resulting from combustion of RDF may differ in quantity (per calorific unit) and in composition from the ash resulting from combustion of other fuels. Some of the ash becomes entrained in the air flow through the kiln and is processed through the air pollution control system of the plant. A research concern, therefore, is whether the differences between RDF and other fuels will affect the amount or composition of ash particles either entering the air pollution control equipment or exiting the control system as emissions from the plant.

Reports on the cofiring of RDF with coal as a boiler fuel suggest that there are increases in total particulate emissions when compared with firing coal alone [25]. It should be noted, however, that the actual moment of particulate emissions may be affected more by site-specific features such as furnace operations and efficiency of air pollution control equipment than by fuel mixture. Also, the RDF's that have been used in these reported cofiring trials were relatively high ash fuels. There is a trend in the design and operation of resource recovery plants towards the production of lower ash RDF and this may affect the amount of fly ash resulting from RDF combustion.

Trials Using RDF in Cement Kilns

Over the past five years, eight portland cement companies have conducted trials in which RDF was used as a fuel in their rotary kilns. Four of the trials lasted for one week or less and did not result in any published reports [26-30]. Among the conclusions from these trials were that pelletized RDF should not be pulverized with coal in a ball mill (the milled pellets swell and clog

the pulverizer; that fluff RDF [particle size less than 2 in. (51 mm)] could be pneumatically fired into a kiln for as long as 72 continuous hours; and that, with RDF supplying up to 30 percent of the energy to the kiln, there were no observed changes either in chemical or physical properties of the clinker or in operating performance of the kilns.

More extensive trials have been – and are continuing to be – conducted at four cement plants, two in the U.S., one in Canada and one in the U.K. These are discussed below.

Blue Circle Group. In the U.K., the Blue Circle Group of the Associated Portland Cement Manufacturers Ltd. has been experimenting with the use of RDF for several years. The Blue Circle Group has patented their process for using RDF in cement kilns but has not published detailed data on the results of their trials [31]. RDF has been used at several of the Blue Circle cement plants and has been reported to produce clinker of satisfactory quality [32, 33, 34].

Experiments at Blue Circle's Westbury plant began in 1974 with trial runs of up to five days. In 1977, the plant contracted with Wiltshire County to receive municipal solid waste on a daily basis. At the cement plant, the refuse is shredded, magnetically separated and pneumatically fed into the coal-fired kiln to provide approximately 14 percent of the kiln's energy requirements. To date, more than 30,000 tons (27,200 t) of RDF have been utilized in this way and no significant buildup of alkali (or other chemical constituent) has been observed.

The RDF produced and used by Blue Circle is generally lower in calorific value and higher in ash (per unit weight) than RDF's produced in the U.S. Consequently, it requires larger quantities of the Blue Circle RDF to supply a given amount of energy to a cement kiln than it would require if a more processed form of RDF were used. This may account for the fact that Blue Circle's practice has been to limit the use of RDF to replacement of 10-20 percent of the primary energy source. The only major problem expressed by Blue Circle has been the need for more reliable shredders – a problem not unique to the use of RDF in kilns.

Canada Cement Lafarge Ltd.   A full year of trials using RDF as 10 to 50 percent of the energy input to a wet process cement kiln is being conducted at a Cement Lafarge plant in Woodstock, Ontario [35]. The kilns at this plant are units fired with coal during the winter (October through March) and natural gas during the summer (April through September). The trials are managed and financially supported by the Ontario Ministry of the Environment.

Refuse derived fuel for the kiln trials is produced at the Toronto resource recovery facility, owned by the Ontario Ministry of the Environment and operated by Browning Ferris Industries. Refuse is shredded to a nominal 6 in. (152 mm) particle size and then air classified. The air-classified lights are then baled and truck hauled to the Woodstock plant. At the cement plant, the bales are broken (using a spike-roll device) and the RDF is then reshredded to a nominal 3 in. (76 mm) size in a modified knife mill. The reshredded fuel is then dropped through an air lock into a pneumatic duct through which the RDF is fed into the kiln. Although the trial has been underway since March of 1979 and RDF has been fired continuously for as long as 72 hours, no data on clinker quality or kiln operation have been released.

Gulf Coast Portland Cement Company.   Browning Ferris Industries, Inc. (BFI) under a contract with the U.S. Department of Energy (DOE), has been investigating the "Cofiring of RDF and Natural Gas in a Cement Kiln." [25] Trials were conducted at the Gulf Coast Portland Cement Co. near Houston, Texas in 1975 and 1977 and are continuing.

RDF for use in these trials was produced in Houston by BFI. Refuse was first shredded to a nominal 3-4 in. size (76-102 mm) then magnetic metals were removed and the non-magnetic fraction air classified in a rotary drum air classifier. Typical ash content of the RDF was 16 percent.

At the Gulf Coast Portland Cement plant, RDF was pneumatically fed into the kiln using a feeding system designed for firing a utility boiler. At feed rates in the range of 5-8 tons/hr (4.5-7.3 t/h), the system worked satisfactorily.

Feeder plugging by large pieces of cloth or paper periodically occurred at feed rates approaching 10 tons/hr (9 t/h).

The 1975 and 1977 trials conducted by BFI were conducted in a wet process, gas-fired cement kiln. For the 1977 trials, RDF was used as 20, 30 and 40 percent of the kiln fuel feed. Detailed analyses of raw materials balance, RDF ash qualtiy, and clinker quality were made as summarized in Table 3. It should be noted that these data are from an interim report and therefore must be considered preliminary results.

At the 20 and 30 percent substitution levels, results were reported to be satisfactory. The chemical components of the clinker were not significantly affected (see Table 3), and specified ASTM restrictions on chemical and physical properties of cement were never exceeded.

X-ray diffraction patterns and petrographic examinations performed on the clinker confirmed that no significant differences between "RDF cement" and regular cement existed. Strength of RDF cement is similar to cement made with 100 percent natural gas (see Table 3). In a number of cases, RDF cement was superior in compressive strength (a phenomenon also reported by the Blue Circle Group in their trials), but the reasons for this increased strength were unexplained. Other physical test data such as air content and autoclave expansion were influenced by the use of RDF but not significantly. It is somewhat puzzling, given the higher sulfur content of RDF over natural gas, that cement made with RDF consistently exhibited shorter set times. In the Gulf Coast trials, the setting time was adjusted by adding gypsum to the cooled, crushed clinker — a normal practice in cement manufacturing.

The trials in which RDF was used as 40 percent of the kiln fuel yielded inconclusive results. Problems of underburning occurred as exhibited by excessive free lime levels in the clinker (see Table 3). It was difficult to maintain adequate kiln temperatures during the 40 percent RDF trials. In part, this was due to a malfunction in the temperature recording device which occurred during this set of trials. It is not certain whether the underburning of the clinker or the inability to control temperature was influenced by the use of RDF.

Stack sampling tests revealed increased levels of controlled particulate emissions when RDF replaced a portion of the natural gas. When RDF was used as 20, 30 and 40 percent of kiln fuel input, particulate emissions increased by 25, 20 and 50 percent respectively as compared with emissions during firing of natural gas alone. Although particulates increased during RDF firing, total particulate emissions remained within

federal standards for cement kilns [(93-94 lb/hr) (12.2-12.6 kg/h)]. During the emissions testing at the Gulf Coast plant, it was noted that the dusts collected by the electrostatic precipitator during RDF firing were coarser than the dusts produced during firing of natural gas alone.

The Gulf Coast/BFI trials have been suspended since 1977, but are scheduled to be continued in 1980, again with the support of the U.S. DOE [36]. Since the last series of trials, the Gulf Coast plant has made the conversion

Table 3. Comparison of Specified Limits with Results of Gulf Coast Cement Co. Trials.

Chemical Properties	Trial Results				ASTM
	0% RDF	20% RDF	30% RDF	40% RDF	Specified Limits
Alkalies (%)	0.04	0.47	0.45	0.11	0.6
Chloride (%)	0.01	0.01	0.01	0.01	2.0
Lead Oxide (%)	negligible	0.01	n.d.*	n.d.*	0.001
Magnesium Oxide (%)	0.74	0.99	0.64	0.78	5.0
Sulfate (SO_3) (%)	0.03	0.03	0.03	0.03	3.0
Free Lime (%)	0.9	n.r.*	n.r.*	2.2	n.r.*

*n.d. = not detected
 n.r. = not reported

Physical Properties					
Min. Compressive Strength (psi)					
1 day	1120	910	1370	1175	–
3	2800	2780	2900	2060	1800
4	4090	4200	4310	3475	2600
14	–	5150	5360	–	–
28	6125	6460	6700	5515	3800
Time of Set (Vicat)					
Initial (min., hrs.)	3.0	2.7	1.2	1.8	0.75
Final (max., hrs.)	4.8	4.0	3.3	2.8	8.0
False set, final penetration (min. %)	73	70	76	72	50
C-185 Air Content, Hydraulic Cement Mortar, (max. %)	6.1	6.5	7.0	7.6	12
Autoclave Expansion (max. %)	0.011	0.078	0.187	0.250	0.8

*n.d. = not detected
 n.r. = not reported

Note: Conversion factor — psi X 6.895 = kPa

from gas to coal as their primary kiln fuel. One objective of the scheduled trials will be to determine whether the problems experienced when RDF was used as 40 percent of the kiln fuel were related to the use of RDF or were simply the result of defective temperature controls within the kiln. The new series of trials will also enable comparisons between using RDF in coal-fired and gas-fired kilns.

Lehigh Portland Cement Co. A series of trials using RDF in a dry process, coal-fired cement kiln began in November, 1979 at the Lehigh Portland Cement Co. plant in Union Bridge, Maryland [37]. The trials were managed by Teledyne National, who also supplied the fuel. Financial support for the trials was from the U.S. Environmental Protection Agency and the Maryland Environmental Service.

The RDF for the trials was produced at the Baltimore County (Md.) resource recovery plant at which refuse is shredded, magnetically separated and the nonmagnetics are air classified. For the cement plant trials, the air classified light fraction was screened in a trommel to recover a 1-1/2 X 1/2 in. (38 X 13 mm) fraction which was re-shredded to a nominal 1 - 1/2 in. (25 - 13 mm) size then transported to the cement plant in compactor trucks. At the cement plant, the RDF was refluffed using rotating lump breakers and fed through an air lock into a 9 in. (229 mm) pneumatic duct leading to the front end of the kiln. Air pressure in the duct was 3/4 - 1 psi (5.3 kPa - 7.1 kPa) and the duct entered the kiln directly below the coal feed pipe. The trial was designed to be a full month of continuous use of RDF. The objective was to use RDF as up to 40 percent of the energy input of the kiln. During the trials, cement chemistry and physical properties were monitored by the Lehigh Co. and by the Portland Cement Association; air pollution monitoring was performed by an EPA contractor. The trial was in progress during the writing of this paper and the results were therefore not available.

LIME

Lime is a chemical used for a variety of applications including steel manufacturing, water and wastewater treatment, chemicals production, and paper manufacturing [38, 39].

Basic Process

The major step in lime production is calcination, which is the controlled heating of carbonate rock to drive off volatile components including carbon dioxide (CO_2) [38]. For lime production, a source of calcium carbonate, either limestone or shell, is fed into a furnace or kiln and heated to 1800–2400 F (480–1300 C) so that calcination can occur [40]. The kiln product, quicklime, can be converted to hydrated lime by adding enough moisture to satisfy the affinity of quicklime for water. The hydrated lime product is a dry, fine powder.

Several types of furnaces or kiln systems are used to produce lime. Approximately 85 percent of the commercial lime produced in the U.S. is made in rotary kilns. Although a variety of fuels can be fired in a rotary lime kiln, the trend here, as in other industries, is to convert from natural gas to coal. The energy consumed in producing lime in a rotary kiln is approximately 7 million Btu/ton (8.1 GJ/t) of lime [8].

The quality and commercial value of quicklime is affected by the amount of impurities present. Chemical specifications differ among the potential uses of lime but, generally speaking, precautions are taken to limit the incorporation of fuel ash into the product and to avoid use of limestone high in silica, alumina or iron oxide. These limestone contaminants may result in the formation of undesirable cementitious products such as calcium silicates, aluminates, and ferrites. Such products may contaminate the lime and/or cause the coating layer within the kiln to build up excessively, resulting in disruption of kiln operation. Impurities such as phosphorous and sulfur may also be present in small quantities in limestone.

The single largest consumer of lime in the U.S. is the steel industry. Most of this lime is used as a flux to purify steel in basic oxygen furnaces (BOF). Any silica, alumina, sulfur, and phosphorous that are originally present in the lime are undesirable and the lime must meet tight chemical specifications to be used for steelmaking.

Major Research Issues

When considering the use of RDF in lime plants, there are two major research issues of interest. These are:

a. Effect of RDF combustion products on kiln coating layer.

b. Effect of RDF ash on the chemical composition of the lime product.

Coating Layer. The coating layer within a lime kiln differs in thickness and chemical composition from that in a cement kiln. Typically, lime kiln coatings are 1/2 in. (13 mm) thick while cement kiln coatings are up to 12 in. (305 mm) thick. Lime kiln coatings are primarily calcium oxide while cement kiln coatings are composed primarily of silicates [41]. The differences in kiln coatings may affect the acceptability of RDF for use in the kiln. As discussed earlier, about 50 percent of the ash from RDF (and also from coal) is silica which, at kiln temperatures reacts with other components of the fuel and feedstock to form silicates. Such silicates are not undesirable in cement kilns because they are chemically compatible with both the clinker and the coatings. Conversely, the incorporation of silicates into the lime kiln coatings (or into the lime itself) is not desirable because the lime kiln coatings are low in silicates and the incorporation of silicates could lead to the formation of rings in the kiln.

A critical factor in determining the effect of using RDF on the coating layer of a lime kiln is the behavior of RDF ash within the kiln. The ash from RDF has been reported to soften at temperatures below flame temperatures in a lime kiln and also below the softening point

of the ash from many coals [2, 5]. Thus, at least within the flame itself, it is probable that RDF ash will be in a softened, if not molten, state. As the ash particles leave the flame zone and proceed towards the back end of the kiln, they are cooled. Although the ash particles tend to be carried along in the gas flow through the kiln, the particles may impact the coating layer at some point in the kiln. If the ash particles are in a softened or molten state when they impact, they are likely to be retained on the coating layer, thus potentially affecting the chemistry and thickness of the coating [42]. If the buildup of ash particles occurs in a localized region of the kiln, rings of deposits may be formed which disrupt kiln operations. It is conceivable that such a ring might form near the hottest area of the kiln, i.e., where there is the shortest distance between the flame and the kiln wall and where the ash is most likely to be molten. This phenomenon could be especially pronounced in newer kilns with narrower kiln diameters and hence more confined heat release zones than some older kilns [43]. Although effects such as deposition of softened RDF ash particles can be hypothesized or speculated upon, there is at present no reported information on actual behavior of RDF ash in a lime kiln (there have been no RDF trials in lime kilns), nor has there been an analysis of the likelihood for RDF ash particles to be softened or melted on contact with kiln coatings.

Effect of RDF on Lime Quality

The value of lime is affected by its chemical purity. Some lime plants use only gas or oil as

Table 4.   Calculated Silica and Metal Oxide (Al_2O_3 Plus Fe_2O_3) Contents of Lime When Using RDF as a Kiln Fuel.*

RDF Ash Content (% by Weight)	Silica Content (% by Weight)	Metal Oxide Content (% by Weight)
10	1.27	0.67
15	1.38	0.72
20	1.50	0.76

*See text for discussion of assumptions

fuels, rather than coal, to minimize the addition of undesirable chemicals (e.g., sulfur, silica). Of particular interest in coal-fired kilns are the effects of increased ash content attributable to the use of a solid fuel. The use of RDF, another solid fuel, would also raise concerns about the effects of ash on the lime making process and product. On a calorific (rather than weight percent) basis, RDF contains more silica, alumina, and iron oxide but less sulfur than coal. The levels of these substances must be minimized for most applications of lime. Investigations are needed to quantify the extent to which ash (either coal or RDF) becomes incorporated into the lime product.

Table 4 presents a simplified analysis of the calculated effects of RDF ash on the silica and metal oxide (Al_2O_3 and Fe_2O_3) contents of lime. The calculations are based on several assumptions described in the following paragraph.

The energy required to produce a ton of lime is approximately 7 million Btu (8.1 GJ/t). Coal and RDF are assumed to have calorific values of 12,000 Btu/lb (28 MJ/kg) and 5500 Btu/lb (13 MJ/kg) respectively. Ash content of coal is assumed to be 10 percent by weight. Although quantities vary with the type of limestone, about 1.7 ton (1.5 t) of limestone are needed to produce 1 ton (0.9 t) of lime [24]. RDF is assumed to provide 30 percent of the energy input to the kiln. Approximately 15 percent of the coal ash and 25 percent of the RDF ash are assumed *not* to be entrained in the flue dust, and may therefore be incorporated into the lime [41]. The silica content of the coal ash is 55 percent, a typical midrange value, and the silica content of the RDF ash is 50 percent. A typical value for the silica content of limestone is 0.5 percent [24]. Typically, coal ash is 22 percent Al_2O_3 and 14 percent Fe_2O_3 [4]. A typical RDF ash might contain 10 percent Al_2O_3 and 4 percent Fe_2O_3 [2, 3, 6].

The use of lime in the manufacture of steel requires that silica (SiO_2) in the lime not exceed 1.5 percent by weight. Other uses of lime do not require such stringent limitations on the silica content. As seen in Table 4, the 1.5 percent limit on silica in lime is reached but not exceeded under the given assumptions.

A reasonable restrictive upper bound on the metal oxide content of lime is the 1 percent (by weight) limit imposed for use in the manufacture of calcium carbide [44]. The calculations reflected in Table 4 suggest that the metal oxides contribution from RDF and coal ash would not, by themselves be expected to cause failure of the lime to meet the 1 percent upper limit.

Table 4 suggests that, when RDF is used as 30 percent or less of the kiln fuel, limits on the silica and metal oxide content of lime can be met. In those cases where the lime product already approaches contaminant limits (due to limestone impurities, for example), the use of RDF could theoretically contribute sufficient impurities to cause the product lime to exceed the limits. The same could also be said of coal ash.

EXPANDED SHALE (LIGHTWEIGHT AGGREGATE)

Lightweight aggregates include a variety of natural (e.g., vermiculite) and manufactured (e.g., expanded shale) mineral and rock materials that, when mixed with cement, are used to form lightweight concrete building blocks and other products. As their name implies, lightweight aggregates are lower in density than sand, gravel, and other mineral aggregates commonly used in construction. "Expanded shale" is a name frequently used to describe shale, clay, and slate processed in a kiln for use as a lightweight aggregate [45]. More than half of the total lightweight aggregate used in the U.S. is expanded shale, most of which is used in construction block [46, 47].

Basic Process

In the U.S., most of the production of expanded shale aggregate is accomplished by the controlled heating of crushed shale, clay or slate in a rotary kiln. In the first section of the kiln, temperatures are maintained in the range 1200–1800 F (650–980 C) so that the material becomes softened and a viscous airtight seal is formed over voids within the clay or shale [46]. Towards the exit end of the kiln (the front end), temperatures rise to 2200 F (1200 C) or so. At these elevated temperatures, heat penetrates the material and gases are generated from certain carbon and sulfur compounds. The escape of these gases, as well as water vapor, is blocked by the airtight coating and "bloating" occurs. As a rule of thumb, the material expands to approximately twice its volume during the bloating process. Before shipment, the material is crushed and graded to a specified size range.

Within the kiln, temperatures and flame length must be maintained in a rather narrow range so as to insure bloating but to prevent fusion of the clay particles. Fusion of the particles leads to formation of large clinkers or rings which disrupt kiln operation and must be removed. As an indication of the importance of temperature control in expanded shale plants, one plant operator reports maintaining the kiln within 10 F of 2100 F (1150 C ± 5.5 C) [48].

The kiln is the major consumer of energy in the expanded shale industry. An average of 2.9 million Btu's (3.1 GJ) is required to produce 1 ton (0.9 t) of expanded shale. As with other industries, expanded shale manufacturers are accelerating the conversion to coal from natural gas and oil. As of 1977, 51 percent of the industry used coal and 42 percent used gas. Oil and waste oil accounted for about 4 percent of the energy consumed.

Major Research Issues

When considering the use of RDF in expanded shale plants, the major issue is the effect of RDF on the ability to closely control kiln temperature. Expanded shale kilns may well be more sensitive to variations in kiln temperatures than either cement kilns or lime kilns. For successful use of a fuel, such as RDF, that varies in moisture content and calorific value, strict monitoring of kiln temperature and control over fuel feed rates would be required.

Generally speaking, the characteristics of the expanded shale itself are not significantly affected by the incorporation of fuel ash into the product. In part, this is because much of the ash is either entrained in the flue dust or screened out of the product during cooling.

Expanded Shale Trials

To date, the only trials in which RDF has been used in an expanded shale kiln took place at the Lehigh Portland Cement Company's plant in Woodsboro, Maryland [48]. The trials were arranged by Teledyne National.

The first trials were conducted in February and March of 1977 in a coal-fired kiln. Shredded, air-classified light fraction was shipped to the expanded shale plant where it was to be reshredded and fired pneumatically into the kiln. Shredder operation at the expanded shale plant was a limiting factor, however, as breakdowns, fires, and maintenance problems kept the system from sustained continuous firing of RDF. During the times that RDF was fired into the kiln, minor problems keeping the flame at a proper length occurred, but there were no problems with product quality or ring formation. RDF supplied 30 percent of the energy for the kiln.

A second series of test runs was conducted in 1978. For this series of trials, secondary shredding of RDF was performed at the resource recovery plant and the RDF was shipped to the expanded shale plant. The RDF was fed through an air lock into a pneumatic duct leading to the kiln. Air pressure within the pneumatic duct was reportedly too high with the result that the flame became too long. Attempts were made to dampen the air flow but the flame continued to be too long which increased the length of the "bloating" zone – an undesirable effect. The final product was judged satisfactory in quality, however, despite the feeding and flame length problems.

OVERALL REVIEW AND CONCLUSIONS

There is no question that the cement, lime and aggregate industries employ energy intensive processes and are in search of cheaper fuels. Much has been learned about the potential for the use of RDF as a kiln fuel through the various trials and other research efforts discussed above. Despite the apparent needs of the industry and despite the trials, however, there are no kilns in the U.S. using RDF on a regular basis.

Table 5. Potential Consumption of RDF/Day.

Assume: 30% substitution of fuel source by RDF

12,000 Btu/lb (27.9 MJ/kg) coal

5500 Btu/lb (12.8 MJ/kg) RDF

plants operate 300 days/yr

Cement Plants — Assume energy consumption of 6 million Btu/ton (7 GJ/t) product

Capacity Tons/Day	No. of Plants	Approx. RDF Requirement Tons/Day
<1350	43	<210
1350–2300	65	210–380
2300–3300	29	380–540
<3300	20	<540

Lime Plants — Assume energy consumption of 7 million Btu/ton (8.1 GJ/t) product

Capacity Tons/Day	No. of Plants	Approx. RDF Requirement Tons/Day
<510	104	<100
510–970	26	100–185
970–2200	26	185–400
<2200	8	<400

Expanded Shale Plants — Assume energy consumption of 2.9 million Btu/ton (3.4 GJ/t) product. Total number of plants is 28.

Capacity Tons/Day	Approx. RDF Requirement Tons/Day
170–340	13–27
340–670	27–55
670–1700	55–135

Note: Conversion factor — tons/day × 0.9 = t/d

The reasons for the failure of RDF to be adopted as a kiln fuel differ among the construction material industries but two general reasons can be given. They are: (a) the limited availability of RDF at reasonable distances from operating kilns; and (b) the need for research and/or demonstrations to establish kiln operator confidence in the use of RDF.

Table 5 presents a summary of the size of the potential market for RDF in cement, lime and expanded shale kilns. The size of the market depends on the number, location and fuel consumption of the kilns in which RDF may be used. As reflected in Table 5, the cement and lime industries offer larger potential markets for use of RDF than the expanded shale industry. There are 157 cement plants, 32 of which are located within 50 miles (80 km) of a major U.S. urban area. On the average and assuming RDF is used as 30 percent of the energy input to the kiln, a cement plant could consume 164 tons/day (149 t/d) (seven day week) of RDF; a lime plant 190 tons (172 t). By contrast, there are only 34 expanded shale plants in the U.S., seven near urban areas. A typical expanded shale plant (say 1000 tons/day (900 t/d) of aggregate) could consume no more than 50 tons/day (45 t/d) of RDF, again assuming 30 percent replacement of the normal kiln fuel.

Table 5 reflects the fact that kilns may provide a large potential market for the future use of RDF. The results of the trials which are now underway together with additional research/demonstration projects (e.g., an RDF trial in a lime kiln) should provide an answer to whether this market potential can be realized.

REFERENCES

1. Renard, M.L., *Refuse-Derived Fuel and Densified Refuse-Derived Fuel,* Washington, D.C., National Center for Resource Recovery, 1978.
2. Gorman, P.G., Shannon, L.J., Schrag, M.P. and Fiscus, D.E., *St. Louis Demonstration Project Final Report: Power Plant Equipment, Facilities, and Environmental Evaluation,* Kansas City, Mo., Midwest Research Institute, 1977.
3. Even, J.C., Adams, S.K., Gheresus, P., Joensen, A.W., Hall, J.L., Fiscus, D.E., and Romine, C.A., *Evaluation of the Ames Solid Waste Recovery System, Part I – Summary of Environmental Emissions: Equipment, Facilities, and Economic Evaluations,* Cincinnati, Ohio, U.S. Environmental Protection Agency, 1977.
4. *Steam: Its Generation and Use,* New York, Babcock and Wilcox Co., 1975.
5. Corey, R.C., "How Coal Properties Influence Handling and Combustion," *Chemical Engineering,* Vol. 85, No. 2 (January, 1978), pp. 111–119.
6. Internal Report on Composition of RDF at New Orleans – Recovery I, National Center for Resource Recovery, Washington, D.C., 1979.
7. Lea, R.M., *The Chemistry of Cement and Concrete,* New York, Chemical Publishing Co., 1971.
8. *Voluntary Business Energy Conservation Program* (Progress Report No. 6), Washington, D.C., U.S. Department of Energy, April, 1978.
9. Hall, W.B. and Ela, R.E., *Cement Mineral Commodity Profiles* (MCP-26), Pittsburgh, Pa., U.S. Bureau of Mines, 1978.
10. McCord, G., (Portland Cement Association), personal communication, December, 1978.
11. *Energy Conservation Potential in the Cement Industry* (Conservation Paper No. 26), Washington, D.C., U.S., Federal Energy Administration, 1975.
12. Taylor, H.F., *Chemistry of Cements,* New York, Academic Press, 1964.
13. Sell, N.J. and Fishbach, F.A., "Energy Conservation and Dust Production in Wet Rotary Cement Kilns," *Resource Recovery and Conservation,* Vol. 2, No. 2, (December 1976), pp. 119–125.
14. "Standard Specifications for Portland Cement (C-150)," *1975 Annual Book of ASTM Standards,* Part 13, Philadelphia, Pa., American Society for Testing and Materials, 1975.
15. Bogue, R.H., *The Chemistry of Portland Cement,* New York, N.Y., Reinhold Publishing Corp., 1955.
16. Stanton, T.E., "Expansion of Concrete Through Reaction Between Cement and Aggregate," *Proceedings,* Am. Soc. Civil Eng., Vol. 66, 1940, pp. 1781–1811.
17. Frohnsdorff, G., Clifton, J.R., Brown, P.W., "History and Status of Standards Relating to Alkalies in Hydraulic Cement," *Cement Standards – History and Trends* (ASTM Special Technical Publication No. 663), Philadelphia, American Society for Testing and Materials, 1979.
18. Vaughan, D.A., Krause, H.H., Cover, P.W., Sexton, R.W., and Boyd, W.K., *Summary Report on Environmental Effects of Utilizing Solid Waste as a Supplementary Power Plant Fuel,* Cincinnati, U.S. EPA, 1978.
19. Petersdorf, R., (Wisconsin Electric Power Co.) personal communication, July 1977.
20. Watkin, C.G.A., (IMI Energy Systems Inc.), personal communication, October 1978.
21. Boley, G.L. (City of Madison), personal communication, April 1979.
22. Reimel, G., (Alpha Portland Cement Co.), personal communication, December 1978.
23. Lapedes, D.N., (ed.), *McGraw-Hill Encyclopedia of Energy,* New York, McGraw-Hill Co., 1976.
24. Boynton, R.S., *Chemistry and Technology of Lime and Limestone,* New York, John Wiley, 1966.
25. Jones, J.R., *Cofiring RDF and Natural Gas in a Cement Kiln,* (A series of unpublished progress reports to the U.S. Dept. of Energy), Houston, Browning-Ferris Industries, Inc., 1975–1977.
26. Wall, R., (Hercules Cement Co.), personal communication, February 1979.
27. Mackenzie, H., (National Resource Recovery Corp.), personal communication, February 1979.
28. Penn-Dixie Cement Corp., *Municipal Solid Waste Fuel as a Supplemental Fuel Source in Cement Kiln Firing* (Report of 1974 Demonstration – Test Program), Nazareth, Pennsylvania, 1974.
29. Bush, C., (Riverside Cement Co.), personal communication, January 1979.
30. Dorn, J., (Southwestern Portland Cement Co.), personal communication, February 1979.
31. Watson, D. and Hood, P., "Portland Cement-Making and Municipal Refuse Conversion," U.S. Patent No. 4,022,630, (issued May 10, 1977), Washington, D.C.
32. Haley, C.A.C., (Blue Circle Group, United Kingdom), personal communication, December 1978.
33. Knights, D., "Domestic Refuse Disposal via Cement Kilns," *Solid Wastes,* (United Kingdom), July 1976, pp. 320–332.

34. Lowes, T.M. and Pennell, A.R., *Use of Low Grade Fuels in Cement Manufacture,* unpublished report, Northfleet, England, Blue Circle Group, March 1978.

35. Provais, P.J., (Ontario Center for Resource Recovery, Toronto, Ontario), personal communication, February 1979.

36. Jones, J.R., (Brown-Ferris Industries, Inc.), personal communication, December 1978.

37. Weinberger, C.R. (Teledyne National Corp.), personal communication, December 1978.

38. Boynton, R.S. and Gutschick, K.A., "Lime," *Industrial Minerals & Rocks,* New York, American Institute of Mining Engineers, 1975, pp. 737–755.

39. U.S. Bureau of Mines, Div. of Nonmetallic Minerals, "Lime Plants in the U.S. in 1977," *Mineral Industry Surveys,* Washington, D.C., U.S. Dept. of Interior, Bureau of Mines, September 1978.

40. *Chemical Lime Facts,* Washington, D.C., National Lime Association, 1973.

41. Schwartzkopf, F., (Kennedy Van Saun Co.), personal communication, February 1979.

42. McManus, W., (U.S. Gypsum Co.), personal communication, January 1979.

43. Sunnergren, C., (Bethlehem Steel Corp.), personal communication, January 1979.

44. "Standard Specification for Quicklime for Calcium Carbide Manufacture (C-258)," *1975 Annual Book of ASTM Standards, Part 13,* Philadelphia, American Society for Testing and Materials, 1975.

45. McCarl, H.N., "Aggregates – Lightweight Aggregates," *Industrial Minerals and Rocks,"* New York, American Institute of Mining Engineers, 1975, pp. 85–94.

46. *Lightweight Concrete,* Bethesda, Maryland, Expanded Shale Clay and Slate Institute, 1971.

47. Robinson, H., (Expanded Shale Clay and Slate Institute), personal communication, December, 1978.

48. Eggert, D., (Lehigh Portland Cement Co.), personal communication, December 1978.

4-18 Converting Solid Waste and Residue into Fuel

Jerry Jones

Source: Adapted from *Chemical Engineering,* Vol. 85, No. 1 (January 2, 1978) pp. 87–94. Reprinted with Permission of McGraw Hill, Inc.

Organic solid wastes and residues* (municipal refuse, tires, sludges, waste plastics and packaging materials, and agricultural and forestry residues) do not offer a complete solution to our energy supply problems, but can be an important energy resource in some regions and for specific processing plants. Energy can be recovered from solid wastes and residues by numerous thermal routes as well as by biochemical conversion.

This article describes the thermal-conversion processes that fall into the categories of pyrolysis, gasification and liquefaction and does not discuss solid-waste incineration or biochemical conversion (see Definitions, and Pyrolysis and Gasification Reactions). We will refer to all processes that involve pyrolysis, thermal gasification or liquefaction of solid wastes as PTGL processes.

Some PTGL processes are designed to discharge product fuel gases directly into the combustion chamber of a steam boiler. Because this type of process reactor (sometimes referred to as a starved-air or partial-combustion chamber) involves solid-waste pyrolysis and gasification, processes of this type will be included in our discussion even though the fuel produced is not stored.

The primary purpose here is to classify the PTGL process options, and to illustrate that:

- Comparisons of PTGL process options should begin with process fundamentals (solids-flow mechanism, bed characteristics, reactor type, etc.).
- The many process options available must be considered on the basis of type of recovered fuel desired and the waste material available.
- PTGL processes are a possible but not necessarily simple solution to energy recovery from solid wastes.
- Second-generation PTGL technologies now emerging will require more research and development work before becoming commercial.

PTGL PROCESS FEATURES

Potential advantages of the PTGL processes, relative to other solid-waste options, generally cited by proponents of PTGL technologies are:

- Production of a storable fuel as opposed to only steam generation from incineration of wastes.
- Recovery of char that can be converted into activated carbon or synthesis gas.
- Lower costs for air pollution control because of the much lower gas volumes requiring cleaning, compared to those for solid-waste combustion in incinerators.

---

*Residues have some positive value (often quite low), as opposed to solid wastes, which represent a disposal cost. In this article, all residues will be referred to as solid wastes. Efforts are also underway to photosynthetically produce feedstocks for energy production. Such biomass materials have the potential to make a much greater contribution to energy supplies than waste materials or residues.

Definitions

Solid-waste incineration. Solid material is completely combusted in a furnace to produce a hot flue gas. The principal way to recover energy is to transfer heat from the gas via a steam boiler. In waterwall incinerators, boiler tubes surround the interior walls of the furnace.

Destructive distillation or pyrolysis (e.g., metallurgical-coke production in vertical-flued ovens). Carbonaceous materials are thermally decomposed into fuels (gases, liquids and char) by indirect heat transfer, with no injection of oxygen, steam or hot CO into the reactor (see Box 2, reactions 1, 2, 3. and 4). Currently, many authors define pyrolysis somewhat differently. By their definition, a pyrolysis process may be autothermic: that is, some of the heat for thermal decomposition is directly transferred from hot gases that are the products of partial combustion of char or gases. This latter definition is not rigorously correct because there is actually a partial-combustion (or starved-air-combustion) zone in the reactor (see Reaction 10).

Gasification. A carbonaceous material is reacted with oxygen, steam or hot CO_2 to produce fuel gas (see Reactions 5, 6, 7 and 8 for examples of char gasification). Gasification reactors may also include a pyrolysis zone in which char is produced. Heat is usually generated within the reactor by partial combustion of the char and is transferred directly from hot combustion-product gases to the solid waste (see Reaction 10).

Liquefaction processes. These yield greater quantities of organic liquids relative to fuel gases. Pyrolysis processes may be designed to produce large quantities of liquids and can therefore be categorized as liquefaction (see Reactions 1 and 2 for examples). Other liquefication processes use solvent hydrogenation, with or without catalysts. In a third type of liquefaction process synthesis gas $(CO + H_2)$ generated and converted catalytically to methanol, polymer gasoline, or other light organic liquids.

Slagging reactor. The reactor temperature exceeds the ash melting point, so that the ash from the reactor can be removed as a molten slag.

Direct heating or firing. Heat is transferred directly from hot combustion-product gases to solid wastes.

Indirect heating or firing. Fuel combustion takes place in a separate chamber, with heat transfer from the hot combustion-product gases to the solid wastes by means of convection and radiation through the reactor wall or fire-tube walls separating the two chambers, or by means of a recirculating heat carrier (hot ceramic balls, hot sand, hot char, molten metal, or molten salts).

- Production of a residue (a glassy aggregate or char) that is environmentally more acceptable than ash from an incinerator.

Many PTGL processes offer some or all of these advantages, but certain problems may develop. For example, a highly concentrated, organically contaminated wastewater stream is sometimes produced. This stream forms in processes where high-moisture-content waste is gasified, the moisture-laden fuel gas cooled, and the moisture condensed (the water comes from the feed material plus water of reaction). Water-soluble oxygenated organics (see Reactions 1 and 2) leave the system in the liquid phase, and a wastewater treatment process is required. The extent of this problem varies from process to process, and depends on the raw-material characteristics and reactor type and design. This problem is avoidable and the technique for prevention will be examined.

Another problem is emission of fine particulates. In slagging reactors having very high temperature zones ($> 2,000°F$), salt vaporization and subsequent condensation in the gas stream cause submicrometer particles to form. This potential problem will be discussed in more detail later.

BASIC PROCESS CHARACTERISTICS

Process options can best be compared by classifying them on the basis of solids-flow mechanism, bed characteristics, reactor type (see below), heat-transfer method, evolved gas flow, temperature profiles, operating pressure, and the

---

Pyrolysis and gassification reactions

1. Carbonaceous solids   *Heat*   High- and moderate-mol. wt. organic liquids (tars and oils, some aromatics)   + char +   Low-mol. wt. organic liquids (many organic acids and aromatics)

$$+ CH_4 + H_2 + H_2O + CO + CO_2$$

$$+ NH_3 + H_2S + COS + HCN$$ Amounts depend on nitrogen and sulfur content in feedstock

2. Organic liquids   *Heat*   Aromatic organics $+ \dfrac{\text{low-mol. wt.}}{\text{organic liquids}} + char + CH_4 + H_2 + H_2O + CO + CO_2$

$$+ NH_3 + H_2S + COS + HCN$$ Amounts depend on nitrogen and sulfur content in feedstock

Pyrolysis gas-phase equilibria

3. $CH_4 + H_2O \rightleftharpoons CO + 3H_2$ (endothermic)*
4. $CO + H_2O \rightleftharpoons CO_2 + H_2$ (slightly exothermic)

Char gasification

5. $C + 2H_2O \rightarrow CO_2 + 2H_2$ ⎫
6. $C + H_2O \rightarrow CO + H_2$ ⎬ (endothermic)**
7. $C + CO_2 \rightarrow 2CO$ ⎭
8. $C + 2H_2 \rightarrow CH_4$ (exothermic)†

Combustion for gasification heat source

9. $C + O_2 \rightarrow CO_2$ (complete combustion)   ⎫ (exothermic)
10. $nC + n/2\ O_2 \rightarrow nCO$ (partial combustion)††   ⎭

*Overall methane yield decreases greatly with increasing temperature because of this reaction.

**High-energy-consuming reactions.

†At atmospheric pressure, the equilibrium conversion to methane is quite low and decreases as temperature rises from $1,000°$ F to $1,500°$ F. High-pressure operation is required to achieve a significant degree of hydrogenation of char or liquid products.

††Also known as starved-air combustion.

---

use of catalysts.* The relationships among these process characteristics — and their impact on product types, product yields, and environmental-control needs — are important to any comparison of processes. For instance, experience with demonstration plants, and analyses of alternative systems presented in the literature, clearly indicate that environmental control needs vary from process to process and represent a large fraction of the system investment and operating costs.

FEEDSTOCK PRETREATMENT

The amount of preprocessing is determined by technical and economic design considerations and varies for different waste materials and types of process reactors. Size reduction may be necessary to (1) ensure troublefree reactor-feeder operation, (2) prevent bridging in certain types of reactors, or (3) increase heat-transfer

---

*The U.S. Dept. of Energy is currently sponsoring research into high-pressure and catalytic liquefaction and gasification of residues. Until recently, most solid-waste-recovery processes were operated at 1 atm. Likewise, the use of catalysts has been limited.

efficiency within a reactor. Size reduction will also aid in metals-recovery and separation of organic fractions from municipal refuse. Densification (cubing or pelletizing) of wastes such as cotton-gin trash or rice straw will increase reactor throughput. Drying is another preliminary processing operation often used to treat high-moisture-content feedstocks and will be discussed later.

REACTOR TYPES AND CHARACTERISTICS

Classification of processes by solids-flow direction and bed conditions in the reactor appears to be the best approach. A number of the reactors that have been drawn are arbitrarily divided into different zones. Only the indirectly-heated reactors without steam or oxygen injection may be described as pyrolysis reactors. The actual length of the solids-drying and heating zone will be a function of feed moisture content and heat-transfer rate. All reactors that contain both gasification and pyrolysis zones are usually directly fired (or autothermic) and may include steam injection for char gasification.

Table 1 lists the basic classes of reactors now being demonstrated or under development and identifies specific characteristics. Table 2 lists several R&D programs that use electrically heated reactors. For commercial applications, electric heating will probably not be economical but this type of reactor is more easily controlled during experimentation.

PREDICTING PRODUCT YIELD AND COMPOSITION

To predict product yield and composition is an extremely complex task, and experimentation may be the only way to accurately correlate individual reactor output with feed composition, feed particle-size characteristics, and reactor operating conditions. Even for a relatively simple case where the physical and chemical characteristics of a dry feedstock are assumed constant, selection of the operating conditions to achieve desired product distribution (gases, oil, and char) and characteristics is not a simple matter. For example, in a packed-bed reactor, the stream flows that must be adjusted include:

- Solid-waste feedrate to top of bed.
- Air or oxygen feed to char gasification zone.
- Steam feed to char gasification zone.
- Char removal rate from bottom of bed.

Once these flowrates are set at levels that allow steady-state operation, certain reactor operating conditions (unique to the flowrates selected) will result:

- Bed depth.
- Temperature profiles (solids and gases).
- Residence times (solids and gases).
- Product yield and composition (oil, gas, char).

Presently, it is difficult to predict the proper operating conditions that achieve specific product yields for most heterogeneous waste materials having variable moisture and ash content. Empirical methods must be used for design.

Even though a quantitative analysis of the many PTGL process options is a complex subject, the general rules outlined below may be useful:

- The yield of condensable organics (oils and tars) is maximized when solids are rapidly heated to a moderate temperature level ($\sim 1,000°F$), and the product gas and vapors immediately quenched. Liquid organics are highly oxygenated if produced from a cellulosic feedstock (CH_2O). Such liquid products, therefore, are partially miscible with water and may contain corrosive organic acids.
- Noncondensable-fulelgas yield (CO, H_2, CH_4) is maximized when the evolved gases and char are held at high temperatures ($1,400°F$) for relatively long residence times. Cocurrent flow of solids and gases allows this condition to exist and may minimize the yield of condensable organics. In cocurrent-flow systems having wet solids feed, moisture driven off in the drying zone flows through the pyrolysis zone. This allows the steam-carbon reactions (see Reactions 5 and 6) to proceed without steam injection and favors high fuel-gas yield. Operation of a

Table 1. Basic Types of Pyrolysis, Thermal Gasification and Liquefaction (PTGL) Reactors New Demonstrated or Under Development.

Solids Flow and Bed Conditions	Typical Reactor Vessels	Heat Transfer	Relative Direction of Gas Flow	Examples of Processes, Developers, R&D Programs	Feedstock	Main Products Fuels or Char Materials	Main Products Stream
I Vertical flow reactors							
A. Moving packed bed (gravity solids flow; also called fixed bed)	Refractory-lined shaft furnace	Direct	Countercurrent	††Forest Fuels Mfg., Inc. (Antrim, (N.H.)	FAR†		X
				Battelle Northwest (Richland, Wash.)	Refuse	X or	X
				American Thermogen (location unknown)	Refuse		X
				††Andco/Torrax Process (Buffalo, N.Y.)	Refuse		X
				H.F. Funk Process* (Murray Hill, N.J.)	Refuse	X	
				††Tech-Air Corp./Georgia Inst. Tech. (Atlanta, Ga.)	FAR	X	
				††Union Carbide Purox Process (Tonawanda, N.Y.)	Refuse, FAR	X	
				††Motala Pyrogas (Sweden)	Refuse	X	
				Urban Research & Development (E. Granby, Conn.)	FAR, sludge	X	
				Wilwardco, Inc. (San Jose, Calif.)	FAR	X	
			Cocurrent	U. of California (Davis, Calif.)	FAR	X	
			Crossflow	Foster Wheeler Power Products (London, England)	Refuse, tires	X	
	Refractory or metal retort	Indirect – wall	Cocurrent	Destrugas Process (Denmark)	Refuse	X	
			Crossflow	Koppleman Process (Encino, Calif.)	FAR	X	
B. Moving stirred bed (gravity solids flow)	Refractory-lined multiple-hearth furnace	Direct	Countercurrent	††BSP/Envirotech (Belmont, Calif.)	Sludge, refuse	X	X
				††Nichols Research & Engr. (Belle Mead, N.J.)	Sludge, wood	X	X
				Garrett Energy Research & Engr. (Claremont, Calif.)	Manure	X	
				Hercules/Black, Crow & Eidsness (Gainesville, Fla.)	Refuse	X	
C. Moving entrained bed (may include mechanical bed transport)	Refractory-lined tubular reactor	Indirect by RHC**	Cocurrent	††Occidental Petroluem Co./Garrett Flash Pyrolysis Process (LaVerne, Calif.)	Refuse	X	
II Fluidized reactors	Refractory-lined or metal-walled vessel	Direct	—	Copeland Systems Inc. (Oak Brook, Ill.)	Sludges	X	
				Coors Brewing Co./U. of Missouri (Rolla, Mo.)	Refuse, FAR	X*	
				Energy Resources Co. (Erco) (Cambridge, Mass.)	Refuse, FAR	X	
				Hercules/Black Crow & Eidsness (Gainesville, Fla.)	Refuse	X	
		Indirect by RHC		Bailie Process/Wheelabrator Incin. Inc. (Pittsburgh, Pa.)	Refuse	X	
				A.D. Little Inc./Combustion Equipment Assoc. (Cambridge, Mass./New York, N.Y.)	Refuse	X	
III Horizontal- and inclined-flow reactors	Rotary kiln or calciner						
A. Tumbling solids bed	Refractory-lined reactor	Direct	Countercurrent	††Devco Management Inc. (New York, N.Y.)	Refuse		X
				††Monsanto Landgard/City of Baltimore, Md.	Refuse	X	X
				Watson Energy Systems (Los Angeles, Calif.)	Refuse		X

Table 1. (continued)

Solids Flow and Bed Concentration	Typical Reactor Vessels	Heat Transfer	Relative Direction of Gas Flow	Examples of Processes, Developers, R&D Programs	Feedstock	Main Products Fuels or Char Materials	Stream
	Metal retort in firebox	Indirect – wall	Countercurrent or cocurrent	Ecology Recycling Unlimited, Inc. (Santa Fe Springs, Calif.)	Refuse	X	
				Pyrolenergy System/Arcalon (Amsterdam)	Refuse, FAR	X	
				Pan American Resources, Inc. (West Covina, Calif.)	Refuse, FAR	X	
				Kobe Steel (Japan)	Tires	X	
				JPL/Orange County, Calif. (Fountain Valley, Calif.)	Sludge	X	
				Rust Engineering (Birmingham, Ala.)	Refuse, sludge	X	
	Metal retort	Indirect by	Cocurrent	Tosco Corp/Goodyear Tire and Rubber (Los Angeles, Calif./Akron, Ohio)	Tires	X	
B. Agitated solids bed	Metal retort (mixing conveyor)	Indirect – wall or fire tubes	–	Deco Energy Co. (Irvine, Calif.)	Tires	X	
				Enterprise Co. (Santa Ana, Calif.)	Refuse	X	
				Kemp Reduction Corp. (Santa Barbara, Calif.)	Refuse, FAR	X	
	Refractory chamber (vibrating conveyor)	Indirect – fire tubes	Cocurrent	PyroSol (Redwood City, Calif.)	Fluff from scrapped autos		X
C. Static solids bed	Metal chamber & conveyor belt	Indirect – fire tubes	Crossflow	Thermex, Inc. (Hayward, Calif.)	Tires	X	
IV Molten metal or salt beds							
A. Floating solids bed (horizontal flow)	Moving molten-lead hearth	Indirect by RHC	–	Michigan Tech. U. (Houghton, Mich.) (Puretec Pyrolysis System)	Refuse, FAR	X	
B. Mixed molten-salt bed (various possible flow schemes)	Vertical shaft or mixed bed	Indirect by RHC	–	Battelle Northwest (Richland, Wash.)	Refuse	X	
				Anti-Polution Systems, Inc. (Pleasantville, N.J.)	Refuse, sludge	X	
V Multiple-reactor systems							
A. Combined entrained-bed/static-bed reactor system	Tubular metal retort and static-hearth refractory chamber	Indirect-wall	Cocurrent	U. of California (Berkeley, Calif.)	Pulping liquor	X	
		Direct	–				
B. Combined moving packed-bed/entrained-bed reactor	Vertical shaft	Direct	Countercurrent	Battelle Columbus Laboratories (Columbus, Ohio)	Paper, biomass	X	
	Vertical shaft (char gasification)	Direct	Cocurrent				

Table 1. (continued)

Solids Flow and Bed Conditions	Typical Reactor Vessels	Heat Transfer	Relative Direction of Gas Flow	Examples of Processes, Developers, R&D Programs	Feedstock	Main Products	
						Fuels or Char Materials	Stream
C. Combined mechanically conveyed static-solids-bed/moving packed-bed reactor	Traveling-grate refractory chamber	Direct	Countercurrent	Mansfield Carbon Products, Inc. (Gallatin, Tenn.)	Refuse	X	
	Refractory-lined shaft furnace	Direct	Countercurrent				

*Pressure above atmoshperic   **A circulating heat carrier   †Forestry and/or agricultural residues   ††At commercial or demonstration scale.

Table 2. Electrically Heated Reactors in the R&D Stage.

Typical Reactor Vessels	Examples of Process, Developers, R&D Programs	Feedstock	Main Products	
			Fuels or Char Materials	Steam
Tubular metal††	Wright-Malta Corp* (supercritical pressure) (Ballston Spa, N.Y.)	FAR†, refuse	X	X (electric power)
Back-mix reactor	Dept. of Energy Wood to Oil Process Development Unit** Bechtel Corp., (Albany, Ore.)	FAR	X	
Tubular quartz reactor††	Princeton U. (Princeton, N.J.)	Manure	X	
Metal retort††	Dept. of Energy/Pittsburgh Energy Research Center (Pittsburgh, Pa.) (Formerly Bureau of Mines)	Refuse	X	
Metal retort††	Stanford U. (Palo Alto, Cal.)	Refuse	X	
Metal retort††	U. of Southern California (Los Angeles, Cal.)	Refuse, sludge	X	
Metal retort††	New York U. (New York, N.Y.)	Refuse	X	
Glass vessel†† (Molten-salt bed)	U. of Tennessee (Knoxville, Tenn.)	Tires, plastics, FAR	X	
Entrained-bed-reactor††				
Fluidized-bed reactor	Texas Tech. U. (Lubbock, Tex.)			
Cyclonic burner††	(All reactors are autothermic)	Manure	X	
Moving packed bed††				

*Pressure above atmospheric   **Sodium carbonate catalyst   †Forestry and/or agricultural residues   ††Bench-scale equipment.

fluidized-bed reactor at high temperature can also give a high gas yield.

Indirectly heated reactors yield a higher-heating-value fuel gas (500 to 800 Btu/scf) than directly fired, air-blown reactors. The latter type produces a fuel gas in the range of 100 to 150 Btu/scf. Oxygen blowing will yield a gas of moderate heat content (250 to 350 Btu/scf). Net energy production, however, may be lower for the indirectly heated reactor system as a result of economic limitations on the use of very large heat-transfer surfaces.

Certain trace components in waste or residues can present design problems relative to corrosion and pollution control. For instance, polyvinyl chloride (PVC) in municipal refuse will cause HCl to form in the product gas of a system. Source separation of PVC can minimize this problem. The reducing atmosphere in the reactor can also yield NH_3, HCN, H_2S from the sulfur and nitrogen compounds in the feed, and these products will be partitioned between the gas phase and liquid phase. The concentration of heavy metals, such as cadmium and mercury, in the feedstock must also be taken into account. Systems must be included to remove these compounds from the air and water effluent streams.

- The temperature profiles in the drying, pyrolysis and gasification zones are extremely important. Water pollution potential is the greatest with countercurrent flow reactors wherever product gases leave the drying zone at a low temperature (500°F), and water is condensed out of the fuel gas. Low temperature results in minimal thermal cracking of high-molecular-weight organic vapors. This condition does yield a somewhat higher overall thermal efficiency for the process, however.
- The condensable organic materials in the product fuel gas may include low-molecular-weight oxygenated organics (acids, ketones and aldehydes), oxygenated aromatics, heavy aromatic oils, and tars. The volume of wastewater condensed from product fuel gas may be in excess of 75 gal/ton of municipal refuse (> 25% moisture in feed), unless the refuse is pre-dried, which is costly. The high water content of many agricultural and forestry residue feedstocks may lead to even greater volumes of wastewater if these feedstocks are not dried prior to processing.
- Only directly fired, moving-packed-bed reactors with countercurrent flow are generally operated in a slagging mode. Slag flow-properties will be determined by feed characteristics such as glass composition and reactor temperature. Submicrometer inorganic particles may be formed by salt condensation from the vapor phase in such systems, and these particles may not be completely removed in the packed bed.

DESIGN CONSIDERATIONS FOR SPECIFIC PRODUCTS

Solid wastes now being considered for feedstocks include municipal refuse, tires, sludges, plastic wastes, forestry-product wastes, agricultural residues such as rice hulls, corn husks, wheat and rice straw, and cattle manure. The feedstock characteristics (C:H:O ratio, cellulose content, lignin content, ash content and composition, water content, particle size, particle flowability) must be considered when selecting a process to produce a fuel gas, oil, or char. It is beyond the scope of this article to discuss this subject in detail. As an example, however, we will discuss a design option for cases where an oil product is desired from a cellulosic (CH_2O) feedstock.

In such a system, the product vapor from pyrolysis of solids will contain oxygenated organic molecules. To maximize the oil yield, it is necessary to minimize the thermal cracking of reactive radicals that are oil precursors. Such cracking can be minimized by immediate and rapid quenching to below the gas dewpoint by means of a cool-oil quench stream, but this technique also condenses the water vapor in the gas stream. As noted earlier, this water comes mainly from the moisture in the solid feed, but also forms as a reaction product. It may be preferable to pre-dry the feed to minimize wastewater treatment problems such as oxygenated-oil removal. However, the costs and possible complications from other environmental problems (odor and particulate control) must be considered before such a decision is made. Some water may also be desirable in the oil to serve as a viscosity modifier.

PROBLEMS IN USE OF RAW FUEL GAS

Reactor selection and operation will depend to a great extent on the form of recovered energy desired from a specific feedstock. Immediate combustion of reactor product gas to generate steam eliminates water pollution resulting from condensation of water from a fuel gas loaded with liquid organics.

It is important, however, to ensure against simply trading an air pollution problem for a water pollution one. Inorganic particulate matter in the fuel gas going to a combustion chamber may vaporize in the hot chamber (about 2,000°F), causing submicrometer particles to form downstream by inorganic-salt condensation. These small particles readily pass through low-efficiency particulate collectors. Where immediate combustion of particulate-laden fuel gas is planned, the problem can be minimized by choosing a reactor that will produce the lowest particulate loading in the exiting fuel gas (for example, a packed bed instead of a tumbling bed, or a stirred bed instead of a fluidized bed).

Reactor choice may not completely solve the problem, though. Submicrometer inorganic particles can also form in the bottom of a high-temperature, directly fired packed-bed reactor. Such particulate-laden streams will not be completely cleaned by passing through a coarse bed of refuse. Cleaning the fuel gas before combustion will minimize this problem; however, such hot-gas cleaning is not a simple process. More work is required to develop an energy-efficient hot-gas-cleaning process.

RECOVERED CHAR

Char recovery is desirable because of the material's potential value as a feedstock for activated-carbon production or as a low-quality absorbent. Char is also a natural binder for water-soluble inorganics, reducing the leaching potential of certain constituents from buried PTGL-reactor residues in landfills, and is a storable solid fuel. However, the practicality of char removal depends on char quantity and characteristics —

which in turn are functions of feedstock conditions, process type and operating conditions — and local demand.

FIRST- AND SECOND-GENERATION PROCESSES

Pyrolysis is applicable to a wide range of materials. Before 1977, only processes using directly fired shaft furnaces and directly fired rotary kilns were being demonstrated in the U.S. for municipal refuse applications with capacities of over 100 tons/day.* Some directly fired reactors are still new relative to producing fuels from wastes. The directly fired multiple hearth furnace, which has long been used for sludge incineration, roasting, and activated-carbon and charcoal production (from pyrolysis of coal and wood wastes), has recently been extensively tested for pyrolysis and gasification of refuse, sludge and manure.

Pyrolysis reactors using indirect heat transfer have not been demonstrated to the same extent as directly fired shaft furnaces and directly fired rotary kilns. They may therefore be classified as second-generation processes. These reactors can yield a higher-Btu-content product gas than can the directly fired first-generation process reactors, but they present some design challenges.

As second-generation processes develop problems that are not of great concern in refractory-lined, directly fired reactors must be addressed. With heat transfer by conduction through a surface such as a wall, for instance, the reactor should ideally have a metal shell with oxidizing conditions on the fire side and reducing conditions (with H_2S and H_2 present) on the other side, requiring the use of expensive, high-nickel alloys such as Inconel. The designer of an indirectly heated reactor may instead select recirculating nongaseous heat carriers that will allow use of a refractory-lined vessel. By such a choice, however, the designer exchanges the problem of using an expensive construction material for the potential operating problem and expense of a recirculating solid or molten heat carrier.

---

*Two of the most important current industrial uses of these types of reactors are as blast furnaces (iron-ore reduction in shaft furnaces) and as cement kilns (directly fired refractory-lined rotary kilns).

4-19 Pyrolysis in Baltimore: From Failure to Success

John C. Even, Jr.

Source: *NCRR Bulletin,* Vol. 10, No. 1 (March 1980) pp. 8–13. **Reprinted with Permission of National Center for Resource Recovery.**

The City of Baltimore Pyrolysis Plant was hailed, when it was first proposed in 1972, as a technological and environmental breakthrough. Designed and to be operated by the Monsanto Enviro-Chem Systems Co., the facility would employ Monsanto's patented Landgard® technique to produce salable steam from the city's solid waste.

Five years later, ironically, the operation was to be considered by many as a technological and environmental failure. Also in 1977, Monsanto withdrew its participation from the project, recommending that the plant either be closed or converted to straight incineration. The city did neither; instead, it elected to not abandon what it felt was basically a sound concept.

Reopened in 1979, the plant is today processing 600 tons of refuse per day — one-fourth of the city's total solid waste — and from it generating steam for sale to the Baltimore Gas and Electric Co.

The Baltimore project was conceived, approved and funded as a demonstration or test program to evaluate the effectiveness of pyrolyzing solid waste for the purpose of generating salable steam while reducing the quantity of refuse to be landfilled.

Extensive national publicity was given to the startup, initial operations and problems encountered. Surprisingly little attention, however, has been paid to the project since it has become an economically sound, productive operation.

While this article is, essentially, of a technical nature, the lessons to be learned from this experience are not. Instead, they are that (1) demonstration programs, particularly of new technologies, should be recognized as such, and that changes in original concepts can and should be expected; (2) there is no substitute for thorough, advanced planning; and (3) the need for open communications and coordination between public and private communities is essential.

Before going back online, the facility underwent a number of modifications aimed primarily at simplifying the pyrolysis process: starved-air incineration of shredded municipal waste in a rotary kiln with after-burner combustion and waste heat recovery. The storage of shredded refuse was eliminated, as was the recovery of ferrous metals and glass. Also, the exhaust gas emissions are now controlled by electrostatic precipitators instead of wet scrubbers, in order to meet emission standards.

The ability to make these necessary modifications, and thereby salvage a significant monetary investment as well as a much needed solid waste disposal alternative, can be traced back to the city's decision in 1977 to continue operating the plant for more than a year after Monsanto personnel had departed. This experience enabled the city to not only develop confidence in the pyrolysis process, but to determine first-hand the changes needed to establish a functional operation that would also meet emission requirements.

Called in to assist the city during the period of reevaluation were the consulting engineering firms of Harrington, Lacey and Associates of

Glen Burnie, Md., and William F. Cosulich Associates of Woodbury, N.Y.

BACKGROUND

Baltimore's Pyrolysis Plant was approved and built as a demonstration facility, with funding by the City of Baltimore, the Maryland Department of Environmental Services and the U.S. Environmental Protection Agency (EPA). The project was intended to demonstrate the feasibility of a 1000 ton-per-day (TPD) pyrolytic conversion process with heat recovery, using municipal solid waste as the only feedstock. Similar Landgard® systems had been successfully operated in smaller scale (35 TPD) pilot plants in St. Louis, Mo., and Kobe, Japan. The Baltimore plant, therefore, was to be a "scale-up" of the basic system.

In operation, refuse was to be processed and stored for subsequent retrieval and pyrolyzing in a rotating reactor kiln operating at 1200°F in an oxygen-deficient (substoichiometric) atmosphere. This was to be followed by the complete combustion of gases in a slagging type of gas purifier.

Heat from the combustion products would then be recovered by two waste heat-to-steam boilers. Cooled exhaust gases would then be passed through a wet gas scrubber system, drawn by an induced draft fan, and directed out into a dehumidifier before being released into the atmosphere. Ferrous metal and glass would be recovered from the slag, with the remaining slag being landfilled. The process, as designed, became operational in 1975.

A detailed study prepared for EPA's Office of Water and Waste Management by the Systems Technology Corp. (SYSTECH) documents the plant's history through this period and into 1978. Copies of this four-volume report (SW175C.2, .3, .4 and SW719) are available

Table 1. Fact Summary; City of Baltimore Pyrolysis Plant.

Official Opening: February 1975

Present Configuration Opening: May 1979

Principals: City of Baltimore, Md. — owns and operates the plant
Baltimore Gas and Electric Co. (BG&E) — purchases the steam
Monsanto Enviro-Chem Systems, Inc. — designed the plant
Leonard Construction, Division of Monsanto Co. — constructed the plant

Volume: Processing 600 TPD on a 3-shift, 6-day-per-week basis

Technology: Shredding; rotary kiln pyrolysis; afterburner gas purification; heat recovery water-tube drum boilers

Product: Steam — delivers about 80,000 lbs./hr. saturated at 350 psig, 415°F to BG&E Lendenhal Station for steam loop heating/air conditioning
Residue — landfilled

Costs: Total capital cost including modifications is $25 million; the City of Baltimore share is $6 million with the rest obtained from various grants, Maryland Environmental Services, U.S. EPA and Monsanto Co.

Costs and Revenue per Input Ton
Based on 8-Month Operation in 1979
(67,409 tons processed)

Costs		*Revenues for Sale of Steam*	
Operating (est.)	$11.87	Steam	$10.58
Kiln refractory replacement	1.00		
Investment (City portion)	5.16		
Totals:	$18.03		$10.58
Net cost per ton:	**$ 7.45**		

from the National Technical Information Service, Springfield, Va. 22161.

SYSTEM MODIFICATIONS

The turnaround of the Baltimore facility from a "failure" to a dependable, effective operational system was due, in the opinion of the city, to the identification and subsequent correction of several major problems. A brief description of these problems and the actions taken to solve them follows.[1]

- *Excessive equipment wear and "plugging" in the refuse storage and retrieval systems* was found to be caused by the "setting up" of the stored shredded waste into an almost unmovable, cohesive mass. Refuse storage was discontinued, and the feed rate changed to match the firing rate of the pyrolytic kiln.
- *Unstable kiln processing and refractory failures* were corrected by substituting a higher temperature-rated refractory lining.
- *Slagging, and consequent "plugging," in the gas purifier (after burner)* was eliminated by exchanging the gas purifier with one that generated fly ash instead of slag.
- *Excessive stack gas particulate emissions, as well as high water vapor content under certain ambient air conditions,* was corrected by replacing the boiler feedwater economizers, the wet scrubber flue gas cleanup and dehumidifier system with an electrostatic precipitator and an induced draft fan for each boiler. Also added was a 220-foot-high exhaust stack, which eliminated icing conditions on an adjacent expressway under "favorable" atmospheric conditions.

The city, in a move to reduce operation costs also eliminated the labor-intensive kiln residue processing facility designed for recovery of ferrous metal and glass.

The above modifications began soon after the plant was closed by the city in February 1978. Up to that time, some 125,000 tons of refuse had been processed.[2]

SYSTEM DESCRIPTION

Incoming waste, delivered by municipal packers, is weighed before being unloaded from the tipping floor into a waste pit. A track-laying type of bulldozer operating in the pit moves the refuse onto one of two shredder infeed conveyors. The two 800 hp, belt-driven Jeffrey Manufacturing Co. shredders, with horizontal shafts and swing hammers, are operated on a daily alternating basis, so that one is always on standby or being serviced.

After shredding, the refuse is conveyed into a hopper which supplies the material to two ram feeders used to charge the pyrolytic kiln. The ram feeders cycle independently at a nominal rate of once each minute pushing the waste into the kiln; the average feed rate is 25 tons per hour (TPH). Thermal reactions begin taking place as soon as the material is dried and heated to a temperature level of about 1800°F, which occurs within a distance of 20 feet from the point of entry. Air admitted through the residue discharge end of the kiln serves to control the combustion and heat release rate of the generated gases; this heat release serves as the energy source for the drying and pyrolytic process.

Combustible gases are removed through the feed end of the kiln. At the 25 TPH feed rate, the reactions are completed in the kiln and the residue exiting the discharge end of the kiln is of an ash-like composition. At higher process rates (the original design specification called for 40 TPH), a considerable amount of unburned, unpyrolyzed material was discharged in the ash.

The 20-foot-diameter, 100-foot-long kiln rotates at nominally one revolution per minute. The kiln, with a castable refractory, was manufactured by the Kennedy Van Saun Corp., Danville, Pa.[3] Supplemental heat (supplied by oil burners) is introduced when the incoming waste is wet, or to keep the kiln operating when refuse is not being processed.

Pyrolytic gases pass from the kiln to the gas purifier or afterburner where, with the introduction of air and sometimes supplemental heat, combustion is completed. The new gas purifier, with its suspended refractory lining, was built by the M.H. Detrick Co., Cornwells Heights, Pa.

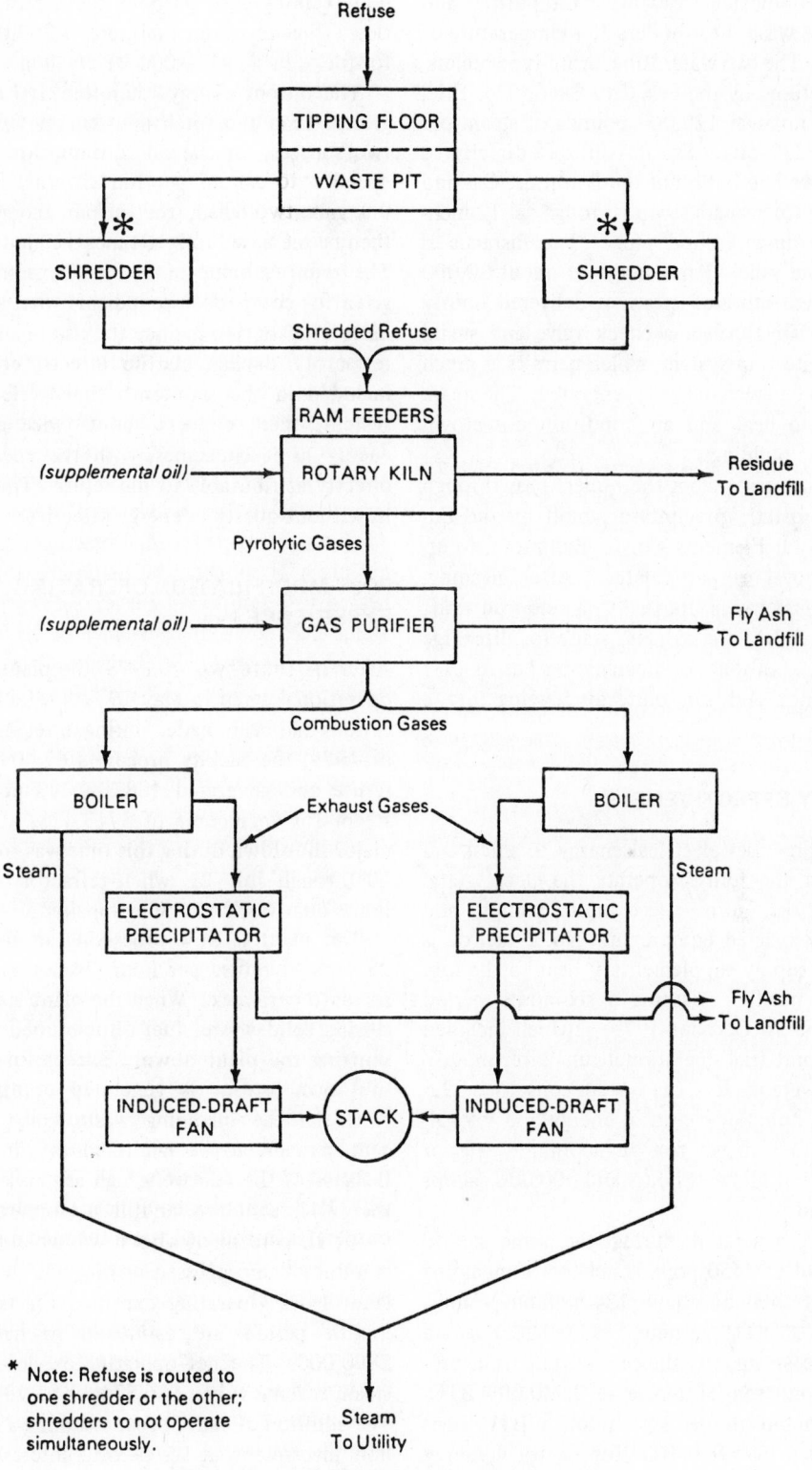

Figure 1. Process flow; Baltimore pyrolysis facility.

The combusted gases leave the purifier and enter the waste heat boilers at a temperature of 1600°F. The two water-tube, drum-type boilers, manufactured by the Erie City Energy Co., Erie, Pa., are rated at 125,000 pounds of steam per hour at 330 psig. Steam is moved directly to the Lendenhal Station of the Baltimore Gas and Electric Co. steam loop through a 12-inch-diameter underground pipe. The distance is about one mile. An average of about 80,000 pounds of saturated steam is delivered hourly at 350 psig through a check valve and steam condensate trap system, which permits as much steam to be delivered as is generated. The steam is used to heat and air condition downtown Baltimore buildings.

Exhaust gases from the boilers pass through an electrostatic precipitator, built by the Environmental Elements Co. of Baltimore, to effect removal of particulates. After cleaning, the exhaust gas is drawn by an induced draft fan and fed to the exhaust stack for discharge into the atmosphere. Each boiler has its own precipitator and fan unit, discharging into a common stock.

ENERGY EFFECTIVENESS

The facility uses electrical energy to shred and transport the refuse, operate the electrostatic precipitators, drive feedwater pumps and power associated equipment. No. 2 fuel oil is used to supply supplementary heat to the kiln and gas purifier. During a six-month period from May to October 1979 — which included startup and trial operational runs after modifications were made — the system consumed 39.5 kilowatt hours of electrical energy and 9.9 gallons of fuel oil per ton of incoming waste, or two million kilowatt hours and 500,000 gallons of fuel oil.

Steam generated during the same period amounted to 2450 pounds per ton of incoming refuse, a total of about 124 million pounds. Using 1200 BTU per pound as the heat released from the steam, the thermal output from processing one ton of refuse is 2,940,000 BTU. Energy input to the system on a BTU basis would be: 395,000 BTU for electrical energy using an equivalency of 10,000 BTU/kilowatt

hour (taking into account the typical generation efficiency from fuel), and 1,363,000 BTU for fuel oil using 138,000 BTU/gallon.

The output energy, therefore, is 1.67 times greater than the total input energy from these two sources. If the oil consumption were reduced to 7 gallons per ton of refuse from the 9.9 gallons burned, the output energy would then be increased to 2.16 times the input energy. The reduced value of fuel oil consumption is given for comparison to indicate what may be a more realistic level, since the use of oil in kiln refractory drying, startup effects, etc., were included in the six-month time period. This system, then, delivers about twice as much energy as it consumes, with the energy gain directly attributable to the refuse. This system is, without question, energy effective.

POST-MODIFICATION OPERATING EXPERIENCE

After its shutdown in 1978, the plant became operational again in May 1979 after all modifications had been made. During the eight months of 1979, the facility processed 67,409 tons of refuse and generated 188,024,000 pounds of steam for an income of $713,426. The only major shutdown during this time was from June 20 through July 21, when refractory material in the duct work was being repaired.[4]

The plant is now processing an average of 25 tons of refuse per hour, 24 hours per day, six days per week. When the plant is not processing solid waste, fuel oil is burned to avoid shutting the plant down. Except for a major shutdown, steam is generated continuously.

Of all the incoming waste, only 25 percent remains to be landfilled as ash residue. Because of the relatively high ash bulk density, the fill rate at the landfill is estimated to be about 10 percent of what it was when the same amount of unprocessed or raw solid waste was landfilled. Operating expenses for the eight-month period are estimated to have been $800,000. The net operating expense (minus steam revenues) was $86,574, or $1.28 per ton. The addition of capital cost assuming a $25 million investment at six percent interest with a 20-year life increases the eight-month cost by some $1.5 million, for a capital cost of $21.55 per ton.

The actual investment in the facility by the City of Baltimore is $6 million (other monies were provided by federal and state grants). At six percent interest over 20 years, the total cost during the eight-month period was $348,000. The resulting capital unit cost was, therefore, $5.16 per ton.

Operating expenses will have a periodic overhaul charge when the kiln refractory requires replacement (similar to grate replacement in incinerator systems). Refractory lining replacement, which is estimated to be necessary after processing about 300,000 tons of refuse, will cost $300,000.[5] This expense will result in an additional $1 per ton charge.

CONCLUSIONS

The application of pyrolysis, in Baltimore and elsewhere, is not unlike any new technology. Research, testing, documentation will be required to make it a practical and economical alternative to the disposal or raw refuse. Despite criticism and recommendations to close the facility, the City of Baltimore had the foresight to see a viable option to disposal and the courage to set about to prove out the system. Although the plant is operating satisfactorily today, the city will continue to look for ways of improving their system, and, thereby, advancing the state-of-the-art of pyrolysis.

The city, for example, is aware that redundancy in the rotary kiln unit would be desirable, since a failure in the kiln requires that the operation be shut down. Two kilns (each of lower capacity) would permit the system to continue operating if one kiln were to be shut down for repair.

This project, as with many other resource recovery systems coming online across the U.S., is successful because of the willingness of the Baltimore City administration to invest the necessary time and money in a concept that it felt offered at least a partial solution to its solid waste disposal problems. It is easy to point out errors or shortcomings in any new venture; the challenge is in correcting them and, thereby, turning failure and defeat into a successful operation.

REFERENCES

1. *A Technical and Economic Evaluation of the Project in Baltimore, Maryland.* Vol. II (SW175C.2). Prepared by Systems Technology Corp. for U.S. Environmental Protection Agency Office of Water and Waste Management. June 1979. pp. 4–5, 315.
2. Rick A. Haverland and David. B. Sussman, "Baltimore: A Lesson in Resource Recovery" (Report SW-712), presented at ASCE Environmental Engineering Division Specialty Conference, July 10–12, 1978. p. 7.
3. Reference 1, p. 92.
4. Edward J. Moore, Head of the Bureau of Solid Waste, City of Baltimore. Letter and personal communication during site visit, Jan. 15, 1980.
5. Jacob J. Bochinski, Chief of Solid Waste Disposal, City of Balitmore. Personal communication, Jan. 18, 1980.

4-20 Predicting Gas Generation from Landfills

Robert H. Ham

Source: *Waste Age,* Vol. 10, No.,11 (November 1979) pp. 50–58. Reprinted with Permission of National Solid Wastes Management Association.

Landfill operators looking to control methane production – either to increase it as a resource, or limit it because of health and safety considerations – should be aware of the factors contributing to methane production.

Gas production by decomposing landfills is complex, involving availability of balanced supplies of decomposable refuse components plus satisfaction of stringent growth condition requirements.

Because of the complex inter-relationships between various micro-organisms leading eventually to methane formation, it is not surprising that a widespread mixture of nutrients and bacterial species is conducive to rapid methane formation.

TOTAL GAS PRODUCTION

The generalized equation describing methane generation is based on a substrate of overall composition. To the extent that various components of waste are made available simultaneously, the overall refuse composition may be inserted into the equation to predict gas composition and total methane formation.

Using this approach, a number of researchers have calculated theoretical gas production for typical urban refuse. The amount calculated is 440 l/kg wet refuse as received. The gas so generated has a composition of 53% methane and 46% carbon dioxide.

This estimate, however, oversimplifies the complex process of solid waste decomposition, and is based on a number of assumptions which are not valid in actual landfill conditions.

- Calculation assumes complete degradation. Such does not happen in any reasonable length of time. Lignin and plastics, for example, are not degradable to any practical extent under anaerobic conditions.

- Calculation assumes that degradation proceeds according to anaerobic conditions so that all organic matter results in methane or carbon dioxide production. Thus, any matter leaving the landfill, either as a gas or leachate, would contain no organic matter except methane, which is not the case in reality.

- Calculation assumes that refuse components are made available such that a balance of substrates and nutrients is available at all times. Again, this is not the case in the real world.

- Calculation assumes no portion of the degraded matter is utilized for cell synthesis. At typical rates of cell synthesis, the error is small, but may be significant in some cases.

Actual total gas production data from decomposition of refuse is difficult to obtain, as is borne out by the lack of such data. Ideally, a landfill would be monitored over its entire decomposition life to determine total gas production. Obviously, the time required to develop such information makes it difficult to obtain, but an additional problem in measuring gas production is the change in landfill conditions brought about by gas collection techniques. If one attempts to enclose a landfill for gas measurement, perhaps by using a wetted clay seal, the decomposition process will be changed, affecting the results directly. Water movement in the landfill, for example, will be unnatural.

Gas (CO_2 and CH_4) Production Rate From Municipal Refuse

Source	Conditions	Basis	Gas Production Rate l/kg Refuse as Received per Year
This Report	After 5 years in landfill	Theoretical	16
Bowerman, et al	Literature and various data sources	Estimated	14
SCS Engineers	Literature and various data sources	Estimated	3.7 to 14
Boyle	Literature	Estimated	3.7 to 14
Merz & Stone	Lysimeter, calculated from 300 days CH_4 production	Measurement	4.9
Streng	Ave, range during active CH_4 prod. for solid waste only lysimeter	Measurement	4.9 to 6.1
Chian & DeWalle	Lysimeter gas prod. over 300 days recalculated for cell 4	Measurement	0.21
Rovers & Farquhar	Lysimeter, maximum production rate observed	Measurement	8.1
Merz	Maximum production in lysimeter at "optimal" temp. and % H_2O	Measurement	32
Ramaswamy	Lysimeter with unusually high food waste content	Measurement	400
Beluche	Cited in literature	Measurement	2.9
Bishop	Pilot-scale landfill, low H_2O content	Measurement	32 to 62
Engineering Science	Test landfill, maximum and minimum observed production on per year basis over 3 year's monitoring	Measurement	16 to 41
Carlson	Estimated during landfill pump tests, varies seasonally	Measurement	3.9 to 39
Mountain View Report	Estimated during landfill pump tests, both values given	Measurement	21 - 29
City of Los Angeles	Theoretical extrapolation of short-term landfill pumping data	Measurement/ Theoretical	11
City of Giondale	Testing of landfill, recalculated for 53% CH_4	Measurement	2.2
Anderson & Callinan	Typical Municipal Refuse	Theoretical	410
Boyle	Typical Municipal Refuse	Theoretical	450
Golueke	Divided organics by component, calculated 550 l/kg dry volatiles	Theoretical	300
Pacey	Weighted organic components by degradability, calculated 62 1 CH_4/kg	Theoretical	120
Klein	Digested refuse with sewage sludge obtained 440 l/kg volatiles destroyed	Lab Measurement	240
Hitte	Cites data for digesting refuse and sewage sludge of 110 1 CH_4/kg refuse and sludge, recalculated assuming wet sludge is negligible	Lab Measurement	210
Pfeffer	Digested refuse at 8% solids, 35°C, 30 day solids ret. time	Lab Measurement	260
Schwegler	370 ft³/lb refuse destroyed, assumes refuse 50% decomposable	"Estimated"	190
Hekimian, et al	"Observed" value for L.A. area	"Estimate"	47
Alpern	Typical Municipal refuse		530

Total Gas (CO_2 and CH_4) Production From Municipal Refuse

Authors	Conditions		Gas Production, l/kg Refuse as Received
City of Los Angeles	Theoretical extrapolation of measured values	Theoretical/ Measurements in Landfill	390
Bowerman, et al	510 l/kg dry refuse, recalculated based on 0.25 kg org. C/kg dry refuse	Theoretical	400
Blanchet	Calculated from landfill test and theoretical extrapolation over 10 years	Measurement/ Theoretical	130
VTN Consolidated, Inc.	"Estimate" for Los Angeles landfills		47
Merz	Refuse in small lysimeters, wetted with digester supernatant	Measurement	13
Merz & Stone	Lysimeter, gas production very low at end of 2-1/2 year study	Measurement	4.1
Rovers & Farquhar	Lysimeter, gas pro. continuing at low level at end of 200-day study	Measurement	3.2
Streng	Lysimeter, gas prod. over approximately 2 years, continuing	Measurement	39
Chian	Small lysimeters, cell 4 only one producing CH_4, gas prod. low after 300 days, recalculated	Measurement	0.47

Small volumes of refuse have been decomposed in containers and the gases measured, but the problem of simulating not only average landfill conditions but also the variations in conditions brought about by climatic events makes the application of such data to full-scale landfills difficult. Many such studies are useless as far as methane production is concerned, because methane production was never achieved. In some cases insufficient time was allowed, but in other cases stable methane production was not obtained, for some unexplained reason.

Summarizing data available in the U.S. on total gas generation from refuse during methane formation reveals higher gas production values based on theoretical rather than measurement approaches. The reason, simply, is that complete decomposition takes a very long time and, in fact, is never attained in practice. One way to avoid this problem is to relate gas production to the amount of refuse actually decomposed (e.g., volatile solids or organic carbon lost) and leave it to the user of the data to determine how much decomposition will be of interest for the particular application or landfill of concern.

Theoretical gas production is approximately 440 l/kg refuse for complete decomposition by methane formers and their associated microbiological coworkers. Variations are due primarily to waste composition differences. Consideration of the decomposability of various waste fractions reduces total gas production to 120-310 l/kg.

The highest measured amounts of gas are produced in digesters in which seeding with sewage sludge; mixing to provide uniformity of conditions, substrate, and nutrients; and control of variables such as temperature, time, and moisture content are practiced to various degrees to promote methane formation. These results may be practical for controlled decomposition of wastes in specially built digesters designed for that purpose, but they are not applicable to landfill conditions except, possibly, as a goal which will probably prove unrealistic even for specially designed and operated landfills.

The most common approach to estimating total gas production entails looking at the available information and estimating a reasonable value for the case in question. One rule of thumb often cited reasons that 370 l/kg is approximately the maximum theoretical gas production from refuse, of which half will not be generated because of imperfections in the various decompositional processes, resulting in incomplete decomposition.

Of this, another half will be lost because it is not produced during the period of active decomposition when gas recovery would be most likely. Finally, only half of that amount will be feasible to recover because the remainder is produced near landfill boundaries or between withdrawal wells, etc., and will, therefore, be lost. The result is that only 47 l/kg refuse is said to be recoverable.

GAS COMPOSITION

Gas composition data is much easier to determine and is, therefore, more readily available than is data on gas production. Figures vary widely, but gas composition in landfills has been recorded from zero to 70% methane and from zero to 90% carbon dioxide. Purely aerobic decomposition should produce equal moles of carbon dioxide as were moles of oxygen consumed, so, theoretically, any carbon dioxide concentration higher than 20% indicates that processes other than aerobic decomposition are involved.

However, carbon dioxide concentrations less than 20% do not necessarily indicate that only aerobic decomposition is occurring. The high solubility of carbon dioxide in water lowers the carbon dioxide concentration in the gas as more moisture is added. During methane formation, carbon dioxide concentrations range generally from 40 to 50%.

The methane concentration is affected more strongly by particular landfill characteristics than is the carbon dioxide concentration, reflecting the narrow range of landfill conditions suitable to methane formers. The methane concentration is normally within the 50 to 70% range with the most common values generally in the 55% range. Variations in methane concentration are often caused by the specific composition of the refuse components being degraded at a particular time, and by carbon dioxide solubility. The importance of refuse composition is illustrated by substituting the elemental analysis of the paper and fat fractions into the equation for methanogenic decomposition. This indicates that the gas produced from paper degradation will be basically 51% methane and 49% carbon dioxide; whereas, from fats, the gas

composition will be 71% methane and 29% carbon dioxide.

RATE OF GAS PRODUCTION

The wide range in decomposibility of matter present in refuse suggests immediately that no simple equation or rate constant will describe adequately the rate of decomposition, or the rate of methane generation, for a landfill. It is clear that readily decomposable substances like sugar and starches will not decompose over the same period as will cellulose.

Since refuse contains materials of such widely differing characteristic rates of decomposition, it is logical to attempt to consider each component individually, using the first order kinetic expression and appropriate constant or half-life values to describe its rate of decomposition independent of the other components. The total landfill decomposition is then described by summing the decomposition of all of the components of interest.

One can divide the organic portion of municipal wastes into three categories grossly described as readily decomposable, moderately decomposable, and, for all practical purposes, non-decomposable. Food wastes are readily decomposable, constitute approximately 12% of the wet weight of refuse and, in absence of data, may be assumed to have a half-life of one year, for example. Similarly, paper, wood, grass, brush, greens, leaves, oils, and paints may be considered moderately decomposable, comprise 57.2% of the refuse on a wet weight basis, and may be assumed to have a half-life of 15 years, for example. Other organic materials, such as plastics, leather, rubber, and rags, are assumed to be undegradable.

Using the overall formula for gas generation for each component (paper, grass, fats, etc.), the amount of gas produced ultimately by the moderately decomposable portion will be 370 l/kg wet refuse which will be 51% methane, and the readily decomposable portion will produce 59 l/kg wet refuse, which will be 64% methane. These totals can be proportioned over the life of the decomposition process using the assumed half-life values and assuming first order kinetics.

There are many assumptions and errors associated with this theoretical approach. The generation rate as calculated represents a maximum value, which may be considerably in error, especially in the early and late years in a landfill decomposition cycle when decomposition products other than methane may become important. One modification of the basic method is to assume a rate of attainment of methane formation conditions to describe the early transition of a landfill to methanogenic decomposition. This reduces the effect of initial portions of the curve, in which very high methane generation rates are shown.

There are other ways by which the rate of gas production may be estimated. These are summarized in the gas production table.

The values given in the table suggest that both from test and full-scale landfill data, a reasonable rate of generation is 3.1 to up to 37 l/kg per year for refuse as received during the more active period of methane production. The range is explained in part by the decompositional age of the refuse at the time of monitoring for gas production rate, by seasonal or climatic variations, involving primarily moisture content, and, to a lesser extent, temperature variations. Values outside this range are generally explainable by unusual refuse composition, lack of formation of a mature methanogenic decomposition process, or very dry refuse.

The period over which methane is produced is unknown. Theoretically, decomposable matter will degrade in a landfill for an infinite period, but, obviously, a point will be reached in practice when so little decomposition takes place that methane production will effectively cease. All of the studies cited cover such a short period of time that little can be said regarding the period of methane production. Several of the lysimeter and test landfill studies did, apparently, extend over the period of active methane production, as production rates were declining or had stopped altogether by the end of the monitoring period. Such studies, however, are probably not representative of full-scale landfills, where methane generation appears to occur over periods much longer than that monitored for the lysimeter or test landfill studies. Those entries which project methane production over a period of time generally assume a period of active methane production on the order of 10 years, which corresponds with the experience of the author.

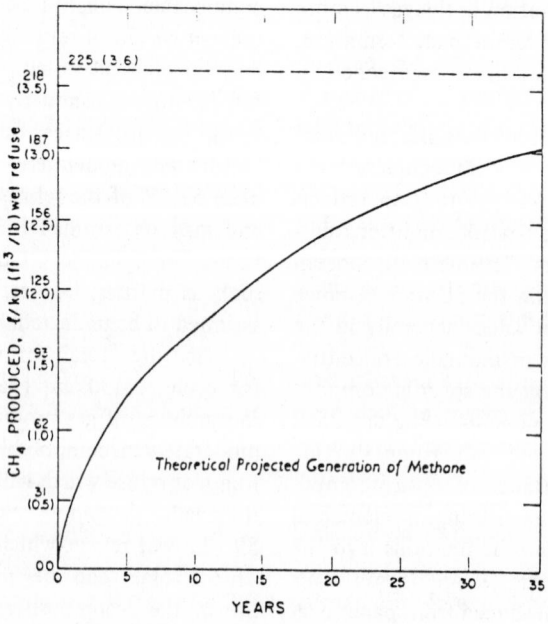

Figure 1.

4-21 The Status of the Pompano Beach Project

Peter J. Ware
Source: Paper Presented at the American Institute of Chemical Engineers, 72nd Annual Conference, San Francicso, California, November 29, 1979, 16 pp. Reprinted with Permission of the Author.

In 1975, the U.S. Department of Energy (formerly ERDA) awarded Waste Management, Inc. a contract to design and construct a "proof-of-concept" experimental facility to demonstrate the biological gasification of urban solid waste and sewage sludge to produce methane-rich gas. Named RefCOM, (Refuse Conversion to Methane) the facility will process between 45 and 90 metric tons per day of shredded urban refuse.

Construction of the facility was completed by May 1st, 1978, and was followed by a six-month start-up phase. The plant has been in daily operation since November, 1978, and is being run in accordance with a predetermined experimental program which will be of two-to-four years' duration.

The Department of Energy (DOE), has other programs underway which support the experimental program at Pompano Beach. These include mixing experiments comparing gas and mechanical agitation, methods for recovering energy from the resultant sludge material, and feedstock preparation by means of high pressure steam explosion. Additional parallel research is proceeding in developing separation systems to separate the methane from the carbon dioxide to render commercially saleable streams. As information is developed in these ancillary projects, the experimental program at Pompano Beach may be modified to incorporate the developments.

Project Background

Recent forecasts of steadily declining supplies of clean fossil fuels have focused attention on the need for development of renewable energy resources. The conversion of biomass (i.e., the organic fraction of urban solid wastes, agricultural residues, and terrestrial and marine energy crops) to synthetic fuels, is such a resource.

Bench-scale studies and analysis by Dr. John T. Pfeffer, of the University of Illinois, Urbana campus, sponsored by the Environmental Protection Agency and the National Science Foundation, under the Research Applied to National Needs (RANN) program, indicated that methane gas produced by anaerobic fermentation of the organic fraction of refuse could be competitive with alternate sources of natural gas. Dr. Pfeffer conducted a series of experiments primarily using refuse-derived fuel (RDF) from St. Louis. Those experiments indicated that 0.057 to 0.07 cubic meters of gas could be produced per kilogram of volatile solids added at mesophilic temperatures (38°C) and with 10 to 30 day sludge retention times. Pfeffer's positive findings led NSF to fund two additional studies: The first by the MITRE Corporation, was a program assessment leading to a recommendation that the next scale of facility should be a 45 to 90 metric ton-per-day plant. The second was an economic and sensitivity analysis of the process by the Dynatech Corporation who developed a preliminary design and an economic model for a full-scale (1000 tons-per-day) digestion plant.

Their economic computations indicated that urban waste methanation would prove technically feasible at a cost competitive with available sources of natural gas. Most of the equipment necessary for operational scale-up of the laboratory benchtop experiments upon which these preliminary designs and cost estimates were based, appeared to be adaptable from other industrial processes, and the investigation had reached the point where pricing of construction and operation of a practical size scale-up was necessary to determine acutal production, purification and distribution prices.

Based on the favorable findings of these two reports, a request for competitive proposals to construct a 45 to 90 metric ton-per-day proof-of-concept plant was issued in March, 1975 by the Energy Research and Development Agency, who had by then assumed the NSF program. Twenty bids were received. The contract was awarded to Waste Management, Inc. (WMI) of Oak Brook, Illinois in June, 1975.

Proof-of-Concept

The generation of pipeline quality gas, if economically viable, will have certain advantages over low-BTU gas or solid fuel products. These advantages include an established market, established transmission and distribution facilities, available combustion technology and an environmentally preferred fuel. As a precursor to commercialization of urban waste methanation, however, a proof-of-concept experiment is needed. This is usually conducted at a "pilot" or "semi-commericial" facility.

The U.S. Department of Energy funded a "proof-of-concept" plant of 90 TPD scale because several process and engineering factors have to be studied before large-scale commercial exploitation of the system can be undertaken. The largest studies to date have been in 0.38 cubic meter fermenters, where the daily refuse feed varied from 2.25 to 4.5 kilograms.

The specific goals of the solid waste to methane proof-of-concept projects are:

1. To establish information concerning the gas product quantities and values.
2. To evaluate process reliability and economics.
3. To determine optimum design and operation parameter values for each process stage and method of operation.
4. To establish a basis for comparing the process to other means of energy production and/or resource recovery from urban waste.
5. To establish the technological and economic bases for commercial utilization of the process.

Site Location

The project is located at an existing facility of Waste Management, Inc. known as the Solid Waste Reduction Center, located in Pompano Beach, Florida. Pompano Beach is a community of about 40,000 inhabitants, situated 16 kilometers north of Ft. Lauderdale in Broward County, Florida.

The Solid Waste Reduction Center, its support services, and adjacent shredded landfill were dedicated in September, 1971. When it went into service, it was the first privately owned and operated facility of its type in the nation. The existing facility consists of a receiving area, including a tipping floor and two receiving pit conveyors, each feeding a vertical-shaft hammermill. One of these units is rated at 13.5 tons per hour, while the other, installed in late 1978, processes 58.5 tons per hour. The combined discharge of these two machines is fed to load-out facilities, from where it is transferred to landfill via high capacity, live bottom trailers. Other existing facilities located at Pompano Beach site include district refuse collection offices, collection equipment maintenance and storage facilities, and a container maintenance shop.

The Microbiological Process

Anaerobic (living in the absence of oxygen) and facultative (living either in the presence or absence of oxygen) bacteria decompose organic material into simpler compounds. The principal products of this process are methane and carbon dioxide. This gas appears naturally as swamp gas in marshy areas, and is the normal product of similar action occurring in sanitary landfills where municipal solid waste and/or sewage sludge is buried.

The process, essentially in three stages, is complex and not totally understood. In the first stage, cellulose and other complex organic compounds are broken down to simple sugars and soluble monomers. In the second stage, a different group of bacteria convert the simple sugars to organic acids, such as acetic and propionic acid. In the third stage, the organic acids are further degraded by yet another group of bacteria, to methane and carbon dioxide.

Design and Construction

Since the in-house capability of Waste Management, Inc. at that time lay primarily in the area of waste collection, transportation and disposal by landfill, Jacobs Constructors, Inc. was retained to execute the detailed mechanical design under WMI supervision, and to manage the construction phase.

Design and construction of the facility was completed in April, 1978, at a final cost of $3.6 million. In addition to normal construction changes and delays associated with any project, complications of this effort included uncertainties in design specifications, changes in subcontract bid packages, and complexities of federal procurement regulations. Problems with engineering management and construction supervision contributed to cost escalation.

Project Schedule Milestones

Award of Proof-of-Concept
Contract   June 23, 1975
Start Construction   February 2, 1977
Complete Construction   April 31, 1978
Complete Start-up (Start Experimental
Program)   November 1, 1978
Complete Program (Current 25 Month
Schedule)   May 31, 1980

Project Budgets
A – Design and Construction

Engineering (Jacobs)	$1,150,000
Equipment	923,000
Construction	2,318,000
Project Management	144,000
Contingency	115,000
Sub-Total	$3,651,000

B – Operations (Proposed Estimate)

Start-Up	$ 396,000
1st Year Balance (1978)	324,000
2nd Year (1979 and to May 1980)	1,476,000
Sub-Total	$2,296,000
Project-Total	$5,847,000

TECHNOLOGY

Process Discription

Briefly, the process consists of the shredding of the urban waste, composed at this plant predominantly of residential waste collected in the local Broward County area, delivered by standard packer trucks to a tipping floor at a rate of over 1000 tons per day. From the tipping floor, the waste processed through the vertical shredders to a nominal 3-in. size and ferrous metal is removed by an electro-magnet. This portion of the facility is owned and operated by Waste Management, Inc., without cost to the proof-of-concept RefCOM plant. The shredded, ferrous-free waste is then split with the bulk transmitted to the sanitary landfill and, depending on the experiment performed, 45-90 tons/day are placed in a storage building for further use in the RefCOM process. The storage building with a maximum capacity of 360 tons of nominal 0.0762 meter size waste serves as a surge system to match the 7/day week RefCOM operation to the 5 1/2 day/week primary shredding operation. An articulating front-end loader is utilized to transfer the shredded material from the surge pile into a 9 tons/hr. capacity pan conveyor for metering to the processing line.

From the storage building, the waste material is fed to a classification building for preprocessing and then to two digesters for biological gasification. In the classification process, the shredded waste passes through a trommel screen to remove inorganic grit and fines, such as glass, silica sands, ash, etc. The material then undergoes secondary shredding to achieve a smaller particle size, and air classification, to separate the light organic fraction from the heavy, generally inorganic fraction.

The light material, which in other resource recovery systems is sometimes referred to as Refuse Derived Fuel, (RDF) is often used as is. In this system it is introduced into a pre-mix tank where it is blended with sewage sludge, recycled filtrate water, nutrients and steam for temperature control. This slurry is then metered into two mechanically agitated anerobic digesters in which the biological (bacterial) process converts approximately 50 per cent methane and 50 percent carbon dioxide. In full-scale commercial operations, this gas can then be upgraded to pipeline quality, using demonstrated gas clean-up or purification techniques. The gas is currently being flared to atmosphere for disposal, but WMI has plans to install a pathological (hospital) waste incineration facility to service the Broward County area, which will utilize approximately 30% of the maximum gas production as auxiliary fuel.

The anticipated optimum digester process conditions will be five days detention and 60°C. The digester residue is dewatered, and the water so separated is recycled back to the digesters as make-up for the feed slurry. Feed solids concentrations on the order of 10 percent are contemplated. The dewatered residue — occupying only 30 percent of the volume of raw refuse — is relatively stable, and can be deposited in a landfill or burned to a sterile ash with the process heat recovered for use in the operation of the digesters. Expected fuel consumption for these conditions is of the order of 15 percent of total gas production, so further energy recovery of this type is highly desirable.

Laboratory — scale studies performed to date by Dr. John Pfeffer of the University of Illinois, who is also technical consultant on this project, indicate that approximately 190 cubic meters of mixed methane and carbon dioxide gas are produced per input of ton of raw refuse; thus, 95 cubic meters of methane (equivalent to pipeline quality gas) per input ton could be produced by this process. Based on an average home gas consumption of 2831 cubic feet per year, a 1,000 ton-per-day plant could serve the gas needs of over 11,000 homes.

Plant Capacity (See attached flow sheet — Figure 1)

The facility is designed to operate within the range of 50–100 tons-per-day.

Most of the project experiments center on the digester performance. Since they are designed to run with a fixed volume, variation of process conditions, such as residence time and solids loading will vary the actual throughput within this range.

Experimental Program

A detailed experimental program has been developed for the facility to evaluate, in phases, several independent variables. The most significant areas to be studeid are: (1) methane production per unit of organic solids fed (2) reduction in solids remaining for ultimate disposal (3) mixing characteristics of the reactor slurry (5) process stability (6) energy requirements for operation, and (7) chemical costs for nutrients and pH control.

The various phases of experimentation will include determination of optimum fermentation temperatures (mesophilic and thermophilic), evaluation of feed preparation, evaluation of feed solid concentration and residue recycle, evaluation of pH and nutrient requirements, residue dewatering, and residue disposal.

The schedule of these activities is attached as Exhibit 2.

OPERATIONS

Start-up

The initial phase was necessary to familiarize the operating personnel with the various subsystems, to check out equipment under load, and to initiate the anaerobic digesters. This included familiarization with the controls, pumps, and valves, with the biochemical requirements such as pH, temperature, and nutrients, and finally with the proposed experimental program. During this period, the digesters were filled and anaerobic fermentation established in a suitable substrate using primary sewage sludge. This allowed final testing of the performance of all equipment and also allowed the operators to

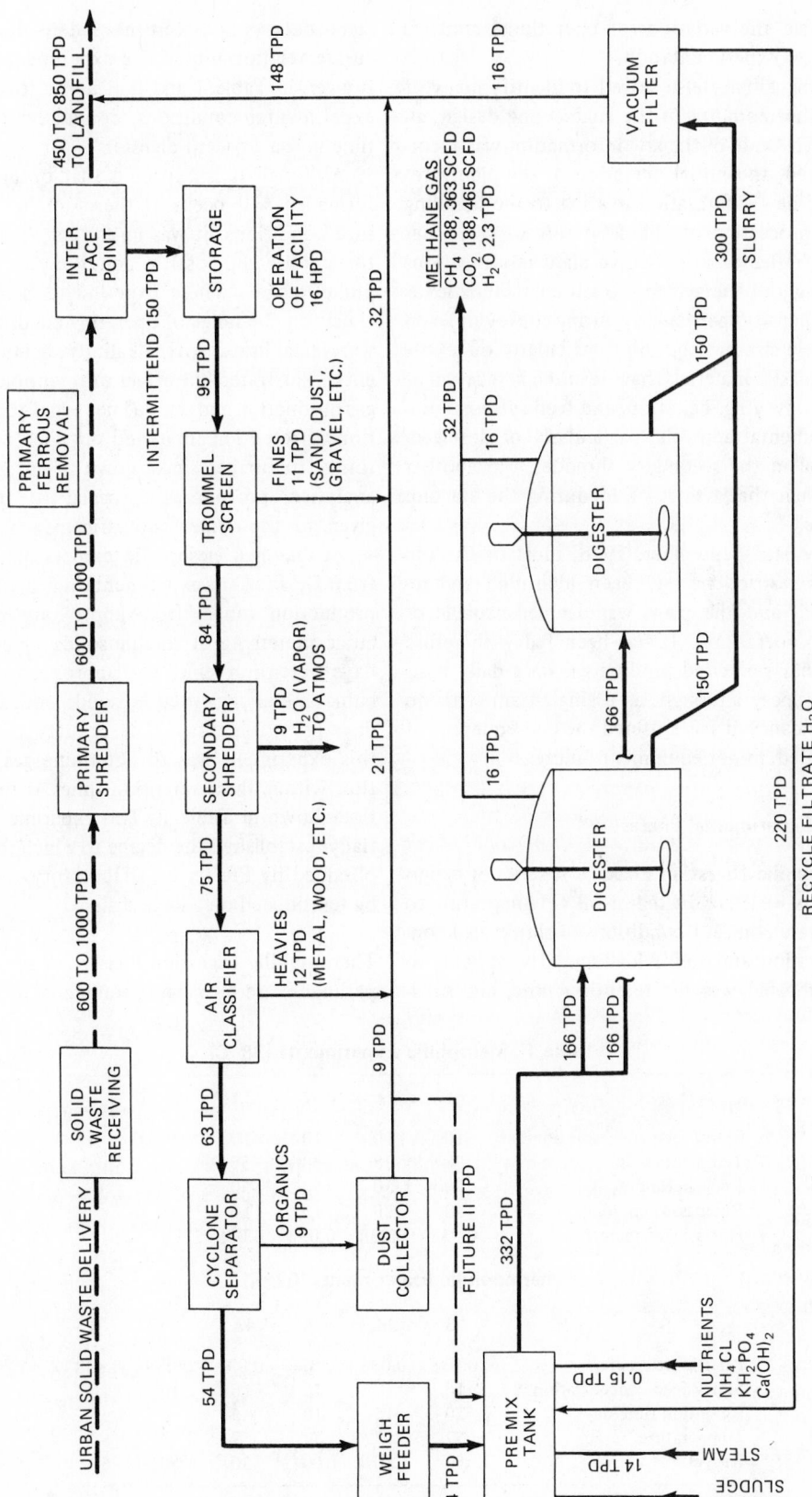

Figure 1.

practice the variations of operational controls prior to experimentation.

This activity also served to identify many of the shortcomings of the engineering design; although 'state-of-the-art' information was incorporated, the initial operation of the plant provided new information relating to the handling and processing of shredded refuse which has been reflected in extensive plant modifications throughout the system. Such characteristics as bulk density (particularly during conveying), and particle size-distribution (particularly of textile and plastic materials) have resulted in redesign of the conveying, agitation, and feed systems. Environmental controls, particularly of dust generated in the secondary shredder, was another problem that was resolved during the start-up phase.

By late September, 1978, most of the obvious restrictions had been identified and resolved, and the plant was deemed capable of daily operation. It has been fed with refuse and has generated product gas on a daily basis ever since, although, as a single-train with no redundancy it has suffered the consequences of repeated, minor equipment failures.

The Experimental Phases

Mesophilic Digestion Phase. A series of experiments were conducted at 38°C temperature to evaluate constant conditions of slurry feed concentration and solids loading. The variable to be adjusted was the retention time, and suffi-

cient data points were needed to develop accurate relationships. The experimental matrix is given in Table 1 and indicates a total of four experimental conditions, conducted two at a time in the adjacent digesters.

Although it is expected that optimum performance will occur at thermophilic temperature conditions, it was important, nonetheless, to establish the baseline condition at the mesophilic range. These experiments served as a check on the range of operating conditions that were established (pH, alkalinity, acidity, nutrients), illustrated the effect of retention time on gas production and showed net benefits as a function of retention time, and provided an opportunity to further shake down the total system analytical procedures. Special attention was given to the degree and efficiency of mixing.

At the 38°C mesophilic temperature, the data from Dr. Pfeffer's experiments indicated that gas production ranges from approximately 0.057 cubic meters/kg of volatile solids added for 10 days retention time to approximately 0.07 cubic meters/kg volatile solids added for 30 days retention time. The primary purpose of this experiment was to determine gas production within these retention times at the condition shown in Table 1. This experiment, essentially, established the degree to which the results obtained by Pfeffer on a laboratory scale could be reproduced on a large scale.

Thermophilic Digestion Phase. A series of experiments are now being conducted at the ther-

Table 1. Mesophilic Experiments (38°C)

	1	1A	2	2A
Slurry feed concentration %	10	10	10	10
Temperature °C	38	38	38	38
Recycle Rate %	50	50	50	50
Retention time/days	30	20	15	10
Particle size/meters	0.038	0.038	0.038	0.038

Thermophilic Experiments (57°C)

	3	3A	4	4A	5	6
Particle size/meters	0.038	0.038	0.038	0.038	0.038	0.038
Slurry feed concentration %	10	10	10	10	10	10
Retention time/days	20	15	10	5	5	5
Temperature °C	57	57	57	57	54	60
Recycle %	50	50	50	50	50	50

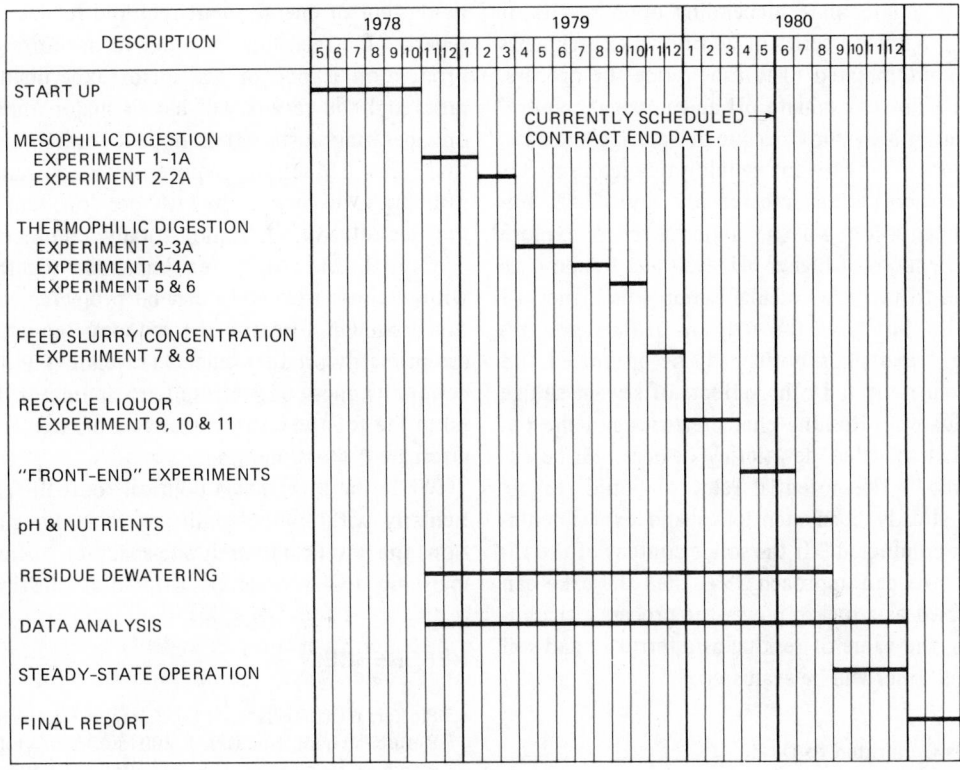

Figure 2.

mophilic temperature range of 55°C to 60°C at various retention times. Constant conditions of size, slurry feed concentration, and recycle will be maintained.

Other Experiments

Having evaluated the performance of the system at thermophilic levels, under constant conditions, various changes in other process variables will be effected to evaluate the system response.

Experiments 7 and 8 will consider feed slurry concentration at higher levels:

Table 2. Feed Slurry Concentration Experiment

	Experiments	
	7	8
Particle size/meters	0.038	0.038
Retention time/days	5	5
Temperature	60°C	60°C
Recycle %	50	50
Feed slurry concentrate %	15	20

Remaining experiments will address the impact of varying recycle ratios of the final filtrate liquor into the process:

Table 3. Recycle Ratios

	9	10	11
Size/inches	0.038	0.038	0.038
Slurry concentration	15	15	15
Retention time/days	5	5	5
Temperature	60°C	60°C	60°C
*Recycle %	50	60	Maximum

* % of make-up water from recycle liquor.

A concurrent series of experiments will be carried out throughout the experimental phase to explore the effect of particle size on the process. At the optimum conditions established, the particle size will be increased to 70% minus 0.08 meters. Following this experiment and attainment of steady state conditions, we will undertake an evaluation of unit operations of the air classifier and the trommel screen.

At a later date, depending upon results of the program, a series of additional experiments are contemplated to further refine the process. These are to evaluate pH and nutrient requirements and to study residue dewatering and uses. Increased activity for cellulolytic organisms has been reported at increased pH (up to 7.5). Experimentation will be undertaken to explore the benefits of higher pH levels and to compare them to the costs of maintaining the higher pH levels. Similarly, the addition of nutrients (nitrogen and phosphorus) will be optimized and the nutrient and other effects of sewage sludge evaluated. Residue characteristics and the potential of other dewatering devices will be explored. The potential value of liquid recycle has already been mentioned and experimentation conducted. If the solids content of the filter cake can approach 35%, then the cake can be used as a fuel to power the process. In addition, the value of residue as a fertilizer and soil conditioner will be evaluated.

Data Generated to Date

As of the date of this paper, only experiments 1 and 2 have been completed. The data is both extensive and complete, but, of course, can serve only as a baseline for current and future experiments, rather than predict optimum conditions.

Process Economics

The RefCOM program is still at least one year away from generating definitive engineering from which a 1000 ton per day facility could be scaled.

Furthermore, operating conditions at thermophilic ranges are speculative. Determining the extent of energy input required to size and separate the feedstock in order to optimize gas production is one of the major experimental tasks and the results will have a major impact on operating costs. It is hoped, for example, that size reduction requirements (currently utilizing in excess of 20 kwh per ton) can be drastically reduced, if not totally eliminated.

Capital and labor requirements, together with maintenance costs can be projected, but the dominant forces in the economic equation are primarily product (energy) revenues and the competitiveness of the resultant tipping or disposal fee for the refuse material compared with alternate disposal methods.

While the former is a political football (particularly with the possibility of price deregulation) the latter is intensely site-specific. Accordingly, no definitive data is offered at this time.

REFERENCES

1. Pfeffer, J.T., "Reclamation of Energy from Organic Refuse," Grant No. EPA-R-80076, Office of Research & Monitoring, U.S. Environmental Protection Agency, National Environmental Research Center, Cincinnati, Ohio (April, 1973).
2. Pfeffer, J.T., and Liebman, J.C., "Biological Conversion of Organic Refuse to Methane," Progress Reports (July, 1973-June, 1974), NSF Grant GL-39191 (July, 1974), January, September, 1975.
3. Kispert, R.G., et al., "Fuel Gas Production from Solid Waste," Final Report, NSF Contract C-827 (January 31, 1975).
4. Bisselle, C., et al., "Urban Trash Methanation Background for a Proof-of-Concept-Experiment," NSF-RA-N-75-002 (February, 1975).
5. University of Miami, Proposal, "Characterization and Environmental Investigation of ERDA's Anaerobic Digestion Facility at Pompano Beach, FL."
6. Walter, D.K., Rines, C., "Status – Refuse Conversion to Methane (RefCOM)," (December, 1978).

4-22 Co-disposal: A Practical Approach to Integrated Waste Management

Richard A. Baldwin, et al

Source: *NCRR Bulletin,* Vol. 9, No. 3 (September 1979) pp. 64–69. Reprinted with Permission of National Center for Resource Recovery.

The concept of codisposal is based on the idea that the simultaneous disposal of solid waste and wastewater treatment sludges can be more efficient under proper circumstances than two separate disposal activities. Interest in the concept has increased as the volume of sludge has grown with more widespread sewage treatment, and as landfill has become a less obvious disposal method in many areas for both solid waste and sludge. At present, it appears that codisposal has entered a new, more promising stage. A number of recent events mark this passage:

- The U.S. Environmental Protection Agency's (EPA) decision to provide Construction Grant funding to the wastewater treatment project now being planned in Memphis, Tenn., which will utilize refuse-derived fuel (RDF) as a fuel in multiple-hearth pyrolysis of sludge. (This is not the first codisposal project to receive EPA funding; projects in Duluth, Minn., and Glen Cove, N.Y., have also received grants. However, the Memphis decision is distinctive because it represents EPA's acceptance of this technology.)
- EPA's recent publication of a draft memorandum analyzing funding policy options for multiple purpose projects such as codisposal. (These options generally make codisposal more attractive than under previous funding schemes.)
- EPA's forthcoming regulations for hazardous waste disposal under the Resource Conservation and Recovery Act of 1976

(RCRA). (It is expected that land disposal of sludge will be more closely controlled than at present. Under other legislation, deadlines have already been set to stop ocean dumping of sludge.)

Table 1 presents a listing of communities currently committed to codisposal projects. In addition, of the 63 resource recovery Urban Grant applications funded by EPA this year, four are pursuing codisposal as their primary approach; many of the other recipients are investigating it as an alternative. With this level of interest, it is appropriate to undertake a brief review of the concept as it stands today.

TECHNOLOGY OVERVIEW

Codisposal can be accomplished in various ways, although there are three basic approaches: landfilling, composting, and thermal destruction. Thermal destruction is the focus of this overview, since it is most compatible with resource recovery and affords significant opportunities for avoiding problems associated with land application.

Four methods of thermal destruction appear promising:

- RDF use in multiple-hearth or fluidized-bed sludge incinerators;
- Sludge in MSW incinerators;
- Sludge in MSW dedicated boilers; and
- Sludge in MSW starved-air combustors.

Table 1. Planned Codisposal Facilities.

Location and Description	Projected Cost (millions)	Status
Ansonia, Conn. About 40 TPD of solid waste and 12.5 TPD dry sludge have been combusted in a retrofitted, refractory lined incinerator. The sludge is dried by passing it through a spray drier which used furnace flue gases.		Stopped operations in 1977 following a shredder explosion. Air pollution equipment being upgraded at this time.
Auburn, Maine. A 150 TPD starved-air combustion system is being designed to accept 10 TPD of dry sludge from the area sewage treatment operation. The sludge will be received and handled separately for controlled feeding and drying prior to being coincinerated. The facility is to produce steam for sale to local industry for process use.	$ 3.5	Groundbreaking sheduled for August 1979. Inclusion of sludge subject to results of ongoing design study by Consumat and City engineering consultants.
Contra Costa County, Calif. About 1,200 TPD of garbage will be processed into 600 TPD of RDF and burned with 96 TPD of sludge in multiple hearth incinerators in the pyrolysis mode.	$50.0	Facility plan completed.
Duluth, Minn. About 70 TPD of dry sludge will be burned in a fluidized bed sludge incinerator using 160 TPD of RDF as the auxiliary fuel source. Because the amount of RDF produced will exceed the amount required for sludge burning, other markets for the excess RDF are being sought. Ferrous metals will be recovered and steam will be used to run the processing facility.	$21.7	Under construction. Expected to start up in Fall 1979.
Glen Cove, N.Y. About 175 TPD of garbage and 25 TPD of sludge (20 percent solids) will be coburned in a garbage incinerator. Waste heat from the incinerator will be used to produce power for the waste-water treatment plant. Ferrous metals will be recovered from the ash.	$10.0	Construction delayed pending further EPA reviews.
Harrisburg, Pa. Some steam from an existing garbage-burning waterwall incinerator will be used to dry sludge to 15 percent solids. The sludge will then be burned with the garbage. The incinerator can process 720 TPD of garbage and 49 TPD of sludge. Ferrous metals recovery is planned.	$ 4.7	Under construction. Estimated completion in October 1979.
Memphis, Tenn. RDF production with ferrous metals recovery. RDF and sludge will be burned in multiple hearth incinerators in the pyrolysis mode. Steam will will be sold to nearby industries. The plant capacity is 2,400 TPD of garbage and 1,225 TPD of sludge.	$140.0	Independent engineering and economic review being undertaken by city. Final decision to proceed to be made in Fall 1979.
Wilmington, Del. About 70 TPD of dry sewage sludge will be composted with RDF. Only a fraction of the 1000 TPD of MSW processed will be composted, and the remainder will be burned in a dedicated boiler. The project is being designed and constructed by Raytheon Service Co.	$51	Ground breaking is expected in September 1979.

Source: General Accounting Office codisposal report and personal communication.

Codisposal in a Multiple-Hearth or Fluidized-Bed Sludge Incinerator

This approach has been the focus of much interest. EPA has funded a demonstration project in Contra Costa County, Calif. Major projects are also planned or under construction for Duluth, Minn., and Memphis, Tenn.

For traditional sludge disposal, multiple-hearth and fluidized-bed furnaces burn oil to dry the dewatered sludge (20–40 percent solids) to the point of selfsustaining combustion. For co-disposal, the system is essentially the same except that processed municipal solid waste (MSW) is used as the fuel. Raw MSW must be passed through an RDF processing train to produce three-to-six-inch particles. Processed refuse and dewatered sludge can be mixed prior to injection or fed separately into the furnace. The rate of mixing depends upon moisture content, heat value and other variables; but it appears that 2.5 or 3 parts RDF to one part sludge will work well.

In incoming air is reduced below stoichiometric proportions, the incinerator will operate as a pyrolysis reactor. The resulting gas has a heat value of up to 130 BTU per standard dry cubic foot (sdcf) and is suitable for combustion for energy recovery. This mode of multiple-hearth furnace operation has been pilot tested for one month at the Contra Costa project.

Fluidized-bed codisposal has also been successfully demonstrated at the Black Clawson hydra-pulping facility in Franklin, Ohio. Start-up and shake-down is about to begin on a 400 ton-per-day (TPD) fluid-bed facility of this type in Duluth.

Existing multiple-hearth furnaces (MHF) and fluidized-bed furnaces (FBF) can be retrofitted to accommodate RDF. The feed system must be adapted to RDF and the air emissions equipment must be modified to handle different and increased off-gas volumes. The Contra Costa facility was a retrofit application and several major MHF and FBF manufacturers (notably Nichols, Envirotech and Dorr-Oliver) feel that their furnaces can be adapted to codisposal.

Sludge in MSW Waterwall Combustion Furnace

Experience in Europe has shown that coincineration in a waterwall furnace is feasible. Prepro-cessing of the MSW is not required. Sludge can be pumped or trucked to the incinerator site as a liquid, then dewatered (20 percent solids) and fed into a steam-heated drier. At 85 percent solids, it is then fired in the combustion chamber. According to one manufacturer, this process can effect a net energy gain.

The refuse-to-sludge ratio in this case is influenced more by practical and economic, rather than technical, considerations. Sludge drying is usually a net consumer of steam, and reductions in steam output from any large scale resource recovery facility would have to be carefully planned. Only ratios greater than 10 parts of MSW to one part of sludge have substantial energy recovery potential.

Sludge in MSW Dedicated Boilers

Dedicated boiler systems, where incoming MSW is processed into RDF prior to combustion, are gaining popularity as an MSW disposal option. Large new facilities are being constructed in Akron, Ohio, and Niagara Falls, N.Y. While neither of these facilities currently plans to include sludge disposal, dedicated boilers are definitely compatible with codisposal. The most significant differences between this system and the waterwall system lie in the higher costs and greater revenue potential of the dedicated boiler, both of which relate to the higher energy transfer efficiencies of the semi-suspension combustion unit.

Sludge in MSW Starved-Air Combustors

This approach differs from other waste incinerators options in both scale and technology. According to systems vendors, codisposal is viable. However, one consideration for codisposal in modular starved-air combustor systems is that the fairly low energy transfer efficiency of the combustion unit would lower the optimum refuse-to-sludge ratio. Thus, the amount of energy left over from sludge drying would also be less than for waterwall systems. In Auburn, Maine, a 150 TPD system of this type is being considered. A design feasibility study, currently underway, will determine whether the concept will be included in the final design and construction.

From a technological standpoint, thermal codisposal is generally a viable process, although it cannot yet be considered ready for an off-the-shelf label. Many of the remaining questions concerning codisposal technology are based on environmental issues. The primary concerns are potential problems with air emission and leachate from the landfilling of combustion residue materials.

ECONOMICS OF CODISPOSAL

By combining disposal operations, codisposal also integrates the economics of resource recovery and wastewater treatment. In resource recovery, the economic objective is to maximize net project revenues, where the costs of constructing, owning and operating the facility are offset by revenues available from tipping fees, sale of recovered materials and sale of recovered energy. The "bottom line" should be a financially self-sufficient facility with a tipping fee that is lower than any other feasible alternative. In general, these facilities must produce sufficient financial returns to liquidate their entire capital debt.

Wastewater treatment, on the other hand, generally produces no revenues apart from the user charges levied within the system. These charges must be sufficient to cover all current costs, as well as to repay the local share of debt incurred to construct the system. The federal share of capital costs need not be repaid, as grant funds are available from EPA to cover a sizeable part of the costs of treatment plant planning, design and construction.

Depending on the scale of the project, codisposal can bring together the revenues available from materials/energy recovery and the grant financing available for waste-water treatment projects. For example, where RDF is used as fuel in a multiple-hearth or fluid-bed sludge incinerator, it is possible that the wastewater treatment plant can generate enough energy to supply some of its own needs or even be an energy exporter. At the least, using RDF as a fuel can help to avoid the rapid increase in fossil fuel costs for sludge incineration.

Where sludge is to be burned in a large-scale MSW resource recovery facility, the service of

sludge disposal becomes another source of revenue to the facility, as does the sale of steam to dry the sludge. Further, the capital costs of sludge transport, dewatering and drying can be borne in part by EPA grant funding.

Relative Costs of Codisposal

In codisposal, the same objective is sought by both the solid waste and the sewage treatment agencies: to carry out their disposal operations at the lowest cost. Unfortunately, there is a lack of empirical cost data for planning and comparing codisposal options. However, the findings of several recent studies indicate that codisposal costs are generally competitive with the combined costs of comparable separate single purpose systems and, under some conditions, could be lower. A 1979 General Accounting Office report[2] summarizes several previous sites specific studies that show codisposal to be more economical than alternative single purpose options. In research carried out by Gordian Associates Inc., for EPA, the generalized costs of single purpose disposal and codisposal were compared for equivalent weights of total solids. Table 2 shows a summary of this comparison. Codisposal cost estimates are generally lower than comparable separate handling options. These comparisons are based on cost data derived from secondary sources and accepted cost estimating methods. As such, they do not necessarily reflect the outcome of any site-specific cost comparison.

Until more empirical data becomes available, it is impossible to make a general statement as to the economic attractiveness of codisposal. However, studies to date show codisposal to be worth considering in any situation where landfill options are not available for sludge and solid waste.

Financing

Capital financing for wastewater collection and treatment is a combination of federal, state and local public funding, plus private contributions for specific elements of the system. For treatment works and major interceptor sewers, eligible capital items may be 75 percent funded by

**Table 2. Comparison of Annual Costs* of Major Thermal Codisposal Options
vs Comparable Single Purpose Alternatives.**

Codisposal Option	Ratio MSW:MSS**	Codisposal Costs	Single Purpose MSW Costs	Single Purpose MSS Costs	Combined Single Purpose Costs
MHF/FBF	250:100	5,250	1,125[†]	4,295[††]	5,420
Waterwall	1000:100	5,600	2,100	4,295[††]	6,395
Dedicated Boiler	1000:100	6,212	2,700	4,295[††]	6,995
Modular Incinerator	100:10	636	330	747[††]	1,077
Pyrolysis	1000:100	6,794	4,200	4,295[††]	8,495

Notes:

*Costs are shown in thousands of 1978 dollars and include capital amortization and debt service. Revenues from recovered energy and materials have been subtracted where applicable.

**Ratios are in dry weights of MSW (Municipal Solid Waste) and MSS (Municipal Sewage Sludge).

[†]Based on a full materials recovery fluff RDF system.

[††]Based on a filter press, MHF incineration system.

Source: *Codisposal of Municipal Solid Waste and Sewage Sludge: An Analysis of Constraints,* Gordian Associates Inc. — an unpublished report prepared for U.S. EPA in 1978.

a federal grant under the Clean Water Act.[3] The remaining 25 percent is provided by state and local sources in shares that vary from state to state. The state share may be provided as a grant or as a low-interest loan, while the local share is in most cases raised by general obligation or revenue bonding. For collection facilities other than major interceptors, funds are also provided locally from bonded indebtedness or from assessments against individual property owners.

Solid waste management activities are financed in a different manner. The most important difference is that limited federal funds are available only for project planning; none are available for capital financing. In addition, there is a greater presence of private risk capital in application to both collection and disposal activities. Thus, the potential capital funding mix includes local public funds, perhaps augmented with state-level funding assistance, and private funds from entrepreneurs operating solid waste handling concerns.

In cases where codisposal appears attractive on the basis of total costs or cost per ton of waste handled, planners will face problems in allocation of capital and operating costs. Each of these cost categories is made up of three components: (1) the costs attributable solely to solid waste handling activities; (2) the costs attributable solely to sludge handling; and (3) the joint costs, which refer to those parts of the process that handle both sludge and solid waste.

The two direct cost components are relatively easy to account for using common sense decision rules. For example, what is the purpose of each process step? If its purpose is to handle one waste stream exclusively, then categorizing the cost of that step is not difficult. Another role might be to ask whether the project depends on the process step in question. In a project using RDF as fuel for a multiple-hearth furnace, it seems clear that the tipping floor is solely a solid waste process necessity, one that would be required for any high-technology MSW facility. Similarly, materials recovery could be classified as related primarily to solid waste management. RDF processing and storage, however, are required in order to have the fuel the facility will use. This step in the process would be a joint cost.

Each project to date uses a unique process train, so no clear-cut set of cost categories has been developed. Nevertheless, if two separate agencies exist, or if the project serves two different populations, the costs must be allocated between the two so that capital financing proportions and user charges can be developed. Capital cost allocation is particularly important is establishing the part of the project funds that can be supported by an EPA Construction Grant.

EPA Multiple Purpose Project Funding

Both the Resource Conservation and Recovery Act and the Clean Water Act explicitly encourage integrated waste disposal. For all projects to date, EPA has provided funds under a multiple purpose funding policy developed in 1976 to address projects in combined sewer overflow, flood control, waste-water reclamation-reuse and codisposal. The 1976 policy was based on complex calculations to prorate joint benefits and costs. It received criticism for effectively reducing the federal share if a project accomplished multiple purposes, thereby favoring single purpose projects. Project funding under the 1976 policy has ranged from 75 percent of all costs in Duluth to about 40 percent of total project cost in Glen Cove.

EPA recently issued a revised policy document for public comment. It offers seven policy alternatives, most of which would result in more favorable treatment for codisposal projects. Under four of the seven policy options, the grant eligible portion of a codisposal project would be 115 percent of the ratio of the most cost-effective, single-purpose sludge disposal option to the cost of the codisposal project. All costs are calculated as the present worth of all capital and operating costs. In some cases, applying the formula may result in a grant eligible amount for codisposal which is less than the sludge-only option's capital cost. If this occurs, a minimum eligibility figure (115 percent of the least costly sludge disposal option's capital cost) would be used. Using this approach, the grant eligible amount for a codisposal project would be significantly higher than under the current prorated formula.

One difficulty in EPA's draft policy analysis is that revenues are not deducted from overall project costs in determining the "present worth cost" to be used in funding calculations. EPA's logic is that projects with any nonmonetary benefits, which cannot be given a dollar value, would be disadvantaged. However, the revenues of codisposal are typically an important aspect of financial feasibility. If they are disregarded in funding decisions, it means that high technology codisposal options will be seen as more costly than they actually are.

INSTITUTIONAL FACTORS AFFECTING CODISPOSAL

Along with technological and economic factors, a third distinct family of institutional considerations is equally important. "Institutional" refers to the complex legal, organizational and administrative factors relating to waste water and solid waste management. These factors, which can become important if a project is technically and economically feasible, fall into three main groups: organizational differences, planning constraints and legal issues.

Organizational Differences

Important differences exist between water and solid waste management programs because solid waste and water quality management have not developed in parallel. Water quality management programs originated as a local public health concern; emphasis shifted later to improvement of the nation's waterways. Particular concern over problems of sludge disposal has emerged recently as a result of continual growth of nationwide treatment capacity.

Municipal wastewater treatment has also evolved as an expensive, publicly-owned function. Widespread secondary treatment requires increasingly costly facilities. To construct these, a sizeable federal grant program was established.[4] Grants under the Federal Water Pollution Control Act are made available to public agencies, with rigorous corollary requirements for planning and management. The effect of these program requirements has been the creation of municipal or regional public bodies, vested with considerable centralized responsibility and authority.

Solid waste management, on the other hand, has progressed along different lines. Waste has traditionally been handled by the individual waste generator — the household, factory, institution, etc. Further, whereas the focus of wastewater treatment is on effluent and stream quality, the focus of solid waste management has been mainly on removal of the waste to a dump or landfill.

With growing population levels and densities, these functions in larger cities and towns had to be performed in some organized manner. This has led to the growth of private waste hauling and disposal industries in the U.S. Unlike wastewater treatment, the different components of solid waste management (*i.e.,* collection, transport, processing, storage, disposal) can be handled by different concerns, and in most places in the U.S. have never been handled by one authority.

A grant program similar to that established for wastewater treatment does not exist for solid waste management, due in part to the far lower levels of capitalization required and to the potential for interference with private operations. Consequently, solid waste management has developed far less centralized activity than wastewater programs. The various planning and financing functions are instead vested in different groups, some public and some private.

Planning Constraints

Wastewater and solid waste management planning activities are guided by different requirements and objectives. For example, both programs are aimed at cost minimization. But since federal grants are available for a significant proportion of capital costs, sewage treatment planning emphasizes minimization of locally supported operating costs, often substituting capital items in favor of added operating expense. On the other hand, most solid waste project costs must be borne locally, so that the emphasis has typically been on the lowest cost mix of capital and other factors of production, often resulting in labor- or land-intensive processes.

This can be a significant barrier, in that co-disposal largely means capital intensity in solid waste handling. The planning process becomes considerably more complex than that required for typical operations, such as landfilling. This additional complexity creates an immediate demand for greater human, technical and data resources, as well as for greater funding levels.

A further problem arises from differences in the geography of solid waste and wastewater management concerns. Not only are wastewater functions planned according to hydrologic boundaries as opposed to municipal ones, but treatment plants are also typically sited downstream from population, near the planned outfall location. Sites available to meet these water-related criteria may not be well located for solid waste handling. The viable scales of operation also do not lend themselves in all cases to servicing the same geographic area or population base. To some extent (*e.g.,* joint siting and the need to organize sewage collection for maximum gravity flow), these are practical problems that can be worked out during planning once a commitment is made to consider codisposal. However, they also represent real institutional issues in that the designation of joint service area boundaries requires an overview level of planning that is not usually found in the individual plans of two separate organizations.

Another major organizational barrier to planning lies in the difference between a completely public wastewater program and a partly public, partly private solid waste activity. This interferes with planning in that private operations have no incentive to plan or operate jointly. Further, public agency planning that has any impact on local private entrepreneurs must be carried out with attention to securing their support and preserving their livelihood.

Consequently, meshing the planning activities of wastewater and solid waste will involve careful coordination at local, state and federal levels. Of these three levels, the local planning agencies are the most important, for two reasons: (1) the motivation for considering codisposal should originate locally; and (2) in the absence of strong solid waste funding programs at both state and federal levels, there may be insufficient staff or incentives to accomplish program coordination. In general, these differences point to joint planning on a regional or areawide level as the appropriate approach to problem resolution.

Legal Issues

Control of the solid waste stream is a critical element in planning codisposal projects. In some municipalities, the collection and disposal of solid waste is a public function; but almost twice as many U.S. cities have their residential refuse collected by private collection firms.[5] In these cases, waste control can be achieved either by offering a lower tipping fee at the public facility or by legislating public control of the municipal waste stream. Flow control is currently the more prevalent method for legislating waste control. It requires solid waste to be delivered to the municipality's facility by private refuse haulers. Such an arrangement has thus far been legislated by the State of Florida; the City of Akron, Ohio; Monroe County, N.Y.; Jefferson County (Louisville), Ky., and the Western Lake Superior Sanitary District in Duluth, Minn.

Another method, which has been legislated in the U.S. only by the State of Wisconsin, is actual municipal ownership of the waste stream. Waste control legislation in effect assures the municipality's access to a steady supply of solid waste for the life of its processing facility.

The waste control issue is presently being challenged in Federal District Court in the case of *Glenwillow Landfill, Inc., et al.* v. *City of Akron et al.*[6] The City of Akron, which enacted flow control legislation in order to facilitate the establishment of an areawide solid waste resource recovery facility, is being challenged by Glenwillow Landfill, Inc., a private landfill operator, as to the constitutionality of its law. A decision is expected later this year.

The above institutional issues have repeatedly proven to be real barriers to the implementation of codisposal. However, the importance of institutional factors depends on whether a project can be seen as technically or economically feasible to begin with.

SUMMARY

In concept, codisposal is an attractive waste management option. Its technology is viable, although it remains to be fully proven and there are several unanswered questions regarding air emissions and leachate from residue disposal. Data available at this time indicate that in those cases where solid waste and wastewater management planning must turn toward high technology disposal methods, codisposal should be included as a major alternative. It appears that codisposal is at least comparable in cost to separate waste handling options. Its economic attractiveness will likely be further enhanced by EPA's forthcoming policies for multiple purpose project funding. Planning and implementation of a codisposal project must be carried out carefully, in light of institutional problems that arise in meshing two dissimilar waste disposal programs. Most of these difficulties can be dealt with by establishing a strong, integrated, local or regional planning program. If these barriers can be overcome, codisposal offers an opportunity to combine the energy and environmental benefits of resource recovery with the financial advantages of wastewater treatment capital funding.

REFERENCES AND NOTES

1. *Strategies for Funding of Multiple-Purpose Projects,* U.S. Environmental Protection Agency, Office of Water and Waste Management, June 1979.
2. *Codisposal of Garbage and Sewage Sludge – A Promising Solution to Two Problems,* Report No. CED-79-59, U.S. General Accounting Office, Washington, D.C., May 16, 1979.
3. Several exceptions to this funding percentage are possible, notably the availability of 85 percent funding for certain innovative or energy-saving treatment processes.
4. Federal Water Pollution Control Act. as amended – Construction grants program P.L. 95-217 (40 CFR 35).
5. E.S. Savas, *Policy Analysis for Local Government: Public* vs. *Private Refuse Collection* (New York: Columbia University, 1977).
6. Case C 78-65A of the Northern District Eastern Division, of the Federal District Court of Ohio.

Index

Abert, James G., 126
Air classification, 277–278, 328
Akron, Ohio, 4, 153–157, 473–479
Albany, N.Y., 4
Al mag. *See* Eddy current separator
Alter, Harvey, 3, 41, 141
Aluminum
  history, 308
  in refuse, 309–310
  mechanical processing, 311–320
  source separation, 311
  see also Eddy current separator
Aluminum Association, 308
Aluminum Co. of America (ALCOA), 315
American Can Co. *See* Americology
American Society for Testing and Materials
    (ASTM), 305, 364
Americology, 115, 121, 289
Ames, Iowa, 4, 120, 195, 511–520
Anderson, Robert C., 23, 85

Ballard, Charles A., 220
Baltimore, Md., 564–569. *See also* Pyrolysis
Bioconversion, 426–427
Biological gasification. *See* Pompano Beach, Fla.
Black Clawson Co., 179, 258, 319. *See also*
    Franklin, Ohio
Bridgeport, Conn., 4, 180
Briquetting. *See* Densified refuse-derived fuel
Buhler, Franchot, 111
Burks, Stephen, 119

California, State of, 27, 29, 101–105
Chase, Richard W., 116
Chicago, Ill., 4
Clean Air Act, 8
Clunie, Jeffrey F., 212
Codisposal
  definition, 61, 583
  economics, 586–588
  methods, 583–586
Cohen, Richard, 153
Combustion Equipment Associates (CEA),
    527–529
Conn, W. David, 27, 101
Connecticut Resource Recovery Authority
    (CRRA), 113, 180, 528

Cyclone separation
  heavy medium, 323–324
  of shredded auto scrap, 326–331
  water-only cyclone, 325

Dade County, Fla., 4, 113, 121, 320
Davis, Robert, 247
Densified refuse-derived fuel (dRDF)
  characteristics, 496–498
  combustion experience, 489–501
  equipment, 493–494
  see also Refuse-derived fuel
Depletion allowance, 23–24
Dower, Roger, 85
Duluth, Minn., 4

Eco-Fuel®
  characteristics, 529–534
  definition, 3
  firing, 528
  markets, 538
  see also Refuse-derived fuel
Eddy-current separator, 277, 313–315
Energy recovery. *See* Waste-to-energy
Equipment Test and Evaluation Facility. *See*
    National Center for Resource Recovery,
    Inc.

Federal Water Pollution Control Act, 8
Ferrous metals, scrap recovery, 299–306
Fiber recovery, 268–273
Flakt Group (Sweden), 275–280
Fluidized bed incinerator, 60
Fly ash, 445–447
Fort Worth, Tex., 234
Franklin, M.A., 58
Franklin, Ohio, 121. *See also* Black Clawson Co.
Franklin, W.E., 58
Freight rates, 16

Garden State Paper Co., 124
Garrett Research and Development Co., 180
Geller, E.S., 240
Gershman, Harvey W., 167
Glass Container Manufacturers Institute (GCMI),
    343

Glass recovery
  characteristics, 346–347
  cullet sorters, 341–342
  electro-optical sorter, 339–341
  froth flotation, 353–360
Gordon, Judith, 80

Hamilton, Ontario (Canada), 4
Hempstead, N.Y., 4, 121, 179, 236, 445
Holcomb, John E., 153

I-95 Complex
  description, 187–188
  Feasibility Study, 193, 199–209
  Markets Study, 192–193, 195–199
  Network Study, 193, 209–210
  see also National Center for Resource Recovery, Inc.
"Indifference value," 194
Industrial Waste Exchange, 18. See also Saint Louis, Mo.
Institute of Paper Chemistry, 258
Institutional barriers, 18
International Iron and Steel Institute, 299

Johnson, Elizabeth, 231

Klee, Albert, 80
Krauss-Maffei AG (Germany), 281–283

Landfill
  gas generation, 570–574
  operation cost, 519–520
  use, 163–164
  see also Methane gas
Lane County, Ore., 121
Lewis, Stephen G., 178
Lorton, Va. See I-95 Complex

Mac Donald, Bruce, 247
Madison, Wis., 4
Mandatory deposit legislation, 16
Marblehead, Mass., 236
Market development, 21. See also National Commission on Materials Policy, National Commission on Supplies and Shortages
Mass burning, 60
Materials recovery, 59. See also Aluminum, Ferrous metals, Glass
Methane gas
  composition, 573
  from landfills, 570–574
  see also Landfill
Mihelich, Donald L., 181
Milwaukee, Wis., 4

Mining and Minerals Policy Act, 17
Modular incinerator, 61
Monroe County, N.Y., 4, 113, 180
Monsanto Enviro-Chem Systems, 119, 179
Municipal Solid Waste (MSW), 3, 52

National Center for Resource Recovery, Inc. (NCRR), 112, 187, 254, 289, 313, 318, 493. See also I-95 Complex, New Orleans, La.
National Commission on Materials Policy, 20–22
National Commission on Supplies and Shortages, 20–22
National Science Foundation (NSF), 254
Nashville, Tenn., 112, 120, 212
Nashville Thermal Transfer Corp. See Nashville, Tenn.
New Orleans, La., 4, 288–289, 293. See also National Center for Resource Recovery, Inc.
New York/New Jersey Port Authority, 71
Niagara Falls, N.Y., 4

Occidental Research Corp., 316

Page, Clint, 119
Paper recovery. See Paper recycling
Paper recycling, 14, 240–245, 247–253, 256–257, 258–261, 275–280. See also Refuse-derived fuel, Densified refuse-derived fuel
Parsons and Wittemore, 113
Particulate matter. See Fly ash
Pelletizing. See Densified refuse-derived fuel
"Piggyback" collection, 234. See also Source separation
Plastics, 368, 370–377
Pompano Beach, Fla., 575–582
"Post-consumer" waste, 52. See also Municipal solid waste
"Prudent innovation," 5
Pyrolysis, 41–42, 61, 371, 380–387, 394, 406, 554, 563. See also Baltimore, Md.

Railroad Revitalization and Regulatory Reform Act, 17, 24
Raytheon Co., 318
Recovery 1. See New Orleans. See also National Center for Resource Recovery, Inc.
Recycling, 8. See also Paper recycling
Recycle Energy System. See Akron, Ohio
Ref Com. See Pompano Beach, Fla.
Refuse-derived fuel (RDF)
  as a kiln fuel, 539–552
  costs, 504–507
  definition, 4, 275, 466–468

Refuse-derived fuel (RDF) (Continued)
    fluff, 59
    powdered, 60
    see also Densified refuse-derived fuel
Refuse Energy Systems Co. (RESCO). *See*
    Saugus, Mass.
Refuse-fired boilers, 429–436
Renard, Marc L., 254
Resource Conservation and Recovery Act
    (RCRA), 17–18, 101, 114, 121
Resource recovery
    as disposal option, 74–77
    as pollution-control device, 80–84
    barriers, 146–152
    definition, 158
    economics, 128–129, 181–185
    financing, 77–78, 220–227
    front-end separation, 103
    IRS regulations, 151
    materials marketing, 167–177
    potential, 67–69
    processes, 158–161
    risks, 126–127, 141–145, 212–219
Resource Recovery Act, 9 n
Resource Recovery Associates, 528
Rotary cylindrical screen. *See* Trommel
Rubber recovery, 377–379. *See also* Tire
    recycling

San Francisco, Calif., 234
Saugus, Mass., 120, 438–443
Scavenging, 236
Scrap futures
    definition, 86–87
    description, 89–94
    benefits, 94–95
Semi-suspension waterwall incinerator, 60
Serper, Allen, 158
Shredding, 328
Smith, Frank Austin, 52
Solid Waste Management and Resource Recovery
    Act, 27. *See also* State of California
Sommerville, Mass., 236–239
Southeast Paper Manufacturing Co., 114
Source separation, 103–104, 124, 231–239,
    247–248. *See also* Paper recycling
Saint Louis, Mo., 18, 119, 189, 450–451
Stoker-fired boilers, 41

Taylor, Robert G., 212
Tax credits, 11, 25–27, 25 n
Technical Association of the Pulp and Paper
    Industry (TAPPI), 254, 293

Tire recycling
    reclaiming, 394–395
    reuse, 393–394
    trends, 391–392
    see also Rubber recovery
Trommel, 277–278, 524–525

Union Electric Co. *See* Saint Louis, Mo.
United Illuminating, 529
UOP, 113
"Urban ore," 7
U.S. Bureau of Mines, 10, 288, 318, 350, 363
U.S. Department of Commerce, 5, 85. *See also*
    U.S. National Bureau of Standards
U.S. Department of Energy (DOE), 5, 115, 575
U.S. Environmental Protection Agency (EPA),
    5, 8, 27, 85, 119, 147, 236, 299–300,
    481, 493, 583–584
U.S. Federal Trade Commission, 13
U.S. National Bureau of Standards, 17

Warren Spring Laboratory (England), 496
Waste glass, 363–366. *See also* Glass recovery
Waste reduction
    approaches, 30
    definition, 27
    policies, 31–36
    see also Resource recovery, Waste-to-energy
Waste-to-energy
    air pollution, 445–453
    amount available, 43–44
    cost, 61–64
    definition, 41–50, 59
    funding, 136–137
    history, 403–404
    maintenance, 135
    markets, 148–149, 407–408
    mass burning in Europe, 417–420
    mass burning in Germany, 421–428
    needs of buyer, 130
    plant considerations, 130–131
    potential savings, 48–49
    pyrolysis, thermal gasification or liquidfica-
        tion (PTGL), 554–563
    technology, 134, 404–407
    see also Pyrolysis, Refuse-derived fuel, Densi-
        fied refuse-derived fuel
Water-wall incinerator, 4
Weber, M.E., 58
Western Michigan University, 234, 286, 290, 293
Wheelabrator-Frye, Inc. *See* Saugus, Mass.
Witmer, J.F., 240
Wright-Patterson AFB, 485–491